Peterson's Guide to

Certificate Programs

at American Colleges and Universities

In cooperation with
nucea National University Continuing Education Association

Peterson's Guide to

Certificate Programs

at American Colleges and Universities

In cooperation with
ᴨᴜᴄᴇᴀ **National University Continuing Education Association**

Editors
George J. Lopos, University of Iowa
Margaret E. Holt, University of Georgia
Richard E. Bohlander, Peterson's Guides
John H. Wells, Peterson's Guides

Peterson's Guides
Princeton, New Jersey

Library of Congress Catalog Card Number: 88-43018
ISBN 0-87866-741-5

Composition and design by Peterson's Guides

Printed in the United States of America

10   9   8   7   6   5   4   3   2   1

Contents

Foreword vii

About Certificate Programs 1

How to Use this Book 3

Certificate Program Profiles 5

Appendixes

NUCEA Member Institutions 322

Classification of Instructional
Programs Taxonomy 323

Indexes

Alphabetical Index by Program
Classification 328

Institutional Index 341

Foreword

Peterson's Guide to Certificate Programs at American Colleges and Universities is designed to help students identify programs that meet their educational objectives, whether they are seeking to advance in their career, acquire new skills and knowledge, or qualify for certification in their field.

The guide was developed by Peterson's, a leading publisher of reference works on education, in cooperation with the National University Continuing Education Association (NUCEA), an association of colleges and universities that are major providers of continuing higher education for adult part-time learners. The two organizations combined their extensive resources to create the first comprehensive directory of certificate programs offered by the nation's four-year institutions of higher education.

Today, 43 percent of the some 12.5 million students in American colleges and universities are enrolled part-time. A growing number of adult part-time learners are pursuing structured, specialized learning programs leading to a certificate.

Recognizing this trend, NUCEA convened an advisory group of experts from colleges and universities, the accrediting agencies, and government to help the association develop a plan for this publication. In addition, representatives of NUCEA's Division of Certificate and Non-Traditional Degree Programs generously contributed their knowledge and time to the preparation of this book.

Two division representatives, George Lopos, associate dean of the Division of Continuing Education at the University of Iowa, and Margaret Holt, associate professor in the College of Education at the University of Georgia, developed the guide's organizational framework and identified the data elements to be collected. As editors of this book, they have sought consistently to include programs with high academic standards and to ensure that the information about each program is comprehensive and useful. They have prepared the following introductory sections to answer frequently asked questions about certificate programs and to offer advice on how to use this book effectively.

About Certificate Programs

What is a Certificate Program?

For the purpose of this guide, a certificate program at an accredited college or university is

a sequence, pattern, or group of courses or contact hours that focus upon an area of specialized knowledge or information and that are developed, administered, and evaluated by the institution's faculty members or by faculty-approved professionals.

Every certificate program listed meets the following criteria: (1) it was developed by and is administered, evaluated, and officially approved by the institution that offers it; (2) each course in the program is designed to meet the occupational, professional, or personal improvement needs of a defined audience; (3) within each course in the program, the student's understanding of the subject matter is evaluated against stated criteria (although courses may or may not confer credit); (4) the program may be taken independently of its being part of a degree program or minor; (5) in its admission policy, the program does not discriminate against any qualified student; and (6) a certificate signifying successful completion of the program is signed by the institution's chief academic officer or representative.

Why Pursue a Certificate Program?

The majority of certificate programs offered by the nation's colleges and universities are professionally oriented. Individuals pursue these programs to prepare for new careers, to qualify for a promotion, to stay current in their field, to satisfy mandated education requirements, or simply to acquire new skills and knowledge.

In many states, a certificate program is a prerequisite for both professional licensure and employment, especially in highly specialized fields such as real estate, insurance, brokerage, and the allied health professions. In some states, certificate programs are also mandated for relicensure purposes. People who work in these states are required to pursue certificate programs either by their professional association or by the state itself.

Certificate programs frequently address the new knowledge areas continually emerging as a result of technological, economic, or legal changes. Colleges and universities seek to respond to these changes by developing relevant certificate programs designed to convey new knowledge to professionals working in the field. This information may not be available through university-sponsored degree programs.

Some individuals enroll in a certificate program as a part of their traditional degree program. They do so to gain expertise in a particular area of study. Others pursue a certificate because they believe it will aid their entry into a professional field. And still others pursue nonacademic certificate programs for self-enrichment.

Who Qualifies for Entry into a Certificate Program?

Most certificate programs have admission requirements; however, requirements vary considerably from program to program. Some programs require applicants to hold particular educational credentials, take an entrance examination, submit transcripts and letters of reference and recommendation, and visit the program coordinator for an interview. Some programs require prospective students to follow the same admission procedure as the sponsoring institution's full-time or part-time students must follow. A few programs have no admission requirements.

The Enrollment Requirements section of each program entry provides a starting point for determining eligibility for specific certificate programs. But because entry requirements differ greatly, those interested should contact individual program administrators for information concerning specific admission requirements and program prerequisites.

How are Certificate Programs Structured?

Certificate programs are usually planned with the needs of working adults in mind. Courses are scheduled at convenient times and locations—sometimes even in the workplace—as well as in concentrated formats suited to the needs of working adults. Program components may be offered through correspondence study or distance learning means such as audiotapes, videotapes, and teleconferences.

The prescribed curriculum for a certificate program typically includes a number of required courses and a few electives. Some programs also require a practicum or internship. Frequently, courses taken as part of a certificate program are applicable to degree programs at the college or university offering the certificate program.

Many certificate programs stand alone, but others are part of an established career ladder in a given profession. In the latter instance, an individual must have a certain level of education and experience to qualify for a given certificate program. The professional association determines what education is fundamental and, in collaboration with a college or university, designs a series of certificate programs to serve the needs of the expert, as well as those of the newcomer. As professionals move up the career ladder, they are encouraged to acquire additional knowledge and skills. Certificate programs assist in this development. They also provide useful benchmarks by which an individual can evaluate how he or she ranks with respect to the established norms of the profession.

What Does a Certificate Signify?

Completion of a certificate program signifies that the certificate holder has acquired certain proficiencies in a specialized area of study through an educational program. The certificate alone does not guarantee improved professional performance. The quality of performance depends upon the applications of the newly acquired knowledge and skills.

It is important to remember that professional associations and state agencies often rely upon certificates as evidence that an individual is eligible for licensure or relicensure in a given profession. The certificate does not, however, guarantee licensure, employment, or promotion unless it has been mandated as the only prerequisite to advancement.

How to Use this Book _____

Organization of the Guide

This book is organized to make your search for an appropriate certificate program as simple as possible. The body of the book is arranged in alphabetical order, first by state, then by institution within the state, and, finally, by program classification. Two appendixes follow the main listing of certificate programs. The first lists NUCEA member institutions that offer programs listed in the guide. The second appendix displays the National Center for Education Statistics' Classification of Instructional Programs (CIP) Taxonomy, as used to categorize individual certificate programs appearing in this reference. Following the appendixes are two indexes. The first is an index of programs arranged alphabetically by CIP program classification and by institution. The final index, the Institutional Index, lists institutions included in the guide and refers to them by page number.

Effective Use of the Guide

How to use this reference depends on how much you know about your program interests, your particular college or university preference, and the distance you can travel to attend a certificate program. For example, if you are interested in finding programs in a specific subject area, you might begin by turning to the Classification of Instructional Programs Taxonomy. Look for the general classification that best represents your interest, as well as for any additional associated classifications that seem potentially relevant. Then turn to the Alphabetical Index by Program Classification where you will find the names of institutions offering appropriate programs in the subject areas you identified previously within the taxonomy. Page numbers given refer you to the first page of a particular institution's program listings, which are organized alphabetically by the program classifications displayed on the first line of each program profile.

To find out where the programs offered by a particular institution are listed, refer to the Institutional Index at the end of the book.

If you want to locate programs geographically, turn directly to the alphabetical listing of programs by state in the main body. Beneath each state heading, you will find program descriptions listed alphabetically by the college or university offering the program and, within that listing, alphabetically by classification.

Whatever method or combination of methods you decide to use, each of the program entries gives detailed information to help you begin your search for the appropriate certificate program.

What Each Program Entry Contains

Each program entry provides you with enough information to decide whether or not a particular certificate program is appropriate for your needs. Each entry includes the CIP subject area and reference number under which the program is listed in the Alphabetical Index and the formal title of the particular certificate program. In addition, each entry includes the following information:

- **General Information** Includes information about the program's content, whether the program confers academic credit, who signs the completion certificate, and whether the program is endorsed by any professional organizations.

- **Program Format** Provides course scheduling information, length of the program, and program completion requirements for the certificate.

- **Evaluation** Provides information about how student learning is evaluated (tests, papers, projects, etc.), the program's grading system, and whether transcripts or other records are kept by the institution.

- **Enrollment Requirements** Lists the prerequisites for entry into the program (e.g., high school diploma, college degree, on-campus residence).

- **Program Costs** Lists the total cost of the certificate program and the cost of individual courses or units within the program.

- **Housing and Student Services** Provides information regarding the availability of on-campus housing and lists the student services offered to program participants (counseling, placement services, etc.).

- **Special Features** Provides information about the distinctive aspects of the particular certificate program.

- **Contact** Lists the program contact person at the college or university, usually the certificate program coordinator or director, and the address and phone number for obtaining the most current information about the program.

The editors have made every effort to ensure that the information provided for each entry is accurate. However, institutions may have changed certain aspects of their program since the book's publication. Therefore, you should always write the contact person at the college or university in question before making a final enrollment decision.

A Note to Foreign Students

If you are not a resident citizen of the United States and you wish to enroll in a certificate program, this guide should prove very helpful. However, you should pay particular attention to each entry's information referring to program availability for foreign students. In addition, note any aspects of the program that are particularly important to foreign students: length of the program, frequency of the program, instructional schedule, and whether scores on the Test of English as a Foreign Language (TOEFL) must accompany your application for enrollment. You should determine the length of time you would have to stay in the United States to complete the certificate program and whether such a stay is possible.

If you have taken into account all of the above and believe that you would be able to attend the certificate program, then you should write to the program's contact person for specific information about how to establish appropriate student status and whether or not housing and student services are available to you. The contact person may also be able to help you with immigration information.

Certificate Program Profiles

ALABAMA

NUCEA MEMBER

AUBURN UNIVERSITY AT MONTGOMERY
Montgomery, Alabama 36193

OFFICE SUPERVISION AND MANAGEMENT (07.04)
Administrative Assistant Certificate

General Information Unit offering the program: Continuing Education. Program content: Time management, professional writing, recruiting and interviewing, business and professional communications, effective management. Available on a non-credit basis. Certificate signed by the Chancellor.

Program Format Evening classes offered. Instructional schedule: Two to four evenings per week. Program cycle: Continuous enrollment. Completion of program requires eight courses, 75% attendance.

Evaluation Student evaluation based on tests, reports. Computer records are kept for each student.

Enrollment Requirements Completion of Secretarial Certificate or equivalent knowledge required. Program is open to non-resident foreign students.

Program Costs $1500 for the program.

Housing and Student Services Housing is not available. Job counseling and placement services are not available.

Special Features Designed to fill need for quality courses for office assistants when the School of Business dropped the Office Management Credit Program. Many of the students are college graduates who are trying to get back in the job market.

Contact Ms. Patricia A. Matthews, Director, Community Services, Montgomery, AL 36193. 205-271-9339.

SECRETARIAL AND RELATED PROGRAMS (07.06)
Secretarial Certificate

General Information Unit offering the program: Continuing Education. Program content: Records management, word processing, bookkeeping, accounting, assertiveness training, office procedures, English, typing, shorthand. Available on a non-credit basis. Certificate signed by the Chancellor.

Program Format Evening classes offered. Instructional schedule: Two to four evenings per week. Program cycle: Continuous enrollment. Completion of program requires 13 courses, 75% attendance.

Evaluation Student evaluation based on tests, reports. Computer records are kept for each student.

Enrollment Requirements Program is open to non-resident foreign students.

Program Costs $1500 for the program.

Housing and Student Services Housing is not available. Job counseling and placement services are not available.

Special Features Designed to fill need for quality courses for office assistants when the School of Business dropped the Office Management Credit Program. Many of the students are college graduates who are trying to get back in the job market.

Contact Ms. Patricia A. Matthews, Director, Community Services, Montgomery, AL 36193. 205-271-9339.

SOUTHEASTERN BIBLE COLLEGE
Birmingham, Alabama 35205

BIBLE STUDIES (39.02)
Bible Certificate

General Information Unit offering the program: Bible. Available for credit. Certificate signed by the President. Certificate applicable to A.A., B.S. in Biblical Studies.

Program Format Correspondence classes offered. Program cycle: Continuous enrollment. Full program cycle lasts 32 credit hours.

Evaluation Student evaluation based on tests, papers, reports, oral assessment by audio or video tapes. Grading system: Letters or numbers. Transcripts are kept for each student.

Enrollment Requirements High school diploma, agreement with doctrinal statement required. Program is not open to non-resident foreign students.

Program Costs $50 per credit hour.

Housing and Student Services Housing is not available. Job counseling and placement services are not available.

Special Features Program began at Dallas Bible College in 1959. Upon closing of Dallas Bible College, program transferred to Southeastern Bible College in 1986. The program is the minimum requirement for workers by many foreign mission boards.

Contact Dr. Ray E. Baughman, Dean of External Studies, 2901 Pawnee Avenue, Birmingham, AL 35205-2099. 205-251-2311.

NUCEA MEMBER

UNIVERSITY OF ALABAMA AT BIRMINGHAM
Birmingham, Alabama 35294

ADVERTISING (09.02)
Advertising and Public Relations

General Information Unit offering the program: Special Studies. Available on a non-credit basis. Certificate signed by the Dean of Special Studies.

Program Format Daytime, evening classes offered. Instructional schedule: One evening per week for two to three hours. Program cycle: Continuous enrollment.

Evaluation Student evaluation based on tests. Grading system: Letters or numbers. Transcripts are kept for each student.

Enrollment Requirements Program is open to non-resident foreign students.

Program Costs $65–$90 per course.

Housing and Student Services Housing is not available. Job counseling and placement services are not available.

Contact Ms. Julia Norment Jones, Certificate and Computer Coordinator, 917 11th Street South, Birmingham, AL 35294. 205-934-3870.

BANKING AND FINANCE (06.03)
Certified Financial Planner

General Information Unit offering the program: Special Studies. Program content: Personal financial planning. Available on a non-credit basis. Certificate signed by the President of College for Financial Planning. Program fulfills requirements for Certified Financial Planning.

Program Format Evening classes offered. Instructional schedule: One evening per week for three hours. Program cycle: Continuous enrollment. Full program cycle lasts 2 years. Completion of program requires six courses.

Evaluation   Student evaluation based on tests. Grading system: Letters or numbers, pass/fail. Transcripts are kept for each student.

Enrollment Requirements   Admission to program through College for Financial Planning required. Program is open to non-resident foreign students.

Program Costs $1575 for the program, $175 per course.

Housing and Student Services   Housing is not available. Job counseling and placement services are not available.

Special Features   Program provides both beginning and established practitioners with practical, hands-on information about critical areas of financial planning. Curriculum continually updated and expanded to reflect changes and innovations. Successful completion of program leads to the widely respected CFP designation. All instructors are CFP's and are approved by the College for Financial Planning.

Contact   Ms. Julia Norment Jones, Certificate and Computer Coordinator, 917 11th Street South, Birmingham, AL 35294. 205-934-3870.

BUSINESS AND MANAGEMENT, GENERAL (06.01)
Business Management Certificate

General Information   Unit offering the program: Special Studies. Program content: Computing, investing, management training. Available on a non-credit basis. Cosponsored by American Management Association. Certificate signed by the Dean of Special Studies.

Program Format   Evening, correspondence classes offered. Instructional schedule: One evening per week for two hours. Program cycle: Continuous enrollment. Completion of program requires seven courses.

Evaluation   Student evaluation based on tests, reports. Grading system: Letters or numbers. Transcripts are kept for each student.

Enrollment Requirements   Program is open to non-resident foreign students.

Program Costs $160 per course.

Housing and Student Services   Housing is not available. Job counseling and placement services are available.

Special Features   Major strength of program is practical information offered about business management.

Contact   Ms. Julia Norment Jones, Certificate and Computer Coordinator, 917 11th Street South, Birmingham, AL 35294. 205-934-3870.

COMPUTER AND INFORMATION SCIENCES, GENERAL (11.01)
Computer Information Processing Certificate

General Information   Unit offering the program: Special Studies. Available on a non-credit basis. Certificate signed by the Dean, Special Studies.

Program Format   Daytime, evening classes offered. Instructional schedule: One evening per week for two to three hours.

Evaluation   Student evaluation based on tests, computer projects. Grading system: Letters or numbers. Transcripts are kept for each student.

Enrollment Requirements   Program is open to non-resident foreign students.

Program Costs $78–$115 per course.

Housing and Student Services   Housing is not available. Job counseling and placement services are not available.

Special Features   Hands-on computer training.

Contact   Ms. Julia Norment Jones, Certificate and Computer Coordinator, 917 11th Street South, Birmingham, AL 35294. 205-934-3870.

LAW (22.01)
Paralegal Studies Series

General Information   Unit offering the program: Special Studies. Program content: Legal research, legal writing, business law, litigation, real estate law. Available on a non-credit basis. Certificate signed by the Dean of Special Studies.

Program Format   Evening classes offered. Instructional schedule: One evening per week. Program cycle: Continuous enrollment. Full program cycle lasts 1 year. Completion of program requires grade of C or better.

Evaluation   Student evaluation based on tests. Grading system: Letters or numbers, pass/fail. Transcripts are kept for each student.

Enrollment Requirements   Program is open to non-resident foreign students.

Program Costs $60–$80 per course.

Housing and Student Services   Housing is not available. Job counseling and placement services are not available.

Special Features   All instructors are from the legal field. Many are attorneys who specialize in the area they are teaching.

Contact   Ms. Julia Norment Jones, Certificate and Computer Coordinator, 917 11th Street South, Birmingham, AL 35294. 205-934-3870.

OFFICE SUPERVISION AND MANAGEMENT (07.04)
Administrative Assistant Certificate Program

General Information   Unit offering the program: Special Studies. Available on a non-credit basis. Certificate signed by the Dean of Special Studies.

Program Format   Daytime, evening, weekend classes offered. Instructional schedule: One evening per week for two hours. Program cycle: Continuous enrollment.

Evaluation   Student evaluation based on tests, reports. Grading system: Letters or numbers. Transcripts are kept for each student.

Enrollment Requirements   Program is open to non-resident foreign students.

Program Costs $65–$90 per course.

Housing and Student Services   Housing is not available. Job counseling and placement services are not available.

Special Features   Courses designed to develop students into top assistant administrative material. Counseling system to tailor-design courses that match students needs and goals.

Contact   Ms. Julia Norment Jones, Certificate and Computer Coordinator, 917 11th Street South, Birmingham, AL 35294. 205-934-3870.

PERSONNEL MANAGEMENT (06.16)
Certified Employee Benefit Specialist Program

General Information   Unit offering the program: Special Studies Noncredit. Program content: Legal, financial and organizational aspects of employee benefit plans. Available on a non-credit basis. Cosponsored by International Foundation of Employee Benefits Plans. Certificate signed by the President of Wharton School, University of Pennsylvania. Program fulfills requirements for Certified Employee Benefit Specialist.

Certified Employee Benefit Specialist Program continued

Program Format Evening classes offered. Instructional schedule: One evening per week for three hours. Program cycle: Continuous enrollment.

Evaluation Student evaluation based on tests. Grading system: Letters or numbers. Transcripts are kept for each student.

Enrollment Requirements Program is open to non-resident foreign students.

Program Costs $700 for the program, $150–$175 per course.

Housing and Student Services Housing is not available. Job counseling and placement services are not available.

Contact Ms. Julia Norment Jones, Certificate and Computer Coordinator, 917 11th South Street, Birmingham, AL 35294. 205-934-3870.

SECRETARIAL AND RELATED PROGRAMS (07.06)
Senior Secretary Certificate Program

General Information Unit offering the program: Special Studies. Program content: Typing, shorthand, bookkeeping report writing. Available on a non-credit basis. Certificate signed by the Dean, Special Studies.

Program Format Daytime, evening, weekend classes offered. Program cycle: Continuous enrollment.

Evaluation Student evaluation based on tests. Grading system: Letters or numbers. Transcripts are kept for each student.

Enrollment Requirements Program is open to non-resident foreign students.

Program Costs $60–$90 per course.

Housing and Student Services Housing is not available. Job counseling and placement services are not available.

Special Features Counseling available to students to tailor program to meet specific needs and goals.

Contact Ms. Julia Norment Jones, Certificate and Computer Coordinator, 917 11th Street South, Birmingham, AL 35294. 205-934-3870.

NUCEA MEMBER
UNIVERSITY OF SOUTH ALABAMA
Mobile, Alabama 36688

LAW (22.01)
Legal Assistants Education Program

General Information Unit offering the program: Department of Conference Activities and Special Programs. Available on a non-credit basis. Endorsed by Alabama Bar Association. Certificate signed by the Dean.

Program Format Evening classes offered. Instructional schedule: Once or twice per week. Program cycle: Continuous enrollment. Completion of program requires 80% attendance.

Evaluation Student evaluation based on tests, papers, reports. Grading system: Letters or numbers, pass/fail. Transcripts are kept for each student.

Enrollment Requirements High school diploma or GED required. Program is open to non-resident foreign students.

Program Costs $1500 for the program, $75 per course.

Housing and Student Services Housing is available. Job counseling and placement services are available.

Special Features Credit for prior experience in specialized areas. Internship program available. Independent study course may be substituted if a student is lacking one course to qualify for graduation.

Contact Ms. Debbie Clolinger, Special Courses Director, 2002 Old Bay Front Drive, Mobile, AL 36615. 205-431-6403.

ALASKA

ALASKA PACIFIC UNIVERSITY
Anchorage, Alaska 99508

BUSINESS AND MANAGEMENT, GENERAL (06.01)
Professional Certificate in Travel Industry Management

General Information Unit offering the program: Travel Industry Management. Available for credit. Certificate signed by the Director of Travel Industry Manangement. Certificate applicable to A.A., B.A. in Travel Industry Management.

Program Format Daytime, evening classes offered. Program cycle: Continuous enrollment. Full program cycle lasts 2 semesters. Completion of program requires 24 credit hours, grade of C or better in each course.

Evaluation Student evaluation based on tests, papers, reports, presentations, practicum. Grading system: Letters or numbers. Transcripts are kept for each student.

Enrollment Requirements High school diploma required. Program is open to non-resident foreign students. English language proficiency required. Students required to live on campus.

Program Costs $4600 for the program, $192 per credit hour.

Housing and Student Services Housing is available. Job counseling and placement services are available.

Special Features Program for adults with a degree or other good basic education now looking for a career change. Excellent training courses often taught by industry leaders will prepare them well for entry-level positions, while management courses will enable them to climb up the career ladder.

Contact Ms. Edith M. Taylor, Director, Travel Industry Management, 4101 University Drive, Anchorage, AK 99508. 907-564-8203.

FOOD PRODUCTION, MANAGEMENT, AND SERVICES (20.04)
Commercial Foodservice Systems

General Information Unit offering the program: Hotel/Foodservice Administration. Program content: Volume food production, purchasing, basic accounting, cost controls. Available for credit. Certificate signed by the Director of Hotel/Foodservice Administration. Certificate applicable to A.A., B.A. in Hotel/Foodservice Administration.

Program Format Daytime, evening classes offered. Instructional schedule: 12 hours per week. Students may enroll fall, spring. Full program cycle lasts 8 courses. Completion of program requires 24 credit hours.

Evaluation Student evaluation based on tests, papers, reports, food production assignments. Grading system: Letters or numbers. Transcripts are kept for each student.

Enrollment Requirements High school diploma or GED required. Program is open to non-resident foreign students. English language proficiency required. Minimum TOEFL score required: 450.

Program Costs $4600–$5800 for the program, $192 per credit hour.

Housing and Student Services Housing is available. Job counseling and placement services are available.

Special Features Courses taken for a certificate program may be applied to degree requirements, should a student decide to continue his or her education. APU awards credit for prior experience and allows students to earn as many as 50 percent of required credits.

Contact   Ms. Susan A. Vaillancourt, Director, Hotel/Foodservice Administration, 4101 University Drive, Anchorage, AK 99508. 907-564-8203.

FOOD SCIENCES AND HUMAN NUTRITION (19.05)
Dietary Foodservice and Sanitation Systems

General Information   Unit offering the program: Hotel/Foodservice Administration. Program content: Food science and sanitation, nutrition, basic food service management, natural science. Available for credit. Certificate signed by the Director of Hotel/Foodservice Administration. Certificate applicable to A.A., B.A. in Hotel/Foodservice Administration.

Program Format   Daytime, evening classes offered. Instructional schedule: 12 hours per week. Students may enroll fall, spring. Full program cycle lasts 8 courses. Completion of program requires 24 credit hours.

Evaluation   Student evaluation based on tests, papers, reports, food production assignments. Grading system: Letters or numbers. Transcripts are kept for each student.

Enrollment Requirements   High school diploma or GED required. Program is open to non-resident foreign students. English language proficiency required. Minimum TOEFL score required: 450.

Program Costs $4600–$5800 for the program, $192 per credit hour.

Housing and Student Services   Housing is available. Job counseling and placement services are available.

Special Features   Courses taken for a certificate program may be applied to degree requirements, should a student decide to continue his or her education. APU awards credit for prior experience and allows students to earn as many as 50 percent of required credits.

Contact   Ms. Susan A. Vaillancourt, Director, Hotel/Foodservice Administration, 4101 University Drive, Anchorage, AK 99508. 907-564-8203.

HOSPITALITY AND RECREATION MARKETING (08.09)
Front Office Reception Systems

General Information   Unit offering the program: Hotel/Foodservice Administration. Program content: Tourism, computers, hotel/food service management, accounting, cost controls, large scale housekeeping and management, human resource management, lodging and foodservice information systems. Available for credit. Certificate signed by the Director of Hotel/Foodservice Administration. Certificate applicable to A.A., B.A. in Hotel/Foodservice Administration.

Program Format   Daytime, evening classes offered. Instructional schedule: 12 hours per week. Students may enroll fall, spring. Full program cycle lasts 8 courses. Completion of program requires 24 credit hours.

Evaluation   Student evaluation based on tests, papers, reports, food production assignments. Grading system: Letters or numbers. Transcripts are kept for each student.

Enrollment Requirements   High school diploma or GED required. Program is open to non-resident foreign students. English language proficiency required. Minimum TOEFL score required: 450.

Program Costs $4600–$5800 for the program, $192 per credit hour.

Housing and Student Services   Housing is available. Job counseling and placement services are available.

Special Features   Courses taken for a certificate program may be applied to degree requirements, should a student decide to continue his or her education. APU awards credit for prior experience and allows students to earn as many as 50 percent of required credits.

Contact   Ms. Susan A. Vaillancourt, Director, Hotel/Foodservice Administration, 4101 University Drive, Anchorage, AK 99508. 907-564-8203.

HOSPITALITY AND RECREATION MARKETING (08.09)
Hotel/Foodservice Sales Systems

General Information   Unit offering the program: Hotel/Foodservice Administration. Program content: Administration, tourism, speech communication, basic accounting, world cuisines, cost controls, marketing. Available for credit. Certificate signed by the Director of Hotel/Foodservice Administration. Certificate applicable to A.A., B.A. in Hotel/Foodservice Administration.

Program Format   Daytime, evening classes offered. Instructional schedule: 12 hours per week. Students may enroll fall, spring. Full program cycle lasts 8 courses. Completion of program requires 24 credit hours.

Evaluation   Student evaluation based on tests, papers, reports, food production assignments. Grading system: Letters or numbers. Transcripts are kept for each student.

Enrollment Requirements   High school diploma or GED required. Program is open to non-resident foreign students. English language proficiency required. Minimum TOEFL score required: 450.

Program Costs $4600–$5800 for the program, $192 per credit hour.

Housing and Student Services   Housing is available. Job counseling and placement services are available.

Special Features   Courses taken for a certificate program may be applied to degree requirements, should a student decide to continue his or her education. APU awards credit for prior experience and allows students to earn as many as 50 percent of required credits.

Contact   Ms. Susan A. Vaillancourt, Director, Hotel/Foodservice Administration, 4101 University Drive, Anchorage, AK 99508. 907-564-8203.

INSTITUTIONAL, HOME MANAGEMENT, AND SUPPORTING SERVICES (20.06)
Large Scale Housekeeping

General Information   Unit offering the program: Hotel/Foodservice Administration. Program content: Computers, hotel/food service administration, food service and sanitation, individual environment, accounting, maintenance, human resource management, hotel/food service design and layout. Available for credit. Certificate signed by the Director of Hotel/Foodservice Administration. Certificate applicable to A.A., B.A. in Hotel/Foodservice Administration.

Program Format   Daytime, evening classes offered. Instructional schedule: 12 hours per week. Students may enroll fall, spring. Full program cycle lasts 8 courses. Completion of program requires 24 credit hours.

Evaluation   Student evaluation based on tests, papers, reports, food production assignments. Grading system: Letters or numbers. Transcripts are kept for each student.

Enrollment Requirements   High school diploma or GED required. Program is open to non-resident foreign students. English language proficiency required. Minimum TOEFL score required: 450.

Program Costs $4600–$5800 for the program, $192 per credit hour.

Housing and Student Services   Housing is available. Job counseling and placement services are available.

Special Features   Courses taken for a certificate program may be applied to degree requirements, should a student decide to continue his or her education. APU awards credit for prior experience and allows students to earn as many as 50 percent of required credits.

Large Scale Housekeeping continued

Contact Ms. Susan A. Vaillancourt, Director, Hotel/Foodservice Administration, 4101 University Drive, Anchorage, AK 99508. 907-564-8203.

ARIZONA

ARIZONA COLLEGE OF THE BIBLE
Phoenix, Arizona 85021

BIBLE STUDIES (39.02)
Certificate in Bible for Graduates

General Information Unit offering the program: Bible. Program content: Old and New Testament, Christian ministries, biblical studies. Available for credit. Certificate signed by the President.

Program Format Daytime, evening classes offered. Program cycle: Continuous enrollment. Full program cycle lasts 32 credit hours. Completion of program requires 2.0 GPA.

Evaluation Student evaluation based on tests, papers, reports. Grading system: Letters or numbers. Transcripts are kept for each student.

Enrollment Requirements Bachelor's degree in a field other than Bible, statement of Christian commitment required. English language proficiency required.

Program Costs $3450 for the program, $144 per credit hour.

Housing and Student Services Housing is available. Job counseling and placement services are available.

Special Features A year of intensive training in Bible, doctrine, and ministry skills for students already holding a bachelor's degree in another vocational field.

Contact Mr. Michael Bechtle, Director of Admissions, 2045 West Northern Avenue, Phoenix, AZ 85021. 602-995-2670.

NUCEA MEMBER
UNIVERSITY OF ARIZONA
Tucson, Arizona 85721

FOREIGN LANGUAGES, MULTIPLE EMPHASIS (16.01)
Successful Completion of the Summer Institute for Court Interpretation

General Information Unit offering the program: Continuing Education. Program content: Specialized vocabulary, simultaneous/consecutive interpretation practice. Available for credit. Certificate signed by the Director, Summer Institute for Court Interpretation.

Program Format Daytime classes offered. Instructional schedule: Monday through Friday. Students enroll in the summer. Full program cycle lasts 3 weeks. Completion of program requires 102 contact hours.

Evaluation Student evaluation based on tests, papers, taped performances. Grading system: Pass/fail. Transcripts are kept for each student.

Enrollment Requirements Excellent Spanish/English proficiency required. Program is open to non-resident foreign students. English language proficiency required.

Program Costs $750 for the program.

Housing and Student Services Housing is available. Job counseling and placement services are available.

Special Features Program, in its seventh year, is the most consistently running institute providing intensive practice in simultaneous and consecutive interpretation, the oral skills necessary to interpret in court. Instructors are among the best federally certified interpreters in the country, and classes are kept small. Course also emphasizes sight translation and specialized vocabulary.

Contact Ms. Roseann D. Gonzalez, Director, Summer Institute for Court Interpretation, Modern Languages, Room 456, Tucson, AZ 85721. 602-621-3687.

INDIVIDUAL AND FAMILY DEVELOPMENT (19.07)
Certificate in Gerontology (Graduate)

General Information Unit offering the program: Committee on Gerontology. Program content: Psychological problems, communicative aspects, economics of aging, human adaptability. Available for credit. Certificate signed by the Dean of the Graduate College.

Program Format Daytime, evening classes offered. Instructional schedule: Classes meet weekly. Program cycle: Continuous enrollment. Full program cycle lasts 18 credit hours. Completion of program requires 3.0 GPA.

Evaluation Student evaluation based on tests, reports, practicum. Grading system: Letters or numbers. Transcripts are kept for each student.

Enrollment Requirements Undergraduate degree, 3.0 GPA required. Program is open to non-resident foreign students.

Program Costs $1134 for the program.

Housing and Student Services Housing is not available. Job counseling and placement services are available.

Special Features Majority of candidates are employed in human services and combine work and study. They are mature and enrich the quality of the classroom experience for all who are enrolled. Courses are all regular University offerings. Program offers semester seminars with guest speakers, opportunity to mingle and meet faculty, other students, and community professionals.

Contact Ms. Margaret Zube, Ph.D., Coordinator, Committee on Gerontology, Anthropology 214, Tucson, AZ 85721. 602-621-4086.

CALIFORNIA

AZUSA PACIFIC UNIVERSITY
Azusa, California 91702

BUSINESS AND MANAGEMENT, GENERAL (06.01)
Certificate of Ministry Management

General Information Unit offering the program: School of Business and Management. Program content: Professional education for managers in churches and parachurches. Available for credit. Endorsed by Christian Ministries Management Association. Certificate signed by the President of the University. Certificate applicable to Master of Ministry Management, M.B.A.

Program Format Weekend classes offered. Instructional schedule: One weekend per month (Friday 4–10 p.m., Saturday 9 a.m. to 12 noon). Program cycle: Continuous enrollment. Full program cycle lasts 9 months. Completion of program requires 3.0 GPA.

Evaluation Student evaluation based on tests, papers, reports, practicum. Grading system: Letters or numbers. Transcripts are kept for each student.

Enrollment Requirements Associate degree required, bachelor's degree preferred. Program is open to non-resident foreign students. English language proficiency required. Minimum TOEFL score required: 500.

Program Costs $1105 for the program, $170 per course.

Housing and Student Services Housing is available. Job counseling and placement services are available.

Special Features Combines the expertise of the Christian academic community with the experience of practitioner/instructors in the process of building a model for effective management of Christian ministries. Bridges the gap between formal graduate degree programs and the brief training offered in workshops, seminars, and institutes.

Contact Mr. Walter A. Hutter, Dean, School of Business and Management, Citrus and Alosta, Azusa, CA 91702. 818-969-3434 Ext. 3083.

TEACHING ENGLISH AS A SECOND LANGUAGE/FOREIGN LANGUAGE (13.14)
Certificate in Teaching English to Speakers of Other Languages

General Information Unit offering the program: Department of International Studies. Program content: Syntax, sociolinguistics, acquisitions, ESL methods and practicum. Available for credit. Certificate signed by the Dean, College of Liberal Arts and Sciences. Certificate applicable to M.A. in TESOL.

Program Format Daytime, evening classes offered. Instructional schedule: Once per week. Students enroll in September. Complete program cycle lasts two to three 9-week terms. Completion of program requires grade of B or better, five courses.

Evaluation Student evaluation based on tests, papers, reports, practicum. Grading system: Letters or numbers. Transcripts are kept for each student.

Enrollment Requirements Bachelor's degree, 3.0 GPA, eight semester units of college-level second-language study required. Program is open to non-resident foreign students. English language proficiency required. Minimum TOEFL score required: 500.

Program Costs $2550 for the program, $170 per unit.

Housing and Student Services Housing is not available. Job counseling and placement services are available.

Special Features Current faculty members have teaching experience in refugee programs, Japanese and Chinese ESL/EFL programs, and California public schools/bilingual programs as well as in two-year- and four-year-college ESL contexts.

Contact Dr. Marvin Mardock, Department Head, International Studies, Azusa, CA 91702. 818-969-3434.

CALIFORNIA STATE UNIVERSITY, BAKERSFIELD
Bakersfield, California 93311

COMPUTER AND INFORMATION SCIENCES, GENERAL (11.01)
Computers in Education

General Information Unit offering the program: Education/Computer Science. Available on either a credit or non-credit basis. Certificate signed by the Dean of Extended Studies.

Program Format Evening, weekend classes offered. Instructional schedule: One evening per week. Program cycle:

Continuous enrollment. Complete program cycle lasts one to two years. Completion of program requires average grade of C or better.

Evaluation Student evaluation based on tests, papers, reports. Grading system: Letters or numbers. Transcripts are kept for each student.

Enrollment Requirements Teaching credential required. Program is open to non-resident foreign students.

Program Costs $750–$1000 for the program, $50–$150 per course.

Housing and Student Services Housing is not available.

Contact Office of Extended Studies, 9001 Stockdale Highway, Bakersfield, CA 93311. 805-833-2208.

LAW (22.01)
Certificate in Attorney Assistantship

General Information Unit offering the program: Political Science. Available for credit. Cosponsored by Local Bar Association. Certificate signed by the Dean of Extended Studies.

Program Format Evening classes offered. Instructional schedule: One evening per week. Program cycle: Continuous enrollment. Complete program cycle lasts 1½ years. Completion of program requires average grade of C or better.

Evaluation Student evaluation based on tests, papers, reports. Grading system: Letters or numbers. Transcripts are kept for each student.

Enrollment Requirements Associate degree or equivalent required. Program is open to non-resident foreign students.

Program Costs $1200 for the program, $100–$150 per course.

Housing and Student Services Housing is not available. Job counseling and placement services are available.

Special Features Instruction comes primarily from local bar association.

Contact Office of Extended Studies, 9001 Stockdale Highway, Bakersfield, CA 93311. 805-833-2208.

MEDICAL LABORATORY TECHNOLOGIES (17.03)
Phlebotomy Certificate Program

General Information Unit offering the program: Clinical Sciences. Program content: Clinical experience in phlebotomy. Available for credit. Endorsed by National Accrediting Agency for Clinical Laboratory Sciences. Certificate signed by the Laboratory Director.

Program Format Daytime classes offered. Instructional schedule: Four hours per day, four days per week. Students enroll in the summer. Full program cycle lasts 9 weeks. Completion of program requires grade of C or better.

Evaluation Student evaluation based on tests, lab practicals. Grading system: Letters or numbers, pass/fail. Transcripts are kept for each student.

Enrollment Requirements Minimum 18 years of age, high school diploma or GED required. Program is open to non-resident foreign students. English language proficiency required.

Program Costs $620 for the program.

Housing and Student Services Housing is not available. Job counseling and placement services are not available.

Special Features Has received accreditation by: NAACLS (National Accrediting Agency for Clinical Laboratory Sciences).

Contact Ms. Landy McBride, Chair, Clinical Sciences, 9001 Stockdale Highway, Bakersfield, CA 93311. 805-833-3143.

NUCEA MEMBER

CALIFORNIA STATE UNIVERSITY, CHICO
Chico, California 95929

ANTHROPOLOGY (45.02)
Certificate in Applied Anthropology: Museology

General Information   Unit offering the program: Anthropology. Program content: Modern museum management, gallery production, public relations, visual and graphic communications, design. Available on either a credit or non-credit basis. Certificate signed by the President of the University. Certificate applicable to B.A., M.A. in Anthropology.

Program Format   Daytime, evening classes offered. Program cycle: Continuous enrollment. Full program cycle lasts 2 semesters. Completion of program requires 26 semester units.

Evaluation   Student evaluation based on papers, museum exhibit, research projects. Transcripts are kept for each student.

Enrollment Requirements   Program is open to non-resident foreign students. English language proficiency required.

Program Costs $245–$377 per semester.

Housing and Student Services   Housing is available. Job counseling and placement services are available.

Special Features   The heart of the program is the Museum of Anthropology. It serves as a showcase for student-curated exhibits and provides an opportunity for practical experience in museum operation. Emphasis is on curatorial research, design, and installation of museum displays. Interdisciplinary courses and an off-campus internship are required.

Contact   Mr. Keith L. Johnson, Director, Museum of Anthropology, Chico, CA 95929. 916-895-6193.

ANTHROPOLOGY (45.02)
Certificate in Applied Cultural Anthropology

General Information   Unit offering the program: Anthropology. Program content: Ethnolinguistics, developing nations, ethnography. Available for credit. Certificate signed by the Dean of Behavioral and Social Sciences.

Program Format   Daytime, evening classes offered. Program cycle: Continuous enrollment. Full program cycle lasts 3 semesters. Completion of program requires internship, average grade of C+ or better.

Evaluation   Student evaluation based on tests, papers, reports. Grading system: Letters or numbers. Transcripts are kept for each student.

Enrollment Requirements   B.A. in Anthropology or coordinator's approval required. Program is open to non-resident foreign students. English language proficiency required. University-administered test.

Program Costs $245–$377 per semester.

Housing and Student Services   Housing is available. Job counseling and placement services are not available.

Contact   Dr. Claire R. Farrer, Coordinator, Applied Cultural Certificate Program, Anthropology Department, 311 Butte Hall, Chico, CA 95929-0400. 916-895-6192.

CITY, COMMUNITY, AND REGIONAL PLANNING (04.03)
Certificate in Cultural Resource Management

General Information   Unit offering the program: Anthropology. Program content: Regulations, procedures, and issues in planning and implementing cultural heritage preservation programs. Available for credit. Certificate signed by the President of the University. Certificate applicable to B.A., M.A. in Anthropology.

Program Format   Daytime, evening, weekend classes offered. Program cycle: Continuous enrollment. Full program cycle lasts 2 years.

Evaluation   Student evaluation based on tests, papers, reports, internship. Grading system: Letters or numbers. Transcripts are kept for each student.

Enrollment Requirements   University admissions required. Program is open to non-resident foreign students. English language proficiency required. Minimum TOEFL score required: 500 for undergraduate students; 550 for graduate students.

Program Costs $245–$377 per semester.

Housing and Student Services   Job counseling and placement services are available.

Special Features   The certificate leads to cultural resource management employment as a private consultant or staff personnel in state, federal, or local agencies in California; primary emphasis on prehistoric archaeological resources with supplementary coverage of historic resources; can be integrated with anthropology B.A. and M.A. programs; on-campus internship provided.

Contact   Dr. Makoto Kowta, Coordinator, Department of Anthropology, Chico, CA 95929. 916-895-6297.

CURRICULUM AND INSTRUCTION (13.03)
Certificate in the Theory and Practice of Basic Writing

General Information   Unit offering the program: Department of English. Program content: Linguistics, tracking composition, literary editing. Available for credit. Certificate signed by the Department Chair. Certificate applicable to M.A. in English.

Program Format   Daytime, evening classes offered. Instructional schedule: Two or three classes per week. Program cycle: Continuous enrollment. Complete program cycle lasts two to four semesters. Completion of program requires seven courses.

Evaluation   Student evaluation based on tests, papers, reports. Grading system: Letters or numbers. Transcripts are kept for each student.

Enrollment Requirements   Bachelor's degree, ENGL 175 or equivalent course (Rhetoric and Writing) required. Program is open to non-resident foreign students. English language proficiency required. Minimum TOEFL score required: 580.

Program Costs $245–$377 per semester.

Housing and Student Services   Housing is not available. Job counseling and placement services are available.

Special Features   A maximum of 6 units of transfer credit may be allowed; a minimum grade point average of 3.0 must be earned; and at least a C must be earned in each course before the certificate is awarded. Students in the M.A. program in English may also complete the certificate. In this case, courses count toward the M.A. and toward the certificate.

Contact   Ms. Karen Hatch, Graduate Adviser, Department of English, College of Humanities and Fine Arts, Chico, CA 95929-0830. 916-895-5289.

HEALTH-RELATED ACTIVITIES (34.01)
Certificate in Exercise Physiology

General Information   Unit offering the program: Department of Physical Education. Program content: Exercise physiology, kinesiology, human performance laboratory, biomechanics, nutrition, sports medicine. Available for credit. Certificate signed by the Dean, College of Education. Certificate applicable to B.A. in Physical Education.

Program Format   Daytime, evening classes offered. Program cycle: Continuous enrollment. Full program cycle lasts 10 courses. Completion of program requires grade of C or better.

Evaluation   Student evaluation based on tests, papers, reports. Grading system: Letters or numbers. Records are kept by College of Education.

Enrollment Requirements   University admissions required. Program is open to non-resident foreign students.

Program Costs $600 for the program.

Housing and Student Services   Housing is not available. Job counseling and placement services are available.

Special Features   Program is professionally staffed with 9 full-time faculty members with expertise in exercise physiology, biomechanics, sports medicine, and related areas. Many of the required courses are taught in a state-of-the-art exercise physiology laboratory with equipment to do computerized measures of important bodily functions, a hydrostatic weighing tank, blood chemical analyzers, and treadmills.

Contact   Dr. Don Lytle, Director of Professional Studies, Department of Physical Education, Chico, CA 95929. 916-895-6373.

INDIVIDUAL AND FAMILY DEVELOPMENT (19.07)
Certificate in Gerontology

General Information   Unit offering the program: Health and Community Services. Program content: Social service for the aging, psychology of aging. Available for credit. Certificate signed by the President. Certificate applicable to B.A. in Community Services.

Program Format   Daytime, evening classes offered. Students may enroll fall, spring. Full program cycle lasts 2 semesters. Completion of program requires 2.5 GPA, 240-hour internship.

Evaluation   Student evaluation based on tests, papers, reports. Grading system: Letters or numbers, pass/fail. Transcripts are kept for each student.

Enrollment Requirements   University admissions required. Program is open to non-resident foreign students.

Program Costs $245–$377 per semester.

Housing and Student Services   Housing is available. Job counseling and placement services are available.

Special Features   Certificate includes core gerontology courses: health and aging, psychology of aging, social gerontology, and elder social services. Includes courses in community mobilization and working with older people. Mandatory internship is 240 total hours working in a community agency. Students from all disciplines are welcome.

Contact   Ms. Armeda F. Ferrini, Ph.D., Chair, Department of Health and Community Services, 607 Butte Hall, Chico, CA 95929. 916-895-6661.

LAW (22.01)
Paralegal

General Information   Unit offering the program: Political Science. Program content: Legal research and analysis, civil rights and liberties, public law. Available for credit. Certificate signed by the President of University. Certificate applicable to B.A. in Political Science, Public Administration, Community Service.

Program Format   Daytime, evening classes offered. Program cycle: Continuous enrollment. Full program cycle lasts 2 semesters. Completion of program requires 26 units, 2.5 GPA.

Evaluation   Student evaluation based on tests, papers. Grading system: Letters or numbers, pass/fail. Transcripts are kept for each student.

Enrollment Requirements   University admissions required. Program is open to non-resident foreign students. Students required to live on campus.

Program Costs $245–$377 per semester.

Housing and Student Services   Housing is available. Job counseling and placement services are available.

Special Features   The Paralegal certificate program is 13 years old and offers sophisticated internships supervised by University faculty. Four full-time faculty members and several attorneys

teach in the program. Upper-division work. Part of regular academic degree program.

Contact   Dr. Teodora De Lorenzo, Coordinator, Public Law, Political Science Department, Chico, CA 95926. 916-895-5301.

LITERATURE, AMERICAN (23.07)
Certificate in Literary Editing and Publishing

General Information   Unit offering the program: Department of English. Program content: Composition, typograph and publication design, graphics, editing, internships. Available for credit. Certificate signed by the Department Chair. Certificate applicable to B.A. in English.

Program Format   Daytime, evening, weekend classes offered. Instructional schedule: Two or three classes per week. Program cycle: Continuous enrollment. Completion of program requires 2.5 GPA, 23–25 units.

Evaluation   Student evaluation based on tests, papers, reports, editing and publishing of literary magazine. Grading system: Letters or numbers. Transcripts are kept for each student.

Enrollment Requirements   Bachelor's degree, 2.5 GPA, faculty permission required. Program is open to non-resident foreign students.

Program Costs $245–$377 per semester.

Housing and Student Services   Housing is not available. Job counseling and placement services are available.

Special Features   An internship with a publication, publisher, or writer is part of the core requirements. The program, although only a few years old, has placed a few of its graduates in publishing houses in San Francisco and New York.

Contact   Dr. Ellen Walker, Coordinator, Literary Editing and Publishing Certificate, Department of English, Chico, CA 95929-0830. 916-895-5165.

PUBLIC ADMINISTRATION (44.04)
Certificate in Public Administration

General Information   Unit offering the program: Political Science. Program content: Local government, political inquiry, organizational theory. Available for credit. Certificate signed by the Coordinator of Public Administration. Certificate applicable to B.A. in Public Administration.

Program Format   Daytime, evening classes offered. Students may enroll fall, spring. Full program cycle lasts 2 years. Completion of program requires 2.0 GPA.

Evaluation   Student evaluation based on tests, papers, reports. Grading system: Letters or numbers. Transcripts are kept for each student.

Enrollment Requirements   High school diploma required. Program is open to non-resident foreign students.

Program Costs $1420 for the program.

Housing and Student Services   Housing is available. Job counseling and placement services are available.

Contact   Dr. Byron M. Jackson, Coordinator of Public Administration, 719 Butte Hall, Chico, CA 95929. 916-895-5737.

TECHNICAL AND BUSINESS WRITING (23.11)
Certificate in Technical Writing

General Information   Unit offering the program: Department of English. Program content: Composition; computer literacy; report, rhetoric, and proposal writing. Available for credit. Certificate signed by the Department Chair. Certificate applicable to B.A. in English.

Program Format   Daytime, evening classes offered. Instructional schedule: Two or three classes per week. Program cycle: Continuous enrollment. Complete program cycle lasts three to four semesters. Completion of program requires 2.5 GPA.

Certificate in Technical Writing continued

Evaluation   Student evaluation based on tests, papers, reports. Grading system: Letters or numbers. Transcripts are kept for each student.

Enrollment Requirements   Program is open to non-resident foreign students.

Program Costs $245–$377 per semester.

Housing and Student Services   Housing is not available. Job counseling and placement services are available.

Special Features   The directors are 7 members of the Society for Technical Communication and regularly attend national conferences to help find jobs for graduates. The faculty sponsors and advises the student chapter of the Society for Technical Communication.

Contact   Dr. Charles Genthe, Coordinator, Technical Writing Certificate, Department of English, College of Humanities and Fine Arts, Chico, CA 95929-0830.

NUCEA MEMBER

CALIFORNIA STATE UNIVERSITY, DOMINGUEZ HILLS
Carson, California 90747

ACCOUNTING, BOOKKEEPING, AND RELATED PROGRAMS (07.01)
Production and Inventory Control Certificate Program

General Information   Unit offering the program: Extended Education, School of Management. Program content: Inventory management, manufacturing resources planning, material requirements planning and purchasing. Available for credit. Cosponsored by Los Angeles Chapter American Production and Inventory Control Society. Certificate signed by the Dean, Extended Education. Certificate applicable to any four-year degree offered at the institution.

Program Format   Evening classes offered. Instructional schedule: Once per week. Program cycle: Continuous enrollment. Full program cycle lasts 4 semesters. Completion of program requires 2.5 GPA.

Evaluation   Student evaluation based on tests. Grading system: Letters or numbers. Transcripts are kept for each student.

Enrollment Requirements   Program is open to non-resident foreign students.

Program Costs $1080 for the program, $216 per course.

Housing and Student Services   Housing is not available. Job counseling and placement services are not available.

Special Features   The program prepares students to pass the test that qualifies them for Certificate in Production and Inventory Control. A series of five practical courses is designed to meet the needs of newcomers to the field and other individuals who work in related areas. A minimum 2.5 grade point average is required.

Contact   Mr. Paul Davis, Program Administrator, 1000 East Victoria Street, Carson, CA 90747. 213-516-3741.

MENTAL HEALTH/HUMAN SERVICES (17.04)
Certificate in Alcoholism/Drug Counseling

General Information   Unit offering the program: Extended Education. Program content: Theories of substance abuse, skills and techniques for counseling. Available for credit. Certificate signed by the Dean, Extended Education. Certificate applicable to any undergraduate degree offered at the institution.

Program Format   Evening classes offered. Instructional schedule: Two evenings per week. Program cycle: Continuous enrollment. Full program cycle lasts 4 semesters. Completion of program requires 400-hour internship.

Evaluation   Student evaluation based on tests, papers, reports, class participation. Grading system: Letters or numbers. Transcripts are kept for each student.

Enrollment Requirements   Two years continuous sobriety; two years of college or experience in human service field required. Program is open to non-resident foreign students.

Program Costs $1584 for the program, $216 per course.

Housing and Student Services   Housing is not available. Job counseling and placement services are not available.

Special Features   This program has been in existence for over ten years, and the certificate is widely recognized by alcoholism treatment centers. The program consists of eight courses designed to prepare individuals to enter the field at a professional level. Minimum cumulative grade point average is 2.5.

Contact   Mr. Paul Davis, Program Administrator, 1000 East Victoria Street, Carson, CA 90747. 213-516-3741.

TEACHER EDUCATION, GENERAL PROGRAMS (13.12)
Early Childhood Certificate Program

General Information   Unit offering the program: Extended Education. Available for credit. Certificate signed by the Dean, Extended Education. Program fulfills requirements for California state licensing for day care and infant care teachers and administrators.

Program Format   Evening classes offered. Instructional schedule: Once per week. Program cycle: Continuous enrollment. Full program cycle lasts 3 semesters.

Evaluation   Student evaluation based on tests, papers, projects, class participation. Grading system: Letters or numbers. Transcripts are kept for each student.

Enrollment Requirements   Program is open to non-resident foreign students.

Program Costs $864–$1080 for the program, $216 per course.

Housing and Student Services   Housing is not available. Job counseling and placement services are not available.

Special Features   All of the program's classes meet in Redondo Beach and offer upper-division degree-applicable academic credit. Option I is for those interested in a teaching permit, and Option II is for those interested in a supervisory permit. Both options offer specialization in either infant or child care.

Contact   Ms. Jennifer Peisch, Coordinator, 1000 East Victoria Street, Carson, CA 90747. 213-516-3741.

NUCEA MEMBER

CALIFORNIA STATE UNIVERSITY, HAYWARD
Hayward, California 94542

CURRICULUM AND INSTRUCTION (13.03)
Microcomputers in Education Certificate Program

General Information   Unit offering the program: Teacher Education, Mathematics, Computer Science. Program content: Developing computer curriculum to instruct students. Available for credit. Certificate signed by the Associate Vice President.

Program Format   Evening classes offered. Instructional schedule: One evening per week. Program cycle: Continuous enrollment. Full program cycle lasts 12 months. Completion of program requires five courses, grade of C or better in each course.

Evaluation   Student evaluation based on tests, projects. Grading system: Letters or numbers. Transcripts are kept for each student.

Enrollment Requirements Program is open to non-resident foreign students.

Program Costs $175 per course.

Housing and Student Services Housing is available. Job counseling and placement services are available.

Special Features As society moves rapidly ahead into the information age, the microcomputer becomes more and more the tool used to understand, analyze, and manipulate the banks of data being generated. Young members of society are expecting, as well as being expected, to begin to use these tools in school. This program was designed to help educators meet these needs in the classrooms.

Contact Mr. Terence Ahern, Program Developer, 25800 Carlos Bee Boulevard, Hayward, CA 94542-3012. 415-881-4076.

LAW (22.01)
Paralegal Certificate Program

General Information Unit offering the program: Political Science, English. Available for credit. Certificate signed by the Associate Vice President.

Program Format Evening classes offered. Instructional schedule: One evening per week. Program cycle: Continuous enrollment. Full program cycle lasts 18 months. Completion of program requires ten courses, grade of C or better in each course.

Evaluation Student evaluation based on tests, papers, reports. Grading system: Letters or numbers. Transcripts are kept for each student.

Enrollment Requirements Eighty-four quarter or 56 semester units required. Program is open to non-resident foreign students.

Program Costs $144 per course.

Housing and Student Services Housing is not available. Job counseling and placement services are available.

Special Features The program prepares students for employment in the public and private sectors of the law profession, the business world (banking, real estate, and insurance), corporate organizations, and administrative agencies. It provides paralegals with a basic understanding of areas of law as well as the actual job responsibilities they will encounter in the profession.

Contact Ms. Carol Mintz, Program Developer, 25800 Carlos Bee Boulevard, Hayward, CA 94546-3012. 415-881-4089.

MENTAL HEALTH/HUMAN SERVICES (17.04)
Certificate in Chemical Dependency

General Information Unit offering the program: Educational Psychology. Available for credit. Certificate signed by the Associate Vice President.

Program Format Evening, weekend classes offered. Program cycle: Continuous enrollment. Full program cycle lasts 9 months. Completion of program requires ten courses, grade of C or better in each course.

Evaluation Student evaluation based on tests, papers, reports. Grading system: Letters or numbers. Transcripts are kept for each student.

Enrollment Requirements Bachelor's degree required. Program is open to non-resident foreign students.

Program Costs $52 per unit.

Housing and Student Services Housing is not available. Job counseling and placement services are available.

Special Features This certificate is designed for individuals interested in obtaining specialized theoretical knowledge and technical skills in order to work with those who have problems with alcohol and other addictive substances. The program is not only for practitioners with little formal training who are interested in the field but also for those with clinical degrees who wish to add skills in this specialized area.

Contact Mr. Terence Ahern, Program Developer, 25800 Carlos Bee Boulevard, Hayward, CA 94542-3012. 415-881-4076.

REAL ESTATE (06.17)
Real Estate Development Certificate Program (Advanced)

General Information Unit offering the program: Management Sciences. Program content: Training for broker's license. Available for credit. Certificate signed by the Associate Vice President.

Program Format Evening classes offered. Instructional schedule: One evening per week. Program cycle: Continuous enrollment. Full program cycle lasts 9 months. Completion of program requires five courses, grade of C or better in each course.

Evaluation Student evaluation based on tests. Grading system: Letters or numbers. Transcripts are kept for each student.

Enrollment Requirements Real estate sales license and two years experience in real estate or a bachelor's degree required. Program is open to non-resident foreign students.

Program Costs $216 per course.

Housing and Student Services Housing is not available. Job counseling and placement services are available.

Special Features This program provides a series of specialized courses for those who wish to sit for the real estate broker's license exam. The courses are theoretically based but presented in practical formats in order to assist the real estate professional to become more knowledgeable and skillful in the field.

Contact Ms. Carol Mintz, Program Developer, 25800 Carlos Bee Boulevard, Hayward, CA 94546-3012. 415-881-4089.

REAL ESTATE (06.17)
Real Estate Development Certificate Program (Basic)

General Information Unit offering the program: Management Sciences. Program content: Training for sales license. Available for credit. Certificate signed by the Associate Vice President.

Program Format Evening classes offered. Instructional schedule: One evening per week. Full program cycle lasts 6 months. Completion of program requires three courses, grade of C or better in each course.

Evaluation Student evaluation based on tests. Grading system: Letters or numbers. Transcripts are kept for each student.

Enrollment Requirements Eighty-four quarter or 56 semester units, or experience in real estate required. Program is open to non-resident foreign students.

Program Costs $48 per unit.

Housing and Student Services Housing is not available. Job counseling and placement services are available.

Special Features This program provides a series of specialized courses for those who wish to sit for the real estate salesperson license exam. The courses are theoretically based but presented in practical formats in order to assist the real estate professional to become more knowledgeable and skillful in the field.

Contact Ms. Carol Mintz, Program Developer, 25800 Carlos Bee Boulevard, Hayward, CA 94542-3012. 415-881-4089.

TEACHER EDUCATION, SPECIFIC SUBJECT AREAS (13.13)
Certificate Program for Teachers of Gifted and Talented

General Information Unit offering the program: Teacher Education. Available for credit. Certificate signed by the Associate Vice Presient.

Program Format Evening, weekend classes offered. Program cycle: Continuous enrollment. Full program cycle lasts 12 months. Completion of program requires grade of C or better in each course.

Certificate Program for Teachers of Gifted and Talented continued

Evaluation   Student evaluation based on tests, papers. Grading system: Letters or numbers. Transcripts are kept for each student.

Enrollment Requirements   Program is open to non-resident foreign students.

Program Costs $48 per unit.

Housing and Student Services   Housing is not available. Job counseling and placement services are available.

Special Features   This certificate program will help teachers at the elementary and secondary levels to plan gifted and talented programs, carry out a valid analysis of varying viewpoints, evaluate the effectiveness of a program, work with parents and other community resources, and serve as a resource to their school and district.

Contact   Mr. Terence Ahern, Program Developer, 25800 Carlos Bee Boulevard, Hayward, CA 94542-3012. 415-881-4076.

TEACHER EDUCATION, SPECIFIC SUBJECT AREAS (13.13)
Certificate Program in Early Childhood Education Studies (Advanced)

General Information   Unit offering the program: Teacher Education. Available for credit. Certificate signed by the Associate Vice President.

Program Format   Evening, weekend classes offered. Program cycle: Continuous enrollment. Full program cycle lasts 12 months. Completion of program requires 15 quarter units, grade of C or better in each course.

Evaluation   Student evaluation based on tests, papers, reports. Grading system: Letters or numbers. Transcripts are kept for each student.

Enrollment Requirements   Program is open to non-resident foreign students.

Program Costs $48 per unit.

Housing and Student Services   Housing is not available. Job counseling and placement services are available.

Special Features   A new 'boom' is being created as mothers return to the work force in greater and greater numbers. There is a growing need for educated personnel who can provide superior child care. The courses in this program were designed for the concerned parent, preschool teacher, aid, or administrator in a child-care environment.

Contact   Mr. Terence Ahern, Program Developer, 25800 Carlos Bee Boulevard, Hayward, CA 94542-3012. 415-881-4076.

TEACHER EDUCATION, SPECIFIC SUBJECT AREAS (13.13)
Certificate Program in Early Childhood Education Studies (Basic)

General Information   Unit offering the program: Teacher Education. Available for credit. Certificate signed by the Associate Vice President.

Program Format   Evening, weekend classes offered. Program cycle: Continuous enrollment. Full program cycle lasts 12 months. Completion of program requires five courses, grade of C or better in each course.

Evaluation   Student evaluation based on tests, papers, reports. Grading system: Letters or numbers. Transcripts are kept for each student.

Enrollment Requirements   Program is open to non-resident foreign students.

Program Costs $48 per unit.

Housing and Student Services   Housing is not available. Job counseling and placement services are available.

Special Features   A new 'boom' is being created as mothers return to the work force in greater and greater numbers. There is a growing need for educated personnel who can provide superior child care. The courses in this program were designed for the concerned parent, preschool teacher, aide, or administrator in a child-care environment.

Contact   Mr. Terence Ahern, Program Developer, 25800 Carlos Bee Boulevard, Hayward, CA 94542-3012. 415-881-4076.

NUCEA MEMBER
CALIFORNIA STATE UNIVERSITY, LONG BEACH
Long Beach, California 90840

BUSINESS AND MANAGEMENT, GENERAL (06.01)
Executive Management Certificate

General Information   Unit offering the program: University Extension Services. Available on a non-credit basis. Certificate signed by the Director, Extension Services.

Program Format   Daytime, evening classes offered. Instructional schedule: Twice per week. Program cycle: Continuous enrollment. Full program cycle lasts 2 semesters.

Evaluation   Student evaluation based on project. Record of completion kept by National Registry of Continuing Education.

Enrollment Requirements   Five years management experience required. Program is open to non-resident foreign students.

Program Costs $625 for the program.

Housing and Student Services   Housing is not available. Job counseling and placement services are available.

Contact   Ms. Lynn Henricks, Director, Extension Services, 1250 Bellflower Boulevard, Long Beach, CA 90840. 714-498-5561.

BUSINESS AND MANAGEMENT, GENERAL (06.01)
Meeting Planners Certificate

General Information   Unit offering the program: University Extension Services. Program content: Resources and references used in planning meetings. Available on a non-credit basis. Certificate signed by the Director, Extension Services.

Program Format   Daytime, evening classes offered. Instructional schedule: Once per week. Full program cycle lasts 1 semester.

Evaluation   Student evaluation based on project. Record of completion kept by National Registry of Continuing Education.

Enrollment Requirements   High school diploma required. Program is open to non-resident foreign students.

Program Costs $55–$95 per course.

Housing and Student Services   Housing is not available. Job counseling and placement services are available.

Contact   Ms. Lynn Henricks, Director, 1250 Bellflower Boulevard, Long Beach, CA 90840. 213-498-8455.

BUSINESS AND MANAGEMENT, GENERAL (06.01)
Organizational Communications Certificate

General Information   Unit offering the program: University Extension Services. Available on a non-credit basis. Certificate signed by the Director, Extension Services.

Program Format   Daytime, evening, weekend classes offered. Instructional schedule: Twice per week or weekends. Program cycle: Continuous enrollment. Full program cycle lasts 1 semester.

Evaluation Student evaluation based on project. Record of completion kept by National Registry of Continuing Education.

Enrollment Requirements High school diploma required. Program is open to non-resident foreign students.

Program Costs $495 for the program.

Housing and Student Services Housing is not available. Job counseling and placement services are available.

Contact Ms. Lynn Henricks, Director, 1250 Bellflower Boulevard, Long Beach, CA 90840. 213-498-8455.

BUSINESS AND MANAGEMENT, GENERAL (06.01)
Supervision Certificate

General Information Unit offering the program: University Extension Services. Program content: Skills to be an effective manager/supervisor. Available on a non-credit basis. Certificate signed by the Director, Extension Services.

Program Format Daytime, evening classes offered. Instructional schedule: Twice per week. Program cycle: Continuous enrollment. Full program cycle lasts 1 semester.

Evaluation Student evaluation based on projects. Record of completion kept by National Registry of Continuing Education.

Enrollment Requirements High school diploma required. Program is open to non-resident foreign students.

Program Costs $495 for the program.

Housing and Student Services Housing is not available. Job counseling and placement services are available.

Contact Ms. Lynn Henricks, Director, 1250 Bellflower Boulevard, Long Beach, CA 90840. 213-498-8455.

CHILD CARE AND GUIDANCE MANAGEMENT AND SERVICES (20.02)
Child Development Certificate

General Information Unit offering the program: University Extension Services. Program content: Guidance techniques, operating and evaluating a child care program. Available for credit. Certificate signed by the Director, Extension Services.

Program Format Daytime, evening classes offered. Students enroll in January. Full program cycle lasts 3 months.

Evaluation Student evaluation based on tests, projects. Grading system: Letters or numbers. Transcripts are kept for each student.

Enrollment Requirements High school diploma required. Program is open to non-resident foreign students.

Program Costs $495 for the program.

Housing and Student Services Housing is not available. Job counseling and placement services are available.

Contact Ms. Christie Dodson, Program Administrator, Extension Services, 1250 Bellflower Boulevard, Long Beach, CA 90840. 213-498-5561.

HEALTH SERVICES ADMINISTRATION (18.07)
Nursing Management Certificate

General Information Unit offering the program: University Extension Services. Program content: Managing people, responsibilities, and budgets. Available on a non-credit basis. Certificate signed by the Director, Extension Services.

Program Format Evening classes offered. Instructional schedule: Two evenings per week for three hours. Program cycle: Continuous enrollment. Full program cycle lasts 1 semester.

Evaluation Student evaluation based on project. Record of completion kept by National Registry of Continuing Education.

Enrollment Requirements High school diploma required. Program is open to non-resident foreign students.

Program Costs $295 for the program.

Housing and Student Services Housing is not available. Job counseling and placement services are available.

Contact Mr. Steve Mirenda, Program Administrator, Extension Services, 1250 Bellflower Boulevard, Long Beach, CA 90840. 213-498-8455.

HUMAN RESOURCES DEVELOPMENT (06.06)
Human Resource Development Certificate

General Information Unit offering the program: University Extension Services. Program content: Awareness, knowledge, and skills for developing a human resource program. Available on a non-credit basis. Certificate signed by the Director, Extension Services.

Program Format Daytime classes offered. Instructional schedule: 9 a.m. to 4 p.m., Thursdays. Program cycle: Continuous enrollment. Full program cycle lasts 1 semester.

Evaluation Student evaluation based on project. Record of completion kept by National Registry of Continuing Education.

Enrollment Requirements High school diploma required. Program is open to non-resident foreign students.

Program Costs $395 for the program.

Housing and Student Services Housing is not available. Job counseling and placement services are available.

Contact Ms. Lynn Henricks, Director, 1250 Bellflower Boulevard, Long Beach, CA 90840. 213-498-8455.

LAW (22.01)
Legal Assistant Certificate

General Information Unit offering the program: University Extension Services. Program content: Research, investigation, interviewing clients, drafting legal memoranda, pleadings, briefs. Available for credit. Certificate signed by the Director, Extension Services.

Program Format Evening classes offered. Students enroll in February. Full program cycle lasts 4 months.

Evaluation Student evaluation based on tests, projects. Grading system: Letters or numbers. Transcripts are kept for each student.

Enrollment Requirements High school diploma required. Program is open to non-resident foreign students.

Program Costs $72–$154 per course.

Housing and Student Services Housing is not available. Job counseling and placement services are available.

Contact Mr. Steve Mirenda, Program Administrator, Extension Services, 1250 Bellflower Boulevard, Long Beach, CA 90840. 213-498-5561.

MICROCOMPUTER APPLICATIONS (11.06)
Computer Excellence Certificate

General Information Unit offering the program: University Extension Services. Program content: Microcomputer usage. Available on a non-credit basis. Certificate signed by the Director, Extension Services.

Program Format Daytime, evening, weekend classes offered. Program cycle: Continuous enrollment. Full program cycle lasts 1 semester.

Evaluation Student evaluation based on projects. Grading system: Letters or numbers. Record of completion kept by National Registry of Continuing Education.

Enrollment Requirements High school diploma required. Program is open to non-resident foreign students.

Program Costs $750 for the program.

Housing and Student Services Housing is not available. Job counseling and placement services are available.

Contact Ms. Lynn Henricks, Director, Extension Services, 1250 Bellflower Boulevard, Long Beach, CA 90840. 714-498-5561.

PERSONNEL AND TRAINING PROGRAMS (07.05)
Training Certificate

General Information Unit offering the program: University Extension Services. Program content: Budgeting and evaluating, training programs. Available on a non-credit basis. Certificate signed by the Director, Extension Services.

Program Format Daytime, evening classes offered. Instructional schedule: Twice per week. Program cycle: Continuous enrollment. Full program cycle lasts 1 semester.

Evaluation Student evaluation based on design, development, and presentation of a training module. Record of completion kept by National Registry of Continuing Education.

Enrollment Requirements High school diploma required. Program is open to non-resident foreign students.

Program Costs $455 for the program.

Housing and Student Services Housing is not available. Job counseling and placement services are available.

Contact Ms. Lynn Henricks, Director, Extension Services, 1250 Bellflower Boulevard, Long Beach, CA 90840. 213-498-5561.

TEACHER EDUCATION, SPECIFIC SUBJECT AREAS (13.13)
Computers in Education Certificate

General Information Unit offering the program: University Extension Services. Program content: Computer applications in elementary and secondary levels. Available for credit. Certificate signed by the Director, Extension Services.

Program Format Daytime, evening, weekend classes offered. Students enroll in January. Full program cycle lasts 1 semester.

Evaluation Student evaluation based on tests, projects. Grading system: Letters or numbers. Transcripts are kept for each student.

Enrollment Requirements High school diploma required. Program is open to non-resident foreign students.

Program Costs $432 for the program.

Housing and Student Services Housing is not available. Job counseling and placement services are available.

Contact Ms. Lynn Henricks, Director, Extension Services, 1250 Bellflower Boulevard, Long Beach, CA 90840. 213-498-5561.

VISUAL AND PERFORMING ARTS, GENERAL (50.01)
Calligraphy Certificate Program

General Information Unit offering the program: University Extension Services. Available for credit. Certificate signed by the Director, Extension Services.

Program Format Daytime, evening, weekend classes offered. Students enroll in January. Full program cycle lasts 1 semester.

Evaluation Student evaluation based on tests, projects. Grading system: Letters or numbers. Transcripts are kept for each student.

Enrollment Requirements Program is open to non-resident foreign students.

Program Costs $144 for the program.

Housing and Student Services Housing is not available. Job counseling and placement services are available.

Contact Ms. Christie Dodson, Program Administrator, Extension Services, 1250 Bellflower Boulevard, Long Beach, CA 90840. 213-498-5561.

WOMEN'S STUDIES (30.07)
Women at Work Certificate Program

General Information Unit offering the program: University Extension Services. Program content: Concerns of contemporary working women. Available on a non-credit basis. Certificate signed by the Director, Extension Services.

Program Format Weekend classes offered. Instructional schedule: 8 a.m. to 1 p.m., Saturdays. Completion of program requires 14 courses.

Evaluation Student evaluation based on projects. Grading system: Pass/fail. Record of completion kept by National Registry of Continuing Education.

Enrollment Requirements High school diploma required. Program is open to non-resident foreign students.

Program Costs $275 for the program.

Housing and Student Services Housing is not available. Job counseling and placement services are available.

Contact Ms. Christie Dodson, Program Administrator, Extension Services, 1250 Bellflower Boulevard, Long Beach, CA 90840. 213-498-8455.

NUCEA MEMBER
CALIFORNIA STATE UNIVERSITY, LOS ANGELES
Los Angeles, California 90032

COMPUTER PROGRAMMING (11.02)
Business Computer Programming

General Information Unit offering the program: Office of Continuing Education, Information Systems Department. Program content: COBOL, systems analysis methods, distributed processing. Available for credit. Certificate signed by the President. Certificate applicable to B.S. in Business Administration.

Program Format Evening, weekend classes offered. Instructional schedule: Once per week for four hours. Quarterly enrollment. Full program cycle lasts 21 months. Completion of program requires 28 quarter units, 2.5 GPA.

Evaluation Student evaluation based on tests. Grading system: Letters or numbers. Transcripts are kept for each student.

Enrollment Requirements Program is open to non-resident foreign students.

Program Costs $1330 for the program, $180–$190 per course.

Housing and Student Services Housing is not available. Job counseling and placement services are not available.

Special Features Program began in the winter of 1982 with 2 instructors and now employs 10 instructors who are programming analysts and computer consultants. Each year, 20 to 50 students are awarded certificates. The majority of the students in the program are from the data-processing industry.

Contact Office of Continuing Education, 5151 State University Drive, Los Angeles, CA 90032. 213-224-3501.

DIAGNOSTIC AND TREATMENT SERVICES (17.02)
Pulmonary Physiology and Technology Certificate Program

General Information Unit offering the program: Office of Continuing Education. Available on a non-credit basis. Cosponsored by Los Angeles County/University of Southern California Medical Center. Certificate signed by the Dean of Continuing Education.

Program Format Evening classes offered. Instructional schedule: Once per week for 3½ hours, labs by arrangement. Quarterly enrollment. Full program cycle lasts 1 year. Completion of program requires 25 units.

Evaluation Student evaluation based on reports, projects. Grading system: Letters or numbers. Transcripts are kept for each student.

Enrollment Requirements One year of college including life science, mathematics, and chemistry courses or equivalent work experience requireed. Program is open to non-resident foreign students.

Program Costs $1500 for the program, $150 per course.

Housing and Student Services Housing is not available. Job counseling and placement services are available.

Special Features Program employs medical doctor and pulmonary physiology lab systems specialist as instructors. Consideration given to applicants with high school diploma and two years of full-time experience in health-care field. Primary audience will be health-care professionals, including respiratory therapists, nurses, physicians, and lab technicians as well as persons from the fields of biology, biochemistry, or biomedical engineering.

Contact Mr. John Hauge, Pulmonary Physiology Lab System Specialist, 1200 North State Street, Room 11721A, LAC/USC Medical Center, Los Angeles, CA 90033. 213-226-7391.

ENTREPRENEURSHIP (08.03)
Certification in Entrepreneurship

General Information Unit offering the program: Office of Continuing Education, Department of Marketing. Program content: Accounting, finance, marketing. Available for credit. Certificate signed by the President. Certificate applicable to B.S. in Business Administration.

Program Format Daytime, evening classes offered. Instructional schedule: Once per week for four hours. Quarterly enrollment. Full program cycle lasts 1 year. Completion of program requires 24 quarter units, grade of C or better in each course.

Evaluation Student evaluation based on tests, papers, reports. Grading system: Letters or numbers. Transcripts are kept for each student.

Enrollment Requirements Program is open to non-resident foreign students.

Program Costs $1080 for the program, $180 per course.

Housing and Student Services Housing is not available. Job counseling and placement services are not available.

Special Features Program designed to prepare students and business people for careers in small companies: starting companies and managing and working in small businesses. Includes instruction on taking a product or service from idea stage through introduction and growth stages and successfully managing the business. Focus on retail marketing of services and products, consulting, accounting, finance, or entrepreneurship.

Contact Dr. Marshall E. Reddick, Professor, Department of Marketing, 5151 State University Drive, Los Angeles, CA 90032. 213-224-4379.

GENERAL MARKETING (08.07)
Certificate Program in Marketing

General Information Unit offering the program: Office of Continuing Education, Department of Marketing. Available for credit. Certificate signed by the President.

Program Format Daytime, evening classes offered. Instructional schedule: Once or twice per week. Quarterly enrollment. Full program cycle lasts 1 year. Completion of program requires 24 quarter units.

Evaluation Student evaluation based on tests. Grading system: Letters or numbers. Transcripts are kept for each student.

Enrollment Requirements Program is open to non-resident foreign students.

Program Costs $720 for the program, $180 per course.

Housing and Student Services Housing is not available. Job counseling and placement services are not available.

Special Features Program prepares non-marketing option business students and non-business students for employment in marketing. It also provides working and professional people with the marketing knowledge necessary for rapid career advancement.

Contact Dr. Henry S. Ang, Professor, Marketing, 5151 State University Drive, Los Angeles, CA 90032. 213-224-2820.

INDUSTRIAL PRODUCTION TECHNOLOGIES (15.06)
Production and Inventory Control

General Information Unit offering the program: Office of Continuing Education. Program content: Manufacturing resource planning, just-in-time total quality control techniques. Available on a non-credit basis. Cosponsored by American Production and Inventory Control Society (APICS). Certificate signed by the Dean of Continuing Education.

Program Format Evening classes offered. Instructional schedule: Once per week for 3½ hours. Students may enroll fall, winter, spring. Complete program cycle lasts up to two years. Completion of program requires six courses, 2.5 GPA.

Evaluation Student evaluation based on tests, reports. Grading system: Letters or numbers. Transcripts are kept for each student.

Enrollment Requirements High school diploma; college-level algebra, mathematics, general education courses required. Program is open to non-resident foreign students.

Program Costs $1808 for the program, $180 per course.

Housing and Student Services Housing is not available. Job counseling and placement services are not available.

Special Features The application of successful production and inventory control principles has made significant impact on many manufacturing companies, resulting in increased profitability, improvement in quality, and more efficient time delivery. Faculty credentials include a baccalaureate degree with a master's degree in an appropriate field, five years of professional experience in the materials field, and the Certified Production Inventory Manager (CPIM) designation.

Contact Dr. Michael Abell, Program Coordinator, 11263 Bertha Street, Cerritos, CA 90701. 714-229-5106.

INTERNATIONAL BUSINESS MANAGEMENT (06.09)
International Business Certificate Program

General Information Unit offering the program: Department of Marketing, Office of Continuing Education, World Trade Education Center. Program content: Finance, management, marketing. Available for credit. Certificate signed by the President. Certificate applicable to B.S. in Business Administration.

Program Format Daytime, evening classes offered. Instructional schedule: Once per week for four hours. Quarterly enrollment. Full program cycle lasts 1 year. Completion of program requires 24 quarter units.

Evaluation Student evaluation based on tests, papers, reports. Grading system: Letters or numbers. Transcripts are kept for each student.

Enrollment Requirements Program is open to non-resident foreign students.

Program Costs $1080 for the program, $180 per course.

Housing and Student Services Housing is not available. Job counseling and placement services are available.

Special Features Annual foreign travel/study tour to visit business firms and public institutions to acquaint students with practices and methods of conducting business in foreign countries and current trends in globalization of all economics.

Contact Dr. M. David Oh, Director of the World Trade Education Center, 5151 State University Drive, Los Angeles, CA 90032. 213-224-2830.

LAW (22.01)
Legal Assistant Certificate Program

General Information   Unit offering the program: Department of Finance and Law, Office of Continuing Education. Available on a non-credit basis. Endorsed by American Bar Association. Certificate signed by the President.

Program Format   Evening classes offered. Instructional schedule: Once per week for 3½ hours. Quarterly enrollment. Full program cycle lasts 1 year. Completion of program requires 32 quarter units of paralegal courses and 58 quarter units of general education and law-related courses, internship.

Evaluation   Student evaluation based on tests, papers, project. Grading system: Letters or numbers. Transcripts are kept for each student.

Enrollment Requirements   High school diploma or equivalent required. Program is open to non-resident foreign students.

Program Costs $1520 for the program, $190 per course.

Housing and Student Services   Housing is not available. Job counseling and placement services are available.

Special Features   The CPLA is a year-round, evening, nondegree credit program taught by lawyers. Fully approved by the ABA since 1978, the program is comprehensive yet flexible enough to accommodate both novices wishing to explore the history, concept, and practice of paralegalism and professionals seeking to upgrade their skills and careers.

Contact   Dr. Udo Heyn, Program Coordinator, CPLA, History Department, 5151 State University Drive, Los Angeles, CA 90032. 213-224-3856.

LAW (22.01)
Legal Interpretation and Translation: English/Spanish

General Information   Unit offering the program: Department of Foreign Languages and Literature, Office of Continuing Education. Program content: Interpreting in criminal actions, civil actions, state administrative hearings; consecutive and simultaneous interpreting techniques. Available on a non-credit basis. Certificate signed by the Dean of Continuing Education.

Program Format   Weekend classes offered. Instructional schedule: Once per week for four hours. Quarterly enrollment. Full program cycle lasts 1 year. Completion of program requires four courses.

Evaluation   Student evaluation based on tests. Grading system: Pass/fail. Transcripts are kept for each student.

Enrollment Requirements   Oral and written examination to verify bilingual and biliterate fluency in both Spanish and English required. Program is open to non-resident foreign students. English language proficiency required.

Program Costs $760 for the program, $190 per course.

Housing and Student Services   Housing is not available. Job counseling and placement services are not available.

Special Features   Program designed to prepare students for county, state, and federal examinations required for employment and to develop skills necessary for satisfactory performance as an interpreter. Program employs 3 instructors who are bilingual and certified to interpret in state and superior courts.

Contact   Ms. Gloria Ramirez, Coordinator, 3117 Sky Court, Simi Valley, CA 93063. 818-356-5259.

LIBRARY ASSISTING (25.03)
Library Technician Certificate Program

General Information   Unit offering the program: School of Education, Office of Continuing Education, Library Services Credential Program. Available on a non-credit basis. Certificate signed by the Dean of Continuing Education.

Program Format   Daytime, evening, weekend classes offered. Instructional schedule: Once per week for four hours. Quarterly enrollment. Full program cycle lasts 1 year. Completion of program requires 24 quarter units, internship.

Evaluation   Student evaluation based on tests. Grading system: Pass/fail. Transcripts are kept for each student.

Enrollment Requirements   High school diploma or equivalent, typing skills (30 words per minute) required. Program is open to non-resident foreign students.

Program Costs $1080 for the program, $135 per course.

Housing and Student Services   Housing is not available. Job counseling and placement services are not available.

Special Features   Program employs 3 to 5 librarians as instructors. Local libraries have been involved with the development of the curriculum, and the classes reflect current practices in the field.

Contact   Dr. Marilyn W. Greenburg, Professor, Division of Curriculum and Instruction, 5151 State University Drive, Los Angeles, CA 90032. 213-224-3762.

MICROCOMPUTER APPLICATIONS (11.06)
Office Systems

General Information   Unit offering the program: Office of Continuing Education, Department of Office Systems and Business Education. Program content: Research and report writing, software applications, human resources. Available for credit. Certificate signed by the President.

Program Format   Daytime, evening classes offered. Instructional schedule: Once or twice per week. Quarterly enrollment. Full program cycle lasts 1 year. Completion of program requires 26 quarter units, 3.0 GPA.

Evaluation   Student evaluation based on tests. Grading system: Letters or numbers. Transcripts are kept for each student.

Enrollment Requirements   Bachelor's degree, completion of Office Organization and Management course or equivalent experience required. Program is open to non-resident foreign students.

Program Costs $1080 for the program, $135–$180 per course.

Housing and Student Services   Housing is not available. Job counseling and placement services are not available.

Special Features   Certificate program provides up-to-date preparation in management of state-of-the-art automated office technology. Study of such office systems as integrated and stand-alone software packages in word processing, electronic spreadsheets, database management systems, telecommunications, and graphics is included. Students learn to master Lotus 1-2-3, WordPerfect, dBase III Plus, and Enable.

Contact   Dr. Ralph Spanswick, Professor, Office Systems and Business Education, 5151 State University Drive, Los Angeles, CA 90032. 213-224-2908.

TEACHER EDUCATION, SPECIFIC SUBJECT AREAS (13.13)
Teaching Microcomputer Business Application

General Information   Unit offering the program: Office of Continuing Education, Department of Office Systems and Business Education. Available for credit. Certificate signed by the President.

Program Format   Daytime, evening classes offered. Instructional schedule: Once or twice per week. Quarterly enrollment. Full program cycle lasts 1 year. Completion of program requires seven courses, 2.5 GPA.

Evaluation   Student evaluation based on tests. Grading system: Letters or numbers. Transcripts are kept for each student.

Enrollment Requirements   Program is open to non-resident foreign students.

Program Costs $1125 for the program, $135–$180 per course.

Housing and Student Services   Housing is not available. Job counseling and placement services are not available.

Special Features Program designed for teachers and trainers in education and industry responsible for teaching students and employees widely used microcomputer business applications. Opportunity to learn integrated and stand-alone software packages in word processing, electronic spreadsheets, database management systems, telecommunications, and graphics. Programs widely used in the business community (Lotus 1-2-3, Enable, WordPerfect, and dBase III Plus) are covered.

Contact Dr. Ralph Spanswick, Professor, Office Systems and Business Education, 5151 University Drive, Los Angeles, CA 90032. 213-224-2908.

NUCEA MEMBER
CALIFORNIA STATE UNIVERSITY, SACRAMENTO
Sacramento, California 95819

COMPUTER AND INFORMATION SCIENCES, GENERAL (11.01)
Computer Science Certificate Program— Levels I, II, and III

General Information Unit offering the program: Computer Science Department. Program content: Use and programming of computers. Available on either a credit or non-credit basis. Endorsed by Association for Computer Sciences. Certificate signed by the Dean of Extended Learning. Certificate applicable to B.S. in Computer Science.

Program Format Evening classes offered. Instructional schedule: Three hours per week. Quarterly enrollment. Completion of program requires grade of C or better, 6 courses (Level I), 9 courses (Level II), 12 courses (Level III).

Evaluation Student evaluation based on tests, papers, reports, programming assignments. Grading system: Letters or numbers. Transcripts are kept for each student.

Enrollment Requirements Program is open to non-resident foreign students.

Program Costs $150–$195 per course.

Housing and Student Services Housing is not available. Job counseling and placement services are available.

Special Features The Certificate Programs in Computer Science may be completed under four different orientations: Data Processing Applications, Educational Applications, Scientific Applications, and Microcomputer Applications. Completion of Level III by students who have a baccalaureate degree with an adequate mathematics background may enable them to meet admissions requirements for the M.S. in Computer Science program at CSUS.

Contact Mr. James W. Kho, Ph.D., Chair, Computer Science Department, 6000 J Street, Sacramento, CA 95819. 916-278-6834.

MENTAL HEALTH/HUMAN SERVICES (17.04)
Chemical Dependency Studies—Alcoholism Certificate Program

General Information Unit offering the program: Extended Learning Programs. Program content: Prevention, intervention, treatment, recovery, relapse prevention, counseling. Available for credit. Endorsed by California Association of Alcohol and Drug Abuse Counselors. Certificate signed by the Dean of Extended Learning. Certificate applicable to M.A., M.S. in Psychology; M.S.W. Program fulfills requirements for California Alcoholism Counselor (CAC).

Program Format Daytime, evening, weekend classes offered. Program cycle: Continuous enrollment. Full program cycle lasts 11 months. Completion of program requires 24 units.

Evaluation Student evaluation based on tests, papers, reports, group work, dyads. Grading system: Letters or numbers, pass/fail. Transcripts are kept for each student.

Enrollment Requirements Program is open to non-resident foreign students.

Program Costs $1680 for the program, $70 per unit.

Housing and Student Services Housing is not available. Job counseling and placement services are available.

Special Features The program's focus is on alcoholism. Participants are professionals in contact with clients who are chemically dependent, chemically dependent people in recovery, co-dependents, and those who wish to learn more about substance abuse and treatment. Issues of prevention, intervention, treatment, recovery, and relapse prevention are addressed. Faculty are selected from both the University and working professionals. Most have a master's degree.

Contact Ms. Jeanette Meeker, Extended Learning Programs, 650 University Avenue, Suite 101A, Sacramento, CA 95825. 916-923-0441.

STUDENT COUNSELING AND PERSONNEL SERVICES (13.11)
Career Development Certificate Program

General Information Unit offering the program: Office of Extended Learning Programs, School of Education. Program content: Personality development, career life planning, group career development. Available for credit. Certificate signed by the Dean of Extended Learning. Certificate applicable to M.A. in Psychology. Program fulfills requirements for recertification contact hours for the National Board for Certified Counselors.

Program Format Evening, weekend classes offered. Program cycle: Continuous enrollment. Full program cycle lasts 3 semesters. Completion of program requires 15 semester units.

Evaluation Student evaluation based on tests, papers, reports. Grading system: Letters or numbers. Transcripts are kept for each student.

Enrollment Requirements Bachelor's degree and two years related experience, or permission of program coordinator required. Program is open to non-resident foreign students.

Program Costs $1050 for the program, $70 per unit.

Special Features The Office of Extended Learning Programs offers a course of study for individuals who wish to develop and/or improve their skills and knowledge in the field of careers development. The seven required and three elective courses can be completed within three semesters.

Contact Ms. Caren McNew-Demetre, Program Coordinator, 6375 Auburn Boulevard, Citrus Heights, CA 95621. 916-969-7068.

TELECOMMUNICATIONS (09.08)
Telecommunications Management Certificate Program

General Information Unit offering the program: Office of Extended Learning Programs. Program content: Voice/data communication, systems selection, telecommunications management and law. Available on a non-credit basis. Certificate signed by the Dean of Extended Learning Programs.

Program Format Evening classes offered. Instructional schedule: Two evenings per week. Program cycle: Continuous enrollment. Full program cycle lasts 1 semester. Completion of program requires 120 contact hours.

Evaluation Student evaluation based on tests, reports, interaction in class. Grading system: Pass/fail. Transcripts are kept for each student.

Enrollment Requirements Managerial experience required. Program is open to non-resident foreign students.

Program Costs $810 for the program, $185 per course.

Housing and Student Services Housing is not available. Job counseling and placement services are not available.

Special Features The program provides career advancement and continuing professional education for those with careers in telecommunications management. The program is offered in

Telecommunications Management Certificate Program continued

cooperation with the University's Departments of Management Information Science and Communication Studies. The instructors are practitioners in the field of telecommunications. The program is intended for middle- and senior-level managers.

Contact Ms. Jackie Branch, Coordinator, Telecommunications Management Program, Telecommunications Division, 650 University Avenue, Suite 101A, Sacramento, CA 95821. 916-923-0282.

TRANSPORTATION AND TRAVEL MARKETING (08.11)
Tourism Certificate Program

General Information Unit offering the program: Extended Learning Programs. Program content: Ticketing; sales techniques; air, sea, and land tourism. Available on a non-credit basis. Endorsed by American Society of Travel Agents (ASTA). Certificate signed by the Dean, Extended Learning Programs.

Program Format Daytime, weekend classes offered. Instructional schedule: 9 a.m. to 5 p.m., Saturdays. Students enroll in September. Full program cycle lasts 11 months. Completion of program requires 11 courses.

Evaluation Student evaluation based on tests, reports. Grading system: Pass/fail. Transcripts are kept for each student.

Enrollment Requirements Program is open to non-resident foreign students.

Program Costs $605 for the program, $55 per course.

Housing and Student Services Housing is not available. Job counseling and placement services are available.

Special Features The program has special appeal for those who anticipate a career change, those who are retired and would like part-time work, and those who wish to combine a special interest with travel skills. A field experience in a travel agency often offers students an employment opportunity. Instructors in the program are working professionals in the travel industry with academic degrees and teaching experience.

Contact Ms. Jeanette Meeker, Extended Learning Programs, 650 University Avenue, Suite 101A, Sacramento, CA 95825. 916-923-0441.

CHAPMAN COLLEGE
Orange, California 92666

HEALTH SERVICES ADMINISTRATION (18.07)
Wellness Coordinator Certificate

General Information Unit offering the program: Continuing Education. Program content: Health promotion and wellness in organizational setting. Available on either a credit or non-credit basis. Endorsed by The California Board of Registered Nurses. Certificate signed by the Regional Dean. Certificate applicable to M.S. in Human Resource Management and Development.

Program Format Weekend classes offered. Instructional schedule: Friday and Saturday classes. Students may enroll twice per year. Complete program cycle lasts eight weekends. Completion of program requires 90 contact hours, 85% attendance.

Evaluation Student evaluation based on tests, papers, reports. Grading system: Letters or numbers, pass/fail. Transcripts are kept for each student.

Enrollment Requirements Prior experience in health-related field required. Program is open to non-resident foreign students.

Program Costs $1295 for the program.

Special Features This program fulfills three different functions. It may be taken for graduate credit toward a master's degree in Human Resource Management and Development or for 6 hours of undergraduate credit. It also stands alone as a certificate with 9 CEUs.

Contact Ms. Cynthia M. Harris, Program Adviser, Hutton Centre, REC 201 East Sandpointe, #250, Santa Ana, CA 92707. 714-662-1986.

HUMAN RESOURCES DEVELOPMENT (06.06)
Human Resource Management and Development Graduate Certificate Program

General Information Unit offering the program: Regional Education Centers. Program content: Management, interpersonal and problem-solving skills, conflict resolution. Available for credit. Certificate signed by the President. Certificate applicable to M.S. in Human Resource Management and Development.

Program Format Evening classes offered. Instructional schedule: Two evenings per week. Program cycle: Continuous enrollment. Full program cycle lasts 1 year. Completion of program requires five courses, 3.0 GPA.

Evaluation Student evaluation based on tests, papers. Grading system: Letters or numbers. Transcripts are kept for each student.

Enrollment Requirements Bachelor's degree required. Program is open to non-resident foreign students.

Program Costs $2250 for the program, $450 per course.

Housing and Student Services Housing is not available. Job counseling and placement services are available.

Special Features Program offered at several of Chapman College's Regional Education Centers.

Contact Ms. Deborah Consalvo, Administrative Assistant, Continuing Education, 333 North Glassell, Orange, CA 92666. 714-997-6728.

LAW (22.01)
Paralegal Certificate

General Information Unit offering the program: Political Science. Program content: Introduction to litigation, legal procedures, business law, family law, constitutional law. Available on either a credit or non-credit basis. Certificate signed by the Vice President of Continuing Education.

Program Format Evening classes offered. Instructional schedule: One evening per week. Program cycle: Continuous enrollment. Completion of program requires eight courses, 3.0 GPA.

Evaluation Student evaluation based on tests, papers, reports. Grading system: Letters or numbers. Transcripts are kept for each student.

Enrollment Requirements Sixty college credits or equivalent, recommendation from an attorney required. Program is not open to non-resident foreign students. English language proficiency required.

Program Costs $2280 for the program, $285 per course.

Housing and Student Services Housing is not available. Job counseling and placement services are not available.

Special Features We will accept 6 credits of transfer course work approved by the Political Science Department to this program. A local advisory group of attorneys designed the program, and it is taught by attorneys as well.

Contact Ms. Dora Robinson, Director, 41-555 Cook Street, Suite 140, Palm Desert, CA 92260. 619-341-8051.

MENTAL HEALTH/HUMAN SERVICES (17.04)
Alcohol and Drug Studies

General Information Unit offering the program: Psychology, Sociology, Biology. Program content: Crisis counseling, family dynamics, sociology, physiology of the chemically dependent. Available for credit. Certificate signed by the Vice President of Continuing Education. Certificate applicable to B.A. in Sociology.

Program Format Evening classes offered. Instructional schedule: One evening per week. Program cycle: Continuous enrollment. Completion of program requires nine courses, 3.0 GPA.

Evaluation Student evaluation based on tests, papers, reports, interview. Grading system: Letters or numbers. Transcripts are kept for each student.

Enrollment Requirements Sixty college credits or equivalent field experience required. Program is not open to non-resident foreign students. English language proficiency required.

Program Costs $3105 for the program, $345 per course.

Housing and Student Services Housing is not available. Job counseling and placement services are not available.

Special Features We will accept 6 credits of transfer course work applicable to this program as approved by the Sociology Department. All instructors have had chemical dependency counseling experience and are academically qualified.

Contact Ms. Dora Robinson, Director, 41-555 Cook Street, Suite 140, Palm Desert, CA 92260. 619-341-8051.

TEACHER EDUCATION, SPECIFIC SUBJECT AREAS (13.13)
Chapman College Summer Science Program for Teachers

General Information Unit offering the program: Continuing Education. Program content: Integration of science with teaching strategies. Available for credit. Certificate signed by the Academic Coordinator.

Program Format Daytime, evening, weekend classes offered. Students enroll in the summer. Completion of program requires eight credit hours.

Evaluation Student evaluation based on tests, papers, reports. Grading system: Letters or numbers. Transcripts are kept for each student.

Enrollment Requirements Teacher credential required. Program is open to non-resident foreign students.

Program Costs $480 for the program.

Housing and Student Services Housing is available. Job counseling and placement services are available.

Special Features The summer science program offers 8 semester units towards the completion of a supplementary authorization in science. The program is designed in conjunction with the California State Department of Education Science Framework and Model Curriculum Standards. Field trips to tide pools, ecological preserves, and other subject-relevant sites are included.

Contact Ms. Deborah Consalvo, Administrative Assistant, Continuing Education, 333 North Glassell, Orange, CA 92666. 714-997-6728.

TEACHER EDUCATION, SPECIFIC SUBJECT AREAS (13.13)
Computer Science Certificate Program for Educators

General Information Unit offering the program: Education, Continuing Education. Program content: Computer education for teachers. Available for credit. Cosponsored by Orange County REC. Certificate signed by the Academic Coordinator.

Program Format Evening, weekend classes offered. Program cycle: Continuous enrollment. Completion of program requires 12 credit hours.

Evaluation Student evaluation based on tests, papers, reports. Grading system: Letters or numbers. Transcripts are kept for each student.

Enrollment Requirements Teaching credential required. Program is open to non-resident foreign students.

Program Costs $90–$180 per course.

Housing and Student Services Housing is not available. Job counseling and placement services are available.

Special Features No previous knowledge or skills in computers required. This program emphasizes the integration of computers in the existing instructional program. All courses are taught hands-on with students having access to microcomputer terminals throughout all phases of instruction.

Contact Ms. Deborah Consalvo, Administrative Assistant, Continuing Education, 333 North Glassell, Orange, CA 92666. 714-997-6728.

COGSWELL POLYTECHNICAL COLLEGE
Cupertino, California 95014

QUALITY CONTROL AND SAFETY TECHNOLOGIES (15.07)
Certificate in Quality Assurance

General Information Unit offering the program: Department of Quality Assurance. Program content: Statistical process control, ergonomics, software QA, automatic test equipment. Available for credit. Certificate signed by the President. Certificate applicable to B.S. in Quality Assurance.

Program Format Evening classes offered. Instructional schedule: One evening per week. Program cycle: Continuous enrollment. Full program cycle lasts 6 courses. Completion of program requires grade of C or better.

Evaluation Student evaluation based on tests, papers, reports. Grading system: Letters or numbers. Transcripts are kept for each student.

Enrollment Requirements Previous quality assurance experience required. Program is open to non-resident foreign students.

Program Costs $4320 for the program, $720 per course.

Housing and Student Services Housing is not available. Job counseling and placement services are available.

Special Features Credits earned through the certificate program may be applied toward a Bachelor of Science degree in quality assurance.

Contact Dr. Ted Kastelic, Director of Science and Engineering, 10420 Bubb Road, Cupertino, CA 95014. 408-252-5550.

COLLEGE OF NOTRE DAME
Belmont, California 94002

REHABILITATION SERVICES (17.08)
Art Therapy Institute

General Information Unit offering the program: Art Therapy Masters Program. Available for credit. Certificate signed by the Graduate Dean. Program fulfills requirements for American Art Therapy Association registration as ATR.

Program Format Evening, weekend classes offered. Program cycle: Continuous enrollment. Completion of program requires 22 semester units, 700 hours of supervised clinical practicum, 75 hours of personal psychotherapy.

Evaluation Student evaluation based on tests, papers, reports. Grading system: Letters or numbers. Transcripts are kept for each student.

Enrollment Requirements Master's degree in related field (art, education, behavioral science) required. Program is open to non-resident foreign students. English language proficiency required. Minimum TOEFL score required: 550.

Program Costs $150 per unit.

Art Therapy Institute continued

Housing and Student Services   Housing is not available. Job counseling and placement services are available.

Special Features   Program is designed for those holding a master's or doctoral degree in a related field (art, education, behavioral science), wishing to meet the American Art Therapy Association requirements for registration as an ATR.

Contact   Ms. Doris Arrington, Directort of Art Therapy Masters Program, 1500 Ralston Avenue, Belmont, CA 94002. 415-593-1601 Ext. 256.

GOLDEN GATE UNIVERSITY
San Francisco, California 94105

ACCOUNTING (06.02)
Certificate in Accounting

General Information   Unit offering the program: School of Accounting. Program content: Financial accounting, cost accounting, taxation, auditing, theory. Available for credit. Certificate signed by the Dean, College of Business Administration.

Program Format   Daytime, evening, weekend classes offered. Instructional schedule: One class per week. Program cycle: Continuous enrollment. Completion of program requires 15 or 30 credit hours, grade of C or better.

Evaluation   Student evaluation based on tests, papers. Grading system: Letters or numbers. Transcripts are kept for each student.

Enrollment Requirements   University admissions required. Program is open to non-resident foreign students. English language proficiency required. Minimum TOEFL score required: 525.

Program Costs $125 per unit.

Housing and Student Services   Housing is not available. Job counseling and placement services are available.

Contact   Mr. Stephen H. Tsih, Assistant Dean, College of Business Administration, 536 Mission Street, San Francisco, CA 94030. 415-442-7225.

ADVERTISING (09.02)
Certificate in Advertising Communications

General Information   Unit offering the program: Marketing Department. Program content: Advertising media, campaigns, copywriting, internship. Available for credit. Certificate signed by the Dean, College of Business Administration.

Program Format   Daytime, evening, weekend classes offered. Instructional schedule: One class per week. Program cycle: Continuous enrollment. Full program cycle lasts 15 credit hours. Completion of program requires grade of C or better.

Evaluation   Student evaluation based on tests, papers. Grading system: Letters or numbers. Transcripts are kept for each student.

Enrollment Requirements   University admissions required. Program is open to non-resident foreign students. English language proficiency required. Minimum TOEFL score required: 525.

Program Costs $125 per unit.

Housing and Student Services   Housing is not available. Job counseling and placement services are available.

Contact   Mr. Stephen H. Tsih, Assistant Dean, College of Business Administration, 536 Mission Street, San Francisco, CA 94030. 415-442-7225.

BANKING AND FINANCE (06.03)
Certificate in Finance

General Information   Unit offering the program: School of Corporate Finance and Financial Banking. Program content: Managerial finance, financial analysis, investments, commercial banking, capital management. Available for credit. Certificate signed by the Dean, College of Business Administration.

Program Format   Daytime, evening, weekend classes offered. Instructional schedule: One class per week. Program cycle: Continuous enrollment. Completion of program requires 15 or 30 credit hours, grade of C or better.

Evaluation   Student evaluation based on tests, papers. Grading system: Letters or numbers. Transcripts are kept for each student.

Enrollment Requirements   University admissions required. Program is open to non-resident foreign students. English language proficiency required. Minimum TOEFL score required: 525.

Program Costs $125 per unit.

Housing and Student Services   Housing is not available. Job counseling and placement services are available.

Contact   Mr. Stephen H. Tsih, Assistant Dean, College of Business Administration, 536 Mission Street, San Francisco, CA 94030. 415-442-7225.

BANKING AND FINANCE (06.03)
Certificate in Financial Services

General Information   Unit offering the program: School of Financial Services. Program content: Financial planning, investment management, real estate. Available for credit. Certificate signed by the Dean, College of Business Administration.

Program Format   Daytime, evening, weekend classes offered. Instructional schedule: One class per week. Program cycle: Continuous enrollment. Full program cycle lasts 15 credit hours. Completion of program requires grade of C or better.

Evaluation   Student evaluation based on tests, papers. Grading system: Letters or numbers. Transcripts are kept for each student.

Enrollment Requirements   University admissions required. Program is open to non-resident foreign students. English language proficiency required. Minimum TOEFL score required: 525.

Program Costs $125 per unit.

Housing and Student Services   Housing is not available. Job counseling and placement services are available.

Contact   Mr. Stephen H. Tsih, Assistant Dean, College of Business Administration, 536 Mission Street, San Francisco, CA 94030. 415-442-7225.

BUSINESS AND MANAGEMENT, GENERAL (06.01)
Certificate in Management

General Information   Unit offering the program: School of Management. Program content: Human resources, labor relations, organizational behavior. Available for credit. Certificate signed by the Dean, College of Business Administration.

Program Format   Daytime, evening, weekend classes offered. Instructional schedule: One class per week. Program cycle: Continuous enrollment. Completion of program requires 15 or 30 credit hours, grade of C or better.

Evaluation   Student evaluation based on tests, papers. Grading system: Letters or numbers. Transcripts are kept for each student.

Enrollment Requirements   University admissions required. Program is open to non-resident foreign students. English language proficiency required. Minimum TOEFL score required: 525.

Program Costs $125 per unit.

Housing and Student Services Housing is not available. Job counseling and placement services are available.

Contact Mr. Stephen H. Tsih, Assistant Dean, College of Business Administration, 536 Mission Street, San Francisco, CA 94030. 415-442-7225.

BUSINESS AND MANAGEMENT, GENERAL (06.01)
Certificate in Office Management

General Information Unit offering the program: School of Management. Program content: Labor relations, human resources, records and information management. Available for credit. Certificate signed by the Dean, College of Business Administration.

Program Format Daytime, evening, weekend classes offered. Instructional schedule: One class per week. Program cycle: Continuous enrollment. Full program cycle lasts 15 credit hours. Completion of program requires grade of C or better.

Evaluation Student evaluation based on tests, papers. Grading system: Letters or numbers. Transcripts are kept for each student.

Enrollment Requirements University admissions required. Program is open to non-resident foreign students. English language proficiency required. Minimum TOEFL score required: 525.

Program Costs $125 per unit.

Housing and Student Services Housing is not available. Job counseling and placement services are available.

Contact Mr. Stephen H. Tsih, Assistant Dean, College of Business Administration, 536 Mission Street, San Francisco, CA 94030. 415-442-7225.

BUSINESS AND MANAGEMENT, GENERAL (06.01)
Certificate in Procurement and Contract Management

General Information Unit offering the program: School of Operations Management. Program content: Contract negotiation; purchasing managemment; government, commercial, and industrial contract administration. Available for credit. Certificate signed by the Dean of the College. Certificate applicable to M.S. in Procurement and Contract Management.

Program Format Daytime, evening, weekend classes offered. Instructional schedule: One class per week. Program cycle: Continuous enrollment. Full program cycle lasts 6 courses. Completion of program requires 18 credit hours, 3.0 GPA.

Evaluation Student evaluation based on tests, papers. Grading system: Letters or numbers. Transcripts are kept for each student.

Enrollment Requirements Bachelor's degree required. Program is open to non-resident foreign students. English language proficiency required. Minimum TOEFL score required: 575.

Program Costs $196 per unit.

Housing and Student Services Housing is not available. Job counseling and placement services are available.

Contact Mr. Stephen H. Tsih, Assistant Dean, College of Business Administration, 536 Mission Street, San Francisco, CA 94030. 415-442-7225.

BUSINESS AND MANAGEMENT, GENERAL (06.01)
Certificate in Security Management

General Information Unit offering the program: School of Management. Program content: Corporate security planning, investigations, retail security, crisis management in the

international environment. Available for credit. Certificate signed by the Dean, College of Business Administration.

Program Format Daytime, evening, weekend classes offered. Instructional schedule: One class per week. Program cycle: Continuous enrollment. Full program cycle lasts 15 credit hours. Completion of program requires grade of C or better.

Evaluation Student evaluation based on tests, papers. Grading system: Letters or numbers. Transcripts are kept for each student.

Enrollment Requirements University admissions required. Program is open to non-resident foreign students. English language proficiency required. Minimum TOEFL score required: 525.

Program Costs $125 per unit.

Housing and Student Services Housing is not available. Job counseling and placement services are available.

Contact Mr. Stephen H. Tsih, Assistant Dean, College of Business Administration, 536 Mission Street, San Francisco, CA 94030. 415-442-7225.

BUSINESS AND MANAGEMENT, GENERAL (06.01)
Certificate in Transit Management

General Information Unit offering the program: School of Operations Management. Program content: Transportation economics, urban planning, labor relations. Available for credit. Certificate signed by the Dean, College of Business Administration.

Program Format Daytime, evening, weekend classes offered. Instructional schedule: One class per week. Program cycle: Continuous enrollment. Full program cycle lasts 30 credit hours. Completion of program requires grade of C or better.

Evaluation Student evaluation based on tests, papers. Grading system: Letters or numbers. Transcripts are kept for each student.

Enrollment Requirements University admissions required. Program is open to non-resident foreign students. English language proficiency required. Minimum TOEFL score required: 525.

Program Costs $125 per unit.

Housing and Student Services Housing is not available. Job counseling and placement services are available.

Contact Mr. Stephen H. Tsih, Assistant Dean, College of Business Administration, 536 Mission Street, San Francisco, CA 94030. 415-442-7225.

BUSINESS AND MANAGEMENT, GENERAL (06.01)
Certificate in Transportation and Distribution Management

General Information Unit offering the program: School of Operations Management. Program content: Business logistics, transportation economics and law, hazardous materials transport, transit operations management. Available for credit. Certificate signed by the Dean, College of Business Administration.

Program Format Daytime, evening, weekend classes offered. Instructional schedule: One class per week. Program cycle: Continuous enrollment. Completion of program requires 15 or 30 credit hours, grade of C or better.

Evaluation Student evaluation based on tests, papers. Grading system: Letters or numbers. Transcripts are kept for each student.

Enrollment Requirements University admissions required. Program is open to non-resident foreign students. English language proficiency required. Minimum TOEFL score required: 525.

Program Costs $125 per unit.

Certificate in Transportation and Distribution Management continued

Housing and Student Services   Housing is not available. Job counseling and placement services are available.

Contact   Mr. Stephen H. Tsih, Assistant Dean, College of Business Administration, 536 Mission Street, San Francisco, CA 94030. 415-442-7225.

BUSINESS AND MANAGEMENT, GENERAL (06.01)
Transportation and Logistics Management

General Information   Unit offering the program: School of Operations Management. Program content: Strategy, legal aspects, cost analysis. Available for credit. Certificate signed by the Dean of the College. Certificate applicable to M.S. in Transportation and Logistics Management.

Program Format   Daytime, evening, weekend classes offered. Instructional schedule: One class per week. Program cycle: Continuous enrollment. Full program cycle lasts 6 courses. Completion of program requires 18 credit hours, 3.0 GPA.

Evaluation   Student evaluation based on tests, papers. Grading system: Letters or numbers. Transcripts are kept for each student.

Enrollment Requirements   Bachelor's degree required. Program is open to non-resident foreign students. English language proficiency required. Minimum TOEFL score required: 575.

Program Costs $196 per unit.

Housing and Student Services   Housing is not available. Job counseling and placement services are available.

Contact   Mr. Stephen H. Tsih, Assistant Dean, College of Business Administration, 536 Mission Street, San Francisco, CA 94030. 415-442-7225.

COMMUNICATIONS TECHNOLOGIES (10.01)
Data Communications

General Information   Unit offering the program: Center for Professional Development. Available on a non-credit basis. Certificate signed by the Director, Center for Professional Development.

Program Format   Daytime, evening, weekend classes offered. Program cycle: Continuous enrollment. Full program cycle lasts 5 courses. Completion of program requires 60 contact hours.

Evaluation   Student evaluation based on tests, computer programs. Grading system: Letters or numbers, pass/fail. Records are kept by Center for Professional Development.

Enrollment Requirements   Program is not open to non-resident foreign students.

Program Costs $1395–$2440 for the program, $185–$750 per course.

Housing and Student Services   Housing is not available. Job counseling and placement services are not available.

Special Features   The program allows the students flexibility in choosing individual classes that best suit their continuing education and/or professional development. Golden Gate University has one of the largest programs in telecommunications in the United States. Instructors are experienced teacher-practitioners.

Contact   Mr. David Gin, Professional Development Programs Coordinator, 536 Mission Street, San Francisco, CA 94105. 415-442-7218.

COMPUTER PROGRAMMING (11.02)
Programming

General Information   Unit offering the program: Center for Professional Development. Program content: Structured techniques of programming. Available on a non-credit basis.

Certificate signed by the Director, Center for Professional Development.

Program Format   Daytime, evening, weekend classes offered. Program cycle: Continuous enrollment. Full program cycle lasts 5 courses. Completion of program requires 60 contact hours.

Evaluation   Student evaluation based on tests, computer programs. Grading system: Letters or numbers, pass/fail. Records are kept by Center for Professional Development.

Enrollment Requirements   Program is not open to non-resident foreign students.

Program Costs $1385–$1995 for the program, $62–$415 per course.

Housing and Student Services   Housing is not available. Job counseling and placement services are not available.

Special Features   The program allows students flexibility in choosing individual classes in the program that most suit their continuing education and/or professional development needs. The instructors are all teacher-practitioners with years of experience. Speciality classes such as JCL and COBOL Maintenance as well as COBOL and Assembler are offered.

Contact   Mr. David Gin, Professional Development Programs Coordinator, 536 Mission Street, San Francisco, CA 94105. 415-442-7218.

HEALTH SERVICES ADMINISTRATION (18.07)
Certificate in Health Services Management

General Information   Unit offering the program: School of Health Services Management. Program content: Hospital administration, health finance, health law, ambulatory and long-term care management. Available for credit. Certificate signed by the Dean, College of Business Administration.

Program Format   Daytime, evening, weekend classes offered. Instructional schedule: One class per week. Program cycle: Continuous enrollment. Complete program cycle lasts 15 or 30 credit hours. Completion of program requires grade of C or better.

Evaluation   Student evaluation based on tests, papers. Grading system: Letters or numbers. Transcripts are kept for each student.

Enrollment Requirements   University admissions required. Program is open to non-resident foreign students. English language proficiency required. Minimum TOEFL score required: 525.

Program Costs $125 per unit.

Housing and Student Services   Housing is not available. Job counseling and placement services are available.

Contact   Mr. Stephen S. Tsih, Assistant Dean, College of Business Administration, 536 Mission Street, San Francisco, CA 94030. 415-442-7225.

HUMAN RESOURCES DEVELOPMENT (06.06)
Certificate in Human Resources Management

General Information   Unit offering the program: Human Resources Management Department. Program content: Supervisory management, personnel recruitment, labor relations. Available for credit. Certificate signed by the Dean, College of Business Administration.

Program Format   Daytime, evening, weekend classes offered. Instructional schedule: One class per week. Program cycle: Continuous enrollment. Completion of program requires 15 or 30 credit hours, grade of C or better.

Evaluation   Student evaluation based on tests, papers. Grading system: Letters or numbers. Transcripts are kept for each student.

Enrollment Requirements   University admissions required. Program is open to non-resident foreign students. English language proficiency required. Minimum TOEFL score required: 525.

Program Costs $125 per unit.

Housing and Student Services   Housing is not available. Job counseling and placement services are available.

Contact   Mr. Stephen H. Tsih, Assistant Dean, College of Business Administration, 536 Mission Street, San Francisco, CA 94030. 415-442-7225.

INFORMATION SCIENCES AND SYSTEMS (11.04)
Certificate in Information Security

General Information   Unit offering the program: Information Systems Department. Program content: EDP auditing, systems security administration, risk management. Available for credit. Certificate signed by the Dean, College of Business Administration.

Program Format   Daytime, evening, weekend classes offered. Instructional schedule: One class per week. Students enroll in September. Full program cycle lasts 3 semesters. Completion of program requires 18 credit hours.

Evaluation   Student evaluation based on tests, papers. Grading system: Letters or numbers. Transcripts are kept for each student.

Enrollment Requirements   Bachelor's degree in computer science or information systems or at least three years of relevant technical computer experience required. Program is open to non-resident foreign students. English language proficiency required. Minimum TOEFL score required: 525.

Program Costs $125 per unit.

Housing and Student Services   Housing is not available. Job counseling and placement services are available.

Contact   Mr. Stephen H. Tsih, Assistant Dean, College of Business Administration, 536 Mission Street, San Francisco, CA 94030. 415-442-7225.

INFORMATION SCIENCES AND SYSTEMS (11.04)
Certificate in Information Systems

General Information   Unit offering the program: Information Systems Department. Program content: Assembler programming, COBOL, Pascal, UNIX programming. Available for credit. Certificate signed by the Dean, College of Business Administration.

Program Format   Daytime, evening, weekend classes offered. Instructional schedule: One class per week. Program cycle: Continuous enrollment. Completion of program requires 15 or 30 credit hours, grade of C or better.

Evaluation   Student evaluation based on tests, papers. Grading system: Letters or numbers. Transcripts are kept for each student.

Enrollment Requirements   University admissions required. Program is open to non-resident foreign students. English language proficiency required. Minimum TOEFL score required: 525.

Program Costs $125 per unit.

Housing and Student Services   Housing is not available. Job counseling and placement services are available.

Contact   Mr. Stephen H. Tsih, Assistant Dean, College of Business Administration, 536 Mission Street, San Francisco, CA 94030. 415-442-7225.

INFORMATION SCIENCES AND SYSTEMS (11.04)
Data Base

General Information   Unit offering the program: Center for Professional Development. Program content: Database products. Available on a non-credit basis. Certificate signed by the Director, Center for Professional Development.

Program Format   Daytime, evening, weekend classes offered. Program cycle: Continuous enrollment. Full program cycle lasts 5 courses. Completion of program requires 60 contact hours.

Evaluation   Student evaluation based on tests, computer programs. Grading system: Letters or numbers, pass/fail. Records are kept by Center for Professional Development.

Enrollment Requirements   Program is not open to non-resident foreign students.

Program Costs $1145–$2145 for the program, $175–$695 per course.

Housing and Student Services   Housing is not available. Job counseling and placement services are not available.

Special Features   The program is unique because it allows the students flexibility in choosing the individual seminars that most suit their needs. The classes range from fundamentals to speciality seminars such as DB2, VSAM, and IMS. The instructors are experienced teacher-practitioners.

Contact   Mr. David Gin, Professional Development Programs Coordinator, 536 Mission Street, San Francisco, CA 94105. 415-442-7218.

INFORMATION SCIENCES AND SYSTEMS (11.04)
Data Base/Data Communications

General Information   Unit offering the program: Center for Professional Development. Available on a non-credit basis. Certificate signed by the Director, Center for Professional Development.

Program Format   Daytime, evening, weekend classes offered. Program cycle: Continuous enrollment. Full program cycle lasts 6 courses. Completion of program requires 60 contact hours.

Evaluation   Student evaluation based on tests, computer programs. Grading system: Letters or numbers, pass/fail. Records are kept by Center for Professional Development.

Enrollment Requirements   Program is not open to non-resident foreign students.

Program Costs $1270–$3435 for the program, $175–$750 per course.

Housing and Student Services   Housing is not available. Job counseling and placement services are not available.

Special Features   The program is unique because it provides the students with a view of database and data communications as well as allows them to choose the individual classes that best suit their continuing education and professional development needs. Instructors are experienced teacher-practitioners.

Contact   Mr. David Gin, Professional Development Program Coordinator, 536 Mission Street, San Francisco, CA 94105. 415-442-7218.

INSTITUTIONAL MANAGEMENT (06.07)
Certificate in Hotel, Restaurant, and Institutional Management

General Information   Unit offering the program: Hotel, Restaurant, and Institutional Management Department. Program content: Front office, food and beverage, hospitality marketing, human relations, tourism, budgeting. Available for credit. Certificate signed by the Dean, College of Business Administration.

Program Format   Daytime, evening, weekend classes offered. Instructional schedule: One class per week. Program cycle: Continuous enrollment. Completion of program requires 15 or 30 credit hours, grade of C or better.

Evaluation   Student evaluation based on tests, papers. Grading system: Letters or numbers. Transcripts are kept for each student.

Enrollment Requirements   University admissions required. Program is open to non-resident foreign students. English language proficiency required. Minimum TOEFL score required: 525.

Certificate in Hotel, Restaurant, and Institutional Management continued

Program Costs $125 per unit.

Housing and Student Services   Housing is not available. Job counseling and placement services are available.

Contact   Mr. Stephen H. Tsih, Assistant Dean, College of Business Administration, 536 Mission Street, San Francisco, CA 94030. 415-442-7225.

INTERNATIONAL BUSINESS MANAGEMENT (06.09)
Certificate in International Management

General Information   Unit offering the program: School of International Management. Program content: International business, accounting and tax, import/export. Available for credit. Certificate signed by the Dean, College of Business Administration.

Program Format   Daytime, evening, weekend classes offered. Instructional schedule: One class per week. Program cycle: Continuous enrollment. Full program cycle lasts 15 credit hours. Completion of program requires grade of C or better.

Evaluation   Student evaluation based on tests, papers. Grading system: Letters or numbers. Transcripts are kept for each student.

Enrollment Requirements   University admissions required. Program is open to non-resident foreign students. English language proficiency required. Minimum TOEFL score required: 525.

Program Costs $125 per unit.

Housing and Student Services   Housing is not available. Job counseling and placement services are available.

Contact   Mr. Stephen H. Tsih, Assistant Dean, College of Business Administration, 536 Mission Street, San Francisco, CA 94030. 415-442-7225.

MANAGEMENT INFORMATION SYSTEMS (06.12)
Computer Systems Management

General Information   Unit offering the program: Center for Professional Development. Program content: Technical management skills. Available on a non-credit basis. Certificate signed by the Director, Center for Professional Development.

Program Format   Daytime, evening, weekend classes offered. Program cycle: Continuous enrollment. Full program cycle lasts 5 courses. Completion of program requires 60 contact hours.

Evaluation   Student evaluation based on tests, computer programs. Grading system: Letters or numbers, pass/fail. Records are kept by Center for Professional Development.

Enrollment Requirements   Program is not open to non-resident foreign students.

Program Costs $1025–$1265 for the program, $175–$305 per course.

Housing and Student Services   Housing is not available. Job counseling and placement services are not available.

Special Features   The program allows the students flexibility in choosing individual classes; topics include project management, computer security, resource planning, computer contracts, artificial intelligence, and data management that best suit their continuing education and/or professional development needs. The instructors are all teacher-practitioners with many years of experience.

Contact   Mr. David Gin, Professional Development Programs Coordinator, 536 Mission Street, San Francisco, CA 94105. 415-442-7218.

MANAGEMENT SCIENCE (06.13)
Certificate in Manufacturing Management

General Information   Unit offering the program: School of Operations Management. Program content: Quality assurance, technological innovation, cost control. Available for credit. Certificate signed by the Dean of the College. Certificate applicable to M.S. in Manufacturing Management.

Program Format   Daytime, evening, weekend classes offered. Instructional schedule: One class per week. Program cycle: Continuous enrollment. Full program cycle lasts 6 courses. Completion of program requires 18 credit hours, 3.0 GPA.

Evaluation   Student evaluation based on tests, papers. Grading system: Letters or numbers. Transcripts are kept for each student.

Enrollment Requirements   Bachelor's degree required. Program is open to non-resident foreign students. English language proficiency required. Minimum TOEFL score required: 575.

Program Costs $196 per unit.

Housing and Student Services   Housing is not available. Job counseling and placement services are available.

Contact   Mr. Stephen H. Tsih, Assistant Dean, College of Business Administration, 536 Mission Street, San Francisco, CA 94030. 415-442-7225.

MARKETING MANAGEMENT AND RESEARCH (06.14)
Certificate in Marketing

General Information   Unit offering the program: Marketing Department. Program content: Marketing principles, research, and management. Available for credit. Certificate signed by the Dean, College of Business Administration.

Program Format   Daytime, evening, weekend classes offered. Instructional schedule: One class per week. Program cycle: Continuous enrollment. Full program cycle lasts 15 credit hours. Completion of program requires grade of C or better.

Evaluation   Student evaluation based on tests, papers. Grading system: Letters or numbers. Transcripts are kept for each student.

Enrollment Requirements   University admissions required. Program is open to non-resident foreign students. English language proficiency required. Minimum TOEFL score required: 525.

Program Costs $125 per unit.

Housing and Student Services   Housing is not available. Job counseling and placement services are available.

Contact   Mr. Stephen H. Tsih, Assistant Dean, College of Business Administration, 536 Mission Street, San Francisco, CA 94030. 415-442-7225.

MATHEMATICS, GENERAL (27.01)
Certificate in Mathematics

General Information   Unit offering the program: Mathematics Department. Program content: Calculus, regression analysis, analysis for management. Available for credit. Certificate signed by the Dean, College of Humanities and Social Sciences.

Program Format   Daytime, evening, weekend classes offered. Instructional schedule: One class per week. Program cycle: Continuous enrollment. Full program cycle lasts 15 credit hours. Completion of program requires grade of C or better.

Evaluation   Student evaluation based on tests, papers. Grading system: Letters or numbers. Transcripts are kept for each student.

Enrollment Requirements   University admissions required. Program is open to non-resident foreign students. English language proficiency required. Minimum TOEFL score required: 525.

Program Costs $125 per unit.

Housing and Student Services   Housing is not available. Job counseling and placement services are available.

Contact   Mr. Stephen H. Tsih, Assistant Dean, College of Business Administration, 536 Mission Street, San Francisco, CA 94030. 415-442-7225.

MICROCOMPUTER APPLICATIONS (11.06)
Certificate in Information Systems— Microcomputers

General Information   Unit offering the program: Information Systems Department. Program content: Database management, ADA, UNIX programming. Available for credit. Certificate signed by the Dean, College of Business Administration.

Program Format   Daytime, evening, weekend classes offered. Instructional schedule: One class per week. Program cycle: Continuous enrollment. Completion of program requires 15 or 30 credit hours, grade of C or better.

Evaluation   Student evaluation based on tests, papers. Grading system: Letters or numbers. Transcripts are kept for each student.

Enrollment Requirements   University admissions required. Program is open to non-resident foreign students. English language proficiency required. Minimum TOEFL score required: 525.

Program Costs $125 per unit.

Housing and Student Services   Housing is not available. Job counseling and placement services are available.

Contact   Mr. Stephen H. Tsih, Assistant Dean, College of Business Administration, 536 Mission Street, San Francisco, CA 94030. 415-442-7225.

POLITICAL SCIENCE AND GOVERNMENT (45.10)
Certificate in Applied Politics

General Information   Unit offering the program: Political Science Department. Program content: Public opinion polling, lobbying, media relations, negotiation. Available for credit. Certificate signed by the Dean, College of Humanities and Social Sciences.

Program Format   Daytime, evening, weekend classes offered. Instructional schedule: One class per week. Program cycle: Continuous enrollment. Full program cycle lasts 15 credit hours. Completion of program requires grade of C or better.

Evaluation   Student evaluation based on tests, papers. Grading system: Letters or numbers. Transcripts are kept for each student.

Enrollment Requirements   University admissions required. Program is open to non-resident foreign students. English language proficiency required. Minimum TOEFL score required: 525.

Program Costs $125 per unit.

Housing and Student Services   Housing is not available. Job counseling and placement services are available.

Contact   Mr. Stephen H. Tsih, Assistant Dean, College of Business Administration, 536 Mission Street, San Francisco, CA 94030. 415-442-7225.

POLITICAL SCIENCE AND GOVERNMENT (45.10)
Certificate in Political Science

General Information   Unit offering the program: Political Science Department. Program content: American government, political ideologies, foreign policy, philosophy of law, negotiation, lobbying. Available for credit. Certificate signed by the Dean, College of Humanities and Social Sciences.

Program Format   Daytime, evening, weekend classes offered. Instructional schedule: One class per week. Program cycle:

Continuous enrollment. Completion of program requires 15 or 30 credit hours, grade of C or better.

Evaluation   Student evaluation based on tests, papers. Grading system: Letters or numbers. Transcripts are kept for each student.

Enrollment Requirements   University admissions required. Program is open to non-resident foreign students. English language proficiency required. Minimum TOEFL score required: 525.

Program Costs $125 per unit.

Housing and Student Services   Housing is not available. Job counseling and placement services are available.

Contact   Mr. Stephen H. Tsih, Assistant Dean, College of Business Administration, 536 Mission Street, San Francisco, CA 94030. 415-442-7225.

PUBLIC AFFAIRS, GENERAL (44.01)
Certificate in Administration of Justice

General Information   Unit offering the program: Political Science Department. Program content: Constitutional law, juvenile justice, social institution, etiology of crime, group violence, police organization. Available for credit. Certificate signed by the Dean, College of Humanities and Social Sciences.

Program Format   Daytime, evening, weekend classes offered. Instructional schedule: One class per week. Program cycle: Continuous enrollment. Completion of program requires 15 or 30 credit hours, grade of C or better.

Evaluation   Student evaluation based on tests, papers. Grading system: Letters or numbers. Transcripts are kept for each student.

Enrollment Requirements   University admissions required. Program is open to non-resident foreign students. English language proficiency required. Minimum TOEFL score required: 525.

Program Costs $125 per unit.

Housing and Student Services   Housing is not available. Job counseling and placement services are available.

Contact   Mr. Stephen H. Tsih, Assistant Dean, College of Business Administration, 536 Mission Street, San Francisco, CA 94030. 415-442-7225.

PUBLIC RELATIONS (09.05)
Certificate in Public Relations

General Information   Unit offering the program: Graduate School of Management. Program content: Theories of communication; business, government, and society; communication and social change. Available for credit. Certificate signed by the Dean of the College. Certificate applicable to M.S. in Public Relations.

Program Format   Daytime, evening, weekend classes offered. Instructional schedule: One class per week. Program cycle: Continuous enrollment. Full program cycle lasts 6 courses. Completion of program requires 18 credit hours, 3.0 GPA.

Evaluation   Student evaluation based on tests, papers. Grading system: Letters or numbers. Transcripts are kept for each student.

Enrollment Requirements   Bachelor's degree required. Program is open to non-resident foreign students. English language proficiency required. Minimum TOEFL score required: 575.

Program Costs $196 per unit.

Housing and Student Services   Housing is not available. Job counseling and placement services are available.

Contact   Mr. Stephen H. Tsih, Assistant Dean, College of Business Administration, 536 Mission Street, San Francisco, CA 94030. 415-442-7225.

REAL ESTATE (06.17)
Certificate in Real Estate

General Information Unit offering the program: School of Financial Services. Program content: Practice, finance, legal aspects, management, investment. Available for credit. Certificate signed by the Dean, College of Business Administration.

Program Format Daytime, evening, weekend classes offered. Instructional schedule: One class per week. Program cycle: Continuous enrollment. Full program cycle lasts 15 credit hours. Completion of program requires grade of C or better.

Evaluation Student evaluation based on tests, papers. Grading system: Letters or numbers. Transcripts are kept for each student.

Enrollment Requirements University admissions required. Program is open to non-resident foreign students. English language proficiency required. Minimum TOEFL score required: 525.

Program Costs $125 per unit.

Housing and Student Services Housing is not available. Job counseling and placement services are available.

Contact Mr. Stephen H. Tsih, Assistant Dean, College of Business Administration, 536 Mission Street, San Francisco, CA 94030. 415-442-7225.

SYSTEMS ANALYSIS (11.05)
Systems and Project Management

General Information Unit offering the program: Center for Professional Development. Program content: Systems analysis and management. Available on a non-credit basis. Certificate signed by the Director, Center for Professional Development.

Program Format Daytime, evening, weekend classes offered. Program cycle: Continuous enrollment. Full program cycle lasts 5 courses. Completion of program requires 60 contact hours.

Evaluation Student evaluation based on tests, computer programs. Grading system: Letters or numbers, pass/fail. Records are kept by Center for Professional Development.

Enrollment Requirements Program is not open to non-resident foreign students.

Program Costs $1435–$1585 for the program, $175–$305 per course.

Housing and Student Services Housing is not available. Job counseling and placement services are not available.

Special Features The program is unique because it provides students with a blend of systems analysis, structured techniques, and project management seminars, as well as the flexibility to choose the individual classes that best suit their continuing education and/or professional development needs. Instructors are experienced teacher-practitioners.

Contact Mr. David Gin, Professional Development Programs Coordinator, 536 Mission Street, San Francisco, CA 94105. 415-442-7218.

TAXATION (06.19)
Certificate in Basic Taxation

General Information Unit offering the program: School of Taxation. Program content: Business law, federal and state taxation. Available for credit. Certificate signed by the Dean, College of Business Administration.

Program Format Daytime, evening, weekend classes offered. Instructional schedule: One class per week. Program cycle: Continuous enrollment. Full program cycle lasts 5 courses. Completion of program requires grade of C or better.

Evaluation Student evaluation based on tests, papers. Grading system: Letters or numbers. Transcripts are kept for each student.

Enrollment Requirements University admissions required. Program is open to non-resident foreign students. English language proficiency required. Minimum TOEFL score required: 525.

Program Costs $139 per unit.

Housing and Student Services Housing is not available. Job counseling and placement services are available.

Contact Mr. Stephen H. Tsih, Assistant Dean, College of Business Administration, 536 Mission Street, San Francisco, CA 94030. 415-442-7225.

TAXATION (06.19)
Certificate in Advanced Taxation

General Information Unit offering the program: School of Taxation. Program content: Procedures and representation, corporate, real and personal property transactions. Available for credit. Certificate signed by the Dean, College of Business Administration.

Program Format Daytime, evening, weekend classes offered. Instructional schedule: One class per week. Program cycle: Continuous enrollment. Full program cycle lasts 15 credit hours. Completion of program requires grade of C or better.

Evaluation Student evaluation based on tests, papers. Grading system: Letters or numbers. Transcripts are kept for each student.

Enrollment Requirements University admissions required. Program is open to non-resident foreign students. English language proficiency required. Minimum TOEFL score required: 525.

Program Costs $139 per unit.

Housing and Student Services Housing is not available. Job counseling and placement services are available.

Contact Mr. Stephen H. Tsih, Assistant Dean, College of Business Administration, 536 Mission Street, San Francisco, CA 94030. 415-442-7225.

TELECOMMUNICATIONS (09.08)
Certificate in Telecommunications

General Information Unit offering the program: School of Telecommunications Management. Program content: Survey of data, legal and regulatory issues, technology and society. Available for credit. Certificate signed by the Dean of the College. Certificate applicable to M.S. in Telecommunications Management.

Program Format Daytime, evening, weekend classes offered. Instructional schedule: One class per week. Program cycle: Continuous enrollment. Full program cycle lasts 18 credit hours. Completion of program requires 3.0 GPA.

Evaluation Student evaluation based on tests, papers. Grading system: Letters or numbers. Transcripts are kept for each student.

Enrollment Requirements Bachelor's degree required. Program is open to non-resident foreign students. English language proficiency required. Minimum TOEFL score required: 575.

Program Costs $196 per unit.

Housing and Student Services Housing is not available. Job counseling and placement services are available.

Contact Mr. Stephen H. Tsih, Assistant Dean, College of Business Administration, 536 Mission Street, San Francisco, CA 94030. 415-442-7225.

TELECOMMUNICATIONS (09.08)
Certificate in Telecommunications Management

General Information Unit offering the program: School of Telecommunications Management. Program content: Data communication, common carrier systems, networking design, video systems, internship. Available for credit. Certificate signed by the Dean, College of Business Administration.

Program Format Daytime, evening, weekend classes offered. Instructional schedule: One class per week. Program cycle: Continuous enrollment. Completion of program requires 15 or 30 credit hours, grade of C or better.

Evaluation Student evaluation based on tests, papers. Grading system: Letters or numbers. Transcripts are kept for each student.

Enrollment Requirements University admissions required. Program is open to non-resident foreign students. English language proficiency required. Minimum TOEFL score required: 525.

Program Costs $125 per unit.

Housing and Student Services Housing is not available. Job counseling and placement services are available.

Contact Mr. Stephen H. Tsih, Assistant Dean, College of Business Administration, 536 Mission Street, San Francisco, CA 94030. 415-442-7225.

TRADE AND INDUSTRIAL SUPERVISION AND MANAGEMENT (06.20)
Certificate in Project and Construction Management

General Information Unit offering the program: School of Operations Management. Program content: Cost estimation, engineering projects, contract administration. Available for credit. Certificate signed by the Dean of the College. Certificate applicable to M.S. in Project and Construction Management.

Program Format Daytime, evening, weekend classes offered. Instructional schedule: One class per week. Program cycle: Continuous enrollment. Full program cycle lasts 6 courses. Completion of program requires 18 credit hours, 3.0 GPA.

Evaluation Student evaluation based on tests, papers. Grading system: Letters or numbers. Transcripts are kept for each student.

Enrollment Requirements Bachelor's degree required. Program is open to non-resident foreign students. English language proficiency required. Minimum TOEFL score required: 575.

Program Costs $196 per unit.

Housing and Student Services Housing is not available. Job counseling and placement services are available.

Contact Mr. Stephen H. Tsih, Assistant Dean, College of Business Administration, 536 Mission Street, San Francisco, CA 94030. 415-442-7225.

HUMPHREYS COLLEGE
Stockton, California 95207

LAW (22.01)
Paralegal

General Information Unit offering the program: Paralegal. Program content: Procedural law. Available for credit. Certificate signed by the Registrar. Certificate applicable to B.S. in Paralegal Studies.

Program Format Evening classes offered. Instructional schedule: One evening per week. Program cycle: Continuous enrollment. Full program cycle lasts 4 quarters. Completion of program requires 32 quarter units.

Evaluation Student evaluation based on tests. Grading system: Letters or numbers. Transcripts are kept for each student.

Enrollment Requirements Program is open to non-resident foreign students.

Program Costs $2280 for the program, $285 per course.

Housing and Student Services Housing is available. Job counseling and placement services are available.

Special Features Program is ten years old and is taught by practicing lawyers and paralegals. Units can be applied to A.A., A.S., or B.S. degrees.

Contact Ms. Rowena Walker, Chair, Paralegal Department, 6650 Inglewood, Stockton, CA 95207. 209-478-0800.

NUCEA MEMBER

LOS ANGELES COLLEGE OF CHIROPRACTIC
Whittier, California 90609

CHIROPRACTIC (18.03)
Chiropractic Orthopedics

General Information Unit offering the program: Postgraduate Division. Available on a non-credit basis. Endorsed by Council on Chiropractic Education, American Board of Chiropractic Orthopedists. Certificate signed by the President. Program fulfills requirements for Chiropractic Orthopedist.

Program Format Weekend classes offered. Instructional schedule: One weekend per month for 12 hours. Program cycle: Continuous enrollment. Full program cycle lasts 27 months. Completion of program requires 300 contact hours, nine examinations, score of 75% or better on each examination.

Evaluation Student evaluation based on tests. Grading system: Letters or numbers. Transcripts are kept for each student.

Enrollment Requirements Doctor of Chiropractic required.

Program Costs $2970–$4050 for the program.

Housing and Student Services Housing is not available. Job counseling and placement services are not available.

Special Features Successful completion of this program leads to eligibility to sit for the examination of the American Board of Chiropractic Orthopedists. Passing this examination leads to status as a diplomate in chiropractic orthopedists. LACC offers this course in eleven cities throughout the United States.

Contact Ms. Janice L. Pratte, Director, Postgraduate Education, 16200 East Amber Valley Drive, P.O. Box 1166, Whittier, CA 90609-1166. 213-947-8755 Ext. 231.

CHIROPRACTIC (18.03)
Sports and Recreational Injuries: Prevention, Evaluation, and Treatment

General Information Unit offering the program: Postgraduate Division. Available on a non-credit basis. Endorsed by Council on Chiropractic Education, ACA Council on Sports Injuries and Physical Fitness. Certificate signed by the President. Program fulfills requirements for Sports Chiropractic Physician.

Program Format Weekend classes offered. Instructional schedule: One weekend per month. Program cycle: Continuous enrollment. Full program cycle lasts 10 months. Completion of program requires 100 hours attendance, minimum 75% on tests.

Evaluation Student evaluation based on tests. Grading system: Letters or numbers, pass/fail. Transcripts are kept for each student.

Enrollment Requirements Doctor of chiropractic required.

Program Costs $1600–$1950 for the program.

Housing and Student Services Housing is not available. Job counseling and placement services are not available.

Special Features Successful completion of this certificate program leads to eligibility to sit for the American Chiropractic Association Council on Sports Injuries and Physical Fitness examination for certification as a chiropractic sports physician.

Contact Ms. Janice L. Pratte, Director, Postgraduate Education, 16200 East Amber Valley Drive P.O. Box 1166, Whittier, CA 90609-1166. 213-947-8755 Ext. 231.

MISCELLANEOUS ALLIED HEALTH SERVICES (17.05)
Chiropractic Assistant

General Information Unit offering the program: Postgraduate Division. Available on a non-credit basis. Certificate signed by the President.

Program Format Weekend classes offered. Instructional schedule: Thirteen Saturdays and two Sundays for 6½ hours per session. Full program cycle lasts 13 weeks. Completion of program requires grade of 70% or better, 86% attendance, CPR certificate.

Evaluation Student evaluation based on tests. Grading system: Letters or numbers. Transcripts are kept for each student.

Enrollment Requirements High school diploma, ability to type 30 words per minute required.

Program Costs $495–$540 for the program.

Housing and Student Services Housing is not available. Job counseling and placement services are available.

Special Features Attendees of this program have an easy time finding job placement.

Contact Dr. Margaret Hamilton, Program Coordinator, 16200 East Amber Valley Drive P.O. Box 1166, Whittier, CA 90609-1166. 213-947-8755 Ext. 233.

MOUNT ST. MARY'S COLLEGE
Los Angeles, California 90049

BUSINESS AND MANAGEMENT, GENERAL (06.01)
Certificate in Management

General Information Unit offering the program: Business Department. Program content: Accounting, marketing, management, economics, business law, organizational behavior, business communications, finance. Available for credit. Certificate signed by the Chair, Business Department. Certificate applicable to B.S. in Business.

Program Format Evening classes offered. Instructional schedule: One evening per week for four hours. Program cycle: Continuous enrollment. Full program cycle lasts 2 years. Completion of program requires grade of C or better in all courses.

Evaluation Student evaluation methods vary by course. Grading system: Letters or numbers. Transcripts are kept for each student.

Enrollment Requirements Full-time employment for at least two years required. Program is not open to non-resident foreign students. English language proficiency required. Departmental writing examination.

Program Costs $550 per course.

Housing and Student Services Housing is not available. Job counseling and placement services are not available.

Special Features All courses are transferable college-level courses. The certificate program leads to our Bachelor of Science degree program, which is an on-going evening program. Mount St. Mary's College also accepts life/work experience up to 30 units.

Contact Ms. Carol Gleckman, Coordinator of Extension Program, 12001 Chalon Road, Los Angeles, CA 90049. 213-476-2237.

NORTHROP UNIVERSITY
Los Angeles, California 90045

ELECTROMECHANICAL INSTRUMENTATION AND MAINTENANCE TECHNOLOGIES (15.04)
Engineering Fundamentals Technology

General Information Unit offering the program: Department of Engineering Technology. Program content: Math, physics, chemistry, mechanics of material, statics, machine shop, English. Available for credit. Certificate signed by the President of the University. Certificate applicable to B.S. in Manufacturing Engineering Technology.

Program Format Daytime, evening, weekend classes offered. Program cycle: Continuous enrollment. Completion of program requires 34–41 credit hours.

Evaluation Student evaluation based on tests, papers, reports. Grading system: Letters or numbers. Transcripts are kept for each student.

Enrollment Requirements Professional experience and above-average academic achievement recommended. Program is open to non-resident foreign students. English language proficiency required. Minimum TOEFL score required: 550.

Program Costs $170 per quarter hour.

Housing and Student Services Housing is available. Job counseling and placement services are available.

Special Features Credit for prior experience. Student input in designing the program. Corporate support and publicity.

Contact Admissions Office, 5800 West Arbor Vitae Street, Los Angeles, CA 90045. 213-337-4404.

ELECTROMECHANICAL INSTRUMENTATION AND MAINTENANCE TECHNOLOGIES (15.04)
Process Engineering Technology

General Information Unit offering the program: Department of Engineering Technology. Program content: Geometry, detail and assembly drafting, assembly tool design, analytical technology, machine design, production cost esimation, English. Available for credit. Certificate signed by the President of the University. Certificate applicable to B.S. in Manufacturing Engineering Technology.

Program Format Daytime, evening, weekend classes offered. Program cycle: Continuous enrollment. Completion of program requires 34–41 credit hours.

Evaluation Student evaluation based on tests, papers, reports. Grading system: Letters or numbers. Transcripts are kept for each student.

Enrollment Requirements Certificate in Tool Design and Engineering Technology required. Program is open to non-resident foreign students. English language proficiency required. Minimum TOEFL score required: 550.

Program Costs $170 per quarter hour.

Housing and Student Services Housing is available. Job counseling and placement services are available.

Special Features Credit for prior experience. Student input in designing the program. Corporate support and publicity.

Contact Admissions Office, 5800 West Arbor Vitae Street, Los Angeles, CA 90045. 213-337-4404.

ELECTROMECHANICAL INSTRUMENTATION AND MAINTENANCE TECHNOLOGIES (15.04)
Productivity Engineering Technology

General Information Unit offering the program: Department of Engineering Technology. Program content: Computers, aerospace vehicle system, industrial observation, technical presentation, analytical technology, numerical control systems, technical writing. Available for credit. Certificate signed by the President of the University. Certificate applicable to B.S. in Manufacturing Engineering Technology.

Program Format Daytime, evening, weekend classes offered. Program cycle: Continuous enrollment. Completion of program requires 34–41 credit hours.

Evaluation Student evaluation based on tests, papers, reports. Grading system: Letters or numbers. Transcripts are kept for each student.

Enrollment Requirements Certificate in Process Engineering Technology required. Program is open to non-resident foreign students. English language proficiency required. Minimum TOEFL score required: 550.

Program Costs $170 per quarter hour.

Housing and Student Services Housing is available. Job counseling and placement services are available.

Special Features Credit for prior experience. Student input in designing the program. Corporate support and publicity.

Contact Admissions Office, 5800 West Arbor Vitae Street, Los Angeles, CA 90045. 213-337-4404.

ELECTROMECHANICAL INSTRUMENTATION AND MAINTENANCE TECHNOLOGIES (15.04)
Tool Design and Engineering Technology

General Information Unit offering the program: Department of Engineering Technology. Program content: Statistics, welding, metallurgy, metrology, industrial safety, quality assurance, mechanical technology, material verification. Available for credit. Certificate signed by the President of the University. Certificate applicable to B.S. in Manufacturing Engineering Technology.

Program Format Daytime, evening, weekend classes offered. Program cycle: Continuous enrollment. Completion of program requires 34–41 credit hours.

Evaluation Student evaluation based on tests, papers, reports. Grading system: Letters or numbers. Transcripts are kept for each student.

Enrollment Requirements Certificate in Engineering Fundamentals Technology required. Program is open to non-resident foreign students. English language proficiency required. Minimum TOEFL score required: 550.

Program Costs $170 per quarter hour.

Housing and Student Services Housing is available. Job counseling and placement services are available.

Special Features Credit for prior experience. Student input in designing the program. Corporate support and publicity.

Contact Admissions Office, 5800 West Arbor Vitae Street, Los Angeles, CA 90045. 213-337-4404.

VEHICLE AND MOBILE EQUIPMENT MECHANICS AND REPAIRERS (47.06)
Airframe/Powerplant Maintenance Technician Certificate

General Information Unit offering the program: Institute of Technology. Program content: Maintaining and repairing jet engines. Available for credit. Endorsed by Federal Aviation Administration. Certificate signed by the President of the University. Certificate applicable to A.S., B.S. in Aerospace Engineering Technology. Program fulfills requirements for FAA Air Agency Certificate Number 3408.

Program Format Daytime, evening, weekend classes offered. Program cycle: Continuous enrollment. Full program cycle lasts 58 weeks.

Evaluation Student evaluation based on tests, papers, reports. Grading system: Letters or numbers. Transcripts are kept for each student.

Enrollment Requirements High school diploma or GED required. Program is open to non-resident foreign students. English language proficiency required. Minimum TOEFL score required: 550.

Program Costs $8300 for the program.

Housing and Student Services Housing is available. Job counseling and placement services are available.

Special Features One of the largest and most reputable FAA-approved aircraft technician programs in the United States.

Contact Admissions Office, 5800 West Arbor Vitae Street, Los Angeles, CA 90045. 213-337-4404.

PATTEN COLLEGE
Oakland, California 94601

RELIGION (38.02)
Certified Christian Worker Program with Evangelical Teacher Training Association

General Information Unit offering the program: Biblical and Professional Departments. Available on a non-credit basis. Endorsed by Evangelical Teacher Training Association. Certificate signed by the President of the College.

Program Format Daytime, evening classes offered. Full program cycle lasts 4 semesters. Completion of program requires 60 units of course work.

Evaluation Student evaluation based on notebook completion. Grading system: Pass/fail. Transcripts are kept for each student.

Enrollment Requirements Program is open to non-resident foreign students. English language proficiency required. Minimum TOEFL score required: 500.

Program Costs $94 per course.

Housing and Student Services Housing is not available. Job counseling and placement services are not available.

Contact Ms. Sharon Hendricks, Director of Admissions, 2433 Coolidge Avenue, Oakland, CA 94601. 415-533-8300 Ext. 238.

NUCEA MEMBER
SAN DIEGO STATE UNIVERSITY
San Diego, California 92182

ACCOUNTING (06.02)
Certificate in Taxation

General Information Unit offering the program: College of Extended Studies, School of Accountancy, College of Business. Program content: Current accounting procedures for tax preparers. Available on a non-credit basis. Certificate signed by the Dean, College of Extended Studies. Program fulfills requirements for Tax Preparer License, State of California.

Program Format Evening classes offered. Instructional schedule: One evening per week for three hours. Students may enroll fall, winter. Full program cycle lasts 3 courses. Completion of program requires 60% attendance.

Evaluation Student evaluation based on tests. Records are kept by College of Extended Studies.

Enrollment Requirements Program is open to non-resident foreign students.

Program Costs $600 for the program, $200 per course.

Housing and Student Services Housing is not available. Job counseling and placement services are available.

Special Features The Certificate in Taxation program is designed for the educational needs of the professional tax preparer. Program represents compilation of most-requested areas of accounting procedures in taxation. The courses, updated with the latest information and techniques, are taught

Certificate in Taxation continued

by faculty members of the highly esteemed School of Accountancy—the first school of accountancy in California.

Contact Ms. Anne Wright, Coordinator, Certificate Programs, College of Extended Studies, San Diego, CA 92182-0723. 619-265-6255.

BANKING AND FINANCE (06.03)
Personal Financial Planning

General Information Unit offering the program: College of Business Administration, Department of Finance. Program content: Investments, estate planning, health and life insurance, employee benefits, finance. Available for credit. Endorsed by International Board of Standards and Practices for Certified Financial Planners. Certificate signed by the President. Certificate applicable to B.S. in Financial Service, M.S. in Financial and Tax Planning.

Program Format Daytime, evening classes offered. Program cycle: Continuous enrollment. Completion of program requires 46 units, grade of C or better.

Evaluation Student evaluation based on tests, papers, reports, cases, practicum. Grading system: Letters or numbers. Transcripts are kept for each student.

Enrollment Requirements Field experience or university enrollment required. Program is open to non-resident foreign students. English language proficiency required.

Program Costs $72–$147 per unit.

Housing and Student Services Housing is available. Job counseling and placement services are available.

Special Features The degree program (and accompanying certificate) is believed to be one of the most advanced and sophisticated courses of study available anywhere for the professional personal financial planner. Because the program is built around a comprehensive and detailed curriculum, graduates have found they have attained excellent preparation for careers in the area.

Contact Mr. Pieter Vandenburg, Chair, Department of Finance, College of Business Administration, San Diego, CA 92182. 619-265-5323.

BUSINESS AND MANAGEMENT, GENERAL (06.01)
Certificate in Management

General Information Unit offering the program: College of Extended Studies. Program content: Finance, accounting, information systems, insurance. Available on a non-credit basis. Certificate signed by the Dean, College of Extended Studies.

Program Format Evening classes offered. Instructional schedule: One evening per week for three hours. Program cycle: Continuous enrollment. Full program cycle lasts 6 courses. Completion of program requires 60% attendance.

Evaluation Student evaluation based on tests, papers, reports. Transcripts are kept for each student.

Enrollment Requirements Program is open to non-resident foreign students.

Program Costs $1080 for the program, $180 per course.

Housing and Student Services Housing is not available. Job counseling and placement services are available.

Special Features SDSU's Professional Development chooses seasoned, knowledgeable business professionals with exceptional teaching abilities to instruct. Courses are scheduled with the busy working professional in mind, and the certificate of completion may be earned in as little as 9 months. Courses are continually updated and new topics developed, based on participant needs.

Contact Ms. Anne Wright, Coordinator, Certificate Programs, College of Extended Studies, San Diego, CA 92182-0723. 619-265-6255.

BUSINESS AND MANAGEMENT, GENERAL (06.01)
Government Contract Management

General Information Unit offering the program: College of Extended Studies, Marketing Department, College of Business. Program content: Legalities, regulations, contract clauses, pricing. Available for credit. Cosponsored by National Contract Management Association, San Diego Chapter. Certificate signed by the President.

Program Format Evening classes offered. Instructional schedule: One evening per week. Students may enroll fall, winter, spring. Complete program cycle lasts one to two years. Completion of program requires 2.0 GPA, six courses.

Evaluation Student evaluation based on tests, reports. Grading system: Letters or numbers. Transcripts are kept for each student.

Enrollment Requirements High school diploma required. Program is open to non-resident foreign students.

Program Costs $1296 for the program, $216 per course.

Housing and Student Services Housing is not available. Job counseling and placement services are available.

Special Features Program provides information on specific facets of government contracting, including legalities, regulations, policies and procedures, contract clauses, pricing, and socioeconomic factors. Program aids in daily professional activities and career advancement. Students participate with others who face similar professional problems and obtain a better overview of the entire operation of contracting with the federal government.

Contact Ms. Anne Wright, Coordinator, Certificate Programs, College of Extended Studies, San Diego, CA 92182-0723. 619-265-6255.

BUSINESS AND MANAGEMENT, GENERAL (06.01)
Materials Management Certificate Program

General Information Unit offering the program: College of Extended Studies, Decision and Information Systems, College of Business. Program content: Production purchasing, materials management, inventory planning, traffic control. Available for credit. Endorsed by American Production and Inventory Control Society, Purchasing Management Association. Certificate signed by the President.

Program Format Evening classes offered. Instructional schedule: One evening per week. Students may enroll fall, winter, spring. Complete program cycle lasts one to four years. Completion of program requires 2.0 GPA, eight courses.

Evaluation Student evaluation based on tests. Grading system: Letters or numbers. Transcripts are kept for each student.

Enrollment Requirements High school diploma required. Program is open to non-resident foreign students.

Program Costs $1728 for the program, $216 per course.

Housing and Student Services Housing is not available. Job counseling and placement services are available.

Special Features Program provides information on specific techniques for production purchasing, materials management, and inventory planning and provides a basic understanding of traffic control, use of systems, and computer and quantitative decision-making techniques.

Contact Ms. Anne Wright, Coordinator, Certificate Programs, College of Extended Studies, San Diego, CA 92182-0723. 619-265-6255.

BUSINESS AND MANAGEMENT, GENERAL (06.01)
Project Management for Design Professionals

General Information Unit offering the program: College of Extended Studies. Program content: Planning, staffing, directing, controlling, evaluating. Available on a non-credit basis. Certificate signed by the Dean, Extended Studies.

Program Format Evening classes offered. Instructional schedule: One evening per week. Students may enroll fall, winter. Full program cycle lasts 2 courses. Completion of program requires 60% attendance.

Evaluation Student evaluation based on tests. Records are kept by College of Extended Studies.

Enrollment Requirements Program is open to non-resident foreign students.

Program Costs $590 for the program, $295 per course.

Housing and Student Services Housing is not available. Job counseling and placement services are available.

Special Features Practicing architects instruct in techniques of project management. Program presents sequential approach from project programming through construction administration. Program explores project management process through development of hypothetical project, focusing on funcions of planning, organizing, staffing, directing, controlling, and evaluating.

Contact Ms. Anne Wright, Coordinator, Certificate Programs, College of Extended Studies, San Diego, CA 92182-0723. 619-265-6255.

CONSTRUCTION TECHNOLOGY (15.10)
Certificate in Construction Practices

General Information Unit offering the program: College of Extended Studies, Civil Engineering and Management, College of Business. Program content: Engineering, information system, management. Available for credit. Endorsed by Associated General Contractors of America, San Diego Chapter. Certificate signed by the President.

Program Format Evening classes offered. Instructional schedule: One evening per week for three hours. Program cycle: Continuous enrollment. Full program cycle lasts 8 courses. Completion of program requires 2.0 GPA.

Evaluation Student evaluation based on tests, reports. Grading system: Letters or numbers. Transcripts are kept for each student.

Enrollment Requirements High school diploma required. Program is open to non-resident foreign students.

Program Costs $1728 for the program, $216 per course.

Housing and Student Services Housing is not available. Job counseling and placement services are available.

Special Features Well-regarded program in engineering and administrative practices of contruction industry is authorized and supported by one of the oldest and most creditable institutions in San Diego. Approved by SDSU's nationally known Colleges of Engineering and Business Administration and maintained under guidance of Construction Practices Advisory Board and the Associated General Contractors, San Diego Chapter.

Contact Ms. Anne Wright, Coordinator, Certificate Programs, College of Extended Studies, San Diego, CA 92182-0723. 619-265-6255.

CONSTRUCTION TECHNOLOGY (15.10)
Construction Inspection Technology
Certificate Program

General Information Unit offering the program: College of Extended Studies. Program content: On-site inspection procedures for concrete, masonary, and structural steel. Available on a non-credit basis. Certificate signed by the Dean, College of Extended Studies.

Program Format Evening classes offered. Instructional schedule: One evening per week for three hours. Students may enroll fall, winter, spring. Full program cycle lasts 3 courses. Completion of program requires 60% attendance.

Evaluation Student evaluation based on tests. Grading system: Pass/fail. Transcripts are kept for each student.

Enrollment Requirements Blueprint literacy required. Program is open to non-resident foreign students.

Program Costs $540 for the program, $180 per course.

Housing and Student Services Housing is not available. Job counseling and placement services are available.

Special Features Upon completion of the program, students should have an understanding of the roles of the building inspector and the special/deputy inspector, knowledge and skill in specific inspection techniques, and familiarity with Uniform Building Code. Program includes on-site and laboratory presentations.

Contact Ms. Anne Wright, Coordinator, Certificate Programs, College of Extended Studies, San Diego, CA 92182-0723. 619-265-6255.

EDUCATIONAL MEDIA (13.05)
Certificate in Instructional Technology

General Information Unit offering the program: Department of Educational Technology. Program content: Instructional design, educational computing, media production. Available for credit. Certificate signed by the Department Chair. Certificate applicable to M.A. in Educational Technology.

Program Format Daytime, modem classes offered. Program cycle: Continuous enrollment. Full program cycle lasts 1 year. Completion of program requires 14 units, grade of B or better.

Evaluation Student evaluation based on tests, papers, reports. Grading system: Letters or numbers. Transcripts are kept for each student.

Enrollment Requirements Letters of recommendation required. Program is open to non-resident foreign students. English language proficiency required.

Program Costs $227–$359 per unit.

Housing and Student Services Housing is available. Job counseling and placement services are available.

Special Features Program features state-of-the-art technology, labs, nationally recognized faculty, and preparation of students for placements in schools, corporations, and social service agencies.

Contact Dr. Allison Rossett, Chair and Professor of Educational Technology, San Diego, CA 92182-0311. 619-265-6718.

FIRE PROTECTION (43.02)
Certificate in Fire Protection Administration

General Information Unit offering the program: College of Extended Studies, School of Public Administration. Program content: Personnel, behavior, management, fiscal and budgetary policy. Available for credit. Endorsed by San Diego and Imperial Counties Fire Science Consortium. Certificate signed by the President. Certificate applicable to B.A. in Public Administration.

Program Format Weekend classes offered. Instructional schedule: 8 a.m. to 5 p.m., Saturdays. Students may enroll fall, winter, spring. Full program cycle lasts 8 courses. Completion of program requires 2.0 GPA.

Evaluation Student evaluation based on tests, papers, reports. Grading system: Letters or numbers. Transcripts are kept for each student.

Enrollment Requirements High school diploma required. Program is open to non-resident foreign students.

Program Costs $1728 for the program, $216 per course.

Housing and Student Services Housing is not available. Job counseling and placement services are available.

Special Features Excellent overview of latest administrative practices in public agencies. Course methods provide better community services at reduced costs, increase administrative efficiency, and broaden managerial options. In-class discussions give opportunity to share with other motivated individuals professional considerations faced by fire chiefs in everyday problem solving and decision making.

Certificate in Fire Protection Administration continued

Contact Ms. Anne Wright, Coordinator, Certificate Programs, College of Extended Studies, San Diego, CA 92182-0723. 619-265-6255.

PERSONNEL MANAGEMENT (06.16)
Personnel and Industrial Relations Certificate Program

General Information Unit offering the program: College of Extended Studies, Management Department, College of Business. Program content: Techniques and legal requirements of personnel administration. Available for credit. Certificate signed by the President.

Program Format Evening, weekend classes offered. Instructional schedule: One evening per week for three hours, one Saturday morning. Program cycle: Continuous enrollment. Full program cycle lasts 12 courses. Completion of program requires 2.0 GPA.

Evaluation Student evaluation based on tests, papers, reports. Grading system: Letters or numbers. Transcripts are kept for each student.

Enrollment Requirements High school diploma required. Program is open to non-resident foreign students.

Program Costs $1728 for the program, $144 per course.

Housing and Student Services Housing is not available. Job counseling and placement services are available.

Special Features Program structured for self-motivated individuals interested in various personnel and industrial relations professional specializations, provides help in daily professional activities and career development. Participation with others who face similar professional problems aids in obtaining a better overview of the personnel and industrial relations field.

Contact Ms. Anne Wright, Coordinator, Certificate Programs, College of Extended Studies, San Diego, CA 92182-0723. 619-265-6255.

TEACHING ENGLISH AS A SECOND LANGUAGE/FOREIGN LANGUAGE (13.14)
Advanced Certificate in Applied Linguistics and ESL

General Information Unit offering the program: Department of Linguistics. Program content: Linguistics acquistion, materials and development, English grammar and phonology, semantics. Available for credit. Certificate signed by the President.

Program Format Daytime, evening classes offered. Program cycle: Continuous enrollment. Full program cycle lasts 4 courses. Completion of program requires grade of C or better, 15 hours of tutoring.

Evaluation Student evaluation based on tests, papers, reports. Grading system: Letters or numbers, pass/fail. Transcripts are kept for each student.

Enrollment Requirements Program is open to non-resident foreign students.

Program Costs $227–$359 per unit.

Housing and Student Services Housing is not available. Job counseling and placement services are available.

Contact Mr. Jeffrey P. Kaplan, Certificate Adviser, Linguistics Department, San Diego, CA 92115. 619-265-5268.

TEACHING ENGLISH AS A SECOND LANGUAGE/FOREIGN LANGUAGE (13.14)
Basic Certificate in Applied Linguistics and ESL

General Information Unit offering the program: Department of Linguistics. Program content: Introductory linguistics, applied linguistics, TESL. Available for credit. Certificate signed by the President.

Program Format Daytime, evening classes offered. Program cycle: Continuous enrollment. Full program cycle lasts 4 courses. Completion of program requires grade of C or better, 15 hours of tutoring.

Evaluation Student evaluation based on tests, papers, reports. Grading system: Letters or numbers, pass/fail. Transcripts are kept for each student.

Enrollment Requirements Program is open to non-resident foreign students.

Program Costs $227–$359 per unit.

Housing and Student Services Housing is not available. Job counseling and placement services are available.

Contact Mr. Jeffrey P. Kaplan, Certificate Adviser, Linguistics Department, San Diego, CA 92115. 619-265-5268.

TECHNICAL AND BUSINESS WRITING (23.11)
Scientific and Technical Writing Certificate

General Information Unit offering the program: English and Comparative Literature. Program content: Advanced compostition, technical communication. Available for credit. Certificate signed by the President of University.

Program Format Daytime, evening classes offered. Program cycle: Continuous enrollment. Full program cycle lasts 21 credit hours.

Evaluation Student evaluation based on tests, papers, reports. Grading system: Letters or numbers. Transcripts are kept for each student.

Enrollment Requirements Program is open to non-resident foreign students. English language proficiency required. Students must pass written examination.

Program Costs $75 per unit.

Housing and Student Services Housing is available. Job counseling and placement services are available.

Special Features Individualized program designed by student and advisor depending on student's background. Internships available.

Contact Ms. Sherry Little, Director, Technical Writing Program, Department of English and Comparative Literature, San Diego, CA 92182. 619-265-6584.

TELECOMMUNICATIONS (09.08)
Telecommunications Certificate Program

General Information Unit offering the program: Colleges of Extended Studies, Business Administration, Engineering, Professional Studies, Fine Arts. Program content: Policy and regulatory principles, voice and data communication, office automation, transmission media. Available on a non-credit basis. Cosponsored by Telecommunications Association, San Diego Chapter. Certificate signed by the Dean, College of Extended Studies.

Program Format Evening classes offered. Instructional schedule: One evening per week for 2½ hours. Program cycle: Continuous enrollment. Full program cycle lasts 7 courses. Completion of program requires 60% attendance.

Evaluation Student evaluation based on tests, papers, reports. Records are kept by College of Extended Studies.

Enrollment Requirements Program is open to non-resident foreign students.

Program Costs $1435 for the program, $205 per course.

Housing and Student Services Housing is not available. Job counseling and placement services are available.

Special Features Voice communication, data communication, office automation, transmission media—telecommunications technologies are developing and merging at a phenomenal rate. Program is multicourse curriculum that integrates telecommunications technologies, and puts them into perspective with management and policy/regulatory principles.

Contact Ms. Anne Wright, Coordinator, Certificate Programs, College of Extended Studies, San Diego, CA 92182-0723. 619-265-6255.

NUCEA MEMBER

SAN FRANCISCO STATE UNIVERSITY
San Francisco, California 94132

CELL AND MOLECULAR BIOLOGY (26.04)
Graduate Certificate Program in Genetic Engineering

General Information Unit offering the program: Department of Biology. Program content: Laboratory and lecture program in recombinant DNA and related techniques. Available for credit. Certificate signed by the Dean of Graduate Studies. Certificate applicable to M.A. in Biology.

Program Format Daytime classes offered. Program cycle: Continuous enrollment. Full program cycle lasts 2 semesters.

Evaluation Student evaluation based on tests. Grading system: Letters or numbers. Transcripts are kept for each student.

Enrollment Requirements Bachelor's degree in biology or biochemistry, specific course background required. Program is open to non-resident foreign students. English language proficiency required. Minimum TOEFL score required: 500.

Program Costs $750 for the program.

Housing and Student Services Housing is available. Job counseling and placement services are available.

Special Features Rigorous program in modern molecular biology designed to prepare students for entry into biotechnology industry and for doctoral programs in molecular biology. Admission requirements include B.A./B.S. degree in biology or biochemistry with rigorous background in genetics, microbiology, and biochemistry. Participants receive hands-on experience in state-of-the-art techniques and course work in fundamentals of the discipline.

Contact Mr. Crellin Pauling, Chairman, Department of Biology, San Francisco, CA 94132. 415-338-1548.

INDIVIDUAL AND FAMILY DEVELOPMENT (19.07)
Applied Gerontology Certificate

General Information Unit offering the program: Extended Education, Gerontology Program. Available for credit. Endorsed by Board of Examiners of Nursing Home Administrators, Board of Registered Nurses. Certificate signed by the Dean. Certificate applicable to M.A. in Gerontology. Program fulfills requirements for BRN, BENHA, 36-hour activity leadership.

Program Format Evening, weekend classes offered. Program cycle: Continuous enrollment. Full program cycle lasts 4 semesters. Completion of program requires 3.0 GPA, 21 units.

Evaluation Student evaluation based on tests, papers, reports. Grading system: Letters or numbers. Transcripts are kept for each student.

Enrollment Requirements Fifty-four semester units required. Program is open to non-resident foreign students. English language proficiency required.

Program Costs $1680 for the program, $80 per unit.

Housing and Student Services Housing is available. Job counseling and placement services are available.

Special Features Part of comprehensive academic program; undergraduate minor, master's degree in gerontology; some financial aid from Sixty Plus of SFSU.

Contact Ms. Anabel O. Pelham, Ph.D., Director, Gerontology Programs, 20 Tapia, San Francisco, CA 94132. 415-338-1684.

LAW (22.01)
Paralegal Studies Certificate Program

General Information Unit offering the program: Extended Education. Program content: Legal skills and substantive law courses. Available for credit. Certificate signed by the Dean.

Program Format Evening classes offered. Students may enroll three times per year. Full program cycle lasts 10 courses. Completion of program requires grade of C or better.

Evaluation Student evaluation based on tests, papers, reports. Grading system: Letters or numbers. Transcripts are kept for each student.

Enrollment Requirements Fifty-six semester units required. Program is open to non-resident foreign students. English language proficiency required.

Program Costs $2400 for the program, $240 per course.

Housing and Student Services Housing is not available. Job counseling and placement services are available.

Contact Ms. Laureen Spini, Program Assistant, Extended Education, 1600 Holloway Avenue, San Francisco, CA 94132. 415-338-1207.

MEDICAL LABORATORY (18.09)
Graduate Certificate in Medical Technology

General Information Unit offering the program: Center for Advanced Medical Technology. Available for credit. Endorsed by American Medical Association's Committee on Allied Health Education and Accreditation. Cosponsored by American Society of Clinical Pathologists (ASCP). Certificate signed by the Dean. Certificate applicable to M.S. in Clinical Science. Program fulfills requirements for Clinical Laboratory Technologists License, Medical Technologist.

Program Format Daytime, evening classes offered. Students may enroll in January and July. Full program cycle lasts 12 months.

Evaluation Student evaluation based on tests, individual laboratory work. Grading system: Letters or numbers, pass/fail. Transcripts are kept for each student.

Enrollment Requirements Bachelor's degree with specific course background, California CLT Trainees License required. Program is open to non-resident foreign students. English language proficiency required. Minimum TOEFL score required: 550.

Program Costs $950 for the program.

Housing and Student Services Housing is available. Job counseling and placement services are available.

Special Features Affiliated with eight hospitals. Accepts up to 16 students per class. Graduates are eligible for NCA and ASCP certification examinations and the California CLT licensure examination. Nine semester units can apply toward the 31-unit MS degree. All phases of medical technology are taught on-campus at the hospitals.

Contact Mr. William N. Bigler, Ph.D., Director, Center for Advanced Medical Technology, San Francisco, CA 94132. 415-338-1696.

MISCELLANEOUS CONSTRUCTION TRADES AND PROPERTY MAINTENANCE (46.04)
Construction Practices Certificate Program

General Information Unit offering the program: Extended Education. Program content: Technical and administrative practices of construction. Available for credit. Certificate signed by the Dean, Extended Education. Certificate applicable to B.S. in Engineering.

Program Format Evening classes offered. Instructional schedule: One evening per week. Program cycle: Continuous enrollment. Full program cycle lasts 8 courses. Completion of program requires 24 units.

Construction Practices Certificate Program continued

Evaluation   Student evaluation based on tests, papers, reports. Grading system: Letters or numbers. Transcripts are kept for each student.

Enrollment Requirements   Fifty-six semester units required. Program is open to non-resident foreign students. English language proficiency required.

Program Costs $240–$255 per course.

Housing and Student Services   Housing is not available. Job counseling and placement services are not available.

Contact   Ms. Mary Pieratt, Coordinator, 1600 Holloway, NAD 153, San Francisco, CA 94132. 415-338-1372.

MUSIC (50.09)
Music/Recording Industry Certificate Program

General Information   Unit offering the program: Extended Education. Program content: History of popular music, legal aspects, publicity, management. Available for credit. Certificate signed by the Dean, Extended Education. Certificate applicable to any four-year degree offered at the institution.

Program Format   Evening, weekend classes offered. Program cycle: Continuous enrollment. Full program cycle lasts 13 courses. Completion of program requires 22 units.

Evaluation   Student evaluation based on tests, papers, reports. Grading system: Letters or numbers, pass/fail. Transcripts are kept for each student.

Enrollment Requirements   Fifty-six semester units required. Program is open to non-resident foreign students. English language proficiency required.

Program Costs $70–$300 per course.

Housing and Student Services   Housing is not available. Job counseling and placement services are available.

Special Features   Program designed to provide professional education in music and recording industry through course of study. Internships are available.

Contact   Ms. Mary Pieratt, Coordinator, 1600 Holloway, NAD 153, San Francisco, CA 94132. 415-338-1372.

TEACHER EDUCATION, SPECIFIC SUBJECT AREAS (13.13)
Graduate Certificate in Teaching Critical Thinking

General Information   Unit offering the program: Department of Philosophy. Available for credit. Certificate signed by the Dean of the Graduate Division. Certificate applicable to M.A. in Philosophy.

Program Format   Daytime, evening classes offered. Full program cycle lasts 2 semesters. Completion of program requires four seminars, grade of B or better, practical teaching experience.

Evaluation   Student evaluation based on tests, papers, reports. Grading system: Letters or numbers. Transcripts are kept for each student.

Enrollment Requirements   Bachelor's degree required. Program is open to non-resident foreign students. English language proficiency required.

Housing and Student Services   Housing is available.

Special Features   The program is designed to be taken along with that for the M.A. in philosophy (some seminars counted for both programs) or independently.

Contact   Chairperson, Department of Philosophy, 1600 Holloway Avenue, San Francisco, CA 94132. 415-338-1596.

TEACHER EDUCATION, SPECIFIC SUBJECT AREAS (13.13)
Preschool—Daycare—Early Childhood Education

General Information   Unit offering the program: Elementary Education. Program content: Requirements for work in preschool and daycare programs. Available for credit. Certificate signed by the Dean, Extended Education. Program fulfills requirements for Regular Instructional Children's Center Permit, Supervisory Children's Center Permit.

Program Format   Evening, weekend classes offered. Program cycle: Continuous enrollment. Full program cycle lasts 3 semesters. Completion of program requires eight courses, 200-hour supervised field experience.

Evaluation   Student evaluation based on papers, reports, field experience. Grading system: Letters or numbers. Transcripts are kept for each student.

Enrollment Requirements   Fifty-six semester units with 2.0 GPA or demonstrated ability to perform upper division work, literacy test required. Program is open to non-resident foreign students. English language proficiency required. JEPET (Junior English Proficiency Essay Test).

Program Costs $1920 for the program, $240 per course.

Housing and Student Services   Housing is not available. Job counseling and placement services are available.

Special Features   For preschool and early childhood students wishing to meet requirements for Children's Center or Licensing permits or continue training. Emphasis on group programs from infancy through school-age day care. The 24 units of required and elective courses offered in evening or weekend sessions for off-campus students. Off-campus courses arranged with agencies as in-service credit training.

Contact   Ms. Lynn Steinman, Certificate Coordinator, Extended Education, 1600 Holloway Avenue, San Francisco, CA 94132. 415-338-1378.

TECHNICAL AND BUSINESS WRITING (23.11)
Career and Technical Writing

General Information   Unit offering the program: Center for Humanistic Studies. Program content: Writing, editing, graphics, production. Available for credit. Certificate signed by the Dean of Undergraduate Studies. Certificate applicable to any four-year degree offered at the institution.

Program Format   Daytime, evening classes offered. Instructional schedule: Three hours per week. Program cycle: Continuous enrollment. Full program cycle lasts 2 semesters. Completion of program requires 24 units.

Evaluation   Student evaluation based on tests, papers, reports, editing/publishing projects, internship. Grading system: Letters or numbers, pass/fail. Transcripts are kept for each student.

Enrollment Requirements   Fifty-six semester units, 2.0 GPA required. Program is open to non-resident foreign students. English language proficiency required. Two semesters of freshman English or equivalent.

Housing and Student Services   Housing is available. Job counseling and placement services are available.

Special Features   Career and Technical Writing program prepares students to be writers and editors in a variety of fields: business, science, engineering, advertising, media, public affairs. Program also useful to persons studying for or already employed in these professions who wish to improve those writing skills necessary for good job performance.

Contact   Ms. Jane Gurko, Coordinator, Career and Technical Writing, San Francisco State University, San Francisco, CA 94132. 415-338-1109.

NUCEA MEMBER
SAN JOSE STATE UNIVERSITY
San Jose, California 95192

COMMUNICATIONS, GENERAL (09.01)
Marketing Communications Certificate Program

General Information Unit offering the program: Extended Education. Program content: Trade shows, news releases, copywriting, visual communications, direct mail, research, strategy. Available on a non-credit basis. Certificate signed by the Director of Extended Education.

Program Format Daytime, evening classes offered. Instructional schedule: 3½ hours per week. Students may enroll fall, spring. Full program cycle lasts 7 courses.

Evaluation Student evaluation based on papers, reports. Grading system: Pass/fail. Transcripts are kept for each student.

Enrollment Requirements Program is open to non-resident foreign students. English language proficiency required. Minimum TOEFL score required: 550.

Program Costs $575 for the program, $55–$165 per course.

Housing and Student Services Housing is not available. Job counseling and placement services are not available.

Contact Continuing Education, One Washington Square, San Jose, CA 95192. 408-277-2182.

LAW (22.01)
Legal Assistant Studies Certificate Program

General Information Unit offering the program: Continuing Education. Available for credit. Certificate signed by the Dean of Continuing Education. Certificate applicable to any four-year degree offered at the institution.

Program Format Evening, weekend classes offered. Program cycle: Continuous enrollment. Complete program cycle lasts two semesters, plus one three-week summer course. Completion of program requires grade of C or better.

Evaluation Student evaluation based on tests, papers, reports. Grading system: Letters or numbers. Transcripts are kept for each student.

Enrollment Requirements Two years of college or minimum three years experience in law required. Program is not open to non-resident foreign students. English language proficiency required.

Program Costs $2550 for the program, $255 per course.

Housing and Student Services Housing is not available. Job counseling and placement services are available.

Special Features The program of study totals 30 semester units. Four courses (12 units) are required of all certificate students; other courses are selected by each student. The four core courses cover the general legal research and support skills needed by all legal assistants. Practicing attorneys teach the courses.

Contact Mr. Robert J. Donovan, Director, Legal Assistant Studies, Continuing Education, San Jose, CA 95192. 408-277-3896.

TECHNICAL AND BUSINESS WRITING (23.11)
Technical Writing Certificate Program

General Information Unit offering the program: English, Continuing Education Division. Available for credit. Certificate signed by the Dean, School of Humanities and Arts. Certificate applicable to any four-year degree offered at the institution.

Program Format Daytime, evening classes offered. Students may enroll fall, spring. Full program cycle lasts 2 semesters. Completion of program requires 18 units, internship.

Evaluation Student evaluation based on tests, papers, reports. Grading system: Letters or numbers. Transcripts are kept for each student.

Enrollment Requirements Two semesters of college English and an introductory computer course required. Program is open to non-resident foreign students. English language proficiency required. Minimum TOEFL score required: 500.

Program Costs $1557 for the program, $255 per course.

Housing and Student Services Housing is not available. Job counseling and placement services are available.

Special Features The internship provides students with an invaluable opportunity to work with a major company in 'Silicon Valley.' Such internships frequently result in students being employed by the company with which they did their internship. Also, completion of program is often a requirement when local companies look to hire technical writers.

Contact Ms. Lois Rew, Coordinator, Technical Writing Program, English Department, San Jose, CA 95192. 408-277-2832.

TRADE AND INDUSTRIAL SUPERVISION AND MANAGEMENT (06.20)
Construction Estimating Certificate Program

General Information Unit offering the program: Extended Education. Program content: Industry's procedures, practices, methods. Available on a non-credit basis. Endorsed by American Society of Professional Estimators, Santa Clara County Chapter. Certificate signed by the Director of Extended Education.

Program Format Evening classes offered. Instructional schedule: Three hours per week. Students may enroll fall, spring. Full program cycle lasts 10 courses.

Evaluation Student evaluation based on tests, papers, reports. Grading system: Pass/fail. Transcripts are kept for each student.

Enrollment Requirements Open enrollment. Program is open to non-resident foreign students. English language proficiency required. Minimum TOEFL score required: 550.

Program Costs $2100 for the program, $210 per course.

Housing and Student Services Housing is not available. Job counseling and placement services are not available.

Contact Continuing Education, One Washington Square, San Jose, CA 95192. 408-277-2182.

TRADE AND INDUSTRIAL SUPERVISION AND MANAGEMENT (06.20)
Construction Management Certificate Program

General Information Unit offering the program: Extended Education. Program content: Training for managers and supervisors. Available on a non-credit basis. Certificate signed by the Director of Extended Education.

Program Format Evening classes offered. Instructional schedule: Three hours per week. Students may enroll fall, spring. Full program cycle lasts 6 courses.

Evaluation Student evaluation based on tests, papers, reports. Grading system: Pass/fail. Transcripts are kept for each student.

Enrollment Requirements Program is open to non-resident foreign students. English language proficiency required. Minimum TOEFL score required: 550.

Program Costs $1260 for the program, $210 per course.

Housing and Student Services Housing is not available. Job counseling and placement services are not available.

Contact Continuing Education, One Washington Square, San Jose, CA 95192. 408-277-2182.

SIMPSON COLLEGE
San Francisco, California 94134

BIBLE STUDIES (39.02)
Biblical Studies Certificate

General Information   Unit offering the program: Bible Department. Program content: Old and New Testament. Available for credit. Certificate signed by the President. Certificate applicable to B.A. in Biblical Studies.

Program Format   Daytime classes offered. Instructional schedule: Monday through Friday. Program cycle: Continuous enrollment. Full program cycle lasts 2 semesters. Completion of program requires 30 credit hours.

Evaluation   Student evaluation based on tests, papers, reports. Grading system: Letters or numbers. Transcripts are kept for each student.

Enrollment Requirements   High school diploma required. Program is open to non-resident foreign students. English language proficiency required. Minimum TOEFL score required: 500.

Program Costs $4200 for the program, $210 per credit hour.

Housing and Student Services   Housing is available. Job counseling and placement services are not available.

Contact   Admissions Office, 801 Silver Avenue, San Francisco, CA 94134. 415-334-7400.

NUCEA MEMBER
UNIVERSITY OF CALIFORNIA AT BERKELEY
Berkeley, California 94720

ACCOUNTING (06.02)
Certificate Program in Accounting

General Information   Unit offering the program: Continuing Education in Business and Management. Available for credit. Certificate signed by the Dean, Continuing Education.

Program Format   Evening, weekend classes offered. Instructional schedule: Three hours per week. Program cycle: Continuous enrollment. Complete program cycle lasts two to three years.

Evaluation   Student evaluation based on tests, papers, reports, projects. Grading system: Letters or numbers. Transcripts are kept for each student.

Enrollment Requirements   College degree or two years business experience required. Program is open to non-resident foreign students.

Program Costs $2000 for the program.

Housing and Student Services   Housing is not available. Job counseling and placement services are not available.

Special Features   The program consists of seven required courses and two elective courses which introduce the student to important theories and practices of modern business accounting. The program can enable mastery of techniques needed for responsible accounting positions in business. It can also help prepare the student for parts of the CPA examination. Instructors are current practicioners in the field.

Contact   Ms. Ray Jean Breckenridge, Certificate Coordinator, University Extension, Department of Business and Management, Berkeley, CA 94720. 415-642-4231.

BANKING AND FINANCE (06.03)
Certificate in Personal Financial Planning

General Information   Unit offering the program: Continuing Education in Business and Management, University Extension. Program content: Income taxes, securities investments, real estate, tax shelters, insurance, employment benefits, estate planning for potential financial planning. Available for credit. Certificate signed by the Dean, University Extension. Program fulfills requirements for registration with International Association for Financial Planning, Atlanta, Georgia.

Program Format   Evening classes offered. Instructional schedule: Three hours per week. Program cycle: Continuous enrollment. Full program cycle lasts 4 years. Completion of program requires eight courses, average grade of B or better, minimum grade of B in case study course.

Evaluation   Student evaluation based on tests, papers, projects. Grading system: Letters or numbers. Transcripts are kept for each student.

Enrollment Requirements   Bachelor's degree; knowledge of financial analysis, economics, and finance required. Program is open to non-resident foreign students.

Program Costs $2500 for the program, $175–$345 per course.

Housing and Student Services   Housing is not available. Job counseling and placement services are not available.

Special Features   The curriculum covers the following aspects of financial planning: income taxes, securities investment, real estate, tax shelters, insurance, employment benefits, and estate planning and integrates all courses in the final course, a case study. Students must meet prerequisites or obtain prior consent for enrollment. Instructors are finance professionals.

Contact   Ms. Ruth Majdrakoff, Director, Certificate in Personal Financial Planning, University Extension - CEBM, 2223 Fulton Street, Berkeley, CA 94720. 415-642-4231.

BUSINESS AND MANAGEMENT, GENERAL (06.01)
Certificate Program in Business Management

General Information   Unit offering the program: Continuing Education in Business and Management. Available for credit. Certificate signed by the Dean, Continuing Education.

Program Format   Evening, weekend classes offered. Instructional schedule: Three hours per week. Program cycle: Continuous enrollment. Complete program cycle lasts two to three years.

Evaluation   Student evaluation based on tests, papers, reports, projects. Grading system: Letters or numbers. Transcripts are kept for each student.

Enrollment Requirements   College degree or two years business experience required.

Program Costs $2000 for the program.

Housing and Student Services   Housing is not available. Job counseling and placement services are not available.

Special Features   The program consists of six required courses and four elective courses which provide an overview of theories and techniques needed to excel in today's business world. These courses provide a secure foundation of business knowledge which can lead students to increased job performance and responsibility.

Contact   Ms. Ray Jean Breckenridge, Certificate Coordinator, University Extension, Department of Business and Management, Berkeley, CA 94720. 415-642-4231.

BUSINESS AND MANAGEMENT, GENERAL (06.01)
Intensive Certificate Program in Purchasing and Materials Management

General Information   Unit offering the program: Business and Management Department. Program content: Price and cost analysis, legal factors, advanced purchasing, materials management, inventory control. Available for credit. Certificate signed by the Department Chairman.

Program Format   Evening, weekend classes offered. Instructional schedule: Twice per week, Saturdays. Program cycle: Continuous enrollment. Full program cycle lasts 9 months.

Completion of program requires 200 contact hours, grade of C or better.

Evaluation Student evaluation based on tests. Grading system: Letters or numbers. Transcripts are kept for each student.

Enrollment Requirements Program is open to non-resident foreign students.

Program Costs $1365 for the program, $195 per course.

Housing and Student Services Housing is not available. Job counseling and placement services are available.

Special Features The program can be completed in 9 months of intensive study.

Contact Mr. William Knickerbocker, Coordinator for Management Development Programs, 2223 Fulton Street, Berkeley, CA 94720. 415-642-4242.

COMMUNICATIONS, GENERAL (09.01)
Certificate in Publishing

General Information Unit offering the program: Continuing Education in Business and Management, University Extension. Program content: Editorial work, production and design, marketing, management. Available for credit. Certificate signed by the Dean, University Extension.

Program Format Evening classes offered. Instructional schedule: Three hours per week. Program cycle: Continuous enrollment. Complete program cycle lasts two to three years. Completion of program requires 210 contact hours, average grade of B or better.

Evaluation Student evaluation based on tests, papers, homework assignments, projects. Grading system: Letters or numbers. Transcripts are kept for each student.

Enrollment Requirements General educational background preferred. Program is open to non-resident foreign students.

Program Costs $2000 for the program.

Housing and Student Services Housing is not available. Job counseling and placement services are not available.

Special Features The curriculum is comprised of four required courses providing an overview of publishing from an editorial standpoint, an introduction to production and marketing, and a familiarity with computers in publishing, plus 90 hours of electives offering detailed instruction in all major areas of publishing. Instructors are publishing professionals.

Contact Ms. Ruth Majdrakoff, Director, Certificate in Publishing, University Extension - CEBM, 2223 Fulton Street, Berkeley, CA 94720. 415-642-4231.

COMPUTER PROGRAMMING (11.02)
Certificate in Business Data Processing

General Information Unit offering the program: Electrical Engineering and Computer Sciences. Program content: Theory and practice for entry-level programming jobs. Available for credit. Certificate signed by the Dean, University of California Extension.

Program Format Evening classes offered. Instructional schedule: Once per week. Program cycle: Continuous enrollment. Complete program cycle lasts four to five semesters. Completion of program requires grade of B or better.

Evaluation Student evaluation based on tests, papers, programming assignments. Grading system: Letters or numbers. Transcripts are kept for each student.

Enrollment Requirements Bachelor's degree recommended. Program is open to non-resident foreign students.

Program Costs $2015 for the program, $210–$315 per course.

Housing and Student Services Housing is not available. Job counseling and placement services are not available.

Special Features All instructors are practicing professionals in the field.

Contact Ms. Bonnie Stiles, Continuing Education Specialist, UNEX, 2223 Fulton Street, Berkeley, CA 94720. 415-642-1061.

FILM ARTS (50.06)
Studies in Commercial Photography

General Information Unit offering the program: Division of Letters and Sciences, University Extension. Program content: Theory, technique, practice of commercial photography. Available on either a credit or non-credit basis. Certificate signed by the Assistant Dean, Division of Letters and Sciences.

Program Format Evening, weekend classes offered. Instructional schedule: Once per week. Program cycle: Continuous enrollment. Full program cycle lasts 7 courses, plus 60-hour internship.

Evaluation Student evaluation based on portfolio of photographs. Grading system: Letters or numbers. Transcripts are kept for each student.

Enrollment Requirements Program is open to non-resident foreign students.

Program Costs $110–$300 per course.

Housing and Student Services Housing is not available. Job counseling and placement services are not available.

Special Features Beginning-level course requirements waived for prior experience. Instructors are practicing professionals. Course schedules geared to needs of working people. Internship provides on-the-job experience with working professional.

Contact Mr. Michael Lesser, Photography Program Coordinator, Berkeley Extension, 55 Laguna Street, San Francisco, CA 94102. 415-642-8840.

FINE ARTS (50.07)
Studies in Art Photography

General Information Unit offering the program: Division of Letters and Sciences, University Extension. Program content: Theory, technique, practice of photography as an art form. Available on either a credit or non-credit basis. Certificate signed by the Assistant Dean, Division of Letters and Sciences.

Program Format Evening, weekend classes offered. Instructional schedule: Once per week. Program cycle: Continuous enrollment. Full program cycle lasts 9 courses.

Evaluation Student evaluation based on portfolio of photographs. Grading system: Letters or numbers, pass/fail. Transcripts are kept for each student.

Enrollment Requirements Program is open to non-resident foreign students.

Program Costs $110–$300 per course.

Housing and Student Services Housing is not available. Job counseling and placement services are not available.

Special Features Beginning course requirement waived for prior experience. Instructors are working artists and professional photographers. Course schedules geared to needs of working people.

Contact Mr. Michael Lesser, Continuing Education Specialist, Berkeley Extension, 55 Laguna Street, San Francisco, CA 94102. 415-642-8840.

GRAPHIC AND PRINTING COMMUNICATIONS (48.02)
Certificate in Graphic Design

General Information Unit offering the program: Letters and Sciences Division. Program content: Developments in graphic studies, portfolio development. Available for credit. Certificate signed by the Director.

Program Format Evening, weekend classes offered. Students may enroll fall, spring, summer. Full program cycle lasts 16 credit hours. Completion of program requires portfolio of work.

Evaluation Student evaluation based on tests, papers, design projects. Grading system: Letters or numbers. Transcripts are kept for each student.

Enrollment Requirements Program is open to non-resident foreign students.

Certificate in Graphic Design continued

Program Costs $170 per course, one day seminar, $65; two day computer workshops, $250.

Housing and Student Services   Housing is not available. Job counseling and placement services are available.

Special Features   The Bay Area is nationally and internationally recognized as a center for the design and illustration of printed matter. Outstanding professionals in the area are instructors and offer technologically current courses such as desktop publishing, microcomputer design, and television design. The program is five years old and continually growing in numbers of course offerings and students.

Contact   Ms. Carol Thompson, Director, Certificate in Graphic Design, University of California Extension 55, Laguna Street, San Francisco, CA 94102. 415-861-7720.

HUMAN RESOURCES DEVELOPMENT (06.06)
Training and Human Resource Development

General Information   Unit offering the program: Continuing Education in Business and Management. Program content: Processes and strategies used in the four phases of training. Available for credit. Certificate signed by the Dean, Continuing Education.

Program Format   Evening, weekend classes offered. Instructional schedule: Three hours per week. Program cycle: Continuous enrollment. Complete program cycle lasts two to three years. Completion of program requires minimum 250 hours of instruction.

Evaluation   Student evaluation based on tests, papers, reports, projects. Grading system: Letters or numbers. Transcripts are kept for each student.

Enrollment Requirements   College degree or two years business experience required. Program is open to non-resident foreign students.

Program Costs $2000 for the program.

Housing and Student Services   Housing is not available. Job counseling and placement services are not available.

Special Features   Seven core courses (210 hours) plus 40 hours of electives. Designed to help HRD professionals and those with training and HRD responsibilities acquire new ideas and network with other professionals; master basic knowledge and skills; develop new competencies; select courses that fit specific HRD needs. Instructors are current practitioners in the field.

Contact   Ms. Evelyn Mosher, Certificate Coordinator, 2223 Fulton, Berkeley, CA 94720. 415-642-4231.

INTERIOR DESIGN (04.05)
Certificate in Interior Design and Interior Architecture

General Information   Unit offering the program: Letters and Sciences Division. Program content: Design, resources, design communication. Available for credit. Certificate signed by the Dean, Continuing Education.

Program Format   Daytime, evening classes offered. Program cycle: Continuous enrollment. Full program cycle lasts 12 semesters. Completion of program requires grade of C or better in all courses.

Evaluation   Student evaluation based on tests, papers, reports. Grading system: Letters or numbers. Transcripts are kept for each student.

Enrollment Requirements   Program is open to non-resident foreign students.

Program Costs $6000 for the program, $185–$500 per course.

Housing and Student Services   Housing is not available. Job counseling and placement services are not available.

Special Features   Courses are open to professionals seeking continuing education as well as persons entering the field. Instructors include top Bay Area designers and architects. Students may waive up to five required courses by transferred courses or field experience. The program is five-years-old with one graduating class.

Contact   Ms. Adena Gilbert, Program Assistant, Berkeley Extension, 2223 Fulton, Berkeley, CA 94720. 415-927-0212.

LANDSCAPE ARCHITECTURE (04.06)
Certificate in Garden Design

General Information   Unit offering the program: University Extension. Program content: Herbaceous plants, methods of changing garden grades and elevations, paving materials, irrigation system. Available on either a credit or non-credit basis. Certificate signed by the Dean, University Extension.

Program Format   Evening, weekend classes offered. Instructional schedule: Once or twice per week, Saturdays. Full program cycle lasts 13 courses. Completion of program requires grade of C or better in credit courses.

Evaluation   Student evaluation based on tests, papers, projects. Grading system: Letters or numbers, pass/fail. Transcripts are kept for each student.

Enrollment Requirements   Bachelor's degree recommended. Program is open to non-resident foreign students.

Program Costs $3300 for the program.

Housing and Student Services   Housing is not available. Job counseling and placement services are not available.

Special Features   Students with successful prior course work in certain subjects can waive some required courses. This curriculum focuses on design education at the residential scale. Some building block courses are the same as those taken by students pursuing the landscape architecture certificate.

Contact   Mr. Robert Scheele, Program Director, University Extension, Berkeley, CA 94720. 415-642-1061.

LANDSCAPE ARCHITECTURE (04.06)
Certificate in Landscape Architecture

General Information   Unit offering the program: Department of Landscape Architecture. Program content: Graphics, plant materials, planning and design, construction, environmental analysis. Available for credit. Endorsed by State Board of Landscape Architects. Certificate signed by the Dean, University Extension. Program fulfills requirements for Licensed Landscape Architect.

Program Format   Evening, weekend classes offered. Instructional schedule: Once or twice per week, Saturdays. Full program cycle lasts 45 credit hours. Completion of program requires grade of C or better in all courses.

Evaluation   Student evaluation based on tests, papers, projects. Grading system: Letters or numbers, pass/fail. Transcripts are kept for each student.

Enrollment Requirements   Bachelor's degree recommended. Program is open to non-resident foreign students.

Program Costs $5700 for the program.

Housing and Student Services   Housing is not available. Job counseling and placement services are not available.

Special Features   Students with successful prior course work in certain subjects can waive some required courses. Instructors are practicing professionals. Many also have taught landscape architecture elsewhere and possess advanced degrees. All courses and instructors are subject to the approval of Department of Landscape Architecture faculty and the Academic Senate.

Contact   Mr. Robert Scheele, Program Director, University Extension, Berkeley, CA 94720. 415-642-1061.

MARKETING MANAGEMENT AND RESEARCH (06.14)
Intensive Certificate Program in Marketing

General Information   Unit offering the program: Business and Management Department. Program content: Research, marketing planning, strategy, consumer behavior. Available for credit. Certificate signed by the Department Chairman.

Program Format   Evening, weekend classes offered. Instructional schedule: Twice per week, Saturdays. Program cycle: Continuous enrollment. Full program cycle lasts 9 months. Completion of program requires 200 classroom hours, grade of C or better.

Evaluation   Student evaluation based on tests, papers, reports. Grading system: Letters or numbers. Transcripts are kept for each student.

Enrollment Requirements   Program is open to non-resident foreign students.

Program Costs $1365 for the program, $195 per course.

Housing and Student Services   Housing is not available. Job counseling and placement services are available.

Special Features   Seven courses required to complete the program—four in required 'core' area of marketing and three elective courses in either marketing management, advertising, sales management, or retail management. Full program can be completed in less than one year of part-time studies.

Contact   Mr. William Knickerbocker, Coordinator for Management Development Programs, 2223 Fulton Street, Berkeley, CA 94720. 415-642-4242.

MENTAL HEALTH/HUMAN SERVICES (17.04)
Alcohol and Drug Abuse Studies

General Information   Unit offering the program: University Extension and School of Public Health. Program content: Fundamentals of abuse and its treatment. Available for credit. Certificate signed by the Dean, University Extension.

Program Format   Daytime, evening, weekend classes offered. Program cycle: Continuous enrollment. Complete program cycle lasts 230 classroom hours. Completion of program requires grade of C or better in all courses.

Evaluation   Student evaluation based on tests, papers, projects, class exercises. Grading system: Letters or numbers. Transcripts are kept for each student.

Enrollment Requirements   Program is open to non-resident foreign students.

Program Costs $1700 for the program, $150 per course.

Housing and Student Services   Housing is not available. Job counseling and placement services are available.

Special Features   The program has a diverse student body of recovering persons and professionals. It is designed to expose students to multiple approaches and techniques. The instructors are mainly professionals working in the field who are also familiar with 12 step and self-help approaches.

Contact   Ms. Helen Diggins, Program Assistant, University Extension, 2223 Fulton Street, Berkeley, CA 94720. 415-643-6901.

OPTOMETRY (18.12)
Certificate of Completion—Optometric Residency Program

General Information   Unit offering the program: School of Optometry. Available for credit. Certificate signed by the Dean, School of Optometry.

Program Format   Daytime, weekend classes offered. Students enroll July 1. Full program cycle lasts 12 months. Completion of program requires 24 units, 3.0 GPA.

Evaluation   Student evaluation based on tests, reports, patient care. Grading system: Letters or numbers, pass/fail. Transcripts are kept for each student.

Enrollment Requirements   O.D. or equivalent degree required. Program is open to non-resident foreign students. English language proficiency required. Minimum TOEFL score required: 550.

Program Costs $47 campus fee per semester.

Housing and Student Services   Housing is not available. Job counseling and placement services are available.

Special Features   The resident can choose one, or combine two, of the following specialty areas: Binocular Vision and/or Pediatric Vision; Contact Lens; Family Practice Optometry; Low Vision Ocular Disease Detection; Visual Functions. The faculty coordinator for that specialty area will work with the resident to select courses, seminar topics, colloquia, clinical work, and research.

Contact   Coordinator, Optometric Residency Program, School of Optometry, Berkeley, CA 94720. 415-642-0945.

PERSONNEL MANAGEMENT (06.16)
Certificate in Personnel Administration

General Information   Unit offering the program: Business and Management. Available for credit. Endorsed by Northern California Human Resources Council. Certificate signed by the Dean, University Extension.

Program Format   Daytime, evening, weekend classes offered. Full program cycle lasts 3 years. Completion of program requires ten courses.

Evaluation   Student evaluation based on tests, papers, reports. Grading system: Letters or numbers. Transcripts are kept for each student.

Enrollment Requirements   Program is open to non-resident foreign students.

Program Costs $2000 for the program, $180 per course.

Contact   Ms. Nikki Fuller, Program Representative, University Extension, 2223 Fulton Street, Berkeley, CA 94720. 415-642-4231.

SYSTEMS ANALYSIS (11.05)
Information Systems: Analysis, Design, and Management

General Information   Unit offering the program: Electrical Engineering and Computer Science. Program content: Theory and practice for systems analysis jobs. Available for credit. Certificate signed by the Dean, University of California Extension.

Program Format   Evening classes offered. Instructional schedule: Once per week. Program cycle: Continuous enrollment. Complete program cycle lasts five to six semesters. Completion of program requires grade of B or better.

Evaluation   Student evaluation based on tests, papers, programming assignments. Grading system: Letters or numbers. Transcripts are kept for each student.

Enrollment Requirements   Bachelor's degree, three years experience required. Program is open to non-resident foreign students.

Program Costs $2395 for the program, $210–$350 per course.

Housing and Student Services   Housing is not available. Job counseling and placement services are not available.

Special Features   All instructors are practicing professionals in the field.

Contact   Ms. Bonnie Stiles, Continuing Education Specialist, UNEX, 2223 Fulton Street, Berkeley, CA 94720. 415-642-1061.

TEACHER EDUCATION, SPECIFIC SUBJECT AREAS (13.13)
Computers in Education

General Information   Unit offering the program: Education Department. Program content: Computers in K–12 education, teaching applications, methodology, hardware and software.

Computers in Education continued

Available for credit. Certificate signed by the Dean, University of California, Berkeley Extension.

Program Format Daytime, evening, weekend classes offered. Program cycle: Continuous enrollment. Full program cycle lasts 16 credit hours. Completion of program requires grade of C or better in each course.

Evaluation Student evaluation based on tests, papers, reports. Grading system: Letters or numbers. Transcripts are kept for each student.

Enrollment Requirements Bachelor's degree and teaching credential, or equivalent professional standing required. Program is open to non-resident foreign students.

Program Costs $1080–$1550 for the program.

Housing and Student Services Housing is not available. Job counseling and placement services are not available.

Special Features The program is under constant appraisal and revision as needed. Feedback from all courses, regular faculty meetings, and contact with advisory board members helps to maintain course quality and appropriateness. New electives are developed each semester. Instructors have all been classroom teachers and are content-area experts with adult teaching experience.

Contact Ms. Jane Fisher, Specialist, Computers in Education, Berkeley Extension, 2223 Fulton Street, Berkeley, CA 94720. 415-642-1171.

TEACHING ENGLISH AS A SECOND LANGUAGE/FOREIGN LANGUAGE (13.14)
Teaching English as a Second Language

General Information Unit offering the program: Education Extension. Program content: Linguistic and second language theories, methods, cross-cultural communication skills, student teaching. Available for credit. Certificate signed by the Dean of Extension.

Program Format Evening, weekend classes offered. Instructional schedule: Once per week. Program cycle: Continuous enrollment. Full program cycle lasts 4 semesters. Completion of program requires grade of B or better for each course.

Evaluation Student evaluation based on tests, papers, reports, student teaching. Grading system: Letters or numbers. Transcripts are kept for each student.

Enrollment Requirements Bachelor's degree required. Program is open to non-resident foreign students. English language proficiency required. Minimum TOEFL score required: 600.

Program Costs $1635 for the program, $175 per course.

Housing and Student Services Housing is not available. Job counseling and placement services are not available.

Special Features The courses in Teaching English as a Second Language combine theory with a strong emphasis on classroom methods and strategies. In addition to learning ESL content and methodologies, students learn fundamental classroom management skills. Program is field-oriented, so students are well prepared for a variety of teaching positions in the public and private sectors, here and abroad.

Contact Ms. Martha O. Egan, Program Coordinator, TESL Certificate Program, Berkeley Extension, 2223 Fulton Street, Berkeley, CA 94720. 415-642-1171.

TELECOMMUNICATIONS (09.08)
Certificate in Telecommunications Engineering

General Information Unit offering the program: Continuing Education in Engineering, University Extension. Program content: Data communication, computer network, digital telephony, communication theory and application, software development. Available for credit. Certificate signed by the Dean, University Extension.

Program Format Evening classes offered. Instructional schedule: Once per week for three hours. Program cycle: Continuous enrollment. Full program cycle lasts 16 credit hours. Completion of program requires average grade of B or better.

Evaluation Student evaluation based on tests, papers, reports, oral presentations. Grading system: Letters or numbers. Transcripts are kept for each student.

Enrollment Requirements Prerequisite of Mathematics for Communications Engineer or equivalent required. Program is open to non-resident foreign students.

Program Costs $1800 for the program, $205–$265 per course.

Housing and Student Services Housing is not available. Job counseling and placement services are available.

Special Features Program is the first such certificate available in California. It was set up in cooperation with Pacific Bell Company with both UC Berkeley and UCLA Extensions. Participants may take course work from Berkeley or UCLA and apply it toward certificates awarded by either institution.

Contact Mr. Richard V. Tsina, Vice Chair, Continuing Education in Engineering, University of California, Berkeley Extension, Berkeley, CA 94720. 415-642-4151.

UNIVERSITY OF CALIFORNIA, DAVIS
Davis, California 95616

COMPUTER AND INFORMATION SCIENCES, GENERAL (11.01)
Certificate Program in Computer Studies

General Information Unit offering the program: University Extension, Division of Computer Science. Program content: Business data processing. Available for credit. Certificate signed by the Dean, University Extension.

Program Format Evening, weekend classes offered. Instructional schedule: One evening per week. Program cycle: Continuous enrollment. Completion of program requires eight courses, 240 classroom hours, grade of C or better.

Evaluation Student evaluation based on tests, papers, reports. Grading system: Letters or numbers, pass/fail. Transcripts are kept for each student.

Enrollment Requirements High school diploma required, bachelor's degree preferred. Program is open to non-resident foreign students.

Program Costs $1500 for the program, $180 per course.

Housing and Student Services Housing is available. Job counseling and placement services are not available.

Special Features Program designed to provide participants with qualifications they need to fill entry-level positions in field of business data processing. Certificate awarded upon satisfactory completion of eight courses-five required and three elective.

Contact Ms. Alice Tom, Continuing Education Specialist, Business and Management, University Extension, Davis, CA 95616. 916-752-7530.

ENVIRONMENTAL CONTROL TECHNOLOGIES (15.05)
Certificate Program in Hazardous Materials Management

General Information Unit offering the program: University Extension, Environmental Toxicology. Program content: Safe management of toxic and hazardous materials. Available for credit. Certificate signed by the Dean, University Extension.

Program Format Evening, weekend classes offered. Instructional schedule: Four days in two-day sessions separated by two to four weeks. Program cycle: Continuous enrollment. Completion of program requires eight courses.

Evaluation Student evaluation based on tests, papers, reports. Grading system: Letters or numbers, pass/fail. Transcripts are kept for each student.

Enrollment Requirements High school diploma required, bachelor's degree preferred. Program is open to non-resident foreign students.

Program Costs $180 per course.

Housing and Student Services Housing is available. Job counseling and placement services are not available.

Special Features Program provides a thorough introduction to the principles, regulation, technologies, laboratory practices, and field methodologies used in hazardous materials management. Teaches state-of-the-art techniques for safe production, use, and disposal of toxic and hazardous materials and practical approaches to meeting government regulations and industry standards related to hazardous materials management.

Contact Ms. Mona Ellerbrock, Continuing Education Specialist, Hazardous Substances, University Extension, Davis, CA 95616. 916-752-6572.

GRAPHIC AND PRINTING COMMUNICATIONS (48.02)
Certificate Program in Graphic Design

General Information Unit offering the program: University Extension, Environmental Design. Program content: Graphic and visual arts. Available for credit. Certificate signed by the Dean, University Extension.

Program Format Evening, weekend classes offered. Instructional schedule: One evening per week. Program cycle: Continuous enrollment. Completion of program requires eight courses, 240 hours of instruction.

Evaluation Student evaluation based on tests, papers, reports. Grading system: Letters or numbers, pass/fail. Transcripts are kept for each student.

Enrollment Requirements High school diploma required, bachelor's degree preferred. Program is open to non-resident foreign students.

Program Costs $1500 for the program, $180 per course.

Housing and Student Services Housing is available. Job counseling and placement services are not available.

Special Features Program offers practical instruction, problem-solving techniques, information on current developments in graphic design, and opportunity to develop portfolio of work. Related courses designed for people with fine art or design backgrounds who need a marketing orientation for their work, those considering entering the commercial art field, or those whose work requires some familiarity with graphic design.

Contact Ms. Catherine Hills, Continuing Education Specialist Education/Liberal Arts, University Extension, Davis, CA 95616. 916-752-8535.

HUMAN RESOURCES DEVELOPMENT (06.06)
Certificate Program in Human Resource Development

General Information Unit offering the program: University Extension, Graduate School of Management. Program content: Knowledge, skills, and effectiveness in management of human resources. Available for credit. Certificate signed by the Dean, University Extension.

Program Format Evening, weekend classes offered. Instructional schedule: One evening per week. Program cycle: Continuous enrollment. Completion of program requires eight courses, 240 classroom hours.

Evaluation Student evaluation based on tests, papers, reports. Grading system: Letters or numbers, pass/fail. Transcripts are kept for each student.

Enrollment Requirements High school diploma required, bachelor's degree preferred. Program is open to non-resident foreign students.

Program Costs $1500 for the program, $180 per course.

Housing and Student Services Housing is available. Job counseling and placement services are not available.

Special Features Program designed to build knowledge, skills, and effectiveness in management of human resources and to improve career opportunities in human resource development, industrial relations, training, personnel administration, or a related area.

Contact Ms. Alice Tom, Continuing Education Specialist, Business and Management, University Extension, Davis, CA 95616. 916-752-7530.

INSURANCE AND RISK MANAGEMENT (06.08)
Certificate Program in Workers' Compensation

General Information Unit offering the program: University Extension, Graduate School of Management. Program content: California workers' compensation system. Available for credit. Certificate signed by the Dean, University Extension.

Program Format Evening, weekend classes offered. Instructional schedule: One evening per week. Program cycle: Continuous enrollment. Completion of program requires seven courses.

Evaluation Student evaluation based on tests, papers, reports. Grading system: Letters or numbers, pass/fail. Transcripts are kept for each student.

Enrollment Requirements High school diploma required, bachelor's degree preferred. Program is open to non-resident foreign students.

Program Costs $180 per course.

Housing and Student Services Housing is available. Job counseling and placement services are not available.

Special Features Program for all professionals involved with workers' compensation. In seven courses, certificate program helps students understand California workers' compensation system and develop effective means for handling cases.

Contact Ms. Alice Tom, Continuing Education Specialist, Business and Management, University Extension, Davis, CA 95616. 916-752-7530.

INVESTMENTS AND SECURITIES (06.10)
Certificate Program in Personal Financial Planning

General Information Unit offering the program: University Extension, Graduate School of Management. Available for credit. Certificate signed by the Dean, University Extension.

Program Format Evening, weekend classes offered. Instructional schedule: One evening per week. Program cycle: Continuous enrollment. Completion of program requires eight courses, 240 classroom hours.

Evaluation Student evaluation based on tests, papers, reports. Grading system: Letters or numbers, pass/fail. Transcripts are kept for each student.

Enrollment Requirements High school diploma required, bachelor's degree preferred. Program is open to non-resident foreign students.

Program Costs $1500 for the program, $180 per course.

Housing and Student Services Housing is available. Job counseling and placement services are not available.

Special Features Certificate Program in Personal Financial Planning provides comprehensive and integrated curriculum of study designed to build on professional expertise of bankers, insurance, real estate and security brokers; trust officers; lawyers; CPA's and investment advisors; and to meet the specialized educational needs of those who have no direct experience in financial planning.

Certificate Program in Personal Financial Planning continued

Contact Ms. Alice Tom, Continuing Education Specialist, Business and Management, University Extension, Davis, CA 95616. 916-752-7530.

LABOR/INDUSTRIAL RELATIONS (06.11)
Certificate Program in Labor-Management Relations

General Information Unit offering the program: University Extension, Political Science. Program content: Negotiating and administrating labor agreements. Available for credit. Certificate signed by the Dean, University Extension.

Program Format Evening, weekend classes offered. Instructional schedule: One evening per week. Program cycle: Continuous enrollment. Completion of program requires six courses.

Evaluation Student evaluation based on tests, papers, reports. Grading system: Letters or numbers, pass/fail. Transcripts are kept for each student.

Enrollment Requirements High school diploma required, bachelor's degree preferred. Program is open to non-resident foreign students.

Program Costs $180 per course.

Housing and Student Services Housing is available. Job counseling and placement services are not available.

Special Features Program designed for managers responsible for negotiating or administering labor agreements and for labor union representatives. Covers material useful to employee-relations officers, personnel administrators, training specialists, and people in related fields. Certificate awarded upon successful completion of five required courses and one elective course.

Contact Ms. Alice Tom, Continuing Education Specialist, Business and Management, University Extension, Davis, CA 95616. 916-752-7530.

LAW (22.01)
Certificate Program in Legal Assisting

General Information Unit offering the program: University Extension, School of Law. Available for credit. Certificate signed by the Dean, University Extension.

Program Format Evening, weekend classes offered. Instructional schedule: One evening per week. Program cycle: Continuous enrollment. Completion of program requires eight courses, 240 classroom hours.

Evaluation Student evaluation based on tests, papers, reports. Grading system: Letters or numbers, pass/fail. Transcripts are kept for each student.

Enrollment Requirements High school diploma required, bachelor's degree preferred. Program is open to non-resident foreign students.

Program Costs $1500 for the program, $180 per course.

Housing and Student Services Housing is available. Job counseling and placement services are not available.

Special Features Program helps students begin a rewarding career as a paralegal, increase promotion potential, refine skills in a specific area of law, and expand knowledge of legal procedures and law office management. Courses emphasize legal concepts and procedures. Curriculum provides basic foundation in substantive and procedural law.

Contact Ms. Wendy Light, Continuing Education Specialist, Business and Management, University Extension, Davis, CA 95616. 916-752-7530.

MANAGEMENT SCIENCE (06.13)
Certificate Program in Management

General Information Unit offering the program: University Extension, Graduate School of Management. Program content: Theory and practical applications of current management

practice. Available for credit. Certificate signed by the Dean, University Extension.

Program Format Evening, weekend classes offered. Instructional schedule: One evening per week. Program cycle: Continuous enrollment. Completion of program requires eight courses, 240 classroom hours.

Evaluation Student evaluation based on tests, papers, reports. Grading system: Letters or numbers, pass/fail. Transcripts are kept for each student.

Enrollment Requirements High school diploma required, bachelor's degree preferred. Program is open to non-resident foreign students.

Program Costs $1500 for the program, $180 per course.

Housing and Student Services Housing is available. Job counseling and placement services are not available.

Special Features Certificate Program in Management designed to respond to current needs of today's manager and provides blend of theory and practical application, analytical and interpersonal skills, and knowledge to enhance professionalism on the job and create career opportunities.

Contact Ms. Alice Tom, Continuing Education Specialist, Business and Management, University Extension, Davis, CA 95616. 916-752-7530.

MISCELLANEOUS CONSTRUCTION TRADES AND PROPERTY MAINTENANCE (46.04)
Certificate Program in Commercial and Industrial Construction Management

General Information Unit offering the program: University Extension, Economics, Civil Engineering, School of Law. Program content: Management techniques for large-scale projects. Available for credit. Certificate signed by the Dean, University Extension.

Program Format Evening, weekend classes offered. Instructional schedule: One evening per week. Program cycle: Continuous enrollment. Completion of program requires eight courses, 240 classroom hours.

Evaluation Student evaluation based on tests, papers, reports. Grading system: Letters or numbers, pass/fail. Transcripts are kept for each student.

Enrollment Requirements High school diploma required, bachelor's degree preferred. Program is open to non-resident foreign students.

Program Costs $1500 for the program, $180 per course.

Housing and Student Services Housing is available. Job counseling and placement services are not available.

Special Features Program offers comprehensive course of study in current industry practices, procedures, problems, and management. Designed to increase effectiveness of contractors, developers, and managers involved in construction of large commercial and residential projects. Through practical instruction in both basic principles and new trends, program provides sound basis for informed day-to-day decision making.

Contact Ms. Alice Tom, Continuing Education Specialist, Business and Management, University Extension, Davis, CA 95616. 916-752-7530.

MISCELLANEOUS CONSTRUCTION TRADES AND PROPERTY MAINTENANCE (46.04)
Certificate Program in Light Construction and Development Management

General Information Unit offering the program: University Extension, Economics, Civil Engineering, School of Law. Program content: Management techniques for light construction projects. Available for credit. Certificate signed by the Dean, University Extension.

Program Format Evening, weekend classes offered. Instructional schedule: One evening per week. Program cycle:

Continuous enrollment. Completion of program requires ten courses.

Evaluation Student evaluation based on tests, papers, reports. Grading system: Letters or numbers, pass/fail. Transcripts are kept for each student.

Enrollment Requirements High school diploma required, bachelor's degree preferred. Program is open to non-resident foreign students.

Program Costs $180 per course.

Housing and Student Services Housing is available. Job counseling and placement services are not available.

Special Features Program helps you learn how to efficiently manage projects and increase profits. Instructors with practical experience cover both basic management principles and actual practices used by successful companies. Homework assignments and tests help you measure your understanding of the material covered. Certificate awarded upon successful completion of eight required courses and two elective courses.

Contact Ms. Alice Tom, Continuing Education Specialist, Business and Management, University Extension, Davis, CA 95616. 916-752-7530.

UNIVERSITY OF CALIFORNIA, LOS ANGELES
Los Angeles, California 90024

ACCOUNTING (06.02)
Award in Accounting

General Information Unit offering the program: Business and Management, UCLA Extension. Available on a non-credit basis. Cosponsored by Los Angeles Chapter of the National Association of Accountants and Southern California Council of NAA Chapters. Certificate signed by the Dean, UCLA Extension.

Program Format Evening classes offered. Instructional schedule: One or two evenings per week. Program cycle: Continuous enrollment. Complete program cycle lasts three to four years. Completion of program requires 13 courses.

Evaluation Student evaluation based on tests, papers, reports, projects. Grading system: Letters or numbers. Transcripts are kept for each student.

Enrollment Requirements Accounting knowledge required. Program is open to non-resident foreign students. English language proficiency required. University-administered test.

Program Costs $2080 for the program, $160 per course.

Housing and Student Services Housing is not available. Job counseling and placement services are not available.

Contact Ms. Bess M. Saito, Coordinator, Certificate Programs, Business and Management Department, 10995 Le Conte Avenue, Suite 515, Los Angeles, CA 90024. 213-825-7031.

ADVERTISING (09.02)
Professional Designation in Advertising

General Information Unit offering the program: Business and Management, UCLA Extension. Available on a non-credit basis. Cosponsored by Western States Advertising Agencies Association (WSAAA). Certificate signed by the Dean, UCLA Extension.

Program Format Evening classes offered. Instructional schedule: One or two evenings per week. Program cycle: Continuous enrollment. Full program cycle lasts 2 years. Completion of program requires eight courses.

Evaluation Student evaluation based on tests, papers, reports, projects. Grading system: Letters or numbers. Transcripts are kept for each student.

Enrollment Requirements Program is open to non-resident foreign students. English language proficiency required. University-administered test.

Program Costs $1280 for the program, $160 per course.

Housing and Student Services Housing is not available. Job counseling and placement services are not available.

Contact Ms. Bess M. Saito, Coordinator, Certificate Programs, Business and Management Department, 10995 Le Conte Avenue, Suite 515, Los Angeles, CA 90024. 213-825-7031.

BANKING AND FINANCE (06.03)
Professional Designation in Personal Financing Planning

General Information Unit offering the program: Business and Management, UCLA Extension. Available on a non-credit basis. Certificate signed by the Dean, UCLA Extension.

Program Format Evening classes offered. Instructional schedule: One or two evenings per week. Program cycle: Continuous enrollment. Full program cycle lasts 2 years. Completion of program requires 32 units.

Evaluation Student evaluation based on tests, papers, reports, projects. Grading system: Letters or numbers. Transcripts are kept for each student.

Enrollment Requirements Completion of Personal Financial Planning 430.31 with grade of C or better required. Program is open to non-resident foreign students. English language proficiency required. University-administered test.

Program Costs $1670 for the program, $165 per course.

Housing and Student Services Housing is not available. Job counseling and placement services are not available.

Contact Ms. Bess M. Saito, Coordinator, Certificate Programs, Business and Management Department, 10995 Le Conte Avenue, Suite 515, Los Angeles, CA 90024. 213-825-7031.

BIOLOGICAL AND PHYSICAL SCIENCES (30.01)
Introductory Science Certificate Program

General Information Unit offering the program: Humanities and Social Science, Division of Science. Program content: Basic science courses in engineering and health related fields. Available for credit. Certificate signed by the Dean, UCLA Extension.

Program Format Evening classes offered. Instructional schedule: One or two evenings per week. Program cycle: Continuous enrollment. Full program cycle lasts 1 year.

Evaluation Student evaluation based on tests, papers, reports. Grading system: Letters or numbers. Transcripts are kept for each student.

Enrollment Requirements Program is open to non-resident foreign students.

Program Costs $2300 for the program, $185 per course.

Housing and Student Services Housing is not available. Job counseling and placement services are not available.

Special Features Designed for individuals returning to school on a part-time basis for job preparation, career change, general enrichment, or preparation for further college study. Degree credit courses are offered in biology, chemistry, mathematics, physics, astronomy, atmospheric sciences, computer sciences, earth and space sciences, geography, and kinesiology. Individual counseling is available to students.

Contact Ms. Eve Haberfield, Ph.D., Assistant Director, Humanities and Social Sciences, UCLA Extension, Division of Sciences, P.O. Box 24901, Los Angeles, CA 90024. 213-825-7093.

BUSINESS ADMINISTRATION AND MANAGEMENT (06.04)
The Business Management Program for Technical Personnel

General Information   Unit offering the program: Business and Management/Contract Programs. Program content: Business and management courses to enhance previous technical education. Available on a non-credit basis. Certificate signed by the Dean, UCLA Extension.

Program Format   Evening classes offered. Instructional schedule: One evening per week for three hours. Program cycle: Continuous enrollment. Full program cycle lasts 8 courses.

Evaluation   Student evaluation based on tests, papers, reports. Grading system: Letters or numbers. Transcripts are kept for each student.

Enrollment Requirements   Undergraduate degree (non-business major) or equivalent experience required. Program is open to non-resident foreign students. English language proficiency required.

Program Costs $1370 for the program, $165 per course.

Housing and Student Services   Housing is not available. Job counseling and placement services are not available.

Special Features   The certificate program was designed to meet the business and management needs of engineers, data processing, research, and other technical personnel needing additional educational skills to improve their management capabilities or prepare them for management positions.

Contact   Ms. Philomene M. Bourbeau, Business Management Program Coordinator, UCLA Extension, 10995 Le Conte Avenue, Suite 515, Los Angeles, CA 90024. 213-206-1548.

BUSINESS AND MANAGEMENT, GENERAL (06.01)
Award in General Business Studies

General Information   Unit offering the program: Business and Management, UCLA Extension. Available on a non-credit basis. Certificate signed by the Dean, UCLA Extension.

Program Format   Evening classes offered. Instructional schedule: One or two evenings per week. Program cycle: Continuous enrollment. Full program cycle lasts 2 years. Completion of program requires eight courses.

Evaluation   Student evaluation based on tests, papers, reports, projects. Grading system: Letters or numbers. Transcripts are kept for each student.

Enrollment Requirements   Program is open to non-resident foreign students. English language proficiency required. University-administered test.

Program Costs $1280 for the program, $160 per course.

Housing and Student Services   Housing is not available. Job counseling and placement services are not available.

Contact   Ms. Bess M. Saito, Coordinator, Certificate Programs, Business and Management Department, 10995 Le Conte Avenue, Suite 515, Los Angeles, CA 90024. 213-825-7031.

BUSINESS AND MANAGEMENT, GENERAL (06.01)
Certificate in Business

General Information   Unit offering the program: Business and Management, UCLA Extension. Program content: Background in business and management, opportunity to specialize in specific field. Available on a non-credit basis. Certificate signed by the Dean, UCLA Extension.

Program Format   Evening, correspondence classes offered. Instructional schedule: One or two evenings per week. Program cycle: Continuous enrollment. Full program cycle lasts 5 years. Completion of program requires 17 courses.

Evaluation   Student evaluation based on tests, papers, reports, projects. Grading system: Letters or numbers. Transcripts are kept for each student.

Enrollment Requirements   Program is open to non-resident foreign students. English language proficiency required. University-administered test.

Program Costs $2800 for the program, $160 per course.

Housing and Student Services   Housing is not available. Job counseling and placement services are not available.

Contact   Ms. Bess M. Saito, Coordinator, Certificate Programs, Business and Management Department, 10995 Le Conte Avenue, Suite 515, Los Angeles, CA 90024. 213-825-7031.

BUSINESS AND MANAGEMENT, GENERAL (06.01)
Professional Designation in Business Management

General Information   Unit offering the program: Business and Management, UCLA Extension. Available on a non-credit basis. Certificate signed by the Dean, UCLA Extension.

Program Format   Evening classes offered. Instructional schedule: One or two evenings per week. Program cycle: Continuous enrollment. Full program cycle lasts 2 years. Completion of program requires eight courses.

Evaluation   Student evaluation based on tests, papers, reports, projects. Grading system: Letters or numbers. Transcripts are kept for each student.

Enrollment Requirements   Program is open to non-resident foreign students. English language proficiency required. University-administered test.

Program Costs $1280 for the program, $160 per course.

Housing and Student Services   Housing is not available. Job counseling and placement services are not available.

Contact   Ms. Bess M. Saito, Coordinator, Certificate Programs, Business and Management Department, 10995 Le Conte Avenue, Suite 515, Los Angeles, CA 90024. 213-825-7031.

BUSINESS AND MANAGEMENT, GENERAL (06.01)
Professional Designation in Government Contract Management

General Information   Unit offering the program: Business and Management, UCLA Extension. Available on a non-credit basis. Cosponsored by National Contract Management Association (NCMA), South Bay Chapter. Certificate signed by the Dean, UCLA Extension.

Program Format   Evening classes offered. Instructional schedule: One or two evenings per week. Program cycle: Continuous enrollment. Full program cycle lasts 2 years. Completion of program requires eight courses.

Evaluation   Student evaluation based on tests, papers, reports, projects. Grading system: Letters or numbers. Transcripts are kept for each student.

Enrollment Requirements   Program is open to non-resident foreign students. English language proficiency required. University-administered test.

Program Costs $1235 for the program, $155 per course.

Housing and Student Services   Housing is not available. Job counseling and placement services are not available.

Contact   Ms. Bess M. Saito, Coordinator, Certificate Programs, Business and Management Department, 10995 Le Conte Avenue, Suite 515, Los Angeles, CA 90024. 213-825-7031.

BUSINESS AND MANAGEMENT, GENERAL (06.01)
Professional Designation in Purchasing and Material Management

General Information Unit offering the program: Business and Management, UCLA Extension. Available on a non-credit basis. Cosponsored by National Association of Purchasing Management; California Association of Public Purchasing Officers (CAPPO); Purchasing Management Association (PMA), Los Angeles Chapter. Certificate signed by the Dean, UCLA Extension.

Program Format Evening classes offered. Instructional schedule: One or two evenings per week. Program cycle: Continuous enrollment. Full program cycle lasts 2 years. Completion of program requires eight courses.

Evaluation Student evaluation based on tests, papers, reports, projects. Grading system: Letters or numbers. Transcripts are kept for each student.

Enrollment Requirements Program is open to non-resident foreign students. English language proficiency required. University-administered test.

Program Costs $1220 for the program, $150 per course.

Housing and Student Services Housing is not available. Job counseling and placement services are not available.

Contact Ms. Bess M. Saito, Coordinator, Certificate Programs, Business and Management Department, 10995 Le Conte Avenue, Suite 515, Los Angeles, CA 90024. 213-825-7031.

CITY, COMMUNITY, AND REGIONAL PLANNING (04.03)
Transportation Demand Management (TDM)

General Information Unit offering the program: Department of Humanities and Social Sciences/Public Policy Program. Program content: Implementation of TDM strategies. Available on a non-credit basis. Endorsed by United States and State of California Department of Transportation. Cosponsored by South Coast Air Quality Management District (SCAQMD), Association for Commuter Transportation. Certificate signed by the Dean.

Program Format Evening classes offered. Instructional schedule: Once per week for three hours. Students may enroll fall, winter, spring. Full program cycle lasts 3 quarters.

Evaluation Student evaluation based on tests, papers, class participation. Grading system: Letters or numbers. Transcripts are kept for each student.

Enrollment Requirements Permission of instructor required.

Program Costs $925 for the program, $295 per quarter.

Housing and Student Services Housing is not available. Job counseling and placement services are not available.

Special Features The three-quarter course is taught and coordinated by a leading transportation planner and supplemented by a series of expert resource people drawn from University faculty and practicing professionals. Those completing the program are prepared to plan and implement transportation demand programs required to meet employer's needs and satisfy government regulations.

Contact Ms. MaBel C. Collins, Program Representative, Public Policy Program, 10995 Le Conte Avenue, Room 731, Los Angeles, CA 90016. 213-825-7885.

COMPUTER AND INFORMATION SCIENCES, GENERAL (11.01)
Certificate Program in Computer Science

General Information Unit offering the program: Department of Engineering, UCLA Extension. Program content: Programming languages, operating systems, compiler construction, machine organization and operation. Available on a non-credit basis. Certificate signed by the Dean, UCLA Extension.

Program Format Evening classes offered. Instructional schedule: Three hours per week. Program cycle: Continuous enrollment. Full program cycle lasts 2 years. Completion of program requires grade of C or better.

Evaluation Student evaluation based on tests, papers, homework, class presentations. Grading system: Letters or numbers. Transcripts are kept for each student.

Enrollment Requirements Bachelor's degree preferred. Program is open to non-resident foreign students. English language proficiency required.

Program Costs $300 per course.

Housing and Student Services Housing is not available. Job counseling and placement services are not available.

Contact Ms. Jeanette Brady, Department Secretary, 10995 Le Conte Avenue, Room 629, Los Angeles, CA 90024. 213-825-4100.

COMPUTER PROGRAMMING (11.02)
Professional Designation in Applications Programming

General Information Unit offering the program: Business and Management, UCLA Extension. Program content: Designing, testing, and debugging computer programs. Available on a non-credit basis. Certificate signed by the Dean, UCLA Extension.

Program Format Evening classes offered. Instructional schedule: One or two evenings per week. Program cycle: Continuous enrollment. Full program cycle lasts 2 years. Completion of program requires seven courses.

Evaluation Student evaluation based on tests, papers, reports, projects. Grading system: Letters or numbers. Transcripts are kept for each student.

Enrollment Requirements Completion of Introduction to Data Processing Concepts or equivalent knowledge required. Program is open to non-resident foreign students. English language proficiency required. University-administered test.

Program Costs $2090 for the program, $260 per course.

Housing and Student Services Housing is not available. Job counseling and placement services are not available.

Contact Ms. Bess M. Saito, Coordinator, Certificate Programs, Business and Management Department, 10995 Le Conte Avenue, Suite 515, Los Angeles, CA 90024. 213-825-7031.

COMPUTER PROGRAMMING (11.02)
Professional Designation in Systems Programming

General Information Unit offering the program: Business and Management, UCLA Extension. Program content: Programming efficiency and conveniences. Available on a non-credit basis. Certificate signed by the Dean, UCLA Extension.

Program Format Evening classes offered. Instructional schedule: One or two evenings per week. Program cycle: Continuous enrollment. Full program cycle lasts 2 years. Completion of program requires seven courses.

Evaluation Student evaluation based on tests, papers, reports, projects. Grading system: Letters or numbers. Transcripts are kept for each student.

Enrollment Requirements Completion of Introduction to Data Processing Concepts or equivalent knowledge required. Program is open to non-resident foreign students. English language proficiency required. University-administered test.

Program Costs $2090 for the program, $260 per course.

Housing and Student Services Housing is not available. Job counseling and placement services are not available.

Contact Ms. Bess M. Saito, Coordinator, Certificate Programs, Business and Management Department, 10995 Le Conte Avenue, Suite 515, Los Angeles, CA 90024. 213-825-7031.

CREATIVE WRITING (23.05)
Designation Program in Creative Writing

General Information   Unit offering the program: The Arts/ Writers' Program. Program content: Fiction, poetry, playwriting, nonfiction. Available for credit. Certificate signed by the Director of the Arts.

Program Format   Daytime, evening, weekend classes offered. Instructional schedule: Once per week for three hours. Program cycle: Continuous enrollment. Full program cycle lasts 12 courses. Completion of program requires 36 units, grade of C or better.

Evaluation   Student evaluation based on short stories, poems, drafts of longer works (both fiction and nonfiction). Grading system: Letters or numbers. Transcripts are kept for each student.

Enrollment Requirements   Program is open to non-resident foreign students.

Program Costs $2500–$3000 for the program.

Housing and Student Services   Housing is not available. Job counseling and placement services are not available.

Special Features   Students may receive credit for similar courses taken at other institutions. Instructors are active in their respective areas, and most possess impressive credentials.

Contact   Mr. John Bradley, Designation Counselor, 10995 Le Conte Avenue, Room 414, Los Angeles, CA 90024. 213-825-9415.

CURRICULUM AND INSTRUCTION (13.03)
Certificate Program in Fitness Instruction

General Information   Unit offering the program: Humanities and Social Sciences, Division of Science. Program content: Basic anatomy, physiology, nutrition, strength training, teaching methods. Available on a non-credit basis. Certificate signed by the Assistant Director, Division of Science.

Program Format   Evening, weekend classes offered. Instructional schedule: Once per week. Program cycle: Continuous enrollment. Complete program cycle lasts one to two years. Completion of program requires comprehensive practical examination/project.

Evaluation   Student evaluation based on tests, papers, reports. Grading system: Letters or numbers. Transcripts are kept for each student.

Enrollment Requirements   Basic course in human biology recommended. Program is open to non-resident foreign students.

Program Costs $1200 for the program, $155 per course.

Housing and Student Services   Housing is not available. Job counseling and placement services are available.

Special Features   Prepares professionals for sports medicine and fitness-related fields. Courses provide information and practical training necessary for the development of safe fitness programs. A comprehensive practical written and oral project is to be done upon completion of all required courses.

Contact   Ms. Eve Haberfield, Ph.D., Assistant Director, Humanities and Social Sciences, UCLA Extension, Division of Sciences, P.O. Box 24901, Los Angeles, CA 90024. 213-825-7093.

DENTAL SERVICES (17.01)
Registered Dental Assistants in Extended Functions

General Information   Unit offering the program: Dentistry, Department of Health Sciences, UCLA Extension. Program content: Didactic and clinical preparation for the RDAEF licensure exam. Available on a non-credit basis. Certificate signed by the Director of Department.

Program Format   Weekend classes offered. Instructional schedule: Saturday and Sunday, alternate weekends. Students may enroll twice per year. Full program cycle lasts 6 weeks.

Evaluation   Student evaluation based on tests, clinical and laboratory work. Grading system: Pass/fail. Transcripts are kept for each student.

Enrollment Requirements   RDA license, certificate in coronal polish, radiation safety, CPR, clinical skills required. Program is not open to non-resident foreign students.

Program Costs $1525 for the program.

Housing and Student Services   Housing is not available. Job counseling and placement services are not available.

Special Features   One of two programs offered in California for RDAEF licensure exam.

Contact   Ms. Jean Abbott, Program Representative, 10995 Le Conte Avenue, Room 614, Los Angeles, CA 90024. 213-825-9187.

DENTISTRY (18.04)
Dental Refresher Program

General Information   Unit offering the program: Dentistry, Department of Health Sciences, UCLA Extension. Program content: Didactic and clinical preparation for California Dental Board Exam. Available on a non-credit basis. Certificate signed by the Director of Department.

Program Format   Evening classes offered. Instructional schedule: Four evenings per week. Students may enroll twice per year. Full program cycle lasts 13 weeks.

Evaluation   Student evaluation based on tests. Transcripts are kept for each student.

Enrollment Requirements   Limited to dental school graduates. Program is open to non-resident foreign students. English language proficiency required.

Program Costs $3325 for the program.

Housing and Student Services   Housing is not available. Job counseling and placement services are not available.

Contact   Ms. Jean Abbott, Program Representative, UCLA Extension, 10995 Le Conte Avenue, Los Angeles, CA 90024. 213-825-9187.

DESIGN (50.04)
Professional Designation Program in Computer Graphics

General Information   Unit offering the program: UCLA Extension, Department of The Arts. Available on a non-credit basis. Certificate signed by the Dean, UCLA Extension.

Program Format   Evening classes offered. Instructional schedule: Once per week for three hours. Program cycle: Continuous enrollment. Complete program cycle lasts one to two years. Completion of program requires grade of C or better in all courses, intermediate and final portfolio review.

Evaluation   Student evaluation based on projects. Grading system: Letters or numbers. Transcripts are kept for each student.

Enrollment Requirements   Art or design background preferred. Program is open to non-resident foreign students. English language proficiency required. University-administered test.

Program Costs $5000–$6000 for the program, $245–$675 per course.

Housing and Student Services   Housing is not available. Job counseling and placement services are not available.

Special Features   Those with substantial background in graphic design or art may be able to waive prerequisites by bringing transcript and portfolio to counseling appointment. Instructors practicing professionals in computer graphics industry. Final class projects designed to be portfolio pieces which can assist employment search process. Students may complete program on full-time, or part-time basis while continuing full-time, regular employment.

Contact Ms. Laura O'Mara, Program Representative, Department of The Arts, UCLA Extension, 10995 Le Conte Avenue, Room 440, Los Angeles, CA 90024-0901. 213-206-8503.

DESIGN (50.04)
Professional Designation Program in Graphic Design/Visual Communication

General Information Unit offering the program: UCLA Extension, Department of The Arts. Available on a non-credit basis. Certificate signed by the Dean, UCLA Extension.

Program Format Evening classes offered. Instructional schedule: Once per week for three hours. Program cycle: Continuous enrollment. Complete program cycle lasts two to three years. Completion of program requires grade of C or better, 25 courses, three portfolio reviews.

Evaluation Student evaluation based on tests, design projects. Grading system: Letters or numbers. Transcripts are kept for each student.

Enrollment Requirements Program is open to non-resident foreign students. English language proficiency required. University-administered test.

Program Costs $6300–$8000 for the program, $245 per course.

Housing and Student Services Housing is not available. Job counseling and placement services are not available.

Special Features Students may qualify for advanced standing because of previous educational experience and can petition to waive certain classes. Courses are taught by professionals in the graphic design industry, including some of Los Angeles' leading graphic designers. Students may complete program on a full-time, or part-time basis while continuing to be employed full-time.

Contact Ms. Laura O'Mara, Program Representative, Department of The Arts, UCLA Extension, 10995 Le Conte Avenue, Room 440, Los Angeles, CA 90024-0901. 213-206-8503.

ELECTRICAL AND ELECTRONIC TECHNOLOGIES (15.03)
Manufacturing Engineering—Electronics Option

General Information Unit offering the program: Department of Engineering, UCLA Extension. Available on a non-credit basis. Cosponsored by The Society of Manufacturing Engineers (SME). Certificate signed by the Dean, UCLA Extension.

Program Format Evening classes offered. Instructional schedule: Three hours per week. Program cycle: Continuous enrollment. Full program cycle lasts 2 years. Completion of program requires grade of C or better in each course.

Evaluation Student evaluation based on tests, papers, homework, class presentations, participation. Grading system: Letters or numbers. Transcripts are kept for each student.

Enrollment Requirements Bachelor's degree preferred. Program is open to non-resident foreign students. English language proficiency required.

Program Costs $300 per course.

Housing and Student Services Housing is not available. Job counseling and placement services are not available.

Contact Mr. Vaughn McBride, Program Representative, Department of Engineering, UCLA Extension, 10995 Le Conte Avenue, Room 629, Los Angeles, CA 90024. 213-825-4100.

ENGINEERING, GENERAL (14.01)
Guidance and Control Engineering

General Information Unit offering the program: Department of Engineering, UCLA Extension. Program content: Theory and methodology necessary to understand, design, and implement control systems. Available on a non-credit basis. Certificate signed by the Dean, UCLA Extension.

Program Format Evening classes offered. Instructional schedule: Three hours per week. Program cycle: Continuous enrollment. Full program cycle lasts 2 years. Completion of program requires grade of C or better.

Evaluation Student evaluation based on tests, papers, homework, class presentations. Grading system: Letters or numbers. Transcripts are kept for each student.

Enrollment Requirements Bachelor's degree preferred. Program is open to non-resident foreign students. English language proficiency required.

Program Costs $300 per course.

Housing and Student Services Housing is not available. Job counseling and placement services are not available.

Contact Mr. Vaughn McBride, Program Representative, Department of Engineering, UCLA Extension, 10995 Le Conte Avenue, Room 629, Los Angeles, CA 90024. 213-825-4100.

ENVIRONMENTAL CONTROL TECHNOLOGIES (15.05)
Toxic and Hazardous Materials Control and Management

General Information Unit offering the program: Humanities and Social Sciences, Division of Science. Program content: Comprehensive and practical curriculum of study in hazardous materials management. Available on a non-credit basis. Certificate signed by the Department Director.

Program Format Evening classes offered. Instructional schedule: One evening per week. Program cycle: Continuous enrollment. Full program cycle lasts 8 courses. Completion of program requires grade of C or better.

Evaluation Student evaluation based on tests, papers, reports. Grading system: Letters or numbers. Transcripts are kept for each student.

Enrollment Requirements Program is open to non-resident foreign students.

Program Costs $260 per course.

Housing and Student Services Housing is not available. Job counseling and placement services are available.

Special Features Program has an advisory board of 23 leaders in the area of hazardous substances that help determine course content. The program is part of the University Extension California Statewide Hazardous Substance Program with courses on eight University of California campuses.

Contact Mr. William Gustafson, Continuing Education Specialist, UCLA Extension, Division of Science, P.O. Box 24901, Los Angeles, CA 90024. 213-825-7093.

FILM ARTS (50.06)
Sequential Program in Motion Picture and Television Arts and Sciences

General Information Unit offering the program: Department of The Arts—Performing and Integrated Arts Division. Program content: Acting, directing, production, post-production for motion pictures and television. Available on a non-credit basis. Certificate signed by the Dean, UCLA Extension.

Program Format Evening, weekend classes offered. Instructional schedule: Once per week. Program cycle: Continuous enrollment. Full program cycle lasts 14 courses. Completion of program requires grade of C or better.

Evaluation Student evaluation based on tests, papers, reports, projects. Grading system: Letters or numbers. Transcripts are kept for each student.

Enrollment Requirements Program is open to non-resident foreign students.

Program Costs $3000–$4500 for the program, $200–$500 per course.

Sequential Program in Motion Picture and Television Arts and Sciences continued

Housing and Student Services Housing is not available. Job counseling and placement services are available.

Special Features Courses are designed in consultation with industry leaders; members of the guilds, academies, and other professional organizations; and UCLA faculty. Instructors and guest speakers are award-winning practicing professionals. Candidates may receive credit for certain classes taken elsewhere.

Contact Mr. Carlo Carlsson, Counselor, Motion Picture and Television Program, 10995 Le Conte Avenue, Room 437, Los Angeles, CA 90024. 213-825-9064.

FILM ARTS (50.06)
Sequential Program in Writing for Film and Television

General Information Unit offering the program: The Arts/Writers' Program. Program content: Screenwriting. Available on a non-credit basis. Certificate signed by the Director of The Arts.

Program Format Daytime, evening, weekend classes offered. Instructional schedule: Once per week for three hours. Program cycle: Continuous enrollment. Full program cycle lasts 12 courses. Completion of program requires 36 units, grade of C or better.

Evaluation Student evaluation based on treatments, outlines, partial and complete scripts. Grading system: Letters or numbers. Transcripts are kept for each student.

Enrollment Requirements Program is open to non-resident foreign students.

Program Costs $3000–$3500 for the program.

Housing and Student Services Housing is not available. Job counseling and placement services are not available.

Special Features Students may receive credit for similar courses taken at other institutions. Instructors are active in the industry and possess impressive credentials. Periodic joint offerings with the Writers Guild of America.

Contact Ms. Darlene Blackburn, Sequential Program Counselor, 10995 Le Conte Avenue, Room 414, Los Angeles, CA 90024. 213-825-9415.

FIRE PROTECTION (43.02)
Certificate Program in Fire Protection Engineering

General Information Unit offering the program: Department of Engineering, UCLA Extension. Program content: Explosions and hazardous materials, building construction, analysis and behavior, suppression systems, life safety factors in building interiors, arson investigation, smoke measurement and coontrol, scientific and technical writing. Available on a non-credit basis. Endorsed by Society of Fire Protection Engineers, Society of Safety Engineers. Certificate signed by the Dean, UCLA Extension.

Program Format Evening classes offered. Instructional schedule: Three hours per week. Program cycle: Continuous enrollment. Full program cycle lasts 2 years. Completion of program requires grade of C or better.

Evaluation Student evaluation based on tests, papers, homework, class presentations. Grading system: Letters or numbers. Transcripts are kept for each student.

Enrollment Requirements Bachelor's degree preferred. Program is open to non-resident foreign students. English language proficiency required.

Program Costs $300 per course.

Housing and Student Services Housing is not available. Job counseling and placement services are not available.

Contact Ms. Caroline Stephens, Senior Clerk Typist, UCLA Extension, 10995 Le Conte Avenue, Los Angeles, CA 90024. 213-825-4100.

GENERAL MARKETING (08.07)
Professional Designation in Marketing and Merchandising

General Information Unit offering the program: Business and Management, UCLA Extension. Available on a non-credit basis. Cosponsored by Sales and Marketing Executives Association of Los Angeles (SME). Certificate signed by the Dean, UCLA Extension.

Program Format Evening classes offered. Instructional schedule: One or two evenings per week. Program cycle: Continuous enrollment. Full program cycle lasts 2 years. Completion of program requires eight courses.

Evaluation Student evaluation based on tests, papers, reports, projects. Grading system: Letters or numbers. Transcripts are kept for each student.

Enrollment Requirements Program is open to non-resident foreign students. English language proficiency required. University-administered test.

Program Costs $1220 for the program, $155 per course.

Housing and Student Services Housing is not available. Job counseling and placement services are not available.

Contact Ms. Bess M. Saito, Coordinator, Certificate Programs, Business and Management Department, 10995 Le Conte Avenue, Suite 515, Los Angeles, CA 90024. 213-825-7031.

HEALTH SERVICES ADMINISTRATION (18.07)
Management and Administration of Health Care Facilities

General Information Unit offering the program: Allied and Public Health, Department of Health Sciences. Program content: Legal, fiscal, and supervisory issues. Available on a non-credit basis. Certificate signed by the Dean, UCLA Extension.

Program Format Evening classes offered. Instructional schedule: One evening per week. Full program cycle lasts 3 quarters.

Evaluation Student evaluation based on tests, papers, reports. Grading system: Letters or numbers. Transcripts are kept for each student.

Enrollment Requirements Limited to managers of health care facility. Program is open to non-resident foreign students.

Program Costs $1650 for the program, $275 per course.

Housing and Student Services Housing is not available. Job counseling and placement services are not available.

Contact Ms. Rina Mark, Program Representative, UCLA Extension, 10995 Le Conte Avenue, Los Angeles, CA 90024. 213-825-5840.

HORTICULTURE (01.06)
Certificate Program in Gardening and Horticulture

General Information Unit offering the program: Humanities and Social Science, Division of Science. Available on a non-credit basis. Certificate signed by the Dean, UCLA Extension.

Program Format Evening, weekend classes offered. Instructional schedule: Once per week. Program cycle: Continuous enrollment. Complete program cycle lasts one to two years.

Evaluation Student evaluation based on tests, papers. Grading system: Letters or numbers. Transcripts are kept for each student.

Enrollment Requirements Program is open to non-resident foreign students.

Program Costs $1800 for the program, $195 per course.

Housing and Student Services Housing is not available. Job counseling and placement services are not available.

Special Features Program conforms to basic training program outlined by the American Association of Botanical Gardens and

Arboreta (AABGA) and partially prepares student for examinations for AABGA North American Certificate in Gardening. Intended for individuals who wish to further career goals in gardening, for practicing gardener, or for those who want to further their knowledge, skills, and enjoyment in gardening and horticulture.

Contact Ms. Eve Haberfield, Ph.D., Assistant Director, Humanities and Social Sciences, UCLA Extension, Division of Science, P.O. Box 24901, Los Angeles, CA 90024. 213-825-7093.

INDIVIDUAL AND FAMILY DEVELOPMENT (19.07)
Studies in Gerontology

General Information Unit offering the program: Allied and Public Health, Continuing Education in Health Sciences, UCLA Extension. Program content: Biology, sociology, psychology, health aspects of aging. Available on a non-credit basis. Certificate signed by the Dean, UCLA Extension.

Program Format Evening, weekend classes offered. Instructional schedule: One evening per week. Full program cycle lasts 1 year. Completion of program requires grade of C or better in all courses.

Evaluation Student evaluation based on tests, papers, reports. Grading system: Letters or numbers. Transcripts are kept for each student.

Enrollment Requirements Bachelor's degree or equivalent required. Program is open to non-resident foreign students.

Program Costs $1600 for the program, $100 per course.

Housing and Student Services Housing is not available. Job counseling and placement services are not available.

Special Features The program is multidisciplinary.

Contact Ms. Janet Frank, Assistant Director, Department of Health Sciences, UCLA Extension, 10995 Le Conte Avenue, Room 614, Los Angeles, CA 90024. 213-825-8423.

INDUSTRIAL PRODUCTION TECHNOLOGIES (15.06)
Manufacturing Engineering—Mechanical Option

General Information Unit offering the program: Department of Engineering, UCLA Extension. Program content: Planning and selection of methods of manufacturing, equipment design, research and development to improve efficiency and productivity of manufacturing techniques. Available on a non-credit basis. Cosponsored by The Society of Manufacturing Engineers (SME). Certificate signed by the Dean, UCLA Extension.

Program Format Evening classes offered. Instructional schedule: Three hours per week. Program cycle: Continuous enrollment. Full program cycle lasts 2 years. Completion of program requires grade of C or better.

Evaluation Student evaluation based on tests, papers, homework, class presentations. Grading system: Letters or numbers. Transcripts are kept for each student.

Enrollment Requirements Bachelor's degree preferred. Program is open to non-resident foreign students. English language proficiency required.

Program Costs $300 per course.

Housing and Student Services Housing is not available. Job counseling and placement services are not available.

Contact Mr. Vaughn McBride, Program Representative, Department of Engineering, UCLA Extension, 10995 Le Conte Avenue, Room 629, Los Angeles, CA 90024. 213-825-4100.

INFORMATION SCIENCES AND SYSTEMS (11.04)
Professional Designation in Systems Analysis

General Information Unit offering the program: Business and Management, UCLA Extension. Program content: Analysis and improvement of business and information systems, data collection, solution designs, implementation and installation of systems. Available on a non-credit basis. Certificate signed by the Dean, UCLA Extension.

Program Format Evening classes offered. Instructional schedule: One or two evenings per week. Program cycle: Continuous enrollment. Full program cycle lasts 2 years. Completion of program requires eight courses.

Evaluation Student evaluation based on tests, papers, reports, projects. Grading system: Letters or numbers. Transcripts are kept for each student.

Enrollment Requirements Program is open to non-resident foreign students. English language proficiency required. University-administered test.

Program Costs $1600 for the program, $180 per course.

Housing and Student Services Housing is not available. Job counseling and placement services are not available.

Contact Ms. Bess M. Saito, Coordinator, Certificate Programs, Business and Management Department, 10995 Le Conte Avenue, Suite 515, Los Angeles, CA 90024. 213-825-7031.

INTERNATIONAL BUSINESS MANAGEMENT (06.09)
Professional Designation in International Business Management

General Information Unit offering the program: Business and Management, UCLA Extension. Available on a non-credit basis. Cosponsored by Foreign Trade Association, Export Managers Association of California, Valley International Trade Association. Certificate signed by the Dean, UCLA Extension.

Program Format Evening classes offered. Instructional schedule: One or two evenings per week. Program cycle: Continuous enrollment. Full program cycle lasts 2 years. Completion of program requires eight courses.

Evaluation Student evaluation based on tests, papers, reports, projects. Grading system: Letters or numbers. Transcripts are kept for each student.

Enrollment Requirements Program is open to non-resident foreign students. English language proficiency required. University-administered test.

Program Costs $1200 for the program, $150 per course.

Housing and Student Services Housing is not available. Job counseling and placement services are not available.

Contact Ms. Bess M. Saito, Coordinator, Certificate Programs, Business and Management Department, 10995 Le Conte Avenue, Suite 515, Los Angeles, CA 90024. 213-825-7031.

INTERNATIONAL BUSINESS MANAGEMENT (06.09)
Professional Designation in International Trade

General Information Unit offering the program: Business and Management, UCLA Extension. Available on a non-credit basis. Cosponsored by Foreign Trade Association, Export Managers Association of California, Valley International Trade Association. Certificate signed by the Dean, UCLA Extension.

Program Format Evening classes offered. Instructional schedule: One or two evenings per week. Program cycle: Continuous enrollment. Full program cycle lasts 18 months. Completion of program requires six courses.

Professional Designation in International Trade continued

Evaluation   Student evaluation based on tests, papers, reports, projects. Grading system: Letters or numbers. Transcripts are kept for each student.

Enrollment Requirements   Program is open to non-resident foreign students. English language proficiency required. University-administered test.

Program Costs $900 for the program, $150 per course.

Housing and Student Services   Housing is not available. Job counseling and placement services are not available.

Contact   Ms. Bess M. Saito, Coordinator, Certificate Programs, Business and Management Department, 10995 Le Conte Avenue, Suite 515, Los Angeles, CA 90024. 213-825-7031.

JOURNALISM (MASS COMMUNICATIONS) (09.04)
Professional Designation in Journalism

General Information   Unit offering the program: Humanities and Social Sciences. Program content: Print and broadcast journalism. Available on a non-credit basis. Endorsed by Los Angeles Press Club Education Foundation. Certificate signed by the Dean, UCLA Extension.

Program Format   Evening, weekend classes offered. Instructional schedule: Once per week for three hours. Program cycle: Continuous enrollment. Completion of program requires nine courses, grade of C or better.

Evaluation   Student evaluation based on tests, papers, reports, class projects and participation. Grading system: Letters or numbers. Transcripts are kept for each student.

Enrollment Requirements   Program is open to non-resident foreign students. English language proficiency required.

Program Costs $1500 for the program, $165 per course.

Housing and Student Services   Housing is not available. Job counseling and placement services are not available.

Special Features   Instructors are professional journalists. Broadcast instructors are leading professional newscasters in the Los Angeles area, all from major television stations. The majority of the print journalists are on the staff of the *Los Angeles Times*. Students have the opportunity to intern in print or broadcast organizations for hands-on experience and the opportunity for employment.

Contact   Ms. Norma Auerbach, Program Representative, UCLA Extension, 10995 Le Conte Avenue, Los Angeles, CA 90024. 213-825-0641.

LABOR/INDUSTRIAL RELATIONS (06.11)
Professional Designation in Industrial Relations

General Information   Unit offering the program: Business and Management, UCLA Extension. Available on a non-credit basis. Certificate signed by the Dean, UCLA Extension.

Program Format   Evening classes offered. Instructional schedule: One or two evenings per week. Program cycle: Continuous enrollment. Full program cycle lasts 2 years. Completion of program requires eight courses.

Evaluation   Student evaluation based on tests, papers, reports, projects. Grading system: Letters or numbers. Transcripts are kept for each student.

Enrollment Requirements   Program is open to non-resident foreign students. English language proficiency required. University-administered test.

Program Costs $1235 for the program, $155 per course.

Housing and Student Services   Housing is not available. Job counseling and placement services are not available.

Contact   Ms. Bess M. Saito, Coordinator, Certificate Programs, Business and Management Department, 10995 Le Conte Avenue, Suite 515, Los Angeles, CA 90024. 213-825-7031.

LANDSCAPE ARCHITECTURE (04.06)
Professional Designation Certificate/ Landscape Architecture

General Information   Unit offering the program: UCLA Extension, Department of The Arts. Program content: Design issues and methodologies. Available on a non-credit basis. Endorsed by California State Board of Landscape Architects. Certificate signed by the Director, Department of The Arts. Program fulfills requirements for Licensed Landscape Architect, State of California.

Program Format   Evening, weekend classes offered. Instructional schedule: Two or three evenings per week for three hours. Full program cycle lasts 4 years. Completion of program requires grade of C or better in 31 courses, two portfolio reviews, final project.

Evaluation   Student evaluation based on tests, papers, studio projects, portfolio. Grading system: Letters or numbers. Transcripts are kept for each student.

Enrollment Requirements   Program is open to non-resident foreign students. English language proficiency required.

Program Costs $9000 for the program, $250–$300 per course.

Housing and Student Services   Housing is not available. Job counseling and placement services are available.

Special Features   The program requires an academically rigorous level of commitment to seeking new answers to the contemporary issues surrounding the natural and built environment while engendering a full understanding of traditional values and methodologies. The faculty is made up of professional landscape architects with outside practices.

Contact   Mr. Thomas A. Lockett, Program Head/Landscape Architecture Program, UCLA Extension, 10995 Le Conte Avenue, Room 414, Los Angeles, CA 90024-0901. 213-825-9414.

LAW (22.01)
Attorney Assistant Training Program

General Information   Unit offering the program: Business and Management, UCLA Extension, School of Law. Program content: Civil or corporate litigation. Available on a non-credit basis. Endorsed by American Bar Association. Certificate signed by the Dean.

Program Format   Daytime, evening classes offered. Instructional schedule: Five days or two evenings per week for three hours. Complete program cycle lasts 18 weeks (day), 12 months (evening). Completion of program requires 3.0/5.0 GPA, 250 classroom hours.

Evaluation   Student evaluation based on tests, papers. Grading system: Pass/fail. Transcripts are kept for each student.

Enrollment Requirements   Bachelor's degree or two years of college and two years of work experience, entrance exam, writing ability required. English language proficiency required. University-administered test.

Program Costs $2750 for the program.

Housing and Student Services   Housing is not available. Job counseling and placement services are available.

Special Features   The AATP was established in 1972 and provides training which blends traditional analytical legal skills with pragmatic knowledge not usually taught in law school. Instructors are selected from the Los Angeles legal community and consist of sole practitioners, partners in large, well-known firms and from the public sector or private businesses, as well as working paralegals. Volunteer internship opportunities are available.

Contact   Mr. Sydney Goines, Administrator, Attorney Assistant Training Program, UCLA Extension, 10995 Le Conte Avenue, Room 517, Los Angeles, CA 90024. 213-825-0741.

MENTAL HEALTH/HUMAN SERVICES (17.04)
Alcohol/Drug Abuse Studies

General Information Unit offering the program: UCLA Extension, Continuing Education in Health Sciences. Available on a non-credit basis. Endorsed by California Association of Alcohol and Drug Abuse Counselors. Certificate signed by the Dean, UCLA Extension.

Program Format Evening classes offered. Instructional schedule: Once per week for three hours. Full program cycle lasts 9 months.

Evaluation Student evaluation based on tests, papers, reports, oral presentations. Grading system: Letters or numbers. Transcripts are kept for each student.

Enrollment Requirements Program is open to non-resident foreign students.

Program Costs $170 per course.

Housing and Student Services Housing is not available. Job counseling and placement services are not available.

Special Features The certificate program is in its fourteenth year.

Contact Ms. Lisa Beillen, Program Assistant, Department of Health Sciences, 10995 Le Conte Avenue, Room 614, Los Angeles, CA 90024. 213-825-6701.

MENTAL HEALTH/HUMAN SERVICES (17.04)
Alcohol/Drug Counseling

General Information Unit offering the program: UCLA Extension, Continuing Education in Health Sciences. Available on a non-credit basis. Endorsed by California Association of Alcohol and Drug Abuse Counselors. Certificate signed by the Dean, UCLA Extension.

Program Format Evening classes offered. Instructional schedule: Once per week for three hours. Full program cycle lasts 12 months. Completion of program requires fieldwork.

Evaluation Student evaluation based on tests, papers, reports. Grading system: Letters or numbers. Transcripts are kept for each student.

Enrollment Requirements One year continuous sobriety required. Program is open to non-resident foreign students.

Program Costs $1360 for the program, $170 per course.

Housing and Student Services Housing is not available. Job counseling and placement services are not available.

Special Features The program gives students the opportunity to obtain the training necessary to be able to effectively counsel substance abusers and their families. The fieldwork practicum class requires an 85-hour practicum that often leads to job opportunities for the students.

Contact Ms. Lisa Beillen, Program Assistant, Department of Health Sciences, 10995 Le Conte Avenue, Room 614, Los Angeles, CA 90024. 213-825-6701.

MENTAL HEALTH/HUMAN SERVICES (17.04)
Alcohol/Drug Program Management

General Information Unit offering the program: UCLA Extension, Continuing Education in Health Sciences. Available on a non-credit basis. Certificate signed by the Dean, UCLA Extension.

Program Format Evening classes offered. Instructional schedule: Once per week for three hours. Full program cycle lasts 9 months.

Evaluation Student evaluation based on tests, papers, reports, oral presentations. Grading system: Letters or numbers. Transcripts are kept for each student.

Enrollment Requirements Prior completion of Alcohol/Drug Certificate or three to five years in the field of chemical dependency required. Program is open to non-resident foreign students.

Program Costs $1080 for the program, $180 per course.

Housing and Student Services Housing is not available. Job counseling and placement services are not available.

Special Features The certificate program is experiencing its first year.

Contact Ms. Lisa Beillen, Program Assistant, Department of Health Sciences, 10995 Le Conte Avenue, Room 614, Los Angeles, CA 90024. 213-825-6701.

MICROCOMPUTER APPLICATIONS (11.06)
Microprocessor Hardware/Software Engineering

General Information Unit offering the program: Department of Engineering, UCLA Extension. Program content: Hardware and software for microcomputers. Available on a non-credit basis. Certificate signed by the Dean, UCLA Extension.

Program Format Evening classes offered. Instructional schedule: Three hours per week. Program cycle: Continuous enrollment. Full program cycle lasts 2 years. Completion of program requires grade of C or better.

Evaluation Student evaluation based on tests, papers, homework, class presentations. Grading system: Letters or numbers. Transcripts are kept for each student.

Enrollment Requirements Bachelor's degree preferred. Program is open to non-resident foreign students. English language proficiency required.

Program Costs $300 per course.

Housing and Student Services Housing is not available. Job counseling and placement services are not available.

Contact Mr. Vaughn McBride, Program Representative, Department of Engineering, UCLA Extension, 10995 Le Conte Avenue, Room 629, Los Angeles, CA 90024. 213-825-4100.

MUSIC (50.09)
Professional Designation in Recording Arts and Sciences

General Information Unit offering the program: Department of The Arts—Performing and Integrated Arts Division. Program content: Artist development, record production, publishing, business and legal aspects, marketing for the music industry. Available on a non-credit basis. Certificate signed by the Dean, UCLA Extension.

Program Format Evening, weekend classes offered. Instructional schedule: Once per week. Program cycle: Continuous enrollment. Full program cycle lasts 12 courses. Completion of program requires grade of C or better in each course.

Evaluation Student evaluation based on tests, papers, reports, projects. Grading system: Letters or numbers. Transcripts are kept for each student.

Enrollment Requirements Program is open to non-resident foreign students.

Program Costs $2500–$3500 for the program, $200–$300 per course.

Housing and Student Services Housing is not available. Job counseling and placement services are available.

Special Features Courses designed in consultation with industry leaders and professional associations and provide students with knowledge and technical training required to advance their careers as artists, producers, engineers, publicists, personal and business managers, music journalists, and executives. Instructors and guest speakers are award-winning practicing professionals. Candidates may receive credit for certain classes taken elsewhere.

Contact Ms. Helen De Witty, Counselor, Recording Arts and Sciences Program, 10995 Le Conte Avenue, Room 437, Los Angeles, CA 90024. 213-825-9064.

MUSIC (50.09)
Professional Designation in Recording Engineering

General Information Unit offering the program: Recording Engineering Program. Program content: Audio technology and equipment, musicianship, business practices for the recording industry. Available on a non-credit basis. Certificate signed by the Dean, UCLA Extension.

Program Format Evening, weekend classes offered. Instructional schedule: One evening per week, Saturday seminars. Program cycle: Continuous enrollment. Full program cycle lasts 9 courses. Completion of program requires grade of C or better in all courses.

Evaluation Student evaluation based on tests, papers, reports, projects. Grading system: Letters or numbers. Transcripts are kept for each student.

Enrollment Requirements College-level intermediate algebra, precalculus, basic physics, and basic electronics required. Program is open to non-resident foreign students.

Program Costs $4500–$6000 for the program, $200–$900 per course.

Housing and Student Services Housing is not available. Job counseling and placement services are available.

Special Features Designed and continually updated in consultation with industry leaders, professional associations, and advisory board composed of engineers, studio owners, record producers, and manufacturer's representatives. Enables future engineer to acquire vision and problem-solving techniques that meet challenge of rapidly evolving technology and dynamic sound recording market. Instructors and guest speakers are award-winning practicing professionals. Candidates may receive credit for prior courses.

Contact Ms. Helen De Witty, Counselor, Recording Engineering Program, 10995 Le Conte Avenue, Room 437, Los Angeles, CA 90024. 213-825-9064.

MUSIC (50.09)
Professional Designation in Songwriting

General Information Unit offering the program: Department of The Arts—Performing and Integrated Arts Division. Program content: Writing melodies and lyrics, producing 'demo' recordings, professional practices for songwriting. Available on a non-credit basis. Cosponsored by National Academy of Songwriters, Society of Composers and Lyricists. Certificate signed by the Dean, UCLA Extension.

Program Format Evening, weekend classes offered. Program cycle: Continuous enrollment. Full program cycle lasts 6 courses. Completion of program requires grade of C or better in all courses.

Evaluation Student evaluation based on tests, individual and collaborative compositions. Grading system: Letters or numbers. Transcripts are kept for each student.

Enrollment Requirements Program is open to non-resident foreign students.

Program Costs $1500–$1800 for the program, $250–$300 per course.

Housing and Student Services Housing is not available. Job counseling and placement services are available.

Special Features Includes courses in melody and lyric writing, song clinic, 'demo' production, and professional practices. Allied courses deal with publishing, record production, legal and business affairs from songwriter's point of view. Instructors and guest speakers are award-winning practicing professionals. No musical prerequisites for admission; classes available to improve musical skills if required. Scholarships are available.

Contact Ms. Helen De Witty, Counselor, Songwriting Program, 10995 Le Conte Avenue, Room 437, Los Angeles, CA 90024. 213-825-9064.

MUSIC (50.09)
Sequential Program in Film Scoring

General Information Unit offering the program: Department of The Arts—Performing and Integrated Arts Division. Program content: Composing, conducting, and orchestrating music for film and television. Available on a non-credit basis. Cosponsored by Society of Composers and Lyricists. Certificate signed by the Dean, UCLA Extension.

Program Format Evening, weekend classes offered. Instructional schedule: Once per week. Program cycle: Continuous enrollment. Full program cycle lasts 5 courses. Completion of program requires grade of C or better in all courses.

Evaluation Student evaluation based on tests, projects, compositions. Grading system: Letters or numbers. Transcripts are kept for each student.

Enrollment Requirements Two years training in college-level music or equivalent professional experience required. Program is open to non-resident foreign students.

Program Costs $2000–$2500 for the program, $275–$350 per course.

Housing and Student Services Housing is not available. Job counseling and placement services are available.

Special Features No comparable curriculum available anywhere in the country. Minimum two years' training in music at college level (or equivalent professional experience) is required for admission. Preparatory courses available outside program that provide additional training in fundamentals. Courses designed and updated by advisory board composed of prominent film composers and executives in film music industry. Limited number scholarships available.

Contact Ms. Helen De Witty, Counselor, Film Scoring Program, 10995 Le Conte Avenue, Room 437, Los Angeles, CA 90024. 213-825-9064.

NURSING (18.11)
Lactation Consultant Training Program

General Information Unit offering the program: Nursing, Department of Health Sciences, UCLA Extension. Program content: Clinical management of breastfeeding problems. Available on a non-credit basis. Certificate signed by the Dean, University Extension. Program fulfills requirements for Board of Registered Nurses.

Program Format Daytime, weekend classes offered. Instructional schedule: All day Thursday and Friday, Saturday morning. Students enroll once per year. Completion of program requires apprenticeship, suckling assessment, community observation, written work, readings.

Evaluation Student evaluation based on papers. Grading system: Letters or numbers, pass/fail. Transcripts are kept for each student.

Enrollment Requirements Program is open to non-resident foreign students.

Program Costs $1350 for the program.

Housing and Student Services Housing is not available. Job counseling and placement services are not available.

Contact Ms. Jean Abbott, Program Representative, UCLA Extension, 10995 Le Conte Avenue, Los Angeles, CA 90024. 213-825-6701.

PERSONNEL MANAGEMENT (06.16)
Professional Designation in Human Resource Management

General Information Unit offering the program: Business and Management, UCLA Extension. Available on a non-credit basis. Certificate signed by the Dean, UCLA Extension.

Program Format Evening classes offered. Instructional schedule: One or two evenings per week. Program cycle:

Continuous enrollment. Full program cycle lasts 2 years. Completion of program requires eight courses.

Evaluation   Student evaluation based on tests, papers, reports, projects. Grading system: Letters or numbers. Transcripts are kept for each student.

Enrollment Requirements   Program is open to non-resident foreign students. English language proficiency required. University-administered test.

Program Costs $1220 for the program, $155 per course.

Housing and Student Services   Housing is not available. Job counseling and placement services are not available.

Contact   Ms. Bess M. Saito, Coordinator, Certificate Programs, Business and Management Department, 10995 Le Conte Avenue, Suite 515, Los Angeles, CA 90024. 213-825-7031.

PUBLIC RELATIONS (09.05)
Professional Designation in Public Relations

General Information   Unit offering the program: Humanities and Social Sciences. Available on a non-credit basis. Endorsed by Public Relations Society of America, Los Angeles Chapter. Certificate signed by the Dean, UCLA Extension.

Program Format   Daytime, evening, weekend classes offered. Instructional schedule: Once per week for three hours. Program cycle: Continuous enrollment. Completion of program requires nine courses, grade of C or better.

Evaluation   Student evaluation based on tests, papers, reports, class projects and participation. Grading system: Letters or numbers. Transcripts are kept for each student.

Enrollment Requirements   Program is open to non-resident foreign students. English language proficiency required.

Program Costs $1500 for the program, $165 per course.

Housing and Student Services   Housing is not available. Job counseling and placement services are not available.

Special Features   Instructors are professionals from major public relations firms in the Los Angeles area. The students have the opportunity to intern in public relations firms for hands-on experience and the opportunity for employment.

Contact   Ms. Norma Auerbach, Program Representative, UCLA Extension, 10995 Le Conte Avenue, Los Angeles, CA 90024. 213-825-0641.

REAL ESTATE (06.17)
Certificate in Real Estate with Specialization in Appraisal, Finance, or Marketing

General Information   Unit offering the program: Business and Management, UCLA Extension. Available on a non-credit basis. Certificate signed by the Dean, UCLA Extension.

Program Format   Evening classes offered. Instructional schedule: One or two evenings per week. Program cycle: Continuous enrollment. Full program cycle lasts 4 years. Completion of program requires eight courses.

Evaluation   Student evaluation based on tests, papers, reports, projects. Grading system: Letters or numbers. Transcripts are kept for each student.

Enrollment Requirements   Course work in real estate practices, finance, appraisal, and law required. Program is open to non-resident foreign students. English language proficiency required. University-administered test.

Program Costs $1950 for the program, $160 per course.

Housing and Student Services   Housing is not available. Job counseling and placement services are not available.

Contact   Ms. Bess M. Saito, Coordinator, Certificate Programs, Business and Management Department, 10995 Le Conte Avenue, Suite 515, Los Angeles, CA 90024. 213-825-7031.

TRADE AND INDUSTRIAL SUPERVISION AND MANAGEMENT (06.20)
Certificate Program in Engineering Management for Construction

General Information   Unit offering the program: Department of Engineering, UCLA Extension. Program content: Construction costs and estimating, planning and management, legal aspects and construction safety. Available on a non-credit basis. Endorsed by American Society of Civil Engineers. Cosponsored by Association of General Contractors. Certificate signed by the Dean, UCLA Extension.

Program Format   Evening classes offered. Instructional schedule: Three hours per week. Program cycle: Continuous enrollment. Full program cycle lasts 2 years. Completion of program requires grade of C or better.

Evaluation   Student evaluation based on tests, papers, homework, class presentations. Grading system: Letters or numbers. Transcripts are kept for each student.

Enrollment Requirements   Bachelor's degree preferred. Program is open to non-resident foreign students. English language proficiency required.

Program Costs $300 per course.

Housing and Student Services   Housing is not available. Job counseling and placement services are not available.

Contact   Ms. Jeanette Brady, Department Secretary, 10995 Le Conte Avenue, Room 629, Los Angeles, CA 90024. 213-825-4100.

UNIVERSITY OF CALIFORNIA, RIVERSIDE
Riverside, California 92521

ACCOUNTING (06.02)
Certificate in Accounting for Governmental and Nonprofit Organizations

General Information   Unit offering the program: University of California Extension, Riverside. Program content: Budgetary process, internal auditing, cost accounting, risk management, system analysis, legal aspects. Available for credit. Certificate signed by the Dean of University Extension.

Program Format   Evening classes offered. Instructional schedule: Three to six hours per week. Program cycle: Continuous enrollment. Full program cycle lasts 6 courses. Completion of program requires grade of C or better.

Evaluation   Student evaluation based on tests. Grading system: Letters or numbers. Transcripts are kept for each student.

Enrollment Requirements   Basic course in accounting or equivalent required. Program is open to non-resident foreign students. English language proficiency required. ESL classes available.

Program Costs $900–$1000 for the program, $160 per course.

Housing and Student Services   Housing is available. Job counseling and placement services are not available.

Special Features   Instructors work in the public accounting field.

Contact   Mr. Sheldon Lisker, Associate Dean, University Extension, Riverside, CA 92521. 714-787-4111.

BIOLOGICAL AND PHYSICAL SCIENCES (30.01)
The Certificate in Field Natural Environment

General Information   Unit offering the program: University of California Extension, Riverside. Program content: Biology, botany, geology, geography, earth sciences, photography,

The Certificate in Field Natural Environment continued
physical education. Available for credit. Certificate signed by the Dean of University Extension.

Program Format Evening, weekend classes offered. Program cycle: Continuous enrollment. Completion of program requires grade of B or better, 30 quarter units.

Evaluation Student evaluation based on tests, field logs. Grading system: Letters or numbers. Transcripts are kept for each student.

Enrollment Requirements Program is open to non-resident foreign students. English language proficiency required.

Program Costs $1200 for the program, $105–$165 per course.

Housing and Student Services Housing is available. Job counseling and placement services are not available.

Special Features Most courses are held primarily in the field.

Contact Mr. Sheldon Lisker, Associate Dean, University Extension, Riverside, CA 92521. 714-787-4111.

BUSINESS ADMINISTRATION AND MANAGEMENT (06.04)
Certificate in Contract Management

General Information Unit offering the program: University of California Extension, Riverside. Program content: Contract law, financial management, negotiations, contract pricing, management. Available for credit. Endorsed by National Contracts Management Association. Certificate signed by the Dean of University Extension.

Program Format Evening classes offered. Instructional schedule: Three to six hours per week. Program cycle: Continuous enrollment. Full program cycle lasts 7 courses. Completion of program requires grade of C or better.

Evaluation Student evaluation based on tests, reports. Grading system: Letters or numbers. Transcripts are kept for each student.

Enrollment Requirements Program is open to non-resident foreign students. English language proficiency required.

Program Costs $1120 for the program, $160 per course.

Housing and Student Services Housing is available. Job counseling and placement services are not available.

Special Features Instructors are professionals in the field.

Contact Mr. Sheldon Lisker, Associate Dean, University Extension, Riverside, CA 92521. 714-787-4111.

BUSINESS ADMINISTRATION AND MANAGEMENT (06.04)
Purchasing Management

General Information Unit offering the program: University of California Extension, Riverside. Program content: Introduction to purchasing and contracting; solicitation, awards, and formation of contracts; contract law, negotiation, and pricing; purchasing; materials management. Available for credit. Endorsed by Inland Empire Chapter of the National Association of Purchasing Management. Certificate signed by the Dean of University Extension.

Program Format Evening classes offered. Instructional schedule: Three to six hours per week. Program cycle: Continuous enrollment. Full program cycle lasts 7 courses. Completion of program requires grade of C or better.

Evaluation Student evaluation based on tests, reports, case studies. Grading system: Letters or numbers. Transcripts are kept for each student.

Enrollment Requirements Program is open to non-resident foreign students. English language proficiency required. ESL classes available.

Program Costs $1100 for the program, $160 per course.

Housing and Student Services Housing is available. Job counseling and placement services are not available.

Special Features Instructors are practicing purchasing professionals.

Contact Mr. Shelly Lisker, Associate Dean, University Extension, Riverside, CA 92521. 714-787-4111.

BUSINESS AND MANAGEMENT, GENERAL (06.01)
Certificate in Management—Graduate Level

General Information Unit offering the program: University of California Extension, Riverside. Program content: Organizational behavior, economic analysis, financial accounting, computer systems, human resources, marketing. Available for credit. Certificate signed by the Dean of University Extension. Certificate applicable to M.B.A.

Program Format Daytime, evening classes offered. Program cycle: Continuous enrollment. Full program cycle lasts 6 courses. Completion of program requires grade of B or better.

Evaluation Student evaluation based on tests, papers, reports. Grading system: Letters or numbers. Transcripts are kept for each student.

Enrollment Requirements Bachelor's degree required. Program is open to non-resident foreign students. English language proficiency required.

Program Costs $1100–$1200 for the program, $195 per course.

Housing and Student Services Housing is available. Job counseling and placement services are not available.

Special Features Courses are regularly scheduled M.B.A. courses offered mainly late afternoons and evenings.

Contact Mr. Sheldon Lisker, Associate Dean, University Extension, Riverside, CA 92521. 714-787-4111.

CIVIL TECHNOLOGIES (15.02)
Certificate in Construction Industry Practice

General Information Unit offering the program: University of California Extension, Riverside. Program content: Accounting, finance, insurance, labor relations, law, project planning. Available for credit. Certificate signed by the Dean of University Extension.

Program Format Evening classes offered. Instructional schedule: Three hours per weekly. Program cycle: Continuous enrollment. Full program cycle lasts 8 courses. Completion of program requires grade of C or better.

Evaluation Student evaluation based on tests, reports. Grading system: Letters or numbers. Transcripts are kept for each student.

Enrollment Requirements Program is open to non-resident foreign students. English language proficiency required.

Program Costs $1200 for the program, $140–$160 per course.

Housing and Student Services Housing is available. Job counseling and placement services are not available.

Special Features Instructors are construction professionals.

Contact Mr. Sheldon Lisker, Associate Dean, University Extension, Riverside, CA 92521. 714-787-4111.

COMPUTER AND INFORMATION SCIENCES, GENERAL (11.01)
Certificate in Computer Studies for Business Data Processing

General Information Unit offering the program: University of California Extension, Riverside. Program content: Data systems, information management, operating systems, programming languages. Available for credit. Certificate signed by the Dean of University Extension.

Program Format Evening classes offered. Instructional schedule: Three hours per week. Program cycle: Continuous enrollment. Full program cycle lasts 8 courses. Completion of program requires grade of C or better.

Evaluation Student evaluation based on tests, reports, computer exercises. Grading system: Letters or numbers. Transcripts are kept for each student.

Enrollment Requirements Program is open to non-resident foreign students. English language proficiency required.

Program Costs $1500 for the program, $160–$195 per course.

Housing and Student Services Housing is available. Job counseling and placement services are not available.

Special Features Covers both mainframe and micro uses.

Contact Mr. Sheldon Lisker, Associate Dean, University Extension, Riverside, CA 92521-0112. 714-787-4111.

COMPUTER AND INFORMATION SCIENCES, GENERAL (11.01)
Educational Computer Resource Specialist

General Information Unit offering the program: University of California Extension, Riverside. Program content: Communication skills, workshop models, curriculum development, staff development, computer graphics. Available for credit. Certificate signed by the Dean of University Extension.

Program Format Daytime, evening, weekend classes offered. Program cycle: Continuous enrollment. Full program cycle lasts 1 year. Completion of program requires grade of B or better.

Evaluation Student evaluation based on tests, papers, reports, hands-on computer activities. Grading system: Letters or numbers. Transcripts are kept for each student.

Enrollment Requirements Bachelor's degree, teaching credential, two years of teaching, completion of Certificate in Microcomputers for Educators, or its equivalent required. Program is open to non-resident foreign students. English language proficiency required.

Program Costs $1500–$1800 for the program, $150 per course.

Housing and Student Services Housing is available. Job counseling and placement services are not available.

Contact Ms. Sue Teele, Director of Education Extension, Bannockburn H101, Riverside, CA 92521-0112. 714-787-4361.

CONSTRUCTION TECHNOLOGY (15.10)
Light Construction and Development Management

General Information Unit offering the program: University of California Extension, Riverside. Program content: Finance and financial controls, project management and feasibility analysis, marketing, urban analysis and development. Available for credit. Cosponsored by Baldy View and Riverside Chapters of Building Industry Association. Certificate signed by the Dean of University Extension. Program fulfills requirements for professional designation of LCDM.

Program Format Evening classes offered. Instructional schedule: Three to six hours per week. Program cycle: Continuous enrollment. Full program cycle lasts 8 courses. Completion of program requires grade of C or better.

Evaluation Student evaluation based on tests, reports, case studies. Grading system: Letters or numbers. Transcripts are kept for each student.

Enrollment Requirements Bachelor's degree, or associate degree with two years of related industry experience, or four years of managerial experience required. Program is open to non-resident foreign students. English language proficiency required. ESL classes available.

Program Costs $1300 for the program, $160 per course.

Housing and Student Services Housing is available. Job counseling and placement services are not available.

Special Features One of few educational programs for residential building industry.

Contact Mr. Shelly Lisker, Associate Dean, University Extension, Riverside, CA 92521. 714-787-4111.

ENVIRONMENTAL CONTROL TECHNOLOGIES (15.05)
Hazardous Materials Management

General Information Unit offering the program: University of California Extension, Riverside. Program content: Environmental toxicology, legal regulations, groundwater hydrology, risk assessment. Available for credit. Certificate signed by the Dean of University Extension.

Program Format Daytime, evening, weekend classes offered. Program cycle: Continuous enrollment. Full program cycle lasts 7 courses. Completion of program requires grade of C or better.

Evaluation Student evaluation based on tests, reports. Grading system: Letters or numbers. Transcripts are kept for each student.

Enrollment Requirements Program is open to non-resident foreign students. English language proficiency required.

Program Costs $1500 for the program, $180–$245 per course.

Housing and Student Services Housing is available. Job counseling and placement services are not available.

Contact Ms. Molly Carpenter, Continuing Education Specialist, University Extension, Riverside, CA 92521. 714-787-5804.

GRAPHIC AND PRINTING COMMUNICATIONS (48.02)
Certificate in Calligraphy

General Information Unit offering the program: University of California Extension, Riverside. Program content: Calligraphy for beginners, intermediate calligraphy I and II, freestyle lettering, brush lettering, advanced seminar. Available for credit. Certificate signed by the Dean of University Extension.

Program Format Evening, weekend classes offered. Program cycle: Continuous enrollment. Full program cycle lasts 7 courses. Completion of program requires grade of C or better.

Evaluation Student evaluation based on tests, reports, presentations. Grading system: Letters or numbers. Transcripts are kept for each student.

Enrollment Requirements Program is open to non-resident foreign students. English language proficiency required. ESL classes available.

Program Costs $1000 for the program, $100–$160 per course.

Housing and Student Services Housing is available. Job counseling and placement services are not available.

Special Features Instructors are practicing artists, calligraphers, etc.

Contact Mr. Sheldon Lisker, Associate Dean, University Extension, Riverside, CA 92521-0112. 714-787-4111.

INDUSTRIAL ENGINEERING (14.17)
Plant Engineering

General Information Unit offering the program: University of California Extension, Riverside. Program content: Design, operation, and maintenance of plants and facilities. Available for credit. Certificate signed by the Dean of University Extension.

Program Format Evening classes offered. Program cycle: Continuous enrollment. Complete program cycle lasts six months to two years. Completion of program requires grade of C or better, six courses.

Evaluation Student evaluation based on tests. Grading system: Letters or numbers. Transcripts are kept for each student.

Enrollment Requirements One year experience in industrial or plant engineering, consent of instructor required. Program is open to non-resident foreign students. English language proficiency required.

Program Costs $1140 for the program, $190 per course.

Plant Engineering continued

Housing and Student Services   Housing is available. Job counseling and placement services are not available.

Contact   Mr. Sheldon Lisker, Associate Dean, University Extension, Riverside, CA 92521. 714-787-4111.

INTERIOR DESIGN (04.05)
Interior Design Certificate Program

General Information   Unit offering the program: University of California Extension, Riverside. Program content: Color theory, drawing, drafting, environmental design, business practices. Available for credit. Certificate signed by the Dean of University Extension.

Program Format   Daytime, evening classes offered. Instructional schedule: Three to nine hours per week. Program cycle: Continuous enrollment. Full program cycle lasts 6 quarters. Completion of program requires grade of C or better.

Evaluation   Student evaluation based on tests, design projects, case studies. Grading system: Letters or numbers. Transcripts are kept for each student.

Enrollment Requirements   Program is open to non-resident foreign students. English language proficiency required.

Program Costs $1500 for the program, $140 per course.

Housing and Student Services   Housing is available. Job counseling and placement services are not available.

Special Features   Conforms to industry standards for entry-level positions in design. Instructors are practicing interior designers.

Contact   Mr. Sheldon Lisker, Associate Dean, University Extension, Riverside, CA 92521-0112. 714-787-4111.

INVESTMENTS AND SECURITIES (06.10)
Certificate in Personal Financial Planning

General Information   Unit offering the program: University of California Extension, Riverside. Program content: Investments, taxation, tax shelters, employment benefits, estate planning. Available for credit. Endorsed by International Association for Financial Planning (IAFP). Certificate signed by the Dean of University Extension.

Program Format   Evening classes offered. Instructional schedule: Three to six hours per week. Program cycle: Continuous enrollment. Full program cycle lasts 9 courses. Completion of program requires grade of B or better.

Evaluation   Student evaluation based on tests, reports, case studies. Grading system: Letters or numbers. Transcripts are kept for each student.

Enrollment Requirements   Elementary knowledge of financial analysis techniques required. Program is open to non-resident foreign students. English language proficiency required.

Program Costs $1500 for the program, $160 per course.

Housing and Student Services   Housing is available. Job counseling and placement services are not available.

Special Features   University-wide program throughout California. Instructors are from various financial planning fields.

Contact   Mr. Sheldon Lisker, Associate Dean, University Extension, Riverside, CA 92521. 714-787-4111.

LABOR/INDUSTRIAL RELATIONS (06.11)
Certificate of Specialization in Worker's Compensation

General Information   Unit offering the program: University of California Extension, Riverside. Program content: Vocational rehabilitation, disability ratings, California Labor Code. Available for credit. Certificate signed by the Dean of University Extension.

Program Format   Evening classes offered. Instructional schedule: Three hours per week. Students may enroll fall, winter, spring. Full program cycle lasts 3 quarters. Completion of program requires grade of C or better, three courses.

Evaluation   Student evaluation based on tests, reports. Grading system: Letters or numbers. Transcripts are kept for each student.

Enrollment Requirements   Program is open to non-resident foreign students. English language proficiency required.

Program Costs $480 for the program, $160 per course.

Housing and Student Services   Housing is available. Job counseling and placement services are not available.

Special Features   Can be completed in one year.

Contact   Mr. Sheldon Lisker, Associate Dean, University Extension, Riverside, CA 92521-0112. 714-787-4111.

LAW (22.01)
Certificate in Legal Assistantship

General Information   Unit offering the program: University of California Extension, Riverside. Program content: Legal research and writing, office management, stress management. Available for credit. Cosponsored by Inland Counties Association of Paralegals, Riverside County Legal Secretaries Association. Certificate signed by the Dean of University Extension.

Program Format   Evening classes offered. Instructional schedule: Three hours per week. Program cycle: Continuous enrollment. Full program cycle lasts 9 courses. Completion of program requires grade of C or better.

Evaluation   Student evaluation based on tests, reports. Grading system: Letters or numbers. Transcripts are kept for each student.

Enrollment Requirements   Bachelor's degree and one year experience, or two years experience as legal secretary or assistant; consent of program coordinator required. Program is open to non-resident foreign students. English language proficiency required.

Program Costs $1200 for the program, $140–$160 per course.

Housing and Student Services   Housing is available. Job counseling and placement services are not available.

Special Features   Instructors are all practicing attorneys or paralegals.

Contact   Mr. Sheldon Lisker, Associate Dean, University Extension, Riverside, CA 92521. 714-787-4111.

MENTAL HEALTH/HUMAN SERVICES (17.04)
Certificate in Alcohol and Drug Studies

General Information   Unit offering the program: University of California Extension, Riverside. Program content: Intervention, criminal justice, pharmacology, co-dependency. Available for credit. Certificate signed by the Dean of University Extension.

Program Format   Evening, weekend classes offered. Program cycle: Continuous enrollment. Completion of program requires grade of C or better, 15 quarter units.

Evaluation   Student evaluation based on tests, reports. Grading system: Letters or numbers. Transcripts are kept for each student.

Enrollment Requirements   Program is open to non-resident foreign students. English language proficiency required.

Program Costs $540 for the program, $60–$140 per course.

Housing and Student Services   Housing is available. Job counseling and placement services are not available.

Contact   Ms. Barbara Moore, Program Coordinator, University Extension, Riverside, CA 92521. 714-787-4102.

MICROCOMPUTER APPLICATIONS (11.06)
Certificate in Microcomputers for Educators

General Information   Unit offering the program: University of California Extension, Riverside. Program content: Introduction, examination, evaluation of software, teaching techniques, programming. Available for credit. Certificate signed by the Dean of University Extension.

Program Format Evening, weekend classes offered. Program cycle: Continuous enrollment. Full program cycle lasts 16 credit hours. Completion of program requires grade of C or better.

Evaluation Student evaluation based on tests. Grading system: Letters or numbers. Transcripts are kept for each student.

Enrollment Requirements Bachelor's degree, teaching credential or sufficient classroom experience required. Program is open to non-resident foreign students. English language proficiency required. ESL classes available.

Program Costs $1015 for the program, $140–$185 per course.

Housing and Student Services Housing is available. Job counseling and placement services are not available.

Contact Ms. Sue Teele, Director of Education Extension, Bannockburn H101, Riverside, CA 92521-0112. 714-787-4361.

PERSONNEL MANAGEMENT (06.16)
Certificate in Personnel Management and Employee Relations

General Information Unit offering the program: University of California Extension, Riverside. Program content: Recruitment, labor relations, compensation administration, employee benefits, information systems, law. Available for credit. Certificate signed by the Dean of University Extension.

Program Format Evening classes offered. Instructional schedule: Three to six hours per week. Program cycle: Continuous enrollment. Full program cycle lasts 2 years. Completion of program requires grade of C or better.

Evaluation Student evaluation based on tests, reports. Grading system: Letters or numbers. Transcripts are kept for each student.

Enrollment Requirements Two years of college or experience in employee relations required. Program is open to non-resident foreign students. English language proficiency required.

Program Costs $1300 for the program, $80–$160 per course.

Housing and Student Services Housing is available. Job counseling and placement services are not available.

Special Features Instructors are in the personnel field.

Contact Mr. Sheldon Lisker, Associate Dean, University Extension, Riverside, CA 92521. 714-787-4111.

PUBLIC RELATIONS (09.05)
The Professional Designation in Public Relations

General Information Unit offering the program: University of California Extension, Riverside. Program content: Writing, editing, advertising, graphics, psychology, sociology. Available for credit. Cosponsored by Public Relations Society of America, California Inland Empire Chapter. Certificate signed by the Dean of University Extension.

Program Format Daytime, evening classes offered. Instructional schedule: One evening per week. Program cycle: Continuous enrollment. Full program cycle lasts 8 courses.

Evaluation Student evaluation based on tests. Grading system: Letters or numbers. Transcripts are kept for each student.

Enrollment Requirements Program is open to non-resident foreign students. English language proficiency required.

Program Costs $1100 for the program, $140 per course.

Housing and Student Services Housing is available. Job counseling and placement services are not available.

Special Features Two courses can be transferred in. Instructors are public relations professionals.

Contact Mr. Clyde Miller, Publications, University of California, Riverside Extension, Riverside, CA 92521-0112. 714-787-3806.

REAL ESTATE (06.17)
Professional Designation in Investment Real Estate

General Information Unit offering the program: University of California Extension, Riverside. Program content: Measure and understand value, risk, return-on-investment, financing, land utilization, market behavior. Available for credit. Certificate signed by the Dean of University Extension.

Program Format Evening classes offered. Instructional schedule: Three to six hours per week. Program cycle: Continuous enrollment. Full program cycle lasts 8 courses. Completion of program requires grade of C or better.

Evaluation Student evaluation based on tests, case studies. Grading system: Letters or numbers. Transcripts are kept for each student.

Enrollment Requirements Intended for those with some real estate experience. Program is open to non-resident foreign students. English language proficiency required. ESL classes available.

Program Costs $1300 for the program, $140–$180 per course.

Housing and Student Services Housing is available. Job counseling and placement services are not available.

Contact Mr. Sheldon Lisker, Associate Dean, University Extension, Riverside, CA 92521-0112. 714-787-4111.

TAXATION (06.19)
Certificate in Taxation

General Information Unit offering the program: University of California Extension, Riverside. Program content: Tax preparation, state income tax, estate planning, penalty provisions, employment taxes. Available for credit. Certificate signed by the Dean of University Extension.

Program Format Evening classes offered. Instructional schedule: Three to six hours per week. Program cycle: Continuous enrollment. Full program cycle lasts 10 courses. Completion of program requires grade of C or better.

Evaluation Student evaluation based on tests. Grading system: Letters or numbers. Transcripts are kept for each student.

Enrollment Requirements Program is open to non-resident foreign students. English language proficiency required.

Program Costs $1500 for the program, $140–$160 per course.

Housing and Student Services Housing is available. Job counseling and placement services are not available.

Special Features Instructors are practitioners, attorneys, accountants, International Revenue Service staff.

Contact Mr. Sheldon Lisker, Associate Dean, University Extension, Riverside, CA 92521. 714-787-4111.

TEACHER EDUCATION, SPECIFIC SUBJECT AREAS (13.13)
Education for the Gifted and Talented

General Information Unit offering the program: University of California Extension, Riverside. Program content: Recent research, curriculum development, computers. Available for credit. Certificate signed by the Dean of University Extension.

Program Format Evening, weekend classes offered. Program cycle: Continuous enrollment. Full program cycle lasts 6 courses. Completion of program requires grade of C or better.

Evaluation Student evaluation based on tests, papers, reports. Grading system: Letters or numbers. Transcripts are kept for each student.

Enrollment Requirements Program is open to non-resident foreign students. English language proficiency required.

Program Costs $840 for the program, $60–$140 per course.

Housing and Student Services Housing is available. Job counseling and placement services are not available.

Education for the Gifted and Talented continued

Special Features The program was developed to meet the in-service requirement mandated by the state of California for teachers of gifted and talented students.

Contact Ms. Sue Teele, Director of Education Extension, Bannockburn H101, Riverside, CA 92521-0112. 714-787-4361.

TEACHER EDUCATION, SPECIFIC SUBJECT AREAS (13.13)
Teaching Language Arts and Writing

General Information Unit offering the program: University of California Extension, Riverside. Program content: Practical application of theories and research, examination of methodologies for classroom, issues affecting teachers. Available for credit. Cosponsored by Inland Area Writing Project. Certificate signed by the Dean of University Extension.

Program Format Evening, weekend classes offered. Program cycle: Continuous enrollment. Completion of program requires grade of C or better, 15 quarter units.

Evaluation Student evaluation based on tests, reports. Grading system: Letters or numbers. Transcripts are kept for each student.

Enrollment Requirements Bachelor's degree, teaching credential or sufficient classroom experience required. Program is open to non-resident foreign students. English language proficiency required.

Program Costs $800 for the program, $60–$140 per course.

Housing and Student Services Housing is available. Job counseling and placement services are not available.

Special Features The program evolved out of the Inland Area Writing Project's expressed need for additional course work in this area.

Contact Ms. Sue Teele, Director of Education Extension, Bannockburn H101, Riverside, CA 92521-0112. 714-787-4361.

TEACHING ENGLISH AS A SECOND LANGUAGE/FOREIGN LANGUAGE (13.14)
Teaching English as a Second Language

General Information Unit offering the program: University of California Extension, Riverside. Program content: Methods, techniques and materials emphasizing American English. Available for credit. Certificate signed by the Dean of University Extension.

Program Format Evening, weekend classes offered. Program cycle: Continuous enrollment. Full program cycle lasts 3 quarters. Completion of program requires 25-quarter-unit program, satisfactory GPA, TOEFL score of 550 for non-native speakers, exit interview.

Evaluation Student evaluation based on tests, papers, reports, oral interviews. Grading system: Letters or numbers. Transcripts are kept for each student.

Enrollment Requirements Written essay examination required. Program is open to non-resident foreign students. English language proficiency required. Minimum TOEFL score required: 500.

Program Costs $60–$160 per course.

Housing and Student Services Housing is available. Job counseling and placement services are not available.

Special Features Program is now in its tenth year. A nice feature of the program is the frequency of guest speakers and teachers from nearby universities, such as the University of Southern California and UCLA. The program is a good balance between theory and practice. Often done in-service in local school districts.

Contact Dr. Sheila Dwight, Director, Intensive English Program, University of California, Riverside Extension, Riverside, CA 92521-0112. 714-787-4346.

URBAN STUDIES (45.12)
Certificate in Land Use Planning and Development Analysis

General Information Unit offering the program: University of California Extension, Riverside. Program content: State law, plan implementation, technical project review, finance, statistics, computer applications. Available for credit. Certificate signed by the Dean of University Extension.

Program Format Evening classes offered. Instructional schedule: Three hours per week. Program cycle: Continuous enrollment. Full program cycle lasts 7 courses. Completion of program requires grade of C or better.

Evaluation Student evaluation based on tests, reports. Grading system: Letters or numbers. Transcripts are kept for each student.

Enrollment Requirements Bachelor's degree or equivalent work experience required. Program is open to non-resident foreign students. English language proficiency required.

Program Costs $1100 for the program, $160 per course.

Housing and Student Services Housing is available. Job counseling and placement services are not available.

Special Features Instructors are professional planners.

Contact Mr. Sheldon Lisker, Associate Dean, University Extension, Riverside, CA 92521-0112. 714-787-4111.

NUCEA MEMBER
UNIVERSITY OF CALIFORNIA, SAN DIEGO
La Jolla, California 92093

ACCOUNTING (06.02)
Professional Certificate in Accounting

General Information Unit offering the program: Business and Management. Program content: Accounting theory and practice, tax principles, computing fundamentals and languages. Available on a non-credit basis. Certificate signed by the Dean, University of California, San Diego Extension.

Program Format Evening classes offered. Instructional schedule: One evening per week. Program cycle: Continuous enrollment. Full program cycle lasts 2 years. Completion of program requires ten courses, projects.

Evaluation Student evaluation based on tests, papers. Grading system: Letters or numbers. Transcripts are kept for each student.

Enrollment Requirements Program is open to non-resident foreign students.

Program Costs $1810 for the program, $165–$185 per course.

Housing and Student Services Housing is not available. Job counseling and placement services are not available.

Special Features Successful completion of the certificate allows student to sit for parts of the CPA exam. A maximum of two courses may be transferred or waived. The units have to be equivalent, and they must have been taken within the last 5 years.

Contact Ms. Cecilia Solis, Manager, Academic Services, University of California, San Diego Extension, X-001, La Jolla, CA 92122. 619-534-5907.

ARCHITECTURE AND ENVIRONMENTAL DESIGN, GENERAL (04.01)
Professional Certificate in Construction and Architectural Engineering Practices

General Information Unit offering the program: Business and Management. Program content: Specifications, contracts, administration, building code. Available on a non-credit basis.

Certificate signed by the Dean, University of California, San Diego Extension.

Program Format   Evening classes offered. Instructional schedule: One evening per week. Program cycle: Continuous enrollment. Completion of program requires nine courses, projects.

Evaluation   Student evaluation based on tests, papers. Grading system: Letters or numbers. Transcripts are kept for each student.

Enrollment Requirements   Program is open to non-resident foreign students.

Program Costs $1665 for the program, $185 per course.

Housing and Student Services   Housing is not available. Job counseling and placement services are not available.

Special Features   A maximum of two courses may be transferred in or waived.

Contact   Ms. Cecilia Solis, Manager, Academic Services, University of California, San Diego Extension, X-001, La Jolla, CA 92122. 619-534-5907.

BANKING AND FINANCE (06.03)
Certificate of Professional Designation in Financial Institution Management

General Information   Unit offering the program: Business and Management. Program content: Accounting issues, marketing strategy, managing human resources, information systems. Available on a non-credit basis. Certificate signed by the Dean, University of California, San Diego Extension.

Program Format   Evening classes offered. Instructional schedule: One evening per week. Program cycle: Continuous enrollment. Full program cycle lasts 2 years. Completion of program requires eight core courses, projects.

Evaluation   Student evaluation based on tests, papers. Grading system: Letters or numbers. Transcripts are kept for each student.

Enrollment Requirements   Program is open to non-resident foreign students.

Program Costs $1480 for the program, $185 per course.

Housing and Student Services   Housing is not available. Job counseling and placement services are not available.

Contact   Ms. Cecilia Solis, Manager, Academic Services, University of California, San Diego Extension, X-001, La Jolla, CA 92122. 619-534-5907.

BANKING AND FINANCE (06.03)
Certificate of Professional Designation in Personal Financial Planning

General Information   Unit offering the program: Business and Management. Program content: Income taxation, tax shelters, investments, estate planning. Available on a non-credit basis. Certificate signed by the Dean, University of California, San Diego Extension.

Program Format   Evening classes offered. Instructional schedule: One evening per week. Program cycle: Continuous enrollment. Full program cycle lasts 2 years. Completion of program requires nine core courses, projects.

Evaluation   Student evaluation based on tests, papers. Grading system: Letters or numbers. Transcripts are kept for each student.

Enrollment Requirements   Program is open to non-resident foreign students.

Program Costs $1850 for the program, $185 per course.

Housing and Student Services   Housing is not available. Job counseling and placement services are not available.

Contact   Ms. Cecilia Solis, Manager, Academic Services, University of California, San Diego Extension, X-001, La Jolla, CA 92122. 619-534-5907.

BUSINESS ADMINISTRATION AND MANAGEMENT (06.04)
Professional Certificate in Business Administration

General Information   Unit offering the program: Business and Management. Program content: Finance, economics, accounting, computing fundamentals, management principles, marketing. Available on a non-credit basis. Certificate signed by the Dean, University of California, San Diego Extension.

Program Format   Evening classes offered. Instructional schedule: One evening per week. Program cycle: Continuous enrollment. Full program cycle lasts 2 years. Completion of program requires ten courses, projects.

Evaluation   Student evaluation based on tests, papers. Grading system: Letters or numbers. Transcripts are kept for each student.

Enrollment Requirements   Program is open to non-resident foreign students.

Program Costs $1850 for the program, $185 per course.

Housing and Student Services   Housing is not available. Job counseling and placement services are not available.

Special Features   A maximum of two courses may be transferred or waived.

Contact   Ms. Cecilia Solis, Manager, Academic Services, University of California, San Diego Extension, X-001, La Jolla, CA 92122. 619-534-5907.

BUSINESS AND MANAGEMENT, GENERAL (06.01)
Professional Certificate in Purchasing Management

General Information   Unit offering the program: Business and Management. Program content: Purchasing, legal analysis for business managers, management principles. Available on a non-credit basis. Certificate signed by the Dean, University of California, San Diego Extension.

Program Format   Evening classes offered. Instructional schedule: One evening per week for three hours. Program cycle: Continuous enrollment. Full program cycle lasts 2 years. Completion of program requires six core courses, three electives, projects.

Evaluation   Student evaluation based on tests, papers. Grading system: Letters or numbers. Transcripts are kept for each student.

Enrollment Requirements   Program is open to non-resident foreign students.

Program Costs $1665 for the program, $185 per course.

Housing and Student Services   Housing is not available. Job counseling and placement services are not available.

Special Features   A maximum of two courses may be transferred or waived.

Contact   Ms. Cecilia Solis, Manager, Academic Services, University of California, San Diego Extension, X-001, La Jolla, CA 92122. 619-534-5907.

CHILD CARE AND GUIDANCE MANAGEMENT AND SERVICES (20.02)
Professional Certificate Program in Early Childhood Development and Education

General Information   Unit offering the program: Education, Behavioral and Health Sciences. Program content: Curriculum modules, human growth and development, teaching in the preschool. Available on a non-credit basis. Certificate signed by the Dean, University of California, San Diego Extension.

Program Format   Evening, weekend classes offered. Instructional schedule: One evening per week, weekend seminars. Program cycle: Continuous enrollment. Full program

Professional Certificate Program in Early Childhood Development and Education continued

cycle lasts 2 years. Completion of program requires 22 quarter units, projects.

Evaluation   Student evaluation based on tests, papers. Grading system: Letters or numbers. Transcripts are kept for each student.

Enrollment Requirements   Program is open to non-resident foreign students.

Program Costs $1017 for the program, $90–$185 per course.

Housing and Student Services   Housing is not available. Job counseling and placement services are not available.

Special Features   Students earn certificate while completing requirements for licensing and certification designated by State Department of Social Services and Commission for Teacher Licensing for employment in licensed preschools and child development centers.

Contact   Ms. Cecilia Solis, Manager, Academic Services, University of California, San Diego Extension, X-001, La Jolla, CA 92122. 619-534-5907.

COMPUTER AND INFORMATION SCIENCES, GENERAL (11.01)
Professional Certificate Program in Computers in Education

General Information   Unit offering the program: Health and Education Department. Program content: Educational software applications, hardware and peripherals, languages and processes. Available on a non-credit basis. Certificate signed by the Dean, University of California, San Diego Extension.

Program Format   Evening classes offered. Instructional schedule: One evening per week. Program cycle: Continuous enrollment. Full program cycle lasts 2 years. Completion of program requires 12 semester units, projects.

Evaluation   Student evaluation based on tests, papers. Grading system: Letters or numbers. Transcripts are kept for each student.

Enrollment Requirements   Program is open to non-resident foreign students.

Program Costs $1850 for the program, $185 per course.

Housing and Student Services   Housing is not available. Job counseling and placement services are not available.

Special Features   Faculty embody a unique combination of computer science knowledge and classroom applications experience. Participants expected to have completed baccalaureate degree or equivalent and hold either a California teaching credential or have sufficient classroom or school site experience.

Contact   Ms. Cecilia Solis, Manager, Academic Services, University of California, San Diego Extension, X-001, La Jolla, CA 92122. 619-534-5907.

COMPUTER ENGINEERING (14.09)
Microcomputer Engineering

General Information   Unit offering the program: Engineering and Applied Computer Sciences. Program content: Digital design, systems engineering, peripheral interfacing, hardware design. Available on a non-credit basis. Certificate signed by the Dean, University of California, San Diego Extension.

Program Format   Evening classes offered. Instructional schedule: One evening per week for three hours. Program cycle: Continuous enrollment. Full program cycle lasts 7 quarters. Completion of program requires five core courses, two electives, projects.

Evaluation   Student evaluation based on tests, papers. Grading system: Letters or numbers. Transcripts are kept for each student.

Enrollment Requirements   Program is open to non-resident foreign students.

Program Costs $1840 for the program, $230 per course.

Housing and Student Services   Housing is not available. Job counseling and placement services are not available.

Special Features   All instructors are professionals in the field.

Contact   Ms. Cecilia Solis, Manager, Academic Services, University of California, San Diego Extension, X-001, La Jolla, CA 92122. 619-534-5907.

COUNSELING PSYCHOLOGY (42.06)
Professional Certificate Program for Counseling Specialists for Adults

General Information   Unit offering the program: Health and Education Department. Program content: Theory and philosophy of counseling, personality types and development, ethics and the law. Available on a non-credit basis. Certificate signed by the Dean, University of California, San Diego Extension.

Program Format   Evening, weekend classes offered. Instructional schedule: One evening per week, one weekend per quarter. Program cycle: Continuous enrollment. Full program cycle lasts 2 years. Completion of program requires practicum, six units of electives, four core courses.

Evaluation   Student evaluation based on tests, papers. Grading system: Letters or numbers. Transcripts are kept for each student.

Enrollment Requirements   Program is open to non-resident foreign students.

Program Costs $1345 for the program, $95–$155 per course.

Housing and Student Services   Housing is not available. Job counseling and placement services are not available.

Contact   Ms. Cecilia Solis, Manager, Academic Services, University of California, San Diego Extension, X-001, La Jolla, CA 92122. 619-534-5907.

ELECTRICAL, ELECTRONICS, AND COMMUNICATIONS ENGINEERING (14.10)
Professional Certificate Program in Communications and Signal Processing

General Information   Unit offering the program: Engineering and Applied Computer Sciences. Program content: Digital and analog transmission systems, communication channel devices and simulation, computer networks. Available on a non-credit basis. Certificate signed by the Dean, University of California, San Diego Extension.

Program Format   Evening classes offered. Instructional schedule: One evening per week for three hours. Program cycle: Continuous enrollment. Full program cycle lasts 7 quarters. Completion of program requires seven courses, projects.

Evaluation   Student evaluation based on tests, papers. Grading system: Letters or numbers. Transcripts are kept for each student.

Enrollment Requirements   Program is open to non-resident foreign students.

Program Costs $1840 for the program, $230 per course.

Housing and Student Services   Housing is not available. Job counseling and placement services are not available.

Special Features   All instructors are professionals in the field.

Contact   Ms. Cecilia Solis, Manager, Academic Services, University of California, San Diego Extension, X-001, La Jolla, CA 92122. 619-534-5907.

ENVIRONMENTAL CONTROL TECHNOLOGIES (15.05)
Energy Management

General Information   Unit offering the program: Engineering and Applied Computer Sciences. Program content: Energy systems, efficient lighting, auditing, cogeneration principles and practices, energy storage. Available on a non-credit basis. Certificate signed by the Dean, University of California, San Diego Extension.

Program Format   Evening classes offered. Instructional schedule: One evening per week for three hours. Program cycle: Continuous enrollment. Full program cycle lasts 6 quarters. Completion of program requires six core courses, projects.

Evaluation   Student evaluation based on tests, papers. Grading system: Letters or numbers. Transcripts are kept for each student.

Enrollment Requirements   Program is open to non-resident foreign students.

Program Costs $1290 for the program, $215 per course.

Housing and Student Services   Housing is not available. Job counseling and placement services are not available.

Special Features   All instructors are professionals in the field.

Contact   Ms. Cecilia Solis, Manager, Academic Services, University of California, San Diego Extension, X-001, La Jolla, CA 92122. 619-534-5907.

ENVIRONMENTAL HEALTH ENGINEERING (14.14)
Professional Certificate in Hazardous Materials Management

General Information   Unit offering the program: Engineering and Applied Computer Sciences. Program content: Regulatory framework, environmental toxicology, technologies for storage, industrial hygiene. Available on a non-credit basis. Certificate signed by the Dean, University of California, San Diego Extension.

Program Format   Evening classes offered. Instructional schedule: One evening per week for three hours. Program cycle: Continuous enrollment. Full program cycle lasts 7 quarters. Completion of program requires seven courses, projects.

Evaluation   Student evaluation based on tests, papers. Grading system: Letters or numbers. Transcripts are kept for each student.

Enrollment Requirements   Program is open to non-resident foreign students.

Program Costs $1290 for the program, $215 per course.

Housing and Student Services   Housing is not available. Job counseling and placement services are not available.

Special Features   All instructors are professionals in the field.

Contact   Ms. Cecilia Solis, Manager, Academic Services, University of California, San Diego Extension, X-001, La Jolla, CA 92122. 619-534-5907.

GENERAL MARKETING (08.07)
Professional Certificate in Marketing Communications

General Information   Unit offering the program: Business and Management, Arts and Sciences. Program content: Contemporary advertising, target marketing, writing, graphic design, promotional strategy management. Available on a non-credit basis. Certificate signed by the Dean, University of California, San Diego Extension.

Program Format   Evening classes offered. Instructional schedule: One evening per week. Program cycle: Continuous enrollment. Completion of program requires eight courses, projects.

Evaluation   Student evaluation based on tests, papers. Grading system: Letters or numbers. Transcripts are kept for each student.

Enrollment Requirements   Prerequisite in marketing or equivalent knowledge required. Program is open to non-resident foreign students.

Program Costs $1665 for the program, $185 per course.

Housing and Student Services   Housing is not available. Job counseling and placement services are not available.

Special Features   A maximum of two courses may be transferred or waived.

Contact   Ms. Cecilia Solis, Manager, Academic Services, University of California, San Diego Extension, X-001, La Jolla, CA 92122. 619-534-5907.

GRAPHIC AND PRINTING COMMUNICATIONS (48.02)
Professional Certificate in Graphic Communications

General Information   Unit offering the program: Integrated Arts and Humanities. Program content: Graphic design, production, commercial lettering. Available on a non-credit basis. Certificate signed by the Dean, University of California, San Diego Extension.

Program Format   Evening, weekend classes offered. Instructional schedule: One evening per week. Program cycle: Continuous enrollment. Full program cycle lasts 2 years. Completion of program requires ten courses, projects.

Evaluation   Student evaluation based on tests, papers. Grading system: Letters or numbers. Transcripts are kept for each student.

Enrollment Requirements   Program is open to non-resident foreign students.

Program Costs $1400 for the program, $135–$145 per course.

Housing and Student Services   Housing is not available. Job counseling and placement services are not available.

Special Features   Prerequisite can be waived if student has prior experience in field. Instructors are all professionals in the graphic design field.

Contact   Ms. Cecilia Solis, Manager, Academic Services, University of California, San Diego Extension, X-001, La Jolla, CA 92122. 619-534-5907.

HEALTH-RELATED ACTIVITIES (34.01)
Professional Certificate Program in Fitness and Health Management Instruction

General Information   Unit offering the program: Education, Behavioral and Health Sciences. Program content: Adult fitness, the human body, physiology of exercise. Available on a non-credit basis. Certificate signed by the Dean, University of California, San Diego Extension.

Program Format   Evening, weekend classes offered. Instructional schedule: One evening per week, Saturdays. Program cycle: Continuous enrollment. Full program cycle lasts 9 months. Completion of program requires 16 quarter units, projects.

Evaluation   Student evaluation based on tests, papers. Grading system: Letters or numbers. Transcripts are kept for each student.

Enrollment Requirements   Program is open to non-resident foreign students.

Program Costs $1040 for the program, $105–$155 per course.

Professional Certificate Program in Fitness and Health Management Instruction continued

Housing and Student Services   Housing is not available. Job counseling and placement services are not available.

Special Features   Participants may request substitution of up to six quarter units of course work. Transfer course work must fulfill the competencies contained in certificate program and should have been taken through a University-level institution within the last two years.

Contact   Ms. Cecilia Solis, Manager, Academic Services, University of California, San Diego Extension, X-001, La Jolla, CA 92122. 619-534-5907.

INFORMATION SCIENCES AND SYSTEMS (11.04)
Professional Certificate in Microcomputers in Business

General Information   Unit offering the program: Business and Management, Engineering and Computer Sciences. Available on a non-credit basis. Certificate signed by the Dean, University of California, San Diego Extension.

Program Format   Evening classes offered. Instructional schedule: One evening per week. Program cycle: Continuous enrollment. Full program cycle lasts 2 years. Completion of program requires three core courses, five electives.

Evaluation   Student evaluation based on tests, papers. Grading system: Letters or numbers. Transcripts are kept for each student.

Enrollment Requirements   Program is open to non-resident foreign students.

Program Costs $1665 for the program, $185 per course.

Housing and Student Services   Housing is not available. Job counseling and placement services are not available.

Special Features   A maximum of two courses may be transferred or waived.

Contact   Ms. Cecilia Solis, Manager, Academic Services, University of California, San Diego Extension, X-001, La Jolla, CA 92122. 619-534-5907.

INFORMATION SCIENCES AND SYSTEMS (11.04)
Professional Certificate in Programming and Development of Business Computer Systems

General Information   Unit offering the program: Business and Management. Program content: Computing fundamentals, program design and analysis, data communications, data structures. Available on a non-credit basis. Certificate signed by the Dean, University of California, San Diego Extension.

Program Format   Evening classes offered. Instructional schedule: One evening per week. Program cycle: Continuous enrollment. Full program cycle lasts 2 years. Completion of program requires four core courses, five electives, projects.

Evaluation   Student evaluation based on tests, papers. Grading system: Letters or numbers. Transcripts are kept for each student.

Enrollment Requirements   Program is open to non-resident foreign students.

Program Costs $1665 for the program, $185 per course.

Housing and Student Services   Housing is not available. Job counseling and placement services are not available.

Special Features   A maximum of two courses may be transferred or waived.

Contact   Ms. Cecilia Solis, Manager, Academic Services, University of California, San Diego Extension, X-001, La Jolla, CA 92122. 619-534-5907.

INSTITUTIONAL MANAGEMENT (06.07)
Professional Certificate in Engineering Management

General Information   Unit offering the program: Business and Management. Program content: Program and product management, product development, marketing issues, writing and presentations. Available on a non-credit basis. Certificate signed by the Dean, University of California, San Diego Extension.

Program Format   Evening classes offered. Instructional schedule: One evening per week. Program cycle: Continuous enrollment. Full program cycle lasts 2 years. Completion of program requires nine core courses, projects.

Evaluation   Student evaluation based on tests, papers. Grading system: Letters or numbers. Transcripts are kept for each student.

Enrollment Requirements   Program is open to non-resident foreign students.

Program Costs $1500 for the program, $145–$185 per course.

Housing and Student Services   Housing is not available. Job counseling and placement services are not available.

Special Features   A maximum of two courses may be transferred or waived.

Contact   Ms. Cecilia Solis, Manager, Academic Services, University of California, San Diego Extension, X-001, La Jolla, CA 92122. 619-534-5907.

INSTITUTIONAL MANAGEMENT (06.07)
Professional Certificate in Management

General Information   Unit offering the program: Business and Management. Program content: Management principles, marketing, business planning, communications, human relations. Available on a non-credit basis. Certificate signed by the Dean, University of California, San Diego Extension.

Program Format   Evening classes offered. Instructional schedule: One evening per week. Program cycle: Continuous enrollment. Full program cycle lasts 2 years. Completion of program requires six core courses, three electives, projects.

Evaluation   Student evaluation based on tests, papers. Grading system: Letters or numbers. Transcripts are kept for each student.

Enrollment Requirements   Program is open to non-resident foreign students.

Program Costs $1665 for the program, $185 per course.

Housing and Student Services   Housing is not available. Job counseling and placement services are not available.

Special Features   A maximum of two courses may be transferred or waived.

Contact   Ms. Cecilia Solis, Manager, Academic Services, University of California, San Diego Extension, X-001, La Jolla, CA 92122. 619-534-5907.

LAW (22.01)
The Legal Assistant Training Program

General Information   Unit offering the program: Integrated Arts and Humanities. Program content: Legal research analysis, legal communications, corporate law, civil litigation, estate planning. Available on a non-credit basis. Certificate signed by the Dean, University of California, San Diego Extension.

Program Format   Evening classes offered. Instructional schedule: One evening per week. Program cycle: Continuous enrollment. Full program cycle lasts 15 months. Completion of program requires ten courses, projects.

Evaluation   Student evaluation based on tests, papers. Grading system: Letters or numbers. Transcripts are kept for each student.

Enrollment Requirements   Bachelor's degree or equivalent experience, letters of reference, grade of C or better in prerequisite required. Program is open to non-resident foreign students.

Program Costs $1800 for the program, $180 per course.

Housing and Student Services Housing is not available. Job counseling and placement services are not available.

Special Features Instructors are all practicing attorneys and working legal assistants.

Contact Ms. Cecilia Solis, Manager, Academic Services, University of California, San Diego Extension, X-001, La Jolla, CA 92122. 619-534-5907.

MANAGEMENT INFORMATION SYSTEMS (06.12)
Professional Certificate in Management and Analysis of Business Computer Systems

General Information Unit offering the program: Business and Management. Available on a non-credit basis. Certificate signed by the Dean, University of California, San Diego Extension.

Program Format Evening classes offered. Instructional schedule: One evening per week. Program cycle: Continuous enrollment. Full program cycle lasts 2 years. Completion of program requires four core courses, five electives, projects.

Evaluation Student evaluation based on tests, papers. Grading system: Letters or numbers. Transcripts are kept for each student.

Enrollment Requirements Program is open to non-resident foreign students.

Program Costs $1665 for the program, $185 per course.

Housing and Student Services Housing is not available. Job counseling and placement services are not available.

Special Features A maximum of two courses may be transferred or waived.

Contact Ms. Cecilia Solis, Manager, Academic Services, University of California, San Diego Extension, X-001, La Jolla, CA 92122. 619-534-5907.

MENTAL HEALTH/HUMAN SERVICES (17.04)
Advanced Mental Health Training

General Information Unit offering the program: Education, Health and Behavioral Science. Program content: Psychopharmacology, somatopsychic disorders, interface with medical practioners. Available on a non-credit basis. Certificate signed by the University of California, San Diego Extension.

Program Format Evening, weekend classes offered. Instructional schedule: One weekend per course per quarter. Program cycle: Continuous enrollment. Full program cycle lasts 9 months. Completion of program requires three core courses, two elective workshops.

Evaluation Student evaluation based on tests, papers. Grading system: Letters or numbers. Transcripts are kept for each student.

Enrollment Requirements Program is open to non-resident foreign students.

Program Costs $565 for the program, $95–$125 per course.

Housing and Student Services Housing is not available. Job counseling and placement services are not available.

Special Features Program is for graduate-level social workers, marriage/family and child counselors, psychologists, psychiatric nurses, and other mental health professionals with a minimum of one year of experience in the field.

Contact Ms. Cecilia Solis, Manager, Academic Services, University of California, San Diego Extension, X-001, La Jolla, CA 92122. 619-534-5907.

MENTAL HEALTH/HUMAN SERVICES (17.04)
Certificate in Alcohol and Other Drug Studies

General Information Unit offering the program: Department of Alcohol and Other Drug Studies. Program content: Issues and attitudes, definitions, concepts, consequences, responses. Available on a non-credit basis. Certificate signed by the Dean, University of California, San Diego Extension. Program fulfills requirements for Board of Registered Nurses, National Association of Social Workers, California Association of Alcohol and Drug Abuse Counselors.

Program Format Evening, weekend, correspondence classes offered. Instructional schedule: One evening per week, weekend seminars. Program cycle: Continuous enrollment. Completion of program requires 20 units, 170 contact hours.

Evaluation Student evaluation based on tests, papers, projects. Grading system: Letters or numbers. Transcripts are kept for each student.

Enrollment Requirements Program is open to non-resident foreign students.

Program Costs $2000–$2250 for the program, $85–$180 per course.

Housing and Student Services Housing is not available. Job counseling and placement services are not available.

Contact Ms. Cecilia Solis, Manager, Academic Services, University of California, San Diego Extension, X-001, La Jolla, CA 92122. 619-534-5907.

MENTAL HEALTH/HUMAN SERVICES (17.04)
Certificate in Recovery Services

General Information Unit offering the program: Department of Alcohol and Other Drug Studies. Available on a non-credit basis. Certificate signed by the Dean, University of California, San Diego Extension. Program fulfills requirements for Board of Registered Nurses, National Association of Social Workers, California Association of Alcohol and Drug Abuse Counselors.

Program Format Evening, weekend classes offered. Instructional schedule: One evening per week, weekend seminars. Program cycle: Continuous enrollment. Completion of program requires four core courses, eight elective units, 153 contact hours.

Evaluation Student evaluation based on tests, papers, projects. Grading system: Letters or numbers. Transcripts are kept for each student.

Enrollment Requirements Program is open to non-resident foreign students.

Program Costs $800–$1000 for the program, $85–$180 per course.

Housing and Student Services Housing is not available. Job counseling and placement services are not available.

Contact Ms. Cecilia Solis, Manager, Academic Services, University of California, San Diego Extension, X-001, La Jolla, CA 92122. 619-534-5907.

PERSONNEL MANAGEMENT (06.16)
Professional Certificate in Personnel Management

General Information Unit offering the program: Business and Management. Program content: Fundamentals of labor relations, personnel recruitment, compensation planning and administration, management principles. Available on a non-credit basis. Certificate signed by the Dean, University of California, San Diego Extension.

Program Format Evening classes offered. Instructional schedule: One evening per week. Program cycle: Continuous enrollment. Full program cycle lasts 2 years. Completion of program requires six core courses, three electives, projects.

Evaluation Student evaluation based on tests, papers. Grading system: Letters or numbers. Transcripts are kept for each student.

Professional Certificate in Personnel Management continued

Enrollment Requirements Program is open to non-resident foreign students.

Program Costs $1665 for the program, $185 per course.

Housing and Student Services Housing is not available. Job counseling and placement services are not available.

Special Features A maximum of two courses may be transferred or waived.

Contact Ms. Cecilia Solis, Manager, Academic Services, University of California, San Diego Extension, X-001, La Jolla, CA 92122. 619-534-5907.

REAL ESTATE (06.17)
Professional Certificate in Real Estate

General Information Unit offering the program: Business and Management. Program content: Practice, appraisal, economics, planning, finance, property management. Available on a non-credit basis. Certificate signed by the Dean, University of California, San Diego Extension.

Program Format Evening, weekend classes offered. Instructional schedule: One evening per week. Program cycle: Continuous enrollment. Full program cycle lasts 2 years. Completion of program requires eight core courses, projects.

Evaluation Student evaluation based on tests, papers. Grading system: Letters or numbers. Transcripts are kept for each student.

Enrollment Requirements Program is open to non-resident foreign students.

Program Costs $1640 for the program, $205 per course.

Housing and Student Services Housing is not available. Job counseling and placement services are not available.

Special Features Successful completion of certificate allows students to sit for the broker's examination. Two courses may be transferred or waived. The units have to be equivalent and must have been taken within the last five years.

Contact Ms. Cecilia Solis, Manager, Academic Services, University of California, San Diego Extension, X-001, La Jolla, CA 92122. 619-534-5907.

REAL ESTATE (06.17)
Professional Certificate in Real Estate Development

General Information Unit offering the program: Business and Management. Program content: Development, economics, feasibility analysis, financing. Available on a non-credit basis. Certificate signed by the Dean, University of California, San Diego Extension.

Program Format Evening classes offered. Instructional schedule: One evening per week. Program cycle: Continuous enrollment. Full program cycle lasts 2 years. Completion of program requires four core courses, five electives, projects.

Evaluation Student evaluation based on tests, papers. Grading system: Letters or numbers. Transcripts are kept for each student.

Enrollment Requirements Program is open to non-resident foreign students.

Program Costs $1800 for the program, $165–$205 per course.

Housing and Student Services Housing is not available. Job counseling and placement services are not available.

Special Features A maximum of two courses may be transferred or waived.

Contact Ms. Cecilia Solis, Manager, Academic Services, University of California, San Diego Extension, X-001, La Jolla, CA 92122. 619-534-5907.

SYSTEMS ANALYSIS (11.05)
Applied Computer Science with Emphasis in Systems Programming

General Information Unit offering the program: Engineering and Applied Computer Sciences. Program content: Planning and evaluation of hardware and software, developing programming standards, computer architecture, data structures. Available on a non-credit basis. Certificate signed by the Dean, University of California, San Diego Extension.

Program Format Evening classes offered. Instructional schedule: One evening per week for three hours. Program cycle: Continuous enrollment. Full program cycle lasts 8 quarters. Completion of program requires eight courses, projects.

Evaluation Student evaluation based on tests, papers. Grading system: Letters or numbers. Transcripts are kept for each student.

Enrollment Requirements Program is open to non-resident foreign students.

Program Costs $1840 for the program, $230 per course.

Housing and Student Services Housing is not available. Job counseling and placement services are not available.

Special Features All instructors are professionals in the field.

Contact Ms. Cecilia Solis, Manager, Academic Services, University of California, San Diego Extension, X-001, La Jolla, CA 92122. 619-534-5907.

TEACHING ENGLISH AS A SECOND LANGUAGE/FOREIGN LANGUAGE (13.14)
Professional Certificate Program in Teaching English as a Second Language

General Information Unit offering the program: Education, Behavioral and Health Sciences. Program content: Language as communication, acquisition, cultural orientation, classroom management techniques. Available on a non-credit basis. Certificate signed by the Dean, University of California, San Diego Extension.

Program Format Evening, weekend classes offered. Instructional schedule: One evening per week, weekend seminars. Program cycle: Continuous enrollment. Full program cycle lasts 1 year. Completion of program requires five core courses, ten units of electives.

Evaluation Student evaluation based on tests, papers. Grading system: Letters or numbers. Transcripts are kept for each student.

Enrollment Requirements Program is open to non-resident foreign students.

Program Costs $1825 for the program, $105–$185 per course.

Housing and Student Services Housing is not available. Job counseling and placement services are not available.

Special Features Applicants who have successfully completed equivalent courses within the last five years may petition for a maximum of six units of credit to be applied to the unit total. Applicants with a minimum of one full-time year of ESL experience may petition for a maximum of six units of credit to be applied to the unit total.

Contact Ms. Cecilia Solis, Manager, Academic Services, University of California, San Diego Extension, X-001, La Jolla, CA 92122. 619-534-5907.

UNIVERSITY OF CALIFORNIA, SANTA BARBARA
Santa Barbara, California 93106

ENVIRONMENTAL DESIGN (04.04)
The Certificate Program in Environmental and Interior Design (Professional Level)

General Information   Unit offering the program: Department of Human Development. Program content: Elements of design, environmental history, environmental and interior design, presentation techniques, environmental lighting. Available for credit. Endorsed by Environmental and Interior Design Advisory Board of Professionals. Certificate signed by the Director, University of California, Santa Barbara Extension.

Program Format   Daytime, evening, weekend classes offered. Program cycle: Continuous enrollment. Complete program cycle lasts 12–18 months. Completion of program requires eight courses, grade of C or better.

Evaluation   Student evaluation based on tests, papers, reports, projects, portfolios, presentations. Grading system: Letters or numbers. Transcripts are kept for each student.

Enrollment Requirements   Completion of Proficiency Certificate or consent of Program Director required. Program is open to non-resident foreign students. English language proficiency required.

Program Costs $3200 for the program, $165–$195 per course.

Housing and Student Services   Housing is not available. Job counseling and placement services are available.

Special Features   The Professional certificate adds to the proficiency-level skills and prepares students to gain knowledge and skills for the design field, master skills and techniques for design creativity, and gain background interior design.

Contact   Ms. Denise Judd, Program Assistant, Department of Human Development, University of California, Santa Barbara Extension, Santa Barbara, CA 93106. 805-961-4717.

ENVIRONMENTAL DESIGN (04.04)
The Certificate Program in Environmental and Interior Design (Proficiency Level)

General Information   Unit offering the program: Department of Human Development. Program content: Drafting, design drawing, color theory and application, materials and processes, professional practice. Available for credit. Endorsed by Environmental and Interior Design Advisory Board of Professionals. Certificate signed by the Director, University of California, Santa Barbara Extension.

Program Format   Daytime, evening, weekend classes offered. Program cycle: Continuous enrollment. Complete program cycle lasts 12–18 months. Completion of program requires nine courses, grade of C or better.

Evaluation   Student evaluation based on tests, papers, reports, projects, portfolios, presentations. Grading system: Letters or numbers. Transcripts are kept for each student.

Enrollment Requirements   Background in art recommended, but not required. Program is open to non-resident foreign students. English language proficiency required.

Program Costs $3200 for the program, $165–$195 per course.

Housing and Student Services   Housing is not available. Job counseling and placement services are available.

Special Features   The proficiency certificate prepares students to gain knowledge for the design field, enhance their competitive position in business, and develop business, drawing, drafting, and research skills.

Contact   Ms. Denise Judd, Program Assistant, Department of Human Development, University of California, Santa Barbara Extension, Santa Barbara, CA 93106. 805-961-4717.

GRAPHIC AND PRINTING COMMUNICATIONS (48.02)
The Certificate in Commercial Design

General Information   Unit offering the program: Human Development. Program content: Layout, paste-up, composition, print technology, design preparation, television and videotape productions. Available for credit. Certificate signed by the Director of Extension.

Program Format   Daytime, evening, weekend classes offered. Program cycle: Continuous enrollment. Full program cycle lasts 1 year.

Evaluation   Student evaluation based on projects, portfolio. Grading system: Letters or numbers. Transcripts are kept for each student.

Enrollment Requirements   English language proficiency required.

Program Costs $1080 for the program, $120 per course.

Housing and Student Services   Housing is not available. Job counseling and placement services are not available.

Special Features   The program presents the basics of commercial design techniques presented by working professionals from a practical point of view. Students acquire skills and vocational knowledge that can be applied to more extensive study and specialization in a two-year design school. All requirements for the Certificate in Commercial Design can be completed within three quarters.

Contact   Human Development Program, University of California, Santa Barbara Extension, Santa Barbara, CA 93106. 805-961-4200.

MENTAL HEALTH/HUMAN SERVICES (17.04)
Alcohol and Drug Counseling Skills Certificate

General Information   Unit offering the program: University of California, Santa Barbara Extension, Department of Human Development. Available for credit. Certificate signed by the Director, University of California, Santa Barbara Extension.

Program Format   Daytime, evening, weekend classes offered. One or two core courses each quarter, electives offered year-round. Full program cycle lasts 1 year. Completion of program requires 24 units.

Evaluation   Student evaluation based on tests, papers, reports. Grading system: Letters or numbers. Transcripts are kept for each student.

Enrollment Requirements   Program is open to non-resident foreign students. English language proficiency required.

Program Costs $1200 for the program.

Housing and Student Services   Housing is not available.

Special Features   Instructors are experienced practitioners and educators in the field. This program in transferable to other UC certificate programs in alcohol and drug studies. Appropriate for medical and mental health professionals who want to augment their training and/or credentials; law enforcement personnel; clergy; educators; professionals and paraprofessionals in social service areas; and persons who want certification to become paraprofessional counselors.

Contact   Department of Human Development, University of California, Santa Barbara Extension, Santa Barbara, CA 93106. 805-961-3695.

MENTAL HEALTH/HUMAN SERVICES (17.04)
Alcohol and Drug Studies Certificate

General Information   Unit offering the program: University of California, Santa Barbara Extension, Department of Human Development. Available for credit. Certificate signed by the Director, University of California, Santa Barbara Extension.

Program Format   Daytime, evening, weekend classes offered. One or two core courses each quarter, electives offered year-

Alcohol and Drug Studies Certificate continued

round. Full program cycle lasts 1 year. Completion of program requires 15 units.

Evaluation Student evaluation based on tests, papers, reports. Grading system: Letters or numbers. Transcripts are kept for each student.

Enrollment Requirements Program is open to non-resident foreign students. English language proficiency required.

Program Costs $955 for the program.

Housing and Student Services Housing is not available.

Special Features Instructors are experienced practitioners and educators in the field. This program is transferable to other UC certificate programs in alcohol and drug studies. Appropriate for medical and mental health professionals who want to augment their training and/or credentials; law enforcements personnel; clergy; educators; professionals and paraprofessionals in social service areas; and persons who want certification to become paraprofessional counselors.

Contact Department of Human Development, University of California, Santa Barbara Extension, Santa Barbara, CA 93106. 805-961-3695.

PSYCHOLOGY, GENERAL (42.01)
Counseling Skills Certificate

General Information Unit offering the program: University of California, Santa Barbara Extension, Human Development Department. Program content: Interviewing skills, counseling models, applying counseling strategies. Available for credit. Certificate signed by the Director, University of California, Santa Barbara Extension.

Program Format Daytime, evening, weekend classes offered. One core course each quarter, electives offered year-round. Full program cycle lasts 1 year. Completion of program requires 15 units.

Evaluation Student evaluation based on tests, papers, reports. Grading system: Letters or numbers. Transcripts are kept for each student.

Enrollment Requirements Instructors' consent and interview required. Program is open to non-resident foreign students. English language proficiency required.

Program Costs $955 for the program.

Housing and Student Services Housing is not available. Job counseling and placement services are available.

Special Features Instructors are practicing professionals in clinical psychology, counseling, or social work. Occasionally, workshops are led by well-known scholars and theoreticians. The program can help develop theoretical knowledge and practical skills applicable to both professional and personal life. Successful completion of the Certificate leads to a position not requiring a degree in counseling.

Contact Human Development Program, University of California, Santa Barbara Extension, Santa Barbara, CA 93106. 805-961-4200.

TEACHING ENGLISH AS A SECOND LANGUAGE/FOREIGN LANGUAGE (13.14)
Certificate in Teaching English as a Second Language

General Information Unit offering the program: Santa Barbara Extension. Available for credit. Certificate signed by the Director, University of California, Santa Barbara Extension.

Program Format Weekend classes offered. Program cycle: Continuous enrollment. Full program cycle lasts 4 quarters. Completion of program requires minimum 24 credit hours, grade of C or better.

Evaluation Student evaluation based on tests, papers, reports. Grading system: Letters or numbers, pass/fail. Transcripts are kept for each student.

Enrollment Requirements Program is open to non-resident foreign students. English language proficiency required. Minimum TOEFL score required: 500.

Program Costs $1200 for the program, $100 per course.

Housing and Student Services Housing is not available. Job counseling and placement services are not available.

Contact Ms. Betty Harris, Director, English Language Program, University of California, Santa Barbara Extension, Santa Barbara, CA 93106. 805-961-3450.

UNIVERSITY OF CALIFORNIA, SANTA CRUZ
Santa Cruz, California 95064

RADIO/TELEVISION, GENERAL (09.07)
Video Arts

General Information Unit offering the program: Arts and Humanities Department, University of California Extension, Santa Cruz. Program content: Equipment use, programming, production techniques. Available for credit. Certificate signed by the Dean, University Extension.

Program Format Evening, weekend classes offered. Program cycle: Continuous enrollment. Full program cycle lasts 24 courses. Completion of program requires 17½ units, grade of B or better.

Evaluation Student evaluation based on papers, video projects. Grading system: Letters or numbers. Transcripts are kept for each student.

Enrollment Requirements Program is open to non-resident foreign students.

Program Costs $2500 for the program.

Housing and Student Services Housing is not available. Job counseling and placement services are not available.

Special Features The program has been designed to accomplish five objectives. Students will have the opportunity to gain knowledge of the technical systems that make video production possible, the techniques involved, the human support systems needed, and peripheral and future technologies. Most important, experience in producing several video programs will be provided. Instructors are working video professionals.

Contact Ms. Jenny Newton, Program Assistant, University of California Extension, Carriage House, Santa Cruz, CA 95064. 408-429-2971.

NUCEA MEMBER
UNIVERSITY OF SOUTHERN CALIFORNIA
Los Angeles, California 90089

AIR TRANSPORTATION (49.01)
Aviation Safety Certificate

General Information Unit offering the program: Safety and Systems Management. Program content: Accident investigation, technology, human factors, safety program management, health, communications. Available on a non-credit basis. Certificate signed by the Director of Institute.

Program Format Daytime classes offered. Students may enroll several times per year.

Evaluation Student evaluation based on tests, case study methods. Transcripts are kept for each student.

Enrollment Requirements Basic knowledge of aviation required. Program is open to non-resident foreign students. English language proficiency required.

Housing and Student Services   Housing is available. Job counseling and placement services are not available.

Special Features   There exists today an increased emphasis on hazard prevention, and it is therefore imperative that the professional in air safety be prepared to deal with these challenges and changing conditions. Program was developed and implemented in 1980 to meet this need. Certification provides professionals with comprehensive knowledge in the field and documentation of their expanding expertise.

Contact   Ms. Loretta Gin, Program Assistant, Professional Programs, SSM 116, MC-0021, Los Angeles, CA 90089-0021. 213-743-6523.

BUSINESS AND MANAGEMENT, GENERAL (06.01)
Certificate in Management Effectiveness

General Information   Unit offering the program: School of Business. Program content: Business math, finance, accounting. Available on a non-credit basis. Certificate signed by the Dean, School of Business.

Program Format   Weekend classes offered. Instructional schedule: 12 Saturdays, 2 intensive weekends. Students enroll in October. Completion of program requires 80% homework completion.

Evaluation   Student evaluation based on group projec. Transcripts are kept for each student.

Enrollment Requirements   Three years experience, undergraduate algebra, interview required. Program is open to non-resident foreign students.

Program Costs $3800 for the program.

Housing and Student Services   Housing is not available. Job counseling and placement services are not available.

Special Features   Founded in 1981, the CME project is offered in two locations: the USC main campus in Los Angeles and USC Orange County Center in Irvine, California. Lectures, study groups, hands-on comparative spreadsheet analysis, video feedback, and required homework are featured.

Contact   Ms. Sally Wright, Program Director, Certificate in Management Effectiveness, DCC-102, Los Angeles, CA 90007-0871. 213-743-5294.

INTERNATIONAL BUSINESS MANAGEMENT (06.09)
International Executive Development Laboratory

General Information   Unit offering the program: School of Public Administration. Program content: Executive development for international executives from government and state-related organizations in the Third World. Available on a non-credit basis. Certificate signed by the Dean, School of Public Administration.

Program Format   Daytime classes offered. Program cycle: Continuous enrollment. Full program cycle lasts 5 weeks.

Evaluation   Student evaluation based on papers, project, class participation. Records are kept by School of Public Administration.

Enrollment Requirements   Undergraduate degree, eight years management experience, command of written and spoken English required. Program is open to non-resident foreign students. English language proficiency required.

Program Costs $4200 for the program.

Housing and Student Services   Housing is available. Job counseling and placement services are available.

Contact   Ms. Pauline Arneberg, Director, Center for International Training and Development, TYL-100, Los Angeles, CA 90089-0041. 213-743-8111.

INTERNATIONAL BUSINESS MANAGEMENT (06.09)
Management Effectiveness Program

General Information   Unit offering the program: School of Public Administration. Program content: Basic management competencies relevant to Third World administration. Available on a non-credit basis. Certificate signed by the Dean, School of Public Administration.

Program Format   Daytime classes offered. Program cycle: Continuous enrollment. Full program cycle lasts 3 weeks.

Evaluation   Student evaluation based on papers, reports, class participation. Records are kept by School of Public Administration.

Enrollment Requirements   Two years management experience required. Program is open to non-resident foreign students.

Program Costs $4000 for the program.

Housing and Student Services   Housing is available. Job counseling and placement services are available.

Contact   Ms. Pauline Arneberg, Director, Center for International Training and Development, School of Public Administration, TYL-100, Los Angeles, CA 90089-0041. 213-743-8111.

MISCELLANEOUS ALLIED HEALTH SERVICES (17.05)
Physician Assistant Program

General Information   Unit offering the program: School of Medicine, Department of Family Medicine. Program content: Training to provide primary-care medical services. Available for credit. Certificate signed by the Dean, School of Medicine. Program fulfills requirements for Physician Assistant.

Program Format   Daytime classes offered. Students may enroll once per year. Full program cycle lasts 2 years.

Evaluation   Student evaluation based on tests, papers, reports, clinical performance. Grading system: Letters or numbers. Transcripts are kept for each student.

Enrollment Requirements   Two years of college including: human anatomy/physiology and lab, microbiology, chemistry, psychology, sociology/cultural anthropology, patient care experience required. Program is open to non-resident foreign students. English language proficiency required.

Program Costs $6500 for the first year, $3500 for the second year.

Housing and Student Services   Housing is not available. Job counseling and placement services are available.

Contact   Mr. Jack Liskin, Program Director, Health Sciences Campus, KAM-B10, Los Angeles, CA 90033. 213-224-7101.

MUSIC (50.09)
Music Recording Certificate Program

General Information   Unit offering the program: School of Music. Program content: Courses in audio engineering. Available on a non-credit basis. Certificate signed by the Dean, School of Music.

Program Format   Evening classes offered. Instructional schedule: Classes meet weekly. Students enroll once per year. Full program cycle lasts 9 months. Completion of program

Music Recording Certificate Program continued

requires 34 units, qualifying examination.

Evaluation   Student evaluation based on tests. Grading system: Letters or numbers. Transcripts are kept for each student.

Enrollment Requirements   Bachelor's degree required, music experience desirable. Program is open to non-resident foreign students.

Housing and Student Services   Housing is not available. Job counseling and placement services are available.

Contact   School of Music, Los Angeles, CA 90089-2991. 213-743-2741.

QUALITY CONTROL AND SAFETY TECHNOLOGIES (15.07)
Occupational Safety and Health Management

General Information   Unit offering the program: Institute of Safety and Systems Management. Available on a non-credit basis. Certificate signed by the Director of Institute.

Program Format   Daytime classes offered. Instructional schedule: One to five days per course. Program cycle: Continuous enrollment. Full program cycle lasts 4 courses.

Evaluation   Student evaluation based on tests. Transcripts are kept for each student.

Enrollment Requirements   Prerequisite courses required. Program is open to non-resident foreign students.

Program Costs $160–$800 per course.

Housing and Student Services   Housing is available. Job counseling and placement services are not available.

Special Features   The Institute of Safety and Systems Management offers two certificate programs in Occupational Safety and Health. Students who complete designated series of courses will be awarded a certificate as a Specialist in the Practice of Occupational Safety and Health or in Occupational Safety and Health Management. Students must complete a minimum of four courses for each certificate.

Contact   Ms. Ramona Cayuela-Petak, Program Director, ISSM UG202, Los Angeles, CA 90089-0024. 213-743-6383.

QUALITY CONTROL AND SAFETY TECHNOLOGIES (15.07)
Specialist in the Practice of Occupational Safety and Health

General Information   Unit offering the program: Institute of Safety and Systems Management. Available on a non-credit basis. Certificate signed by the Director of Institute.

Program Format   Daytime classes offered. Instructional schedule: One to five days per course. Full program cycle lasts 4 courses.

Evaluation   Student evaluation based on tests. Transcripts are kept for each student.

Enrollment Requirements   Prerequisite courses required. Program is open to non-resident foreign students.

Program Costs $160–$800 per course.

Housing and Student Services   Housing is available. Job counseling and placement services are not available.

Special Features   The Institute of Safety and Systems Management offers two certificate programs in Occupational Safety and Health. Students who complete the designated series of courses will be awarded a certificate as a specialist in the practice of Occupational Safety and Health or in Occupational Safety and Health Management. Students must complete a minimum of four courses for each certificate.

Contact   Ms. Ramona Cayuela-Petek, Program Director, ISSM UG 202, Los Angeles, CA 90089-0021. 213-743-6383.

COLORADO

NUCEA MEMBER
COLORADO STATE UNIVERSITY
Fort Collins, Colorado 80523

COMMUNICATIONS, GENERAL (09.01)
Work-Related Writing Certificate Program

General Information   Unit offering the program: Division of Continuing Education. Program content: Grammar, sentence structures, punctuation, proofreading, editing, updated writing. Available on a non-credit basis. Certificate signed by the Assistant Academic Vice President.

Program Format   Daytime, evening, weekend classes offered. Program cycle: Continuous enrollment. Complete program cycle lasts one to two semesters. Completion of program requires four courses.

Evaluation   Student evaluation based on tests, class performance. Grading system: Pass/fail. Transcripts are kept for each student.

Enrollment Requirements   Program is open to non-resident foreign students.

Housing and Student Services   Housing is not available. Job counseling and placement services are not available.

Contact   Ms. Naomi DiBona, Associate Director, Division of Continuing Education, Fort Collins, CO 80523. 303-491-5288.

MICROCOMPUTER APPLICATIONS (11.06)
Microcomputer Applications Certificate Program

General Information   Unit offering the program: Division of Continuing Education. Program content: Electronic spreadsheet, introduction to BASIC, word processing, database management, personal computer communications. Available on a non-credit basis. Certificate signed by the Assistant Academic Vice President.

Program Format   Daytime, evening, weekend classes offered. Program cycle: Continuous enrollment. Complete program cycle lasts up to three years. Completion of program requires five courses.

Evaluation   Student evaluation based on tests, class performance. Grading system: Pass/fail. Transcripts are kept for each student.

Enrollment Requirements   Program is open to non-resident foreign students.

Housing and Student Services   Housing is not available. Job counseling and placement services are not available.

Contact   Ms. Naomi DiBona, Associate Director, Division of Continuing Education, Fort Collins, CO 80523. 303-491-5288.

OFFICE SUPERVISION AND MANAGEMENT (07.04)
Supervisor's Development Certificate Program

General Information   Unit offering the program: Division of Continuing Education. Program content: Personal supervisory style, transition into supervision, written and oral communications, organization, delegation, performance appraisal, problem solving. Available on a non-credit basis. Certificate signed by the Assistant Academic Vice President.

Program Format Daytime, evening, weekend classes offered. Program cycle: Continuous enrollment. Complete program cycle lasts up to three years. Completion of program requires six required courses, electives, 110 contact hours.

Evaluation Student evaluation based on tests, class performance. Grading system: Pass/fail. Transcripts are kept for each student.

Enrollment Requirements Program is open to non-resident foreign students.

Housing and Student Services Housing is not available. Job counseling and placement services are not available.

Contact Ms. Naomi DiBona, Associate Director, Division of Continuing Education, Fort Collins, CO 80523. 303-491-5288.

PERSONNEL MANAGEMENT (06.16)
Certified Employee Benefits Specialist Program

General Information Unit offering the program: Division of Continuing Education. Program content: Life, health, group benefit programs, pension plans, social security, savings plans, management principles, legal environment, accounting and information systems, asset management, personnel and labor relations. Available on a non-credit basis. Endorsed by International Foundation of Employee Benefit Plans. Certificate signed by the Assistant Academic Vice President.

Program Format Daytime, evening, weekend classes offered. Program cycle: Continuous enrollment. Complete program cycle lasts up to five years. Completion of program requires ten courses, written examination.

Evaluation Student evaluation based on tests, class performance. Grading system: Pass/fail. Transcripts are kept for each student.

Enrollment Requirements Program is open to non-resident foreign students.

Housing and Student Services Housing is not available. Job counseling and placement services are not available.

Contact Ms. Naomi DiBona, Associate Director, Division of Continuing Education, Fort Collins, CO 80523. 303-491-5288.

COLORADO TECHNICAL COLLEGE
Colorado Springs, Colorado 80907

ELECTRICAL AND ELECTRONIC TECHNOLOGIES (15.03)
Electronic Engineering Technology Certificate

General Information Unit offering the program: Electronics Engineering Technology Department. Program content: Electronics, mathematics, physics. Available for credit. Certificate signed by the President of College. Certificate applicable to A.S., B.S. in Electronic Engineering Technology.

Program Format Daytime, evening classes offered. Program cycle: Continuous enrollment. Full program cycle lasts 1 year. Completion of program requires 2.0 GPA.

Evaluation Student evaluation based on tests, papers, reports. Grading system: Letters or numbers. Transcripts are kept for each student.

Enrollment Requirements English and mathematics tests required. Program is open to non-resident foreign students. English language proficiency required. Minimum TOEFL score required: 500.

Program Costs $100 per quarter hour.

Housing and Student Services Housing is not available. Job counseling and placement services are available.

Contact Office of Admissions, 4435 North Chestnut, Colorado Springs, CO 80907-3896. 303-598-0200.

NUCEA MEMBER

UNIVERSITY OF COLORADO AT BOULDER
Boulder, Colorado 80309

CHILD CARE AND GUIDANCE MANAGEMENT AND SERVICES (20.02)
Certificate in Preschool Administration

General Information Unit offering the program: Division of Continuing Education. Program content: Nutrition, personnel organization, management. Available on a non-credit basis. Endorsed by Colorado Department of Social Services, Licensing Unit. Certificate signed by the Director, Division of Continuing Education. Program fulfills requirements for Day-Care Administrator.

Program Format Correspondence classes offered. Program cycle: Continuous enrollment. Full program cycle lasts 3 courses.

Evaluation Student evaluation based on tests, papers. Grading system: Pass/fail. Record of CEUs kept for each student.

Enrollment Requirements Open enrollment. Program is open to non-resident foreign students. English language proficiency required.

Program Costs $240 for the program, $80 per course.

Special Features Credit by examination available upon approval by program manager.

Contact Mr. John R. Dunn, Program Manager, Independent Study, Division of Continuing Education, Box 178, Boulder, CO 80309. 800-332-5839.

CHILD CARE AND GUIDANCE MANAGEMENT AND SERVICES (20.02)
Certificate in Preschool Teaching

General Information Unit offering the program: Division of Continuing Education. Program content: Early childhood development, guidance techniques, curriculum planning. Available on a non-credit basis. Endorsed by Colorado Department of Social Services, Licensing Unit. Certificate signed by the Director, Division of Continuing Education. Program fulfills requirements for Day-Care Teacher.

Program Format Correspondence classes offered. Program cycle: Continuous enrollment. Full program cycle lasts 5 courses.

Evaluation Student evaluation based on tests, papers. Grading system: Pass/fail. Record of CEUs kept for each student.

Enrollment Requirements Open admissions. Program is open to non-resident foreign students. English language proficiency required.

Program Costs $480 for the program, $120 per course.

Special Features Credit by examination is available with permission of program manager.

Contact Mr. John R. Dunn, Program Manager, Independent Study, Division of Continuing Education, Box 178, Boulder, CO 80309. 800-332-5839.

MICROCOMPUTER APPLICATIONS (11.06)
Certificate in Computer Applications

General Information Unit offering the program: Continuing Education. Program content: Business and personal computer use. Available on a non-credit basis. Certificate signed by the Director, Continuing Education.

Program Format Daytime, evening, weekend classes offered. Program cycle: Continuous enrollment. Full program cycle lasts 1 year.

Evaluation Student evaluation based on reports. Grading system: Pass/fail. Transcripts are kept for each student.

Enrollment Requirements Program is open to non-resident foreign students.

Certificate in Computer Applications continued

Housing and Student Services   Housing is available. Job counseling and placement services are available.

Special Features   Computer instruction as it applies to a wide variety of professions; most applications range from computer graphics and CAD to business office uses like word processing, accounting, and database study.

Contact   Mr. Peter Seward, Academic Coordinator, Continuing Education, Campus 178, Boulder, CO 80309. 303-492-6226.

REAL ESTATE (06.17)
Certificate of Achievement in Real Estate (Broker)

General Information   Unit offering the program: Division of Continuing Education. Program content: Principles, law, contracts, appraisal, finance. Available on a non-credit basis. Endorsed by Colorado Real Estate Commission. Certificate signed by the Director, Division of Continuing Education. Program fulfills requirements for Colorado Brokers License.

Program Format   Daytime, evening, correspondence classes offered. Program cycle: Continuous enrollment. Completion of program requires 48 classroom hours.

Evaluation   Student evaluation based on tests, papers. Grading system: Pass/fail. Record of CEUs kept for each student.

Enrollment Requirements   Program is open to non-resident foreign students. English language proficiency required.

Program Costs $280 for the program, $140 per course.

Housing and Student Services   Housing is not available. Job counseling and placement services are not available.

Special Features   Applicants for licensing are encouraged to contact the Colorado Real Estate Commission for licensing requirements.

Contact   Mr. John Dunn, Program Manager, Division of Continuing Education, Box 178, Boulder, CO 80309. 800-332-5839.

REAL ESTATE (06.17)
Certificate of Achievement in Real Estate (Sales)

General Information   Unit offering the program: Division of Continuing Education. Program content: Principles, law, contracts, appraisal, finance. Available on a non-credit basis. Endorsed by Colorado Real Estate Commission. Certificate signed by the Director, Division of Continuing Education. Program fulfills requirements for Colorado Sales License.

Program Format   Daytime, evening, correspondence classes offered. Program cycle: Continuous enrollment. Full program cycle lasts 3 courses. Completion of program requires 78 classroom hours.

Evaluation   Student evaluation based on tests, papers. Grading system: Pass/fail. Record of CEUs kept for each student.

Enrollment Requirements   Program is open to non-resident foreign students. English language proficiency required.

Program Costs $420 for the program, $140 per course.

Housing and Student Services   Housing is not available. Job counseling and placement services are not available.

Special Features   Applicants for licensing are encouraged to contact the Colorado Real Estate Commission for licensing requirements.

Contact   Mr. John Dunn, Program Manager, Division of Continuing Education, Box 178, Boulder, CO 80309. 800-332-5839.

COMMUNICATIONS, GENERAL (09.01)
Certificate in Corporate Communication

General Information   Unit offering the program: Applied Communication Division, University College. Program content: Communication skills for business professionals. Available for credit. Certificate signed by the Dean, University College. Certificate applicable to Master of Special Studies.

Program Format   Evening, weekend classes offered. Program cycle: Continuous enrollment. Completion of program requires 3.0 GPA, 27 credit hours.

Evaluation   Student evaluation based on tests, papers, reports, projects. Grading system: Letters or numbers. Transcripts are kept for each student.

Enrollment Requirements   Bachelor's degree, 3.0 GPA, or equivalent knowledge required. Program is open to non-resident foreign students. English language proficiency required. Minimum TOEFL score required: 550.

Program Costs $3915 for the program.

Housing and Student Services   Housing is not available. Job counseling and placement services are not available.

Special Features   Courses are experientially based and are taught by working professionals in their area of expertise who also have the requisite academic credentials.

Contact   Dr. Jacqueline Frischknecht, Division Director of Applied Communication, University College, Denver, CO 80208. 303-871-3217.

COMPUTER AND INFORMATION SCIENCES, GENERAL (11.01)
Certificate in Artificial Intelligence

General Information   Unit offering the program: Computer Information Division, University College. Available for credit. Certificate signed by the Dean, University College. Certificate applicable to Master of Computer Information Systems.

Program Format   Evening classes offered. Instructional schedule: One evening per week. Program cycle: Continuous enrollment. Completion of program requires five courses.

Evaluation   Student evaluation based on tests, papers, computer programs. Grading system: Letters or numbers. Transcripts are kept for each student.

Enrollment Requirements   Knowledge of programming language required. Program is open to non-resident foreign students. English language proficiency required. Minimum TOEFL score required: 550.

Program Costs $480 per course.

Housing and Student Services   Job counseling and placement services are not available.

Special Features   Courses are taught by working professionals from industry.

Contact   Mr. Don King, Director, Computer Information Systems Division, University College, Denver, CO 80208. 303-871-3241.

COMPUTER AND INFORMATION SCIENCES, GENERAL (11.01)
Certificate in Computer Information Systems

General Information   Unit offering the program: Computer Information Division, University College. Available for credit.

Certificate signed by the Dean, University College. Certificate applicable to Master of Computer Information Systems.

Program Format Evening classes offered. Instructional schedule: One evening per week. Program cycle: Continuous enrollment. Completion of program requires five courses.

Evaluation Student evaluation based on tests, papers, computer programs. Grading system: Letters or numbers. Transcripts are kept for each student.

Enrollment Requirements Basic computer programming knowledge required. Program is open to non-resident foreign students. English language proficiency required. Minimum TOEFL score required: 550.

Program Costs $480 per course.

Housing and Student Services Housing is not available. Job counseling and placement services are not available.

Special Features Courses are taught by working professionals from industry.

Contact Mr. Don King, Director, Computer Information Systems Division, University College, Denver, CO 80208. 303-871-3241.

COMPUTER AND INFORMATION SCIENCES, GENERAL (11.01)
Certificate in Data Processing Management

General Information Unit offering the program: Computer Informations Division, University College. Program content: Computer management techniques. Available for credit. Certificate signed by the Dean, University College. Certificate applicable to Master of Computer Information Systems.

Program Format Evening classes offered. Program cycle: Continuous enrollment. Completion of program requires five courses, 3.0 GPA.

Evaluation Student evaluation based on tests, papers, computer programs. Grading system: Letters or numbers. Transcripts are kept for each student.

Enrollment Requirements Basic knowledge of computers required. Program is open to non-resident foreign students. English language proficiency required. Minimum TOEFL score required: 550.

Program Costs $480 per course.

Housing and Student Services Housing is not available. Job counseling and placement services are not available.

Contact Mr. Don King, Director, Computer Information Systems Division, University College, Denver, CO 80208. 303-871-3241.

COMPUTER PROGRAMMING (11.02)
Certificate of Advanced Computer Programming

General Information Unit offering the program: Women in Computer Science Division, University College. Program content: VMS, COBOL, UNIX and C programming, basics of software design and database programming. Available for credit. Certificate signed by the Dean, University College.

Program Format Evening classes offered. Students enroll in September. Completion of program requires six courses.

Evaluation Student evaluation based on tests, reports, computer programs. Grading system: Letters or numbers. Transcripts are kept for each student.

Enrollment Requirements Bachelor's degree required. Program is open to non-resident foreign students. English language proficiency required. Minimum TOEFL score required: 550.

Program Costs $800 per course.

Housing and Student Services Housing is not available. Job counseling and placement services are not available.

Special Features Established by National Science Foundation in 1981. Course sequence provides a recognized opportunity for women to switch their careers to computers or to enhance their current careers with significant computer skills.

Contact Mr. Don King, Director, Computer Information Systems Division, University College, Denver, CO 80208. 303-871-3241.

PUBLIC RELATIONS (09.05)
Certificate in Public Relations

General Information Unit offering the program: Applied Communication Division, University College. Available for credit. Certificate signed by the Dean, University College. Certificate applicable to Master of Special Studies.

Program Format Evening, weekend classes offered. Program cycle: Continuous enrollment. Completion of program requires 3.0 GPA, 27 credit hours.

Evaluation Student evaluation based on tests, papers, reports, projects. Grading system: Letters or numbers. Transcripts are kept for each student.

Enrollment Requirements Program is open to non-resident foreign students. English language proficiency required. Minimum TOEFL score required: 550.

Program Costs $3915 for the program.

Housing and Student Services Housing is not available. Job counseling and placement services are not available.

Special Features Courses designed in cooperation with working public relations professionals and are taught by them.

Contact Dr. Jacqueline Frischknecht, Division Director of Applied Communication, University College, Denver, CO 80208. 303-871-3217.

NUCEA MEMBER
UNIVERSITY OF NORTHERN COLORADO
Greeley, Colorado 80639

INDIVIDUAL AND FAMILY DEVELOPMENT (19.07)
Graduate Certificate in Gerontology

General Information Unit offering the program: Department of Human Services, Gerontology Program. Program content: Issues facing older adults. Available for credit. Certificate signed by the Dean, College of Health and Human Services. Certificate applicable to M.A. in Gerontology.

Program Format Daytime, evening classes offered. Instructional schedule: Once per week for three hours. Program cycle: Continuous enrollment. Full program cycle lasts 2 semesters. Completion of program requires 3.0 GPA.

Evaluation Student evaluation based on tests, papers, presentations. Grading system: Letters or numbers. Transcripts are kept for each student.

Enrollment Requirements Bachelor's degree required. Program is open to non-resident foreign students.

Housing and Student Services Housing is available. Job counseling and placement services are available.

Special Features The certificate provides the student with a broad overview of the field of gerontology. It is designed for individuals with a master's degree in a different discipline or other professional designation (i.e., RN; BSW) or a bachelor's degree and several years of experience in the human services field.

Contact Ms. Karen A. Roberto, Ph.D., Assistant Professor and Coordinator of Gerontology Program, Department of Human Services, Greeley, CO 80631. 303-351-1585.

CONNECTICUT

ALBERTUS MAGNUS COLLEGE
New Haven, Connecticut 06511

BUSINESS AND MANAGEMENT, GENERAL (06.01)
Certificate in Business Administration

General Information   Unit offering the program: Business and Economics. Available for credit. Certificate signed by the Dean of Continuing Education. Certificate applicable to B.A. in Business and Economics.

Program Format   Daytime, evening classes offered. Instructional schedule: Two evenings per week. Program cycle: Continuous enrollment. Complete program cycle lasts one to two years. Completion of program requires eight courses.

Evaluation   Student evaluation based on tests, papers, reports. Transcripts are kept for each student.

Enrollment Requirements   Program is not open to non-resident foreign students. English language proficiency required.

Program Costs $3500 for the program, $420 per course.

Housing and Student Services   Housing is not available. Job counseling and placement services are available.

Contact   Ms. Elaine S. Lewis, Dean of Continuing Education, 700 Prospect Street, New Haven, CT 06517. 203-773-8505.

PAIER COLLEGE OF ART, INC.
Hamden, Connecticut 06511

DESIGN (50.04)
Certificate in Technical Illustration

General Information   Unit offering the program: Illustration. Program content: Detailed art work of manufactured articles. Available for credit. Certificate signed by the President. Certificate applicable to B.F.A.

Program Format   Daytime, evening classes offered. Students may enroll August, January. Full program cycle lasts 6 semesters. Completion of program requires 22 semester hours.

Evaluation   Student evaluation based on tests, drawings. Grading system: Letters or numbers. Transcripts are kept for each student.

Enrollment Requirements   High school diploma, portfolio, interview, two recommendations required. Program is open to non-resident foreign students. English language proficiency required.

Program Costs $4884 for the program.

Housing and Student Services   Housing is not available. Job counseling and placement services are available.

Special Features   All faculty are art professionals. Preparation for immediate employment with instructional standards geared to market requirements. Transfer credit for comparable courses in other accredited colleges. All credits are applicable to more extensive diploma or degree programs in illustration.

Contact   Mr. Sante Graziani, Academic Dean, 6 Prospect Court, Hamden, CT 06511. 203-777-7319.

FINE ARTS (50.07)
Certificate in Portrait/Figure Painting

General Information   Unit offering the program: Fine Arts. Program content: Head/figure painting in oils. Available for credit. Certificate signed by the President. Certificate applicable to B.F.A.

Program Format   Daytime, evening classes offered. Students may enroll August, January. Full program cycle lasts 4 semesters. Completion of program requires 28 semester hours.

Evaluation   Student evaluation based on tests, drawings, paintings. Grading system: Letters or numbers. Transcripts are kept for each student.

Enrollment Requirements   High school diploma, portfolio reflecting freshman drawing/painting skills, interview required. Program is open to non-resident foreign students. English language proficiency required.

Program Costs $6216 for the program.

Housing and Student Services   Housing is not available. Job counseling and placement services are available.

Special Features   All faculty are art professionals. Preparation for immediate employment with instructional standards geared to market requirements. Transfer credit for comparable courses in other accredited colleges. All credits applicable to more extensive diploma or degree programs in fine arts.

Contact   Mr. Sante Graziani, Academic Dean, 6 Prospect Court, Hamden, CT 06511. 203-777-7319.

FINE ARTS (50.07)
Certificate in Sharp Focus/Trompe L'Oeil Painting

General Information   Unit offering the program: Fine Arts. Available for credit. Certificate signed by the President. Certificate applicable to B.F.A.

Program Format   Daytime, evening classes offered. Students may enroll August, January. Full program cycle lasts 4 semesters. Completion of program requires 30 semester hours.

Evaluation   Student evaluation based on tests, drawings, paintings. Grading system: Letters or numbers. Transcripts are kept for each student.

Enrollment Requirements   High school diploma, portfolio, interview, two recommendations required. Program is open to non-resident foreign students. English language proficiency required.

Program Costs $6660 for the program.

Housing and Student Services   Housing is not available. Job counseling and placement services are available.

Special Features   All faculty are art professionals. Preparation for immediate employment with instructional standards geared to market requirements. Transfer credit for comparable courses in other accredited colleges. All credits are applicable to more extensive diploma or degree programs in fine arts.

Contact   Mr. Sante Graziani, Academic Dean, 6 Prospect Court, Hamden, CT 06511. 203-777-7319.

GRAPHIC AND PRINTING COMMUNICATIONS (48.02)
Certificate in Graphic Production

General Information   Unit offering the program: Graphic Design. Program content: Art work for printing. Available for credit. Certificate signed by the President. Certificate applicable to B.F.A.

Program Format   Daytime, evening classes offered. Students may enroll August, January. Full program cycle lasts 4 semesters. Completion of program requires 27 semester hours.

Evaluation   Student evaluation based on tests, laboratory work, completed examples. Grading system: Letters or numbers. Transcripts are kept for each student.

Enrollment Requirements   High school diploma, portfolio, interview, two recommendations required. Program is open to non-resident foreign students. English language proficiency required.

Program Costs $5994 for the program.

Housing and Student Services   Housing is not available. Job counseling and placement services are available.

Special Features All faculty are art professionals. Preparation is for immediate employment with instructional standards geared to market requirements. Transfer credit for comparable credit courses in other accredited colleges. All credits applicable to more extensive diploma or degree programs in graphic design.

Contact Mr. Sante Graziani, Academic Dean, 6 Prospect Court, Hamden, CT 06511. 203-777-7319.

INTERIOR DESIGN (04.05)
Certificate in Interior Design for Retailing

General Information Unit offering the program: Interior Design. Program content: Consultation/selling interiors materials. Available for credit. Certificate signed by the President. Certificate applicable to B.F.A.

Program Format Daytime, evening classes offered. Students may enroll August, January. Full program cycle lasts 4 semesters. Completion of program requires 28 semester hours.

Evaluation Student evaluation based on tests, drawings, design projects. Grading system: Letters or numbers. Transcripts are kept for each student.

Enrollment Requirements High school diploma, portfolio, interview, two recommendations required. Program is open to non-resident foreign students. English language proficiency required.

Program Costs $6216 for the program.

Housing and Student Services Housing is not available. Job counseling and placement services are available.

Special Features All faculty are art professionals. Preparation for immediate employment with instructional standards geared to market requirements. Transfer credit for comparable courses in other accredited colleges. All credits applicable to more extensive diploma or degree programs in interior design.

Contact Mr. Sante Graziani, Academic Dean, 6 Prospect Court, Hamden, CT 06511. 203-777-7319.

SACRED HEART UNIVERSITY
Bridgeport, Connecticut 06606

BUSINESS AND MANAGEMENT, GENERAL (06.01)
Administrative Assistant Certificate Program

General Information Unit offering the program: Management, Economics, and Office Administration Departments. Program content: Business, communication, economics, office management. Available for credit. Certificate signed by the Dean, College of Business and Professional Studies. Certificate applicable to A.S. in Office Administration, B.S. in Business Administration.

Program Format Daytime, evening classes offered. Instructional schedule: One evening per week. Program cycle: Continuous enrollment. Full program cycle lasts 2 semesters.

Evaluation Student evaluation based on tests, papers. Grading system: Letters or numbers. Transcripts are kept for each student.

Enrollment Requirements High school diploma required. Program is not open to non-resident foreign students.

Program Costs $1980 for the program, $495 per course.

Housing and Student Services Housing is not available. Job counseling and placement services are available.

Special Features Some credit for prior experience is available.

Contact Mr. Ed Donato, Associate Dean of Continuing Education, P.O. Box 6460, Bridgeport, CT 06606. 203-371-7830.

COMPUTER AND INFORMATION SCIENCES, GENERAL (11.01)
Computer Science Certificate Program

General Information Unit offering the program: Computer Science Department. Program content: Computer science from the scientific or data processing area. Available for credit. Certificate signed by the Dean, College of Arts and Sciences. Certificate applicable to B.S. in Computer Science.

Program Format Daytime, evening classes offered. Instructional schedule: One evening per week. Program cycle: Continuous enrollment. Full program cycle lasts 2 years.

Evaluation Student evaluation based on tests, papers. Grading system: Letters or numbers. Transcripts are kept for each student.

Enrollment Requirements High school diploma required. Program is not open to non-resident foreign students.

Program Costs $3300 for the program, $165 per credit hour.

Housing and Student Services Housing is not available. Job counseling and placement services are available.

Special Features Some credit for prior experience is available.

Contact Mr. Ed Donato, Associate Dean of Continuing Education, P.O. Box 6460, Bridgeport, CT 06606. 203-371-7830.

TRANSPORTATION AND TRAVEL MARKETING (08.11)
Travel Agent Certificate Program

General Information Unit offering the program: Continuing Education Department. Program content: SABRE ticketing, world travel. Available on a non-credit basis. Certificate signed by the Dean of Continuing Education.

Program Format Evening classes offered. Instructional schedule: One or two evenings per week. Program cycle: Continuous enrollment. Full program cycle lasts 1 semester.

Evaluation Student evaluation based on tests. Grading system: Pass/fail. Record of completion kept for each student.

Enrollment Requirements Limited to students 18 years of age or older. Program is not open to non-resident foreign students.

Program Costs $690 for the program.

Housing and Student Services Housing is not available. Job counseling and placement services are available.

Contact Mr. Ed Donato, Associate Dean of Continuing Education, P.O. Box 6460, Bridgeport, CT 06606. 203-371-7830.

WORD PROCESSING (07.08)
Word Processing Certificate Program

General Information Unit offering the program: Office Administration Department. Program content: Business, English, word processing. Available for credit. Certificate signed by the Dean, College of Business and Professional studies. Certificate applicable to A.S. in Office Administration.

Program Format Daytime, evening classes offered. Instructional schedule: One evening per week. Program cycle: Continuous enrollment. Full program cycle lasts 2 semesters.

Evaluation Student evaluation based on tests, papers. Grading system: Letters or numbers. Transcripts are kept for each student.

Enrollment Requirements High school diploma required. Program is not open to non-resident foreign students.

Program Costs $1980 for the program, $495 per course.

Housing and Student Services Housing is not available. Job counseling and placement services are available.

Special Features Some credit for prior experience is available.

Contact Mr. Ed Donato, Associate Dean of Continuing Education, P.O. Box 6460, Bridgeport, CT 06606. 203-371-7830.

UNIVERSITY OF CONNECTICUT
Storrs, Connecticut 06268

PERSONNEL AND TRAINING PROGRAMS (07.05)
Systematic Design and Management of Training

General Information   Unit offering the program: Institute of Public Service International, Extended and Continuing Education. Program content: Design of training programs. Available on a non-credit basis. Certificate signed by the President.

Program Format   Daytime classes offered. Instructional schedule: Monday through Friday. Program cycle: Continuous enrollment. Full program cycle lasts 10 weeks. Completion of program requires improvement project.

Evaluation   Student evaluation based on papers, reports, individual and group exercises. Grading system: Letters or numbers. Transcripts are kept for each student.

Enrollment Requirements   Bachelor's degree preferred, experience in public service required. Program is open to non-resident foreign students. English language proficiency required. Minimum TOEFL score required: 500.

Program Costs $4900 for the program.

Housing and Student Services   Housing is available. Job counseling and placement services are not available.

Special Features   Program is for practicing public managers from developing counties. It is a tailored program for public managers.

Contact   Ms. Josephine Mavromatis, Associate Professor, 1800 Asylum Avenue, Fourth Floor, West Hartford, CT 06117. 203-241-4924.

PUBLIC ADMINISTRATION (44.04)
Fundamentals of Management

General Information   Unit offering the program: Institute of Public Service International. Program content: Managerial responsibilities and learning needs. Available on a non-credit basis. Certificate signed by the President.

Program Format   Daytime classes offered. Instructional schedule: Monday through Friday. Program cycle: Continuous enrollment. Full program cycle lasts 6 weeks.

Evaluation   Student evaluation based on papers, reports, individual and group exercises. Grading system: Letters or numbers. Transcripts are kept for each student.

Enrollment Requirements   Bachelor's degree preferred, experience in public sector required. Program is open to non-resident foreign students. English language proficiency required. Minimum TOEFL score required: 500.

Program Costs $4400 for the program.

Housing and Student Services   Housing is available. Job counseling and placement services are not available.

Special Features   Program designed to upgrade management skills of participants. Requires that participants come from a public-sector institution.

Contact   Ms. Josephine Mavromatis, Associate Professor, 1800 Asylum Avenue, Fourth Floor, West Hartford, CT 06117. 203-241-4924.

PUBLIC ADMINISTRATION (44.04)
Public Management Development Program

General Information   Unit offering the program: Institute of Public Service International. Program content: Concepts and skills for public managers. Available on a non-credit basis. Certificate signed by the President. Certificate applicable to M.P.A.

Program Format   Daytime classes offered. Instructional schedule: Monday through Friday. Students enroll in September. Full program cycle lasts 28 weeks. Completion of program requires average grade of B or better, project.

Evaluation   Student evaluation based on papers, reports. Grading system: Letters or numbers. Transcripts are kept for each student.

Enrollment Requirements   Limited to public managers. Program is open to non-resident foreign students. English language proficiency required. Minimum TOEFL score required: 500.

Program Costs $7500 for the program.

Housing and Student Services   Housing is available. Job counseling and placement services are not available.

Special Features   Two-part program (management core and specialization) offers opportunity to public managers to upgrade their skills in public management and then in one of three areas of interest: human resource management, financial management, or project analysis and implementation.

Contact   Ms. Josephine Mavromatis, Associate Professor, 1800 Asylum Avenue, Fourth Floor, West Hartford, CT 06117. 203-241-4924.

UNIVERSITY OF NEW HAVEN
West Haven, Connecticut 06516

APPLIED MATHEMATICS (27.03)
Quantitative Analysis

General Information   Unit offering the program: Department of Management. Program content: Statistics, quantitative methods. Available on either a credit or non-credit basis. Certificate signed by the Dean, School of Professional Studies and Continuing Education. Certificate applicable to B.S. in Business Administratio, Management Science.

Program Format   Daytime, evening classes offered. Program cycle: Continuous enrollment. Full program cycle lasts 1 year. Completion of program requires 2.0 GPA, five courses.

Evaluation   Student evaluation based on tests, papers. Grading system: Letters or numbers. Transcripts are kept for each student.

Enrollment Requirements   High school diploma or GED required. Program is open to non-resident foreign students. English language proficiency required. Minimum TOEFL score required: 500. Students required to live on campus.

Program Costs $2145 for the program, $429 per course.

Housing and Student Services   Housing is available. Job counseling and placement services are available.

Special Features   UNH does not grant credit for life or prior experience. The courses are part of regular University offerings and taught by regular full-time faculty.

Contact   Dr. Wilfred Harricharan, Chairman, Department of Management, 300 Orange Avenue, West Haven, CT 06516. 203-932-7126.

BUSINESS ECONOMICS (06.05)
Economics

General Information   Unit offering the program: Department of Economics. Program content: Economics, economic analysis and banking. Available on either a credit or non-credit basis. Certificate signed by the Dean, School of Professional Studies and Continuing Education. Certificate applicable to B.S. in Business Economics.

Program Format   Daytime, evening classes offered. Program cycle: Continuous enrollment. Full program cycle lasts 1 year. Completion of program requires 2.0 GPA, five courses.

Evaluation Student evaluation based on tests, papers. Grading system: Letters or numbers. Transcripts are kept for each student.

Enrollment Requirements High school diploma or GED required. Program is open to non-resident foreign students. English language proficiency required. Minimum TOEFL score required: 500.

Program Costs $2145 for the program, $429 per course.

Housing and Student Services Housing is available. Job counseling and placement services are available.

Special Features UNH does not award life experience credits. Transfer credits from other institutions are accepted if the grade of "C" or better was earned. The courses are regular offerings, taught by regular full-time faculty.

Contact Mr. John Teluk, Chairman, Department of Economics, 300 Orange Avenue, West Haven, CT 06516. 203-932-7347.

CRIMINAL JUSTICE (43.01)
Law Enforcement Science

General Information Unit offering the program: Forensic Science. Program content: Fingerprints, forensic science laboratory, criminal investigation, crime scene technology. Available for credit. Certificate signed by the Dean, School of Professional Studies and Continuing Education. Certificate applicable to B.S. in Law Enforcement Science, Forensic Science.

Program Format Daytime, evening classes offered. Program cycle: Continuous enrollment. Full program cycle lasts 4 semesters. Completion of program requires 2.0 GPA, six courses.

Evaluation Student evaluation based on tests, papers. Grading system: Letters or numbers. Transcripts are kept for each student.

Enrollment Requirements High school diploma or GED required. Program is open to non-resident foreign students. English language proficiency required. Minimum TOEFL score required: 500.

Program Costs $2574 for the program, $429 per course.

Housing and Student Services Housing is available. Job counseling and placement services are available.

Special Features UNH does not award life experience credit. Courses are part of regular University offerings and taught by regular full-time faculty. Program provides minimal training for police technicians.

Contact Dr. R. E. Gaensslen, Director, Forensic Science, 300 Orange Avenue, West Haven, CT 06516. 203-932-7116.

CRIMINAL JUSTICE (43.01)
Security Management

General Information Unit offering the program: Public Management. Program content: Industrial security, legal issues, arson investigation. Available for credit. Certificate signed by the Dean, School of Professional Studies and Continuing Education. Certificate applicable to B.S. in Security Management.

Program Format Daytime, evening classes offered. Program cycle: Continuous enrollment. Full program cycle lasts 3 semesters. Completion of program requires 2.0 GPA, six courses.

Evaluation Student evaluation based on tests, papers. Grading system: Letters or numbers. Transcripts are kept for each student.

Enrollment Requirements High school diploma or GED required. Program is open to non-resident foreign students. English language proficiency required. Minimum TOEFL score required: 500.

Program Costs $2574 for the program, $429 per course.

Housing and Student Services Housing is not available. Job counseling and placement services are available.

Special Features UNH does not grant credit for life or prior experience. The courses are part of regular University offerings and taught by regular full-time faculty.

Contact Mr. David A. Maxwell, Chairman, Department of Public Management, 300 Orange Avenue, West Haven, CT 06516. 203-932-7369.

FIRE PROTECTION (43.02)
Arson Investigation

General Information Unit offering the program: Professional Studies. Program content: Fire investigation, criminal justice. Available for credit. Certificate signed by the Dean of Professional Studies. Certificate applicable to B.S. in Arson Investigation, Fire Science Technology, Fire Science Administration.

Program Format Daytime, evening classes offered. Program cycle: Continuous enrollment. Full program cycle lasts 1 year. Completion of program requires 2.0 GPA, 30 credit hours.

Evaluation Student evaluation based on tests, papers. Grading system: Letters or numbers. Transcripts are kept for each student.

Enrollment Requirements High school diploma or GED required. Program is open to non-resident foreign students. English language proficiency required.

Program Costs $429 per course.

Housing and Student Services Housing is available. Job counseling and placement services are available.

Contact Dr. Frederick Mercilliott, Director, Fire Science, 300 Orange Avenue, West Haven, CT 06516. 203-932-7239.

FIRE PROTECTION (43.02)
Fire Prevention

General Information Unit offering the program: Professional Studies. Program content: Fire science. Available for credit. Certificate signed by the Dean of Professional Studies. Certificate applicable to B.S. in Arson Investigation, Fire Science Technology, Fire Science Administration.

Program Format Daytime, evening classes offered. Program cycle: Continuous enrollment. Full program cycle lasts 1 year. Completion of program requires 2.0 GPA, 21 credit hours.

Evaluation Student evaluation based on tests, papers. Grading system: Letters or numbers. Transcripts are kept for each student.

Enrollment Requirements High school diploma or GED required. Program is open to non-resident foreign students. English language proficiency required.

Program Costs $429 per course.

Housing and Student Services Housing is available. Job counseling and placement services are available.

Contact Dr. Frederick Mercilliott, Director, Fire Science, 300 Orange Avenue, West Haven, CT 06516. 203-932-7239.

FIRE PROTECTION (43.02)
Hazardous Materials

General Information Unit offering the program: Professional Studies. Program content: Fire science, chemistry. Available for credit. Certificate signed by the Dean of Professional Studies. Certificate applicable to B.S. in Arson Investigation, Fire Science Technology, Fire Science Administration.

Program Format Daytime, evening classes offered. Program cycle: Continuous enrollment. Full program cycle lasts 1 year. Completion of program requires 2.0 GPA, 21 credit hours.

Evaluation Student evaluation based on tests, papers. Grading system: Letters or numbers. Transcripts are kept for each student.

Enrollment Requirements High school diploma or GED required. Program is open to non-resident foreign students. English language proficiency required.

Program Costs $429 per course.

Housing and Student Services Housing is available. Job counseling and placement services are available.

Hazardous Materials continued

Contact Dr. Frederick Mercilliott, Director, Fire Science, 300 Orange Avenue, West Haven, CT 06516. 203-932-7239.

FIRE PROTECTION (43.02)
Health Care and Hospital Fire Safety and Security

General Information Unit offering the program: Professional Studies. Program content: Fire science. Available for credit. Certificate signed by the Dean of Professional Studies. Certificate applicable to B.S. in Arson Investigation, Fire Science Technology, Fire Science Administration.

Program Format Daytime, evening classes offered. Program cycle: Continuous enrollment. Full program cycle lasts 1 year. Completion of program requires 2.0 GPA, 15 credit hours.

Evaluation Student evaluation based on tests, papers. Grading system: Letters or numbers. Transcripts are kept for each student.

Enrollment Requirements High school diploma or GED required. Program is open to non-resident foreign students. English language proficiency required.

Program Costs $429 per course.

Housing and Student Services Housing is available. Job counseling and placement services are available.

Contact Dr. Frederick Mercilliott, Director, Fire Science, 300 Orange Avenue, West Haven, CT 06516. 203-932-7239.

FIRE PROTECTION (43.02)
Industrial Fire Protection

General Information Unit offering the program: Professional Studies. Program content: Fire science, safety. Available for credit. Certificate signed by the Dean of Professional Studies. Certificate applicable to B.S. in Arson Investigation, Fire Science Technology, Fire Science Administration.

Program Format Daytime, evening classes offered. Program cycle: Continuous enrollment. Full program cycle lasts 1 year. Completion of program requires 2.0 GPA, 24 credit hours.

Evaluation Student evaluation based on tests, papers. Grading system: Letters or numbers. Transcripts are kept for each student.

Enrollment Requirements High school diploma or GED required. Program is open to non-resident foreign students. English language proficiency required.

Program Costs $429 per course.

Housing and Student Services Housing is available. Job counseling and placement services are available.

Contact Dr. Frederick Mercilliott, Director, Fire Science, 300 Orange Avenue, West Haven, CT 06516. 203-932-7239.

FOOD PRODUCTION, MANAGEMENT, AND SERVICES (20.04)
Culinary Arts

General Information Unit offering the program: Hotel and Restaurant Management. Program content: Volume food purchasing, production, service, garde-manager, pastry and dessert preparation. Available for credit. Certificate signed by the Dean. Certificate applicable to B.S. in Hotel and Restaurant Management.

Program Format Daytime, evening classes offered. Instructional schedule: Three hours per week. Program cycle: Continuous enrollment. Full program cycle lasts 2 semesters. Completion of program requires 2.0 GPA, six courses.

Evaluation Student evaluation based on tests, papers, reports. Grading system: Letters or numbers. Transcripts are kept for each student.

Enrollment Requirements High school diploma or GED required. Program is open to non-resident foreign students.

English language proficiency required. Minimum TOEFL score required: 550. Students required to live on campus.

Program Costs $429 per course.

Housing and Student Services Housing is available. Job counseling and placement services are available.

Contact Mr. Linsley T. DeVeau, Chairman, Hotel and Restaurant Management, 300 Orange Avenue, West Haven, CT 06516. 203-932-7356.

FOOD PRODUCTION, MANAGEMENT, AND SERVICES (20.04)
Food Service Education

General Information Unit offering the program: Hotel and Restaurant Management. Program content: Food production, service and purchasing, food and labor costs. Available for credit. Certificate signed by the Dean. Certificate applicable to B.S. in Hotel and Restaurant Management.

Program Format Daytime, evening classes offered. Instructional schedule: Three hours per week. Program cycle: Continuous enrollment. Full program cycle lasts 2 semesters. Completion of program requires 2.0 GPA, six courses.

Evaluation Student evaluation based on tests, papers, reports. Grading system: Letters or numbers. Transcripts are kept for each student.

Enrollment Requirements High school diploma or GED required. Program is open to non-resident foreign students. English language proficiency required. Minimum TOEFL score required: 550. Students required to live on campus.

Program Costs $429 per course.

Housing and Student Services Housing is available. Job counseling and placement services are available.

Contact Mr. Linsley T. DeVeau, Chairman, Hotel and Restaurant Management, 300 Orange Avenue, West Haven, CT 06516. 203-932-7356.

FOOD PRODUCTION, MANAGEMENT, AND SERVICES (20.04)
Hotel and Restaurant Management

General Information Unit offering the program: Hotel and Restaurant Management. Program content: Accounting, auditing, food and labor cost controls, personnel management, systems, operations, equipment, layout design. Available for credit. Certificate signed by the Dean. Certificate applicable to B.S. in Hotel and Restaurant Management.

Program Format Daytime, evening classes offered. Instructional schedule: Three hours per week. Program cycle: Continuous enrollment. Full program cycle lasts 2 semesters. Completion of program requires 2.0 GPA, six courses.

Evaluation Student evaluation based on tests, papers, reports. Grading system: Letters or numbers. Transcripts are kept for each student.

Enrollment Requirements High school dipolma or GED required. Program is open to non-resident foreign students. English language proficiency required. Minimum TOEFL score required: 550. Students required to live on campus.

Program Costs $429 per course.

Housing and Student Services Housing is available. Job counseling and placement services are available.

Contact Mr. Linsley T. DeVeau, Chairman, Hotel and Restaurant Management, 300 Orange Avenue, West Haven, CT 06516. 203-932-7356.

FOOD PRODUCTION, MANAGEMENT, AND SERVICES (20.04)
Restaurant Management

General Information Unit offering the program: Hotel and Restaurant Management. Program content: Food and labor cost controls, personnel management, systems, operations, equipment, layout design. Available for credit. Certificate signed by the Dean. Certificate applicable to B.S. in Hotel and Restaurant Management.

Program Format   Daytime, evening classes offered. Instructional schedule: Three hours per week. Program cycle: Continuous enrollment. Full program cycle lasts 2 semesters. Completion of program requires 2.0 GPA, six courses.

Evaluation   Student evaluation based on tests, papers, reports. Grading system: Letters or numbers. Transcripts are kept for each student.

Enrollment Requirements   High school diploma or GED required. Program is open to non-resident foreign students. English language proficiency required. Minimum TOEFL score required: 550. Students required to live on campus.

Program Costs $429 per course.

Housing and Student Services   Housing is available. Job counseling and placement services are available.

Contact   Mr. Linsley T. DeVeau, Chairman, Hotel and Restaurant Management, 300 Orange Avenue, West Haven, CT 06516. 203-932-7356.

INSTITUTIONAL MANAGEMENT (06.07)
Bar Management

General Information   Unit offering the program: Hotel and Restaurant Management. Program content: Wine appreciation, marketing, sales promotion, food and labor cost controls, systems, operations, equipment, layout design. Available for credit. Certificate signed by the Dean. Certificate applicable to B.S. in Hotel and Restaurant Management.

Program Format   Daytime, evening classes offered. Instructional schedule: Three hours per week. Program cycle: Continuous enrollment. Full program cycle lasts 2 semesters. Completion of program requires 2.0 GPA, six courses.

Evaluation   Student evaluation based on tests, papers, reports. Grading system: Letters or numbers. Transcripts are kept for each student.

Enrollment Requirements   High school diploma or GED required. Program is open to non-resident foreign students. English language proficiency required. Minimum TOEFL score required: 550. Students required to live on campus.

Program Costs $429 per course.

Housing and Student Services   Housing is available. Job counseling and placement services are available.

Contact   Mr. Linsley T. DeVeau, Chairman, Hotel and Restaurant Management, 300 Orange Avenue, West Haven, CT 06516. 203-932-7356.

INSTITUTIONAL MANAGEMENT (06.07)
Casino Management

General Information   Unit offering the program: Hotel and Restaurant Management. Program content: Laws, security, computer systems, marketing, sales promotion, personnel. Available for credit. Certificate signed by the Dean. Certificate applicable to B.S. in Hotel and Restaurant Management.

Program Format   Daytime, evening classes offered. Instructional schedule: Three hours per week. Program cycle: Continuous enrollment. Full program cycle lasts 2 semesters. Completion of program requires 2.0 GPA, six courses.

Evaluation   Student evaluation based on tests, papers, reports. Grading system: Letters or numbers. Transcripts are kept for each student.

Enrollment Requirements   High school diploma or GED required. Program is open to non-resident foreign students. English language proficiency required. Minimum TOEFL score required: 550. Students required to live on campus.

Program Costs $429 per course.

Housing and Student Services   Housing is available. Job counseling and placement services are available.

Contact   Mr. Linsley T. DeVeau, Chairman, Hotel and Restaurant Management, 300 Orange Avenue, West Haven, CT 06516. 203-932-7356.

INSTITUTIONAL MANAGEMENT (06.07)
Club Management

General Information   Unit offering the program: Hotel and Restaurant Management. Program content: Operations, property and banquet management, private club administration, committee policies and procedures. Available for credit. Certificate signed by the Dean. Certificate applicable to B.S. in Hotel and Restaurant Management.

Program Format   Daytime, evening classes offered. Instructional schedule: Three hours per week. Program cycle: Continuous enrollment. Full program cycle lasts 2 semesters. Completion of program requires 2.0 GPA, six courses.

Evaluation   Student evaluation based on tests, papers, reports. Grading system: Letters or numbers. Transcripts are kept for each student.

Enrollment Requirements   High school diploma or GED required. Program is open to non-resident foreign students. English language proficiency required. Minimum TOEFL score required: 550. Students required to live on campus.

Program Costs $429 per course.

Housing and Student Services   Housing is available. Job counseling and placement services are available.

Contact   Mr. Linsley T. DeVeau, Chairman, Hotel and Restaurant Management, 300 Orange Avenue, West Haven, CT 06516. 203-932-7356.

INSTITUTIONAL MANAGEMENT (06.07)
Hotel Management

General Information   Unit offering the program: Hotel and Restaurant Management. Program content: Front office systems, laws, accounting, auditing, marketing, promotions, personnel, systems, operations. Available for credit. Certificate signed by the Dean. Certificate applicable to B.S. in Hotel and Restaurant Management.

Program Format   Daytime, evening classes offered. Instructional schedule: Three hours per week. Program cycle: Continuous enrollment. Full program cycle lasts 2 semesters. Completion of program requires 2.0 GPA, six courses.

Evaluation   Student evaluation based on tests, papers, reports. Grading system: Letters or numbers. Transcripts are kept for each student.

Enrollment Requirements   High school diploma or GED required. Program is open to non-resident foreign students. English language proficiency required. Minimum TOEFL score required: 550. Students required to live on campus.

Program Costs $429 per course.

Housing and Student Services   Housing is available. Job counseling and placement services are available.

Contact   Mr. Linsley T. DeVeau, Chairman, Hotel and Restaurant Management, 300 Orange Avenue, West Haven, CT 06516. 203-932-7356.

LAW (22.01)
Paralegal Studies Certificate

General Information   Unit offering the program: Department of Political Science. Program content: Legal research, procedure, bibliography, resources. Available for credit. Certificate signed by the Dean of Arts and Sciences. Certificate applicable to B.A. in Political Science.

Program Format   Evening classes offered. Instructional schedule: One evening per week. Program cycle: Continuous enrollment. Complete program cycle lasts three to four semesters. Completion of program requires grade of C or better, six courses.

Paralegal Studies Certificate continued

Evaluation   Student evaluation based on tests, papers, reports, research, library skills. Grading system: Letters or numbers. Transcripts are kept for each student.

Enrollment Requirements   High school diploma required. Program is open to non-resident foreign students.

Program Costs $2574 for the program, $429 per course.

Housing and Student Services   Housing is available. Job counseling and placement services are available.

Special Features   In general, instructors are experienced lawyers, many with extensive teaching experience. The program has provided training for scores of already-employed paralegals (often financially supported by their law firms) and has served as a starting point for many who pursue professional legal degrees. Some courses are required in the department's pre-law concentration for four-year majors.

Contact   Dr. James Dull, Chairman, Department of Political Science, 300 Orange Avenue, West Haven, CT 06516. 203-932-7247.

QUALITY CONTROL AND SAFETY TECHNOLOGIES (15.07)
Industrial Hygiene

General Information   Unit offering the program: Occupational Safety and Health. Program content: Radiation safety, OSHA legal standards. Available for credit. Certificate signed by the Dean. Certificate applicable to B.S. in Occupational Safety and Health.

Program Format   Daytime, evening classes offered. Program cycle: Continuous enrollment. Full program cycle lasts 18 credit hours. Completion of program requires 2.0 GPA.

Evaluation   Student evaluation based on tests, papers, reports. Grading system: Letters or numbers. Transcripts are kept for each student.

Enrollment Requirements   High school diploma or GED required. Program is open to non-resident foreign students. English language proficiency required. Minimum TOEFL score required: 550.

Program Costs $600 per course.

Housing and Student Services   Housing is not available. Job counseling and placement services are available.

Contact   Mr. Brad T. Garber, Ph.D., Professor, 300 Orange Avenue, West Haven, CT 06516. 203-932-7175.

QUALITY CONTROL AND SAFETY TECHNOLOGIES (15.07)
Occupational Safety

General Information   Unit offering the program: Occupational Safety and Health. Program content: Fire chemistry, accidents. Available for credit. Certificate signed by the Dean. Certificate applicable to B.S. in Occupational Safety and Health.

Program Format   Daytime, evening classes offered. Program cycle: Continuous enrollment. Full program cycle lasts 18 credit hours. Completion of program requires 2.0 GPA.

Evaluation   Student evaluation based on tests, papers, reports. Grading system: Letters or numbers. Transcripts are kept for each student.

Enrollment Requirements   High school diploma or GED required. Program is open to non-resident foreign students. English language proficiency required. Minimum TOEFL score required: 550.

Program Costs $600 per course.

Housing and Student Services   Housing is not available. Job counseling and placement services are available.

Contact   Mr. Brad T. Garber, Ph.D., Professor, 300 Orange Avenue, West Haven, CT 06516. 203-932-7175.

QUALITY CONTROL AND SAFETY TECHNOLOGIES (15.07)
Occupational Safety and Health

General Information   Unit offering the program: Occupational Safety and Health. Program content: Fire detection, industrial hygiene, noise, requirements of OSHA law. Available on either a credit or non-credit basis. Certificate signed by the Dean. Certificate applicable to B.S. in Occupational Safety and Health.

Program Format   Daytime, evening classes offered. Program cycle: Continuous enrollment. Full program cycle lasts 18 credit hours. Completion of program requires 2.0 GPA.

Evaluation   Student evaluation based on tests, papers, reports. Grading system: Letters or numbers. Transcripts are kept for each student.

Enrollment Requirements   High school diploma or GED required. Program is open to non-resident foreign students. English language proficiency required. Minimum TOEFL score required: 550.

Program Costs $429 per course.

Housing and Student Services   Housing is not available. Job counseling and placement services are available.

Contact   Mr. Brad T. Garber, Ph.D., Professor, 300 Orange Avenue, West Haven, CT 06516. 203-932-7175.

QUALITY CONTROL AND SAFETY TECHNOLOGIES (15.07)
Occupational Safety and Health Management

General Information   Unit offering the program: Occupational Safety and Health. Program content: Accident conditions and controls, industrial hygiene, noise, fire detection, OSHA standards. Available for credit. Certificate signed by the Dean. Certificate applicable to B.S. in Occupational Safety and Health.

Program Format   Daytime, evening classes offered. Program cycle: Continuous enrollment. Full program cycle lasts 18 credit hours. Completion of program requires 2.0 GPA.

Evaluation   Student evaluation based on tests, papers, reports. Grading system: Letters or numbers. Transcripts are kept for each student.

Enrollment Requirements   High school diploma or GED required. Program is open to non-resident foreign students. English language proficiency required. Minimum TOEFL score required: 550.

Program Costs $600 per course.

Housing and Student Services   Housing is not available. Job counseling and placement services are available.

Contact   Mr. Brad T. Garber, Ph.D., Professor, 300 Orange Avenue, West Haven, CT 06516. 203-932-7175.

RADIO/TELEVISION, GENERAL (09.07)
Mass Communication

General Information   Unit offering the program: Communication. Program content: TV, radio, interpersonal communication. Available for credit. Certificate signed by the Dean, School of Professional Studies and Continuing Education. Certificate applicable to B.S., B.A. in Communication.

Program Format   Daytime, evening classes offered. Program cycle: Continuous enrollment. Full program cycle lasts 1 year. Completion of program requires 2.0 GPA, five courses.

Evaluation   Student evaluation based on tests, papers. Grading system: Letters or numbers. Transcripts are kept for each student.

Enrollment Requirements   High school diploma or GED required. Program is open to non-resident foreign students. English language proficiency required. Minimum TOEFL score required: 500. Students required to live on campus.

Program Costs $2145 for the program, $429 per course.

Housing and Student Services   Housing is available. Job counseling and placement services are available.

Special Features   UNH does not grant credit for life or prior experience. The program consists of regular University offerings taught by regular full-time faculty. There are three required courses, and the remaining two courses may be used to specialize in radio, television, writing for media, or interpersonal communication.

Contact   Dr. Steven Raucher, Chairman, Department of Communication, 300 Orange Avenue, West Haven, CT 06516. 203-932-7209.

TRADE AND INDUSTRIAL SUPERVISION AND MANAGEMENT (06.20)
Executive Housekeeping Administration

General Information   Unit offering the program: Hotel and Restaurant Management. Program content: Accounting, auditing, food and labor costs, personnel, environmental services, systems, operations. Available for credit. Certificate signed by the Dean. Certificate applicable to B.S. in Hotel and Restaurant Management.

Program Format   Daytime, evening classes offered. Instructional schedule: Three hours per week. Program cycle: Continuous enrollment. Full program cycle lasts 2 semesters. Completion of program requires 2.0 GPA, six courses.

Evaluation   Student evaluation based on tests, papers, reports. Grading system: Letters or numbers. Transcripts are kept for each student.

Enrollment Requirements   High school diploma or GED required. Program is open to non-resident foreign students. English language proficiency required. Minimum TOEFL score required: 550. Students required to live on campus.

Program Costs $429 per course.

Housing and Student Services   Housing is available. Job counseling and placement services are available.

Contact   Mr. Linsley T. DeVeau, Chairman, Hotel and Restaurant Management, 300 Orange Avenue, West Haven, CT 06516. 203-932-7356.

DELAWARE

GOLDEY BEACOM COLLEGE
Wilmington, Delaware 19808

COMPUTER AND INFORMATION SCIENCES, GENERAL (11.01)
Computer Information Systems Certificate

General Information   Unit offering the program: Accounting/Computer Information Systems Department. Program content: Pascal, COBOL, assembler programming. Available for credit. Certificate signed by the President of the College. Certificate applicable to A.S., B.S. in Computer Information Systems.

Program Format   Daytime, evening classes offered. Program cycle: Continuous enrollment. Full program cycle lasts 32 credit hours. Completion of program requires 2.0 GPA.

Evaluation   Student evaluation based on tests, papers, reports, projects. Grading system: Letters or numbers. Transcripts are kept for each student.

Enrollment Requirements   Bachelor's degree (in a field other than computer science) required. Program is open to non-resident foreign students. English language proficiency required. Minimum TOEFL score required: 475.

Program Costs $125 per credit hour.

Housing and Student Services   Housing is available. Job counseling and placement services are available.

Contact   Ms. Sherry Connell, Dean of Admissions, 4701 Limestone Road, Wilmington, DE 19808. 302-998-8814.

SECRETARIAL AND RELATED PROGRAMS (07.06)
General Business Certificate

General Information   Unit offering the program: Office Technologies and Administration. Program content: Computer applications, word processing, accounting. Available for credit. Certificate signed by the President of the College. Certificate applicable to A.S. in Executive, Legal, or Medical Secretary.

Program Format   Daytime, evening classes offered. Program cycle: Continuous enrollment. Full program cycle lasts 34 credit hours. Completion of program requires 2.0 GPA.

Evaluation   Student evaluation based on tests, papers, reports. Grading system: Letters or numbers. Transcripts are kept for each student.

Enrollment Requirements   High school diploma or equivalent required. Program is open to non-resident foreign students. English language proficiency required. Minimum TOEFL score required: 475.

Program Costs $130 per credit hour (day); $125 per credit hour (evening).

Housing and Student Services   Housing is available. Job counseling and placement services are available.

Contact   Ms. Sherry Connell, Dean of Admissions, 4701 Limestone Road, Wilmington, DE 19808. 302-998-8814.

TYPING, GENERAL OFFICE, AND RELATED PROGRAMS (07.07)
General Clerical Certificate

General Information   Unit offering the program: Office Technologies and Administration. Program content: Word processing, typing, English. Available for credit. Certificate signed by the President of the College. Certificate applicable to associate or bachelor's degree in office technologies and administration.

Program Format   Daytime, evening classes offered. Program cycle: Continuous enrollment. Full program cycle lasts 26 credit hours. Completion of program requires 2.0 GPA.

Evaluation   Student evaluation based on tests, papers, reports. Grading system: Letters or numbers. Transcripts are kept for each student.

Enrollment Requirements   High school diploma or equivalent required. Program is open to non-resident foreign students. English language proficiency required. Minimum TOEFL score required: 475.

Program Costs $130 per credit hour (day); $125 per credit hour (evening).

Housing and Student Services   Housing is available. Job counseling and placement services are available.

Contact   Ms. Sherry Connell, Dean of Admissions, 4701 Limestone Road, Wilmington, DE 19808. 302-998-8814.

TYPING, GENERAL OFFICE, AND RELATED PROGRAMS (07.07)
Stenographic Certificate

General Information   Unit offering the program: Office Technologies and Administration. Program content: Shorthand, typing, word processing, English. Available for credit. Certificate signed by the President of the College. Certificate applicable to A.S. in Executive Secretary.

Program Format   Daytime, evening classes offered. Program cycle: Continuous enrollment. Full program cycle lasts 35 credit hours. Completion of program requires 2.0 GPA.

Stenographic Certificate continued

Evaluation Student evaluation based on tests, papers, reports. Grading system: Letters or numbers. Transcripts are kept for each student.

Enrollment Requirements High school diploma or equivalent required. Program is open to non-resident foreign students. English language proficiency required. Minimum TOEFL score required: 475.

Program Costs $130 per credit hour (day); $125 per credit hour (evening).

Housing and Student Services Housing is available. Job counseling and placement services are available.

Contact Ms. Sherry Connell, Dean of Admissions, 4701 Limestone Road, Wilmington, DE 19808. 302-998-8814.

WORD PROCESSING (07.08)
Word/Information Processing Certificate

General Information Unit offering the program: Office Technologies and Administration. Program content: Word processing, typing, computer applications, English. Available for credit. Certificate signed by the President of the College. Certificate applicable to A.S. in Word/Information Processing.

Program Format Daytime, evening classes offered. Program cycle: Continuous enrollment. Full program cycle lasts 34 credit hours. Completion of program requires 2.0 GPA.

Evaluation Student evaluation based on tests, papers, reports. Grading system: Letters or numbers. Transcripts are kept for each student.

Enrollment Requirements High school diploma or equivalent required. Program is open to non-resident foreign students. English language proficiency required. Minimum TOEFL score required: 475.

Program Costs $130 per credit hour (day); $125 per credit hour (evening).

Housing and Student Services Housing is available. Job counseling and placement services are available.

Contact Ms. Sherry Connell, Dean of Admissions, 4701 Limestone Road, Wilmington, DE 19808. 302-998-8814.

UNIVERSITY OF DELAWARE
Newark, Delaware 19716

GRAPHIC AND PRINTING COMMUNICATIONS (48.02)
Commercial Art and Design

General Information Unit offering the program: Division of Continuing Education, Department of Art and Communication. Available on a non-credit basis. Certificate signed by the Associate Director.

Program Format Evening classes offered. Instructional schedule: One evening per week (academic year); two evenings per week (summer). Program cycle: Continuous enrollment. Completion of program requires six courses.

Evaluation Student evaluation based on artwork and projects. Grading system: excellent/superior/satisfactory/unsatisfactory. Transcripts are kept for each student.

Housing and Student Services Housing is not available. Job counseling and placement services are not available.

Special Features A six-course certificate program designed to help students develop latent talent. Program serves the returning student well—provides a nonthreatening atmosphere and a supportive learning environment. All faculty members are professionals working in the commercial art field.

Contact Mr. Matthew M. Shipp, Program Specialist, 2800 Pennsylvania Avenue, Wilmington, DE 19806. 302-573-4435.

LAW (22.01)
Legal Assistant

General Information Unit offering the program: Division of Continuing Education. Available on a non-credit basis. Endorsed by American Bar Association, Delaware Bar Association, Delaware Paralegal Association. Certificate signed by the Associate Director.

Program Format Evening classes offered. Program cycle: Continuous enrollment. Completion of program requires grade of C or better in six courses.

Evaluation Student evaluation based on tests, papers. Grading system: Letters or numbers. Transcripts are kept for each student.

Enrollment Requirements Forty-two college credits required. Program is open to non-resident foreign students.

Program Costs $1560 for the program, $260 per course.

Housing and Student Services Housing is not available. Job counseling and placement services are available.

Special Features A six-course evening program given at the Wilmington campus only. Program designed for the part-time student as a result of a needs assessment survey. Has a 15-person advisory board made up of practicing paralegals, attorneys, judges, business persons, and college professors. All faculty are practicing attorneys. Placement service available.

Contact Mr. Matthew M. Shipp, Program Director, 2800 Pennsylvania Avenue, Wilmington, DE 19806. 302-573-4435.

DISTRICT OF COLUMBIA

AMERICAN UNIVERSITY
Washington, District of Columbia 20016

ACCOUNTING (06.02)
Graduate Certificate in Accounting

General Information Unit offering the program: Kogod College of Business Administration—Accounting Department. Available for credit. Certificate signed by the Vice Provost for University Programs. Certificate applicable to M.S. in Accounting, M.B.A. with accounting concentration.

Program Format Daytime, evening classes offered. Instructional schedule: 2½ hours per week. Program cycle: Continuous enrollment. Full program cycle lasts 30 credit hours.

Evaluation Student evaluation based on tests. Grading system: Letters or numbers. Transcripts are kept for each student.

Enrollment Requirements Satisfactory GMAT score or successful completion of CPA, and 2.75 GPA for last 60 hours of undergraduate work required. Program is open to non-resident foreign students. English language proficiency required. Minimum TOEFL score required: 600, or satisfactory score on English placement exam.

Program Costs $9690 for the program, $969 per course.

Housing and Student Services Housing is not available. Job counseling and placement services are available.

Contact University Programs Advisement Center, McKinley Building, Room 153, Washington, DC 20016. 202-885-2500.

BALTO-SLAVIC LANGUAGES (16.04)
Certificate in Translation (Russian)

General Information Unit offering the program: Department of Language and Foreign Studies. Program content: Conversation, composition. Available for credit. Certificate signed by the Vice Provost for University Programs. Certificate applicable to B.A. in Russian, M.A. in Russian Studies.

Program Format   Daytime, evening classes offered. Program cycle: Continuous enrollment. Full program cycle lasts 15 credit hours.

Evaluation   Student evaluation based on tests, papers, reports. Grading system: Letters or numbers. Transcripts are kept for each student.

Enrollment Requirements   Advanced language standing required. Program is open to non-resident foreign students. English language proficiency required. Minimum TOEFL score required: 600.

Program Costs $323–$339 per semester hour.

Housing and Student Services   Housing is available. Job counseling and placement services are not available.

Contact   University Programs Advisement Center, McKinley Building, Room 153, Washington, DC 20016. 202-885-2500.

BUSINESS ADMINISTRATION AND MANAGEMENT (06.04)
Graduate Certificate in Business Management

General Information   Unit offering the program: Kogod College of Business Administration. Program content: Organizational theory, economics, marketing, accounting. Available for credit. Certificate signed by the Vice Provost for University Programs. Certificate applicable to M.B.A.

Program Format   Daytime, evening classes offered. Program cycle: Continuous enrollment. Full program cycle lasts 15 credit hours.

Evaluation   Student evaluation based on tests, papers. Grading system: Letters or numbers. Transcripts are kept for each student.

Enrollment Requirements   Satisfactory GMAT score, 2.75 GPA in last 60 hours of undergraduate work required. Program is open to non-resident foreign students. English language proficiency required. Minimum TOEFL score required: 600, or satisfactory score on English placement exam.

Program Costs $4845 for the program, $969 per course.

Housing and Student Services   Housing is not available. Job counseling and placement services are available.

Contact   University Programs Advisement Center, McKinley Building, Room 153, Washington, DC 20016. 202-885-2500.

BUSINESS ADMINISTRATION AND MANAGEMENT (06.04)
Graduate Certificate in Procurement Management

General Information   Unit offering the program: Kogod College of Business Administration. Program content: Federal procurement law and policy, contract administration, materials management, purchasing, cost and price analysis. Available for credit. Certificate signed by the Vice Provost for University Programs. Certificate applicable to M.S. in Procurement Management, M.B.A. with Procurement Management concentration.

Program Format   Evening classes offered. Program cycle: Continuous enrollment. Full program cycle lasts 18 credit hours.

Evaluation   Student evaluation based on tests, papers. Grading system: Letters or numbers. Transcripts are kept for each student.

Enrollment Requirements   Satisfactory GMAT score, 2.75 GPA for last 60 hours of undergraduate work required. Program is open to non-resident foreign students. English language proficiency required. Minimum TOEFL score required: 600, or satisfactory score on English placement exam.

Program Costs $5814 for the program, $969 per course.

Housing and Student Services   Housing is not available. Job counseling and placement services are available.

Contact   University Programs Advisement Center, McKinley Building, Room 153, Washington, DC 20016. 202-885-2500.

BUSINESS AND MANAGEMENT, GENERAL (06.01)
Graduate Certificate in Arts Management

General Information   Unit offering the program: Office of Continuing Studies. Program content: Arts management, public relations, fund-raising, supervisory skills. Available on either a credit or non-credit basis. Certificate signed by the Vice Provost for University Programs. Certificate applicable to M.A. in Arts Management.

Program Format   Daytime, evening classes offered. Instructional schedule: 2½ hours per week. Program cycle: Continuous enrollment. Completion of program requires five courses, two noncredit workshops.

Evaluation   Student evaluation based on tests, papers, reports. Grading system: Letters or numbers. Transcripts are kept for each student.

Enrollment Requirements   Bachelor's degree with 3.0 GPA for last two years of study required. Program is open to non-resident foreign students. English language proficiency required. Evaluation by department.

Program Costs $5045 for the program, $969 per course, $100 per workshop.

Housing and Student Services   Housing is not available. Job counseling and placement services are available.

Special Features   The program has been designed in response to the growing need for professional management in the arts.

Contact   University Programs Advisement Center, McKinley Building, Room 153, Washington, DC 20016. 202-885-2500.

COMPUTER AND INFORMATION SCIENCES, GENERAL (11.01)
Graduate Certificate in Computer Systems Applications

General Information   Unit offering the program: Computer Science and Information Systems. Program content: Technologies, issues, and management concerns of computer and telecommunications systems applications. Available for credit. Certificate signed by the Vice Provost for University Programs. Certificate applicable to M.S. in Technology of Management.

Program Format   Evening classes offered. Instructional schedule: One evening per week. Program cycle: Continuous enrollment. Full program cycle lasts 15 credit hours. Completion of program requires 3.0 GPA.

Evaluation   Student evaluation based on tests, papers, reports. Grading system: Letters or numbers. Transcripts are kept for each student.

Enrollment Requirements   Bachelor's degree required. Program is open to non-resident foreign students. English language proficiency required. Evaluation by department.

Program Costs $4845 for the program, $969 per course.

Housing and Student Services   Housing is not available. Job counseling and placement services are available.

Special Features   Nine semester hours of foundation work or evidence of appropriate experience is required in addition to the required 15 credit hours. Instructors are University faculty or adjunct faculty who are working in the field.

Contact   University Programs Advisement Center, McKinley Building, Room 153, Washington, DC 20016. 202-885-2500.

COMPUTER AND INFORMATION SCIENCES, GENERAL (11.01)
Graduate Certificate in Management Information Systems

General Information   Unit offering the program: Computer Science and Information Systems. Program content: Design, implementation, and management of complex information

Graduate Certificate in Management Information Systems continued

systems. Available for credit. Certificate signed by the Vice Provost for University Programs. Certificate applicable to M.S. in Technology of Management.

Program Format Evening classes offered. Instructional schedule: One evening per week. Program cycle: Continuous enrollment. Full program cycle lasts 15 credit hours. Completion of program requires 3.0 GPA.

Evaluation Student evaluation based on tests, papers, reports. Grading system: Letters or numbers. Transcripts are kept for each student.

Enrollment Requirements Bachelor's degree, completion of foundation courses required. Program is open to non-resident foreign students. English language proficiency required. Evaluation by department.

Program Costs $4845 for the program, $969 per course.

Housing and Student Services Housing is not available. Job counseling and placement services are available.

Special Features Nine semesters of foundation work or evidence of appropriate experience is required in addition to the required 15 credit hours. Instructors are University faculty or adjunct faculty who are working in the field.

Contact University Programs Advisement Center, McKinley Building, Room 153, Washington, DC 20016. 202-885-2500.

ECONOMICS (45.06)
Graduate Certificate in Applied Economics

General Information Unit offering the program: Economics. Program content: Theoretical and practical aspects of economics. Available for credit. Certificate signed by the Vice Provost for University Programs. Certificate applicable to M.A. in Economics, M.A. in Development Banking.

Program Format Evening classes offered. Program cycle: Continuous enrollment. Full program cycle lasts 21 credit hours. Completion of program requires seven courses, 3.0 GPA.

Evaluation Student evaluation based on tests, papers, reports. Grading system: Letters or numbers. Transcripts are kept for each student.

Enrollment Requirements Bachelor's degree required. Program is open to non-resident foreign students. English language proficiency required. Minimum TOEFL score required: 600, or satisfactory score on English placement exam.

Program Costs $6741 for the program, $969 per course.

Housing and Student Services Housing is not available. Job counseling and placement services are available.

Special Features Prerequisite course may be exempted for well-qualified individuals with comparable prior education or experience. Certificate students have access to all computer facilities, including time-sharing terminals connected to the mainframe and several microcomputer labs on campus.

Contact University Programs Advisement Center, McKinley Building, Room 153, Washington, DC 20016. 202-885-2500.

GERMANIC LANGUAGES (16.05)
Certificate in Translation (German)

General Information Unit offering the program: Department of Language and Foreign Studies. Program content: Conversation, composition. Available for credit. Certificate signed by the Vice Provost for University Programs. Certificate applicable to B.A. in German.

Program Format Daytime, evening classes offered. Program cycle: Continuous enrollment. Full program cycle lasts 15 credit hours.

Evaluation Student evaluation based on tests, papers, reports. Grading system: Letters or numbers. Transcripts are kept for each student.

Enrollment Requirements Advanced language standing required. Program is open to non-resident foreign students.

English language proficiency required. Minimum TOEFL score required: 600.

Program Costs $323–$339 per semester hour.

Housing and Student Services Housing is available. Job counseling and placement services are not available.

Contact University Programs Advisement Center, McKinley Building, Room 153, Washington, DC 20016. 202-885-2500.

HUMAN RESOURCES DEVELOPMENT (06.06)
Professional Certificate in Volunteer Management

General Information Unit offering the program: Office of Continuing Studies. Available on a non-credit basis. Endorsed by Association for Volunteer Administration. Certificate signed by the Vice Provost for University Programs.

Program Format Evening, weekend classes offered. Program cycle: Continuous enrollment. Full program cycle lasts 2 semesters. Completion of program requires five seminars, two workshops.

Evaluation Student evaluation based on papers, reports. Grading system: Pass/fail. Records are kept by Office of Continuing Studies.

Enrollment Requirements Program is open to non-resident foreign students.

Program Costs $710 for the program, $110–$180 per course.

Housing and Student Services Housing is not available. Job counseling and placement services are not available.

Contact Ms. Debra G. Rapone, Program Manager, Office of Continuing Studies, Nebraska Hall, 4400 Massachusetts Avenue, NW, Washington, DC 20016. 202-885-3970.

ITALIC LANGUAGES (16.09)
Certificate in Translation (French)

General Information Unit offering the program: Department of Language and Foreign Studies. Program content: Conversation, composition. Available for credit. Certificate signed by the Vice Provost for University Programs. Certificate applicable to B.A., M.A. in French.

Program Format Daytime, evening classes offered. Program cycle: Continuous enrollment. Full program cycle lasts 15 credit hours.

Evaluation Student evaluation based on tests, papers, reports. Grading system: Letters or numbers. Transcripts are kept for each student.

Enrollment Requirements Advanced language standing required. Program is open to non-resident foreign students. English language proficiency required. Minimum TOEFL score required: 600.

Program Costs $323–$339 per semester hour.

Housing and Student Services Housing is available. Job counseling and placement services are not available.

Contact University Programs Advisement Center, McKinley Building, Room 153, Washington, DC 20016. 202-885-2500.

ITALIC LANGUAGES (16.09)
Certificate in Translation (Spanish)

General Information Unit offering the program: Department of Language and Foreign Studies. Program content: Conversation, composition. Available for credit. Certificate signed by the Vice Provost for University Programs. Certificate applicable to B.A. in Spanish, M.A. in Spanish Studies.

Program Format Daytime, evening classes offered. Program cycle: Continuous enrollment. Full program cycle lasts 15 credit hours.

Evaluation Student evaluation based on tests, papers, reports. Grading system: Letters or numbers. Transcripts are kept for each student.

Enrollment Requirements Advanced language standing required. Program is open to non-resident foreign students. English language proficiency required. Minimum TOEFL score required: 600.

Program Costs $323–$339 per semester hour.

Housing and Student Services Housing is available. Job counseling and placement services are not available.

Contact University Programs Advisement Center, McKinley Building, Room 153, Washington, DC 20016. 202-885-2500.

LIBERAL/GENERAL STUDIES (24.01)
Graduate Certificate in Professional Development

General Information Unit offering the program: University Programs Advisement Center. Available for credit. Certificate signed by the Vice Provost for University Programs.

Program Format Daytime, evening classes offered. Instructional schedule: 2½ hours per week. Program cycle: Continuous enrollment. Complete program cycle lasts 15–18 credit hours.

Evaluation Student evaluation based on tests, papers. Grading system: Letters or numbers. Transcripts are kept for each student.

Enrollment Requirements Bachelor's degree required. Program is open to non-resident foreign students. English language proficiency required. Evaluation by English Language Institute.

Program Costs $4845–$5814 for the program, $969 per course.

Housing and Student Services Housing is not available. Job counseling and placement services are not available.

Special Features The program is designed by the student and his or her academic/faculty adviser to meet the student's professional needs. The program must be approved by the appropriate department.

Contact University Programs Advisement Center, McKinley Building, Room 153, Washington, DC 20016. 202-885-2500.

LIBERAL/GENERAL STUDIES (24.01)
Undergraduate Certificate in Career Development

General Information Unit offering the program: University Programs Advisement Center. Available for credit. Certificate signed by the Vice Provost for University Programs. Certificate applicable to any two- or four-year degree offered at the institution.

Program Format Daytime, evening classes offered. Instructional schedule: 2½ hours per week. Program cycle: Continuous enrollment. Full program cycle lasts 30 credit hours.

Evaluation Student evaluation based on tests, papers. Grading system: Letters or numbers. Transcripts are kept for each student.

Enrollment Requirements High school diploma or equivalent required. Program is open to non-resident foreign students. English language proficiency required. Evaluation by English Language Institute.

Program Costs $9690 for the program, $969–$1292 per course.

Housing and Student Services Housing is not available. Job counseling and placement services are not available.

Special Features The program is designed by the student and his or her academic/faculty adviser to meet the student's professional needs. The program outline must be approved by the appropriate department.

Contact University Programs Advisement Center, McKinley Building, Room 153, Washington, DC 20016. 202-885-2500.

PUBLIC ADMINISTRATION (44.04)
Graduate Certificate in Governmental Management

General Information Unit offering the program: Office of Continuing Studies. Program content: Public administration, management. Available for credit. Certificate signed by the Vice Provost for University Programs. Certificate applicable to M.A. in Public Administration.

Program Format Daytime, evening classes offered. Instructional schedule: 2½ hours per week. Program cycle: Continuous enrollment. Full program cycle lasts 5 courses.

Evaluation Student evaluation based on tests, papers, reports. Grading system: Letters or numbers. Transcripts are kept for each student.

Enrollment Requirements Bachelor's degree required. Program is open to non-resident foreign students. English language proficiency required. Minimum TOEFL score required: 600.

Program Costs $4845 for the program, $969 per course.

Housing and Student Services Housing is not available. Job counseling and placement services are available.

Contact University Programs Advisement Center, McKinley Building, Room 153, Washington, DC 20016. 202-885-2500.

PUBLIC ADMINISTRATION (44.04)
Graduate Certificate in Public Financial Management

General Information Unit offering the program: Office of Continuing Studies. Available for credit. Certificate signed by the Vice Provost for University Programs. Certificate applicable to M.P.F.M.

Program Format Evening classes offered. Instructional schedule: 2½ hours per week. Program cycle: Continuous enrollment. Full program cycle lasts 5 courses.

Evaluation Student evaluation based on tests, papers, reports. Grading system: Letters or numbers. Transcripts are kept for each student.

Enrollment Requirements Bachelor's degree required. Program is open to non-resident foreign students. English language proficiency required. Minimum TOEFL score required: 600.

Program Costs $969 per course.

Housing and Student Services Housing is not available. Job counseling and placement services are available.

Special Features The programs have been developed by the U.S. Joint Financial Management Improvement Program and the American University in order to strengthen the financial management techniques and skills needed for more effective management of government-sponsored programs and services.

Contact University Programs Advisement Center, McKinley Building, Room 153, Washington, DC 20016. 202-885-2500.

PUBLIC ADMINISTRATION (44.04)
Graduate Certificate in Public Management

General Information Unit offering the program: Office of Continuing Studies. Program content: Public administration, management. Available for credit. Certificate signed by the Vice Provost for University Programs. Certificate applicable to M.P.A.

Program Format Daytime, evening classes offered. Instructional schedule: 2½ hours per week. Program cycle: Continuous enrollment. Full program cycle lasts 5 courses.

Evaluation Student evaluation based on tests, papers, reports. Grading system: Letters or numbers. Transcripts are kept for each student.

Enrollment Requirements Bachelor's degree required. Program is open to non-resident foreign students. English language proficiency required. Minimum TOEFL score required: 600.

Graduate Certificate in Public Management continued

Program Costs $4845 for the program, $969 per course.

Housing and Student Services Housing is not available. Job counseling and placement services are available.

Special Features The certificate program allows students a great deal of latitude in course selection.

Contact University Programs Advisement Center, McKinley Building, Room 153, Washington, DC 20016. 202-885-2500.

REAL ESTATE (06.17)
Graduate Certificate in Real Estate and Urban Development

General Information Unit offering the program: Kogod College of Business Administration. Available for credit. Certificate signed by the Vice Provost for University Programs. Certificate applicable to M.S. in Real Estate and Urban Development, M.B.A.

Program Format Daytime, evening classes offered. Program cycle: Continuous enrollment. Completion of program requires nine courses.

Evaluation Student evaluation based on tests, papers, reports. Grading system: Letters or numbers. Transcripts are kept for each student.

Enrollment Requirements Satisfactory GMAT score, 2.75 GPA for last 60 hours of undergraduate work required. Program is open to non-resident foreign students. English language proficiency required. Minimum TOEFL score required: 600, or satisfactory score on English placement exam.

Program Costs $8721 for the program, $969 per course.

Housing and Student Services Housing is not available. Job counseling and placement services are available.

Contact University Programs Advisement Center, McKinley Building, Room 153, Washington, DC 20016. 202-885-2500.

SMALL BUSINESS MANAGEMENT AND OWNERSHIP (06.18)
Professional Development Certificate in Entrepreneurship

General Information Unit offering the program: Office of Continuing Studies. Program content: Specific skills necessary to start and run a small business. Available on a non-credit basis. Certificate signed by the Vice Provost for University Programs.

Program Format Daytime, evening, weekend classes offered. Instructional schedule: Once per week for two hours or Saturdays. Program cycle: Continuous enrollment. Full program cycle lasts 2 semesters. Completion of program requires five courses, two workshops.

Evaluation Student evaluation based on reports. Records are kept by Office of Continuing Studies.

Enrollment Requirements Program is open to non-resident foreign students.

Program Costs $915 for the program, $80–$195 per course.

Housing and Student Services Housing is not available. Job counseling and placement services are not available.

Contact Ms. Debra G. Rapone, Program Manager, Office of Continuing Studies, 4400 Massachusetts Avenue, Washington, DC 20016. 202-885-3970.

STATISTICS (27.05)
Graduate Certificate in Applied Statistics

General Information Unit offering the program: Mathematics and Statistics. Available for credit. Certificate signed by the Vice Provost for University Programs. Certificate applicable to M.A. in Statistics, M.S. in Statistical Computing.

Program Format Daytime, evening classes offered. Program cycle: Continuous enrollment. Full program cycle lasts 15 credit hours. Completion of program requires five courses, 3.0 GPA.

Evaluation Student evaluation based on tests. Grading system: Letters or numbers. Transcripts are kept for each student.

Enrollment Requirements Bachelor's degree, satisfactory completion of prerequisites required. Program is open to non-resident foreign students. English language proficiency required. Minimum TOEFL score required: 600, or satisfactory score on English placement exam.

Program Costs $4845 for the program, $969 per course.

Housing and Student Services Housing is not available. Job counseling and placement services are available.

Special Features The computer center at the University serves the ongoing computer research and instructional needs of the students 24 hours a day. In addition to time-sharing terminals connected to the mainframe, there are several microcomputer laboratories on campus.

Contact University Programs Advisement Center, McKinley Building, Room 153, Washington, DC 20016. 202-885-2500.

STATISTICS (27.05)
Undergraduate Certificate in Applied Statistics

General Information Unit offering the program: Mathematics and Statistics. Program content: Computing, calculus, statistics. Available for credit. Certificate signed by the Vice Provost for University Programs.

Program Format Daytime, evening classes offered. Program cycle: Continuous enrollment. Full program cycle lasts 5 courses. Completion of program requires 2.0 GPA.

Evaluation Student evaluation based on tests. Grading system: Letters or numbers. Transcripts are kept for each student.

Enrollment Requirements High school diploma or GED required. Program is open to non-resident foreign students. English language proficiency required. Minimum TOEFL score required: 600, or satisfactory score on English placement exam.

Program Costs $5814 for the program, $969–$1292 per course.

Housing and Student Services Housing is not available. Job counseling and placement services are available.

Special Features The computer center at the University serves the ongoing computer research and instructional needs of the students 24 hours a day. In addition to time-sharing terminals connected to the mainframe, there are several microcomputer laboratories on campus.

Contact University Programs Advisement Center, McKinley Building, Room 153, Washington, DC 20016. 202-885-2500.

TEACHING ENGLISH AS A SECOND LANGUAGE/FOREIGN LANGUAGE (13.14)
Graduate Certificate in Teaching English to Speakers of Other Languages (TESOL)

General Information Unit offering the program: Department of Language and Foreign Studies. Program content: Theory and methodology required for teaching English. Available for credit. Certificate signed by the Vice Provost for University Programs. Certificate applicable to M.A. in Linguistics.

Program Format Evening classes offered. Instructional schedule: 2½ hours per week. Program cycle: Continuous enrollment. Full program cycle lasts 15 credit hours.

Evaluation Student evaluation based on tests, papers, reports. Grading system: Letters or numbers. Transcripts are kept for each student.

Enrollment Requirements Bachelor's degree required. Program is open to non-resident foreign students. English language proficiency required. Minimum TOEFL score required: 600.

Program Costs $4845 for the program, $969 per course.

Housing and Student Services Housing is not available. Job counseling and placement services are available.

Contact University Programs Advisement Center, McKinley Building, Room 153, Washington, DC 20016. 202-885-2500.

TECHNICAL AND BUSINESS WRITING (23.11)
Graduate Certificate in Technical Writing

General Information Unit offering the program: Office of Continuing Studies. Program content: Technical and report writing, computer applications, communications. Available on either a credit or non-credit basis. Certificate signed by the Vice Provost for University Programs. Certificate applicable to M.A. in Literature, M.S. in Computer Science.

Program Format Evening, weekend classes offered. Instructional schedule: 2½ hours per week. Program cycle: Continuous enrollment. Full program cycle lasts 5 courses. Completion of program requires portfolio of documents, two workshops.

Evaluation Student evaluation based on tests, papers. Grading system: Letters or numbers. Transcripts are kept for each student.

Enrollment Requirements Bachelor's degree required. Program is open to non-resident foreign students. English language proficiency required. Evaluation by English Language Institute.

Program Costs $5045 for the program, $969 per course, $200 for workshops.

Housing and Student Services Housing is not available. Job counseling and placement services are not available.

Special Features The program is interdisciplinary and includes courses in computer science, statistics, literature, and communication.

Contact University Programs Advisement Center, McKinley Building, Room 153, Washington, DC 20016. 202-885-2500.

TECHNICAL AND BUSINESS WRITING (23.11)
Undergraduate Certificate in Technical Writing

General Information Unit offering the program: Office of Continuing Studies. Available on either a credit or non-credit basis. Certificate signed by the Vice Provost for University Programs. Certificate applicable to any two- or four-year degree offered at the institution.

Program Format Daytime, evening, weekend classes offered. Instructional schedule: 2½ hours per week. Program cycle: Continuous enrollment. Full program cycle lasts 6 courses. Completion of program requires portfolio of documents, one workshop.

Evaluation Student evaluation based on tests, papers. Grading system: Letters or numbers. Transcripts are kept for each student.

Enrollment Requirements High school diploma or equivalent required. Program is open to non-resident foreign students. English language proficiency required. Evaluation by English Language Institute.

Program Costs $6137 for the program, $969–$1292 per course.

Housing and Student Services Housing is not available. Job counseling and placement services are not available.

Special Features The program is interdisciplinary and includes courses in computer science, statistics, literature, and communication.

Contact University Programs Advisement Center, McKinley Building, Room 153, Washington, DC 20016. 202-885-2500.

GEORGE WASHINGTON UNIVERSITY
Washington, District of Columbia 20052

BUSINESS AND MANAGEMENT, GENERAL (06.01)
Administrative Manager Program

General Information Unit offering the program: Center for Career Education and Workshops. Program content: Management theories, effective written and oral communication, managerial accounting and budgeting, marketing, computing, organizational dynamics, personnel administration, statistics, economics, strategic planning. Available on a non-credit basis. Certificate signed by the Dean, Division of Continuing Education.

Program Format Evening classes offered. Instructional schedule: One evening per week. Program cycle: Continuous enrollment. Complete program cycle lasts one to two years. Completion of program requires average grade pf B or better, 80% attendance.

Evaluation Student evaluation based on tests, papers, reports, class presentations. Grading system: Letters or numbers. Transcripts are kept for each student.

Enrollment Requirements Transcripts, statement of interest, two letters of recommendation, personal interview required. Program is open to non-resident foreign students.

Program Costs $2500–$2900 for the program, $290 per course.

Housing and Student Services Housing is not available. Job counseling and placement services are available.

Special Features Designed to benefit current or prospective middle-management and supervisory-level professionals. Participants increase their personal and organizational effectiveness by developing quantitative and qualitative management skills. Instructors are professionals chosen from the profit and nonprofit sectors—business and industry, associations, and government.

Contact Ms. Cynthia M. Beres, Director, Management and Public Relations Programs, 801 22nd Street, NW, Suite T-409, Washington, DC 20052. 202-994-8065.

BUSINESS AND MANAGEMENT, GENERAL (06.01)
Association Executive Program

General Information Unit offering the program: Center for Career Education and Workshops. Program content: Association law and regulation, membership promotion and services, conference and meeting planning, management training, computer applications, public relations. Available on a non-credit basis. Certificate signed by the Dean, Division of Continuing Education.

Program Format Evening classes offered. Instructional schedule: One evening per week. Program cycle: Continuous enrollment. Complete program cycle lasts one to two years. Completion of program requires average grade of B or better, 80% attendance.

Evaluation Student evaluation based on tests, papers, reports, class presentations. Grading system: Letters or numbers. Transcripts are kept for each student.

Enrollment Requirements Transcripts, statement of interest, two letters of recommendation, personal interview required. Program is open to non-resident foreign students.

Program Costs $2500–$2900 for the program, $290 per course.

Housing and Student Services Housing is not available. Job counseling and placement services are available.

Special Features Offers students specialized training needed to enter or advance in association management careers. Instructors are skilled professionals who combine diverse specialty areas with association management expertise. Under

Association Executive Program continued

supervision of instructors, students formulate projects to be applied at current or prospective jobs.

Contact   Ms. Cynthia M. Beres, Director, Management and Public Relations Programs, 801 22nd Street, NW, Suite T-409, Washington, DC 20052. 202-994-8065.

BUSINESS AND MANAGEMENT, GENERAL (06.01)
Fund Raising Administrator

General Information   Unit offering the program: Center for Career Education and Workshops. Program content: Strategic planning, donor research, proposal design, volunteer recruitment, supervision, promotional and public relations efforts, grantsmanship, direct mail, planned giving, board development and training, computer applications. Available on a non-credit basis. Certificate signed by the Dean, Division of Continuing Education.

Program Format   Evening classes offered. Instructional schedule: One evening per week. Program cycle: Continuous enrollment. Complete program cycle lasts one to two years. Completion of program requires average grade of B or better, 80% attendance.

Evaluation   Student evaluation based on tests, papers, reports, class presentations. Grading system: Letters or numbers. Transcripts are kept for each student.

Enrollment Requirements   Transcripts, statement of interest, two letters of recommendation, personal interview required. Program is open to non-resident foreign students.

Program Costs $2500–$2900 for the program, $290 per course.

Housing and Student Services   Housing is not available. Job counseling and placement services are available.

Special Features   Introduced in 1978 in response to an increasing need for highly trained personnel to sustain the programs of nonprofit organizations. Provides pratical skills needed to enter or advance in careers in fund-raising and development as either general managers or specialists.

Contact   Ms. Cynthia M. Beres, Director, Management and Public Relations Programs, 801 22nd Street, NW Suite T-409, Washington, DC 20052. 202-994-8065.

COMMUNICATIONS TECHNOLOGIES (10.01)
Publication Specialist

General Information   Unit offering the program: Center for Career Education and Workshops. Program content: Editorial, graphic arts and production, marketing, management. Available on a non-credit basis. Certificate signed by the Dean, Department of Continuing Education.

Program Format   Evening, weekend classes offered. Instructional schedule: Monday through Thursday, Saturday classes and workshops. Program cycle: Continuous enrollment. Full program cycle lasts 10 courses. Completion of program requires 240 contact hours.

Evaluation   Student evaluation based on tests, papers, reports, projects. Grading system: Letters or numbers. Transcripts are kept for each student.

Enrollment Requirements   College degree, two letters of recommendation required. Program is open to non-resident foreign students. English language proficiency required. University of Illinois English Rhetoric Placement Test administered.

Program Costs $2560 for the program.

Housing and Student Services   Housing is not available. Job counseling and placement services are available.

Special Features   Offers practical training with over thirty courses to choose among. Instructors are leading editors, writers, publishers, publications managers, designers, typographers, printers, and advertising, marketing, and public relations

professionals. A graduate is exposed to the entire publications field, and must take courses in the editorial, design and production, management, and marketing areas.

Contact   Ms. Dee Buchanan, Director, Publication Specialist Program, 801 22nd Street, Suite T-409, Washington, DC 20052. 202-994-7273.

LANDSCAPE ARCHITECTURE (04.06)
Certificate in Landscape Design

General Information   Unit offering the program: Center for Continuing Education and Workshops. Program content: Graphics, design, construction and site engineering, horticulture. Available on a non-credit basis. Certificate signed by the Dean, Division of Continuing Education.

Program Format   Daytime, evening, weekend classes offered. Instructional schedule: Two or three hours per week. Program cycle: Continuous enrollment. Full program cycle lasts 2 years. Completion of program requires 350 class hours, average grade of B or better, comprehensive examination, independent design project.

Evaluation   Student evaluation based on tests, reports, design projects. Grading system: Letters or numbers. Transcripts are kept for each student.

Enrollment Requirements   Bachelor's degree or equivalent work experience required. Program is open to non-resident foreign students. English language proficiency required.

Program Costs $4000 for the program, $225–$350 per course.

Housing and Student Services   Housing is not available. Job counseling and placement services are available.

Special Features   Emphasizes residential landscape design. Instructors are professionals designers, landscape architects and horticulturalists. A full-time student takes two courses at a time, each meeting once a week for eight weeks in order to complete the sixteen required courses within two years. Other schedules may be arranged.

Contact   Ms. Frances Lumbard, Director, Landscape Design Program, 801 22nd Street, NW, Suite T-409, Washington, DC 20052. 202-994-8069.

LAW (22.01)
Legal Assistant

General Information   Unit offering the program: Center for Continuing Education and Workshops. Program content: Practical and theoretical skills in law practice for paralegals. Available on a non-credit basis. Endorsed by American Bar Association. Certificate signed by the Dean, Division of Continuing Education.

Program Format   Evening classes offered. Instructional schedule: Two evenings per week. Program cycle: Continuous enrollment. Full program cycle lasts 3 semesters. Completion of program requires average grade of B or better.

Evaluation   Student evaluation based on tests, papers, reports, oral presentation. Grading system: Letters or numbers. Transcripts are kept for each student.

Enrollment Requirements   Undergraduate degree required. Program is open to non-resident foreign students. English language proficiency required.

Program Costs $2400 for the program.

Housing and Student Services   Housing is not available. Job counseling and placement services are available.

Special Features   Provides legal training in research, writing, procedure, and substantive and administrative law. Taught by practicing attorneys and legal assistants, students learn practical skills which enhance employability and job advancement.

Contact   Ms. Carol M. Dietrich, Director, Legal Assistant Program, 801 22nd Street, NW, Suite T-409, Washington, DC 20052. 202-994-7095.

MANAGEMENT INFORMATION SYSTEMS (06.12)
Information Systems Specialist Program

General Information   Unit offering the program: Center for Continuing Education and Workshops. Program content: Computer and information systems, management, programming, software applications, telecommunications. Available on a non-credit basis. Certificate signed by the Dean, Division of Continuing Education.

Program Format   Evening, weekend classes offered. Instructional schedule: One evening per week. Program cycle: Continuous enrollment. Complete program cycle lasts one to two years. Completion of program requires average grade of B or better.

Evaluation   Student evaluation based on tests, papers, reports, programming assignments. Grading system: Letters or numbers. Transcripts are kept for each student.

Enrollment Requirements   Transcripts, two letters of recommendation, statement of interest, interview with director required. Program is open to non-resident foreign students.

Program Costs $2900–$3450 for the program, $345–$690 per course.

Housing and Student Services   Housing is not available. Job counseling and placement services are available.

Special Features   Students learn from professional practitioners and experts in the field of information management and education. Students develop skills and techniques for computer programming and systems design and management. Concentration of course work in information management, programming languages, telecommunications, or software applications.

Contact   Mr. James G. Hudson, Director, Information Systems Specialist Program, 801 22nd Street, NW, Suite T-409, Washington, DC 20052. 202-994-8533.

ORGANIZATIONAL BEHAVIOR (06.15)
International Management Development Certificate

General Information   Unit offering the program: Graduate School of Arts and Sciences, International Programs. Program content: Organizational, human resources, information management. Available for credit. Endorsed by United States Department of Agriculture. Certificate signed by the Director, Graduate School. Certificate applicable to M.A. in Administrative Sciences.

Program Format   Daytime, evening classes offered. Instructional schedule: Four days per week. Program cycle: Continuous enrollment. Full program cycle lasts 12 months. Completion of program requires 13 courses, comprehensive exam.

Evaluation   Student evaluation based on tests, papers, reports. Grading system: Letters or numbers. Transcripts are kept for each student.

Enrollment Requirements   Bachelor's degree or equivalent required. Program is open to non-resident foreign students. English language proficiency required. Minimum TOEFL score required: 500.

Program Costs $11,500 for the program, $1500 per course.

Housing and Student Services   Housing is available. Job counseling and placement services are available.

Special Features   The International Management Development Program was begun in 1972. Designed specifically for international participants, the program has trained managers from more than seventy countries. The program emphasizes home-country applications of training. Two specialty tracks, organizational management and management information systems, are available.

Contact   Ms. J. Jenkins, IMDP Coordinator, Graduate School, USDA, Room 134, 600 Maryland Avenue, SW, Washington, DC 20024. 202-447-7476.

POLITICAL SCIENCE AND GOVERNMENT (45.10)
The Washington Representative

General Information   Unit offering the program: Division of Continuing Education, Center for Career Education and Workshops. Program content: Government relations, lobbying, grass-roots coalition through legislative and executive branch. Available on a non-credit basis. Certificate signed by the Dean, Division of Continuing Education.

Program Format   Evening, weekend classes offered. Instructional schedule: Two evenings per week. Program cycle: Continuous enrollment. Full program cycle lasts 11 months. Completion of program requires average grade of B or better, 80% attendance.

Evaluation   Student evaluation based on tests, papers, reports, class participation. Grading system: Letters or numbers. Transcripts are kept for each student.

Enrollment Requirements   Bachelor's degree and/or relevant experience, writing skills required. Program is open to non-resident foreign students.

Program Costs $2500 for the program, $145–$395 per course.

Housing and Student Services   Housing is not available. Job counseling and placement services are available.

Special Features   Relies on, and takes advantage of the Washington political and power structure. Instructors are highly placed practitioners in political scene whose expertise comes from both theoretical, and practical perspectives. Students learn how government operates from the local level, through all aspects of the federal level, including regulatory and Congressional processes, through the executive branch, and how that process may be influenced.

Contact   Ms. Nancy Hearn Aronson, Director, Washington Representative Program, 801 22nd Street, NW, Suite T-409, Washington, DC 20052. 202-994-7216.

PUBLIC RELATIONS (09.05)
Public Relations and Advanced Public Relations Professional Programs

General Information   Unit offering the program: Center for Career Education and Workshops. Program content: Public relations/communications theory, effective writing styles, marketing strategies, publicity and promotion, media relations, public affairs, communication law, broadcasting, management. Available on a non-credit basis. Endorsed by Public Relations Society of America (PRSA), National Capital Chapter; International Association of Business Communicators (IABC), Washington, D.C. Chapter. Certificate signed by the Dean, Division of Continuing Education.

Program Format   Evening classes offered. Instructional schedule: One evening per week for three hours. Program cycle: Continuous enrollment. Complete program cycle lasts one to two years. Completion of program requires average grade of B or better, 80% attendance.

Evaluation   Student evaluation based on tests, papers, reports, class presentations. Grading system: Letters or numbers. Transcripts are kept for each student.

Enrollment Requirements   Transcripts, statement of interest, two letters of recommendation, personal interview required. Program is open to non-resident foreign students. English language proficiency required.

Program Costs $2600–$3000 for the program, $290 per course.

Housing and Student Services   Housing is not available. Job counseling and placement services are available.

Special Features   Offers comprehensive training in planning, implementing, and evaluating public relations programs in profit and nonprofit settings. Emphasizes the managerial and counselor roles of the public relations professional. Practical workshops are conducted in areas of resume and portfolio

Public Relations and Advanced Public Relations Professional Programs continued

preparation, job-search strategies, and employment opportunities.

Contact Ms. Cynthia M. Beres, Director, Management and Public Relations Program, 801 22nd Street, NW, Suite T-409, Washington, DC 20052. 202-994-8065.

FLORIDA

BAPTIST BIBLE INSTITUTE
Graceville, Florida 32440

RELIGIOUS EDUCATION (39.04)
Diploma in Religious Education

General Information Unit offering the program: Interdepartmental. Program content: Religious education, psychology, theology, general core courses. Available for credit. Certificate signed by the President. Certificate applicable to Bachelor of Religious Education.

Program Format Daytime, evening classes offered. Full program cycle lasts 3 years. Completion of program requires 98 semester hours, 2.0 GPA.

Evaluation Student evaluation based on tests, papers, reports. Grading system: Letters or numbers. Transcripts are kept for each student.

Enrollment Requirements High school diploma or GED required. Program is not open to non-resident foreign students. English language proficiency required.

Program Costs $33 per semester hour.

Housing and Student Services Housing is available. Job counseling and placement services are available.

Special Features This is a three-year academic program that prepares students for the ministry. There is a strong biblical core of 24 semester hours.

Contact Mr. Walter D. Draughon Jr., Dean, 1306 College Drive, Graceville, FL 32440. 904-263-3261.

RELIGIOUS MUSIC (39.05)
Diploma in Music Ministry

General Information Unit offering the program: Interdepartmental. Program content: Church music, theory, pedagogy, conducting, theological and general core courses. Available for credit. Certificate signed by the President. Certificate applicable to Bachelor of Music Ministry.

Program Format Daytime, evening classes offered. Full program cycle lasts 3 years. Completion of program requires 98 semester hours, 2.0 GPA.

Evaluation Student evaluation based on tests, papers, reports. Grading system: Letters or numbers. Transcripts are kept for each student.

Enrollment Requirements High school diploma or GED required. Program is not open to non-resident foreign students. English language proficiency required.

Program Costs $33 per semester hour.

Housing and Student Services Housing is available. Job counseling and placement services are available.

Special Features This is a three-year academic program that prepares students for the ministry. There is a strong biblical core of 24 semester hours.

Contact Mr. Walter D. Draughon Jr., Dean, 1306 College Drive, Graceville, FL 32440. 904-263-3261.

THEOLOGICAL STUDIES (39.06)
Diploma in Ministry with Religious Education/ Music

General Information Unit offering the program: Interdepartmental. Program content: Religious education, psychology, music theory, ensemble, conducting, theology, general core courses. Available for credit. Certificate signed by the President. Certificate applicable to Bachelor of Ministry with Religious Education/Music.

Program Format Daytime, evening classes offered. Full program cycle lasts 3 years. Completion of program requires 98 semester hours, 2.0 GPA.

Evaluation Student evaluation based on tests, papers, reports. Grading system: Letters or numbers. Transcripts are kept for each student.

Enrollment Requirements High school diploma or GED required. Program is not open to non-resident foreign students. English language proficiency required.

Program Costs $33 per semester hour.

Housing and Student Services Housing is available. Job counseling and placement services are available.

Special Features This is a three-year academic program that prepares students for the ministry. There is a strong biblical core of 24 semester hours.

Contact Mr. Walter D. Draughon Jr., Dean, 1306 College Drive, Graceville, FL 32440. 904-263-3261.

THEOLOGICAL STUDIES (39.06)
Diploma in Theology

General Information Unit offering the program: Interdepartmental. Program content: Bible, denominational and societal orientation, evangelism, homiletics, missions, pastoral ministry, religious education. Available for credit. Certificate signed by the President. Certificate applicable to Bachelor of Theology.

Program Format Daytime, evening classes offered. Full program cycle lasts 3 years. Completion of program requires 98 semester hours, 2.0 GPA.

Evaluation Student evaluation based on tests, papers, reports. Grading system: Letters or numbers. Transcripts are kept for each student.

Enrollment Requirements High school diploma or GED required. Program is not open to non-resident foreign students. English language proficiency required.

Program Costs $33 per semester hour.

Housing and Student Services Housing is available. Job counseling and placement services are available.

Special Features This is a three-year academic program that prepares students for the ministry. There is a strong biblical core of 24 semester hours.

Contact Mr. Walter D. Draughon Jr., Dean, 1306 College Drive, Graceville, FL 32440. 904-263-3261.

NUCEA MEMBER
BARRY UNIVERSITY
Miami Shores, Florida 33161

LAW (22.01)
Certificate of Achievement for Completion of Legal Assistant Program

General Information Unit offering the program: School of Adult and Continuing Education. Program content: Introduction to legal systems, litigation, criminal law, estate managing, legal research, torts. Available on either a credit or non-credit basis. Certificate signed by the Dean, School of Adult and Continuing Education. Certificate applicable to B.A. in Liberal Arts, B.P.S.

Program Format Evening, weekend classes offered. Instructional schedule: Two evenings per week, alternate Saturdays. Program cycle: Continuous enrollment. Full program cycle lasts 13 months. Completion of program requires ten courses, grade of C or better in each course.

Evaluation Student evaluation based on tests, papers. Grading system: Letters or numbers. Transcripts are kept for each student.

Enrollment Requirements One year of college or two years professional work experience required. Program is open to non-resident foreign students. English language proficiency required.

Program Costs $2415 for the program, $210–$315 per course.

Housing and Student Services Housing is not available. Job counseling and placement services are available.

Special Features Instructors are all local lawyers or judges specializing in the field of instruction; several instructors are from the University of Miami School of Law. The program is working toward application for accreditation by the American Bar Association.

Contact Ms. Marni Pilafian Lee, Director, Legal Assistant Program, 11300 NE Second Avenue, Miami Shores, FL 33161. 800-842-1000.

NUCEA MEMBER
FLORIDA INTERNATIONAL UNIVERSITY
Miami, Florida 33199

HUMAN RESOURCES DEVELOPMENT (06.06)
Certificate in Training and Human Resources Development

General Information Unit offering the program: Center for Management Development, College of Business Administration. Available on a non-credit basis. Endorsed by American Society for Training and Development (ASTD), Miami and Broward Chapters. Certificate signed by the Dean.

Program Format Evening, weekend classes offered. Instructional schedule: One evening per week, two Saturdays. Students enroll once per year. Full program cycle lasts 2 semesters. Completion of program requires 100 contact hours.

Evaluation Student evaluation based on projects, presentations, class participation. Records are kept by College of Business Administration.

Enrollment Requirements College degree or two years experience as a trainer required. Program is not open to non-resident foreign students. English language proficiency required.

Program Costs $1200 for the program.

Housing and Student Services Housing is not available. Job counseling and placement services are available.

Special Features We believe this to be the largest noncredit program in the country. Partnership with ASTD has resulted in national training "superstars" attending and speaking at graduation (as a gift to program), and ASTD professional internship opportunities. Conversion to credit in University's College of Education at graduate or Ph.D. level available.

Contact Ms. Willabeth Jordan, Director, North Miami, FL 33181. 305-940-5825.

LAW (22.01)
Legal Assistant Certificate Program

General Information Unit offering the program: Division of Continuing Education. Program content: Concepts for performance within a legal, government, or business environment. Available on a non-credit basis. Endorsed by National Association of Legal Assistants, American Bar Association. Cosponsored by Center for Legal Studies.

Certificate signed by the Dean, Division of Continuing Education. Program fulfills requirements for Certified Legal Assistant.

Program Format Evening, weekend classes offered. Instructional schedule: Two evenings per week, Saturdays. Program cycle: Continuous enrollment. Complete program cycle lasts three to four semesters.

Evaluation Student evaluation based on tests, papers. Grading system: Letters or numbers. Transcripts are kept for each student.

Enrollment Requirements High school diploma, writing skills test, two employer references required. Program is open to non-resident foreign students. English language proficiency required.

Program Costs $100 per course, $40 for monthly seminar.

Housing and Student Services Job counseling and placement services are available.

Contact Ms. Barbara A. Saucedo, Acting Director, Conferences and Short Courses Department, Division of Continuing Education, North Miami, FL 33181. 305-940-5669.

WOMEN'S STUDIES (30.07)
Women's Studies Certificate Program

General Information Unit offering the program: College of Arts and Sciences. Program content: Women in a social and historical context. Available for credit. Certificate signed by the Dean.

Program Format Daytime, evening classes offered. Program cycle: Continuous enrollment. Full program cycle lasts 18 credit hours. Completion of program requires grade of C or better.

Evaluation Student evaluation based on tests, papers, reports. Grading system: Letters or numbers. Transcripts are kept for each student.

Enrollment Requirements University admissions required. Program is open to non-resident foreign students. English language proficiency required.

Program Costs $31 per semester hour.

Housing and Student Services Housing is available.

Special Features Students enrolled in any FIU program may take electives in women's studies. Courses are taught by faculty in various disciplines and colleges and are coordinated by the Women's Studies Center, which also provides extracurricular opportunities, such as visiting scholar lecture series, conferences, research resources, and related activities and events.

Contact Ms. Marilyn Hoder-Salmon, Director, University Park, Miami, FL 33199. 305-554-2408.

NUCEA MEMBER
FLORIDA STATE UNIVERSITY
Tallahassee, Florida 32306

CRIMINAL JUSTICE (43.01)
Certificate in Corrections

General Information Unit offering the program: School of Criminology. Program content: Law enforcement, the court system and corrections, probation, pardon, parole, theories of offender treatment. Available for credit. Certificate signed by the Dean, School of Criminology. Certificate applicable to bachelor's degree in criminology.

Program Format Daytime, evening, correspondence classes offered. Program cycle: Continuous enrollment. Full program cycle lasts 7 courses. Completion of program requires 21 semester hours, internship.

Evaluation Student evaluation based on tests, papers, reports. Grading system: Letters or numbers, pass/fail. Transcripts are kept for each student.

Enrollment Requirements High school diploma required. Program is open to non-resident foreign students. English

Certificate in Corrections continued

language proficiency required. Minimum TOEFL score required: 550.

Program Costs $37 per semester hour (state residents); $125 per semester hour (nonresidents).

Housing and Student Services Housing is available. Job counseling and placement services are available.

Contact Mr. Stephen S. Chapman, Associate Director, Continuing Studies, Center for Professional Development, Tallahassee, FL 32312-2027. 904-644-3801.

CRIMINAL JUSTICE (43.01)
Certificate in Law Enforcement

General Information Unit offering the program: School of Criminology. Program content: Crime detection and investigation, police problems and practices, legal aspects, the court system. Available for credit. Certificate signed by the Dean, School of Criminology. Certificate applicable to bachelor's degree in criminology.

Program Format Daytime, evening classes offered. Program cycle: Continuous enrollment. Full program cycle lasts 7 courses. Completion of program requires 21 semester hours, internship.

Evaluation Student evaluation based on tests, papers, reports. Grading system: Letters or numbers. Transcripts are kept for each student.

Enrollment Requirements High school diploma required. Program is open to non-resident foreign students. English language proficiency required. Minimum TOEFL score required: 550.

Program Costs $37 per semester hour (state residents); $124 per semester hour (nonresidents).

Housing and Student Services Housing is available. Job counseling and placement services are available.

Contact Mr. Stephen S. Chapman, Associate Director, Continuing Studies, Center for Professional Development, Tallahassee, FL 32312-2027. 904-644-3801.

HUMAN RESOURCES DEVELOPMENT (06.06)
Certificate in Human Resource Development

General Information Unit offering the program: Educational Foundations and Policy Studies. Program content: Staff training and development, adult learning theory, program needs assessment and evaluation. Available for credit. Certificate signed by the Dean, College of Education.

Program Format Evening classes offered. Program cycle: Continuous enrollment. Full program cycle lasts 15 credit hours. Completion of program requires five courses, 135 contact hours.

Evaluation Student evaluation based on tests, papers, reports. Grading system: Letters or numbers. Transcripts are kept for each student.

Enrollment Requirements Bachelor's degree required. Program is open to non-resident foreign students. English language proficiency required. Minimum TOEFL score required: 550.

Program Costs $65 per semester hour (state residents); $190 per semester hour (nonresidents).

Housing and Student Services Housing is available. Job counseling and placement services are available.

Special Features The program features a multidisciplinary program of studies. Roles and competencies covered by the courses are consistent with human resource development functions identified by the leading professional organizations in training and development. Selection of courses can be made within individual professional interest. Participants may register as special students and complete certificate requirements without requesting formal admission to Florida State University.

Contact Mr. Irwin Jahns, Associate Coordinator, College of Education, 113 Stone Building, Tallahassee, FL 32306. 904-644-4594.

INDIVIDUAL AND FAMILY DEVELOPMENT (19.07)
Graduate Certificate in Gerontology

General Information Unit offering the program: Multidisciplinary Center on Gerontology. Program content: Aging and old age—demographics, politics, policies; program planning—analysis and implementation; nutrition; housing; healthcare. Available for credit. Certificate signed by the Dean, College of Social Sciences.

Program Format Daytime, evening classes offered. Program cycle: Continuous enrollment. Full program cycle lasts 3 courses, plus 100-hour field experience. Completion of program requires grade of C or better.

Evaluation Student evaluation based on tests, papers, reports. Grading system: Letters or numbers, pass/fail. Transcripts are kept for each student.

Enrollment Requirements Bachelor's degree required. Program is open to non-resident foreign students. English language proficiency required. Minimum TOEFL score required: 550.

Program Costs $65 per semester hour (state residents); $190 per semester hour (nonresidents).

Housing and Student Services Housing is not available. Job counseling and placement services are available.

Special Features Students take all 9 hours in one semester or spread the course work out over two or more terms. Courses in more than thirteen departments may be used towards the certificate. The program features an eminent scholar chair in gerontology.

Contact Dr. Marie Cowart, Director, Multidisciplinary Center on Gerontology, 647 Bellamy Building, Tallahassee, FL 32306. 904-644-2832.

INDIVIDUAL AND FAMILY DEVELOPMENT (19.07)
Undergraduate Certificate in Gerontology

General Information Unit offering the program: Multidisciplinary Center on Gerontology. Program content: Dynamics of aging, demographics, economics, leisure and services for the aged. Available for credit. Certificate signed by the Dean, College of Social Sciences.

Program Format Daytime, evening classes offered. Program cycle: Continuous enrollment. Full program cycle lasts 3 courses, plus 100-hour field experience. Completion of program requires grade of C or better.

Evaluation Student evaluation based on tests, papers, reports. Grading system: Letters or numbers, pass/fail. Transcripts are kept for each student.

Enrollment Requirements High school diploma required. Program is open to non-resident foreign students. English language proficiency required. Minimum TOEFL score required: 550.

Program Costs $37 per semester hour (state residents); $125 per semester hour (nonresidents).

Housing and Student Services Housing is not available. Job counseling and placement services are available.

Special Features Students may take all 9 courses in one semester or spread the course work out over two or more terms. Courses in more than thirteen departments may be used towards the certificate. The program features an eminent scholar chair in gerontology.

Contact Dr. Marie Cowart, Director, Multidisciplinary Center on Gerontology, 647 Bellamy Building, Tallahassee, FL 32306. 904-644-2832.

PUBLIC ADMINISTRATION (44.04)
Graduate Certificate in Public Management

General Information Unit offering the program: Department of Public Administration. Program content: Financial resources and administration, fiscal impact analysis, managing public financial resources. Available for credit. Certificate signed by the Dean, College of Social Sciences. Certificate applicable to M.P.A.

Program Format Evening, weekend classes offered. Program cycle: Continuous enrollment. Full program cycle lasts 6 courses. Completion of program requires 18 semester hours.

Evaluation Student evaluation based on tests, papers, reports. Grading system: Letters or numbers. Transcripts are kept for each student.

Enrollment Requirements Bachelor's degree required. Program is open to non-resident foreign students. English language proficiency required. Minimum TOEFL score required: 550.

Program Costs $65 per semester hour (state residents); $190 per semester hour (nonresidents).

Housing and Student Services Housing is available. Job counseling and placement services are available.

Contact Mr. Stephen S. Chapman, Associate Director, Continuing Studies, Center for Professional Development, Tallahassee, FL 32312-2027. 904-644-3801.

PUBLIC ADMINISTRATION (44.04)
Public Administration Certificate in Executive Development

General Information Unit offering the program: Department of Public Administration. Program content: Public policy development and administration, managing human resources, organizational theory. Available for credit. Certificate signed by the Dean, College of Social Sciences. Certificate applicable to M.P.A.

Program Format Evening classes offered. Program cycle: Continuous enrollment. Full program cycle lasts 6 courses. Completion of program requires 18 semester hours.

Evaluation Student evaluation based on tests, papers, reports. Grading system: Letters or numbers. Transcripts are kept for each student.

Enrollment Requirements Bachelor's degree required. Program is open to non-resident foreign students. English language proficiency required. Minimum TOEFL score required: 550.

Program Costs $65 per semester hour (state residents); $190 per semester hour (nonresidents).

Housing and Student Services Housing is available. Job counseling and placement services are available.

Contact Mr. Stephen S. Chapman, Associate Director, Continuing Studies, Center for Professional Development, Tallahassee, FL 32312-2027. 904-644-3801.

JONES COLLEGE
Jacksonville, Florida 32211

TRANSPORTATION AND TRAVEL MARKETING (08.11)
Travel and Tourism Diploma Program

General Information Program content: Travel agency management. Available for credit. Certificate signed by the President of the College.

Program Format Daytime, evening classes offered. Instructional schedule: Three or four days per week. Quarterly enrollment. Full program cycle lasts 4 quarters.

Evaluation Student evaluation based on tests, assignments. Grading system: Letters or numbers. Transcripts are kept for each student.

Enrollment Requirements College admissions required. Program is open to non-resident foreign students. English language proficiency required. Minimum TOEFL score required: 450.

Program Costs $2595 for the program.

Housing and Student Services Housing is not available. Job counseling and placement services are available.

Contact Mr. Raymond Gross, Dean, 5353 Arlington Expressway, Jacksonville, FL 32211. 904-743-1122.

TYPING, GENERAL OFFICE, AND RELATED PROGRAMS (07.07)
Computer Data Entry Diploma

General Information Program content: Data entry, typing, English, office skills. Available for credit. Certificate signed by the President. Certificate applicable to associate or bachelor's degree in marketing.

Program Format Daytime classes offered. Instructional schedule: Four days per week. Quarterly enrollment. Full program cycle lasts 3 months.

Evaluation Student evaluation based on tests, assignments. Grading system: Letters or numbers. Transcripts are kept for each student.

Enrollment Requirements College admissions required. Program is open to non-resident foreign students. English language proficiency required. Minimum TOEFL score required: 450.

Program Costs $2995 for the program.

Housing and Student Services Housing is not available. Job counseling and placement services are available.

Contact Mr. Raymond Gross, Dean of the College, 5353 Arlington Expressway, Jacksonville, FL 32211. 904-743-1122.

WORD PROCESSING (07.08)
Word Processing Certificate

General Information Program content: Word processing, typing, English. Available for credit. Certificate signed by the Dean of the College. Certificate applicable to B.S. in Marketing/Management.

Program Format Evening classes offered. Instructional schedule: Three evenings per week. Quarterly enrollment. Full program cycle lasts 3 months.

Evaluation Student evaluation based on tests, assignments. Grading system: Letters or numbers. Transcripts are kept for each student.

Enrollment Requirements College admissions required. Program is open to non-resident foreign students. English language proficiency required. Minimum TOEFL score required: 450.

Program Costs $754 for the program.

Housing and Student Services Housing is not available. Job counseling and placement services are available.

Contact Mr. Raymond Gross, Dean of the College, 5353 Arlington Expressway, Jacksonville, FL 32211. 904-743-1122.

NUCEA MEMBER
NOVA UNIVERSITY
Fort Lauderdale, Florida 33314

AUDIOLOGY AND SPEECH PATHOLOGY
(18.01)
Speech Correction

General Information Unit offering the program: Program in Speech Language Pathology of CAE. Program content: Language disorders, audiology, anatomy, physiology. Available for credit. Certificate applicable to M.S. in Speech Language Pathology. Program fulfills requirements for Certificate of Clinical Competence/American Speech-Language Hearing Association.

Program Format Evening, weekend classes offered. Instructional schedule: Three to six hours per week. Program cycle: Continuous enrollment. Complete program cycle lasts 2½ years. Completion of program requires 3.0 GPA, 45 credit hours, 300 clinical hours.

Evaluation Student evaluation based on tests, papers, reports, clinical performance. Grading system: Letters or numbers. Transcripts are kept for each student.

Enrollment Requirements Bachelor's degree required. Program is open to non-resident foreign students.

Program Costs $8775 for the program, $195 per course.

Housing and Student Services Housing is not available. Job counseling and placement services are available.

Special Features Provides necessary course work and clinical experience for Florida certification in Speech-Language Pathology. Prepares for Certificate of Clinical Competence awarded by American Speech-Language-Hearing Association (ASHA). Requirements for Certification for Speech Correction by Florida State Department of Education also available. Undergraduate clinical clock hours (150) and 6 hours of graduate credits may be transferred, however, no credit given for experience.

Contact Dr. Jack Mills, Program Director, 3375 Southwest 75 Avenue, Fort Lauderdale, FL 33314.

BANKING AND FINANCE (06.03)
Banking and Finance Specialty

General Information Unit offering the program: Business and Administrative Studies. Program content: Monetary theory and policy, business cycles and forecasting, financial management, banking and financial institutions, investments. Available for credit. Certificate signed by the Dean, College for Career Development. Certificate applicable to B.S. in Business Administration.

Program Format Evening classes offered. Instructional schedule: Once per week for four hours. Program cycle: Continuous enrollment. Full program cycle lasts 1 year. Completion of program requires five courses, 2.25 GPA.

Evaluation Student evaluation based on tests, papers, reports. Grading system: Letters or numbers. Transcripts are kept for each student.

Enrollment Requirements High school diploma, prerequisites required. Program is open to non-resident foreign students. English language proficiency required. Minimum TOEFL score required: 550.

Program Costs $465 per course.

Housing and Student Services Housing is available. Job counseling and placement services are available.

Contact Business and Administrative Studies, 3301 College Avenue, Fort Lauderdale, FL 33314. 305-475-7357.

BUSINESS AND MANAGEMENT, GENERAL
(06.01)
Business Specialty

General Information Unit offering the program: Business and Administrative Studies. Program content: General business and management. Available for credit. Certificate signed by the Dean, College for Career Development. Certificate applicable to B.S. in Professional Management.

Program Format Evening, weekend classes offered. Enrollment offered as need arises. Full program cycle lasts 1 year. Completion of program requires five courses, 2.25 GPA.

Evaluation Student evaluation based on tests, papers, reports. Grading system: Letters or numbers. Transcripts are kept for each student.

Enrollment Requirements Forty-five college credits required. Program is open to non-resident foreign students. English language proficiency required. Minimum TOEFL score required: 550.

Program Costs $2325 for the program, $465 per course.

Housing and Student Services Housing is available. Job counseling and placement services are available.

Contact College for Career Development, 3301 College Avenue, Fort Lauderdale, FL 33314. 305-475-7034.

BUSINESS AND MANAGEMENT, GENERAL
(06.01)
Hotel and Restaurant Management Specialty

General Information Unit offering the program: Business and Administrative Studies. Available for credit. Certificate signed by the Dean, College for Career Development. Certificate applicable to B.S. in Business Administration.

Program Format Evening classes offered. Instructional schedule: Once per week for four hours. Program cycle: Continuous enrollment. Full program cycle lasts 1 year. Completion of program requires five courses, 2.25 GPA.

Evaluation Student evaluation based on tests, papers, reports. Grading system: Letters or numbers. Transcripts are kept for each student.

Enrollment Requirements High school diploma, prerequisites required. Program is open to non-resident foreign students. English language proficiency required. Minimum TOEFL score required: 550.

Program Costs $465 per course.

Housing and Student Services Housing is available. Job counseling and placement services are available.

Contact Business and Administrative Studies, 3301 College Avenue, Fort Lauderdale, FL 33314. 305-475-7357.

CLINICAL PSYCHOLOGY (42.02)
Certification in Psychoanalytic Psychotherapy

General Information Unit offering the program: School of Psychology. Available for credit. Certificate signed by the Director of Postdoctoral Institute.

Program Format Evening, weekend classes offered. Instructional schedule: Three classes per week. Program cycle: Continuous enrollment. Full program cycle lasts 4 years. Completion of program requires course work, supervised psychoanalytic psychotherapy, two years of personal analysis.

Evaluation Student evaluation based on tests, papers, reports. Grading system: Pass/fail. Transcripts are kept for each student.

Enrollment Requirements Limited to licensed and practicing clinicians in Florida; doctorate in psychology, medicine, or allied mental health required. Program is not open to non-resident foreign students.

Program Costs $1500 per year.

Housing and Student Services Housing is not available. Job counseling and placement services are not available.

Special Features Credit is offered for pervious study and/or personal therapy.

Contact Dr. Harold Lindner, Director, Postdoctoral Institute, 3301 College Avenue, Fort Lauderdale, FL 33314. 305-486-8947.

COMPUTER AND INFORMATION SCIENCES, GENERAL (11.01)
Computer Applications Specialty

General Information Unit offering the program: Business and Administrative Studies. Program content: Computers in decision making, information management, office automation. Available for credit. Certificate signed by the Dean, College for Career Development. Certificate applicable to B.S. in Professional Management.

Program Format Evening, weekend classes offered. Enrollment offered as need arises. Full program cycle lasts 1 year. Completion of program requires five courses, 2.25 GPA.

Evaluation Student evaluation based on tests, papers, reports. Grading system: Letters or numbers. Transcripts are kept for each student.

Enrollment Requirements Forty-five college credits required. Program is open to non-resident foreign students. English language proficiency required. Minimum TOEFL score required: 550.

Program Costs $2385 for the program, $465–$525 per course.

Housing and Student Services Housing is available. Job counseling and placement services are available.

Contact College for Career Development, 3301 College Avenue, Fort Lauderdale, FL 33314. 305-475-7034.

COMPUTER AND INFORMATION SCIENCES, GENERAL (11.01)
Computer Science Specialty

General Information Unit offering the program: Center for Computer Education. Program content: Introduction to computer organization and programming, BASIC, COBOL, management information systems. Available for credit. Certificate signed by the Dean, College for Career Development. Certificate applicable to B.S. in Business Administration.

Program Format Daytime, evening classes offered. Program cycle: Continuous enrollment. Full program cycle lasts 1 year. Completion of program requires five courses, 2.25 GPA.

Evaluation Student evaluation based on tests, papers, reports. Grading system: Letters or numbers. Transcripts are kept for each student.

Enrollment Requirements High school diploma, prerequisites required. Program is open to non-resident foreign students. English language proficiency required. Minimum TOEFL score required: 550.

Program Costs $525 per course.

Housing and Student Services Housing is available. Job counseling and placement services are available.

Contact Business and Administrative Studies, 3301 College Avenue, Fort Lauderdale, FL 33314. 305-475-7357.

CRIMINAL JUSTICE (43.01)
Criminal Justice Specialty

General Information Unit offering the program: College for Career Development. Program content: Juvenile crime and justice, ethical and moral judgements, public policy, organizational behavior, interviewing, psychology. Available for credit. Certificate signed by the Dean, College for Career Development. Certificate applicable to B.S. in Community Psychology, General Psychology, Administrative Studies.

Program Format Evening classes offered. Instructional schedule: Once per week. Program cycle: Continuous enrollment. Completion of program requires six courses, final examinations.

Evaluation Student evaluation based on tests. Grading system: Letters or numbers. Transcripts are kept for each student.

Enrollment Requirements High school diploma or equivalent required. English language proficiency required. Minimum TOEFL score required: 550.

Program Costs $2790 for the program, $465 per course.

Housing and Student Services Job counseling and placement services are available.

Special Features Program provides broad behaviorial science base for those who have an interest in the criminal justice system. Particularly appropriate for those who intend to pursue careers in law enforcement, rehabilitation, or community services.

Contact Mr. William P. Cahill, Director, Behavioral Sciences, Fort Lauderdale, FL 33314. 305-475-7353.

ENGLISH AS A SECOND LANGUAGE (23.12)
Intensive English and Intensive Language

General Information Unit offering the program: College for Career Development. Program content: English as a second language, other languages. Available on either a credit or non-credit basis. Certificate signed by the Institute Director. Certificate applicable to any four-year degree offered at the institution.

Program Format Daytime classes offered. Program cycle: Continuous enrollment. Full program cycle lasts 16 weeks.

Evaluation Student evaluation based on tests, papers. Grading system: Letters or numbers. Transcripts are kept for each student.

Enrollment Requirements Placement exam required. Program is open to non-resident foreign students.

Program Costs $1350 per semester.

Housing and Student Services Housing is available. Job counseling and placement services are available.

Special Features Approximately 120 students from many countries progress through a four-level program.

Contact Ms. Janet Travis, Director, Intensive Language Program, 3301 College Avenue, Fort Lauderdale, FL 33314.

GENERAL MARKETING (08.07)
Marketing Specialty

General Information Unit offering the program: Business and Administrative Studies. Program content: Channels of distribution, advertising and sales, consumer behavior, marketing strategy, special topics. Available for credit. Certificate signed by the Dean, College for Career Development. Certificate applicable to B.S. in Business Administration.

Program Format Evening classes offered. Instructional schedule: Once per week for four hours. Program cycle: Continuous enrollment. Full program cycle lasts 1 year. Completion of program requires five courses, 2.25 GPA.

Evaluation Student evaluation based on tests, papers, reports. Grading system: Letters or numbers. Transcripts are kept for each student.

Enrollment Requirements High school diploma, prerequisites required. Program is open to non-resident foreign students. English language proficiency required. Minimum TOEFL score required: 550.

Program Costs $465 per course.

Housing and Student Services Housing is available. Job counseling and placement services are available.

Contact Business and Administrative Studies, 3301 College Avenue, Fort Lauderdale, FL 33314. 305-475-7357.

HEALTH SERVICES ADMINISTRATION (18.07)
Health Care Services Specialty

General Information Unit offering the program: Business and Administrative Studies. Available for credit. Certificate signed by

Health Care Services Specialty continued

the Dean, College for Career Development. Certificate applicable to B.S. in Professional Management.

Program Format Evening, weekend classes offered. Enrollment offered as need arises. Full program cycle lasts 1 year. Completion of program requires five courses, 2.25 GPA.

Evaluation Student evaluation based on tests, papers, reports. Grading system: Letters or numbers. Transcripts are kept for each student.

Enrollment Requirements Forty-five college credits required. Program is open to non-resident foreign students. English language proficiency required. Minimum TOEFL score required: 550.

Program Costs $2385 for the program, $465–$525 per course.

Housing and Student Services Housing is available. Job counseling and placement services are available.

Contact College for Career Development, 3301 College Avenue, Fort Lauderdale, FL 33314. 305-475-7034.

INTERNATIONAL BUSINESS MANAGEMENT (06.09)
International Business Specialty

General Information Unit offering the program: Business and Administrative Studies. Program content: International economics, finance, management, marketing, export/import marketing. Available for credit. Certificate signed by the Dean, College for Career Development. Certificate applicable to B.S. in Business Administration.

Program Format Evening classes offered. Instructional schedule: Once per week for four hours. Program cycle: Continuous enrollment. Full program cycle lasts 1 year. Completion of program requires five courses, 2.25 GPA.

Evaluation Student evaluation based on tests, papers, reports. Grading system: Letters or numbers. Transcripts are kept for each student.

Enrollment Requirements High school diploma, prerequisites required. Program is open to non-resident foreign students. English language proficiency required. Minimum TOEFL score required: 550.

Program Costs $465 per course.

Housing and Student Services Housing is available. Job counseling and placement services are available.

Contact Business and Administrative Studies, 3301 College Avenue, Fort Lauderdale, FL 33314. 305-475-7357.

LAW (22.01)
Legal Assistant/Paralegal Certificate

General Information Unit offering the program: Behavioral Science/Legal Assistant–Career Division. Program content: Substantive law, legal applications and procedures. Available for credit. Certificate signed by the Dean. Certificate applicable to B.S. in Legal Studies. Program fulfills requirements for Certified Legal Assistant.

Program Format Evening classes offered. Instructional schedule: Two evenings per week for four hours. Program cycle: Continuous enrollment. Full program cycle lasts 6 months. Completion of program requires six courses.

Evaluation Student evaluation based on tests, papers. Grading system: Letters or numbers. Transcripts are kept for each student.

Enrollment Requirements High school diploma required. Program is open to non-resident foreign students. English language proficiency required.

Program Costs $2800 for the program, $465 per course.

Housing and Student Services Housing is available. Job counseling and placement services are available.

Special Features All instructors are practicing attorneys. Program includes on-sight Lexis training and computer courses

for the legal profession. Students have full use of law school library resources.

Contact Mr. Peter Skolnik, Coordinator, 3301 College Avenue, Parker Building, Fort Lauderdale, FL 33314. 305-476-8936.

LAW (22.01)
Legal Assistant/Paralegal Studies Specialty

General Information Unit offering the program: College for Career Development. Program content: Legal research, constitutional history, economics. Available for credit. Certificate signed by the Undergraduate Dean. Certificate applicable to any four-year degree offered at the institution. Program fulfills requirements for Certified Legal Assistant.

Program Format Evening classes offered. Instructional schedule: Four hours per week. Program cycle: Continuous enrollment. Full program cycle lasts 6 months. Completion of program requires six required courses.

Evaluation Student evaluation based on tests, papers, class participation. Grading system: Letters or numbers. Transcripts are kept for each student.

Enrollment Requirements High school diploma required. Program is open to non-resident foreign students. English language proficiency required. Minimum TOEFL score required: 550.

Program Costs $2790 for the program, $465 per course.

Housing and Student Services Housing is available. Job counseling and placement services are available.

Special Features Courses are offered in the evenings for college credit. The required courses and approved electives may be applied toward a degree. All courses are taught by attorneys, trained legal assistants and/or University faculty members. Students have full access to University facilities including computer resources, law school library, and writing and reading lab.

Contact Mr. Peter Skolnik, Coordinator, 3301 College Avenue, Parker Building, Fort Lauderdale, FL 33314. 305-476-8936.

MENTAL HEALTH/HUMAN SERVICES (17.04)
Substance Abuse Specialty

General Information Unit offering the program: College for Career Development. Program content: Effects on family and business, psychology, physiology, rehabilitation strategies, self-help groups. Available on either a credit or non-credit basis. Certificate signed by the Dean, College for Career Development. Certificate applicable to B.S. in Community Psychology, General Psychology, Administrative Studies.

Program Format Weekend classes offered. Instructional schedule: All day Saturday. Program cycle: Continuous enrollment. Completion of program requires six courses.

Evaluation Student evaluation based on tests, papers, reports. Grading system: Letters or numbers. Transcripts are kept for each student.

Enrollment Requirements High school diploma or equivalent required. Program is open to non-resident foreign students. English language proficiency required. Minimum TOEFL score required: 550.

Program Costs $2790 for the program, $465 per course.

Housing and Student Services Housing is available. Job counseling and placement services are available.

Special Features Designed to familiarize students with the field of chemical dependency treatment. Courses cover the psychology and physiology of substance abuse, family problems, effects upon business and industry, rehabilitation strategies, and the self-help group movement.

Contact Mr. William P. Cahill, Director, Behavioral Sciences, Fort Lauderdale, FL 33314. 305-475-7353.

MENTAL HEALTH/HUMAN SERVICES (17.04)
Substance Abuse Studies

General Information Unit offering the program: College of Career Development, Behavioral Sciences. Program content: Psychology, physiology, rehabilitation strategies, self-help groups. Available on either a credit or non-credit basis. Certificate signed by the Dean. Certificate applicable to B.S. in Psychology.

Program Format Evening, weekend classes offered. Program cycle: Continuous enrollment. Full program cycle lasts 48 weeks. Completion of program requires 2.0 GPA.

Evaluation Student evaluation based on tests, papers, reports. Grading system: Letters or numbers. Transcripts are kept for each student.

Enrollment Requirements Univerisity admissions required. Program is open to non-resident foreign students. English language proficiency required. Minimum TOEFL score required: 550.

Program Costs $455 per course.

Housing and Student Services Housing is available. Job counseling and placement services are available.

Special Features Program works actively with community agencies. Enrollment is made up of profesionals and regular students, about half of whom are seeking degrees.

Contact Dr. William Cahill, Director, Undergraduate Behavioral Sciences, 3301 College Avenue, Fort Lauderdale, FL 33314.

MISCELLANEOUS SPECIALIZED AREAS, LIFE SCIENCES (26.06)
Institute of Marine and Coastal Studies

General Information Unit offering the program: Oceanographic Center. Program content: Marine biology, coastal zone management, oceanography. Available for credit. Certificate signed by the Associate Director. Certificate applicable to M.S. and Ph.D. in Ocean Sciences.

Program Format Evening classes offered. Program cycle: Continuous enrollment. Complete program cycle lasts six to seven quarters. Completion of program requires 10–12 courses, thesis.

Evaluation Student evaluation based on tests, papers, reports. Grading system: Letters or numbers, pass/fail. Transcripts are kept for each student.

Enrollment Requirements Bachelor's degree, three letters of recommendation, GRE scores required. Program is open to non-resident foreign students. English language proficiency required. Minimum TOEFL score required: 550.

Program Costs $170 per credit hour.

Housing and Student Services Housing is available. Job counseling and placement services are not available.

Special Features Ph.D. degree in oceanography in highly tutorial mode. M.S. degree in ocean sciences with specialities in marine biology traditional program and coastal zone management trains students to manage coastal resources. Evening classes and weekend field trips allow student to be employed.

Contact Dr. Richard Dodge, Director, 8000 North Ocean Drive, Dania, FL 33004. 305-920-1909.

PERSONNEL MANAGEMENT (06.16)
Human Resource Management Specialty

General Information Unit offering the program: Business and Administrative Studies. Program content: Organizational theory and communication, labor relations. Available for credit. Certificate signed by the Dean, College for Career Development. Certificate applicable to B.S. in Business Administration.

Program Format Evening classes offered. Instructional schedule: Once per week for four hours. Program cycle: Continuous enrollment. Full program cycle lasts 1 year. Completion of program requires five courses, 2.25 GPA.

Evaluation Student evaluation based on tests, papers, reports. Grading system: Letters or numbers. Transcripts are kept for each student.

Enrollment Requirements High school diploma, prerequisites required. Program is open to non-resident foreign students. English language proficiency required. Minimum TOEFL score required: 550.

Program Costs $465 per course.

Housing and Student Services Housing is available. Job counseling and placement services are available.

Contact Business and Administrative Studies, 3301 College Avenue, Fort Lauderdale, FL 33314. 305-475-7357.

RINGLING SCHOOL OF ART AND DESIGN
Sarasota, Florida 34234

DESIGN (50.04)
Computer Design Certificate

General Information Unit offering the program: Computer Design. Program content: Drawing, lettering, basic computers, art history, electronic printing, photography, computer-aided design. Available for credit. Certificate signed by the President of the College. Certificate applicable to B.F.A.

Program Format Daytime classes offered. Students enroll in the fall. Full program cycle lasts 3 years. Completion of program requires 2.0 GPA, 90 credit hours.

Evaluation Student evaluation based on projects. Grading system: Letters or numbers. Transcripts are kept for each student.

Enrollment Requirements High school diploma or GED, portfolio required. Program is open to non-resident foreign students. English language proficiency required.

Program Costs $6000 per academic year, $225 per credit hour.

Housing and Student Services Housing is available. Job counseling and placement services are available.

Contact Mr. James H. Dean, Director of Admissions, 1111 27th Street, Sarasota, FL 34234. 813-351-4614.

DESIGN (50.04)
Graphic Design Certificate

General Information Unit offering the program: Graphic Design. Program content: Drawing, lettering, color and design, figure, art history, computer graphics, photography, marketing. Available for credit. Certificate signed by the President of the College. Certificate applicable to B.F.A.

Program Format Daytime classes offered. Students enroll in the fall. Full program cycle lasts 90 credit hours. Completion of program requires 2.0 GPA, 90 credit hours.

Evaluation Student evaluation based on projects. Grading system: Letters or numbers. Transcripts are kept for each student.

Enrollment Requirements High school diploma or GED, portfolio required. Program is open to non-resident foreign students. English language proficiency required.

Program Costs $6000 per academic year, $225 per credit hour.

Housing and Student Services Housing is available. Job counseling and placement services are available.

Contact Mr. James H. Dean, Director of Admissions, 1111 27th Street, Sarasota, FL 34234. 813-351-4614.

Ringling School of Art and Design

DESIGN (50.04)
Illustration Certificate

General Information   Unit offering the program: Illustration. Program content: Drawing, color and design, figure, modeling, art history, visual communications, photography, painting, portfolio. Available for credit. Certificate signed by the President of the College. Certificate applicable to B.F.A.

Program Format   Daytime classes offered. Students enroll in the fall. Full program cycle lasts 3 years. Completion of program requires 2.0 GPA, 90 credit hours.

Evaluation   Student evaluation based on projects. Grading system: Letters or numbers. Transcripts are kept for each student.

Enrollment Requirements   High school diploma or GED, portfolio required. Program is open to non-resident foreign students. English language proficiency required.

Program Costs $6000 per academic year, $225 per credit hour.

Housing and Student Services   Housing is available. Job counseling and placement services are available.

Contact   Mr. James H. Dean, Director of Admissions, 1111 27th Street, Sarasota, FL 34234. 813-351-4614.

FINE ARTS (50.07)
Fine Arts Certificate

General Information   Unit offering the program: Fine Arts. Program content: Drawing, figure, color and design, model, art history, printmaking, sculpture, painting, drafting, computer graphics. Available for credit. Certificate signed by the President of the College. Certificate applicable to B.F.A.

Program Format   Daytime classes offered. Students enroll in the fall. Full program cycle lasts 3 years. Completion of program requires 2.0 GPA, 90 credit hours.

Evaluation   Student evaluation based on projects. Grading system: Letters or numbers. Transcripts are kept for each student.

Enrollment Requirements   High school diploma or GED, portfolio required. Program is open to non-resident foreign students. English language proficiency required.

Program Costs $6000 per academic year, $225 per credit hour.

Housing and Student Services   Housing is available. Job counseling and placement services are available.

Contact   Mr. James H. Dean, Director of Admissions, 1111 27th Street, Sarasota, FL 34234. 813-351-4614.

INTERIOR DESIGN (04.05)
Interior Design Certificate

General Information   Unit offering the program: Interior Design. Program content: Drafting, color and design, history of architecture, drawing, art history, fabrics and finishes, construction and lighting. Available for credit. Certificate signed by the President of the College. Certificate applicable to B.F.A.

Program Format   Daytime classes offered. Students enroll in the fall. Full program cycle lasts 3 years. Completion of program requires 2.0 GPA, 90 credit hours.

Evaluation   Student evaluation based on projects. Grading system: Letters or numbers. Transcripts are kept for each student.

Enrollment Requirements   High school diploma or GED, portfolio required. Program is open to non-resident foreign students. English language proficiency required.

Program Costs $6000 per academic year, $225 per credit hour.

Housing and Student Services   Housing is available. Job counseling and placement services are available.

Contact   Mr. James H. Dean, Director of Admissions, 1111 27th Street, Sarasota, FL 34234. 813-351-4614.

ST. JOHN VIANNEY COLLEGE SEMINARY
Miami, Florida 33165

PHILOSOPHY (38.01)
Certificate in Pre-Theology Studies

General Information   Program content: Philosophy, theology, spiritual formation. Available for credit. Certificate signed by the Chairman of the Board of Trustees.

Program Format   Daytime classes offered. Full program cycle lasts 9 months.

Evaluation   Student evaluation based on tests, papers. Grading system: Pass/fail. Transcripts are kept for each student.

Enrollment Requirements   Bachelor's degree required. Program is open to non-resident foreign students. Students required to live on campus.

Program Costs $5950 for the program.

Housing and Student Services   Housing is available. Job counseling and placement services are not available.

Special Features   Most of the faculty hold doctorates. Spiritual direction and vocation discernment are provided by ordained priests. In-service ministry opportunities are given, and community life is provided.

Contact   Sr. Trinita Flood, Academic Dean, 2900 S.W. 87 Avenue, Miami, FL 33165. 305-223-4561.

NUCEA MEMBER
UNIVERSITY OF MIAMI
Coral Gables, Florida 33124

BUSINESS AND MANAGEMENT, GENERAL (06.01)
Certificate in Management

General Information   Unit offering the program: Management Institute. Program content: Accounting, marketing, finance, business communication, employee relations, customer service, budget control, microcomputer applications. Available on a non-credit basis. Certificate signed by the Dean, School of Continuing Studies.

Program Format   Daytime, evening, weekend classes offered. Program cycle: Continuous enrollment. Completion of program requires six courses.

Evaluation   Student evaluation based on tests. Grading system: Letters or numbers. Transcripts are kept for each student.

Enrollment Requirements   Program is open to non-resident foreign students.

Program Costs $2070 for the program, $185–$345 per course.

Housing and Student Services   Housing is not available. Job counseling and placement services are not available.

Special Features   Courses can be taken to earn a Certificate in Management or taken individually to enhance professional skills. Students may choose from courses in their line of work or try to make the step up to management.

Contact   Dr. Melanie McKay, Assistant Dean, School of Continuing Studies, James L. Knight Center, 4th Floor, 400 SE 2nd Avenue, Miami, FL 33131. 305-372-0140.

BUSINESS AND PERSONAL SERVICES MARKETING (08.02)
Certificate in Sales

General Information   Unit offering the program: Sales Institute. Program content: Fundamentals of sales, skill enhancement, time management, phone sales, sales management. Available on a non-credit basis. Certificate signed by the Dean, School of Continuing Studies.

Program Format Daytime, evening, weekend classes offered. Instructional schedule: One- and two-day seminars. Program cycle: Continuous enrollment. Completion of program requires six courses.

Evaluation Student evaluation based on tests. Grading system: Pass/fail. Transcripts are kept for each student.

Enrollment Requirements Program is open to non-resident foreign students.

Program Costs $1630 for the program, $165–$325 per course.

Housing and Student Services Housing is not available. Job counseling and placement services are not available.

Special Features The Sales Institute is designed to help improve selling and sales management techniques. Students learn how to scout for new clients, come face-to-face with key decision makers, make an impressive presentation, identify and use motivational factors, overcome objections, and close the order.

Contact Dr. Melanie McKay, Assistant Dean, School of Continuing Studies, James L. Knight Center, 4th Floor, 400 SE 2nd Avenue, Miami, FL 33131. 305-372-0140.

LAW (22.01)
Certificate in Paralegal Studies

General Information Unit offering the program: Paralegal Institute. Program content: Legal research and writing, estate planning and probate law, civil litigation, real property law, constitutional law. Available on either a credit or non-credit basis. Certificate signed by the Dean, School of Continuing Studies.

Program Format Daytime, evening, weekend classes offered. Program cycle: Continuous enrollment. Full program cycle lasts 2 years.

Evaluation Student evaluation based on tests. Grading system: Letters or numbers. Transcripts are kept for each student.

Enrollment Requirements Entrance examination in grammar required. Program is open to non-resident foreign students.

Program Costs $4380 for the program, $315–$375 per course.

Housing and Student Services Housing is not available. Job counseling and placement services are available.

Special Features The Paralegal Institute has trained more than 4,000 students for exciting careers as paralegals during the past decade.

Contact Ms. Kathleen Long, Director, Paralegal Institute, James L. Knight Center, 4th Floor, 400 SE 2nd Avenue, Miami, FL 33131. 305-372-0140.

MENTAL HEALTH/HUMAN SERVICES (17.04)
Certificate of Proficiency in Chemical Dependency/Counseling

General Information Unit offering the program: Chemical Dependency Institute. Program content: Drug and disease, theoretical principles and practices, treatment planning, sexuality, chemically dependent family. Available on a non-credit basis. Certificate signed by the Dean, School of Continuing Studies.

Program Format Daytime, evening, weekend classes offered. Program cycle: Continuous enrollment. Full program cycle lasts 10 months. Completion of program requires six courses, grade of C or better; three practica (Counseling certificate only).

Evaluation Student evaluation based on tests. Grading system: Letters or numbers. Transcripts are kept for each student.

Enrollment Requirements Program is open to non-resident foreign students.

Program Costs $2065 for the program, $295 per course.

Housing and Student Services Housing is not available. Job counseling and placement services are not available.

Special Features The Chemical Dependency Certificate programs combine two proven educational approaches: the didactic method, which provides solid grounding in theory and knowledge, and the experiential approach, which develops the actual counseling skills necessary to treat chemically dependent individuals. The courses are offered in both English and Spanish and meet the needs of Miami's multilingual population.

Contact Dr. Melanie McKay, Assistant Dean, School of Continuing Studies, James L. Knight Center, 4th Floor, 400 SE 2nd Avenue, Miami, FL 33131. 305-372-0140.

TELECOMMUNICATIONS (09.08)
Certificate in Telecommunications

General Information Unit offering the program: Telecommunications Institute. Program content: Voice, data, service, operations, networks. Available on a non-credit basis. Endorsed by Telecommunications Advisory Board, Southeastern Telecommunications Association. Certificate signed by the Dean, School of Continuing Studies.

Program Format Daytime, evening classes offered. Program cycle: Continuous enrollment. Completion of program requires six courses.

Evaluation Student evaluation based on tests. Grading system: Letters or numbers. Transcripts are kept for each student.

Enrollment Requirements Program is open to non-resident foreign students.

Program Costs $2250 for the program, $375 per course.

Housing and Student Services Housing is not available. Job counseling and placement services are not available.

Special Features Developed by the School of Continuing Studies in conjunction with the Telecommunications Advisory Board, a group of South Florida professionals with extensive experience in the field. Program was recently recognized as "excellent" by Southeastern Telecommunications Association.

Contact Dr. Melanie McKay, Assistant Dean, School of Continuing Studies, James L. Knight Center, 4th Floor, 400 SE 2nd Avenue, Miami, FL 33131. 305-372-0140.

NUCEA MEMBER
UNIVERSITY OF SOUTH FLORIDA
Tampa, Florida 33620

GENERAL MARKETING (08.07)
Direct Marketing

General Information Unit offering the program: Division of Lifelong Learning. Available on a non-credit basis. Certificate signed by the Director, Lifelong Learning.

Program Format Evening classes offered. Instructional schedule: One evening per week. Program cycle: Continuous enrollment. Full program cycle lasts 2 semesters. Completion of program requires three courses.

Evaluation Student evaluation based on tests. Grading system: Pass/fail. Transcripts are kept for each student.

Enrollment Requirements Program is open to non-resident foreign students.

Program Costs $360 for the program.

Housing and Student Services Housing is not available. Job counseling and placement services are not available.

Contact Dr. Cheryl M. Burbano, Program Coordinator, LLL 012, Tampa, FL 33620. 813-974-2403.

GRAPHIC AND PRINTING COMMUNICATIONS (48.02)
Commercial Design Certificate Program

General Information Unit offering the program: Division of Lifelong Learning. Available on a non-credit basis. Certificate signed by the Director, Lifelong Learning.

Program Format Evening, weekend classes offered. Students may enroll three times per year. Full program cycle lasts 3 semesters. Completion of program requires six courses.

Evaluation Student evaluation based on portfolio review. Transcripts are kept for each student.

Enrollment Requirements Program is not open to non-resident foreign students. English language proficiency required.

Program Costs $840 for the program, $140 per course.

Housing and Student Services Housing is available. Job counseling and placement services are available.

Special Features Courses include Commercial Art I and II, Professional Illustration Techniques, Professional Cartooning, The Artists Goes to Market, Quick Sketch Techniques, Computer Graphics, Packaging Graphics, and selected special topics. Instructors include University faculty and commercial design professionals.

Contact Ms. Lee Leavengood, Director, Division of Lifelong Learning, LLL 012, Tampa, FL 33620. 813-974-2403.

LANDSCAPE ARCHITECTURE (04.06)
Landscape Design

General Information Unit offering the program: Division of Lifelong Learning. Program content: Plant identification, landscape design, ornamental horticulture, landscape construction. Available on a non-credit basis. Certificate signed by the Director, Lifelong Learning.

Program Format Evening classes offered. Instructional schedule: One evening per week. Program cycle: Continuous enrollment. Full program cycle lasts 2 semesters. Completion of program requires four courses.

Evaluation Student evaluation based on tests. Grading system: Pass/fail. Transcripts are kept for each student.

Enrollment Requirements Program is open to non-resident foreign students.

Program Costs $695 for the program.

Housing and Student Services Housing is not available. Job counseling and placement services are not available.

Special Features Optional laboratory sessions are also available.

Contact Dr. Cheryl M. Burbano, Program Coordinator, LLL 012, Tampa, FL 33620. 813-974-2403.

LEISURE AND RECREATIONAL ACTIVITIES (36.01)
Travel and Tourism

General Information Unit offering the program: Division of Lifelong Learning. Available on a non-credit basis. Certificate signed by the Director, Lifelong Learning.

Program Format Evening classes offered. Instructional schedule: One evening per week. Program cycle: Continuous enrollment. Full program cycle lasts 1 semester. Completion of program requires three courses.

Evaluation Student evaluation based on tests. Grading system: Pass/fail. Transcripts are kept for each student.

Enrollment Requirements Program is open to non-resident foreign students.

Program Costs $425 for the program.

Housing and Student Services Housing is not available. Job counseling and placement services are not available.

Contact Dr. Cheryl M. Burbano, Program Coordinator, LLL 012, Tampa, FL 33620. 813-974-2403.

PRECISION WORK, ASSORTED MATERIALS (48.06)
Gemology

General Information Unit offering the program: Division of Lifelong Learning. Program content: Diamond identification, jewelry history, gemstones and metals, pearls and corals. Available on a non-credit basis. Certificate signed by the Director, Lifelong Learning.

Program Format Evening classes offered. Instructional schedule: One evening per week. Program cycle: Continuous enrollment. Full program cycle lasts 2 semesters. Completion of program requires four courses.

Evaluation Student evaluation based on tests, reports. Grading system: Pass/fail. Transcripts are kept for each student.

Enrollment Requirements Program is open to non-resident foreign students.

Program Costs $695 for the program.

Housing and Student Services Housing is not available. Job counseling and placement services are not available.

Contact Dr. Cheryl M. Burbano, Program Coordinator, LLL 012, Tampa, FL 33620. 813-974-2403.

TECHNICAL AND BUSINESS WRITING (23.11)
Writing and Communication Certificate Program

General Information Unit offering the program: Division of Lifelong Learning. Available on a non-credit basis. Certificate signed by the Director, Lifelong Learning.

Program Format Evening classes offered. Students may enroll three times per year. Completion of program requires six courses.

Evaluation Student evaluation based on reports. Transcripts are kept for each student.

Enrollment Requirements Program is open to non-resident foreign students.

Program Costs $85 per course.

Housing and Student Services Housing is not available. Job counseling and placement services are not available.

Contact Ms. Lagretta Lenkur, Program Coordinator, LLL 012, Tampa, FL 33620. 813-974-2403.

URBAN STUDIES (45.12)
Graduate Certificate in Public Management

General Information Unit offering the program: Public Administration Department. Program content: Urban management, city planning, public budgeting, policy analysis, program evaluation, intergovernmental relations. Available for credit. Certificate signed by the Dean, College of Social and Behavioral Sciences. Certificate applicable to M.P.A.

Program Format Evening classes offered. Instructional schedule: One class per week. Program cycle: Continuous enrollment. Full program cycle lasts 1 year. Completion of program requires 18 credit hours.

Evaluation Student evaluation based on tests, papers, reports. Grading system: Letters or numbers. Transcripts are kept for each student.

Enrollment Requirements Bachelor's degree, assessment of career history required. Program is open to non-resident foreign students. English language proficiency required. Minimum TOEFL score required: 550.

Program Costs $169 per course (state residents); $510 per course (nonresidents).

Contact Director, Public Administration Program, SOC 107, 4203 East Fowler Avenue, Tampa, FL 33620. 813-974-3496.

GEORGIA

NUCEA MEMBER
COLUMBUS COLLEGE
Columbus, Georgia 31993

LAW (22.01)
Paralegal Training Program

General Information   Unit offering the program: Division of Continuing Education. Program content: Legal skills, legal research, family law, wills and estates, litigation. Available on a non-credit basis. Certificate signed by the College President.

Program Format   Evening classes offered. Instructional schedule: One evening per week. Program cycle: Continuous enrollment. Complete program cycle lasts 15–18 months. Completion of program requires 160 contact hours.

Evaluation   Student evaluation based on papers, assignments. Grading system: Pass/fail. Transcripts are kept for each student.

Enrollment Requirements   Program is open to non-resident foreign students.

Program Costs $80 per course.

Housing and Student Services   Housing is not available. Job counseling and placement services are not available.

Special Features   The program consists of thirteen courses of which students must complete and pass ten in order to receive a certificate of completion and continuing education credit. The courses are taught by lawyers in the community who specialize in the particular subject matter being offered. Two paralegal programs (or courses) are offered each quarter.

Contact   Ms. Darlene Oakley, Program Coordinator, Division of Continuing Education, Columbus, GA 31993-2399. 404-568-2023.

NUCEA MEMBER
GEORGIA INSTITUTE OF TECHNOLOGY
Atlanta, Georgia 30332

ENGLISH AS A SECOND LANGUAGE (23.12)
Completion of English Study (Levels 1–6)

General Information   Unit offering the program: Education Extension. Program content: English for non-native speakers. Available on a non-credit basis. Certificate signed by the President.

Program Format   Daytime classes offered. Instructional schedule: Four hours per day, five days per week. Program cycle: Continuous enrollment. Complete program cycle lasts one quarter per level. Completion of program requires class work, labs, conferences.

Evaluation   Student evaluation based on tests, papers, reports. Grading system: Letters or numbers. Transcripts are kept for each student.

Enrollment Requirements   Two years high school English required. Program is open to non-resident foreign students.

Program Costs $950 per quarter.

Housing and Student Services   Housing is available. Job counseling and placement services are available.

Special Features   Since 1958, participants have included foreign students and business and professional people from all over the world. Grammar, reading, writing, pronunciation, and English for specific purposes are studied. Upon completion of the program, a certificate is awarded.

Contact   Mr. Charles Windish, Acting Director, The Language Institute, Education Extension, Atlanta, GA 30332. 404-894-2425.

ENVIRONMENTAL HEALTH ENGINEERING (14.14)
Supervision of Asbestos Abatement Contracts

General Information   Unit offering the program: Education Extension. Program content: How to remove asbestos. Available on a non-credit basis. Endorsed by Environmental Protection Agency (EPA). Certificate signed by the President. Program fulfills requirements for Asbestos Removal for Contractors.

Program Format   Daytime classes offered. Instructional schedule: Two to five days per week. Program cycle: Continuous enrollment. Full program cycle lasts 2 weeks.

Evaluation   Student evaluation based on tests. Grading system: Letters or numbers. Transcripts are kept for each student.

Enrollment Requirements   Program is open to non-resident foreign students.

Program Costs $1020 for the program.

Housing and Student Services   Housing is not available. Job counseling and placement services are not available.

Special Features   Georgia Institute of Technology was the first educational institution sanctioned by the U.S. Environmental Protection Agency (EPA) to offer program to fulfill licensure requirement.

Contact   Dr. Clifford R. Bragdon, Director, Education Extension, Atlanta, GA 30332-0385. 404-894-2402.

NUCEA MEMBER
UNIVERSITY OF GEORGIA
Athens, Georgia 30602

BANKING AND FINANCE (06.03)
Certified Finance Officer

General Information   Unit offering the program: Governmental Training Division. Program content: Financial management. Available on a non-credit basis. Cosponsored by Georgia Municipal Association, Association of County Commissioners of Georgia. Certificate signed by the Director.

Program Format   Daytime classes offered. Instructional schedule: Once per week. Program cycle: Continuous enrollment.

Evaluation   Student evaluation based on tests, case study. Grading system: Pass/fail. Transcripts are kept for each student.

Enrollment Requirements   Program is open to non-resident foreign students.

Program Costs $10 per course.

Housing and Student Services   Housing is not available. Job counseling and placement services are not available.

Special Features   Courses conducted at locations throughout the state. There are currently 270 certified finance officers in Georgia. Six core courses (budget preparation and control, introductory accounting, capital improvements programming, debt administration, purchasing, and payroll administration) and either an exam or a case study at the end of each course are required for certification.

Contact   Mr. Paul Glick, Financial Management Association, 1260 South Lumpkin Street, Athens, GA 30602. 404-542-1450.

CHILD CARE AND GUIDANCE MANAGEMENT AND SERVICES (20.02)
Certified Child Caregiver

General Information   Unit offering the program: Program Development/Home Economics Public Service Unit. Available on a non-credit basis. Endorsed by Georgia Department of

Certified Child Caregiver continued

Human Resources–Child Care Licensing Section. Certificate signed by the Director, Georgia Center for Continuing Education. Program fulfills requirements for Georgia Child Care Worker.

Program Format Daytime, evening, weekend, correspondence classes offered. Program cycle: Continuous enrollment. Completion of program requires 100 classroom hours.

Evaluation Student evaluation based on papers, laboratory work. Grading system: Pass/fail. Record of CEUs kept for each student.

Enrollment Requirements Minimum age of 17, literacy required. Program is open to non-resident foreign students.

Housing and Student Services Housing is available. Job counseling and placement services are not available.

Special Features Program requires care-givers to work directly with children, under supervision, throughout the training. Student may take this certificate as an independent study with some group work or as a class offering. Contact with professional organizations and other child-care training programs is part of the certificate requirements.

Contact Mr. Scott Lane, Program Development Specialist: Child Development, Room 231, Georgia Center for Continuing Education, Athens, GA 30602. 404-542-2100.

CITY, COMMUNITY, AND REGIONAL PLANNING (04.03)
Historic Preservation Studies

General Information Unit offering the program: School of Environmental Design. Program content: Theory, practices, criteria, law, planning, architectural history. Available for credit. Certificate signed by the Dean, School of Environmental Design.

Program Format Daytime classes offered. Instructional schedule: Two or three classes per week. Program cycle: Continuous enrollment. Full program cycle lasts 6 courses. Completion of program requires 3.0 GPA, 30 credit hours.

Evaluation Student evaluation based on tests, papers, reports. Grading system: Letters or numbers. Transcripts are kept for each student.

Enrollment Requirements Bachelor's degree required. Program is not open to non-resident foreign students. English language proficiency required. Minimum TOEFL score required: 550.

Program Costs $1818 for the program, $303 per course (state residents); $4248 for the program, $708 per course (nonresidents).

Housing and Student Services Housing is available. Job counseling and placement services are available.

Special Features The certificate program is drawn from the Master of Historic Preservation curriculum, and students share classes with MHP majors. The certificate program can serve as a minor for majors in other areas and will prepare individuals for service in preservation organizations or agencies or leadership in community preservation efforts.

Contact Mr. John C. Waters, Coordinator, Graduate Studies in Historic Preservation, Calwell Hall, School of Environmental Design, Athens, GA 30602. 404-542-4706.

FOOD PRODUCTION, MANAGEMENT, AND SERVICES (20.04)
Dietary Manager Independent Study Course

General Information Unit offering the program: Home Economics and Personal Adult Learning Services, Public Service Unit. Program content: Nutrition, food production and service, human relations, food service management. Available on a non-credit basis. Endorsed by Dietary Managers Association. Certificate signed by the Director, Georgia Center for Continuing Education. Program fulfills requirements for Dietary Managers Association.

Program Format Correspondence classes offered. Program cycle: Continuous enrollment. Full program cycle lasts 12 months.

Evaluation Student evaluation based on tests, assignments. Grading system: Pass/fail. Record of CEUs kept for each student.

Enrollment Requirements High school diploma or GED, endorsement of a food service administrator and laboratory preceptor required. Program is not open to non-resident foreign students.

Program Costs $165 for the program.

Housing and Student Services Housing is not available. Job counseling and placement services are not available.

Special Features Dietary Manager Independent Study Course was developed to provide instructional program for individuals desiring to work in institutional food service manangement. Reading assignments and practical exercise monitored by a preceptor are designed to promote development of skills needed in food service management positions.

Contact Ms. Trudy Cain, Program Specialist in Home Economics, Georgia Center for Continuing Education, Athens, GA 30602. 404-542-2069.

HEALTH SERVICES ADMINISTRATION (18.07)
Patient Relations Specialist Certificate Program

General Information Unit offering the program: Program Development. Program content: Interpersonal skills for health-care workers. Available on a non-credit basis. Certificate signed by the Director.

Program Format Daytime, evening, weekend, correspondence, video teleconference (with two-way audio) classes offered. Instructional schedule: Self-study with two 3-day workshop sessions. Program cycle: Continuous enrollment. Full program cycle lasts 6 months.

Evaluation Student evaluation based on project completion, behavioral assessment. Transcripts are kept for each student.

Enrollment Requirements Limited to health-care employees. Program is open to non-resident foreign students. English language proficiency required.

Housing and Student Services Housing is available. Job counseling and placement services are not available.

Special Features Highly emotionally charged situations are inherent in health-care institutions. This certificate program is designed to teach advanced interpersonal skills that will allow health-care personnel to deal confidently with most interactions that occur. Scheduling is flexible and program is modularized for convenience of working persons.

Contact Mr. William C. Childers, Ph.D., Senior Public Service Associate, Georgia Center for Continuing Education, Athens, GA 30602. 404-542-4766.

HUMANITIES AND SOCIAL SCIENCES (30.04)
Certificate in Environmental Ethics

General Information Unit offering the program: Interdepartmental. Program content: Philosophy, ecology, law, geography, art, zoology, forestry. Available for credit. Certificate signed by the President of the University.

Program Format Daytime classes offered. Program cycle: Continuous enrollment. Full program cycle lasts 3 quarters. Completion of program requires 30 credit hours.

Evaluation Student evaluation based on tests, papers, internship. Grading system: Letters or numbers. Transcripts are kept for each student.

Enrollment Requirements Master's degree required. Program is open to non-resident foreign students. English language proficiency required. Minimum TOEFL score required: 550.

Program Costs $590 per semester (state residents); $1563 per semester (nonresidents).

Housing and Student Services Housing is available. Job counseling and placement services are available.

Special Features Thirty-member faculty of Environmental Ethics is drawn from twenty different departments, schools, and programs of the University. These faculty members are prepared to teach certificate candidates in a large variety of elective courses, depending on other graduate interests. Regular evening seminars, guest speakers, other activities.

Contact Mr. Frederick Ferré, Department Head, Philosophy, Athens, GA 30602. 404-542-2823.

INDIVIDUAL AND FAMILY DEVELOPMENT (19.07)
Certificate in Basic Gerontology

General Information Unit offering the program: Gerontology Program, Georgia Center for Continuing Education. Program content: Biology, sociology, and psychology of aging. Available on a non-credit basis. Certificate signed by the Director, Georgia Center for Continuing Education.

Program Format Correspondence classes offered. Program cycle: Continuous enrollment. Full program cycle lasts 3 quarters.

Evaluation Student evaluation based on tests, papers. Grading system: Pass/fail. Transcripts are kept for each student.

Enrollment Requirements Program is open to non-resident foreign students. English language proficiency required. Minimum TOEFL score required: 520.

Housing and Student Services Job counseling and placement services are not available.

Special Features New program for personnel of network on aging.

Contact Ms. Marietta P. Suhart, Program Specialist in Gerontology, Georgia Center for Continuing Education, Athens, GA 30602. 404-542-1272.

INDIVIDUAL AND FAMILY DEVELOPMENT (19.07)
Graduate Certificate of Gerontology

General Information Unit offering the program: Gerontology Center. Program content: Nutrition, housing, psychology, recreation, sociology, physiology. Available for credit. Certificate signed by the Director, Gerontology Center.

Program Format Daytime, evening classes offered. Program cycle: Continuous enrollment. Completion of program requires 30 credit hours, thesis or practicum.

Evaluation Student evaluation based on tests, papers. Transcripts are kept for each student.

Enrollment Requirements Bachelor's degree required. Program is open to non-resident foreign students. English language proficiency required.

Program Costs $590 per semester (state residents); $1563 per semester (nonresidents).

Housing and Student Services Housing is available. Job counseling and placement services are available.

Special Features Designed to provide interdisciplinary training in field of aging and to complement rather than supplant master's- or doctoral-level work within a specific discipline including psychology, adult education, social work, child and family development, pharmacy, and recreation and leisure. Students must take a gerontology seminar and complete a practicum or thesis in gerontology. They must also take additional courses with aging content from two or more disciplines.

Contact Dr. Denise Park, Associate Director, Gerontology Center, Athens, GA 30602. 404-542-3954.

MENTAL HEALTH/HUMAN SERVICES (17.04)
Pre-Professional Certificate in Marriage and Family Therapy

General Information Unit offering the program: School of Social Work, College of Home Economics, College of Education. Program content: Historical, ethical, and legal issues. Available for credit. Certificate signed by the President of the University. Certificate applicable to M.S.W. Program fulfills requirements for Marriage and Family Therapy licensure.

Program Format Daytime, evening classes offered. Instructional schedule: Once or twice per week. Program cycle: Continuous enrollment. Full program cycle lasts 40 credit hours. Completion of program requires 3.0 GPA.

Evaluation Student evaluation based on tests, papers, reports. Grading system: Letters or numbers. Transcripts are kept for each student.

Enrollment Requirements Master's degree in related field required. Program is not open to non-resident foreign students. English language proficiency required.

Program Costs $554 per quarter.

Housing and Student Services Housing is available. Job counseling and placement services are available.

Special Features The interdisciplinary feature of the program adds to the depth and breadth of the educational experience for students. Academic requirements for licensure in the state are met by the program although additional experience and supervision are needed. Most instructors are on the graduate faculty with diversified areas of expertise.

Contact Ms. Allie C. Kilpatrick, Associate Professor, School of Social Work, Athens, GA 30602. 404-542-5455.

PUBLIC AFFAIRS, GENERAL (44.01)
Certified Municipal Clerk for State of Georgia

General Information Unit offering the program: Governmental Training Division. Program content: Public administration, social and interpersonal concerns. Available on a non-credit basis. Certificate signed by the Director, Carl Vinson Institute of Government. Program fulfills requirements for Certified Municipal Clerk.

Program Format Daytime classes offered. Instructional schedule: Two- to three-day courses. Students may enroll in February, September. Completion of program requires 100 classroom hours, comprehensive written examination.

Evaluation Student evaluation based on tests. Grading system: Pass/fail. Computer transcript kept for each student.

Enrollment Requirements Limited to members of the Georgia Municipal Clerks and Finance Officers Association. Program is open to non-resident foreign students.

Program Costs $115 per course.

Housing and Student Services Housing is available. Job counseling and placement services are not available.

Contact Dr. Joan Curtis, Head, Management Development Program, Georgia Center for Continuing Education, Athens, GA 30602. 404-542-1450.

NUCEA MEMBER
WEST GEORGIA COLLEGE
Carrollton, Georgia 30118

ORGANIZATIONAL BEHAVIOR (06.15)
Basic Leadership Skills Certificate Program

General Information Unit offering the program: Division of Continuing Education/Public Services, School of Business. Program content: Management, motivation, communication. Available on a non-credit basis. Certificate signed by the Dean, School of Business.

Basic Leadership Skills Certificate Program continued

Program Format   Daytime, evening classes offered. Instructional schedule: Once per week for three hours. Program cycle: Continuous enrollment. Full program cycle lasts 15 weeks. Completion of program requires 45 contact hours.

Evaluation   Student evaluation based on tests, class participation on projects. Grading system: Pass/fail. Transcripts are kept for each student.

Enrollment Requirements   Program is open to non-resident foreign students.

Program Costs $330 for the program.

Housing and Student Services   Housing is not available. Job counseling and placement services are not available.

Special Features   Program uses only instructors who are competent in area of expertise, able to communicate subject matter to all types of individuals, and have worked in industry/business sector as worker or consultant.

Contact   Mr. Tom Johnson, Assistant Director, Division of Continuing Education/Public Services, Carrollton, GA 30118. 404-836-6610.

HAWAII

HAWAII PACIFIC COLLEGE
Honolulu, Hawaii 96813

COMPUTER AND INFORMATION SCIENCES, GENERAL (11.01)
Certificate in Computer Science

General Information   Unit offering the program: Special Programs Department. Available for credit. Certificate signed by the President of the College. Certificate applicable to A.S. in Data Processing Technology, B.S. in Computer Science.

Program Format   Daytime, evening, weekend classes offered. Program cycle: Continuous enrollment. Full program cycle lasts 30 credit hours. Completion of program requires ten courses.

Evaluation   Student evaluation based on tests, papers, reports. Grading system: Letters or numbers. Transcripts are kept for each student.

Enrollment Requirements   Program is open to non-resident foreign students.

Program Costs $213 per course.

Housing and Student Services   Housing is available. Job counseling and placement services are available.

Special Features   The certificate program is primarily offered to off-campus students on military bases. The certificate is awarded in computer science for successful completion of ten specific classes, ranging from introductory computer work to advanced hardware technology.

Contact   Dr. Helen G. Chapin, Associate Vice President and Dean for Special Programs, 1166 Fort Street, Honolulu, HI 96813. 808-544-0215.

SYSTEMS ANALYSIS (11.05)
Certificate in Systems Analysis

General Information   Unit offering the program: Special Programs Department. Available for credit. Certificate signed by the President of the College. Certificate applicable to A.S. in Data Processing Technology, B.S. in Computer Science.

Program Format   Daytime, evening, weekend classes offered. Program cycle: Continuous enrollment. Full program cycle lasts 9 credit hours. Completion of program requires three courses.

Evaluation   Student evaluation based on tests, papers, reports. Grading system: Letters or numbers. Transcripts are kept for each student.

Enrollment Requirements   Program is open to non-resident foreign students.

Program Costs $213 per course.

Housing and Student Services   Housing is available. Job counseling and placement services are available.

Special Features   The certificate program is primarily offered to off-campus students on military bases. The certificate is awarded in computer science for successful completion of three specific advanced courses in systems analysis.

Contact   Dr. Helen G. Chapin, Associate Vice President and Dean for Special Programs, 1166 Fort Street, Honolulu, HI 96813. 808-544-0215.

NUCEA MEMBER
UNIVERSITY OF HAWAII AT MANOA
Honolulu, Hawaii 96822

PUBLIC ADMINISTRATION (44.04)
Certificate in Public Administration

General Information   Unit offering the program: College of Continuing Education and Community Service, Department of Political Science. Program content: Government-private sector relations; economic, policy, and organizational processes. Available for credit. Certificate signed by the University President.

Program Format   Evening, weekend classes offered. Instructional schedule: Tuesday and Thursday 6–9 p.m.; Saturday 8 a.m. to 12 noon. Program cycle: Continuous enrollment. Full program cycle lasts 12 months. Completion of program requires 15 credit hours, practicum.

Evaluation   Student evaluation based on tests, papers, reports. Grading system: Letters or numbers, pass/fail. Transcripts are kept for each student.

Enrollment Requirements   Bachelor's degree, statement of career goals, personal interview required. Program is not open to non-resident foreign students. English language proficiency required. Minimum TOEFL score required: 600.

Program Costs $675 for the program, $135 per course.

Housing and Student Services   Housing is available. Job counseling and placement services are not available.

Special Features   Participants move through a common curriculum over two semesters and one summer. Students create relationships expected to last after the program has ended. Twelve credits of course work and 3 credits in a capstone seminar with a practicum. On occasion, special weekend sessions bring in speakers to focus on a specific topic.

Contact   Mr. Richard Pratt, Program Director, Political Science Department, Porteus Hall, Room 631B, Honolulu, HI 96822. 808-948-8620.

ILLINOIS

COLLEGE OF ST. FRANCIS
Joliet, Illinois 60435

COMPUTER AND INFORMATION SCIENCES, GENERAL (11.01)
Computer Science Certificate

General Information   Unit offering the program: Computer Science. Program content: Advanced microcomputers, data structures, theory of programming languages, assembler. Available for credit. Certificate signed by the President. Certificate applicable to B.S. in Computer Science.

Program Format Daytime, evening classes offered. Program cycle: Continuous enrollment. Full program cycle lasts 6 semesters.

Evaluation Student evaluation based on tests, programs. Grading system: Letters or numbers. Transcripts are kept for each student.

Enrollment Requirements Competency in algebra and programming language required. English language proficiency required.

Program Costs $2550 for the program, $510 per course.

Housing and Student Services Housing is not available. Job counseling and placement services are available.

Special Features Credit will be given for prior experience. Program content is flexible to meet individual needs.

Contact Ms. Sheryl Paul, Transfer Coordinator, 500 Wilcox, Joliet, IL 60435. 815-740-3400.

COMPUTER AND INFORMATION SCIENCES, GENERAL (11.01)
Computer Science Certificate

General Information Unit offering the program: Computer Science. Program content: Management information system design, operating systems, software engineering, database management. Available for credit. Certificate signed by the President. Certificate applicable to B.S. in Computer Science.

Program Format Daytime, evening classes offered. Program cycle: Continuous enrollment. Full program cycle lasts 6 semesters.

Evaluation Student evaluation based on tests, programs. Grading system: Letters or numbers. Transcripts are kept for each student.

Enrollment Requirements Competency in algebra and programming language required. English language proficiency required.

Program Costs $2550 for the program, $510 per course.

Housing and Student Services Housing is not available. Job counseling and placement services are available.

Special Features Credit will be given for prior experience. Program content is flexible to meet individual needs.

Contact Ms. Sheryl Paul, Transfer Coordinator, 500 Wilcox, Joliet, IL 60435. 815-740-3400.

MENTAL HEALTH/HUMAN SERVICES (17.04)
Chemical Dependency

General Information Unit offering the program: Psychology. Program content: Psychology, chemical dependency, group dynamics, family therapy, counseling. Available for credit. Certificate signed by the President. Certificate applicable to B.A. in Psychology.

Program Format Daytime, evening classes offered. Program cycle: Continuous enrollment. Complete program cycle lasts four to five semesters. Completion of program requires practicum, grade of C or better in each course.

Evaluation Student evaluation based on tests, papers, reports. Grading system: Letters or numbers. Transcripts are kept for each student.

Enrollment Requirements High school diploma or equivalent required.

Program Costs $4250 for the program, $510 per course.

Housing and Student Services Housing is available. Job counseling and placement services are available.

Contact Ms. Sheryl Paul, Transfer Coordinator, 500 Wilcox, Joliet, IL 60435. 815-740-3400.

NUCEA MEMBER
ELMHURST COLLEGE
Elmhurst, Illinois 60126

BUSINESS ADMINISTRATION AND MANAGEMENT (06.04)
Elmhurst Management Program

General Information Unit offering the program: Center for Business and Economics, Evening Session. Available for credit. Certificate signed by the Director, Evening Session and Continuing Education. Certificate applicable to B.S. in Business Administration.

Program Format Evening, weekend classes offered. Instructional schedule: One evening per week or Saturday morning. Students may enroll September, January, March, May. Full program cycle lasts 46 weeks. Completion of program requires presentations, homework assignments, grade of C or better.

Evaluation Student evaluation based on tests, papers, reports, class participation. Grading system: Letters or numbers. Transcripts are kept for each student.

Enrollment Requirements Forty-eight semester hours; course work in economics, accounting, math; business experience required. Program is not open to non-resident foreign students.

Program Costs $5920 for the program.

Housing and Student Services Housing is not available. Job counseling and placement services are available.

Special Features Seminar/workshop; professional business faculty; experiential learning; CLEP option; course material work-related and applicable to on-the-job responsibilities.

Contact Ms. Cynthia Crissman, Recruitment Coordinator, Elmhurst Management Program, 190 Prospect, Elmhurst, IL 60126. 312-617-3030.

HARRINGTON INSTITUTE OF INTERIOR DESIGN
Chicago, Illinois 60605

INTERIOR DESIGN (04.05)
Professional Diploma of Interior Design

General Information Unit offering the program: Evening Division. Program content: Interior design, space planning, drafting, rendering. Available for credit. Certificate signed by the Dean. Certificate applicable to A.A.S. in Interior Design.

Program Format Evening classes offered. Instructional schedule: Twice per week for three hours. Program cycle: Continuous enrollment. Full program cycle lasts 3 years. Completion of program requires 2.0 GPA.

Evaluation Student evaluation based on tests, projects, portfolio. Grading system: Letters or numbers. Transcripts are kept for each student.

Enrollment Requirements High school diploma, interview required. Program is open to non-resident foreign students. English language proficiency required. Minimum TOEFL score required: 500, also written essay.

Program Costs $1392 per semester.

Housing and Student Services Housing is not available. Job counseling and placement services are available.

Special Features All instructors are professionals (i.e., architects, designers, etc.) Program teaches all the skills to those who wish to be professional designers.

Contact Office of Admissions, 410 South Michigan Avenue, Chicago, IL 60605. 312-939-4975.

ILLINOIS BENEDICTINE COLLEGE
Lisle, Illinois 60532

BUSINESS AND MANAGEMENT, GENERAL (06.01)
Certificate of Management

General Information Unit offering the program: Institute for Management. Program content: Written communication, psychology, ethics in business policy, marketing, group process, decision making. Available for credit. Certificate signed by the Chairman, Board of Trustees. Certificate applicable to any four-year degree offered at the institution.

Program Format Evening classes offered. Instructional schedule: One evening per week. Program cycle: Continuous enrollment. Full program cycle lasts 12 courses.

Evaluation Student evaluation based on tests, papers, reports, case studies. Grading system: Letters or numbers. Transcripts are kept for each student.

Enrollment Requirements Program is open to non-resident foreign students. English language proficiency required. Minimum TOEFL score required: 550.

Program Costs $510 per course.

Housing and Student Services Housing is not available. Job counseling and placement services are available.

Special Features The Institute was founded in 1964 to give men and women with middle and senior management abilities an opportunity to broaden their background and achieve their real potential. The Institute's faculty of business executives with formal graduate education is dedicated to the development of others, and by 1987 over 1,000 men and women had successfully completed the program.

Contact Mr. Donald L. Juday, Director, Institute for Management, Lisle, IL 60532. 312-960-1500 Ext. 320.

HEALTH SERVICES ADMINISTRATION (18.07)
Health Service Administration Certificate

General Information Unit offering the program: Department of Management and Organizational Behavior. Program content: Managerial capacity instruction for health care areas. Available for credit. Certificate signed by the President. Certificate applicable to M.S. in Management and Organizational Behavior.

Program Format Weekend classes offered. Instructional schedule: Three hours Friday evening, all day Saturday and Sunday. Program cycle: Continuous enrollment. Complete program cycle lasts three months to one year. Completion of program requires 12 credit hours.

Evaluation Student evaluation based on papers. Grading system: Letters or numbers. Transcripts are kept for each student.

Enrollment Requirements Program is open to non-resident foreign students.

Program Costs $155 per credit hour.

Housing and Student Services Housing is not available. Job counseling and placement services are available.

Contact Dr. Peter F. Sorensen Jr., Department of Management and Organizational Behavior, 5700 College Road-BEN 211, Lisle, IL 60532. 312-960-1500 Ext. 491.

MANAGEMENT SCIENCE (06.13)
Human Service Adminstration Certificate

General Information Unit offering the program: Department of Management and Organizational Behavior. Program content: Administration for not-for-profit organizations and community service. Available for credit. Certificate signed by the President. Certificate applicable to M.S. in Management and Organizational Behavior.

Program Format Weekend classes offered. Instructional schedule: Three hours Friday evening, all day Saturday and Sunday. Program cycle: Continuous enrollment. Complete program cycle lasts three months to one year. Completion of program requires 12 credit hours.

Evaluation Student evaluation based on papers. Grading system: Letters or numbers. Transcripts are kept for each student.

Enrollment Requirements Program is open to non-resident foreign students.

Program Costs $155 per credit hour.

Housing and Student Services Housing is not available. Job counseling and placement services are available.

Contact Dr. Peter F. Sorensen Jr., Department of Management and Organizational Behavior, 5700 College Road-BEN 211, Lisle, IL 60532. 312-960-1500 Ext. 491.

MANAGEMENT SCIENCE (06.13)
Management/Organizational Behavior Certificate

General Information Unit offering the program: Department of Management and Organizational Behavior. Program content: Contemporary topics in management. Available for credit. Certificate signed by the President. Certificate applicable to M.S. in Management and Organizational Behavior.

Program Format Weekend classes offered. Instructional schedule: Three hours Friday evening, all day Saturday and Sunday. Program cycle: Continuous enrollment. Complete program cycle lasts three months to one year. Completion of program requires 12 credit hours.

Evaluation Student evaluation based on papers. Grading system: Letters or numbers. Transcripts are kept for each student.

Enrollment Requirements Program is open to non-resident foreign students.

Program Costs $155 per credit hour.

Housing and Student Services Housing is not available. Job counseling and placement services are available.

Contact Dr. Peter F. Sorensen Jr., Department of Management and Organizational Behavior, 5700 College Road-BEN 211, Lisle, IL 60532. 312-960-1500 Ext. 491.

ORGANIZATIONAL BEHAVIOR (06.15)
Organizational Development Certificate

General Information Unit offering the program: Department of Management and Organizational Behavior. Program content: Organizational and management improvement skills. Available for credit. Certificate signed by the President. Certificate applicable to M.S. in Management and Organizational Behavior.

Program Format Weekend classes offered. Instructional schedule: Three hours Friday evening, all day Saturday and Sunday. Program cycle: Continuous enrollment. Complete program cycle lasts three months to one year. Completion of program requires 12 credit hours.

Evaluation Student evaluation based on papers. Grading system: Letters or numbers. Transcripts are kept for each student.

Enrollment Requirements Program is open to non-resident foreign students.

Program Costs $155 per credit hour.

Housing and Student Services Housing is not available. Job counseling and placement services are available.

Contact Dr. Peter F. Sorensen Jr., Department of Management and Organizational Behavior, 5700 College Road - BEN 211, Lisle, IL 60532. 312-960-1500 Ext. 491.

PERSONNEL MANAGEMENT (06.16)
Human Resource Management Certificate

General Information Unit offering the program: Department of Management and Organizational Behavior. Program content: Personnel professionalism. Available for credit. Certificate signed by the President. Certificate applicable to M.S. in Management and Organizational Behavior.

Program Format Weekend classes offered. Instructional schedule: Three hours Friday evening, all day Saturday and Sunday. Program cycle: Continuous enrollment. Complete program cycle lasts three months to one year. Completion of program requires 12 credit hours.

Evaluation Student evaluation based on papers. Grading system: Letters or numbers. Transcripts are kept for each student.

Enrollment Requirements Program is open to non-resident foreign students.

Program Costs $155 per credit hour.

Housing and Student Services Housing is not available. Job counseling and placement services are available.

Contact Dr. Peter F. Sorensen Jr., Department of Management and Organizational Behavior, 5700 College Road-BEN 211, Lisle, IL 60532. 312-960-1500 Ext. 491.

NUCEA MEMBER
LOYOLA UNIVERSITY OF CHICAGO
Chicago, Illinois 60611

COMPUTER PROGRAMMING (11.02)
Certificate in Computer Science

General Information Unit offering the program: University College, Department of Mathematical Sciences. Program content: Pascal, assembly, and other languages. Available for credit. Certificate signed by the Dean, University College.

Program Format Daytime, evening classes offered. Program cycle: Continuous enrollment. Full program cycle lasts 15 credit hours. Completion of program requires grade of C or better in all courses.

Evaluation Student evaluation based on tests, papers, reports. Grading system: Letters or numbers. Transcripts are kept for each student.

Enrollment Requirements University admissions required. Program is open to non-resident foreign students.

Program Costs $450 per course.

Housing and Student Services Housing is not available. Job counseling and placement services are available.

Contact Mr. Mark E. Wolff, Assistant Dean, University College, 820 North Michigan Avenue, Chicago, IL 60611. 312-670-3016.

RELIGION (38.02)
Certificate in Theology

General Information Unit offering the program: University College, Department of Theology. Program content: Old Testament, New Testament, moral problem, Jesus Christ, church and sacrament. Available for credit. Certificate signed by the Dean, University College.

Program Format Daytime, evening classes offered. Program cycle: Continuous enrollment. Full program cycle lasts 15 credit hours. Completion of program requires grade of C or better in all courses.

Evaluation Student evaluation based on tests, papers, reports. Grading system: Letters or numbers. Transcripts are kept for each student.

Enrollment Requirements University admissions required. Program is open to non-resident foreign students.

Program Costs $450 per course.

Housing and Student Services Housing is not available. Job counseling and placement services are available.

Contact Mr. Mark E. Wolff, Assistant Dean, University College, 820 North Michigan Avenue, Chicago, IL 60611. 312-670-3016.

MUNDELEIN COLLEGE
Chicago, Illinois 60660

TELECOMMUNICATIONS (09.08)
Telecommunications Management

General Information Unit offering the program: Telecommunications. Program content: Telecommunication, business administration. Available for credit. Certificate signed by the President. Certificate applicable to B.S. in Telecommunications Management.

Program Format Weekend classes offered. Instructional schedule: Alternate weekends. Program cycle: Continuous enrollment. Full program cycle lasts 63 credit hours. Completion of program requires 2.0 GPA.

Evaluation Student evaluation based on tests, papers, reports. Grading system: Letters or numbers. Transcripts are kept for each student.

Enrollment Requirements High school diploma or 2.0 GPA in college credits required. Program is open to non-resident foreign students. English language proficiency required. Minimum TOEFL score required: 500.

Program Costs $639 per course.

Housing and Student Services Housing is available. Job counseling and placement services are available.

Special Features Credit for previous experience is determined by chair of the department after the student has completed 9 semester hours of work at Mundelein. Instructers are well-qualified with required degrees.

Contact Mr. James Waring, Director of Telecommunications Management Department, 6363 Sheridan Road, Chicago, IL 60660. 312-262-8100 Ext. 520.

NATIONAL COLLEGE OF EDUCATION
Evanston, Illinois 60201

BUSINESS DATA PROCESSING AND RELATED PROGRAMS (07.03)
Business Education for Career Advancement

General Information Unit offering the program: Business. Program content: Introduction to data processing and accounting. Available for credit. Certificate signed by the President of the College. Certificate applicable to B.A. in Business Administration, Computer Information Systems and Management, Accounting.

Program Format Daytime, evening, weekend classes offered. Program cycle: Continuous enrollment. Full program cycle lasts 4 quarters. Completion of program requires 49 credit hours, 2.0 GPA.

Evaluation Student evaluation based on tests, papers, reports. Grading system: Letters or numbers. Transcripts are kept for each student.

Enrollment Requirements High school diploma required. Program is open to non-resident foreign students.

Program Costs $122 per quarter hour.

Housing and Student Services Housing is not available. Job counseling and placement services are available.

Contact Ms. Laura Ashby, Associate Director of Admissions, 18 South Michigan Avenue, Chicago, IL 60603. 312-621-9650.

CURRICULUM AND INSTRUCTION (13.03)
Certificate of Advanced Study (Curriculum and Instruction)

General Information Unit offering the program: Division of Applied Behavioral Sciences. Available for credit. Certificate signed by the Registrar.

Program Format Evening classes offered. Program cycle: Continuous enrollment. Full program cycle lasts 30 credit hours. Completion of program requires 3.0 GPA.

Evaluation Student evaluation based on tests, papers, reports. Grading system: Letters or numbers. Transcripts are kept for each student.

Enrollment Requirements Master's degree required. Program is open to non-resident foreign students. English language proficiency required. Minimum TOEFL score required: 550.

Program Costs $185 per semester hour.

Housing and Student Services Housing is available. Job counseling and placement services are available.

Contact Ms. Margaret McClory, Director, Graduate Admissions, 2840 Sheridan Road, Evanston, IL 60201. 312-475-1100 Ext. 2477.

EDUCATION ADMINISTRATION (13.04)
Certificate of Advanced Study (Educational Leadership)

General Information Unit offering the program: Division of Applied Behavioral Sciences. Available for credit. Certificate signed by the Registrar.

Program Format Evening classes offered. Program cycle: Continuous enrollment. Full program cycle lasts 30 credit hours. Completion of program requires 3.0 GPA.

Evaluation Student evaluation based on tests, papers, reports. Grading system: Letters or numbers. Transcripts are kept for each student.

Enrollment Requirements Master's degree required. Program is open to non-resident foreign students. English language proficiency required. Minimum TOEFL score required: 550.

Program Costs $185 per semester hour.

Housing and Student Services Housing is available. Job counseling and placement services are available.

Contact Ms. Margaret McClory, Director, Graduate Admissions, 2840 Sheridan Road, Evanston, IL 60201. 312-475-1100 Ext. 2477.

INDIVIDUAL AND FAMILY DEVELOPMENT (19.07)
Gerontology Administration

General Information Unit offering the program: Division of Human Services. Program content: Health care, programs and policies, management of community programs, administration of volunteer programs. Available for credit. Certificate signed by the Program Advisor. Certificate applicable to B.S. in Human Services.

Program Format Evening classes offered. Program cycle: Continuous enrollment. Full program cycle lasts 4 quarters.

Evaluation Student evaluation based on tests, papers, reports. Grading system: Letters or numbers. Transcripts are kept for each student.

Enrollment Requirements College admissions required. Program is open to non-resident foreign students. English language proficiency required. Certification by college-based language institute required.

Program Costs $122 per semester hour.

Housing and Student Services Housing is available. Job counseling and placement services are available.

Contact Ms. Michela Jones, Assistant Director of Admissions, 2840 Sheridan Road, Evanston, IL 60201. 312-475-1100.

INDIVIDUAL AND FAMILY DEVELOPMENT (19.07)
Gerontology Counseling Studies

General Information Unit offering the program: Division of Human Services. Program content: Interpersonal communications, theory and techniques, health care, programs and policies, counseling processes. Available for credit. Certificate signed by the Program Advisor. Certificate applicable to B.S. in Human Services.

Program Format Evening classes offered. Program cycle: Continuous enrollment. Full program cycle lasts 4 quarters.

Evaluation Student evaluation based on tests, papers, reports. Grading system: Letters or numbers. Transcripts are kept for each student.

Enrollment Requirements College admissions required. Program is open to non-resident foreign students. English language proficiency required. Certification by college-based language institute required.

Program Costs $122 per semester hour.

Housing and Student Services Housing is available. Job counseling and placement services are available.

Contact Ms. Michela Jones, Assistant Director of Admissions, 2840 Sheridan Road, Evanston, IL 60201. 312-475-1100.

INDIVIDUAL AND FAMILY DEVELOPMENT (19.07)
Gerontology Generalist Studies

General Information Unit offering the program: Division of Human Services. Program content: Health care, programs and policies, families, counseling, management of community programs, administration of volunteer programs. Available for credit. Certificate signed by the Program Advisor.

Program Format Evening classes offered. Program cycle: Continuous enrollment. Full program cycle lasts 4 quarters.

Evaluation Student evaluation based on tests, papers, reports. Grading system: Letters or numbers. Transcripts are kept for each student.

Enrollment Requirements College admissions required. Program is open to non-resident foreign students. English language proficiency required. Certification by college-based language institute required.

Program Costs $122 per semester hour.

Housing and Student Services Housing is available. Job counseling and placement services are available.

Contact Ms. Michela Jones, Assistant Director of Admissions, 2840 Sheridan Road, Evanston, IL 60201. 312-475-1100.

MENTAL HEALTH/HUMAN SERVICES (17.04)
Addictions Administration

General Information Unit offering the program: Division of Human Services. Program content: History, sociology, and theories of addictions, administration of treatment and nonprofit organizations. Available for credit. Certificate signed by the Program Advisor. Certificate applicable to B.S. in Human Services.

Program Format Evening classes offered. Program cycle: Continuous enrollment. Full program cycle lasts 4 quarters.

Evaluation Student evaluation based on tests, papers, reports. Grading system: Letters or numbers. Transcripts are kept for each student.

Enrollment Requirements College admissions required. Program is open to non-resident foreign students. English language proficiency required. Certification by college-based language institute required.

Program Costs $122 per semester hour.

Housing and Student Services Housing is available. Job counseling and placement services are available.

Contact Ms. Michela Jones, Assistant Director of Admissions, 2840 Sheridan Road, Evanston, IL 60201. 312-475-1100.

MENTAL HEALTH/HUMAN SERVICES (17.04)
Addictions Counseling (Graduate)

General Information Unit offering the program: Division of Human Services. Program content: History and trends in addictions, theory and technique of counseling, clinical intervention, internships. Available for credit. Endorsed by Illinois Certification Board and Illinois Alcohol Counseling Certification Board. Certificate signed by the Program Advisor. Certificate applicable to M.S. in Human Services.

Program Format Evening classes offered. Program cycle: Continuous enrollment. Full program cycle lasts 4 quarters.

Evaluation Student evaluation based on tests, papers, reports. Grading system: Letters or numbers. Transcripts are kept for each student.

Enrollment Requirements Bachelor's degree required. Program is open to non-resident foreign students. English language proficiency required. Certification by college-based language institute required.

Program Costs $185 per semester hour.

Housing and Student Services Housing is available. Job counseling and placement services are available.

Contact Ms. Michela Jones, Assistant Director of Admissions, 2840 Sheridan Road, Evanston, IL 60201. 312-475-1100.

MENTAL HEALTH/HUMAN SERVICES (17.04)
Addictions Counseling (Undergraduate)

General Information Unit offering the program: Division of Human Services. Program content: History and trends in addictions, theory and technique of counseling, clinical intervention, internships. Available for credit. Endorsed by Illinois Certification Board and Illinois Alcohol Counseling Certification Board. Certificate signed by the Program Advisor. Certificate applicable to B.S. in Human Services.

Program Format Evening classes offered. Program cycle: Continuous enrollment. Full program cycle lasts 4 quarters.

Evaluation Student evaluation based on tests, papers, reports. Grading system: Letters or numbers. Transcripts are kept for each student.

Enrollment Requirements Program is open to non-resident foreign students. English language proficiency required. Certification by college-based language institute required.

Program Costs $122 per semester hour.

Housing and Student Services Housing is available. Job counseling and placement services are available.

Contact Ms. Michela Jones, Assistant Director of Admissions, 2840 Sheridan Road, Evanston, IL 60201. 312-475-1100.

MENTAL HEALTH/HUMAN SERVICES (17.04)
Addictions Treatment Studies

General Information Unit offering the program: Division of Human Services. Program content: History, sociology, theories and physiology of addictions, administration of treatment, clinical intervention. Available for credit. Certificate signed by the Program Advisor. Certificate applicable to B.S. in Human Services.

Program Format Evening classes offered. Program cycle: Continuous enrollment. Full program cycle lasts 4 quarters.

Evaluation Student evaluation based on tests, papers, reports. Grading system: Letters or numbers. Transcripts are kept for each student.

Enrollment Requirements College admissions required. Program is open to non-resident foreign students. English language proficiency required. Certification by college-based language institute required.

Program Costs $122 per semester hour.

Housing and Student Services Housing is available. Job counseling and placement services are available.

Contact Ms. Michela Jones, Assistant Director of Admissions, 2840 Sheridan Road, Evanston, IL 60201. 312-475-1100.

MENTAL HEALTH/HUMAN SERVICES (17.04)
Employee Assistance Program (Substance Abuse Specific)

General Information Unit offering the program: Division of Human Services. Program content: Labor and management, assessment skills, substance abuse. Available for credit. Endorsed by Illinois Certification Board. Certificate signed by the Program Advisor. Certificate applicable to M.S. in Human Services.

Program Format Evening classes offered. Program cycle: Continuous enrollment. Full program cycle lasts 4 quarters.

Evaluation Student evaluation based on tests, papers, reports. Grading system: Letters or numbers. Transcripts are kept for each student.

Enrollment Requirements Bachelor's degree required. Program is open to non-resident foreign students. English language proficiency required. Certification by college-based language institute required.

Housing and Student Services Housing is available. Job counseling and placement services are available.

Contact Ms. Michela Jones, Assistant Director of Admissions, 2840 Sheridan Road, Evanston, IL 60201. 312-475-1100.

MENTAL HEALTH/HUMAN SERVICES (17.04)
Mental Health Counseling Studies

General Information Unit offering the program: Division of Human Services. Program content: Counseling, theories and techniques of group communications, family therapy. Available for credit. Certificate signed by the Program Advisor.

Program Format Evening classes offered. Program cycle: Continuous enrollment. Full program cycle lasts 4 quarters.

Evaluation Student evaluation based on tests, papers, reports. Grading system: Letters or numbers. Transcripts are kept for each student.

Enrollment Requirements College admissions required. Program is open to non-resident foreign students. English language proficiency required. Certification by college-based language institute required.

Program Costs $122 per semester hour.

Housing and Student Services Housing is available. Job counseling and placement services are available.

Contact Ms. Michela Jones, Assistant Director of Admissions, 2840 Sheridan Road, Evanston, IL 60201. 312-475-1100.

MENTAL HEALTH/HUMAN SERVICES (17.04)
Substance Abuse Prevention Professional Certificate

General Information Unit offering the program: Division of Human Services. Program content: Program development, prevention models, substances. Available for credit. Endorsed by Illinois Certification Board. Certificate signed by the Program Advisor. Certificate applicable to M.S. in Human Services.

Program Format Evening classes offered. Program cycle: Continuous enrollment. Full program cycle lasts 4 quarters.

Evaluation Student evaluation based on tests, papers, reports. Grading system: Letters or numbers. Transcripts are kept for each student.

Enrollment Requirements Bachelor's degree required. Program is open to non-resident foreign students. English language proficiency required. Certification by college-based language institute required.

Program Costs $185 per semester hour.

Substance Abuse Prevention Professional Certificate continued

Housing and Student Services   Housing is available. Job counseling and placement services are available.

Contact   Ms. Michela Jones, Assistant Director of Admissions, 2840 Sheridan Road, Evanston, IL 60201. 312-475-1100.

SCHOOL PSYCHOLOGY (13.08)
Certificate of Advanced Study (School Psychology)

General Information   Unit offering the program: Division of Applied Behavioral Sciences. Available for credit. Certificate signed by the Registrar.

Program Format   Evening classes offered. Program cycle: Continuous enrollment. Full program cycle lasts 30 credit hours. Completion of program requires 3.0 GPA.

Evaluation   Student evaluation based on tests, papers, reports. Grading system: Letters or numbers. Transcripts are kept for each student.

Enrollment Requirements   Master's degree required. Program is open to non-resident foreign students. English language proficiency required. Minimum TOEFL score required: 550.

Program Costs $185 per semester hour.

Housing and Student Services   Housing is available. Job counseling and placement services are available.

Contact   Ms. Margaret McClory, Director, Graduate Admissions, 2840 Sheridan Road, Evanston, IL 60201. 312-475-1100 Ext. 2477.

SPECIAL EDUCATION (13.10)
Certificate of Advanced Study (Special Education)

General Information   Unit offering the program: Division of Applied Behavioral Sciences. Available for credit. Certificate signed by the Registrar.

Program Format   Evening classes offered. Program cycle: Continuous enrollment. Full program cycle lasts 30 credit hours. Completion of program requires 3.0 GPA.

Evaluation   Student evaluation based on tests, papers, reports. Grading system: Letters or numbers. Transcripts are kept for each student.

Enrollment Requirements   Master's degree required. Program is open to non-resident foreign students. English language proficiency required. Minimum TOEFL score required: 550.

Program Costs $185 per semester hour.

Housing and Student Services   Housing is available. Job counseling and placement services are available.

Contact   Ms. Margaret McClory, Director, Graduate Admissions, 2840 Sheridan Road, Evanston, IL 60201. 312-475-1100 Ext. 2477.

TEACHER EDUCATION, SPECIFIC SUBJECT AREAS (13.13)
Certificate of Advanced Study (Computer Education)

General Information   Unit offering the program: Division of Applied Behavioral Sciences. Available for credit. Certificate signed by the Registrar.

Program Format   Evening classes offered. Program cycle: Continuous enrollment. Full program cycle lasts 30 credit hours. Completion of program requires 3.0 GPA.

Evaluation   Student evaluation based on tests, papers, reports. Grading system: Letters or numbers. Transcripts are kept for each student.

Enrollment Requirements   Master's degree required. Program is open to non-resident foreign students. English language proficiency required. Minimum TOEFL score required: 550.

Program Costs $185 per semester hour.

Housing and Student Services   Housing is available. Job counseling and placement services are available.

Contact   Ms. Margaret McClory, Director, Graduate Admissions, 2840 Sheridan Road, Evanston, IL 60201. 312-475-1100 Ext. 2477.

TEACHER EDUCATION, SPECIFIC SUBJECT AREAS (13.13)
Certificate of Advanced Study (Early Childhood Education)

General Information   Unit offering the program: Division of Applied Behavioral Sciences. Available for credit. Certificate signed by the Registrar.

Program Format   Evening classes offered. Program cycle: Continuous enrollment. Full program cycle lasts 30 credit hours. Completion of program requires 3.0 GPA.

Evaluation   Student evaluation based on tests, papers, reports. Grading system: Letters or numbers. Transcripts are kept for each student.

Enrollment Requirements   Master's degree required. Program is open to non-resident foreign students. English language proficiency required. Minimum TOEFL score required: 550.

Program Costs $185 per semester hour.

Housing and Student Services   Housing is available. Job counseling and placement services are available.

Contact   Ms. Margaret McClory, Director, Graduate Admissions, 2840 Sheridan Road, Evanston, IL 60201. 312-475-1100 Ext. 2477.

TEACHER EDUCATION, SPECIFIC SUBJECT AREAS (13.13)
Certificate of Advanced Study (Mathematics Education)

General Information   Unit offering the program: Division of Applied Behavioral Sciences. Available for credit. Certificate signed by the Registrar.

Program Format   Evening classes offered. Program cycle: Continuous enrollment. Full program cycle lasts 30 credit hours. Completion of program requires 3.0 GPA.

Evaluation   Student evaluation based on tests, papers, reports. Grading system: Letters or numbers. Transcripts are kept for each student.

Enrollment Requirements   Master's degree required. Program is open to non-resident foreign students. English language proficiency required. Minimum TOEFL score required: 550.

Program Costs $185 per semester hour.

Housing and Student Services   Housing is available. Job counseling and placement services are available.

Contact   Ms. Margaret McClory, Director, Graduate Admissions, 2840 Sheridan Road, Evanston, IL 60201. 312-475-1100 Ext. 2477.

TEACHER EDUCATION, SPECIFIC SUBJECT AREAS (13.13)
Certificate of Advanced Study (Reading and Language)

General Information   Unit offering the program: Division of Applied Behavioral Sciences. Available for credit. Certificate signed by the Registrar.

Program Format   Evening classes offered. Program cycle: Continuous enrollment. Full program cycle lasts 30 credit hours. Completion of program requires 3.0 GPA.

Evaluation   Student evaluation based on tests, papers, reports. Grading system: Letters or numbers. Transcripts are kept for each student.

Enrollment Requirements Master's degree required. Program is open to non-resident foreign students. English language proficiency required. Minimum TOEFL score required: 550.

Program Costs $185 per semester hour.

Housing and Student Services Housing is available. Job counseling and placement services are available.

Contact Ms. Margaret McClory, Director, Graduate Admissions, 2840 Sheridan Road, Evanston, IL 60201. 312-475-1100 Ext. 2477.

TEACHER EDUCATION, SPECIFIC SUBJECT AREAS (13.13)
Certificate of Advanced Study (Science Education)

General Information Unit offering the program: Division of Applied Behavioral Sciences. Available for credit. Certificate signed by the Registrar.

Program Format Evening classes offered. Program cycle: Continuous enrollment. Full program cycle lasts 30 credit hours. Completion of program requires 3.0 GPA.

Evaluation Student evaluation based on tests, papers, reports. Grading system: Letters or numbers. Transcripts are kept for each student.

Enrollment Requirements Master's degree required. Program is open to non-resident foreign students. English language proficiency required. Minimum TOEFL score required: 550.

Program Costs $185 per semester hour.

Housing and Student Services Housing is available. Job counseling and placement services are available.

Contact Ms. Margaret McClory, Director, Graduate Admissions, 2840 Sheridan Road, Evanston, IL 60201. 312-475-1100 Ext. 2477.

NUCEA MEMBER
NORTHERN ILLINOIS UNIVERSITY
De Kalb, Illinois 60115

INDIVIDUAL AND FAMILY DEVELOPMENT (19.07)
Gerontology Certificate

General Information Unit offering the program: International and Special Programs, Gerontology Program. Program content: Graduate course work in the field of aging. Available for credit. Certificate signed by the Dean, International and Special Programs.

Program Format Daytime, evening classes offered. Program cycle: Continuous enrollment. Full program cycle lasts 15 credit hours.

Evaluation Student evaluation based on tests, papers, reports. Grading system: Letters or numbers. Transcripts are kept for each student.

Enrollment Requirements Bachelor's degree required. Program is open to non-resident foreign students.

Program Costs $893 for the program, $60 per credit hour.

Housing and Student Services Housing is available. Job counseling and placement services are available.

Special Features Northern's Gerontology Program offers undergraduate and graduate interdisciplinary study in the field of aging. The certificate program is designed to meet the educational and continuing education needs of those interested in, working in, or researching the field of aging. Courses are offered on campus, and off campus in the Chicago western suburbs.

Contact Dr. Ken Ferraro, Director, Gerontology Program, Social Science Research Institute, De Kalb, IL 60115. 815-753-1940.

OLIVET NAZARENE UNIVERSITY
Kankakee, Illinois 60901

RELIGION (38.02)
Church Management Program for Ministers of the Gospel

General Information Unit offering the program: Continuing Education Department, Graduate School. Program content: Church organization and management. Available on either a credit or non-credit basis. Certificate signed by the University President. Certificate applicable to master's degree in church management.

Program Format Daytime, evening classes offered. Instructional schedule: One-week seminars. Program cycle: three seminars each year in January, May, and September. Full program cycle lasts 30 credit hours. Completion of program requires eight seminars, special project.

Evaluation Student evaluation based on papers, reports, thesis when earning credit. Grading system: Letters or numbers. Transcripts are kept for each student.

Enrollment Requirements Undergraduate degree (16 credit hours in religion and 2.3 GPA), church ministry activities required. Program is open to non-resident foreign students. English language proficiency required.

Program Costs $1500–$1970 for the program, $150–$198 per course.

Housing and Student Services Housing is not available. Job counseling and placement services are not available.

Special Features Instructors chosen on an ecumenical basis in the various fields of study. Program, in progress since 1976, enables pastors to increase, update, and enhance their ministry and earn a certificate or master's degree while continuing to pastor. It is open to all faiths and denominations, all creeds and colors.

Contact Dr. Joseph F. Nielson, Coordinator, Box 123, Kankakee, IL 60901. 815-939-5132.

NUCEA MEMBER
ROOSEVELT UNIVERSITY
Chicago, Illinois 60605

PERSONNEL MANAGEMENT (06.16)
Certified Employee Benefits Specialist

General Information Unit offering the program: Division of Non-Credit Programs. Program content: Legal, financial, organizational issues relating to the employee benefit field. Available on a non-credit basis. Endorsed by International Foundation of Employee Benefit Plans; University of Pennsylvania, Wharton School. Certificate signed by the Dean of the Wharton School.

Program Format Daytime, evening, correspondence classes offered. Instructional schedule: One evening per week for 2½ hours. Students may enroll fall, spring. Full program cycle lasts 2½ to 5 years. Completion of program requires ten national examinations.

Evaluation Student evaluation based on tests. Grading system: Pass/fail. Records are kept by University of Pennsylvania, Wharton School.

Enrollment Requirements Program is open to non-resident foreign students.

Certified Employee Benefits Specialist continued

Housing and Student Services   Housing is not available. Job counseling and placement services are not available.

Special Features   The CEBS program covers the legal, financial, and organizational framework within which employee benefit plans function. The twelve-year-old program has experienced rapid growth; there are presently 27,000 candidates and over 1,800 graduates.

Contact   Ms. Susan Zemelman, Director, Non-Credit Programs, 430 South Michigan Avenue, Chicago, IL 60605. 312-341-3637.

SAINT XAVIER COLLEGE
Chicago, Illinois 60655

ACCOUNTING (06.02)
Accounting Certificate Program

General Information   Unit offering the program: Graham School of Management. Program content: Basic accounting. Available for credit. Certificate signed by the Dean, Graham School of Management. Certificate applicable to any four-year degree offered at the institution.

Program Format   Daytime, evening classes offered. Program cycle: Continuous enrollment. Full program cycle lasts 30 credit hours. Completion of program requires 2.0 GPA.

Evaluation   Student evaluation based on tests, papers. Transcripts are kept for each student.

Enrollment Requirements   Bachelor's degree required. Program is open to non-resident foreign students. English language proficiency required. Minimum TOEFL score required: 550.

Program Costs $612 per course.

Housing and Student Services   Housing is available. Job counseling and placement services are available.

Contact   Sr. Evelyn McKenna, Director of Admissions, 3700 West 103rd Street, Chicago, IL 60426. 312-779-3300.

BUSINESS AND MANAGEMENT, GENERAL (06.01)
Business Certificate Program

General Information   Unit offering the program: Graham School of Management. Program content: Economics, accounting, business law, marketing, finance, management information systems. Available for credit. Certificate signed by the Dean, Graham School of Management. Certificate applicable to any four-year degree offered at the institution.

Program Format   Daytime, evening, weekend classes offered. Program cycle: Continuous enrollment. Full program cycle lasts 30 credit hours. Completion of program requires 2.0 GPA.

Evaluation   Student evaluation based on tests, papers. Transcripts are kept for each student.

Enrollment Requirements   Bachelor's degree (non-business major) required. Program is open to non-resident foreign students. English language proficiency required. Minimum TOEFL score required: 550.

Program Costs $612 per course.

Housing and Student Services   Housing is available. Job counseling and placement services are available.

Contact   Sr. Evelyn McKenna, Director of Admissions, 3700 West 103rd Street, Chicago, IL 60655. 312-779-3300.

SOUTHERN ILLINOIS UNIVERSITY AT EDWARDSVILLE
Edwardsville, Illinois 62026

ENVIRONMENTAL CONTROL TECHNOLOGIES (15.05)
Certificate of Completion in Water Quality Control Operations

General Information   Unit offering the program: Environmental Resources Training Center. Program content: Water supply and wastewater treatment operations. Available on a non-credit basis. Endorsed by Illinois Environmental Protection Agency. Certificate signed by the President.

Program Format   Daytime classes offered. Instructional schedule: 35–40 hours per week. Students enroll in September. Full program cycle lasts 4 quarters. Completion of program requires 3.0/5.0 GPA.

Evaluation   Student evaluation based on tests, papers, reports. Grading system: Letters or numbers. Transcripts are kept for each student.

Enrollment Requirements   Three references; high school diploma or GED is recommended but not absolutely required. Program is open to non-resident foreign students. English language proficiency required. Minimum TOEFL score required: 550.

Program Costs $2720 for the program, $680 per quarter.

Housing and Student Services   Housing is available. Job counseling and placement services are available.

Special Features   The last quarter of the program consists of supervised work-study in a water supply and/or wastewater treatment plant. Program graduates satisfy the education/experience requirements to take exams for entry-level certification in Illinois as public water supply operator and wastewater treatment operator.

Contact   Ms. Nancy Harris, Administrative Aide, Box 1075, Edwardsville, IL 62026-1075. 618-692-2030.

INDIVIDUAL AND FAMILY DEVELOPMENT (19.07)
Interdisciplinary Graduate Certificate in Gerontology

General Information   Unit offering the program: Gerontology Program. Program content: Aging process, characteristics and problems of the aging, programs and services. Available for credit. Certificate signed by the President. Certificate applicable to any graduate degree offered at the institution.

Program Format   Daytime, evening classes offered. Instructional schedule: Four hours per week. Program cycle: Continuous enrollment. Full program cycle lasts 4 courses.

Evaluation   Student evaluation based on tests, papers, reports, field practicum. Grading system: Letters or numbers. Transcripts are kept for each student.

Enrollment Requirements   Bachelor's degree, admission to graduate school required. Program is open to non-resident foreign students. English language proficiency required. Minimum TOEFL score required: 550.

Program Costs $740 for the program, $185 per course (state residents); $1773 for the program, $443 per course (nonresidents).

Housing and Student Services   Housing is available. Job counseling and placement services are available.

Special Features   Provides students and professionals from diverse disciplinary backgrounds and professional programs with a working knowledge of the basic processes of aging; the needs, characteristics, and problems of the aging; programs, services, and resources available to the aging; and a practicum experience utilizing programs, agencies, and institutions serving the aging.

Contact   Mr. Anthony Traxler, Ph.D., Professor and Director, Gerontology Program, Edwardsville, IL 62026-1127. 618-692-3454.

NUCEA MEMBER
UNIVERSITY OF ILLINOIS AT URBANA-CHAMPAIGN
Urbana, Illinois 61801

INTERNATIONAL BUSINESS MANAGEMENT (06.09)
Program for International Managers

General Information   Unit offering the program: Executive Development Center. Available on a non-credit basis. Certificate signed by the Dean of College.

Program Format   Daytime classes offered. Program cycle: Continuous enrollment. Full program cycle lasts 1 year.

Evaluation   Student evaluation based on tests, papers, reports. Grading system: Letters or numbers, pass/fail. Transcripts are kept for each student.

Enrollment Requirements   Bachelor's degree required. Program is open to non-resident foreign students. English language proficiency required. Minimum TOEFL score required: 520. Students required to live on campus.

Program Costs $16,000 for the program.

Housing and Student Services   Housing is available. Job counseling and placement services are not available.

Special Features   Provides familiarity with American and international business practices and ensures adequate English skills to conduct business in the international business community. Participants attend regular University courses in accounting, finance, business administration, and economics. In addition, they attend specially designed management seminars and meet with visiting executives of American corporations. They visit industrial, financial, and commercial organizations both locally and in major U.S. cities.

Contact   Ms. Carolyn M. Pribble, Program Manager, 205 David Kinley Hall, 1407 West Gregory Drive, Urbana, IL 61801. 217-333-2571.

WHEATON COLLEGE
Wheaton, Illinois 60187

AREA STUDIES (05.01)
Certificate of Chinese Studies

General Information   Unit offering the program: Missons/Intercultural Studies, Institute for Chinese Studies. Program content: Missions/intercultural studies of the Chinese. Available for credit. Certificate signed by the President. Certificate applicable to M.A. in Missions/Intercultural Studies.

Program Format   Daytime, evening classes offered. Program cycle: Continuous enrollment. Full program cycle lasts 1 year. Completion of program requires 24 semester hours.

Evaluation   Student evaluation based on tests, papers, reports. Grading system: Letters or numbers. Transcripts are kept for each student.

Enrollment Requirements   Bachelor's degree, biblical knowledge required. Program is open to non-resident foreign students. English language proficiency required. Test of Spoken English (TSE).

Program Costs $4848 for the program.

Housing and Student Services   Housing is available. Job counseling and placement services are available.

Special Features   The program meets the needs of Christian professionals heading for service in China, missionaries to work among the Chinese, Chinese pastors and lay persons ministering among their own people, and persons desiring intercultural experience and service among the Chinese populatons of Western countries.

Contact   Mr. Ludwig Anderson, Associate Director of Graduate Admissions, Wheaton, IL 60187-5593. 312-260-5195.

INDIANA

ANDERSON UNIVERSITY
Anderson, Indiana 46012

THEOLOGICAL STUDIES (39.06)
Theological Studies Certificate

General Information   Unit offering the program: School of Theology. Available for credit. Certificate signed by the Vice President.

Program Format   Daytime, evening, weekend classes offered. Instructional schedule: One evening or two afternoons per week, Saturdays. Program cycle: Continuous enrollment. Full program cycle lasts 24 credit hours. Completion of program requires 2.5 GPA.

Evaluation   Student evaluation based on tests, papers, reports. Grading system: Letters or numbers. Transcripts are kept for each student.

Enrollment Requirements   Bachelor's degree or demonstation of sufficient academic ability required. Program is open to non-resident foreign students.

Program Costs $1800 for the program.

Housing and Student Services   Housing is available. Job counseling and placement services are not available.

Contact   Mr. John H. Aukerman, Assistant Professor, School of Theology, Anderson, IN 46012. 317-641-4530.

NUCEA MEMBER
BALL STATE UNIVERSITY
Muncie, Indiana 47306

COMPUTER PROGRAMMING (11.02)
Computing

General Information   Unit offering the program: Department of Computer Science, School of Continuing Education. Program content: Discrete structures, Pascal, COBOL, computer hardware systems, comparative operating systems. Available for credit. Certificate signed by the Dean, Continuing Education.

Program Format   Daytime, evening classes offered. Program cycle: Continuous enrollment. Completion of program requires six courses, 3.0 GPA.

Evaluation   Student evaluation based on tests, papers, reports. Grading system: Letters or numbers. Transcripts are kept for each student.

Enrollment Requirements   Program is open to non-resident foreign students. English language proficiency required.

Program Costs $212 per course.

Housing and Student Services   Housing is available. Job counseling and placement services are available.

Contact   Dr. Clint Fuelling, Chairperson, Department of Computer Science, Muncie, IN 47306. 317-285-8641.

HISTORY (45.08)
Modern Military History

General Information Unit offering the program: Department of History, School of Continuing Education. Program content: War: 390 B.C. to 1648 A.D., Civil War and reconstruction, diplomatic history, World War I, World War II, Europe since 1945, America and Vietnam. Available for credit. Certificate signed by the Dean, Continuing Education. Certificate applicable to B.S., M.A. in History.

Program Format Evening classes offered. Instructional schedule: One evening per week. Full program cycle lasts 15 months. Completion of program requires five courses, grade of C or better.

Evaluation Student evaluation based on tests. Grading system: Letters or numbers. Transcripts are kept for each student.

Enrollment Requirements University admissions required. Program is open to non-resident foreign students.

Program Costs $222–$240 per course.

Housing and Student Services Housing is available. Job counseling and placement services are available.

Contact Dr. James Danglade, Assistant Dean for Credit Programs, School of Continuing Education, Muncie, IN 47306. 317-285-1581.

INDIVIDUAL AND FAMILY DEVELOPMENT (19.07)
Gerontology

General Information Unit offering the program: Institute for Gerontology, Center for Lifelong Education, School of Continuing Education. Program content: Health and aging, psychology, social gerontology, death and dying, development of exercise programs, educating society, counseling. Available for credit. Certificate signed by the Dean, Continuing Education. Certificate applicable to B.S. in General Arts; M.A. in Gerontology, Adult Education.

Program Format Evening classes offered. Instructional schedule: One evening per week. Full program cycle lasts 15 months. Completion of program requires five courses, grade of C or better.

Evaluation Student evaluation based on tests. Grading system: Letters or numbers. Transcripts are kept for each student.

Enrollment Requirements University admissions required. Program is open to non-resident foreign students.

Program Costs $222–$240 per course.

Housing and Student Services Housing is available. Job counseling and placement services are available.

Contact Mr. Thomas Ray, Director, Administrative Services, School of Continuing Education, Muncie, IN 47306. 317-285-1581.

INDUSTRIAL PRODUCTION TECHNOLOGIES (15.06)
Computer-Aided Drafting and Machining (CAD/CAM)

General Information Unit offering the program: Department of Industry and Technology, School of Continuing Education. Program content: Introduction to computer-aided drafting and manufacturing, problems in computer graphics, manufacturing design, fundamentals of computerized numerical control. Available for credit. Certificate signed by the Dean, Continuing Education. Certificate applicable to A.S. in Manufacturing Technology.

Program Format Daytime, evening classes offered. Program cycle: Continuous enrollment. Completion of program requires five course, 2.0 GPA.

Evaluation Student evaluation based on tests, papers, reports. Grading system: Letters or numbers. Transcripts are kept for each student.

Enrollment Requirements Course work in Manufacturing Materials and Process, Technical Drawing and Print Reading, Advanced Technical Drawing, Metal Machining, Intermediate Algebra, Trigonometry or equivalent knowledge required. Program is open to non-resident foreign students. English language proficiency required.

Program Costs $196 per course.

Housing and Student Services Housing is available. Job counseling and placement services are available.

Contact Dr. Donald F. Smith, Chairman, Department of Industry and Technology, P.A. Building, Muncie, IN 47306. 317-285-5641.

MENTAL HEALTH/HUMAN SERVICES (17.04)
Drug Abuse Counseling

General Information Unit offering the program: Departments of Counseling Psychology Guidance Services, Educational Psychology, Physiology and Health Science, Psychological Science; School of Continuing Education. Program content: Alcohol problems; drug dependence and abuse; adolescent, adult, and abnormal psychology; counseling. Available for credit. Endorsed by Indiana Counselors' Association on Alcohol and Drug Abuse (ICAADA). Certificate signed by the Dean, Continuing Education.

Program Format Daytime, evening classes offered. Program cycle: Continuous enrollment. Completion of program requires five courses, 2.0 GPA.

Evaluation Student evaluation based on tests, papers, reports. Grading system: Letters or numbers. Transcripts are kept for each student.

Enrollment Requirements Basic course work in psychology, behavioral science required. Program is open to non-resident foreign students. English language proficiency required.

Program Costs $196 per course.

Housing and Student Services Housing is available. Job counseling and placement services are available.

Contact Mr. Thomas Ray, Director, Administrative Services, School of Continuing Education, Muncie, IN 47306. 317-285-1581.

CALUMET COLLEGE OF SAINT JOSEPH
Whiting, Indiana 46394

ACCOUNTING (06.02)
Certificate in Accounting (One Year)

General Information Unit offering the program: Division of Management. Program content: Accounting, management, computer information systems, economics. Available for credit. Certificate signed by the President. Certificate applicable to A.S. in Accounting.

Program Format Daytime, evening, weekend classes offered. Program cycle: Continuous enrollment. Full program cycle lasts 1 year. Completion of program requires 15 credit hours.

Evaluation Student evaluation based on tests, papers, reports. Grading system: Letters or numbers. Transcripts are kept for each student.

Enrollment Requirements High school/college transcripts, GED scores required. English language proficiency required.

Program Costs $285 per course.

Housing and Student Services Housing is not available. Job counseling and placement services are available.

Contact Ms. Sharon J. Sweeney, Director of Admissions/Financial Aid, 2400 New York Avenue, Whiting, IN 46394. 219-473-4215.

BUSINESS AND MANAGEMENT, GENERAL (06.01)
Certificate in Management (One Year)

General Information Unit offering the program: Division of Management. Program content: Management, economics, computer information systems, communication arts. Available for credit. Certificate signed by the President. Certificate applicable to A.S. in Management.

Program Format Daytime, evening, weekend classes offered. Program cycle: Continuous enrollment. Full program cycle lasts 1 year. Completion of program requires 15 credit hours.

Evaluation Student evaluation based on tests, papers, reports. Grading system: Letters or numbers. Transcripts are kept for each student.

Enrollment Requirements High school/college transcripts, GED scores required. English language proficiency required.

Program Costs $285 per course.

Housing and Student Services Housing is not available. Job counseling and placement services are available.

Contact Ms. Sharon J. Sweeney, Director of Admissions/Financial Aid, 2400 New York Avenue, Whiting, IN 46394. 219-473-4215.

BUSINESS DATA PROCESSING AND RELATED PROGRAMS (07.03)
Certificate in Business Data Processing (One Year)

General Information Unit offering the program: Division of Management. Program content: Computer information systems, management, accounting. Available for credit. Certificate signed by the President.

Program Format Daytime, evening, weekend classes offered. Program cycle: Continuous enrollment. Full program cycle lasts 1 year. Completion of program requires 15 credit hours.

Evaluation Student evaluation based on tests, papers, reports. Grading system: Letters or numbers. Transcripts are kept for each student.

Enrollment Requirements High school/college transcripts, GED scores required. English language proficiency required.

Program Costs $285 per course.

Housing and Student Services Housing is not available. Job counseling and placement services are available.

Contact Ms. Sharon J. Sweeney, Director of Admissions/Financial Aid, 2400 New York Avenue, Whiting, IN 46394. 219-473-4215.

CHEMISTRY (40.05)
Certificate in Chemistry (One Year)

General Information Unit offering the program: Division of Science and Mathematics. Program content: Chemistry, computer information systems, library science, mathematics, physics. Available for credit. Certificate signed by the President. Certificate applicable to A.S. in Chemistry.

Program Format Daytime, evening, weekend classes offered. Program cycle: Continuous enrollment. Full program cycle lasts 1 year. Completion of program requires 15 credit hours.

Evaluation Student evaluation based on tests, papers, reports. Grading system: Letters or numbers. Transcripts are kept for each student.

Enrollment Requirements High school/college transcripts, GED scores required. English language proficiency required.

Program Costs $285 per course.

Housing and Student Services Housing is not available. Job counseling and placement services are available.

Contact Ms. Sharon J. Sweeney, Director of Admissions/Financial Aid, 2400 New York Avenue, Whiting, IN 46394. 219-473-4215.

COMMUNICATIONS, GENERAL (09.01)
Certificate in Communication Arts/ Photography Concentration (One Year)

General Information Unit offering the program: Division of Communication and Fine Arts. Program content: Communication arts, fine arts, photography. Available for credit. Certificate signed by the President. Certificate applicable to A.S. in Communication Arts.

Program Format Daytime, evening, weekend classes offered. Program cycle: Continuous enrollment. Full program cycle lasts 1 year. Completion of program requires 15 credit hours.

Evaluation Student evaluation based on tests, papers, reports. Grading system: Letters or numbers. Transcripts are kept for each student.

Enrollment Requirements High school/college transcripts, GED scores required. English language proficiency required.

Program Costs $285 per course.

Housing and Student Services Housing is not available. Job counseling and placement services are available.

Contact Ms. Sharon J. Sweeney, Director of Admissions/Financial Aid, 2400 New York Avenue, Whiting, IN 46394. 219-473-4215.

CRIMINAL JUSTICE (43.01)
Certificate in Criminal Justice (One Year)

General Information Unit offering the program: Division of Social and Behavioral Sciences. Program content: Criminal justice, political science, psychology, sociology. Available for credit. Certificate signed by the President. Certificate applicable to A.S. in Criminal Justice.

Program Format Daytime, evening, weekend classes offered. Program cycle: Continuous enrollment. Full program cycle lasts 1 year. Completion of program requires 15 credit hours.

Evaluation Student evaluation based on tests, papers, reports. Grading system: Letters or numbers. Transcripts are kept for each student.

Enrollment Requirements High school/college transcripts, GED scores required. English language proficiency required.

Program Costs $285 per course.

Housing and Student Services Housing is not available. Job counseling and placement services are available.

Contact Ms. Sharon J. Sweeney, Director of Admissions/Financial Aid, 2400 New York Avenue, Whiting, IN 46394. 219-473-4215.

JOURNALISM (MASS COMMUNICATIONS) (09.04)
Certificate in Communication Arts/Journalism Concentration (One Year)

General Information Unit offering the program: Division of Communication and Fine Arts. Program content: Communication arts and fine arts. Available for credit. Certificate signed by the President. Certificate applicable to A.S. in Communication Arts.

Program Format Daytime, evening, weekend classes offered. Program cycle: Continuous enrollment. Full program cycle lasts 1 year. Completion of program requires 15 credit hours.

Evaluation Student evaluation based on tests, papers, reports. Grading system: Letters or numbers. Transcripts are kept for each student.

Enrollment Requirements High school/college transcripts, GED scores required. English language proficiency required.

Program Costs $285 per course.

Housing and Student Services Housing is not available. Job counseling and placement services are available.

Contact Ms. Sharon J. Sweeney, Director of Admissions/Financial Aid, 2400 New York Avenue, Whiting, IN 46394. 219-473-4215.

RELIGIOUS EDUCATION (39.04)
Certificate in Religious Studies (One Year)

General Information Unit offering the program: Division of Humanities. Program content: Theology, education. Available for credit. Certificate signed by the President. Certificate applicable to A.S. in Religious Studies.

Program Format Daytime, evening, weekend classes offered. Program cycle: Continuous enrollment. Full program cycle lasts 1 year. Completion of program requires 15 credit hours.

Evaluation Student evaluation based on tests, papers, reports. Grading system: Letters or numbers. Transcripts are kept for each student.

Enrollment Requirements High school/college transcripts, GED scores required. English language proficiency required.

Program Costs $285 per course.

Housing and Student Services Housing is not available. Job counseling and placement services are available.

Contact Ms. Sharon J. Sweeney, Director of Admissions/Financial Aid, 2400 New York Avenue, Whiting, IN 46394. 219-473-4215.

SECRETARIAL AND RELATED PROGRAMS (07.06)
Certificate in Professional Secretarial Science (One Year)

General Information Unit offering the program: Division of Management. Program content: Business education, communication arts, management, English. Available for credit. Certificate signed by the President. Certificate applicable to A.S. in Professional Secretarial Science.

Program Format Daytime, evening, weekend classes offered. Program cycle: Continuous enrollment. Full program cycle lasts 1 year. Completion of program requires 15 credit hours.

Evaluation Student evaluation based on tests, papers, reports. Grading system: Letters or numbers. Transcripts are kept for each student.

Enrollment Requirements High school/college transcripts, GED scores required. English language proficiency required.

Program Costs $285 per course.

Housing and Student Services Housing is not available. Job counseling and placement services are available.

Contact Ms. Sharon J. Sweeney, Director of Admissions/Financial Aid, 2400 New York Avenue, Whiting, IN 46394. 219-473-4215.

FORT WAYNE BIBLE COLLEGE
Fort Wayne, Indiana 46807

BIBLE STUDIES (39.02)
Christian Workers Certificate (One Year Program)

General Information Unit offering the program: Department of Correspondence Studies. Program content: Bible, ministry-oriented studies. Available for credit. Certificate signed by the President. Certificate applicable to any four-year degree offered at the institution.

Program Format Correspondence classes offered. Program cycle: Continuous enrollment. Full program cycle lasts 32 credit hours.

Evaluation Student evaluation based on tests, papers. Grading system: Letters or numbers. Transcripts are kept for each student.

Enrollment Requirements High school diploma required. Program is open to non-resident foreign students. English language proficiency required.

Program Costs $40 per credit hour.

Housing and Student Services Housing is not available. Job counseling and placement services are not available.

Special Features All courses are designed and graded by faculty of Fort Wayne Bible College.

Contact Mr. Douglas A. Barcalow, Ed.D., Director of Correspondence Studies, 1025 West Rudisill Boulevard, Fort Wayne, IN 46807. 219-456-2111 Ext. 305.

HUNTINGTON COLLEGE
Huntington, Indiana 46750

RELIGIOUS EDUCATION (39.04)
Diploma in Foundations in Christian Leadership

General Information Unit offering the program: Bible Department. Program content: Bible, Christian education, general studies. Available for credit. Certificate signed by the President. Certificate applicable to B.A. in Bible and Religion, B.S. in Christian Education.

Program Format Daytime classes offered. Students may enroll fall, spring. Full program cycle lasts 2 semesters. Completion of program requires 32 semester hours (at least 24 in residence), 2.0 GPA, English competency examination.

Evaluation Student evaluation based on tests, papers, reports. Grading system: Letters or numbers. Transcripts are kept for each student.

Enrollment Requirements College admissions required. Program is open to non-resident foreign students. English language proficiency required. Minimum TOEFL score required: 450.

Program Costs $5400 for the program.

Housing and Student Services Housing is available. Job counseling and placement services are available.

Contact Mr. Chantler Thompson, Director of Admissions, 2303 College Avenue, Huntington, IN 46750. 219-356-6000.

SECRETARIAL AND RELATED PROGRAMS (07.06)
Diploma in Secretarial Science

General Information Unit offering the program: Business. Program content: Basic business, office management, secretarial studies. Available for credit. Certificate signed by the President. Certificate applicable to A.A. in Secretarial Science.

Program Format Daytime, evening classes offered. Students may enroll fall, spring. Full program cycle lasts 2 semesters. Completion of program requires 32 semester hours (at least 24 in residence), 2.0 GPA, English competency examination.

Evaluation Student evaluation based on tests, papers, reports. Grading system: Letters or numbers. Transcripts are kept for each student.

Enrollment Requirements College admissions required. Program is open to non-resident foreign students. English language proficiency required. Minimum TOEFL score required: 450.

Program Costs $5400 for the program.

Housing and Student Services Housing is available. Job counseling and placement services are available.

Contact Mr. Chantler Thompson, Director of Admissions, Huntington, IN 46750. 219-356-6000.

INDIANA INSTITUTE OF TECHNOLOGY
Fort Wayne, Indiana 46803

ELECTRICAL AND ELECTRONICS EQUIPMENT REPAIR (47.01)
Diploma in Computer Repair Technology

General Information Unit offering the program: Computer Science/Mathematics. Program content: Repair of computing and peripheral equipment. Available for credit. Certificate signed by the President of the College. Certificate applicable to associate or bachelor's degree in business administration, computer information systems.

Program Format Daytime, evening classes offered. Instructional schedule: Four hours per day, five days per week. Program cycle: Continuous enrollment. Full program cycle lasts 9 months. Completion of program requires 2.0 GPA.

Evaluation Student evaluation based on tests. Grading system: Letters or numbers. Transcripts are kept for each student.

Enrollment Requirements High school diploma or GED required. Program is open to non-resident foreign students. English language proficiency required. Minimum TOEFL score required: 500.

Program Costs $6498 for the program.

Housing and Student Services Housing is available. Job counseling and placement services are available.

Special Features Students build 16-bit microcomputer as course/lab requirement. Machine is student's property at completion. Credit transfers into business or computer information systems programs at IIT (associate or bachelor's level).

Contact Mr. Kenneth W. Nicolet, Director of Student Development, 1600 East Washington Boulevard, Fort Wayne, IN 46803. 219-422-5561 Ext. 251.

NUCEA MEMBER
INDIANA STATE UNIVERSITY
Terre Haute, Indiana 47809

LAW (22.01)
Paralegal Studies Certificate Program

General Information Unit offering the program: Conferences and Non-Credit Programs. Available on a non-credit basis. Certificate signed by the Dean, Instructional Services.

Program Format Evening classes offered. Instructional schedule: Three hours per week. Students may enroll twice per year. Full program cycle lasts 2 years. Completion of program requires six courses, five half-day seminars.

Evaluation Student evaluation based on tests. Grading system: Letters or numbers. Transcripts are kept for each student.

Enrollment Requirements 60 credit hours, 2.5 GPA required. Program is open to non-resident foreign students.

Program Costs $1200 for the program, $200 per course, $25 per seminar.

Housing and Student Services Housing is not available. Job counseling and placement services are available.

Special Features Courses taught by local attorneys, seminars taught by paralegals.

Contact Mr. Michael Williamson, Director, Conferences and Non-Credit Programs, 240 Alumni Center, Terre Haute, IN 47809. 812-237-2522.

NUCEA MEMBER
INDIANA UNIVERSITY AT SOUTH BEND
South Bend, Indiana 46634

BUSINESS AND MANAGEMENT, GENERAL (06.01)
Management Certificate

General Information Unit offering the program: Division of Continuing Education. Program content: Planning and policy decisions. Available on a non-credit basis. Certificate signed by the Chancellor.

Program Format Daytime, evening classes offered. Instructional schedule: Once per week. Students may enroll fall, spring. Full program cycle lasts 2 years. Completion of program requires project.

Evaluation Student evaluation methods vary by course. Transcripts are kept for each student.

Enrollment Requirements Program is open to non-resident foreign students.

Program Costs $199 per course.

Housing and Student Services Housing is not available. Job counseling and placement services are not available.

Special Features Program developed with recommendation of an advisory committee from business, industry, and education, that meets annually to assess content and make further recommendations. Now beginning its fourth year. The certificate is awarded upon completion of 18 CEU's to individuals who seek to move beyond the supervisory level. Faculty are regionally recognized for their expertise and leadership in the business community.

Contact Ms. Suzanne Z. Miller, Associate Director, Division of Continuing Education, P.O. Box 7111, South Bend, IN 46634. 219-237-4261.

FOOD PRODUCTION, MANAGEMENT, AND SERVICES (20.04)
Hotel and Restaurant Management Certificate

General Information Unit offering the program: Division of Continuing Education. Available on a non-credit basis. Cosponsored by Educational Institute of the American Hotel and Motel Association. Certificate signed by the Chancellor.

Program Format Evening classes offered. Instructional schedule: One evening per week. Students may enroll fall, spring. Full program cycle lasts 2 years.

Evaluation Student evaluation based on tests. Transcripts are kept for each student.

Enrollment Requirements Program is open to non-resident foreign students.

Program Costs $119–$139 per course.

Housing and Student Services Housing is not available. Job counseling and placement services are not available.

Special Features Program approved by the American Hotel and Motel Association. Each course leading to the IUSB certificate also leads to an AHMA certificate upon successful completion. Program was developed with the assistance of an advisory committee of managers of restaurants, hotels, and motels recognized worldwide; instructors are practicing professionals and use industry-specific and approved instructional materials.

Contact Ms. Norma Singleton, Program Administrator, P.O. Box 7111, South Bend, IN 46634. 219-237-4261.

LAW (22.01)
Paralegal Studies Certificate

General Information Unit offering the program: Division of Continuing Education. Available on either a credit or non-credit basis. Certificate signed by the Chancellor. Certificate applicable to B.G.S.

Program Format Daytime, evening, weekend classes offered. Instructional schedule: Twice per week. Students may enroll fall, spring. Full program cycle lasts 2 years. Completion of program requires test scores of 75% or better.

Evaluation Student evaluation based on tests, papers. Grading system: Letters or numbers. Transcripts are kept for each student.

Enrollment Requirements Program is open to non-resident foreign students. English language proficiency required. Test of Standard Written English (TSWE).

Program Costs $225 per course.

Housing and Student Services Housing is not available. Job counseling and placement services are available.

Special Features The program publishes names of graduates, keeps résumés on file, and makes information available to prospective employers. Program is recognized as the premier regional program by attorneys; curriculum is developed and administered by attorneys widely respected for their knowledge and expertise. Instructors are area attorneys who are excellent teachers and experts in their field. Program is recognized by American Association of Paralegal Education.

Contact Ms. Jane Robinson, Director, Division of Continuing Education, P.O. Box 7111, South Bend, IN 46634. 219-237-4261.

TRADE AND INDUSTRIAL SUPERVISION AND MANAGEMENT (06.20)
Production and Inventory Management Certificate

General Information Unit offering the program: Division of Continuing Education. Program content: Production and inventory control concepts, purchasing, quality assurance, computer-based MIS. Available on a non-credit basis. Endorsed by American Production and Inventory Control Society. Certificate signed by the Chancellor.

Program Format Evening classes offered. Instructional schedule: One evening per week. Students may enroll fall, spring. Full program cycle lasts 2 years.

Evaluation Student evaluation based on tests. Grading system: Pass/fail. Transcripts are kept for each student.

Enrollment Requirements Program is open to non-resident foreign students.

Program Costs $119–$199 per course.

Housing and Student Services Housing is not available. Job counseling and placement services are not available.

Contact Ms. Jane Robinson, Director, Division of Continuing Education, P.O. Box 7111, South Bend, IN 46634. 219-237-4261.

NUCEA MEMBER

INDIANA UNIVERSITY BLOOMINGTON
Bloomington, Indiana 47405

ELECTRICAL AND ELECTRONIC TECHNOLOGIES (15.03)
Certificate in Communication Electronics

General Information Unit offering the program: Division of Continuing Studies. Program content: Basic electronics, active device fundamentals, electronic circuits, communication electronics. Available on a non-credit basis. Certificate signed by the Director, Division of Continuing Studies.

Program Format Evening, weekend classes offered. Instructional schedule: Once or twice per week. Students may enroll fall, spring. Full program cycle lasts 2 years. Completion of program requires 360 classroom hours.

Evaluation Student evaluation based on tests. Grading system: Letters or numbers. Transcripts are kept for each student.

Enrollment Requirements Program is open to non-resident foreign students.

Program Costs $272 per course.

Housing and Student Services Housing is not available. Job counseling and placement services are not available.

Special Features This is a laboratory-oriented course of study emphasizing trouble-shooting techniques. Advanced placement is possible for those with prior electrical training.

Contact Ms. Barbara Jones, Assistant Director, 620 Union Drive - UN 101, Indianapolis, IN 46202. 317-274-5051.

ELECTRICAL AND ELECTRONIC TECHNOLOGIES (15.03)
Certificate in Industrial Electronics

General Information Unit offering the program: Division of Continuing Studies. Program content: Basic electronics, active device fundamentals, electronic circuits, industrial control circuits. Available on a non-credit basis. Certificate signed by the Director, Division of Continuing Studies.

Program Format Evening, weekend classes offered. Instructional schedule: Once or twice per week. Students may enroll fall, spring. Full program cycle lasts 2 years. Completion of program requires 360 classroom hours.

Evaluation Student evaluation based on tests. Grading system: Letters or numbers. Transcripts are kept for each student.

Enrollment Requirements Program is open to non-resident foreign students.

Program Costs $272 per course.

Housing and Student Services Housing is not available. Job counseling and placement services are not available.

Special Features This is a laboratory-oriented course of study emphasizing trouble-shooting techniques. Advanced placement is possible for those with prior electrical training.

Contact Ms. Barbara Jones, Assistant Director, 620 Union Drive-UN 101, Indianapolis, IN 46202. 317-274-5051.

ELECTRICAL AND ELECTRONIC TECHNOLOGIES (15.03)
Certificate in Microprocessor Electronics

General Information Unit offering the program: Division of Continuing Studies. Program content: Basic electronics, active device fundamentals, electronic circuits, workshop for technicians. Available on a non-credit basis. Certificate signed by the Director, Division of Continuing Studies.

Program Format Evening, weekend classes offered. Instructional schedule: Once or twice per week. Students may enroll fall, spring. Full program cycle lasts 2 years. Completion of program requires 360 classrooms hours.

Evaluation Student evaluation based on tests. Grading system: Letters or numbers. Transcripts are kept for each student.

Enrollment Requirements Program is open to non-resident foreign students.

Program Costs $272 per course.

Housing and Student Services Housing is not available. Job counseling and placement services are not available.

Special Features This is a laboratory-oriented course of study emphasizing trouble-shooting techniques. Advanced placement is possible for those with prior electrical training.

Contact Ms. Barbara Jones, Assistant Director, 620 Union Drive-UN 101, Indianapolis, IN 46202. 317-274-5051.

LABOR/INDUSTRIAL RELATIONS (06.11)
Certificate in Labor Studies

General Information   Unit offering the program: Division of Labor Studies, School of Continuing Studies. Program content: Labor studies, unions, collective bargaining. Available for credit. Certificate signed by the President. Certificate applicable to A.S., B.S. in Labor Studies.

Program Format   Daytime, evening, weekend, correspondence classes offered. Program cycle: Continuous enrollment. Full program cycle lasts 30 credit hours. Completion of program requires 18 credits in labor studies, 12 additional credits.

Evaluation   Student evaluation based on tests, papers, reports. Grading system: Letters or numbers. Transcripts are kept for each student.

Enrollment Requirements   High school diploma or GED required. Program is open to non-resident foreign students.

Program Costs $55–$65 per credit hour.

Housing and Student Services   Housing is not available. Job counseling and placement services are available.

Special Features   The program is available through correspondence, and provisions have been made for credit through the college-level examination program and for military service. The instructors are the division faculty who generally have union experience as well as academic training in labor studies. The program provides a firm foundation in the core courses of the labor studies curriculum.

Contact   Mr. Lee Balliet, Director, Division of Labor Studies, Poplars 630, Bloomington, IN 47405. 812-335-9082.

LAW (22.01)
Paralegal Studies Certificate Program

General Information   Unit offering the program: Division of Continuing Studies. Program content: Law and legal procedures. Available on a non-credit basis. Certificate signed by the Director, Division of Continuing Studies.

Program Format   Evening classes offered. Instructional schedule: Once per week. Program cycle: Continuous enrollment. Full program cycle lasts 12 courses. Completion of program requires 2.0 GPA.

Evaluation   Student evaluation based on tests, papers. Grading system: Letters or numbers. Transcripts are kept for each student.

Enrollment Requirements   Program is open to non-resident foreign students.

Program Costs $145 per course.

Housing and Student Services   Housing is not available. Job counseling and placement services are not available.

Special Features   The Paralegal Studies Certificate Program consists of nine required and three elective courses. Among the electives is a paralegal internship. Part-time students can expect to complete the program in approximately two calendar years.

Contact   Ms. Barbara Jones, Assistant Director, 620 Union Drive - UN 101, Indianapolis, IN 46202. 317-274-5047.

OFFICE SUPERVISION AND MANAGEMENT (07.04)
Basic Supervision Certificate

General Information   Unit offering the program: Division of Continuing Studies, Indiana University Southeast. Program content: Business administration, interpersonal communication, personnel supervision, production supervision, labor relations. Available on either a credit or non-credit basis. Certificate signed by the Chancellor. Certificate applicable to associate or bachelor's degree in general studies.

Program Format   Evening, weekend classes offered. Instructional schedule: 2½ hours per week. Students may enroll fall, spring. Full program cycle lasts 5 courses.

Evaluation   Student evaluation based on tests, papers, reports, projects. Grading system: Letters or numbers. Transcripts are kept for each student.

Enrollment Requirements   University admissions required. Program is open to non-resident foreign students.

Program Costs $782 for the program, $156 per course.

Housing and Student Services   Housing is not available. Job counseling and placement services are available.

Special Features   Students who have completed the same or comparable courses at other accredited institutions may substitute those courses for the W100 Business Administration course or the S122 Interpersonal Communication course. The other three supervisory courses must be taken on the Indiana University Southeast campus.

Contact   Ms. Saundra Brown, General Studies Counselor, 4201 Grant Line Road, New Albany, IN 47150. 812-945-2731 Ext. 314.

NUCEA MEMBER
INDIANA UNIVERSITY NORTHWEST
Gary, Indiana 46408

ACCOUNTING (06.02)
Postbaccalaureate Certificate in Accounting

General Information   Unit offering the program: Division of Business and Economics. Program content: Accounting and related fields in preparation for CPA exam. Available for credit. Certificate signed by the President.

Program Format   Daytime, evening classes offered. Instructional schedule: Once or twice per week. Program cycle: Continuous enrollment. Full program cycle lasts 14 courses. Completion of program requires 42 credit hours, 2.0 GPA.

Evaluation   Student evaluation based on tests, papers, reports. Grading system: Letters or numbers. Transcripts are kept for each student.

Enrollment Requirements   Bachelor's degree required. Program is open to non-resident foreign students.

Program Costs $2877 for the program, $205 per course.

Housing and Student Services   Housing is not available. Job counseling and placement services are available.

Contact   Mr. William Lee, Admissions Officer, 3400 Broadway, Gary, IN 46408. 219-980-6821.

BUSINESS AND MANAGEMENT, GENERAL (06.01)
Certificate in Business Studies

General Information   Unit offering the program: Division of Business and Economics. Program content: English, math, accounting, economics, business law, statistics. Available for credit. Certificate signed by the President. Certificate applicable to B.S. in Business.

Program Format   Daytime, evening, weekend classes offered. Program cycle: Continuous enrollment. Completion of program requires 2.0 GPA, 60 credit hours.

Evaluation   Student evaluation based on tests, papers, reports. Grading system: Letters or numbers. Transcripts are kept for each student.

Enrollment Requirements   University admissions required. Program is open to non-resident foreign students.

Program Costs $50 per credit hour (state residents); $124 per credit hour (nonresidents).

Housing and Student Services   Housing is not available. Job counseling and placement services are available.

Special Features   No credit for prior experience. All courses are regular college courses applicable toward four-year degree.

Contact   Mr. William Lee, Admissions Officer, 3400 Broadway, Gary, IN 46408. 219-980-6821.

DATA PROCESSING (11.03)
Postbaccalaureate Certificate in Data Processing and Information Systems

General Information Unit offering the program: Data Processing and Information Systems Department. Program content: COBOL, programming, data structures, information systems design, data processing management, computer simulation and modeling. Available for credit. Certificate signed by the President. Certificate applicable to B.S. in Data Processing and Information Systems.

Program Format Daytime, evening, weekend classes offered. Program cycle: Continuous enrollment. Full program cycle lasts 2 semesters. Completion of program requires 30 credit hours.

Evaluation Student evaluation based on tests, computer programs. Grading system: Letters or numbers. Transcripts are kept for each student.

Enrollment Requirements Bachelor's degree required. Program is open to non-resident foreign students.

Program Costs $50 per credit hour (state residents); $124 per credit hour (nonresidents).

Housing and Student Services Housing is not available. Job counseling and placement services are available.

Contact Dr. Robert Votaw, Acting Chairman, 3400 Broadway, Gary, IN 46408. 219-980-6638.

DENTAL SERVICES (17.01)
Certificate in Dental Assisting

General Information Unit offering the program: Dental Auxiliary Education. Program content: Microbiology, pathology, physiology, anatomy, history, embryology, radiology, clinical science, ethics, behavioral science. Available for credit. Certificate signed by the Dean, School of Dentistry. Certificate applicable to A.S., B.S. in General Studies.

Program Format Daytime classes offered. Instructional schedule: Monday through Friday. Students enroll in August. Full program cycle lasts 2 semesters. Completion of program requires 32 credit hours.

Evaluation Student evaluation based on tests, papers, reports. Grading system: Letters or numbers. Transcripts are kept for each student.

Enrollment Requirements High school diploma or GED, 2.5 GPA, typing course required. Program is open to non-resident foreign students. English language proficiency required.

Program Costs $2764 for the program, $50 per credit hour.

Housing and Student Services Housing is not available. Job counseling and placement services are available.

Special Features Program in existence since 1976; graduates placed within two months of graduation. Because of university setting, graduates can return to campus and pursue advanced degrees. Faculty members include diverse group of educators and private practitioners.

Contact Ms. Kathleen J. Hinshaw, Program Supervisor, 3223 Broadway, Gary, IN 46409. 219-980-6770.

LABOR/INDUSTRIAL RELATIONS (06.11)
Certificate in Labor Studies

General Information Unit offering the program: Division of Labor Studies. Program content: Role of organized labor in contemporary society. Available for credit. Certificate signed by the Director, Division of Labor Studies. Certificate applicable to A.S., B.S. in Labor Studies.

Program Format Daytime, evening, correspondence classes offered. Instructional schedule: Classes meet weekly. Program cycle: Continuous enrollment. Full program cycle lasts 10 courses. Completion of program requires 30 credit hours, 2.0 GPA.

Evaluation Student evaluation based on tests, papers, reports. Grading system: Letters or numbers. Transcripts are kept for each student.

Enrollment Requirements High school diploma or GED required. Program is open to non-resident foreign students. English language proficiency required.

Program Costs $1600 for the program, $160 per course.

Housing and Student Services Housing is not available. Job counseling and placement services are available.

Special Features There is credit for prior experience, and 'testing out' of certain courses.

Contact Mr. Bruce Nissen, Associate Professor, 3400 Broadway, Gary, IN 46408. 219-980-6825.

PUBLIC ADMINISTRATION (44.04)
Certificate in Public Management (Graduate)

General Information Unit offering the program: School of Public and Environmental Affairs. Program content: Public management, finance, personnel, budgeting. Available for credit. Certificate signed by the President. Certificate applicable to M.P.A.

Program Format Evening, weekend classes offered. Instructional schedule: 2¾ hours per week. Program cycle: Continuous enrollment. Completion of program requires 15 credit hours. 3.0 GPA.

Evaluation Student evaluation based on tests, papers, reports. Grading system: Letters or numbers. Transcripts are kept for each student.

Enrollment Requirements Bachelor's degree required. Program is open to non-resident foreign students.

Program Costs $990 for the program, $198 per course (state residents); $2212 for the program, $442 per course (nonresidents).

Housing and Student Services Housing is not available. Job counseling and placement services are available.

Contact Mr. Philip J. Rutledge, Director of Public and Environmental Affairs, 3400 Broadway, Gary, IN 46408. 219-980-6695.

OAKLAND CITY COLLEGE
Oakland City, Indiana 47660

COMPUTER PROGRAMMING (11.02)
Computer Science

General Information Unit offering the program: Mathematics/Computing Science. Program content: Computer organization, programming, data and file structures. Available for credit. Certificate signed by the President of the College. Certificate applicable to A.S. in Computer Technology.

Program Format Daytime classes offered. Program cycle: Continuous enrollment. Full program cycle lasts 4 semesters. Completion of program requires 2.0 GPA.

Evaluation Student evaluation based on tests, papers, reports, programming projects. Grading system: Letters or numbers. Transcripts are kept for each student.

Enrollment Requirements College admissions required. Program is open to non-resident foreign students. English language proficiency required.

Program Costs $5568 for the program, $174 per credit hour.

Housing and Student Services Housing is available. Job counseling and placement services are available.

Special Features The program was developed to recognize those students who might want to take computer science courses but not complete a degree that would include general education courses. The candidates would be enrolled as part-time students.

Contact   Admissions Office, Oakland City College, Oakland City, IN 47660. 812-749-1222.

HEATING, AIR CONDITIONING, AND REFRIGERATION MECHANICS (47.02)
Heating and Air Conditioning and Refrigeration

General Information   Unit offering the program: Technical Division. Program content: Residential and commercial heating, air-conditioning, refrigeration. Available on either a credit or non-credit basis. Certificate signed by the President. Certificate applicable to Associate in Applied Science.

Program Format   Daytime classes offered. Instructional schedule: Four hours per day, five days per week. Students may enroll summer, fall. Full program cycle lasts 1 year. Completion of program requires grade of D (70%) or better.

Evaluation   Student evaluation based on tests, shop performance. Grading system: Letters or numbers. Transcripts are kept for each student.

Enrollment Requirements   High school diploma or GED required. Program is open to non-resident foreign students. English language proficiency required.

Program Costs $6950 for the program, $175 per credit hour.

Housing and Student Services   Housing is available. Job counseling and placement services are available.

Special Features   Since 1984, the Heating, Air-Conditioning, and Refrigeration Department of Oakland City College has provided industry with job-entry-level graduates. Students are encouraged to receive credit for prior achievements by successfully passing appropriate omissions examinations.

Contact   Admissions Office, 143 North Lucretia, Oakland City, IN 47660. 812-749-4781.

PRECISION METAL WORK (48.05)
Welding

General Information   Unit offering the program: Technical Division. Program content: Four-position gas and arc welding, blueprint reading, metallurgy. Available on either a credit or non-credit basis. Certificate signed by the President. Certificate applicable to Associate in Applied Science.

Program Format   Daytime, evening classes offered. Instructional schedule: Four hours per day, five days per week. Students may enroll summer, fall. Full program cycle lasts 1 year. Completion of program requires grade of D (70%) or better.

Evaluation   Student evaluation based on tests, shop performance. Grading system: Letters or numbers. Transcripts are kept for each student.

Enrollment Requirements   High school diploma or GED required. Program is open to non-resident foreign students. English language proficiency required.

Program Costs $6950 for the program, $175 per credit hour.

Housing and Student Services   Housing is available. Job counseling and placement services are available.

Special Features   Since 1974, the Welding Department of Oakland City College has been providing AWS-certified welders to industry. Students are encouraged to receive credit for prior achievements by successfully passing appropriate omissions examination.

Contact   Admissions Office, 143 North Lucretia, Oakland City, IN 47660. 812-749-4781.

TYPING, GENERAL OFFICE, AND RELATED PROGRAMS (07.07)
Secretarial Science

General Information   Unit offering the program: Business Division. Program content: English grammar, composition, typewriting, shorthand, business electives. Available for credit.

Certificate signed by the President. Certificate applicable to A.S., B.S. in Accounting, Business Administration, Business Education.

Program Format   Daytime classes offered. Instructional schedule: Three hours per day, five days per week. Students enroll in the fall. Full program cycle lasts 40 credit hours. Completion of program requires grade of D (70%) or better.

Evaluation   Student evaluation based on tests, papers, reports. Grading system: Letters or numbers. Transcripts are kept for each student.

Enrollment Requirements   High school diploma or GED required. Program is open to non-resident foreign students. English language proficiency required.

Program Costs $5568 for the program, $174 per credit hour.

Housing and Student Services   Housing is available. Job counseling and placement services are available.

Contact   Admissions Office, 143 North Lucretia, Oakland City, IN 47660. 812-749-4781.

VEHICLE AND MOBILE EQUIPMENT MECHANICS AND REPAIRERS (47.06)
Auto and Diesel Mechanics

General Information   Unit offering the program: Technical Division. Program content: Automotive and diesel engine mechanics, brakes, transmissions. Available on either a credit or non-credit basis. Certificate signed by the President. Certificate applicable to Associate in Applied Science.

Program Format   Daytime classes offered. Instructional schedule: Four hours per day, five days per week. Students may enroll summer, fall. Full program cycle lasts 1 year. Completion of program requires grade of D (70%) or better.

Evaluation   Student evaluation based on tests, shop performance. Grading system: Letters or numbers. Transcripts are kept for each student.

Enrollment Requirements   High school diploma or GED required. Program is open to non-resident foreign students. English language proficiency required.

Program Costs $6950 for the program, $175 per credit hour.

Housing and Student Services   Housing is available. Job counseling and placement services are available.

Special Features   Since 1974, the Automotive/Diesel Department of Oakland City College has been providing industry with qualified job-entry-level graduates. The twelve courses in the program provide an in-depth and well-rounded education. Students are encouraged to receive credit for prior achievements by successfully passing appropriate omissions examinations.

Contact   Admissions Office, 143 North Lucretia, Oakland City, IN 47660. 812-749-4781.

NUCEA MEMBER

PURDUE UNIVERSITY
West Lafayette, Indiana 47907

COMPUTER AND INFORMATION SCIENCES, GENERAL (11.01)
Achieving Foodservice Excellence: Computer Applications in Foodservice

General Information   Unit offering the program: Restaurant, Hotel, and Institutional Management Institute. Program content: Computers as an aid in food service planning, budgeting, staffing, cost control, purchasing, and menu planning. Available on a non-credit basis. Certificate signed by the Director, Continuing Education. Program fulfills requirements for Dietary Managers Association, American Culinary Federation, American School Food Service Association, International Foodservice Executives Association.

Program Format   Correspondence classes offered. Program cycle: Continuous enrollment. Full program cycle lasts 1 year.

Achieving Foodservice Excellence: Computer Applications in Foodservice continued

Completion of program requires grade of 70% or better on final examination.

Evaluation Student evaluation based on tests. Grading system: Letters or numbers. Records are kept for each student.

Enrollment Requirements Program is open to non-resident foreign students.

Program Costs $249 per course.

Housing and Student Services Housing is not available. Job counseling and placement services are not available.

Special Features Program developed by the internationally-known Restaurant, Hotel, and Institutional Management Institute at Purdue University. Through considerable experience in continuing education programs like this one, RHIMI has helped countless food service professionals improve their facility's operation and advance their own careers. The Institute draws upon faculty nationally to develop specific course content.

Contact Mr. Wayne J. Berning, Director of Restaurant, Hotel, and Institutional Management, 101 Young Graduate House, West Lafayette, IN 47907. 317-494-2749.

FOOD PRODUCTION, MANAGEMENT, AND SERVICES (20.04)
Achieving Foodservice Excellence: Food Purchasing, Selection, and Procurement

General Information Unit offering the program: Restaurant, Hotel, and Institutional Management Institute. Program content: Negotiating better prices and service from food service suppliers and setting up internal procedures for streamlining the purchasing process. Available on a non-credit basis. Certificate signed by the Director, Continuing Education. Program fulfills requirements for Dietary Managers Association, American Culinary Federation, International Foodservice Executives Association, American School Foodservice Association.

Program Format Correspondence classes offered. Program cycle: Continuous enrollment. Full program cycle lasts 1 year. Completion of program requires grade of 70% or better on final examination.

Evaluation Student evaluation based on tests. Grading system: Letters or numbers. Records are kept for each student.

Enrollment Requirements Program is open to non-resident foreign students.

Program Costs $229 per course.

Housing and Student Services Housing is not available. Job counseling and placement services are not available.

Special Features Program was developed by the internationally-known Restaurant, Hotel, and Institutional Management Institute at Purdue University. Through considerable experience in continuing education programs like this one, RHIMI has helped countless food service professionals improve their facility's operation and advance their own careers. The Institute draws upon faculty nationally to develop specific course content.

Contact Mr. Wayne J. Berning, Director of Restaurant, Hotel, and Institutional Management, 101 Young Graduate House, West Lafayette, IN 47907. 317-494-2749.

FOOD PRODUCTION, MANAGEMENT, AND SERVICES (20.04)
Achieving Foodservice Excellence: Professional Cooking and Foodservice Standards

General Information Unit offering the program: Restaurant, Hotel, and Institutional Management Institute. Available on a non-credit basis. Cosponsored by Dietary Managers Association. Certificate signed by the Director, Continuing Education. Program fulfills requirements for Dietary Managers Association, American Culinary Federation, International Foodservice Executives

Association, American School Food Service Association, Society for Food Service Management, American College of Nursing Home Administrators.

Program Format Correspondence classes offered. Program cycle: Continuous enrollment. Full program cycle lasts 1 year. Completion of program requires grade of 70% or better on final examination.

Evaluation Student evaluation based on tests. Grading system: Letters or numbers. Records are kept for each student.

Enrollment Requirements Program is open to non-resident foreign students.

Program Costs $229 per course.

Housing and Student Services Housing is not available. Job counseling and placement services are not available.

Special Features Program was developed by the internationally-known Restaurant, Hotel, and Institutional Management Institute at Purdue University. Through considerable experience in continuing education programs like this one, RHIMI has helped countless food service professionals improve their facility's operation and advance their own careers. The Institute draws upon faculty nationally to develop specific course content.

Contact Mr. Wayne J. Berning, Director of Restaurant, Hotel, and Institutional Management, 101 Young Graduate House, West Lafayette, IN 47907. 317-494-2749.

HEALTH SERVICES ADMINISTRATION (18.07)
Central Service Technical Training

General Information Unit offering the program: Center for Professional Correspondence Study. Program content: Central service processes, technological advances, processing techniques. Available on a non-credit basis. Cosponsored by International Association of Hospital Central Service Management. Certificate signed by the Director, Continuing Education. Program fulfills requirements for International Association of Hospital Central Service Management Certified Registered Central Service Technician.

Program Format Correspondence classes offered. Program cycle: Continuous enrollment. Full program cycle lasts 1 year. Completion of program requires grade of 75% or better on final examination.

Evaluation Student evaluation based on tests. Grading system: Letters or numbers. Records are kept for each student.

Enrollment Requirements Program is open to non-resident foreign students.

Program Costs $295 per course.

Housing and Student Services Housing is not available. Job counseling and placement services are not available.

Special Features Center for Professional Correspondence Study was established in 1985 to serve educational/training requirements of individuals and associations on both a national and international dimension. Center is committed to trend of "life-long learning" as an outreach extension to enhance professional growth of people interested in individualized learning. Center draws upon faculty nationally to develop specific course content.

Contact Mr. Wayne J. Berning, Director, Center for Professional Correspondence Study, 101 Young Graduate House, West Lafayette, IN 47907. 317-494-2749.

HEALTH SERVICES ADMINISTRATION (18.07)
Principles of Management and Supervision for Central Service Personnel

General Information Unit offering the program: Center for Professional Correspondence Study. Program content: Management skills in central service. Available on a non-credit basis. Cosponsored by International Association of Hospital Central Service Management. Certificate signed by the Director, Continuing Education. Program fulfills requirements for International Association of Hospital Central Service

Management Certification in Central Service Management Concepts.

Program Format   Correspondence classes offered. Program cycle: Continuous enrollment. Full program cycle lasts 1 year. Completion of program requires grade of 80% or better on final examination.

Evaluation   Student evaluation based on tests. Grading system: Letters or numbers. Records are kept for each student.

Enrollment Requirements   Program is open to non-resident foreign students.

Program Costs $395 per course.

Housing and Student Services   Housing is not available. Job counseling and placement services are not available.

Special Features   Center for Professional Correspondence Study was established in 1985 to serve educational/training requirements of individuals and associations on both a national and international dimension. Center is committed to trend of "life-long learning" as an outreach extension to enhance professional growth of people interested in individualized learning. Center draws upon faculty nationally to develop specific course content.

Contact   Mr. Wayne J. Berning, Director, Center for Professional Correspondence Study, 101 Young Graduate House, West Lafayette, IN 47907. 317-494-2749.

TRADE AND INDUSTRIAL SUPERVISION AND MANAGEMENT (06.20)
Achieving Foodservice Excellence: Management and Supervision—Keys to Organizational Success

General Information   Unit offering the program: Restaurant, Hotel, and Institutional Management Institute. Program content: Food service operation. Available on a non-credit basis. Certificate signed by the Director, Continuing Education. Program fulfills requirements for Dietary Managers Association, American Culinary Federation, American School Food Service Association, International Foodservice Executives Association, Society for Food Service Management, American College of Nursing Home Administrators.

Program Format   Correspondence classes offered. Program cycle: Continuous enrollment. Full program cycle lasts 1 year. Completion of program requires grade of 70% or better on final examination.

Evaluation   Student evaluation based on tests. Grading system: Letters or numbers. Records are kept for each student.

Enrollment Requirements   Program is open to non-resident foreign students.

Program Costs $229 per course.

Housing and Student Services   Housing is not available. Job counseling and placement services are not available.

Special Features   Program was developed by the internationally-known Restaurant, Hotel, and Institutional Management Institute at Purdue University. Through considerable experience in continuing education programs like this one, RHIMI has helped countless food service professionals improve their facility's operation and advance their own careers. The Institute draws upon faculty nationally to develop specific course content.

Contact   Mr. Wayne J. Berning, Director of Restaurant, Hotel, and Institutional Management, 101 Young Graduate House, West Lafayette, IN 47907. 317-494-2749.

TRANSPORTATION AND TRAVEL MARKETING (08.11)
Achieving Professional Excellence: Travel and Tourism Marketing Management

General Information   Unit offering the program: Restaurant, Hotel, and Institutional Management Institute. Program content: Motivation for travel, geography of travel, modes of travel, travel

trade packaging and programming. Available on a non-credit basis. Certificate signed by the Director, Continuing Education.

Program Format   Correspondence classes offered. Program cycle: Continuous enrollment. Full program cycle lasts 1 year. Completion of program requires grade of 70% or better on final examination.

Evaluation   Student evaluation based on tests. Grading system: Letters or numbers. Records are kept for each student.

Enrollment Requirements   Program is open to non-resident foreign students.

Program Costs $225 per course.

Housing and Student Services   Housing is not available. Job counseling and placement services are not available.

Special Features   Program developed by internationally-known Restaurant, Hotel, and Institutional Management Institute at Purdue University. Committed to trend toward "lifelong learning" and continuing career development, RHIMI provides national educational program dedicated to enhancing hospitality and travel industry. RHIMI identifies and assesses learning needs of professionals in hospitality, travel, and allied fields, and develops education seminars, self-study courses, and training programs to meet those needs.

Contact   Mr. Wayne J. Berning, Director of Restaurant, Hotel, and Institutional Management, 101 Young Graduate House, West Lafayette, IN 47907. 317-494-2749.

PURDUE UNIVERSITY CALUMET
Hammond, Indiana 46323

BUSINESS AND MANAGEMENT, GENERAL (06.01)
Certificate in Professional Supervision

General Information   Unit offering the program: Supervision. Program content: Industrial organization, human relations, public speaking. Available for credit. Endorsed by American Society of Professional Supervision. Certificate signed by the Chancellor. Certificate applicable to A.A.S., B.S. in Supervision.

Program Format   Daytime, evening, weekend classes offered. Program cycle: Continuous enrollment. Complete program cycle lasts one to two years. Completion of program requires 24 credit hours.

Evaluation   Student evaluation based on tests. Grading system: Letters or numbers. Transcripts are kept for each student.

Enrollment Requirements   Two years supervisory experience required. Program is open to non-resident foreign students.

Program Costs $3600 for the program, $150 per course.

Housing and Student Services   Housing is not available. Job counseling and placement services are available.

Special Features   Approximately 900 graduates of the program employed in over one hundred businesses since program established in 1956. Current graduation rate is 25 students per year.

Contact   Mr. Carl F. Jenks, Professor, METS, Purdue Calumet, Hammond, IN 46323. 219-989-2280.

COMPUTER PROGRAMMING (11.02)
Post Baccalaureate Certificate

General Information   Unit offering the program: Information Systems and Computer Programming Department. Program content: Computer programming, computer systems analysis. Available for credit. Certificate signed by the Chancellor. Certificate applicable to A.A.S. in Computer Technology.

Program Format   Daytime, evening, weekend classes offered. Program cycle: Continuous enrollment. Full program cycle lasts 8 courses. Completion of program requires grade of C or better.

Post Baccalaureate Certificate continued

Evaluation Student evaluation based on tests, reports, laboratory exercises. Grading system: Letters or numbers. Transcripts are kept for each student.

Enrollment Requirements Bachelor's degree required. Program is open to non-resident foreign students.

Program Costs $1300 for the program, $150 per course.

Housing and Student Services Housing is not available. Job counseling and placement services are available.

Special Features Professionally experienced faculty. Several current texts in wide use authored by faculty. Courses are directly transferrable to degree programs. Program has excellent reputation.

Contact Mr. A. J. Adams, Professor and Department Head, Hammond, IN 46323. 219-989-2412.

SAINT MEINRAD COLLEGE
Saint Meinrad, Indiana 47577

THEOLOGICAL STUDIES (39.06)
College Graduate Program

General Information Program content: Philosophy, theology, ethics, scripture, spirituality, metaphysics, church history. Available for credit. Certificate signed by the President.

Program Format Daytime classes offered. Instructional schedule: Monday through Friday. Students enroll in the fall. Full program cycle lasts 2 semesters.

Evaluation Student evaluation based on tests, papers, reports. Transcripts are kept for each student.

Enrollment Requirements Undergraduate degree required. Program is open to non-resident foreign students. English language proficiency required. Demonstrated proficiency acceptable. Students required to live on campus.

Program Costs $6974 for the program.

Housing and Student Services Housing is available. Job counseling and placement services are available.

Contact Rev. Matthias Neuman, OSB, Faculty Moderator of the College Graduate Program, St. Meinrad, IN 47577. 812-357-6662.

UNIVERSITY OF INDIANAPOLIS
Indianapolis, Indiana 46227

BUSINESS AND MANAGEMENT, GENERAL (06.01)
Certificate in Management Development

General Information Unit offering the program: Center for Continuing Education and Management Development. Program content: Communications, leadership, human relations, understanding human behavior, stress, assertiveness, self-understanding. Available on a non-credit basis. Certificate signed by the President of the University.

Program Format Evening, weekend classes offered. Program cycle: Continuous enrollment. Complete program cycle lasts one to five years. Completion of program requires eight courses.

Evaluation Student evaluation based on reports. Grading system: Pass/fail. Transcripts are kept for each student.

Enrollment Requirements Program is not open to non-resident foreign students. English language proficiency required.

Program Costs $800–$1500 for the program, $100–$150 per course.

Housing and Student Services Housing is not available. Job counseling and placement services are not available.

Special Features Taught by qualified practicing managers. Stresses practical skills, not just theories. Students are treated with respect as guests of the University.

Contact Ms. Judy Hasselkus, Assistant Director, Center for Management Development, 1400 East Hanna Avenue, Indianapolis, IN 46227. 317-788-3442.

NUCEA MEMBER
UNIVERSITY OF SOUTHERN INDIANA
Evansville, Indiana 47712

ACCOUNTING (06.02)
Post-Baccalaureate Certificate in Professional Accountancy

General Information Unit offering the program: Division of Business. Program content: Accounting, economics, business law, business electives. Available for credit. Certificate signed by the Vice President for Academic Affairs. Certificate applicable to B.S. in Accounting.

Program Format Daytime, evening classes offered. Students may enroll fall, spring, summer. Full program cycle lasts 40 credit hours. Completion of program requires 3.0 GPA.

Evaluation Student evaluation based on tests. Grading system: Letters or numbers. Transcripts are kept for each student.

Enrollment Requirements Admission to the university as a special student required. Program is open to non-resident foreign students.

Program Costs $1920 for the program, $144 per course.

Housing and Student Services Housing is available. Job counseling and placement services are available.

Contact Dr. Kenneth B. Settle, Chairman, Division of Business, Evansville, IN 47712. 812-464-1718.

COMMUNICATIONS, GENERAL (09.01)
The Writing Concentration

General Information Unit offering the program: English Department. Program content: Advanced composition, critical and investigative writing, history of rhetoric, writing for the professions. Available for credit. Certificate signed by the Chair, Division of Humanities. Certificate applicable to B.S. in English (writing emphasis).

Program Format Daytime, evening classes offered. Program cycle: Continuous enrollment. Full program cycle lasts 4 semesters. Completion of program requires 15 credit hours.

Evaluation Student evaluation based on tests, papers, reports. Grading system: Letters or numbers. Transcripts are kept for each student.

Enrollment Requirements College degree, writing classes 101 and 201 required. Program is open to non-resident foreign students.

Program Costs $720 for the program, $48 per credit hour.

Housing and Student Services Housing is available. Job counseling and placement services are available.

Special Features Students can use their own work/career experience for internship. There is a History of Rhetoric or History of English Language requirement. The program is three years old. Graduates have all received employment due to their skills as writers. Staffed by regular writing faculty and specialists who visit seminar classes as part of professional obligation.

Contact Mr. Thomas M. Rivers, Professor of English, English Department, Evansville, IN 47712. 812-464-1734.

IOWA

FAITH BAPTIST BIBLE COLLEGE AND SEMINARY
Ankeny, Iowa 50021

BIBLE STUDIES (39.02)
Basic Bible Program (One Year Certificate)

General Information Program content: Bible survey courses, book analysis, principles of Bible study. Available for credit. Certificate signed by the President. Certificate applicable to any two- or four-year degree offered at the institution.

Program Format Daytime classes offered. Program cycle: Continuous enrollment. Full program cycle lasts 1 year. Completion of program requires 32 credit hours, average grade of C or better.

Evaluation Student evaluation based on tests, papers, reports. Grading system: Letters or numbers. Transcripts are kept for each student.

Enrollment Requirements College admissions required. Program is open to non-resident foreign students. English language proficiency required.

Program Costs $3320 for the program.

Housing and Student Services Housing is available. Job counseling and placement services are available.

Contact Ms. Sally Snedigar, Registrar, 1900 NW 4th Street, Ankeny, IA 50021. 515-964-0601.

MARYCREST COLLEGE
Davenport, Iowa 52804

LAW (22.01)
Legal Assistant Training Program

General Information Unit offering the program: Graduate and Adult Programs. Program content: Legal research and writing, business law, legal concepts. Available for credit. Certificate signed by the Senior Vice President.

Program Format Evening classes offered. Program cycle: Continuous enrollment. Full program cycle lasts 33 credit hours. Completion of program requires 2.5 GPA.

Evaluation Student evaluation based on tests, papers, reports. Grading system: Letters or numbers. Transcripts are kept for each student.

Enrollment Requirements High school diploma or GED required. Program is open to non-resident foreign students. English language proficiency required. Minimum TOEFL score required: 550.

Program Costs $60 per credit hour.

Housing and Student Services Housing is available. Job counseling and placement services are available.

Contact Ms. Neala McCarthy, Administrative Assistant, 1607 West 12th Street, Davenport, IA 52804. 319-326-9581.

MENTAL HEALTH/HUMAN SERVICES (17.04)
Substance Abuse Counselor Training Program

General Information Unit offering the program: Office of Graduate and Adult Programs. Program content: Counseling skills; physiological, psychological, and sociological aspects of substance abuse. Available for credit. Certificate signed by the Senior Vice President.

Program Format Evening classes offered. Program cycle: Continuous enrollment. Full program cycle lasts 48 credit hours. Completion of program requires 640-hour practicum, 2.5 GPA.

Evaluation Student evaluation based on tests, papers, reports. Grading system: Letters or numbers. Transcripts are kept for each student.

Enrollment Requirements High school diploma or GED required. Program is open to non-resident foreign students. English language proficiency required. Minimum TOEFL score required: 550.

Program Costs $60 per credit hour.

Housing and Student Services Housing is available. Job counseling and placement services are available.

Special Features A 640-hour practicum is required for all students.

Contact Ms. Salome Raheim, Substance Abuse Counselor Training Program Coordinator, 1607 West 12th Street, Davenport, IA 52804. 319-326-9581.

UNIVERSITY OF DUBUQUE
Dubuque, Iowa 52001

COMPUTER PROGRAMMING (11.02)
Certificate in Computer Programming

General Information Unit offering the program: Department of Computer Science. Program content: Assembly language, Pascal, FORTRAN, COBOL, math, speech, English. Available for credit. Certificate signed by the President of the University. Certificate applicable to B.S. in Computer/Information Science.

Program Format Daytime, evening classes offered. Program cycle: Continuous enrollment. Completion of program requires ten courses.

Evaluation Student evaluation based on tests, reports. Grading system: Letters or numbers. Transcripts are kept for each student.

Enrollment Requirements University admissions required. Program is open to non-resident foreign students.

Program Costs $5850 for the program, $585 per course.

Housing and Student Services Housing is available. Job counseling and placement services are available.

Contact Dr. Dale Fransson, Chair, Department of Computer Science, 2000 University Avenue, Dubuque, IA 52001. 319-589-3276.

NUCEA MEMBER
UNIVERSITY OF IOWA
Iowa City, Iowa 52242

DIAGNOSTIC AND TREATMENT SERVICES (17.02)
Diagnostic Ultrasonography Program

General Information Unit offering the program: Department of Radiology, University of Iowa Hospitals and Clinics. Program content: Ultrasound. Available on a non-credit basis. Certificate signed by the Director, University Hospitals and Clinics.

Program Format Daytime classes offered. Instructional schedule: 40 hours per week. Students may enroll March, September. Full program cycle lasts 12 months. Completion of program requires competency examination.

Evaluation Student evaluation based on tests, papers, reports. Grading system: Letters or numbers. Certificate of completion kept for each student.

Enrollment Requirements Limited to graduates of a two-year, AMA-approved program in radiologic technology, nursing or

Diagnostic Ultrasonography Program continued

medical technology. Program is open to non-resident foreign students.

Program Costs $240 for the program.

Housing and Student Services   Housing is available. Job counseling and placement services are available.

Contact   Mr. Dann Cohrs, Program Director, Department of Radiology, S 717 GH, Universtiy of Iowa Hospital and Clinics, Iowa City, IA 52242. 319-356-4871.

DIAGNOSTIC AND TREATMENT SERVICES
(17.02)
Nuclear Medicine Technology

General Information   Unit offering the program: Department of Radiology, University of Iowa Hospitals and Clinics. Available on either a credit or non-credit basis. Endorsed by Committee on Allied Health Education and Accreditation (CAHEA). Certificate signed by the Director, University Hospitals and Clinics. Program fulfills requirements for Certified Nuclear Medicine Technologist (CNMT).

Program Format   Daytime classes offered. Instructional schedule: Monday through Friday. Program cycle: Continuous enrollment. Full program cycle lasts 12 months.

Evaluation   Student evaluation based on tests, papers, reports, clinical competency. Grading system: Letters or numbers, pass/fail. Transcripts are kept for each student.

Enrollment Requirements   Graduate of two-year CAHEA program, bachelor's degree with basic sciences required. Program is open to non-resident foreign students. English language proficiency required. Minimum TOEFL score required: 480.

Program Costs   Noncredit: $240 for the program, Credit: $1564 for the program (state residents); $4900 for the program (nonresidents).

Housing and Student Services   Housing is available. Job counseling and placement services are available.

Special Features   This is the only nuclear medicine technology program in Iowa. A total of 112 people have graduated from the program since it began in 1967. In July, 1987, the program was awarded continuing accreditation for five years.

Contact   Mr. Kenneth A. Holmes, Program Director, Nuclear Medicine Technology Program, University of Iowa Hospitals and Clinics, Iowa City, IA 52242. 319-356-2954.

DIAGNOSTIC AND TREATMENT SERVICES
(17.02)
Program in Magnetic Resonance Imaging Technology

General Information   Unit offering the program: Department of Radiology, University of Iowa Hospitals and Clinics. Available on a non-credit basis. Certificate signed by the Director and Assistant to the President for Statewide Health Services, University of Iowa Hospitals and Clinics.

Program Format   Daytime classes offered. Instructional schedule: Five days per week. Students may enroll March, September. Full program cycle lasts 6 months. Completion of program requires average grade of C or better.

Evaluation   Student evaluation based on tests, papers, reports. Grading system: Letters or numbers. Transcripts are kept for each student.

Enrollment Requirements   Graduate of CAHEA accredited program in Radiologic Technology, certification with the American Registry of Radiologic Technologists required.

Program is open to non-resident foreign students. English language proficiency required. Minimum TOEFL score required: 500.

Program Costs $1000 for the program.

Housing and Student Services   Housing is available. Job counseling and placement services are available.

Contact   Ms. Marilyn Holland, Director, Radiologic Technology Education, University of Iowa Hsopitals and Clinics, Iowa City, IA 52242. 319-356-4332.

DIAGNOSTIC AND TREATMENT SERVICES
(17.02)
Program in Radiologic Technology

General Information   Unit offering the program: Department of Radiology, University of Iowa Hospitals and Clinics. Program content: Radiographic technique, radiation biology, radiographic physics, anatomy and physiology. Available on a non-credit basis. Endorsed by Committee on Allied Health Education and Accreditation (CAHEA). Certificate signed by the Director and Assistant to the President for Statewide Health Services, University of Iowa Hospitals and Clinics.

Program Format   Daytime classes offered. Instructional schedule: Five days per week. Students enroll in July. Full program cycle lasts 24 months. Completion of program requires grade of C or better in all courses.

Evaluation   Student evaluation based on tests, papers, reports. Grading system: Letters or numbers. Transcripts are kept for each student.

Enrollment Requirements   High school diploma; course work in algebra, biology, and chemistry; ACT scores required. Program is open to non-resident foreign students. English language proficiency required. Minimum TOEFL score required: 500.

Program Costs $980 for the program.

Housing and Student Services   Housing is available. Job counseling and placement services are available.

Contact   Ms. Marilyn Holland, Director, Radiologic Technology Education, University of Iowa Hospitals and Clinics, Iowa City, IA 52242. 319-356-4332.

DIAGNOSTIC AND TREATMENT SERVICES
(17.02)
Program in Vascular Imaging Technology

General Information   Unit offering the program: Department of Radiology, University of Iowa Hospitals and Clinics. Available on a non-credit basis. Certificate signed by the Director and Assistant to the President for Statewide Health Services, University of Iowa Hospitals and Clinics.

Program Format   Daytime classes offered. Instructional schedule: Five days per week. Students may enroll March, September. Full program cycle lasts 6 months. Completion of program requires average grade of C or better.

Evaluation   Student evaluation based on tests, papers, reports. Grading system: Letters or numbers. Transcripts are kept for each student.

Enrollment Requirements   Graduate of CAHEA accredited program in Radiologic Technology, certification with the American Registry of Radiologic Technologists required. Program is open to non-resident foreign students. English language proficiency required. Minimum TOEFL score required: 500.

Program Costs $1000 for the program.

Housing and Student Services   Housing is available. Job counseling and placement services are available.

Contact   Ms. Marilyn Holland, Director, Radiologic Technology Education, University of Iowa Hospitals and Clinics, Iowa City, IA 52242. 319-356-4332.

DIAGNOSTIC AND TREATMENT SERVICES (17.02)
Radiation Therapy Technology

General Information Unit offering the program: Department of Radiology–Division of Radiation Oncology, University of Iowa Hospitals and Clinics. Program content: Physics of radiation therapy, physiology and pathology of cancer, medical management of the cancer patient, treatment techniques using ionizing radiation. Available on a non-credit basis. Endorsed by Council on Allied Health Education and Accreditation. Certificate signed by the Department Director.

Program Format Daytime classes offered. Instructional schedule: Monday through Friday. Students enroll in September. Full program cycle lasts 12 months.

Evaluation Student evaluation based on tests, clinical competency. Grading system: Letters or numbers, pass/fail. Transcripts are kept for each student.

Enrollment Requirements Certification as a radiographer required. Program is open to non-resident foreign students.

Program Costs $240 for the program.

Housing and Student Services Housing is available. Job counseling and placement services are available.

Special Features Twelve-month program in radiation therapy technology offers certified radiographer opportunity to enter different area of patient service with program concentrated in techniques of treatment of cancer with ionizing radiation sources. The combination of formal classroom instruction and supervised clinical experience prepares graduate to assume work responsibilites after graduation after short period of orientation.

Contact Ms. Elona McLees, Program Director, Radiation Oncology, C 142 GH, University of Iowa Hospitals and Clinics, Iowa City, IA 52242-1059. 319-356-2253.

FOOD SCIENCES AND HUMAN NUTRITION (19.05)
Dietetic Intern

General Information Unit offering the program: Dietary Department, University of Iowa Hospitals and Clinics. Program content: Seminar, research, analysis of food service systems, hospital dietary administration. Available on either a credit or non-credit basis. Endorsed by American Dietetic Association. Certificate signed by the President of the University. Program fulfills requirements for Registered Dietitian/Licensed Dietitian.

Program Format Daytime classes offered. Instructional schedule: 40 hours per week. Students enroll in August. Full program cycle lasts 44 weeks.

Evaluation Student evaluation based on tests, papers, reports. Grading system: Letters or numbers. Transcripts are kept for each student.

Enrollment Requirements Successfull completion of ADA Plan IV Requirements, bachelor's degree required. Program is open to non-resident foreign students. English language proficiency required.

Program Costs $1550 for the program.

Housing and Student Services Housing is available. Job counseling and placement services are available.

Special Features University of Iowa Hospitals and Clinics Dietetic Internship is a postbaccalaureate generalist program coupled with additional graduate study. Learning experiences provided by classes, conferences, seminars, projects, and individual instruction. Criteria for acceptance into one of the 16 positions include such qualities as superior scholarship, interest in completing graduate work, varied work experiences, and ability to relate well to others.

Contact Ms. Suzanne Koury, Dietetic Internship Director, Dietary Department, University of Iowa Hospitals and Clinics, Iowa City, IA 52242. 319-356-2692.

HEALTH SERVICES ADMINISTRATION (18.07)
Surveillance, Prevention, and Control of Nosocomial Infections

General Information Unit offering the program: Program of Hospital Epidemiology, University of Iowa Hospitals and Clinics. Program content: Identify, evaluate, and prevent nosocomial infections; institutional compliance of regulatory/advisory agency standards. Available on a non-credit basis. Certificate signed by the Hospital Chief Executive Officer.

Program Format Daytime, weekend classes offered. Instructional schedule: Monday through Friday, and one Saturday morning. Students may enroll twice per year. Full program cycle lasts 2 weeks.

Evaluation Student evaluation based on tests, epidemic evaluation simulation. Record of CEUs kept for each student.

Enrollment Requirements Program is open to RN, LPN, medical technician, or MD with infection-control or hospital epidemiology responsibility. Program is open to non-resident foreign students. English language proficiency required.

Program Costs $250–$350 for the program.

Housing and Student Services Housing is available. Job counseling and placement services are not available.

Special Features Program is mixture of didactic and practical application training experiences designed to provide foundation of skills and knowledge for beginning infection-control practitioners. Offered by the University of Iowa Hospitals and Clinics since 1977 and similar to courses offered by the Centers for Disease Control. Small class size enables specialized tailoring of the program to suit individual needs.

Contact Mr. Stephen A. Streed, Education and Epidemiology Systems Coordinator, C-41-N GH, University of Iowa Hospitals and Clinics, Iowa City, IA 52242. 319-356-2828.

MEDICAL LABORATORY TECHNOLOGIES (17.03)
Certificate in Medical Technology

General Information Unit offering the program: Medical Technology Program, University of Iowa Hospitals and Clinics. Program content: Prepares graduates to work in hospital and other health care laboratories. Available for credit. Endorsed by National Accrediting Agency for Clinical Laboratory Sciences. Certificate signed by the President of the University of Iowa. Certificate applicable to B.S. in Medical Technology. Program fulfills requirements for Medical Technologist (ASCP) and Clinical Laboratory Scientist (NCA).

Program Format Daytime classes offered. Instructional schedule: Monday through Friday. Full program cycle lasts 2 semesters. Completion of program requires comprehensive examination.

Evaluation Student evaluation based on tests, clinical performance. Grading system: Letters or numbers. Transcripts are kept for each student.

Enrollment Requirements Completion of prerequisite courses and three years of college required. Program is open to non-resident foreign students. English language proficiency required.

Program Costs $2000–$4500 for the program.

Housing and Student Services Housing is available. Job counseling and placement services are available.

Special Features Program cosponsored by University of Iowa College of Medicine, University of Iowa Hospitals and Clinics, and Iowa City Veterans Administration Medical Center. Graduates well prepared for and have easily found jobs in hospital, research, and environmental laboratories and in blood banks, educational institutions, and health laboratory–related industry. Some pursue further study in cytogenetics, cytotechnology, microbiology, biochemistry, hematology, or medicine.

Contact Ms. Marian Schwabbauer, Director, Clinical Laboratory Sciences Program, 160 Med Labs, Iowa City, IA 52242. 319-335-8248.

KANSAS

KANSAS NEWMAN COLLEGE
Wichita, Kansas 67213

NURSING-RELATED SERVICES (17.06)
Surgical Technology

General Information Unit offering the program: Health Science. Program content: Operating-room technician program. Available for credit. Cosponsored by St. Francis Regional Medical Center. Certificate signed by the Chairman, Department of Health Science.

Program Format Daytime classes offered. Program cycle: Continuous enrollment. Full program cycle lasts 10 months.

Evaluation Student evaluation based on tests, papers, reports. Grading system: Letters or numbers. Transcripts are kept for each student.

Enrollment Requirements High school diploma required. Program is open to non-resident foreign students. English language proficiency required. Minimum TOEFL score required: 540.

Program Costs $3068 for the program.

Housing and Student Services Housing is available. Job counseling and placement services are available.

Contact Director of Admissions, Wichita, KS 67213. 316-942-4291.

NUCEA MEMBER
KANSAS STATE UNIVERSITY
Manhattan, Kansas 66506

AGRICULTURAL PRODUCTS AND PROCESSING (01.04)
Certificate of Accomplishment

General Information Unit offering the program: Animal Sciences and Industry, Foods and Nutrition, Chemistry. Program content: Food science course work. Available for credit. Endorsed by USDA Food Safety and Inspection Service–Meat and Poultry Division. Certificate signed by the Dean. Certificate applicable to B.S. in Food Science. Program fulfills requirements for 1382 Series, Food Technologist, USDA-FSIS-MPI.

Program Format Videotape, audiotape, one-week laboratory classes offered. Program cycle: Continuous enrollment. Full program cycle lasts 2 years.

Evaluation Student evaluation based on tests, papers, reports, lab results. Grading system: Letters or numbers. Records are kept by Division of Continuing Education.

Enrollment Requirements High school diploma or GED required. Program is open to non-resident foreign students.

Program Costs $1960 for the program, $98 per semester hour.

Housing and Student Services Housing is available. Job counseling and placement services are available.

Special Features Quiz-outs allowed in some courses. Brochure available with biographical data about instructors, structure of the program, and USDA stipulations for completion.

Contact Mr. William E. Lockhart, Ph.D., Coordinator, Food Science Program, 314 Umberger Hall, Manhattan, KS 66506. 913-532-5686.

NUCEA MEMBER
PITTSBURG STATE UNIVERSITY
Pittsburg, Kansas 66762

DRAFTING (48.01)
Technical Education Center Certificate of Completion (Drafting Technology)

General Information Unit offering the program: Engineering Technology Department. Program content: Mathematics; machine, structural, and pipe drafting; computer-aided drafting. Available on either a credit or non-credit basis. Cosponsored by Kansas Board of Regents. Certificate signed by the President of the University.

Program Format Daytime, evening classes offered. Instructional schedule: Six hours per day, five days per week. Program cycle: Continuous enrollment. Full program cycle lasts 2 years.

Evaluation Student evaluation based on tests, papers, reports, hands-on practical performance. Grading system: Letters or numbers. Transcripts are kept for each student.

Enrollment Requirements Minimum 17 years of age, high school diploma required. Program is open to non-resident foreign students. English language proficiency required. Minimum TOEFL score required: 520.

Program Costs $1297–$2175 for the program.

Housing and Student Services Housing is available. Job counseling and placement services are available.

Special Features Technical Education Center is unique in Kansas and rare in the United States. Center provides intensive training in nine vocational and technical programs that are designed to prepare youth and adults for successful rewarding employment in industry as skilled technicians in their field. Instructors have extensive industrial work experience in their particular trade area.

Contact Dr. Jesse L. Hudson, Assistant Dean, School of Technology, School of Technology and Applied Sciences, 115 Willard Hall, Pittsburg, KS 66762. 316-231-7000 Ext. 4631.

ELECTRICAL AND ELECTRONICS EQUIPMENT REPAIR (47.01)
Technical Education Center Certificate of Completion (Electricity)

General Information Unit offering the program: Technical Education Department. Program content: Electric motor rebuilding, wiring, mathematics, raceway installation, blueprint reading. Available on either a credit or non-credit basis. Cosponsored by Kansas Board of Regents. Certificate signed by the President of the University.

Program Format Daytime, evening classes offered. Instructional schedule: Six hours per day, five days per week. Program cycle: Continuous enrollment. Full program cycle lasts 2 years.

Evaluation Student evaluation based on tests, papers, reports, hands-on practical performance. Grading system: Letters or numbers. Transcripts are kept for each student.

Enrollment Requirements Minimum 17 years of age, high school diploma required. Program is open to non-resident foreign students. English language proficiency required. Minimum TOEFL score required: 520.

Program Costs $1297–$2175 for the program.

Housing and Student Services Housing is available. Job counseling and placement services are available.

Special Features Technical Education Center is unique in Kansas and rare in the United States. Center provides intensive training in nine vocational and technical programs that are designed to prepare youth and adults for successful rewarding employment in industry as skilled technicians in their field. Instructors have extensive industrial work experience in their particular trade area.

Contact Dr. Jesse L. Hudson, Assistant Dean, School of Technology, School of Technology and Applied Sciences, 115 Willard Hall, Pittsburg, KS 66762. 316-231-7000 Ext. 4631.

ELECTRICAL AND ELECTRONICS EQUIPMENT REPAIR (47.01)
Technical Education Center Certificate of Completion (Electronics)

General Information Unit offering the program: Engineering Technology Department. Program content: Electronic devices, circuits, and systems; radio communications; AM, FM, and microwave circuits; consumer electronics. Available on either a credit or non-credit basis. Cosponsored by Kansas Board of Regents. Certificate signed by the President of the University.

Program Format Daytime, evening classes offered. Instructional schedule: Six hours per day, five days per week. Program cycle: Continuous enrollment. Full program cycle lasts 2 years.

Evaluation Student evaluation based on tests, papers, reports, hands-on practical performance. Grading system: Letters or numbers. Transcripts are kept for each student.

Enrollment Requirements Minimum 17 years of age, high school diploma required. Program is open to non-resident foreign students. English language proficiency required. Minimum TOEFL score required: 520.

Program Costs $1297–$2175 for the program.

Housing and Student Services Housing is available. Job counseling and placement services are available.

Special Features Technical Education Center is unique in Kansas and rare in the United States. Center provides intensive training in nine vocational and technical programs that are designed to prepare youth and adults for successful rewarding employment in industry as skilled technicians in their field. Instructors have extensive industrial work experience in their particular trade area.

Contact Dr. Jesse L. Hudson, Assistant Dean, School of Technology, School of Technology and Applied Sciences, 115 Willard Hall, Pittsburg, KS 66762. 316-231-7000 Ext. 4631.

HEATING, AIR CONDITIONING, AND REFRIGERATION MECHANICS (47.02)
Technical Education Center Certificate of Completion (Air Conditioning and Refrigeration)

General Information Unit offering the program: Technical Education Department. Program content: Refrigeration, mathematics, electrical schematics, trouble shooting, design, blueprint reading, commercial controls, electrical wiring. Available on either a credit or non-credit basis. Cosponsored by Kansas Board of Regents. Certificate signed by the President of the University.

Program Format Daytime, evening classes offered. Instructional schedule: Six hours per day, five days per week. Program cycle: Continuous enrollment. Full program cycle lasts 2 years.

Evaluation Student evaluation based on tests, papers, reports, hands-on practical performance. Grading system: Letters or numbers. Transcripts are kept for each student.

Enrollment Requirements Minimum 17 years of age, high school diploma required. Program is open to non-resident foreign students. English language proficiency required. Minimum TOEFL score required: 520.

Program Costs $1297–$2175 for the program.

Housing and Student Services Housing is available. Job counseling and placement services are available.

Special Features Technical Education Center is unique in Kansas and rare in the United States. Center provides intensive training in nine vocational and technical programs that are designed to prepare youth and adults for successful rewarding

employment in industry as skilled technicians in their field. Instructors have extensive industrial work experience in their particular trade area.

Contact Dr. Jesse L. Hudson, Assistant Dean, School of Technology, School of Technology and Applied Sciences, 115 Willard Hall, Pittsburg, KS 66762. 316-231-7000 Ext. 4631.

INDUSTRIAL EQUIPMENT MAINTENANCE AND REPAIR (47.03)
Technical Education Center Certificate of Completion (Machine Shop Technology)

General Information Unit offering the program: Engineering Technology Department. Program content: Mathematics, blueprint reading, metallurgy, tools and fixtures, welding. Available on either a credit or non-credit basis. Cosponsored by Kansas Board of Regents. Certificate signed by the President of the University.

Program Format Daytime, evening classes offered. Instructional schedule: Six hours per day, five days per week. Program cycle: Continuous enrollment. Full program cycle lasts 2 years.

Evaluation Student evaluation based on tests, papers, reports, hands-on practical performance. Grading system: Letters or numbers. Transcripts are kept for each student.

Enrollment Requirements Minimum 17 years of age, high school diploma required. Program is open to non-resident foreign students. English language proficiency required. Minimum TOEFL score required: 520.

Program Costs $1297–$2175 for the program.

Housing and Student Services Housing is available. Job counseling and placement services are available.

Special Features Technical Education Center is unique in Kansas and rare in the United States. Center provides intensive training in nine vocational and technical programs that are designed to prepare youth and adults for successful rewarding employment in industry as skilled technicians in their field. Instructors have extensive industrial work experience in their particular trade area.

Contact Dr. Jesse L. Hudson, Assistant Dean, School of Technology, School of Technology and Applied Sciences, 115 Willard Hall, Pittsburg, KS 66762. 316-231-7000 Ext. 4631.

PRECISION METAL WORK (48.05)
Technical Education Center Certificate of Completion (Welding)

General Information Unit offering the program: Technical Education Department. Program content: Drafting, mathematics, layout, technical information, blueprint reading. Available on either a credit or non-credit basis. Cosponsored by Kansas Board of Regents. Certificate signed by the President of the University.

Program Format Daytime, evening classes offered. Instructional schedule: Six hours per day, five days per week. Program cycle: Continuous enrollment. Full program cycle lasts 2 years.

Evaluation Student evaluation based on tests, papers, reports, hands-on practical performance. Grading system: Letters or numbers. Transcripts are kept for each student.

Enrollment Requirements Minimum 17 years of age, high school diploma required. Program is open to non-resident foreign students. English language proficiency required. Minimum TOEFL score required: 520.

Program Costs $1297–$2175 for the program.

Housing and Student Services Housing is available. Job counseling and placement services are available.

Special Features Technical Education Center is unique in Kansas and rare in the United States. Center provides intensive training in nine vocational and technical programs that are designed to prepare youth and adults for successful rewarding employment in industry as skilled technicians in their field.

Technical Education Center Certificate of Completion (Welding) continued

Instructors have extensive industrial work experience in their particular trade area.

Contact Dr. Jesse L. Hudson, Assistant Dean, School of Technology, School of Technology and Applied Sciences, 115 Willard Hall, Pittsburg, KS 66762. 316-231-7000 Ext. 4631.

VEHICLE AND MOBILE EQUIPMENT MECHANICS AND REPAIRERS (47.06)
Technical Education Center Certificate of Completion (Auto Body Repair)

General Information Unit offering the program: Industrial Arts and Technology Department. Available on either a credit or non-credit basis. Cosponsored by Kansas Board of Regents. Certificate signed by the President of the University.

Program Format Daytime, evening classes offered. Instructional schedule: Six hours per day, five days per week. Program cycle: Continuous enrollment. Full program cycle lasts 11 months.

Evaluation Student evaluation based on tests, papers, reports, hands-on practical performance. Grading system: Letters or numbers. Transcripts are kept for each student.

Enrollment Requirements Minimum 17 years of age, high school diploma required. Program is open to non-resident foreign students. English language proficiency required. Minimum TOEFL score required: 520.

Program Costs $1297–$2175 for the program.

Housing and Student Services Housing is available. Job counseling and placement services are available.

Special Features Technical Education Center is unique in Kansas and rare in the United States. Center provides intensive training in nine vocational and technical programs that are designed to prepare youth and adults for successful rewarding employment in industry as skilled technicians in their field. Instructors have extensive industrial work experience in their particular trade area.

Contact Dr. Jesse L. Hudson, Assistant Dean, School of Technology, School of Technology and Applied Sciences, 115 Willard Hall, Pittsburg, KS 66762. 316-231-7000 Ext. 4631.

VEHICLE AND MOBILE EQUIPMENT MECHANICS AND REPAIRERS (47.06)
Technical Education Center Certificate of Completion (Auto Mechanics)

General Information Unit offering the program: Industrial Arts and Technology Department. Program content: Automotive electricity and mathematics, power plant diagnosis, automatic transmission, air conditioning. Available on either a credit or non-credit basis. Cosponsored by Kansas Board of Regents. Certificate signed by the President of the University.

Program Format Daytime, evening classes offered. Instructional schedule: Six hours per day, five days per week. Program cycle: Continuous enrollment. Full program cycle lasts 2 years.

Evaluation Student evaluation based on tests, papers, reports, hands-on practical performance. Grading system: Letters or numbers. Transcripts are kept for each student.

Enrollment Requirements Minimum 17 years of age, high school diploma required. Program is open to non-resident foreign students. English language proficiency required. Minimum TOEFL score required: 520.

Program Costs $1297–$2175 for the program.

Housing and Student Services Housing is available. Job counseling and placement services are available.

Special Features Technical Education Center is unique in Kansas and rare in the United States. Center provides intensive training in nine vocational and technical programs that are designed to prepare youth and adults for successful rewarding

employment in industry as skilled technicians in their field. Instructors have extensive industrial work experience in their particular trade area.

Contact Dr. Jesse L. Hudson, Assistant Dean, School of Technology, School of Technology and Applied Sciences, 115 Willard Hall, Pittsburg, KS 66762. 316-231-7000 Ext. 4631.

WOODWORKING (48.07)
Technical Education Center Certificate of Completion (Cabinet and Furniture Making)

General Information Unit offering the program: Industrial Arts and Technology Department. Program content: Upholstery, woodwork, shop sketching, blueprint reading, carpentry, mathematics, maintenance problems. Available on either a credit or non-credit basis. Cosponsored by Kansas Board of Regents. Certificate signed by the President of the University.

Program Format Daytime, evening classes offered. Instructional schedule: Six hours per day, five days per week. Program cycle: Continuous enrollment. Full program cycle lasts 2 years.

Evaluation Student evaluation based on tests, papers, reports, hands-on practical performance. Grading system: Letters or numbers. Transcripts are kept for each student.

Enrollment Requirements Minimum 17 years of age, high school diploma required. Program is open to non-resident foreign students. English language proficiency required. Minimum TOEFL score required: 520.

Program Costs $1297–$2175 for the program.

Housing and Student Services Housing is available. Job counseling and placement services are available.

Special Features Technical Education Center is unique in Kansas and rare in the United States. Center provides intensive training in nine vocational and technical programs that are designed to prepare youth and adults for successful rewarding employment in industry as skilled technicians in their field. Instructors have extensive industrial work experience in their particular trade area.

Contact Dr. Jesse L. Hudson, Assistant Dean, School of Technology, School of Technology and Applied Sciences, 115 Willard Hall, Pittsburg, KS 66762. 316-231-7000 Ext. 4631.

SOUTHWESTERN COLLEGE
Winfield, Kansas 67156

DIAGNOSTIC AND TREATMENT SERVICES (17.02)
Emergency Mobile Intensive Care Training

General Information Unit offering the program: Division of Natural Sciences, Department of Biology. Program content: Hospital clinical rotation, field internship, registry test preparation. Available for credit. Cosponsored by William Newton Memorial Hospital. Certificate signed by the President of the College. Certificate applicable to B.A. in Biology. Program fulfills requirements for Emergency Mobile Intensive Care Training (State of Kansas).

Program Format Daytime, evening classes offered. Instructional schedule: 30–40 hours per week. Students enroll in August. Full program cycle lasts 12 months. Completion of program requires written and practical tests in anatomy and physiology, state examination, internship.

Evaluation Student evaluation based on tests, internship, case studies, term paper. Grading system: Letters or numbers. Transcripts are kept for each student.

Enrollment Requirements Letter of reference, interview, EMT certification plus one year experience or medical background, related college work required. Program is open to non-resident foreign students. English language proficiency required. Minimum TOEFL score required: 450.

Program Costs $3936 for the program.

Housing and Student Services Housing is available. Job counseling and placement services are available.

Special Features The course instructor is an R.N., certified in critical care, and is herself an EMICT. All of the adjunct faculty members are either R.N.'s or hold paramedic certification/experience. Approximately 90 percent of those completing the program pass the state registry the first time they take it. (100 percent eventually pass the state registry.).

Contact Ms. Marilyn Crowley, Coordinator, EMICT, 100 College Street, Winfield, KS 67156. 316-221-4150.

KENTUCKY

NUCEA MEMBER
NORTHERN KENTUCKY UNIVERSITY
Highland Heights, Kentucky 41076

ACCOUNTING (06.02)
IRS Accounting Certificate

General Information Unit offering the program: Credit Continuing Education, Department of Accounting. Program content: Accounting courses and business law. Available for credit. Endorsed by Internal Revenue Service. Certificate signed by the Director, Credit Continuing Education. Certificate applicable to B.S. in Accounting.

Program Format Evening classes offered. Instructional schedule: One evening per week. Full program cycle lasts 3 semesters. Completion of program requires grade of C or better in all required courses.

Evaluation Student evaluation based on tests. Grading system: Letters or numbers. Transcripts are kept for each student.

Enrollment Requirements Limited to IRS employees. Program is not open to non-resident foreign students.

Program Costs $987 for the program, $141 per course (state residents); $2793 for the program, $399 per course (nonresidents).

Housing and Student Services Housing is not available. Job counseling and placement services are not available.

Contact Dr. Susan Kemper, Director, Credit Continuing Education, 1401 Dixie Highway, Covington, KY 41011. 606-572-5601.

SPALDING UNIVERSITY
Louisville, Kentucky 40203

FOOD PRODUCTION, MANAGEMENT, AND SERVICES (20.04)
Dietary Manager Certificate

General Information Unit offering the program: Community Education Office. Program content: Food service management, nutrition care. Available on a non-credit basis. Endorsed by Dietary Managers Association. Cosponsored by Martha Gregory Associates. Certificate signed by the Program Director. Program fulfills requirements for Dietary Managers Association.

Program Format Daytime classes offered. Instructional schedule: Three hours per week. Students enroll in September. Full program cycle lasts 2 semesters. Completion of program requires grade of C or better, 150 contact hours in health care facility.

Evaluation Student evaluation based on tests, papers, reports, practicum. Grading system: Letters or numbers. Records are kept for each student.

Enrollment Requirements Limited to persons presently working in health care institution with an R.D. Program is open to non-resident foreign students.

Program Costs $450 for the program.

Housing and Student Services Housing is not available. Job counseling and placement services are not available.

Special Features New program started in 1985 and has 5-year approval from Dietary Managers' Association.

Contact Ms. Susan Wood, Assistant to the Provost, Community Education, Louisville, KY 40203. 502-585-9911 Ext. 298.

THOMAS MORE COLLEGE
Crestview Hills, Kentucky 41017

ACCOUNTING (06.02)
Accounting Certificate

General Information Unit offering the program: Accountancy. Program content: Accounting, business law. Available for credit. Certificate signed by the President.

Program Format Daytime, evening, weekend classes offered. Program cycle: Continuous enrollment. Full program cycle lasts 42 credit hours.

Evaluation Student evaluation based on tests. Grading system: Letters or numbers. Transcripts are kept for each student.

Enrollment Requirements College admissions required. Program is open to non-resident foreign students.

Program Costs $7010–$7770 for the program, $491–$555 per course.

Housing and Student Services Housing is available. Job counseling and placement services are available.

Contact Mr. Thomas J. Gilday, Chairperson, Department of Accountancy, Crestview Hills, KY 41017. 606-341-5800.

BUSINESS AND MANAGEMENT, GENERAL (06.01)
Certificate in Business Administration

General Information Unit offering the program: Business Administration. Program content: Accountancy, economics, computer science, business law. Available for credit. Certificate signed by the President. Certificate applicable to A.A., B.A., A.E.S., B.E.S. in Business Administration.

Program Format Daytime, evening, weekend classes offered. Program cycle: Continuous enrollment. Full program cycle lasts 36 credit hours. Completion of program requires 2.0 GPA.

Evaluation Student evaluation based on tests, papers, reports, case analysis. Grading system: Letters or numbers. Transcripts are kept for each student.

Enrollment Requirements College admissions required. Program is open to non-resident foreign students.

Program Costs $6660 for the program, $555 per course.

Housing and Student Services Housing is available. Job counseling and placement services are available.

Special Features Credit for experience is available through the RECALL option. Work experience is available through the COOP option.

Contact Admissions Office, Crestview Hills, KY 41017. 606-341-5800.

MANAGEMENT INFORMATION SYSTEMS
(06.12)
Computer Management

General Information Unit offering the program: Computer Science. Program content: Computer science, accounting, business administration. Available for credit. Certificate signed by the President. Certificate applicable to B.A. in Computer Information Systems.

Program Format Daytime, evening, weekend classes offered. Program cycle: Continuous enrollment. Full program cycle lasts 4 semesters.

Evaluation Student evaluation based on tests, papers, reports. Grading system: Letters or numbers. Transcripts are kept for each student.

Enrollment Requirements College admissions required. Program is open to non-resident foreign students.

Program Costs $5550 for the program, $555 per course.

Housing and Student Services Housing is available. Job counseling and placement services are available.

Special Features Students may obtain credit for prior learning through the College's "Recall" program. Program emphasizes business aspects of computers.

Contact Mr. Kenneth Taylor, Chairman, Computer Science, Crestview Hills, KY 41017. 606-344-3417.

NUCEA MEMBER
UNIVERSITY OF KENTUCKY
Lexington, Kentucky 40506

COMPUTER AND INFORMATION SCIENCES, GENERAL (11.01)
University of Kentucky Computer Certificate Program

General Information Unit offering the program: Community Education. Program content: Microcomputers, word processing, BASIC programming, data management, electronic spreadsheets. Available on a non-credit basis. Certificate signed by the Dean, University of Kentucky Extension.

Program Format Daytime, evening, weekend classes offered. Program cycle: Continuous enrollment. Full program cycle lasts 5 courses. Completion of program requires grade of 70% or better.

Evaluation Student evaluation based on tests. Grading system: Letters or numbers. Transcripts are kept for each student.

Enrollment Requirements Program is open to non-resident foreign students.

Program Costs $525 for the program.

Housing and Student Services Housing is not available. Job counseling and placement services are not available.

Contact Ms. Valerie Summers, Director, 205 Frazee Hall, Lexington, KY 40506-0031. 800-325-2766.

TRANSPORTATION AND TRAVEL MARKETING
(08.11)
Travel Agent Career Training

General Information Unit offering the program: Community Education. Program content: Introduction to the travel agency, cruises, air travel, tours and packages, travel geography. Available on a non-credit basis. Certificate signed by the Dean, University of Kentucky Extension.

Program Format Evening classes offered. Students may enroll three times per year. Completion of program requires five courses.

Evaluation Student evaluation based on tests, papers, reports. Grading system: Letters or numbers. Transcripts are kept for each student.

Enrollment Requirements Minimum 16 years of age required. Program is open to non-resident foreign students.

Program Costs $260 for the program.

Housing and Student Services Housing is not available. Job counseling and placement services are not available.

Contact Ms. Valerie Summers, Director of Community Education, 205 Frazee Hall, Lexington, KY 40506-0031. 606-257-3294.

LOUISIANA

NUCEA MEMBER
LOUISIANA STATE UNIVERSITY AND AGRICULTURAL AND MECHANICAL COLLEGE
Baton Rouge, Louisiana 70803

ACCOUNTING (06.02)
CPA Preparation Program

General Information Unit offering the program: Accounting. Program content: Financial accounting, income tax, cost accounting, auditing. Available for credit. Certificate signed by the Dean of Continuing Education.

Program Format Evening classes offered. Instructional schedule: Two evenings per week. Program cycle: Continuous enrollment. Full program cycle lasts 18 months. Completion of program requires eight accounting courses.

Evaluation Student evaluation based on tests. Grading system: Letters or numbers. Transcripts are kept for each student.

Enrollment Requirements Bachelor's degree required. Program is open to non-resident foreign students. English language proficiency required.

Program Costs $2000 for the program, $250 per course.

Housing and Student Services Housing is not available. Job counseling and placement services are not available.

Special Features Courses offered to satisfy requirements of students taking the CPA exam. Classes taught by regular accounting department faculty. The program has been in existence for 10 years.

Contact Mr. Edward L. Simon, Department Head, Extramural Teaching, 112 Pleasant Hall, Baton Rouge, LA 70803. 504-388-5213.

BUSINESS AND MANAGEMENT, GENERAL
(06.01)
Business Application Specialist in Computers (BASIC)

General Information Unit offering the program: Continuing Education Short Courses and Conferences. Program content: Word processing, spreadsheets, database management, programming. Available on a non-credit basis. Certificate signed by the Dean, Division of Continuing Education.

Program Format Daytime, evening, weekend classes offered. Program cycle: Continuous enrollment. Full program cycle lasts 2 semesters. Completion of program requires examination.

Evaluation Student evaluation based on tests. Grading system: Pass/fail. Transcripts are kept for each student.

Enrollment Requirements Program is not open to non-resident foreign students.

Program Costs $1200 for the program, $135 per course.

Housing and Student Services Housing is available. Job counseling and placement services are not available.

Special Features Business Application Specialist in Computer (BASIC) is a program designed for those who need computer knowledge and training to keep pace with the competitive business environment. A wide range of courses from introductory to advanced levels, including DOS, word processing, database management systems, financial spreadsheets, computer programming, and business computer applications are offered.

Contact Mr. Tom Atkinson, Director of Computer Instruction and Support, 177 Pleasant Hall, Baton Rouge, LA 70803. 504-388-6314.

INDUSTRIAL ENGINEERING (14.17)
Engineering Management

General Information Unit offering the program: Industrial Engineering. Program content: Finance, management theory, law. Available on either a credit or non-credit basis. Endorsed by Louisiana Engineering Society. Certificate signed by the Dean, Division of Continuing Education.

Program Format Evening classes offered. Instructional schedule: One evening per week. Students may enroll fall, spring. Full program cycle lasts 4 semesters. Completion of program requires four courses.

Evaluation Student evaluation based on tests, papers, reports. Grading system: Letters or numbers. Transcripts are kept for each student.

Enrollment Requirements Limited to professional engineers. Program is open to non-resident foreign students. English language proficiency required.

Program Costs $1200 for the program, $300 per course.

Housing and Student Services Housing is not available. Job counseling and placement services are not available.

Special Features Courses seek to improve managerial skills of professional engineers by offering them classes in finance, management, law, etc. The program has been in existence for 20 years and is state-wide in scope.

Contact Mr. Edward L. Simon, Department Head, Extramural Teaching, 112 Pleasant Hall, Baton Rouge, LA 70803. 504-388-5213.

LAW (22.01)
Paralegal Studies Institute

General Information Unit offering the program: Division of Continuing Education. Program content: Legal research and analysis. Available on a non-credit basis. Endorsed by American Association for Paralegal Education/American Bar Association. Certificate signed by the Dean, Division of Continuing Education. Program fulfills requirements for Certified Legal Assistant.

Program Format Evening classes offered. Instructional schedule: One evening per week for three hours. Program cycle: Continuous enrollment. Full program cycle lasts 8 courses. Completion of program requires grade of B or better.

Evaluation Student evaluation based on tests, papers, reports, legal document preparation. Grading system: Letters or numbers. Transcripts are kept for each student.

Enrollment Requirements College degree or high school/GED plus B average required. Program is open to non-resident foreign students.

Program Costs $1760 for the program, $220 per course.

Housing and Student Services Housing is not available. Job counseling and placement services are available.

Special Features The Paralegal Studies Institute offers continuing professional education for practicing paralegals and a certificate program for entry-level paralegals. Special features include a placement office, two levels of internships (beginning and advanced), programs for attorneys, and the National Association of Legal Secretaries basic course sequence. This allows training of the whole legal team.

Contact Mr. Herbert E. Carter, Director, Paralegal Studies Institute, 177 Pleasant Hall, Baton Rouge, LA 70803. 504-388-6621.

SAINT JOSEPH SEMINARY COLLEGE
Saint Benedict, Louisiana 70457

RELIGIOUS EDUCATION (39.04)
Religious Studies Institute

General Information Unit offering the program: Philosophy and Religion. Program content: Ministry and leadership for lay church leaders. Available for credit. Certificate signed by the President.

Program Format Weekend classes offered. Students enroll in August. Full program cycle lasts 2 years.

Evaluation Student evaluation based on tests, papers, reports, class participation. Grading system: Letters or numbers. Transcripts are kept for each student.

Enrollment Requirements Program is open to non-resident foreign students. English language proficiency required. Minimum TOEFL score required: 550.

Program Costs $670 for the program, $45 per credit hour.

Housing and Student Services Housing is not available. Job counseling and placement services are not available.

Special Features The program provides the opportunity for growth in the practical as well as the spiritual components of church service.

Contact Mr. Thomas A. Siegrist, Director of Admissions/Registrar, St. Benedict, LA 70457. 504-892-1800.

NUCEA MEMBER
UNIVERSITY OF NEW ORLEANS
New Orleans, Louisiana 70148

LAW (22.01)
Certificate of Paralegal Studies

General Information Unit offering the program: Metropolitan College, Paralegal Institute. Program content: Substantive and procedural law. Available on a non-credit basis. Certificate signed by the Director.

Program Format Daytime, evening classes offered. Program cycle: Continuous enrollment. Full program cycle lasts 12 months. Completion of program requires eight courses, 2.0 GPA.

Evaluation Student evaluation based on tests, papers, reports. Grading system: Letters or numbers. Transcripts are kept for each student.

Enrollment Requirements Bachelor's degree or three years legal experience or admission examination required. Program is open to non-resident foreign students. English language proficiency required. Diagnostic assessment of language skills and writing sample.

Program Costs $2360 for the program, $295 per course.

Housing and Student Services Housing is not available. Job counseling and placement services are available.

Special Features UNO Paralegal Institute, established in 1981, offers a noncredit certificate program in paralegal studies, consisting of 8 courses combining instruction in substantive law with training in legal procedural skills, that can be completed in 12 months. Instruction offered by practicing attorneys and paralegals with extensive teaching and legal practice experience.

Certificate of Paralegal Studies continued

Contact Mr. James W. Sexton, Director, Paralegal Institute, 226 Carondelet Street, 3rd Floor, New Orleans, LA 70130. 504-523-6859.

MICROCOMPUTER APPLICATIONS (11.06)
Microcomputer Certificate Program

General Information Unit offering the program: Personal Computer Learning Center. Program content: DOS, Lotus, dBase III+, WordPerfect electives, practicum. Available on a non-credit basis. Certificate signed by the Chancellor.

Program Format Daytime, evening, weekend classes offered. Instructional schedule: Once per week for three hours. Program cycle: Continuous enrollment. Full program cycle lasts 2 years. Completion of program requires 96 contact hours.

Evaluation Student evaluation based on tests. Grading system: Pass/fail. Transcripts are kept for each student.

Enrollment Requirements Admission examination required. Program is open to non-resident foreign students.

Program Costs $2000 for the program, $215 per course.

Housing and Student Services Job counseling and placement services are not available.

Special Features MCP requirements include completion of a predetermined core set of courses (4 courses); completion of Levels II and III, area of specialization; 1 elective; and applied practicum project, which includes a "real world" microcomputer application. All levels require satisfactory performance on testing procedures before advancement to subsequent levels.

Contact Ms. Jane E. Prudhomme, Director, Personal Computer Learning Center, Downtown Center, 226 Carondelet Street, New Orleans, LA 70501. 504-523-6859 Ext. 15.

MARYLAND

EASTERN CHRISTIAN COLLEGE
Bel Air, Maryland 21014

BIBLE STUDIES (39.02)
Certificate in Biblical Studies

General Information Unit offering the program: Bible and Practical Ministries Departments. Program content: Bible, practical ministries. Available for credit. Certificate signed by the President. Certificate applicable to any two- or four-year degree offered at the institution.

Program Format Daytime classes offered. Full program cycle lasts 2 semesters.

Evaluation Student evaluation based on tests, papers, reports. Grading system: Letters or numbers. Transcripts are kept for each student.

Enrollment Requirements High school diploma, recommendations, ACT scores required. Program is open to non-resident foreign students. English language proficiency required. Minimum TOEFL score required: 450.

Program Costs $48 per credit hour.

Housing and Student Services Housing is available. Job counseling and placement services are available.

Contact Mr. Frank Harris, Dean of Students, P.O. Box 629, Bel Air, MD 21014. 301-734-7727.

FROSTBURG STATE UNIVERSITY
Frostburg, Maryland 21532

BUSINESS AND MANAGEMENT, GENERAL (06.01)
Certificate in Management Studies

General Information Unit offering the program: Center for Management Development. Available for credit. Certificate signed by the Dean of Graduate Studies. Certificate applicable to M.S. in Management.

Program Format Evening classes offered. Instructional schedule: One evening per week. Program cycle: Continuous enrollment. Completion of program requires 2.5 GPA, 24 credit hours.

Evaluation Student evaluation based on tests, papers, reports. Grading system: Letters or numbers. Transcripts are kept for each student.

Enrollment Requirements Administrative/supervisory experience and/or college experience required. Program is open to non-resident foreign students. English language proficiency required. Minimum TOEFL score required: 560.

Program Costs $1896 for the program, $273 per course.

Housing and Student Services Job counseling and placement services are not available.

Contact Dr. Robert S. Donnelly, Director, Center for Management Development, Frostburg, MD 21532-1099. 301-689-4375.

NUCEA MEMBER
JOHNS HOPKINS UNIVERSITY
Baltimore, Maryland 21218

EDUCATION ADMINISTRATION (13.04)
Certificate of Advanced Study in Education (Administration and Supervision)

General Information Unit offering the program: Education. Program content: Conceptual and theortical basis, effective leadership, foundations in supervision. Available for credit. Certificate signed by the Dean. Certificate applicable to doctoral degree.

Program Format Evening classes offered. Instructional schedule: Once per week for 1 hour, 55 minutes in fall and spring semesters; twice per week for 2 hours in summer semester. Program cycle: Continuous enrollment. Full program cycle lasts 30 credit hours. Completion of program requires grade of B or better.

Evaluation Student evaluation based on tests, papers, presentations or graduate project/thesis. Grading system: Letters or numbers. Transcripts are kept for each student.

Enrollment Requirements Master's degree required. Program is not open to non-resident foreign students.

Program Costs $4350 for the program, $435 per course, $145 per credit hour.

Housing and Student Services Housing is not available. Job counseling and placement services are available.

Contact Dr. Ralph Fessler, Director, Division of Education, 101 Whitehead Hall, School of Continuing Studies, Baltimore, MD 21218. 301-338-8273.

EDUCATIONAL MEDIA (13.05)
Certificate of Advanced Study in Education (Education Technology)

General Information Unit offering the program: Education. Program content: Programming and education, educational use of micro-technology. Available for credit. Certificate signed by the Dean. Certificate applicable to doctoral degree.

Program Format   Evening classes offered. Instructional schedule: Once per week for 1 hour, 55 minutes in fall and spring semesters; twice per week for 2 hours in summer semester. Program cycle: Continuous enrollment. Full program cycle lasts 30 credit hours. Completion of program requires grade of B or better in all courses.

Evaluation   Student evaluation based on tests, papers, presentations or graduate project/thesis. Grading system: Letters or numbers. Transcripts are kept for each student.

Enrollment Requirements   Master's degree required. Program is not open to non-resident foreign students.

Program Costs $4350 for the program, $435 per course, $145 per credit hour.

Housing and Student Services   Housing is not available. Job counseling and placement services are available.

Contact   Dr. Ralph Fessler, Director, Division of Education, 101 Whitehead Hall, School of Continuing Studies, Baltimore, MD 21218. 301-338-8273.

EVALUATION AND RESEARCH (13.06)
Certificate of Advanced Study in Education (Research and Measurement)

General Information   Unit offering the program: Education. Program content: Computer applications, measurement and evaluation, statistics, behavioral research. Available for credit. Certificate signed by the Dean. Certificate applicable to doctoral degree.

Program Format   Evening classes offered. Instructional schedule: Once per week for 1 hour, 55 minutes in fall and spring semesters; twice per week for 2 hours in summer semester. Program cycle: Continuous enrollment. Full program cycle lasts 30 credit hours. Completion of program requires grade of B or better in all courses.

Evaluation   Student evaluation based on tests, papers, presentations or graduate project/thesis. Grading system: Letters or numbers. Transcripts are kept for each student.

Enrollment Requirements   Master's degree required. Program is not open to non-resident foreign students.

Program Costs $4350 for the program, $435 per course, $145 per credit hour.

Housing and Student Services   Housing is not available. Job counseling and placement services are available.

Contact   Dr. Ralph Fessler, Director, Division of Education, 101 Whitehead Hall, School of Continuing Studies, Baltimore, MD 21218. 301-338-8273.

LIBERAL/GENERAL STUDIES (24.01)
Certificate of Advanced Study in Liberal Arts

General Information   Unit offering the program: School of Continuing Studies, Arts and Sciences Division. Available for credit. Certificate signed by the Chairman, Board of Trustees.

Program Format   Evening classes offered. Program cycle: Continuous enrollment. Full program cycle lasts 30 credit hours. Completion of program requires grade of B or better in all courses.

Evaluation   Student evaluation methods vary by course. Grading system: Letters or numbers. Transcripts are kept for each student.

Enrollment Requirements   M.F.A. required. Program is open to non-resident foreign students.

Program Costs $435–$465 per course.

Housing and Student Services   Job counseling and placement services are not available.

Contact   Mr. David B. House, Director, Arts and Sciences, 204 Shaffer Hall, Baltimore, MD 21218. 301-338-7191.

REAL ESTATE (06.17)
The Real Estate Development Process

General Information   Unit offering the program: Office of Business and Professional Development, School of Continuing Studies. Available on a non-credit basis. Certificate signed by the Dean. Program fulfills requirements for Brokers license and Sales Agent license.

Program Format   Evening classes offered. Full program cycle lasts 1 year.

Evaluation   Student evaluation based on reports, class presentations. Transcripts are kept for each student.

Enrollment Requirements   Two years experience in real estate, letter from current employer required. Program is open to non-resident foreign students.

Program Costs $1600 for the program.

Housing and Student Services   Housing is not available. Job counseling and placement services are not available.

Special Features   Designed for real estate professionals, the program stresses how the development process operates. Seasoned specialists present case studies based on current real estate projects. Approach is from perspective of private sector interests—developer, lender or investor, managing operator, and executor of the project. Attention given to how public sector regulations and policies create opportunities or constraints in the development process.

Contact   Mr. Craig Weidemann, Director, Business and Professional Development Programs, School of Continuing Studies, Baltimore, MD 21218. 301-338-8500.

SCHOOL PSYCHOLOGY (13.08)
Certificate of Advanced Study in Education (Counseling and Clinical Supervision)

General Information   Unit offering the program: Education. Program content: Techniques in couple and family therapy, psycho-diagnostics, fieldwork. Available for credit. Certificate signed by the Dean. Certificate applicable to doctoral degree.

Program Format   Evening classes offered. Instructional schedule: Once per week for 1 hour, 55 minutes in fall and spring semesters; twice per week for 2 hours in summer semester. Program cycle: Continuous enrollment. Full program cycle lasts 30 credit hours. Completion of program requires grade of B or better in all courses.

Evaluation   Student evaluation based on tests, papers, presentations or graduate project/thesis. Grading system: Letters or numbers. Transcripts are kept for each student.

Enrollment Requirements   Master's degree required. Program is not open to non-resident foreign students.

Program Costs $4350 for the program, $435 per course, $145 per credit hour.

Housing and Student Services   Housing is not available. Job counseling and placement services are available.

Contact   Dr. Ralph Fessler, Director, Division of Education, 101 Whitehead Hall, School of Continuing Studies, Baltimore, MD 21218. 301-338-8273.

SPECIAL EDUCATION (13.10)
Certificate of Advanced Study in Education (Special Education and Rehabilitation)

General Information Unit offering the program: Education. Program content: Mild and moderate handicapping conditions, mainstreaming, corroborative programming, legal aspects. Available for credit. Certificate signed by the Dean. Certificate applicable to doctoral degree.

Program Format Evening classes offered. Instructional schedule: Once per week for 1 hour, 55 minutes in fall and spring semesters; twice per week for 2 hours in summer semester. Program cycle: Continuous enrollment. Full program cycle lasts 30 credit hours. Completion of program requires grade of B or better.

Evaluation Student evaluation based on tests, papers, presentations or graduate project/thesis. Grading system: Letters or numbers. Transcripts are kept for each student.

Enrollment Requirements Master's degree required. Program is not open to non-resident foreign students.

Program Costs $4350 for the program, $435 per course, $145 per credit hour.

Housing and Student Services Housing is not available. Job counseling and placement services are available.

Contact Dr. Ralph Fessler, Director, Division of Education, 101 Whitehead Hall, School of Continuing Studies, Baltimore, MD 21218. 301-338-8273.

STUDENT COUNSELING AND PERSONNEL SERVICES (13.11)
Certificate of Advanced Study in Education (Career Counseling)

General Information Unit offering the program: Education. Program content: Guidance programs, career development, group counseling, statistics. Available for credit. Certificate signed by the Dean. Certificate applicable to doctoral degree.

Program Format Evening classes offered. Instructional schedule: Once per week for 1 hour, 55 minutes in fall and spring semesters; twice per week for 2 hours in summer semester. Program cycle: Continuous enrollment. Full program cycle lasts 30 credit hours. Completion of program requires grade of B or better in all courses.

Evaluation Student evaluation based on tests, papers, presentations or graduate project/thesis. Grading system: Letters or numbers. Transcripts are kept for each student.

Enrollment Requirements Master's degree required. Program is not open to non-resident foreign students.

Program Costs $4350 for the program, $435 per course, $145 per credit hour.

Housing and Student Services Housing is not available. Job counseling and placement services are available.

Contact Dr. Ralph Fessler, Director, Division of Education, 101 Whitehead Hall, School of Continuing Studies, Baltimore, MD 21218. 301-338-8273.

STUDENT COUNSELING AND PERSONNEL SERVICES (13.11)
Certificate of Advanced Study in Education (Human Resources Counseling)

General Information Unit offering the program: Education. Program content: Organizational behavior, adult learning, group counseling, statistics. Available for credit. Certificate signed by the Dean. Certificate applicable to doctoral degree.

Program Format Evening classes offered. Instructional schedule: Once per week for 1 hour, 55 minutes in fall and spring semesters; twice per week for 2 hours in summer semester. Program cycle: Continuous enrollment. Full program cycle lasts 30 credit hours. Completion of program requires grade of B or better in all courses.

Evaluation Student evaluation based on tests, papers, presentations or graduate project/thesis. Grading system: Letters or numbers. Transcripts are kept for each student.

Enrollment Requirements Master's degree required. Program is not open to non-resident foreign students.

Program Costs $4350 for the program, $435 per course, $145 per credit hour.

Housing and Student Services Housing is not available. Job counseling and placement services are available.

Contact Dr. Ralph Fessler, Director, Division of Education, 101 Whitehead Hall, School of Continuing Studies, Baltimore, MD 21218. 301-338-8273.

TEACHER EDUCATION, SPECIFIC SUBJECT AREAS (13.13)
Certificate in Economic Education

General Information Unit offering the program: School of Continuing Studies, Administration and Business Division. Program content: Economics, teacher training skills, information technology. Available for credit. Endorsed by Black and Decker. Cosponsored by Chessie System. Certificate signed by the Dean, School of Continuing Studies. Certificate applicable to M.S. in Economic Education.

Program Format Daytime, evening, weekend classes offered. Instructional schedule: Once per week. Program cycle: Continuous enrollment. Full program cycle lasts 6 semesters. Completion of program requires six courses, grade of B or better.

Evaluation Student evaluation based on tests, papers, reports, curriculum writing, computer program construction. Grading system: Letters or numbers. Transcripts are kept for each student.

Enrollment Requirements Master's degree or 3.0 GPA for last two years of undergraduate degree required. Program is not open to non-resident foreign students.

Program Costs $2600–$2800 for the program, $435–$465 per course.

Housing and Student Services Housing is not available. Job counseling and placement services are available.

Special Features Tuition assistance program. Internship program (student placement in private sector or federal or state government employment for credit). Affiliation with national networks for the study of economics and economic education. Full economic education resource library including written, audiovisual, and computer materials.

Contact Ms. Margaret M. Murphy, Ph.D., Program Director, Suite 202, Overlook Center, 5457 Twin Knolls Road, Columbia, MD 21045.

TEACHER EDUCATION, SPECIFIC SUBJECT AREAS (13.13)
Certificate of Advanced Study in Education (Reading)

General Information Unit offering the program: Education. Program content: Teaching comprehension, abilities and techniques, reading disabilities and diagnosis, adult literacy. Available for credit. Certificate signed by the Dean. Certificate applicable to doctoral degree.

Program Format Evening classes offered. Instructional schedule: Once per week for 1 hour, 55 minutes in fall and spring semesters; twice per week for 2 hours in summer semester. Program cycle: Continuous enrollment. Full program cycle lasts 30 credit hours. Completion of program requires grade of B or better in all courses.

Evaluation Student evaluation based on tests, papers, presentations or graduate project/thesis. Grading system: Letters or numbers. Transcripts are kept for each student.

Enrollment Requirements   Master's degree required. Program is not open to non-resident foreign students.

Program Costs $4350 for the program, $435 per course, $145 per credit hour.

Housing and Student Services   Housing is not available. Job counseling and placement services are available.

Contact   Dr. Ralph Fessler, Director, Division of Education, 101 Whitehead Hall, School of Continuing Studies, Baltimore, MD 21218. 301-338-8273.

UNIVERSITY OF BALTIMORE
Baltimore, Maryland 21201

ACCOUNTING (06.02)
Certificate in Accounting

General Information   Unit offering the program: Accounting. Program content: Accounting and business law. Available for credit. Certificate signed by the University President. Certificate applicable to B.S. in Business, Accounting.

Program Format   Daytime, evening classes offered. Instructional schedule: 2½ hours per week. Program cycle: Continuous enrollment. Completion of program requires 2.25 GPA.

Evaluation   Student evaluation based on tests, papers. Grading system: Letters or numbers. Transcripts are kept for each student.

Enrollment Requirements   Fifty-six college credits, 2.25 GPA required. Program is not open to non-resident foreign students. English language proficiency required. Minimum TOEFL score required: 550.

Program Costs $2448 for the program, $204 per course.

Housing and Student Services   Housing is not available. Job counseling and placement services are available.

Contact   Dr. Paul Davis, Chairman, Accounting Department, 1420 North Charles Street, Baltimore, MD 21201. 301-625-3214.

COMPUTER AND INFORMATION SCIENCES, GENERAL (11.01)
Certificate in Computer Information Systems

General Information   Unit offering the program: Information and Quantitative Sciences, School of Business. Program content: Accounting, quantitative techniques, information systems. Available for credit. Certificate signed by the University President. Certificate applicable to B.S. in Business Administration.

Program Format   Daytime, evening classes offered. Instructional schedule: 2½ hours per week. Students may enroll fall, spring. Completion of program requires 36 credit hours, 2.0 GPA.

Evaluation   Student evaluation based on tests, papers, reports. Grading system: Letters or numbers. Transcripts are kept for each student.

Enrollment Requirements   Fifty-six college credits, 2.0 GPA required. Program is not open to non-resident foreign students. English language proficiency required. Minimum TOEFL score required: 550.

Program Costs $2448 for the program, $204 per course.

Housing and Student Services   Housing is not available. Job counseling and placement services are available.

Special Features   Only students with 56 transferable college credits are admitted. Students take the same courses required for B.S. degree. No credit is given for experience. Students must complete 36 credit hours at the University. Courses taught by full-time faculty (80 percent with doctoral degrees). A few courses taught by adjunct faculty.

Contact   Dr. R. Rao Vemuganti, Chairman, Information and Quantitative Sciences, 1420 North Charles Street, Baltimore, MD 21201. 301-625-3304.

MASSACHUSETTS

ANNA MARIA COLLEGE FOR MEN AND WOMEN
Paxton, Massachusetts 01612

BUSINESS AND MANAGEMENT, GENERAL (06.01)
Accounting/Finance

General Information   Unit offering the program: MBA Program. Available for credit. Certificate signed by the Program Director. Certificate applicable to M.A. in Management.

Program Format   Evening classes offered. Instructional schedule: 3½ hours per week. Program cycle: Continuous enrollment. Full program cycle lasts 18 credit hours.

Evaluation   Student evaluation based on tests, papers, reports. Grading system: Letters or numbers. Transcripts are kept for each student.

Enrollment Requirements   Bachelor's degree required. Program is open to non-resident foreign students. English language proficiency required. Minimum TOEFL score required: 500.

Program Costs $360 per course.

Housing and Student Services   Housing is not available. Job counseling and placement services are available.

Special Features   Certificate program enhances professional credentials and meets the needs of the student as yet undecided about earning the master's degree. Course earns graduate credit and can be applied later to both the M.A. in management and the M.B.A. in leadership degree programs.

Contact   Dr. Norman Woodin, Director, MBA Program, Sunset Lane, Paxton, MA 01612. 617-757-4586.

BUSINESS AND MANAGEMENT, GENERAL (06.01)
Economics/Statistics

General Information   Unit offering the program: MBA Program. Available for credit. Certificate signed by the Program Director. Certificate applicable to M.A. in Management.

Program Format   Evening classes offered. Instructional schedule: 3½ hours per week. Program cycle: Continuous enrollment. Full program cycle lasts 18 credit hours.

Evaluation   Student evaluation based on tests, papers, reports. Grading system: Letters or numbers. Transcripts are kept for each student.

Enrollment Requirements   Bachelor's degree required. Program is open to non-resident foreign students. English language proficiency required. Minimum TOEFL score required: 500.

Program Costs $360 per course.

Housing and Student Services   Housing is not available. Job counseling and placement services are available.

Special Features   Certificate program enhances professional credentials and meets the needs of the student as yet undecided about earning the master's degree. Course earns graduate credit and can be applied later to both the M.A. in management and the M.B.A. in leadership degree programs.

Contact   Dr. Norman Woodin, Director, MBA Program, Sunset Lane, Paxton, MA 01612. 617-757-4586.

BUSINESS AND MANAGEMENT, GENERAL (06.01)
Management/Marketing

General Information   Unit offering the program: MBA Program. Available for credit. Certificate signed by the Program Director. Certificate applicable to M.A. in Management.

Program Format   Evening classes offered. Instructional schedule: 3½ hours per week. Program cycle: Continuous enrollment. Full program cycle lasts 18 credit hours.

Evaluation   Student evaluation based on tests, papers, reports. Grading system: Letters or numbers. Transcripts are kept for each student.

Enrollment Requirements   Bachelor's degree required. Program is open to non-resident foreign students. English language proficiency required. Minimum TOEFL score required: 500.

Program Costs $360 per course.

Housing and Student Services   Housing is not available. Job counseling and placement services are available.

Special Features   Certificate program enhances professional credentials and meets the needs of the student as yet undecided about earning the master's degree. Course earns graduate credit and can be applied later to both the M.A. in management and the M.B.A. in leadership degree programs.

Contact   Dr. Norman Woodin, Director, MBA Program, Sunset Lane, Paxton, MA 01612. 617-757-4586.

ASSUMPTION COLLEGE
Worcester, Massachusetts 01609

HUMAN RESOURCES DEVELOPMENT (06.06)
Human Resources Management

General Information   Unit offering the program: Center for Continuing and Professional Education. Program content: Management, employment law, interviewing, environments of business, organization and human behavior. Available for credit. Certificate signed by the Dean of Graduate Studies and Continuing Education.

Program Format   Evening classes offered. Program cycle: Continuous enrollment. Full program cycle lasts 7 courses. Completion of program requires grade of C or better in all courses.

Evaluation   Student evaluation based on tests, papers, reports. Grading system: Letters or numbers. Transcripts are kept for each student.

Enrollment Requirements   Program is open to non-resident foreign students. English language proficiency required.

Program Costs $264 per course.

Housing and Student Services   Housing is not available. Job counseling and placement services are not available.

Contact   Dr. Marjorie A. Nickel, Dean of Graduate Studies and Continuing Education, 500 Salisbury Street, Worcester, MA 01615-0005. 617-752-5615.

LAW (22.01)
Paralegal Studies

General Information   Unit offering the program: Center for Continuing and Profession Education. Program content: Legal research and writing; litigation; corporations; estates and trusts; family, consumer, and real estate law; criminal law and procedures. Available for credit. Certificate signed by the Dean of Graduate Studies and Continuing Education.

Program Format   Evening classes offered. Program cycle: Continuous enrollment. Full program cycle lasts 8 courses. Completion of program requires 2.0 GPA.

Evaluation   Student evaluation based on tests, papers, reports. Grading system: Letters or numbers. Transcripts are kept for each student.

Enrollment Requirements   High school diploma, two years of college or equivalent work experience required. Program is open to non-resident foreign students. English language proficiency required.

Program Costs $264 per course.

Housing and Student Services   Housing is not available. Job counseling and placement services are not available.

Contact   Dr. Marjorie A. Nickel, Dean of Graduate Studies and Continuing Education, 500 Salisbury Street, Worcester, MA 01615-0005. 617-752-5615.

BENTLEY COLLEGE
Waltham, Massachusetts 02254

ACCOUNTING (06.02)
Certificate in Accountancy

General Information   Unit offering the program: Department of Accountancy, School of Continuing and Professional Studies. Program content: Cost accounting, income taxes, auditing, accounting information systems. Available for credit. Certificate signed by the Vice President, Academic Affairs. Certificate applicable to B.S. in Accountancy.

Program Format   Daytime, evening, weekend classes offered. Instructional schedule: Once per week. Program cycle: Continuous enrollment. Full program cycle lasts 10 courses. Completion of program requires 30 semester hours, 2.0 GPA.

Evaluation   Student evaluation based on tests, papers, reports. Grading system: Letters or numbers. Transcripts are kept for each student.

Enrollment Requirements   Completion of two accountancy courses with 1.7 GPA required. Program is not open to non-resident foreign students. English language proficiency required. Minimum TOEFL score required: 550.

Program Costs $4500 for the program, $450 per course.

Housing and Student Services   Housing is not available. Job counseling and placement services are available.

Special Features   Students may transfer credit for up to four courses into the certificate's ten-course program. Proficiency examinations are available in all required courses. Students acquire an accountancy background as preparation for the CPA examination. Founding program at Bentley College, then Bentley School of Accounting and Finance.

Contact   Ms. Margaret R. Conner, Director, Academic Support Services, School of Continuing and Professional Studies, Waltham, MA 02254. 617-891-2901.

ACCOUNTING, BOOKKEEPING, AND RELATED PROGRAMS (07.01)
Accounting Assistant Certificate

General Information   Unit offering the program: School of Continuing and Professional Studies. Available on a non-credit basis. Certificate signed by the President.

Program Format   Evening classes offered. Instructional schedule: One evening per week for 2½ hours. Program cycle: Continuous enrollment. Complete program cycle lasts one to eight semesters. Completion of program requires eight 7-week modules.

Evaluation   Student evaluation based on tests. Grading system: Letters or numbers. Transcripts are kept for each student.

Enrollment Requirements   Program is open to non-resident foreign students. English language proficiency required.

Program Costs $1800 for the program, $225 per course.

Housing and Student Services Housing is not available. Job counseling and placement services are available.

Special Features The school may waive up to two modules of this certificate program if students can demonstrate proficiency by passing a written examination. Also, successful completion of a similar course at another institution is accepted upon receipt of transcript.

Contact Ms. Joan S. Pizzano, Program Director, Accounting Assistant Program, Beaver and Forest Streets, Waltham, MA 02254. 617-891-2135.

BANKING AND FINANCE (06.03)
Certified Financial Planner

General Information Unit offering the program: School of Continuing and Professional Studies. Program content: Risk management, investments, tax planning, employee benefits, state planning. Available for credit. Endorsed by International Board of Standards and Practices for Certified Financial Planners. Cosponsored by The College For Financial Planning in Denver, Colorado. Certificate signed by the International Board of Standards and Practices for Certified Financial Planners.

Program Format Evening, correspondence classes offered. Instructional schedule: One evening per week for 2½ hours. Program cycle: Continuous enrollment. Full program cycle lasts 6 courses. Completion of program requires national exam via College For Financial Planning in Denver.

Evaluation Student evaluation based on tests. Grading system: Pass/fail. Transcripts are kept for each student.

Enrollment Requirements Enrollment at the College For Financial Planning in Denver required. Program is open to non-resident foreign students.

Program Costs $1950 for the program, $325 per course.

Housing and Student Services Housing is not available. Job counseling and placement services are available.

Special Features Students must be enrolled in the College for Financial Planning in Denver, Colorado, through which all materials and textbooks are sent to students. National exams are scheduled three times per year at the end of each course. Faculty is hand chosen from Certified Financial Planners in the Boston area. Review sessions for exams are offered as part of course schedule.

Contact Mr. Stephen Sullivan, Program Director, School of Continuing and Professional Studies, Waltham, MA 02154. 617-891-2135.

BUSINESS AND MANAGEMENT, GENERAL (06.01)
Certificate in Meeting Management

General Information Unit offering the program: School of Continuing and Professional Studies. Program content: Skills to be a successful meeting planner. Available for credit. Endorsed by Meeting Planners International. Certificate signed by the President of the College.

Program Format Evening classes offered. Instructional schedule: One evening per week for two hours. Program cycle: Continuous enrollment. Full program cycle lasts 6 courses.

Evaluation Student evaluation based on papers, class participation. Grading system: Pass/fail. Transcripts are kept for each student.

Enrollment Requirements Program is open to non-resident foreign students.

Program Costs $1290 for the program, $215 per course.

Housing and Student Services Housing is not available. Job counseling and placement services are available.

Special Features The program is geared to students who wish to develop their abilities, enhance their credentials, or change their career into the area of meeting management. The courses are taught by practitioners of meeting management and are directed by an advisory board of additional practitioners. A student attending one course per course scheduling can complete the certificate program in less than one year.

Contact Mr. Stephen Sullivan, Program Director, School of Continuing and Professional Studies, Waltham, MA 02154. 617-891-2135.

COMMUNICATIONS, GENERAL (09.01)
Business Communication Certificate

General Information Unit offering the program: School of Continuing and Professional Studies. Program content: Two tracks in technical communication and public relations/journalism. Available for credit. Certificate signed by the Vice President, Academic Affairs. Certificate applicable to B.S. in Professional Studies, Business Communications; B.A. in Liberal Arts.

Program Format Daytime, evening, weekend classes offered. Program cycle: Continuous enrollment. Full program cycle lasts 10 courses. Completion of program requires 30 semester hours, 2.0 GPA.

Evaluation Student evaluation based on tests, papers, reports. Grading system: Letters or numbers. Transcripts are kept for each student.

Enrollment Requirements Associate degree or 60 credit hours of college work including six hours of college math and six hours of compositionrequired. Program is not open to non-resident foreign students. English language proficiency required. Minimum TOEFL score required: 550.

Program Costs $4500 for the program, $450 per course.

Housing and Student Services Housing is not available. Job counseling and placement services are available.

Special Features Free academic advising and career planning assistance available. Internships in technical writing or public relations arranged. Generous elective options available from business departments at Bentley in accounting, computer information systems, management, marketing, and the like. Transfer credit accepted as applicable. Financial aid available.

Contact Ms. Margaret R. Conner, Director, Academic Support Services, School of Continuing and Professional Studies, Waltham, MA 02254. 617-891-2903.

HUMAN RESOURCES DEVELOPMENT (06.06)
Human Resources Management Certificate Program

General Information Unit offering the program: School of Continuing and Professional Studies. Program content: Recruiting and hiring, benefits administration, compensation, affirmative action, training, employee relations. Available on a non-credit basis. Certificate signed by the President of the College.

Program Format Evening classes offered. Instructional schedule: One or two evenings per week. Program cycle: Continuous enrollment. Full program cycle lasts 5 courses.

Evaluation Student evaluation based on tests, papers, reports. Grading system: Letters or numbers, pass/fail. Transcripts are kept for each student.

Enrollment Requirements Program is open to non-resident foreign students.

Program Costs $1650 for the program, $240–$380 per course.

Housing and Student Services Housing is not available. Job counseling and placement services are available.

Special Features The required introductory course may be waived based on prior experience in human resources. Instructors are professionals who hold full-time positions in human resources management and teach in the program at night. One- or two-day seminars are offered to supplement knowledge gained in evening courses. The Human Resources Management Roundtable Series presents current topics in a 2-hour evening format.

Human Resources Management Certificate Program continued

Contact Ms. Karen A. Scibinico, Program Director, School of Continuing and Professional Studies, Morison Hall, Waltham, MA 02254. 617-891-2135.

INFORMATION SCIENCES AND SYSTEMS (11.04)
Certificate in Computer Information Systems

General Information Unit offering the program: Department of Computer Information Systems, School of Continuing and Professional Studies. Program content: Application of computers in accounting, management, business, finance. Available for credit. Certificate signed by the Vice President, Academic Affairs.

Program Format Daytime, evening, weekend classes offered. Program cycle: Continuous enrollment. Full program cycle lasts 12 courses. Completion of program requires 36 semester hours, 2.0 GPA.

Evaluation Student evaluation based on tests, papers, reports. Grading system: Letters or numbers. Transcripts are kept for each student.

Enrollment Requirements Bachelor's degree, completion of two computer science courses with minimum 2.0 GPA required. Program is not open to non-resident foreign students. English language proficiency required. Minimum TOEFL score required: 550.

Program Costs $5200 for the program, $450 per course.

Housing and Student Services Housing is not available. Job counseling and placement services are available.

Special Features Course work includes extensive use of computer resources: 300 Hewlett-Packard desktop microcomputers, 1,800 Hewlett-Packard portable microcomputers, 20 IBM personal computers, a four-terminal DEC MicroVAX II, and a fully equipped graphics/microcomputer lab, all of which help prepare students to interact effectively with business organizational functions and computer technology. Free academic advising and career planning assistance.

Contact Ms. Margaret R. Conner, Director, Academic Support Services, School of Continuing and Professional Studies, Waltham, MA 02254. 617-891-2903.

LAW (22.01)
Certificate in Paralegal Studies

General Information Unit offering the program: School of Continuing and Professional Studies. Program content: Litigation and legal research, communication skills workshop, paralegal electives. Available on a non-credit basis. Endorsed by American Bar Association. Certificate signed by the President. Certificate applicable to associate degree in paralegal studies.

Program Format Daytime, evening classes offered. Program cycle: Continuous enrollment. Complete program cycle lasts one to five semesters.

Evaluation Student evaluation based on tests, papers. Grading system: Letters or numbers. Transcripts are kept for each student.

Enrollment Requirements Forty-five college credits, 2.3 GPA required. Program is open to non-resident foreign students. English language proficiency required.

Program Costs $2410 for the program, $450 per course.

Housing and Student Services Housing is not available. Job counseling and placement services are available.

Special Features The program was established in 1973 and received approval from the American Bar Association in 1975. It was the first program in New England to receive such approval and until August 1987 was the only ABA-approved program in

Massachusetts. Applicants may receive advanced standing in the program if they can demonstrate extensive related work experience and successfully complete a written proficiency examination.

Contact Ms. Joan S. Pizzano, Program Director, Institute of Paralegal Studies, Beaver and Forest Streets, Waltham, MA 02254. 617-891-2135.

PERSONNEL MANAGEMENT (06.16)
Pension and Employee Benefits Administration Certificate Program

General Information Unit offering the program: School of Continuing and Professional Studies. Program content: Benefits design, funding law, tax requirements and finance. Available on a non-credit basis. Endorsed by New England Employee Benefits Council (NEEBC). Certificate signed by the President of the College.

Program Format Evening classes offered. Instructional schedule: One or two evenings per week. Program cycle: Continuous enrollment. Full program cycle lasts 5 courses.

Evaluation Student evaluation based on tests, papers, reports, class projects. Grading system: Letters or numbers, pass/fail. Transcripts are kept for each student.

Enrollment Requirements Program is open to non-resident foreign students.

Program Costs $1650 for the program, $240–$380 per course.

Housing and Student Services Housing is not available. Job counseling and placement services are available.

Special Features Instructors are full-time professionals in the field of pension and benefits and teach in the program at night. A Human Resources Management Program course may be applied toward the pension and benefits certificate. NEEBC members receive a 10% tuition discount. One- or two-day seminars are offered to supplement evening courses. The Employee Benefits Breakfast Lecture Series presents current topics in a 2-hour format.

Contact Ms. Karen A. Scibinico, Program Director, School of Continuing and Professional Studies, Morison Hall, Waltham, MA 02254. 617-891-2135.

REAL ESTATE (06.17)
BOMI—Real Property Administration (RPA) Certificate

General Information Unit offering the program: School of Continuing and Professional Studies. Program content: Real estate appraisal, real property administration, investment and finance. Available on a non-credit basis. Endorsed by Building Owners and Manager Institute International. Certificate signed by the Dean.

Program Format Evening classes offered. Instructional schedule: Once per week for 2½ hours. Program cycle: Continuous enrollment. Complete program cycle lasts one to two years. Completion of program requires seven national examinations.

Evaluation Student evaluation based on tests. Grading system: Pass/fail. Transcripts are kept for each student.

Enrollment Requirements Program is not open to non-resident foreign students.

Housing and Student Services Housing is not available. Job counseling and placement services are available.

Special Features The program consists of a series of seven national courses, each with its own final exam, that are designed for a generalist in the commercial property management field.

Contact Mr. Thomas McCarron, Program Director, Morison Hall, Waltham, MA 02254. 617-891-2135.

BOSTON ARCHITECTURAL CENTER
Boston, Massachusetts 02115

INTERIOR DESIGN (04.05)
Certificate in Interior Design

General Information Unit offering the program: Continuing Education Program. Program content: Design, history, technical skills, presentation skills. Available for credit. Certificate signed by the Dean. Program fulfills requirements for Foundation for Interior Design Research (FIDER).

Program Format Evening classes offered. Instructional schedule: Two to three evenings per week. Program cycle: Continuous enrollment. Completion of program requires 54 academic credits, 27 work credits, thesis.

Evaluation Student evaluation based on portfolio review. Grading system: Letters or numbers. Transcripts are kept for each student.

Enrollment Requirements High school diploma or equivalent required. Program is not open to non-resident foreign students.

Program Costs $275–$395 per course.

Housing and Student Services Housing is not available. Job counseling and placement services are available.

Special Features This is an evening work/study program. Students work concurrently in professional offices during the day. They are assisted with career placement through the Work Curriculum Office. Instuctors are practicing professionals in architecture and interior design.

Contact Ms. Denise A. Bell, Director of Continuing Education, 320 Newbury Street, Boston, MA 02115. 617-536-3170.

BRIDGEWATER STATE COLLEGE
Bridgewater, Massachusetts 02324

ACCOUNTING (06.02)
Graduate Certificate Program in Accounting/ Finance Management

General Information Unit offering the program: Accounting/ Finance Management. Program content: Accounting, auditing, budgeting, investments, finance, business law, business data processing. Available for credit. Certificate signed by the Chairman, Board of Trustees.

Program Format Evening classes offered. Program cycle: Continuous enrollment. Full program cycle lasts 8 courses. Completion of program requires 2.5 GPA.

Evaluation Student evaluation based on tests, papers. Grading system: Letters or numbers. Transcripts are kept for each student.

Enrollment Requirements Bachelor's degree required. Program is open to non-resident foreign students.

Program Costs $180 per course.

Housing and Student Services Housing is not available. Job counseling and placement services are available.

Contact Mr. Henry J. Fanning, Dean, Continuing Education, Bridgewater, MA 02324. 617-697-1259.

ACCOUNTING (06.02)
Undergraduate Certificate Program in Accounting/Finance Management

General Information Unit offering the program: Accounting/ Finance Management. Program content: General accounting, tax returns, production and inventory records, budgets, investment plans, financial planning. Available for credit. Certificate signed by the Chairman, Board of Trustees.

Program Format Evening classes offered. Program cycle: Continuous enrollment. Full program cycle lasts 8 courses. Completion of program requires 2.5 GPA.

Evaluation Student evaluation based on tests, papers. Grading system: Letters or numbers. Transcripts are kept for each student.

Enrollment Requirements High school diploma or equivalent required. Program is open to non-resident foreign students.

Program Costs $180 per course.

Housing and Student Services Housing is not available. Job counseling and placement services are available.

Contact Mr. Henry J. Fanning, Dean, Continuing Education, Bridgewater, MA 02324. 617-697-1260.

BUSINESS AND MANAGEMENT, GENERAL (06.01)
Graduate Certificate Program in Operations Management

General Information Unit offering the program: Operations Management. Program content: Management, budgeting, finance, accounting, data processing. Available for credit. Certificate signed by the Chairman, Board of Trustees.

Program Format Evening classes offered. Program cycle: Continuous enrollment. Full program cycle lasts 8 courses. Completion of program requires 2.5 GPA.

Evaluation Student evaluation based on tests, papers. Grading system: Letters or numbers. Transcripts are kept for each student.

Enrollment Requirements Bachelor's degree required. Program is open to non-resident foreign students.

Program Costs $180 per course.

Housing and Student Services Housing is not available. Job counseling and placement services are available.

Contact Mr. Henry J. Fanning, Dean, Continuing Education, Bridgewater, MA 02324. 617-697-1260.

COMPUTER AND INFORMATION SCIENCES, GENERAL (11.01)
Undergraduate Certificate Program in Computer Science

General Information Unit offering the program: Computer Science. Program content: Pascal, COBOL, assembly language, data structures, algorithms, sytems analysis and design. Available for credit. Certificate signed by the Chairman, Board of Trustees.

Program Format Evening classes offered. Program cycle: Continuous enrollment. Full program cycle lasts 8 courses. Completion of program requires 2.5 GPA.

Evaluation Student evaluation based on tests, papers. Grading system: Letters or numbers. Transcripts are kept for each student.

Enrollment Requirements High school diploma or equivalent required. Program is open to non-resident foreign students.

Program Costs $180 per course.

Housing and Student Services Housing is not available. Job counseling and placement services are available.

Contact Mr. Henry J. Fanning, Dean, Continuing Education, Bridgewater, MA 02324. 617-697-1260.

LAW (22.01)
Undergraduate Certificate Program in Paralegal Studies

General Information Unit offering the program: Paralegal Studies. Program content: Substantive, criminal, family, and tenant law; legal research and writing; litigation; real estate;

Undergraduate Certificate Program in Paralegal Studies continued

estates. Available for credit. Certificate signed by the Chairman, Board of Trustees.

Program Format   Evening classes offered. Program cycle: Continuous enrollment. Full program cycle lasts 8 courses. Completion of program requires 2.5 GPA.

Evaluation   Student evaluation based on tests, papers. Grading system: Letters or numbers. Transcripts are kept for each student.

Enrollment Requirements   High school diploma or equivalent required. Program is open to non-resident foreign students.

Program Costs $180 per course.

Housing and Student Services   Housing is not available. Job counseling and placement services are available.

Contact   Mr. Henry J. Fanning, Dean, Continuing Education, Bridgewater, MA 02324. 617-697-1260.

MANAGEMENT INFORMATION SYSTEMS (06.12)
Graduate Certificate Program in Information Systems Management

General Information   Unit offering the program: Information Systems Management. Program content: Systems analysis, data processing, information systems management. Available for credit. Certificate signed by the Chairman, Board of Trustees.

Program Format   Evening classes offered. Program cycle: Continuous enrollment. Full program cycle lasts 8 courses. Completion of program requires 2.5 GPA.

Evaluation   Student evaluation based on tests, papers. Grading system: Letters or numbers. Transcripts are kept for each student.

Enrollment Requirements   Bachelor's degree required. Program is open to non-resident foreign students.

Program Costs $180 per course.

Housing and Student Services   Housing is not available. Job counseling and placement services are available.

Contact   Mr. Henry J. Fanning, Dean, Continuing Education, Bridgewater, MA 02324. 617-697-1260.

MARKETING MANAGEMENT AND RESEARCH (06.14)
Graduate Certificate Program in Marketing Management

General Information   Unit offering the program: Marketing Management. Program content: Business law, advertising, marketing, data processing, sales management. Available for credit. Certificate signed by the Chairman, Board of Trustees.

Program Format   Evening classes offered. Program cycle: Continuous enrollment. Full program cycle lasts 8 courses. Completion of program requires 2.5 GPA.

Evaluation   Student evaluation based on tests, papers. Grading system: Letters or numbers. Transcripts are kept for each student.

Enrollment Requirements   Bachelor's degree required. Program is open to non-resident foreign students.

Program Costs $180 per course.

Housing and Student Services   Housing is not available. Job counseling and placement services are available.

Contact   Mr. Henry J. Fanning, Dean, Continuing Education, Bridgewater, MA 02324. 617-697-1260.

MARKETING MANAGEMENT AND RESEARCH (06.14)
Undergraduate Certificate Program in Marketing Management

General Information   Unit offering the program: Marketing Management. Program content: Marketing, advertising, management. Available for credit. Certificate signed by the Chairman, Board of Trustees.

Program Format   Evening classes offered. Program cycle: Continuous enrollment. Full program cycle lasts 8 courses. Completion of program requires 2.5 GPA.

Evaluation   Student evaluation based on tests, papers. Grading system: Letters or numbers. Transcripts are kept for each student.

Enrollment Requirements   High school diploma or equivalent required. Program is open to non-resident foreign students.

Program Costs $180 per course.

Housing and Student Services   Housing is not available. Job counseling and placement services are available.

Contact   Mr. Henry J. Fanning, Dean, Continuing Education, Bridgewater, MA 02324. 617-697-1259.

PUBLIC RELATIONS (09.05)
Undergraduate Certificate Program in Media Studies

General Information   Unit offering the program: Media and Librarianship. Program content: Instructional media, basic photography, script writing, production, graphics, cinematography. Available for credit. Certificate signed by the Chairman, Board of Trustees.

Program Format   Evening classes offered. Program cycle: Continuous enrollment. Full program cycle lasts 8 courses. Completion of program requires 2.5 GPA.

Evaluation   Student evaluation based on tests, papers. Grading system: Letters or numbers. Transcripts are kept for each student.

Enrollment Requirements   High school diploma or equivalent required. Program is open to non-resident foreign students.

Program Costs $180 per course.

Housing and Student Services   Housing is not available. Job counseling and placement services are available.

Contact   Mr. Henry J. Fanning, Dean, Continuing Education, Bridgewater, MA 02324. 617-697-1260.

TEACHER EDUCATION, GENERAL PROGRAMS (13.12)
Undergraduate Certificate Program in Substitute Teachers and Instructional School Aides—Early Childhood Level

General Information   Unit offering the program: Substitute Teachers and Instructional School Aides—Early Childhood Level. Program content: Child psychology, early childhood education, kindergarden theory and methods, beginning reading, methods and materials, managing classroom behavior. Available for credit. Certificate signed by the Chairman, Board of Trustees.

Program Format   Evening classes offered. Program cycle: Continuous enrollment. Full program cycle lasts 8 courses. Completion of program requires 2.5 GPA.

Evaluation   Student evaluation based on tests, papers. Grading system: Letters or numbers. Transcripts are kept for each student.

Enrollment Requirements   High school diploma or equivalent required. Program is open to non-resident foreign students.

Program Costs $180 per course.

Housing and Student Services   Housing is not available. Job counseling and placement services are available.

Contact Mr. Henry J. Fanning, Dean, Continuing Education, Bridgewater, MA 02324. 617-697-1260.

TEACHER EDUCATION, GENERAL PROGRAMS (13.12)
Undergraduate Certificate Program in Substitute Teachers and Instructional School Aides—Elementary Level

General Information Unit offering the program: Substitute Teachers and Instructional School Aides—Elementary Level. Program content: Strategies of teaching, elementary school curriculum, managing classroom behavior, child psychology, methods and materials, special needs learners, computers in the classroom. Available for credit. Certificate signed by the Chairman, Board of Trustees.

Program Format Evening classes offered. Program cycle: Continuous enrollment. Full program cycle lasts 8 courses. Completion of program requires 2.5 GPA.

Evaluation Student evaluation based on tests, papers. Grading system: Letters or numbers. Transcripts are kept for each student.

Enrollment Requirements High school diploma or equivalent required. Program is open to non-resident foreign students.

Program Costs $180 per course.

Housing and Student Services Housing is not available. Job counseling and placement services are available.

Contact Mr. Henry J. Fanning, Dean, Continuing Education, Bridgewater, MA 02324. 617-697-1260.

NUCEA MEMBER
CLARK UNIVERSITY
Worcester, Massachusetts 01610

TECHNICAL AND BUSINESS WRITING (23.11)
Certificate in Technical Writing

General Information Unit offering the program: College of Professional and Continuing Education. Available on a non-credit basis. Certificate signed by the Director, College of Professional and Continuing Education.

Program Format Evening classes offered. Students enroll in the fall. Full program cycle lasts 3 semesters. Completion of program requires five courses, three workshops.

Evaluation Student evaluation based on projects. Grading system: Letters or numbers, pass/fail. Transcripts are kept for each student.

Enrollment Requirements Bachelor's degree, writing samples, interview required. Program is open to non-resident foreign students.

Program Costs $950 per trimester.

Housing and Student Services Housing is not available. Job counseling and placement services are available.

Special Features The one-year program includes courses in technical writing skills, computing and programming skills, and a management development seminar. Focus is on operating systems, programming, and their application. Faculty is drawn from both academic and business worlds (high technology, insurance companies, etc.).

Contact Ms. Laura Myers, Director, College of Professional and Continuing Education, 950 Main Street, Worcester, MA 01610. 617-793-7408.

ELMS COLLEGE
Chicopee, Massachusetts 01013

LAW (22.01)
Certificate of Advanced Paralegal Studies

General Information Unit offering the program: Paralegal. Program content: Legal research, preparation of legal documents, analysis of procedures and transactions. Available on either a credit or non-credit basis. Endorsed by American Bar Association. Certificate signed by the President of the College. Certificate applicable to A.A., B.A. in Paralegal Studies.

Program Format Daytime, evening, weekend classes offered. Program cycle: Continuous enrollment. Full program cycle lasts 25 credit hours. Completion of program requires grade of C or better.

Evaluation Student evaluation based on tests, papers, reports. Grading system: Letters or numbers. Transcripts are kept for each student.

Enrollment Requirements Forty-five general education credits required. Program is open to non-resident foreign students.

Program Costs $4500 for the program, $180 per credit hour.

Housing and Student Services Housing is available. Job counseling and placement services are available.

Special Features Students complete core of required courses to ensure grasp of basics of legal system, forms and sources of system of justice, key research tools for locating and understanding legislation, skills for accurate legal writing and reasoning, and ethical role and limitations of the paralegal. Many legal specialty courses are offered. Taught by area attorneys and knowledgeable professionals.

Contact Mrs. Maria Silvestri, Paralegal Coordinator, Elms Paralegal Institute, Chicopee, MA 01013-2839. 413-594-2761 Ext. 300.

NUCEA MEMBER
EMMANUEL COLLEGE
Boston, Massachusetts 02115

HEALTH SERVICES ADMINISTRATION (18.07)
Health Administration Certificate Program

General Information Unit offering the program: Health Administration Program. Program content: Accounting, economics, law, ethics, marketing. Available on either a credit or non-credit basis. Certificate signed by the President.

Program Format Evening classes offered. Instructional schedule: Three hours per week. Program cycle: Continuous enrollment. Full program cycle lasts 14 weeks.

Evaluation Student evaluation based on tests, papers, reports. Grading system: Letters or numbers. Transcripts are kept for each student.

Enrollment Requirements Bachelor's degree required. Program is open to non-resident foreign students. English language proficiency required. Minimum TOEFL score required: 500.

Program Costs $464 per course.

Housing and Student Services Housing is not available. Job counseling and placement services are available.

Contact Dr. Frances Donahue, SND, Coordinator, Health Administration Program, 400 The Fenway, Boston, MA 02115. 617-735-9827.

INDIVIDUAL AND FAMILY DEVELOPMENT (19.07)
Certificate in Gerontology

General Information   Unit offering the program: Department of Psychology. Program content: Studies in aging from psychological, biological, sociological, and spiritual perspectives. Available for credit. Certificate signed by the Associate Dean. Certificate applicable to B.S. in Developmental Psychology.

Program Format   Daytime, evening classes offered. Program cycle: Continuous enrollment. Full program cycle lasts 8 courses.

Evaluation   Student evaluation based on tests, papers, reports. Grading system: Letters or numbers. Transcripts are kept for each student.

Enrollment Requirements   Undergraduate degree required. Program is open to non-resident foreign students. English language proficiency required. Minimum TOEFL score required: 500.

Program Costs $464 per course.

Housing and Student Services   Housing is available. Job counseling and placement services are available.

Special Features   Students enrolled as psychology majors in developmental psychology or rehabilitation counseling may be simultaneously enrolled in gerontology certificate program. Courses taught by full-time faculty. Gerontology has been a major track since 1978, housed in psychology department. Internship placements by psychology department. Concentration in elderly care (rehabilitative) or managerial and policy aspects.

Contact   Dr. Carson C. Johnson, Chairman, Psychology Department, 400 The Fenway, Boston, MA 02115. 617-735-9978.

REHABILITATION SERVICES (17.08)
Certification in Music Therapy—Equivalency Program

General Information   Unit offering the program: Music Department. Program content: Theory, clinical models, client assessment, creative treatment. Available on either a credit or non-credit basis. Endorsed by American Association for Music Therapy. Certificate signed by the Director of Music Therapy. Certificate applicable to B.A. in Music Therapy. Program fulfills requirements for Certified Music Therapist.

Program Format   Daytime, evening classes offered. Program cycle: Continuous enrollment. Completion of program requires grade of C or better in 9–20 courses, 800 hours clinical fieldwork, instrumental competency examination.

Evaluation   Student evaluation based on tests, papers, reports, clinical fieldwork. Grading system: Letters or numbers. Transcripts are kept for each student.

Enrollment Requirements   Musical competency (piano, voice, guitar), bachelor's degree required. Program is open to non-resident foreign students. English language proficiency required.

Program Costs $464 per course.

Special Features   Program approved by American Association for Music Therapy; awards certification (CMT) at successful completion. Faculty of nationally recognized authors and clinical experts provides direction through personal advising, course work, and rigorous off-campus internships training. Excellent clinical apprenticeship opportunities (psychiatric, gerontology, hospice, mental retardation, multi-handicaps, private practice, etc.) available in Boston.

Contact   Ms. Donna Chadwick, Director of Music Therapy, 400 The Fenway, Boston, MA 02115. 617-735-9944.

RELIGIOUS EDUCATION (39.04)
Educational and Pastoral Ministry Certificate Program

General Information   Unit offering the program: Educational and Pastoral Ministry Programs (Graduate). Program content: Biblical, theological, sociological, and counseling courses. Available for credit. Certificate signed by the Academic Dean. Certificate applicable to M.A. in Educational and Pastoral Ministry.

Program Format   Daytime, evening, weekend classes offered. Program cycle: Continuous enrollment. Full program cycle lasts 18 credit hours.

Evaluation   Student evaluation based on tests, papers, reports. Grading system: Letters or numbers. Transcripts are kept for each student.

Enrollment Requirements   Bachelor's degree or pertinent life experience required. Program is open to non-resident foreign students. English language proficiency required.

Program Costs $226 per credit hour.

Housing and Student Services   Housing is available. Job counseling and placement services are available.

Contact   Sr. Claudia Blanchette, SND, Director, Educational and Pastoral Ministry, 400 The Fenway, Boston, MA 02115. 617-735-9936.

RELIGIOUS EDUCATION (39.04)
Pastoral Counseling Certificate Program

General Information   Unit offering the program: Educational and Pastoral Ministry Programs (Graduate). Program content: Counseling families, groups, individuals. Available for credit. Certificate signed by the Academic Dean. Certificate applicable to M.A. in Pastoral Counseling.

Program Format   Daytime, evening, weekend classes offered. Program cycle: Continuous enrollment. Full program cycle lasts 18 credit hours.

Evaluation   Student evaluation based on tests, papers, reports. Grading system: Letters or numbers. Transcripts are kept for each student.

Enrollment Requirements   Master's degree in related field required. Program is open to non-resident foreign students. English language proficiency required.

Program Costs $226 per credit hour.

Housing and Student Services   Housing is available. Job counseling and placement services are available.

Contact   Sr. Claudia Blanchette, SND, Director, Educational and Pastoral Ministry, 400 The Fenway, Boston, MA 02115. 617-735-9936.

FITCHBURG STATE COLLEGE
Fitchburg, Massachusetts 01420

COMPUTER AND INFORMATION SCIENCES, GENERAL (11.01)
Certificate Program in Computer Hardware

General Information   Unit offering the program: Division of Graduate and Continuing Education. Program content: Digital electronics, computer organization. Available for credit. Certificate signed by the Dean, Division of Graduate and Continuing Education. Certificate applicable to B.S. in Computer Science.

Program Format   Evening classes offered. Instructional schedule: One evening per week. Program cycle: Continuous enrollment. Full program cycle lasts 12 credit hours. Completion of program requires 3.0 GPA.

Evaluation   Student evaluation based on tests, papers. Grading system: Letters or numbers. Transcripts are kept for each student.

Enrollment Requirements   High school diploma, knowledge of high school algebra required. Program is open to non-resident foreign students.

Program Costs $660–$840 for the program, $165–$210 per course.

Housing and Student Services Housing is not available. Job counseling and placement services are available.

Contact Mr. Franz A. Nowotny, Dean, Graduate and Continuing Education, Fitchburg, MA 01420-2697. 617-345-7207.

COMPUTER PROGRAMMING (11.02)
Certificate Program in Computer Language

General Information Unit offering the program: Division of Graduate and Continuing Education. Program content: Literacy in Pascal, FORTRAN, COBOL. Available for credit. Certificate signed by the Dean, Graduate and Continuing Education. Certificate applicable to B.S. in Computer Science.

Program Format Evening classes offered. Instructional schedule: One evening per week. Program cycle: Continuous enrollment. Full program cycle lasts 9 credit hours. Completion of program requires 3.0 GPA.

Evaluation Student evaluation based on tests. Grading system: Letters or numbers. Transcripts are kept for each student.

Enrollment Requirements Program is open to non-resident foreign students.

Program Costs $495–$630 for the program, $165–$210 per course.

Housing and Student Services Housing is not available. Job counseling and placement services are available.

Special Features Provides necessary instruction to assist students in becoming more literate in one or more of the following computer languages: Pascal, FORTRAN, and COBOL. Each language certificate requires three courses (9 credits) to complete.

Contact Mr. Franz A. Nowotny, Dean, Graduate and Continuing Education, Fitchburg, MA 01420-2697. 617-345-7207.

CONSTRUCTION TECHNOLOGY (15.10)
Certificate Program in On-Site Construction Management

General Information Unit offering the program: Division of Graduate and Continuing Education. Program content: Worker coordination, materials, subcontractors, regulatory agencies. Available on either a credit or non-credit basis. Certificate signed by the Dean, Graduate and Continuing Education.

Program Format Evening classes offered. Instructional schedule: One evening per week. Program cycle: Continuous enrollment. Full program cycle lasts 12 credit hours. Completion of program requires 3.0 GPA.

Evaluation Student evaluation based on tests, papers, reports. Grading system: Letters or numbers. Transcripts are kept for each student.

Enrollment Requirements Program is open to non-resident foreign students.

Program Costs $660–$840 for the program, $165–$210 per course.

Housing and Student Services Housing is not available. Job counseling and placement services are available.

Special Features The program is designed to provide information to enable construction personnel to function more effectively in management-related activities. Successful completion of the certificate program enables an individual to function more effectively and become cognizant of on-site construction management activities and objectives.

Contact Mr. Franz A. Nowotny, Dean, Graduate and Continuing Education, Fitchburg, MA 01420-2697. 617-345-7207.

INDUSTRIAL PRODUCTION TECHNOLOGIES (15.06)
Certificate Program in Computer Aided Manufacturing

General Information Unit offering the program: Division of Graduate and Continuing Education. Program content: Technical updating, application and decision-making information. Available for credit. Certificate signed by the Dean, Graduate and Continuing Education. Certificate applicable to Master of Occupational Education.

Program Format Evening classes offered. Instructional schedule: One evening per week. Program cycle: Continuous enrollment. Full program cycle lasts 12 credit hours. Completion of program requires 3.0 GPA.

Evaluation Student evaluation based on tests. Grading system: Letters or numbers. Transcripts are kept for each student.

Enrollment Requirements Program is open to non-resident foreign students.

Program Costs $780–$960 for the program, $195–$240 per course.

Housing and Student Services Housing is not available. Job counseling and placement services are available.

Special Features Provides technical updating and information in the high-tech areas of Computer Aided Manufacturing (CAM). Intended for those involved in technical education at various levels and for those seeking technical updating and information for application and decision making.

Contact Mr. Franz A. Nowotny, Dean, Graduate and Continuing Education, Fitchburg, MA 01420-2697. 617-345-7207.

INDUSTRIAL PRODUCTION TECHNOLOGIES (15.06)
Certificate Program in Plastic Technology

General Information Unit offering the program: Division of Graduate and Continuing Education. Program content: Quality control, molding, tests and analysis, hydraulics, pneumatics, robotic interface. Available for credit. Cosponsored by NYPRO Industries. Certificate signed by the Dean, Graduate and Continuing Education.

Program Format Evening classes offered. Instructional schedule: One evening per week. Program cycle: Continuous enrollment. Full program cycle lasts 24 credit hours. Completion of program requires 2.0 GPA.

Evaluation Student evaluation based on tests, papers, reports. Grading system: Letters or numbers. Transcripts are kept for each student.

Enrollment Requirements Program is open to non-resident foreign students.

Program Costs $1320–$1680 for the program, $165–$210 per course.

Housing and Student Services Housing is not available. Job counseling and placement services are available.

Special Features In cooperation with NYPRO, the college offers a Certificate Program in Plastic Technology. The certificate program, which is open to area residents, is offered at the NYPRO plant in Clinton, Massachusetts.

Contact Mr. Franz A. Nowotny, Dean, Graduate and Continuing Education, Fitchburg, MA 01420-2697. 617-345-7207.

TEACHER EDUCATION, GENERAL PROGRAMS (13.12)
Certificate of Advanced Graduate Study: Career/Occupational Education

General Information Unit offering the program: Division of Graduate and Continuing Education. Program content: Theories, research, analysis of career programs, curriculum development. Available for credit. Certificate signed by the Dean, Graduate and Continuing Education.

Program Format Evening classes offered. Instructional schedule: One evening per week. Program cycle: Continuous enrollment. Full program cycle lasts 33 credit hours. Completion of program requires 3.0 GPA.

Certificate of Advanced Graduate Study: Career/Occupational Education continued

Evaluation Student evaluation based on tests, papers, reports. Grading system: Letters or numbers. Transcripts are kept for each student.

Enrollment Requirements Bachelor's degree, MAT or GMAT scores required. Program is open to non-resident foreign students.

Program Costs $2145–$2640 for the program, $195–$240 per course.

Housing and Student Services Housing is not available. Job counseling and placement services are available.

Special Features The program is designed to prepare students for successful and rewarding lives by improving their basis for making any occupational choice, by facilitating their acquisition of occupational skills, by enhancing their aspirations, and by increasing their awareness of choices they have among the many different occupations open to them.

Contact Mr. Franz A. Nowotny, Dean, Graduate and Continuing Education, Fitchburg, MA 01420-2697. 617-345-7207.

TEACHER EDUCATION, GENERAL PROGRAMS (13.12)
Certificate Program in Education Technology

General Information Unit offering the program: Division of Graduate and Continuing Education. Program content: Computer use in classrooms. Available for credit. Certificate signed by the Dean, Graduate and Continuing Education. Certificate applicable to M.Ed. in Leadership and Management.

Program Format Evening classes offered. Instructional schedule: One evening per week. Program cycle: Continuous enrollment. Full program cycle lasts 18 credit hours. Completion of program requires 3.0 GPA.

Evaluation Student evaluation based on tests, papers, reports. Grading system: Letters or numbers. Transcripts are kept for each student.

Enrollment Requirements Valid Massachusetts teaching certificate, bachelor's degree, Miller Analogies Test score required. Program is open to non-resident foreign students.

Program Costs $1170–$1440 for the program, $195–$240 per course.

Housing and Student Services Housing is not available. Job counseling and placement services are available.

Special Features The program is designed to allow educators in three specific areas to integrate modern educational technology into the classroom and the curriculum. These areas, which each have 18 hours of required courses specific to the area, are elementary education, secondary education, and special education.

Contact Mr. Franz A. Nowotny, Dean, Graduate and Continuing Education, Fitchburg, MA 01420-2697. 617-345-7207.

TEACHER EDUCATION, SPECIFIC SUBJECT AREAS (13.13)
Fine Arts Director Certificate Program

General Information Unit offering the program: Division of Graduate and Continuing Education. Program content: Creative arts curriculum, philosophy and current issues in arts education. Available for credit. Certificate signed by the Dean, Graduate and Continuing Education. Certificate applicable to M.Ed. in Leadership and Management.

Program Format Daytime classes offered. Instructional schedule: Two 2-week summer sessions. Students enroll in July. Complete program cycle lasts two summers. Completion of program requires 3.0 GPA, four courses.

Evaluation Student evaluation based on tests, papers, reports. Grading system: Letters or numbers. Transcripts are kept for each student.

Enrollment Requirements Valid teaching certificate in the arts required. Program is open to non-resident foreign students.

Program Costs $800 for the program.

Housing and Student Services Housing is not available. Job counseling and placement services are available.

Special Features The program is designed for those responsible for supervision of fine arts programs or teachers entering into these areas.

Contact Mr. Franz A. Nowotny, Dean, Graduate and Continuing Education, Fitchburg, MA 01420-2697. 617-345-7207.

NUCEA MEMBER
HARVARD UNIVERSITY
Cambridge, Massachusetts 02138

BUSINESS AND MANAGEMENT, GENERAL (06.01)
Certificate of Special Studies in Administration and Management

General Information Unit offering the program: University Extension. Program content: Policy, planning, operations, human resources development, finance and control, quantitative methods, communications. Available for credit. Certificate signed by the Dean of University Extension and Continuing Education.

Program Format Evening classes offered. Instructional schedule: Once per week for two hours. Program cycle: Continuous enrollment. Full program cycle lasts 8 courses. Completion of program requires grade of B- or better for each course.

Evaluation Student evaluation based on tests, papers, reports, cases. Grading system: Letters or numbers. Transcripts are kept for each student.

Enrollment Requirements Bachelor's degree required. Program is open to non-resident foreign students. English language proficiency required. Minimum TOEFL score required: 550.

Program Costs $3300 for the program, $400 per course.

Housing and Student Services Housing is not available. Job counseling and placement services are not available.

Special Features The program began in 1980, and there are over 600 graduates to date. Designed for students with some managerial experience who wish to improve their skills through formal academic training and for those with little or no experience in management who wish to acquire an academic background in this area.

Contact Mr. Raymond F. Comeau, Assistant Dean of University Extension, 20 Garden Street, Cambridge, MA 02138. 617-495-4005.

COMPUTER AND INFORMATION SCIENCES, GENERAL (11.01)
Certificate of Advanced Study in Applied Sciences

General Information Unit offering the program: University Extension. Program content: Software engineering, applied electronics, decision science, computer science, technical writing. Available for credit. Certificate signed by the Dean of University Extension and Continuing Education.

Program Format Evening classes offered. Instructional schedule: Once per week for two hours. Program cycle: Continuous enrollment. Full program cycle lasts 8 courses. Completion of program requires grade of B- or better for each course.

Evaluation Student evaluation based on tests, papers, reports. Grading system: Letters or numbers. Transcripts are kept for each student.

Enrollment Requirements Bachelor's degree required. Program is open to non-resident foreign students. English language proficiency required.

Program Costs $3200–$4000 for the program, $400–$500 per course.

Housing and Student Services Housing is not available. Job counseling and placement services are not available.

Special Features The program is designed for students with a modest academic background in science or math who need formal traning in applied science for their career goals. The CAS program includes a number of specialized courses of immediate relevance to today's high-technology industry. Instructors are both high-tech industry professionals and University educators.

Contact Mr. Henry H. Leitner, Assistant Director of Science Instruction, Continuing Education, 20 Garden Street, Cambridge, MA 02138. 617-495-4024.

HEALTH SERVICES ADMINISTRATION (18.07)
Certificate in Public Health

General Information Unit offering the program: University Extension, School of Public Health. Available for credit. Certificate signed by the Dean of University Extension.

Program Format Evening classes offered. Instructional schedule: Once per week for two hours. Program cycle: Continuous enrollment. Full program cycle lasts 8 courses. Completion of program requires grade of B- or better for each course, 32 credit hours.

Evaluation Student evaluation based on tests, papers, reports, cases. Grading system: Letters or numbers. Transcripts are kept for each student.

Enrollment Requirements Bachelor's degree required. Program is open to non-resident foreign students. English language proficiency required. Minimum TOEFL score required: 550.

Program Costs $3700 for the program, $400–$525 per course.

Housing and Student Services Housing is not available. Job counseling and placement services are not available.

Special Features Designed to meet the educational needs of a wide range of health professionals, from physicians, administrators, and staff working in environmental, occupational, and public health agencies to those working in private hospitals and health clinics. The program will also be of interest to students wishing to explore the field of public health.

Contact Mr. Raymond Comeau, Assistant Dean of University Extension, 20 Garden Street, Cambridge, MA 02138. 617-495-4005.

MOUNT IDA COLLEGE
Newton Centre, Massachusetts 02159

LAW (22.01)
Certificate Program in Paralegal Studies

General Information Unit offering the program: Continuing Education Division. Program content: Civil litigation, criminal law, probate. Available for credit. Certificate signed by the Director, Continuing Education Division. Certificate applicable to A.A. in Paralegal Studies.

Program Format Evening classes offered. Instructional schedule: Once per week for 2½ hours. Students enroll in September. Full program cycle lasts 6 courses. Completion of program requires 18 credit hours.

Evaluation Student evaluation based on tests, papers, reports. Grading system: Letters or numbers. Transcripts are kept for each student.

Enrollment Requirements High school diploma or GED required.

Program Costs $1080 for the program, $180 per course.

Housing and Student Services Housing is not available. Job counseling and placement services are available.

Special Features All instructors are practicing attorneys. A short, intensive six-week winter term allows students to fit in three terms of study during an academic year and still have summers free for leisure activities, if desired.

Contact Dr. Susan C. Holton, Director, Continuing Education Division, 777 Dedham Street, Newton Centre, MA 02159. 617-969-7000 Ext. 168.

OFFICE SUPERVISION AND MANAGEMENT (07.04)
Office Management Certificate Program

General Information Unit offering the program: Continuing Education Division. Program content: Supervisory skills, understanding the nature of business organizations. Available for credit. Certificate signed by the Director, Continuing Education Division. Certificate applicable to A.S. in Business Administration.

Program Format Evening classes offered. Instructional schedule: Once per week for 2½ hours. Students enroll in September. Full program cycle lasts 6 courses. Completion of program requires 18 credit hours.

Evaluation Student evaluation based on tests, papers, reports. Grading system: Letters or numbers. Transcripts are kept for each student.

Enrollment Requirements High school diploma or GED required.

Program Costs $1080 for the program, $180 per course.

Housing and Student Services Housing is not available. Job counseling and placement services are available.

Special Features The program provides a vehicle to re-enter the work force or to advance in one's present place of employment. Three credits may be granted for life (work) experience. A fall, winter (short, intensive winter term), and spring term schedule permits students to have summer free, if desired.

Contact Dr. Susan C. Holton, Director, Continuing Education Division, 777 Dedham Street, Newton Centre, MA 02159. 617-969-7000 Ext. 168.

NORTH ADAMS STATE COLLEGE
North Adams, Massachusetts 01247

ACCOUNTING (06.02)
Certificate in Accounting

General Information Unit offering the program: Program of Continuing Education. Available for credit. Certificate signed by the Dean of Community, Continuing, and Graduate Education. Certificate applicable to B.S. in Business Administration.

Program Format Evening classes offered. Instructional schedule: One evening per week. Program cycle: Continuous enrollment. Full program cycle lasts 24 credit hours. Completion of program requires 2.0 GPA.

Evaluation Student evaluation based on tests, papers, reports. Grading system: Letters or numbers. Transcripts are kept for each student.

Enrollment Requirements High school diploma required, related work experience preferred. Program is open to non-resident foreign students.

Program Costs $1288 for the program, $161 per course.

Housing and Student Services Housing is not available. Job counseling and placement services are available.

Contact Office of Continuing Education, Church Street, North Adams, MA 01247. 413-664-4511.

CHILD CARE AND GUIDANCE MANAGEMENT AND SERVICES (20.02)
Certificate in Day Care, Head Teacher Program

General Information Unit offering the program: Program of Continuing Education. Available for credit. Certificate signed by the Dean of Community, Continuing, and Graduate Education. Certificate applicable to any four-year degree offered at the institution. Program fulfills requirements for Head Teacher.

Program Format Evening classes offered. Instructional schedule: One evening per week. Program cycle: Continuous enrollment. Full program cycle lasts 12 credit hours. Completion of program requires 2.0 GPA.

Evaluation Student evaluation based on tests, papers, reports. Grading system: Letters or numbers. Transcripts are kept for each student.

Enrollment Requirements High school diploma required, experience with young children preferred.

Program Costs $664 for the program, $166 per course.

Housing and Student Services Housing is not available. Job counseling and placement services are not available.

Contact Office of Continuing Education, Church Street, North Adams, MA 01247. 413-664-4511.

PINE MANOR COLLEGE
Chestnut Hill, Massachusetts 02167

ENGLISH AS A SECOND LANGUAGE (23.12)
Certificate for Study in the Pine Manor Language Institute

General Information Unit offering the program: Pine Manor Language Institute. Program content: English as a second language for non-native speakers. Available on a non-credit basis. Certificate signed by the Program Director.

Program Format Daytime classes offered. Students may enroll September, January, March, June. Full program cycle lasts 4 semesters. Completion of program requires 80% attendance, grade of C or better.

Evaluation Student evaluation based on tests, compositions, participation, attendance, homework assignments. Grading system: Letters or numbers. Transcripts are kept for each student.

Enrollment Requirements Program open to women only, high school diploma required. Program is open to non-resident foreign students.

Program Costs $2026–$3800 per semester.

Housing and Student Services Housing is available. Job counseling and placement services are not available.

Special Features Program provides intensive ESL course work to women. Small classes (generally 5–8 students), so students receive personal attention. Instructors have master's degrees in ESL or linguistics. Twenty hours/week in grammar, listening, reading, writing, vocabulary, and conversation. Students meet 2 hours/week with United States conversation partner during academic year. Wide variety of field trips and activities to introduce students to United States culture.

Contact Ms. Sharon Morrison, International Admissions Director, 400 Heath Street, Chestnut Hill, MA 02167. 617-731-7104.

ST. HYACINTH COLLEGE AND SEMINARY
Granby, Massachusetts 01033

PHILOSOPHY (38.01)
Pre-Theological Certificate

General Information Program content: Philosophy, theology, classical languages, character and spiritual development. Available on either a credit or non-credit basis. Certificate signed by the President of the College. Program fulfills requirements for Program of Priestly Formation.

Program Format Daytime classes offered. Students enroll once per year. Full program cycle lasts 4 semesters. Completion of program requires 2.0 GPA, Formation approval.

Evaluation Student evaluation based on tests, papers, reports, apostolic and Formation evaluation. Grading system: Letters or numbers. Transcripts are kept for each student.

Enrollment Requirements Sponsorship and a bachelor's degree required. Program is open to non-resident foreign students. English language proficiency required.

Program Costs $100 per credit hour.

Housing and Student Services Housing is available. Job counseling and placement services are not available.

Contact Rev. Jude Winkler, Admissions Officer, 66 School Street, Granby, MA 01033. 413-467-7191.

SMITH COLLEGE
Northampton, Massachusetts 01063

AREA STUDIES (05.01)
Diploma Program in American Studies

General Information Program content: American culture and institutions. Available for credit. Certificate signed by the President.

Program Format Daytime, evening classes offered. Students enroll in the fall. Full program cycle lasts 2 semesters. Completion of program requires 24 credit hours (including two 4-credit seminars), 3.0 GPA.

Evaluation Student evaluation based on tests, papers. Grading system: Letters or numbers. Transcripts are kept for each student.

Enrollment Requirements Limited to college-level foreign students; some knowledge of American history or literature preferred. Program is open to non-resident foreign students. English language proficiency required.

Program Costs $16,000 for the program.

Housing and Student Services Housing is available. Job counseling and placement services are available.

Special Features Students receive individual supervision for their final paper and have access to all Smith College facilities. This coeducational program is the only one exclusively for foreign students.

Contact Dr. Peter I. Rose, Director, Diploma Program in American Studies, 103 Wright Hall, Northampton, MA 01063. 413-584-2700.

STONEHILL COLLEGE
North Easton, Massachusetts 02357

BUSINESS AND MANAGEMENT, GENERAL (06.01)
The Certificate in Management

General Information Unit offering the program: Community and Professional Education. Program content: Courses in management for supervisory personnel. Available on a non-credit basis. Certificate signed by the Associate Academic Dean for Continuing Education.

Program Format Evening classes offered. Instructional schedule: One evening per week. Students may enroll September, February, April. Full program cycle lasts 3 semesters. Completion of program requires six courses.

Evaluation Student evaluation methods vary by course. Grading system: Pass/fail. Transcripts are kept for each student.

Enrollment Requirements Program is open to non-resident foreign students. English language proficiency required.

Program Costs $1590 for the program, $265 per course.

Housing and Student Services Housing is not available. Job counseling and placement services are not available.

Special Features The Management Certificate Program is designed to introduce, improve, and develop supervisory and management skills for participants who are either on-line supervisors and interested in improving their skills or participants who are interested in pursuing positions in leadership. The courses are designed for practitioners looking for practical applications.

Contact Ms. Sherry E. Pinter, Director, Community and Professional Education, Washington Street, North Easton, MA 02357. 617-238-1081.

INDIVIDUAL AND FAMILY DEVELOPMENT (19.07)
Certificate in Gerontology

General Information Unit offering the program: Sociology/Evening Division. Available for credit. Certificate signed by the Associate Academic Dean. Certificate applicable to any degree offered by the Evening Division.

Program Format Evening classes offered. Program cycle: Continuous enrollment. Full program cycle lasts 18 credit hours. Completion of program requires 2.0 GPA, six courses.

Evaluation Student evaluation based on tests, papers, reports. Grading system: Letters or numbers. Transcripts are kept for each student.

Enrollment Requirements High school diploma required. Program is open to non-resident foreign students. English language proficiency required.

Program Costs $2010 for the program, $335 per course.

Housing and Student Services Housing is not available. Job counseling and placement services are available.

Special Features The Evening Division offers a six-course program which provides students with a broad theoretical background in gerontology and assists them in developing practical skills for working with the elderly. These courses are designed primarily to assist human service workers, nursing home staff members, health care professionals, and others to develop and/or improve their skills in serving the elderly.

Contact Mr. Richard Shankar, Professor of Sociology, Washington Street, North Easton, MA 02357. 617-238-1081 Ext. 272.

LAW (22.01)
Certificate in Paralegal Studies

General Information Unit offering the program: Evening Division. Available for credit. Certificate signed by the Associate Academic Dean. Certificate applicable to any four-year degree offered at the institution.

Program Format Evening classes offered. Instructional schedule: One evening per week. Program cycle: Continuous enrollment. Full program cycle lasts 21 credit hours. Completion of program requires 2.0 GPA.

Evaluation Student evaluation based on tests, papers, reports. Grading system: Letters or numbers. Transcripts are kept for each student.

Enrollment Requirements High school diploma required. Program is open to non-resident foreign students. English language proficiency required.

Program Costs $2345 for the program, $335 per course.

Housing and Student Services Housing is not available. Job counseling and placement services are available.

Special Features The purpose of this program is to prepare students for entry-level positions as legal assistants in a general law practice, or in one of two specialty areas: health care law, or litigation.

Contact Mr. George Rogers, Assistant Academic Dean for Continuing Education, Washington Street, North Easton, MA 02357. 617-238-1081 Ext. 470.

MENTAL HEALTH/HUMAN SERVICES (17.04)
Certificate in Alcoholism Counseling

General Information Unit offering the program: Evening Division. Available for credit. Certificate signed by the President of the College. Certificate applicable to any degree offered by the Evening Division.

Program Format Evening classes offered. Instructional schedule: One evening per week. Program cycle: Continuous enrollment. Full program cycle lasts 15 credit hours. Completion of program requires 2.0 GPA, four courses, 100-hour practicum.

Evaluation Student evaluation based on tests, papers, reports, practicum. Grading system: Letters or numbers. Transcripts are kept for each student.

Enrollment Requirements High school diploma required. Program is open to non-resident foreign students. English language proficiency required.

Program Costs $1675 for the program, $335 per course.

Housing and Student Services Housing is not available. Job counseling and placement services are not available.

Special Features Stonehill Evening Division offers a five-course program to train students in the skill of counseling alcoholics. These courses are primarily designed to assist human service workers, health professionals, alcoholism counselors, and volunteers to improve their skills in working with alcoholics.

Contact Mr. David Mulligan, Director of Alcoholism Counseling Program, Evening Division, North Easton, MA 02357. 617-238-1081 Ext. 470.

PERSONNEL AND TRAINING PROGRAMS (07.05)
The Certificate in Personnel Practices

General Information Unit offering the program: Community and Professional Education. Available on a non-credit basis. Certificate signed by the Associate Academic Dean for Continuing Education.

Program Format Evening classes offered. Instructional schedule: One evening per week. Students may enroll September, February, April. Full program cycle lasts 3 semesters. Completion of program requires five courses.

Evaluation Student evaluation methods vary by course. Grading system: Pass/fail. Transcripts are kept for each student.

Enrollment Requirements Program is open to non-resident foreign students. English language proficiency required.

Program Costs $1300 for the program, $260 per course.

The Certificate in Personnel Practices continued

Housing and Student Services Housing is not available. Job counseling and placement services are not available.

Special Features The Certificate in Personnel Practices program is designed primarily for the prospective or entry-level professional who wants to become successful in the personnel field. The program has been developed to address the demanding and sophisticated personnel function including human relations, compensation and benefits, and discrimination laws.

Contact Ms. Sherry E. Pinter, Director, Community and Professional Education, Washington Street, North Easton, MA 02357. 617-238-1081.

RELIGIOUS EDUCATION (39.04)
Certificate in Religious Education

General Information Unit offering the program: Evening Division. Available for credit. Certificate signed by the Dean of Continuing Education. Certificate applicable to any degree offered by the Evening Division.

Program Format Evening classes offered. Instructional schedule: One evening per week. Program cycle: Continuous enrollment. Full program cycle lasts 15 credit hours. Completion of program requires 2.0 GPA, five courses.

Evaluation Student evaluation based on tests, papers, reports. Grading system: Letters or numbers. Transcripts are kept for each student.

Enrollment Requirements High school diploma required. Program is open to non-resident foreign students. English language proficiency required.

Program Costs $1675 for the program, $335 per course.

Housing and Student Services Housing is not available.

Special Features The Evening Division offers a five-course program leading to a certificate in religious education. Although open for all students who wish to achieve a deeper understanding of Christian tradition, the program is specifically designed for CCD and parochial school teachers.

Contact Rev. Richard Mazziotta, Director of Religious Education Program, Washington Street, North Easton, MA 02357. 617-238-1081 Ext. 487.

SECRETARIAL AND RELATED PROGRAMS (07.06)
The Secretary/Administrative Assistant Certificate

General Information Unit offering the program: Community and Professional Education. Available on a non-credit basis. Certificate signed by the Associate Academic Dean for Continuing Education.

Program Format Evening classes offered. Instructional schedule: One evening per week. Students may enroll September, February, April. Full program cycle lasts 3 semesters. Completion of program requires five courses.

Evaluation Student evaluation methods vary by course. Grading system: Pass/fail. Record of completion kept in course files.

Enrollment Requirements Program is open to non-resident foreign students. English language proficiency required.

Program Costs $635 for the program, $95–$165 per course.

Housing and Student Services Housing is not available. Job counseling and placement services are not available.

Special Features The Secretary/Administrative Assistant Certificate Program will improve participants decision-making and problem-solving skills. Students will gain greater self-confidence and learn techniques for better written and spoken communications. Courses cover assertiveness, management, writing and speaking, and supervisory skills.

Contact Ms. Sherry E. Pinter, Director, Community and Professional Education, Washington Street, North Easton, MA 02357. 617-238-1081.

UNIVERSITY OF LOWELL
Lowell, Massachusetts 01854

MANAGEMENT SCIENCE (06.13)
Advanced Certificate in Management for Engineers

General Information Unit offering the program: College of Management Science, Division of Continuing Education. Available on either a credit or non-credit basis. Certificate signed by the Vice President for Academic Affairs. Certificate applicable to M.B.A.

Program Format Evening classes offered. Instructional schedule: Two evenings per week. Program cycle: Continuous enrollment. Full program cycle lasts 2 semesters. Completion of program requires eight modules, 2.5 GPA.

Evaluation Student evaluation based on tests, papers, reports. Grading system: Letters or numbers. Transcripts are kept for each student.

Enrollment Requirements Bachelor's degree in engineering or science or employment in engineering or science with bachelor's degree required. Program is open to non-resident foreign students. English language proficiency required. Students submit writing sample.

Program Costs $3600 for the program, $450 per course.

Housing and Student Services Housing is available. Job counseling and placement services are available.

Special Features Specifically designed for engineers, scientists, project leaders, and technical staff who have recently become, or who are interested in becoming, managers in their organizations. Instructors are primarily full-time faculty in the College of Management Science experienced in working with and teaching engineers in management.

Contact Dr. Dirk Messelaar, Assistant Director, Continuing Education, One University Avenue, Lowell, MA 01854. 617-454-4664.

TECHNICAL AND BUSINESS WRITING (23.11)
Certificate in Technical Communications

General Information Unit offering the program: English Department, Division of Continuing Education. Program content: Software writing, computer programming. Available for credit. Endorsed by Wang Labs, Digital Equipment Corporation, Apollo Computer. Certificate signed by the Vice President for Academic Affairs.

Program Format Evening classes offered. Instructional schedule: Two evenings per week. Program cycle: Continuous enrollment. Full program cycle lasts 4 semesters. Completion of program requires eight courses, 2.5 GPA.

Evaluation Student evaluation based on tests, papers, reports. Grading system: Letters or numbers. Transcripts are kept for each student.

Enrollment Requirements Bachelor's degree, completion of one college-level programming course required. Program is open to non-resident foreign students. English language proficiency required.

Program Costs $1751 for the program, $235 per course.

Housing and Student Services Housing is available. Job counseling and placement services are available.

Special Features The University of Lowell's Technical Communications Program prepares adults with bachelor's degrees to become software writers in the computer industry. The program was developed with the assistance of local high-technology companies; program instructors are all working professionals from local computer companies.

Contact Dr. Dirk Messelaar, Assistant Director, Continuing Education, One University Avenue, Lowell, MA 01854. 617-454-4664.

WESTERN NEW ENGLAND COLLEGE
Springfield, Massachusetts 01119

COMPUTER PROGRAMMING (11.02)
Certificate in Computer Information Systems

General Information Unit offering the program: School of Business, School of Continuing Higher Education. Available for credit. Certificate signed by the President.

Program Format Daytime, evening, weekend classes offered. Program cycle: Continuous enrollment. Full program cycle lasts 18 credit hours. Completion of program requires 2.0 GPA.

Evaluation Student evaluation based on tests, papers, computer programming assignments. Grading system: Letters or numbers. Transcripts are kept for each student.

Enrollment Requirements Sixty college credits with a 2.0 GPA required. Program is not open to non-resident foreign students. English language proficiency required.

Program Costs $180 per credit hour.

Housing and Student Services Housing is not available. Job counseling and placement services are available.

Special Features Students have access to modern computational facilities. The computer center is equipped with an IBM-System 36 and three Data General Corporation computer systems: two MV8000's and an MV4000. Microcomputer facilities include a laboratory with 36 general instructional microcomputers and a Writing Center with 40 microcomputers dedicated to word processing.

Contact School of Continuing Education, Herman Hall, 1215 Wilbraham Road, Springfield, MA 01119. 413-782-1249.

NUCEA MEMBER
WORCESTER STATE COLLEGE
Worcester, Massachusetts 01602

BUSINESS ADMINISTRATION AND MANAGEMENT (06.04)
Management and Supervision

General Information Unit offering the program: Business Administration and Economics. Program content: Business administration. Available for credit. Certificate signed by the Dean. Certificate applicable to B.S. in Business Administration.

Program Format Evening classes offered. Instructional schedule: Once or twice per week. Program cycle: Continuous enrollment. Full program cycle lasts 2 years. Completion of program requires seven courses, exit interview.

Evaluation Student evaluation based on tests, papers, reports. Grading system: Letters or numbers. Transcripts are kept for each student.

Enrollment Requirements Forty-eight college credits or equivalent work experience required. Program is open to non-resident foreign students. English language proficiency required.

Program Costs $165–$207 per course.

Housing and Student Services Housing is not available. Job counseling and placement services are available.

Special Features Program designed with input from business community. Instructors selected from qualified individuals with strong business background. Graduates have demonstrated the

usefulness of the program through career changes and upgrading of professional positions.

Contact Dr. Robert Hartwig, Chair, Business Administration and Economics Department, 486 Chandler Street, Worcester, MA 01602. 617-793-8091.

DATA PROCESSING (11.03)
Certificate Program in Data Processing

General Information Unit offering the program: Mathematics/Computer Science Department. Available for credit. Certificate signed by the Dean. Certificate applicable to bachelor's degree in computer science.

Program Format Evening classes offered. Program cycle: Continuous enrollment. Full program cycle lasts 2 years. Completion of program requires nine courses, exit interview.

Evaluation Student evaluation methods vary by course. Grading system: Letters or numbers. Transcripts are kept for each student.

Enrollment Requirements Three semester hours of college algebra, introduction to computer science or BASIC required. Program is open to non-resident foreign students. English language proficiency required.

Program Costs $165–$207 per course.

Housing and Student Services Housing is not available. Job counseling and placement services are available.

Special Features Program provides a solid foundation for entering the field of computer science or pursuing more advanced study.

Contact Mr. Kenneth Schoen, Chair, Mathematics/Computer Science Department, 486 Chandler Street, Worcester, MA 01602. 617-793-8000.

MICHIGAN

JORDAN COLLEGE
Cedar Springs, Michigan 49319

BUSINESS ADMINISTRATION AND MANAGEMENT (06.04)
Business Administration

General Information Unit offering the program: Business Division. Program content: Accounting, English, economics, business law, data processing. Available for credit. Certificate signed by the President. Certificate applicable to A.A.S. in Business Administration.

Program Format Daytime, evening classes offered. Students may enroll fall, spring, summer. Full program cycle lasts 2 semesters. Completion of program requires 30 semester hours, general education requirements, 2.0 GPA.

Evaluation Student evaluation based on tests, papers, reports. Grading system: Letters or numbers. Transcripts are kept for each student.

Enrollment Requirements Official transcripts required. Program is not open to non-resident foreign students.

Program Costs $3900 for the program, $495–$660 per course.

Housing and Student Services Housing is not available. Job counseling and placement services are available.

Contact Mr. Charles Conboy, Office of Admissions, 360 West Pine, Cedar Springs, MI 49319. 616-696-1180.

BUSINESS DATA PROCESSING AND RELATED PROGRAMS (07.03)
Computerized Accounting

General Information   Unit offering the program: Business Division. Program content: Accounting, business, computers. Available for credit. Certificate signed by the President. Certificate applicable to A.A.S. in Computerized Accounting.

Program Format   Daytime, evening classes offered. Students may enroll fall, spring, summer. Full program cycle lasts 3 semesters. Completion of program requires 37–38 semester hours, general education requirements, 2.0 GPA.

Evaluation   Student evaluation based on tests, papers, reports. Grading system: Letters or numbers. Transcripts are kept for each student.

Enrollment Requirements   Official transcripts required. Program is not open to non-resident foreign students.

Program Costs $5910 for the program, $495–$660 per course.

Housing and Student Services   Housing is not available. Job counseling and placement services are available.

Contact   Mr. Charles Conboy, Office of Admissions, 360 West Pine, Cedar Springs, MI 49319. 616-696-1180.

CHILD CARE AND GUIDANCE MANAGEMENT AND SERVICES (20.02)
Child Development

General Information   Unit offering the program: Social Science Division. Program content: Psychology, child development courses. Available for credit. Certificate signed by the President. Certificate applicable to A.A.S. in Child Development.

Program Format   Daytime, evening classes offered. Students may enroll fall, spring, summer. Full program cycle lasts 2 semesters. Completion of program requires 30 semester hours, general education requirements, 2.0 GPA.

Evaluation   Student evaluation based on tests, papers, reports. Grading system: Letters or numbers. Transcripts are kept for each student.

Enrollment Requirements   Official transcripts required. Program is not open to non-resident foreign students.

Program Costs $3900 for the program, $495–$660 per course.

Housing and Student Services   Housing is not available. Job counseling and placement services are available.

Contact   Mr. Charles Conboy, Office of Admissions, 360 West Pine, Cedar Springs, MI 49319. 616-696-1180.

COMPUTER PROGRAMMING (11.02)
Computer Programming

General Information   Unit offering the program: Business Division. Program content: Business, computers, general education. Available for credit. Certificate signed by the President. Certificate applicable to A.A.S. in Computer Programming.

Program Format   Daytime, evening classes offered. Students may enroll fall, spring, summer. Full program cycle lasts 3 semesters. Completion of program requires 36 semester hours, general education requirements, 2.0 GPA or better.

Evaluation   Student evaluation based on tests, papers, reports. Grading system: Letters or numbers. Transcripts are kept for each student.

Enrollment Requirements   Official transcripts required. Program is not open to non-resident foreign students.

Program Costs $5950 for the program, $495–$660 per course.

Housing and Student Services   Housing is not available. Job counseling and placement services are available.

Contact   Mr. Charles Conboy, Office of Admissions, 360 West Pine, Cedar Springs, MI 49319. 616-696-1180.

INFORMATION SCIENCES AND SYSTEMS (11.04)
Computer Information/Business Administration

General Information   Unit offering the program: Business Division. Program content: Accounting, business, computers. Available for credit. Certificate signed by the President. Certificate applicable to A.A.S. in Computer Information/ Business Administration.

Program Format   Daytime, evening classes offered. Students may enroll fall, spring, summer. Full program cycle lasts 3 semesters. Completion of program requires 38 semester hours, general education requirements, 2.0 GPA.

Evaluation   Student evaluation based on tests, papers, reports. Grading system: Letters or numbers. Transcripts are kept for each student.

Enrollment Requirements   Official transcripts required. Program is not open to non-resident foreign students.

Program Costs $5910 for the program, $495–$660 per course.

Housing and Student Services   Housing is not available. Job counseling and placement services are available.

Contact   Mr. Charles Conboy, Office of Admissions, 360 West Pine, Cedar Springs, MI 49319. 616-696-1180.

MICROCOMPUTER APPLICATIONS (11.06)
Computer Applications

General Information   Unit offering the program: Business Division. Program content: Accounting, business, computers. Available for credit. Certificate signed by the President. Certificate applicable to A.A.S. in Computer Applications.

Program Format   Daytime, evening classes offered. Students may enroll fall, spring, summer. Full program cycle lasts 3 semesters. Completion of program requires 36–37 semester hours, general education requirements, 2.0 GPA.

Evaluation   Student evaluation based on tests, papers, reports. Grading system: Letters or numbers. Transcripts are kept for each student.

Enrollment Requirements   Official transcripts required. Program is not open to non-resident foreign students.

Program Costs $5970 for the program, $495–$660 per course.

Housing and Student Services   Housing is not available. Job counseling and placement services are available.

Contact   Mr. Charles Conboy, Office of Admissions, 360 West Pine, Cedar Springs, MI 49319. 616-696-1180.

MISCELLANEOUS ALLIED HEALTH SERVICES (17.05)
Group Care Worker

General Information   Unit offering the program: Social Science Division. Program content: Psychology, health care courses. Available for credit. Certificate signed by the President.

Program Format   Daytime, evening classes offered. Students may enroll fall, spring, summer. Full program cycle lasts 2 semesters. Completion of program requires 30 semester hours, general education requirements, 2.0 GPA.

Evaluation   Student evaluation based on tests, papers, reports. Grading system: Letters or numbers. Transcripts are kept for each student.

Enrollment Requirements   Official transcripts required. Program is not open to non-resident foreign students.

Program Costs $3900 for the program, $495–$660 per course.

Housing and Student Services   Housing is not available. Job counseling and placement services are available.

Contact   Mr. Charles Conboy, Office of Admissions, 360 West Pine, Cedar Springs, MI 49319. 616-696-1180.

MISCELLANEOUS ALLIED HEALTH SERVICES (17.05)
Home Health Aide

General Information   Unit offering the program: Social Science Division. Program content: First aid, nutrition, anatomy, psychology. Available for credit. Certificate signed by the President.

Program Format   Daytime, evening classes offered. Students may enroll fall, spring, summer. Full program cycle lasts 2 semesters. Completion of program requires 30 semester hours, general education requirements, 2.0 GPA.

Evaluation   Student evaluation based on tests, papers, reports. Grading system: Letters or numbers. Transcripts are kept for each student.

Enrollment Requirements   Official transcripts required. Program is not open to non-resident foreign students.

Program Costs $3900 for the program, $495–$660 per course.

Housing and Student Services   Housing is not available. Job counseling and placement services are available.

Contact   Mr. Charles Conboy, Office of Admissions, 360 West Pine, Cedar Springs, MI 49319. 616-696-1180.

PERSONAL SERVICES (12.04)
Cosmetology

General Information   Unit offering the program: Science and Technology. Program content: Theory and methods, public speaking. Available for credit. Certificate signed by the President. Certificate applicable to A.A.S. in Cosmetology.

Program Format   Daytime, evening classes offered. Students may enroll fall, spring, summer. Full program cycle lasts 2 semesters. Completion of program requires 30 semester hours, general education requirements, 2.0 GPA.

Evaluation   Student evaluation based on tests, papers, reports. Grading system: Letters or numbers. Transcripts are kept for each student.

Enrollment Requirements   Official transcripts required. Program is not open to non-resident foreign students.

Program Costs $3900 for the program, $495–$660 per course.

Housing and Student Services   Housing is not available. Job counseling and placement services are available.

Contact   Mr. Charles Conboy, Office of Admissions, 360 West Pine, Cedar Springs, MI 49319. 616-696-1180.

RENEWABLE NATURAL RESOURCES, GENERAL (03.01)
Energy Management

General Information   Unit offering the program: Science and Technology Division. Program content: Power production, electricity, HVAC systems. Available for credit. Certificate signed by the President.

Program Format   Daytime, evening classes offered. Students may enroll fall, spring, summer. Full program cycle lasts 3 semesters. Completion of program requires 36–37 semester hours, general education requirements, 2.0 GPA.

Evaluation   Student evaluation based on tests, papers, reports. Grading system: Letters or numbers. Transcripts are kept for each student.

Enrollment Requirements   Official transcripts required. Program is open to non-resident foreign students. English language proficiency required. Minimum TOEFL score required: 500.

Program Costs $5915 for the program, $495–$660 per course.

Housing and Student Services   Housing is not available. Job counseling and placement services are available.

Contact   Mr. Charles Conboy, Office of Admissions, 360 West Pine, Cedar Springs, MI 49319. 616-696-1180.

RENEWABLE NATURAL RESOURCES, GENERAL (03.01)
Solar Retrofit Technology

General Information   Unit offering the program: Science and Technology. Program content: Renewable energy, technology courses. Available for credit. Certificate signed by the President.

Program Format   Daytime, evening classes offered. Students may enroll fall, spring, summer. Full program cycle lasts 3 years. Completion of program requires 39 semester hours, general education requirements, 2.0 GPA.

Evaluation   Student evaluation based on tests, papers, reports. Grading system: Letters or numbers. Transcripts are kept for each student.

Enrollment Requirements   Official transcripts required. Program is open to non-resident foreign students. English language proficiency required. Minimum TOEFL score required: 500.

Program Costs $5950 for the program, $495–$660 per course.

Housing and Student Services   Housing is not available. Job counseling and placement services are available.

Contact   Mr. Charles Conboy, Office of Admissions, 360 West Pine, Cedar Springs, MI 49319. 616-696-1180.

SECRETARIAL AND RELATED PROGRAMS (07.06)
Secretarial Science/Executive Secretary

General Information   Unit offering the program: Business Division. Program content: Accounting, shorthand, technical writing, office management. Available for credit. Certificate signed by the President. Certificate applicable to A.A.S. in Secretarial Science/Executive Secretary.

Program Format   Daytime, evening classes offered. Students may enroll fall, spring, summer. Full program cycle lasts 3 semesters. Completion of program requires 45 semester hours, general education requirements, 2.0 GPA.

Evaluation   Student evaluation based on tests, papers, reports. Grading system: Letters or numbers. Transcripts are kept for each student.

Enrollment Requirements   Official transcripts required. Program is not open to non-resident foreign students.

Program Costs $6030 for the program, $495–$660 per course.

Housing and Student Services   Housing is not available. Job counseling and placement services are available.

Contact   Mr. Charles Conboy, Office of Admissions, 360 West Pine, Cedar Springs, MI 49319. 616-696-1180.

SECRETARIAL AND RELATED PROGRAMS (07.06)
Secretarial Science/Legal Secretary

General Information   Unit offering the program: Business Division. Program content: Technical writing, legal terminology, computers, office procedures. Available for credit. Certificate signed by the President. Certificate applicable to A.A.S. in Secretarial Science/Legal Secretary.

Program Format   Daytime, evening classes offered. Students may enroll fall, spring, summer. Full program cycle lasts 3 semesters. Completion of program requires 45 semester hours, general education requirements, 2.0 GPA.

Evaluation   Student evaluation based on tests, papers, reports. Grading system: Letters or numbers. Transcripts are kept for each student.

Enrollment Requirements   Official transcripts required. Program is not open to non-resident foreign students.

Program Costs $6030 for the program, $495–$660 per course.

Housing and Student Services   Housing is not available. Job counseling and placement services are available.

Secretarial Science/Legal Secretary continued

Contact Mr. Charles Conboy, Office of Admissions, 360 West Pine, Cedar Springs, MI 49319. 616-696-1180.

SECRETARIAL AND RELATED PROGRAMS (07.06)
Secretarial Science/Medical Secretary

General Information Unit offering the program: Business Division. Program content: Typing, transcription, word processing, technical writing, medical terminology. Available for credit. Certificate signed by the President. Certificate applicable to A.A.S. in Secretarial Science/Medical Secretary.

Program Format Daytime, evening classes offered. Students may enroll fall, spring, summer. Full program cycle lasts 3 semesters. Completion of program requires 45 semester hours, general education requirements, 2.0 GPA.

Evaluation Student evaluation based on tests, papers, reports. Grading system: Letters or numbers. Transcripts are kept for each student.

Enrollment Requirements Official transcripts required. Program is not open to non-resident foreign students.

Program Costs $6030 for the program, $495–$660 per course.

Housing and Student Services Housing is not available. Job counseling and placement services are available.

Contact Mr. Charles Conboy, Office of Admissions, 360 West Pine, Cedar Springs, MI 49319. 616-696-1180.

WORD PROCESSING (07.08)
Word Processing

General Information Unit offering the program: Business Division. Program content: Computers, typing. Available for credit. Certificate signed by the President. Certificate applicable to A.A.S. in Word Processing.

Program Format Daytime, evening classes offered. Students may enroll fall, spring, summer. Full program cycle lasts 3 semesters. Completion of program requires 45 semester hours, general education requirements, 2.0 GPA.

Evaluation Student evaluation based on tests, papers, reports. Grading system: Letters or numbers. Transcripts are kept for each student.

Enrollment Requirements Official transcripts required. Program is not open to non-resident foreign students.

Program Costs $6010 for the program, $495–$660 per course.

Housing and Student Services Housing is not available. Job counseling and placement services are available.

Contact Mr. Charles Conboy, Office of Admissions, 360 West Pine, Cedar Springs, MI 49319. 616-696-1180.

MARYGROVE COLLEGE
Detroit, Michigan 48221

BUSINESS AND MANAGEMENT, GENERAL (06.01)
Certificate of Completion—Business

General Information Unit offering the program: Department of Business. Program content: Accounting, marketing, management, finance, business law. Available for credit. Certificate signed by the President of College. Certificate applicable to B.A., B.B.A.

Program Format Daytime, evening classes offered. Program cycle: Continuous enrollment. Full program cycle lasts 20 credit hours. Completion of program requires 2.0 GPA.

Evaluation Student evaluation based on tests, papers, reports. Grading system: Letters or numbers. Transcripts are kept for each student.

Enrollment Requirements Bachelor's degree required. Program is open to non-resident foreign students. English language proficiency required.

Program Costs $3400 for the program.

Housing and Student Services Housing is available. Job counseling and placement services are available.

Special Features Taught by all full-time faculty. The courses are part of a bachelor's degree program. The certificate may be earned while pursuing a second major or a second degree. Designed for individuals seeking business skills after having earned a bachelor's degree in a nonbusiness field.

Contact Mr. John S. Barbour, Department Head, Business, 8425 West McNichols, Detroit, MI 48221. 313-862-8000.

COMPUTER PROGRAMMING (11.02)
Certificate of Completion in Computer Science Post-Degree Program

General Information Unit offering the program: Computer Science Department. Program content: Computer programming application. Available for credit. Certificate signed by the Academic Dean.

Program Format Daytime, weekend classes offered. Program cycle: Continuous enrollment. Full program cycle lasts 4 semesters. Completion of program requires 2.0 GPA.

Evaluation Student evaluation based on tests, papers, computer programs. Grading system: Letters or numbers. Transcripts are kept for each student.

Enrollment Requirements Bachelor's degree, college admissions required. Program is open to non-resident foreign students. English language proficiency required.

Program Costs $3042 for the program, $507 per course.

Housing and Student Services Housing is available. Job counseling and placement services are available.

Contact Ms. Judy Gold, Department Chair, Computer Science Department, 8425 West McNichols, Detroit, MI 48221. 313-862-8000.

DIAGNOSTIC AND TREATMENT SERVICES (17.02)
Completion of the Diagnostic Medical Sonography Program

General Information Unit offering the program: Allied Health. Program content: Physics, anatomy, pathology, clinical practicum. Available for credit. Certificate signed by the Academic Dean. Certificate applicable to B.A. in Allied Health. Program fulfills requirements for American Registry of Diagnostic Medical Sonography.

Program Format Daytime, evening classes offered. Instructional schedule: Clinical practicum three to four days per week; didactic classes once or twice per week. Students enroll in January. Full program cycle lasts 12 months. Completion of program requires 2.0 GPA, 480 contact hours.

Evaluation Student evaluation based on tests, papers, reports, clinical competency evaluations. Grading system: Letters or numbers. Transcripts are kept for each student.

Enrollment Requirements Associate degree in allied health profession, minimum 18 years of age, 2.0 GPA required. Program is open to non-resident foreign students.

Program Costs $169 per credit hour.

Housing and Student Services Housing is available. Job counseling and placement services are available.

Contact Ms. Dana Quinn-Reid, Program Director, Diagnostic Medical Sonography, 8425 West McNichols, Detroit, MI 48221. 313-862-8000 Ext. 259.

FOREIGN LANGUAGES, MULTIPLE EMPHASIS (16.01)
Marygrove Translator's Certificate

General Information Unit offering the program: Modern Languages. Program content: Translation and interpretation in French, German, or Spanish. Available for credit. Certificate signed by the Coordinator of Translation Programs. Certificate applicable to B.A. in English, Language Arts; M.Ed.

Program Format Daytime classes offered. Instructional schedule: Three classes per week. Students may enroll every other year. Full program cycle lasts 2 semesters. Completion of program requires three courses, grade of B or better.

Evaluation Student evaluation based on tests, papers, written assignments. Grading system: Letters or numbers. Transcripts are kept for each student.

Enrollment Requirements Intermediate proficiency in the language to be studied required. Program is open to non-resident foreign students. English language proficiency required.

Program Costs $1521 for the program, $507 per course.

Housing and Student Services Housing is available. Job counseling and placement services are available.

Special Features The program was designed according to specifications of the American Translator's Association. It maintains national proficiency standards.

Contact Dr. E. DuBruck, Coordinator, 8425 West McNichols, Detroit, MI 48221. 313-972-8000 Ext. 284.

MISCELLANEOUS ALLIED HEALTH SERVICES (17.05)
Medical Clinical Assistant

General Information Unit offering the program: Division of Allied Health. Program content: Theory, laboratory experience, clinical externship. Available for credit. Certificate signed by the Academic Dean. Certificate applicable to A.S. in Medical Clinical Assistant. Program fulfills requirements for American Medical Association.

Program Format Daytime, evening classes offered. Program cycle: Continuous enrollment. Full program cycle lasts 10 months. Completion of program requires 160-hour externship.

Evaluation Student evaluation based on tests, simulation. Grading system: Letters or numbers. Transcripts are kept for each student.

Enrollment Requirements College admissions required. Program is open to non-resident foreign students. English language proficiency required.

Program Costs $5000 for the program.

Housing and Student Services Housing is available. Job counseling and placement services are available.

Special Features The program is integrated into the rest of the regular college courses. Classes taken qualify for college credit and can be applied to Associate of Science programs and toward a major in allied health (BA). Students are placed in an externship that often leads to employment opportunities.

Contact Ms. Amber Patterson, Director of Admissions, 8425 West McNichols, Detroit, MI 48221. 313-862-8000.

MUSIC (50.09)
Certificate Program in Sacred Music

General Information Unit offering the program: Music. Program content: Church music. Available on either a credit or non-credit basis. Certificate signed by the Department Chair, Department of Music. Certificate applicable to bachelor's degree in sacred music.

Program Format Daytime, weekend classes offered. Instructional schedule: Monday through Thursday during academic year, three days in the summer. Program cycle: Continuous enrollment. Full program cycle lasts 37 credit hours. Completion of program requires demonstration of proficiency.

Evaluation Student evaluation based on tests, papers, performance in organ, voice, and choir. Grading system: Letters or numbers. Transcripts are kept for each student.

Enrollment Requirements College admissions, audition required. Program is open to non-resident foreign students. English language proficiency required.

Program Costs $6950 for the program.

Housing and Student Services Housing is available. Job counseling and placement services are available.

Special Features The music faculty at Marygrove College includes many highly qualified musicians. Included in the roster is Huw Lewis, an internationally acclaimed concert organist. Mr. Lewis holds the performing and teaching diplomas of the Royal College of Music and the Royal Academy of Music in London and a master's degree from the University of Michigan, where he is presently involved in doctoral studies.

Contact Ms. Elaine Grover, Assistant Professor of Music, 8425 West McNichols, Detroit, MI 48221. 313-862-8000 Ext. 354.

WORD PROCESSING (07.08)
Word Processing Pre-Baccalaureate Certificate

General Information Unit offering the program: Special Projects and Business. Program content: Word processing, business communications, business math, shorthand, typing, office procedures, introduction to business. Available for credit. Cosponsored by City of Detroit. Certificate signed by the Dean, Continuing Education.

Program Format Daytime classes offered. Students enroll once per year. Full program cycle lasts 7 months.

Evaluation Student evaluation based on tests, papers, reports. Grading system: Letters or numbers. Transcripts are kept for each student.

Enrollment Requirements College admissions required. Program is not open to non-resident foreign students. English language proficiency required. Level 9 on TABE test.

Program Costs Program is federally funded through the state of Michigan and the city of Detroit.

Housing and Student Services Housing is available. Job counseling and placement services are available.

Special Features The program gives the students college credit, provides them with a marketable skill, and gives them a base in order to further their education. The city of Detroit combines its funds with the excellent Marygrove facility to provide one of the best training programs in the area.

Contact Ms. Barbara Barnaby, Director of Word Processing Program, 8425 West McNichols, Detroit, MI 48221. 313-862-8000 Ext. 425.

NORTHWOOD INSTITUTE
Midland, Michigan 48640

BUSINESS ADMINISTRATION AND MANAGEMENT (06.04)
Professional Development Certification

General Information Unit offering the program: Business Division of Continuing Education. Program content: Decision making, problem solving, customer relations. Available on a non-credit basis. Cosponsored by Dow Corning Company, Ford Motor Company. Certificate signed by the Dean, Continuing Education.

Program Format Daytime classes offered. Students may enroll fall, spring, summer. Full program cycle lasts 3 months.

Evaluation Student evaluation based on individual and group work assignments. Transcripts are kept for each student.

Professional Development Certification continued

Enrollment Requirements Middle- to upper-management work experience required. Program is open to non-resident foreign students.

Program Costs $120–$225 for the program, $40–$75 per course.

Housing and Student Services Housing is available.

Special Features Current pragmatic approach to problems associated with middle to upper management. Good, effective carry-over skills.

Contact Mr. Joseph Lughermo, Special Projects Director, Continuing Education, 3225 Cook Road, Midland, MI 48640. 517-832-4326.

NUCEA MEMBER
OAKLAND UNIVERSITY
Rochester, Michigan 48063

ACCOUNTING (06.02)
Accounting Assistant Program

General Information Unit offering the program: Division of Continuing Education. Program content: Principles of practical accounting; payroll systems; tax; managerial, computer-based, and applied financial accounting; ten-key calculator; accounting systems and internal control. Available on a non-credit basis.

Program Format Evening classes offered. Students may enroll in September, January, April, June. Full program cycle lasts 15 months. Completion of program requires 80-hour internship.

Evaluation Student evaluation based on tests, projects. Grading system: Letters or numbers. Transcripts are kept for each student.

Enrollment Requirements High school diploma or equivalent required. Program is open to non-resident foreign students.

Program Costs $1210 for the program, $65–$155 per course.

Housing and Student Services Housing is not available. Job counseling and placement services are available.

Contact Ms. Carmen A. Thomas, Program Manager, Continuing Education, Rochester, MI 48309. 313-370-3120.

NUCEA MEMBER
WESTERN MICHIGAN UNIVERSITY
Kalamazoo, Michigan 49008

INDIVIDUAL AND FAMILY DEVELOPMENT (19.07)
Graduate Specialty in Gerontology

General Information Unit offering the program: Gerontology Program. Available for credit. Certificate signed by the President. Certificate applicable to any graduate degree offered at the institution.

Program Format Daytime, evening, weekend classes offered. Instructional schedule: Daytime classes two to three times per week; evening classes once per week; workshops four hours per day for ten days. Program cycle: Continuous enrollment. Full program cycle lasts 1 year. Completion of program requires 20 credit hours.

Evaluation Student evaluation based on tests, papers, reports. Grading system: Letters or numbers. Transcripts are kept for each student.

Enrollment Requirements Master's degree required. Program is open to non-resident foreign students. English language proficiency required. Minimum TOEFL score required: 550, English qualifying exam.

Program Costs $75 per credit hour.

Housing and Student Services Housing is available. Job counseling and placement services are available.

Special Features Graduate Specialty Program in Gerontology is available to students holding or seeking graduate degrees in any field. Multidisciplinary in nature, it provides academic instruction in gerontology, along with practical field experience and/or thesis/dissertation research in the major field on an approved gerontological topic.

Contact Ms. Ellen K. Page-Robin, Ph.D., Director, Gerontology Program, College of Health and Human Services, Kalamazoo, MI 49008-3899. 616-383-1747.

MENTAL HEALTH/HUMAN SERVICES (17.04)
Specialty Certificate in Alcohol and Drug Abuse

General Information Unit offering the program: College of Health and Human Services. Program content: Clinical, administration, and research of alcohol and drug abuse treatment and prevention. Available for credit. Cosponsored by Michigan Office of Substance Abuse. Certificate signed by the President. Certificate applicable to M.A. in Counseling, Biology, Psychology, Occupational Therapy, Sociology, Education Counseling, Public Administration. Program fulfills requirements for Certified Addiction Counselor.

Program Format Daytime, evening classes offered. Full program cycle lasts 1 year. Completion of program requires academic and internship course work.

Evaluation Student evaluation based on tests, papers, reports, internship. Grading system: Letters or numbers, pass/fail. Transcripts are kept for each student.

Enrollment Requirements Graduate degree required. Program is open to non-resident foreign students. English language proficiency required. Minimum TOEFL score required: 550, English qualifying exam.

Program Costs $75 per credit hour.

Housing and Student Services Housing is available. Job counseling and placement services are available.

Special Features The Specialty Program in Alcohol and Drug Abuse was established in 1973 as an interdisciplinary program. Focus of program is to allow current and former graduate students to specialize their practice in the clinical, administrative, or research aspects of alcohol and drug abuse.

Contact Program Advisor, Specialty Program in Alcohol and Drug Abuse, Kalamazoo, MI 49008. 616-383-8186.

MISCELLANEOUS ALLIED HEALTH SERVICES (17.05)
Specialty Certification in Holistic Health Care

General Information Unit offering the program: College of Health and Human Services. Program content: Holistic approaches to health. Available for credit. Certificate signed by the President of the University. Certificate applicable to any graduate degree offered at the institution.

Program Format Evening, weekend classes offered. Program cycle: Continuous enrollment. Full program cycle lasts 3 semesters. Completion of program requires 15 credit hours, field experience.

Evaluation Student evaluation based on tests, papers, reports. Grading system: Letters or numbers. Transcripts are kept for each student.

Enrollment Requirements Master's degree, two letters of recommendation, transcripts required. Program is open to non-resident foreign students. English language proficiency required. Minimum TOEFL score required: 550, English qualifying exam.

Program Costs $75–$84 per credit hour.

Housing and Student Services   Housing is available. Job counseling and placement services are available.

Special Features   One of the few accredited training programs in the United States on holistic health care.

Contact   Director, Specialty Programs in Holistic Health Care, College of Health and Human Services, Kalamazoo, MI 49008. 616-383-8116.

SOCIAL WORK (44.07)
Certificate in Policy, Planning, and Administration

General Information   Unit offering the program: School of Social Work. Program content: Management training for social work practitioners. Available for credit. Certificate signed by the President.

Program Format   Evening classes offered. Instructional schedule: One evening per week. Program cycle: Continuous enrollment. Full program cycle lasts 18 credit hours. Completion of program requires six courses.

Evaluation   Student evaluation based on tests, papers. Grading system: Letters or numbers. Transcripts are kept for each student.

Enrollment Requirements   M.S.W. required. Program is open to non-resident foreign students.

Program Costs $75 per credit hour.

Housing and Student Services   Housing is not available. Job counseling and placement services are not available.

Special Features   Intended for experienced social workers who have an M.S.W. Students integrated into classes with M.S.W. degree students. Students develop learning contracts with course instructors and programs are tailored to meet student's needs.

Contact   Ms. Beverly Moore, Director of Admissions and Student Services, School of Social Work, Kalamazoo, MI 49008-5034. 616-383-0974.

MINNESOTA

NORTH CENTRAL BIBLE COLLEGE
Minneapolis, Minnesota 55404

BIBLE STUDIES (39.02)
One-Year Bible Certificate

General Information   Unit offering the program: Pastoral Studies Department. Program content: Bible and Bible-related subjects. Available for credit. Certificate signed by the President of the College. Certificate applicable to bachelor's degree in pastoral studies.

Program Format   Daytime, evening, weekend classes offered. Program cycle: Continuous enrollment. Full program cycle lasts 1 year. Completion of program requires 30 credit hours.

Evaluation   Student evaluation based on tests, papers, reports. Grading system: Letters or numbers. Transcripts are kept for each student.

Enrollment Requirements   High school transcript, ACT scores, pastor's reference required. Program is open to non-resident foreign students. English language proficiency required. Students required to live on campus.

Program Costs $110 per course.

Housing and Student Services   Housing is available. Job counseling and placement services are available.

Special Features   Courses in the one-year Bible Certificate program are taught by regular faculty. Program is new this year and is specifically structured to give a well-rounded experience within this area.

Contact   Ms. Cheryl A. Book, Director of Admissions and Records, 910 Elliot Avenue South, Minneapolis, MN 55404. 800-433-3959.

MUSIC (50.09)
Music Performance Certificate

General Information   Unit offering the program: Music Department. Available for credit. Certificate signed by the President of the College. Certificate applicable to bachelor's degree in sacred music.

Program Format   Daytime, evening, weekend classes offered. Program cycle: Continuous enrollment. Full program cycle lasts 1 year. Completion of program requires 30 credit hours.

Evaluation   Student evaluation based on tests, papers, reports. Grading system: Letters or numbers. Transcripts are kept for each student.

Enrollment Requirements   High school transcript, ACT scores, pastor's reference required. Program is open to non-resident foreign students. English language proficiency required. Students required to live on campus.

Program Costs $110 per course.

Housing and Student Services   Housing is available. Job counseling and placement services are available.

Special Features   Courses in the Music Performance Certificate are taught by regular faculty. Program is new this year, and is specifically structured to give a well-rounded experience within this area.

Contact   Ms. Cheryl A. Book, Director of Admissions and Records, 910 Elliot Avenue South, Minneapolis, MN 55404. 800-433-3959.

ST. CLOUD STATE UNIVERSITY
St. Cloud, Minnesota 56301

MENTAL HEALTH/HUMAN SERVICES (17.04)
Chemical Dependency

General Information   Unit offering the program: Health/Traffic Safety, Psychology. Program content: Physical and psychological implications of physical dependency. Available for credit. Certificate signed by the Dean of Education. Certificate applicable to B.A. in Psychology.

Program Format   Daytime classes offered. Program cycle: Continuous enrollment. Completion of program requires 64 credit hours.

Evaluation   Student evaluation based on tests, papers, reports, internship. Grading system: Letters or numbers. Transcripts are kept for each student.

Enrollment Requirements   Departmental approval required. Program is open to non-resident foreign students. English language proficiency required. Students required to live on campus.

Program Costs $1987–$2669 for the program, $124–$167 per course.

Housing and Student Services   Housing is available. Job counseling and placement services are available.

Contact   Dr. Frank P. Osendorf, Professor of Health Education and Traffic Safety, St. Cloud, MN 56301. 612-255-4251.

ST. PAUL BIBLE COLLEGE
St. Bonifacius, Minnesota 55375

BIBLE STUDIES (39.02)
Bible Certificate

General Information Unit offering the program: Bible and Theology. Program content: Bible study, Old and New Testament, Christian doctrine and ministries, evangelism. Available for credit. Certificate signed by the President. Certificate applicable to B.A. in Pastoral Ministries.

Program Format Daytime classes offered. Full program cycle lasts 2 semesters. Completion of program requires 32 credit hours, 2.0 GPA, one semester of Christian service.

Evaluation Student evaluation based on tests, papers, reports. Grading system: Letters or numbers. Transcripts are kept for each student.

Enrollment Requirements College admissions required. Program is open to non-resident foreign students. English language proficiency required.

Program Costs $130 per credit hour.

Housing and Student Services Housing is available.

Special Features The Bible Certificate one-year program is an attempt to provide short-term bible education for those desiring a college-level experience but having no interest in a bachelor's degree. Instructors are those regularly engaged in College teaching.

Contact Mr. Art Figurski, Dean of Admissions, 6425 County Road 30, St. Bonifacius, MN 55375. 612-446-1411.

RELIGIOUS EDUCATION (39.04)
Christian Education Certificate

General Information Unit offering the program: Christian Education Department. Program content: Methods of Bible study, Old and New Testament, Christian doctrine, evangelism, educational work of the church, speech, counseling, human relations. Available for credit. Certificate signed by the President. Certificate applicable to B.S. in Christian Education. Program fulfills requirements for Evangelical Teacher Training Association.

Program Format Daytime, evening classes offered. Program cycle: Continuous enrollment. Full program cycle lasts 2 semesters. Completion of program requires 32 credit hours, 2.0 GPA, one semester of Christian service.

Evaluation Student evaluation based on tests, papers, reports. Grading system: Letters or numbers. Transcripts are kept for each student.

Enrollment Requirements College admissions required. Program is open to non-resident foreign students. English language proficiency required.

Program Costs $3750 for the program, $375 per course.

Housing and Student Services Housing is available. Job counseling and placement services are available.

Special Features Program prepares lay leadership for local church educational ministry.

Contact Mr. Art Figurski, Dean of Admissions, 6425 County Road 30, St. Bonifacius, MN 55375. 612-446-1411.

SCHOOL OF THE ASSOCIATED ARTS
St. Paul, Minnesota 55102

DESIGN (50.04)
Illustration

General Information Unit offering the program: Illustration Department. Program content: Studio credits. Available for credit. Cosponsored by International Council of Design Schools.

Certificate signed by the Chairman of the Board of Trustees. Certificate applicable to B.F.A.

Program Format Daytime classes offered. Students may enroll fall, spring. Full program cycle lasts 3 years. Completion of program requires final project, portfolio review, final show, 105 credit hours, 2.0 GPA.

Evaluation Student evaluation based on tests, papers, reports, portfolios. Grading system: Letters or numbers. Transcripts are kept for each student.

Enrollment Requirements High school diploma or equivalent, average grade of C or better required. Program is open to non-resident foreign students. English language proficiency required.

Program Costs $4300 for the program.

Housing and Student Services Housing is not available. Job counseling and placement services are available.

Special Features Same studio arts requirements as bachelor's candidates. B.F.A. requires 36 liberal arts semester credits. Certificate candidates need only 6 liberal arts semester credits in art history. All courses are taught by professionals in their respective fields.

Contact Mr. Robert E. Hankey, Dean, 344 Summit Avenue, St. Paul, MN 55102. 612-224-3416.

FINE ARTS (50.07)
Fine Arts

General Information Unit offering the program: Fine Arts Department. Program content: Studio credits and art history. Available for credit. Cosponsored by International Council of Design Schools. Certificate signed by the Chairman of the Board of Trustees. Certificate applicable to B.F.A.

Program Format Daytime classes offered. Students may enroll fall, spring. Full program cycle lasts 3 years. Completion of program requires final project, portfolio review, final show, 105 credit hours, 2.0 GPA.

Evaluation Student evaluation based on tests, papers, reports, portfolios. Grading system: Letters or numbers. Transcripts are kept for each student.

Enrollment Requirements High school diploma or equivalent, average grade of C or better required. Program is open to non-resident foreign students. English language proficiency required.

Program Costs $4300 for the program.

Housing and Student Services Housing is not available. Job counseling and placement services are available.

Special Features Same studio arts requirements as bachelor's candidates. B.F.A. requires 36 liberal arts semester credits. Certificate candidates need only 6 liberal arts semester credits in art history. All courses are taught by professionals in their respective fields.

Contact Mr. Robert E. Hankey, Dean, 344 Summit Avenue, St. Paul, MN 55102. 612-224-3416.

GRAPHIC AND PRINTING COMMUNICATIONS (48.02)
Communication Design

General Information Unit offering the program: Communication Design Department. Program content: Studio credits and art history. Available for credit. Cosponsored by International Council of Design Schools. Certificate signed by the Chairman of the Board of Trustees. Certificate applicable to B.F.A.

Program Format Daytime classes offered. Students may enroll fall, spring. Full program cycle lasts 3 years. Completion of program requires final project, portfolio review, final show, 105 credit hours, 2.0 GPA.

Evaluation Student evaluation based on tests, papers, reports, portfolios. Grading system: Letters or numbers. Transcripts are kept for each student.

Enrollment Requirements High school diploma or equivalent, average grade of C or better required. Program is open to non-resident foreign students. English language proficiency required.

Program Costs $4300 for the program.

Housing and Student Services Housing is not available. Job counseling and placement services are available.

Special Features Same studio arts requirements as bachelor's candidates. B.F.A. requires 36 liberal arts semester credits. Certificate candidates need only 6 liberal arts semester credits in art history. All courses are taught by professionals in their respective fields.

Contact Mr. Robert E. Hankey, Dean, 344 Summit Avenue, St. Paul, MN 55102. 612-224-3416.

NUCEA MEMBER

UNIVERSITY OF MINNESOTA, MORRIS
Morris, Minnesota 56267

BUSINESS ADMINISTRATION AND MANAGEMENT (06.04)
Associate in Management of Administrative Services Certificate

General Information Unit offering the program: University of Minnesota Continuing Education and Extension. Program content: Accounting, business law, economics, mathematics, managerial statistics, introduction to computers and data processing. Available for credit. Certificate signed by the President of University. Certificate applicable to many four-year degrees offered by the School of Management.

Program Format Daytime, evening, correspondence classes offered. Quarterly enrollment. Completion of program requires 51–55 credit hours.

Evaluation Student evaluation methods vary by course. Grading system: Letters or numbers, pass/fail. Transcripts are kept for each student.

Housing and Student Services Housing is available. Job counseling and placement services are available.

Contact Ms. Karla M. Klinger, Program Director, Morris Learning Center, Morris, MN 56267. 612-589-2211 Ext. 6456.

BUSINESS ADMINISTRATION AND MANAGEMENT (06.04)
Junior Business Administration Certificate

General Information Unit offering the program: University of Minnesota Continuing Education and Extension. Program content: Financial accounting, economics, data analysis, statistics, computer information and technology. Available for credit. Certificate signed by the President of University. Certificate applicable to B.S. in Business.

Program Format Daytime, evening, correspondence classes offered. Quarterly enrollment. Completion of program requires 49–52 credit hours.

Evaluation Student evaluation methods vary by course. Grading system: Letters or numbers, pass/fail. Transcripts are kept for each student.

Enrollment Requirements University admissions required.

Housing and Student Services Housing is available. Job counseling and placement services are available.

Contact Ms. Karla M. Klinger, Program Director, Morris Learning Center, Morris, MN 56267. 612-589-2211 Ext. 6456.

BUSINESS ADMINISTRATION AND MANAGEMENT (06.04)
Senior Business Administration Certificate

General Information Unit offering the program: University of Minnesota Continuing Education and Extension. Program content: Accounting, economics, marketing, business law, risk and logistics management. Available for credit. Certificate signed by the President of University. Certificate applicable to B.S. in Business.

Program Format Daytime, evening, correspondence classes offered. Quarterly enrollment. Completion of program requires 90 credit hours.

Evaluation Student evaluation methods vary by course. Grading system: Letters or numbers, pass/fail. Transcripts are kept for each student.

Enrollment Requirements University admissions required.

Housing and Student Services Housing is available. Job counseling and placement services are available.

Contact Ms. Karla M. Klinger, Program Director, Morris Learning Center, Morris, MN 56267. 612-589-2211 Ext. 6456.

ENGINEERING, GENERAL (14.01)
Undergraduate Development Certificate in Engineering and Science

General Information Unit offering the program: University of Minnesota Continuing Education and Extension. Program content: Mathematics, physics, technical communication, graphics. Available for credit. Certificate signed by the President of University. Certificate applicable to bachelor's degree in engineering or science.

Program Format Daytime, evening, correspondence classes offered. Quarterly enrollment. Completion of program requires 45 or 90 credit hours.

Evaluation Student evaluation methods vary by course. Grading system: Letters or numbers, pass/fail. Transcripts are kept for each student.

Enrollment Requirements High school diploma or equivalent, two years of algebra and geometry/trigonometry required.

Housing and Student Services Housing is available. Job counseling and placement services are available.

Contact Ms. Karla M. Klinger, Program Director, Morris Learning Center, Morris, MN 56267. 612-589-2211 Ext. 6456.

LIBERAL/GENERAL STUDIES (24.01)
Liberal Arts Certificate

General Information Unit offering the program: University of Minnesota Continuing Education and Extension. Program content: Composition, logic, language, mathematics, physical and biological sciences. Available for credit. Certificate signed by the President of University. Certificate applicable to any four-year degree offered at the institution.

Program Format Daytime, evening, correspondence classes offered. Quarterly enrollment. Completion of program requires 45 credit hours.

Evaluation Student evaluation methods vary by course. Grading system: Letters or numbers, pass/fail. Transcripts are kept for each student.

Housing and Student Services Housing is available. Job counseling and placement services are available.

Contact Ms. Karla M. Klinger, Program Director, Morris Learning Center, Morris, MN 56267. 612-589-2211 Ext. 6456.

MATHEMATICS, GENERAL (27.01)
Mathematics and Science Certificate

General Information Unit offering the program: University of Minnesota Continuing Education and Extension. Program content: Calculus, physical and biological sciences. Available for credit. Certificate signed by the President of University.

Program Format Daytime, evening, correspondence classes offered. Quarterly enrollment. Completion of program requires 45 credit hours.

Mathematics and Science Certificate continued

Evaluation Student evaluation methods vary by course. Grading system: Letters or numbers, pass/fail. Transcripts are kept for each student.

Enrollment Requirements Two years of algebra and geometry/trigonometry required.

Housing and Student Services Housing is available. Job counseling and placement services are available.

Contact Ms. Karla M. Klinger, Program Director, Morris Learning Center, Morris, MN 56267. 612-589-2211 Ext. 6456.

NUCEA MEMBER

UNIVERSITY OF MINNESOTA, TWIN CITIES CAMPUS
Minneapolis, Minnesota 55455

ACCOUNTING (06.02)
Junior Accounting Certificate

General Information Unit offering the program: Accounting, Continuing Education and Extension. Program content: Cost accounting, information systems, financial and managerial accounting. Available for credit. Certificate signed by the President of University. Certificate applicable to B.S. in Business.

Program Format Evening classes offered. Instructional schedule: One or two evenings per week. Program cycle: Continuous enrollment. Full program cycle lasts 2 years. Completion of program requires 59–68 credit hours.

Evaluation Student evaluation based on tests, papers, reports. Grading system: Letters or numbers, pass/fail. Transcripts are kept for each student.

Enrollment Requirements Twelve college-level credits, minimum 2.2 GPA required. Program is not open to non-resident foreign students. English language proficiency required. MELAB score 70.

Program Costs $3440 for the program, $215 per course.

Housing and Student Services Housing is not available. Job counseling and placement services are available.

Contact Academic Adviser, CEE Counseling Department, 315 Pillsbury Drive, SE, Minneapolis, MN 55455. 612-625-2500.

ACCOUNTING (06.02)
Senior Accounting Certificate

General Information Unit offering the program: Accounting, Continuing Education and Extension. Program content: Business law, risk management, marketing, business policy. Available for credit. Certificate signed by the President of University. Certificate applicable to B.S. in Business.

Program Format Evening classes offered. Instructional schedule: One or two evenings per week. Program cycle: Continuous enrollment. Complete program cycle lasts four to six years. Completion of program requires 87–96 credit hours.

Evaluation Student evaluation based on tests, papers, reports. Grading system: Letters or numbers, pass/fail. Transcripts are kept for each student.

Enrollment Requirements Twelve college-level credits, minimum 2.2 GPA required. Program is not open to non-resident foreign students. English language proficiency required. MELAB score 70.

Program Costs $4945 for the program, $215 per course.

Housing and Student Services Housing is not available. Job counseling and placement services are available.

Special Features Courses provide some beginning background in accounting practice and theory that is available to students who graduate with a four-year degree with a specialization in this field. Recommended for students who have completed a bachelor degree program in another field.

Contact Academic Adviser, CEE Counseling Department, 315 Pillsbury Drive, SE, Minneapolis, MN 55455. 612-625-2500.

BUSINESS AND MANAGEMENT, GENERAL (06.01)
Junior Business Administration Certificate

General Information Unit offering the program: School of Management, Continuing Education and Extension. Program content: Financial accounting, economics, data analysis, statistics, computer and information technology. Available for credit. Certificate signed by the President of University. Certificate applicable to B.S. in Business.

Program Format Evening classes offered. Instructional schedule: One or two evenings per week. Program cycle: Continuous enrollment. Complete program cycle lasts two to four years. Completion of program requires 49–52 credit hours.

Evaluation Student evaluation based on tests, papers, reports. Grading system: Letters or numbers, pass/fail. Transcripts are kept for each student.

Enrollment Requirements Twelve college-level credits, minimum 2.2 GPA required. Program is not open to non-resident foreign students. English language proficiency required. MELAB score 70.

Program Costs $2580 for the program, $215 per course.

Housing and Student Services Housing is not available. Job counseling and placement services are available.

Contact Academic Adviser, CEE Counseling Department, 315 Pillsbury Drive, SE, Minneapolis, MN 55455. 612-625-2500.

BUSINESS AND MANAGEMENT, GENERAL (06.01)
Senior Business Administration Certificate

General Information Unit offering the program: School of Management, Continuing Education and Extension. Program content: Accounting, economics, marketing, business law, risk and logistics management. Available for credit. Certificate signed by the President of University. Certificate applicable to B.S. in Business.

Program Format Evening classes offered. Instructional schedule: One or two evenings per week. Program cycle: Continuous enrollment. Complete program cycle lasts four to six years. Completion of program requires 90 credit hours.

Evaluation Student evaluation based on tests, papers, reports. Grading system: Letters or numbers, pass/fail. Transcripts are kept for each student.

Enrollment Requirements Twelve college-level credits, minimum 2.2 GPA required. Program is not open to non-resident foreign students. English language proficiency required. MELAB score 70.

Program Costs $3225 for the program, $215 per course.

Housing and Student Services Housing is not available. Job counseling and placement services are available.

Contact Academic Adviser, CEE Counseling Department, 315 Pillsbury Drive, SE, Minneapolis, MN 55455. 612-625-2500.

COMMUNITY PSYCHOLOGY (42.04)
Behavior Analyst in Community Environments

General Information Unit offering the program: Continuing Education and Extension, Department of Educational Psychology. Program content: Training in behavior analysis and therapy. Available for credit. Certificate signed by the President of University.

Program Format Evening classes offered. Instructional schedule: One or two evenings per week. Program cycle: Continuous enrollment. Full program cycle lasts 1 year. Completion of program requires 30–33 quarter units, practicum.

Evaluation Student evaluation based on course work and practicum completion. Grading system: Letters or numbers, pass/fail. Transcripts are kept for each student.

Enrollment Requirements College degree, 3.0 GPA, psychology course work required. Program is not open to non-resident foreign students. English language proficiency required. MELAB score 70 or better.

Program Costs $1300 for the program, $177 per course.

Housing and Student Services Housing is available. Job counseling and placement services are not available.

Contact Ms. Jacquelyn Henning, Senior Academic Adviser, 314 Nolte Center, 315 Pillsbury Drive, SE, Minneapolis, MN 55455. 612-625-2500.

COMPUTER AND INFORMATION SCIENCES, GENERAL (11.01)
Undergraduate Development Certificate in Computer Science

General Information Unit offering the program: Computer Science, Continuing Education and Extension. Program content: Programming, computer languages, software systems, structures of computer systems. Available for credit. Certificate signed by the President of University. Certificate applicable to bachelor's degree in computer science.

Program Format Evening classes offered. Instructional schedule: One or two evenings per week. Program cycle: Continuous enrollment. Full program cycle lasts 1 year. Completion of program requires 45 credit hours.

Evaluation Student evaluation based on tests, papers, reports. Grading system: Letters or numbers, pass/fail. Transcripts are kept for each student.

Enrollment Requirements Twelve college-level credits, minimum 2.2 GPA required. Program is not open to non-resident foreign students. English language proficiency required. MELAB score 70.

Program Costs $2400 for the program, $215 per course.

Housing and Student Services Housing is not available. Job counseling and placement services are not available.

Special Features Program can be first step toward degree or provide means of broadening perspectives and skills of persons already employed at the programmer or technician level.

Contact Academic Adviser, CEE Counseling Department, 315 Pillsbury Drive, SE, Minneapolis, MN 55455. 612-625-2500.

ENGINEERING, GENERAL (14.01)
Undergraduate Development Certificate in Engineering and Science

General Information Unit offering the program: Institute of Technology, Continuing Education and Extension. Program content: Mathematics, physics, technical communication, graphics. Available for credit. Certificate signed by the President of University. Certificate applicable to bachelor's degree in engineering, science.

Program Format Evening classes offered. Instructional schedule: One or two evenings per week. Program cycle: Continuous enrollment. Complete program cycle lasts four to six years.

Evaluation Student evaluation based on tests, papers, reports. Grading system: Letters or numbers, pass/fail. Transcripts are kept for each student.

Enrollment Requirements Twelve college-level credits, minimum 2.2 GPA required. Program is not open to non-resident foreign students. English language proficiency required. MELAB score 70.

Program Costs $3225 for the program, $215 per course.

Housing and Student Services Housing is not available. Job counseling and placement services are available.

Contact Academic Adviser, CEE Counseling Department, 315 Pillsbury Drive, SE, Minneapolis, MN 55455. 612-625-2500.

LABOR/INDUSTRIAL RELATIONS (06.11)
Industrial Relations Certificate

General Information Unit offering the program: Industrial Relations Center. Program content: Collective bargaining, labor relations, federal regulations, wages, psychology. Available for credit. Certificate signed by the President of University. Certificate applicable to any four-year degree offered at the institution.

Program Format Evening, correspondence classes offered. Instructional schedule: One or two evenings per week. Program cycle: Continuous enrollment. Full program cycle lasts 2 years. Completion of program requires 45 credit hours.

Evaluation Student evaluation based on tests, papers, reports. Grading system: Letters or numbers, pass/fail. Transcripts are kept for each student.

Enrollment Requirements Twelve college-level credits with 2.2 GPA required. Program is not open to non-resident foreign students. English language proficiency required. MELAB score of 70.

Program Costs $2000 for the program, $167–$205 per course.

Housing and Student Services Housing is not available. Job counseling and placement services are available.

Special Features Recommended for students who have completed a bachelor's degree.

Contact Academic Adviser, CEE Counseling Department, 315 Pillsbury Drive, SE, Minneapolis, MN 55455. 612-625-2500.

LIBERAL/GENERAL STUDIES (24.01)
Liberal Arts Certificate

General Information Unit offering the program: College of Liberal Arts, Continuing Education and Extension. Program content: Composition, logic, language, mathematics, physical and biological sciences. Available for credit. Certificate signed by the President of University. Certificate applicable to any four-year degree offered at the institution.

Program Format Evening, correspondence classes offered. Instructional schedule: One or two evenings per week. Program cycle: Continuous enrollment. Full program cycle lasts 2 years. Completion of program requires 45 credit hours.

Evaluation Student evaluation based on tests, papers, reports. Grading system: Letters or numbers, pass/fail. Transcripts are kept for each student.

Enrollment Requirements Twelve college-level credits, 2.2 GPA required. Program is not open to non-resident foreign students. English language proficiency required. MELAB score of 70.

Program Costs $2000 for the program, $167–$205 per course.

Housing and Student Services Housing is not available. Job counseling and placement services are available.

Contact Academic Adviser, CEE Counseling Department, 315 Pillsbury Drive, SE, Minneapolis, MN 55455. 612-625-2500.

MENTAL HEALTH/HUMAN SERVICES (17.04)
Alcohol and Drug Counseling Education Certificate

General Information Unit offering the program: Family Social Science Department, Continuing Education and Extension. Program content: Pharmacology, counseling skills, assessment, group therapy theory. Available for credit. Certificate signed by the President of University. Certificate applicable to any four-year degree offered at the institution.

Program Format Evening classes offered. Instructional schedule: One or two evenings per week. Program cycle: Continuous enrollment. Complete program cycle lasts two to four years. Completion of program requires 48–51 credits, field experience.

Alcohol and Drug Counseling Education Certificate continued

Evaluation   Student evaluation based on tests, papers, reports. Grading system: Letters or numbers, pass/fail. Transcripts are kept for each student.

Enrollment Requirements   Interview, period of sobriety required. Program is not open to non-resident foreign students. English language proficiency required. MELAB score 70.

Program Costs $2186 for the program, $229 per course.

Housing and Student Services   Housing is not available. Job counseling and placement services are available.

Contact   Academic Adviser, CEE Counseling Department, 315 Pillsbury Drive, SE, Minneapolis, MN 55455. 612-625-2500.

OPHTHALMIC SERVICES (17.07)
Ophthalmology Technician Certificate

General Information   Unit offering the program: Opthalmology, Continuing Education and Extension. Program content: Technical and mechanical skills, treatment and diagnosis of eye diseases. Available for credit. Cosponsored by St. Paul Ramsey Medical Center. Certificate signed by the President of University. Program fulfills requirements for Certified Ophthalmic Technologist or Certified Ophthalmic Technician.

Program Format   Daytime classes offered. Students enroll once per year. Full program cycle lasts 21 months. Completion of program requires 75 credits of courses, approval of medical director.

Evaluation   Student evaluation based on tests, papers, reports, clinical performance evaluations. Grading system: Letters or numbers, pass/fail. Transcripts are kept for each student.

Enrollment Requirements   High school/college credits and grades, references, autobiographical sketch, interviews required. Program is open to non-resident foreign students. English language proficiency required.

Program Costs $3500 for the program.

Housing and Student Services   Housing is not available. Job counseling and placement services are not available.

Contact   Ms. Nancy J. Weber, Program Administrator, School for Ophthalmic Technicians, 640 Jackson Street, St. Paul, MN 55101. 612-221-3000.

MISSISSIPPI

MILLSAPS COLLEGE
Jackson, Mississippi 39210

ACCOUNTING, BOOKKEEPING, AND RELATED PROGRAMS (07.01)
Postbaccalaureate Certificate in Accounting

General Information   Unit offering the program: Else School of Management. Available for credit. Certificate signed by the Dean, Else School of Management.

Program Format   Daytime, evening classes offered. Program cycle: Continuous enrollment. Full program cycle lasts 33 credit hours.

Evaluation   Student evaluation based on tests, papers, reports. Grading system: Letters or numbers. Transcripts are kept for each student.

Enrollment Requirements   Bachelor's degree required. Program is open to non-resident foreign students. English language proficiency required. Minimum TOEFL score required: 550.

Program Costs $645 per course.

Housing and Student Services   Housing is available. Job counseling and placement services are available.

Special Features   Taught by full-time faculty of Millsaps College. Courses are part of curriculum of the College. Other students in the courses are not necessarily in the certification program but are taking the courses for academic credit.

Contact   Ms. Kay Mortimer, Assistant Dean, Else School of Management, 1701 North State Street, Jackson, MS 39210. 601-354-5201 Ext. 286.

NUCEA MEMBER
UNIVERSITY OF MISSISSIPPI
University, Mississippi 38677

LAW (22.01)
Certificate in Paralegal Studies

General Information   Unit offering the program: Court Education Programs. Available on either a credit or non-credit basis. Certificate signed by the Chancellor.

Program Format   Evening classes offered. Instructional schedule: One evening per week. Program cycle: Continuous enrollment. Completion of program requires 30 credit hours of general education and business-related courses, 36 credit hours of legal specialty courses, grade of C or better.

Evaluation   Student evaluation based on tests, papers. Grading system: Letters or numbers. Records are kept or each student.

Enrollment Requirements   University admissions required. Program is open to non-resident foreign students.

Program Costs $150 per course (Tupelo); $165 per course (Jackson).

Housing and Student Services   Housing is not available. Job counseling and placement services are available.

Special Features   Program offered off campus at two locations: Tupelo and Jackson. Designed to qualify students for law-related occupations, including public and private law practices and/or corporate or government law-related activities. Leads to legal assistant certification. Training benefits legal secretaries and other paralegal personnel, students desiring to prepare for careers as legal assistants, and people in other occupations and professions who need support courses.

Contact   Ms. Krista Johns, Associate Director for Court Education Programs, 101 Universities Center, 3825 Ridgewood Road, Jackson, MS 39211. 601-982-6590.

WESLEY COLLEGE
Florence, Mississippi 39073

RELIGIOUS EDUCATION (39.04)
Certificate in Ministerial Studies

General Information   Unit offering the program: Bible. Program content: English, speech, communication skills, Bible/pastoral studies. Available for credit. Endorsed by Congregational Methodist Church. Certificate signed by the President. Certificate applicable to B.S. in Biblical Literature, Pastoral Studies.

Program Format   Daytime classes offered. Program cycle: Continuous enrollment. Full program cycle lasts 4 semesters. Completion of program requires 2.0 GPA.

Evaluation   Student evaluation based on tests, papers, reports. Grading system: Letters or numbers. Transcripts are kept for each student.

Enrollment Requirements   High school diploma or GED required. Program is not open to non-resident foreign students.

Program Costs $60 per credit hour for part-time students, $700 per semester for full-time students.

Housing and Student Services   Housing is available. Job counseling and placement services are available.

Special Features   The program is designed for the adult who has received a call to the ministry and needs courses to help him in ministering to his church.

Contact   Ms. Patsy Gilmore, Director of Admissions, P.O. Box 70, Florence, MS 39073. 601-845-2265.

MISSOURI

CALVARY BIBLE COLLEGE
Kansas City, Missouri 64147

BIBLE STUDIES (39.02)
Advanced Biblical Studies Certificate

General Information   Program content: Theology, Bible, and Bible-related subjects. Available for credit. Certificate signed by the Academic Dean.

Program Format   Daytime classes offered. Program cycle: Continuous enrollment. Full program cycle lasts 1 year.

Evaluation   Student evaluation based on tests, papers, reports. Grading system: Letters or numbers. Transcripts are kept for each student.

Enrollment Requirements   College degree, pastor's reference, transcripts required. Program is not open to non-resident foreign students. English language proficiency required. Students required to live on campus.

Program Costs $80 per credit hour.

Housing and Student Services   Housing is available. Job counseling and placement services are not available.

Contact   Ms. Deidre Schimek, Director of Admissions, 15800 Calvary Road, Kansas City, MO 64147. 816-322-0110.

CONCEPTION SEMINARY COLLEGE
Conception, Missouri 64433

PHILOSOPHY (38.01)
Certificate of Completion of Pre-Theological
Studies

General Information   Unit offering the program: Interdepartmental. Program content: Basic philosophical and theological courses. Available for credit. Certificate signed by the Chancellor.

Program Format   Daytime classes offered. Program cycle: Continuous enrollment. Full program cycle lasts 4 semesters. Completion of program requires all course work, participation in personal formation.

Evaluation   Student evaluation based on tests, papers, reports. Grading system: Letters or numbers, pass/fail. Transcripts are kept for each student.

Enrollment Requirements   Bachelor's degree, sponsorship of a Roman Catholic diocese required. Program is not open to non-resident foreign students. English language proficiency required. Students required to live on campus.

Program Costs $12,000 for the program.

Housing and Student Services   Housing is available. Job counseling and placement services are not available.

Special Features   This is a two-year course of study and personal and spiritual formation for Roman Catholic men interested in the priesthood and who have B.A./B.S. degrees but

not sufficient philosophical/theological background for admission to a graduate school of theology.

Contact   Rev. Gregory Polan, OSB, Director of Admissions, Conception, MO 64433. 816-944-2218.

LINDENWOOD COLLEGE
St. Charles, Missouri 63301

INDIVIDUAL AND FAMILY DEVELOPMENT
(19.07)
Graduate Certificate in Gerontology

General Information   Unit offering the program: Division of Graduate Studies. Program content: Sociological, psychological, physiological, political, and economic aspects of aging. Available for credit. Certificate signed by the President of the College. Certificate applicable to M.A. in Gerontology.

Program Format   Evening classes offered. Instructional schedule: One evening per week. Program cycle: Continuous enrollment. Full program cycle lasts 3 quarters. Completion of program requires oral and written presentations based on readings and seminar discussions.

Evaluation   Student evaluation based on papers, oral presentations. Grading system: Letters or numbers. Transcripts are kept for each student.

Enrollment Requirements   Undergraduate or graduate degree required. Program is open to non-resident foreign students. English language proficiency required. Minimum TOEFL score required: 450.

Program Costs $4590 for the program, $510 per course.

Housing and Student Services   Housing is available. Job counseling and placement services are available.

Special Features   The program is designed for human service specialists, health practitioners, and public policymakers. The courses are offered in small group seminars taught by leaders in gerontological service and research. Graduates of the program hold major posts in the various services and research institutions across the United States.

Contact   Ms. Arlene Taich, Ph.D., Dean of Graduate Studies, St. Charles, MO 63301. 314-949-2000 Ext. 275.

NORTHWEST MISSOURI STATE
UNIVERSITY
Maryville, Missouri 64468

AGRICULTURAL PRODUCTION (01.03)
Farm Operations

General Information   Unit offering the program: Department of Agriculture. Program content: Plant and animal science, agricultural mechanization and economics, soils. Available for credit. Certificate signed by the President of the University. Certificate applicable to any four-year degree offered at the institution.

Program Format   Daytime, evening classes offered. Program cycle: Continuous enrollment. Full program cycle lasts 2 years. Completion of program requires 60 credit hours.

Evaluation   Student evaluation methods vary by course. Grading system: Letters or numbers. Transcripts are kept for each student.

Enrollment Requirements   University admissions required. Program is open to non-resident foreign students. English language proficiency required. Minimum TOEFL score required: 500.

Program Costs $36 per credit hour.

Farm Operations continued

Housing and Student Services Housing is available. Job counseling and placement services are available.

Contact Admissions Office, Maryville, MO 64468. 816-562-1562.

CHILD CARE AND GUIDANCE MANAGEMENT AND SERVICES (20.02)
Child Care Administrator

General Information Unit offering the program: Department of Home Economics. Program content: Family relationships, motor development, parenthood education, first aid, administration, oral communication, human development and nutrition. Available for credit. Certificate signed by the President of the University. Certificate applicable to any four-year degree offered at the institution.

Program Format Daytime, evening classes offered. Program cycle: Continuous enrollment. Full program cycle lasts 2 years. Completion of program requires 60 credit hours, 2.0 GPA, practicum.

Evaluation Student evaluation methods vary by course. Grading system: Letters or numbers. Transcripts are kept for each student.

Enrollment Requirements University admissions required. Program is open to non-resident foreign students. English language proficiency required. Minimum TOEFL score required: 500.

Program Costs $36 per credit hour.

Housing and Student Services Housing is available. Job counseling and placement services are available.

Contact Admissions Office, Maryville, MO 64468. 816-562-1562.

CONSTRUCTION TECHNOLOGY (15.10).
Building Construction Technology

General Information Unit offering the program: Department of Technology. Program content: Wood technology, construction techniques, drafting, surveying, construction management and estimating. Available for credit. Certificate signed by the President of the University. Certificate applicable to any four-year degree offered at the institution.

Program Format Daytime, evening classes offered. Program cycle: Continuous enrollment. Full program cycle lasts 2 years. Completion of program requires 60 credit hours.

Evaluation Student evaluation methods vary by course. Grading system: Letters or numbers. Transcripts are kept for each student.

Enrollment Requirements University admissions required. Program is open to non-resident foreign students. English language proficiency required. Minimum TOEFL score required: 500.

Program Costs $36 per credit hour.

Housing and Student Services Housing is available. Job counseling and placement services are available.

Contact Admissions Office, Maryville, MO 64468. 816-562-1562.

DRAFTING (48.01)
Drafting Technology

General Information Unit offering the program: Department of Technology. Program content: Technical and architectural drawing, drafting, surveying, metal technology. Available for credit. Certificate signed by the President of the University. Certificate applicable to any four-year degree offered at the institution.

Program Format Daytime, evening classes offered. Program cycle: Continuous enrollment. Full program cycle lasts 2 years. Completion of program requires 60 credit hours.

Evaluation Student evaluation methods vary by course. Grading system: Letters or numbers. Transcripts are kept for each student.

Enrollment Requirements University admissions required. Program is open to non-resident foreign students. English language proficiency required. Minimum TOEFL score required: 500.

Program Costs $36 per credit hour.

Housing and Student Services Housing is available. Job counseling and placement services are available.

Contact Admissions Office, Maryville, MO 64468. 816-562-1562.

DRAFTING (48.01)
Drafting Technology

General Information Unit offering the program: Department of Technology. Program content: Architectural and technical drawing, metals, architectural and machine drafting, surveying. Available for credit. Certificate signed by the President of the University. Certificate applicable to any four-year degree offered at the institution.

Program Format Daytime, evening classes offered. Program cycle: Continuous enrollment. Full program cycle lasts 1 year. Completion of program requires 30 credit hours.

Evaluation Student evaluation methods vary by course. Grading system: Letters or numbers. Transcripts are kept for each student.

Enrollment Requirements University admissions required. Program is open to non-resident foreign students. English language proficiency required. Minimum TOEFL score required: 500.

Program Costs $36 per credit hour.

Housing and Student Services Housing is available. Job counseling and placement services are available.

Contact Admissions Office, Maryville, MO 64468. 816-562-1562.

ELECTRICAL AND ELECTRONIC TECHNOLOGIES (15.03)
Electronic Technology

General Information Unit offering the program: Department of Technology. Program content: Digital electronics, solid state, communication systems, AC and DC machines, computers. Available for credit. Certificate signed by the President of the University. Certificate applicable to any four-year degree offered at the institution.

Program Format Daytime, evening classes offered. Program cycle: Continuous enrollment. Full program cycle lasts 2 years. Completion of program requires 60 credit hours.

Evaluation Student evaluation methods vary by course. Grading system: Letters or numbers. Transcripts are kept for each student.

Enrollment Requirements University admissions required. Program is open to non-resident foreign students. English language proficiency required. Minimum TOEFL score required: 500.

Program Costs $36 per credit hour.

Housing and Student Services Housing is available. Job counseling and placement services are available.

Contact Admissions Office, Maryville, MO 64468. 816-562-1562.

MECHANICAL AND RELATED TECHNOLOGIES (15.08)
Metal Technology

General Information Unit offering the program: Department of Technology. Program content: Metal technology, industrial

166

plastics, welding, drafting, chemistry. Available for credit. Certificate signed by the President of the University. Certificate applicable to any four-year degree offered at the institution.

Program Format   Daytime, evening classes offered. Program cycle: Continuous enrollment. Full program cycle lasts 2 years. Completion of program requires 60 credit hours.

Evaluation   Student evaluation methods vary by course. Grading system: Letters or numbers. Transcripts are kept for each student.

Enrollment Requirements   University admissions required. Program is open to non-resident foreign students. English language proficiency required. Minimum TOEFL score required: 500.

Program Costs $36 per credit hour.

Housing and Student Services   Housing is available. Job counseling and placement services are available.

Contact   Admissions Office, Maryville, MO 64468. 816-562-1562.

SECRETARIAL AND RELATED PROGRAMS
(07.06)
Medical Secretarial Certificate

General Information   Unit offering the program: Business, Biological Sciences. Program content: Word processing, shorthand, communications, medical terminology, chemistry, zoology, microbiology. Available for credit. Certificate signed by the President of the University. Certificate applicable to any four-year degree offered at the institution.

Program Format   Daytime, evening classes offered. Program cycle: Continuous enrollment. Full program cycle lasts 2 years. Completion of program requires 60 credit hours, 2.0 GPA.

Evaluation   Student evaluation methods vary by course. Grading system: Letters or numbers. Transcripts are kept for each student.

Enrollment Requirements   University admissions required. Program is open to non-resident foreign students. English language proficiency required. Minimum TOEFL score required: 500.

Program Costs $36 per credit hour.

Housing and Student Services   Housing is available. Job counseling and placement services are available.

Contact   Admissions Office, Maryville, MO 64468. 816-562-1562.

SECRETARIAL AND RELATED PROGRAMS
(07.06)
One Year Secretarial Certificate

General Information   Unit offering the program: Business. Program content: Business machines, typing, shorthand, accounting, business. Available for credit. Certificate signed by the President of the University. Certificate applicable to any four-year degree offered at the institution.

Program Format   Daytime, evening classes offered. Program cycle: Continuous enrollment. Full program cycle lasts 1 year. Completion of program requires 27 credit hours, 2.0 GPA.

Evaluation   Student evaluation methods vary by course. Grading system: Letters or numbers. Transcripts are kept for each student.

Enrollment Requirements   University admissions required. Program is open to non-resident foreign students. English language proficiency required. Minimum TOEFL score required: 500.

Program Costs $36 per credit hour.

Housing and Student Services   Housing is available. Job counseling and placement services are available.

Contact   Admissions Office, Maryville, MO 64468. 816-562-1562.

SECRETARIAL AND RELATED PROGRAMS
(07.06)
Two Year Secretarial Certificate

General Information   Unit offering the program: Business. Program content: Shorthand, typing, word processing, management, business law, executive office procedures, business communication. Available for credit. Certificate signed by the President of the University. Certificate applicable to any four-year degree offered at the institution.

Program Format   Daytime, evening classes offered. Program cycle: Continuous enrollment. Full program cycle lasts 2 years. Completion of program requires 55 credit hours, 2.0 GPA.

Evaluation   Student evaluation methods vary by course. Grading system: Letters or numbers. Transcripts are kept for each student.

Enrollment Requirements   University admissions required. Program is open to non-resident foreign students. English language proficiency required. Minimum TOEFL score required: 500.

Program Costs $36 per credit hour.

Housing and Student Services   Housing is available. Job counseling and placement services are available.

Contact   Admissions Office, Maryville, MO 64468. 816-562-1562.

SAINT LOUIS CONSERVATORY OF MUSIC
St. Louis, Missouri 63130

MUSIC (50.09)
Artist's Certificate

General Information   Available for credit. Endorsed by National Association of Schools of Music. Certificate signed by the Chairman of the Board.

Program Format   Daytime classes offered. Program cycle: Continuous enrollment. Complete program cycle lasts two to four semesters. Completion of program requires 18 credit hours, four recitals.

Evaluation   Student evaluation based on recitals. Grading system: Letters or numbers. Transcripts are kept for each student.

Enrollment Requirements   Audition required. Program is open to non-resident foreign students. English language proficiency required. Minimum TOEFL score required: 500.

Program Costs $7250 for the program.

Housing and Student Services   Housing is not available. Job counseling and placement services are available.

Special Features   The conservatory has an extraordinary artist-faculty who serve as ideal models for talented young performers of music. The certificate program is meant for the best young students who are ready to embark on a career and need refinement and experience. Only the best are admitted to this competitive program.

Contact   Mr. Michael Christopher, Associate Dean, 560 Trinity, St. Louis, MO 63130. 314-863-3033.

NUCEA MEMBER

SAINT LOUIS UNIVERSITY
St. Louis, Missouri 63103

ACCOUNTING (06.02)
Accounting Certificate

General Information Unit offering the program: Metropolitan College. Program content: Financial, intermediate, managerial, and cost accounting; budgeting for profit; auditing; accounting information systems; tax. Available for credit. Certificate signed by the Dean of Metropolitan College.

Program Format Evening, weekend classes offered. Instructional schedule: Once per week. Program cycle: Continuous enrollment. Completion of program requires 24 credit hours.

Evaluation Student evaluation based on tests, papers, reports. Grading system: Letters or numbers. Transcripts are kept for each student.

Enrollment Requirements Admission to Metropolitan College, transcripts required. Program is open to non-resident foreign students. English language proficiency required.

Program Costs $125 per credit hour.

Housing and Student Services Housing is available. Job counseling and placement services are available.

Special Features All courses must be completed with an average grade of C or better within five years of initial enrollment. Up to 12 hours of transfer work from accredited colleges and universities may be used as transfer credit and applied to course work for the certificate.

Contact Metropolitan College, 221 North Grand Boulevard, St. Louis, MO 63103. 314-658-2330.

BANKING AND FINANCE (06.03)
Certificate in Finance

General Information Unit offering the program: Metropolitan College. Program content: Business finance, financial institutions. Available for credit. Certificate signed by the Dean of Metropolitan College.

Program Format Evening, weekend classes offered. Instructional schedule: Once per week. Program cycle: Continuous enrollment. Completion of program requires 30 credit hours.

Evaluation Student evaluation based on tests, papers, reports. Grading system: Letters or numbers. Transcripts are kept for each student.

Enrollment Requirements Admission to Metropolitan College, transcripts required. Program is open to non-resident foreign students. English language proficiency required.

Program Costs $125 per credit hour.

Housing and Student Services Housing is available. Job counseling and placement services are available.

Special Features All courses must be completed with an average grade of C or better within five years of initial enrollment. Up to 12 hours of transfer work from accredited colleges and universities may be used as transfer credit and applied to course work for the certificate.

Contact Metropolitan College, 221 North Grand Boulevard, St. Louis, MO 63103. 314-658-2330.

BUSINESS ADMINISTRATION AND MANAGEMENT (06.04)
Certificate in General Business

General Information Unit offering the program: Metropolitan College. Program content: Accounting, economics, finance, marketing, management information systems, legal environment. Available for credit. Certificate signed by the Dean of Metropolitan College.

Program Format Evening, weekend classes offered. Instructional schedule: Once per week. Program cycle: Continuous enrollment. Completion of program requires 30 credit hours.

Evaluation Student evaluation based on tests, papers, reports. Grading system: Letters or numbers. Transcripts are kept for each student.

Enrollment Requirements Admission to Metropolitan College, transcripts required. Program is open to non-resident foreign students. English language proficiency required.

Program Costs $125 per credit hour.

Housing and Student Services Housing is available. Job counseling and placement services are available.

Special Features All courses must be completed with an average grade of C or better within five years of initial enrollment. Up to 12 hours of transfer work from accredited colleges and universities may be used as transfer credit and applied to course work for the certificate.

Contact Metropolitan College, 221 North Grand Boulevard, St. Louis, MO 63103. 314-658-2330.

BUSINESS DATA PROCESSING AND RELATED PROGRAMS (07.03)
Credit Management Certificate

General Information Unit offering the program: Metropolitan College. Program content: Financial accounting and analysis, presentations, economics, business finance, principles of credit. Available for credit. Cosponsored by St. Louis Association of Credit Management. Certificate signed by the Dean of Metropolitan College.

Program Format Evening, weekend classes offered. Instructional schedule: Once per week. Program cycle: Continuous enrollment. Completion of program requires 27 credit hours.

Evaluation Student evaluation based on tests, papers, reports. Grading system: Letters or numbers. Transcripts are kept for each student.

Enrollment Requirements Admission to Metropolitan College, transcripts required. Program is open to non-resident foreign students. English language proficiency required.

Program Costs $125 per credit hour.

Housing and Student Services Housing is available. Job counseling and placement services are available.

Special Features All courses must be completed with an average grade of C or better within five years of initial enrollment. Up to 12 hours of transfer work from accredited colleges and universities may be used as transfer credit and applied to course work for the certificate.

Contact Metropolitan College, 221 North Grand Boulevard, St. Louis, MO 63103. 314-658-2330.

COMPUTER AND INFORMATION SCIENCES, GENERAL (11.01)
Certificate of Computer Science

General Information Unit offering the program: Metropolitan College. Program content: Algebra, BASIC, data processing, systems analysis, COBOL, FORTRAN, Pascal, statistics, microprocessing, comparative languages, computer logic design. Available for credit. Certificate signed by the Dean of Metropolitan College.

Program Format Evening, weekend classes offered. Instructional schedule: Once per week. Program cycle: Continuous enrollment. Completion of program requires 30 credit hours.

Evaluation Student evaluation based on tests, papers, reports. Grading system: Letters or numbers. Transcripts are kept for each student.

Enrollment Requirements Admission to Metropolitan College, transcripts required. Program is open to non-resident foreign students. English language proficiency required.

Program Costs $125 per credit hour.

Housing and Student Services Housing is available. Job counseling and placement services are available.

Special Features All courses must be completed with an average grade of C or better within five years of initial enrollment. Up to 12 hours of transfer work from accredited colleges and universities may be used as transfer credit and applied to course work for the certificate.

Contact Metropolitan College, 221 North Grand Boulevard, St. Louis, MO 63103. 314-658-2330.

LABOR/INDUSTRIAL RELATIONS (06.11)
Industrial Relations Certificate

General Information Unit offering the program: Metropolitan College. Program content: Labor markets, wage and salary administration, governmental regulation of labor, collective bargaining and arbitration, use and development of manpower resources. Available for credit. Certificate signed by the Dean of Metropolitan College.

Program Format Evening, weekend classes offered. Instructional schedule: Once per week. Program cycle: Continuous enrollment. Completion of program requires 30 credit hours.

Evaluation Student evaluation based on tests, papers, reports. Grading system: Letters or numbers. Transcripts are kept for each student.

Enrollment Requirements Admission to Metropolitan College, transcripts required. Program is open to non-resident foreign students. English language proficiency required.

Program Costs $125 per credit hour.

Housing and Student Services Housing is available. Job counseling and placement services are available.

Special Features All courses must be completed with an average grade of C or better within five years of initial enrollment. Up to 12 hours of transfer work from accredited colleges and universities may be used as transfer credit and applied to course work for the certificate.

Contact Metropolitan College, 221 North Grand Boulevard, St. Louis, MO 63103. 314-658-2330.

MANAGEMENT SCIENCE (06.13)
Certificate in Management and Organization Theory

General Information Unit offering the program: Metropolitan College. Program content: Group dynamics, organizational communication, problem solving, supervision and management. Available for credit. Certificate signed by the Dean of Metropolitan College.

Program Format Evening, weekend classes offered. Instructional schedule: Once per week. Program cycle: Continuous enrollment. Completion of program requires 30 credit hours.

Evaluation Student evaluation based on tests, papers, reports. Grading system: Letters or numbers. Transcripts are kept for each student.

Enrollment Requirements Admission to Metropolitan College, transcripts required. Program is open to non-resident foreign students. English language proficiency required.

Program Costs $125 per credit hour.

Housing and Student Services Housing is available. Job counseling and placement services are available.

Special Features All courses must be completed with an average grade of C or better within five years of initial enrollment. Up to 12 hours of transfer work from accredited colleges and universities may be used as transfer credit and applied to course work for the certificate.

Contact Metropolitan College, 221 North Grand Boulevard, St. Louis, MO 63103. 314-658-2330.

MARKETING MANAGEMENT AND RESEARCH (06.14)
Certificate in Marketing

General Information Unit offering the program: Metropolitan College. Program content: Business and professional presentations, economics, research, public relations, consumer behavior, sales management. Available for credit. Certificate signed by the Dean of Metropolitan College.

Program Format Evening, weekend classes offered. Instructional schedule: Once per week. Program cycle: Continuous enrollment. Completion of program requires 24 credit hours.

Evaluation Student evaluation based on tests, papers, reports. Grading system: Letters or numbers. Transcripts are kept for each student.

Enrollment Requirements Admission to Metropolitan College, transcripts required. Program is open to non-resident foreign students. English language proficiency required.

Program Costs $125 per credit hour.

Housing and Student Services Housing is available. Job counseling and placement services are available.

Special Features All courses must be completed with an average grade of C or better within five years of initial enrollment. Up to 12 hours of transfer work from accredited colleges and universities may be used as transfer credit and applied to course work for the certificate.

Contact Metropolitan College, 221 North Grand Boulevard, St. Louis, MO 63103. 314-658-2330.

REAL ESTATE (06.17)
Certificate in Real Estate

General Information Unit offering the program: Metropolitan College. Program content: Finance, accounting, economics, appraising, inferential statistics. Available for credit. Endorsed by Society of Real Estate Appraisers. Certificate signed by the Dean of Metropolitan College.

Program Format Evening, weekend classes offered. Instructional schedule: Once per week. Program cycle: Continuous enrollment. Completion of program requires 30 credit hours.

Evaluation Student evaluation based on tests, papers, reports. Grading system: Letters or numbers. Transcripts are kept for each student.

Enrollment Requirements Admission to Metropolitan College, transcripts required. Program is open to non-resident foreign students. English language proficiency required.

Program Costs $125 per credit hour.

Housing and Student Services Housing is available. Job counseling and placement services are available.

Special Features All courses must be completed with an average grade of C or better within five years of initial enrollment. Up to 12 hours of transfer work from accredited colleges and universities may be used as transfer credit and applied to course work for the certificate.

Contact Metropolitan College, 221 North Grand Boulevard, St. Louis, MO 63103. 314-658-2330.

SCHOOL OF THE OZARKS
Point Lookout, Missouri 65726

COUNSELING PSYCHOLOGY (42.06)
Paraprofessional Counseling Certificate

General Information Unit offering the program: Psychology. Program content: Psychology, abnormal psychology, human relations, group dynamics, counseling, personality development, practicum and/or internship. Available for credit. Certificate signed by the Director, Counseling Center. Certificate applicable to bachelor's degree in psychology.

Program Format Daytime, evening classes offered. Program cycle: Continuous enrollment. Full program cycle lasts 3 semesters.

Evaluation Student evaluation based on tests, papers, oral examination. Grading system: Letters or numbers. Record of completion kept by department.

Enrollment Requirements College admissions, successful completion of introduction to psychology, human relations, and group dynamics courses required. Program is open to non-resident foreign students.

Housing and Student Services Housing is available. Job counseling and placement services are available.

Special Features Students who complete the program often work in counseling settings, such as half-way houses, drug-abuse rehabilitation, or mental hospitals.

Contact Mr. John Goodwin, Ph.D., Chair, Psychology, School of the Ozarks, Point Lookout, MO 65726. 417-334-6411 Ext. 226.

STEPHENS COLLEGE
Columbia, Missouri 65215

HEALTH SERVICES ADMINISTRATION (18.07)
Certificate in Health Information Management

General Information Unit offering the program: Health Information Management. Program content: Quality assurance, computers, statistics, legal aspects, anatomy, physiology. Available for credit. Endorsed by American Medical Association; American Medical Records Association. Certificate signed by the President of the College.

Program Format Daytime, correspondence classes offered. Instructional schedule: Independent study, five-day on-site requirement. Program cycle: Continuous enrollment. Full program cycle lasts 51 credit hours. Completion of program requires assignments, final exams, 17 courses.

Evaluation Student evaluation based on tests, papers, reports. Grading system: Letters or numbers. Transcripts are kept for each student.

Enrollment Requirements Bachelor's degree, Accredited Record Technician certification required. Program is not open to non-resident foreign students. English language proficiency required. Minimum TOEFL score required: 500.

Program Costs $535 per course.

Housing and Student Services Housing is available. Job counseling and placement services are available.

Special Features Program is first external degree progression program for Accredited Record Technicians who wish to become Registered Record Administrators. Offered through Stephens College Without Walls program, independent study baccalaureate degree program for adults who for various reasons cannot attend courses offered in residential format. Students come from every state in the country and Puerto Rico.

Contact Ms. Joan T. Rines, Director, Health Information Management Program, Campus Box 2083, Columbia, MO 65215. 314-876-7283.

NUCEA MEMBER
UNIVERSITY OF MISSOURI–COLUMBIA
Columbia, Missouri 65211

LIBRARY SCIENCE (25.04)
Certificate of Professional Studies

General Information Unit offering the program: School of Library and Informational Science. Program content: Library management, library automation, or library services. Available on a non-credit basis. Certificate signed by the Dean.

Program Format Daytime, evening, weekend classes offered. Program cycle: Continuous enrollment. Completion of program requires 12 CEUs.

Evaluation Student evaluation methods vary by course. Records are kept in Continuing Library Education Office.

Enrollment Requirements Program is open to non-resident foreign students.

Housing and Student Services Housing is available. Job counseling and placement services are available.

Special Features An organized continuing education program for personnel in libraries and other information agencies and for individuals who can benefit. The curriculum is designed to address in-depth skill development through a choice of three core areas: Library Management, Library Automation, Library Services.

Contact Mr. Frederick J. Raithel, Director of Continuing Library Education/Extension, 104 Stewart Hall, Columbia, MO 65211. 314-882-1709.

WILLIAM JEWELL COLLEGE
Liberty, Missouri 64068

LAW (22.01)
Paralegal Certificate

General Information Unit offering the program: Evening Division. Program content: Research, litigation, corporate law, computers, English composition. Available for credit. Certificate signed by the President of the College. Certificate applicable to any four-year degree offered at the institution.

Program Format Evening classes offered. Program cycle: Continuous enrollment. Completion of program requires grade of C or better in all courses.

Evaluation Student evaluation based on tests, papers, reports. Grading system: Letters or numbers. Transcripts are kept for each student.

Enrollment Requirements Program is open to non-resident foreign students. English language proficiency required. Students must pass college writing test.

Program Costs $1820 for the program. $70 per credit hour.

Housing and Student Services Housing is not available. Job counseling and placement services are available.

Contact Dr. Steve Schwegler, Associate Dean, Liberty, MO 64068. 816-781-7700.

MONTANA

NUCEA MEMBER
WESTERN MONTANA COLLEGE
Dillon, Montana 59725

CHILD CARE AND GUIDANCE MANAGEMENT AND SERVICES (20.02)
CDA Credential (Child Development Associate)

General Information Unit offering the program: Education. Available for credit. Endorsed by Council for Early Childhood Professional Recognition. Certificate signed by the Director, Council for Early Childhood Professional Recognition.

Program Format Daytime, evening classes offered. Instructional schedule: Class lecture three hours per week; field experience ten hours per week. Program cycle: Continuous enrollment. Full program cycle lasts 4 semesters. Completion of program requires 640 contact hours.

Evaluation Student evaluation based on tests, papers, reports, assessments, journals. Grading system: Letters or numbers. Transcripts are kept for each student.

Enrollment Requirements High school diploma or GED, ACT or SAT scores required. Program is not open to non-resident foreign students. English language proficiency required.

Program Costs $74–$246 for one to six credit hours.

Housing and Student Services Housing is available. Job counseling and placement services are available.

Special Features This program is designed to meet the training needs of the early childhood teacher or student. There is a two-track system: on-the-job training and pre-employment training. The training model emphasizes the individual's strengths and works toward advancing skills in weak areas through a combination of class lectures, readings, and supervised field experience.

Contact Ms. Colleen McGuire, Instructor and Program Coordinator, Box 31, Dillon, MT 59725. 406-683-7176.

NEBRASKA

COLLEGE OF SAINT MARY
Omaha, Nebraska 68124

HEALTH SERVICES ADMINISTRATION (18.07)
Certificate of Completion of Health Information Management Program

General Information Unit offering the program: Health Information Management, Health Science Division. Program content: Disease processes, records management, information processing, management, health care delivery system. Available for credit. Certificate signed by the Division Chair, Health Science Division. Certificate applicable to B.S. in Health Information Management. Program fulfills requirements for Registered Record Administrator.

Program Format Daytime classes offered. Program cycle: Continuous enrollment. Full program cycle lasts 2 years. Completion of program requires 76 credit hours.

Evaluation Student evaluation based on tests, papers, clinical competence. Grading system: Letters or numbers. Transcripts are kept for each student.

Enrollment Requirements Bachelor's degree required. Program is open to non-resident foreign students.

Program Costs $174 per credit hour.

Housing and Student Services Housing is available. Job counseling and placement services are available.

Contact Ms. Ellen Jacobs, Director, Health Information Management Program, 1901 South 72nd Street, Omaha, NE 68124. 402-399-2611.

LAW (22.01)
Certificate in Paralegal Studies

General Information Unit offering the program: Business. Program content: Law and supporting course work. Available for credit. Certificate signed by the President. Certificate applicable to B.A. in Paralegal Studies.

Program Format Daytime, evening, weekend classes offered. Instructional schedule: Daytime classes three times per week; evening classes once per week; weekend classes on alternate weekends. Program cycle: Continuous enrollment. Full program cycle lasts 32 credit hours. Completion of program requires 2.0 GPA.

Evaluation Student evaluation based on tests, papers, reports. Grading system: Letters or numbers. Transcripts are kept for each student.

Enrollment Requirements Bachelor's degree or employed as paralegal required.

Program Costs $174 per credit hour.

Housing and Student Services Housing is available. Job counseling and placement services are available.

Special Features Admittance on basis of on-going or past work and educational experiences. Core of general law courses complimented by specialized law courses. Credit for Extra College Learning - allowing for CLEP, Challenge, and Portfolio development as alternatives to traditional course work. Internships for qualifying students with placement in local law firms.

Contact Ms. Barb Zieg-Hansen, Associate Director, Paralegal Studies, 1901 South 72nd Street, Omaha, NE 68124. 402-399-2413.

TELECOMMUNICATIONS (09.08)
Telecommunications Systems Management

General Information Unit offering the program: Business Division. Program content: Communications management. Available for credit. Certificate signed by the President.

Program Format Evening, weekend classes offered. Instructional schedule: Three hours per week. Program cycle: Continuous enrollment. Full program cycle lasts 6 courses. Completion of program requires 18 credit hours, grade of C or better.

Evaluation Student evaluation based on tests, papers. Grading system: Letters or numbers. Transcripts are kept for each student.

Enrollment Requirements Program is open to non-resident foreign students. English language proficiency required. Minimum TOEFL score required: 500.

Program Costs $3132 for the program, $522 per course.

Housing and Student Services Housing is available. Job counseling and placement services are available.

Special Features Innovative curriculum responds to the demands of the future. Work/career-oriented and designed for the working adult student. Credit earned without formal enrollment in courses by Examination or Challenge Examination. Courses taught by mix of full-time instructors and adjunct faculty from local telecommunication companies providing for well-grounded program with "state-of-the-art" and "real-time" input.

Contact Ms. Rayda J. Santrach, Director, Telecommunications Systems Management, 1901 South 72nd Street, Omaha, NE 68124. 402-399-2672.

CREIGHTON UNIVERSITY
Omaha, Nebraska 68178

ATMOSPHERIC SCIENCES AND METEOROLOGY (40.04)
Certificate of Atmospheric Sciences

General Information   Unit offering the program: Department of Atmospheric Sciences. Program content: Meteorology, calculus, physics. Available for credit. Certificate signed by the Dean, University College. Certificate applicable to B.S. in Atmospheric Sciences.

Program Format   Evening classes offered. Instructional schedule: One or two evenings per week. Program cycle: Continuous enrollment. Full program cycle lasts 37 credit hours. Completion of program requires grade of C or better in all courses.

Evaluation   Student evaluation based on tests. Grading system: Letters or numbers. Transcripts are kept for each student.

Enrollment Requirements   Program is open to non-resident foreign students. English language proficiency required. Minimum TOEFL score required: 500.

Program Costs $127–$190 per credit hour.

Housing and Student Services   Housing is not available. Job counseling and placement services are available.

Special Features   Advanced placement is available to students who qualify, particularly for those with meteorological training with the aviation industry, the National Weather Service, or branches of the military.

Contact   Mr. Arthur V. Douglas, Ph.D., Chair, Department of Atmospheric Sciences, Omaha, NE 68178. 402-280-2641.

BUSINESS AND MANAGEMENT, GENERAL (06.01)
Certificate of Business Administration

General Information   Unit offering the program: University College. Program content: Business administration, accounting, economics, finance, management, marketing, systems. Available for credit. Certificate signed by the Dean, University College. Certificate applicable to B.S. in Business Administration.

Program Format   Evening classes offered. Instructional schedule: One evening per week. Program cycle: Continuous enrollment. Full program cycle lasts 33 credit hours. Completion of program requires grade of C or better in all courses.

Evaluation   Student evaluation based on tests, papers, reports. Grading system: Letters or numbers. Transcripts are kept for each student.

Enrollment Requirements   Program is open to non-resident foreign students. English language proficiency required. Minimum TOEFL score required: 500.

Program Costs $127–$190 per credit hour.

Housing and Student Services   Housing is not available. Job counseling and placement services are available.

Special Features   Successful completion of the courses required for the Certificate of Business Administration introduces the student to the six functional areas of business: accounting, economics, finance, marketing, management, and systems; and are prerequisite courses for admission to the graduate program leading to the degree of Master of Business Administration (MBA).

Contact   Ms. Barbara H. Angus, Assistant to the Dean, University College, Omaha, NE 68178. 402-280-2424.

COMMUNICATIONS, GENERAL (09.01)
Certificate of Organizational Communication

General Information   Unit offering the program: Department of English/Speech. Program content: Principles of organizational communication, interviewing, theory and practice in group communications. Available for credit. Certificate signed by the Dean, University College. Certificate applicable to B.A. in Speech.

Program Format   Evening classes offered. Instructional schedule: One evening per week. Program cycle: Continuous enrollment. Full program cycle lasts 36 credit hours. Completion of program requires grade of C or better in all courses.

Evaluation   Student evaluation based on tests, papers, reports, internship. Grading system: Letters or numbers. Transcripts are kept for each student.

Enrollment Requirements   Program is open to non-resident foreign students. English language proficiency required. Minimum TOEFL score required: 500.

Program Costs $127–$190 per credit hour.

Housing and Student Services   Housing is not available. Job counseling and placement services are available.

Special Features   Credit may be given for prior experience in certain areas. Instructors are regular full-time faculty from the Department of English/Speech. Courses are rotated each semester in the evening program, but students may also take day courses. At least half of the course work must be completed at Creighton.

Contact   Mr. Donald D. Yoder, Ph.D., Coordinator, Department of English/Speech, Omaha, NE 68178. 402-280-2822.

COMPUTER PROGRAMMING (11.02)
Certificate of Computer Science

General Information   Unit offering the program: Department of Mathematics/Computer Science. Program content: Computer organization, programming languages, computer systems. Available for credit. Certificate signed by the Dean, University College. Certificate applicable to B.S. in Computer Sciences.

Program Format   Evening classes offered. Instructional schedule: One evening per week. Program cycle: Continuous enrollment. Complete program cycle lasts 27–30 credit hours. Completion of program requires grade of C or better in all courses.

Evaluation   Student evaluation based on tests, student-designed programs. Grading system: Letters or numbers. Transcripts are kept for each student.

Enrollment Requirements   Program is open to non-resident foreign students. English language proficiency required. Minimum TOEFL score required: 500.

Program Costs $127–$190 per credit hour.

Housing and Student Services   Housing is not available. Job counseling and placement services are available.

Special Features   Credit for experience possible.

Contact   Mr. John A. Mordeson, Chair, Department of Mathematics/Computer Science, Omaha, NE 68178. 402-280-2827.

HISTORY (45.08)
Certificate of History

General Information   Unit offering the program: Department of History. Program content: Western heritage, European culture, U.S. history. Available for credit. Certificate signed by the Dean, University College. Certificate applicable to B.A. in History.

Program Format   Evening classes offered. Instructional schedule: One evening per week. Program cycle: Continuous enrollment. Full program cycle lasts 34 credit hours. Completion of program requires grade of C or better in all courses.

Evaluation   Student evaluation based on tests, papers, reports. Grading system: Letters or numbers. Transcripts are kept for each student.

Enrollment Requirements   Program is open to non-resident foreign students. English language proficiency required. Minimum TOEFL score required: 500.

Program Costs $127–$190 per credit hour.

Housing and Student Services   Housing is not available. Job counseling and placement services are available.

Special Features   Credit by examination (CLEP, DANTES) possible. Good preparation for law school.

Contact   Mr. Warren G. Kneer, Chair, Department of History, Omaha, NE 68178. 402-280-2884.

MATHEMATICS, GENERAL (27.01)
Certificate of Mathematics

General Information   Unit offering the program: Department of Mathematics/Computer Science. Program content: Algebra, calculus, statistics, probability. Available for credit. Certificate signed by the Dean, University College. Certificate applicable to B.S. in Mathematics.

Program Format   Evening classes offered. Instructional schedule: One or two evenings per week. Program cycle: Continuous enrollment. Full program cycle lasts 30 credit hours. Completion of program requires grade of C or better in all courses.

Evaluation   Student evaluation based on tests, homework assignments. Grading system: Letters or numbers. Transcripts are kept for each student.

Enrollment Requirements   Program is open to non-resident foreign students. English language proficiency required. Minimum TOEFL score required: 500.

Program Costs $127–$190 per credit hour.

Housing and Student Services   Housing is not available. Job counseling and placement services are available.

Special Features   Credit by examination (CLEP, DANTES, departmental exam) possible.

Contact   Mr. John N. Mordeson, Ph.D., Chair, Department of Mathematics, Omaha, NE 68178. 402-280-2827.

PSYCHOLOGY, GENERAL (42.01)
Certificate of Psychology

General Information   Unit offering the program: Department of Psychology. Program content: Introduction to psychology, experimental, statistics. Available for credit. Certificate signed by the Dean, University College. Certificate applicable to B.A. in Psychology.

Program Format   Evening classes offered. Instructional schedule: One or two evenings per week. Program cycle: Continuous enrollment. Full program cycle lasts 31 credit hours. Completion of program requires grade of C or better in all courses.

Evaluation   Student evaluation based on tests, papers, reports, internship. Grading system: Letters or numbers. Transcripts are kept for each student.

Enrollment Requirements   Program is open to non-resident foreign students. English language proficiency required. Minimum TOEFL score required: 500.

Program Costs $127–$190 per credit hour.

Housing and Student Services   Housing is not available. Job counseling and placement services are available.

Special Features   Credit for experience possible.

Contact   Ms. Elizabeth A. Dahl, Ph.D., Chair, Department of Psychology, Omaha, NE 68178. 402-280-2821.

PUBLIC RELATIONS (09.05)
Certificate of Public Relations

General Information   Unit offering the program: Department of Journalism and Mass Communication. Program content: News reporting, principles of public relations, law of mass communication. Available for credit. Certificate signed by the Dean, University College. Certificate applicable to B.A. in Journalism.

Program Format   Evening classes offered. Instructional schedule: One evening per week. Program cycle: Continuous enrollment. Complete program cycle lasts 28–29 credit hours. Completion of program requires grade of C or better in all courses.

Evaluation   Student evaluation based on tests, papers, reports. Grading system: Letters or numbers. Transcripts are kept for each student.

Enrollment Requirements   Program is open to non-resident foreign students. English language proficiency required. Minimum TOEFL score required: 500.

Program Costs $127–$190 per credit hour.

Housing and Student Services   Housing is not available. Job counseling and placement services are available.

Special Features   Credit for prior experience possible. Courses offering practical experience available (e.g., internship).

Contact   Mr. David A. Haberman, Chair, Department of Journalism and Mass Communication, Omaha, NE 68178. 402-280-2825.

RELIGION (38.02)
Certificate of Ministry

General Information   Unit offering the program: Department of Theology. Program content: Introduction to Bible, Christian ministry, ethics. Available for credit. Certificate signed by the Dean, University College. Certificate applicable to B.A. in Ministry.

Program Format   Evening classes offered. Instructional schedule: One evening per week. Program cycle: Continuous enrollment. Full program cycle lasts 28 credit hours. Completion of program requires grade of C or better in all courses.

Evaluation   Student evaluation based on tests, papers, reports, portfolio of life experiences. Grading system: Letters or numbers. Transcripts are kept for each student.

Enrollment Requirements   Program is open to non-resident foreign students. English language proficiency required. Minimum TOEFL score required: 500.

Program Costs $127–$190 per credit hour.

Housing and Student Services   Housing is not available. Job counseling and placement services are available.

Special Features   Credit for experience possible. Program open to persons of all denominations who desire a curriculum with a solid theological base and practical application in church ministry.

Contact   Ms. Patricia R. Callone, Assistant Dean, University College, Omaha, NE 68178. 402-280-2888.

RELIGION (38.02)
Diploma in Ministry

General Information   Unit offering the program: Department of Theology. Program content: Introduction to Bible, Christian ministry, ethics. Available on a non-credit basis. Certificate signed by the Dean, University College.

Program Format   Evening classes offered. Instructional schedule: One evening per week. Program cycle: Continuous enrollment. Full program cycle lasts 28 credit hours. Completion of program requires grade of C or better in all courses.

Evaluation   Student evaluation based on tests, papers, reports, portfolio of life experiences. Grading system: Letters or numbers, grades are AUDIT. Transcripts are kept for each student.

Enrollment Requirements   Program is open to non-resident foreign students. English language proficiency required. Minimum TOEFL score required: 500.

Program Costs $64–$95 per credit hour.

Diploma in Ministry continued

Housing and Student Services   Housing is not available. Job counseling and placement services are available.

Special Features   Credit for experience possible. Program open to persons of all denominations who desire a curriculum with a solid theological base and practical application in church ministry.

Contact   Ms. Patricia R. Callone, Assistant Dean, University College, Omaha, NE 68178. 402-280-2888.

STATISTICS (27.05)
Certificate of Statistics

General Information   Unit offering the program: Department of Mathematics/Computer Science. Program content: Mathematical statistics, analysis of varients, linear statistical models. Available for credit. Certificate signed by the Dean, University College. Certificate applicable to B.S. in Mathematics.

Program Format   Evening classes offered. Program cycle: Continuous enrollment. Full program cycle lasts 26 credit hours. Completion of program requires grade of C or better in all courses.

Evaluation   Student evaluation based on tests, homework assignments. Grading system: Letters or numbers. Transcripts are kept for each student.

Enrollment Requirements   Program is open to non-resident foreign students. English language proficiency required. Minimum TOEFL score required: 500.

Program Costs $127–$190 per credit hour.

Housing and Student Services   Housing is not available. Job counseling and placement services are available.

Special Features   Credit on the basis of CLEP, Dantes, or departmental exam possible.

Contact   Mr. John A. Mordeson, Ph.D., Chair, Department of Mathematics/Computer Sciences, Omaha, NE 68178. 402-280-2827.

PERU STATE COLLEGE
Peru, Nebraska 68421

DIAGNOSTIC AND TREATMENT SERVICES (17.02)
Emergency Medical Technician—Ambulance

General Information   Unit offering the program: Division of Continuing Education. Available for credit. Endorsed by Nebraska Department of Health. Certificate signed by the President of the College. Program fulfills requirements for Emergency Medical Technician–Ambulance.

Program Format   Evening classes offered. Instructional schedule: One evening per week. Students may enroll fall, spring. Full program cycle lasts 27 weeks. Completion of program requires passing state-established examination.

Evaluation   Student evaluation based on tests, practical examination. Grading system: Letters or numbers. Transcripts are kept for each student.

Enrollment Requirements   Recommendation from local agency required. Program is not open to non-resident foreign students. English language proficiency required.

Program Costs $100 for the program.

Housing and Student Services   Housing is available. Job counseling and placement services are not available.

Contact   Mr. Robert Baker, Dean, Peru, NE 68421. 402-872-3815.

NUCEA MEMBER

UNIVERSITY OF NEBRASKA–LINCOLN
Lincoln, Nebraska 68588

MISCELLANEOUS CONSTRUCTION TRADES AND PROPERTY MAINTENANCE (46.04)
Building Inspection

General Information   Unit offering the program: Division of Continuing Studies—Independent Study Department. Program content: Building code requirements, structural inspection, plan review. Available on a non-credit basis. Endorsed by International Conference of Building Officials. Certificate signed by the Director, Independent Study.

Program Format   Correspondence classes offered. Program cycle: Continuous enrollment. Complete program cycle lasts five months to one year. Completion of program requires three written assignments, two examinations.

Evaluation   Student evaluation based on tests, papers. Record of completion kept by Division of Continuing Studies.

Enrollment Requirements   Program is open to non-resident foreign students. English language proficiency required.

Program Costs $120 per course.

Housing and Student Services   Housing is not available. Job counseling and placement services are not available.

Special Features   The Building Inspection and Plan Review course is a cooperative effort between the University of Nebraska–Lincoln Division of Continuing Studies and the International Conference of Building Officials. The UNL Independent Study program has been awarded 26 NUCEA awards for excellence in course design in the past thirteen years.

Contact   Mr. L. David Allen, Coordinator, College Instruction, 269 Nebraska Center for Continuing Education, Lincoln, NE 68583-0900. 402-472-1932.

NEW HAMPSHIRE

FRANKLIN PIERCE COLLEGE
Rindge, New Hampshire 03461

ACCOUNTING (06.02)
Accounting Certificate

General Information   Unit offering the program: Division of Continuing Education. Available for credit. Certificate signed by the Dean of Continuing Education. Certificate applicable to A.A., B.S. in Accounting.

Program Format   Evening, weekend classes offered. Instructional schedule: Two evenings per week or five hours Friday evening or Saturday. Program cycle: Continuous enrollment. Completion of program requires 2.0 GPA, ten courses.

Evaluation   Student evaluation based on tests, papers, reports, presentations, projects. Grading system: Letters or numbers. Transcripts are kept for each student.

Enrollment Requirements   High school diploma or GED required. Program is open to non-resident foreign students. English language proficiency required. Students reviewed on individual basis.

Program Costs $1710 for the program, $285 per course.

Housing and Student Services   Housing is not available. Job counseling and placement services are available.

Contact   Mr. Walter Antoniotti, Dean of Continuing Education, 472 Amherst Street, Nashua, NH 03063. 603-889-6146.

BUSINESS AND MANAGEMENT, GENERAL (06.01)
Management Certificate

General Information   Unit offering the program: Division of Continuing Education. Available for credit. Certificate signed by the Dean of Continuing Education. Certificate applicable to A.A., B.S. in Business Management.

Program Format   Evening, weekend classes offered. Instructional schedule: Two evenings per week or five hours Friday evening or Saturday. Program cycle: Continuous enrollment. Completion of program requires 2.0 GPA, ten courses.

Evaluation   Student evaluation based on tests, papers, reports, presentations, projects. Grading system: Letters or numbers. Transcripts are kept for each student.

Enrollment Requirements   High school diploma or GED required. Program is open to non-resident foreign students. English language proficiency required. Students reviewed on individual basis.

Program Costs $1710 for the program, $285 per course.

Housing and Student Services   Housing is not available. Job counseling and placement services are available.

Contact   Mr. Walter Antoniotti, Dean of Continuing Education, 472 Amherst Street, Nashua, NH 03063. 603-889-6146.

COMPUTER AND INFORMATION SCIENCES, GENERAL (11.01)
Computer Science Certificate

General Information   Unit offering the program: Division of Continuing Education. Available for credit. Certificate signed by the Dean of Continuing Education. Certificate applicable to A.A., B.S. in Computer Science.

Program Format   Evening, weekend classes offered. Instructional schedule: Two evenings per week or five hours Friday evening or Saturday. Program cycle: Continuous enrollment. Completion of program requires 2.0 GPA, ten courses.

Evaluation   Student evaluation based on tests, papers, reports, presentations, projects. Grading system: Letters or numbers. Transcripts are kept for each student.

Enrollment Requirements   High school diploma or GED required. Program is open to non-resident foreign students. English language proficiency required. Students reviewed on individual basis.

Program Costs $1710 for the program, $285 per course.

Housing and Student Services   Housing is not available. Job counseling and placement services are available.

Contact   Mr. Walter Antoniotti, Dean of Continuing Education, 472 Amherst Street, Nashua, NH 03063. 603-889-6146.

GENERAL MARKETING (08.07)
Marketing Certificate

General Information   Unit offering the program: Division of Continuing Education. Available for credit. Certificate signed by the Dean of Continuing Education. Certificate applicable to A.A., B.S. in Marketing.

Program Format   Evening, weekend classes offered. Instructional schedule: Two evenings per week or five hours Friday evening or Saturday. Program cycle: Continuous enrollment. Completion of program requires 2.0 GPA, ten courses.

Evaluation   Student evaluation based on tests, papers, reports, presentations, projects. Grading system: Letters or numbers. Transcripts are kept for each student.

Enrollment Requirements   High school diploma or GED required. Program is open to non-resident foreign students. English language proficiency required. Students reviewed on individual basis.

Program Costs $1710 for the program, $285 per course.

Housing and Student Services   Housing is not available. Job counseling and placement services are available.

Contact   Mr. Walter Antoniotti, Dean of Continuing Education, 472 Amherst Street, Nashua, NH 03063. 603-889-6146.

NEW HAMPSHIRE COLLEGE
Manchester, New Hampshire 03104

ACCOUNTING (06.02)
Certificate in Accounting

General Information   Unit offering the program: Continuing Education Centers. Available for credit. Certificate signed by the Dean, Undergraduate School of Business. Certificate applicable to B.S. in Business Administration, Accounting, Management Information Systems.

Program Format   Evening, weekend classes offered. Instructional schedule: Two evenings per week or weekends. Program cycle: Continuous enrollment. Full program cycle lasts 1 year. Completion of program requires 13 courses, 40 contact hours per course.

Evaluation   Student evaluation based on tests, papers, reports. Grading system: Letters or numbers. Transcripts are kept for each student.

Enrollment Requirements   High school diploma, prerequisites required. Program is open to non-resident foreign students. English language proficiency required.

Program Costs $270 per course.

Housing and Student Services   Housing is not available. Job counseling and placement services are available.

Special Features   Credit is given for prior experience.

Contact   Mr. George Perraudin, Director, Manchester Center, 2500 North River Road, Manchester, NH 03104. 603-668-2211.

BANKING AND FINANCE (06.03)
Certificate in Business Finance

General Information   Unit offering the program: Continuing Education Centers. Available for credit. Certificate signed by the Dean, Undergraduate School of Business. Certificate applicable to B.S. in Business Administration, Accounting, Management Information Systems.

Program Format   Evening, weekend classes offered. Instructional schedule: Two evenings per week or weekends. Program cycle: Continuous enrollment. Full program cycle lasts 1 year. Completion of program requires 12 courses, 40 contact hours per course.

Evaluation   Student evaluation based on tests, papers, reports. Grading system: Letters or numbers. Transcripts are kept for each student.

Enrollment Requirements   High school diploma, prerequisites required. Program is open to non-resident foreign students.

Program Costs $270 per course.

Housing and Student Services   Housing is not available. Job counseling and placement services are available.

Special Features   Credit is given for prior experience.

Contact   Mr. George Perraudin, Director, Manchester Center, 2500 North River Road, Manchester, NH 03104. 603-668-2211.

BUSINESS ADMINISTRATION AND MANAGEMENT (06.04)
Materials Management Certificate

General Information   Unit offering the program: Continuing Education Centers. Available for credit. Certificate signed by the Dean, Undergraduate School of Business. Certificate applicable

Materials Management Certificate continued

to B.S. in Business Administration, Accounting, Management Information Systems.

Program Format Evening, weekend classes offered. Instructional schedule: Two evenings per week or weekends. Program cycle: Continuous enrollment. Full program cycle lasts 1 year. Completion of program requires six courses, 40 contact hours per course.

Evaluation Student evaluation based on tests, papers, reports. Grading system: Letters or numbers. Transcripts are kept for each student.

Enrollment Requirements High school diploma, prerequisites required. Program is open to non-resident foreign students.

Program Costs $270 per course.

Housing and Student Services Housing is not available. Job counseling and placement services are available.

Special Features Credit is given for prior experience.

Contact Mr. George Perraudin, Director, Manchester Center, 2500 North River Road, Manchester, NH 03104. 603-668-2211.

BUSINESS AND MANAGEMENT, GENERAL (06.01)
Certificate in Business Administration

General Information Unit offering the program: Continuing Education Centers. Available for credit. Certificate signed by the Dean, Undergraduate School of Business. Certificate applicable to B.S. in Business Administration, Accounting, Management Information Systems.

Program Format Evening, weekend classes offered. Instructional schedule: Two evenings per week or weekends. Program cycle: Continuous enrollment. Full program cycle lasts 1 year. Completion of program requires 12 courses, 40 contact hours per course.

Evaluation Student evaluation based on tests, papers, reports. Grading system: Letters or numbers. Transcripts are kept for each student.

Enrollment Requirements High school diploma, prerequisites required. Program is open to non-resident foreign students. English language proficiency required.

Program Costs $270 per course.

Housing and Student Services Housing is not available. Job counseling and placement services are available.

Special Features Credit is given for prior experience.

Contact Mr. George Perraudin, Director, Manchester Center, 2500 North River Road, Manchester, NH 03104. 603-668-2211.

COMPUTER PROGRAMMING (11.02)
Certificate in Computer Programming

General Information Unit offering the program: Continuing Education Centers. Available for credit. Certificate signed by the Dean, Undergraduate School of Business. Certificate applicable to B.S. in Business Administration, Accounting, Management Information Systems.

Program Format Evening, weekend classes offered. Instructional schedule: Two evenings per week or weekends. Program cycle: Continuous enrollment. Full program cycle lasts 1 year. Completion of program requires 13 courses, 40 contact hours per course.

Evaluation Student evaluation based on tests, papers, reports. Grading system: Letters or numbers. Transcripts are kept for each student.

Enrollment Requirements High school diploma, prerequisites required. Program is open to non-resident foreign students. English language proficiency required.

Program Costs $270 per course.

Housing and Student Services Housing is not available. Job counseling and placement services are available.

Special Features Credit is given for prior experience.

Contact Mr. George Perraudin, Director, Manchester Center, 2500 North River Road, Manchester, NH 03104. 603-668-2211.

GENERAL MARKETING (08.07)
Certificate in Salesmanship

General Information Unit offering the program: Continuing Education Centers. Available for credit. Certificate signed by the Dean, Undergraduate School of Business. Certificate applicable to B.S. in Business Administration, Accounting, Management Information Systems.

Program Format Evening, weekend classes offered. Instructional schedule: Two evenings per week or weekends. Program cycle: Continuous enrollment. Full program cycle lasts 1 year. Completion of program requires 12 courses, 40 contact hours per course.

Evaluation Student evaluation based on tests, papers, reports. Grading system: Letters or numbers. Transcripts are kept for each student.

Enrollment Requirements High school diploma, prerequisites required. Program is open to non-resident foreign students. English language proficiency required.

Program Costs $270 per course.

Housing and Student Services Housing is not available. Job counseling and placement services are available.

Special Features Credit is given for prior experience.

Contact Mr. George Perraudin, Director, Manchester Center, 2500 North River Road, Manchester, NH 03104. 603-668-2211.

HUMAN RESOURCES DEVELOPMENT (06.06)
Certificate in Human Resources Management

General Information Unit offering the program: Continuing Education Centers. Available for credit. Certificate signed by the Dean, Undergraduate School of Business. Certificate applicable to B.S. in Business Administration, Accounting, Management Information Systems.

Program Format Evening, weekend classes offered. Instructional schedule: Two evenings per week or weekends. Program cycle: Continuous enrollment. Full program cycle lasts 1 year. Completion of program requires 13 courses, 40 contact hours per course.

Evaluation Student evaluation based on tests, papers, reports. Grading system: Letters or numbers. Transcripts are kept for each student.

Enrollment Requirements High school diploma, prerequisites required. Program is open to non-resident foreign students. English language proficiency required.

Program Costs $270 per course.

Housing and Student Services Housing is not available. Job counseling and placement services are available.

Special Features Credit is given for prior experience.

Contact Mr. George Perraudin, Director, Manchester Center, 2500 North River Road, Manchester, NH 03104. 603-668-2211.

RIVIER COLLEGE
Nashua, New Hampshire 03060

CHILD CARE AND GUIDANCE MANAGEMENT AND SERVICES (20.02)
Certificate in Early Childhood Education

General Information Unit offering the program: Early Childhood Education Program. Program content: Theory and practice. Available for credit. Certificate signed by the Dean of Continuing Education. Certificate applicable to A.A., B.A. in Early

Childhood Education. Program fulfills requirements for New Hampshire and Massachusetts Child Care Licensing.

Program Format   Daytime, evening, weekend classes offered. Program cycle: Continuous enrollment. Full program cycle lasts 1 year. Completion of program requires five courses.

Evaluation   Student evaluation based on tests, papers, reports. Grading system: Letters or numbers. Transcripts are kept for each student.

Enrollment Requirements   High school diploma or GED required. Program is open to non-resident foreign students. English language proficiency required. Minimum TOEFL score required: 500.

Program Costs $1485 for the program, $297 per course.

Housing and Student Services   Housing is available. Job counseling and placement services are available.

Contact   Dr. Daniel Anker, Dean, School of Continuing Education, 420 South Main Street, Nashua, NH 03060. 603-888-1311 Ext. 228.

DESIGN (50.04)
Certificate in Communication Graphics

General Information   Unit offering the program: Art and Music. Program content: Drawing, design, graphic production. Available for credit. Certificate signed by the President. Certificate applicable to A.A. in Communications Graphics.

Program Format   Evening classes offered. Full program cycle lasts 10 courses.

Evaluation   Student evaluation based on studio projects. Grading system: Letters or numbers. Transcripts are kept for each student.

Enrollment Requirements   High school diploma or GED required. Program is open to non-resident foreign students. English language proficiency required. Minimum TOEFL score required: 500.

Program Costs $3000 for the program, $297 per course.

Housing and Student Services   Housing is available. Job counseling and placement services are available.

Contact   Sr. Marie Couture, Co-Chair, Art and Music Department, 420 South Main Street, Nashua, NH 03060. 603-888-1311 Ext. 275.

LAW (22.01)
Certificate in Paralegal Studies

General Information   Unit offering the program: Paralegal Studies Department. Program content: Legal research and writing, real estate law, civil litigation, estate planning, accounting, math, word processing. Available for credit. Endorsed by American Bar Association. Certificate signed by the Dean of Continuing Education. Certificate applicable to B.S. in Paralegal Studies.

Program Format   Evening classes offered. Instructional schedule: One class per week. Program cycle: Continuous enrollment. Complete program cycle lasts four to five semesters. Completion of program requires 2.0 GPA, 46 credit hours.

Evaluation   Student evaluation based on tests, papers, reports. Grading system: Letters or numbers. Transcripts are kept for each student.

Enrollment Requirements   Bachelor's degree required. Program is open to non-resident foreign students. English language proficiency required. Minimum TOEFL score required: 500.

Program Costs $4500 for the program, $297 per course.

Housing and Student Services   Housing is available. Job counseling and placement services are available.

Special Features   The certificate in paralegal studies is offered to those who already possess a bachelor's degree. The program has been approved by the American Bar Association since 1979. All courses are taught by attorneys with experience working with paralegals. Students are assisted in finding internships and in finding employment after graduation.

Contact   Dr. Maryann Civitello, Chair, Department of Paralegal Studies, 420 South Main Street, Nashua, NH 03060. 603-888-1311.

OFFICE SUPERVISION AND MANAGEMENT (07.04)
Information Processing Management/Office Technology

General Information   Unit offering the program: Business. Available for credit. Certificate signed by the President. Certificate applicable to B.S. in Information Processing Management/Office Technology.

Program Format   Daytime, evening classes offered. Complete program cycle lasts 12–18 months.

Evaluation   Student evaluation based on tests, papers, reports. Grading system: Letters or numbers. Transcripts are kept for each student.

Enrollment Requirements   High school diploma or GED, keyboard experience required. Program is open to non-resident foreign students. English language proficiency required. Minimum TOEFL score required: 500.

Program Costs $2400 for the program, $297 per course.

Housing and Student Services   Housing is available. Job counseling and placement services are available.

Contact   Dr. Joseph Allard, Director, Information Processing Programs, 420 South Main Street, Nashua, NH 03060. 603-888-1311 Ext. 287.

PUBLIC RELATIONS (09.05)
Certificate in Public Relations

General Information   Unit offering the program: English and Communications. Program content: Writing, editing, design, advertising. Available for credit. Certificate signed by the President.

Program Format   Daytime, evening classes offered. Program cycle: Continuous enrollment. Complete program cycle lasts 1½ years.

Evaluation   Student evaluation based on tests, papers, reports. Grading system: Letters or numbers. Transcripts are kept for each student.

Enrollment Requirements   Bachelor's degree required. Program is open to non-resident foreign students. English language proficiency required. Minimum TOEFL score required: 500.

Program Costs $1800 for the program, $297 per course.

Housing and Student Services   Housing is available. Job counseling and placement services are available.

Contact   Dr. Paul Lizotte, Chairperson, English and Communications Department, 420 South Main Street, Nashua, NH 03060. 603-888-1311 Ext. 267.

SECRETARIAL AND RELATED PROGRAMS (07.06)
Word/Information Processing

General Information   Unit offering the program: Business. Program content: Technology and procedures in the office environment. Certificate signed by the President. Certificate applicable to B.S. in Information Processing Management/Office Technology.

Program Format   Daytime, evening classes offered. Program cycle: Continuous enrollment. Complete program cycle lasts 1–1½ years.

Evaluation   Student evaluation based on tests, papers, reports. Grading system: Letters or numbers. Transcripts are kept for each student.

Word/Information Processing continued

Enrollment Requirements High school diploma or GED, keyboard experience required. Program is open to non-resident foreign students. English language proficiency required. Minimum TOEFL score required: 500.

Program Costs $2100 for the program, $297 per course.

Housing and Student Services Housing is available. Job counseling and placement services are available.

Contact Dr. Joseph Allard, Director, Information Processing Programs, 420 South Main Street, Nashua, NH 03060. 603-888-1311 Ext. 287.

NUCEA MEMBER

SCHOOL FOR LIFELONG LEARNING OF THE UNIVERSITY SYSTEM OF NEW HAMPSHIRE
Durham, New Hampshire 03824

BUSINESS AND MANAGEMENT, GENERAL (06.01)
Postal Management Certificate Program

General Information Program content: Postal operations, overview of concepts, management practices. Available for credit. Certificate signed by the Associate Dean.

Program Format Daytime, evening, weekend classes offered. Instructional schedule: Twice per week. Program cycle: Continuous enrollment.

Evaluation Student evaluation based on tests, papers, reports. Grading system: Letters or numbers. Transcripts are kept for each student.

Enrollment Requirements Program is open to non-resident foreign students.

Program Costs $70–$280 per course, $70 per credit hour.

Housing and Student Services Housing is not available. Job counseling and placement services are not available.

Special Features Time limits do not exist in regards to the completion of each program. Learners also have the option of petitioning to have a course dropped from the requirements of a certificate.

Contact Certificate Coordinator, School for Lifelong Learning, Dunlap Center, Durham, NH 03824. 603-862-1692.

CHILD CARE AND GUIDANCE MANAGEMENT AND SERVICES (20.02)
Child Care Family Based Certificate Program

General Information Program content: Relationships between parent/provider, strategies for working with preschool children. Available for credit. Certificate signed by the Associate Dean.

Program Format Daytime, evening, weekend classes offered. Instructional schedule: Twice per week. Program cycle: Continuous enrollment. Completion of program requires three courses.

Evaluation Student evaluation based on tests, papers, reports. Grading system: Letters or numbers. Transcripts are kept for each student.

Enrollment Requirements Program is open to non-resident foreign students.

Program Costs $70–$280 per course, $70 per credit hour.

Housing and Student Services Housing is not available. Job counseling and placement services are not available.

Special Features Time limits do not exist in regards to the completion of each program. Learners also have the option of petitioning to have a course dropped from the requirements of a certificate.

Contact Certificate Coordinator, School for Lifelong Learning, Dunlap Center, Durham, NH 03824. 603-862-1692.

CHILD CARE AND GUIDANCE MANAGEMENT AND SERVICES (20.02)
Child Care Group Based Certificate Program

General Information Program content: Fundamentals of the group child-care environment. Available for credit. Certificate signed by the Associate Dean.

Program Format Daytime, evening, weekend classes offered. Instructional schedule: Twice per week. Program cycle: Continuous enrollment. Completion of program requires three courses.

Evaluation Student evaluation based on tests, papers, reports. Grading system: Letters or numbers. Transcripts are kept for each student.

Enrollment Requirements Program is open to non-resident foreign students.

Program Costs $70–$280 per course, $70 per credit hour.

Housing and Student Services Housing is not available. Job counseling and placement services are not available.

Special Features Time limits do not exist in regards to the completion of each program. Learners also have the option of petitioning to have a course dropped from the requirments of a certificate.

Contact Certificate Coordinator, School for Lifelong Learning, Dunlap Center, Durham, NH 03824. 603-862-1692.

COMPUTER PROGRAMMING (11.02)
Computer Literacy Certificate Program

General Information Program content: History of computer systems, creation of programs. Available for credit. Certificate signed by the Asssociate Dean.

Program Format Daytime, evening, weekend classes offered. Instructional schedule: Twice per week. Program cycle: Continuous enrollment. Completion of program requires six courses.

Evaluation Student evaluation based on tests, papers, reports. Grading system: Letters or numbers. Transcripts are kept for each student.

Enrollment Requirements Program is open to non-resident foreign students.

Program Costs $70–$280 per course, $70 per credit hour.

Housing and Student Services Housing is not available. Job counseling and placement services are not available.

Special Features Time limits do not exist in regards to the completion of each program. Learners also have the option of petitioning to have a course dropped from the requirements of a certificate. CLEP Exams (College Level Examination Programs) can be counted toward the elimination of one course in the Computer Literacy Program.

Contact Certificate Coordinator, School for Lifelong Learning, Dunlap Center, Durham, NH 03824. 603-862-1692.

INTERPERSONAL SKILLS (35.01)
Effective Communication Certificate Program

General Information Available for credit. Certificate signed by the Associate Dean.

Program Format Daytime, evening, weekend classes offered. Instructional schedule: Twice per week. Program cycle: Continuous enrollment. Completion of program requires six courses.

Evaluation Student evaluation based on tests, papers, reports. Grading system: Letters or numbers. Transcripts are kept for each student.

Enrollment Requirements Program is open to non-resident foreign students.

Program Costs $70–$280 per course, $70 per credit hour.

Housing and Student Services Housing is not available. Job counseling and placement services are not available.

Special Features Time limits do not exist in regards to the completion of each program. Learners also have the option of petitioning to have a course dropped from the requirements of a certificate program.

Contact Certificate Coordinator, School for Lifelong Learning, Dunlap Center, Durham, NH 03824. 603-862-1692.

LIBRARY ASSISTING (25.03)
Library Techniques Certificate Program

General Information Available for credit. Certificate signed by the Associate Dean. Program fulfills requirements for certification from New Hampshire State Library.

Program Format Daytime, evening, weekend classes offered. Instructional schedule: Twice per week. Program cycle: Continuous enrollment. Completion of program requires eight courses.

Evaluation Student evaluation based on tests, papers, reports. Grading system: Letters or numbers. Transcripts are kept for each student.

Enrollment Requirements Program is open to non-resident foreign students.

Program Costs $70–$280 per course, $70 per credit hour.

Housing and Student Services Housing is not available. Job counseling and placement services are not available.

Special Features Time limits do not exist in regards to the completion of each program. Learners also have the option of petitioning to have a course dropped from the requirements of a certificate.

Contact Certificate Coordinator, School for Lifelong Learning, Dunlap Center, Durham, NH 03824. 603-862-1692.

MICROCOMPUTER APPLICATIONS (11.06)
Microcomputer Applications Certificate Program

General Information Available for credit. Certificate signed by the Associate Dean.

Program Format Daytime, evening, weekend classes offered. Instructional schedule: Twice per week. Program cycle: Continuous enrollment. Completion of program requires three courses.

Evaluation Student evaluation based on tests, papers, reports. Grading system: Letters or numbers. Transcripts are kept for each student.

Enrollment Requirements Completion of Computer Literacy Certificate required. Program is open to non-resident foreign students.

Program Costs $70–$280 per course, $70 per credit hour.

Housing and Student Services Housing is not available. Job counseling and placement services are not available.

Special Features Time limits do not exist in regards to the completion of each program. Learners also have the option of petitioning to have a course dropped from the requirements of a certificate.

Contact Certificate Coordinator, School for Lifelong Learning, Dunlap Center, Durham, NH 03824. 603-862-1692.

QUALITY CONTROL AND SAFETY TECHNOLOGIES (15.07)
Quality Control Certificate Program

General Information Available for credit. Certificate signed by the Associate Dean.

Program Format Daytime, evening, weekend classes offered. Instructional schedule: Twice per week. Program cycle:

Continuous enrollment. Completion of program requires six courses.

Evaluation Student evaluation based on tests, papers, reports. Grading system: Letters or numbers. Transcripts are kept for each student.

Enrollment Requirements Program is open to non-resident foreign students.

Program Costs $70–$280 per course, $70 per credit hour.

Housing and Student Services Housing is not available. Job counseling and placement services are not available.

Special Features Time limits do not exist in regards to the completion of each program. Learners also have the option of petitioning to have a course dropped from the requirements of a certificate.

Contact Certificate Coordinator, School for Lifelong Learning, Dunlap Center, Durham, NH 03824. 603-862-1692.

SECRETARIAL AND RELATED PROGRAMS (07.06)
The Secretary as a Professional Certificate Program

General Information Program content: Management and administrative practices, oral and written communications. Available for credit. Certificate signed by the Associate Dean.

Program Format Daytime, evening, weekend classes offered. Instructional schedule: Twice per week. Program cycle: Continuous enrollment. Completion of program requires three courses.

Evaluation Student evaluation based on tests, papers, reports. Grading system: Letters or numbers. Transcripts are kept for each student.

Enrollment Requirements Program is open to non-resident foreign students.

Program Costs $70–$280 per course, $70 per credit hour.

Housing and Student Services Housing is not available. Job counseling and placement services are not available.

Special Features Time limits do not exist in regards to the completion of each program. Learners also have the option of petitioning to have a course dropped from the requirements of a certificate.

Contact Certificate Coordinator, School for Lifelong Learning, Dunlap Center, Durham, NH 03824. 603-862-1692.

NUCEA MEMBER
UNIVERSITY OF NEW HAMPSHIRE
Durham, New Hampshire 03824

LAW (22.01)
Paralegal Studies

General Information Unit offering the program: Division of Continuing Education. Program content: Family law, estates, trusts, wills, litigation, research, tax, accounting. Available on a non-credit basis. Certificate signed by the Diector, Division of Continuing Education.

Program Format Evening classes offered. Instructional schedule: One evening per week. Program cycle: Continuous enrollment. Full program cycle lasts 2 years.

Evaluation Student evaluation based on tests, papers, reports, class participation. Grading system: Letters or numbers. Transcripts are kept for each student.

Enrollment Requirements High school diploma, two years work experience required. Program is open to non-resident foreign students.

Program Costs $1200 for the program.

Housing and Student Services Housing is not available.

Paralegal Studies continued

Special Features   Program offered state-wide through the University system.

Contact   Ms. Linda Durant, Staff Associate, Division of Continuing Education, Brook House, Durham, NH 03824. 603-862-1088.

NEW JERSEY

COLLEGE OF SAINT ELIZABETH
Convent Station, New Jersey 07961

ACCOUNTING (06.02)
Certificate in Accounting

General Information   Unit offering the program: Weekend College Office. Program content: Financial accounting, managerial accounting, business administration. Available for credit. Certificate signed by the Dean of Studies. Certificate applicable to B.S. in Business Administration.

Program Format   Weekend classes offered. Instructional schedule: Alternate weekends. Program cycle: Continuous enrollment. Full program cycle lasts 24 credit hours. Completion of program requires grade of C or better.

Evaluation   Student evaluation based on tests, papers. Grading system: Letters or numbers. Transcripts are kept for each student.

Enrollment Requirements   High school diploma or GED required.

Program Costs $600 per course.

Housing and Student Services   Housing is not available. Job counseling and placement services are not available.

Special Features   The Weekend College curricula offerings are designed with the employed person in mind. They extend to men and women the opportunity to earn a Bachelor of Arts degree in English or a Bachelor of Science degree in Business Administration with a concentration in accounting, computer information systems, management, or marketing.

Contact   Sr. Marie Jonathon Bulisok, Associate Dean, Center for Lifelong Learning, Convent Station, NJ 07961. 201-292-6348.

BUSINESS AND MANAGEMENT, GENERAL (06.01)
Certificate in Management

General Information   Unit offering the program: Weekend College Office. Program content: Marketing, organizational behavior, finance. Available for credit. Certificate signed by the Dean of Studies. Certificate applicable to B.S. in Business Administration.

Program Format   Weekend classes offered. Instructional schedule: Alternate weekends. Program cycle: Continuous enrollment. Full program cycle lasts 24 credit hours. Completion of program requires grade of C or better.

Evaluation   Student evaluation based on tests, papers. Grading system: Letters or numbers. Transcripts are kept for each student.

Enrollment Requirements   High school diploma or GED required.

Program Costs $600 per course.

Housing and Student Services   Housing is not available. Job counseling and placement services are not available.

Special Features   The Weekend College curricula offerings are designed with the employed person in mind. They extend to men and women the opportunity to earn a Bachelor of Arts degree in English or a Bachelor of Science degree in Business Administration with a concentration in accounting, computer information systems, management, or marketing.

Contact   Sr. Marie Jonathon Bulisok, Associate Dean, Center for Lifelong Learning, Convent Station, NJ 07961. 201-292-6348.

COMPUTER AND INFORMATION SCIENCES, GENERAL (11.01)
Certificate in Computer Information Systems

General Information   Unit offering the program: Weekend College Office. Program content: Business applications software, COBOL. Available for credit. Certificate signed by the Dean of Studies. Certificate applicable to B.S. in Business Administration.

Program Format   Weekend classes offered. Instructional schedule: Alternate weekends. Program cycle: Continuous enrollment. Full program cycle lasts 24 credit hours. Completion of program requires grade of C or better.

Evaluation   Student evaluation based on tests, papers. Grading system: Letters or numbers. Transcripts are kept for each student.

Enrollment Requirements   Secondary school diploma or GED required.

Program Costs $600 per course.

Housing and Student Services   Housing is not available. Job counseling and placement services are not available.

Special Features   The Weekend College curricula offerings are designed with the employed person in mind. They extend to men and women the opportunity to earn a Bachelor of Arts degree in English or a Bachelor of Science degree in Business Administration with a concentration in accounting, computer information systems, management, or marketing.

Contact   Sr. Marie Jonathon Bulisok, Associate Dean, Center for Lifelong Learning, Convent Station, NJ 07961. 201-292-6348.

INDIVIDUAL AND FAMILY DEVELOPMENT (19.07)
Gerontology Program

General Information   Unit offering the program: Gerontology Program. Program content: Aging and the individual, social gerontology, programs and services for the aged. Available for credit. Certificate signed by the Director, Gerontology Program. Certificate applicable to any four-year degree offered at the institution.

Program Format   Evening classes offered. Complete program cycle lasts five to seven semesters. Completion of program requires grade of C or better in all courses.

Evaluation   Student evaluation based on tests, papers, reports. Transcripts are kept for each student.

Enrollment Requirements   College admission, letter of reference required. Program is open to non-resident foreign students. English language proficiency required. Minimum TOEFL score required: 500.

Program Costs $200 per course.

Housing and Student Services   Housing is available. Job counseling and placement services are available.

Contact   Sr. Ellen M. Desmond, Ph.D., Director, Gerontology Program, Convent Station, NJ 07961. 201-292-6386.

MARKETING MANAGEMENT AND RESEARCH (06.14)
Certificate in Marketing

General Information   Unit offering the program: Weekend College Office. Program content: Research, advertising and promotion, computers. Available for credit. Certificate signed by the Dean of Studies. Certificate applicable to B.S. in Business Administration.

Program Format Weekend classes offered. Instructional schedule: Alternate weekends. Program cycle: Continuous enrollment. Full program cycle lasts 24 credit hours. Completion of program requires grade of C or better.

Evaluation Student evaluation based on tests, papers. Grading system: Letters or numbers. Transcripts are kept for each student.

Enrollment Requirements High school diploma or GED required.

Program Costs $600 per course.

Housing and Student Services Housing is not available. Job counseling and placement services are not available.

Special Features The Weekend College curricula offerings are designed with the employed person in mind. They extend to men and women the opportunity to earn a Bachelor of Arts degree in English or a Bachelor of Science degree in Business Administration with a concentration in accounting, computer information systems, management, or marketing.

Contact Sr. Marie Jonathon Bulisok, Associate Dean, Center for Lifelong Learning, Convent Station, NJ 07961. 201-292-6348.

RELIGIOUS EDUCATION (39.04)
Certificate for Coordinators of Religious Education

General Information Unit offering the program: Office of Ministry Programs with Religious Studies and Education Departments. Available on either a credit or non-credit basis. Endorsed by Office of Evangelization/Education of the Diocese of Paterson. Certificate signed by the President.

Program Format Daytime classes offered. Instructional schedule: Once per week for 2½ hours. Program cycle: Continuous enrollment. Full program cycle lasts 4 years. Completion of program requires grade of C or better.

Evaluation Student evaluation based on tests, papers, reports. Grading system: Letters or numbers. Transcripts are kept for each student.

Enrollment Requirements College admissions required. Program is open to non-resident foreign students. English language proficiency required.

Program Costs $600 per course, five workshops at $68.

Housing and Student Services Housing is not available. Job counseling and placement services are not available.

Special Features Most candidates are presently working as coordinators of religious education programs in their parishes. The program was designed to meet their needs for greater knowledge of the areas of religious studies taught in their parishes. It also assists them, through the education department offerings, in helping their teachers better communicate religious knowledge to the different grade levels.

Contact Sr. Joanne Picciurro, Assistant Director, Parish Catechetics Division, Office of Evangelization/Education, 777 Valley Road, Clifton, NJ 07013. 201-777-8818.

RELIGIOUS EDUCATION (39.04)
Certificate in Ministry

General Information Unit offering the program: Office of Ministry Programs and Religious Studies Department. Program content: Credit and noncredit training in hospital and social justice experience. Available on either a credit or non-credit basis. Endorsed by Diocese of Metuchen. Certificate signed by the President.

Program Format Evening classes offered. Instructional schedule: Once per week for 2½ hours. Program cycle: Continuous enrollment. Full program cycle lasts 4 years. Completion of program requires grade of C or better.

Evaluation Student evaluation based on tests, papers. Grading system: Letters or numbers. Transcripts are kept for each student.

Enrollment Requirements Approval of diocese required. Program is not open to non-resident foreign students. English language proficiency required.

Program Costs $600 per course, workshops - $187.

Housing and Student Services Housing is not available. Job counseling and placement services are not available.

Special Features Students may have up to 12 credits accepted from another accredited college if taken within last ten years. All faculty members are regular full-time members of this college or adjunct instructors/professors hired for a particular course. The Diocese of Metuchen uses this program as principal means of educating permanent deacons for ordination. Diocese covers spiritual/personal and apostolic components of program.

Contact Rev. Herb Stab, Director, Permanent Diaconate, Our Lady of Fatima Church, 501 New Market Street, Piscataway, NJ 08854. 201-968-5555.

RELIGIOUS EDUCATION (39.04)
Certificate in Pastoral Ministry

General Information Unit offering the program: Office of Ministry Programs; Religious Studies, Psychology, and Sociology Departments. Available on either a credit or non-credit basis. Certificate signed by the President.

Program Format Evening classes offered. Instructional schedule: Once per week for 2½ hours. Program cycle: Continuous enrollment. Full program cycle lasts 4 years. Completion of program requires grade of C or better.

Evaluation Student evaluation based on tests, papers, reports. Grading system: Letters or numbers. Transcripts are kept for each student.

Enrollment Requirements College admissions required. Program is not open to non-resident foreign students. English language proficiency required.

Program Costs $600 per course, six workshops at $95.

Housing and Student Services Housing is not available. Job counseling and placement services are not available.

Special Features Designed to equip and assist laymen, women, and the religious who want to update themselves and enter into ministerial roles within the Church. All professors are regular faculty or adjunct.

Contact Rev. John G. Pisarcik, Director, Office of Ministry Programs, Convent Station, NJ 07961. 201-292-6305.

RELIGIOUS EDUCATION (39.04)
Certificate in Training in Pastoral Leadership (for Hispanics)

General Information Unit offering the program: Office of Ministry Programs; Religious Studies, Philosophy, and Sociology Departments. Program content: Taught completely in Spanish for present and future leaders of the community. Endorsed by Diocese of Paterson. Certificate signed by the President.

Program Format Evening classes offered. Instructional schedule: Once per week for 2½ hours. Program cycle: Continuous enrollment. Full program cycle lasts 4 years. Completion of program requires grade of C or better.

Evaluation Student evaluation based on tests, papers, reports. Grading system: Letters or numbers. Transcripts are kept for each student.

Enrollment Requirements College admissions required. Program is not open to non-resident foreign students.

Program Costs $600 per course, seven workshops at $87.

Housing and Student Services Housing is not available. Job counseling and placement services are not available.

Special Features Designed in conjunction with the Diocese of Paterson to meet the needs of the growing Hispanic community. The program equips students to share new knowledge in parish/diocese settings. All professors in the program are fluent in Spanish and English. Courses are taught on campus or at our extension site in the inner-city.

Certificate in Training in Pastoral Leadership (for Hispanics) continued

Contact Rev. John G. Pisarcik, Director, Office of Ministry Programs, Convent Station, NJ 07961. 201-292-6305.

FELICIAN COLLEGE
Lodi, New Jersey 07644

ACCOUNTING (06.02)
Accounting Systems Management

General Information Unit offering the program: Business. Program content: Accounting, business communication. Available for credit. Certificate signed by the Director of Adult Education. Certificate applicable to B.A. in Social and Behavioral Sciences.

Program Format Daytime, evening, weekend classes offered. Program cycle: Continuous enrollment. Full program cycle lasts 24 credit hours.

Evaluation Student evaluation based on tests, papers, reports, journals. Grading system: Letters or numbers. Transcripts are kept for each student.

Enrollment Requirements Program is open to non-resident foreign students. English language proficiency required.

Program Costs $480 per course.

Housing and Student Services Housing is not available. Job counseling and placement services are available.

Contact Director of Adult Education, Lodi, NJ 07644. 201-778-1190.

BUSINESS AND MANAGEMENT, GENERAL (06.01)
Business Administration

General Information Unit offering the program: Business. Program content: Business communications, marketing, management. Available for credit. Certificate signed by the Director of Adult Education. Certificate applicable to B.A. in Social and Behavioral Sciences.

Program Format Daytime, evening, weekend classes offered. Program cycle: Continuous enrollment. Full program cycle lasts 24 credit hours.

Evaluation Student evaluation based on tests, papers, reports, journals. Grading system: Letters or numbers. Transcripts are kept for each student.

Enrollment Requirements Program is open to non-resident foreign students. English language proficiency required.

Program Costs $480 per course.

Housing and Student Services Housing is not available. Job counseling and placement services are available.

Contact Director of Adult Education, Lodi, NJ 07644. 201-778-1190.

BUSINESS AND MANAGEMENT, GENERAL (06.01)
High Tech Office Management

General Information Unit offering the program: Business. Program content: Business communication, word processing, computer science. Available for credit. Certificate signed by the Director of Adult Education. Certificate applicable to B.A. in Social and Behavioral Sciences.

Program Format Daytime, evening, weekend classes offered. Program cycle: Continuous enrollment. Full program cycle lasts 24 credit hours.

Evaluation Student evaluation based on tests, papers, reports, journals. Grading system: Letters or numbers. Transcripts are kept for each student.

Enrollment Requirements Program is open to non-resident foreign students. English language proficiency required.

Program Costs $480 per course.

Housing and Student Services Housing is not available. Job counseling and placement services are available.

Contact Director of Adult Education, Lodi, NJ 07644. 201-778-1190.

COMPUTER PROGRAMMING (11.02)
Computer Programming

General Information Unit offering the program: Computer Science. Program content: Programming languages, digital electronics, systems analysis and design, data processing. Available for credit. Certificate signed by the Director of Adult Education. Certificate applicable to B.A. in Natural Science, Mathematics.

Program Format Daytime, evening, weekend classes offered. Program cycle: Continuous enrollrnent. Full program cycle lasts 4 semesters. Completion of program requires 24 credit hours.

Evaluation Student evaluation based on tests, papers, reports, journals. Grading system: Letters or numbers. Transcripts are kept for each student.

Enrollment Requirements Program is open to non-resident foreign students. English language proficiency required.

Program Costs $480 per course.

Housing and Student Services Housing is not available. Job counseling and placement services are available.

Contact Director of Adult Education, Lodi, NJ 07644. 201-778-1190.

DATA PROCESSING (11.03)
Data Processing

General Information Unit offering the program: Computer Science. Program content: Management information systems, programming languages, systems analysis and design. Available for credit. Certificate signed by the Director of Adult Education. Certificate applicable to B.A. in Natural Science, Mathematics.

Program Format Daytime, evening, weekend classes offered. Program cycle: Continuous enrollment. Full program cycle lasts 4 semesters. Completion of program requires 24 credit hours.

Evaluation Student evaluation based on tests, papers, reports, journals. Grading system: Letters or numbers. Transcripts are kept for each student.

Enrollment Requirements Program is open to non-resident foreign students. English language proficiency required.

Program Costs $480 per course.

Housing and Student Services Housing is not available. Job counseling and placement services are available.

Contact Director of Adult Education, Lodi, NJ 07644. 201-778-1190.

PERSONNEL MANAGEMENT (06.16)
Human Resource Administration

General Information Unit offering the program: Business. Program content: Human resource administration, individual and group processes, business communication. Available for credit. Certificate signed by the Director of Adult Education. Certificate applicable to B.A. in Social and Behavioral Sciences.

Program Format Daytime, evening, weekend classes offered. Program cycle: Continuous enrollment. Full program cycle lasts 24 credit hours.

Evaluation Student evaluation based on tests, papers, reports, journals. Grading system: Letters or numbers. Transcripts are kept for each student.

Enrollment Requirements Program is open to non-resident foreign students. English language proficiency required.

Program Costs $480 per course.

Housing and Student Services Housing is not available. Job counseling and placement services are available.

Contact Director of Adult Education, Lodi, NJ 07644. 201-778-1190.

PSYCHOLOGY, GENERAL (42.01)
Handwriting Analysis

General Information Unit offering the program: Psychology. Program content: Psychology of handwriting analysis, pathology, validation. Available for credit. Certificate signed by the Director of Adult Education. Certificate applicable to B.A. in Psychology.

Program Format Daytime, evening, weekend classes offered. Program cycle: Continuous enrollment. Full program cycle lasts 2 semesters. Completion of program requires 24 credit hours, research project.

Evaluation Student evaluation based on tests, papers, reports, journals. Grading system: Letters or numbers. Transcripts are kept for each student.

Enrollment Requirements Program is open to non-resident foreign students. English language proficiency required.

Program Costs $480 per course.

Housing and Student Services Housing is not available. Job counseling and placement services are available.

Contact Director of Adult Education, Lodi, NJ 07644. 201-778-1190.

RELIGION (38.02)
Religious Studies

General Information Unit offering the program: Department of Religious Studies. Program content: Old and New Testament, world religions, contemporary moral issues, psychology of religion. Available for credit. Cosponsored by Diocese of Metuchen. Certificate signed by the Director of Adult Education. Certificate applicable to B.A. in Religious Studies.

Program Format Daytime, evening, weekend classes offered. Program cycle: Continuous enrollment. Complete program cycle lasts two to five years. Completion of program requires grade of C or better, 24 credit hours.

Evaluation Student evaluation based on tests, papers, reports, journals. Grading system: Letters or numbers. Transcripts are kept for each student.

Enrollment Requirements Program is open to non-resident foreign students. English language proficiency required.

Program Costs $480 per course.

Housing and Student Services Housing is not available. Job counseling and placement services are available.

Contact Director of Adult Education, Lodi, NJ 07644. 201-778-1190.

NUCEA MEMBER
RUTGERS, THE STATE UNIVERSITY OF NEW JERSEY, COOK COLLEGE
New Brunswick, New Jersey 08903

LABOR/INDUSTRIAL RELATIONS (06.11)
Union Leadership Academy Diploma

General Information Unit offering the program: Labor Education Department. Program content: Labor leadership, trade union administration, labor law, labor and society, labor and the economy, labor and the government, theories of labor movement, contemporary labor problems. Available on a non-credit basis. Cosponsored by Labor Studies Departments of Pennsylvania State University, West Virginia Univesity, Essex County College. Certificate signed by the Director, Institute of Management and Labor Relations.

Program Format Evening classes offered. Program cycle: Continuous enrollment. Full program cycle lasts 4 semesters. Completion of program requires eight courses.

Evaluation Student evaluation based on papers, reports. Transcripts are kept for each student.

Enrollment Requirements Program is open to non-resident foreign students.

Program Costs $200 for the program, $25 per course.

Housing and Student Services Housing is not available. Job counseling and placement services are not available.

Contact Mr. Robert A. Steffen, Extension Specialist, Labor Education Center, Cook Campus, New Brunswick, NJ 08903. 201-932-9503.

RUTGERS, THE STATE UNIVERSITY OF NEW JERSEY, NEW BRUNSWICK
New Brunswick, New Jersey 08903

COMMUNITY SERVICES (44.02)
Certificate in Volunteer Management

General Information Unit offering the program: Continuing Education Program, School of Social Work. Program content: Personnel and fiscal management, organization design, marketing, program evaluation. Available on a non-credit basis. Certificate signed by the Director, Continuing Education Program, School of Social Work.

Program Format Daytime classes offered. Program cycle: Continuous enrollment. Full program cycle lasts 2 years.

Evaluation Student evaluation based on work flows, training designs, budget preparation. Record of CEUs kept for each student.

Enrollment Requirements Program is open to non-resident foreign students. English language proficiency required.

Housing and Student Services Housing is not available. Job counseling and placement services are not available.

Contact Ms. Patricia C. Dunn, Ed.D., Director, Continuing Education and School of Social Work, Building 4087, Kilmer Campus, New Brunswick, NJ 08903. 201-932-3178.

INDIVIDUAL AND FAMILY DEVELOPMENT (19.07)
Post-Master's Certificate in Gerontology

General Information Unit offering the program: Continuing Education Program, School of Social Work. Program content: Research, intervention with elderly. Available on either a credit or non-credit basis. Certificate signed by the Director, Continuing Education Program, School of Social Work.

Program Format Daytime, evening classes offered. Program cycle: Continuous enrollment. Completion of program requires six credit hours, 66 contact hours, 120 hours of practicum.

Evaluation Student evaluation based on tests, practicum. Grading system: Pass/fail. Record of CEUs kept for each student.

Enrollment Requirements Master's degree required. Program is open to non-resident foreign students. English language proficiency required.

Housing and Student Services Housing is not available. Job counseling and placement services are not available.

Contact Ms. Patricia C. Dunn, Ed.D., Director, Continuing Education and School of Social Work, Building 4087, Kilmer Campus, New Brunswick, NJ 08903. 201-932-3178.

LIBRARY AND ARCHIVAL SCIENCES, GENERAL (25.01)
Sixth-Year Specialist Program in Library Service

General Information   Unit offering the program: Professional Development Studies; School of Communication, Information, and Library Studies. Program content: Program planning and evaluating, research methods. Available for credit. Certificate signed by the Dean.

Program Format   Daytime, evening classes offered. Program cycle: Continuous enrollment. Full program cycle lasts 24 credit hours. Completion of program requires thesis.

Evaluation   Student evaluation based on papers. Grading system: Letters or numbers. Transcripts are kept for each student.

Enrollment Requirements   M.L.S., two years experience, statement of objectives, independent study proposal required. Program is open to non-resident foreign students. English language proficiency required. Minimum TOEFL score required: 600.

Program Costs $3300 for the program, $126 per credit hour.

Housing and Student Services   Housing is not available. Job counseling and placement services are available.

Contact   Ms. Jana Varless, Director, Professional Development Studies, School of Communication, Information, and Library Studies, 4 Huntington Street, New Brunswick, NJ 08903. 201-932-7169.

PUBLIC ADMINISTRATION (44.04)
Certificate for Municipal Welfare Directors

General Information   Unit offering the program: Continuing Education Program, School of Social Work. Program content: Counseling techniques; roles, function, and values of welfare directors; handling crisis situation. Available on a non-credit basis. Endorsed by Municipal Welfare Directors' Association of New Jersey. Cosponsored by New Jersey Division of Public Welfare, Department of Human Services. Certificate signed by the Director, Continuing Education Program, School of Social Work.

Program Format   Daytime classes offered. Program cycle: Continuous enrollment. Full program cycle lasts 2 years. Completion of program requires five workshops, one elective.

Evaluation   Student evaluation based on assignments. Record of CEUs kept for each student.

Enrollment Requirements   Limited to municipal welfare directors. Program is not open to non-resident foreign students. English language proficiency required.

Housing and Student Services   Housing is not available. Job counseling and placement services are not available.

Contact   Ms. Patricia C. Dunn, Ed.D., Director, Continuing Education Program, School of Social Work, Building 4087, Kilmer Campus, New Brunswick, NJ 08903. 201-932-3178.

PUBLIC ADMINISTRATION (44.04)
Post-Master's Certificate in Human Service Administration

General Information   Unit offering the program: Continuing Education Program, School of Social Work. Program content: Management and administration. Available for credit. Certificate signed by the Director, Continuing Education Program, School of Social Work. Certificate applicable to M.S.W.

Program Format   Daytime classes offered. Program cycle: Continuous enrollment. Full program cycle lasts 4 semesters.

Evaluation   Student evaluation based on tests, papers. Grading system: Letters or numbers. Transcripts are kept for each student.

Enrollment Requirements   Master's degree required. Program is open to non-resident foreign students. English language proficiency required.

Housing and Student Services   Housing is not available. Job counseling and placement services are not available.

Contact   Ms. Patricia C. Dunn, Ed.D., Director, Continuing Education and School of Social Work, Building 4087, Kilmer Campus, New Brunswick, NJ 08903. 201-932-3178.

SAINT PETER'S COLLEGE
Jersey City, New Jersey 07306

BUSINESS AND MANAGEMENT, GENERAL (06.01)
Business Management Certificate

General Information   Unit offering the program: Department of Marketing and Management. Program content: Business communication, management, organizational behavior, marketing, general survey and contracts, computers, information processing, accounting. Available for credit. Certificate signed by the Academic Dean, Evening Session. Certificate applicable to B.S. in Business Management.

Program Format   Evening, weekend classes offered. Instructional schedule: Two evenings per week or Saturdays. Program cycle: Continuous enrollment. Full program cycle lasts 10 courses. Completion of program requires 2.0 GPA.

Evaluation   Student evaluation methods vary by course. Grading system: Letters or numbers. Transcripts are kept for each student.

Enrollment Requirements   Bachelor's degree (non-business major) required. Program is open to non-resident foreign students. English language proficiency required. College-administered exam.

Program Costs $172 per credit hour.

Housing and Student Services   Housing is available. Job counseling and placement services are available.

Contact   Ms. Judy Casey, Director of Evening Admissions, 2641 Kennedy Boulevard, Jersey City, NJ 07306. 201-333-4400 Ext. 504.

BUSINESS AND MANAGEMENT, GENERAL (06.01)
General Business Certificate

General Information   Unit offering the program: Department of Marketing and Management. Program content: Business communications, management, marketing, economics, accounting, introduction to computers and information processing, general surveys and contracts. Available for credit. Certificate signed by the Academic Dean, Evening Session. Certificate applicable to A.A., B.S. in Business Management.

Program Format   Evening, weekend classes offered. Instructional schedule: Two evenings per week or Saturdays. Program cycle: Continuous enrollment. Full program cycle lasts 11 courses. Completion of program requires 2.0 GPA.

Evaluation   Student evaluation methods vary by course. Grading system: Letters or numbers. Transcripts are kept for each student.

Enrollment Requirements   Bachelor's degree (non-business major) required. Program is open to non-resident foreign students. English language proficiency required. College-administered exam.

Program Costs $172 per credit hour.

Housing and Student Services   Housing is available. Job counseling and placement services are available.

Contact Ms. Judy Casey, Director of Evening Admissions, 2641 Kennedy Boulevard, Jersey City, NJ 07306. 201-333-4400 Ext. 504.

BUSINESS AND MANAGEMENT, GENERAL (06.01)
Management Certificate

General Information Unit offering the program: Department of Marketing and Management. Program content: Organizational behavior, accounting, management, marketing, introduction to computers and information processing, general survey and contracts. Available for credit. Certificate signed by the Academic Dean, Evening Session. Certificate applicable to A.A., B.S. in Business Management.

Program Format Evening, weekend classes offered. Instructional schedule: Two evenings per week or Saturdays. Program cycle: Continuous enrollment. Full program cycle lasts 10 courses. Completion of program requires 2.0 GPA.

Evaluation Student evaluation methods vary by course. Grading system: Letters or numbers. Transcripts are kept for each student.

Enrollment Requirements College admissions required. Program is open to non-resident foreign students. English language proficiency required. College-administered exam.

Program Costs $172 per credit hour.

Housing and Student Services Housing is available. Job counseling and placement services are available.

Contact Ms. Judy Casey, Director of Evening Admissions, 2641 Kennedy Boulevard, Jersey City, NJ 07306. 201-333-4400 Ext. 504.

BUSINESS DATA PROCESSING AND RELATED PROGRAMS (07.03)
Business Systems Certificate

General Information Unit offering the program: Computer Science. Program content: Business information systems, systems analysis, COBOL, report-generating software for managers, accounting. Available for credit. Certificate signed by the Academic Dean, Evening Session. Certificate applicable to A.A. in Data Processing, B.S. in Computer Science.

Program Format Evening, weekend classes offered. Instructional schedule: Two evenins per week or Saturdays. Program cycle: Continuous enrollment. Full program cycle lasts 11 courses. Completion of program requires 2.0 GPA.

Evaluation Student evaluation methods vary by course. Grading system: Letters or numbers. Transcripts are kept for each student.

Enrollment Requirements College admissions required. Program is open to non-resident foreign students. English language proficiency required. College-administered exam.

Program Costs $172 per credit hour.

Housing and Student Services Housing is available. Job counseling and placement services are available.

Contact Ms. Judy Casey, Director of Evening Admissions, 2641 Kennedy Boulevard, Jersey City, NJ 07306. 201-333-4400 Ext. 504.

COMPUTER PROGRAMMING (11.02)
Computer Programming Certificate

General Information Unit offering the program: Computer Science. Program content: COBOL, business information systems, information processing, accounting, report generating software, 360 BAL programming. Available for credit. Certificate

signed by the Academic Dean, Evening Session. Certificate applicable to A.A. in Data Processing, B.S. in Computer Science.

Program Format Evening, weekend classes offered. Instructional schedule: Two evenings per week or Saturdays. Program cycle: Continuous enrollment. Full program cycle lasts 11 courses. Completion of program requires 2.0 GPA.

Evaluation Student evaluation methods vary by course. Grading system: Letters or numbers. Transcripts are kept for each student.

Enrollment Requirements College admissions required. Program is open to non-resident foreign students. English language proficiency required. College-administered exam.

Program Costs $5676 for the program, $172 per credit hour.

Housing and Student Services Housing is available. Job counseling and placement services are available.

Special Features Previous college courses, CLEP, learning experiences, and portfolio evaluation may account for 15 credits in this program, but 12 credits minimum in data processing and computer science must be earned at Saint Peter's College.

Contact Ms. Judy Casey, Director of Evening Admissions, 2641 Kennedy Boulevard, Jersey City, NJ 07306. 201-333-4400 Ext. 504.

FOOD MARKETING (08.06)
World-Wide Food Marketing Certificate

General Information Unit offering the program: Department of Marketing and Management. Program content: Business communication, food marketing, procurement and distribution of food, consumption patterns and purchasing behavior. Available for credit. Certificate signed by the Academic Dean, Evening Session. Certificate applicable to A.A., B.S. in Marketing Management.

Program Format Evening, weekend classes offered. Instructional schedule: Two nights per week or Saturdays. Program cycle: Continuous enrollment. Full program cycle lasts 11 courses. Completion of program requires 2.0 GPA.

Evaluation Student evaluation methods vary by course. Grading system: Letters or numbers. Transcripts are kept for each student.

Enrollment Requirements College admissions required. Program is open to non-resident foreign students. English language proficiency required. College-administered exam.

Program Costs $172 per credit hour.

Housing and Student Services Housing is available. Job counseling and placement services are available.

Contact Ms. Judy Casey, Director of Evening Admissions, 2641 Kennedy Boulevard, Jersey City, NJ 07306. 201-333-4400 Ext. 504.

HEALTH SERVICES ADMINISTRATION (18.07)
Health Care Management Certificate

General Information Unit offering the program: Program in Health Care Management. Program content: Business communications, health care management, marketing concepts in health care, hospital organizational behavior, accounting and budgeting for nonprofit organizations, legal aspects of health care, elementary Spanish. Available for credit. Certificate signed by the Academic Dean, Evening Session. Certificate applicable to B.S. in Health Care Management.

Program Format Evening, weekend classes offered. Instructional schedule: Two nights per week or Saturdays. Program cycle: Continuous enrollment. Full program cycle lasts 10 courses. Completion of program requires 2.0 GPA.

Evaluation Student evaluation methods vary by course. Grading system: Letters or numbers. Transcripts are kept for each student.

Health Care Management Certificate continued

Enrollment Requirements Bachelor's degree in an allied health field or nursing required. Program is open to non-resident foreign students. English language proficiency required. College-administered exam.

Program Costs $172 per credit hour.

Housing and Student Services Housing is available. Job counseling and placement services are available.

Contact Ms. Judy Casey, Director of Evening Admissions, 2641 Kennedy Boulevard, Jersey City, NJ 07306. 201-333-4400 Ext. 504.

MARKETING MANAGEMENT AND RESEARCH (06.14)
Marketing Certificate

General Information Unit offering the program: Department of Marketing and Management. Program content: Marketing, management, organizational behavior, general survey and contracts, introduction to computers and information processing, accounting. Available for credit. Certificate signed by the Academic Dean, Evening Session. Certificate applicable to A.A., B.S. in Business Management.

Program Format Evening, weekend classes offered. Instructional schedule: Two nights per week or Saturdays. Program cycle: Continuous enrollment. Full program cycle lasts 10 courses. Completion of program requires 2.0 GPA.

Evaluation Student evaluation methods vary by course. Grading system: Letters or numbers. Transcripts are kept for each student.

Enrollment Requirements College admissions required. Program is open to non-resident foreign students. English language proficiency required. College-administered exam.

Program Costs $172 per credit hour.

Housing and Student Services Housing is available. Job counseling and placement services are available.

Contact Ms. Judy Casey, Director of Evening Admissions, 2641 Kennedy Boulevard, Jersey City, NJ 07306. 201-333-4400 Ext. 504.

MARKETING MANAGEMENT AND RESEARCH (06.14)
Marketing Management Certificate

General Information Unit offering the program: Department of Marketing and Management. Program content: Marketing, business communication, consumer behavior, management, accounting, computers and information processing, general survey and contracts. Available for credit. Certificate signed by the Academic Dean, Evening Session. Certificate applicable to A.A., B.S. in Marketing Management.

Program Format Evening, weekend classes offered. Instructional schedule: Two nights per week or Saturdays. Program cycle: Continuous enrollment. Full program cycle lasts 10 courses. Completion of program requires 2.0 GPA.

Evaluation Student evaluation methods vary by course. Grading system: Letters or numbers. Transcripts are kept for each student.

Enrollment Requirements Bachelor's degree (non-business major) required. Program is open to non-resident foreign students. English language proficiency required. College-administered exam.

Program Costs $172 per credit hour.

Housing and Student Services Housing is available. Job counseling and placement services are available.

Contact Ms. Judy Casey, Director of Evening Admissions, 2641 Kennedy Boulevard, Jersey City, NJ 07306. 201-333-4400 Ext. 504.

STEVENS INSTITUTE OF TECHNOLOGY
Hoboken, New Jersey 07030

BUSINESS ADMINISTRATION AND MANAGEMENT (06.04)
Engineering Management

General Information Unit offering the program: Department of Management. Program content: Managerial accouting, management science models, organizational behavior and theory, project management. Available for credit. Certificate signed by the President. Certificate applicable to M.S. in Information Management.

Program Format Evening classes offered. Instructional schedule: 2½ hours per week. Students may enroll fall, spring. Full program cycle lasts 2 semesters. Completion of program requires final examinations.

Evaluation Student evaluation based on tests, papers, reports, projects. Grading system: Letters or numbers. Transcripts are kept for each student.

Enrollment Requirements Bachelor's degree required. Program is open to non-resident foreign students. English language proficiency required.

Program Costs $3750 for the program, $375 per credit hour.

Housing and Student Services Housing is not available. Job counseling and placement services are available.

Special Features Lawrence Schacht Management Laboratory with seminar room; conference rooms tied together with flexible audiovisual system enabling monitoring and remote control. Lab is augmented by computer lab.

Contact Dr. Arthur Shapiro, Coordinator of Management Programs, Department of Management, Stevens Institute of Technology, Hoboken, NJ 07030. 201-420-5384.

CELL AND MOLECULAR BIOLOGY (26.04)
Chemical Physiology

General Information Unit offering the program: Chemistry. Program content: Physiology, biochemistry and laboratory, drug action. Available for credit. Certificate signed by the President. Certificate applicable to M.S. in Chemical Biology.

Program Format Evening classes offered. Instructional schedule: Two evenings per week. Program cycle: Continuous enrollment. Full program cycle lasts 2 semesters. Completion of program requires four courses.

Evaluation Student evaluation based on tests, papers, reports. Grading system: Letters or numbers. Transcripts are kept for each student.

Enrollment Requirements Bachelor's degree in biology or chemistry required. Program is open to non-resident foreign students. English language proficiency required. Minimum TOEFL score required: 500.

Program Costs $3750 for the program, $938 per course.

Housing and Student Services Housing is available. Job counseling and placement services are available.

Contact Dr. Ronald S. Kane, Dean of Graduate Studies and Continuing Education, Hoboken, NJ 07030. 201-420-5234.

CHEMICAL ENGINEERING (14.07)
Fundamentals of Modern Chemical Engineering

General Information Unit offering the program: Chemical Engineering. Program content: Computer modeling and elements of mass/energy balancing, reactor design and separations. Available on a non-credit basis. Certificate signed by the President. Certificate applicable to M.E. in Chemical Engineering.

Program Format Evening classes offered. Instructional schedule: Two evenings per week. Program cycle: Continuous enrollment. Full program cycle lasts 2 semesters.

Evaluation Student evaluation based on tests, papers, reports. Grading system: Letters or numbers. Transcripts are kept for each student.

Enrollment Requirements Bachelor's degree in science or engineering required. Program is open to non-resident foreign students. English language proficiency required. Minimum TOEFL score required: 500.

Program Costs $3750 for the program, $938 per course.

Housing and Student Services Housing is available. Job counseling and placement services are available.

Special Features The program has successfully prepared many chemists, physicists, and mechanical or civil engineers for graduate study in chemical engineering. It has also permitted practicing chemical engineers to up-date their expertise in modern chemical engineering to make use of computational methods and some of the new high technology areas of chemical engineering.

Contact Dr. Ronald S. Kane, Dean of Graduate Studies and Continuing Education, Hoboken, NJ 07030. 201-420-5234.

CHEMISTRY (40.05)
Bio-Medical Chemistry

General Information Unit offering the program: Chemistry. Program content: Drug action, medicinal chemistry, bio-organic and physical organic chemistry. Available for credit. Certificate signed by the President. Certificate applicable to M.S. in Chemistry.

Program Format Evening classes offered. Instructional schedule: Two evenings per week. Program cycle: Continuous enrollment. Full program cycle lasts 2 semesters.

Evaluation Student evaluation based on tests, papers, reports. Grading system: Letters or numbers. Transcripts are kept for each student.

Enrollment Requirements Bachelor's degree in chemistry required. Program is open to non-resident foreign students. English language proficiency required. Minimum TOEFL score required: 500.

Program Costs $3750 for the program, $938 per course.

Housing and Student Services Housing is available. Job counseling and placement services are available.

Contact Dr. Ronald S. Kane, Dean of Graduate Studies and Continuing Education, Hoboken, NJ 07030. 201-420-5234.

CHEMISTRY (40.05)
Instrumental Analysis

General Information Unit offering the program: Chemistry. Program content: Chemical analysis theory and laboratory, instrument design, spectroscopy. Available for credit. Certificate signed by the President. Certificate applicable to M.S. in Chemistry.

Program Format Evening classes offered. Instructional schedule: Two evenings per week. Program cycle: Continuous enrollment. Full program cycle lasts 2 semesters.

Evaluation Student evaluation based on tests, papers, reports. Grading system: Letters or numbers. Transcripts are kept for each student.

Enrollment Requirements Bachelor's degree in chemistry required. Program is open to non-resident foreign students. English language proficiency required. Minimum TOEFL score required: 500.

Program Costs $3750 for the program, $938 per course.

Housing and Student Services Housing is available. Job counseling and placement services are available.

Special Features The highly focused grouping of courses is aimed at understanding the theoretical and practical bases of chemical instrumentation and how it is used. Laboratory provides hands-on experience in instrumentation design and in the operation of sophisticated instruments such as NMR, GC-MS, etc.

Contact Dr. Ronald S. Kane, Dean of Graduate Studies and Continuing Education, Hoboken, NJ 07030. 201-420-5234.

ELECTRICAL AND ELECTRONIC TECHNOLOGIES (15.03)
Certificate of Special Study in Control Systems

General Information Unit offering the program: Electrical Engineering and Computer Science. Available for credit. Certificate signed by the Dean of Graduate School. Certificate applicable to M.E. in Electrical Engineering.

Program Format Evening classes offered. Instructional schedule: One evening per week. Program cycle: Continuous enrollment. Complete program cycle lasts two to four semesters. Completion of program requires homework, written examinations.

Evaluation Student evaluation based on tests. Grading system: Letters or numbers. Transcripts are kept for each student.

Enrollment Requirements Bachelor's degree in electrical engineering, B average in major required. Program is open to non-resident foreign students. English language proficiency required. Minimum TOEFL score required: 500.

Housing and Student Services Housing is available. Job counseling and placement services are available.

Special Features Courses taught by Stevens' electrical engineering faculty. Many students enrolled in these courses are working toward a master's degree, and these courses can be used as credit toward a master's or Ph.D. by any student. The courses are Analog and Digital Control Theory I and II, Digital Controls, and Selected Topics in Modern Control.

Contact Dr. Francis T. Boesch, Department Head, Electrical Engineering and Computer Science, Hoboken, NJ 07030. 201-420-5623.

ELECTRICAL AND ELECTRONIC TECHNOLOGIES (15.03)
Certificate of Special Study in Instrumentation

General Information Unit offering the program: Electrical Engineering and Computer Science. Available for credit. Certificate signed by the Dean of Graduate School. Certificate applicable to M.E. in Electrical Engineering.

Program Format Evening classes offered. Instructional schedule: One evening per week. Program cycle: Continuous enrollment. Complete program cycle lasts two to four semesters. Completion of program requires homework, written examinations.

Evaluation Student evaluation based on tests. Grading system: Letters or numbers. Transcripts are kept for each student.

Enrollment Requirements Bachelor's degree in electrical engineering, B average in major required. Program is open to non-resident foreign students. English language proficiency required. Minimum TOEFL score required: 500.

Housing and Student Services Housing is available. Job counseling and placement services are available.

Special Features Courses taught by Stevens' electrical engineering faculty. Many students enrolled in these courses are working toward a master's degree, and these courses can be used as credit toward a master's or Ph.D. by any student. The courses are Data Acquisition and Processing I and II, Microprocessor and Microcomputer Systems I, Digital Control Theory.

Contact Dr. Francis T. Boesch, Department Head, Electrical Engineering and Computer Science, Hoboken, NJ 07030. 201-420-5623.

ELECTRICAL AND ELECTRONIC TECHNOLOGIES (15.03)
Certificate of Special Study in Modern Filter Synthesis

General Information Unit offering the program: Electrical Engineering and Computer Science. Available for credit. Certificate signed by the Dean of Graduate School. Certificate applicable to M.E. in Electrical Engineering.

Program Format Evening classes offered. Instructional schedule: One evening per week. Program cycle: Continuous enrollment. Complete program cycle lasts two to four semesters. Completion of program requires homework, written examinations.

Evaluation Student evaluation based on tests. Grading system: Letters or numbers. Transcripts are kept for each student.

Enrollment Requirements Bachelor's degree in electrical engineering, B average in major required. Program is open to non-resident foreign students. English language proficiency required. Minimum TOEFL score required: 500.

Housing and Student Services Housing is available. Job counseling and placement services are available.

Special Features Courses taught by Stevens' electrical engineering faculty. Many students enrolled in these courses are working toward a master's degree, and these courses can be used as credit toward a master's or Ph.D by any student. The courses are Active and Passive Distributed Signal Processing I and II, and Digital Signal Processing I and II.

Contact Dr. Francis T. Boesch, Department Head, Electrical Engineering and Computer Science, Hoboken, NJ 07030. 201-420-5623.

MATERIALS ENGINEERING (14.18)
Polymer Processing

General Information Unit offering the program: Chemical Engineering. Program content: Transport process, rheology, processing. Available for credit. Certificate signed by the President. Certificate applicable to M.E. in Chemical Engineering.

Program Format Evening classes offered. Instructional schedule: Two evenings per week. Program cycle: Continuous enrollment. Full program cycle lasts 2 semesters.

Evaluation Student evaluation based on tests, papers, reports. Grading system: Letters or numbers. Transcripts are kept for each student.

Enrollment Requirements Bachelor's degree in science or engineering required. Program is open to non-resident foreign students. English language proficiency required. Minimum TOEFL score required: 500.

Program Costs $3750 for the program, $938 per course.

Housing and Student Services Housing is available. Job counseling and placement services are available.

Contact Dr. Ronald S. Kane, Dean of Graduate Studies and Continuing Education, Hoboken, NJ 07030. 201-420-5234.

MATHEMATICS AND COMPUTER SCIENCE (30.08)
Certificate in Computer Mathematics

General Information Unit offering the program: Mathematics. Program content: Mathematics and computer programming. Available on a non-credit basis. Certificate signed by the Director of Certificate Program in Computer Mathematics.

Program Format Daytime, evening classes offered. Instructional schedule: One evening per week (academic year); five days per week (summer). Students enroll July 1. Full program cycle lasts 15 months.

Evaluation Student evaluation based on tests, projects. Grading system: Pass/fail. Record of completion kept by Mathematics Department.

Enrollment Requirements Limited to New Jersey high school math teachers. Program is not open to non-resident foreign students.

Program Costs Summer tuition free, $600 for the academic year.

Housing and Student Services Housing is available. Job counseling and placement services are not available.

Special Features Program enhances math skills of teachers and gives them the wherewithal to teach all high school computing courses. Participants are taught precalculus, calculus, computer mathematics, BASIC, and Pascal.

Contact Dr. L. E. Levine, Director, Certificate Program in Computer Math, Hoboken, NJ 07030. 201-420-5427.

MECHANICAL AND RELATED TECHNOLOGIES (15.08)
Mini-Graduate Program—Structural Analysis of Materials

General Information Unit offering the program: Materials and Metallurgical Engineering. Program content: X-ray, electron diffraction, and microscopy in the characterization of materials. Available for credit. Certificate signed by the President. Certificate applicable to M.S. in Materials.

Program Format Evening classes offered. Instructional schedule: One evening per week. Courses offered once per year or alternate years. Full program cycle lasts 4 semesters. Completion of program requires average grade of B or better, four courses, ten credit hours.

Evaluation Student evaluation based on tests. Grading system: Letters or numbers. Transcripts are kept for each student.

Enrollment Requirements Bachelor's degree in science or engineering required. Program is open to non-resident foreign students. English language proficiency required. Minimum TOEFL score required: 500.

Housing and Student Services Housing is available. Job counseling and placement services are available.

Contact Mr. Rolf Weil, Professor of Materials and Metallurgical Engineering, Hoboken, NJ 07030. 201-420-5257.

MECHANICAL AND RELATED TECHNOLOGIES (15.08)
Mini-Graduate Program—Surface Modification of Materials

General Information Unit offering the program: Materials and Metallurgical Engineering. Program content: Basic aspects of material surfaces and their modification for engineering applications. Available for credit. Certificate signed by the President. Certificate applicable to M.S. in Materials.

Program Format Evening classes offered. Instructional schedule: One evening per week. Courses offered once per year of alternate years. Full program cycle lasts 4 semesters. Completion of program requires ten credits, average grade of B or better.

Evaluation Student evaluation based on tests. Grading system: Letters or numbers. Transcripts are kept for each student.

Enrollment Requirements Bachelor's degree in science or engineering required. Program is open to non-resident foreign students. English language proficiency required. Minimum TOEFL score required: 500.

Housing and Student Services Housing is available. Job counseling and placement services are available.

Contact Mr. Rolf Weil, Professor of Materials and Metallurgical Engineering, Hoboken, NJ 07030. 201-420-5257.

NEW MEXICO

NUCEA MEMBER
UNIVERSITY OF NEW MEXICO
Albuquerque, New Mexico 87131

BUSINESS AND MANAGEMENT, GENERAL (06.01)
The Certificate in Management Program

General Information Unit offering the program: Continuing Education. Available on a non-credit basis. Cosponsored by American Management Association. Certificate signed by the Dean, Continuing Education.

Program Format Daytime, evening, weekend classes offered. Program cycle: Continuous enrollment. Complete program cycle lasts one to two years.

Evaluation Student evaluation based on tests, papers, reports. Records are kept for each student.

Enrollment Requirements Program is open to non-resident foreign students. English language proficiency required.

Program Costs $165 per course.

Contact Mr. Dick Croghon, Associate Director, 1634 University Boulevard, NE, Albuquerque, NM 87131. 505-277-2511.

NEW YORK

ADELPHI UNIVERSITY
Garden City, New York 11530

TAXATION (06.19)
Professional Diploma in Financial Planning

General Information Unit offering the program: University College. Program content: Management of personal financial affairs, technical and professional skills, guidelines for ethical standards. Available on either a credit or non-credit basis. Endorsed by International Board of Standards and Practices for Certified Financial Planners, New York State Board of Accountancy. Certificate signed by the Dean. Certificate applicable to B.S. in Management and Communications.

Program Format Evening, weekend classes offered. Instructional schedule: Once per week. Students may enroll fall, spring, summer. Completion of program requires six courses, 3.0 GPA.

Evaluation Student evaluation based on tests, papers, reports, case studies, quizzes. Grading system: Letters or numbers. Transcripts are kept for each student.

Enrollment Requirements Twenty-one years of age, ability to perform college-level work required. Program is open to non-resident foreign students.

Program Costs $515 per course.

Housing and Student Services Housing is not available. Job counseling and placement services are available.

Special Features Comprehensive nondegree, postbaccalaureate-level program consisting of six practical business-oriented courses. Designed to aid professionals in developing overall financial strategies for clients. Faculty is composed of distinguished attorneys, securities brokers, bankers, and insurance executives, who bring their expertise and experience to the classroom. Thirteen hundred students have graduated from the program.

Contact Ms. Christina Muccioli, Coordinator of Special Programs, South Avenue, Garden City, NY 11530. 516-663-1045.

BARUCH COLLEGE OF THE CITY UNIVERSITY OF NEW YORK
New York, New York 10010

BUSINESS ADMINISTRATION AND MANAGEMENT (06.04)
Purchasing Management Certificate

General Information Unit offering the program: Continuing Studies. Program content: Professional level purchasing education. Available on a non-credit basis. Endorsed by National Association of Purchasing Management. Certificate signed by the Director of Continuing Studies. Program fulfills requirements for Certified Purchasing Manager (CPM).

Program Format Evening classes offered. Instructional schedule: One evening per week. Program cycle: Continuous enrollment. Full program cycle lasts 6 courses.

Evaluation Student evaluation based on tests, papers, reports. Grading system: Letters or numbers. Transcripts are kept for each student.

Enrollment Requirements Program is open to non-resident foreign students.

Program Costs $930 for the program, $155 per course.

Housing and Student Services Housing is not available. Job counseling and placement services are not available.

Special Features The Purchasing Management Certificate Program offers professional level education to current practitioners and career aspirants. Instructors are senior managers and have many years of practical experience. The curriculum covers vendor relations, materials/inventory management, negotiations, economics, legalities/ethics, and computers. Two Certified Purchasing Manager (CPM) points are awarded upon completion of each course.

Contact Mr. John Maxwell, Business Programs Manager, 17 Lexington Avenue, Box 391, New York, NY 10010. 212-725-7172.

BUSINESS AND MANAGEMENT, GENERAL (06.01)
Business Management Certificate

General Information Unit offering the program: Continuing Studies. Available on a non-credit basis. Cosponsored by Education Services/Citibank, N.A. Certificate signed by the Director of Continuing Studies.

Program Format Evening, weekend classes offered. Instructional schedule: One evening per week. Program cycle: Continuous enrollment. Full program cycle lasts 6 courses.

Evaluation Student evaluation based on tests, papers, reports, projects. Grading system: Letters or numbers, pass/fail. Transcripts are kept for each student.

Enrollment Requirements Program is open to non-resident foreign students.

Program Costs $930 for the program, $155 per course.

Housing and Student Services Housing is not available. Job counseling and placement services are not available.

Special Features The Business Management Certificate offers a curriculum which includes: advertising, accounting, finance, investments, international business, human resources, management, marketing, sales, and writing. Instructors are primarily drawn from senior positions in industry. A general program of study or one which is concentrated in a specific area of inquiry may be pursued.

Business Management Certificate continued

Contact Mr. John Maxwell, Business Programs Manager, 17 Lexington Avenue, Box 391, New York, NY 10010. 212-725-7172.

COMPUTER AND INFORMATION SCIENCES, GENERAL (11.01)
Comprehensive Microcomputer Training Program

General Information Unit offering the program: Continuing Studies. Program content: DOS, Lotus 1-2-3, dBase III Plus. Available on a non-credit basis. Certificate signed by the Director of Continuing Studies.

Program Format Daytime, evening classes offered. Instructional schedule: Two evenings or four days per week or all day Saturday. Students may enroll October, March, June. Complete program cycle lasts six months (day), one year (evening or weekend).

Evaluation Student evaluation based on tests, computer assignments and lab work. Grading system: Letters or numbers. Transcripts are kept for each student.

Enrollment Requirements College experience helpful but not required. Program is open to non-resident foreign students.

Program Costs $2800 for the program, $475 per course.

Housing and Student Services Housing is not available. Job counseling and placement services are available.

Special Features The program was developed to provide entry-level skills in microcomputer programming and covers DOS, Lotus 1-2-3, dBase III Plus, survey of word processors, the BASIC language, and advanced topics such as networking and current trends. Instructors represent the business community. Program changes to meet trends. Students use IBM equipment.

Contact Ms. Randi Baker, Manager, Computer Programs, 17 Lexington Avenue, Box 391, New York, NY 10010. 212-725-7172.

COMPUTER PROGRAMMING (11.02)
Comprehensive Computer Programming Training Program

General Information Unit offering the program: Continuing Studies. Program content: COBOL/assembler training for business on IBM equipment. Available on a non-credit basis. Certificate signed by the Director of Continuing Studies.

Program Format Daytime, evening classes offered. Instructional schedule: Four days or two evenings per week. Students may enroll October, March, June. Complete program cycle lasts eight months (day), fifteen months (evening). Completion of program requires average grade of C or better.

Evaluation Student evaluation based on tests, computer programming assignments, labwork. Grading system: Letters or numbers. Transcripts are kept for each student.

Enrollment Requirements College degree helpful but not required. Program is open to non-resident foreign students.

Program Costs $2800 for the program, $375 per course.

Housing and Student Services Housing is not available. Job counseling and placement services are available.

Special Features Program is ten years old and well respected by many banks, corporations, and businesses. Course focuses on COBOL using IBM equipment but includes Assembler, microcomputers, and OS/JCL. Instructors are from the business community, and many have advanced degrees. Program changes to meet current trends.

Contact Ms. Randi Baker, Manager, Computer Programs, 17 Lexington Avenue, Box 391, New York, NY 10010. 212-725-7172.

DATA PROCESSING (11.03)
Data Processing Certificate Program

General Information Unit offering the program: Continuing Studies. Program content: Computer applications specializing in data processing. Available on a non-credit basis. Certificate signed by the Director of Continuing Studies.

Program Format Daytime, evening, weekend classes offered. Instructional schedule: Once per week for two hours. Students may enroll January, March, May, June, October.

Evaluation Student evaluation based on tests, reports. Grading system: Letters or numbers, pass/fail. Transcripts are kept for each student.

Enrollment Requirements Program is open to non-resident foreign students.

Program Costs $1050–$1500 for the program, $30–$375 per course.

Housing and Student Services Housing is not available. Job counseling and placement services are not available.

Special Features Students may select from a wide range of courses: introductory courses to state-of-the-art languages, such as FOCUS, C, Microcomputer Hardware, and Networking. Instructors are generally from the business community reflecting the most up-to-date computer know-how. The introductory course requirement is waived if students can demonstrate they have taken an equivalent course though they must still take a total of six courses. Courses taken on a space-available basis in the professional certificate programs can be counted toward this certificate if the professional certificate program is not completed.

Contact Ms. Randi Baker, Manager, Computer Programs, 17 Lexington Avenue, Box 391, New York, NY 10010. 212-725-7172.

LAW (22.01)
Baruch College Paralegal Certificate Program

General Information Unit offering the program: Continuing Studies. Program content: Law and paralegalism, litigation, legal research, business entities, real property, wills, estates, trusts, domestic relations. Available on a non-credit basis. Certificate signed by the Director of Continuing Studies.

Program Format Daytime, evening classes offered. Students may enroll three times per year. Full program cycle lasts 5 months. Completion of program requires test scores of 70% or better, seven courses.

Evaluation Student evaluation based on tests. Grading system: Letters or numbers. Transcripts are kept for each student.

Enrollment Requirements Sixty college credits or six years work experience, recommendations, interview required. Program is open to non-resident foreign students. English language proficiency required.

Program Costs $1350 for the program.

Housing and Student Services Housing is not available. Job counseling and placement services are available.

Special Features The Baruch College Paralegal Certificate Program was designed to train individuals to enter the legal community. Instructors in the program are practicing attorneys with ten or more years legal experience.

Contact Mrs. Jeanette Payne, Manager of Professional Programs, 17 Lexington Avenue, Box 409, New York, NY 10010. 212-725-7172.

MICROCOMPUTER APPLICATIONS (11.06)
Certificate Program in Microcomputer Technology

General Information Unit offering the program: Continuing Studies. Program content: Microcomputer hardware and software training. Available on a non-credit basis. Certificate signed by the Director of Continuing Studies.

Program Format Daytime, evening classes offered. Instructional schedule: Four days or two evenings per week. Students may enroll October, March. Complete program cycle lasts six months (day), ten months (evening).

Evaluation Student evaluation based on tests, computer assignment, lab work. Grading system: Letters or numbers. Transcripts are kept for each student.

Enrollment Requirements Successful completion of the first two courses required. Program is open to non-resident foreign students.

Program Costs $3150 for the program, $425 per course.

Housing and Student Services Housing is not available. Job counseling and placement services are available.

Special Features Program developed to meet current needs of computer field. Successful graduate is capable of managing microcomputer services in business or educational environment. Course includes an internship. Microcomputer hardware as well as software knowledge is provided.

Contact Ms. Randi Baker, Manager, Computer Programs, 17 Lexington Avenue, Box 391, New York, NY 10010. 212-725-7172.

TRANSPORTATION AND TRAVEL MARKETING (08.11)
Travel and Tourism Certificate Program

General Information Unit offering the program: Continuing Studies. Program content: Overview of the travel industry with emphasis on geography. Available on a non-credit basis. Cosponsored by New York chapter of the American Society of Travel Agents (NYASTA). Certificate signed by the Director of Continuing Studies.

Program Format Evening classes offered. Instructional schedule: 60 lecture hours. Students may enroll fall, spring. Full program cycle lasts 10 weeks. Completion of program requires test scores of 70% or better.

Evaluation Student evaluation based on tests. Grading system: Letters or numbers. Transcripts are kept for each student.

Enrollment Requirements Program is open to non-resident foreign students. English language proficiency required.

Program Costs $557 for the program.

Housing and Student Services Housing is not available. Job counseling and placement services are available.

Special Features The Travel and Tourism Certificate Program was designed to train individuals to become entry-level travel agents.

Contact Mrs. Jeanette Payne, Manager of Professional Programs, 17 Lexington Avenue, Box 409, New York, NY 10010. 212-725-7172.

DOMINICAN COLLEGE OF BLAUVELT
Orangeburg, New York 10962

BUSINESS AND MANAGEMENT, GENERAL (06.01)
Certificate in Management

General Information Unit offering the program: Business Administration Department. Program content: Marketing, macroeconomics, human resources, computer systems. Available for credit. Certificate signed by the Academic Dean. Certificate applicable to any four-year degree offered at the institution.

Program Format Daytime, evening, weekend classes offered. Program cycle: Continuous enrollment. Full program cycle lasts 4 courses. Completion of program requires 2.5 GPA.

Evaluation Student evaluation based on tests, papers, reports, final exam. Grading system: Letters or numbers. Transcripts are kept for each student.

Enrollment Requirements Program is open to non-resident foreign students. English language proficiency required. Minimum TOEFL score required: 525.

Program Costs $145 per credit hour.

Housing and Student Services Housing is not available. Job counseling and placement services are not available.

Special Features Taught primarily by full-time faculty.

Contact Mr. Harry White, Director of Admissions, 10 Western Highway, Orangeburg, NY 10962. 914-359-7800.

COMPUTER AND INFORMATION SCIENCES, GENERAL (11.01)
Computer Information Systems

General Information Unit offering the program: Business Administration Department. Program content: COBOL, management applications of microcomputers, systems analysis and design, database organization. Available for credit. Certificate signed by the Academic Dean. Certificate applicable to any four-year degree offered at the institution.

Program Format Daytime, evening, weekend classes offered. Program cycle: Continuous enrollment. Full program cycle lasts 30 credit hours. Completion of program requires 2.5 GPA.

Evaluation Student evaluation based on tests, papers, reports. Grading system: Letters or numbers. Transcripts are kept for each student.

Enrollment Requirements Program is open to non-resident foreign students. English language proficiency required. Minimum TOEFL score required: 525.

Program Costs $145 per credit hour.

Housing and Student Services Housing is not available. Job counseling and placement services are not available.

Special Features Taught primarily by full-time faculty.

Contact Mr. Harry White, Director of Admissions, 10 Western Highway, Orangeburg, NY 10962. 914-359-7800.

COMPUTER PROGRAMMING (11.02)
Computer Programming

General Information Unit offering the program: Business Administration Department. Program content: COBOL, business applications, system design and analysis, database organization and management. Available for credit. Certificate signed by the Academic Dean.

Program Format Daytime, evening, weekend classes offered. Program cycle: Continuous enrollment. Full program cycle lasts 33 credit hours. Completion of program requires 2.5 GPA.

Evaluation Student evaluation based on tests, papers, reports. Grading system: Letters or numbers. Transcripts are kept for each student.

Enrollment Requirements Program is open to non-resident foreign students. English language proficiency required. Minimum TOEFL score required: 525.

Program Costs $145 per credit hour.

Housing and Student Services Housing is not available. Job counseling and placement services are not available.

Special Features Taught primarily by full-time faculty.

Contact Mr. Harry White, Director of Admissions, 10 Western Highway, Orangeburg, NY 10962. 914-359-7800.

INSTITUTIONAL MANAGEMENT (06.07)
Community Residence Management

General Information Unit offering the program: Business Administration Department. Program content: Managing the mentally retarded in a community residence. Available for credit.

Community Residence Management continued
Certificate signed by the Academic Dean. Certificate applicable to any four-year degree offered at the institution.

Program Format   Daytime, evening, weekend classes offered. Program cycle: Continuous enrollment. Completion of program requires 2.5 GPA.

Evaluation   Student evaluation based on tests, papers, reports. Grading system: Letters or numbers. Transcripts are kept for each student.

Enrollment Requirements   Program is open to non-resident foreign students. English language proficiency required. Minimum TOEFL score required: 525.

Program Costs $145 per credit hour.

Housing and Student Services   Housing is not available. Job counseling and placement services are not available.

Special Features   Taught primarily by full-time faculty.

Contact   Mr. Harry White, Director of Admissions, 10 Western Highway, Orangeburg, NY 10962. 914-359-7800.

DOWLING COLLEGE
Oakdale, New York 11769

INFORMATION SCIENCES AND SYSTEMS (11.04)
Certificate in Computer Information Systems

General Information   Unit offering the program: Business Administration Division. Program content: Systems analysis, systems design, computer programming. Available for credit. Certificate signed by the President of the College.

Program Format   Evening classes offered. Program cycle: Continuous enrollment. Full program cycle lasts 2 years. Completion of program requires 36 credit hours.

Evaluation   Student evaluation based on tests, papers, reports. Grading system: Letters or numbers. Transcripts are kept for each student.

Enrollment Requirements   Bachelor's degree required. Program is open to non-resident foreign students. English language proficiency required.

Program Costs $6000 for the program, $495 per course.

Housing and Student Services   Housing is not available. Job counseling and placement services are available.

Contact   Mrs. Gloria Christopher, Director of Admissions, Oakdale, NY 11769. 516-244-3030.

TEACHER EDUCATION, SPECIFIC SUBJECT AREAS (13.13)
Advanced Certificate in Computers in Education

General Information   Unit offering the program: Education Division. Program content: Applications of computer technology to learning environments. Available for credit. Certificate signed by the President of the College. Certificate applicable to M.S. in Education.

Program Format   Evening classes offered. Program cycle: Continuous enrollment. Full program cycle lasts 1 year. Completion of program requires 18 credit hours.

Evaluation   Student evaluation based on tests, papers. Grading system: Letters or numbers. Transcripts are kept for each student.

Enrollment Requirements   Bachelor's degree, provisional teacher certification required. Program is open to non-resident foreign students. English language proficiency required.

Program Costs $3240 for the program, $540 per course.

Housing and Student Services   Housing is not available. Job counseling and placement services are available.

Contact   Dr. Elaine Kaplan, Dean of Graduate Education Programs, Oakdale, NY 11769. 516-244-3296.

TEACHER EDUCATION, SPECIFIC SUBJECT AREAS (13.13)
Certificate in Coaching

General Information   Unit offering the program: Education Division. Program content: Coaching principles, organization, safety. Available for credit. Certificate signed by the President of the College. Certificate applicable to any four-year degree offered at the institution.

Program Format   Evening classes offered. Program cycle: Continuous enrollment. Full program cycle lasts 8 months. Completion of program requires six to nine credits.

Evaluation   Student evaluation based on tests, practicum. Grading system: Letters or numbers. Transcripts are kept for each student.

Enrollment Requirements   Program is open to non-resident foreign students. English language proficiency required.

Program Costs $1000–$1500 for the program, $495 per course.

Housing and Student Services   Housing is not available. Job counseling and placement services are available.

Contact   Mr. Robert Kopelman, Assistant Professor of Physical Education, Oakdale, NY 11769. 516-244-3289.

LONG ISLAND UNIVERSITY, C. W. POST CAMPUS
Brookville, New York 11548

ACCOUNTING, BOOKKEEPING, AND RELATED PROGRAMS (07.01)
Accounting Assistant

General Information   Unit offering the program: Continuing Education, School of Professional Accountancy. Program content: Accounting, payroll, taxes, computer applications. Available on a non-credit basis. Certificate signed by the Director of Continuing Education.

Program Format   Evening classes offered. Instructional schedule: One evening per week. Program cycle: Continuous enrollment. Full program cycle lasts 6 courses.

Evaluation   Student evaluation based on tests. Grading system: Pass/fail. Transcripts are kept for each student.

Enrollment Requirements   High school diploma or equivalent required. Program is not open to non-resident foreign students.

Program Costs $300 per course.

Housing and Student Services   Housing is not available. Job counseling and placement services are available.

Special Features   The C.W. Post Accounting Assistant Certificate Program offers students several key advantages, including classes in an academic atmosphere and access to all the facilities of a beautiful 400-acre campus, an outstanding faculty drawn from our prestigious School of Accountancy, and reasonable tuition of $300 per course.

Contact   Mr. Louis J. Cino, Associate Director, Continuing Education, Brookville, NY 11548. 516-299-2236.

BUSINESS AND MANAGEMENT, GENERAL (06.01)
Graduate Business Certificate Program

General Information   Unit offering the program: Continuing Education. Program content: Accounting, finance, management, marketing. Available for credit. Certificate signed by the University Dean. Certificate applicable to M.B.A.

Program Format Evening classes offered. Instructional schedule: Two evenings per week. Program cycle: Continuous enrollment. Full program cycle lasts 14 weeks.

Evaluation Student evaluation based on tests, papers, reports. Grading system: Letters or numbers. Transcripts are kept for each student.

Enrollment Requirements Bachelor's degree (3.0 GPA) in field other than business required. Program is open to non-resident foreign students. English language proficiency required.

Program Costs $2100 for the program.

Housing and Student Services Housing is not available. Job counseling and placement services are available.

Special Features A graduate-level program for nonbusiness majors who can receive 12 graduate credits in a semester that can be applied towards an MBA.

Contact Ms. Barbara Berman, Director, Brookville, NY 11548. 516-229-2236.

FINE ARTS (50.07)
Art and Antique Appraisal

General Information Unit offering the program: Continuing Education. Program content: Introduction to the field of appraising. Available on a non-credit basis. Endorsed by Long Island Chapter of the American Society of Appraisers. Certificate signed by the Director of Continuing Education.

Program Format Evening classes offered. Instructional schedule: One evening per week. Program cycle: Continuous enrollment. Full program cycle lasts 8 courses.

Evaluation Student evaluation based on papers. Grading system: Pass/fail. Transcripts are kept for each student.

Enrollment Requirements Program is not open to non-resident foreign students.

Program Costs $150 per course.

Housing and Student Services Housing is not available. Job counseling and placement services are available.

Special Features Courses may be taken individually or in pursuit of the Art and Antiques Appraisal Certificate. To attain the certificate, students must successfully complete six of eight required courses and two of five electives, submit class assignments, and undertake a sample appraisal. Visits to auction rooms, museums, furniture showrooms, and art galleries are conducted as part of the curriculum.

Contact Mr. Louis J. Cino, Associate Director, Continuing Education, Brookville, NY 11548. 516-299-2236.

LAW (22.01)
Long Island University Paralegal Studies Program (Generalist)

General Information Unit offering the program: Continuing Education. Program content: Background in several areas of law. Available on a non-credit basis. Endorsed by American Bar Association. Certificate signed by the Director, Continuing Education.

Program Format Evening classes offered. Students may enroll fall, spring, summer. Full program cycle lasts 6 months. Completion of program requires average grade of 73% or better.

Evaluation Student evaluation based on tests. Grading system: Letters or numbers. Transcripts are kept for each student.

Enrollment Requirements Bachelor's degree preferred; associate degree or equivalent credits required. Program is open to non-resident foreign students.

Program Costs $2100 for the program.

Housing and Student Services Housing is available. Job counseling and placement services are available.

Special Features The Paralegal Studies Program at LIU has been approved by the American Bar Association and has

developed a comprehensive curriculum to train paralegals. Classes are taught by practicing attorneys. Internship program provides students with an opportunity to gain first-hand experience in the legal field while attending classes. Employment assistance is available to all graduates.

Contact Ms. Carol P. Jockle, Coordinator, Paralegal Studies Program, Brookville, NY 11548. 516-299-2238.

LAW (22.01)
Long Island University Paralegal Studies Program (Specialist)

General Information Unit offering the program: Continuing Education. Program content: Exposure to a single area of law. Available on a non-credit basis. Endorsed by American Bar Association. Certificate signed by the Director, Continuing Education.

Program Format Daytime classes offered. Students may enroll fall, spring, summer. Full program cycle lasts 3 months. Completion of program requires average grade of 73% or better.

Evaluation Student evaluation based on tests. Grading system: Letters or numbers. Transcripts are kept for each student.

Enrollment Requirements Bachelor's degree preferred; associate degree or equivalent credits required. Program is open to non-resident foreign students.

Program Costs $2100 for the program.

Housing and Student Services Housing is available. Job counseling and placement services are available.

Special Features The Paralegal Studies Program at LIU has been approved by the American Bar Association and has developed a comprehensive curriculum to train paralegals. Classes are taught by practicing attorneys. Internship program provides students with an opportunity to gain first-hand experience in the legal field while attending classes. Employment assistance is available to all graduates.

Contact Ms. Carol P. Jockle, Coordinator, Paralegal Studies Program, Brookville, NY 11548. 516-299-2238.

MENTAL HEALTH/HUMAN SERVICES (17.04)
Alcoholism Counseling

General Information Unit offering the program: Continuing Education. Available on a non-credit basis. Endorsed by New York Federation of Alcoholism Counseling. Certificate signed by the Director of Continuing Education. Program fulfills requirements for Certified Alcoholism Counselor/New York State Division of Alcoholism and Alcohol Abuse.

Program Format Evening classes offered. Instructional schedule: One evening per week. Program cycle: Continuous enrollment. Full program cycle lasts 5 courses. Completion of program requires average grade of B or better.

Evaluation Student evaluation based on tests, papers. Grading system: Letters or numbers. Transcripts are kept for each student.

Enrollment Requirements High school diploma required. Program is not open to non-resident foreign students.

Program Costs $250 per course.

Housing and Student Services Housing is not available. Job counseling and placement services are available.

Special Features Assists professionals in meeting the standards of competency required by the New York State Division of Alcoholism and Alcohol Abuse for acquiring credentials in the field. Course content includes the theories and the techniques of counseling, rehabilitation issues and employee assistance, and the psychological, pharmacological and sociological implications of the problem.

Contact Mr. Louis J. Cino, Associate Director, Continuing Education, Brookville, NY 11548. 516-299-2236.

MANHATTANVILLE COLLEGE
Purchase, New York 10577

BANKING AND FINANCE (06.03)
Certificate in Finance

General Information   Unit offering the program: Office of Adult and Special Programs. Program content: Accounting, statistics, corporation finance, investment analysis. Available for credit. Certificate signed by the Dean of Adult and Special Programs. Certificate applicable to B.A. in Finance.

Program Format   Daytime, evening classes offered. Instructional schedule: Two evenings per week. Full program cycle lasts 7 courses. Completion of program requires grade of C or better.

Evaluation   Student evaluation based on tests, papers, reports. Grading system: Letters or numbers. Transcripts are kept for each student.

Enrollment Requirements   Program is open to non-resident foreign students. English language proficiency required.

Program Costs $156 per credit hour.

Housing and Student Services   Housing is not available. Job counseling and placement services are available.

Special Features   All instructors are Manhattanville undergraduate faculty.

Contact   Ms. Ruth Dowd, Dean of Adult and Special Programs, Purchase, NY 10577. 914-694-3425.

BUSINESS AND MANAGEMENT, GENERAL (06.01)
Certificate in Management

General Information   Unit offering the program: Office of Adult and Special Programs. Program content: Accounting, marketing, human resources. Available for credit. Certificate signed by the Dean of Adult and Special Programs. Certificate applicable to B.A. in Management.

Program Format   Daytime, evening classes offered. Full program cycle lasts 5 courses. Completion of program requires grade of C or better.

Evaluation   Student evaluation based on tests, papers, reports. Grading system: Letters or numbers. Transcripts are kept for each student.

Enrollment Requirements   Program is open to non-resident foreign students. English language proficiency required.

Program Costs $156 per credit hour.

Housing and Student Services   Housing is not available. Job counseling and placement services are available.

Special Features   All instructors are Manhattanville undergraduate faculty.

Contact   Ms. Ruth Dowd, Dean of Adult and Special Programs, Purchase, NY 10577. 914-694-3425.

COMPUTER AND INFORMATION SCIENCES, GENERAL (11.01)
Certificate in Computer Science

General Information   Unit offering the program: Office of Adult and Special Programs. Program content: Computer and data processing, programming, data structures. Available for credit. Certificate signed by the Dean of Adult and Special Programs. Certificate applicable to B.A. in Computer Science.

Program Format   Daytime, evening classes offered. Instructional schedule: Two evenings per week. Full program cycle lasts 5 courses. Completion of program requires grade of C or better.

Evaluation   Student evaluation based on tests, papers, reports. Grading system: Letters or numbers. Transcripts are kept for each student.

Enrollment Requirements   Program is open to non-resident foreign students. English language proficiency required.

Program Costs $156 per credit hour.

Housing and Student Services   Housing is not available. Job counseling and placement services are available.

Special Features   All instructors are Manhattanville undergraduate faculty.

Contact   Ms. Ruth Dowd, Dean of Adult and Special Programs, Purchase, NY 10577. 914-694-3425.

LAW (22.01)
Paralegal

General Information   Unit offering the program: Office of Adult and Special Programs. Program content: Legal research and writing, litigation, trusts, estates. Available on a non-credit basis. Certificate signed by the Dean of Adult and Special Programs.

Program Format   Evening classes offered. Instructional schedule: Two evenings per week. Program cycle: Continuous enrollment. Full program cycle lasts 5 courses. Completion of program requires grade of C or better.

Evaluation   Student evaluation based on tests, papers, reports. Grading system: Letters or numbers. Transcripts are kept for each student.

Enrollment Requirements   Forty-five college credits required. Program is open to non-resident foreign students. English language proficiency required.

Program Costs $1620 for the program.

Housing and Student Services   Housing is not available. Job counseling and placement services are available.

Special Features   All instructors are practicing attorneys.

Contact   Ms. Ruth Dowd, Dean of Adult and Special Programs, Purchase, NY 10577. 914-694-3425.

MANNES COLLEGE OF MUSIC
New York, New York 10024

MUSIC (50.09)
The Diploma Program of the Extension Division

General Information   Unit offering the program: Extension Division. Program content: Instrument, voice, composition, music theory, ear training, music history. Available for credit. Certificate signed by the President.

Program Format   Daytime, evening classes offered. Students may enroll fall, spring, summer. Full program cycle lasts 3 years. Completion of program requires 72 credit hours, graduation jury or two to three original compositions.

Evaluation   Student evaluation based on tests, papers, performance juries, compositions. Grading system: Letters or numbers. Transcripts are kept for each student.

Enrollment Requirements   Audition in proposed major (instrument, voice, compositions); placement tests in theory, ear training, dictation required. Program is open to non-resident foreign students. English language proficiency required.

Program Costs $4000 per year.

Housing and Student Services   Housing is not available. Job counseling and placement services are available.

Special Features   The Diploma Program offers students an opportunity to study music at the college level in an intensive and systematic fashion, with flexibility to accommodate students at varying levels of ability. Students placing on an advanced level in theory and ear training in the entrance exams receive advanced credit.

Contact Ms. Diane Newman, Director, Extension Division, 150 West 85th Street, New York, NY 10024. 212-580-0210.

MEDGAR EVERS COLLEGE OF THE CITY UNIVERSITY OF NEW YORK
Brooklyn, New York 11225

INDIVIDUAL AND FAMILY DEVELOPMENT (19.07)
Certificate in Gerontology

General Information Unit offering the program: Health Science Division. Program content: Fundamental concepts of gerontology, biological processes of aging, cross-cultural aspects. Available for credit. Certificate signed by the President of the College.

Program Format Daytime, evening, weekend classes offered. Program cycle: Continuous enrollment. Full program cycle lasts 6 courses. Completion of program requires 2.0 GPA, 20 credit hours.

Evaluation Student evaluation based on tests, papers, reports, field practicum. Grading system: Letters or numbers. Transcripts are kept for each student.

Enrollment Requirements High school diploma or equivalent required. Program is open to non-resident foreign students. English language proficiency required.

Program Costs $800 for the program, $120 per course.

Housing and Student Services Housing is not available. Job counseling and placement services are available.

Special Features The certificate was developed through funding from the Administration on Aging (1980-82). Focus is on enhancing the skills of persons whose primary goal is to improve the quality of services for aging individuals and families of diverse socio-cultural and ethnic backgrounds. Provides a perspective of aging individuals in the philosophical, humanistic, anthropological, and historical contexts.

Contact Dr. Bertie Gilmore, Chairperson, Health Science Division, 1150 Carroll Street, Brooklyn, NY 11225. 718-735-1931.

WORD PROCESSING (07.08)
Certificate in Word Processing

General Information Unit offering the program: Business Administration. Program content: Secretarial science, word processing. Available for credit. Certificate signed by the President of the College. Certificate applicable to A.A.S. in Secretarial Science.

Program Format Daytime, evening classes offered. Program cycle: Continuous enrollment. Full program cycle lasts 2 semesters. Completion of program requires 2.0 GPA, 30 credit hours.

Evaluation Student evaluation based on tests, reports. Grading system: Letters or numbers. Transcripts are kept for each student.

Enrollment Requirements Ability to type 35 words per minute required. Program is open to non-resident foreign students. English language proficiency required.

Program Costs $1280 for the program, $40 per credit hour.

Housing and Student Services Housing is not available. Job counseling and placement services are available.

Special Features Instructors in the program meet the requirements needed for teaching at the college level—they possess doctorates or MBA degrees. Some courses may be waived if student has sufficient prior experience on equipment.

Contact Ms. Ola M. Hightower, Deputy Chairperson, Business Administration, 1150 Carroll Street, Brooklyn, NY 11225. 718-735-1814.

MERCY COLLEGE
Dobbs Ferry, New York 10522

ACCOUNTING (06.02)
Accounting

General Information Unit offering the program: Accounting Department. Program content: Accounting, auditing, taxation, statistics, algebra. Available for credit. Certificate signed by the President of the College. Certificate applicable to any two- or four-year degree offered at the institution.

Program Format Daytime, evening, weekend classes offered. Program cycle: Continuous enrollment. Complete program cycle lasts one to three years. Completion of program requires 2.0 GPA, 36 credit hours.

Evaluation Student evaluation based on tests, papers, reports. Grading system: Letters or numbers. Transcripts are kept for each student.

Enrollment Requirements Math and English placement tests, high school diploma required. Program is not open to non-resident foreign students. English language proficiency required.

Program Costs $495 per course.

Housing and Student Services Housing is not available. Job counseling and placement services are available.

Contact Ms. Paula Donegan, Assistant to the Dean for Academic Administration, 555 Broadway, Dobbs Ferry, NY 10522. 914-693-4500.

BUSINESS AND MANAGEMENT, GENERAL (06.01)
General Business Administration

General Information Unit offering the program: Business Administration Department. Program content: Accounting, business law, statistics, economics, finance, algebra, marketing. Available for credit. Certificate signed by the President of the College. Certificate applicable to any two- or four-year degree offered at the institution.

Program Format Daytime, evening, weekend classes offered. Program cycle: Continuous enrollment. Complete program cycle lasts one to three years. Completion of program requires 2.0 GPA, 30 credit hours.

Evaluation Student evaluation based on tests, papers, reports. Grading system: Letters or numbers. Transcripts are kept for each student.

Enrollment Requirements Math and English placement tests, high school diploma required. Program is not open to non-resident foreign students. English language proficiency required.

Program Costs $495 per course.

Housing and Student Services Housing is not available. Job counseling and placement services are available.

Contact Ms. Paula Donegan, Assistant to the Dean for Academic Administration, 555 Broadway, Dobbs Ferry, NY 10522. 914-693-4500.

BUSINESS AND MANAGEMENT, GENERAL (06.01)
Management

General Information Unit offering the program: Business Administration Department. Program content: Algebra, computers, statistics, organizational behavior, industrial psychology, marketing, sales. Available for credit. Certificate signed by the President of the College. Certificate applicable to any two- or four-year degree offered at the institution.

Program Format Daytime, evening, weekend classes offered. Program cycle: Continuous enrollment. Complete program cycle lasts one to three years. Completion of program requires 2.0 GPA, 33 credit hours.

Management continued

Evaluation   Student evaluation based on tests, papers, reports. Grading system: Letters or numbers. Transcripts are kept for each student.

Enrollment Requirements   Math and English placement tests, high school diploma required. Program is not open to non-resident foreign students. English language proficiency required.

Program Costs $495 per course.

Housing and Student Services   Housing is not available. Job counseling and placement services are available.

Contact   Ms. Paula Donegan, Assistant to the Dean for Academic Administration, 555 Broadway, Dobbs Ferry, NY 10522. 914-693-4500.

COMPUTER AND INFORMATION SCIENCES, GENERAL (11.01)
Computer Science

General Information   Unit offering the program: Mathematics and Computer Information Science Department. Program content: Computers and programming, Pascal, assembly language. Available for credit. Certificate signed by the President of the College. Certificate applicable to any two- or four-year degree offered at the institution.

Program Format   Daytime, evening, weekend classes offered. Program cycle: Continuous enrollment. Complete program cycle lasts one to three years. Completion of program requires 2.0 GPA, 15 credit hours.

Evaluation   Student evaluation based on tests, papers, reports. Grading system: Letters or numbers. Transcripts are kept for each student.

Enrollment Requirements   Math and English placement tests, high school diploma required. Program is not open to non-resident foreign students. English language proficiency required.

Program Costs $495 per course.

Housing and Student Services   Housing is not available. Job counseling and placement services are available.

Contact   Ms. Paula Donegan, Assistant to the Dean for Academic Administration, 555 Broadway, Dobbs Ferry, NY 10522. 914-693-4500.

COMPUTER AND INFORMATION SCIENCES, GENERAL (11.01)
Computer Science

General Information   Unit offering the program: Mathematics and Computer Information Science Department. Program content: Data structures, operating systems, programming languages, computer architecture, discrete structures, calculus and geometry. Available for credit. Certificate signed by the President of the College. Certificate applicable to any two- or four-year degree offered at the institution.

Program Format   Daytime, evening, weekend classes offered. Program cycle: Continuous enrollment. Complete program cycle lasts one to three years. Completion of program requires 2.0 GPA, 22 credit hours.

Evaluation   Student evaluation based on tests, papers, reports. Grading system: Letters or numbers. Transcripts are kept for each student.

Enrollment Requirements   Math and English placement tests, high school diploma required. Program is not open to non-resident foreign students. English language proficiency required.

Program Costs $495 per course.

Housing and Student Services   Housing is not available. Job counseling and placement services are available.

Contact   Ms. Paula Donegan, Assistant to the Dean for Academic Administration, 555 Broadway, Dobbs Ferry, NY 10522. 914-693-4500.

CRIMINAL JUSTICE (43.01)
Criminal Justice

General Information   Unit offering the program: Law, Criminal Justice, and Safety Administration Department. Program content: Constitutional law, corrections, criminal justice system. Available for credit. Certificate signed by the President of the College. Certificate applicable to any two- or four-year degree offered at the institution.

Program Format   Daytime, evening, weekend classes offered. Program cycle: Continuous enrollment. Complete program cycle lasts one to three years. Completion of program requires 2.0 GPA, 15 credit hours.

Evaluation   Student evaluation based on tests, papers, reports. Grading system: Letters or numbers. Transcripts are kept for each student.

Enrollment Requirements   Math and English placement tests, high school diploma required. Program is not open to non-resident foreign students. English language proficiency required.

Program Costs $495 per course.

Housing and Student Services   Housing is not available. Job counseling and placement services are available.

Contact   Ms. Paula Donegan, Assistant to the Dean for Academic Administration, 555 Broadway, Dobbs Ferry, NY 10522. 914-693-4500.

CRIMINAL JUSTICE (43.01)
Private Security

General Information   Unit offering the program: Law, Criminal Justice, and Safety Administration Department. Program content: Legal aspects, fire prevention and protection systems, criminal law, arson and criminal investigation, constitutional law. Available for credit. Certificate signed by the President of the College. Certificate applicable to any two- or four-year degree offered at the institution.

Program Format   Daytime, evening, weekend classes offered. Program cycle: Continuous enrollment. Complete program cycle lasts one to three years. Completion of program requires 2.0 GPA, 15 credit hours.

Evaluation   Student evaluation based on tests, papers, reports. Grading system: Letters or numbers. Transcripts are kept for each student.

Enrollment Requirements   Math and English placement tests, high school diploma required. Program is not open to non-resident foreign students. English language proficiency required.

Program Costs $495 per course.

Housing and Student Services   Housing is not available. Job counseling and placement services are available.

Contact   Ms. Paula Donegan, Assistant to the Dean for Academic Administration, 555 Broadway, Dobbs Ferry, NY 10522. 914-693-4500.

DESIGN (50.04)
Graphic Design

General Information   Unit offering the program: Art and Photography Department. Program content: Two- or three-dimensional design, drawing, photography, color and design, lettering and typography. Available for credit. Certificate signed by the President of the College. Certificate applicable to any two- or four-year degree offered at the institution.

Program Format   Daytime, evening, weekend classes offered. Program cycle: Continuous enrollment. Complete program cycle lasts one to three years. Completion of program requires 2.0 GPA, 18 credit hours.

Evaluation   Student evaluation based on tests, papers, reports. Grading system: Letters or numbers. Transcripts are kept for each student.

Enrollment Requirements   Math and English placement tests, high school diploma required. Program is not open to non-resident foreign students. English language proficiency required.

Program Costs $495 per course.

Housing and Student Services   Housing is not available. Job counseling and placement services are available.

Contact   Ms. Paula Donegan, Assistant to the Dean for Academic Administration, 555 Broadway, Dobbs Ferry, NY 10522. 914-693-4500.

FILM ARTS (50.06)
Photography

General Information   Unit offering the program: Art and Photography Department. Program content: Two-dimensional design, history of photography, color and forensic photography, materials and techniques. Available for credit. Certificate signed by the President of the College. Certificate applicable to any two- or four-year degree offered at the institution.

Program Format   Daytime, evening, weekend classes offered. Program cycle: Continuous enrollment. Complete program cycle lasts one to three years. Completion of program requires 2.0 GPA, 18 credit hours.

Evaluation   Student evaluation based on tests, papers, reports. Grading system: Letters or numbers. Transcripts are kept for each student.

Enrollment Requirements   Math and English placement tests, high school diploma required. Program is not open to non-resident foreign students. English language proficiency required.

Program Costs $495 per course.

Housing and Student Services   Housing is not available. Job counseling and placement services are available.

Contact   Ms. Paula Donegan, Assistant to the Dean for Academic Administration, 555 Broadway, Dobbs Ferry, NY 10522. 914-693-4500.

FIRE PROTECTION (43.02)
Fire Science

General Information   Unit offering the program: Law, Criminal Justice, and Safety Administration Department. Program content: Prevention and protection systems, principles and practices, arson investigation. Available for credit. Certificate signed by the President of the College. Certificate applicable to any two- or four-year degree offered at the institution.

Program Format   Daytime, evening, weekend classes offered. Program cycle: Continuous enrollment. Complete program cycle lasts one to three years. Completion of program requires 2.0 GPA, 15 credit hours.

Evaluation   Student evaluation based on tests, papers, reports. Grading system: Letters or numbers. Transcripts are kept for each student.

Enrollment Requirements   Math and English placement tests, high school diploma required. Program is not open to non-resident foreign students. English language proficiency required.

Program Costs $495 per course.

Housing and Student Services   Housing is not available. Job counseling and placement services are available.

Contact   Ms. Paula Donegan, Assistant to the Dean for Academic Administration, 555 Broadway, Dobbs Ferry, NY 10522. 914-693-4500.

FIRE PROTECTION (43.02)
Public Safety

General Information   Unit offering the program: Law, Criminal Justice, and Safety Administration Department. Program content: Safety management, fire prevention, protection systems. Available for credit. Certificate signed by the President of the College. Certificate applicable to any two- or four-year degree offered at the institution.

Program Format   Daytime, evening, weekend classes offered. Program cycle: Continuous enrollment. Complete program cycle

lasts one to three years. Completion of program requires 2.0 GPA, 15 credit hours.

Evaluation   Student evaluation based on tests, papers, reports. Grading system: Letters or numbers. Transcripts are kept for each student.

Enrollment Requirements   Math and English placement tests, high school diploma required. Program is not open to non-resident foreign students. English language proficiency required.

Program Costs $495 per course.

Housing and Student Services   Housing is not available. Job counseling and placement services are available.

Contact   Ms. Paula Donegan, Assistant to the Dean for Academic Administration, 555 Broadway, Dobbs Ferry, NY 10522. 914-693-4500.

GENERAL MARKETING (08.07)
Marketing

General Information   Unit offering the program: Business Administration Department. Program content: Statistics, algebra, organizational behavior, research, management, sales, advertising. Available for credit. Certificate signed by the President of the College. Certificate applicable to any two- or four-year degree offered at the institution.

Program Format   Daytime, evening, weekend classes offered. Program cycle: Continuous enrollment. Complete program cycle lasts one to three years. Completion of program requires 2.0 GPA, 33 credit hours.

Evaluation   Student evaluation based on tests, papers, reports. Grading system: Letters or numbers. Transcripts are kept for each student.

Enrollment Requirements   Math and English placement tests, high school diploma required. Program is not open to non-resident foreign students. English language proficiency required.

Program Costs $495 per course.

Housing and Student Services   Housing is not available. Job counseling and placement services are available.

Contact   Ms. Paula Donegan, Assistant to the Dean for Academic Administration, 555 Broadway, Dobbs Ferry, NY 10522. 914-693-4500.

INDIVIDUAL AND FAMILY DEVELOPMENT (19.07)
Gerontology

General Information   Unit offering the program: Behavioral Science Department. Program content: Personality development, aging and mental health, social psychology, medical sociology. Available for credit. Certificate signed by the President of the College. Certificate applicable to any two- or four-year degree offered at the institution.

Program Format   Daytime, evening, weekend classes offered. Program cycle: Continuous enrollment. Complete program cycle lasts one to three years. Completion of program requires 2.0 GPA, 18 credit hours.

Evaluation   Student evaluation based on tests, papers, reports. Grading system: Letters or numbers. Transcripts are kept for each student.

Enrollment Requirements   Math and English placement tests, high school diploma required. Program is not open to non-resident foreign students. English language proficiency required.

Program Costs $495 per course.

Housing and Student Services   Housing is not available. Job counseling and placement services are available.

Contact   Ms. Paula Donegan, Assistant to the Dean for Academic Administration, 555 Broadway, Dobbs Ferry, NY 10522. 914-693-4500.

INFORMATION SCIENCES AND SYSTEMS (11.04)
Computer Information Systems

General Information   Unit offering the program: Mathematics and Computer Information Science Department. Program content: COBAL, systems analysis, principles of management, management information systems. Available for credit. Certificate signed by the President of the College. Certificate applicable to any two- or four-year degree offered at the institution.

Program Format   Daytime, evening, weekend classes offered. Program cycle: Continuous enrollment. Complete program cycle lasts one to three years. Completion of program requires 2.0 GPA, 18 credit hours.

Evaluation   Student evaluation based on tests, papers, reports. Grading system: Letters or numbers. Transcripts are kept for each student.

Enrollment Requirements   Math and English placement tests, high school diploma required. Program is not open to non-resident foreign students. English language proficiency required.

Program Costs $495 per course.

Housing and Student Services   Housing is not available. Job counseling and placement services are available.

Contact   Ms. Paula Donegan, Assistant to the Dean for Academic Administration, 555 Broadway, Dobbs Ferry, NY 10522. 914-693-4500.

ITALIC LANGUAGES (16.09)
French Language and Culture

General Information   Unit offering the program: Foreign Languages, Literature, and Linguistics Department. Program content: Area studies, culture, literature. Available for credit. Certificate signed by the President of the College. Certificate applicable to any two- or four-year degree offered at the institution.

Program Format   Daytime, evening, weekend classes offered. Program cycle: Continuous enrollment. Complete program cycle lasts one to three years. Completion of program requires 2.0 GPA, 18 credit hours.

Evaluation   Student evaluation based on tests, papers, reports. Grading system: Letters or numbers. Transcripts are kept for each student.

Enrollment Requirements   Math and English placement tests, high school diploma, one to two years of French studies required. Program is not open to non-resident foreign students. English language proficiency required.

Program Costs $495 per course.

Housing and Student Services   Housing is not available. Job counseling and placement services are available.

Contact   Ms. Paula Donegan, Assistant to the Dean for Academic Administration, 555 Broadway, Dobbs Ferry, NY 10522. 914-693-4500.

ITALIC LANGUAGES (16.09)
Italian Language and Culture

General Information   Unit offering the program: Foreign Languages, Literature, and Linguistics Department. Program content: Area studies, culture, literature. Available for credit. Certificate signed by the President of the College. Certificate applicable to any two- or four-year degree offered at the institution.

Program Format   Daytime, evening, weekend classes offered. Program cycle: Continuous enrollment. Complete program cycle lasts one to three years. Completion of program requires 2.0 GPA, 18 credit hours.

Evaluation   Student evaluation based on tests, papers, reports. Grading system: Letters or numbers. Transcripts are kept for each student.

Enrollment Requirements   Math and English placement tests, high school diploma, one to two years of Italian studies required. Program is not open to non-resident foreign students. English language proficiency required.

Program Costs $495 per course.

Housing and Student Services   Housing is not available. Job counseling and placement services are available.

Contact   Ms. Paula Donegan, Assistant to the Dean for Academic Administration, 555 Broadway, Dobbs Ferry, NY 10522. 914-693-4500.

ITALIC LANGUAGES (16.09)
Spanish Language and Culture

General Information   Unit offering the program: Foreign Languages, Literature, and Linguistics Department. Program content: Area studies, culture, literature. Available for credit. Certificate signed by the President of the College. Certificate applicable to any two- or four-year degree offered at the institution.

Program Format   Daytime, evening, weekend classes offered. Program cycle: Continuous enrollment. Complete program cycle lasts one to three years. Completion of program requires 2.0 GPA, 18 credit hours.

Evaluation   Student evaluation based on tests, papers, reports. Grading system: Letters or numbers. Transcripts are kept for each student.

Enrollment Requirements   Math and English placement tests, high school diploma required. Program is not open to non-resident foreign students. English language proficiency required.

Program Costs $495 per course.

Housing and Student Services   Housing is not available. Job counseling and placement services are available.

Contact   Ms. Paula Donegan, Assistant to the Dean for Academic Administration, 555 Broadway, Dobbs Ferry, NY 10522. 914-693-4500.

JOURNALISM (MASS COMMUNICATIONS) (09.04)
Journalism and Media

General Information   Unit offering the program: English Literature, Humanities and Journalism Department. Program content: Rhetoric and exposition, news reporting, copy editing and graphics, magazine editing and production, media, sports reporting. Available for credit. Certificate signed by the President of the College. Certificate applicable to any two- or four-year degree offered at the institution.

Program Format   Daytime, evening, weekend classes offered. Program cycle: Continuous enrollment. Complete program cycle lasts one to three years. Completion of program requires 2.0 GPA, 24 credit hours.

Evaluation   Student evaluation based on tests, papers, reports. Grading system: Letters or numbers. Transcripts are kept for each student.

Enrollment Requirements   Math and English placement tests, high school diploma required. Program is not open to non-resident foreign students. English language proficiency required.

Program Costs $495 per course.

Housing and Student Services   Housing is not available. Job counseling and placement services are available.

Contact   Ms. Paula Donegan, Assistant to the Dean for Academic Administration, 555 Broadway, Dobbs Ferry, NY 10522. 914-693-4500.

LIBERAL/GENERAL STUDIES (24.01)
Liberal Studies

General Information   Unit offering the program: English, Mathematics, Behavioral Science, Art Departments. Program content: English, history, math, economics, psychology or sociology, art, music, philosophy or religion, foreign language. Available for credit. Certificate signed by the President of the College. Certificate applicable to any two- or four-year degree offered at the institution.

Program Format   Daytime, evening, weekend classes offered. Program cycle: Continuous enrollment. Complete program cycle lasts one to three years. Completion of program requires 2.0 GPA, 24 credit hours.

Evaluation   Student evaluation based on tests, papers, reports. Grading system: Letters or numbers. Transcripts are kept for each student.

Enrollment Requirements   Math and English placement tests, high school diploma required. Program is not open to non-resident foreign students. English language proficiency required.

Program Costs $495 per course.

Housing and Student Services   Housing is not available. Job counseling and placement services are available.

Contact   Ms. Paula Donegan, Assistant to the Dean for Academic Administration, 555 Broadway, Dobbs Ferry, NY 10522. 914-693-4500.

PERSONNEL MANAGEMENT (06.16)
Personnel Management

General Information   Unit offering the program: Business Administration Department. Program content: Principles of management, group dynamics, industrial psychology, organizational behavior, psychology of crisis and communication. Available for credit. Certificate signed by the President of the College. Certificate applicable to any two- or four-year degree offered at the institution.

Program Format   Daytime, evening, weekend classes offered. Program cycle: Continuous enrollment. Complete program cycle lasts one to three years. Completion of program requires 2.0 GPA, 18 credit hours.

Evaluation   Student evaluation based on tests, papers, reports. Grading system: Letters or numbers. Transcripts are kept for each student.

Enrollment Requirements   Math and English placement tests, high school diploma required. Program is not open to non-resident foreign students. English language proficiency required.

Program Costs $495 per course.

Housing and Student Services   Housing is not available. Job counseling and placement services are available.

Contact   Ms. Paula Donegan, Assistant to the Dean for Academic Administration, 555 Broadway, Dobbs Ferry, NY 10522. 914-693-4500.

QUALITY CONTROL AND SAFETY TECHNOLOGIES (15.07)
OSHA: Occupational Safety and Health Administration

General Information   Unit offering the program: Law, Criminal Justice, and Safety Administration Department. Program content: Safety management, OSHA significance and application, organization and supervision of safety programs. Available for credit. Certificate signed by the President of the College. Certificate applicable to any two- or four-year degree offered at the institution.

Program Format   Daytime, evening, weekend classes offered. Program cycle: Continuous enrollment. Complete program cycle lasts one to three years. Completion of program requires 2.0 GPA, 15 credit hours.

Evaluation   Student evaluation based on tests, papers, reports. Grading system: Letters or numbers. Transcripts are kept for each student.

Enrollment Requirements   Math and English placement tests, high school diploma required. Program is not open to non-resident foreign students. English language proficiency required.

Program Costs $495 per course.

Housing and Student Services   Housing is not available. Job counseling and placement services are available.

Contact   Ms. Paula Donegan, Assistant to the Dean for Academic Administration, 555 Broadway, Dobbs Ferry, NY 10522. 914-693-4500.

REHABILITATION SERVICES (17.08)
Pet Assisted Therapy Facilitation

General Information   Unit offering the program: Veterinary Technology Department. Program content: Animal behavior, psychology. Available for credit. Certificate signed by the President of the College. Certificate applicable to any two- or four-year degree offered at the institution.

Program Format   Daytime, evening, weekend classes offered. Program cycle: Continuous enrollment. Complete program cycle lasts one to three years. Completion of program requires 2.0 GPA, 21 credit hours.

Evaluation   Student evaluation based on tests, papers, reports. Grading system: Letters or numbers. Transcripts are kept for each student.

Enrollment Requirements   Math and English placement tests, high school diploma required. Program is not open to non-resident foreign students. English language proficiency required.

Program Costs $495 per course.

Housing and Student Services   Housing is not available. Job counseling and placement services are available.

Contact   Ms. Paula Donegan, Assistant to the Dean for Academic Administration, 555 Broadway, Dobbs Ferry, NY 10522. 914-693-4500.

SOCIAL SCIENCES, GENERAL (45.01)
Human Behavior

General Information   Unit offering the program: Behavioral Science Department. Program content: Sociology, psychology. Available for credit. Certificate signed by the President of the College. Certificate applicable to any two- or four-year degree offered at the institution.

Program Format   Daytime, evening, weekend classes offered. Program cycle: Continuous enrollment. Complete program cycle lasts one to three years. Completion of program requires 2.0 GPA, 18 credit hours.

Evaluation   Student evaluation based on tests, papers, reports. Grading system: Letters or numbers. Transcripts are kept for each student.

Enrollment Requirements   Math and English placement tests, high school diploma required. Program is not open to non-resident foreign students. English language proficiency required.

Program Costs $495 per course.

Housing and Student Services   Housing is not available. Job counseling and placement services are available.

Contact   Ms. Paula Donegan, Assistant to the Dean for Academic Administration, 555 Broadway, Dobbs Ferry, NY 10522. 914-693-4500.

NEW YORK INSTITUTE OF TECHNOLOGY
Old Westbury, New York 11568

BUSINESS ADMINISTRATION AND MANAGEMENT (06.04)
Business Management

General Information   Unit offering the program: School of Management. Program content: Accounting, business law, economics, personnel, business organization. Available for

Business Management continued

credit. Certificate signed by the Dean, School of Management. Certificate applicable to B.S. in Business Administration.

Program Format   Daytime, evening classes offered. Instructional schedule: Three days or two evenings per week. Full program cycle lasts 18 credit hours.

Evaluation   Student evaluation based on tests, papers, reports. Grading system: Letters or numbers. Transcripts are kept for each student.

Enrollment Requirements   High school diploma required. Program is open to non-resident foreign students. English language proficiency required. Minimum TOEFL score required: 500.

Program Costs $2880 for the program, $480 per course.

Housing and Student Services   Housing is not available. Job counseling and placement services are available.

Contact   Dr. Carol Schwartz, Dean, School of Management, Wheatley Road, Old Westbury, NY 11568. 516-686-7554.

BUSINESS ADMINISTRATION AND MANAGEMENT (06.04)
Energy Management

General Information   Unit offering the program: School of Business, Energy Center. Program content: Conservation, architecture. Available for credit. Cosponsored by Consolidated Edison. Certificate signed by the Dean. Certificate applicable to M.S. in Energy Management.

Program Format   Daytime, evening classes offered. Instructional schedule: Weekly seminars. Program cycle: Continuous enrollment. Full program cycle lasts 18 credit hours.

Evaluation   Student evaluation based on tests, papers, reports. Grading system: Letters or numbers. Transcripts are kept for each student.

Enrollment Requirements   Bachelor's degree required. Program is open to non-resident foreign students. English language proficiency required. Minimum TOEFL score required: 500.

Program Costs $3150 for the program, $525 per course.

Housing and Student Services   Housing is not available. Job counseling and placement services are available.

Contact   Dr. Carol Schwartz, Dean, School of Management, Wheatley Road, Old Westbury, NY 11568. 516-686-7554.

BUSINESS ADMINISTRATION AND MANAGEMENT (06.04)
Public Transportation Management

General Information   Unit offering the program: School of Management, Labor Center. Program content: Labor relations law, marketing management, innovations. Available for credit. Certificate signed by the Dean.

Program Format   Evening classes offered. Program cycle: Continuous enrollment. Full program cycle lasts 18 credit hours.

Evaluation   Student evaluation based on tests, papers, reports. Grading system: Letters or numbers. Transcripts are kept for each student.

Enrollment Requirements   Bachelor's degree required. Program is open to non-resident foreign students. English language proficiency required. Minimum TOEFL score required: 500.

Program Costs $3150 for the program, $525 per course.

Housing and Student Services   Housing is not available. Job counseling and placement services are available.

Contact   Dr. Richard Dibble, Director, Center for Labor and Industrial Relations, Wheatley Road, Old Westbury, NY 11568. 516-686-7722.

BUSINESS DATA PROCESSING AND RELATED PROGRAMS (07.03)
Data Processing

General Information   Unit offering the program: Computer Science. Program content: Programming language, systems design, data structures, database management. Available for credit. Certificate signed by the Dean, Center for Engineering and Technology. Certificate applicable to B.S. in Computer Science.

Program Format   Daytime, evening classes offered. Program cycle: Continuous enrollment. Full program cycle lasts 18 credit hours.

Evaluation   Student evaluation based on tests. Grading system: Letters or numbers. Transcripts are kept for each student.

Enrollment Requirements   High school diploma required. Program is open to non-resident foreign students. English language proficiency required. Minimum TOEFL score required: 500.

Program Costs $2880 for the program, $480 per course.

Housing and Student Services   Housing is available. Job counseling and placement services are available.

Contact   Dr. T. Teng, Chair, Computer Science Department, Wheatley Road, Old Westbury, NY 11568. 516-686-7516.

CLINICAL PSYCHOLOGY (42.02)
Human Relations

General Information   Unit offering the program: School of Humanities. Program content: Assessment, group dynamics, behavior modification, crisis intervention, psychotherapy. Available for credit. Certificate signed by the Dean. Certificate applicable to B.S. in Human Relations.

Program Format   Daytime, evening classes offered. Program cycle: Continuous enrollment. Full program cycle lasts 18 credit hours.

Evaluation   Student evaluation based on tests, reports. Grading system: Letters or numbers. Transcripts are kept for each student.

Enrollment Requirements   High school diploma required. Program is open to non-resident foreign students. English language proficiency required. Minimum TOEFL score required: 500.

Program Costs $2880 for the program, $480 per course.

Housing and Student Services   Housing is available. Job counseling and placement services are available.

Contact   Dr. Robert Goldblatt, Chair, Human Relations Department, Wheatley Road, Old Westbury, NY 11568. 516-686-7728.

CLOTHING, APPAREL, AND TEXTILES MANAGEMENT, PRODUCTION, AND SERVICES (20.03)
Fashion Retailing and Merchandising

General Information   Unit offering the program: Division of Continuing Professional Education. Program content: Forecasting, fiber, importing, art design, display, promotional advertising. Available on a non-credit basis. Certificate signed by the Dean, Office of Institutional Liaison.

Program Format   Daytime, evening classes offered. Instructional schedule: Once per week for two hours. Full program cycle lasts 3 semesters. Completion of program requires mid-term and final examinations.

Evaluation   Student evaluation based on tests, papers, reports. Grading system: Pass/fail. Transcripts are kept for each student.

Enrollment Requirements   Open enrollment. Program is open to non-resident foreign students. English language proficiency required. Students should be reading at a minimum twelfth-grade level.

Program Costs $660 for the program, $110 per course.

Housing and Student Services   Housing is not available. Job counseling and placement services are available.

Special Features   The program is offered both day and evening at NYIT's Central Islip Campus.

Contact   Dr. Louis J. Traina, Director, Division of Continuing Professional Education, Carleton Avenue, Building 66, Room 212, Central Islip, NY 11722. 516-348-3325.

INDUSTRIAL PRODUCTION TECHNOLOGIES (15.06)
Industrial Technology

General Information   Unit offering the program: School of Engineering and Technology. Program content: Operation management, statistical design, quality control, production planning. Available for credit. Certificate signed by the Dean, Center for Engineering and Technology. Certificate applicable to B.S. in Industrial Technology.

Program Format   Daytime, evening classes offered. Program cycle: Continuous enrollment. Full program cycle lasts 18 credit hours.

Evaluation   Student evaluation based on tests. Grading system: Letters or numbers. Transcripts are kept for each student.

Enrollment Requirements   High school diploma required. Program is open to non-resident foreign students. English language proficiency required. Minimum TOEFL score required: 500.

Program Costs $2880 for the program, $480 per course.

Housing and Student Services   Housing is available. Job counseling and placement services are available.

Contact   Dr. Gotleib Koenig, Chair, Industrial Engineering Department, Wheatley Road, Old Westbury, NY 11568. 516-686-7516.

INTERIOR DESIGN (04.05)
Interior Design

General Information   Unit offering the program: Division of Continuing Professional Education. Program content: Drawing, rendering, lighting, stuctures, color. Available on a non-credit basis. Certificate signed by the Dean, Office of Institutional Liaison.

Program Format   Daytime, evening classes offered. Instructional schedule: 2½ hours per week. Full program cycle lasts 3 semesters. Completion of program requires mid-term and final examinations.

Evaluation   Student evaluation based on tests, papers, reports. Grading system: Pass/fail. Transcripts are kept for each student.

Enrollment Requirements   Open enrollment. Program is open to non-resident foreign students. English language proficiency required. Students should be reading at a minimum twelfth-grade level.

Program Costs $1170 for the program, $195 per course.

Housing and Student Services   Housing is not available. Job counseling and placement services are available.

Special Features   For the past ten years, NYIT has been offering a noncredit Interior Design Certificate Program which is endorsed by the American Society of Interior Designers (ASID). This program, because of its flexible schedule and its inexpensive fees, offers an option to NYIT's Bachelor of Science program in Interior Design.

Contact   Dr. Louis J. Traina, Director, Division of Continuing Professional Education, Carleton Avenue, Building 66, Room 212, Central Islip, NY 11722. 516-348-3325.

LABOR/INDUSTRIAL RELATIONS (06.11)
Labor Relations

General Information   Unit offering the program: School of Management, Labor Center. Program content: Collective bargaining, arbitration, mediation, union organization and administration. Available for credit. Certificate signed by the Dean. Certificate applicable to M.S. in Labor and Industrial Relations.

Program Format   Evening classes offered. Program cycle: Continuous enrollment. Full program cycle lasts 18 credit hours.

Evaluation   Student evaluation based on tests, papers, reports. Grading system: Letters or numbers. Transcripts are kept for each student.

Enrollment Requirements   Bachelor's degree required. Program is open to non-resident foreign students. English language proficiency required. Minimum TOEFL score required: 500.

Program Costs $3150 for the program, $525 per course.

Housing and Student Services   Housing is not available. Job counseling and placement services are available.

Contact   Dr. Richard Dibble, Director, Center for Labor and Industrial Relations, Wheatley Road, Old Westbury, NY 11568. 516-686-7722.

MENTAL HEALTH/HUMAN SERVICES (17.04)
Alcoholism Counseling

General Information   Unit offering the program: School of Humanities. Program content: Crisis intervention, etiology of substance abuse, group therapy, counseling techniques. Available for credit. Certificate signed by the Dean.

Program Format   Evening classes offered. Program cycle: Continuous enrollment. Full program cycle lasts 18 credit hours.

Evaluation   Student evaluation based on tests, papers, reports. Grading system: Letters or numbers. Transcripts are kept for each student.

Enrollment Requirements   Bachelor's degree required. Program is open to non-resident foreign students. English language proficiency required. Minimum TOEFL score required: 500.

Program Costs $3150 for the program, $525 per course.

Housing and Student Services   Housing is not available. Job counseling and placement services are available.

Contact   Dr. Robert Goldblatt, Chair, Human Relations Department, Wheatley Road, Old Westbury, NY 11568. 516-686-7728.

REAL ESTATE (06.17)
Real Estate Appraisal

General Information   Unit offering the program: Division of Continuing Professional Education. Program content: Property description, evaluation report, depreciation, market approaches, data assembly. Available on a non-credit basis. Endorsed by New York State Division of Licensing, American Association of Real Estate Appraisers. Certificate signed by the Director, Division of Continuing Professional Education. Program fulfills requirements for Residential-1, Certified Appraiser–Residential.

Program Format   Daytime, evening, weekend classes offered. Students may enroll fall, spring, summer. Complete program cycle lasts 90 classroom hours. Completion of program requires final examination.

Evaluation   Student evaluation based on tests, papers, reports. Grading system: Pass/fail. Transcripts are kept for each student.

Enrollment Requirements   Open enrollment. Program is open to non-resident foreign students. English language proficiency required. Students should be reading at a minumum twelfth-grade level.

Program Costs $590 for the program, $295 per course.

Housing and Student Services   Housing is not available. Job counseling and placement services are available.

Real Estate Appraisal continued

Special Features   Students can pursue either the R-1 Designation or the CA-R Certification from the American Association of Real Estate Appraisers. Courses are also recognized by the New York State Division of Licensing as a Continuing Education Course required for Real Estate Salespersons/Brokers licensing renewal.

Contact   Dr. Louis Traina, Director, Division of Continuing Professional Education, Carleton Avenue, Building 66, Room 212, Central Islip, NY 11722. 516-348-3325.

TECHNICAL AND BUSINESS WRITING (23.11)
Technical Writing

General Information   Unit offering the program: School of Humanities. Program content: Composition, computer science, engineering. Available for credit. Certificate signed by the Dean, Center for General Studies. Certificate applicable to B.S. in Technical Writing.

Program Format   Daytime, evening classes offered. Program cycle: Continuous enrollment. Full program cycle lasts 18 credit hours.

Evaluation   Student evaluation based on papers, reports. Grading system: Letters or numbers. Transcripts are kept for each student.

Enrollment Requirements   High school diploma required. Program is open to non-resident foreign students. English language proficiency required. Minimum TOEFL score required: 500.

Program Costs $2880 for the program, $480 per course.

Housing and Student Services   Housing is available. Job counseling and placement services are available.

Contact   Dr. Edward Gulliano, Program Director, Technical Writing, Wheatley Road, Old Westbury, NY 11568. 516-686-7516.

TRANSPORTATION AND TRAVEL MARKETING (08.11)
Travel and Tourism

General Information   Unit offering the program: Division of Continuing Professional Education. Program content: Tour packaging, advertising, promotion, public relations, marketing, airlines, agency management. Available on a non-credit basis. Endorsed by Long Island Travel and Tourism Board. Certificate signed by the Dean, Office of Institutional Liaison.

Program Format   Daytime, evening classes offered. Instructional schedule: Once per week for two hours. Students may enroll fall, spring, summer. Full program cycle lasts 6 courses. Completion of program requires mid-term and final examinations.

Evaluation   Student evaluation based on tests, papers, reports. Grading system: Pass/fail. Transcripts are kept for each student.

Enrollment Requirements   Open enrollment. Program is open to non-resident foreign students. English language proficiency required. Students should be reading at a minimum twelfth-grade level.

Program Costs $660 for the program, $110 per course.

Housing and Student Services   Housing is not available. Job counseling and placement services are available.

Special Features   NYIT offers a six-course certificate program for participants in the travel and tourism field who wish to update their skills, as well as for those interested in entering the field. Courses are offered both day and evening to accommodate the adult student's busy schedule.

Contact   Dr. Louis J. Traina, Director, Division of Continuing Professional Education, Carleton Avenue, Building 66, Room 212, Central Islip, NY 11722. 516-348-3325.

NUCEA MEMBER
NEW YORK UNIVERSITY
New York, New York 10011

ACCOUNTING, BOOKKEEPING, AND RELATED PROGRAMS (07.01)
Certificate in Bookkeeping

General Information   Unit offering the program: Information Technologies Institute. Program content: Journalizing transactions, ledger, payroll, financial statements, business papers, sales returns. Available on a non-credit basis. Certificate signed by the Dean, School of Continuing Education.

Program Format   Evening classes offered. Program cycle: Continuous enrollment. Complete program cycle lasts 56 classroom hours. Completion of program requires two courses, 2.0 GPA.

Evaluation   Student evaluation methods vary by course. Grading system: Letters or numbers. Transcripts are kept for each student.

Enrollment Requirements   Program is open to non-resident foreign students.

Program Costs $325 per course.

Housing and Student Services   Housing is not available. Job counseling and placement services are not available.

Contact   Certificate in Bookkeeping, Information Technologies, School of Continuing Education, 48 Cooper Square, Room 104, New York, NY 10003. 212-998-7190.

ACCOUNTING, BOOKKEEPING, AND RELATED PROGRAMS (07.01)
Certificate in Business Statistics

General Information   Unit offering the program: Real Estate Institute. Program content: Basic statistics for management, ANOVA, SPSS/PC+. Available on a non-credit basis. Certificate signed by the Dean, School of Continuing Education.

Program Format   Evening classes offered. Program cycle: Continuous enrollment. Complete program cycle lasts 50 classroom hours. Completion of program requires two courses, average grade of B- or better.

Evaluation   Student evaluation methods vary by course. Grading system: Letters or numbers. Transcripts are kept for each student.

Enrollment Requirements   Program is open to non-resident foreign students.

Program Costs $290 per course.

Housing and Student Services   Housing is not available. Job counseling and placement services are not available.

Contact   Certificate in Business Statistics, Midtown Center, 11 West 42nd Street, New York, NY 10036. 212-790-1300.

ADVERTISING (09.02)
Certificate in Marketing/Advertising

General Information   Unit offering the program: Management Institute. Program content: Marketing planning and communications, advertising, promotion, sales, copywriting. Available on a non-credit basis. Certificate signed by the Dean, School of Continuing Education.

Program Format   Evening classes offered. Program cycle: Continuous enrollment. Complete program cycle lasts 106–148 classroom hours. Completion of program requires six courses, average grade of B or better.

Evaluation   Student evaluation methods vary by course. Grading system: Letters or numbers. Transcripts are kept for each student.

Enrollment Requirements   Program is open to non-resident foreign students.

Program Costs $110–$375 per course.

Housing and Student Services   Housing is not available. Job counseling and placement services are not available.

Contact   Certificate in Marketing/Advertising, School of Continuing Education, 48 Cooper Square, Room 108, New York, NY 10003. 212-998-7215.

BANKING AND FINANCE (06.03)
Certificate in Banking Management

General Information   Unit offering the program: Banking and Finance. Program content: Money and banking, bank operations management, corporate cash management, financial statements, international banking. Available on a non-credit basis. Certificate signed by the Dean, School of Continuing Education.

Program Format   Evening classes offered. Program cycle: Continuous enrollment. Complete program cycle lasts 122–150 classroom hours. Completion of program requires six courses, 2.0 GPA.

Evaluation   Student evaluation methods vary by course. Grading system: Letters or numbers. Transcripts are kept for each student.

Enrollment Requirements   Limited to those employed in the field. Program is open to non-resident foreign students.

Program Costs $305–$360 per course.

Housing and Student Services   Housing is not available. Job counseling and placement services are not available.

Contact   Certificate in Banking Management, School of Continuing Education, 48 Cooper Square, Room 107, New York, NY 10003. 212-998-7210.

BANKING AND FINANCE (06.03)
Certificate in Credit and Financial Analysis

General Information   Unit offering the program: Banking and Finance. Program content: Financial statement analysis, risk, lending, marketing, money and banking, accounting. Available on a non-credit basis. Certificate signed by the Dean, School of Continuing Education.

Program Format   Evening classes offered. Program cycle: Continuous enrollment. Complete program cycle lasts 95–152 classroom hours. Completion of program requires six courses, 2.0 GPA.

Evaluation   Student evaluation methods vary by course. Grading system: Letters or numbers. Transcripts are kept for each student.

Enrollment Requirements   Limited to those employed in the field. Program is open to non-resident foreign students.

Program Costs $260–$360 per course.

Housing and Student Services   Housing is not available. Job counseling and placement services are not available.

Contact   Certificate in Credit and Financial Analysis, School of Continuing Education, 48 Cooper Square, Room 107, New York, NY 10003. 212-998-7210.

BANKING AND FINANCE (06.03)
Certificate in Financial Controls

General Information   Unit offering the program: Banking and Finance. Program content: Accounting for the non-financial manager, financial statements, analysis of financial data, cost accounting, internal auditing, cash management, corporate finance. Available on a non-credit basis. Certificate signed by the Dean, School of Continuing Education.

Program Format   Evening classes offered. Program cycle: Continuous enrollment. Complete program cycle lasts 102–142 classroom hours. Completion of program requires six courses, 2.0 GPA.

Evaluation   Student evaluation methods vary by course. Grading system: Letters or numbers. Transcripts are kept for each student.

Enrollment Requirements   Program is open to non-resident foreign students.

Program Costs $235–$305 per course.

Housing and Student Services   Housing is not available. Job counseling and placement services are not available.

Contact   Certificate in Financial Controls, School of Continuing Education, 48 Cooper Square, Room 107, New York, NY 10003. 212-998-7210.

BANKING AND FINANCE (06.03)
Certificate in Financial Planning

General Information   Unit offering the program: Banking and Finance. Program content: Risk management, investments, employee benefits, taxes, retirement, estate planning. Available on a non-credit basis. Certificate signed by the Dean, School of Continuing Education.

Program Format   Evening classes offered. Program cycle: Continuous enrollment. Complete program cycle lasts 156 classroom hours. Completion of program requires six courses, 2.0 GPA.

Evaluation   Student evaluation methods vary by course. Grading system: Letters or numbers. Transcripts are kept for each student.

Enrollment Requirements   Program is open to non-resident foreign students.

Program Costs $400 per course.

Housing and Student Services   Housing is not available. Job counseling and placement services are not available.

Contact   Certificate in Financial Planning, School of Continuing Education, 48 Cooper Square, Room 107, New York, NY 10003. 212-998-7210.

BANKING AND FINANCE (06.03)
Certificate in Mortgage-Backed Securities

General Information   Unit offering the program: Real Estate Institute. Program content: Marketing strategies, second mortgages, structures. Available on a non-credit basis. Certificate signed by the Dean, School of Continuing Education.

Program Format   Evening classes offered. Program cycle: Continuous enrollment. Complete program cycle lasts 86–123 classroom hours. Completion of program requires six courses, 2.0 GPA.

Evaluation   Student evaluation methods vary by course. Grading system: Letters or numbers. Transcripts are kept for each student.

Enrollment Requirements   Limited to those in the industry. Program is open to non-resident foreign students.

Program Costs $190–$320 per course.

Housing and Student Services   Housing is not available. Job counseling and placement services are not available.

Contact   Certificate Clerk, The Real Estate Institute, Midtown Center, 11 West 42nd Street, New York, NY 10036. 212-790-1300.

BANKING AND FINANCE (06.03)
Certificate in Mortgage Banking

General Information   Unit offering the program: Real Estate Institute. Program content: Functions and operations of the mortgage banker. Available on a non-credit basis. Certificate signed by the Dean, School of Continuing Education.

Program Format   Evening classes offered. Program cycle: Continuous enrollment. Complete program cycle lasts 98–125 classroom hours. Completion of program requires six courses, 2.0 GPA.

Certificate in Mortgage Banking continued

Evaluation Student evaluation methods vary by course. Grading system: Letters or numbers. Transcripts are kept for each student.

Enrollment Requirements Program is open to non-resident foreign students.

Program Costs $190–$320 per course.

Housing and Student Services Housing is not available. Job counseling and placement services are not available.

Contact Certificate Clerk, The Real Estate Institute, Midtown Center, 11 West 42nd Street, New York, NY 10036. 212-790-1300.

BUSINESS AND MANAGEMENT, GENERAL (06.01)
Certificate in Management Practices

General Information Unit offering the program: Management Institute. Program content: Time management, planning, organizing, directing, evaluating work, communication, leadership. Available on a non-credit basis. Certificate signed by the Dean, School of Continuing Education.

Program Format Evening classes offered. Complete program cycle lasts 129–165 classroom hours. Completion of program requires six courses, average grade of B or better.

Evaluation Student evaluation methods vary by course. Grading system: Letters or numbers. Transcripts are kept for each student.

Enrollment Requirements Program is open to non-resident foreign students.

Program Costs $160–$335 per course.

Housing and Student Services Housing is not available. Job counseling and placement services are not available.

Contact Certificate in Management Practices, School of Continuing Education, 48 Cooper Square, Room 108, New York, NY 10003. 212-998-7215.

BUSINESS AND PERSONAL SERVICES MARKETING (08.02)
Certificate in Meeting and Conference Management

General Information Unit offering the program: Management Institute. Program content: Meeting management, budget controls, legal requirements, resources and supplier relations. Available on a non-credit basis. Certificate signed by the Dean, School of Continuing Education.

Program Format Evening classes offered. Program cycle: Continuous enrollment. Complete program cycle lasts 74–95 classroom hours. Completion of program requires five courses, average grade of B or better.

Evaluation Student evaluation methods vary by course. Grading system: Letters or numbers. Transcripts are kept for each student.

Enrollment Requirements Program is open to non-resident foreign students.

Program Costs $160–$305 per course.

Housing and Student Services Housing is not available. Job counseling and placement services are not available.

Contact Certificate in Meeting and Conference Management, School of Continuing Education, 48 Cooper Square, Room 108, New York, NY 10003. 212-998-7215.

BUSINESS DATA PROCESSING AND RELATED PROGRAMS (07.03)
Certificate in Applied Business Concepts

General Information Unit offering the program: Information Technologies Institute. Program content: Accounting fundamentals, written and verbal communication, management techniques, computers, word processing. Available on a non-credit basis. Certificate signed by the Dean, School of Continuing Education.

Program Format Evening classes offered. Program cycle: Continuous enrollment. Complete program cycle lasts 160 classroom hours. Completion of program requires six courses, 2.0 GPA.

Evaluation Student evaluation methods vary by course. Grading system: Letters or numbers. Transcripts are kept for each student.

Enrollment Requirements Program is open to non-resident foreign students.

Program Costs $300–$325 per course.

Housing and Student Services Housing is not available. Job counseling and placement services are not available.

Contact Applied Business Concepts, Information Technologies, School of Continuing Education, 48 Cooper Square, Room 104, New York, NY 10003. 212-998-7190.

BUSINESS DATA PROCESSING AND RELATED PROGRAMS (07.03)
Certificate in Office Automation

General Information Unit offering the program: Information Technologies Institute. Program content: Word processing, electronic mail, personal business computing, integrated voice/data telephone systems. Available on a non-credit basis. Certificate signed by the Dean, School of Continuing Education.

Program Format Evening classes offered. Program cycle: Continuous enrollment. Complete program cycle lasts 192 classroom hours. Completion of program requires six courses, 2.0 GPA.

Evaluation Student evaluation methods vary by course. Grading system: Letters or numbers. Transcripts are kept for each student.

Enrollment Requirements Intended for office employees. Program is open to non-resident foreign students.

Program Costs $375–$395 per course.

Housing and Student Services Housing is not available. Job counseling and placement services are not available.

Contact Certificate Applications, Information Technologies, School of Continuing Education, 48 Cooper Square, Room 104, New York, NY 10003. 212-998-7190.

COMMUNICATIONS, GENERAL (09.01)
Certificate in Book Publishing

General Information Unit offering the program: Management Institute. Program content: Production, marketing, business aspects, copyediting, proofreading, design, management. Available on a non-credit basis. Certificate signed by the Dean, School of Continuing Education.

Program Format Evening classes offered. Program cycle: Continuous enrollment. Complete program cycle lasts 82–122 classroom hours. Completion of program requires five courses, average grade of B or better.

Evaluation Student evaluation methods vary by course. Grading system: Letters or numbers. Transcripts are kept for each student.

Enrollment Requirements Program is open to non-resident foreign students.

Program Costs $160–$305 per course.

Housing and Student Services Housing is not available. Job counseling and placement services are not available.

Contact Certificate in Book Publishing, School of Continuing Education, 48 Cooper Square, Room 108, New York, NY 10003. 212-998-7215.

COMMUNICATIONS, GENERAL (09.01)
Certificate in Copywriting

General Information   Unit offering the program: Management Institute. Program content: Advertising copywriting, TV commercials, medical and business copywriting, circulation promotion. Available on a non-credit basis. Certificate signed by the Dean, School of Continuing Education.

Program Format   Evening classes offered. Program cycle: Continuous enrollment. Complete program cycle lasts 97–120 classroom hours. Completion of program requires five courses, average grade of B or better.

Evaluation   Student evaluation methods vary by course. Grading system: Letters or numbers. Transcripts are kept for each student.

Enrollment Requirements   Program is open to non-resident foreign students.

Program Costs $195–$330 per course.

Housing and Student Services   Housing is not available. Job counseling and placement services are not available.

Contact   Certificate in Copywriting, School of Continuing Education, 48 Cooper Square, Room 108, New York, NY 10003. 212-998-7215.

COMPUTER AND INFORMATION SCIENCES, GENERAL (11.01)
Certificate in MVS Console Operations

General Information   Unit offering the program: Information Technologies Institute. Program content: Concepts and skills for the IBM MVS computer. Available on a non-credit basis. Certificate signed by the Dean, School of Continuing Education.

Program Format   Evening classes offered. Program cycle: Continuous enrollment. Complete program cycle lasts 180 classroom hours. Completion of program requires two courses, 2.0 GPA.

Evaluation   Student evaluation methods vary by course. Grading system: Letters or numbers. Transcripts are kept for each student.

Enrollment Requirements   Program is open to non-resident foreign students.

Program Costs $750 per course.

Housing and Student Services   Housing is not available. Job counseling and placement services are not available.

Contact   Certificate Applications, Information Technologies, School of Continuing Education, 48 Cooper Square, Room 104, New York, NY 10003. 212-998-7190.

COMPUTER ENGINEERING (14.09)
Certificate in Software Engineering

General Information   Unit offering the program: Information Technologies Institute. Program content: Managing software development, file and database design, performance evaluation, testing, design, requirements analysis. Available on a non-credit basis. Certificate signed by the Dean, School of Continuing Education.

Program Format   Evening classes offered. Program cycle: Continuous enrollment. Complete program cycle lasts 252 classroom hours. Completion of program requires six courses, 2.0 GPA.

Evaluation   Student evaluation methods vary by course. Grading system: Letters or numbers. Transcripts are kept for each student.

Enrollment Requirements   Three years working experience with COBOL, PL/I, FORTRAN, C or Ada required. Program is open to non-resident foreign students.

Program Costs $395 per course.

Housing and Student Services   Housing is not available. Job counseling and placement services are not available.

Contact   Certificate Applications, Information Technologies, School of Continuing Education, 48 Cooper Square, Room 104, New York, NY 10003. 212-998-7190.

COMPUTER PROGRAMMING (11.02)
Certificate in Applications Programming

General Information   Unit offering the program: Information Technologies Institute. Program content: Computer programming concepts, problem analysis, COBOL programming, operating system concepts and IBM MVS, OS/VS job control language. Available on a non-credit basis. Certificate signed by the Dean, School of Continuing Education.

Program Format   Evening classes offered. Program cycle: Continuous enrollment. Complete program cycle lasts 252 classroom hours. Completion of program requires six courses, 2.0 GPA.

Evaluation   Student evaluation methods vary by course. Grading system: Letters or numbers. Transcripts are kept for each student.

Enrollment Requirements   Program is open to non-resident foreign students.

Program Costs $390–$395 per course.

Housing and Student Services   Housing is not available. Job counseling and placement services are not available.

Contact   Certificate Applications, Information Technologies, School of Continuing Education, 48 Cooper Square, Room 104, New York, NY 10003. 212-998-7190.

DATA PROCESSING (11.03)
Certificate in Data Base Technology

General Information   Unit offering the program: Information Technologies Institute. Program content: Database concepts, techniques, applications. Available on a non-credit basis. Certificate signed by the Dean, School of Continuing Education.

Program Format   Evening classes offered. Program cycle: Continuous enrollment. Complete program cycle lasts 120–132 classroom hours. Completion of program requires four courses, 2.0 GPA.

Evaluation   Student evaluation methods vary by course. Grading system: Letters or numbers. Transcripts are kept for each student.

Enrollment Requirements   Programming knowledge required. Program is open to non-resident foreign students.

Program Costs $375–$415 per course.

Housing and Student Services   Housing is not available. Job counseling and placement services are not available.

Contact   Certificate Applications, Information Technologies, School of Continuing Education, 48 Cooper Square, Room 104, New York, NY 10003. 212-998-7190.

DATA PROCESSING (11.03)
Certificate in Data Communications

General Information   Unit offering the program: Information Technologies Institute. Program content: Data communications systems, SNA architecture, communications protocols, networks. Available on a non-credit basis. Certificate signed by the Dean, School of Continuing Education.

Program Format   Evening classes offered. Program cycle: Continuous enrollment. Complete program cycle lasts 184–198 classroom hours. Completion of program requires five courses, 2.0 GPA.

Evaluation   Student evaluation methods vary by course. Grading system: Letters or numbers. Transcripts are kept for each student.

Enrollment Requirements   Program is open to non-resident foreign students.

Program Costs $375–$415 per course.

Certificate in Data Communications continued

Housing and Student Services   Housing is not available. Job counseling and placement services are not available.

Contact   Certificate Applications, Information Technologies, School of Continuing Education, 48 Cooper Square, Room 104, New York, NY 10003. 212-998-7190.

ELECTRICAL AND ELECTRONIC TECHNOLOGIES (15.03)
Certificate in Electronics

General Information   Unit offering the program: Information Technologies Institute. Program content: Electrical circuit theory, digital electronics. Available on a non-credit basis. Certificate signed by the Dean, School of Continuing Education.

Program Format   Evening classes offered. Program cycle: Continuous enrollment. Complete program cycle lasts 120 classroom hours. Completion of program requires two courses, 2.0 GPA.

Evaluation   Student evaluation methods vary by course. Grading system: Letters or numbers. Transcripts are kept for each student.

Enrollment Requirements   Program is open to non-resident foreign students.

Program Costs $450 per course.

Housing and Student Services   Housing is not available. Job counseling and placement services are not available.

Contact   Certificate Applications, Information Technologies, School of Continuing Education, 48 Cooper Square, Room 104, New York, NY 10003. 212-998-7190.

ELECTRICAL AND ELECTRONIC TECHNOLOGIES (15.03)
PC Technician Certificate

General Information   Unit offering the program: Information Technologies Institute. Program content: Theory, applications, troubleshooting, and repair of IBM PC, XT, and AT computers and compatibles. Available on a non-credit basis. Certificate signed by the Dean, School of Continuing Education.

Program Format   Evening classes offered. Program cycle: Continuous enrollment. Complete program cycle lasts 180 classroom hours. Completion of program requires three courses, 2.0 GPA.

Evaluation   Student evaluation methods vary by course. Grading system: Letters or numbers. Transcripts are kept for each student.

Enrollment Requirements   Background in electrical circuit theory and digital electronics required. Program is open to non-resident foreign students.

Program Costs $900 per course.

Housing and Student Services   Housing is not available. Job counseling and placement services are not available.

Contact   Certificate Applications, Information Technologies, School of Continuing Education, 48 Cooper Square, Room 104, New York, NY 10003. 212-998-7190.

ELECTRICAL AND POWER TRANSMISSION INSTALLATION (46.03)
Certificate in Building Electrical Systems Design

General Information   Unit offering the program: Real Estate Institute. Program content: Electrical theory, wiring devices, feeder design, grounding, emergency systems, ground fault, short circuits. Available on a non-credit basis. Certificate signed by the Dean, School of Continuing Education.

Program Format   Evening classes offered. Program cycle: Continuous enrollment. Complete program cycle lasts 96–104 classroom hours. Completion of program requires four courses, 2.0 GPA.

Evaluation   Student evaluation methods vary by course. Grading system: Letters or numbers. Transcripts are kept for each student.

Enrollment Requirements   Program is open to non-resident foreign students.

Program Costs $275 per course.

Housing and Student Services   Housing is not available. Job counseling and placement services are not available.

Contact   Certificate Clerk, The Real Estate Institute, Midtown Center, 11 West 42nd Street, New York, NY 10036. 212-790-1300.

ELECTRICAL AND POWER TRANSMISSION INSTALLATION (46.03)
Certificate in Lighting Systems Design

General Information   Unit offering the program: Real Estate Institute. Program content: Lighting technology, controls, energy conservation, system design criteria. Available on a non-credit basis. Certificate signed by the Dean, School of Continuing Eduction.

Program Format   Evening classes offered. Program cycle: Continuous enrollment. Complete program cycle lasts 52 classroom hours. Completion of program requires two courses, 2.0 GPA.

Evaluation   Student evaluation methods vary by course. Grading system: Letters or numbers. Transcripts are kept for each student.

Enrollment Requirements   Program is open to non-resident foreign students.

Program Costs $275 per course.

Housing and Student Services   Housing is not available. Job counseling and placement services are not available.

Contact   Certificate Clerk, The Real Estate Institute, Midtown Center, 11 West 42nd Street, New York, NY 10036. 212-790-1300.

ENVIRONMENTAL CONTROL TECHNOLOGIES (15.05)
Certificate in HVAC Systems and Equipment

General Information   Unit offering the program: Real Estate Institute. Program content: Principles of air-conditioning and refrigeration, systems and equipment, controls, air distribution, piping design. Available on a non-credit basis. Certificate signed by the Dean, School of Continuing Education.

Program Format   Evening classes offered. Program cycle: Continuous enrollment. Complete program cycle lasts 91–110 classroom hours. Completion of program requires four courses, 2.0 GPA.

Evaluation   Student evaluation methods vary by course. Grading system: Letters or numbers. Transcripts are kept for each student.

Enrollment Requirements   Intended for those in consulting, contracting, construction, or management. Program is open to non-resident foreign students.

Program Costs $260–$290 per course.

Housing and Student Services   Housing is not available. Job counseling and placement services are not available.

Contact   Certificate Clerk, The Real Estate Institute, Midtown Center, 11 West 42nd Street, New York, NY 10036. 212-790-1300.

FILM ARTS (50.06)
Certificate in Filmmaking

General Information   Unit offering the program: The Filmmaking Program. Program content: Production, lighting, editing, budgeting, directing, writing. Available on a non-credit basis. Certificate signed by the Dean, School of Continuing Education.

Program Format Daytime, evening, weekend classes offered. Program cycle: Continuous enrollment. Complete program cycle lasts 272–389 classroom hours. Completion of program requires eight courses, 80% attendance, average grade of B or better.

Evaluation Student evaluation methods vary by course. Grading system: Letters or numbers. Transcripts are kept for each student.

Enrollment Requirements Program is open to non-resident foreign students.

Program Costs $260–$650 per course.

Housing and Student Services Housing is not available. Job counseling and placement services are not available.

Special Features The Daytime Intensive Program is an 11-week intensive course of study. All requirements are the same as the regular certificate program. The Summer Intensive Program is a special five-week intensive program. Admission by application only. Financial aid available only for daytime intensive and summer intensive programs.

Contact The Filmmaking Program, School of Continuing Education, 332 Shimkin Hall, New York, NY 10003. 212-998-7140.

FINE ARTS (50.07)
Certificate in Appraisal Studies

General Information Unit offering the program: Division of Arts, Sciences and Humanities. Program content: Personal property damage, elements of multi-specialty appraising, IRS legal guidelines, ethics. Available on a non-credit basis. Certificate signed by the Dean, School of Continuing Education.

Program Format Evening classes offered. Program cycle: Continuous enrollment. Complete program cycle lasts 61–89 classroom hours. Completion of program requires one seminar, eight courses, 2.0 GPA.

Evaluation Student evaluation methods vary by course. Grading system: Letters or numbers. Transcripts are kept for each student.

Enrollment Requirements Program is open to non-resident foreign students.

Program Costs $100–$240 per course.

Housing and Student Services Housing is not available. Job counseling and placement services are not available.

Contact Appraisal Studies Certificate, School of Continuing Education, 332 Shimkin Hall, New York, NY 10003. 212-998-7130.

FOOD PRODUCTION, MANAGEMENT, AND SERVICES (20.04)
Certificate in Food and Beverage Management

General Information Unit offering the program: Management Institute. Program content: Management, menu planning, food purchasing and storage, kitchen planning, food and beverage control, staffing, payroll. Available on a non-credit basis. Certificate signed by the Dean, School of Continuing Education.

Program Format Evening classes offered. Instructional schedule: Two evenings per week. Program cycle: Continuous enrollment. Complete program cycle lasts 55 classroom hours. Completion of program requires grade of B or better.

Evaluation Student evaluation methods vary by course. Grading system: Letters or numbers. Transcripts are kept for each student.

Enrollment Requirements Program is open to non-resident foreign students.

Program Costs $375 for the program.

Housing and Student Services Housing is not available. Job counseling and placement services are not available.

Contact Certificate in Food and Beverage Management, School of Continuing Education, 48 Cooper Square, Room 108, New York, NY 10003. 212-998-7215.

FOREIGN LANGUAGES, MULTIPLE EMPHASIS (16.01)
Certificate in Foreign Language

General Information Unit offering the program: Foreign Language Department. Program content: Conversational communication skills in languages. Available on a non-credit basis. Certificate signed by the Dean, School of Continuing Education.

Program Format Evening classes offered. Program cycle: Continuous enrollment. Complete program cycle lasts 80–120 classroom hours. Completion of program requires four to six courses, 2.0 GPA.

Evaluation Student evaluation methods vary by course. Grading system: Letters or numbers. Transcripts are kept for each student.

Enrollment Requirements Program is open to non-resident foreign students.

Program Costs $265–$475 per course.

Housing and Student Services Housing is not available. Job counseling and placement services are not available.

Contact Foreign Language Department, School of Continuing Education, 2 University Place, Room 55, New York, NY 10003. 212-998-7030.

FOREIGN LANGUAGES, MULTIPLE EMPHASIS (16.01)
Certificate in Translation

General Information Unit offering the program: Foreign Language Department. Program content: Theory and practice of translation. Available on a non-credit basis. Certificate signed by the Dean, School of Continuing Education.

Program Format Evening classes offered. Program cycle: Continuous enrollment. Complete program cycle lasts 120 classroom hours. Completion of program requires six courses, 2.0 GPA.

Evaluation Student evaluation methods vary by course. Grading system: Letters or numbers. Transcripts are kept for each student.

Enrollment Requirements Degree or advanced study in a foreign language, completion of Theory and Practice course required. Program is open to non-resident foreign students.

Program Costs $350 per course.

Housing and Student Services Housing is not available. Job counseling and placement services are not available.

Contact Foreign Language Department, School of Continuing Education, 2 University Place, Room 55, New York, NY 10003. 212-998-7030.

HEALTH SERVICES ADMINISTRATION (18.07)
Certificate in Health Care Administration

General Information Unit offering the program: Information Technologies Institute. Program content: Budgeting and practical accounting, supervision, current legal issues, automation in health care administration. Available on a non-credit basis. Certificate signed by the Dean, School of Continuing Education.

Program Format Evening classes offered. Program cycle: Continuous enrollment. Complete program cycle lasts 85 classroom hours. Completion of program requires four courses, 2.0 GPA.

Evaluation Student evaluation methods vary by course. Grading system: Letters or numbers. Transcripts are kept for each student.

Enrollment Requirements Program is open to non-resident foreign students.

Certificate in Health Care Administration continued

Program Costs $300–$375 per course.

Housing and Student Services Housing is not available. Job counseling and placement services are not available.

Contact Certificate in Health Care Administration, School of Continuing Education, 48 Cooper Square, Room 104, New York, NY 10003. 212-998-7190.

HOSPITALITY AND RECREATION MARKETING (08.09)
Certificate in Sports and Special Event Management

General Information Unit offering the program: Management Institute. Program content: Promotion, marketing, public relations, communications. Available on a non-credit basis. Certificate signed by the Dean, School of Continuing Education.

Program Format Evening classes offered. Program cycle: Continuous enrollment. Complete program cycle lasts 80–86 classroom hours. Completion of program requires five courses, average grade of B or better.

Evaluation Student evaluation methods vary by course. Grading system: Letters or numbers. Transcripts are kept for each student.

Enrollment Requirements Program is open to non-resident foreign students.

Program Costs $175–$295 per course.

Housing and Student Services Housing is not available. Job counseling and placement services are not available.

Contact Certificate in Sports and Special Event Management, School of Continuing Education, 48 Cooper Square, Room 108, New York, NY 10003. 212-998-7215.

INFORMATION SCIENCES AND SYSTEMS (11.04)
Certificate in Artificial Intelligence

General Information Unit offering the program: Information Technologies Institute. Program content: Introduction to artificial intelligence, natural language processing, knowledge engineering for business, PROLOG, LISP. Available on a non-credit basis. Certificate signed by the Dean, School of Continuing Education.

Program Format Evening classes offered. Program cycle: Continuous enrollment. Complete program cycle lasts 168 classroom hours. Completion of program requires four courses, 2.0 GPA.

Evaluation Student evaluation methods vary by course. Grading system: Letters or numbers. Transcripts are kept for each student.

Enrollment Requirements Program is open to non-resident foreign students.

Program Costs $395 per course.

Housing and Student Services Housing is not available. Job counseling and placement services are not available.

Contact Certificate Applications, Information Technologies, School of Continuing Education, 48 Cooper Square, Room 104, New York, NY 10003. 212-998-7190.

INFORMATION SCIENCES AND SYSTEMS (11.04)
Certificate in CICS

General Information Unit offering the program: Information Technologies Institute. Program content: Command level application programming, CCIS concepts and facilities, internals, architecture. Available on a non-credit basis. Certificate signed by the Dean, School of Continuing Education.

Program Format Evening classes offered. Program cycle: Continuous enrollment. Complete program cycle lasts 156 classroom hours. Completion of program requires four courses, 2.0 GPA.

Evaluation Student evaluation methods vary by course. Grading system: Letters or numbers. Transcripts are kept for each student.

Enrollment Requirements Professional experience in COBOL or BAL required. Program is open to non-resident foreign students.

Program Costs $390–$415 per course.

Housing and Student Services Housing is not available. Job counseling and placement services are not available.

Contact Certificate Applications, Information Technologies, School of Continuing Education, 48 Cooper Square, Room 104, New York, NY 10003. 212-998-7190.

INFORMATION SCIENCES AND SYSTEMS (11.04)
Certificate in PC Software Development

General Information Unit offering the program: Information Technologies Institute. Program content: C programming for the IBM PC, 8086/8088 assembler programming, advanced topics. Available on a non-credit basis. Certificate signed by the Dean, School of Continuing Education.

Program Format Evening classes offered. Program cycle: Continuous enrollment. Complete program cycle lasts 252 classroom hours. Completion of program requires six courses, 2.0 GPA.

Evaluation Student evaluation methods vary by course. Grading system: Letters or numbers. Transcripts are kept for each student.

Enrollment Requirements Knowledge of PC DOS, PC applications, and a high-level language required. Students must have access to an IBM PC, 8086/8088 macro assembler, and C compiler. Program is open to non-resident foreign students.

Program Costs $395–$415 per course.

Housing and Student Services Housing is not available. Job counseling and placement services are not available.

Contact Certificate Applications, Information Technologies, School of Continuing Education, 48 Cooper Square, Room 104, New York, NY 10003. 212-998-7190.

INFORMATION SCIENCES AND SYSTEMS (11.04)
Certificate in Systems Programming

General Information Unit offering the program: Information Technologies Institute. Program content: Advanced techniques in assembler, OS/VS supervisor services and macros, MVS analysis. Available on a non-credit basis. Certificate signed by the Dean, School of Continuing Education.

Program Format Evening classes offered. Program cycle: Continuous enrollment. Complete program cycle lasts 252 classroom hours. Completion of program requires six courses, 2.0 GPA.

Evaluation Student evaluation methods vary by course. Grading system: Letters or numbers. Transcripts are kept for each student.

Enrollment Requirements Limited to those working in data processing using assembler. Program is open to non-resident foreign students.

Program Costs $395–$415 per course.

Housing and Student Services Housing is not available. Job counseling and placement services are not available.

Contact Certificate Applications, Information Technologies, School of Continuing Education, 48 Cooper Square, Room 104, New York, NY 10003. 212-998-7190.

INFORMATION SCIENCES AND SYSTEMS (11.04)
Certificate in UNIX/C

General Information   Unit offering the program: Information Technologies Institute. Program content: UNIX operating system, programming tools, C programming, system internals, administration. Available on a non-credit basis. Certificate signed by the Dean, School of Continuing Education.

Program Format   Evening classes offered. Program cycle: Continuous enrollment. Complete program cycle lasts 186 classroom hours. Completion of program requires five courses, 2.0 GPA.

Evaluation   Student evaluation methods vary by course. Grading system: Letters or numbers. Transcripts are kept for each student.

Enrollment Requirements   Program is open to non-resident foreign students.

Program Costs $390–$415 per course.

Housing and Student Services   Housing is not available. Job counseling and placement services are not available.

Contact   Certificate Applications, Information Technologies, School of Continuing Education, 48 Cooper Square, Room 104, New York, NY 10003. 212-998-7190.

INFORMATION SCIENCES AND SYSTEMS (11.04)
Certificate in VAX/VMS Computer Systems

General Information   Unit offering the program: Information Technologies Institute. Program content: Concepts and facilities, architecture, programming services, system management. Available on a non-credit basis. Certificate signed by the Dean, School of Continuing Education.

Program Format   Evening classes offered. Program cycle: Continuous enrollment. Complete program cycle lasts 168 classroom hours. Completion of program requires four courses, 2.0 GPA.

Evaluation   Student evaluation methods vary by course. Grading system: Letters or numbers. Transcripts are kept for each student.

Enrollment Requirements   Program is open to non-resident foreign students.

Program Costs $395 per course.

Housing and Student Services   Housing is not available. Job counseling and placement services are not available.

Contact   Certificate Applications, Information Technologies, School of Continuing Education, 48 Cooper Square, Room 104, New York, NY 10003. 212-998-7190.

INSTITUTIONAL MANAGEMENT (06.07)
Certificate in Fund-Raising Management

General Information   Unit offering the program: Management Institute. Program content: Fund-raising concepts and practices, writing, information systems, direct mail, publicity and promotion. Available on a non-credit basis. Certificate signed by the Dean, School of Continuing Education.

Program Format   Evening classes offered. Program cycle: Continuous enrollment. Complete program cycle lasts 56–72 classroom hours. Completion of program requires four courses, average grade of B or better.

Evaluation   Student evaluation methods vary by course. Grading system: Letters or numbers. Transcripts are kept for each student.

Enrollment Requirements   Program is open to non-resident foreign students.

Program Costs $135–$225 per course.

Housing and Student Services   Housing is not available. Job counseling and placement services are not available.

Contact   Certificate in Fund-Raising Management, School of Continuing Education, 48 Cooper Square, Room 108, New York, NY 10003. 212-998-7215.

INSTITUTIONAL MANAGEMENT (06.07)
Certificate in Hotel and Motel Management

General Information   Unit offering the program: Management Institute. Program content: Rooms, food and beverage, personnel, accounting, sales and marketing, engineering. Available on a non-credit basis. Certificate signed by the Dean, School of Continuing Education.

Program Format   Evening classes offered. Instructional schedule: Two evenings per week. Program cycle: Continuous enrollment. Complete program cycle lasts 65 classroom hours. Completion of program requires grade of B or better.

Evaluation   Student evaluation methods vary by course. Grading system: Letters or numbers. Transcripts are kept for each student.

Enrollment Requirements   Program is open to non-resident foreign students.

Program Costs $550 for the program.

Housing and Student Services   Housing is not available. Job counseling and placement services are not available.

Contact   Certificate in Hotel and Motel Management, School of Continuing Education, 48 Cooper Square, Room 108, New York, NY 10003. 212-998-7215.

INTERNATIONAL BUSINESS MANAGEMENT (06.09)
Certificate in Foreign Exchange and Money Market Trading

General Information   Unit offering the program: Banking and Finance. Program content: Fundamentals of foreign exchange, foreign currency, futures and options trading, money market trading and domestic funding, risk management, exposure, trading techniques. Available on a non-credit basis. Certificate signed by the Dean, School of Continuing Education.

Program Format   Evening classes offered. Program cycle: Continuous enrollment. Complete program cycle lasts 58–78 classroom hours. Completion of program requires four courses, 2.0 GPA.

Evaluation   Student evaluation methods vary by course. Grading system: Letters or numbers. Transcripts are kept for each student.

Enrollment Requirements   Program is open to non-resident foreign students.

Program Costs $240–$305 per course.

Housing and Student Services   Housing is not available. Job counseling and placement services are not available.

Contact   Certificate in Foreign Exchange and Money Market Trading, School of Continuing Education, 48 Cooper Square, Room 107, New York, NY 10003. 212-998-7210.

INTERNATIONAL BUSINESS MANAGEMENT (06.09)
Certificate in International Banking

General Information   Unit offering the program: Banking and Finance. Program content: Practices and techniques of international banking, international money and capital markets, lending analysis, foreign exchange. Available on a non-credit basis. Certificate signed by the Dean, School of Continuing Education.

Certificate in International Banking continued

Program Format   Evening classes offered. Program cycle: Continuous enrollment. Complete program cycle lasts 97–142 classroom hours. Completion of program requires six courses, 2.0 GPA.

Evaluation   Student evaluation methods vary by course. Grading system: Letters or numbers. Transcripts are kept for each student.

Enrollment Requirements   Basic accounting knowledge required. Program is open to non-resident foreign students.

Program Costs $305 per course.

Housing and Student Services   Housing is not available. Job counseling and placement services are not available.

Contact   Certificate in International Banking, School of Continuing Education, 48 Cooper Square, Room 107, New York, NY 10003. 212-998-7210.

INTERNATIONAL BUSINESS MANAGEMENT (06.09)
Certificate in International Business and Finance

General Information   Unit offering the program: Banking and Finance. Program content: International money and capital markets, marketing, financing, legal aspects, taxation, quality management, cross-cultural strategies. Available on a non-credit basis. Certificate signed by the Dean, School of Continuing Education.

Program Format   Evening classes offered. Program cycle: Continuous enrollment. Complete program cycle lasts 89–110 classroom hours. Completion of program requires six courses, 2.0 GPA.

Evaluation   Student evaluation methods vary by course. Grading system: Letters or numbers. Transcripts are kept for each student.

Enrollment Requirements   Basic accounting knowledge required. Program is open to non-resident foreign students.

Program Costs $210–$305 per course.

Housing and Student Services   Housing is not available. Job counseling and placement services are not available.

Contact   Certificate in International Business and Finance, School of Continuing Education, 48 Cooper Square, Room 107, New York, NY 10003. 212-998-7210.

INTERNATIONAL BUSINESS MANAGEMENT (06.09)
Certificate in International Trade

General Information   Unit offering the program: Real Estate Institute. Program content: Principles of international traffic and trade, minimizing customs duties, logistics management, import/export. Available on a non-credit basis. Certificate signed by the Dean, School of Continuing Education.

Program Format   Evening classes offered. Program cycle: Continuous enrollment. Complete program cycle lasts 96 classroom hours. Completion of program requires four courses, 2.0 GPA.

Evaluation   Student evaluation methods vary by course. Grading system: Letters or numbers. Transcripts are kept for each student.

Enrollment Requirements   Program is open to non-resident foreign students.

Program Costs $210–$240 per course.

Housing and Student Services   Housing is not available. Job counseling and placement services are not available.

Contact   Certificate in International Trade, Midtown Center, 11 West 42nd Street, New York, NY 10036. 212-790-1300.

INTERNATIONAL BUSINESS MANAGEMENT (06.09)
Certificate in International Traffic Management

General Information   Unit offering the program: Real Estate Institute. Program content: Import/export, customhouse brokerage, air cargo, credit instruments for international trade. Available on a non-credit basis. Certificate signed by the Dean, School of Continuing Education.

Program Format   Evening classes offered. Program cycle: Continuous enrollment. Complete program cycle lasts 79–94 classroom hours. Completion of program requires four courses, 2.0 GPA.

Evaluation   Student evaluation methods vary by course. Grading system: Letters or numbers. Transcripts are kept for each student.

Enrollment Requirements   Program is open to non-resident foreign students.

Program Costs $150–$245 per course.

Housing and Student Services   Housing is not available. Job counseling and placement services are not available.

Contact   Certificate in International Traffic Management, Midtown Center, 11 West 42nd Street, New York, NY 10036. 212-790-1300.

INVESTMENTS AND SECURITIES (06.10)
Certificate in Capital Markets

General Information   Unit offering the program: Banking and Finance. Program content: Corporate finance, investment banking, mergers and acquisitions, venture capital, corporate strategic planning, interest rate swaps, money market and futures trading. Available on a non-credit basis. Certificate signed by the Dean, School of Continuing Education.

Program Format   Evening classes offered. Program cycle: Continuous enrollment. Complete program cycle lasts 120–144 classroom hours. Completion of program requires six courses, 2.0 GPA.

Evaluation   Student evaluation methods vary by course. Grading system: Letters or numbers. Transcripts are kept for each student.

Enrollment Requirements   Program is open to non-resident foreign students.

Program Costs $260–$305 per course.

Housing and Student Services   Housing is not available. Job counseling and placement services are not available.

Contact   Certificate in Capital Markets, School of Continuing Education, 48 Cooper Square, Room 107, New York, NY 10003. 212-998-7210.

INVESTMENTS AND SECURITIES (06.10)
Certificate in Commodities Trading

General Information   Unit offering the program: Banking and Finance. Program content: Commodities trading, techniques of hedging, futures markets, exchange traded commodities futures options, futures trading. Available on a non-credit basis. Certificate signed by the Dean, School of Continuing Education.

Program Format   Evening classes offered. Program cycle: Continuous enrollment. Complete program cycle lasts 37–62 classroom hours. Completion of program requires three courses, 2.0 GPA.

Evaluation   Student evaluation methods vary by course. Grading system: Letters or numbers. Transcripts are kept for each student.

Enrollment Requirements   Program is open to non-resident foreign students.

Program Costs $170–$295 per course.

Housing and Student Services   Housing is not available. Job counseling and placement services are not available.

Contact Certificate in Commodities Trading, School of Continuing Education, 48 Cooper Square, Room 107, New York, NY 10003. 212-998-7210.

INVESTMENTS AND SECURITIES (06.10)
Certificate in Financial Markets

General Information Unit offering the program: Banking and Finance. Program content: Management of investment portfolio, regulations, options market, stock market timing, securities analysis. Available on a non-credit basis. Certificate signed by the Dean, School of Continuing Education.

Program Format Evening classes offered. Program cycle: Continuous enrollment. Complete program cycle lasts 69–115 classroom hours. Completion of program requires six courses, 2.0 GPA.

Evaluation Student evaluation methods vary by course. Grading system: Letters or numbers. Transcripts are kept for each student.

Enrollment Requirements Designed for securities dealers, corporate treasury personnel, bankers and investors. Program is open to non-resident foreign students.

Program Costs $170–$305 per course.

Housing and Student Services Housing is not available. Job counseling and placement services are not available.

Contact Certificate in Financial Markets, School of Continuing Education, 48 Cooper Square, Room 107, New York, NY 10003. 212-998-7210.

LAW (22.01)
Certificate in Real Property Law

General Information Unit offering the program: Real Estate Institute. Program content: Contracts, transactions, regulations, real estate litigation. Available on a non-credit basis. Certificate signed by the Dean, School of Continuing Education.

Program Format Evening classes offered. Program cycle: Continuous enrollment. Complete program cycle lasts 51–84 classroom hours. Completion of program requires four courses, 2.0 GPA.

Evaluation Student evaluation methods vary by course. Grading system: Letters or numbers. Transcripts are kept for each student.

Enrollment Requirements Intended for attorneys. Program is open to non-resident foreign students.

Program Costs $175–$385 per course.

Housing and Student Services Housing is not available. Job counseling and placement services are not available.

Contact Certificate Clerk, The Real Estate Institute, Midtown Center, 11 West 42nd Street, New York, NY 10036. 212-790-1300.

MISCELLANEOUS CONSTRUCTION TRADES AND PROPERTY MAINTENANCE (46.04)
Advanced Certificate in HVAC Design

General Information Unit offering the program: Real Estate Institute. Program content: Psychometric principles, computation of loads, basic steam and water design, economic analysis. Available on a non-credit basis. Certificate signed by the Dean, School of Continuing Education.

Program Format Evening classes offered. Program cycle: Continuous enrollment. Complete program cycle lasts 112 classroom hours. Completion of program requires four courses, 2.0 GPA.

Evaluation Student evaluation methods vary by course. Grading system: Letters or numbers. Transcripts are kept for each student.

Enrollment Requirements Bachelor's degree in engineering or four to five years consulting experience required. Program is open to non-resident foreign students.

Program Costs $330 per course.

Housing and Student Services Housing is not available. Job counseling and placement services are not available.

Contact Certificate Clerk, The Real Estate Institute, Midtown Center, 11 West 42nd Street, New York, NY 10036. 212-790-1300.

MISCELLANEOUS CONSTRUCTION TRADES AND PROPERTY MAINTENANCE (46.04)
Certificate in Building Construction

General Information Unit offering the program: Real Estate Institute. Program content: Construction management, estimating, construction technology, field supervision, systems design, renovation construction, building codes and regulations. Available on a non-credit basis. Certificate signed by the Dean, School of Continuing Education.

Program Format Evening classes offered. Program cycle: Continuous enrollment. Complete program cycle lasts 105–169 classroom hours. Completion of program requires six courses, 2.0 GPA.

Evaluation Student evaluation methods vary by course. Grading system: Letters or numbers. Transcripts are kept for each student.

Enrollment Requirements Program is open to non-resident foreign students.

Program Costs $250–$330 per course.

Housing and Student Services Housing is not available. Job counseling and placement services are not available.

Contact Certificate Clerk, The Real Estate Institute, Midtown Center, 11 West 42nd Street, New York, NY 10036. 212-790-1300.

MISCELLANEOUS CONSTRUCTION TRADES AND PROPERTY MAINTENANCE (46.04)
Certificate in Construction Management

General Information Unit offering the program: Real Estate Institute. Program content: Construction law, accounting and records, managing interior work, estimating, scheduling. Available on a non-credit basis. Certificate signed by the Dean, School of Continuing Education.

Program Format Evening classes offered. Program cycle: Continuous enrollment. Complete program cycle lasts 124–152 classroom hours. Completion of program requires six courses, 2.0 GPA.

Evaluation Student evaluation methods vary by course. Grading system: Letters or numbers. Transcripts are kept for each student.

Enrollment Requirements Program is open to non-resident foreign students.

Program Costs $250–$305 per course.

Housing and Student Services Housing is not available. Job counseling and placement services are not available.

Contact Certificate Clerk, The Real Estate Institute, Midtown Center, 11 West 42nd Street, New York, NY 10036. 212-790-1300.

MISCELLANEOUS CONSTRUCTION TRADES AND PROPERTY MAINTENANCE (46.04)
Certificate in Construction Technology

General Information Unit offering the program: Real Estate Institute. Program content: Construction practices and materials, building systems, construction cost estimating, blueprints, structural technology. Available on a non-credit basis. Certificate signed by the Dean, School of Continuing Education.

Program Format Evening classes offered. Program cycle: Continuous enrollment. Complete program cycle lasts 148–166

Certificate in Construction Technology continued

classroom hours. Completion of program requires six courses, 2.0 GPA.

Evaluation Student evaluation methods vary by course. Grading system: Letters or numbers. Transcripts are kept for each student.

Enrollment Requirements Program is open to non-resident foreign students.

Program Costs $260–$305 per course.

Housing and Student Services Housing is not available. Job counseling and placement services are not available.

Contact Certificate Clerk, The Real Estate Institute, Midtown Center, 11 West 42nd Street, New York, NY 10036. 212-790-1300.

MISCELLANEOUS CONSTRUCTION TRADES AND PROPERTY MAINTENANCE (46.04)
Certificate in Field Supervision

General Information Unit offering the program: Real Estate Institute. Program content: Structural technology, construction field management, inspection, safety, documentation and records. Available on a non-credit basis. Certificate signed by the Dean, School of Continuing Education.

Program Format Evening classes offered. Program cycle: Continuous enrollment. Complete program cycle lasts 114 classroom hours. Completion of program requires six courses, 2.0 GPA.

Evaluation Student evaluation methods vary by course. Grading system: Letters or numbers. Transcripts are kept for each student.

Enrollment Requirements Program is open to non-resident foreign students.

Program Costs $255–$275 per course.

Housing and Student Services Housing is not available. Job counseling and placement services are not available.

Contact Certificate Clerk, The Real Estate Institute, Midtown Center, 11 West 42nd Street, New York, NY 10036. 212-790-1300.

MISCELLANEOUS CONSTRUCTION TRADES AND PROPERTY MAINTENANCE (46.04)
Certificate in Fire Protection Systems

General Information Unit offering the program: Real Estate Institute. Program content: Fire protection systems, alarms, fire codes, protection devices. Available on a non-credit basis. Certificate signed by the Dean, School of Continuing Education.

Program Format Evening classes offered. Program cycle: Continuous enrollment. Complete program cycle lasts 51–61 classroom hours. Completion of program requires three courses, 2.0 GPA.

Evaluation Student evaluation methods vary by course. Grading system: Letters or numbers. Transcripts are kept for each student.

Enrollment Requirements Intended for those with a basic knowledge of fire protection design. Program is open to non-resident foreign students.

Program Costs $255–$270 per course.

Housing and Student Services Housing is not available. Job counseling and placement services are not available.

Contact Certificate Clerk, The Real Estate Institute, Midtown Center, 11 West 42nd Street, New York, NY 10036. 212-790-1300.

MISCELLANEOUS CONSTRUCTION TRADES AND PROPERTY MAINTENANCE (46.04)
Certificate in Renovation Construction

General Information Unit offering the program: Real Estate Institute. Program content: City codes, management, historic restoration projects, inspection, decisions. Available on a non-credit basis. Certificate signed by the Dean, School of Continuing Education.

Program Format Evening classes offered. Program cycle: Continuous enrollment. Complete program cycle lasts 93–186 classroom hours. Completion of program requires six courses, 2.0 GPA.

Evaluation Student evaluation methods vary by course. Grading system: Letters or numbers. Transcripts are kept for each student.

Enrollment Requirements Program is open to non-resident foreign students.

Program Costs $190–$330 per course.

Housing and Student Services Housing is not available. Job counseling and placement services are not available.

Contact Certificate Clerk, The Real Estate Institute, Midtown Center, 11 West 42nd Street, New York, NY 10036. 212-790-1300.

OFFICE SUPERVISION AND MANAGEMENT (07.04)
Administrative Assistant Certificate

General Information Unit offering the program: Information Technologies Institute. Program content: Administrative assisting, written and verbal communication, office automation. Available on a non-credit basis. Certificate signed by the Dean, School of Continuing Education.

Program Format Evening classes offered. Program cycle: Continuous enrollment. Complete program cycle lasts 122–124 classroom hours. Completion of program requires four courses, 2.0 GPA.

Evaluation Student evaluation methods vary by course. Grading system: Letters or numbers. Transcripts are kept for each student.

Enrollment Requirements Program is open to non-resident foreign students.

Program Costs $300–$375 per course.

Housing and Student Services Housing is not available. Job counseling and placement services are not available.

Contact Administrative Assistant Certificate, School of Continuing Education, 48 Cooper Square, Room 104, New York, NY 10003. 212-998-7190.

PERSONNEL MANAGEMENT (06.16)
Certificate in Compensation and Employee Benefits Management

General Information Unit offering the program: Management Institute. Program content: Salary administration, benefits, pensions, health insurance, executive compensation, worker's compensation law. Available on a non-credit basis. Certificate signed by the Dean, School of Continuing Education.

Program Format Evening classes offered. Program cycle: Continuous enrollment. Complete program cycle lasts 66–108 classroom hours. Completion of program requires five courses, average grade of B or better.

Evaluation Student evaluation methods vary by course. Grading system: Letters or numbers. Transcripts are kept for each student.

Enrollment Requirements Program is open to non-resident foreign students.

Program Costs $125–$300 per course.

Housing and Student Services   Housing is not available. Job counseling and placement services are not available.

Contact   Certificate in Compensation and Employee Benefits, School of Continuing Education, 48 Cooper Square, Room 108, New York, NY 10003. 212-998-7215.

PERSONNEL MANAGEMENT (06.16)
Certificate in Personnel Practices

General Information   Unit offering the program: Management Institute. Program content: Interviewing, job analysis and evaluation, benefits, training and development, conflict resolution. Available on a non-credit basis. Certificate signed by the Dean, School of Continuing Education.

Program Format   Evening classes offered. Program cycle: Continuous enrollment. Complete program cycle lasts 78–164 classroom hours. Completion of program requires six courses, average grade of B or better.

Evaluation   Student evaluation methods vary by course. Grading system: Letters or numbers. Transcripts are kept for each student.

Enrollment Requirements   Program is open to non-resident foreign students.

Program Costs $125–$375 per course.

Housing and Student Services   Housing is not available. Job counseling and placement services are not available.

Contact   Certificate in Personnel Practices, School of Continuing Education, 48 Cooper Square, Room 108, New York, NY 10003. 212-998-7215.

PLUMBING, PIPEFITTING, AND STEAMFITTING (46.05)
Certificate in Basic Plumbing Design

General Information   Unit offering the program: Real Estate Institute. Program content: Fluid mechanics and dynamics, pump curves, distribution, drainage systems, materials. Available on a non-credit basis. Certificate signed by the Dean, School of Continuing Education.

Program Format   Evening classes offered. Program cycle: Continuous enrollment. Complete program cycle lasts 98 classroom hours. Completion of program requires four courses, 2.0 GPA.

Evaluation   Student evaluation methods vary by course. Grading system: Letters or numbers. Transcripts are kept for each student.

Enrollment Requirements   Program is open to non-resident foreign students.

Program Costs $295 per course.

Housing and Student Services   Housing is not available. Job counseling and placement services are not available.

Contact   Certificate Clerk, The Real Estate Institute, Midtown Center, 11 West 42nd Street, New York, NY 10036. 212-790-1300.

PUBLIC RELATIONS (09.05)
Certificate in Public Relations

General Information   Unit offering the program: Management Institute. Program content: Public relations, publicity techniques, writing, broadcast communication, project management. Available on a non-credit basis. Certificate signed by the Dean, School of Continuing Education.

Program Format   Evening classes offered. Program cycle: Continuous enrollment. Complete program cycle lasts 73–104 classroom hours. Completion of program requires five courses, average grade of B or better.

Evaluation   Student evaluation methods vary by course. Grading system: Letters or numbers. Transcripts are kept for each student.

Enrollment Requirements   Program is open to non-resident foreign students.

Program Costs $140–$310 per course.

Housing and Student Services   Housing is not available. Job counseling and placement services are not available.

Contact   Certificate in Public Relations, School of Continuing Education, 48 Cooper Square, Room 108, New York, NY 10003. 212-998-7215.

REAL ESTATE (06.17)
Certificate in Building and Property Management

General Information   Unit offering the program: Real Estate Institute. Program content: Investment and finance, insurance, administration, accounting, design, operation, maintenance. Available on a non-credit basis. Certificate signed by the Dean, School of Continuing Education.

Program Format   Evening classes offered. Program cycle: Continuous enrollment. Complete program cycle lasts 84–143 classroom hours. Completion of program requires six courses, 2.0 GPA.

Evaluation   Student evaluation methods vary by course. Grading system: Letters or numbers. Transcripts are kept for each student.

Enrollment Requirements   Program is open to non-resident foreign students.

Program Costs $180–$330 per course.

Housing and Student Services   Housing is not available. Job counseling and placement services are not available.

Contact   Certificate Clerk, The Real Estate Institute, Midtown Center, 11 West 42nd Street, New York, NY 10036. 212-790-1300.

REAL ESTATE (06.17)
Certificate in Cooperative and Condominium Management

General Information   Unit offering the program: Real Estate Institute. Program content: Management fundamentals, financial management, legal and environmental issues, operations and maintenance. Available on a non-credit basis. Certificate signed by the Dean, School of Continuing Education.

Program Format   Evening classes offered. Program cycle: Continuous enrollment. Complete program cycle lasts 96–120 classroom hours. Completion of program requires six courses, 2.0 GPA.

Evaluation   Student evaluation methods vary by course. Grading system: Letters or numbers. Transcripts are kept for each student.

Enrollment Requirements   Intended for professional managing agents. Program is open to non-resident foreign students.

Program Costs $180–$330 per course.

Housing and Student Services   Housing is not available. Job counseling and placement services are not available.

Contact   Certificate Clerk, The Real Estate Institute, Midtown Center, 11 West 42nd Street, New York, NY 10036. 212-790-1300.

REAL ESTATE (06.17)
Certificate in Corporate Real Estate

General Information   Unit offering the program: Real Estate Institute. Program content: Acquisition, finance, management, environmental regulations. Available on a non-credit basis. Certificate signed by the Dean, School of Continuing Education.

Program Format   Evening classes offered. Program cycle: Continuous enrollment. Complete program cycle lasts 68–91 classroom hours. Completion of program requires four courses, 2.0 GPA.

Certificate in Corporate Real Estate continued

Evaluation Student evaluation methods vary by course. Grading system: Letters or numbers. Transcripts are kept for each student.

Enrollment Requirements Intended for corporate officers and real estate professionals. Program is open to non-resident foreign students.

Program Costs $185–$280 per course.

Housing and Student Services Housing is not available. Job counseling and placement services are not available.

Contact Certificate Clerk, The Real Estate Institute, Midtown Center, 11 West 42nd Street, New York, NY 10036. 212-790-1300.

REAL ESTATE (06.17)
Certificate in Real Estate Accounting and Reporting

General Information Unit offering the program: Real Estate Institute. Program content: Accounting and reporting for income producing properties, taxation, auditing. Available on a non-credit basis. Certificate signed by the Dean, School of Continuing Education.

Program Format Evening classes offered. Program cycle: Continuous enrollment. Complete program cycle lasts 68–90 classroom hours. Completion of program requires four courses, 2.0 GPA.

Evaluation Student evaluation methods vary by course. Grading system: Letters or numbers. Transcripts are kept for each student.

Enrollment Requirements Program is open to non-resident foreign students.

Program Costs $265–$285 per course.

Housing and Student Services Housing is not available. Job counseling and placement services are not available.

Contact Certificate Clerk, The Real Estate Institute, Midtown Center, 11 West 42nd Street, New York, NY 10036. 212-790-1300.

REAL ESTATE (06.17)
Certificate in Real Estate Appraisal

General Information Unit offering the program: Real Estate Institute. Program content: Appraisal and valuation principles, forms, market analysis, case studies. Available on a non-credit basis. Certificate signed by the Dean, School of Continuing Education.

Program Format Evening classes offered. Program cycle: Continuous enrollment. Complete program cycle lasts 97–145 classroom hours. Completion of program requires six courses, 2.0 GPA.

Evaluation Student evaluation methods vary by course. Grading system: Letters or numbers. Transcripts are kept for each student.

Enrollment Requirements Basic knowledge of math, calculators, and computers required. Program is open to non-resident foreign students.

Program Costs $190–$330 per course.

Housing and Student Services Housing is not available. Job counseling and placement services are not available.

Contact Certificate Clerk, The Real Estate Institute, Midtown Center, 11 West 42nd Street, New York, NY 10036. 212-790-1300.

REAL ESTATE (06.17)
Certificate in Real Estate Development

General Information Unit offering the program: Real Estate Institute. Program content: Development fundamentals, planning, reconstruction, commercial development. Available on a non-credit basis. Certificate signed by the Dean, School of Continuing Education.

Program Format Evening classes offered. Program cycle: Continuous enrollment. Complete program cycle lasts 88–127 classroom hours. Completion of program requires six courses, 2.0 GPA.

Evaluation Student evaluation methods vary by course. Grading system: Letters or numbers. Transcripts are kept for each student.

Enrollment Requirements Program is open to non-resident foreign students.

Program Costs $190–$330 per course.

Housing and Student Services Housing is not available. Job counseling and placement services are not available.

Contact Certificate Clerk, The Real Estate Institute, Midtown Center, 11 West 42nd Street, New York, NY 10036. 212-790-1300.

REAL ESTATE (06.17)
Certificate in Real Estate Finance

General Information Unit offering the program: Real Estate Institute. Program content: Financial structuring, case studies, construction lending, joint ventures. Available on a non-credit basis. Certificate signed by the Dean, School of Continuing Education.

Program Format Evening classes offered. Program cycle: Continuous enrollment. Complete program cycle lasts 92–137 classroom hours. Completion of program requires four courses, 2.0 GPA.

Evaluation Student evaluation methods vary by course. Grading system: Letters or numbers. Transcripts are kept for each student.

Enrollment Requirements Program is open to non-resident foreign students.

Program Costs $190–$320 per course.

Housing and Student Services Housing is not available. Job counseling and placement services are not available.

Contact Certificate Clerk, The Real Estate Institute, Midtown Center, 11 West 42nd Street, New York, NY 10036. 212-790-1300.

REAL ESTATE (06.17)
Certificate in Real Estate Studies

General Information Unit offering the program: Real Estate Institute. Program content: Selling and leasing techniques, financing, appraisal, investment, development, management, title search. Available on a non-credit basis. Certificate signed by the Dean, School of Continuing Education.

Program Format Evening classes offered. Program cycle: Continuous enrollment. Complete program cycle lasts 72–180 classroom hours. Completion of program requires six courses, 2.0 GPA.

Evaluation Student evaluation methods vary by course. Grading system: Letters or numbers. Transcripts are kept for each student.

Enrollment Requirements Program is open to non-resident foreign students.

Program Costs $175–$385 per course.

Housing and Student Services Housing is not available. Job counseling and placement services are not available.

Contact Certificate in Real Estate Studies, Midtown Center, 11 West 42nd Street, New York, NY 10036. 212-790-1300.

REAL ESTATE (06.17)
Certificate in Title Examination

General Information Unit offering the program: Real Estate Institute. Program content: Real property law, abstracting, underwriting concepts and practices in title insurance. Available on a non-credit basis. Certificate signed by the Dean, School of Continuing Education.

Program Format   Evening classes offered. Program cycle: Continuous enrollment. Complete program cycle lasts 116 classroom hours. Completion of program requires four courses, 2.0 GPA.

Evaluation   Student evaluation methods vary by course. Grading system: Letters or numbers. Transcripts are kept for each student.

Enrollment Requirements   Program is open to non-resident foreign students.

Program Costs $300 per course.

Housing and Student Services   Housing is not available. Job counseling and placement services are not available.

Contact   Certificate Clerk, The Real Estate Institute, Midtown Center, 11 West 42nd Street, New York, NY 10036. 212-790-1300.

REAL ESTATE (06.17)
The Intensive Program in Real Estate

General Information   Unit offering the program: Real Estate Institute. Program content: Real estate law, finance, appraisal, investment techniques. Available on a non-credit basis. Certificate signed by the Dean, School of Continuing Education.

Program Format   Evening classes offered. Instructional schedule: Two evenings per week. Program cycle: Continuous enrollment. Full program cycle lasts 1 semester. Completion of program requires grade of C or better, 72 classroom hours.

Evaluation   Student evaluation methods vary by course. Grading system: Letters or numbers. Transcripts are kept for each student.

Enrollment Requirements   Program is open to non-resident foreign students.

Program Costs $835 for the program.

Housing and Student Services   Housing is not available. Job counseling and placement services are not available.

Contact   Certificate Clerk, The Real Estate Institute, Midtown Center, 11 West 42nd Street, New York, NY 10036. 212-790-1300.

SMALL BUSINESS MANAGEMENT AND OWNERSHIP (06.18)
Certificate in Small Business Management

General Information   Unit offering the program: Management Institute. Program content: Business plans, capital, marketing strategies, legal and tax aspects, ownership, employee management, new technologies, selling techniques, new product development. Available on a non-credit basis. Certificate signed by the Dean, School of Continuing Education.

Program Format   Evening classes offered. Program cycle: Continuous enrollment. Complete program cycle lasts 72–84 classroom hours. Completion of program requires four courses, average grade of B or better.

Evaluation   Student evaluation methods vary by course. Grading system: Letters or numbers. Transcripts are kept for each student.

Enrollment Requirements   Program is open to non-resident foreign students.

Program Costs $195–$270 per course.

Housing and Student Services   Housing is not available. Job counseling and placement services are not available.

Contact   Certificate in Small Business Management, School of Continuing Education, 48 Cooper Square, Room 108, New York, NY 10003. 212-998-7215.

TAXATION (06.19)
Certificate in Taxation

General Information   Unit offering the program: The Taxation Program. Program content: Individual and corporate income tax, estate planning, state and local taxation, legislative changes. Available on a non-credit basis. Certificate signed by the Dean, School of Continuing Education.

Program Format   Evening classes offered. Program cycle: Continuous enrollment. Completion of program requires 12 CEUs.

Evaluation   Student evaluation methods vary by course. Grading system: Letters or numbers. Transcripts are kept for each student.

Enrollment Requirements   Intended for tax practitioners. Program is open to non-resident foreign students.

Program Costs $175–$280 per course.

Housing and Student Services   Housing is not available. Job counseling and placement services are not available.

Contact   Continuing Education in Law and Taxation, Midtown Center, Room 429, 11 West 42nd Street, New York, NY 10036. 212-790-1320.

TELECOMMUNICATIONS (09.08)
Certificate in Telecommunications Analysis

General Information   Unit offering the program: Information Technologies Institute. Program content: Data communication, telephony, electronics, finance, digital PBX, LAN, voice network design. Available on a non-credit basis. Certificate signed by the Dean, School of Continuing Education.

Program Format   Evening classes offered. Program cycle: Continuous enrollment. Complete program cycle lasts 228 classroom hours. Completion of program requires eight courses, 2.0 GPA.

Evaluation   Student evaluation methods vary by course. Grading system: Letters or numbers. Transcripts are kept for each student.

Enrollment Requirements   Program is open to non-resident foreign students.

Program Costs $375–$395 per course.

Housing and Student Services   Housing is not available. Job counseling and placement services are not available.

Contact   Certificate Applications, Information Technologies, School of Continuing Education, 48 Cooper Square, Room 104, New York, NY 10003. 212-998-7190.

TELECOMMUNICATIONS (09.08)
Certificate in Telecommunications Management

General Information   Unit offering the program: Information Technologies Institute. Program content: Network management and design, satellite systems, policy issues, financial tools, ISDN. Available on a non-credit basis. Certificate signed by the Dean, School of Continuing Education.

Program Format   Evening classes offered. Program cycle: Continuous enrollment. Complete program cycle lasts 192–204 classroom hours. Completion of program requires six courses, 2.0 GPA.

Evaluation   Student evaluation methods vary by course. Grading system: Letters or numbers. Transcripts are kept for each student.

Enrollment Requirements   Certificate in Telecommunications Analysis or equivalent experience required. Program is open to non-resident foreign students.

Program Costs $375–$395 per course.

Housing and Student Services   Housing is not available. Job counseling and placement services are not available.

Certificate in Telecommunications Management continued

Contact Certificate Applications, Information Technologies, School of Continuing Education, 48 Cooper Square, Room 104, New York, NY 10003. 212-998-7190.

TRANSPORTATION AND TRAVEL MARKETING (08.11)
Certificate in Travel and Tourism

General Information Unit offering the program: Management Institute. Program content: Reference materials, writing airline tickets, tours, special forms, group travel, travel geography. Available on a non-credit basis. Certificate signed by the Dean, School of Continuing Education.

Program Format Evening, weekend classes offered. Instructional schedule: Two evenings per week or Saturdays. Program cycle: Continuous enrollment. Complete program cycle lasts 60 classroom hours. Completion of program requires grade of B or better.

Evaluation Student evaluation methods vary by course. Grading system: Letters or numbers. Transcripts are kept for each student.

Enrollment Requirements Program is open to non-resident foreign students.

Program Costs $520 for the program.

Housing and Student Services Housing is not available. Job counseling and placement services are not available.

Contact Certificate in Travel and Tourism, School of Continuing Education, 48 Cooper Square, Room 108, New York, NY 10003. 212-998-7215.

PACE UNIVERSITY, PLEASANTVILLE/ BRIARCLIFF CAMPUS
Pleasantville, New York 10570

ACCOUNTING (06.02)
Basic Accounting

General Information Unit offering the program: Lubin School of Business Administration. Program content: Financial, managerial, and cost accounting. Available for credit. Certificate signed by the University Registrar. Certificate applicable to any two- or four-year degree offered at the institution.

Program Format Daytime, evening classes offered. Program cycle: Continuous enrollment. Complete program cycle lasts one to two years. Completion of program requires 2.0 GPA, 17 credit hours.

Evaluation Student evaluation based on tests, papers, reports. Grading system: Letters or numbers. Transcripts are kept for each student.

Enrollment Requirements Sixty-four college credits required. Program is open to non-resident foreign students. English language proficiency required.

Program Costs $195 per credit hour.

Housing and Student Services Housing is not available. Job counseling and placement services are available.

Special Features Designed to help students reach a specific goal in a relatively short time. Credits earned in certificate programs may be used toward associate and bachelor's degrees. Only one course may be transferred from another accredited institution.

Contact Dr. M. Berchmans Coyle, Director, Division of General Studies, Pleasantville, NY 10570. 914-741-3424.

ACCOUNTING (06.02)
Financial Accounting

General Information Unit offering the program: Lubin School of Business Administration. Program content: Financial accounting, intermediate and advanced accounting, accounting theory and problems. Available for credit. Certificate signed by the University Registrar. Certificate applicable to any two- or four-year degree offered at the institution.

Program Format Daytime, evening classes offered. Program cycle: Continuous enrollment. Complete program cycle lasts one to two years. Completion of program requires 2.0 GPA, 19 credit hours.

Evaluation Student evaluation based on tests, papers, reports. Grading system: Letters or numbers. Transcripts are kept for each student.

Enrollment Requirements Sixty-four college credits required. Program is open to non-resident foreign students. English language proficiency required.

Program Costs $195 per credit hour.

Housing and Student Services Housing is not available. Job counseling and placement services are available.

Special Features Designed to help students reach a specific goal in a relatively short time. Credits earned in certificate programs may be used toward associate and bachelor's degrees. Only one course may be transferred from another accredited institution.

Contact Dr. M. Berchmans Coyle, Director, Division of General Studies, Bedford Road, Pleasantville, NY 10570. 914-741-3424.

ACCOUNTING (06.02)
Financial Accounting Certificate

General Information Unit offering the program: Lubin School of Business Administration. Program content: Accounting, accounting theory problems, auditing, federal income tax law and practice. Available for credit. Certificate signed by the University Registrar. Certificate applicable to any two- or four-year degree offered at the institution.

Program Format Daytime, evening classes offered. Program cycle: Continuous enrollment. Complete program cycle lasts one to two years. Completion of program requires 2.0 GPA, 16 credit hours.

Evaluation Student evaluation based on tests, papers, reports. Grading system: Letters or numbers. Transcripts are kept for each student.

Enrollment Requirements Sixty-four college credits, Basic Accounting Certificate required. Program is open to non-resident foreign students. English language proficiency required.

Program Costs $195 per credit hour.

Housing and Student Services Housing is not available. Job counseling and placement services are available.

Contact Dr. M. Berchmans Coyle, Director, Division of General Studies, Pleasantville, NY 10570. 914-741-3424.

ACCOUNTING (06.02)
Internal Auditing Standards and Techniques

General Information Unit offering the program: Lubin School of Business Administration. Program content: Internal accounting control, computer sampling techniques in auditing, internal and operational auditing. Available for credit. Certificate signed by the University Registrar. Certificate applicable to any two- or four-year degree offered at the institution.

Program Format Daytime, evening classes offered. Program cycle: Continuous enrollment. Complete program cycle lasts one to two years. Completion of program requires 2.0 GPA, 12 credit hours.

Evaluation Student evaluation based on tests, papers, reports. Grading system: Letters or numbers. Transcripts are kept for each student.

Enrollment Requirements   Bachelor's degree recommended. Program is open to non-resident foreign students. English language proficiency required.

Program Costs $195 per credit hour.

Housing and Student Services   Housing is not available. Job counseling and placement services are available.

Contact   Dr. M. Berchmans Coyle, Director, Division of General Studies, Bedford Road, Pleasantville, NY 10570. 914-741-3424.

ACCOUNTING (06.02)
Management Accounting

General Information   Unit offering the program: Lubin School of Business Administration. Program content: Managerial accounting, cost accounting, advanced problems in managerial accounting, accounting information systems, managerial and organizational concepts. Available for credit. Certificate signed by the University Registrar. Certificate applicable to any two- or four-year degree offered at the institution.

Program Format   Daytime, evening classes offered. Program cycle: Continuous enrollment. Complete program cycle lasts one to two years. Completion of program requires 2.0 GPA, 16 credit hours.

Evaluation   Student evaluation based on tests, papers, reports. Grading system: Letters or numbers. Transcripts are kept for each student.

Enrollment Requirements   Sixty-four college credits, financial accounting prerequisite required. Program is open to non-resident foreign students. English language proficiency required.

Program Costs $195 per credit hour.

Housing and Student Services   Housing is not available. Job counseling and placement services are available.

Special Features   Designed to help students reach a specific goal in a relatively short time. Credits earned in certificate programs may be used toward associate and bachelor's degrees. Only one course may be transferred from another accredited institution.

Contact   Dr. M. Berchmans Coyle, Director, Division of General Studies, Bedford Road, Pleasantville, NY 10570. 914-741-3424.

ACCOUNTING (06.02)
Management Accounting

General Information   Unit offering the program: Lubin School of Business Administration. Program content: Internal and external reporting, problems of managerial accounting, periodic financial reporting, managerial and organizational concepts. Available for credit. Certificate signed by the University Registrar. Certificate applicable to any two- or four-year degree offered at the institution.

Program Format   Daytime, evening classes offered. Program cycle: Continuous enrollment. Complete program cycle lasts one to two years. Completion of program requires 2.0 GPA, 15 credit hours.

Evaluation   Student evaluation based on tests, papers, reports. Grading system: Letters or numbers. Transcripts are kept for each student.

Enrollment Requirements   Sixty-four college credits, Basic Accounting Certificate required. Program is open to non-resident foreign students. English language proficiency required.

Program Costs $195 per credit hour.

Housing and Student Services   Housing is not available. Job counseling and placement services are available.

Contact   Dr. M. Berchmans Coyle, Director, Division of General Studies, Pleasantville, NY 10570. 914-741-3424.

AGRICULTURAL BUSINESS AND MANAGEMENT (01.01)
Equine Studies Track I: Assistant Riding Instructor

General Information   Unit offering the program: Dyson College of Arts and Sciences. Program content: Equitation, equine science, theory of equitation, instructional methods in equitation, equitation clinic, the horse show. Available for credit. Certificate signed by the University Registrar. Certificate applicable to any two- or four-year degree offered at the institution.

Program Format   Daytime, evening classes offered. Program cycle: Continuous enrollment. Complete program cycle lasts one to two years. Completion of program requires 2.0 GPA, 16 credit hours.

Evaluation   Student evaluation based on tests, papers, reports. Grading system: Letters or numbers. Transcripts are kept for each student.

Enrollment Requirements   Program is open to non-resident foreign students. English language proficiency required.

Program Costs $195 per credit hour.

Housing and Student Services   Housing is not available. Job counseling and placement services are available.

Contact   Dr. M. Berchmans Coyle, Director, Division of General Studies, Bedford Road, Pleasantville, NY 10570. 914-741-3424.

AGRICULTURAL BUSINESS AND MANAGEMENT (01.01)
Equine Studies Track II: Stable Management

General Information   Unit offering the program: Dyson College of Arts and Sciences. Program content: Veterinary medicine, internship, the horse show, horse judging. Available for credit. Certificate signed by the University Registrar. Certificate applicable to any two- or four-year degree offered at the institution.

Program Format   Daytime, evening classes offered. Program cycle: Continuous enrollment. Complete program cycle lasts one to two years. Completion of program requires 2.0 GPA, 18 credit hours.

Evaluation   Student evaluation based on tests, papers, reports. Grading system: Letters or numbers. Transcripts are kept for each student.

Enrollment Requirements   Program is open to non-resident foreign students. English language proficiency required.

Program Costs $195 per credit hour.

Housing and Student Services   Housing is not available. Job counseling and placement services are available.

Contact   Dr. M. Berchmans Coyle, Director, Division of General Studies, Bedford Road, Pleasantville, NY 10570. 914-741-3424.

BANKING AND FINANCE (06.03)
Finance

General Information   Unit offering the program: Lubin School of Business Administration. Program content: Financial management, managerial economics, advanced financial analysis, money and capital markets, principles of investment. Available for credit. Certificate signed by the University Registrar. Certificate applicable to any two- or four-year degree offered at the institution.

Program Format   Daytime, evening classes offered. Program cycle: Continuous enrollment. Complete program cycle lasts one to two years. Completion of program requires 2.0 GPA, 16 credit hours.

Evaluation   Student evaluation based on tests, papers, reports. Grading system: Letters or numbers. Transcripts are kept for each student.

Enrollment Requirements   Sixty-four college credits required. Program is open to non-resident foreign students. English language proficiency required.

Finance continued

Program Costs $195 per credit hour.

Housing and Student Services   Housing is not available. Job counseling and placement services are available.

Special Features   Designed to help students reach a specific goal in a relatively short time. Credits earned in certificate programs may be used toward associate and bachelor's degrees. Only one course may be transferred from another accredited institution.

Contact   Dr. M. Berchmans Coyle, Director, Division of General Studies, Bedford Road, Pleasantville, NY 10570. 914-741-3424.

BUSINESS AND MANAGEMENT, GENERAL (06.01)
General Business

General Information   Unit offering the program: Lubin School of Business Administration. Program content: Computing, principles of economics, financial accounting, business law, marketing, managerial and organizational concepts. Available for credit. Certificate signed by the University Registrar. Certificate applicable to any two- or four-year degree offered at the institution.

Program Format   Daytime, evening classes offered. Program cycle: Continuous enrollment. Complete program cycle lasts one to two years. Completion of program requires 2.0 GPA, 19 credit hours.

Evaluation   Student evaluation based on tests, papers, reports. Grading system: Letters or numbers. Transcripts are kept for each student.

Enrollment Requirements   Program is open to non-resident foreign students. English language proficiency required.

Program Costs $195 per credit hour.

Housing and Student Services   Housing is not available. Job counseling and placement services are available.

Contact   Dr. M. Berchmans Coyle, Director, Division of General Studies, Pleasantville, NY 10570. 914-741-3424.

COMPUTER PROGRAMMING (11.02)
Applications Programming

General Information   Unit offering the program: School of Computer Science and Information Systems. Program content: Computer studies, COBOL programming, assembly language program, information systems concepts. Available for credit. Certificate signed by the University Registrar. Certificate applicable to any two- or four-year degree offered at the institution.

Program Format   Daytime, evening classes offered. Program cycle: Continuous enrollment. Complete program cycle lasts one to two years. Completion of program requires 2.0 GPA, 15 credit hours.

Evaluation   Student evaluation based on tests, papers, reports. Grading system: Letters or numbers. Transcripts are kept for each student.

Enrollment Requirements   Program is open to non-resident foreign students. English language proficiency required.

Program Costs $195 per credit hour.

Housing and Student Services   Housing is not available. Job counseling and placement services are available.

Special Features   Designed to help students reach a specific goal in a relatively short time. Credits earned in certificate programs may be used toward associate and bachelor's degrees. Only one course may be transferred from another accredited institution.

Contact   Dr. M. Berchmans Coyle, Director, Division of General Studies, Bedford Road, Pleasantville, NY 10570. 914-741-3424.

DESIGN (50.04)
Scientific Illustration

General Information   Unit offering the program: Dyson College of Arts and Sciences. Program content: Graphics for science, graphic design. Available for credit. Certificate signed by the University Registrar. Certificate applicable to any two- or four-year degree offered at the institution.

Program Format   Daytime, evening classes offered. Program cycle: Continuous enrollment. Complete program cycle lasts one to two years. Completion of program requires 2.0 GPA, 15 credit hours.

Evaluation   Student evaluation based on tests, papers, reports. Grading system: Letters or numbers. Transcripts are kept for each student.

Enrollment Requirements   Program is open to non-resident foreign students. English language proficiency required.

Program Costs $195 per credit hour.

Housing and Student Services   Housing is not available. Job counseling and placement services are available.

Contact   Dr. M. Berchmans Coyle, Director, Division of General Studies, Bedford Road, Pleasantville, NY 10570. 914-741-3424.

FINE ARTS (50.07)
Art History

General Information   Unit offering the program: Dyson College of Arts and Sciences. Program content: History and appreciation of architecture; fine arts; American, modern, and Oriental art. Available for credit. Certificate signed by the University Registrar. Certificate applicable to any two- or four-year degree offered at the institution.

Program Format   Daytime, evening classes offered. Program cycle: Continuous enrollment. Complete program cycle lasts one to two years. Completion of program requires 2.0 GPA, 15 credit hours.

Evaluation   Student evaluation based on tests, papers, reports. Grading system: Letters or numbers. Transcripts are kept for each student.

Enrollment Requirements   Program is open to non-resident foreign students. English language proficiency required.

Program Costs $195 per credit hour.

Housing and Student Services   Housing is not available. Job counseling and placement services are available.

Special Features   Designed to help students reach a specific goal in a relatively short time. Credits earned in certificate programs may be used toward associate and bachelor's degrees. Only one course may be transferred from another accredited institution.

Contact   Dr. M. Berchmans Coyle, Director, Division of General Studies, Bedford Road, Pleasantville, NY 10570. 914-741-3424.

GERMANIC LANGUAGES (16.05)
German

General Information   Unit offering the program: Dyson College of Arts and Sciences. Program content: Commercial German, German culture and literature, conversation, diction, phonetics, advanced German composition. Available for credit. Certificate signed by the University Registrar. Certificate applicable to any two- or four-year degree offered at the institution.

Program Format   Daytime, evening classes offered. Program cycle: Continuous enrollment. Complete program cycle lasts one to two years. Completion of program requires 2.0 GPA, 24 credit hours.

Evaluation   Student evaluation based on tests, papers, reports. Grading system: Letters or numbers. Transcripts are kept for each student.

Enrollment Requirements   Program is open to non-resident foreign students. English language proficiency required.

Program Costs $195 per credit hour.

Housing and Student Services Housing is not available. Job counseling and placement services are available.

Special Features Designed to help students reach a specific goal in a relatively short time. Credits earned in certificate programs may be used toward associate and bachelor's degrees. Only one course may be transferred from another accredited institution.

Contact Dr. M. Berchmans Coyle, Director, Division of General Studies, Bedford Road, Pleasantville, NY 10570. 914-741-3424.

GRAPHIC AND PRINTING COMMUNICATIONS (48.02)
Commercial Art

General Information Unit offering the program: Dyson College of Arts and Sciences. Program content: Illustration, principles of design, graphic design, typography, special techniques workshop. Available for credit. Certificate signed by the University Registrar. Certificate applicable to any two- or four-year degree offered at the institution.

Program Format Daytime, evening classes offered. Program cycle: Continuous enrollment. Complete program cycle lasts one to two years. Completion of program requires 2.0 GPA, 15 credit hours.

Evaluation Student evaluation based on tests, papers, reports. Grading system: Letters or numbers. Transcripts are kept for each student.

Enrollment Requirements Program is open to non-resident foreign students. English language proficiency required.

Program Costs $195 per credit hour.

Housing and Student Services Housing is not available. Job counseling and placement services are available.

Contact Dr. M. Berchmans Coyle, Director, Division of General Studies, Bedford Road, Pleasantville, NY 10570. 914-741-3424.

HORTICULTURE (01.06)
Horticulture and Nursery Management

General Information Unit offering the program: Dyson College of Arts and Sciences. Program content: Marketing, financial accounting, horticulture, botany, plant physiology, internship in biology. Available for credit. Certificate signed by the University Registrar. Certificate applicable to any two- or four-year degree offered at the institution.

Program Format Daytime, evening classes offered. Program cycle: Continuous enrollment. Complete program cycle lasts one to two years. Completion of program requires 2.0 GPA, 21 credit hours.

Evaluation Student evaluation based on tests, papers, reports. Grading system: Letters or numbers. Transcripts are kept for each student.

Enrollment Requirements One year of biology required. Program is open to non-resident foreign students. English language proficiency required.

Program Costs $195 per credit hour.

Housing and Student Services Housing is not available. Job counseling and placement services are available.

Contact Dr. M. Berchmans Coyle, Director, Division of General Studies, Bedford Road, Pleasantville, NY 10570. 914-741-3424.

INFORMATION SCIENCES AND SYSTEMS (11.04)
Information Systems

General Information Unit offering the program: School of Computer Science and Information Systems. Program content: Computer studies, COBOL programming, information systems concepts and design, complex information systems. Available for credit. Certificate signed by the University Registrar. Certificate applicable to any two- or four-year degree offered at the institution.

Program Format Daytime, evening classes offered. Program cycle: Continuous enrollment. Complete program cycle lasts one to two years. Completion of program requires 2.0 GPA, 15 credit hours.

Evaluation Student evaluation based on tests, papers, reports. Grading system: Letters or numbers. Transcripts are kept for each student.

Enrollment Requirements Program is open to non-resident foreign students. English language proficiency required.

Program Costs $195 per credit hour.

Housing and Student Services Housing is not available. Job counseling and placement services are available.

Special Features Designed to help students reach a specific goal in a relatively short time. Credits earned in certificate programs may be used toward associate and bachelor's degrees. Only one course may be transferred from another accredited institution.

Contact Dr. M. Berchmans Coyle, Director, Division of General Studies, Bedford Road, Pleasantville, NY 10570. 914-741-3424.

INTERIOR DESIGN (04.05)
Interior Design

General Information Unit offering the program: Dyson College of Arts and Sciences. Program content: Architectural renderings and graphics, color workshop, styles and interiors, history and appreciation of architecture. Available for credit. Certificate signed by the University Registrar. Certificate applicable to any two- or four-year degree offered at the institution.

Program Format Daytime, evening classes offered. Program cycle: Continuous enrollment. Complete program cycle lasts one to two years. Completion of program requires 2.0 GPA, 15 credit hours.

Evaluation Student evaluation based on tests, papers, reports. Grading system: Letters or numbers. Transcripts are kept for each student.

Enrollment Requirements Program is open to non-resident foreign students. English language proficiency required.

Program Costs $195 per credit hour.

Housing and Student Services Housing is not available. Job counseling and placement services are available.

Contact Dr. M. Berchmans Coyle, Director, Division of General Studies, Bedford Road, Pleasantville, NY 10570. 914-741-3424.

ITALIC LANGUAGES (16.09)
Italian

General Information Unit offering the program: Dyson College of Arts and Sciences. Program content: Commercial Italian, Italian culture and literature, conversation, diction, phonetics, advanced Italian composition. Available for credit. Certificate signed by the University Registrar. Certificate applicable to any two- or four-year degree offered at the institution.

Program Format Daytime, evening classes offered. Program cycle: Continuous enrollment. Complete program cycle lasts one to two years. Completion of program requires 2.0 GPA, 24 credit hours.

Evaluation Student evaluation based on tests, papers, reports. Grading system: Letters or numbers. Transcripts are kept for each student.

Enrollment Requirements Program is open to non-resident foreign students. English language proficiency required.

Program Costs $195 per credit hour.

Housing and Student Services Housing is not available. Job counseling and placement services are available.

Special Features Designed to help students reach a specific goal in a relatively short time. Credits earned in certificate programs may be used toward associate and bachelor's degrees. Only one course may be transferred from another accredited institution.

Italian continued

Contact   Dr. M. Berchmans Coyle, Director, Division of General Studies, Bedford Road, Pleasantville, NY 10570. 914-741-3424.

ITALIC LANGUAGES (16.09)
Proficiency in French

General Information   Unit offering the program: Dyson College of Arts and Sciences. Program content: Conversation, composition, French for industry and the professions, French culture and civilization, French literature. Available for credit. Certificate signed by the University Registrar. Certificate applicable to any two- or four-year degree offered at the institution.

Program Format   Daytime, evening classes offered. Program cycle: Continuous enrollment. Complete program cycle lasts one to two years. Completion of program requires 2.0 GPA, 18–24 credit hours.

Evaluation   Student evaluation based on tests, papers, reports. Grading system: Letters or numbers. Transcripts are kept for each student.

Enrollment Requirements   Program is open to non-resident foreign students. English language proficiency required.

Program Costs $195 per credit hour.

Housing and Student Services   Housing is not available. Job counseling and placement services are available.

Contact   Dr. M. Berchmans Coyle, Director, Division of General Studies, Bedford Road, Pleasantville, NY 10570. 914-741-3424.

ITALIC LANGUAGES (16.09)
Proficiency in Spanish

General Information   Unit offering the program: Dyson College of Arts and Sciences. Program content: Latin American culture, conversation, diction, phonetics, professional communication, translation, interpretation. Available for credit. Certificate signed by the University Registrar. Certificate applicable to any two- or four-year degree offered at the institution.

Program Format   Daytime, evening classes offered. Program cycle: Continuous enrollment. Complete program cycle lasts one to two years. Completion of program requires 2.0 GPA, 18–24 credit hours.

Evaluation   Student evaluation based on tests, papers, reports. Grading system: Letters or numbers. Transcripts are kept for each student.

Enrollment Requirements   Program is open to non-resident foreign students. English language proficiency required.

Program Costs $195 per credit hour.

Housing and Student Services   Housing is not available. Job counseling and placement services are available.

Contact   Dr. M. Berchmans Coyle, Director, Division of General Studies, Bedford Road, Pleasantville, NY 10570. 914-741-3424.

LABOR/INDUSTRIAL RELATIONS (06.11)
Labor Management Relations

General Information   Unit offering the program: Lubin School of Business Administration. Program content: American labor history, law of administrative and regulatory agencies, law of labor management relations, collective bargaining and arbitration, public sector and labor relations, discrimination in employment and affirmative action. Available for credit. Certificate signed by the University Registrar. Certificate applicable to any two- or four-year degree offered at the institution.

Program Format   Daytime, evening classes offered. Program cycle: Continuous enrollment. Complete program cycle lasts one to two years. Completion of program requires 2.0 GPA, 18 credit hours.

Evaluation   Student evaluation based on tests, papers, reports. Grading system: Letters or numbers. Transcripts are kept for each student.

Enrollment Requirements   Sixty-four college credits required. Program is open to non-resident foreign students. English language proficiency required.

Program Costs $195 per credit hour.

Housing and Student Services   Housing is not available. Job counseling and placement services are available.

Special Features   Designed to help students reach a specific goal in a relatively short time. Credits earned in certificate programs may be used toward associate and bachelor's degrees. Only one course may be transferred from another accredited institution.

Contact   Dr. M. Berchmans Coyle, Director, Division of General Studies, Bedford Road, Pleasantville, NY 10570. 914-741-3424.

MANAGEMENT SCIENCE (06.13)
Management

General Information   Unit offering the program: Lubin School of Business Administration. Program content: Organizational behavior, productivity in business, management science and production management, human resources management, training and development, organizational theory and development, leadership principles and practice. Available for credit. Certificate signed by the University Registrar. Certificate applicable to any two- or four-year degree offered at the institution.

Program Format   Daytime, evening classes offered. Program cycle: Continuous enrollment. Complete program cycle lasts one to two years. Completion of program requires 2.0 GPA, 15 credit hours.

Evaluation   Student evaluation based on tests, papers, reports. Grading system: Letters or numbers. Transcripts are kept for each student.

Enrollment Requirements   Sixty-four college credits required. Program is open to non-resident foreign students. English language proficiency required.

Program Costs $195 per credit hour.

Housing and Student Services   Housing is not available. Job counseling and placement services are available.

Contact   Dr. M. Berchmans Coyle, Director, Division of General Studies, Pleasantville, NY 10570. 914-741-3424.

MARKETING MANAGEMENT AND RESEARCH (06.14)
International Marketing Management

General Information   Unit offering the program: Lubin School of Business Administration. Program content: International marketing, financial aspects, export and import policies and practices. Available for credit. Certificate signed by the University Registrar. Certificate applicable to any two- or four-year degree offered at the institution.

Program Format   Daytime, evening classes offered. Program cycle: Continuous enrollment. Complete program cycle lasts one to two years. Completion of program requires 2.0 GPA, 12 credit hours.

Evaluation   Student evaluation based on tests, papers, reports. Grading system: Letters or numbers. Transcripts are kept for each student.

Enrollment Requirements   Sixty-four college credits required. Program is open to non-resident foreign students. English language proficiency required.

Program Costs $195 per credit hour.

Housing and Student Services   Housing is not available. Job counseling and placement services are available.

Special Features   Designed to help students reach a specific goal in a relatively short time. Credits earned in certificate programs may be used toward associate and bachelor's degrees. Only one course may be transferred from another accredited institution.

Contact   Dr. M. Berchmans Coyle, Director, Division of General Studies, Bedford Road, Pleasantville, NY 10570. 914-741-3424.

MARKETING MANAGEMENT AND RESEARCH (06.14)
International Marketing Management

General Information   Unit offering the program: Lubin School of Business Administration. Program content: Advertising and promotion, export and import policies, international economic problems. Available for credit. Certificate signed by the University Registrar. Certificate applicable to any two- or four-year degree offered at the institution.

Program Format   Daytime, evening classes offered. Program cycle: Continuous enrollment. Complete program cycle lasts one to two years. Completion of program requires 2.0 GPA, 15 credit hours.

Evaluation   Student evaluation based on tests, papers, reports. Grading system: Letters or numbers. Transcripts are kept for each student.

Enrollment Requirements   Sixty-four college credits required. Program is open to non-resident foreign students. English language proficiency required.

Program Costs $195 per credit hour.

Housing and Student Services   Housing is not available. Job counseling and placement services are available.

Contact   Dr. M. Berchmans Coyle, Director, Division of General Studies, Pleasantville, NY 10570. 914-741-3424.

MEDICAL LABORATORY TECHNOLOGIES (17.03)
Laboratory Animal Technology

General Information   Unit offering the program: Dyson College of Arts and Sciences. Program content: Veterinary medicine, animal behavior, primate behavior, laboratory animal science, laboratory animal health and disease, internship in biology. Available for credit. Certificate signed by the University Registrar. Certificate applicable to any two- or four-year degree offered at the institution.

Program Format   Daytime, evening classes offered. Program cycle: Continuous enrollment. Complete program cycle lasts one to two years. Completion of program requires 2.0 GPA, 17 credit hours.

Evaluation   Student evaluation based on tests, papers, reports. Grading system: Letters or numbers. Transcripts are kept for each student.

Enrollment Requirements   One year of general biology required. Program is open to non-resident foreign students. English language proficiency required.

Program Costs $195 per credit hour.

Housing and Student Services   Housing is not available. Job counseling and placement services are available.

Contact   Dr. M. Berchmans Coyle, Director, Division of General Studies, Bedford Road, Pleasantville, NY 10570. 914-741-3424.

MICROCOMPUTER APPLICATIONS (11.06)
Personal Computer Applications

General Information   Unit offering the program: School of Computer Science and Information Systems. Program content: Personal computer applications, telecommunications applications for microcomputer, electronic business communications. Available for credit. Certificate signed by the University Registrar. Certificate applicable to any two- or four-year degree offered at the institution.

Program Format   Daytime, evening classes offered. Program cycle: Continuous enrollment. Complete program cycle lasts one to two years. Completion of program requires 2.0 GPA, 12 credit hours.

Evaluation   Student evaluation based on tests, papers, reports. Grading system: Letters or numbers. Transcripts are kept for each student.

Enrollment Requirements   Program is open to non-resident foreign students. English language proficiency required.

Program Costs $195 per credit hour.

Housing and Student Services   Housing is not available. Job counseling and placement services are available.

Special Features   Designed to help students reach a specific goal in a relatively short time. Credits earned in certificate programs may be used toward associate and bachelor's degrees. Only one course may be transferred from another accredited institution.

Contact   Dr. M. Berchmans Coyle, Director, Division of General Studies, Bedford Road, Pleasantville, NY 10570. 914-741-3424.

PHYSICS (40.08)
Applied Physics

General Information   Unit offering the program: Dyson College of Arts and Sciences. Program content: Digital electronics systems, general physics, electromagnetism, electronics. Available for credit. Certificate signed by the University Registrar. Certificate applicable to any two- or four-year degree offered at the institution.

Program Format   Daytime, evening classes offered. Program cycle: Continuous enrollment. Complete program cycle lasts one to two years. Completion of program requires 2.0 GPA, 24 credit hours.

Evaluation   Student evaluation based on tests, papers, reports. Grading system: Letters or numbers. Transcripts are kept for each student.

Enrollment Requirements   Program is open to non-resident foreign students. English language proficiency required.

Program Costs $195 per credit hour.

Housing and Student Services   Housing is not available. Job counseling and placement services are available.

Special Features   Designed to give practical experience in fundamental laboratory and research procedures. Recommended for those seeking entry-level laboratory positions in industry, government, or nonprofit organizations.

Contact   Dr. M. Berchmans Coyle, Director, Division of General Studies, Bedford Road, Pleasantville, NY 10570. 914-741-3424.

POLITICAL SCIENCE AND GOVERNMENT (45.10)
Politics

General Information   Unit offering the program: Dyson College of Arts and Sciences. Program content: Politics, public myth, twenty-first century politics, revolution or reform, political workshops. Available for credit. Certificate signed by the University Registrar. Certificate applicable to any two- or four-year degree offered at the institution.

Program Format   Daytime, evening classes offered. Program cycle: Continuous enrollment. Complete program cycle lasts one to two years. Completion of program requires 2.0 GPA, 15 credit hours.

Evaluation   Student evaluation based on tests, papers, reports. Grading system: Letters or numbers. Transcripts are kept for each student.

Enrollment Requirements   Program is open to non-resident foreign students. English language proficiency required.

Program Costs $195 per credit hour.

Housing and Student Services   Housing is not available. Job counseling and placement services are available.

Special Features   Designed to help students reach a specific goal in a relatively short time. Credits earned in certificate programs may be used toward associate and bachelor's degrees.

Politics continued

Only one course may be transferred from another accredited institution.

Contact Dr. M. Berchmans Coyle, Director, Division of General Studies, Bedford Road, Pleasantville, NY 10570. 914-741-3424.

SECRETARIAL AND RELATED PROGRAMS (07.06)
Administrative Office Skills

General Information Unit offering the program: School of Computer Science and Information Systems. Program content: Word processing, office automation and administration, automated office systems and operations, word/information processing applications. Available for credit. Certificate signed by the University Registrar. Certificate applicable to any two- or four-year degree offered at the institution.

Program Format Daytime, evening classes offered. Program cycle: Continuous enrollment. Complete program cycle lasts one to two years. Completion of program requires 2.0 GPA, 15 credit hours.

Evaluation Student evaluation based on tests, papers, reports. Grading system: Letters or numbers. Transcripts are kept for each student.

Enrollment Requirements Program is open to non-resident foreign students. English language proficiency required.

Program Costs $195 per credit hour.

Housing and Student Services Housing is not available. Job counseling and placement services are available.

Special Features Designed to help students reach a specific goal in a relatively short time. Credits earned in certificate programs may be used toward associate and bachelor's degrees. Only one course may be transferred from another accredited institution.

Contact Dr. M. Berchmans Coyle, Director, Division of General Studies, Bedford Road, Pleasantville, NY 10570. 914-741-3424.

SECRETARIAL AND RELATED PROGRAMS (07.06)
Secretarial Office Skills

General Information Unit offering the program: School of Computer Science and Information Systems. Program content: Shorthand theory and dictation, transcription, keyboarding, business communications, advanced typewriting and machine transcription, executive secretarial administration. Available for credit. Certificate signed by the University Registrar. Certificate applicable to any two- or four-year degree offered at the institution.

Program Format Daytime, evening classes offered. Program cycle: Continuous enrollment. Complete program cycle lasts one to two years. Completion of program requires 2.0 GPA, 16 credit hours.

Evaluation Student evaluation based on tests, papers, reports. Grading system: Letters or numbers. Transcripts are kept for each student.

Enrollment Requirements Program is open to non-resident foreign students. English language proficiency required.

Program Costs $195 per credit hour.

Housing and Student Services Housing is not available. Job counseling and placement services are available.

Special Features Designed to help students reach a specific goal in a relatively short time. Credits earned in certificate programs may be used toward associate and bachelor's degrees. Only one course may be transferred from another accredited institution.

Contact Dr. M. Berchmans Coyle, Director, Division of General Studies, Bedford Road, Pleasantville, NY 10570. 914-741-3424.

TAXATION (06.19)
Taxation

General Information Unit offering the program: Lubin School of Business Administration. Program content: Financial accounting, federal income tax law and practice, state and municipal taxation, tax research, estate and gift taxation. Available for credit. Certificate signed by the University Registrar. Certificate applicable to any two- or four-year degree offered at the institution.

Program Format Daytime, evening classes offered. Program cycle: Continuous enrollment. Complete program cycle lasts one to two years. Completion of program requires 2.0 GPA, 16 credit hours.

Evaluation Student evaluation based on tests, papers, reports. Grading system: Letters or numbers. Transcripts are kept for each student.

Enrollment Requirements Sixty-four college credits required. Program is open to non-resident foreign students. English language proficiency required.

Program Costs $195 per credit hour.

Housing and Student Services Housing is not available. Job counseling and placement services are available.

Contact Dr. M. Berchmans Coyle, Director, Division of General Studies, Pleasantville, NY 10570. 914-741-3424.

TYPING, GENERAL OFFICE, AND RELATED PROGRAMS (07.07)
Legal Office Training

General Information Unit offering the program: School of Computer Science and Information Systems. Program content: Litigation, word processing, business law. Available for credit. Certificate signed by the University Registrar. Certificate applicable to any two- or four-year degree offered at the institution.

Program Format Daytime, evening classes offered. Program cycle: Continuous enrollment. Complete program cycle lasts one to two years. Completion of program requires 2.0 GPA, 15 credit hours.

Evaluation Student evaluation based on tests, papers, reports. Grading system: Letters or numbers. Transcripts are kept for each student.

Enrollment Requirements Minimum stenography and typewriting speeds required. Program is open to non-resident foreign students. English language proficiency required.

Program Costs $195 per credit hour.

Housing and Student Services Housing is not available. Job counseling and placement services are available.

Special Features Designed to help students reach a specific goal in a relatively short time. Credits earned in certificate programs may be used toward associate and bachelor's degrees. Only one course may be transferred from another accredited institution.

Contact Dr. M. Berchmans Coyle, Director, Division of General Studies, Bedford Road, Pleasantville, NY 10570. 914-741-3424.

PRATT INSTITUTE
Brooklyn, New York 11205

DESIGN (50.04)
Certificate Program in Computer Graphics

General Information Unit offering the program: Division of Continuing Education. Program content: Electronic illustration, computer graphics, video animation, desktop publishing. Available on a non-credit basis. Certificate signed by the Associate Director, Continuing Education.

Program Format Evening, weekend classes offered. Instructional schedule: Three hours per week. Students may enroll fall, spring, summer. Full program cycle lasts 11 courses. Completion of program requires grade of C or better in all courses.

Evaluation Student evaluation based on tests, assignments. Grading system: Letters or numbers. Transcripts are kept for each student.

Enrollment Requirements Understanding of design concepts required. Program is open to non-resident foreign students.

Program Costs $80–$450 per course.

Housing and Student Services Housing is not available. Job counseling and placement services are available.

Special Features Pratt Institute has been involved in various aspects of graphic design for all of its 100-year history. The offerings of the Certificate in Computer Graphics are steeped in this tradition. The course work is centered around issues of design, but the tools are necessarily wedded to modern microcomputer technology.

Contact Ms. Karen Adler Miletsky, Associate Director, Continuing Education, 295 Lafayette Street, New York, NY 10012. 212-925-8481.

INTERIOR DESIGN (04.05)
Interior Design Certificate

General Information Unit offering the program: Division of Continuing Education. Program content: Design studios, drafting, materials and finishes, color theory, mechanical systems, lighting design, professional relations, history. Available on a non-credit basis. Certificate signed by the Associate Director, Continuing Education.

Program Format Evening, weekend classes offered. Instructional schedule: Three hours per week. Students may enroll fall, spring, summer. Full program cycle lasts 12 courses. Completion of program requires grade of C or better in all courses.

Evaluation Student evaluation based on tests, papers, assignments, portfolio. Grading system: Letters or numbers. Transcripts are kept for each student.

Enrollment Requirements Program is open to non-resident foreign students.

Program Costs $3000 for the program, $250 per course.

Housing and Student Services Housing is not available. Job counseling and placement services are available.

Special Features The program offers students the opportunity to review the needs of both contract and residential interior design. The curriculum provides the requisite education and training to actively participate in this profession. The faculty are practicing interior designers and architects.

Contact Ms. Karen Adler Miletsky, Associate Director, Continuing Education, 295 Lafayette Street, New York, NY 10012. 212-925-8481.

NUCEA MEMBER
ROCHESTER INSTITUTE OF TECHNOLOGY
Rochester, New York 14623

BUSINESS AND MANAGEMENT, GENERAL (06.01)
Customer and Consumer Service

General Information Unit offering the program: Business and The Arts, Academic Division, College of Continuing Education. Program content: Organizational and communication theory and skills for improving quality and customer satisfaction. Available for credit. Certificate signed by the Dean of the College. Certificate applicable to A.A.S., B.S. in Applied Arts and Science.

Program Format Evening, weekend classes offered. Instructional schedule: One to three evenings per week, five alternate Saturdays. Program cycle: Continuous enrollment. Full program cycle lasts 5 courses. Completion of program requires 2.0 GPA.

Evaluation Student evaluation based on tests, papers, reports, projects. Grading system: Letters or numbers. Transcripts are kept for each student.

Enrollment Requirements Program is open to non-resident foreign students.

Program Costs $3060 for the program.

Housing and Student Services Housing is available. Job counseling and placement services are available.

Special Features Program covers characteristics of the service economy, organizational systems that improve quality and customer satisfaction, interpersonal communication theory and skills, management techniques for customer service personnel, and information processes for customer/consumer services, focusing on providing competitive advantage. Faculty are academically qualified professionals who teach what they do.

Contact Dr. Lynda Rummel, Director, Business and The Arts, Academic Division, College of Continuing Education, 50 West Main Street, Rochester, NY 14614. 716-475-4999.

BUSINESS AND MANAGEMENT, GENERAL (06.01)
Management Certificate

General Information Unit offering the program: Business and The Arts, Academic Division, College of Continuing Education. Program content: Management theory and supervisory techniques for frontline and emerging managers. Available for credit. Certificate signed by the Chairman of the Board of Trustees. Certificate applicable to A.A.S., B.S. in Business Administration, Management, Applied Arts and Science; A.A. in General Education.

Program Format Evening, weekend classes offered. Instructional schedule: One evening per week or five alternate Saturdays, special variable length programs. Program cycle: Continuous enrollment. Full program cycle lasts 3 courses. Completion of program requires 2.0 GPA.

Evaluation Student evaluation based on tests, papers, reports, team projects. Grading system: Letters or numbers. Transcripts are kept for each student.

Enrollment Requirements Program is open to non-resident foreign students. English language proficiency required.

Program Costs $1836 for the program, $612 per course.

Housing and Student Services Housing is available. Job counseling and placement services are available.

Special Features Faculty are academically qualified experienced managers who teach what they do. Program was developed with assistance of advisory group of prominent business leaders. Program includes assessment of individual management style and extensive practice in practical management skills.

Contact Dr. Lynda Rummel, Director, Business and The Arts, College of Continuing Education, 50 West Main Street, Rochester, NY 14614. 716-475-4999.

BUSINESS AND MANAGEMENT, GENERAL (06.01)
Management Diploma

General Information Unit offering the program: Business and The Arts, Academic Division, College of Continuing Education. Program content: Marketing, personnel management, traffic and transportation management, accounting, industrial management, real estate, or general management. Available for credit. Certificate signed by the Chairman of the Board of Trustees. Certificate applicable to A.A.S., B.S. in Business Administration, Accounting, Management, Applied Arts and Science.

Management Diploma continued

Program Format Evening, weekend classes offered. Instructional schedule: One or two evenings per week or five alternate Saturdays. Program cycle: Continuous enrollment. Full program cycle lasts 4 courses. Completion of program requires 2.0 GPA.

Evaluation Student evaluation based on tests, papers, reports, projects. Grading system: Letters or numbers. Transcripts are kept for each student.

Enrollment Requirements Management Certificate or equivalent required. Program is open to non-resident foreign students.

Program Costs $2448 for the program.

Housing and Student Services Housing is available. Job counseling and placement services are available.

Special Features Allows students to concentrate studies in a specific area of business or management that may have immediate relevance to their careers or jobs. Developed with advisory group of business leaders.

Contact Dr. Lynda Rummel, Director, Business and The Arts, College of Continuing Education, 50 West Main Street, Rochester, NY 14614. 716-475-4999.

COMMUNICATIONS, GENERAL (09.01)
Business and Career Communication

General Information Unit offering the program: Business and The Arts, Academic Division, College of Continuing Education. Program content: Theory and skills for professional presentations, leadership of business groups, written communications. Available for credit. Certificate signed by the Dean of the College. Certificate applicable to A.A.S., B.S. in Applied Arts and Science; A.A. in General Education.

Program Format Evening, weekend, telecommunications classes offered. Instructional schedule: Once or twice per week, or five alternate Saturdays. Program cycle: Continuous enrollment. Full program cycle lasts 3 courses. Completion of program requires 2.0 GPA.

Evaluation Student evaluation based on tests, papers, reports, projects. Grading system: Letters or numbers. Transcripts are kept for each student.

Enrollment Requirements Program is open to non-resident foreign students. English language proficiency required.

Program Costs $1836 for the program, $612 per course.

Housing and Student Services Housing is available. Job counseling and placement services are available.

Special Features Courses taught by practicing professionals selected for their expertise and ability to teach. Program provides comprehensive education in theory and skills of effective communication in business settings.

Contact Dr. Lynda Rummel, Director, Business and The Arts, College of Continuing Education, 50 West Main Street, Rochester, NY 14614. 716-475-4999.

COMMUNICATIONS, GENERAL (09.01)
Certificate in Advanced Technical Communication

General Information Unit offering the program: Business and The Arts, Academic Division, College of Continuing Education. Program content: Specialized skills and knowledge in advanced, professional areas of technical communication. Available for credit. Endorsed by Society for Technical Communication, Rochester Chapter. Certificate signed by the Chairman of the Board of Trustees. Certificate applicable to A.A.S., B.S. in Applied Arts and Science; B.S. in Professional and Technical Communication; A.A. in General Education.

Program Format Evening classes offered. Instructional schedule: Two to three evenings per week or special variable length programs. Program cycle: Continuous enrollment, spring quarter enrollment preferred. Full program cycle lasts 6 courses. Completion of program requires 2.0 GPA.

Evaluation Student evaluation based on tests, papers, reports, projects. Grading system: Letters or numbers. Transcripts are kept for each student.

Enrollment Requirements Certificate in Basic Technical Communication or equivalent required. Program is open to non-resident foreign students. English language proficiency required.

Program Costs $1836 for the program.

Housing and Student Services Housing is available. Job counseling and placement services are available.

Special Features Program provides advanced instruction and professional development in science writing, oral communication, online communication, promotional writing, audiovisual presentations, and managing the communication project; access to Computer Applications Lab; faculty are academically qualified professionals who do what they teach; credit for college-level learning; development assistance from Society for Technical Communication, Rochester chapter.

Contact Dr. Lynda Rummel, Director, Business and The Arts, Academic Division, College of Continuing Education, 50 West Main Street, Rochester, NY 14614. 716-475-4999.

COMMUNICATIONS, GENERAL (09.01)
Certificate in Basic Technical Communication

General Information Unit offering the program: Business and The Arts, Academic Division, College of Continuing Education. Available for credit. Endorsed by Society for Technical Communication, Rochester Chapter. Certificate signed by the Chairman of the Board of Trustees. Certificate applicable to A.A.S., B.S. in Applied Arts and Science; B.S. in Professional and Technical Communication; A.A. in General Education.

Program Format Evening classes offered. Instructional schedule: Two to three evenings per week or special variable length programs. Fall enrollment preferred. Full program cycle lasts 5 courses. Completion of program requires 2.0 GPA.

Evaluation Student evaluation based on tests, papers, reports, documentation projects. Grading system: Letters or numbers. Transcripts are kept for each student.

Enrollment Requirements Program is open to non-resident foreign students. English language proficiency required. Portfolio assessment and/or placement test.

Program Costs $1836 for the program.

Housing and Student Services Housing is available. Job counseling and placement services are available.

Special Features Program developed with assistance of Rochester chapter, Society for Technical Communication; faculty are professionals selected for their expertise and ability to teach; access to Computer Applications Laboratory; program designed to provide fundamental skills and knowledge in writing, editing, research, instructional and document design; credit for college-level learning.

Contact Dr. Lynda Rummel, Director, Business and The Arts, College of Continuing Education, 50 West Main Street, Rochester, NY 14614. 716-475-4999.

CRAFTS (50.02)
Crafts Diploma

General Information Unit offering the program: Business and The Arts, Academic Division, College of Continuing Education. Program content: Basic drawing, design, art appreciation, crafts. Available for credit. Certificate signed by the Chairman of the Board of Trustees. Certificate applicable to A.A.S., B.S. in Applied Arts and Science.

Program Format Evening, weekend classes offered. Instructional schedule: One to three evenings per week or alternate Saturdays. Completion of program requires 2.0 GPA, 26 courses.

Evaluation Student evaluation based on tests, papers, reports, portfolio. Grading system: Letters or numbers. Transcripts are kept for each student.

Enrollment Requirements High school diploma or equivalent required. Program is open to non-resident foreign students.

Program Costs $7704 for the program, $153 per credit hour.

Housing and Student Services Housing is available. Job counseling and placement services are available.

Special Features Up to 12 credits may be transferred into program with approval of advisor. Students need not attend each quarter. Option exists for independent study. Students build portfolios that can be used for job applications or for application to B.S./B.F.A. programs.

Contact Mr. Eric L. Bellman, Arts Chairperson, College of Continuing Education, 50 West Main, Rochester, NY 14614. 716-475-4977.

DESIGN (50.04)
Advertising Design Diploma

General Information Unit offering the program: Business and The Arts, Academic Division, College of Continuing Education. Program content: Basic drawing, design, art appreciation, advertising design. Available for credit. Certificate signed by the Chairman of the Board of Trustees. Certificate applicable to A.A.S., B.S. in Applied Arts and Science.

Program Format Evening, weekend classes offered. Instructional schedule: One to three evenings per week or alternate Saturdays. Completion of program requires 2.0 GPA, 26 courses.

Evaluation Student evaluation based on tests, papers, reports, portfolio. Grading system: Letters or numbers. Transcripts are kept for each student.

Enrollment Requirements High school diploma or equivalent required. Program is open to non-resident foreign students.

Program Costs $7704 for the program, $153 per credit hour.

Housing and Student Services Housing is available. Job counseling and placement services are available.

Special Features Up to 12 credits may be transferred into program with approval of advisor. Students need not attend each quarter. Option exists for independent study. Students build portfolios that can be used for job applications or for application to B.S./B.F.A. programs.

Contact Mr. Eric L. Bellman, Arts Chairperson, College of Continuing Education, 50 West Main, Rochester, NY 14614. 716-475-4977.

DESIGN (50.04)
Fashion Illustration Diploma

General Information Unit offering the program: Business and The Arts, Academic Division, College of Continuing Education. Program content: Basic drawing, design, art appreciation, illustration. Available for credit. Certificate signed by the Chairman of the Board of Trustees. Certificate applicable to A.A.S., B.S. in Applied Arts and Science.

Program Format Evening, weekend classes offered. Instructional schedule: One to three evenings per week or alternate Saturdays. Completion of program requires 2.0 GPA, 26 courses.

Evaluation Student evaluation based on tests, papers, reports, portfolio. Grading system: Letters or numbers. Transcripts are kept for each student.

Enrollment Requirements High school diploma or equivalent required. Program is open to non-resident foreign students.

Program Costs $7704 for the program, $153 per credit hour.

Housing and Student Services Housing is available. Job counseling and placement services are available.

Special Features Up to 12 credits may be transferred into program with approval of advisor. Students need not attend each quarter. Option exists for independent study. Students build portfolios that can be used for job applications or for application to B.S./B.F.A. programs.

Contact Mr. Eric L. Bellman, Arts Chairperson, College of Continuing Education, 50 West Main, Rochester, NY 14614. 716-475-4977.

FILM ARTS (50.06)
Photography Diploma

General Information Unit offering the program: Business and The Arts, Academic Division, College of Continuing Education. Program content: Technical education in professional photography combined with human relations. Available for credit. Certificate signed by the Chairman of the Board of Trustees. Certificate applicable to A.A.S., B.S. in Applied Arts and Science; A.A.S. in Professional Photography; B.S. in Graphic Arts.

Program Format Evening classes offered. Instructional schedule: One to three evenings per week. Fall enrollment preferred. Full program cycle lasts 16 courses.

Evaluation Student evaluation based on tests, papers, reports, projects. Grading system: Letters or numbers. Transcripts are kept for each student.

Enrollment Requirements Program is open to non-resident foreign students.

Program Costs $7497 for the program, $153 per quarter hour.

Housing and Student Services Housing is available. Job counseling and placement services are available.

Special Features Faculty are professional photographers or faculty with RIT's world renowned College of Graphic Arts and Photography. RIT's facilities are excellent.

Contact Mr. Andrew Davidhazy, Coordinator, Photography Programs, College of Graphic Arts and Photography, One Lomb Memorial Drive, Rochester, NY 14623. 716-475-2592.

FINE ARTS (50.07)
Fine Arts Diploma

General Information Unit offering the program: Business and The Arts, Academic Division, College of Continuing Education. Program content: Basic drawing, design, art appreciation. Available for credit. Certificate signed by the Chairman of the Board of Trustees. Certificate applicable to A.A.S., B.S. in Applied Arts and Science.

Program Format Evening, weekend classes offered. Instructional schedule: One to three evenings per week or alternate Saturdays. Completion of program requires 2.0 GPA, 26 courses.

Evaluation Student evaluation based on tests, papers, reports, portfolio. Grading system: Letters or numbers. Transcripts are kept for each student.

Enrollment Requirements High school diploma or equivalent required. Program is open to non-resident foreign students.

Program Costs $7704 for the program, $153 per credit hour.

Housing and Student Services Housing is available. Job counseling and placement services are available.

Special Features Up to 12 credits may be transferred into program with approval of advisor. Students need not attend each quarter. Option exists for independent study. Students build portfolios that can be used for job applications or for application to B.S./B.F.A. programs.

Contact Mr. Eric L. Bellman, Arts Chairperson, College of Continuing Education, 50 West Main, Rochester, NY 14614. 716-475-4977.

GRAPHIC AND PRINTING COMMUNICATIONS (48.02)
Printing Diploma

General Information Unit offering the program: Business and The Arts, Academic Division, College of Continuing Education. Program content: Specialized areas of printing, practical understanding of printing process. Available for credit. Certificate signed by the Chairman of the Board of Trustees. Certificate

Printing Diploma continued

applicable to A.A.S., B.S. in Graphic Arts, Applied Arts and Science.

Program Format Evening classes offered. Instructional schedule: One to three evenings per week. Fall enrollment preferred. Completion of program requires 2.0 GPA, 21 courses.

Evaluation Student evaluation based on tests, papers, reports, projects. Grading system: Letters or numbers. Transcripts are kept for each student.

Enrollment Requirements Program is open to non-resident foreign students.

Program Costs $6879 for the program, $153 per quarter hour.

Housing and Student Services Housing is available. Job counseling and placement services are available.

Special Features Broad range of printing technologies. Taught in excellent facilities of School of Printing Management and Sciences. Faculty are from internationally known RIT College of Graphic Arts and Photography.

Contact Ms. Linda Tolan, College of Graphic Arts and Photography, One Lomb Memorial Drive, Rochester, NY 14623. 716-475-5955.

INTERIOR DESIGN (04.05)
Interior Design Diploma

General Information Unit offering the program: Business and The Arts, Academic Division, College of Continuing Education. Program content: Basic drawing, design, art appreciation, interior design. Available for credit. Certificate signed by the Chairman of the Board of Trustees. Certificate applicable to A.A.S., B.S. in Applied Arts and Science.

Program Format Evening, weekend classes offered. Instructional schedule: One to three evenings per week or alternate Saturdays. Completion of program requires 2.0 GPA, 26 courses.

Evaluation Student evaluation based on tests, papers, reports, portfolio. Grading system: Letters or numbers. Transcripts are kept for each student.

Enrollment Requirements High school diploma or equivalent required. Program is open to non-resident foreign students.

Program Costs $7704 for the program, $153 per credit hour.

Housing and Student Services Housing is available. Job counseling and placement services are available.

Special Features Up to 12 credits may be transferred into program with approval of advisor. Students need not attend each quarter. Option exists for independent study. Students build portfolios that can be used for job applications or for application to B.S./B.F.A. programs.

Contact Mr. Eric L. Bellman, Arts Chairperson, College of Continuing Education, 50 West Main, Rochester, NY 14614. 716-475-4977.

LIBERAL/GENERAL STUDIES (24.01)
Diploma, Applied Arts and Science

General Information Unit offering the program: College of Continuing Education. Program content: Student's plan of study approved by program committee. Available for credit. Certificate signed by the Chairman of the Board of Trustees. Certificate applicable to A.A.S., B.S. in Applied Arts and Science.

Program Format Daytime, evening, weekend classes offered. Program cycle: Continuous enrollment. Completion of program requires 2.0 GPA, 36 quarter units.

Evaluation Student evaluation methods vary by course. Grading system: Letters or numbers. Transcripts are kept for each student.

Enrollment Requirements Plan of study approval required. Program is open to non-resident foreign students. English language proficiency required.

Program Costs $5508 for the program, $153 per quarter hour.

Housing and Student Services Housing is not available. Job counseling and placement services are available.

Special Features Personalized plan of study reflecting career goals. Credit is sometimes given for college-level learning and/or experience.

Contact Ms. Bette Anne Winston, Academic Advising Coordinator, College of Continuing Education, 1 Lomb Memorial Drive, Rochester, NY 14623-9979. 716-475-2218.

PRECISION METAL WORK (48.05)
Automatic Screwmachine, Setup and Operate Diploma

General Information Unit offering the program: Science and Technology, Academic Division, College of Continuing Education. Program content: Hand screw machine, automatic screw machine, blueprint reading, human relations, mathematics. Available for credit. Certificate signed by the Chairman of the Board of Trustees. Certificate applicable to associate degree in industrial technologies.

Program Format Evening classes offered. Instructional schedule: Two evenings per week. Program cycle: Continuous enrollment. Completion of program requires 2.0 GPA, 30 quarter units.

Evaluation Student evaluation based on tests. Grading system: Letters or numbers. Transcripts are kept for each student.

Enrollment Requirements Program is open to non-resident foreign students.

Program Costs $4590 for the program, $153 per quarter hour.

Housing and Student Services Housing is available. Job counseling and placement services are available.

Special Features Excellent support facilities.

Contact Mr. Henry Cooke, Director, Science and Technology, College of Continuing Education, 50 West Main Street, Rochester, NY 14614. 716-475-5021.

PRECISION METAL WORK (48.05)
Instrument Making and Experimental Work Diploma

General Information Unit offering the program: Science and Technology, Academic Division, College of Continuing Education. Program content: Instrument making, trigonometry, heat treatment, mathematics, lab, blueprint reading, human relations. Available for credit. Certificate signed by the Chairman of the Board of Trustees. Certificate applicable to two-year degree in industrial technologies.

Program Format Evening classes offered. Instructional schedule: Two evenings per week. Program cycle: Continuous enrollment. Completion of program requires 2.0 GPA, 40 quarter units.

Evaluation Student evaluation based on tests. Grading system: Letters or numbers. Transcripts are kept for each student.

Enrollment Requirements Program is open to non-resident foreign students.

Program Costs $6120 for the program, $153 per quarter hour.

Housing and Student Services Housing is available. Job counseling and placement services are available.

Special Features Excellent facilities.

Contact Mr. Henry Cooke, Director, Science and Technology, College of Continuing Education, 50 West Main Street, Rochester, NY 14614. 716-475-5021.

PRECISION METAL WORK (48.05)
Machine Shop Diploma

General Information Unit offering the program: Science and Technology, Academic Division, College of Continuing Education. Program content: Engineering drawing, precision measurement, blueprint reading, lab, heat treatment, human relations. Available for credit. Certificate signed by the Chairman of the Board of Trustees. Certificate applicable to associate degree in industrial technologies.

Program Format   Evening classes offered. Instructional schedule: Two evenings per week. Program cycle: Continuous enrollment. Completion of program requires 2.0 GPA, 30 quarter units.

Evaluation   Student evaluation based on tests. Grading system: Letters or numbers. Transcripts are kept for each student.

Enrollment Requirements   Program is open to non-resident foreign students.

Program Costs $4590 for the program, $153 per quarter hour.

Housing and Student Services   Housing is available. Job counseling and placement services are available.

Special Features   Excellent support facilities.

Contact   Mr. Henry Cooke, Director, Science and Technology, College of Continuing Education, 50 West Main Street, Rochester, NY 14614. 716-475-5021.

PRECISION METAL WORK (48.05)
Tool and Die Making Diploma

General Information   Unit offering the program: Science and Technology, Academic Division, College of Continuing Education. Program content: Tool and die, trigonometry, blueprint reading, heat treatment, human relations, lab. Available for credit. Certificate signed by the Chairman of the Board of Trustees. Certificate applicable to associate degree in industrial technologies.

Program Format   Evening classes offered. Instructional schedule: Two evenings per week. Program cycle: Continuous enrollment. Completion of program requires 2.0 GPA, 30 quarter units.

Evaluation   Student evaluation based on tests. Grading system: Letters or numbers. Transcripts are kept for each student.

Enrollment Requirements   Program is open to non-resident foreign students.

Program Costs $6120 for the program, $153 per quarter hour.

Housing and Student Services   Housing is available. Job counseling and placement services are available.

Special Features   Excellent physical support facilities.

Contact   Mr. Henry Cooke, Director, Science and Technology, College of Continuing Education, 50 West Main Street, Rochester, NY 14614. 716-475-5021.

PUBLIC RELATIONS (09.05)
Certificate in Public Relations Communications—Graphic Communication

General Information   Unit offering the program: Business and The Arts, Academic Division, College of Continuing Education. Program content: Foundation skills and knowledge in public relations, concentration in graphic communication. Available for credit. Certificate signed by the Chairman of the Board of Trustees. Certificate applicable to A.A.S., B.S. in Applied Arts and Science; A.A. in General Education.

Program Format   Evening classes offered. Instructional schedule: Two to three evenings per week or special variable length programs. Program cycle: Continuous enrollment, fall enrollment preferred. Full program cycle lasts 7 courses. Completion of program requires 2.0 GPA.

Evaluation   Student evaluation based on tests, papers, reports, projects. Grading system: Letters or numbers. Transcripts are kept for each student.

Enrollment Requirements   Program is open to non-resident foreign students. English language proficiency required. Portfolio assessment and/or placement test.

Program Costs $2907 for the program.

Housing and Student Services   Housing is available. Job counseling and placement services are available.

Special Features   Program provides foundation knowledge of public relations, advertising evaluation and techniques, psychology of persuasion, and managing the communication project. Develops skills in graphic communication and art for reproduction. Faculty are practicing professionals selected for expertise and ability to teach. Developed with assistance of advisory group of professionals. College-level credit available.

Contact   Dr. Lynda Rummel, Director, Business and The Arts, Academic Division, College of Continuing Education, 50 West Main Street, Rochester, NY 14614. 716-475-4999.

PUBLIC RELATIONS (09.05)
Certificate in Public Relations Communications—Professional Writing

General Information   Unit offering the program: Business and The Arts, Academic Division, College of Continuing Education. Program content: Foundation skills and knowledge in public relations, concentration in professional writing. Available for credit. Certificate signed by the Chairman of the Board of Trustees. Certificate applicable to A.A.S., B.S. in Applied Arts and Science; A.A. in General Education.

Program Format   Evening classes offered. Instructional schedule: Two to three evenings per week or special variable length programs. Program cycle: Continuous enrollment, fall enrollment recommended. Full program cycle lasts 8 courses. Completion of program requires 2.0 GPA.

Evaluation   Student evaluation based on tests, papers, reports, projects. Grading system: Letters or numbers. Transcripts are kept for each student.

Enrollment Requirements   Program is open to non-resident foreign students. English language proficiency required. Portfolio assessment and/or placement test.

Program Costs $3060 for the program.

Housing and Student Services   Housing is available. Job counseling and placement services are available.

Special Features   Program provides foundation knowledge in public relations, advertising evaluation and techniques, psychology of persuasion, and managing the communication project; and skills and knowledge in writing for the organization, promotional writing, and scripting and speechwriting; credit for college-level learning; faculty are practicing professionals; developed with assistance of advisory group.

Contact   Dr. Lynda Rummel, Director, Business and The Arts, Academic Division, College of Continuing Education, 50 West Main Street, Rochester, NY 14614. 716-475-4999.

SMALL BUSINESS·MANAGEMENT AND OWNERSHIP (06.18)
Small Business Management

General Information   Unit offering the program: Business and The Arts, Academic Division, College of Continuing Education. Program content: Entrepreneurial theory and skills in new venture development, small business planning, financing and marketing. Available for credit. Certificate signed by the Dean of the College. Certificate applicable to A.A.S., B.S. in Business Administration, Management, Applied Arts and Science.

Program Format   Evening, weekend classes offered. Instructional schedule: One evening per week or five alternate Saturdays. Program cycle: Continuous enrollment. Full program cycle lasts 3 courses. Completion of program requires 2.0 GPA.

Evaluation   Student evaluation based on tests, papers, reports, projects. Grading system: Letters or numbers. Transcripts are kept for each student.

Enrollment Requirements   Program is open to non-resident foreign students.

Program Costs $1836 for the program, $612 per course.

Housing and Student Services   Housing is available. Job counseling and placement services are available.

Small Business Management continued

Special Features   Development of business action plan. Faculty are academically qualified successful entrepreneurs.

Contact   Dr. Lynda Rummel, Director, Business and The Arts, College of Continuing Education, 50 West Main Street, Rochester, NY 14614. 716-475-4999.

RUSSELL SAGE COLLEGE
Troy, New York 12180

LAW (22.01)
Certificate Program in Paralegal Education

General Information   Unit offering the program: Legal Assistant Program. Available for credit. Certificate signed by the Dean of Continuing Education. Certificate applicable to A.A.S. in Legal Assistant.

Program Format   Evening classes offered. Instructional schedule: Once per week. Program cycle: Continuous enrollment. Full program cycle lasts 2 years. Completion of program requires nine courses.

Evaluation   Student evaluation based on tests, papers. Grading system: Letters or numbers. Transcripts are kept for each student.

Enrollment Requirements   Open admissions but not recommended for students directly from high school. Program is open to non-resident foreign students.

Program Costs $150 per credit hour.

Housing and Student Services   Housing is available. Job counseling and placement services are available.

Special Features   Certificate is offered by Legal Assistant Program, which began in 1975. All instructors are practicing attorneys. No credit for prior job experience. Courses designed to teach practical paralegal skills in a number of legal areas.

Contact   Mr. Michael J. Smith, Director of Paralegal Education, Junior College of Albany, 140 New Scotland Avenue, Albany, NY 12208. 518-445-1729.

ST. BONAVENTURE UNIVERSITY
St. Bonaventure, New York 14778

RELIGIOUS EDUCATION (39.04)
Leadership Development for the Church of the Southern Tier

General Information   Unit offering the program: Communiversity Program for Lifelong Learning. Program content: Instruction for lay leaders. Available on a non-credit basis. Endorsed by Diocese of Buffalo. Certificate signed by the Dean, Graduate School.

Program Format   Weekend classes offered. Instructional schedule: 24 weekends per year. Program cycle: Continuous enrollment. Full program cycle lasts 2 years. Completion of program requires 96 study hours, practicum.

Evaluation   Student evaluation based on practicum. Records are kept for each student.

Enrollment Requirements   Program is open to non-resident foreign students. English language proficiency required.

Program Costs $700 for the program.

Housing and Student Services   Housing is not available. Job counseling and placement services are not available.

Contact   Ms. Ann Lehman, Coordinator, P.O. Box 146, St. Bonaventure, NY 14760. 716-375-2111 Ext. 46.

ST. FRANCIS COLLEGE
Brooklyn Heights, New York 11201

ACCOUNTING (06.02)
Advanced Business Certificate in Corporate Accounting

General Information   Unit offering the program: Department of Accounting and Business Law. Program content: Elementary accounting, introduction to computers, organization and management, cost accounting, taxation, business communication. Available for credit. Certificate signed by the President.

Program Format   Daytime, evening classes offered. Program cycle: Continuous enrollment. Full program cycle lasts 21 credit hours. Completion of program requires 2.0 GPA.

Evaluation   Student evaluation based on tests, papers, reports. Grading system: Letters or numbers. Transcripts are kept for each student.

Enrollment Requirements   High school diploma or equivalent required. Program is open to non-resident foreign students. English language proficiency required. Minimum TOEFL score required: 500.

Program Costs $3170 for the program, $450 per course.

Housing and Student Services   Housing is not available. Job counseling and placement services are available.

Contact   Ms. Susan MacDonnell, Director of Admissions for Continuing Education, 180 Remsen Street, Brooklyn Heights, NY 11201. 718-522-2300.

BANKING AND FINANCE (06.03)
Advanced Business Certificate in Finance

General Information   Unit offering the program: Management Department. Program content: Introduction to accounting and computers, business communications, corporate and managerial finance. Available for credit. Certificate signed by the President.

Program Format   Daytime, evening classes offered. Program cycle: Continuous enrollment. Full program cycle lasts 21 credit hours. Completion of program requires 2.0 GPA.

Evaluation   Student evaluation based on tests, papers, reports. Grading system: Letters or numbers. Transcripts are kept for each student.

Enrollment Requirements   High school diploma or equivalent required. Program is open to non-resident foreign students. English language proficiency required. Minimum TOEFL score required: 500.

Program Costs $3170 for the program, $450 per course.

Housing and Student Services   Housing is not available. Job counseling and placement services are available.

Contact   Ms. Susan MacDonnell, Director of Admissions for Continuing Education, 180 Remsen Street, Brooklyn Heights, NY 11201. 718-522-2300.

BUSINESS AND MANAGEMENT, GENERAL (06.01)
Advanced Business Certificate in General Business

General Information   Unit offering the program: Management Department. Program content: Introduction to accounting and computers, organization and management, business communications, basic marketing, macroeconomics. Available for credit. Certificate signed by the President.

Program Format   Daytime, evening classes offered. Program cycle: Continuous enrollment. Full program cycle lasts 18 credit hours. Completion of program requires 2.0 GPA.

Evaluation   Student evaluation based on tests, papers, reports. Grading system: Letters or numbers. Transcripts are kept for each student.

Enrollment Requirements High school diploma or equivalent required. Program is open to non-resident foreign students. English language proficiency required. Minimum TOEFL score required: 500.

Program Costs $2720 for the program, $450 per course.

Housing and Student Services Housing is not available. Job counseling and placement services are available.

Contact Ms. Susan MacDonnell, Director of Admissions for Continuing Education, 180 Remsen Street, Brooklyn Heights, NY 11201. 718-522-2300.

GENERAL MARKETING (08.07)
Advanced Business Certificate in Marketing

General Information Unit offering the program: Management Department. Program content: Accounting, computers, marketing, business communication, organization and management, marketing management. Available for credit. Certificate signed by the President.

Program Format Daytime, evening classes offered. Program cycle: Continuous enrollment. Full program cycle lasts 18 credit hours. Completion of program requires 2.0 GPA.

Evaluation Student evaluation based on tests, papers, reports. Grading system: Letters or numbers. Transcripts are kept for each student.

Enrollment Requirements High school diploma or equivalent required. Program is open to non-resident foreign students. English language proficiency required.

Program Costs $2720 for the program, $450 per course.

Housing and Student Services Housing is not available. Job counseling and placement services are available.

Contact Ms. Susan MacDonnell, Director of Admissions for Continuing Education, 180 Remsen Street, Brooklyn Heights, NY 11201. 718-522-2300.

MANAGEMENT INFORMATION SYSTEMS (06.12)
Advanced Business Certificate in Electronic Data Processing

General Information Unit offering the program: Management Department. Program content: Introduction to accounting and computers, organization and management, systems analysis, COBOL. Available for credit. Certificate signed by the President.

Program Format Daytime, evening classes offered. Program cycle: Continuous enrollment. Full program cycle lasts 18 credit hours. Completion of program requires 2.0 GPA.

Evaluation Student evaluation based on tests, papers, reports. Grading system: Letters or numbers. Transcripts are kept for each student.

Enrollment Requirements High school diploma or equivalent required. Program is open to non-resident foreign students. English language proficiency required. Minimum TOEFL score required: 500.

Program Costs $2720 for the program, $450 per course.

Housing and Student Services Housing is not available. Job counseling and placement services are available.

Contact Ms. Susan MacDonnell, Director of Admissions for Continuing Education, 180 Remsen Street, Brooklyn Heights, NY 11201. 718-522-2300.

PERSONNEL MANAGEMENT (06.16)
Advanced Business Certificate in Human Resources

General Information Unit offering the program: Management Department. Program content: Introduction to accounting and computers, organization and management, business communications, behavioral science, personnel management. Available for credit. Certificate signed by the President.

Program Format Daytime, evening classes offered. Program cycle: Continuous enrollment. Full program cycle lasts 18 credit hours. Completion of program requires 2.0 GPA.

Evaluation Student evaluation based on tests, papers, reports. Grading system: Letters or numbers. Transcripts are kept for each student.

Enrollment Requirements High school diploma or equivalent required. Program is open to non-resident foreign students. English language proficiency required. Minimum TOEFL score required: 500.

Program Costs $2720 for the program, $450 per course.

Housing and Student Services Housing is not available. Job counseling and placement services are available.

Contact Ms. Susan MacDonnell, Director of Admissions for Continuing Education, 180 Remsen Street, Brooklyn Heights, NY 11201. 718-522-2300.

NUCEA MEMBER
ST. JOHN FISHER COLLEGE
Rochester, New York 14618

ACCOUNTING, BOOKKEEPING, AND RELATED PROGRAMS (07.01)
Certificate in Credit Administration

General Information Unit offering the program: Professional Development Office. Available on a non-credit basis. Endorsed by National Association of Credit Management, Rochester. Cosponsored by National Institute of Credit. Certificate signed by the Registrar. Program fulfills requirements for Certificate in Credit Administration (CCA).

Program Format Evening classes offered. Instructional schedule: Classes meet weekly. Program cycle: Continuous enrollment. Full program cycle lasts 10 months. Completion of program requires four courses.

Evaluation Student evaluation based on tests. Grading system: Pass/fail. Transcripts are kept for each student.

Enrollment Requirements Some financial background required. Program is not open to non-resident foreign students.

Program Costs $840 for the program, $210 per course.

Housing and Student Services Housing is not available. Job counseling and placement services are not available.

Special Features This program, which leads to a Certificate in Credit Administration (CCA), is designed to meet the needs of business credit professionals who seek ways to develop and sharpen the skills necessary to make use of changing credit trends for the benefit of the companies they represent.

Contact Ms. Gail Bober, Director of Professional Development, 3690 East Avenue, Rochester, NY 14618. 716-385-8320.

BUSINESS AND MANAGEMENT, GENERAL (06.01)
Certificate in Business Management

General Information Unit offering the program: Professional Development Office. Available on a non-credit basis. Cosponsored by American Management Association. Certificate signed by the Registrar.

Program Format Evening classes offered. Instructional schedule: Classes meet weekly. Program cycle: Continuous enrollment. Full program cycle lasts 2 years.

Evaluation Student evaluation based on tests, papers, reports, case studies. Grading system: Pass/fail. Transcripts are kept for each student.

Enrollment Requirements Program is open to non-resident foreign students. English language proficiency required.

Program Costs $1140 for the program, $190 per course.

Certificate in Business Management continued

Housing and Student Services Housing is not available. Job counseling and placement services are not available.

Special Features Most instructors are working in the local business community, and they emphasize practical application. This certificate program is especially useful for those men and women who are looking to advance their careers, to sharpen a specific skill, to become more familiar with a function area, or to acquire the versatile expertise upper-level professionals must have.

Contact Ms. Gail Bober, Director of Professional Development, 3690 East Avenue, Rochester, NY 14618. 716-385-8320.

INDIVIDUAL AND FAMILY DEVELOPMENT (19.07)
Certificate Program in Gerontology

General Information Unit offering the program: Professional Development Office. Program content: Concerns and needs of the aging. Available on a non-credit basis. Certificate signed by the Registrar.

Program Format Evening classes offered. Instructional schedule: 4–6 p.m., weekly. Program cycle: Continuous enrollment. Full program cycle lasts 2 years. Completion of program requires 24 courses.

Evaluation Student evaluation based on tests, reports. Grading system: Pass/fail. Transcripts are kept for each student.

Enrollment Requirements Program is not open to non-resident foreign students.

Program Costs $1404 for the program, $81 per course.

Housing and Student Services Housing is not available. Job counseling and placement services are not available.

Special Features The program provides the opportunity to develop understanding and skills needed to work with older individuals whether as an administrator in an extended-care facility, as a director of an agency for the elderly, as one who delivers primary service, or simply as someone caring for an older relative or friend.

Contact Ms. Gail Bober, Director of Professional Development, 3690 East Avenue, Rochester, NY 14618. 716-385-8320.

TRANSPORTATION AND TRAVEL MARKETING (08.11)
Certificate in Travel Agency Business

General Information Unit offering the program: Professional Development Office. Available on a non-credit basis. Endorsed by Borelli Travel Agency. Certificate signed by the Registrar.

Program Format Evening classes offered. Program cycle: Continuous enrollment. Full program cycle lasts 2 semesters. Completion of program requires five courses.

Evaluation Student evaluation based on tests, papers, reports. Grading system: Pass/fail. Transcripts are kept for each student.

Enrollment Requirements Program is not open to non-resident foreign students.

Program Costs $1180 for the program.

Housing and Student Services Housing is not available. Job counseling and placement services are available.

Special Features The program is designed to develop a greater understanding of the travel business and is intended both for those planning to enter the field or those thinking of opening their own agency. An optional internship is available.

Contact Ms. Gail Bober, Director of Professional Development, 3690 East Avenue, Rochester, NY 14618. 716-385-8320.

ST. JOSEPH'S COLLEGE
Brooklyn, New York 11205

BUSINESS ADMINISTRATION AND MANAGEMENT (06.04)
Certificate in Management

General Information Unit offering the program: Division of General Studies, College of Arts and Sciences. Program content: Management of organizations in business, nonprofit, or public sector. Available for credit. Certificate signed by the President. Certificate applicable to B.S. in Management of Human Resources, Business Education, Health Administration.

Program Format Daytime, evening, weekend classes offered. Program cycle: Continuous enrollment. Full program cycle lasts 27 credit hours. Completion of program requires 2.0 GPA.

Evaluation Student evaluation based on tests, papers, reports. Grading system: Letters or numbers. Transcripts are kept for each student.

Enrollment Requirements High school diploma required. Program is open to non-resident foreign students. English language proficiency required. College-administered writing assessment.

Program Costs $3996 for the program, $444 per course.

Housing and Student Services Housing is not available. Job counseling and placement services are available.

Contact Admissions Counselor, Division of General Studies, 245 Clinton Avenue, Brooklyn, NY 11205. 718-622-4690.

COMPUTER AND INFORMATION SCIENCES, GENERAL (11.01)
Certificate in Data and Information Processing

General Information Unit offering the program: Division of General Studies, College of Arts and Sciences. Available for credit. Certificate signed by the President. Certificate applicable to B.S. in Management of Human Resources, Business Administration.

Program Format Daytime, evening, weekend classes offered. Program cycle: Continuous enrollment. Full program cycle lasts 12 credit hours. Completion of program requires 2.0 GPA.

Evaluation Student evaluation based on tests, papers, reports. Grading system: Letters or numbers. Transcripts are kept for each student.

Enrollment Requirements High school diploma required. Program is open to non-resident foreign students. English language proficiency required. College-administered writing assessment.

Program Costs $1776 for the program, $444 per course.

Housing and Student Services Housing is not available. Job counseling and placement services are available.

Contact Admissions Counselor, Division of General Studies, 245 Clinton Avenue, Brooklyn, NY 11205. 718-622-4690.

CRIMINAL JUSTICE (43.01)
Certificate in Criminal Justice

General Information Unit offering the program: College of Arts and Sciences. Program content: Theoretical and practical exposure to criminal justice system. Available for credit. Certificate signed by the President. Certificate applicable to B.A. in Human Relations, Social Science.

Program Format Daytime, evening classes offered. Program cycle: Continuous enrollment. Full program cycle lasts 24 credit hours. Completion of program requires 2.0 GPA.

Evaluation Student evaluation based on tests, papers, reports. Grading system: Letters or numbers. Transcripts are kept for each student.

Enrollment Requirements High school diploma required. Program is open to non-resident foreign students. English language proficiency required. College-administered writing assessment.

Program Costs $3552 for the program, $444 per course.

Housing and Student Services   Housing is not available. Job counseling and placement services are available.

Contact   Ms. Eileen Mullen, Director of Admissions, 245 Clinton Avenue, Brooklyn, NY 11205. 718-636-6800.

HUMAN RESOURCES DEVELOPMENT (06.06)
Certificate in Leadership and Human Resources Development

General Information   Unit offering the program: Division of General Studies, College of Arts and Sciences. Program content: Supervisory and managerial effectiveness. Available for credit. Certificate signed by the President. Certificate applicable to B.S. in Management of Human Resources, Business Administration, Health Administration.

Program Format   Daytime, evening, weekend classes offered. Program cycle: Continuous enrollment. Full program cycle lasts 12 credit hours. Completion of program requires 2.0 GPA.

Evaluation   Student evaluation based on tests, papers, reports. Grading system: Letters or numbers. Transcripts are kept for each student.

Enrollment Requirements   High school diploma required. Program is open to non-resident foreign students. English language proficiency required. College-administered writing assessment.

Program Costs $1776 for the program, $444 per course.

Housing and Student Services   Housing is not available. Job counseling and placement services are available.

Contact   Admissions Counselor, Division of General Studies, 245 Clinton Avenue, Brooklyn, NY 11205. 718-622-4690.

INDIVIDUAL AND FAMILY DEVELOPMENT (19.07)
Certificate in Gerontology

General Information   Unit offering the program: Division of General Studies, College of Arts and Sciences. Program content: Understanding and serving an older clientele. Available for credit. Certificate signed by the President. Certificate applicable to B.S. in Community Health, Health Administration, Recreation; B.A. in Psychology, Social Science, Human Relations.

Program Format   Daytime, evening, weekend classes offered. Program cycle: Continuous enrollment. Full program cycle lasts 12 credit hours. Completion of program requires 2.0 GPA.

Evaluation   Student evaluation based on tests, papers, reports. Grading system: Letters or numbers. Transcripts are kept for each student.

Enrollment Requirements   High school diploma required. Program is open to non-resident foreign students. English language proficiency required. College-administered writing assessment.

Program Costs $1776 for the program, $444 per course.

Housing and Student Services   Housing is not available. Job counseling and placement services are available.

Special Features   Practicum is required.

Contact   Admissions Counselor, Division of General Studies, 245 Clinton Boulevard, Brooklyn, NY 11205. 718-622-4690.

MISCELLANEOUS ALLIED HEALTH SERVICES (17.05)
Certificate in Health Counseling

General Information   Unit offering the program: Division of General Studies. Program content: Counseling theory and techniques to meet client needs in variety of health settings. Available for credit. Certificate signed by the President.

Certificate applicable to B.S. in Community Health, Health Administration.

Program Format   Daytime, evening, weekend classes offered. Program cycle: Continuous enrollment. Full program cycle lasts 12 credit hours. Completion of program requires 2.0 GPA.

Evaluation   Student evaluation based on tests, papers, reports. Grading system: Letters or numbers. Transcripts are kept for each student.

Enrollment Requirements   High school diploma, experience in health field required. Program is open to non-resident foreign students. English language proficiency required. College-administered writing assessment.

Program Costs $1776 for the program, $444 per course.

Housing and Student Services   Housing is not available. Job counseling and placement services are available.

Contact   Admissions Counselor, Division of General Studies, 245 Clinton Avenue, Brooklyn, NY 11205. 718-622-4690.

MISCELLANEOUS ALLIED HEALTH SERVICES (17.05)
Certificate in Health Instruction

General Information   Unit offering the program: Division of General Studies. Program content: Plan, implement, and evaluate health education programs for health consumers in the hospital and community. Available for credit. Certificate signed by the President. Certificate applicable to B.S. in Community Health, Health Administration.

Program Format   Daytime, evening, weekend classes offered. Program cycle: Continuous enrollment. Full program cycle lasts 12 credit hours. Completion of program requires 2.0 GPA.

Evaluation   Student evaluation based on tests, papers, reports. Grading system: Letters or numbers. Transcripts are kept for each student.

Enrollment Requirements   High school diploma, experience in health field required. Program is open to non-resident foreign students. English language proficiency required. College-administered writing assessment.

Program Costs $1776 for the program, $444 per course.

Housing and Student Services   Housing is not available. Job counseling and placement services are available.

Special Features   Practicum is required.

Contact   Admissions Counselor, Division of General Studies, 245 Clinton Avenue, Brooklyn, NY 11205. 718-622-4690.

MISCELLANEOUS ALLIED HEALTH SERVICES (17.05)
Certificate in Health Staff Development

General Information   Unit offering the program: Division of General Studies. Program content: Plan, implement, and evaluate in-service and training programs in health care facilities. Available for credit. Certificate signed by the President. Certificate applicable to B.S. in Community Health, Health Administration.

Program Format   Daytime, evening, weekend classes offered. Program cycle: Continuous enrollment. Full program cycle lasts 12 credit hours. Completion of program requires 2.0 GPA.

Evaluation   Student evaluation based on tests, papers, reports. Grading system: Letters or numbers. Transcripts are kept for each student.

Enrollment Requirements   High school diploma, experience in health field required. Program is open to non-resident foreign students. English language proficiency required. College-administered writing assessment.

Program Costs $1776 for the program, $444 per course.

Housing and Student Services   Housing is not available. Job counseling and placement services are available.

Special Features   Practicum is required.

Certificate in Health Staff Development continued

Contact   Admissions Counselor, Division of General Studies, 245 Clinton Avenue, Brooklyn, NY 11205. 718-622-4690.

MISCELLANEOUS ALLIED HEALTH SERVICES (17.05)
Certificate in Home Care Administration

General Information   Unit offering the program: Division of General Studies. Available for credit. Certificate signed by the President. Certificate applicable to B.S. in Community Health, Health Administration.

Program Format   Daytime, evening, weekend classes offered. Program cycle: Continuous enrollment. Full program cycle lasts 18 credit hours. Completion of program requires 2.0 GPA.

Evaluation   Student evaluation based on tests, papers, reports. Grading system: Letters or numbers. Transcripts are kept for each student.

Enrollment Requirements   High school diploma, experience in health field required. Program is open to non-resident foreign students. English language proficiency required. College-administered writing assessment.

Program Costs $2664 for the program, $444 per course.

Housing and Student Services   Housing is not available. Job counseling and placement services are available.

Contact   Admissions Counselor, Division of General Studies, 245 Clinton Avenue, Brooklyn, NY 11205. 718-622-4690.

ST. JOSEPH'S COLLEGE, SUFFOLK CAMPUS
Patchogue, New York 11772

BUSINESS ADMINISTRATION AND MANAGEMENT (06.04)
Certificate in Management

General Information   Unit offering the program: Division of General Studies, College of Arts and Sciences. Program content: Management of organizations in business, nonprofit, or public sector. Available for credit. Certificate signed by the President. Certificate applicable to B.S. in Management of Human Resources, Business Education, Health Administration.

Program Format   Daytime, evening, weekend classes offered. Program cycle: Continuous enrollment. Full program cycle lasts 27 credit hours. Completion of program requires 2.0 GPA.

Evaluation   Student evaluation based on tests, papers, reports. Grading system: Letters or numbers. Transcripts are kept for each student.

Enrollment Requirements   High school diploma required. Program is open to non-resident foreign students. English language proficiency required. College-administered writing assessment.

Program Costs $3996 for the program, $444 per course.

Housing and Student Services   Housing is not available. Job counseling and placement services are available.

Contact   Admissions Counselor, Division of General Studies, 155 Roe Boulevard, Patchogue, NY 11772. 516-654-3200.

COMPUTER AND INFORMATION SCIENCES, GENERAL (11.01)
Certificate in Data and Information Processing

General Information   Unit offering the program: Division of General Studies, College of Arts and Sciences. Program content: Computer applications. Available for credit. Certificate signed by the President. Certificate applicable to B.S. in Management of Human Resources, Business Administration.

Program Format   Daytime, evening, weekend classes offered. Program cycle: Continuous enrollment. Full program cycle lasts 12 credit hours. Completion of program requires 2.0 GPA.

Evaluation   Student evaluation based on tests, papers, reports. Grading system: Letters or numbers. Transcripts are kept for each student.

Enrollment Requirements   High school diploma required. Program is open to non-resident foreign students. English language proficiency required. College-administered writing assessment.

Program Costs $1776 for the program, $444 per course.

Housing and Student Services   Housing is not available. Job counseling and placement services are available.

Contact   Admissions Counselor, Division of General Studies, 155 Roe Boulevard, Patchogue, NY 11772. 516-654-3200.

CRIMINAL JUSTICE (43.01)
Certificate in Criminal Justice

General Information   Unit offering the program: College of Arts and Sciences. Program content: Theoretical and practical exposure to criminal justice system. Available for credit. Certificate signed by the President. Certificate applicable to B.A. in Human Relations, Social Science.

Program Format   Daytime, evening classes offered. Program cycle: Continuous enrollment. Full program cycle lasts 24 credit hours. Completion of program requires 2.0 GPA.

Evaluation   Student evaluation based on tests, papers, reports. Grading system: Letters or numbers. Transcripts are kept for each student.

Enrollment Requirements   High school diploma required. Program is open to non-resident foreign students. English language proficiency required. College-administered writing assessment.

Program Costs $3552 for the program, $444 per course.

Housing and Student Services   Housing is not available. Job counseling and placement services are available.

Contact   Ms. Marion Salgado, Director of Admissions, 155 Roe Boulevard, Patchogue, NY 11772. 516-654-3200.

HUMAN RESOURCES DEVELOPMENT (06.06)
Certificate in Leadership and Human Resources Development

General Information   Unit offering the program: Division of General Studies, College of Arts and Sciences. Program content: Supervisory and managerial effectiveness. Available for credit. Certificate signed by the President. Certificate applicable to B.S. in Management of Human Resources, Business Administration, Health Administration.

Program Format   Daytime, evening, weekend classes offered. Program cycle: Continuous enrollment. Full program cycle lasts 12 credit hours. Completion of program requires 2.0 GPA.

Evaluation   Student evaluation based on tests, papers, reports. Grading system: Letters or numbers. Transcripts are kept for each student.

Enrollment Requirements   High school diploma required. Program is open to non-resident foreign students. English language proficiency required. College-administered writing assessment.

Program Costs $1776 for the program, $444 per course.

Housing and Student Services   Housing is not available. Job counseling and placement services are available.

Contact   Admissions Counselor, Division of General Studies, 155 Roe Boulevard, Patchogue, NY 11772. 516-654-3200.

INDIVIDUAL AND FAMILY DEVELOPMENT (19.07)
Certificate in Gerontology

General Information   Unit offering the program: Division of General Studies, College of Arts and Sciences. Program content: Knowledge essential to understanding and serving an older clientele. Available for credit. Certificate signed by the President. Certificate applicable to B.S. in Community Health, Health Administration, Recreation; B.A. in Psychology, Social Science, Human Relations.

Program Format   Daytime, evening, weekend classes offered. Program cycle: Continuous enrollment. Full program cycle lasts 12 credit hours. Completion of program requires 2.0 GPA.

Evaluation   Student evaluation based on tests, papers, reports. Grading system: Letters or numbers. Transcripts are kept for each student.

Enrollment Requirements   High school diploma required. Program is open to non-resident foreign students. English language proficiency required. College-administered writing assessment.

Program Costs $1776 for the program, $444 per course.

Housing and Student Services   Housing is not available. Job counseling and placement services are available.

Special Features   Practicum is required.

Contact   Admissions Counselor, Division of General Studies, 155 Roe Boulevard, Patchogue, NY 11772. 516-654-3200.

MISCELLANEOUS ALLIED HEALTH SERVICES (17.05)
Certificate in Health Counseling

General Information   Unit offering the program: Division of General Studies. Program content: Counseling theory and techniques to meet client needs in variety of health settings. Available for credit. Certificate signed by the President. Certificate applicable to B.S. in Community Health, Health Administration.

Program Format   Daytime, evening, weekend classes offered. Program cycle: Continuous enrollment. Full program cycle lasts 12 credit hours. Completion of program requires 2.0 GPA.

Evaluation   Student evaluation based on tests, papers, reports. Grading system: Letters or numbers. Transcripts are kept for each student.

Enrollment Requirements   High school diploma, experience in health field required. Program is open to non-resident foreign students. English language proficiency required. College-administered writing assessment.

Program Costs $1776 for the program, $444 per course.

Housing and Student Services   Housing is not available. Job counseling and placement services are available.

Contact   Admissions Counselor, Division of General Studies, 155 Roe Boulevard, Patchogue, NY 11772. 516-654-3200.

MISCELLANEOUS ALLIED HEALTH SERVICES (17.05)
Certificate in Health Instruction

General Information   Unit offering the program: Division of General Studies. Program content: Plan, implement, and evaluate health education programs for health consumers in the hospital and community. Available for credit. Certificate signed by the President. Certificate applicable to B.S. in Community Health, Health Administration.

Program Format   Daytime, evening, weekend classes offered. Program cycle: Continuous enrollment. Full program cycle lasts 12 credit hours. Completion of program requires 2.0 GPA.

Evaluation   Student evaluation based on tests, papers, reports. Grading system: Letters or numbers. Transcripts are kept for each student.

Enrollment Requirements   High school diploma, experience in health field required. Program is open to non-resident foreign students. English language proficiency required. College-administered writing assessment.

Program Costs $1776 for the program, $444 per course.

Housing and Student Services   Housing is not available. Job counseling and placement services are available.

Special Features   Practicum is required.

Contact   Admissions Counselor, Division of General Studies, 155 Roe Boulevard, Patchogue, NY 11772. 516-654-3200.

MISCELLANEOUS ALLIED HEALTH SERVICES (17.05)
Certificate in Health Staff Development

General Information   Unit offering the program: Division of General Studies. Program content: Plan, implement, and evaluate in-service and training programs in health care facilities. Available for credit. Certificate signed by the President. Certificate applicable to B.S. in Community Health, Health Administration.

Program Format   Daytime, evening, weekend classes offered. Program cycle: Continuous enrollment. Full program cycle lasts 12 credit hours. Completion of program requires 2.0 GPA.

Evaluation   Student evaluation based on tests, papers, reports. Grading system: Letters or numbers. Transcripts are kept for each student.

Enrollment Requirements   High school diploma, experience in health field required. Program is open to non-resident foreign students. English language proficiency required. College-administered writing assessment.

Program Costs $1776 for the program, $444 per course.

Housing and Student Services   Housing is not available. Job counseling and placement services are available.

Special Features   Practicum is required.

Contact   Admissions Counselor, Division of General Studies, 155 Roe Boulevard, Patchogue, NY 11772. 516-654-3200.

MISCELLANEOUS ALLIED HEALTH SERVICES (17.05)
Certificate in Home Care Administration

General Information   Unit offering the program: Division of General Studies. Available for credit. Certificate signed by the President. Certificate applicable to B.S. in Community Health, Health Administration.

Program Format   Daytime, evening, weekend classes offered. Program cycle: Continuous enrollment. Full program cycle lasts 18 credit hours. Completion of program requires 2.0 GPA.

Evaluation   Student evaluation based on tests, papers, reports. Grading system: Letters or numbers. Transcripts are kept for each student.

Enrollment Requirements   High school diploma, experience in health field required. Program is open to non-resident foreign students. English language proficiency required. College-administered writing assessment.

Program Costs $2664 for the program, $444 per course.

Housing and Student Services   Housing is not available. Job counseling and placement services are available.

Contact   Admissions Counselor, Division of General Studies, 155 Roe Boulevard, Patchogue, NY 11772. 516-654-3200.

SOCIOLOGY (45.11)
Certificate in Applied Sociology

General Information   Unit offering the program: College of Arts and Sciences. Program content: Social science theories and research methods for organizational needs, issues, policy and planning decisions. Available for credit. Certificate signed by the

Certificate in Applied Sociology continued
President. Certificate applicable to B.S. in Social Science, Human Relations.

Program Format Daytime, evening classes offered. Program cycle: Continuous enrollment. Full program cycle lasts 24 credit hours. Completion of program requires 2.0 GPA.

Evaluation Student evaluation based on tests, papers, reports. Grading system: Letters or numbers. Transcripts are kept for each student.

Enrollment Requirements High school diploma required. Program is open to non-resident foreign students. English language proficiency required. College-administered writing assessment.

Program Costs $3552 for the program, $444 per course.

Housing and Student Services Housing is not available. Job counseling and placement services are available.

Contact Ms. Marion Salgado, Director of Admissions, 155 Roe Boulevard, Patchogue, NY 11772. 516-654-3200.

NUCEA MEMBER
ST. THOMAS AQUINAS COLLEGE
Sparkill, New York 10976

INDIVIDUAL AND FAMILY DEVELOPMENT (19.07)
Certificate in Gerontology

General Information Unit offering the program: Social Sciences Division. Available for credit. Certificate signed by the Chairman, Board of Trustees.

Program Format Daytime, evening classes offered. Full program cycle lasts 30 credit hours.

Evaluation Student evaluation based on tests, papers, reports. Grading system: Letters or numbers. Transcripts are kept for each student.

Enrollment Requirements Intended for those working in programs for the elderly. Program is not open to non-resident foreign students.

Program Costs $435 per course.

Housing and Student Services Housing is not available. Job counseling and placement services are available.

Contact Ms. Andrea Kraeft, Director of Admissions, Route 340, Sparkill, NY 10976. 914-359-9500 Ext. 252.

NUCEA MEMBER
STATE UNIVERSITY OF NEW YORK AT ALBANY
Albany, New York 12222

AREA STUDIES (05.01)
Latin American and Caribbean Studies

General Information Unit offering the program: Department of Latin American and Caribbean Studies. Program content: Latin American culture, literature, societies. Available for credit. Certificate signed by the Chancellor of SUNY system.

Program Format Daytime, evening classes offered. Program cycle: Continuous enrollment. Full program cycle lasts 2 semesters. Completion of program requires 3.0 GPA, 12 credit hours.

Evaluation Student evaluation based on tests, papers, reports. Grading system: Letters or numbers, pass/fail. Transcripts are kept for each student.

Enrollment Requirements Bachelor's degree, GRE scores required. Program is open to non-resident foreign students. English language proficiency required. Minimum TOEFL score required: 550.

Program Costs $1092 for the program (state residents); $1880 for the program (nonresidents).

Housing and Student Services Housing is not available. Job counseling and placement services are available.

Contact Mr. Jeff Collins, Assistant Director of Graduate Admissions, 1400 Washington Avenue, Albany, NY 12222. 518-442-3980.

BALTO-SLAVIC LANGUAGES (16.04)
Russian Translation

General Information Unit offering the program: Department of Slavic Languages and Literatures. Program content: Advanced Russian. Available for credit. Certificate signed by the Chancellor of SUNY system.

Program Format Daytime, evening classes offered. Program cycle: Continuous enrollment. Complete program cycle lasts two to three semesters. Completion of program requires grade of B or better in all courses, 30 credit hours.

Evaluation Student evaluation based on tests, papers, reports, field exam, oral exam. Grading system: Letters or numbers, pass/fail. Transcripts are kept for each student.

Enrollment Requirements M.A. in Russian or Slavic language required. Program is open to non-resident foreign students. English language proficiency required. Minimum TOEFL score required: 550.

Program Costs $2730 for the program (state residents); $4710 for the program (nonresidents).

Housing and Student Services Housing is available. Job counseling and placement services are available.

Contact Mr. Jeff Collins, Assistant Director of Graduate Admissions, 1400 Washington Avenue, Albany, NY 12222. 518-442-3980.

COMMUNICATIONS, GENERAL (09.01)
Educational Communications

General Information Unit offering the program: Department of Program Development and Evaluation. Program content: Educational communications, media design, production. Available for credit. Certificate signed by the Chancellor of SUNY system.

Program Format Daytime, evening classes offered. Program cycle: Continuous enrollment. Complete program cycle lasts four to five semesters. Completion of program requires 3.0 GPA, 60 credit hours.

Evaluation Student evaluation based on tests, papers, reports, internship, practicum, comprehensive exam. Grading system: Letters or numbers, pass/fail. Transcripts are kept for each student.

Enrollment Requirements Bachelor's degree, GRE scores required. Program is open to non-resident foreign students. English language proficiency required. Minimum TOEFL score required: 550.

Program Costs $5460 for the program, $273 per course (state residents); $9400 for the program, $470 per course (nonresidents).

Housing and Student Services Housing is available. Job counseling and placement services are available.

Contact Mr. Jeff Collins, Assistant Director of Graduate Admissions, 1400 Washington Avenue, Albany, NY 12222. 518-442-3980.

COUNSELING PSYCHOLOGY (42.06)
Counseling

General Information Unit offering the program: Department of Counseling Psychology. Program content: Counseling, behavioral and social sciences. Available for credit. Certificate signed by the Chancellor of SUNY system. Program fulfills requirements for School Counselor.

Program Format Daytime, evening classes offered. Program cycle: Continuous enrollment. Complete program cycle lasts four to five semesters. Completion of program requires 3.0 GPA, 60 credit hours.

Evaluation Student evaluation based on tests, papers, reports, fieldwork, comprehensive exam. Grading system: Letters or numbers, pass/fail. Transcripts are kept for each student.

Enrollment Requirements Bachelor's degree, GRE scores, 15 credit hours in Psychology required. Program is open to non-resident foreign students. English language proficiency required. Minimum TOEFL score required: 550.

Program Costs $5460 for the program, $273 per course (state residents); $9400 for the program, $470 per course (nonresidents).

Housing and Student Services Housing is available. Job counseling and placement services are available.

Contact Mr. Jeff Collins, Assistant Director of Graduate Admissions, 1400 Washington Avenue, Albany, NY 12222. 518-442-3980.

CURRICULUM AND INSTRUCTION (13.03)
Curriculum-Instruction

General Information Unit offering the program: Department of Program Development and Evaluation. Program content: Curriculum, instruction, supervision, program evaluation and development. Available for credit. Certificate signed by the Chancellor of SUNY system. Certificate applicable to D.Ed. in Curriculum-Instruction.

Program Format Daytime, evening classes offered. Program cycle: Continuous enrollment. Complete program cycle lasts four to five semesters. Completion of program requires 3.0 GPA, 60 credit hours.

Evaluation Student evaluation based on tests, papers, reports, internship, comprehensive exam. Grading system: Letters or numbers, pass/fail. Transcripts are kept for each student.

Enrollment Requirements Bachelor's degree, GRE scores required. Program is open to non-resident foreign students. English language proficiency required. Minimum TOEFL score required: 550.

Program Costs $5460 for the program, $273 per course (state residents); $9400 for the program, $470 per course (nonresidents).

Housing and Student Services Housing is available. Job counseling and placement services are available.

Special Features Teacher education instruction specialization is available.

Contact Mr. Jeff Collins, Assistant Director of Graduate Admissions, 1400 Washington Avenue, Albany, NY 12222. 518-442-3980.

DEMOGRAPHY (45.05)
Demography

General Information Unit offering the program: Department of Sociology. Program content: Sociology and statistics. Available for credit. Certificate signed by the Chancellor of SUNY system. Certificate applicable to M.A., Ph.D. in Sociology.

Program Format Daytime, evening classes offered. Program cycle: Continuous enrollment. Full program cycle lasts 2 semesters. Completion of program requires 3.0 GPA, 18 credit hours.

Evaluation Student evaluation based on tests, papers, reports. Grading system: Letters or numbers, pass/fail. Transcripts are kept for each student.

Enrollment Requirements Bachelor's degree in a social science required. Program is open to non-resident foreign students. English language proficiency required. Minimum TOEFL score required: 550.

Program Costs $1618 for the program (state residents); $2820 for the program (nonresidents).

Housing and Student Services Housing is not available. Job counseling and placement services are available.

Contact Mr. Jeff Collins, Assistant Director of Graduate Admissions, 1400 Washington Avenue, Albany, NY 12222. 518-442-3980.

EDUCATION ADMINISTRATION (13.04)
Educational Administration

General Information Unit offering the program: Department of Educational Administration and Policy Studies. Program content: Educational administration, policy, management. Available for credit. Certificate signed by the Chancellor of SUNY system. Certificate applicable to D.Ed. in Educational Administration. Program fulfills requirements for School Administrator and Superintendent.

Program Format Daytime, evening classes offered. Program cycle: Continuous enrollment. Full program cycle lasts 4 semesters. Completion of program requires 3.0 GPA, 60 credit hours.

Evaluation Student evaluation based on tests, papers, reports, internship, comprehensive exam. Grading system: Letters or numbers, pass/fail. Transcripts are kept for each student.

Enrollment Requirements Bachelor's degree, GRE scores required. Program is open to non-resident foreign students. English language proficiency required. Minimum TOEFL score required: 550.

Program Costs $5460 for the program, $273 per course (state residents); $9400 for the program, $470 per course (nonresidents).

Housing and Student Services Housing is available. Job counseling and placement services are available.

Contact Mr. Jeff Collins, Assistant Director of Graduate Admissions, 1400 Washington Avenue, Albany, NY 12222. 518-442-3980.

EVALUATION AND RESEARCH (13.06)
Educational Research

General Information Unit offering the program: Department of Educational Psychology and Statistics. Program content: Educational psychology, measurement, statistics, research design. Available for credit. Certificate signed by the Chancellor of SUNY system. Certificate applicable to Ph.D. in Educational Psychology.

Program Format Daytime, evening classes offered. Program cycle: Continuous enrollment. Complete program cycle lasts four to five semesters. Completion of program requires 3.0 GPA, 60 credit hours, established New York residency.

Evaluation Student evaluation based on tests, papers, reports, comprehensive exam. Grading system: Letters or numbers, pass/fail. Transcripts are kept for each student.

Enrollment Requirements Bachelor's degree, knowledge of algebra, GRE scores, 18 credit hours in psychology required. Program is open to non-resident foreign students. English language proficiency required. Minimum TOEFL score required: 550.

Program Costs $5460 for the program, $273 per course (state residents); $9400 for the program, $470 per course (nonresidents).

Housing and Student Services Housing is available. Job counseling and placement services are available.

Contact Mr. Jeff Collins, Assistant Director of Graduate Admissions, 1400 Washington Avenue, Albany, NY 12222. 518-442-3980.

LIBRARY AND ARCHIVAL SCIENCES, GENERAL (25.01)
Information and Library Science

General Information Unit offering the program: School of Information Science and Policy. Program content: Proseminar, directed readings, library research. Available for credit. Certificate signed by the Chancellor of SUNY system.

Program Format Daytime, evening classes offered. Program cycle: Continuous enrollment. Complete program cycle lasts two to three semesters. Completion of program requires 3.0 GPA, 30 credit hours.

Evaluation Student evaluation based on tests, papers, reports, internship, comprehensive exam. Grading system: Letters or numbers, pass/fail. Transcripts are kept for each student.

Enrollment Requirements Master's degree in library or information science required. Program is open to non-resident foreign students. English language proficiency required. Minimum TOEFL score required: 550.

Program Costs $2730 for the program (state residents); $4730 for the program (nonresidents).

Housing and Student Services Housing is available. Job counseling and placement services are available.

Contact Mr. Jerry Parker, Assistant Provost, GSPA, 1400 Washington Avenue, Albany, NY 12222. 518-442-5200.

PUBLIC ADMINISTRATION (44.04)
Advanced Public Management

General Information Unit offering the program: Department of Public Administration, School of Social Welfare. Program content: Public administration, program development and evaluation. Available for credit. Certificate signed by the Chancellor of SUNY system. Certificate applicable to M.P.A., D.P.A.

Program Format Daytime, evening classes offered. Program cycle: Continuous enrollment. Full program cycle lasts 2 semesters. Completion of program requires 3.0 GPA, five courses.

Evaluation Student evaluation based on tests, papers, reports. Grading system: Letters or numbers, pass/fail. Transcripts are kept for each student.

Enrollment Requirements Bachelor's degree required. Program is open to non-resident foreign students. English language proficiency required. Minimum TOEFL score required: 550.

Program Costs $1547–$1820 for the program (state residents); $2669–$3140 for the program (nonresidents).

Housing and Student Services Housing is available. Job counseling and placement services are available.

Contact Mr. Jerry Parker, Assistant Provost, 1400 Washington Avenue, Albany, NY 12222. 518-442-5200.

PUBLIC ADMINISTRATION (44.04)
Public Sector Management

General Information Unit offering the program: Department of Public Administration. Program content: Public administration, management. Available for credit. Certificate signed by the Chancellor of SUNY system. Certificate applicable to M.P.A., D.P.A.

Program Format Daytime, evening classes offered. Program cycle: Continuous enrollment. Full program cycle lasts 2 semesters. Completion of program requires 3.0 GPA, 20 credit hours.

Evaluation Student evaluation based on tests, papers, reports. Grading system: Letters or numbers, pass/fail. Transcripts are kept for each student.

Enrollment Requirements Bachelor's degree required. Program is open to non-resident foreign students. English

language proficiency required. Minimum TOEFL score required: 550.

Program Costs $1820 for the program (state residents); $3140 for the program (nonresidents).

Housing and Student Services Housing is available. Job counseling and placement services are available.

Contact Mr. Jerry Parker, Assistant Provost, Graduate School of Public Administration, 1400 Washington Avenue, Albany, NY 12222. 518-442-5200.

PUBLIC ADMINISTRATION (44.04)
Regulatory Economics

General Information Unit offering the program: Department of Economics. Program content: Economics of the public sector with emphasis on quantitative. Available for credit. Certificate signed by the Chancellor of SUNY system. Certificate applicable to M.A., Ph.D. in Economics.

Program Format Daytime, evening classes offered. Program cycle: Continuous enrollment. Full program cycle lasts 1 semester. Completion of program requires four courses, average grade of B or better.

Evaluation Student evaluation based on tests, papers, reports. Grading system: Letters or numbers, pass/fail. Transcripts are kept for each student.

Enrollment Requirements Bachelor's degree required. Program is open to non-resident foreign students. English language proficiency required. Minimum TOEFL score required: 550.

Program Costs $1090 for the program (state residents); $1880 for the program (nonresidents).

Housing and Student Services Housing is not available. Job counseling and placement services are available.

Contact Mr. Jeff Collins, Assistant Director of Graduate Admissions, 1400 Washington Avenue, Albany, NY 12222. 518-442-3980.

SCHOOL PSYCHOLOGY (13.08)
School Psychology

General Information Unit offering the program: Departments of Psychology, Educational Psychology, Statistics. Program content: Theoretical and experimental. Available for credit. Certificate signed by the Chancellor of SUNY system. Certificate applicable to Psy.D. in School Psychology. Program fulfills requirements for School Psychologist.

Program Format Daytime, evening classes offered. Program cycle: Continuous enrollment. Complete program cycle lasts four to five semesters. Completion of program requires 3.0 GPA, 60 credit hours, established New York residency.

Evaluation Student evaluation based on tests, papers, reports, internship, comprehensive exam. Grading system: Letters or numbers, pass/fail. Transcripts are kept for each student.

Enrollment Requirements Bachelor's degree, GRE scores, 18 credit hours in Psychology required. Program is open to non-resident foreign students. English language proficiency required. Minimum TOEFL score required: 550.

Program Costs $5460 for the program, $273 per course (state residents); $9400 for the program, $470 per course (nonresidents).

Housing and Student Services Housing is available. Job counseling and placement services are available.

Contact Mr. Jeff Collins, Assistant Director of Graduate Admissions, 1400 Washington Avenue, Albany, NY 12222. 518-442-3980.

SYSTEMS SCIENCE (30.06)
Planning and Policy Analysis

General Information Unit offering the program: Graduate School of Public Affairs. Program content: Research designs and methods, statistics, program evaluation, systems analysis. Available for credit. Certificate signed by the Chancellor of SUNY system. Certificate applicable to D.P.A. in Public Administration.

Program Format Daytime, evening classes offered. Program cycle: Continuous enrollment. Full program cycle lasts 4 semesters. Completion of program requires 3.0 GPA, 48 credit hours.

Evaluation Student evaluation based on tests, papers, reports, internship. Grading system: Letters or numbers, pass/fail. Transcripts are kept for each student.

Enrollment Requirements Bachelor's degree required. Program is open to non-resident foreign students. English language proficiency required. Minimum TOEFL score required: 550.

Program Costs $4368 for the program (state residents); $7520 for the program (nonresidents).

Housing and Student Services Housing is available. Job counseling and placement services are available.

Contact Mr. Jerry Parker, Assistant Provost, GSPA, 1400 Washington Avenue, Albany, NY 12222. 518-442-5200.

TEACHER EDUCATION, SPECIFIC SUBJECT AREAS (13.13)
Reading

General Information Unit offering the program: Department of Reading. Program content: Psycholinguistics, literacy. Available for credit. Certificate signed by the Chancellor of SUNY system. Certificate applicable to D.Ed. in Reading. Program fulfills requirements for Reading.

Program Format Daytime, evening classes offered. Program cycle: Continuous enrollment. Complete program cycle lasts four to five semesters. Completion of program requires 3.0 GPA, 60 credit hours.

Evaluation Student evaluation based on papers, reports, fieldwork, comprehensive exam. Grading system: Letters or numbers, pass/fail. Transcripts are kept for each student.

Enrollment Requirements Bachelor's degree, GRE scores required. Program is open to non-resident foreign students. English language proficiency required. Minimum TOEFL score required: 550.

Program Costs $5460 for the program, $273 per course (state residents); $9400 for the program, $470 per course (nonresidents).

Housing and Student Services Housing is available. Job counseling and placement services are available.

Contact Mr. Jeff Collins, Assistant Director of Graduate Admissions, 1400 Washington Avenue, Albany, NY 12222. 518-442-3980.

TELECOMMUNICATIONS (09.08)
Certificate Program in Telecommunications Management

General Information Unit offering the program: Office of Public Service. Program content: Introduction to telephony, data communications, integration. Available on either a credit or non-credit basis. Cosponsored by Central New York Communications Association. Certificate signed by the Associate Vice President for Public Service.

Program Format Daytime classes offered. Instructional schedule: Three days per month. Full program cycle lasts 6 months. Completion of program requires six courses.

Evaluation Student evaluation based on project. Records are kept for each student.

Enrollment Requirements Limited to practitioners in telecommunications. Program is open to non-resident foreign students.

Program Costs $2100 for the program, $350 per course.

Housing and Student Services Housing is not available. Job counseling and placement services are not available.

Special Features The program meets the expressed needs of telecommunications managers for an applied, practical program. Instructors are practicing professionals in user and vendor organizations. There are three classes a month for six months, allowing time to integrate instruction and work. A unique feature is the requirement that participants complete a project acceptable to their work supervisor.

Contact Mr. Norman D. Kurland, Program Director, 135 Western Avenue, Husted 201, Albany, NY 12222. 518-442-5150.

URBAN STUDIES (45.12)
Urban Policy

General Information Unit offering the program: Sociology, Geography, Planning Departments. Program content: Policy, urban and regional development. Available for credit. Certificate signed by the Chancellor of SUNY system. Certificate applicable to M.A., Ph.D. in Sociology; M.A. in Geography; M.R.P. in Planning.

Program Format Daytime, evening classes offered. Program cycle: Continuous enrollment. Complete program cycle lasts one to two semesters. Completion of program requires 3.0 GPA, 15–18 credit hours.

Evaluation Student evaluation based on tests, papers, reports. Grading system: Letters or numbers, pass/fail. Transcripts are kept for each student.

Enrollment Requirements Bachelor's degree required. Program is open to non-resident foreign students. English language proficiency required. Minimum TOEFL score required: 550.

Program Costs $1365–$1638 for the program (state residents); $2350–$2820 for the program (nonresidents).

Housing and Student Services Housing is available. Job counseling and placement services are available.

Contact Mr. Jeff Collins, Assistant Director of Graduate Admissions, 1400 Washington Avenue, Albany, NY 12222. 518-442-3980.

WOMEN'S STUDIES (30.07)
Women and Public Policy

General Information Unit offering the program: Program in Women's Studies, Graduate School of Public Affairs. Program content: Women's studies, public policy issues, skills. Available for credit. Certificate signed by the Chancellor of SUNY system. Certificate applicable to M.A. in Public Affairs.

Program Format Daytime, evening classes offered. Program cycle: Continuous enrollment. Completion of program requires 3.0 GPA, 12–16 credit hours.

Evaluation Student evaluation based on tests, papers, reports. Grading system: Letters or numbers, pass/fail. Transcripts are kept for each student.

Enrollment Requirements Bachelor's degree required. Program is open to non-resident foreign students. English language proficiency required. Minimum TOEFL score required: 550.

Program Costs $1092–$1365 for the program (state residents); $1880–$2350 for the program (nonresidents).

Housing and Student Services Housing is available. Job counseling and placement services are available.

Contact Mr. Jeff Collins, Assistant Director of Graduate Admissions, 1400 Washington Avenue, Albany, NY 12222. 518-442-3980.

STATE UNIVERSITY OF NEW YORK AT BUFFALO
Buffalo, New York 14260

TAXATION (06.19)
Graduate Tax Certificate Program

General Information   Unit offering the program: Center for Management Development, School of Management. Program content: Corporate taxation, tax research and ethics, property transactions. Available on a non-credit basis. Certificate signed by the Chairman, Department of Operations Analysis. Program fulfills requirements for New York State Board of Accountancy's Continuing Professional Education credits for CPA's.

Program Format   Evening classes offered. Instructional schedule: One evening per week. Students may enroll three times per year. Full program cycle lasts 9 courses. Completion of program requires 2.5 GPA.

Evaluation   Student evaluation based on tests, reports. Grading system: Letters or numbers. Records are kept for each student.

Enrollment Requirements   Bachelor's degree or equivalent experience in accounting required. Program is open to non-resident foreign students.

Program Costs $250 per course.

Housing and Student Services   Housing is not available. Job counseling and placement services are not available.

Special Features   The program was initiated in 1985 by area law and accounting firms who provide guidance and instructors.

Contact   Ms. Carolyn Shadle, Program Administrator, 108 Jacobs Management Center, Buffalo, NY 14260. 716-636-3200.

STATE UNIVERSITY OF NEW YORK COLLEGE OF TECHNOLOGY AT UTICA/ROME
Utica, New York 13504

BUSINESS AND MANAGEMENT, GENERAL (06.01)
Certificate of Advanced Management

General Information   Unit offering the program: School of Business and Public Management. Program content: Organizational behavior, management accounting, finance, managerial economics, marketing, policy. Available on a non-credit basis. Certificate signed by the Campus President.

Program Format   Evening classes offered. Instructional schedule: Once per week for three hours. Students enroll in September. Full program cycle lasts 2 years.

Evaluation   Student evaluation based on tests, reports, class participation. Grading system: Pass/fail. Record of CEUs kept for each student.

Enrollment Requirements   Endorsement by employer required. Program is open to non-resident foreign students. English language proficiency required.

Program Costs $1800 for the program, $300 per course.

Housing and Student Services   Housing is not available. Job counseling and placement services are not available.

Special Features   Designed for currently employed managers or soon-to-be managers without formal schooling in program topics. Materials at the graduate course level but without the formal aspects of credit courses. Program enrolls a small class of approximately 15 participants each year.

Contact   Mr. Albert Mario, Director, P.O. Box 3050, Utica, NY 13504. 315-792-7432.

SYRACUSE UNIVERSITY
Syracuse, New York 13244

HUMAN ENVIRONMENT AND HOUSING (19.06)
Home Furnishings and Decoration Certificate Program

General Information   Unit offering the program: University College. Available on a non-credit basis. Certificate signed by the Dean of Syracuse University College.

Program Format   Daytime classes offered. Instructional schedule: Twice per week for three hours. Students enroll once per year. Full program cycle lasts 2 semesters. Completion of program requires eight modules, internship.

Evaluation   Student evaluation based on tests, lab projects, internship. Grading system: Pass/fail. Transcripts are kept for each student.

Enrollment Requirements   High school diploma, 500 word essay required. Program is not open to non-resident foreign students. English language proficiency required.

Program Costs $2025 for the program.

Housing and Student Services   Housing is not available. Job counseling and placement services are available.

Special Features   Program has a lecture/lab format where students either complete a project in class or at home. There are a significant number of on-site lectures during field trips to various businesses. The students' culminating experience is a 4-week internship of a minimum of six hours per week where they choose a work environment in the aspect of interior decorating that most interests them.

Contact   Ms. Phyllis R. Chase, Director, Home Furnishing and Decoration Program, 610 East Fayette Street, Syracuse, NY 13244-6020. 315-423-4116.

LAW (22.01)
The Legal Assistant Program

General Information   Unit offering the program: University College. Program content: Basic concepts of substantive and procedural law. Available on a non-credit basis. Endorsed by American Bar Association. Certificate signed by the Dean of Syracuse University College.

Program Format   Evening classes offered. Instructional schedule: Two evenings per week for three hours. Students enroll once per year. Full program cycle lasts 2 semesters. Completion of program requires 12 courses.

Evaluation   Student evaluation based on tests, papers. Grading system: Pass/fail. Transcripts are kept for each student.

Enrollment Requirements   Bachelor's degree preferred, minimum of 45 college credits required. Program is not open to non-resident foreign students. English language proficiency required. Composition demonstrating English ability.

Program Costs $2200 for the program.

Housing and Student Services   Housing is not available. Job counseling and placement services are available.

Special Features   The program is taught by local practicing attorneys who are themselves, for the most part, supervising paralegals in the work place. Emphasis is on practical skills. Many of the students are currently working in the legal community and use this to further career growth. The ABA approval enhances and maintains its credibility.

Contact   Ms. Phyllis R. Chase, Director, Legal Assistant Program, 610 East Fayette Street, Syracuse, NY 13244-6020. 315-423-4116.

LAW (22.01)
The Legal Assistant Program (Summer)

General Information   Unit offering the program: University College. Program content: Basic concepts of substantive and procedural law. Available on a non-credit basis. Endorsed by American Bar Association. Certificate signed by the Dean of Syracuse University College.

Program Format   Daytime, evening classes offered. Instructional schedule: Four to five days per week. Students enroll in June. Full program cycle lasts 3 months. Completion of program requires 12 courses.

Evaluation   Student evaluation based on tests, papers, reports. Grading system: Pass/fail. Transcripts are kept for each student.

Enrollment Requirements   Bachelor's degree required. Program is not open to non-resident foreign students. English language proficiency required. Composition demonstrating English ability.

Program Costs $2200 for the program.

Housing and Student Services   Housing is available. Job counseling and placement services are available.

Special Features   This is a 3-month intensive career certificate program designed for those students who have completed a bachelor's degree and now want focused training for a career in the legal community or legal aspect of business. Courses are taught by local practicing attorneys who emphasize the practical skills necessary to function as a paralegal.

Contact   Ms. Phyllis R. Chase, Director, Legal Assistant Program, 610 East Fayette Street, Syracuse, NY 13244-6020. 315-423-4116.

YESHIVA UNIVERSITY
New York, New York 10033

INDIVIDUAL AND FAMILY DEVELOPMENT (19.07)
Post-Master's Certificate in Gerontological Practice

General Information   Unit offering the program: Brookdale Institute for the Study of Gerontonlogy, Wurzweiler School of Social Work. Program content: Social policy, medical and psychological aspects of aging, retirement, ethnicity and culture, management functions, counseling. Available for credit. Certificate signed by the President. Certificate applicable to Ph.D. or D.S.W.

Program Format   Evening classes offered. Instructional schedule: One evening per week. Students enroll in September. Full program cycle lasts 32 weeks.

Evaluation   Student evaluation based on papers. Grading system: Pass/fail. Transcripts are kept for each student.

Enrollment Requirements   Master's degree or equivalent required. Program is open to non-resident foreign students. English language proficiency required. Minimum TOEFL score required: 550.

Program Costs $3060 for the program, $375 per course.

Housing and Student Services   Housing is not available. Job counseling and placement services are available.

Contact   Dr. Celia B. Weisman, Director, Gerontological Institute, 2495 Amsterdam Avenue, New York, NY 10033. 212-960-0808.

NORTH CAROLINA

MARS HILL COLLEGE
Mars Hill, North Carolina 28754

BUSINESS AND MANAGEMENT, GENERAL (06.01)
Management

General Information   Unit offering the program: Division of Business, Center for Continuing Education. Program content: Business management, human resources administration. Available for credit. Certificate signed by the President. Certificate applicable to B.A. in Liberal Arts, Business.

Program Format   Daytime, evening classes offered. Instructional schedule: One evening per week. Program cycle: Continuous enrollment. Full program cycle lasts 5 courses. Completion of program requires grade of C or better in each course.

Evaluation   Student evaluation based on tests, papers, reports. Grading system: Letters or numbers. Transcripts are kept for each student.

Enrollment Requirements   College admissions required. Program is open to non-resident foreign students. English language proficiency required. Minimum TOEFL score required: 500.

Program Costs $750 for the program, $150 per course.

Housing and Student Services   Housing is available. Job counseling and placement services are available.

Special Features   Credit for work experience is available either through testing or preparation of a learning portfolio.

Contact   Ms. Wilma Carlisle, Admissions Counselor, Center for Continuing Education, Mars Hill, NC 28754. 704-689-1166.

INDIVIDUAL AND FAMILY DEVELOPMENT (19.07)
Gerontology

General Information   Unit offering the program: Social and Behavioral Sciences, Center for Continuing Education. Program content: Aging services with a family systems orientation. Available for credit. Certificate signed by the President. Certificate applicable to B.S.W.

Program Format   Daytime, evening, weekend classes offered. Instructional schedule: One weekend (Friday evening, Saturday 9 a.m. to 5 p.m.) per month or one evening per week. Full program cycle lasts 6 courses. Completion of program requires grade of C or better in each course.

Evaluation   Student evaluation based on tests, papers, reports, internship. Grading system: Letters or numbers. Transcripts are kept for each student.

Enrollment Requirements   College admissions required. Program is open to non-resident foreign students. English language proficiency required. Minimum TOEFL score required: 500.

Program Costs $900 for the program, $150 per course.

Housing and Student Services   Housing is available. Job counseling and placement services are available.

Special Features   Interdisciplinary faculty representing social work, sociology, gerontology, political science, medicine, and long-term care administration. Credit for previous experience available either through testing or preparation of a learning portfolio. One course each semester offered in a weekend format.

Contact   Ms. Juliana Cooper-Goldenberg, Director of the Gerontology Center, Mars Hill, NC 28754. 704-689-1331.

NUCEA MEMBER

NORTH CAROLINA STATE UNIVERSITY AT RALEIGH
Raleigh, North Carolina 27695

COMMUNICATIONS, GENERAL (09.01)
Human Communication Certificate Program

General Information Unit offering the program: Speech-Communications. Program content: Public speaking, communication theory, business and professional communication. Available for credit. Certificate signed by the Department Head. Certificate applicable to B.A. in Speech-Communication.

Program Format Daytime, evening classes offered. Instructional schedule: Twice per week. Program cycle: Continuous enrollment. Full program cycle lasts 3 semesters. Completion of program requires five courses, grade of C or better.

Evaluation Student evaluation based on tests, papers, reports. Grading system: Letters or numbers. Transcripts are kept for each student.

Enrollment Requirements High school diploma required. Program is not open to non-resident foreign students.

Program Costs $640 for the program, $128 per course.

Housing and Student Services Housing is not available. Job counseling and placement services are available.

Special Features The Human Communication Certificate Program consists of 15 credit hours of communication courses. Three of the courses are specified and two are chosen from a set of restricted electives. The purpose of the program is to expose students to a basic understanding of human communication skills and theories.

Contact Dr. Raymond S. Rodgers, Assistant Department Head, Box 8104, Raleigh, NC 27695-8104. 919-737-3204.

COMPUTER PROGRAMMING (11.02)
Certificate of Computer Programming

General Information Unit offering the program: Computer Science Department. Program content: Calculus, programming, data structures, management information systems. Available for credit. Endorsed by Veterans Administration. Certificate signed by the Dean, School of Physical and Mathematical Sciences. Certificate applicable to B.S. in Computer Science.

Program Format Daytime, evening classes offered. Students may enroll fall, spring, summer. Full program cycle lasts 3 semesters. Completion of program requires seven courses, grade of C or better.

Evaluation Student evaluation based on tests, computer programs. Grading system: Letters or numbers. Transcripts are kept for each student.

Enrollment Requirements Bachelor's degree required. Program is not open to non-resident foreign students.

Program Costs $750 for the program, $125 per course.

Housing and Student Services Housing is not available. Job counseling and placement services are available.

Special Features The Certificate of Computer Programming allows a person to minor in computer science after having finished a degree, obtain the remedial courses needed before going on to a master's degree in computer science, get in on the programming job market, and work full-time and take evening classes each semester.

Contact Ms. Joyce Hatch, Assistant Department Head, Computer Science Department, Box 8206, Raleigh, NC 27695-8206. 919-737-7027.

INDIVIDUAL AND FAMILY DEVELOPMENT (19.07)
Studies in Gerontology

General Information Unit offering the program: Adult and Community College Education. Program content: Psychology, sociology, methodology. Available for credit. Certificate signed by the Department Head.

Program Format Evening classes offered. Instructional schedule: One or two evenings per week. Program cycle: Continuous enrollment. Full program cycle lasts 18 credit hours.

Evaluation Student evaluation based on tests, papers, reports. Grading system: Letters or numbers. Transcripts are kept for each student.

Enrollment Requirements Bachelor's degree, B average in undergraduate major or in previous graduate work required. Program is not open to non-resident foreign students. English language proficiency required. Minimum TOEFL score required: 550.

Program Costs $768 for the program, $128 per course.

Housing and Student Services Housing is not available. Job counseling and placement services are available.

Special Features The certificate program is interdisciplinary. Students can select courses most suitable to their vocational and career goals. Most courses are offered during late afternoon and evening hours.

Contact Dr. J. Conrad Glass Jr., Professor, 310 Poe Hall, Box 7801, Raleigh, NC 27695-7801. 919-737-3590.

PERSONNEL AND TRAINING PROGRAMS (07.05)
Trainer Development

General Information Unit offering the program: Occupational Education. Program content: Media and instructional technology, methods and materials, psychology. Available for credit. Certificate signed by the Dean, School of Education.

Program Format Evening classes offered. Instructional schedule: One or two evenings per week. Program cycle: Continuous enrollment. Full program cycle lasts 5 courses.

Evaluation Student evaluation based on tests, papers, reports, oral presentations. Grading system: Letters or numbers, pass/fail. Transcripts are kept for each student.

Enrollment Requirements High school diploma or equivalent required; bachelor's degree preferred. Program is open to non-resident foreign students.

Program Costs $640 for the program, $128 per course.

Housing and Student Services Housing is not available. Job counseling and placement services are available.

Special Features Prescribed set of courses agreed upon in advance and set down in a contract. Student takes active role in determining course work that will best provide for his/her desired professional growth. When course work has been completed, student is asked to take oral examination, designed to include a component that establishes plan for further study and evaluates learning experience nondegree certificate program has offered.

Contact Dr. Linda Dillon, Associate Professor, Box 7801, Raleigh, NC 27695-7801. 919-737-2234.

PUBLIC ADMINISTRATION (44.04)
Management Development: Administration of Justice

General Information Unit offering the program: Political Science, Public Administration. Program content: Crime causation, criminal justice systems, sociology. Available for credit. Certificate signed by the Department Head. Certificate applicable to M.P.A.

Program Format Evening classes offered. Instructional schedule: One or two evenings per week. Program cycle:

Continuous enrollment. Full program cycle lasts 4 semesters. Completion of program requires 9–12 credit hours.

Evaluation   Student evaluation based on tests, papers, reports. Grading system: Letters or numbers. Records are kept in department files.

Enrollment Requirements   Undergraduate degree with 3.0 GPA required. Program is not open to non-resident foreign students.

Program Costs $384–$512 for the program, $128 per course.

Housing and Student Services   Housing is available. Job counseling and placement services are available.

Contact   Program Manager, Political Science and Public Administration, Box 8102, Raleigh, NC 27695-8102. 919-737-2481.

PUBLIC ADMINISTRATION (44.04)
Management Development: Adult and Community College Administration

General Information   Unit offering the program: Political Science, Public Administration. Program content: Legal issues, administration and supervision, comparative education. Available for credit. Certificate signed by the Department Head. Certificate applicable to M.P.A.

Program Format   Evening classes offered. Instructional schedule: One or two evenings per week. Program cycle: Continuous enrollment. Full program cycle lasts 4 semesters. Completion of program requires 9–12 credit hours.

Evaluation   Student evaluation based on tests, papers, reports. Grading system: Letters or numbers. Records are kept in department files.

Enrollment Requirements   Undergraduate degree with 3.0 GPA required. Program is not open to non-resident foreign students.

Program Costs $384–$512 for the program, $128 per course.

Housing and Student Services   Housing is available. Job counseling and placement services are available.

Contact   Program Manager, Political Science and Public Administration, Box 8102, Raleigh, NC 27695-8102. 919-737-2481.

PUBLIC ADMINISTRATION (44.04)
Management Development: Data Management

General Information   Unit offering the program: Political Science, Public Administration. Program content: Processing techniques, computer organization, databases, files. Available for credit. Certificate signed by the Department Head. Certificate applicable to M.P.A.

Program Format   Evening classes offered. Instructional schedule: One or two evenings per week. Program cycle: Continuous enrollment. Full program cycle lasts 4 semesters. Completion of program requires 9–12 credit hours.

Evaluation   Student evaluation based on tests, papers, reports. Grading system: Letters or numbers. Records are kept in department files.

Enrollment Requirements   Undergraduate degree with 3.0 GPA required. Program is not open to non-resident foreign students.

Program Costs $384–$512 for the program, $128 per course.

Housing and Student Services   Housing is available. Job counseling and placement services are available.

Contact   Program Manager, Political Science and Public Administration, Box 8102, Raleigh, NC 27695-8102. 919-737-2481.

PUBLIC ADMINISTRATION (44.04)
Management Development: Financial Management

General Information   Unit offering the program: Political Science, Public Administration. Program content: Theory, methodology, and current issues in financial accounting. Available for credit. Certificate signed by the Department Head. Certificate applicable to M.P.A.

Program Format   Evening classes offered. Instructional schedule: One or two evenings per week. Program cycle: Continuous enrollment. Full program cycle lasts 4 semesters. Completion of program requires 9–12 credit hours.

Evaluation   Student evaluation based on tests, papers, reports. Grading system: Letters or numbers. Records are kept in department files.

Enrollment Requirements   Undergraduate degree with 3.0 GPA required. Program is not open to non-resident foreign students.

Program Costs $384–$512 for the program, $128 per course.

Housing and Student Services   Housing is available. Job counseling and placement services are available.

Contact   Program Manager, Political Science and Public Administration, Box 8102, Raleigh, NC 27695-8102. 919-737-2481.

PUBLIC ADMINISTRATION (44.04)
Management Development: Human Resources Management

General Information   Unit offering the program: Political Science, Public Administration. Program content: Psychology, research methods, analysis, skills, practicum. Available for credit. Certificate signed by the Department Head. Certificate applicable to M.P.A.

Program Format   Evening classes offered. Instructional schedule: One or two evenings per week. Program cycle: Continuous enrollment. Full program cycle lasts 4 semesters. Completion of program requires 9–12 credit hours.

Evaluation   Student evaluation based on tests, papers, reports. Grading system: Letters or numbers. Records are kept in department files.

Enrollment Requirements   Undergraduate degree with 3.0 GPA required. Program is not open to non-resident foreign students.

Program Costs $384–$512 for the program, $128 per course.

Housing and Student Services   Housing is available. Job counseling and placement services are available.

Contact   Program Manager, Political Science and Public Administration, Box 8102, Raleigh, NC 27695-8102. 919-737-2481.

PUBLIC ADMINISTRATION (44.04)
Management Development: Management Control Systems

General Information   Unit offering the program: Political Science, Public Administration. Program content: Information systems and resources, policy and applications of operations management. Available for credit. Certificate signed by the Department Head. Certificate applicable to M.P.A.

Program Format   Evening classes offered. Instructional schedule: One or two evenings per week. Program cycle: Continuous enrollment. Full program cycle lasts 4 semesters. Completion of program requires 9–12 credit hours.

Evaluation   Student evaluation based on tests, papers, reports. Grading system: Letters or numbers. Records are kept in department files.

Enrollment Requirements   Undergraduate degree with 3.0 GPA required. Program is not open to non-resident foreign students.

Management Development: Management Control Systems continued

Program Costs $384–$512 for the program, $128 per course.

Housing and Student Services   Housing is available. Job counseling and placement services are available.

Contact   Program Manager, Political Science and Public Administration, Box 8102, Raleigh, NC 27695-8102. 919-737-2481.

PUBLIC ADMINISTRATION (44.04)
Management Development: Program Evaluation

General Information   Unit offering the program: Political Science, Public Administration. Program content: Research and analysis. Available for credit. Certificate signed by the Department Head. Certificate applicable to M.P.A.

Program Format   Evening classes offered. Instructional schedule: One or two evenings per week. Program cycle: Continuous enrollment. Full program cycle lasts 4 semesters. Completion of program requires 9–12 credit hours.

Evaluation   Student evaluation based on tests, papers, reports. Grading system: Letters or numbers. Records are kept in department files.

Enrollment Requirements   Undergraduate degree with 3.0 GPA required. Program is not open to non-resident foreign students.

Program Costs $384–$512 for the program, $128 per course.

Housing and Student Services   Housing is available. Job counseling and placement services are available.

Contact   Program Manager, Political Science and Public Administration, Box 8102, Raleigh, NC 27695-8102. 919-737-2481.

PUBLIC ADMINISTRATION (44.04)
Management Development: Public Affairs

General Information   Unit offering the program: Political Science, Public Administration. Program content: Planning techniques, project management and appraisal. Available for credit. Certificate signed by the Department Head. Certificate applicable to M.P.A.

Program Format   Evening classes offered. Instructional schedule: One or two evenings per week. Program cycle: Continuous enrollment. Full program cycle lasts 4 semesters. Completion of program requires 9–12 credit hours.

Evaluation   Student evaluation based on tests, papers, reports. Grading system: Letters or numbers. Records are kept in department files.

Enrollment Requirements   Undergraduate degree with 3.0 GPA required. Program is not open to non-resident foreign students.

Program Costs $384–$512 for the program, $128 per course.

Housing and Student Services   Housing is available. Job counseling and placement services are available.

Contact   Program Manager, Political Science and Public Administration, Box 8102, Raleigh, NC 27695-8102. 919-737-2481.

PUBLIC ADMINISTRATION (44.04)
Management Development: Recreation Resources Management

General Information   Unit offering the program: Political Science, Public Administration. Program content: Leadership supervision, park finance, facility and site planning. Available for credit. Certificate signed by the Department Head. Certificate applicable to M.P.A.

Program Format   Evening classes offered. Instructional schedule: One or two evenings per week. Program cycle:

Continuous enrollment. Full program cycle lasts 4 semesters. Completion of program requires 9–12 credit hours.

Evaluation   Student evaluation based on tests, papers, reports. Grading system: Letters or numbers. Records are kept in department files.

Enrollment Requirements   Undergraduate degree with 3.0 GPA required. Program is not open to non-resident foreign students.

Program Costs $384–$512 for the program, $128 per course.

Housing and Student Services   Housing is available. Job counseling and placement services are available.

Contact   Program Manager, Political Science and Public Administration, Box 8102, Raleigh, NC 27695-8102. 919-737-2481.

PUBLIC ADMINISTRATION (44.04)
Management Development: Urban Administration

General Information   Unit offering the program: Political Science, Public Administration. Program content: Public policy, planning and government, spatial structure, environmental systems analysis. Available for credit. Certificate signed by the Department Head. Certificate applicable to M.P.A.

Program Format   Evening classes offered. Instructional schedule: One or two evenings per week. Program cycle: Continuous enrollment. Full program cycle lasts 4 semesters. Completion of program requires 9–12 credit hours.

Evaluation   Student evaluation based on tests, papers, reports. Grading system: Letters or numbers. Records are kept in department files.

Enrollment Requirements   Undergraduate degree with 3.0 GPA required. Program is not open to non-resident foreign students.

Program Costs $384–$512 for the program, $128 per course.

Housing and Student Services   Housing is available. Job counseling and placement services are available.

Contact   Program Manager, Political Science and Public Administration, Box 8102, Raleigh, NC 27695-8102. 919-737-2481.

TECHNICAL AND BUSINESS WRITING (23.11)
Professional Writing

General Information   Unit offering the program: English. Program content: Copyediting, composition, communication of technical information. Available for credit. Certificate signed by the Department Head.

Program Format   Daytime, evening classes offered. Instructional schedule: Three classes per week. Program cycle: Continuous enrollment. Full program cycle lasts 4 semesters. Completion of program requires grade of C or better.

Evaluation   Student evaluation based on tests, papers, reports. Grading system: Letters or numbers. Records are kept in department files.

Enrollment Requirements   Completion of two semesters college English, high school diploma required. Program is open to non-resident foreign students. English language proficiency required.

Program Costs $508 for the program, $127 per course.

Housing and Student Services   Housing is not available. Job counseling and placement services are not available.

Special Features   The Professional Writing Certificate provides basic education for entry-level positions in journalism, public relations, information services, and technical writing.

Contact   Mr. David H. Covington, Director, Professional Writing Certificate Program, Box 8105, Department of English, Raleigh, NC 27695-8105. 919-737-3854.

TEXTILE ENGINEERING (14.28)
Textile Certificate in Apparel Production

General Information Unit offering the program: School of Textiles. Program content: Soft goods marketing. Available for credit. Certificate signed by the Dean, School of Textiles.

Program Format Off-campus televised classes offered. Program cycle: Continuous enrollment. Full program cycle lasts 5 courses. Completion of program requires 15 credit hours.

Evaluation Student evaluation based on tests, papers, reports. Grading system: Letters or numbers. Transcripts are kept for each student.

Enrollment Requirements Bachelor's degree required. Program is not open to non-resident foreign students.

Program Costs $1000–$1500 for the program, $200–$300 per course.

Housing and Student Services Housing is not available. Job counseling and placement services are available.

Special Features Entire certificate can be earned off-campus via TOTE. Courses can be applied to more than one certificate.

Contact Mr. T. L. Russell, Instructional Technologist, Box 8301, Raleigh, NC 27695-8301. 919-737-3761.

TEXTILE ENGINEERING (14.28)
Textile Certificate in Dyeing and Finishing

General Information Unit offering the program: School of Textiles. Program content: Color science, technology and methods. Available for credit. Certificate signed by the Dean, School of Textiles.

Program Format Off-campus televised classes offered. Program cycle: Continuous enrollment. Full program cycle lasts 5 courses. Completion of program requires 15 credit hours.

Evaluation Student evaluation based on tests, papers, reports. Grading system: Letters or numbers. Transcripts are kept for each student.

Enrollment Requirements Bachelor's degree required. Program is not open to non-resident foreign students.

Program Costs $1000–$1500 for the program, $200–$300 per course.

Housing and Student Services Housing is not available. Job counseling and placement services are available.

Special Features Entire certificate can be earned off-campus via TOTE. Courses can be applied to more than one certificate.

Contact Mr. T. L. Russell, Instructional Technologist, Box 8301, Raleigh, NC 27695-8301. 919-737-3761.

TEXTILE ENGINEERING (14.28)
Textile Certificate in Fabric Production

General Information Unit offering the program: School of Textiles. Program content: Knitting and weaving systems, formation and structures. Available for credit. Certificate signed by the Dean, School of Textiles.

Program Format Off-campus televised classes offered. Program cycle: Continuous enrollment. Full program cycle lasts 5 courses. Completion of program requires 15 credit hours.

Evaluation Student evaluation based on tests, papers, reports. Grading system: Letters or numbers. Transcripts are kept for each student.

Enrollment Requirements Bachelor's degree required. Program is not open to non-resident foreign students.

Program Costs $1000–$1500 for the program, $200–$300 per course.

Housing and Student Services Housing is not available. Job counseling and placement services are available.

Special Features Entire certificate can be earned off-campus via TOTE. Courses can be applied to more than one certificate.

Contact Mr. T. L. Russell, Instructional Technologist, Box 8301, Raleigh, NC 27695-8301. 919-737-3761.

TEXTILE ENGINEERING (14.28)
Textile Certificate in Fiber Science for Textile Conservatives

General Information Unit offering the program: School of Textiles. Program content: Polymer chemistry, fiber science. Available for credit. Certificate signed by the Dean, School of Textiles.

Program Format Off-campus televised classes offered. Program cycle: Continuous enrollment. Full program cycle lasts 5 courses. Completion of program requires 15 credit hours.

Evaluation Student evaluation based on tests, papers, reports. Grading system: Letters or numbers. Transcripts are kept for each student.

Enrollment Requirements Bachelor's degree required. Program is not open to non-resident foreign students.

Program Costs $1000–$1500 for the program, $200–$300 per course.

Housing and Student Services Housing is not available. Job counseling and placement services are available.

Special Features Entire certificate can be earned off-campus via TOTE. Courses can be applied to more than one certificate.

Contact Mr. T. L. Russell, Instructional Technologist, Box 8301, Raleigh, NC 27695-8301. 919-737-3761.

TEXTILE ENGINEERING (14.28)
Textile Certificate in Textile Administration

General Information Unit offering the program: School of Textiles. Program content: Industry supervision, management, and control. Available for credit. Certificate signed by the Dean, School of Textiles.

Program Format Off-campus televised classes offered. Program cycle: Continuous enrollment. Full program cycle lasts 5 courses. Completion of program requires 15 credit hours.

Evaluation Student evaluation based on tests, papers, reports. Grading system: Letters or numbers. Transcripts are kept for each student.

Enrollment Requirements Bachelor's degree required. Program is not open to non-resident foreign students.

Program Costs $1000–$1500 for the program, $200–$300 per course.

Housing and Student Services Housing is not available. Job counseling and placement services are available.

Special Features Entire certificate can be earned off-campus via TOTE. Courses can be applied to more than one certificate.

Contact Mr. T. L. Russell, Instructional Technologist, Box 8301, Raleigh, NC 27695-8301. 919-737-3761.

TEXTILE ENGINEERING (14.28)
Textile Certificate in Textile Fibers and Polymers

General Information Unit offering the program: School of Textiles. Program content: Physical properties, fiber forming polymers, fiber science. Available for credit. Certificate signed by the Dean, School of Textiles.

Program Format Off-campus televised classes offered. Program cycle: Continuous enrollment. Full program cycle lasts 5 courses. Completion of program requires 15 credit hours.

Evaluation Student evaluation based on tests, papers, reports. Grading system: Letters or numbers. Transcripts are kept for each student.

Enrollment Requirements Bachelor's degree required. Program is not open to non-resident foreign students.

Program Costs $1000–$1500 for the program, $200–$300 per course.

Textile Certificate in Textile Fibers and Polymers continued

Housing and Student Services Housing is not available. Job counseling and placement services are available.

Special Features Entire certificate can be earned off-campus via TOTE. Courses can be applied to more than one certificate.

Contact Mr. T. L. Russell, Instructional Technologist, Box 8301, Raleigh, NC 27695-8301. 919-737-3761.

TEXTILE ENGINEERING (14.28)
Textile Certificate in Textile Fundamentals

General Information Unit offering the program: School of Textiles. Program content: Fiber science, yarn production systems. Available for credit. Certificate signed by the Dean, School of Textiles.

Program Format Off-campus televised classes offered. Program cycle: Continuous enrollment. Full program cycle lasts 5 courses. Completion of program requires 15 credit hours.

Evaluation Student evaluation based on tests, papers, reports. Grading system: Letters or numbers. Transcripts are kept for each student.

Enrollment Requirements Bachelor's degree required. Program is not open to non-resident foreign students.

Program Costs $1000–$1500 for the program, $200–$300 per course.

Housing and Student Services Housing is not available. Job counseling and placement services are available.

Special Features Entire certificate can be earned off-campus via TOTE. Courses can be applied to more than one certificate.

Contact Mr. T. L. Russell, Instructional Technologist, Box 8301, Raleigh, NC 27695-8301. 919-737-3761.

TEXTILE ENGINEERING (14.28)
Textile Certificate in Yarn Manufacturing

General Information Unit offering the program: School of Textiles. Program content: Yarn production systems, modern development. Available for credit. Certificate signed by the Dean, School of Textiles.

Program Format Off-campus televised classes offered. Program cycle: Continuous enrollment. Full program cycle lasts 5 courses. Completion of program requires 15 credit hours.

Evaluation Student evaluation based on tests, papers, reports. Grading system: Letters or numbers. Transcripts are kept for each student.

Enrollment Requirements Bachelor's degree required. Program is not open to non-resident foreign students.

Program Costs $1000–$1500 for the program, $200–$300 per course.

Housing and Student Services Housing is not available. Job counseling and placement services are available.

Special Features Entire certificate can be earned off-campus via TOTE. Courses can be applied to more than one certificate.

Contact Mr. T. L. Russell, Instructional Technologist, Box 8301, Raleigh, NC 27695-8301. 919-737-3761.

UNIVERSITY OF NORTH CAROLINA AT CHAPEL HILL
Chapel Hill, North Carolina 27514

DENTAL SERVICES (17.01)
Certificate in Dental Assisting

General Information Unit offering the program: Department of Dental Ecology, School of Dentistry. Program content: Biomedical sciences, dental sciences, human behavior, communication. Available on a non-credit basis. Certificate signed by the Dean, School of Dentistry.

Program Format Daytime classes offered. Students enroll in the fall. Full program cycle lasts 10 months. Completion of program requires 2.0 GPA.

Evaluation Student evaluation based on tests, papers, reports, clinical exams, proficiencies. Grading system: Letters or numbers. Transcripts are kept for each student.

Enrollment Requirements High school diploma or equivalent, grade of 2.0. Program is open to non-resident foreign students.

Program Costs $1023 for the program.

Housing and Student Services Housing is available. Job counseling and placement services are available.

Contact Ms. Mary George, Director, Dental Auxiliary Programs, School of Dentistry, Chapel Hill, NC 27514. 919-966-2800.

DIAGNOSTIC AND TREATMENT SERVICES (17.02)
Diagnostic Medical Sonography

General Information Unit offering the program: Department of Radiology. Program content: Ultrasound physics, general ultrasound, OB/GYN ultrasound, lab. Available on a non-credit basis. Endorsed by North Carolina Memorial Hospital. Certificate signed by the Dean of Medical School.

Program Format Daytime classes offered. Instructional schedule: 40 hours per week. Students enroll in August. Full program cycle lasts 12 months.

Evaluation Student evaluation based on tests, papers, competency evaluations. Grading system: Letters or numbers. Transcripts are kept for each student.

Enrollment Requirements Completion of accredited two-year program in Radiologic Technology required. Program is open to non-resident foreign students. English language proficiency required.

Program Costs $600 for the program.

Housing and Student Services Housing is not available. Job counseling and placement services are not available.

Special Features One of two programs in the state. One to one student-technologist ratio.

Contact Ms. Janice Keene, Associate Professor, Division of Radiologic Science, Department of Medical Allied Health Professions, Chapel Hill, NC 27514. 919-966-5146.

DIAGNOSTIC AND TREATMENT SERVICES (17.02)
Nuclear Medicine Technology

General Information Unit offering the program: Imaging Division, Department of Radiology. Program content: Clinical nuclear medicine, radiopharmacy, instrumentation. Available on a non-credit basis. Endorsed by North Carolina Memorial Hospital. Certificate signed by the Dean, School of Medicine.

Program Format Daytime classes offered. Instructional schedule: 40 hours per week. Program cycle: Continuous enrollment. Full program cycle lasts 1 year. Completion of program requires grade of C or better.

Evaluation Student evaluation based on tests, papers, clinical evaluations. Grading system: Letters or numbers. Transcripts are kept for each student.

Enrollment Requirements Limited to registered radiologic or medical technician with bachelor's degree in a biological or natural science. Program is open to non-resident foreign students. English language proficiency required.

Program Costs $750 for the program.

Housing and Student Services Housing is available. Job counseling and placement services are available.

Special Features The program is sponsored by the North Carolina Memorial Hospital and the UNC School of Medicine through the Imaging Division of the Department of Radiology. Instructors include radiologists, technologists, physicists, and radiopharmacists of the Imaging Division. Graduates are eligible for national certification by the American Registry of Radiologic Technologists in Nuclear Medicine and the Nuclear Medicine Technology Certification Board.

Contact Ms. Marilyn W. Parrish, Educational Coordinator, Imaging Division, Radiology, Chapel Hill, NC 27514. 919-966-5233.

EDUCATION ADMINISTRATION (13.04)
Certificate of Graduate Study in Education

General Information Unit offering the program: Program in Educational Administration. Program content: Administration, supervision. Available for credit. Certificate signed by the Chancellor. Certificate applicable to Ed.D., Ph.D. in Educational Administration. Program fulfills requirements for North Carolina Advanced Administrator Certificate.

Program Format Evening classes offered. Instructional schedule: One class per week. Program cycle: Continuous enrollment. Full program cycle lasts 30 credit hours. Completion of program requires written comprehensive examination.

Evaluation Student evaluation based on tests, papers, internship. Grading system: Letters or numbers. Transcripts are kept for each student.

Enrollment Requirements Master's degree, GRE scores, letters of recommedation required. Program is open to non-resident foreign students. English language proficiency required. Minimum TOEFL score required: 550.

Program Costs $882–$1260 for the program, $126 per course.

Housing and Student Services Housing is available. Job counseling and placement services are available.

Contact Mr. Richard A. King, Chair, Program in Educational Administration, Peabody Hall, CB 3500, Chapel Hill, NC 27599. 919-966-1354.

MEDICAL LABORATORY (18.09)
Cytotechnology

General Information Unit offering the program: Department of Medical Allied Health Professions. Program content: Study of cells, early detection and diagnosis of cancer. Available on a non-credit basis. Cosponsored by North Carolina Memorial Hospital. Certificate signed by the Dean of the Medical School.

Program Format Daytime classes offered. Instructional schedule: Monday through Friday. Program cycle: Continuous enrollment. Full program cycle lasts 12 months. Completion of program requires minimum score of 75%, 80% on graded activities.

Evaluation Student evaluation based on tests, papers, reports, clinical laboratory assignments. Records kept for each student.

Enrollment Requirements Bachelor's degree; courses in chemistry, math, and biology required. Program is open to non-resident foreign students. English language proficiency required.

Program Costs $500 for the program.

Housing and Student Services Housing is available. Job counseling and placement services are available.

Special Features The Division of Cytotechnology is one of seven health-related educational programs in the Department of Medical Allied Health Professions, UNC-CH School of Medicine. The program was established in 1952. It is located in the cytology laboratory, North Carolina Memorial Hospital, where student cytotechnologists receive excellent clinical experience.

Contact Ms. Sandra M. Renwiek, Program Director, Cytotechnology Division, CB 7120 Medical School, Chapel Hill, NC 27599-7120. 919-966-2339.

MISCELLANEOUS ALLIED HEALTH SERVICES (17.05)
Radiation Therapy Technology

General Information Unit offering the program: Department of Radiation Oncology. Program content: Radiation physics, dosimetry, patient interactions, oncology, nursing, radiobiology, radiation safety. Available on a non-credit basis. Endorsed by North Carolina Memorial Hospital. Certificate signed by the Dean, School of Medicine. Program fulfills requirements for American Registry of Radiologic Technologists (ART).

Program Format Daytime classes offered. Instructional schedule: Five days per week. Students may enroll once per year. Full program cycle lasts 12 months. Completion of program requires 2.0 GPA.

Evaluation Student evaluation based on tests, papers, clinical competency exams, clinical rating scales. Grading system: Letters or numbers. Transcripts are kept for each student.

Enrollment Requirements Certification in diagnostic radiologic technology required. Program is open to non-resident foreign students. English language proficiency required.

Program Costs $1000–$1500 for the program.

Housing and Student Services Housing is available. Job counseling and placement services are available.

Contact Ms. Amy Lindsey, Program Director, Manning Drive, Chapel Hill, NC 27514. 919-966-1101.

UNIVERSITY OF NORTH CAROLINA AT CHARLOTTE
Charlotte, North Carolina 28223

INSTITUTIONAL MANAGEMENT (06.07)
Not-For-Profit Management Certificate Program

General Information Unit offering the program: Office of Continuing Education and College of Business. Program content: Staff and volunteer management, finances, strategic planning. Available on a non-credit basis. Certificate signed by the Dean, College of Business.

Program Format Daytime, evening classes offered. Instructional schedule: Twice per week for 2½ hours. Students enroll in January. Full program cycle lasts 9 weeks.

Evaluation Student evaluation based on reports, presentations, class participation. Grading system: Pass/fail. Transcripts are kept for each student.

Enrollment Requirements Limited to administrators in a nonprofit agency. Program is open to non-resident foreign students. English language proficiency required.

Program Costs $750 for the program, $250 per course.

Housing and Student Services Housing is not available. Job counseling and placement services are not available.

Special Features Taught by a six-member team of faculty, all with extensive theoretical and practical experience with NFPS.

Contact Dr. R. Oakley Winters, Director, Continuing Education, 208 King, Charlotte, NC 28223. 704-547-2424.

TRADE AND INDUSTRIAL SUPERVISION AND MANAGEMENT (06.20)
Engineering Management Certificate Program

General Information Unit offering the program: Office of Continuing Education, College of Business, College of Engineering. Program content: Capital expenditures, projects and programs, business planning, people skills. Available on a non-credit basis. Certificate signed by the Deans of Business and Engineering.

Engineering Management Certificate Program continued

Program Format Evening classes offered. Instructional schedule: Two evenings per week. Students may enroll twice per year. Full program cycle lasts 12 weeks.

Evaluation Student evaluation based on reports, class participation. Grading system: Pass/fail. Transcripts are kept for each student.

Enrollment Requirements Limited to engineers with management responsibilities. Program is open to non-resident foreign students. English language proficiency required.

Program Costs $1000 for the program, $250 per course.

Housing and Student Services Housing is not available. Job counseling and placement services are not available.

Special Features Taught by a faculty team of 11 persons, 5 of whom have degrees and experience in both management and engineering.

Contact Dr. R. Oakley Winters, Director, Continuing Education, 208 King, Charlotte, NC 28223. 704-547-2424.

NUCEA MEMBER
WESTERN CAROLINA UNIVERSITY
Cullowhee, North Carolina 28723

FAMILY AND COMMUNITY SERVICES (19.03)
Advanced Family Service Associate

General Information Unit offering the program: Social Work Department. Program content: Social welfare policies, programs, and services; families; topics; person, environment, culture; internship. Available for credit. Certificate signed by the Director of Continuing Education and Summer School.

Program Format Daytime classes offered. Program cycle: Continuous enrollment. Full program cycle lasts 2 years. Completion of program requires five courses, final examination.

Evaluation Student evaluation based on tests, papers, reports. Grading system: Letters or numbers. Transcripts are kept for each student.

Enrollment Requirements Completion of Basic Family Service Assistant Certificate required. Program is open to non-resident foreign students.

Program Costs $975 for the program, $195 per course.

Housing and Student Services Housing is not available. Job counseling and placement services are not available.

Contact Dr. Wilburn Hayden, Department Head, Social Work, School of Arts and Sciences, Cullowhee, NC 28723. 704-227-7112.

FAMILY AND COMMUNITY SERVICES (19.03)
Basic Family Service Assistant

General Information Unit offering the program: Social Work Department. Program content: Foundations of family service skills, basic competence skills for social service providers. Available for credit. Certificate signed by the Director of Continuing Education and Summer School.

Program Format Daytime classes offered. Instructional schedule: Classes meet Thursday and Friday. Program cycle: Continuous enrollment. Full program cycle lasts 2 semesters. Completion of program requires two courses, final examination.

Evaluation Student evaluation based on tests. Grading system: Letters or numbers. Transcripts are kept for each student.

Enrollment Requirements High school diploma required. Program is open to non-resident foreign students.

Program Costs $390 for the program, $195 per course.

Housing and Student Services Housing is not available. Job counseling and placement services are not available.

Contact Dr. Wilburn Hayden, Department Head, Social Work, School of Arts and Sciences, Cullowhee, NC 28723. 704-227-7112.

NORTH DAKOTA

TRINITY BIBLE COLLEGE
Ellendale, North Dakota 58436

RELIGIOUS EDUCATION (39.04)
One Year Bible Certificate

General Information Unit offering the program: Biblical Studies Department. Program content: Bible, theology, general education. Certificate signed by the President of the College. Certificate applicable to B.A. in Biblical Studies.

Program Format Daytime classes offered. Program cycle: Continuous enrollment. Full program cycle lasts 2 semesters.

Evaluation Student evaluation based on tests, papers, reports. Grading system: Letters or numbers. Transcripts are kept for each student.

Enrollment Requirements High school diploma required. Program is open to non-resident foreign students.

Program Costs $79 per credit hour.

Housing and Student Services Housing is available. Job counseling and placement services are not available.

Special Features A two-semester, 32-hour program designed to give participants a year's study in a Bible College atmosphere. Classes are part of the normal curriculum, taught by regular appointed faculty.

Contact Dr. Dayton Kingsriter, Academic Dean, Ellendale, ND 58436. 701-349-3621.

OHIO

BALDWIN-WALLACE COLLEGE
Berea, Ohio 44017

ACCOUNTING (06.02)
Accounting

General Information Unit offering the program: Business Administration. Program content: Basic foundation in accounting functions. Available for credit. Certificate signed by the Vice President for Academic Affairs. Certificate applicable to any four-year degree offered at the institution.

Program Format Daytime, evening, weekend classes offered. Program cycle: Continuous enrollment. Full program cycle lasts 30 credit hours. Completion of program requires 2.0 GPA.

Evaluation Student evaluation based on tests, papers, reports. Grading system: Letters or numbers. Transcripts are kept for each student.

Enrollment Requirements College admissions required. Program is open to non-resident foreign students. English language proficiency required. Minimum TOEFL score required: 500.

Program Costs $100 per credit hour.

Housing and Student Services Housing is not available. Job counseling and placement services are available.

Special Features The program is designed to provide participants with the knowledge and skills that will permit them to carry out accounting tasks critical to any organization. The program of study includes both courses at the preparatory level and specialized courses in the student's area of particular interest. Academic credit for prior experience is possible.

Contact Ms. Jane Cavanaugh, Director of Admission for Continuing Education, 275 Eastland Road, Berea, OH 44017. 216-826-2222.

BUSINESS AND MANAGEMENT, GENERAL (06.01)
Human Resources Management

General Information Unit offering the program: Business Administration, Sociology, Psychology, Speech Communications. Program content: Management-related course work for newly appointed managers. Available for credit. Certificate signed by the Vice President for Academic Affairs. Certificate applicable to any four-year degree offered at the institution.

Program Format Daytime, evening, weekend classes offered. Program cycle: Continuous enrollment. Completion of program requires 2.0 GPA, 28–30 credit hours.

Evaluation Student evaluation based on tests, papers, reports. Grading system: Letters or numbers. Transcripts are kept for each student.

Enrollment Requirements College admissions required. Program is open to non-resident foreign students. English language proficiency required. Minimum TOEFL score required: 500.

Program Costs $100 per credit hour.

Housing and Student Services Housing is not available. Job counseling and placement services are available.

Special Features The program is designed primarily for new or prospective managers who need some assistance with the development of managerial skills. This is an interdisciplinary program that can be completed within one academic year or less. Academic credit for prior experience is possible.

Contact Ms. Jane Cavanaugh, Director of Admission for Continuing Education, 275 Eastland Road, Berea, OH 44017. 216-826-2222.

COMMUNICATIONS, GENERAL (09.01)
Communications

General Information Unit offering the program: Business Administration, English, Speech Communication. Program content: Interdisciplinary course work in written and oral communications. Available for credit. Certificate signed by the Vice President for Academic Affairs. Certificate applicable to any four-year degree offered at the institution.

Program Format Daytime, evening, weekend classes offered. Program cycle: Continuous enrollment. Completion of program requires 2.0 GPA, 24–26 credit hours.

Evaluation Student evaluation based on tests, papers, reports. Grading system: Letters or numbers. Transcripts are kept for each student.

Enrollment Requirements College admissions required. Program is open to non-resident foreign students. English language proficiency required. Minimum TOEFL score required: 500.

Program Costs $100 per credit hour.

Housing and Student Services Housing is not available. Job counseling and placement services are available.

Special Features The program is designed to provide participants with the skills and insights that will make them more effective communicators in a variety of organizational settings, such as business, industry, service agencies, and government. Academic credit for prior experience is possible.

Contact Ms. Jane Cavanaugh, Director of Admission for Continuing Education, 275 Eastland Road, Berea, OH 44017. 216-826-2222.

COMPUTER AND INFORMATION SCIENCES, GENERAL (11.01)
Computer Information Systems

General Information Unit offering the program: Business Administration, Computer Science, Mathematics. Available for credit. Certificate signed by the Vice President for Academic Affairs. Certificate applicable to any four-year degree offered at the institution.

Program Format Daytime, evening, weekend classes offered. Program cycle: Continuous enrollment. Full program cycle lasts 45 credit hours. Completion of program requires 2.0 GPA.

Evaluation Student evaluation based on tests, papers, reports. Grading system: Letters or numbers. Transcripts are kept for each student.

Enrollment Requirements College admissions required. Program is open to non-resident foreign students. English language proficiency required. Minimum TOEFL score required: 500.

Program Costs $100 per credit hour.

Housing and Student Services Housing is not available. Job counseling and placement services are available.

Special Features The program is designed to prepare the participant for an entry-level position as a programmer/analyst in the information systems department of an organization. The curriculum focuses on the information needs of organizations and the tools frequently used by programmers to meet these needs. Academic credit for prior experience is possible.

Contact Ms. Jane Cavanaugh, Director of Admission for Continuing Education, 275 Eastland Road, Berea, OH 44017. 216-826-2222.

COMPUTER AND INFORMATION SCIENCES, GENERAL (11.01)
Computer Literacy

General Information Unit offering the program: Computer Science, Mathematics. Program content: Fundamentals of data processing and computer literacy. Available for credit. Certificate signed by the Vice President for Academic Affairs. Certificate applicable to any four-year degree offered at the institution.

Program Format Daytime, evening, weekend classes offered. Program cycle: Continuous enrollment. Full program cycle lasts 20 credit hours. Completion of program requires 2.0 GPA.

Evaluation Student evaluation based on tests, papers, reports. Grading system: Letters or numbers. Transcripts are kept for each student.

Enrollment Requirements College admissions required. Program is open to non-resident foreign students. English language proficiency required. Minimum TOEFL score required: 500.

Program Costs $100 per credit hour.

Housing and Student Services Housing is not available. Job counseling and placement services are available.

Special Features Digital and personal computers are used in a hands-on approach to familiarize students with techniques such as input, output, memory, storage devices, and flowcharts. The computer language BASIC is taught and used to run simple programs. Fourth-generation software such as Lotus 1-2-3;s also covered. Academic credit for prior experience is possible.

Contact Ms. Jane Cavanaugh, Director of Admission for Continuing Education, 275 Eastland Road, Berea, OH 44017. 216-826-2222.

COMPUTER AND INFORMATION SCIENCES, GENERAL (11.01)
Computer Science

General Information   Unit offering the program: Computer Science. Program content: Computer architecture, methods of data acceptance, storage and processing. Available for credit. Certificate signed by the Vice President for Academic Affairs. Certificate applicable to any four-year degree offered at the institution.

Program Format   Daytime, evening, weekend classes offered. Program cycle: Continuous enrollment. Full program cycle lasts 35 credit hours. Completion of program requires 2.0 GPA.

Evaluation   Student evaluation based on tests, papers, reports. Grading system: Letters or numbers. Transcripts are kept for each student.

Enrollment Requirements   College admissions required. Program is open to non-resident foreign students. English language proficiency required. Minimum TOEFL score required: 500.

Program Costs $100 per credit hour.

Housing and Student Services   Housing is not available. Job counseling and placement services are available.

Special Features   The program accepts students with a good aptitude in computer programming but little or no training. Upon successful completion of the certificate program, the participant will have the necessary skills for continuing study or for an entry-level position as a programmer/analyst. Academic credit for prior experience is possible.

Contact   Ms. Jane Cavanaugh, Director of Admission for Continuing Education, 275 Eastland Road, Berea, OH 44017. 216-826-2222.

COLLEGE OF MOUNT ST. JOSEPH
Cincinnati, Ohio 45051

CHILD CARE AND GUIDANCE MANAGEMENT AND SERVICES (20.02)
Child Care Professional Studies

General Information   Unit offering the program: Division of Continuing Education. Program content: Theory and practice of child care professional studies. Available for credit. Endorsed by American Council of Nannies. Certificate signed by the Director, Child Care Professional Studies Program. Certificate applicable to any two- or four-year degree offered at the institution. Program fulfills requirements for American Council of Nannies.

Program Format   Daytime, evening classes offered. Program cycle: Continuous enrollment. Full program cycle lasts 2 semesters. Completion of program requires 20 semester hours.

Evaluation   Student evaluation based on tests, papers, reports. Grading system: Letters or numbers. Transcripts are kept for each student.

Enrollment Requirements   High school diploma required.

Program Costs $147 per credit hour.

Housing and Student Services   Housing is available. Job counseling and placement services are available.

Contact   Dr. Jane Link, Director, Child Care Professional Studies Program, Division of Continuing Education, Mount St. Joseph, OH 45051. 513-244-4481.

DESIGN (50.04)
Certificate in Graphic Design

General Information   Unit offering the program: Art Department. Program content: Advertising production, illustration, typography, photography, figure drawing, color theory, graphic design. Available for credit. Certificate signed by the Art Department Chairperson.

Program Format   Daytime, evening classes offered. Program cycle: Continuous enrollment. Completion of program requires 51 semester hours.

Evaluation   Student evaluation based on tests, papers, projects. Grading system: Letters or numbers. Transcripts are kept for each student.

Enrollment Requirements   Bachelor's degree in field other than graphic arts required. Program is open to non-resident foreign students.

Program Costs $146 per credit hour.

Housing and Student Services   Housing is available. Job counseling and placement services are available.

Contact   Ms. Betty Brothers, Chairperson, Art Department, Mount St. Joseph, OH 45051. 513-244-4420.

INDIVIDUAL AND FAMILY DEVELOPMENT (19.07)
Certificate in Gerontological Studies

General Information   Unit offering the program: Behavioral Sciences Department. Program content: Biology of aging, fitness, retirement and leisure, nutrition, mental health, adult development, social aspects of aging. Available for credit. Certificate signed by the Director of Gerontological Studies Program.

Program Format   Daytime, weekend classes offered. Program cycle: Continuous enrollment. Completion of program requires 33 semester hours.

Evaluation   Student evaluation based on tests, papers, reports. Grading system: Letters or numbers. Transcripts are kept for each student.

Enrollment Requirements   High school diploma required.

Program Costs $146 per credit hour.

Housing and Student Services   Housing is available. Job counseling and placement services are available.

Contact   Mr. Richard Haubner, Director, Gerontological Studies Program, Mount St. Joseph, OH 45051. 513-244-4523.

INTERIOR DESIGN (04.05)
Certificate in Interior Design

General Information   Unit offering the program: Art Department. Program content: Architectural drawing, furniture, lighting, finishes and textiles, watercolor, management, procedure, theory of interior design. Available for credit. Certificate signed by the Art Department Chairperson.

Program Format   Daytime, evening classes offered. Program cycle: Continuous enrollment. Completion of program requires 47 semester hours.

Evaluation   Student evaluation based on tests, papers, projects. Grading system: Letters or numbers. Transcripts are kept for each student.

Enrollment Requirements   Bachelor's degree in field other than interior design required.

Program Costs $146 per credit hour.

Housing and Student Services   Housing is available. Job counseling and placement services are available.

Contact   Ms. Betty Brothers, Chairperson, Art Department, Mount St. Joseph, OH 45051. 513-244-4420.

LAW (22.01)
Certificate in Paralegal Studies

General Information   Unit offering the program: Behavioral Sciences Department. Available for credit. Certificate signed by the Director of Paralegal Studies Program. Certificate applicable to A.A., B.A. in Paralegal Studies.

OHIO
Notre Dame College of Ohio

Program Format Evening classes offered. Program cycle: Continuous enrollment. Full program cycle lasts 4 semesters. Completion of program requires 32 semester hours.

Evaluation Student evaluation based on tests, papers, reports, class participation. Grading system: Letters or numbers. Transcripts are kept for each student.

Enrollment Requirements Associate or bachelor's degree required.

Program Costs $146 per credit hour.

Housing and Student Services Housing is available. Job counseling and placement services are available.

Special Features The paralegal program was established in 1976 to provide a quality liberal arts education with a paralegal career orientation for its students. Our small class size and dedicated faculty see to it that the quality remains high.

Contact Mr. Jay Johnson, Director, Paralegal Studies Program, Mount St. Joseph, OH 45051. 513-244-4392.

MARIETTA COLLEGE
Marietta, Ohio 45750

ACCOUNTING (06.02)
Accounting Certificate

General Information Unit offering the program: Office of Continuing Education. Program content: Information systems, business law, finance, auditing, cost accounting. Available for credit. Certificate signed by the President.

Program Format Evening classes offered. Instructional schedule: One evening per week. Program cycle: Continuous enrollment. Full program cycle lasts 6 semesters. Completion of program requires grade of C or better.

Evaluation Student evaluation based on tests, papers, reports. Grading system: Letters or numbers. Transcripts are kept for each student.

Enrollment Requirements College admissions required. Program is not open to non-resident foreign students.

Program Costs $3600 for the program, $300 per course.

Housing and Student Services Housing is not available. Job counseling and placement services are available.

Special Features The certificate is designed to be coupled with an undergraduate degree in an unrelated field.

Contact Mr. George Banziger, Dean of Continuing Education, Marietta, OH 45750-3031. 614-374-4732.

BUSINESS ADMINISTRATION AND MANAGEMENT (06.04)
Pre-MBA Certificate

General Information Unit offering the program: Office of Continuing Education. Program content: Economics, business law, marketing, information systems, operations, statistics. Available for credit. Certificate signed by the President. Certificate applicable to M.B.A. from Ohio University.

Program Format Evening, weekend classes offered. Instructional schedule: One evening per week. Program cycle: Continuous enrollment. Full program cycle lasts 10 semesters. Completion of program requires grade of C or better.

Evaluation Student evaluation based on tests, papers, reports. Grading system: Letters or numbers. Transcripts are kept for each student.

Enrollment Requirements College admissions required. Program is open to non-resident foreign students.

Program Costs $12,600 for the program, $300 per course.

Housing and Student Services Housing is not available. Job counseling and placement services are available.

Special Features Credit for life experience may be obtained via portfolio assessment. Courses may be transferred.

Contact Mr. George Banziger, Dean of Continuing Education, Marietta, OH 45750-3031. 614-374-4732.

MICROCOMPUTER APPLICATIONS (11.06)
Microcomputer Systems Specialist Certificate

General Information Unit offering the program: Office of Continuing Education. Program content: Software applications, database design, operating systems, programming, information systems. Available for credit. Certificate signed by the President.

Program Format Evening, weekend classes offered. Instructional schedule: One evening per week or Saturday. Program cycle: Continuous enrollment. Full program cycle lasts 4 semesters. Completion of program requires grade of C or better.

Evaluation Student evaluation based on tests, papers, reports. Grading system: Letters or numbers. Transcripts are kept for each student.

Enrollment Requirements College admissions required. Program is open to non-resident foreign students.

Program Costs $2400 for the program, $300 per course.

Housing and Student Services Housing is not available. Job counseling and placement services are available.

Special Features A large microcomputer laboratory is available. Individual advising is provided.

Contact Mr. George Banziger, Dean of Continuing Education, Marietta, OH 45750-3031. 614-374-4732.

NOTRE DAME COLLEGE OF OHIO
Cleveland, Ohio 44121

ACCOUNTING (06.02)
Accounting

General Information Unit offering the program: Business Administration. Program content: Business communications and law, cost accounting, auditing, taxes, finance, management and organization. Available for credit. Certificate signed by the Dean of Academic Affairs. Certificate applicable to B.A. in Business Administration.

Program Format Daytime, evening, weekend classes offered. Program cycle: Continuous enrollment. Full program cycle lasts 30 credit hours. Completion of program requires 2.0 GPA.

Evaluation Student evaluation based on tests, papers, reports. Grading system: Letters or numbers. Transcripts are kept for each student.

Enrollment Requirements High school diploma required, bachelor's degree recommended, women only. Program is open to non-resident foreign students. English language proficiency required. Minimum TOEFL score required: 575.

Program Costs $135 per credit hour.

Housing and Student Services Housing is available. Job counseling and placement services are available.

Special Features CLEP exams and college-designed challenge exams used to assess prior experience. Most instructors have business experience as well as academic preparation for teaching. Accounting program prepares for CPA exam. Weekend college is specifically for the woman over age 25 and working who seeks a degree for a career change. She should have strong academic ability, be highly motivated, and an independent learner.

Contact Dr. Madeline Columbro, Dean of Academic Affairs, 4545 College Road, Cleveland, OH 44121. 216-381-1680.

249

BANKING AND FINANCE (06.03)
Management in Financial Institutions

General Information   Unit offering the program: Business Administration. Program content: Basic accounting and computers, marketing, finance, business communications, management and organization, taxes, investments, business and government, business law, money and banking. Available for credit. Certificate signed by the Dean of Academic Affairs. Certificate applicable to B.A. in Business Administration.

Program Format   Daytime, evening, weekend classes offered. Program cycle: Continuous enrollment. Full program cycle lasts 30 credit hours. Completion of program requires 2.0 GPA.

Evaluation   Student evaluation based on tests, papers, reports. Grading system: Letters or numbers. Transcripts are kept for each student.

Enrollment Requirements   High school diploma required, bachelor's degree recommended, women only. Program is open to non-resident foreign students. English language proficiency required. Minimum TOEFL score required: 575.

Program Costs $135 per credit hour.

Housing and Student Services   Housing is available. Job counseling and placement services are available.

Special Features   CLEP exams and college-designed challenge exams used to assess prior experience. Most instructors have business experience as well as academic preparation for teaching. Weekend college is specifically for the woman over age 25 and working who seeks a degree for a career change. She should have strong academic ability, be highly motivated, and an independent learner.

Contact   Dr. Madeline Columbro, Dean of Academic Affairs, 4545 College Road, Cleveland, OH 44121. 216-381-1680.

BUSINESS AND MANAGEMENT, GENERAL (06.01)
Management

General Information   Unit offering the program: Business Administration. Program content: Basic accounting, entrepreneurship, marketing, computers, business communications and law, supervision, management and organization, finance, human resources, organizational behavior. Available for credit. Certificate signed by the Dean of Academic Affairs. Certificate applicable to B.A. in Business Administration.

Program Format   Daytime, evening, weekend classes offered. Program cycle: Continuous enrollment. Full program cycle lasts 30 credit hours. Completion of program requires 2.0 GPA.

Evaluation   Student evaluation based on tests, papers, reports. Grading system: Letters or numbers. Transcripts are kept for each student.

Enrollment Requirements   High school diploma required, bachelor's degree recommended, women only. Program is open to non-resident foreign students. English language proficiency required. Minimum TOEFL score required: 575.

Program Costs $135 per credit hour.

Housing and Student Services   Housing is available. Job counseling and placement services are available.

Special Features   CLEP exams and college-designed challenge exams used to assess prior experience. Most instructors have business experience as well as academic preparation for teaching. Weekend college is specifically for the woman over age 25 and working who seeks a degree for a career change. She should have strong academic ability, be highly motivated, and an independent learner.

Contact   Dr. Madeline Columbro, Dean of Academic Affairs, 4545 College Road, Cleveland, OH 44121. 216-381-1680.

ITALIC LANGUAGES (16.09)
Professional Translating (French)

General Information   Unit offering the program: Modern Language Department. Program content: Principles, procedures, and tools for professional translation; commercial translation; practicum in general translation. Available for credit. Certificate signed by the Dean of Academic Affairs. Certificate applicable to B.A. in Modern Languages. Program fulfills requirements for membership in the American Translators Association.

Program Format   Evening classes offered. Instructional schedule: One evening per week. Program cycle: Continuous enrollment. Full program cycle lasts 4 semesters. Completion of program requires 2.0 GPA, four courses.

Evaluation   Student evaluation based on tests, papers, reports. Grading system: Letters or numbers. Transcripts are kept for each student.

Enrollment Requirements   Limited to those proficient in French. Program is open to non-resident foreign students. English language proficiency required. College-administered test.

Program Costs $135 per credit hour.

Housing and Student Services   Housing is available. Job counseling and placement services are available.

Contact   Sr. Maryann Weber, Assistant Professor of French and Spanish, 4545 College Road, Cleveland, OH 44121. 216-381-1680.

ITALIC LANGUAGES (16.09)
Professional Translating (Spanish)

General Information   Unit offering the program: Modern Language Department. Program content: Principles, procedures, and tools for professional translation; commercial translation; practicum in general translation. Available for credit. Certificate signed by the Dean of Academic Affairs. Certificate applicable to B.A. in Modern Languages. Program fulfills requirements for membership in the American Translators Association.

Program Format   Evening classes offered. Instructional schedule: One evening per week. Program cycle: Continuous enrollment. Full program cycle lasts 4 semesters. Completion of program requires 2.0 GPA, four courses.

Evaluation   Student evaluation based on tests, papers, reports. Grading system: Letters or numbers. Transcripts are kept for each student.

Enrollment Requirements   Limited to those proficient in Spanish. Program is open to non-resident foreign students. English language proficiency required. College-administered test.

Program Costs $135 per credit hour.

Housing and Student Services   Housing is available. Job counseling and placement services are available.

Contact   Ms. Clara Thurner, Associate Professor of German and Spanish, 4545 College Road, Cleveland, OH 44121. 216-381-1680.

MARKETING MANAGEMENT AND RESEARCH (06.14)
Marketing

General Information   Unit offering the program: Business Administration. Program content: Basic accounting, computers, business communications, management and organization, consumer behavior, finance, research, advertising, international marketing. Available for credit. Certificate signed by the Dean of Academic Affairs. Certificate applicable to B.A. in Business Administration.

Program Format   Daytime, evening, weekend classes offered. Program cycle: Continuous enrollment. Full program cycle lasts 30 credit hours. Completion of program requires 2.0 GPA.

Evaluation   Student evaluation based on tests, papers, reports. Grading system: Letters or numbers. Transcripts are kept for each student.

Enrollment Requirements High school diploma required, bachelor's degree recommended, women only. Program is open to non-resident foreign students. English language proficiency required. Minimum TOEFL score required: 575.

Program Costs $135 per credit hour.

Housing and Student Services Housing is available. Job counseling and placement services are available.

Special Features CLEP exams and college-designed challenge exams used to assess prior experience. Most instructors have business experience as well as academic preparation for teaching. Weekend college is specifically for the woman over age 25 and working who seeks a degree for a career change. She should have strong academic ability, be highly motivated, and an independent learner.

Contact Dr. Madeline Columbro, Dean of Academic Affairs, 4545 College Road, Cleveland, OH 44121. 216-381-1680.

RELIGION (38.02)
Certificate in Pastoral Ministry

General Information Unit offering the program: Center for Catechetics and Ministry. Program content: Scripture, theology, spirituality, counseling skills, ministry and liturgy, planning for parish ministry. Available for credit. Certificate signed by the Dean of Academic Affairs. Certificate applicable to B.A. in Catechetics.

Program Format Evening classes offered. Students may enroll September, January. Full program cycle lasts 6 courses. Completion of program requires 2.0 GPA.

Evaluation Student evaluation based on tests, papers, reports. Grading system: Letters or numbers. Transcripts are kept for each student.

Enrollment Requirements High school diploma, letter of recommendation, ministry involvement in parish or community required. Program is open to non-resident foreign students. English language proficiency required. Minimum TOEFL score required: 575.

Program Costs $135 per credit hour.

Housing and Student Services Housing is available. Job counseling and placement services are available.

Contact Center for Catechetics and Ministry, 4545 College Road, Cleveland, OH 44121. 216-381-1680.

RELIGIOUS EDUCATION (39.04)
Certificate in Catechetics

General Information Unit offering the program: Center for Catechetics and Ministry. Program content: Theology, philosophy, psychology, education. Available for credit. Certificate signed by the Dean of Academic Affairs. Certificate applicable to B.A. in Catechetics.

Program Format Evening classes offered. Program cycle: Continuous enrollment. Full program cycle lasts 20 courses. Completion of program requires 2.0 GPA.

Evaluation Student evaluation based on tests, papers, reports. Grading system: Letters or numbers. Transcripts are kept for each student.

Enrollment Requirements High school diploma, letter of recommendation, interview required. Program is open to non-resident foreign students. English language proficiency required. Minimum TOEFL score required: 575.

Program Costs $135 per credit hour.

Housing and Student Services Housing is available. Job counseling and placement services are available.

Contact Center for Catechetics and Ministry, 4545 College Road, Cleveland, OH 44121. 216-381-1680.

NUCEA MEMBER
OHIO STATE UNIVERSITY
Columbus, Ohio 43210

INTERNATIONAL RELATIONS (45.09)
Undergraduate Certificate–Area Studies Program

General Information Unit offering the program: University Center for International Studies. Program content: Instruction in East Asia, Eastern Europe, Latin America, Middle East. Available for credit. Certificate signed by the Director, University Center for International Studies. Certificate applicable to bachelor's degree in international studies.

Program Format Daytime, evening classes offered. Program cycle: Continuous enrollment. Completion of program requires 50 credit hours (20 must be taken in a foreign language).

Evaluation Student evaluation based on tests, papers, reports. Grading system: Letters or numbers. Transcripts are kept for each student.

Enrollment Requirements High school diploma or GED required. Program is open to non-resident foreign students. English language proficiency required.

Program Costs $100 per credit hour (part-time).

Housing and Student Services Housing is available. Job counseling and placement services are available.

Special Features The International Studies Certificates can be an adjunct to the student's regular major. A student can receive a certificate in the following areas: Asian studies, Latin America, Middle East, or Slavic and East European studies.

Contact Dr. Alam Rayind, Assistant Director, Center for International Studies, 308 Dulles Hall, 230 West 17th Avenue, Columbus, OH 43210-1311. 614-292-9660.

NUCEA MEMBER
OHIO UNIVERSITY–CHILLICOTHE
Chillicothe, Ohio 45601

TYPING, GENERAL OFFICE, AND RELATED PROGRAMS (07.07)
General Secretarial Technology

General Information Unit offering the program: Office Administration Technology. Program content: Typing and general office work. Available for credit. Certificate signed by the Dean of University College. Certificate applicable to A.A.B. in General Secretarial Technology.

Program Format Daytime, evening, weekend classes offered. Program cycle: Continuous enrollment. Full program cycle lasts 49 credit hours. Completion of program requires 15 courses.

Evaluation Student evaluation based on tests, papers, reports. Grading system: Letters or numbers. Transcripts are kept for each student.

Enrollment Requirements High school diploma required. Program is open to non-resident foreign students. English language proficiency required.

Program Costs $57 per credit hour.

Housing and Student Services Housing is not available. Job counseling and placement services are available.

Special Features The student may eliminate required courses by passing an omissions test, or he/she may submit experience documents for evaluation of credit.

Contact Mr. David Gigley, Coordinator, Office Administration, P.O. Box 629, Chillicothe, OH 45601. 614-775-9500.

OTTERBEIN COLLEGE
Westerville, Ohio 43081

ACCOUNTING (06.02)
Certificate in Accounting

General Information Unit offering the program: Department of Business Administration, Economics and Accounting. Available for credit. Certificate signed by the President of the College. Certificate applicable to any four-year degree offered at the institution.

Program Format Daytime, evening classes offered. Program cycle: Continuous enrollment. Completion of program requires 62 quarter units, 2.0 GPA.

Evaluation Student evaluation based on tests, papers, reports. Grading system: Letters or numbers. Transcripts are kept for each student.

Enrollment Requirements High school diploma required. Program is open to non-resident foreign students. English language proficiency required.

Program Costs $99 per quarter hour.

Housing and Student Services Job counseling and placement services are available.

Contact Mr. Greg Longacre, Director of Continuing Education, Westerville, OH 43081. 614-898-1356.

BUSINESS ADMINISTRATION AND MANAGEMENT (06.04)
Certificate in Business Administration— General

General Information Unit offering the program: Department of Business Administration, Economics and Accounting. Available for credit. Certificate signed by the President of the College. Certificate applicable to any four-year degree offered at the institution.

Program Format Daytime, evening, weekend classes offered. Program cycle: Continuous enrollment. Completion of program requires 62 quarter units, 2.0 GPA.

Evaluation Student evaluation based on tests, papers, reports. Grading system: Letters or numbers. Transcripts are kept for each student.

Enrollment Requirements High school diploma required. Program is open to non-resident foreign students. English language proficiency required.

Program Costs $99 per quarter hour.

Housing and Student Services Job counseling and placement services are available.

Contact Mr. Greg Longacre, Director of Continuing Education, Westerville, OH 43081. 614-898-1356.

BUSINESS ADMINISTRATION AND MANAGEMENT (06.04)
Certificate in Business Administration— Management

General Information Unit offering the program: Department of Business Administration, Economics and Accounting. Available for credit. Certificate signed by the President of the College. Certificate applicable to any four-year degree offered at the institution.

Program Format Daytime, evening, weekend classes offered. Program cycle: Continuous enrollment. Completion of program requires 62 quarter units, 2.0 GPA.

Evaluation Student evaluation based on tests, papers, reports. Grading system: Letters or numbers. Transcripts are kept for each student.

Enrollment Requirements High school diploma required. Program is open to non-resident foreign students. English language proficiency required.

Program Costs $99 per quarter hour.

Housing and Student Services Job counseling and placement services are available.

Contact Mr. Greg Longacre, Director of Continuing Education, Westerville, OH 43081. 614-898-1356.

COMPUTER AND INFORMATION SCIENCES, GENERAL (11.01)
Certificate in Computer Science

General Information Unit offering the program: Department of Math and Computer Science. Available for credit. Certificate signed by the President of the College. Certificate applicable to any four-year degree offered at the institution.

Program Format Daytime, evening classes offered. Program cycle: Continuous enrollment. Completion of program requires 62 quarter units, 2.0 GPA.

Evaluation Student evaluation based on tests, papers, reports. Grading system: Letters or numbers. Transcripts are kept for each student.

Enrollment Requirements High school diploma required. Program is open to non-resident foreign students. English language proficiency required.

Program Costs $99 per quarter hour.

Housing and Student Services Job counseling and placement services are available.

Contact Mr. Greg Longacre, Director of Continuing Education, Westerville, OH 43081. 614-898-1356.

NUCEA MEMBER
UNIVERSITY OF AKRON
Akron, Ohio 44325

CHILD CARE AND GUIDANCE MANAGEMENT AND SERVICES (20.02)
Child Care Worker

General Information Unit offering the program: Community and Technical College. Program content: Vocational training for child care workers. Available for credit. Certificate signed by the Coordinator/Senior Vice President.

Program Format Daytime, evening classes offered. Program cycle: Continuous enrollment. Completion of program requires 2.0 GPA for undergraduate programs, 3.0 GPA for graduate programs.

Evaluation Student evaluation based on tests, papers, reports. Grading system: Letters or numbers, pass/fail. Transcripts are kept for each student.

Enrollment Requirements University admissions required. Program is open to non-resident foreign students.

Program Costs $75–$151 per credit hour.

Housing and Student Services Housing is not available. Job counseling and placement services are available.

Contact University Admissions/University Registrar, East Buchtel Avenue, Akron, OH 44325. 216-375-7100.

CITIZENSHIP/CIVIC ACTIVITIES (33.01)
Volunteer Program Management

General Information Unit offering the program: Community and Technical College. Program content: Managing a volunteer program in the public sector. Available for credit. Certificate signed by the Coordinator/Senior Vice President.

Program Format Daytime, evening classes offered. Program cycle: Continuous enrollment.

Evaluation Student evaluation based on tests, papers, reports. Grading system: Letters or numbers, pass/fail. Transcripts are kept for each student.

Enrollment Requirements University admissions required. Program is open to non-resident foreign students.

Program Costs $75–$151 per credit hour.

Housing and Student Services Housing is not available. Job counseling and placement services are available.

Contact University Admissions/University Registrar, East Buchtel Avenue, Akron, OH 44325. 216-375-7100.

CITY, COMMUNITY, AND REGIONAL PLANNING (04.03)
Planning with an Emphasis on City or Regional Resource Studies

General Information Unit offering the program: Geography. Program content: Economic analysis and geography, metropolitan politics, urban planning. Available for credit. Certificate signed by the Coordinator/Senior Vice President.

Program Format Daytime, evening classes offered. Program cycle: Continuous enrollment. Full program cycle lasts 11 courses. Completion of program requires grade of C or better in all courses; average grade of B or better in five core courses.

Evaluation Student evaluation based on tests, papers, reports. Grading system: Letters or numbers, pass/fail. Transcripts are kept for each student.

Enrollment Requirements Bachelor's degree, statement of intent required. Program is open to non-resident foreign students.

Program Costs $75–$151 per credit hour.

Housing and Student Services Housing is not available. Job counseling and placement services are available.

Contact University Admissions/University Registrar, East Buchtel Avenue, Akron, OH 44325. 216-375-7100.

COMMUNICATIONS, GENERAL (09.01)
Professional Communication

General Information Unit offering the program: Speech Department. Program content: Effective communication of business and technical information. Available for credit. Certificate signed by the Coordinator/Senior Vice President.

Program Format Daytime, evening classes offered. Program cycle: Continuous enrollment.

Evaluation Student evaluation based on tests, papers, reports. Grading system: Letters or numbers, pass/fail. Transcripts are kept for each student.

Enrollment Requirements University admissions required. Program is open to non-resident foreign students.

Program Costs $75–$151 per credit hour.

Housing and Student Services Housing is not available. Job counseling and placement services are available.

Contact University Admissions/University Registrar, East Buchtel Avenue, Akron, OH 44325. 216-375-7100.

COMPOSITION (23.04)
Composition

General Information Unit offering the program: Arts and Science College, Department of English. Program content: Linguistics, research, theory, teaching, history of English language. Available for credit. Certificate signed by the Coordinator/Senior Vice President.

Program Format Daytime, evening classes offered. Program cycle: Continuous enrollment.

Evaluation Student evaluation based on tests, papers, reports. Grading system: Letters or numbers, pass/fail. Transcripts are kept for each student.

Enrollment Requirements Bachelor's degree required. Program is open to non-resident foreign students.

Program Costs $75–$151 per credit hour.

Housing and Student Services Housing is not available. Job counseling and placement services are available.

Contact University Admissions/University Registrar, East Buchtel Avenue, Akron, OH 44325. 216-375-7100.

CRIMINAL JUSTICE (43.01)
Criminal Justice/Security Emphasis

General Information Unit offering the program: Community and Technical College. Program content: Fire prevention practices, hazardous materials, safety procedures, administration and supervision for public service. Available for credit. Certificate signed by the Coordinator/Senior Vice President.

Program Format Daytime, evening classes offered. Program cycle: Continuous enrollment. Full program cycle lasts 6 courses.

Evaluation Student evaluation based on tests, papers, reports. Grading system: Letters or numbers, pass/fail. Transcripts are kept for each student.

Enrollment Requirements University admissions required. Program is open to non-resident foreign students.

Program Costs $75–$151 per credit hour.

Housing and Student Services Housing is not available. Job counseling and placement services are available.

Contact University Admissions/University Registrar, East Buchtel Avenue, Akron, OH 44325. 216-375-7100.

EDUCATION ADMINISTRATION (13.04)
Higher Education

General Information Unit offering the program: College of Education, Department of Higher Education. Available for credit. Certificate signed by the Coordinator/Senior Vice President.

Program Format Daytime, evening classes offered. Program cycle: Continuous enrollment. Full program cycle lasts 15 credit hours. Completion of program requires 3.0 GPA.

Evaluation Student evaluation based on tests, papers, reports. Grading system: Letters or numbers, pass/fail. Transcripts are kept for each student.

Enrollment Requirements Master's degree required. Program is open to non-resident foreign students.

Program Costs $75–$151 per credit hour.

Housing and Student Services Housing is not available. Job counseling and placement services are available.

Contact University Admissions/University Registrar, East Buchtel Avenue, Akron, OH 44325. 216-375-7100.

ETHNIC STUDIES (05.02)
Afro-American Studies

General Information Unit offering the program: Community and Technical College. Program content: History and overview of Afro-American contributions and interactions in American culture. Available for credit. Certificate signed by the Coordinator/Senior Vice President.

Program Format Daytime, evening classes offered. Program cycle: Continuous enrollment. Completion of program requires 2.0 GPA.

Evaluation Student evaluation based on tests, papers, reports. Grading system: Letters or numbers, pass/fail. Transcripts are kept for each student.

Enrollment Requirements University admissions required. Program is open to non-resident foreign students.

Program Costs $75–$151 per credit hour.

Housing and Student Services Housing is not available. Job counseling and placement services are available.

Afro-American Studies continued

Contact University Admissions/University Registrar, East Buchtel Avenue, Akron, OH 44325. 216-375-7100.

FIRE PROTECTION (43.02)
Fire Protection Technology

General Information Unit offering the program: Community and Technical College. Program content: Detection, suppression, and investigative methods; safety in building design and construction. Available for credit. Certificate signed by the Coordinator/Senior Vice President.

Program Format Daytime, evening classes offered. Program cycle: Continuous enrollment. Full program cycle lasts 22 credit hours. Completion of program requires 2.0 GPA.

Evaluation Student evaluation based on tests, papers, reports. Grading system: Letters or numbers, pass/fail. Transcripts are kept for each student.

Enrollment Requirements University admissions required. Program is open to non-resident foreign students.

Program Costs $75–$151 per credit hour.

Housing and Student Services Housing is not available. Job counseling and placement services are available.

Contact University Admissions/University Registrar, East Buchtel Avenue, Akron, OH 44325. 216-375-7100.

HOSPITALITY AND RECREATION MARKETING (08.09)
Hospitality Management

General Information Unit offering the program: Community and Technical College. Program content: Hotel/motel option and restaurant option. Available for credit. Certificate signed by the Coordinator/Senior Vice President.

Program Format Daytime, evening classes offered. Program cycle: Continuous enrollment.

Evaluation Student evaluation based on tests, papers, reports. Grading system: Letters or numbers, pass/fail. Transcripts are kept for each student.

Enrollment Requirements University admissions required. Program is open to non-resident foreign students.

Program Costs $75–$151 per credit hour.

Housing and Student Services Housing is not available. Job counseling and placement services are available.

Contact University Admissions/University Registrar, East Buchtel Avenue, Akron, OH 44325. 216-375-7100.

HUMAN ENVIRONMENT AND HOUSING (19.06)
Interior Design

General Information Unit offering the program: Departments of Home Economics, Family Ecology, Art. Available for credit. Certificate signed by the Coordinator/Senior Vice President. Certificate applicable to bachelor's degree in clothing and textiles, graphic design.

Program Format Daytime, evening classes offered. Program cycle: Continuous enrollment.

Evaluation Student evaluation based on tests, papers, reports. Grading system: Letters or numbers, pass/fail. Transcripts are kept for each student.

Enrollment Requirements Bachelor's degree required. Program is open to non-resident foreign students.

Program Costs $75–$151 per credit hour.

Housing and Student Services Housing is not available. Job counseling and placement services are available.

Contact University Admissions/University Registrar, East Buchtel Avenue, Akron, OH 44325. 216-375-7100.

INDIVIDUAL AND FAMILY DEVELOPMENT (19.07)
Aging Services

General Information Unit offering the program: Community and Technical College. Program content: Technical report writing, community work, senior citizen and social services. Available for credit. Certificate signed by the Coordinator/Senior Vice President.

Program Format Daytime, evening classes offered. Full program cycle lasts 8 courses.

Evaluation Student evaluation based on tests, papers, reports. Grading system: Letters or numbers, pass/fail. Transcripts are kept for each student.

Enrollment Requirements University admissions required. Program is open to non-resident foreign students.

Program Costs $75–$151 per credit hour.

Housing and Student Services Housing is not available. Job counseling and placement services are available.

Contact University Admissions/University Registrar, East Buchtel Avenue, Akron, OH 44325. 216-375-7100.

INDIVIDUAL AND FAMILY DEVELOPMENT (19.07)
Gerontology

General Information Unit offering the program: Community and Technical College. Available for credit. Certificate signed by the Coordinator/Senior Vice President.

Program Format Daytime, evening classes offered. Program cycle: Continuous enrollment.

Evaluation Student evaluation based on tests, papers, reports. Grading system: Letters or numbers, pass/fail. Transcripts are kept for each student.

Enrollment Requirements Bachelor's degree, interview required. Program is open to non-resident foreign students.

Program Costs $75–$151 per credit hour.

Housing and Student Services Housing is not available. Job counseling and placement services are available.

Contact University Admissions/University Registrar, East Buchtel Avenue, Akron, OH 44325. 216-375-7100.

LINGUISTICS (INCLUDES PHONETICS, SEMANTICS, AND PHILOLOGY) (23.06)
Linguistic Studies

General Information Unit offering the program: English Department. Program content: Linguistics, communications, logic. Available for credit. Certificate signed by the Coordinator/Senior Vice President.

Program Format Daytime, evening classes offered. Program cycle: Continuous enrollment. Full program cycle lasts 6 courses. Completion of program requires two semesters of language.

Evaluation Student evaluation based on tests, papers, reports. Grading system: Letters or numbers, pass/fail. Transcripts are kept for each student.

Enrollment Requirements Consent of program director required. Program is open to non-resident foreign students.

Program Costs $75–$151 per credit hour.

Housing and Student Services Housing is not available. Job counseling and placement services are available.

Contact University Admissions/University Registrar, East Buchtel Avenue, Akron, OH 44325. 216-375-7100.

MENTAL HEALTH/HUMAN SERVICES (17.04)
Alcohol Services Aide

General Information Unit offering the program: Community and Technical College. Program content: Technical report writing; alcohol use, abuse, and treatment; techniques of community work; helping skills. Available for credit. Certificate signed by the Coordinator/Senior Vice President.

Program Format   Daytime, evening classes offered. Program cycle: Continuous enrollment. Full program cycle lasts 8 courses.

Evaluation   Student evaluation based on tests, papers, reports. Grading system: Letters or numbers, pass/fail. Transcripts are kept for each student.

Enrollment Requirements   University admissions required. Program is open to non-resident foreign students.

Program Costs $75–$151 per credit hour.

Housing and Student Services   Housing is not available. Job counseling and placement services are available.

Contact   University Admissions/University Registrar, East Buchtel Avenue, Akron, OH 44325. 216-375-7100.

POLITICAL SCIENCE AND GOVERNMENT (45.10)
Applied Politics

General Information   Unit offering the program: Political Science Department. Program content: History, organization, and management of campaigns. Available for credit. Certificate signed by the Coordinator/Senior Vice President. Certificate applicable to B.S., B.A. in Public Policy Management.

Program Format   Daytime, evening classes offered. Program cycle: Continuous enrollment.

Evaluation   Student evaluation based on tests, papers, reports. Grading system: Letters or numbers, pass/fail. Transcripts are kept for each student.

Enrollment Requirements   University admissions required. Program is open to non-resident foreign students.

Program Costs $75–$151 per credit hour.

Housing and Student Services   Housing is not available. Job counseling and placement services are available.

Contact   University Admissions/University Registrar, East Buchtel Avenue, Akron, OH 44325. 216-375-7100.

SECRETARIAL AND RELATED PROGRAMS (07.06)
Office Administration/Administrative Secretarial

General Information   Unit offering the program: Community and Technical College. Program content: Typing, letter writing, operating office machines. Available for credit. Certificate signed by the Coordinator/Senior Vice President.

Program Format   Daytime, evening classes offered. Program cycle: Continuous enrollment. Full program cycle lasts 2 semesters.

Evaluation   Student evaluation based on tests, papers, reports. Grading system: Letters or numbers, pass/fail. Transcripts are kept for each student.

Enrollment Requirements   Two years of college required. Program is open to non-resident foreign students.

Program Costs $75–$151 per credit hour.

Housing and Student Services   Housing is not available. Job counseling and placement services are available.

Contact   University Admissions/University Registrar, East Buchtel Avenue, Akron, OH 44325. 216-375-7100.

SMALL BUSINESS MANAGEMENT AND OWNERSHIP (06.18)
Small Business Management

General Information   Unit offering the program: Community and Technical College, Business Management Technology Department. Program content: Accounting; math; English; small business development, management, and operations. Available

for credit. Certificate signed by the Coordinator/Senior Vice President.

Program Format   Daytime, evening classes offered. Program cycle: Continuous enrollment.

Evaluation   Student evaluation based on tests, papers, reports. Grading system: Letters or numbers, pass/fail. Transcripts are kept for each student.

Enrollment Requirements   University admissions required. Program is open to non-resident foreign students.

Program Costs $75–$151 per credit hour.

Housing and Student Services   Housing is not available. Job counseling and placement services are available.

Contact   University Admissions/University Registrar, East Buchtel Avenue, Akron, OH 44325. 216-375-7100.

SPEECH, DEBATE, AND FORENSICS (23.10)
Manual Communication

General Information   Unit offering the program: Speech Department. Program content: Communicating with the deaf population. Available for credit. Certificate signed by the Coordinator/Senior Vice President.

Program Format   Daytime, evening classes offered. Program cycle: Continuous enrollment. Full program cycle lasts 8 courses.

Evaluation   Student evaluation based on tests, papers, reports. Grading system: Letters or numbers, pass/fail. Transcripts are kept for each student.

Enrollment Requirements   Bachelor's degree required. Program is open to non-resident foreign students.

Program Costs $75–$151 per credit hour.

Housing and Student Services   Housing is not available. Job counseling and placement services are available.

Contact   University Admissions/University Registrar, East Buchtel Avenue, Akron, OH 44325. 216-375-7100.

TEACHING ENGLISH AS A SECOND LANGUAGE/FOREIGN LANGUAGE (13.14)
Teaching English as a Second Language

General Information   Unit offering the program: English Department. Available for credit. Certificate signed by the Coordinator/Senior Vice President.

Program Format   Daytime, evening classes offered. Program cycle: Continuous enrollment. Full program cycle lasts 18 credit hours. Completion of program requires 2.0 GPA.

Evaluation   Student evaluation based on tests, papers, reports. Grading system: Letters or numbers, pass/fail. Transcripts are kept for each student.

Enrollment Requirements   Two years of college-level foreign language required. Program is open to non-resident foreign students. English language proficiency required. Minimum TOEFL score required: 550.

Program Costs $75–$151 per credit hour.

Housing and Student Services   Housing is not available. Job counseling and placement services are available.

Contact   University Admissions/University Registrar, East Buchtel Avenue, Akron, OH 44325. 216-375-7100.

URBAN STUDIES (45.12)
Mid-Career Program in Urban Studies

General Information   Unit offering the program: Department of Urban Studies. Program content: Public administration, research methods, planning, service systems. Available for credit. Certificate signed by the Coordinator/Senior Vice President.

Program Format   Daytime, evening classes offered. Program cycle: Continuous enrollment. Full program cycle lasts 16 credit hours.

Mid-Career Program in Urban Studies continued

Evaluation Student evaluation based on tests, papers, reports. Grading system: Letters or numbers, pass/fail. Transcripts are kept for each student.

Enrollment Requirements Bachelor's degree, five years professional experience required. Program is open to non-resident foreign students.

Program Costs $75–$151 per credit hour.

Housing and Student Services Housing is not available. Job counseling and placement services are available.

Contact University Admissions/University Registrar, East Buchtel Avenue, Akron, OH 44325. 216-375-7100.

WOMEN'S STUDIES (30.07)
Women's Studies

General Information Unit offering the program: University College. Program content: Sex roles, sex differences, concepts of masculinity and femininity. Available for credit. Certificate signed by the Coordinator/Senior Vice President.

Program Format Daytime, evening classes offered. Program cycle: Continuous enrollment. Full program cycle lasts 19 credit hours.

Evaluation Student evaluation based on tests, papers, reports. Grading system: Letters or numbers, pass/fail. Transcripts are kept for each student.

Enrollment Requirements University admissions required. Program is open to non-resident foreign students.

Program Costs $75–$151 per credit hour.

Housing and Student Services Housing is not available. Job counseling and placement services are available.

Contact University Admissions/University Registrar, East Buchtel Avenue, Akron, OH 44325. 216-375-7100.

WORD PROCESSING (07.08)
Office Administration/Word Processing

General Information Unit offering the program: Community and Technical College. Program content: Business machines and communications, information management, word processing equipment and applications. Available for credit. Certificate signed by the Coordinator/Senior Vice President. Certificate applicable to A.S. in Secretarial Science.

Program Format Daytime, evening classes offered. Program cycle: Continuous enrollment.

Evaluation Student evaluation based on tests, papers, reports. Grading system: Letters or numbers, pass/fail. Transcripts are kept for each student.

Enrollment Requirements University admissions required. Program is open to non-resident foreign students.

Program Costs $75–$151 per credit hour.

Housing and Student Services Housing is not available. Job counseling and placement services are available.

Contact University Admissions/University Registrar, East Buchtel Avenue, Akron, OH 44325. 216-375-7100.

NUCEA MEMBER
UNIVERSITY OF CINCINNATI
Cincinnati, Ohio 45221

ACCOUNTING (06.02)
Accountancy

General Information Unit offering the program: Business. Program content: Accounting, business law, cost and tax accounting, finance, spreadsheets, business applications of computers. Available for credit. Certificate signed by the College Dean.

Program Format Daytime, evening classes offered. Program cycle: Continuous enrollment. Full program cycle lasts 3 quarters. Completion of program requires 48 quarter units, 2.0 GPA.

Evaluation Student evaluation based on tests. Grading system: Letters or numbers. Transcripts are kept for each student.

Enrollment Requirements Bachelor's degree required. Program is open to non-resident foreign students. English language proficiency required. Minimum TOEFL score required: 515.

Program Costs $2359 for the program (state residents); $5400 for the program (nonresidents).

Housing and Student Services Housing is not available. Job counseling and placement services are available.

Contact Dr. Robert Howell, Assistant Dean, 9555 Plainfield Road, Cincinnati, OH 45236. 513-745-5700.

BIOLOGICAL TECHNOLOGIES (41.01)
Industrial Laboratory Technology (Environmental Control Protection Technology Option)

General Information Unit offering the program: Biology. Program content: Chemical analysis, biological water sampling, organic chemistry, wastewater engineering, solid and hazardous waste. Available for credit. Certificate signed by the College Dean.

Program Format Daytime classes offered. Program cycle: Continuous enrollment. Full program cycle lasts 3 quarters. Completion of program requires 47 quarter units, 2.0 GPA.

Evaluation Student evaluation based on tests, papers, reports. Grading system: Letters or numbers. Transcripts are kept for each student.

Enrollment Requirements Bachelor's degree required. Program is open to non-resident foreign students. English language proficiency required. Minimum TOEFL score required: 515.

Program Costs $2359 for the program (state residents); $5400 for the program (nonresidents).

Housing and Student Services Housing is not available. Job counseling and placement services are available.

Contact Dr. Robert Howell, Assistant Dean, 9555 Plainfield Road, Cincinnati, OH 45236. 513-745-5700.

BUSINESS AND MANAGEMENT, GENERAL (06.01)
Business

General Information Unit offering the program: Business. Program content: Economics, accounting, marketing, finance, management, computers in business, business law. Available for credit. Certificate signed by the College Dean.

Program Format Daytime, evening classes offered. Program cycle: Continuous enrollment. Full program cycle lasts 3 quarters. Completion of program requires 45 quarter units, 2.0 GPA.

Evaluation Student evaluation based on tests. Grading system: Letters or numbers. Transcripts are kept for each student.

Enrollment Requirements Bachelor's degree required. English language proficiency required. Minimum TOEFL score required: 515.

Program Costs $2359 for the program (state residents); $5400 for the program (nonresidents).

Housing and Student Services Housing is not available. Job counseling and placement services are available.

Contact Dr. Robert Howell, Assistant Dean, 9555 Plainfield Road, Cincinnati, OH 45236. 513-745-5700.

BUSINESS AND MANAGEMENT, GENERAL (06.01)
Business Management

General Information   Unit offering the program: Clermont College, Business Division. Program content: Human resources management, administrative leadership, business communication, accounting, oral presentation, psychology. Available for credit. Certificate signed by the Dean, Clermont College. Certificate applicable to A.A.B. in Business Management Technology.

Program Format   Daytime, evening, weekend classes offered. Program cycle: Continuous enrollment. Completion of program requires 45 quarter units, 2.0 GPA.

Evaluation   Student evaluation based on tests, papers, reports. Grading system: Letters or numbers. Transcripts are kept for each student.

Enrollment Requirements   Program is open to non-resident foreign students.

Program Costs $2259 for the program.

Housing and Student Services   Housing is not available. Job counseling and placement services are available.

Contact   Mr. Dan Dell, Chair, Business Division, College Drive, Batavia, OH 45103. 513-732-5252.

BUSINESS AND MANAGEMENT, GENERAL (06.01)
Retail Management

General Information   Unit offering the program: Business. Program content: Economics, accounting, marketing, management, retailing, business law. Available for credit. Certificate signed by the College Dean.

Program Format   Daytime, evening classes offered. Program cycle: Continuous enrollment. Full program cycle lasts 3 quarters. Completion of program requires 48 quarter units, 2.0 GPA.

Evaluation   Student evaluation based on tests. Grading system: Letters or numbers. Transcripts are kept for each student.

Enrollment Requirements   Bachelor's degree required. Program is open to non-resident foreign students. English language proficiency required. Minimum TOEFL score required: 515.

Program Costs $2359 for the program (state residents); $5400 for the program (nonresidents).

Housing and Student Services   Housing is not available. Job counseling and placement services are available.

Contact   Dr. Robert Howell, Assistant Dean, 9555 Plainfield Road, Cincinnati, OH 45236. 513-745-5700.

COMPUTER PROGRAMMING (11.02)
Computer Programming

General Information   Unit offering the program: Math Department. Program content: Computer science, mathematics for computer logic, computer organization, data structures, assembly language, systems analysis, database management programming. Available for credit. Certificate signed by the College Dean.

Program Format   Daytime, evening classes offered. Program cycle: Continuous enrollment. Full program cycle lasts 5 quarters. Completion of program requires 55 quarter units (40 must be in computer science).

Evaluation   Student evaluation based on tests. Grading system: Letters or numbers. Transcripts are kept for each student.

Enrollment Requirements   Bachelor's degree required. Program is open to non-resident foreign students. English language proficiency required. Minimum TOEFL score required: 515.

Program Costs $2359 for the program (state residents); $5400 for the program (nonresidents).

Housing and Student Services   Housing is not available. Job counseling and placement services are available.

Contact   Dr. Robert Howell, Assistant Dean, 9555 Plainfield Road, Cincinnati, OH 45236. 513-745-3707.

COMPUTER PROGRAMMING (11.02)
Computer Programming Professional Certificate

General Information   Unit offering the program: Math and Applied Sciences. Program content: Data processing, calculus, speech, technical writing. Available on either a credit or non-credit basis. Certificate signed by the Dean of University College. Certificate applicable to A.A.B. in Computer Programming Technology.

Program Format   Daytime classes offered. Program cycle: Continuous enrollment. Full program cycle lasts 3 quarters. Completion of program requires 48 quarter units.

Evaluation   Student evaluation based on tests, reports. Grading system: Letters or numbers. Transcripts are kept for each student.

Enrollment Requirements   Bachelor's degree required. Program is open to non-resident foreign students. English language proficiency required.

Housing and Student Services   Housing is available. Job counseling and placement services are available.

Contact   Mr. James Maratta, Department Head, Mail location 168, Cincinnati, OH 45221. 513-475-5770.

COMPUTER PROGRAMMING (11.02)
Computer Programming Technical Certificate

General Information   Unit offering the program: Math and Applied Sciences. Program content: Data processing, college algebra, statistics, economics, accounting, English. Available on either a credit or non-credit basis. Certificate signed by the Dean of University College. Certificate applicable to A.A.B. in Computer Programming Technology.

Program Format   Daytime classes offered. Program cycle: Continuous enrollment. Full program cycle lasts 3 quarters. Completion of program requires 48 quarter units.

Evaluation   Student evaluation based on tests, papers, reports. Grading system: Letters or numbers. Transcripts are kept for each student.

Enrollment Requirements   High school diploma required. Program is open to non-resident foreign students. English language proficiency required.

Housing and Student Services   Housing is available. Job counseling and placement services are available.

Contact   Mr. James Maratta, Department Head, Mail location 168, Cincinnati, OH 45221. 513-475-5770.

DATA PROCESSING (11.03)
Computer Operations

General Information   Unit offering the program: Clermont College, Business Division. Program content: Information processing, accounting, VAX, applications, programming, technical writing. Available for credit. Certificate signed by the Dean, Clermont College. Certificate applicable to A.A.B. in Computer Programming Technology.

Program Format   Daytime, evening, weekend classes offered. Program cycle: Continuous enrollment. Full program cycle lasts 3 quarters. Completion of program requires 47–49 quarter units.

Evaluation   Student evaluation based on tests, papers, reports. Grading system: Letters or numbers. Transcripts are kept for each student.

Enrollment Requirements   Program is open to non-resident foreign students.

Program Costs $2259 for the program.

Computer Operations continued

Housing and Student Services   Housing is not available. Job counseling and placement services are available.

Contact   Mr. Dan Dell, Chair, Business Division, College Drive, Batavia, OH 45103. 513-732-5252.

GENERAL MARKETING (08.07)
Sales/Marketing

General Information   Unit offering the program: Business. Program content: Marketing, management, public relations, finance, selling, economics, accounting, business law, advertising, computers. Available for credit. Certificate signed by the College Dean.

Program Format   Daytime, evening classes offered. Program cycle: Continuous enrollment. Full program cycle lasts 3 quarters. Completion of program requires 51 quarter units, 2.0 GPA.

Evaluation   Student evaluation based on tests. Grading system: Letters or numbers. Transcripts are kept for each student.

Enrollment Requirements   Bachelor's degree required. Program is open to non-resident foreign students. English language proficiency required. Minimum TOEFL score required: 515.

Program Costs $2359 for the program (state residents); $5400 for the program (nonresidents).

Housing and Student Services   Housing is not available. Job counseling and placement services are available.

Contact   Dr. Robert Howell, Assistant Dean, 9555 Plainfield Road, Cincinnati, OH 45236. 513-745-5700.

GRAPHIC AND PRINTING COMMUNICATIONS (48.02)
Commercial Art

General Information   Unit offering the program: History. Program content: Layout, illustration, lettering, package design, photography, promotion design. Available for credit. Certificate signed by the College Dean.

Program Format   Daytime, evening classes offered. Program cycle: Continuous enrollment. Full program cycle lasts 2 years. Completion of program requires 41 quarter units, 2.0 GPA. Students who have not earned their bachelor's degree in art must complete an additional 15 quarter hours in drawing and art history.

Evaluation   Student evaluation based on tests. Grading system: Letters or numbers. Transcripts are kept for each student.

Enrollment Requirements   Bachelor's degree required. Program is open to non-resident foreign students. English language proficiency required. Minimum TOEFL score required: 515.

Program Costs $2359 for the program (state residents); $5400 for the program (nonresidents).

Housing and Student Services   Housing is available. Job counseling and placement services are available.

Contact   Dr. Robert Howell, Assistant Dean, 9555 Plainfield Road, Cincinnati, OH 45236. 513-745-5700.

INDUSTRIAL PRODUCTION TECHNOLOGIES (15.06)
Facilities Planning

General Information   Unit offering the program: Industrial Engineering Technology Program. Program content: Plant equipment, department, and layout. Available for credit. Certificate signed by the Dean. Certificate applicable to A.A.S. in Industrial Engineering Technology.

Program Format   individualized study method. Instructional schedule: Student selects schedule. Program cycle: Continuous enrollment. Full program cycle lasts 2 quarters.

Evaluation   Student evaluation based on tests, papers, reports. Grading system: Letters or numbers. Transcripts are kept for each student.

Enrollment Requirements   High school diploma or GED required. Program is open to non-resident foreign students. English language proficiency required.

Program Costs $63 per quarter hour, $753 per quarter.

Housing and Student Services   Housing is not available. Job counseling and placement services are available.

Special Features   The program is administered under the individualized study system. All materials and equipment are located in a learning center, and students may use this resource during day and evening hours and four hours on Saturdays.

Contact   Industrial Engineering Technology Program, Clermont College, College Drive, Batavia, OH 45103. 513-732-5200.

INDUSTRIAL PRODUCTION TECHNOLOGIES (15.06)
Methods Study

General Information   Unit offering the program: Industrial Engineering Technology Program. Program content: Operations analysis and work measurement. Available for credit. Certificate signed by the Dean. Certificate applicable to A.A.S. in Industrial Engineering Technology.

Program Format   individualized study method. Instructional schedule: Student selects schedule. Program cycle: Continuous enrollment. Full program cycle lasts 2 quarters.

Evaluation   Student evaluation based on tests, papers, reports. Grading system: Letters or numbers. Transcripts are kept for each student.

Enrollment Requirements   High school diploma or GED required. Program is open to non-resident foreign students. English language proficiency required.

Program Costs $63 per quarter hour, $753 per quarter.

Housing and Student Services   Housing is not available. Job counseling and placement services are available.

Special Features   The program is administered under the individualized study system. All materials and equipment are located in a learning center, and students may use this resource during day and evening hours and four hours on Saturdays.

Contact   Industrial Engineering Technology Program, Clermont College, College Drive, Batavia, OH 45103. 513-732-5200.

INDUSTRIAL PRODUCTION TECHNOLOGIES (15.06)
Production Planning

General Information   Unit offering the program: Industrial Engineering Technology Program. Program content: Production and inventory control. Available for credit. Certificate signed by the Dean. Certificate applicable to A.A.S. in Industrial Engineering Technology.

Program Format   individualized study method. Instructional schedule: Student selects schedule. Program cycle: Continuous enrollment. Full program cycle lasts 2 quarters.

Evaluation   Student evaluation based on tests, papers, reports. Grading system: Letters or numbers. Transcripts are kept for each student.

Enrollment Requirements   High school diploma or GED required. Program is open to non-resident foreign students. English language proficiency required.

Program Costs $63 per quarter hour, $753 per quarter.

Housing and Student Services   Housing is not available. Job counseling and placement services are available.

Special Features   The program is administered under the individualized study system. All materials and equipment are located in a learning center, and students may use this resource during day and evening hours and four hours on Saturdays.

Contact Industrial Engineering Technology Program, Clermont College, College Drive, Batavia, OH 45103. 513-732-5200.

LAW (22.01)
Legal Assisting (Paralegal) Professional Certificate

General Information Unit offering the program: Business Technologies. Program content: Legal principles, litigation, estates and probate, tax law, domestic relations, debt collection practices. Available on either a credit or non-credit basis. Certificate signed by the Dean of University College. Certificate applicable to A.A.B. in Legal Assisting (Paralegal) Technology.

Program Format Daytime classes offered. Program cycle: Continuous enrollment. Full program cycle lasts 3 quarters. Completion of program requires 45 quarter units.

Evaluation Student evaluation based on tests, papers, reports. Grading system: Letters or numbers. Transcripts are kept for each student.

Enrollment Requirements Bachelor's degree, 3.0 GPA required. Program is open to non-resident foreign students. English language proficiency required.

Housing and Student Services Housing is available. Job counseling and placement services are available.

Contact Mr. Herman Pfaltzgraff, Department Head, Mail location 207, Cincinnati, OH 45221. 513-475-3227.

LIBRARY SCIENCE (25.04)
Library/Instructional Media

General Information Unit offering the program: Library. Program content: Library technology, technical services, on-line systems, audiovisual equipment, microcomputer office applications. Available for credit. Certificate signed by the College Dean.

Program Format Daytime, evening classes offered. Program cycle: Continuous enrollment. Full program cycle lasts 3 quarters. Completion of program requires 45 quarter units, 2.0 GPA.

Evaluation Student evaluation based on tests. Grading system: Letters or numbers. Transcripts are kept for each student.

Enrollment Requirements Bachelor's degree required. Program is open to non-resident foreign students. English language proficiency required. Minimum TOEFL score required: 515.

Program Costs $2359 for the program (state residents); $5400 for the program (nonresidents).

Housing and Student Services Housing is not available. Job counseling and placement services are available.

Contact Dr. Robert Howell, Assistant Dean, 9555 Plainfield Road, Cincinnati, OH 45236. 513-745-5700.

MECHANICAL AND RELATED TECHNOLOGIES (15.08)
Automation Software Professional Certificate

General Information Unit offering the program: Math and Applied Sciences. Program content: Electrical circuits, electronics, equipment repair, computer electronics, computer programming, manufacturing methods, robotics. Available on either a credit or non-credit basis. Certificate signed by the Dean of University College. Certificate applicable to A.A.B. in Automated Software Technology.

Program Format Daytime classes offered. Program cycle: Continuous enrollment. Full program cycle lasts 3 quarters. Completion of program requires 45 quarter units.

Evaluation Student evaluation based on tests, papers, reports. Grading system: Letters or numbers. Transcripts are kept for each student.

Enrollment Requirements Bachelor's degree, 2.5 GPA required. Program is open to non-resident foreign students. English language proficiency required.

Housing and Student Services Housing is available. Job counseling and placement services are available.

Contact Mr. James Maratta, Department Head, Mail location 168, Cincinnati, OH 45221. 513-475-5770.

OFFICE SUPERVISION AND MANAGEMENT (07.04)
Office Services Management

General Information Unit offering the program: Clermont College, Business Division. Program content: Typing, office machines, business documentation, management. Available for credit. Certificate signed by the Dean, Clermont College. Certificate applicable to A.A.B. in Business and Office Administration.

Program Format Daytime, evening classes offered. Program cycle: Continuous enrollment. Completion of program requires 45 quarter units, 2.0 GPA.

Evaluation Student evaluation based on tests, papers, reports. Grading system: Letters or numbers. Transcripts are kept for each student.

Enrollment Requirements Program is open to non-resident foreign students.

Program Costs $2259 for the program.

Housing and Student Services Housing is not available. Job counseling and placement services are available.

Contact Mr. Dan Dell, Chair, Business Division, College Drive, Batavia, OH 45103. 513-732-5252.

PHYSICAL SCIENCE TECHNOLOGIES (41.03)
Industrial Laboratory Technology (General Option)

General Information Unit offering the program: Chemistry. Program content: Chemical analysis, biological lab techniques, organic chemistry, microbiology, histology, computer science, laboratory technology orientation. Available for credit. Certificate signed by the College Dean.

Program Format Daytime classes offered. Program cycle: Continuous enrollment. Full program cycle lasts 3 quarters. Completion of program requires 45 quarter units, 2.0 GPA.

Evaluation Student evaluation based on tests. Grading system: Letters or numbers. Transcripts are kept for each student.

Enrollment Requirements Bachelor's degree required. Program is open to non-resident foreign students. English language proficiency required. Minimum TOEFL score required: 515.

Program Costs $2359 for the program (state residents); $5400 for the program (nonresidents).

Housing and Student Services Housing is not available. Job counseling and placement services are available.

Contact Dr. Robert Howell, Assistant Dean, 9555 Plainfield Road, Cincinnati, OH 45236. 513-745-5700.

REAL ESTATE (06.17)
Real Estate

General Information Unit offering the program: Business. Program content: Brokerage, law, finance, appraising, economics, accounting, marketing. Available for credit. Certificate signed by the College Dean.

Program Format Daytime, evening classes offered. Program cycle: Continuous enrollment. Full program cycle lasts 3 quarters. Completion of program requires 48 credit hours, 2.0 GPA.

Evaluation Student evaluation based on tests. Grading system: Letters or numbers. Transcripts are kept for each student.

Enrollment Requirements Bachelor's degree required. Program is open to non-resident foreign students. English language proficiency required. Minimum TOEFL score required: 515.

Real Estate continued

Program Costs $2359 for the program (state residents); $5400 for the program (nonresidents).

Housing and Student Services Housing is not available.

Contact Dr. Robert Howell, Assistant Dean, 9555 Plainfield Road, Cincinnati, OH 45236. 513-745-5700.

REAL ESTATE (06.17)
Real Estate Certificate

General Information Unit offering the program: Business Division. Program content: Law, appraisal, finance, business law, management, selling, accounting. Available for credit. Certificate signed by the Dean of Clermont College.

Program Format Daytime, evening, weekend classes offered. Program cycle: Continuous enrollment. Completion of program requires 45 quarter units, 2.0 GPA.

Evaluation Student evaluation methods vary by course. Grading system: Letters or numbers. Transcripts are kept for each student.

Enrollment Requirements Program is open to non-resident foreign students.

Program Costs $2259 for the program.

Housing and Student Services Housing is not available. Job counseling and placement services are available.

Contact Mr. Dan Dell, Chair, Business Division, College Drive, Batavia, OH 45103. 513-732-5252.

SECRETARIAL AND RELATED PROGRAMS (07.06)
Medical Transcription Technology

General Information Unit offering the program: Office Administration. Program content: English, typing, medical front office management, machine and medical transcription, medical terminology, survey of anatomy and physiology, word processing. Available for credit. Certificate signed by the College Dean. Certificate applicable to A.A.B. in Office Administration.

Program Format Daytime, evening classes offered. Program cycle: Continuous enrollment. Full program cycle lasts 3 quarters. Completion of program requires 51 quarter units, 2.0 GPA.

Evaluation Student evaluation based on tests. Grading system: Letters or numbers. Transcripts are kept for each student.

Enrollment Requirements High school diploma or GED required. Program is open to non-resident foreign students. English language proficiency required. Minimum TOEFL score required: 515.

Program Costs $2359 for the program (state residents); $5400 for the program (nonresidents).

Housing and Student Services Housing is not available. Job counseling and placement services are available.

Contact Dr. Robert Howell, Assistant Dean, 9555 Plainfield Road, Cincinnati, OH 45236. 513-745-5700.

TEACHER EDUCATION, SPECIFIC SUBJECT AREAS (13.13)
Orff-Schulwerk Certification Program–Level I, II, III

General Information Unit offering the program: Continuing Education, Division of Music Education. Program content: Philosophy and pedagogy of the Orff-Schulwerk process. Available on either a credit or non-credit basis. Endorsed by American Orff-Schulwerk Association. Certificate signed by the Chairperson, Division of Music Education. Certificate applicable to master's degree in music education (Orff cognate).

Program Format Daytime classes offered. Instructional schedule: 8:30 a.m. to 4:30 p.m., two weeks in the summer. Students enroll in the summer. Complete program cycle lasts three summers.

Evaluation Student evaluation based on tests, papers, practicum, homework assignments. Grading system: Letters or numbers. Transcripts are kept for each student.

Enrollment Requirements Limited to those with degree in music education or certification to teach K–12 music. Program is open to non-resident foreign students.

Program Costs $270–$534 per course.

Housing and Student Services Housing is available. Job counseling and placement services are not available.

Special Features University of Cincinnati's Orff-Schulwerk faculty consists of nationally known clinicians, most of whom have served as organizers of American Orff-Schulwerk Association. The College-Conservatory of Music provides well-equipped, air-conditioned facility located close to downtown Cincinnati, providing workshop participants with opportunities to hear music and attend festivals sponsored by variety of ethnic groups throughout the summer.

Contact Ms. Rene Boyer-White, Director, Orff-Schulwerk Certification Program, College-Conservatory of Music, Cincinnati, OH 45221. 513-475-4409.

WOMEN'S STUDIES (30.07)
Women's Studies

General Information Unit offering the program: History. Program content: Women in society, literature, and the business world; sexual behavior; philosophy of women. Available for credit. Certificate signed by the College Dean.

Program Format Daytime, evening classes offered. Program cycle: Continuous enrollment. Full program cycle lasts 3 quarters. Completion of program requires 45 quarter units.

Evaluation Student evaluation based on tests, papers. Grading system: Letters or numbers. Transcripts are kept for each student.

Enrollment Requirements High school diploma or GED required. Program is open to non-resident foreign students. English language proficiency required. Minimum TOEFL score required: 515.

Program Costs $2359 for the program (state residents); $5400 for the program (nonresidents).

Housing and Student Services Housing is not available. Job counseling and placement services are available.

Contact Dr. Robert Howell, Assistant Dean, 9555 Plainfield Road, Cincinnati, OH 45236. 513-745-5700.

WORD PROCESSING (07.08)
Office Automation

General Information Unit offering the program: Clermont College, Business Division. Program content: Typing, office machines, word processing, business communication, management. Available for credit. Certificate signed by the Dean, Clermont College. Certificate applicable to A.A.B. in Business and Office Administration.

Program Format Daytime, evening classes offered. Program cycle: Continuous enrollment. Full program cycle lasts 45 credit hours. Completion of program requires 45 quarter units, 2.0 GPA.

Evaluation Student evaluation based on tests, papers, reports. Grading system: Letters or numbers. Transcripts are kept for each student.

Enrollment Requirements Program is open to non-resident foreign students.

Program Costs $2259 for the program.

Housing and Student Services Housing is not available. Job counseling and placement services are available.

Contact Mr. Dan Dell, Chair, Business Division, College Drive, Batavia, OH 45103. 513-732-5252.

WORD PROCESSING (07.08)
Word Processing Technology

General Information Unit offering the program: Office Administration. Program content: English, machine transcription, typing, business communication, office systems, word processing. Available for credit. Certificate signed by the College Dean. Certificate applicable to A.A.B. in Office Administration.

Program Format Daytime, evening classes offered. Program cycle: Continuous enrollment. Full program cycle lasts 3 quarters. Completion of program requires 51 quarter units, 2.0 GPA.

Evaluation Student evaluation based on tests. Grading system: Letters or numbers. Transcripts are kept for each student.

Enrollment Requirements High school diploma or GED required. Program is open to non-resident foreign students. English language proficiency required. Minimum TOEFL score required: 515.

Program Costs $2359 for the program (state residents); $5400 for the program (nonresidents).

Housing and Student Services Housing is not available. Job counseling and placement services are available.

Contact Dr. Robert Howell, Assistant Dean, 9555 Plainfield Road, Cincinnati, OH 45236. 513-745-5700.

URSULINE COLLEGE
Pepper Pike, Ohio 44124

BUSINESS AND MANAGEMENT, GENERAL (06.01)
Women in Management

General Information Unit offering the program: Business Department. Program content: Business, communication skills, marketing, statistics, organizational behavior and the practice of management. Available for credit. Certificate signed by the President. Certificate applicable to A.A. in Business, B.A. in Business Administration.

Program Format Daytime, evening, weekend classes offered. Program cycle: Continuous enrollment. Full program cycle lasts 21 credit hours.

Evaluation Student evaluation based on tests, papers, reports. Grading system: Letters or numbers. Transcripts are kept for each student.

Enrollment Requirements College admissions required. Program is open to non-resident foreign students. English language proficiency required. Minimum TOEFL score required: 500.

Program Costs $3360 for the program, $480 per course.

Housing and Student Services Housing is available. Job counseling and placement services are available.

Special Features Women in Management sequence is a series of seven courses in business designed to acquaint women with basic principles of management. At least six of the seven courses must be taken at Ursuline. Taught by qualified business instructors.

Contact Mrs. Lindsay English, Chairman of the Business Department, 2550 Lander Road, Pepper Pike, OH 44124. 216-449-4200 Ext. 214.

COMPUTER AND INFORMATION SCIENCES, GENERAL (11.01)
Computer Science

General Information Unit offering the program: Computer Science. Program content: Introduction to computers, BASIC, systems analysis, academic internship. Available for credit. Certificate signed by the President. Certificate applicable to A.A. in Computer Science.

Program Format Daytime, evening classes offered. Program cycle: Continuous enrollment. Full program cycle lasts 24 credit hours.

Evaluation Student evaluation based on tests, reports, lab assignments. Grading system: Letters or numbers. Transcripts are kept for each student.

Enrollment Requirements College admissions required. Program is open to non-resident foreign students. English language proficiency required. Minimum TOEFL score required: 500.

Program Costs $3840 for the program, $480 per course.

Housing and Student Services Housing is available. Job counseling and placement services are available.

Special Features The Computer Science program is designed for those students who are completing or have completed an associate or baccalaureate concentration outside of the computer science area, but wish to develop an expertise in the computer field. At least six of the eight courses must be taken at Ursuline. Some limited credit for prior experience possible. Taught by qualified computer science instructors.

Contact Sr. Ann Gertrude Hill, OSU, Chairman of Computer Science, 2550 Lander Road, Pepper Pike, OH 44124. 216-449-4200 Ext. 261.

INDIVIDUAL AND FAMILY DEVELOPMENT (19.07)
Family Studies

General Information Unit offering the program: Division of Natural and Social Sciences. Program content: Nursing, philosophy, psychology, religious studies, sociology. Available for credit. Certificate signed by the President. Certificate applicable to B.A. in Family Studies.

Program Format Daytime, evening classes offered. Program cycle: Continuous enrollment. Full program cycle lasts 39 credit hours.

Evaluation Student evaluation based on tests, papers, reports, class participation, internship. Grading system: Letters or numbers. Transcripts are kept for each student.

Enrollment Requirements College admissions required. Program is open to non-resident foreign students. English language proficiency required. Minimum TOEFL score required: 500.

Program Costs $6240 for the program, $480 per course.

Housing and Student Services Housing is available. Job counseling and placement services are available.

Special Features This interdisciplinary program is designed to provide students with the knowledge and experience needed to understand the challenges of family living. Prior life experience credits may be awarded. Academic internship off campus in some family-related agency required. Taught by qualified instructors and headed by the chairman of the Department of Sociology.

Contact Mr. Gary Polster, Ph.D., Chairman of Department of Sociology, 2550 Lander Road, Pepper Pike, OH 44124. 216-449-4200 Ext. 229.

REHABILITATION SERVICES (17.08)
Art Therapy

General Information Unit offering the program: Art Department. Program content: Drawing, printing, sculpture, psychology, abnormal psychology, theories of personality. Available for credit. Endorsed by American Art Therapy Association. Certificate signed by the Director of Art Therapy Program.

Program Format Daytime, evening classes offered. Program cycle: Continuous enrollment. Full program cycle lasts 18 credit hours.

Art Therapy continued

Evaluation Student evaluation based on tests, papers, reports, observation, field work. Grading system: Letters or numbers. Transcripts are kept for each student.

Enrollment Requirements University admissions required. Program is open to non-resident foreign students. English language proficiency required. Minimum TOEFL score required: 500.

Program Costs $2880 for the program, $480 per course.

Housing and Student Services Housing is available. Job counseling and placement services are available.

Special Features The Art Therapy sequence is a series of undergraduate courses in art and psychology designed to introduce the student to field of art therapy and to prepare for graduate study. Some limited credit for prior experience is possible. Taught by instructors qualified in art and psychology and headed by a registered art therapist.

Contact Sr. Kathleen Burke, OSU, Director of Art Therapy, 2550 Lander Road, Pepper Pike, OH 44124. 216-449-4200 Ext. 275.

RELIGIOUS EDUCATION (39.04)
Religious Education

General Information Unit offering the program: Religious Studies. Program content: Doctrine, scripture, liturgy, sacraments, morality, methods. Available on either a credit or non-credit basis. Endorsed by Religious Education Office, Diocese of Cleveland. Certificate signed by the President. Certificate applicable to B.A. in Religious Studies.

Program Format Daytime, evening classes offered. Program cycle: Continuous enrollment. Full program cycle lasts 6 courses.

Evaluation Student evaluation based on tests, papers, reports, assignments. Grading system: Letters or numbers. Transcripts are kept for each student.

Enrollment Requirements College admissions required. Program is open to non-resident foreign students. English language proficiency required. Minimum TOEFL score required: 500.

Program Costs $1920 for the program.

Housing and Student Services Housing is available. Job counseling and placement services are available.

Special Features The Religious Education Program is designed to assist teachers in Catholic schools acquire diocesan certification in religion. A sequence of six courses is offered at the main campus as well as at selected off-campus sites. Taught by qualified religious studies instructors.

Contact Sr. Maureen McCarthy, OSU, Chairman of the Religious Studies Department, 2550 Lander Road, Pepper Pike, OH 44124. 216-449-4200 Ext. 249.

NUCEA MEMBER
WRIGHT STATE UNIVERSITY
Dayton, Ohio 45435

CITY, COMMUNITY, AND REGIONAL PLANNING (04.03)
Certificate in Urban Planning

General Information Unit offering the program: Geography. Program content: Technologies to describe, evaluate, and change urban environments; planning methods. Available for credit. Certificate signed by the Dean, College of Liberal Arts.

Program Format Daytime, evening classes offered. Program cycle: Continuous enrollment. Completion of program requires 22 credit hours, 2.0 GPA, portfolio, oral defense of project.

Evaluation Student evaluation based on tests, papers, reports. Transcripts are kept for each student.

Enrollment Requirements University admissions required. Program is open to non-resident foreign students.

Program Costs $60 per credit hour.

Special Features University's urban environment provides opportunities for student research.

Contact Dr. Kenji K. Oshiro, Chairer, Department of Geography, Colonel Glenn Highway, Dayton, OH 45435. 513-873-2845.

DRAMATIC ARTS (50.05)
Theatre Technology Certificate

General Information Unit offering the program: Theatre. Program content: Theatre technologies, professional standards. Available for credit. Certificate signed by the Dean, College of Liberal Arts. Certificate applicable to B.F.A. in Design/Technology.

Program Format Daytime classes offered. Program cycle: Continuous enrollment. Full program cycle lasts 1 year. Completion of program requires on-the-job training, 18 quarter units.

Evaluation Student evaluation based on tests, papers, portfolio, practicum. Transcripts are kept for each student.

Enrollment Requirements Bachelor's degree, portfolio required. Program is open to non-resident foreign students.

Program Costs $60 per quarter hour.

Housing and Student Services Job counseling and placement services are available.

Special Features Program emphasizes professional theatre production technique. Specific areas of study include costume, scenic, and stage property technology as well as scenic painting. Up-to-date equipment and opportunity to work with practicing professionals available. Productions include university and professional theatre, ballet, and opera.

Contact Chairer, Department of Theatre, Colonel Glenn Highway, Dayton, OH 45429. 513-873-3072.

ENGLISH AS A SECOND LANGUAGE (23.12)
Certificate in TESOL (Teaching English to Speakers of Other Languages)

General Information Unit offering the program: Department of English Language and Literatures. Available for credit. Certificate signed by the Dean, College of Liberal Arts.

Program Format Daytime, evening classes offered. Program cycle: Continuous enrollment. Completion of program requires five courses, 3.0 GPA, practicum.

Evaluation Student evaluation based on tests, papers, reports, exit exam, practicum. Transcripts are kept for each student.

Enrollment Requirements University admissions, completion of upper-division introductory linguistics course required. Program is open to non-resident foreign students.

Program Costs $240 per course.

Special Features Students may transfer up to two courses, subject to approval. Several practicum options are available, including a six-month internship in Japan for qualified students.

Contact Dr. Marguerite MacDonald, Director of TESOL/ESL, Colonel Glenn Highway, Dayton, OH 45435. 513-873-2470.

GEOGRAPHY (45.07)
Certificate in Cartography, Photogrammetry, and Remote Sensing

General Information Unit offering the program: Geography. Program content: Data collection, aerial and space photography, mapping and computer mapping. Available for credit. Certificate signed by the Dean, College of Liberal Arts. Certificate applicable to B.A. in Geography.

Program Format Daytime, evening classes offered. Program cycle: Continuous enrollment. Completion of program requires five courses, 2.0 GPA, portfolio.

Evaluation Student evaluation based on tests, papers, reports, portfolio. Grading system: Letters or numbers. Transcripts are kept for each student.

Enrollment Requirements University admissions required. Program is open to non-resident foreign students.

Program Costs $60 per credit hour.

Special Features Students have access to advanced equipment in the cartography and remote sensing laboratory. The geography department has a library of imagery to serve student needs, including standard aerial photography, aircraft photography, and satellite imagery.

Contact Dr. Kenji K. Oshiro, Chairer, Department of Geography, Colonel Glenn Highway, Dayton, OH 45435. 513-873-2845.

INDIVIDUAL AND FAMILY DEVELOPMENT (19.07)
Certificate in Gerontology

General Information Unit offering the program: College of Liberal Arts. Program content: Aging process, social and health policies, skills to work with older people. Available for credit. Certificate signed by the Dean, College of Liberal Arts.

Program Format Daytime, evening classes offered. Program cycle: Continuous enrollment. Completion of program requires five courses, 3.0 GPA, 200-hour practicum.

Evaluation Student evaluation based on tests, papers, reports, oral examination. Transcripts are kept for each student.

Enrollment Requirements University admissions required. Program is open to non-resident foreign students.

Program Costs $60 per credit hour.

Special Features Multidisciplinary program involves cooperative efforts of professionals from wide range of fields. Practicum allows students to test concepts and skills learned in the classroom in a work setting.

Contact Dr. Bela J. Bognar, Associate Professor of Social Work and Medicine in Society, Department of Sociology, Colonel Glenn Highway, Dayton, OH 45435. 513-873-2585.

SECRETARIAL AND RELATED PROGRAMS (07.06)
One-Year Certificate in Secretarial Technology

General Information Unit offering the program: Office Administration Technology–Secretarial. Available for credit. Certificate signed by the Dean of Lake Campus. Certificate applicable to A.A.B. in Secretarial Technology.

Program Format Daytime classes offered. Program cycle: Continuous enrollment. Full program cycle lasts 1 year. Completion of program requires 50 quarter units, 2.0 GPA.

Evaluation Student evaluation based on tests, papers, reports. Grading system: Letters or numbers. Transcripts are kept for each student.

Enrollment Requirements Program is open to non-resident foreign students. English language proficiency required.

Program Costs $2700 for the program, $54 per quarter hour.

Housing and Student Services Housing is not available. Job counseling and placement services are available.

Special Features Certificate program encompasses necessary office skills for entry-level secretarial positions while giving student well-rounded background in secretarial field. Students

completing certificate program well prepared to meet challenges of today's office world.

Contact Mr. H. Roger Fulk, Director, Office Administration Technology, Lake Campus, 7600 SR 703, Celina, OH 45822. 419-586-2365 Ext. 237.

TECHNICAL AND BUSINESS WRITING (23.11)
Certificate in Professional Writing

General Information Unit offering the program: Department of English Language and Literatures. Available for credit. Certificate signed by the Dean, College of Liberal Arts. Certificate applicable to B.A. in English, Communication.

Program Format Daytime, evening classes offered. Program cycle: Continuous enrollment. Complete program cycle lasts up to five quarters. Completion of program requires five courses, grade of B or better.

Evaluation Student evaluation based on writing assignments. Transcripts are kept for each student.

Enrollment Requirements University admissions required. Program is open to non-resident foreign students.

Program Costs $240 per course.

Special Features Students may transfer up to two courses, subject to approval. Persons employed in writing-related positions may apply for waiver of the internship, thereby reducing course requirements by one. Business, technical, journalism, and creative writing courses are included as possibilities within the program.

Contact Mr. Peter S. Bracher, Chairer, Department of English Language and Literatures, Colonel Glenn Highway, Dayton, OH 45435. 513-873-3136.

OKLAHOMA

HILLSDALE FREE WILL BAPTIST COLLEGE
Moore, Oklahoma 73153

BIBLE STUDIES (39.02)
Certificate in Bible

General Information Available for credit. Certificate signed by the President of the College.

Program Format Daytime, evening, correspondence classes offered. Students may enroll fall, spring. Full program cycle lasts 31 credit hours.

Evaluation Student evaluation based on tests, papers, reports. Grading system: Letters or numbers. Transcripts are kept for each student.

Enrollment Requirements Limited to ordained and licensed ministers over age 30. Program is open to non-resident foreign students.

Program Costs $1860 for the program, $180 per course.

Housing and Student Services Housing is available. Job counseling and placement services are available.

Special Features Certificate can be completed in residence, by correspondence, or through a combination of the two.

Contact Dr. Thomas L. Marberry, Vice President of Academic Affairs, P.O. Box 7208, Moore, OK 73153. 405-794-6661.

SOUTHWESTERN OKLAHOMA STATE UNIVERSITY
Weatherford, Oklahoma 73096

GRAPHIC AND PRINTING COMMUNICATIONS (48.02)
Commercial Art Certificate

General Information   Unit offering the program: Art. Program content: Painting, design, advertising layout, graphic techniques. Available for credit. Certificate signed by the President. Certificate applicable to Bachelor of Commercial Art.

Program Format   Daytime, evening classes offered. Program cycle: Continuous enrollment. Full program cycle lasts 60 credit hours. Completion of program requires 2.0 GPA.

Evaluation   Student evaluation methods vary by course. Grading system: Letters or numbers. Transcripts are kept for each student.

Enrollment Requirements   University admissions required. Program is open to non-resident foreign students.

Program Costs $1440–$1560 for the program, $24–$26 per credit hour.

Housing and Student Services   Housing is available. Job counseling and placement services are available.

Special Features   Courses taught by regular faculty. Program permits students to take a concentrated 60 hours in commercial art—and since they are the courses taught for the undergraduate and graduate programs, students can continue in a degree program, if they desire.

Contact   Mr. James Terrell, Chairman, Art Department, Weatherford, OK 73096. 405-772-6611.

SECRETARIAL AND RELATED PROGRAMS (07.06)
Business Proficiency Certificate

General Information   Unit offering the program: Office of Administration and Business Education. Program content: English, business math, typing, accounting, Displaywriter, WordStar. Available for credit. Certificate signed by the President. Certificate applicable to any four-year degree offered by the School of Business.

Program Format   Daytime, evening classes offered. Program cycle: Continuous enrollment. Full program cycle lasts 40 credit hours. Completion of program requires 2.0 GPA.

Evaluation   Student evaluation based on tests. Grading system: Letters or numbers. Transcripts are kept for each student.

Enrollment Requirements   University admissions required. Program is open to non-resident foreign students.

Program Costs $1440–$1560 for the program, $24–$26 per credit hour.

Housing and Student Services   Housing is available. Job counseling and placement services are available.

Special Features   Secretarial—emphasis in shorthand and information processing with special advisement available in 60-hour programs in medical and legal specialization; clerical—emphasis in accounting. Student may continue in degree program.

Contact   Dr. Amanda Copeland, Chairman, Office Administration/Business Education Department, Weatherford, OK 73096. 405-772-6611.

NUCEA MEMBER
UNIVERSITY OF OKLAHOMA
Norman, Oklahoma 73069

BUSINESS AND MANAGEMENT, GENERAL (06.01)
Economic Development Management Certificate Program

General Information   Unit offering the program: Center for Economic and Community Development. Available on either a credit or non-credit basis. Endorsed by Board of Regents of the American Economic Development Council. Certificate signed by the President.

Program Format   Daytime, weekend classes offered. Program cycle: Continuous enrollment. Complete program cycle lasts up to five years. Completion of program requires eight courses.

Evaluation   Student evaluation based on laboratory in management practice. Transcripts are kept for each student.

Enrollment Requirements   Limited to Economic Development Institute graduate or Certified Industrial Developer, or persons with eight years of unbroken experience in economic development. Program is open to non-resident foreign students. English language proficiency required.

Program Costs $3000–$5000 for the program, $300–$500 per course, $45–$200 facilities fee for each course.

Housing and Student Services   Housing is available. Job counseling and placement services are not available.

Contact   Ms. June Wilmot, Director, Center for Economic and Community Development, 1700 Asp Avenue, Norman, OK 73037. 405-325-3891.

OREGON

EUGENE BIBLE COLLEGE
Eugene, Oregon 97405

BIBLE STUDIES (39.02)
One Year Bible Certificate

General Information   Program content: Bible, theology. Available for credit. Certificate signed by the President. Certificate applicable to any four-year degree offered at the institution.

Program Format   Daytime, correspondence classes offered. Program cycle: Continuous enrollment. Complete program cycle lasts three quarters (on-campus), fourteen courses (correspondence). Completion of program requires 2.0 GPA.

Evaluation   Student evaluation based on tests, papers, reports. Grading system: Letters or numbers. Transcripts are kept for each student.

Enrollment Requirements   College admissions required. Program is open to non-resident foreign students. English language proficiency required. Students required to live on campus.

Program Costs $2625 for the program (on-campus); $1960 for the program (correspondence).

Housing and Student Services   Housing is available. Job counseling and placement services are not available.

Contact   Mr. Dennis Schmidt, Director of External Studies, 2155 Bailey Hill Road, Eugene, OR 97405. 503-345-8680.

NUCEA MEMBER
MARYLHURST COLLEGE
Marylhurst, Oregon 97036

RELIGIOUS MUSIC (39.05)
Music Ministry

General Information   Unit offering the program: Religion and Ministry Department, Music Department. Program content: Liturgy, music, practicum. Available for credit. Certificate signed by the Vice President for Academic Affairs.

Program Format   Daytime, evening, weekend classes offered. Program cycle: Continuous enrollment. Full program cycle lasts 45 credit hours.

Evaluation   Student evaluation based on papers, reports. Grading system: Letters or numbers. Transcripts are kept for each student.

Enrollment Requirements   Program is open to non-resident foreign students. English language proficiency required.

Program Costs $125 per credit hour.

Housing and Student Services   Housing is available. Job counseling and placement services are not available.

Special Features   Program intended to train lay people to be church professionals in the field of music ministry.

Contact   Ms. Elaine Kraft, SNJM, Chair, Religion and Ministry Department, Marylhurst, OR 97036. 503-636-8141 Ext. 351.

TELECOMMUNICATIONS (09.08)
Telecommunications Systems Management

General Information   Unit offering the program: Business and Management. Available for credit. Endorsed by Tektronix. Cosponsored by Pacific NW Bell. Certificate signed by the Chairman, Business and Management. Certificate applicable to B.S. in Business and Management.

Program Format   Evening, weekend classes offered. Instructional schedule: One evening per week. Program cycle: Continuous enrollment. Full program cycle lasts 1 year. Completion of program requires 24 credit hours, 240 classroom hours.

Evaluation   Student evaluation based on tests, papers, reports, oral presentations. Grading system: Letters or numbers. Transcripts are kept for each student.

Enrollment Requirements   Completion of prerequisite business courses or equivalent required. Program is open to non-resident foreign students.

Program Costs $3000 for the program, $375 per course.

Housing and Student Services   Housing is available. Job counseling and placement services are available.

Special Features   Telecommunication System Management (TSM) program is in third year of existence. Sponsors have included all major utilities in Portland area. Most certificate students have or are pursuing a degree. A TC certificate is available at the master's level.

Contact   Mr. Ronald W. Adams, Program Director, Telecommunications Systems Management, Marylhurst, OR 97036. 503-636-8141.

THEOLOGICAL STUDIES (39.06)
Certificate in Pastoral Ministries

General Information   Unit offering the program: Religion and Ministry Department. Program content: Theology, psychology, practicum, spirituality. Available for credit. Certificate signed by the Vice President for Academic Affairs.

Program Format   Evening, weekend classes offered. Instructional schedule: One evening per week. Program cycle: Continuous enrollment. Completion of program requires 22 core credits, electives.

Evaluation   Student evaluation based on papers, reports. Grading system: Letters or numbers. Transcripts are kept for each student.

Enrollment Requirements   Program is open to non-resident foreign students. English language proficiency required.

Program Costs $125 per credit hour.

Housing and Student Services   Housing is available. Job counseling and placement services are not available.

Special Features   Program intended to train lay people to be church professionals.

Contact   Ms. Elaine Kraft, SNJM, Chair, Religion and Ministry Department, Marylhurst, OR 97036. 503-636-8141 Ext. 351.

PACIFIC NORTHWEST COLLEGE OF ART, OREGON ART INSTITUTE
Portland, Oregon 97205

DESIGN (50.04)
Certificate Award Program (Design)

General Information   Unit offering the program: Extension Program. Program content: Choice of graphic, illustration, or computer design. Available on a non-credit basis. Certificate signed by the Director of the Extension Program. Certificate applicable to B.F.A.

Program Format   Evening, weekend classes offered. Instructional schedule: Once per week for three hours. Program cycle: Continuous enrollment. Complete program cycle lasts two to three years. Completion of program requires 90% attendance.

Evaluation   Student evaluation based on portfolio review. Grading system: Letters or numbers. Records are kept in Extension Office.

Enrollment Requirements   Portfolio required. Program is open to non-resident foreign students. English language proficiency required.

Program Costs $130 per course.

Housing and Student Services   Housing is not available.

Special Features   Open to all without prerequisite. Noncredit certificate awarded in fine arts and design. Must complete the required ten classes within a two-year period. Instructors hired for the quality of their work as artists, professionalism, and expertise in field of instruction. Certificate students have opportunity to work in studios of professional art college under guidance of working artists and designers.

Contact   Ms. Robyn P. Starbuck, Extension Program Director, 1219 SW Park Avenue, Portland, OR 97205. 503-226-0462.

FINE ARTS (50.07)
Certificate Award Program (Fine Arts)

General Information   Unit offering the program: Extension Program. Program content: Painting, print making, sculpture, photography, ceramics, drawing. Available on a non-credit basis. Certificate signed by the Director of the Extension Program. Certificate applicable to B.F.A.

Program Format   Evening, weekend classes offered. Instructional schedule: Once per week for three hours. Program cycle: Continuous enrollment. Full program cycle lasts 2 years. Completion of program requires 90% attendance.

Evaluation   Student evaluation based on portfolio review. Grading system: Letters or numbers. Records are kept in Extension Office.

Enrollment Requirements   Portfolio required. Program is open to non-resident foreign students. English language proficiency required.

Program Costs $130 per course.

Housing and Student Services   Housing is not available.

Certificate Award Program (Fine Arts) continued

Special Features Open to all without prerequisite. Noncredit certificates awarded in Fine Arts and Design. Must complete the required ten classes within a two-year period. Instructors hired for the quality of their work as artists, professionalism, and expertise in field of instruction. Certificate students have opportunity to work in studios of professional art college under guidance of working artists and designers.
Contact Ms. Robyn P. Starbuck, Extension Program Director, 1219 SW Park Avenue, Portland, OR 97205. 503-226-0462.

NUCEA MEMBER
SOUTHERN OREGON STATE COLLEGE
Ashland, Oregon 97520

BUSINESS ADMINISTRATION AND MANAGEMENT (06.04)
Western Arts Management Institute: Certificate of Arts Management

General Information Unit offering the program: Division of Continuing Education. Program content: Grant writing, marketing, management, law. Available on either a credit or non-credit basis. Endorsed by Arts Council of Southern Oregon. Certificate signed by the Director, Division of Continuing Education.

Program Format Daytime, evening classes offered. Students enroll in the summer. Full program cycle lasts 2 weeks. Completion of program requires eight courses, internship.

Evaluation Student evaluation based on reports. Grades given with credit option. Transcripts are kept for each student.

Enrollment Requirements Program is open to non-resident foreign students.

Program Costs $500 for the program, $80 per course, $145 internship fee.

Housing and Student Services Housing is available. Job counseling and placement services are not available.

Special Features WAMI is a two-week intensive course of study designed for arts administrators, museum and gallery directors, college faculty, nonprofit board members, and people interested in a career working with cultural organizations. WAMI provides training important to anyone involved with arts councils, performing arts groups, and exhibiting institutions.
Contact Mr. Donovan Gray, Director, Arts Council of Southern Oregon, 236 East Main, Ashland, OR 97520. 503-482-5594.

WESTERN BAPTIST COLLEGE
Salem, Oregon 97301

BIBLE STUDIES (39.02)
Biblical Studies Certificate

General Information Unit offering the program: Biblical Studies Department. Program content: Biblical literature and doctines, missiology, Christian life and witness, Bible study methods. Available for credit. Certificate signed by the College President. Certificate applicable to A.A., B.S. in Bible Studies.

Program Format Daytime classes offered. Full program cycle lasts 1 year. Completion of program requires 48 units, two quarters of field education.

Evaluation Student evaluation based on tests, papers, reports. Grading system: Letters or numbers. Transcripts are kept for each student.

Enrollment Requirements College admissions required. Program is open to non-resident foreign students. English language proficiency required. Minimum TOEFL score required: 500.
Program Costs $5157 for the program.
Housing and Student Services Housing is available. Job counseling and placement services are not available.
Contact Admissions, 5000 Deer Park Drive, SE, Salem, OR 97301-9392. 503-581-8600.

WILLAMETTE UNIVERSITY
Salem, Oregon 97301

LAW (22.01)
Certificate in Dispute Resolution

General Information Unit offering the program: Center for Dispute Resolution, College of Law. Program content: Solving conflict among people or organizations through client counseling, negotiation, mediation, arbitration, and trial advocacy. Available for credit. Certificate signed by the President. Certificate applicable to J.D.

Program Format Daytime, evening classes offered. Program cycle: Continuous enrollment. Full program cycle lasts 18 credit hours. Completion of program requires average grade of 70% or better.

Evaluation Student evaluation based on tests, papers, independent study, research projects. Grading system: Letters or numbers, pass/fail. Transcripts are kept for each student.

Enrollment Requirements Bachelor's degree required. Program is open to non-resident foreign students.

Program Costs $4860 for the program, $270 per credit hour.

Housing and Student Services Housing is not available. Job counseling and placement services are available.

Special Features Inaugurated in 1985, the program is open to law and nontraditional students holding undergraduate degrees. All classes are part of the regular law school curriculum, taught by law professors. Summer school features distinguished visiting faculty.
Contact Ms. Patricia E. Scheidt, Program Coordinator, Center for Dispute Resolution, 900 State Street, Salem, OR 97301. 503-370-6046.

PENNSYLVANIA

ALBRIGHT COLLEGE
Reading, Pennsylvania 19612

ACCOUNTING (06.02)
Certificate of Professional Studies in Accounting

General Information Unit offering the program: Office of Continuing Education. Program content: Accounting principles, auditing, fund accounting, taxation, cost accounting, business combinations. Available for credit. Certificate signed by the Dean of Continuing Education. Certificate applicable to B.S. in Accounting.

Program Format Evening classes offered. Program cycle: Continuous enrollment. Full program cycle lasts 36 credit hours. Completion of program requires 2.0 GPA.

Evaluation Student evaluation based on tests, papers, reports. Grading system: Letters or numbers. Transcripts are kept for each student.

Enrollment Requirements   High school and college transcripts required. Program is open to non-resident foreign students.

Program Costs $130 per credit hour.

Housing and Student Services   Housing is not available. Job counseling and placement services are available.

Special Features   The certificate programs were designed to provide an excellent collegiate educational experience and to award a certificate to those who find their personal or educational goals at this time do not include the traditional college degree. They are also attractive to individuals who may already have a degree and seek additional studies to complement their education.

Contact   Ms. Sylvia K. Kane, Coordinator of Evening Programs, Office of Continuing Education, P.O. Box 15234, Reading, PA 19612-5234. 215-921-2381 Ext. 203.

BUSINESS AND MANAGEMENT, GENERAL (06.01)
Certificate of Professional Studies in Business Management

General Information   Unit offering the program: Office of Continuing Education. Program content: Management principles, financial management, accounting, economics, organizational behavior, marketing, information systems and microcomputers, industrial relations. Available for credit. Certificate signed by the Dean of Continuing Education. Certificate applicable to B.S. in Business Administration.

Program Format   Evening classes offered. Program cycle: Continuous enrollment. Full program cycle lasts 36 credit hours. Completion of program requires 2.0 GPA.

Evaluation   Student evaluation based on tests, papers, reports. Grading system: Letters or numbers. Transcripts are kept for each student.

Enrollment Requirements   High school and college transcripts required. Program is open to non-resident foreign students.

Program Costs $130 per credit hour.

Housing and Student Services   Housing is not available. Job counseling and placement services are available.

Special Features   The certificate programs were designed to provide an excellent collegiate educational experience and to award a certificate to those who find their personal or educational goals at this time do not include the traditional college degree. They are also attractive to individuals who may already have a degree and seek additional studies to complement their education.

Contact   Ms. Sylvia K. Kane, Coordinator of Evening Programs, Office of Continuing Education, P.O. Box 15234, Reading, PA 19612-5234. 215-921-2381 Ext. 203.

COMPUTER AND INFORMATION SCIENCES, GENERAL (11.01)
Certificate of Professional Studies in Computer Science

General Information   Unit offering the program: Office of Continuing Education. Program content: Discrete mathematics, assembly language, computer organization, software engineering, algorithms, operating systems. Available for credit. Certificate signed by the Dean of Continuing Education. Certificate applicable to B.S. in Computer Science.

Program Format   Evening classes offered. Program cycle: Continuous enrollment. Full program cycle lasts 37 credit hours. Completion of program requires 2.0 GPA.

Evaluation   Student evaluation based on tests, papers, reports. Grading system: Letters or numbers. Transcripts are kept for each student.

Enrollment Requirements   High school and college transcripts required. Program is open to non-resident foreign students.

Program Costs $130 per credit hour.

Housing and Student Services   Housing is not available. Job counseling and placement services are available.

Special Features   The certificate programs were designed to provide an excellent collegiate educational experience and to award a certificate to those who find their personal or educational goals at this time do not include the traditional college degree. They are also attractive to individuals who may already have a degree and seek additional studies to complement their education.

Contact   Ms. Sylvia K. Kane, Coordinator of Evening Programs, Office of Continuing Education, P.O. Box 15234, Reading, PA 19612-5234. 215-921-2381 Ext. 203.

DATA PROCESSING (11.03)
Certificate of Professional Studies in Data Processing

General Information   Unit offering the program: Office of Continuing Education. Program content: Discrete mathematics, information systems and microcomputers, system development, assembly language, database management, computer organization, applications programming and file processing. Available for credit. Certificate signed by the Dean of Continuing Education. Certificate applicable to B.S. in Computer Science.

Program Format   Evening classes offered. Program cycle: Continuous enrollment. Full program cycle lasts 37 credit hours. Completion of program requires 2.0 GPA.

Evaluation   Student evaluation based on tests, papers, reports. Grading system: Letters or numbers. Transcripts are kept for each student.

Enrollment Requirements   High school and college transcripts required. Program is open to non-resident foreign students.

Program Costs $130 per credit hour.

Housing and Student Services   Housing is not available. Job counseling and placement services are available.

Special Features   The certificate programs were designed to provide an excellent collegiate educational experience and to award a certificate to those who find their personal or educational goals at this time do not include the traditional college degree. They are also attractive to individuals who may already have a degree and seek additional studies to complement their education.

Contact   Ms. Sylvia K. Kane, Coordinator of Evening Programs, Office of Continuing Education, P.O. Box 15234, Reading, PA 19612-5234. 215-921-2381 Ext. 203.

MARKETING MANAGEMENT AND RESEARCH (06.14)
Certificate of Professional Studies in Business Marketing

General Information   Unit offering the program: Office of Continuing Education. Program content: Marketing, management principles, market research, marketing management, financial management, economics, accounting. Available for credit. Certificate signed by the Dean of Continuing Education. Certificate applicable to B.S. in Business Administration.

Program Format   Evening classes offered. Program cycle: Continuous enrollment. Full program cycle lasts 36 credit hours. Completion of program requires 2.0 GPA.

Evaluation   Student evaluation based on tests, papers, reports. Grading system: Letters or numbers. Transcripts are kept for each student.

Enrollment Requirements   High school and college transcripts required. Program is open to non-resident foreign students.

Program Costs $130 per credit hour.

Housing and Student Services   Housing is not available. Job counseling and placement services are available.

Special Features   The certificate programs were designed to provide an excellent collegiate educational experience and to award a certificate to those who find their personal or educational

Certificate of Professional Studies in Business Marketing continued

goals at this time do not include the traditional college degree. They are also attractive to individuals who may already have a degree and seek additional studies to complement their education.

Contact   Ms. Sylvia K. Kane, Coordinator of Evening Programs, Office of Continuing Education, P.O. Box 15234, Reading, PA 19612-5234. 215-921-2381 Ext. 203.

ALVERNIA COLLEGE
Reading, Pennsylvania 19607

ACCOUNTING (06.02)
Certificate in Accounting

General Information   Unit offering the program: Continuing Education, Evening Division. Program content: Accounting, finance, cost accounting, economics, personal income tax, internal auditing, business law, modern management and business organization. Available for credit. Certificate signed by the President. Certificate applicable to B.A. in Accounting.

Program Format   Weekend classes offered. Instructional schedule: Once per week for three hours. Program cycle: Continuous enrollment. Completion of program requires 36 credit hours, 2.0 GPA.

Evaluation   Student evaluation based on tests, papers. Grading system: Letters or numbers. Transcripts are kept for each student.

Enrollment Requirements   High school diploma required. Program is open to non-resident foreign students. English language proficiency required. Minimum TOEFL score required: 500.

Program Costs $115 per credit hour.

Housing and Student Services   Housing is available. Job counseling and placement services are not available.

Special Features   Up to 9 credits may be transferred from another accredited institution.

Contact   Mr. Daniel A. Casciano, Director, Reading, PA 19607. 215-777-5411.

BANKING AND FINANCE (06.03)
Certificate in Banking and Finance

General Information   Unit offering the program: Continuing Education, Evening Division. Program content: Bank operations, business law, financial management, economics, dynamics of banking, finance, accounting, money and banking, modern management and business organization. Available for credit. Certificate signed by the President. Certificate applicable to B.A. in Banking and Finance.

Program Format   Weekend classes offered. Instructional schedule: Once per week for three hours. Program cycle: Continuous enrollment. Completion of program requires 36 credit hours, 2.0 GPA.

Evaluation   Student evaluation based on tests, papers. Grading system: Letters or numbers. Transcripts are kept for each student.

Enrollment Requirements   High school diploma required. Program is open to non-resident foreign students. English language proficiency required. Minimum TOEFL score required: 500.

Program Costs $115 per credit hour.

Housing and Student Services   Housing is available. Job counseling and placement services are not available.

Special Features   Up to 9 credits may be transferred from another accredited institution.

Contact   Mr. Daniel A. Casciano, Director, Reading, PA 19607. 215-777-5411.

BUSINESS ADMINISTRATION AND MANAGEMENT (06.04)
Certificate in Business Management/ Administration

General Information   Unit offering the program: Continuing Education, Evening Division. Program content: Management, business financial management, business law, data processing, marketing, economics, finance, accounting , modern management and business organization. Available for credit. Certificate signed by the President. Certificate applicable to B.A. in Business Management/Administration.

Program Format   Weekend classes offered. Instructional schedule: Once per week for three hours. Program cycle: Continuous enrollment. Completion of program requires 36 credit hours, 2.0 GPA.

Evaluation   Student evaluation based on tests, papers. Grading system: Letters or numbers. Transcripts are kept for each student.

Enrollment Requirements   High school diploma required. Program is open to non-resident foreign students. English language proficiency required. Minimum TOEFL score required: 500.

Program Costs $115 per credit hour.

Housing and Student Services   Housing is available. Job counseling and placement services are not available.

Special Features   Up to 9 credits may be transferred from another accredited institution.

Contact   Mr. Daniel A. Casciano, Director, Reading, PA 19607. 215-777-5411.

BEAVER COLLEGE
Glenside, Pennsylvania 19038

BUSINESS ADMINISTRATION AND MANAGEMENT (06.04)
Post-Baccalaureate Certificate in Business Administration

General Information   Unit offering the program: Department of Business Administration and Economics. Program content: Computers, economics, mathematics, business. Available for credit. Certificate signed by the Dean of Continuing Education. Certificate applicable to B.S. in Business Administration.

Program Format   Daytime, evening classes offered. Program cycle: Continuous enrollment. Full program cycle lasts 2 years. Completion of program requires 12 courses, average grade of C or better.

Evaluation   Student evaluation based on tests, papers, reports. Grading system: Letters or numbers. Transcripts are kept for each student.

Enrollment Requirements   Bachelor's degree required. Program is open to non-resident foreign students. English language proficiency required. Minimum TOEFL score required: 500.

Program Costs $390 per course.

Housing and Student Services   Housing is not available. Job counseling and placement services are available.

Special Features Credit for up to five courses may be granted based upon prior undergraduate work. Courses may be waived through CLEP, ACT-PEP, DANTES, and PONSI examinations and evaluations. The program meets the first-year M.B.A. requirements for many graduate schools. The program may be tailored to students' individual needs.

Contact Dr. William D. Biggs, Dean of Continuing Education, Glenside, PA 19038. 215-572-2998.

COMPUTER AND INFORMATION SCIENCES, GENERAL (11.01)
Post-Baccalaureate Certificate in Computer Science—Major

General Information Unit offering the program: Department of Computer Science. Available for credit. Certificate signed by the Dean of Continuing Education. Certificate applicable to B.S. in Computer Science.

Program Format Daytime, evening classes offered. Program cycle: Continuous enrollment. Full program cycle lasts 2 years. Completion of program requires 12 courses, average grade of C or better.

Evaluation Student evaluation based on tests, papers, reports. Grading system: Letters or numbers. Transcripts are kept for each student.

Enrollment Requirements Bachelor's degree required. Program is open to non-resident foreign students. English language proficiency required. Minimum TOEFL score required: 500.

Program Costs $390 per course.

Housing and Student Services Housing is not available. Job counseling and placement services are available.

Special Features Credit for up to five courses may be granted based upon prior undergraduate work. Courses may be waived through CLEP, ACT-PEP, DANTES, PONSI and challenge examinations and evaluations.

Contact Dr. William D. Biggs, Dean of Continuing Education, Glenside, PA 19038. 215-572-2998.

COMPUTER AND INFORMATION SCIENCES, GENERAL (11.01)
Post-Baccalaureate Certificate in Computer Science—Minor

General Information Unit offering the program: Department of Computer Science. Available for credit. Certificate signed by the Dean of Continuing Education. Certificate applicable to B.S. in Computer Science.

Program Format Daytime, evening classes offered. Program cycle: Continuous enrollment. Full program cycle lasts 1 year. Completion of program requires six courses, average grade of C or better.

Evaluation Student evaluation based on tests, papers, reports. Grading system: Letters or numbers. Transcripts are kept for each student.

Enrollment Requirements Bachelor's degree required. Program is open to non-resident foreign students. English language proficiency required.

Program Costs $390 per course.

Housing and Student Services Housing is not available. Job counseling and placement services are available.

Special Features Credit for up to two courses may be granted based upon prior undergraduate work. Courses may be waived through CLEP, DANTES, ACT-PEP, PONSI and challenge examinations and evaluations.

Contact Dr. William D. Biggs, Dean of Continuing Education, Glenside, PA 19038. 215-572-2998.

CEDAR CREST COLLEGE
Allentown, Pennsylvania 18104

COMPUTER AND INFORMATION SCIENCES, GENERAL (11.01)
Certificate in Computer Science

General Information Unit offering the program: Computer Science and Mathematics Departments. Program content: Computer programming, computer science, information science. Available for credit. Certificate signed by the Vice President for Academic Affairs.

Program Format Daytime, evening, weekend classes offered. Instructional schedule: One evening per week or alternate weekends. Program cycle: Continuous enrollment. Full program cycle lasts 27 credit hours. Completion of program requires 2.0 GPA.

Evaluation Student evaluation based on tests, papers, reports, class participation, presentations, final exam, computer lab work, programming. Grading system: Letters or numbers. Transcripts are kept for each student.

Enrollment Requirements Bachelor's degree required. Program is open to non-resident foreign students. English language proficiency required. Minimum TOEFL score required: 525.

Program Costs $3753 for the program, $417 per course.

Housing and Student Services Housing is not available. Job counseling and placement services are available.

Contact Continuing Education Office, Allentown, PA 18104. 215-437-4471 Ext. 355.

INDIVIDUAL AND FAMILY DEVELOPMENT (19.07)
Certificate Program in Social Gerontology

General Information Unit offering the program: Sociology/Gerontology. Program content: Biology, nursing, psychology, sociology. Available for credit. Certificate signed by the Vice President for Academic Affairs. Certificate applicable to any four-year degree offered at the institution.

Program Format Daytime, evening, weekend classes offered. Instructional schedule: One evening per week or alternate weekends. Program cycle: Continuous enrollment. Full program cycle lasts 21 credit hours. Completion of program requires 2.0 GPA.

Evaluation Student evaluation based on tests, papers, class participation, presentations, final exam. Grading system: Letters or numbers. Transcripts are kept for each student.

Enrollment Requirements Bachelor's degree required. Program is open to non-resident foreign students. English language proficiency required. Minimum TOEFL score required: 525.

Program Costs $2919 for the program, $417 per course.

Housing and Student Services Housing is not available. Job counseling and placement services are available.

Contact Continuing Education Office, Allentown, PA 18104. 215-437-4471 Ext. 355.

LAW (22.01)
Paralegal Studies Certificate

General Information Unit offering the program: Paralegal Studies Department. Program content: Communications, economics and business, mathematics, social sciences, paralegal studies. Available for credit. Endorsed by American Bar Association. Certificate signed by the Vice President for Academic Affairs. Certificate applicable to any four-year degree in liberal arts offered at the institution.

Program Format Evening, weekend classes offered. Instructional schedule: One evening per week or alternate

Paralegal Studies Certificate continued

weekends. Program cycle: Continuous enrollment. Full program cycle lasts 69 credit hours. Completion of program requires 2.5 GPA.

Evaluation Student evaluation based on tests, papers, class participation, presentations, final exam. Grading system: Letters or numbers. Transcripts are kept for each student.

Enrollment Requirements Bachelor's degree required. Program is open to non-resident foreign students. English language proficiency required. Minimum TOEFL score required: 525.

Program Costs $417 per course, $139 per credit hour.

Housing and Student Services Housing is not available. Job counseling and placement services are available.

Contact Mr. Gary M. Glascom, Program Director for Paralegal Studies, Allentown, PA 18104. 215-437-4471 Ext. 412.

NUCEA MEMBER
FRANKLIN AND MARSHALL COLLEGE
Lancaster, Pennsylvania 17604

ACCOUNTING (06.02)
Certificate of Achievement in Accounting

General Information Unit offering the program: Office of Continuing Education. Program content: Financial, cost, and managerial accounting; finance; auditing; taxes. Available for credit. Certificate signed by the President. Certificate applicable to A.A. in Business Administration.

Program Format Evening classes offered. Instructional schedule: One evening per week for three hours. Students may enroll September, February, June. Full program cycle lasts 27 credit hours.

Evaluation Student evaluation based on tests, papers. Grading system: Letters or numbers. Transcripts are kept for each student.

Enrollment Requirements High school diploma or equivalent required. Program is open to non-resident foreign students.

Program Costs $3240 for the program, $360 per course.

Housing and Student Services Housing is not available. Job counseling and placement services are not available.

Special Features The Certificate of Achievement in Accounting is not a professional license. It indicates that the successful student has been exposed to the proper foundations, perspectives, and skills required by the accounting profession. This background serves as excellent preparation for the various professional certification programs including the CPA and the CMA.

Contact Mr. Russ J. Burke, Director of Continuing Education, P.O. Box 3003, Lancaster, PA 17604-3003. 717-291-4001.

BANKING AND FINANCE (06.03)
Certificate of Achievement in Finance

General Information Unit offering the program: Office of Continuing Education. Program content: Business finance, investments, money and banking, economics, basic accounting, finite mathematics. Available for credit. Certificate signed by the President. Certificate applicable to A.A. in Business Administration.

Program Format Evening classes offered. Instructional schedule: One evening per week for three hours. Students may enroll September, February, June. Full program cycle lasts 24 credit hours.

Evaluation Student evaluation based on tests. Grading system: Letters or numbers. Transcripts are kept for each student.

Enrollment Requirements High school diploma or equivalent required. Program is open to non-resident foreign students.

Program Costs $2720 for the program, $340 per course.

Housing and Student Services Housing is not available. Job counseling and placement services are not available.

Special Features Certificate of Achievement in Finance program designed to provide sound theoretical and functional background to nature and mechanics of finance involving acquisition and management of money, assets, and investments.

Contact Mr. Russ J. Burke, Director of Continuing Education, P.O. Box 3003, Lancaster, PA 17604-3003. 717-291-4001.

BUSINESS AND MANAGEMENT, GENERAL (06.01)
Certificate of Achievement in Management

General Information Unit offering the program: Office of Continuing Education. Program content: Organizational management, business finance, marketing, basic accounting, composition, personnel management, industrial relations. Available for credit. Certificate signed by the President. Certificate applicable to A.A. in Business Administration.

Program Format Evening classes offered. Instructional schedule: One evening per week for three hours. Students may enroll September, February, June. Full program cycle lasts 24 credit hours.

Evaluation Student evaluation based on tests. Grading system: Letters or numbers. Transcripts are kept for each student.

Enrollment Requirements High school diploma or equivalent required. Program is open to non-resident foreign students.

Program Costs $2720 for the program, $340 per course.

Housing and Student Services Housing is not available. Job counseling and placement services are not available.

Special Features Certificate of Achievement in Management program is designed to provide a general introduction to management topics. The diversity of topics covered helps to insure a breadth of understanding so important in an age of increasing specialization.

Contact Mr. Russ J. Burke, Director of Continuing Education, P.O. Box 3003, Lancaster, PA 17604-3003. 717-291-4001.

BUSINESS DATA PROCESSING AND RELATED PROGRAMS (07.03)
Certificate of Achievement in Data Processing

General Information Unit offering the program: Office of Continuing Education. Program content: Data processing, communications, COBOL, RPG II. Available for credit. Certificate signed by the President.

Program Format Evening classes offered. Instructional schedule: One evening per week for three hours. Students may enroll September, February, June. Full program cycle lasts 27 credit hours.

Evaluation Student evaluation based on tests. Grading system: Letters or numbers. Transcripts are kept for each student.

Enrollment Requirements High school diploma or equivalent required. Program is open to non-resident foreign students.

Program Costs $3060 for the program, $340 per course.

Housing and Student Services Housing is not available. Job counseling and placement services are not available.

Special Features Prescribed data processing curriculum offers instruction in general principles of data processing, communications, and specifics of selected computer languages. Required courses include advanced-level work intended to provide broad understanding of major elements of data processing for business applications: data integrity, system utiltity, and efficient operation.

Contact Mr. Russ J. Burke, Director of Continuing Education, P.O. Box 3003, Lancaster, PA 17604-3003. 717-291-4001.

COMMUNICATIONS, GENERAL (09.01)
Certificate of Achievement in Communications

General Information Unit offering the program: Office of Continuing Education. Program content: Compostion, literary analysis, critical thinking, public address, persuasion. Available for credit. Certificate signed by the President. Certificate applicable to A.A. in Business Administration.

Program Format Evening classes offered. Instructional schedule: One evening per week for three hours. Students may enroll September, February, June. Full program cycle lasts 24 credit hours.

Evaluation Student evaluation based on tests, papers. Grading system: Letters or numbers. Transcripts are kept for each student.

Enrollment Requirements High school diploma or equivalent required. Program is open to non-resident foreign students.

Program Costs $2720 for the program, $340 per course.

Housing and Student Services Housing is not available. Job counseling and placement services are not available.

Special Features Certificate of Achievement in Communications program helps students improve abilities to sort, understand, apply, and share information. It permits students to tailor course selection to meet personal interests or goals. Students may prepare for further studies in the liberal arts, explore critically a particular literary or artistic genre, or gain experience in applying communication skills to business problems.

Contact Mr. Russ J. Burke, Director of Continuing Education, P.O. Box 3003, Lancaster, PA 17604-3003. 717-291-4001.

GENERAL MARKETING (08.07)
Certificate of Achievement in Marketing

General Information Unit offering the program: Office of Continuing Education. Program content: Marketing, sales, advertising, consumer behavior, communications, public address. Available for credit. Certificate signed by the President. Certificate applicable to A.A. in Business Administration.

Program Format Evening classes offered. Instructional schedule: One evening per week for three hours. Students may enroll September, February, June. Full program cycle lasts 24 credit hours.

Evaluation Student evaluation based on tests, papers. Grading system: Letters or numbers. Transcripts are kept for each student.

Enrollment Requirements High school diploma or equivalent required. Program is open to non-resident foreign students.

Program Costs $2720 for the program, $340 per course.

Housing and Student Services Housing is not available. Job counseling and placement services are not available.

Special Features Through the Certificate of Achievement in Marketing program, students are taught basic concepts in marketing, sales, and advertising as well as how to speak and write better. The knowledge acquired can be applied to any profit or nonprofit business or organization.

Contact Mr. Russ J. Burke, Director of Continuing Education, P.O. Box 3003, Lancaster, PA 17604-3003. 717-291-4001.

TRADE AND INDUSTRIAL SUPERVISION AND MANAGEMENT (06.20)
Certificate of Achievement in Supervision

General Information Unit offering the program: Office of Continuing Education. Program content: Supervisory and organization management, composition, professional and interpersonal communication, sociology. Available for credit. Certificate signed by the President. Certificate applicable to A.A. in Business Administration.

Program Format Evening classes offered. Instructional schedule: One evening per week for three hours. Students may enroll September, February, June. Full program cycle lasts 24 credit hours.

Evaluation Student evaluation based on tests, papers, reports. Grading system: Letters or numbers. Transcripts are kept for each student.

Enrollment Requirements High school diploma or equivalent required. Program is open to non-resident foreign students.

Program Costs $2720 for the program, $340 per course.

Housing and Student Services Housing is not available. Job counseling and placement services are not available.

Special Features Today's manager must deal not only with machine, monetary, and material resources but with human resources as well in an age of change, cultural diversity, and a more demanding and vocal work force. The study of supervision—behavioral theory in the workplace—has grown and been refined significantly as its essential and strategic impact on productivity is recognized.

Contact Mr. Russ J. Burke, Director of Continuing Education, P.O. Box 3003, Lancaster, PA 17604-3003. 717-291-4001.

NUCEA MEMBER
INDIANA UNIVERSITY OF PENNSYLVANIA
Indiana, Pennsylvania 15705

CRIMINAL JUSTICE (43.01)
Pennsylvania Municipal Police Officer

General Information Unit offering the program: School of Continuing Education. Program content: Firearms training, techniques of arrest, first aid and CPR, motor vehicle code, public safety. Available on a non-credit basis. Endorsed by Pennsylvania Municipal Police Officer's Education and Training Commission. Certificate signed by the Dean, School of Continuing Education. Program fulfills requirements for Pennsylvania Municipal Police Officer.

Program Format Daytime, evening, weekend classes offered. Program cycle: Continuous enrollment. Complete program cycle lasts twelve weeks (full-time) or ten months (part-time).

Evaluation Student evaluation based on tests. Grading system: Letters or numbers. Transcripts are kept for each student.

Enrollment Requirements High school diploma or equivalent, record without conviction required. Program is not open to non-resident foreign students. English language proficiency required. Minimum TOEFL score required: 500.

Program Costs $1500 for the program.

Housing and Student Services Housing is available. Job counseling and placement services are available.

Contact Mr. Gary M. Welsh, Director, Criminal Justice Training Center, Indiana, PA 15705. 412-357-3989.

KUTZTOWN UNIVERSITY OF PENNSYLVANIA
Kutztown, Pennsylvania 19530

BUSINESS AND MANAGEMENT, GENERAL (06.01)
Continuing Education Certificate Program— C.B.K. (Common Body of Knowledge) Program

General Information Unit offering the program: College of Business, Office of Continuing Education. Program content: Accounting, economics, statistics, mathematics, marketing,

Continuing Education Certificate Program—C.B.K. (Common Body of Knowledge) Program continued

computers. Available on a non-credit basis. Certificate signed by the President of the University.

Program Format Daytime, evening, weekend classes offered. Program cycle: Continuous enrollment. Full program cycle lasts 6 months. Completion of program requires eight 16-hour seminars, examination after each course.

Evaluation Student evaluation based on tests. Grading system: Pass/fail. Records are kept in Continuing Education Office.

Enrollment Requirements Program is open to non-resident foreign students.

Program Costs $1400 for the program, $175 per course.

Housing and Student Services Housing is not available. Job counseling and placement services are available.

Special Features Program designed for people interested in MBA whose undergraduate major did not provide them with the prerequisite business courses. Opportunity for highly motivated students to take short (16 hours) noncredit courses in accounting, economics, statistics, calculus, marketing, and microcomputer applications. Those who pass a 1-3 hour exemption exam after each short course are given a waiver of its undergraduate credit equivalent.

Contact Mr. Charles E. O'Loughlin, Dean of Continuing Education, Kutztown, PA 19530. 215-683-4250.

MORAVIAN COLLEGE
Bethlehem, Pennsylvania 18018

HUMAN RESOURCES DEVELOPMENT (06.06)
Human Resources Administration

General Information Unit offering the program: Division of Continuing Studies. Program content: Modern management practices in human resources field. Available for credit. Endorsed by American Society of Personnel Administrators, Lehigh Valley Chapter. Certificate signed by the President. Certificate applicable to B.A. in Management, Psychology.

Program Format Evening classes offered. Instructional schedule: Two evenings per week. Program cycle: Continuous enrollment. Full program cycle lasts 36 credit hours. Completion of program requires 2.0 GPA.

Evaluation Student evaluation based on tests, papers, reports. Grading system: Letters or numbers. Transcripts are kept for each student.

Enrollment Requirements College background or work experience in personnel field required. Program is not open to non-resident foreign students.

Program Costs $3888 for the program, $108 per credit hour.

Housing and Student Services Housing is not available. Job counseling and placement services are available.

Special Features Program consists of a combination of regular college credit courses and specialized professional courses also offered for college credit.

Contact Dr. Linda Heindel, Associate Dean, Division of Continuing Studies, Bethlehem, PA 18018. 215-861-1386.

INDIVIDUAL AND FAMILY DEVELOPMENT (19.07)
Gerontology

General Information Unit offering the program: Division of Continuing Studies. Program content: Psychological, sociological, biological foundations to understand elderly. Available for credit. Certificate signed by the President. Certificate applicable to B.A. in Sociology, Psychology.

Program Format Evening classes offered. Program cycle: Continuous enrollment. Full program cycle lasts 28 credit hours. Completion of program requires 2.0 GPA.

Evaluation Student evaluation based on tests, papers, reports. Grading system: Letters or numbers. Transcripts are kept for each student.

Enrollment Requirements College experience or work in gerontology required. Program is not open to non-resident foreign students.

Program Costs $3024 for the program, $108 per course.

Housing and Student Services Housing is not available. Job counseling and placement services are available.

Special Features The program was designed by Lehigh Valley professionals in the field of aging. A professional advisory group oversees and supports curriculum development and job placement opportunities.

Contact Dr. Linda Heindel, Associate Dean, Bethlehem, PA 18018. 215-861-1386.

JOURNALISM (MASS COMMUNICATIONS) (09.04)
Business Communication

General Information Unit offering the program: Division of Continuing Studies. Program content: Writing, art, business. Available for credit. Endorsed by International Association of Business Communicators, Lehigh Valley Chapter. Certificate signed by the President. Certificate applicable to B.A. in Journalism, Graphic Arts.

Program Format Evening classes offered. Program cycle: Continuous enrollment. Full program cycle lasts 28 credit hours. Completion of program requires 2.0 GPA.

Evaluation Student evaluation based on tests, papers, reports. Grading system: Letters or numbers. Transcripts are kept for each student.

Enrollment Requirements College experience, basic writing course required. Program is not open to non-resident foreign students.

Program Costs $3024 for the program, $108 per credit hour.

Housing and Student Services Housing is not available. Job counseling and placement services are available.

Special Features Very flexible program permitting emphasis through electives in graphic arts or writing.

Contact Dr. Linda Heindel, Associate Dean, Bethlehem, PA 18018. 215-861-1386.

NEUMANN COLLEGE
Aston, Pennsylvania 19014

ACCOUNTING (06.02)
Accounting

General Information Unit offering the program: Continuing Education. Program content: Financial, managerial, cost, and tax accounting; auditing. Available for credit. Certificate signed by the Assistant Vice President for Academic Affairs. Certificate applicable to any four-year degree offered at the institution.

Program Format Daytime, evening, weekend classes offered. Program cycle: Continuous enrollment. Completion of program requires 18 credit hours.

Evaluation Student evaluation based on tests, papers, reports. Grading system: Letters or numbers. Transcripts are kept for each student.

Enrollment Requirements High school diploma or GED required, students must be 21 years of age at completion of program. Program is not open to non-resident foreign students. English language proficiency required. Minimum TOEFL score required: 550.

Program Costs $155 per credit hour.

Housing and Student Services   Housing is not available. Job counseling and placement services are available.

Special Features   Program designed to assist adult students to achieve upward job mobility by earning college credits which lead to certificate. Credits obtained through CLEP tests and challenge examinations applicable. Neumann College's AIM Program, of which Accounting Certificate is a component, offers option of applying credits toward an associate and/or baccalaureate degree. Courses taught by college instructors.

Contact   Mr. Alfred Hanley, Ph.D., Director of Continuing Education, Aston, PA 19014. 215-459-0905.

BUSINESS AND MANAGEMENT, GENERAL (06.01)
General Business

General Information   Unit offering the program: Continuing Education. Program content: Management and organization, market theory and application, financial accounting, software application, economics, business policy. Available for credit. Certificate signed by the Assistant Vice President for Academic Affairs. Certificate applicable to any four-year degree offered at the institution.

Program Format   Daytime, evening, weekend classes offered. Program cycle: Continuous enrollment. Full program cycle lasts 28 credit hours.

Evaluation   Student evaluation based on tests, papers, reports. Grading system: Letters or numbers. Transcripts are kept for each student.

Enrollment Requirements   High school diploma or GED required, students must be 21 years of age at completion of program. Program is not open to non-resident foreign students. English language proficiency required. Minimum TOEFL score required: 550.

Program Costs $155 per credit hour.

Housing and Student Services   Housing is not available. Job counseling and placement services are available.

Special Features   Program designed to assist adult students to achieve upward job mobility by earning college credits which lead to certificate. Credits obtained through CLEP tests and challenge exams applicable. Neumann College's AIM Program, of which the General Business Certificate is a component, offers option of applying credits toward an associate and/or baccalaureate degree. Courses taught by college instructors.

Contact   Mr. Alfred Hanley, Ph.D., Director of Continuing Education, Aston, PA 19014. 215-459-0905.

GENERAL MARKETING (08.07)
Marketing

General Information   Unit offering the program: Continuing Education. Program content: Market research, retail marketing, consumer behavior, strategy/policy, promotion, sales force. Available for credit. Certificate signed by the Assistant Vice President for Academic Affairs. Certificate applicable to any four-year degree offered at the institution.

Program Format   Daytime, evening, weekend classes offered. Program cycle: Continuous enrollment. Full program cycle lasts 24 credit hours.

Evaluation   Student evaluation based on tests, papers, reports. Grading system: Letters or numbers. Transcripts are kept for each student.

Enrollment Requirements   High school diploma or GED required, students must be 21 years of age at completion of program. Program is not open to non-resident foreign students. English language proficiency required. Minimum TOEFL score required: 550.

Program Costs $155 per credit hour.

Housing and Student Services   Housing is not available. Job counseling and placement services are available.

Special Features   Program designed to assist adult students to achieve upward job mobility by earning college credits which lead to certificate. Credits obtained through CLEP tests and challenge exams are applicable. Neumann College's AIM Program, of which the Marketing Certificate is a component, offers the student the optionn of applying credits toward an associate and/or baccalaureate degree. Courses taught by college instructors.

Contact   Mr. Alfred Hanley, Ph.D., Director of Continuing Education, Aston, PA 19014. 215-459-0905.

HEALTH SERVICES ADMINISTRATION (18.07)
Health Care Administration

General Information   Unit offering the program: Continuing Education. Program content: Personnel administration, business management and organization, public policy, legal aspects, health planning. Available for credit. Certificate signed by the Assistant Vice President for Academic Affairs. Certificate applicable to any four-year degree offered at the institution.

Program Format   Daytime, evening, weekend classes offered. Program cycle: Continuous enrollment. Full program cycle lasts 24 credit hours.

Evaluation   Student evaluation based on tests, papers, reports. Grading system: Letters or numbers. Transcripts are kept for each student.

Enrollment Requirements   High school diploma or GED required, students must be 21 years of age at completion of program. Program is not open to non-resident foreign students. English language proficiency required. Minimum TOEFL score required: 550.

Program Costs $155 per credit hour.

Housing and Student Services   Housing is not available. Job counseling and placement services are available.

Special Features   Program designed to assist adult student to achieve upward job mobility by earning college credits which lead to certificate. Credits obtained through CLEP tests and challenge exams applicable. Neumann College's AIM Program, of which the Health Care Administration Certificate is a component, offers option of applying credits toward an associate and/or baccalaureate degree. Courses taught by college instructors.

Contact   Mr. Alfred Hanley, Ph.D., Director of Continuing Education, Aston, PA 19014. 215-459-0905.

HUMAN RESOURCES DEVELOPMENT (06.06)
Human Resource Development

General Information   Unit offering the program: Continuing Education. Program content: Organizational behavior, personnel, staffing, training, development, labor relations, compensation and benefits, appraisal and counseling. Available for credit. Certificate signed by the Assistant Vice President for Academic Affairs. Certificate applicable to any four-year degree offered at the institution.

Program Format   Daytime, evening, weekend classes offered. Program cycle: Continuous enrollment. Full program cycle lasts 24 credit hours.

Evaluation   Student evaluation based on tests, papers, reports. Grading system: Letters or numbers. Transcripts are kept for each student.

Enrollment Requirements   High school diploma or GED required, students must be 21 years of age at completion of program. Program is not open to non-resident foreign students. English language proficiency required. Minimum TOEFL score required: 550.

Program Costs $155 per credit hour.

Housing and Student Services   Housing is not available. Job counseling and placement services are available.

Special Features   Program designed to assist adult students to achieve upward job mobility by earning college credits which lead to certificate. Credits obtained through CLEP tests and challenge exams applicable. Neumann College's AIM Program,

Human Resource Development continued

of which Human Resource Development Certificate is a component, offers option of applying credits toward an associate and/or baccalaureate degree. Courses taught by college instructors.

Contact   Mr. Alfred Hanley, Ph.D., Director of Continuing Education, Aston, PA 19014. 215-459-0905.

INFORMATION SCIENCES AND SYSTEMS (11.04)
Computer and Information Management

General Information   Unit offering the program: Continuing Education. Program content: Database program development; analysis; problem solving in BASIC; software applications; information, computer, and office systems. Available for credit. Certificate signed by the Assistant Vice President for Academic Affairs. Certificate applicable to any four-year degree offered at the institution.

Program Format   Daytime, evening, weekend classes offered. Program cycle: Continuous enrollment. Full program cycle lasts 19 credit hours.

Evaluation   Student evaluation based on tests, papers, reports. Grading system: Letters or numbers. Transcripts are kept for each student.

Enrollment Requirements   High school diploma or GED required, students must be 21 years of age at completion of program. Program is not open to non-resident foreign students. English language proficiency required. Minimum TOEFL score required: 550.

Program Costs $155 per credit hour.

Housing and Student Services   Housing is not available. Job counseling and placement services are available.

Special Features   Program designed to assist adult students to achieve upward job mobility by earning college credits which lead to certificate. Credits obtained through CLEP tests and challenge exams applicable. Neumann College's AIM Program, of which the Computer and Information Management Certificate is a component, offers student option of applying credits toward an associate and/or baccalaureate degree. Courses taught by college instructors.

Contact   Mr. Alfred Hanley, Ph.D., Director of Continuing Education, Aston, PA 19014. 215-459-0905.

LIBERAL/GENERAL STUDIES (24.01)
Humanities

General Information   Unit offering the program: Continuing Education. Program content: Writing, literature, communications, art, English, languages, music, philosophy, religion. Available for credit. Certificate signed by the Assistant Vice President for Academic Affairs. Certificate applicable to any four-year degree offered at the institution.

Program Format   Daytime, evening, weekend classes offered. Program cycle: Continuous enrollment. Full program cycle lasts 27 credit hours.

Evaluation   Student evaluation based on tests, papers, reports. Grading system: Letters or numbers. Transcripts are kept for each student.

Enrollment Requirements   High school diploma or GED required, students must be 21 years of age at completion of program. Program is not open to non-resident foreign students. English language proficiency required. Minimum TOEFL score required: 550.

Program Costs $155 per credit hour.

Housing and Student Services   Housing is not available. Job counseling and placement services are available.

Special Features   Program designed to assist adult students to achieve upward job mobility by earning college credits which lead to a certificate. Credits obtained through CLEP tests and challenge exams applicable toward certificate. Neumann

College's AIM Program, of which Humanities Certificate is a component, offers student option of applying certificate credits toward associate and/or baccalaureate degree. Courses taught by college instructors.

Contact   Mr. Alfred Hanley, Ph.D., Director of Continuing Education, Aston, PA 19014. 215-459-0905.

PSYCHOLOGY, GENERAL (42.01)
Behavioral Science

General Information   Unit offering the program: Continuing Education. Program content: Human condition, statistics, behavioral science methods, life span development, psychology, sociology. Available for credit. Certificate signed by the Assistant Vice President for Academic Affairs. Certificate applicable to any four-year degree offered at the institution.

Program Format   Daytime, evening, weekend classes offered. Program cycle: Continuous enrollment. Full program cycle lasts 27 credit hours.

Evaluation   Student evaluation based on tests, papers, reports. Grading system: Letters or numbers. Transcripts are kept for each student.

Enrollment Requirements   High school diploma or GED required, students must be 21 years of age at completion of program. Program is not open to non-resident foreign students. English language proficiency required. Minimum TOEFL score required: 550.

Program Costs $155 per credit hour.

Housing and Student Services   Housing is not available. Job counseling and placement services are available.

Special Features   Program designed to assist adult students to achieve upward job mobility by earning college credits which lead to certificate. Credits obtained through CLEP tests and challenge exams applicable. Neumann College's AIM Program, of which the Behavioral Science Certificate is a component, offers the student the option of applying credits toward an associate and/or baccalaureate degree. Courses taught by college instructors.

Contact   Mr. Alfred Hanley, Ph.D., Director of Continuing Education, Aston, PA 19014. 215-459-0905.

PHILADELPHIA COLLEGE OF BIBLE
Langhorne, Pennsylvania 19047

BIBLE STUDIES (39.02)
Evening School Diploma

General Information   Unit offering the program: School of Continuing Education. Program content: Bible studies. Available on a non-credit basis. Certificate signed by the President.

Program Format   Evening classes offered. Instructional schedule: Three evenings per week. Program cycle: Continuous enrollment. Full program cycle lasts 4 years. Completion of program requires 48 credit hours, 2.0 GPA.

Evaluation   Student evaluation based on tests, papers, reports. Grading system: Letters or numbers. Transcripts are kept for each student.

Enrollment Requirements   Program is open to non-resident foreign students.

Program Costs $2200 for the program, $45 per course.

Housing and Student Services   Housing is not available. Job counseling and placement services are available.

Special Features   Classes taught by resident and adjunct faculty. Credit may be given for work taken elsewhere up to one-half of total CEUs. Evening School has been in operation since beginning of Philadelphia College of Bible.

Contact   Mr. David Smith, Director of Admissions and Records, Langhorne Manor, Langhorne, PA 19047. 215-752-5800.

NUCEA MEMBER
PHILADELPHIA COLLEGE OF TEXTILES AND SCIENCE
Philadelphia, Pennsylvania 19144

ACCOUNTING (06.02)
Accounting

General Information   Unit offering the program: Continuing Education. Program content: Accounting, business law, taxes, auditing. Available for credit. Certificate signed by the Dean, Continuing Education. Certificate applicable to B.S. in Accounting.

Program Format   Evening, weekend classes offered. Instructional schedule: One evening per week. Program cycle: Continuous enrollment. Complete program cycle lasts one to two years. Completion of program requires ten courses.

Evaluation   Student evaluation based on tests, papers, reports. Grading system: Letters or numbers. Transcripts are kept for each student.

Enrollment Requirements   Bachelor's degree required. Program is open to non-resident foreign students.

Program Costs $414 per course.

Housing and Student Services   Housing is not available. Job counseling and placement services are available.

Special Features   The Postbaccalaureate Program is intended to provide participants holding bachelor's degrees in other disciplines to broaden their educational background by studying in fields in which they anticipate employment or are currently employed. Students have access to all college resources and the most current theory and applications in the field.

Contact   Mr. Robert Cotter, Director, Information and Marketing, Philadelphia, PA 19144. 215-951-2900.

APPAREL AND ACCESSORIES MARKETING (08.01)
Apparel Management

General Information   Unit offering the program: Continuing Education. Program content: Survey of apparel and textile industry, production, quality control, merchandising management, technology of fabrication, flat pattern, basic construction. Available for credit. Certificate signed by the Dean, Continuing Education. Certificate applicable to B.S. in Apparel Management.

Program Format   Evening, weekend classes offered. Instructional schedule: One evening per week. Program cycle: Continuous enrollment. Complete program cycle lasts one to two years. Completion of program requires seven courses.

Evaluation   Student evaluation based on tests, papers, reports. Grading system: Letters or numbers. Transcripts are kept for each student.

Enrollment Requirements   Bachelor's degree required. Program is open to non-resident foreign students.

Program Costs $414 per course.

Housing and Student Services   Housing is not available. Job counseling and placement services are available.

Special Features   The Postbaccalaureate Program is intended to provide participants holding bachelor's degrees in other disciplines to broaden their educational background by studying in fields in which they anticipate employment or are currently employed. Students have access to all college resources and the most current theory and applications in the field.

Contact   Mr. Robert Cotter, Director, Information and Marketing, Philadelphia, PA 19144. 215-951-2900.

COMPUTER AND INFORMATION SCIENCES, GENERAL (11.01)
Computer Science

General Information   Unit offering the program: Continuing Education. Program content: Programming, COBOL, Pascal, algorithms and data structures, database management, assembly, computer organizations, calculus, statistics. Available for credit. Certificate signed by the Dean, Continuing Education. Certificate applicable to B.S. in Computer Science.

Program Format   Evening, weekend classes offered. Instructional schedule: One evening per week. Complete program cycle lasts one to two years. Completion of program requires 16 courses.

Evaluation   Student evaluation based on tests, papers, reports. Grading system: Letters or numbers. Transcripts are kept for each student.

Enrollment Requirements   Bachelor's degree required. Program is open to non-resident foreign students.

Program Costs $414 per course.

Housing and Student Services   Housing is not available. Job counseling and placement services are available.

Special Features   The Postbaccalaureate Program is intended to provide participants holding bachelor's degrees in other disciplines to broaden their educational background by studying in fields in which they anticipate employment or are currently employed. Students have access to all college resources and the most current theory and applications in the field.

Contact   Mr. Robert Cotter, Director, Information and Marketing, Philadelphia, PA 19144. 215-951-2900.

DATA PROCESSING (11.03)
Computer/Data Processing

General Information   Unit offering the program: Continuing Education. Program content: Introduction to information systems, programming, COBOL, systems analysis, database management, management information systems, simulation and modeling, applied management science, Pascal. Available for credit. Certificate signed by the Dean, Continuing Education. Certificate applicable to B.S. in Computer Science.

Program Format   Evening, weekend classes offered. Instructional schedule: One evening per week. Program cycle: Continuous enrollment. Complete program cycle lasts one to two years. Completion of program requires 11 courses.

Evaluation   Student evaluation based on tests, papers, reports. Grading system: Letters or numbers. Transcripts are kept for each student.

Enrollment Requirements   Bachelor's degree required. Program is open to non-resident foreign students.

Program Costs $414 per course.

Housing and Student Services   Housing is not available. Job counseling and placement services are available.

Special Features   The Postbaccalaureate Program is intended to provide participants holding bachelor's degrees in other disciplines to broaden their educational background by studying in fields in which they anticipate employment or are currently employed. Students have access to all college resources and the most current theory and applications in the field.

Contact   Mr. Robert Cotter, Director, Information and Marketing, Philadelphia, PA 19144. 215-951-2900.

ENTREPRENEURSHIP (08.03)
Entrepreneurship

General Information   Unit offering the program: Continuing Education. Program content: Introduction to information systems, management, marketing, finance, accounting, consumer behavior, business law, human resources, advertising, retail strategy, merchandise buying. Available for credit. Certificate signed by the Dean, Continuing Education. Certificate applicable to any four-year degree offered at the institution.

Entrepreneurship continued

Program Format Evening, weekend classes offered. Instructional schedule: One evening per week. Program cycle: Continuous enrollment. Complete program cycle lasts one to two years. Completion of program requires 14 courses.

Evaluation Student evaluation based on tests, papers, reports. Grading system: Letters or numbers. Transcripts are kept for each student.

Enrollment Requirements Bachelor's degree required. Program is open to non-resident foreign students.

Program Costs $414 per course.

Housing and Student Services Housing is not available. Job counseling and placement services are available.

Special Features The Postbaccalaureate Program is intended to provide participants holding bachelor's degrees in other disciplines to broaden their educational background by studying in fields in which they anticipate employment or are currently employed. Students have access to all college resources and the most current theory and applications in the field.

Contact Mr. Robert Cotter, Director, Information and Marketing, Philadelphia, PA 19144. 215-951-2900.

GENERAL MARKETING (08.07)
Fashion Merchandising

General Information Unit offering the program: Continuing Education. Program content: Introduction to information systems, marketing, consumer behavior, retail, buying, accounting, survey of textile and apparel industry, fabrics. Available for credit. Certificate signed by the Dean, Continuing Education. Certificate applicable to B.S. in Fashion Merchandising.

Program Format Evening, weekend classes offered. Instructional schedule: One evening per week. Program cycle: Continuous enrollment. Complete program cycle lasts one to two years. Completion of program requires 12 courses.

Evaluation Student evaluation based on tests, papers, reports. Grading system: Letters or numbers. Transcripts are kept for each student.

Enrollment Requirements Bachelor's degree required. Program is open to non-resident foreign students.

Program Costs $414 per course.

Housing and Student Services Housing is not available. Job counseling and placement services are available.

Special Features The Postbaccalaureate Program is intended to provide participants holding bachelor's degrees in other disciplines to broaden their educational background by studying in fields in which they anticipate employment or are currently employed. Students have access to all college resources and the most current theory and applications in the field.

Contact Mr. Robert Cotter, Director, Information and Marketing, Philadelphia, PA 19144. 215-951-2900.

INTERIOR DESIGN (04.05)
Interior Design

General Information Unit offering the program: Continuing Education. Program content: Math, fabrics, computer-aided design, art and design, color theory, drawing, architectural graphics, interior construction and materials presentation techniques, western art, history of architecture and interiors. Available for credit. Certificate signed by the Dean, Continuing Education. Certificate applicable to B.S. in Interior Design.

Program Format Evening, weekend classes offered. Instructional schedule: One evening per week. Program cycle: Continuous enrollment. Complete program cycle lasts one to two years. Completion of program requires 13–20 courses.

Evaluation Student evaluation based on tests, papers, reports. Grading system: Letters or numbers. Transcripts are kept for each student.

Enrollment Requirements Bachelor's degree required. Program is open to non-resident foreign students.

Program Costs $414 per course.

Housing and Student Services Housing is not available. Job counseling and placement services are available.

Special Features The Postbaccalaureate Program is intended to provide participants holding bachelor's degrees in other disciplines to broaden their educational background by studying in fields in which they anticipate employment or are currently employed. Students have access to all college resources and the most current theory and applications in the field.

Contact Mr. Robert Cotter, Director, Information and Marketing, Philadelphia, PA 19144. 215-951-2900.

MANAGEMENT SCIENCE (06.13)
M.B.A. Preparation

General Information Unit offering the program: Continuing Education. Program content: Information systems, management concepts, mathematical analysis, marketing, financial and managerial accounting, economic analysis. Available for credit. Certificate signed by the Dean, Continuing Education. Certificate applicable to any four-year degree offered at the institution.

Program Format Evening, weekend classes offered. Instructional schedule: One evening per week. Program cycle: Continuous enrollment. Complete program cycle lasts one to two years. Completion of program requires 7–12 courses.

Evaluation Student evaluation based on tests, papers, reports. Grading system: Letters or numbers. Transcripts are kept for each student.

Enrollment Requirements Bachelor's degree required. Program is open to non-resident foreign students.

Program Costs $414 per course.

Housing and Student Services Housing is not available. Job counseling and placement services are available.

Special Features The Postbaccalaureate Program is intended to provide participants holding bachelor's degrees in other disciplines to broaden their educational background by studying in fields in which they anticipate employment or are currently employed. Students have access to all college resources and the most current theory and applications in the field.

Contact Mr. Robert Cotter, Director, Information and Marketing, Philadelphia, PA 19144. 215-951-2900.

TEXTILES AND CLOTHING (19.09)
Fashion Design

General Information Unit offering the program: Continuing Education. Program content: Survey of textile and apparel industry, fabrics, art and design, fashion/figure drawing, flat pattern and construction design, draping and menswear design. Available for credit. Certificate signed by the Dean, Continuing Education. Certificate applicable to B.S. in Fashion Design.

Program Format Evening, weekend classes offered. Instructional schedule: One evening per week. Complete program cycle lasts one to two years. Completion of program requires 13 courses.

Evaluation Student evaluation based on tests, papers, reports. Grading system: Letters or numbers. Transcripts are kept for each student.

Enrollment Requirements Bachelor's degree required. Program is open to non-resident foreign students.

Program Costs $414 per course.

Housing and Student Services Housing is not available. Job counseling and placement services are available.

Special Features The Postbaccalaureate Program is intended to provide participants holding bachelor's degrees in other disciplines to broaden their educational background by studying in fields in which they anticipate employment or are currently employed. Students have access to all college resources and the most current theory and applications in the field.

Contact Mr. Robert Cotter, Director, Information and Marketing, Philadelphia, PA 19144. 215-951-2900.

TEXTILES AND CLOTHING (19.09)
Textile Design

General Information Unit offering the program: Continuing Education. Program content: Printing, weaving, or knitting. Available for credit. Certificate signed by the Dean, Continuing Education. Certificate applicable to B.S. in Textile Design.

Program Format Evening, weekend classes offered. Instructional schedule: One evening per week. Program cycle: Continuous enrollment. Complete programs cycle last one to two years. Completion of program requires 10–16 courses.

Evaluation Student evaluation based on tests, papers, reports. Grading system: Letters or numbers. Transcripts are kept for each student.

Enrollment Requirements Bachelor's degree required. Program is open to non-resident foreign students.

Program Costs $414 per course.

Housing and Student Services Housing is not available. Job counseling and placement services are available.

Special Features The Postbaccalaureate Program is intended to provide participants holding bachelor's degrees in other disciplines to broaden their educational background by studying in fields in which they anticipate employment or are currently employed. Students have access to all college resources and the most current theory and applications in the field.

Contact Mr. Robert Cotter, Director, Information and Marketing, Philadelphia, PA 19144. 215-951-2900.

ROBERT MORRIS COLLEGE
Coraopolis, Pennsylvania 15108

ACCOUNTING (06.02)
Accounting

General Information Unit offering the program: School of Continuing Education, School of Business Administration. Program content: Cost accounting, taxes, auditing. Available on either a credit or non-credit basis. Certificate signed by the Dean, School of Continuing Education. Certificate applicable to B.S. in Business Administration.

Program Format Daytime, evening classes offered. Full program cycle lasts 9 courses. Completion of program requires 2.5 GPA.

Evaluation Student evaluation based on tests, papers, reports. Grading system: Letters or numbers. Transcripts are kept for each student.

Enrollment Requirements Bachelor's degree or 90 undergraduate credits required. Program is open to non-resident foreign students. English language proficiency required. Minimum TOEFL score required: 500.

Program Costs $372 per course.

Housing and Student Services Housing is available. Job counseling and placement services are available.

Special Features Courses clustered in specialization groups and each reflects range from introductory to advanced study. All programs are built upon current theory and practice relevant to the discipline. Program designed to keep students abreast of new developments in field or to prepare for career advancement or change. Programs available on part-time basis to enable participants to expand business backgrounds while continuing their careers.

Contact Dr. Helen Mullen, Dean, School of Continuing Education, Narrows Run Road, Coraopolis, PA 15108. 412-262-8442.

BUSINESS AND MANAGEMENT, GENERAL (06.01)
Management

General Information Unit offering the program: School of Continuing Education, School of Business Administration. Program content: Labor relations, personnel, purchasing, compensation. Available on either a credit or non-credit basis. Certificate signed by the Dean, School of Continuing Education. Certificate applicable to B.S. in Business Administration.

Program Format Daytime, evening classes offered. Full program cycle lasts 6 courses. Completion of program requires 2.5 GPA.

Evaluation Student evaluation based on tests, papers, reports. Grading system: Letters or numbers. Transcripts are kept for each student.

Enrollment Requirements Bachelor's degree or 90 undergraduate credits required. Program is open to non-resident foreign students. English language proficiency required. Minimum TOEFL score required: 500.

Program Costs $372 per course.

Housing and Student Services Housing is available. Job counseling and placement services are available.

Special Features Courses clustered in specialization groups and each reflects range from introductory to advanced study. All programs are built upon current theory and practice relevant to the discipline. Program designed to keep students abreast of new developments in field or to prepare for career advancement or change. Programs available on part-time basis to enable participants to expand business backgrounds while continuing their careers.

Contact Dr. Helen Mullen, Dean, School of Continuing Education, Narrows Run Road, Coraopolis, PA 15108. 412-262-8442.

COMPUTER AND INFORMATION SCIENCES, GENERAL (11.01)
Computer Competency

General Information Unit offering the program: School of Continuing Education, School of Business Administration. Program content: Data processing, BASIC applications, microcomputer software applications. Available on either a credit or non-credit basis. Certificate signed by the Dean, School of Continuing Education. Certificate applicable to B.S. in Business Administration.

Program Format Daytime, evening classes offered. Full program cycle lasts 3 courses. Completion of program requires 2.5 GPA.

Evaluation Student evaluation based on tests, papers, reports. Grading system: Letters or numbers. Transcripts are kept for each student.

Enrollment Requirements Bachelor's degree or 90 undergraduate credits required. Program is open to non-resident foreign students. English language proficiency required. Minimum TOEFL score required: 500.

Program Costs $372 per course.

Housing and Student Services Housing is available. Job counseling and placement services are available.

Special Features Courses clustered in specialization groups and each reflects range from introductory to advanced study. All programs are built upon current theory and practice relevant to the discipline. Program designed to keep students abreast of new developments in field or to prepare for career advancement or change. Programs available on part-time basis to enable participants to expand business backgrounds while continuing their careers.

Contact Dr. Helen Mullen, Dean, School of Continuing Education, Narrows Run Road, Coraopolis, PA 15108. 412-262-8442.

DATA PROCESSING (11.03)
Data Processing

General Information Unit offering the program: School of Continuing Education, School of Business Administration. Program content: Programming, systems analysis, file management, on-line design. Available on either a credit or non-credit basis. Certificate signed by the Dean, School of Continuing Education. Certificate applicable to B.S. in Business Administration.

Program Format Daytime, evening classes offered. Full program cycle lasts 5 courses. Completion of program requires 2.5 GPA.

Evaluation Student evaluation based on tests, papers, reports. Grading system: Letters or numbers. Transcripts are kept for each student.

Enrollment Requirements Bachelor's degree or 90 undergraduate credits required. Program is open to non-resident foreign students. English language proficiency required. Minimum TOEFL score required: 500.

Program Costs $372 per course.

Housing and Student Services Housing is available. Job counseling and placement services are available.

Special Features Courses clustered in specialization groups and each reflects range from introductory to advanced study. All programs are built upon current theory and practice relevant to the discipline. Program designed to keep students abreast of new developments in field or to prepare for career advancement or change. Programs available on part-time basis to enable participants to expand business backgrounds while continuing their careers.

Contact Dr. Helen Mullen, Dean, School of Continuing Education, Narrows Run Road, Coraopolis, PA 15108. 412-262-8442.

GENERAL MARKETING (08.07)
Marketing

General Information Unit offering the program: School of Continuing Education, School of Business Administration. Program content: Product development, planning, strategy, consumer behavior, sales. Available on either a credit or non-credit basis. Certificate signed by the Dean, School of Continuing Education. Certificate applicable to B.S. in Business Administration.

Program Format Daytime, evening classes offered. Full program cycle lasts 6 courses. Completion of program requires 2.5 GPA.

Evaluation Student evaluation based on tests, papers, reports. Grading system: Letters or numbers. Transcripts are kept for each student.

Enrollment Requirements Bachelor's degree or 90 undergraduate credits required. Program is open to non-resident foreign students. English language proficiency required. Minimum TOEFL score required: 500.

Program Costs $372 per course.

Housing and Student Services Housing is available. Job counseling and placement services are available.

Special Features Courses clustered in specialization groups and each reflects range from introductory to advanced study. All programs are built upon current theory and practice relevant to the discipline. Program designed to keep students abreast of new developments in field or to prepare for career advancement or change. Programs available on part-time basis to enable participants to expand business backgrounds while continuing their careers.

Contact Dr. Helen Mullen, Dean, School of Continuing Education, Narrows Run Road, Coraopolis, PA 15108. 412-262-8442.

LAW (22.01)
Legal Assistant Certificate Program

General Information Unit offering the program: School of Continuing Education. Program content: Litigation, general and bankruptcy law, wills, estates, trusts, torts, legal research. Available on a non-credit basis. Certificate signed by the Dean, School of Continuing Education.

Program Format Evening classes offered. Instructional schedule: Three hours per week. Program cycle: Continuous enrollment. Full program cycle lasts 4 quarters. Completion of program requires eight courses.

Evaluation Student evaluation based on tests, papers, reports, forms work. Grading system: Letters or numbers. Transcripts are kept for each student.

Enrollment Requirements Associate or bachelor's degree, or three years working experience required. Program is open to non-resident foreign students.

Program Costs $1600 for the program, $200 per course.

Housing and Student Services Housing is not available. Job counseling and placement services are available.

Special Features The program has a tradition of excellence in training paralegas in the Pittsburgh community. The majority of active legal assistants in the Pittsburgh legal community have received training at Robert Morris College. Instructors consist of practicing attorney, law librarian and a few paralegals.

Contact Mr. Ronald A. Cammarata, Director of Continuing Education, Fifth Avenue at Sixth, Pittsburgh, PA 15219. 412-227-6823.

REAL ESTATE (06.17)
Certificate in Real Estate

General Information Unit offering the program: School of Continuing Education. Program content: Transactions, appraisal, finance, law, investment, property management, salesmanship. Available on a non-credit basis. Certificate signed by the Dean, School of Continuing Education. Program fulfills requirements for Real Estate Salesperson; Real Estate Broker.

Program Format Daytime, evening classes offered. Instructional schedule: Once or twice per week. Program cycle: Continuous enrollment. Full program cycle lasts 8 courses. Completion of program requires 80% attendance.

Evaluation Student evaluation based on tests, reports, projects. Grading system: Pass/fail. Transcripts are kept for each student.

Enrollment Requirements Program is open to non-resident foreign students.

Program Costs $130 per course.

Housing and Student Services Housing is not available. Job counseling and placement services are not available.

Special Features Courses approved by the Pennsylvania Real Estate Commission to meet educational requirements for Salesperson and Broker Licensure in Pennsylvania. Of value to investors, consumers, or for furthering employment opportunities in real estate-related fields. Many instructors are real estate licensees, chosen for their effectiveness in classroom. Of 16 approved credits, 10, including last 2, must be earned at Robert Morris College.

Contact Department of Continuing Education, Fifth Avenue at Sixth, Pittsburgh, PA 15219. 412-227-6813.

TECHNICAL AND BUSINESS WRITING (23.11)
Professional Writing

General Information Unit offering the program: School of Continuing Education, School of Business Administration. Program content: Document design, publications production, business reports. Available on either a credit or non-credit basis. Certificate signed by the Dean, School of Continuing Education. Certificate applicable to B.S. in Business Administration.

Program Format   Daytime, evening classes offered. Full program cycle lasts 4 courses. Completion of program requires 2.5 GPA.

Evaluation   Student evaluation based on tests, papers, reports. Grading system: Letters or numbers. Transcripts are kept for each student.

Enrollment Requirements   Bachelor's degree or 90 undergraduate credits required. Program is open to non-resident foreign students. English language proficiency required. Minimum TOEFL score required: 500.

Program Costs $372 per course.

Housing and Student Services   Housing is available. Job counseling and placement services are available.

Special Features   Courses clustered in specialization groups and each reflects range from introductory to advanced study. All programs are built upon current theory and practice relevant to the discipline. Program designed to keep students abreast of new developments in field or to prepare for career advancement or change. Programs available on part-time basis to enable participants to expand business backgrounds while continuing their careers.

Contact   Dr. Helen Mullen, Dean, School of Continuing Education, Narrows Run Road, Coraopolis, PA 15108. 412-262-8442.

WORD PROCESSING (07.08)
Word Processing Certificate Program

General Information   Unit offering the program: Continuing Education. Program content: Typewriting skills, dictaphone, communication skills, word processor. Available on a non-credit basis. Certificate signed by the Department Chairperson. Certificate applicable to A.A., A.S. in Administrative Services.

Program Format   Daytime, evening classes offered. Program cycle: Continuous enrollment. Full program cycle lasts 10 weeks. Completion of program requires 150 contact hours.

Evaluation   Student evaluation based on tests. Records are kept for each student.

Enrollment Requirements   Ability to type 40 words per minute required. Program is not open to non-resident foreign students. English language proficiency required.

Program Costs $1200 for the program.

Housing and Student Services   Housing is not available. Job counseling and placement services are available.

Contact   Dr. Helen Mullen, Dean, Continuing Education, Fifth Avenue at Sixth, Pittsburgh, PA 15219. 412-262-8442.

ST. CHARLES BORROMEO SEMINARY
Philadelphia, Pennsylvania 19151

THEOLOGICAL STUDIES (39.06)
Certificate of Proficiency in Religious Studies (Graduate)

General Information   Unit offering the program: Religious Studies Division. Program content: Religious studies, theology. Available on either a credit or non-credit basis. Endorsed by Archdiocese of Philadelphia, PA. Cosponsored by Congregation for Clergy, Rome. Certificate signed by the President.

Program Format   Daytime, evening classes offered. Program cycle: Continuous enrollment. Completion of program requires 18 credit hours.

Evaluation   Student evaluation based on tests, papers, reports. Grading system: Letters or numbers. Transcripts are kept for each student.

Enrollment Requirements   Bachelor's degree with 18 undergraduate credits in religious studies required. Program is

open to non-resident foreign students. English language proficiency required.

Program Costs $4050 for the program, $225 per course.

Housing and Student Services   Housing is not available. Job counseling and placement services are not available.

Special Features   The program offers courses at both the graduate and undergraduate levels and awards certificates at each level. The program has been in operation for over 20 years and has provided instruction for teachers of religion from around the world. The certification program serves as a part of a full Master of Arts program.

Contact   Rev. Arthur E. Rodgers, Academic Dean, Philadelphia, PA 19151. 215-839-3760.

THEOLOGICAL STUDIES (39.06)
Certificate of Proficiency in Religious Studies (Undergraduate)

General Information   Unit offering the program: Religious Studies Division. Program content: Religious studies, theology. Available on either a credit or non-credit basis. Endorsed by Archdiocese of Philadelphia, PA. Cosponsored by Congregation for Clergy, Rome. Certificate signed by the President.

Program Format   Daytime, evening classes offered. Program cycle: Continuous enrollment. Completion of program requires 18 credit hours.

Evaluation   Student evaluation based on tests, papers, reports. Grading system: Letters or numbers. Transcripts are kept for each student.

Enrollment Requirements   Program is open to non-resident foreign students. English language proficiency required.

Program Costs $1890 for the program, $105 per course.

Housing and Student Services   Housing is not available. Job counseling and placement services are not available.

Special Features   The program offers courses at both the graduate and undergraduate levels and awards certificates at each level. The program has been in operation for over 20 years and has provided instruction for teachers of religion from around the world. The certification program serves as a part of a full Master of Arts program.

Contact   Rev. Arthur E. Rodgers, Academic Dean, Philadelphia, PA 19151. 215-839-3760.

SAINT VINCENT COLLEGE
Latrobe, Pennsylvania 15650

BUSINESS AND MANAGEMENT, GENERAL (06.01)
Management Science

General Information   Unit offering the program: Continuing Education. Program content: Accounting, human resources, business communication, organizational behavior, industrial psychology, personnel administration. Available for credit. Certificate signed by the President. Certificate applicable to B.S. in Management or Business Administration.

Program Format   Daytime, evening, weekend classes offered. Program cycle: Continuous enrollment. Full program cycle lasts 1 year. Completion of program requires 2.0 GPA, 30 credit hours.

Evaluation   Student evaluation based on tests, papers. Grading system: Letters or numbers. Transcripts are kept for each student.

Enrollment Requirements   Program is open to non-resident foreign students.

Program Costs $6060 for the program, $606 per course. Tuition reduced 50% for students with bachelor's degree.

Management Science continued

Housing and Student Services   Housing is available. Job counseling and placement services are available.

Contact   Mr. Jay Truxal, Director, Career Development, Latrobe, PA 15650. 412-539-9761.

COMPUTER PROGRAMMING (11.02)
Certificate in Computing Science

General Information   Unit offering the program: Continuing Education. Program content: Computer architecture, assembly language, language and rhetoric, accounting, social sciences. Available for credit. Certificate signed by the President. Certificate applicable to B.S. in Computing and Information Science, Business Computer Systems Analysis.

Program Format   Daytime, evening, weekend classes offered. Program cycle: Continuous enrollment. Full program cycle lasts 1 year. Completion of program requires 2.0 GPA, 30 credit hours.

Evaluation   Student evaluation based on tests, papers, computer programs. Grading system: Letters or numbers. Transcripts are kept for each student.

Enrollment Requirements   Program is open to non-resident foreign students.

Program Costs $6310 for the program, $606 per course, tuition 50% less for students with bachelor's degree.

Housing and Student Services   Housing is available. Job counseling and placement services are available.

Special Features   Up to 15 credits from other college work (including credit for life experience and CLEP) are transferable.

Contact   Mr. Jay Truxal, Director, Career Development, Latrobe, PA 15650. 412-539-9761.

LAW (22.01)
Paralegal Certificate Program

General Information   Unit offering the program: Continuing Education. Available on a non-credit basis. Certificate signed by the Director of Continuing Education.

Program Format   Evening, weekend classes offered. Program cycle: Continuous enrollment. Full program cycle lasts 16 months. Completion of program requires 2.0 GPA.

Evaluation   Student evaluation based on tests, papers, presentations. Grading system: Letters or numbers. Transcripts are kept for each student.

Enrollment Requirements   Program is open to non-resident foreign students.

Program Costs $1505 for the program, $175 per course, $40 per workshop.

Housing and Student Services   Housing is not available. Job counseling and placement services are available.

Contact   Mr. Jay Truxal, Director, Career Development, Latrobe, PA 15650. 412-539-9761.

NUCEA MEMBER
SETON HILL COLLEGE
Greensburg, Pennsylvania 15601

BUSINESS AND MANAGEMENT, GENERAL (06.01)
Management Certificate Program

General Information   Unit offering the program: Continuing Education and Management Department. Program content: Accounting, BASIC, communications, human resources, financial management, data management, marketing, sales. Available for credit. Certificate signed by the President of College. Certificate applicable to B.A. in Management.

Program Format   Daytime, evening, weekend classes offered. Program cycle: Continuous enrollment. Full program cycle lasts

2 semesters. Completion of program requires 24 credit hours, grade of C or better in each course.

Evaluation   Student evaluation based on tests, papers, reports. Grading system: Letters or numbers. Transcripts are kept for each student.

Enrollment Requirements   High school diploma or GED required. Program is open to non-resident foreign students. English language proficiency required. Minimum TOEFL score required: 500.

Program Costs $4368 for the program, $546 per course.

Housing and Student Services   Housing is available. Job counseling and placement services are available.

Contact   Ms. Martha Raak, Director, Continuing Education, Greensburg, PA 15601. 412-838-4209.

CHILD CARE AND GUIDANCE MANAGEMENT AND SERVICES (20.02)
Child Care Certificate Program

General Information   Unit offering the program: Continuing Education and Home Economics Department. Program content: Parenting, nutrition, day care administration. Available for credit. Certificate signed by the President of College. Certificate applicable to B.A. in Home Economics. Program fulfills requirements for Assistant Group Supervisor.

Program Format   Daytime classes offered. Students may enroll fall, spring. Full program cycle lasts 2 semesters. Completion of program requires 15 credit hours with grade of C or better in all courses.

Evaluation   Student evaluation based on tests, papers, reports. Grading system: Letters or numbers. Transcripts are kept for each student.

Enrollment Requirements   High school diploma or GED required. Program is open to non-resident foreign students. English language proficiency required. Minimum TOEFL score required: 500.

Program Costs $2730 for the program, $546 per course.

Housing and Student Services   Housing is available. Job counseling and placement services are available.

Special Features   This program is for those who want to work in a child-care setting. Credits earned may be applied toward a degree. All instructors are highly qualified members of the Seton Hill College faculty.

Contact   Ms. Martha Raak, Director, Continuing Education, Greensburg, PA 15601. 412-838-4209.

COMPUTER PROGRAMMING (11.02)
Computer Certificate Program

General Information   Unit offering the program: Continuing Education and Math/Computer Science Departments. Program content: Finite mathematics, microcomputer concepts, BASIC, COBOL, business communications. Available for credit. Certificate signed by the President of College. Certificate applicable to bachelor's degree in math/computer science.

Program Format   Daytime, evening classes offered. Program cycle: Continuous enrollment. Full program cycle lasts 25 credit hours. Completion of program requires grade of C or better in each course.

Evaluation   Student evaluation based on tests, papers, reports. Grading system: Letters or numbers. Transcripts are kept for each student.

Enrollment Requirements   High school diploma or GED required. English language proficiency required. Minimum TOEFL score required: 500.

Program Costs $5000 for the program, $546 per course.

Housing and Student Services   Housing is available. Job counseling and placement services are available.

Contact   Ms. Martha Raak, Director, Continuing Education, Greensburg, PA 15601. 412-838-4209.

FOREIGN LANGUAGES, MULTIPLE EMPHASIS (16.01)
Foreign Language and Culture

General Information   Unit offering the program: Continuing Education, French and Spanish Departments. Program content: Spoken French or Spanish, with business or cultural option. Available for credit. Certificate signed by the President of College.

Program Format   Daytime, evening classes offered. Program cycle: Continuous enrollment. Full program cycle lasts 20 credit hours.

Evaluation   Student evaluation based on tests, papers, reports. Grading system: Letters or numbers. Transcripts are kept for each student.

Enrollment Requirements   High school diploma or GED required. Program is open to non-resident foreign students. English language proficiency required. Minimum TOEFL score required: 500.

Program Costs $3750 for the program, $542 per course.

Housing and Student Services   Housing is available. Job counseling and placement services are available.

Contact   Ms. Martha Raak, Director, Continuing Education, Greensburg, PA 15601. 412-838-4209.

GENERAL MARKETING (08.07)
Retail Management

General Information   Unit offering the program: Continuing Education and Home Economics Department. Program content: Economics, computers, marketing, communications, industrial psychology, selling. Available for credit. Certificate signed by the President of College. Certificate applicable to bachelor's degree in home economics with a retail emphasis.

Program Format   Daytime, evening classes offered. Program cycle: Continuous enrollment. Full program cycle lasts 23 credit hours.

Evaluation   Student evaluation based on tests, papers, reports. Grading system: Letters or numbers. Transcripts are kept for each student.

Enrollment Requirements   High school diploma or GED required. Program is open to non-resident foreign students. English language proficiency required. Minimum TOEFL score required: 500.

Program Costs $4200 for the program, $542 per course.

Housing and Student Services   Housing is available. Job counseling and placement services are available.

Contact   Ms. Martha Raak, Director, Continuing Education, Greensburg, PA 15601. 412-838-4209.

INTERIOR DESIGN (04.05)
Interior Decorator Certificate

General Information   Unit offering the program: Continuing Education and Home Economics Department. Program content: Art, design, textiles, housing and interior design, technical drawing, accounting, selling, computer concepts. Available for credit. Certificate signed by the President of College. Certificate applicable to bachelor's degree in home economics/interior design.

Program Format   Daytime, evening classes offered. Program cycle: Continuous enrollment. Full program cycle lasts 2 years.

Evaluation   Student evaluation based on tests, papers, reports. Grading system: Letters or numbers. Transcripts are kept for each student.

Enrollment Requirements   High school diploma or GED required. English language proficiency required. Minimum TOEFL score required: 500.

Program Costs $5000 for the program, $546 per course.

Housing and Student Services   Housing is available. Job counseling and placement services are available.

Contact   Ms. Martha Raak, Director, Continuing Education, Greensburg, PA 15601. 412-838-4209.

PUBLIC RELATIONS (09.05)
Advertising and Public Relations

General Information   Unit offering the program: Continuing Education and Communications Department. Program content: Business communications, graphic design, photojournalism, advanced composition, speaking, speech writing. Available for credit. Certificate signed by the President of College.

Program Format   Daytime, evening, weekend classes offered. Program cycle: Continuous enrollment. Full program cycle lasts 24 credit hours.

Evaluation   Student evaluation based on tests, papers, reports. Grading system: Letters or numbers. Transcripts are kept for each student.

Enrollment Requirements   High school diploma or GED required. Program is open to non-resident foreign students. English language proficiency required. Minimum TOEFL score required: 500.

Program Costs $4500 for the program, $542 per course.

Housing and Student Services   Housing is available. Job counseling and placement services are available.

Contact   Ms. Martha Raak, Director, Continuing Education, Greensburg, PA 15601. 412-838-4209.

RELIGIOUS MUSIC (39.05)
Sacred Music

General Information   Unit offering the program: Continuing Education and Music. Program content: Harmony, aural theory, choral conducting, Christian hymnody, organ in worship. Available for credit. Certificate signed by the President of College. Certificate applicable to B.Mus. in Sacred Music.

Program Format   Daytime, evening classes offered. Program cycle: Continuous enrollment. Full program cycle lasts 25 credit hours.

Evaluation   Student evaluation based on tests, papers, reports, demonstration of proficiencies. Grading system: Letters or numbers. Transcripts are kept for each student.

Enrollment Requirements   High school diploma or GED, musical proficiency required. Program is open to non-resident foreign students. English language proficiency required. Minimum TOEFL score required: 500.

Program Costs $5000 for the program, $542 per course.

Housing and Student Services   Housing is available. Job counseling and placement services are available.

Contact   Ms. Martha Raak, Director, Continuing Education, Greensburg, PA 15601. 412-838-4209.

THEOLOGICAL STUDIES (39.06)
Certificate in Ministry Program

General Information   Unit offering the program: Theology and Continuing Education. Program content: Scripture, doctrine, music, pastoral ministry. Available for credit. Certificate signed by the President of College.

Program Format   Daytime, evening classes offered. Program cycle: Continuous enrollment. Full program cycle lasts 40 credit hours. Completion of program requires internship.

Evaluation   Student evaluation based on tests, papers, reports. Grading system: Letters or numbers. Transcripts are kept for each student.

Enrollment Requirements   High school diploma required. Program is open to non-resident foreign students. English language proficiency required. Minimum TOEFL score required: 500.

Program Costs $542 per course.

Housing and Student Services   Housing is available. Job counseling and placement services are available.

Certificate in Ministry Program continued
Contact   Ms. Martha Raak, Director, Continuing Education, Greensburg, PA 15601. 412-838-4209.

UNITED WESLEYAN COLLEGE
Allentown, Pennsylvania 18103

BIBLE STUDIES (39.02)
Certificate in Biblical Studies

General Information   Unit offering the program: Biblical Studies, Missiology. Program content: Understanding the Bible, course work in liberal arts. Available for credit. Certificate signed by the President. Certificate applicable to A.S., B.S. in Missions, Pastoral Ministry, English Bible and Theology.

Program Format   Daytime, evening classes offered. Program cycle: Continuous enrollment. Full program cycle lasts 1 year. Completion of program requires 2.0 GPA.

Evaluation   Student evaluation based on tests, papers, reports. Grading system: Letters or numbers. Transcripts are kept for each student.

Enrollment Requirements   High school diploma or GED, references required. Program is open to non-resident foreign students. English language proficiency required.

Program Costs $4690 for the program.

Housing and Student Services   Housing is available. Job counseling and placement services are available.

Contact   Rev. David Keith, Director of Admissions, 1414 East Cedar Street, Allentown, PA 18103. 215-439-8709.

NUCEA MEMBER
UNIVERSITY OF PENNSYLVANIA
Philadelphia, Pennsylvania 19104

COMMUNICATIONS, GENERAL (09.01)
The Publishing Institute

General Information   Unit offering the program: College of General Studies/Special Programs. Program content: Overview of book publishing, issues facing the industry. Available on a non-credit basis. Certificate signed by the Director, College of General Studies.

Program Format   Evening classes offered. Instructional schedule: Classes meet weekly. Students enroll in the fall. Full program cycle lasts 1 year. Completion of program requires 75% attendance, final paper, two courses.

Evaluation   Student evaluation based on papers. Records are kept in Special Programs Office.

Enrollment Requirements   Program is open to non-resident foreign students.

Program Costs $650 for the program.

Housing and Student Services   Housing is not available. Job counseling and placement services are not available.

Special Features   Courses taught by leading professionals who describe their career paths, discuss specific aspects and problems encountered in their jobs, and usually provide brief reading or writing assignments. A unique opportunity to learn about publishing and to become aware of career possibilities. This is the fourth year the program has been offered and its reputation has grown significantly in the Delaware Valley.

Contact   Ms. Joanne M. Hanna, Program Coordinator, Special Programs, 3808 Walnut Street, Philadelphia, PA 19104-6136. 215-898-6479.

TEACHING ENGLISH AS A SECOND LANGUAGE/FOREIGN LANGUAGE (13.14)
Proficiency Certificate

General Information   Unit offering the program: English Language Programs. Program content: English for non-native speakers. Available on a non-credit basis. Certificate signed by the Director.

Program Format   Daytime classes offered. Instructional schedule: Full-time study is 20 hours per week. Program cycle: Continuous enrollment. Full program cycle lasts 8 weeks.

Evaluation   Student evaluation based on tests, reports. Records are kept for each student.

Enrollment Requirements   Minimum 17 years of age, visa required. Program is open to non-resident foreign students.

Program Costs $965 for the program.

Housing and Student Services   Housing is available. Job counseling and placement services are available.

Special Features   Offering English language training to international students, professionals, and scholars for the past twenty-five years. In addition to our regularly scheduled Intensive Program, the ELP has provided special contract programs to many groups.

Contact   Ms. Nancy Overholt, Admissions Coordinator, English Language Programs, 21 Bennett Hall, 34th and Walnut Streets, Philadelphia, PA 19104. 215-898-8681.

NUCEA MEMBER
UNIVERSITY OF PITTSBURGH
Pittsburgh, Pennsylvania 15260

ACCOUNTING (06.02)
Accounting

General Information   Unit offering the program: Graduate School of Business, College of General Studies. Program content: Taxes, auditing. Available on a non-credit basis. Endorsed by Pennsylvania Institute of Certified Public Accountants. Certificate signed by the Dean, College of General Studies.

Program Format   Evening classes offered. Instructional schedule: One evening per week for 2½ hours. Program cycle: Continuous enrollment. Full program cycle lasts 6 semesters. Completion of program requires 24 credit hours, 2.0 GPA.

Evaluation   Student evaluation based on tests, papers. Grading system: Letters or numbers. Transcripts are kept for each student.

Enrollment Requirements   High school diploma required. Program is open to non-resident foreign students.

Program Costs $2712 for the program, $339 per course.

Housing and Student Services   Housing is not available. Job counseling and placement services are available.

Contact   Mr. Richard L. Baird, Academic Advisor, 458 Cathedral of Learning, Pittsburgh, PA 15260. 412-624-1070.

ACCOUNTING (06.02)
Accounting

General Information   Unit offering the program: Titusville Campus. Available for credit. Certificate signed by the Executive Dean.

Program Format   Evening classes offered. Instructional schedule: One evening per week for three hours. Program cycle: Continuous enrollment. Full program cycle lasts 24 credit hours. Completion of program requires 2.0 GPA.

Evaluation   Student evaluation based on tests. Grading system: Letters or numbers. Transcripts are kept for each student.

Enrollment Requirements   High school diploma required. Program is open to non-resident foreign students.

Program Costs $318 per course.

Housing and Student Services Housing is available. Job counseling and placement services are available.

Contact Mr. Gerald Lazzaro, Program Adviser, P.O. Box 287, Titusville, PA 16354. 814-827-2702.

BUSINESS AND MANAGEMENT, GENERAL (06.01)
Business

General Information Unit offering the program: Graduate School of Business, College of General Studies. Program content: Financial accounting, human resources, organizational behavior, cost accounting. Available on a non-credit basis. Certificate signed by the Dean, College of General Studies.

Program Format Evening classes offered. Instructional schedule: One evening per week for 2½ hours. Program cycle: Continuous enrollment. Full program cycle lasts 4 semesters. Completion of program requires 24 credit hours, 2.0 GPA.

Evaluation Student evaluation based on tests, papers, reports. Grading system: Letters or numbers. Transcripts are kept for each student.

Enrollment Requirements High school diploma required. Program is open to non-resident foreign students.

Program Costs $2712 for the program, $339 per course.

Housing and Student Services Housing is not available. Job counseling and placement services are not available.

Contact Mr. Richard L. Baird, Academic Adviser, 458 Cathedral of Learning, Pittsburgh, PA 15260. 412-624-1670.

COMMUNITY SERVICES (44.02)
Community Information Management

General Information Unit offering the program: Graduate School of Public and International Affairs, School of Social Work, School of Library and Information Science. Program content: Skills and technological understanding of information needs of community and government organizations. Available for credit. Certificate signed by the Dean. Certificate applicable to M.U.R.P., M.P.A.

Program Format Daytime, evening classes offered. Instructional schedule: Once per week for three hours. Program cycle: Continuous enrollment. Full program cycle lasts 15 credit hours.

Evaluation Student evaluation methods vary by course. Grading system: Letters or numbers. Transcripts are kept for each student.

Enrollment Requirements University admissions required. Program is open to non-resident foreign students. English language proficiency required. Minimum TOEFL score required: 550.

Program Costs $2550–$5100 for the program, $510–$1020 per course.

Housing and Student Services Housing is not available. Job counseling and placement services are available.

Special Features Degree candidates may apply for advanced standing based on prior experience. Internships and practica are available for students in the certificate program.

Contact Ms. Jane E. Lohman, Assistant Dean, Graduate School of Public and International Affairs, Pittsburgh, PA 15260. 412-648-7640.

CREATIVE WRITING (23.05)
Writing

General Information Unit offering the program: College of General Studies. Program content: Creative, fiction, poetry, news, magazine writing. Available for credit. Certificate signed by the Dean, College of General Studies. Certificate applicable to B.A. in English.

Program Format Evening classes offered. Instructional schedule: One evening per week for 2½ hours. Program cycle: Continuous enrollment. Full program cycle lasts 21 credit hours. Completion of program requires grade of C or better.

Evaluation Student evaluation based on tests, papers. Grading system: Letters or numbers. Transcripts are kept for each student.

Enrollment Requirements Admission to College of General Studies required. Program is open to non-resident foreign students. English language proficiency required. Minimum TOEFL score required: 500.

Program Costs $2373 for the program, $339 per course.

Housing and Student Services Housing is available. Job counseling and placement services are available.

Contact Director of Admissions, College of General Studies, 407 Cathedral of Learning, Pittsburgh, PA 15260. 412-624-6600.

FOREIGN LANGUAGES, MULTIPLE EMPHASIS (16.01)
Professional Translation

General Information Unit offering the program: College of General Studies. Program content: Technical aspects of language translation for government, business. Available for credit. Certificate signed by the Dean, College of General Studies. Certificate applicable to B.A., B.S. in Languages.

Program Format Evening classes offered. Instructional schedule: One class per week. Program cycle: Continuous enrollment. Full program cycle lasts 21 credit hours. Completion of program requires proficiency on qualifying exam.

Evaluation Student evaluation based on tests. Grading system: Letters or numbers. Transcripts are kept for each student.

Enrollment Requirements Five college semesters in two languages (Spanish, French, Italian, German) required. Program is open to non-resident foreign students. English language proficiency required. Minimum TOEFL score required: 500.

Program Costs $2373 for the program, $339 per course.

Housing and Student Services Housing is available. Job counseling and placement services are not available.

Contact Director of Admissions, College of General Studies, 407 Cathedral of Learning, Pittsburgh, PA 15260. 412-624-6600.

HISTORY (45.08)
Conceptual Foundations of Medicine

General Information Unit offering the program: Department of History and Philosophy of Science. Program content: Multi-disciplinary perspective on foundations of modern medicine. Available for credit. Certificate signed by the President of the University.

Program Format Daytime classes offered. Program cycle: Continuous enrollment. Full program cycle lasts 6 courses. Completion of program requires grade of C+ or better.

Evaluation Student evaluation methods vary by course. Grading system: Letters or numbers. Transcripts are kept for each student.

Enrollment Requirements Completion of HPS course numbers 12 and 13 with grade of C or better required. Program is open to non-resident foreign students.

Program Costs $510–$1020 per course.

Housing and Student Services Housing is available. Job counseling and placement services are not available.

Contact Department Secretary, Department of History and Philosophy of Science, Pittsburgh, PA 15260. 412-624-5896.

HISTORY (45.08)
Medieval and Renaissance Studies

General Information Unit offering the program: Medieval and Renaissance Studies Program. Program content: Aspects of

Medieval and Renaissance Studies continued

Medieval or Renaissance culture. Available for credit. Certificate signed by the Professor. Certificate applicable to B.A. in Languages.

Program Format   Daytime classes offered. Program cycle: Continuous enrollment. Full program cycle lasts 24 credit hours. Completion of program requires eight courses, reading knowledge of modern foreign language or Latin.

Evaluation   Student evaluation methods vary by course. Grading system: Letters or numbers. Transcripts are kept for each student.

Enrollment Requirements   Program is open to non-resident foreign students. English language proficiency required.

Program Costs $510–$1020 per course.

Housing and Student Services   Housing is not available. Job counseling and placement services are not available.

Special Features   Program supplies focus for undergraduate studies in arts and sciences; emphasizes political and social history of premodern era and some of the outstanding institutions and achievements (artistic and intellectual) of period from c. 500 to c. 1500 A.D. Also provides a larger context to the usual departmental major in history, literature, art history, etc.

Contact   Dr. Barbara N. Sargent-Baur, Director, Medieval and Renaissance Studies Program, 1328 Cathedral of Learning, Pittsburgh, PA 15260. 412-624-6224.

HUMAN RESOURCES DEVELOPMENT (06.06)
Human Resources Management

General Information   Unit offering the program: Graduate School of Business, College of General Studies. Program content: Concepts, techniques, and functions of human resources. Available on a non-credit basis. Certificate signed by the Dean, College of General Studies.

Program Format   Evening classes offered. Instructional schedule: One evening per week for 2½ hours. Program cycle: Continuous enrollment. Full program cycle lasts 1 year. Completion of program requires 18 credit hours, 2.0 GPA.

Evaluation   Student evaluation based on tests. Grading system: Letters or numbers. Transcripts are kept for each student.

Enrollment Requirements   High school diploma required. Program is open to non-resident foreign students.

Program Costs $2034 for the program, $339 per course.

Housing and Student Services   Housing is not available. Job counseling and placement services are not available.

Contact   Mr. Richard L. Baird, Academic Adviser, 458 Cathedral of Learning, Pittsburgh, PA 15260. 412-624-1670.

INSURANCE AND RISK MANAGEMENT (06.08)
Insurance

General Information   Unit offering the program: Graduate School of Business, College of General Studies. Program content: Fundamental understanding of insurance. Available on a non-credit basis. Endorsed by Insurance Institute of America. Certificate signed by the Dean, College of General Studies.

Program Format   Evening classes offered. Instructional schedule: One evening per week. Program cycle: Continuous enrollment. Full program cycle lasts 1 year. Completion of program requires six credit hours, 2.0 GPA.

Evaluation   Student evaluation based on tests, papers, reports. Grading system: Letters or numbers. Transcripts are kept for each student.

Enrollment Requirements   High school diploma required. Program is open to non-resident foreign students. English language proficiency required.

Program Costs $678 for the program.

Housing and Student Services   Housing is not available. Job counseling and placement services are not available.

Contact   Mr. Richard L. Baird, Academic Adviser, 458 Cathedral of Learning, Pittsburgh, PA 15260. 412-624-1670.

INTERNATIONAL PUBLIC SERVICE (44.03)
International Securities Studies

General Information   Unit offering the program: Graduate School of Public and International Affairs. Program content: Analysis of economic, social, political, military, and technical aspects of arms control and international security affairs. Available for credit. Certificate signed by the Dean. Certificate applicable to M.P.I.A.

Program Format   Daytime classes offered. Instructional schedule: Once per week for three hours. Program cycle: Continuous enrollment. Full program cycle lasts 18 credit hours.

Evaluation   Student evaluation methods vary by course. Grading system: Letters or numbers. Transcripts are kept for each student.

Enrollment Requirements   University admissions required. Program is open to non-resident foreign students. English language proficiency required. Minimum TOEFL score required: 550.

Program Costs $2550–$5100 for the program, $510–$1020 per course.

Housing and Student Services   Housing is not available. Job counseling and placement services are available.

Special Features   Degree candidates may apply for advanced standing based on prior experience. Internships and practica are available for students in the certificate program.

Contact   Ms. Jane E. Lohman, Assistant Dean, Graduate School of Public and International Affairs, Pittsburgh, PA 15260. 412-648-7640.

LAW (22.01)
Paralegal Studies

General Information   Unit offering the program: Department of Interdisciplinary Studies in Law and Justice, College of General Studies. Program content: Legal research and writing. Available on either a credit or non-credit basis. Certificate signed by the Department Chairman. Certificate applicable to any four-year degree offered at the institution.

Program Format   Daytime, evening, weekend classes offered. Program cycle: Continuous enrollment. Full program cycle lasts 60 credit hours. Completion of program requires competency examination, 2.5 GPA.

Evaluation   Student evaluation based on tests, papers, reports. Grading system: Letters or numbers. Transcripts are kept for each student.

Enrollment Requirements   High school diploma or GED, previous college work with 2.5 GPA required. Program is open to non-resident foreign students. English language proficiency required. Minimum TOEFL score required: 500.

Program Costs $6780 for the program, $339 per course.

Housing and Student Services   Housing is available. Job counseling and placement services are available.

Special Features   Advanced standing credits are evaluated for previous college work. CLEP credits accepted though only applicable toward general education requirement. Internships available. Students may choose from six track areas: General Practice, Business Practice, Criminal Practice, Estates and Trusts, Litigation, and Real Estate Practice.

Contact   Director of Admissions, College of General Studies, 407 Cathedral of Learning, Pittsburgh, PA 15260. 412-624-6600.

MARKETING MANAGEMENT AND RESEARCH (06.14)
Marketing

General Information   Unit offering the program: Graduate School of Business, College of General Studies. Program content: Marketing process. Available on a non-credit basis. Certificate signed by the Dean, College of General Studies.

Program Format Evening classes offered. Instructional schedule: One evening per week for 2½ hours. Program cycle: Continuous enrollment. Full program cycle lasts 1 year. Completion of program requires 15 credit hours, 2.0 GPA.

Evaluation Student evaluation based on tests, papers. Grading system: Letters or numbers. Transcripts are kept for each student.

Enrollment Requirements High school diploma required. Program is open to non-resident foreign students. English language proficiency required.

Program Costs $1695 for the program, $339 per course.

Housing and Student Services Housing is not available. Job counseling and placement services are not available.

Contact Mr. Richard L. Baird, Academic Adviser, 458 Cathedral of Learning, Pittsburgh, PA 15260. 412-624-1670.

PUBLIC AFFAIRS, GENERAL (44.01)
City Management

General Information Unit offering the program: Graduate School of Public and International Affairs. Program content: Administrative skills at policy-making and managerial levels of local, county, regional governments. Available for credit. Certificate signed by the Dean. Certificate applicable to M.P.A., M.U.R.P.

Program Format Daytime, evening classes offered. Instructional schedule: Once per week for three hours. Program cycle: Continuous enrollment. Full program cycle lasts 15 credit hours.

Evaluation Student evaluation methods vary by course. Grading system: Letters or numbers. Transcripts are kept for each student.

Enrollment Requirements University admissions required. Program is open to non-resident foreign students. English language proficiency required. Minimum TOEFL score required: 550.

Program Costs $2550–$5100 for the program, $510–$1020 per course.

Housing and Student Services Housing is not available. Job counseling and placement services are available.

Special Features Degree candidates may apply for advanced standing based on prior experience. Internships and practica are available for students in the certificate program.

Contact Ms. Jane E. Lohman, Assistant Dean, Graduate School of Public and International Affairs, Pittsburgh, PA 15260. 412-648-7640.

PUBLIC AFFAIRS, GENERAL (44.01)
Financial Management

General Information Unit offering the program: Graduate School of Public and International Affairs. Program content: Issues, policies, and analytical skills for fiscal management in public sector. Available for credit. Certificate signed by the Dean. Certificate applicable to M.P.A.

Program Format Daytime, evening, weekend classes offered. Instructional schedule: Once per week for three hours. Program cycle: Continuous enrollment. Full program cycle lasts 15 credit hours.

Evaluation Student evaluation methods vary by course. Grading system: Letters or numbers. Transcripts are kept for each student.

Enrollment Requirements University admissions required. Program is open to non-resident foreign students. English language proficiency required. Minimum TOEFL score required: 550.

Program Costs $2550 for the program, $510 per course (state residents); $5100 for the program, $1020 per course (nonresidents).

Housing and Student Services Housing is not available. Job counseling and placement services are available.

Special Features Degree candidates may apply for advanced standing based on prior experience. Internships and practica are available for students in the certificate program.

Contact Ms. Jane E. Lohman, Assistant Dean, Graduate School of Public and International Affairs, Pittsburgh, PA 15260. 412-648-7640.

PUBLIC AFFAIRS, GENERAL (44.01)
Information Services Management

General Information Unit offering the program: Graduate School of Public and International Affairs. Program content: Policy management of urban or governmental information and communication services. Available for credit. Certificate signed by the Dean. Certificate applicable to M.P.A.

Program Format Daytime, evening, weekend classes offered. Instructional schedule: Once per week for three hours. Program cycle: Continuous enrollment. Full program cycle lasts 15 credit hours.

Evaluation Student evaluation methods vary by course. Grading system: Letters or numbers. Transcripts are kept for each student.

Enrollment Requirements University admissions required. Program is open to non-resident foreign students. English language proficiency required. Minimum TOEFL score required: 550.

Program Costs $2550 for the program, $510 per course (state residents); $5100 for the program, $1020 per course (nonresidents).

Housing and Student Services Housing is not available. Job counseling and placement services are available.

Special Features Degree candidates may apply for advanced standing based on prior experience. Internships and practica are available for students in the certificate program.

Contact Ms. Jane E. Lohman, Assistant Dean, Graduate School of Public and International Affairs, Pittsburgh, PA 15260. 412-648-7640.

PUBLIC AFFAIRS, GENERAL (44.01)
Management Science

General Information Unit offering the program: Graduate School of Public and International Affairs. Program content: Systematic and analytic problem solving through quantitative techniques. Available for credit. Certificate signed by the Dean. Certificate applicable to M.P.A.

Program Format Daytime, evening, weekend classes offered. Instructional schedule: Once per week for three hours. Program cycle: Continuous enrollment. Full program cycle lasts 15 credit hours.

Evaluation Student evaluation methods vary by course. Grading system: Letters or numbers. Transcripts are kept for each student.

Enrollment Requirements University admissions required. Program is open to non-resident foreign students. English language proficiency required. Minimum TOEFL score required: 550.

Program Costs $2550 for the program, $510 per course (state residents); $5100 for the program, $1020 per course (nonresidents).

Housing and Student Services Housing is not available. Job counseling and placement services are available.

Special Features Degree candidates may apply for advanced standing based on prior experience. Internships and practica are available for students in the certificate program.

Contact Ms. Jane E. Lohman, Assistant Dean, Graduate School of Public and International Affairs, Pittsburgh, PA 15260. 412-648-7640.

PUBLIC AFFAIRS, GENERAL (44.01)
Personnel and Labor Relations

General Information   Unit offering the program: Graduate School of Public and International Affairs. Program content: Personnel administration, collective bargaining, productivity, effective management. Available for credit. Certificate signed by the Dean. Certificate applicable to M.P.A.

Program Format   Daytime, evening, weekend classes offered. Instructional schedule: Once per week for three hours. Program cycle: Continuous enrollment. Full program cycle lasts 15 credit hours.

Evaluation   Student evaluation methods vary by course. Grading system: Letters or numbers. Transcripts are kept for each student.

Enrollment Requirements   University admissions required. Program is open to non-resident foreign students. English language proficiency required. Minimum TOEFL score required: 550.

Program Costs $2550 for the program, $510 per course (state residents); $5100 for the program, $1020 per course (nonresidents).

Housing and Student Services   Housing is not available. Job counseling and placement services are available.

Special Features   Degree candidates may apply for advanced standing based on prior experience. Internships and practica are available for students in the certificate program.

Contact   Ms. Jane E. Lohman, Assistant Dean, Graduate School of Public and International Affairs, Pittsburgh, PA 15260. 412-648-7640.

PUBLIC AFFAIRS, GENERAL (44.01)
Urban and Regional Development

General Information   Unit offering the program: Graduate School of Public and International Affairs. Program content: Basic concepts, problem-solving skills, practical experience in integrated community and economic development. Available for credit. Certificate signed by the Dean. Certificate applicable to M.U.R.P., M.P.A.

Program Format   Daytime, evening classes offered. Instructional schedule: Once per week for three hours. Program cycle: Continuous enrollment. Full program cycle lasts 15 credit hours.

Evaluation   Student evaluation methods vary by course. Grading system: Letters or numbers. Transcripts are kept for each student.

Enrollment Requirements   University admissions required. Program is open to non-resident foreign students. English language proficiency required. Minimum TOEFL score required: 550.

Program Costs $2550 for the program, $510 per course (state residents); $5100 for the program, $1020 per course (nonresidents).

Housing and Student Services   Housing is not available. Job counseling and placement services are available.

Special Features   Degree candidates may apply for advanced standing based on prior experience. Internships and practica are available for students in the certificate program.

Contact   Ms. Jane E. Lohman, Assistant Dean, Graduate School of Public and International Affairs, Pittsburgh, PA 15260. 412-648-7640.

PUBLIC POLICY STUDIES (44.05)
Applied Policy Analysis

General Information   Unit offering the program: Graduate School of Public and International Affairs. Program content: Develop, implement, and evaluate solutions to current government problems. Available for credit. Certificate signed by the Dean. Certificate applicable to M.P.A.

Program Format   Daytime, evening, weekend classes offered. Instructional schedule: Once per week for three hours. Program cycle: Continuous enrollment. Full program cycle lasts 18 credit hours. Completion of program requires practicum.

Evaluation   Student evaluation methods vary by course. Grading system: Letters or numbers. Transcripts are kept for each student.

Enrollment Requirements   University admissions required. Program is open to non-resident foreign students. English language proficiency required. Minimum TOEFL score required: 550.

Program Costs $2550–$5100 for the program, $510–$1020 per course.

Housing and Student Services   Housing is not available. Job counseling and placement services are available.

Special Features   Degree candidates may apply for advanced standing based on prior experience. Internships and practica are available for students in the certificate program.

Contact   Ms. Jane E. Lohman, Assistant Dean, Graduate School of Public and International Affairs, Pittsburgh, PA 15260. 412-648-7640.

REAL ESTATE (06.17)
Real Estate

General Information   Unit offering the program: Graduate School of Business, College of General Studies. Available on a non-credit basis. Endorsed by Pennsylvania Real Estate Commission. Certificate signed by the Dean, College of General Studies.

Program Format   Evening classes offered. Program cycle: Continuous enrollment. Full program cycle lasts 2 years. Completion of program requires 16 credit hours, 2.0 GPA.

Evaluation   Student evaluation based on tests, papers. Grading system: Letters or numbers. Transcripts are kept for each student.

Enrollment Requirements   High school diploma required. Program is open to non-resident foreign students.

Program Costs $226 per two-credit course.

Housing and Student Services   Housing is not available. Job counseling and placement services are not available.

Contact   Mr. Richard L. Baird, Academic Adviser, 458 Cathedral of Learning, Pittsburgh, PA 15260. 412-624-1670.

SOCIAL WORK (44.07)
Family and Marital Therapy

General Information   Unit offering the program: School of Social Work. Program content: Integration of theory and practice for family and marital therapists. Available for credit. Certificate signed by the Dean, School of Social Work.

Program Format   Evening classes offered. Program cycle: Continuous enrollment. Full program cycle lasts 4 semesters. Completion of program requires 22 credit hours.

Evaluation   Student evaluation based on papers, reports. Grading system: Letters or numbers. Transcripts are kept for each student.

Enrollment Requirements   Master's degree in social work or related field required. Program is not open to non-resident foreign students.

Program Costs $3740 for the program, $340 per course.

Housing and Student Services   Housing is not available. Job counseling and placement services are not available.

Special Features   The post-master's Family Therapy Certificate program has been jointly designed by family therapy educators and practitioners to provide a planned sequence of courses and clinical supervision that will promote integration of theory and practice and enhance competency for practitioners of family and marital therapy.

Contact Mr. Rick Wells, Professor, 2327 Cathedral of Learning, Pittsburgh, PA 15260. 412-624-6320.

SPEECH, DEBATE, AND FORENSICS (23.10)
Communication

General Information Unit offering the program: College of General Studies. Program content: Public speaking, composition, theories. Available for credit. Certificate signed by the Dean, College of General Studies. Certificate applicable to B.A., B.S. in Communications.

Program Format Daytime, evening, weekend, correspondence classes offered. Instructional schedule: Once per week for 2½ hours. Program cycle: Continuous enrollment. Full program cycle lasts 24 credit hours. Completion of program requires grade of C or better.

Evaluation Student evaluation based on tests, papers, reports. Grading system: Letters or numbers. Transcripts are kept for each student.

Enrollment Requirements Admission to College of General Studies required. Program is open to non-resident foreign students. English language proficiency required. Minimum TOEFL score required: 500.

Program Costs $2712 for the program, $339 per course.

Housing and Student Services Housing is available. Job counseling and placement services are available.

Contact Director of Admissions, College of General Studies, 407 Cathedral of Learning, Pittsburgh, PA 15260. 412-624-6624.

WOMEN'S STUDIES (30.07)
Women's Studies

General Information Unit offering the program: Women's Studies Program. Program content: Anthropology; English literature; writing; fine arts; history; psychology; sociology; philosophy of social, political, and economic equality. Available for credit. Certificate signed by the Dean, College of Arts and Sciences.

Program Format Daytime, evening, weekend, correspondence classes offered. Instructional schedule: Once per week for 2½ hours. Program cycle: Continuous enrollment. Full program cycle lasts 18 credit hours. Completion of program requires 2.0 GPA.

Evaluation Student evaluation based on tests, papers, reports. Grading system: Letters or numbers, pass/fail. Transcripts are kept for each student.

Enrollment Requirements Program is open to non-resident foreign students.

Program Costs $339 per course.

Housing and Student Services Housing is not available. Job counseling and placement services are not available.

Special Features Field placement gives 3 credits for working in an organization off campus. Paper is required.

Contact Dr. Irene Frieze, Director, Women's Studies Program, Pittsburgh, PA 15260. 412-624-6485.

WASHINGTON AND JEFFERSON COLLEGE
Washington, Pennsylvania 15301

BUSINESS ADMINISTRATION AND MANAGEMENT (06.04)
Management Proficiency Program for Industrial Managers

General Information Unit offering the program: Business/Economics. Program content: Communications, finance, marketing, accounting, employee relations, data processing, business law. Available for credit. Cosponsored by Washington County Manufacturers' Association. Certificate signed by the President. Certificate applicable to associate degree in industrial supervision.

Program Format Daytime, evening classes offered. Instructional schedule: Once per week. Program cycle: Continuous enrollment. Full program cycle lasts 4 courses.

Evaluation Student evaluation based on tests. Grading system: Letters or numbers, pass/fail. Transcripts are kept for each student.

Enrollment Requirements Program is not open to non-resident foreign students.

Program Costs $350 per course.

Housing and Student Services Housing is not available. Job counseling and placement services are not available.

Special Features Courses are offered day and evening so shift workers can attend each week.

Contact Mr. William W. Leake, Dean, Institutional Research, Washington, PA 15301. 412-223-6006.

BUSINESS ADMINISTRATION AND MANAGEMENT (06.04)
Management Training Program for Industrial Supervisors

General Information Unit offering the program: Business/Economics. Program content: Principles of management; economics for supervisors; industrial motivation, communications, and productivity; grievance and contract administration. Available for credit. Cosponsored by Washington County Manufacturers' Association. Certificate signed by the President. Certificate applicable to associate degree in industrial supervision.

Program Format Daytime, evening classes offered. Instructional schedule: Once per week. Program cycle: Continuous enrollment. Full program cycle lasts 4 courses.

Evaluation Student evaluation based on tests. Grading system: Letters or numbers, pass/fail. Transcripts are kept for each student.

Enrollment Requirements Program is not open to non-resident foreign students.

Program Costs $350 per course.

Housing and Student Services Housing is not available. Job counseling and placement services are not available.

Special Features Courses are offered day and evening so shift workers can attend each week.

Contact Mr. William W. Leake, Dean, Institutional Research, Washington, PA 15301. 412-223-6006.

NUCEA MEMBER
WIDENER UNIVERSITY, PENNSYLVANIA CAMPUS
Chester, Pennsylvania 19013

ACCOUNTING (06.02)
Certificate in Accounting

General Information Unit offering the program: University College. Program content: Accounting, economics, mathematics, computers, business law. Available for credit. Certificate signed by the Dean of University College. Certificate applicable to A.S., B.S. in Business Administration.

Program Format Evening, weekend classes offered. Instructional schedule: Once per week. Program cycle: Continuous enrollment. Full program cycle lasts 30 credit hours. Completion of program requires 2.0 GPA.

Certificate in Accounting continued

Evaluation Student evaluation based on tests, reports. Grading system: Letters or numbers. Transcripts are kept for each student.

Enrollment Requirements Program is not open to non-resident foreign students.

Program Costs $127 per credit hour.

Housing and Student Services Housing is not available. Job counseling and placement services are available.

Special Features CLEP credit permitted. Portfolio assessment.

Contact Mr. Joseph A. DiAngelo, D.Ed., Dean of University College, Chester, PA 19013. 215-499-4334.

BUSINESS AND MANAGEMENT, GENERAL (06.01)
Certificate in Management

General Information Unit offering the program: University College. Program content: Accounting, economics, communications, labor relations, computers, mathematics. Available for credit. Certificate signed by the Dean of University College. Certificate applicable to A.S., B.S. in Business Administration.

Program Format Evening, weekend classes offered. Instructional schedule: Once per week. Program cycle: Continuous enrollment. Full program cycle lasts 30 credit hours. Completion of program requires 2.0 GPA.

Evaluation Student evaluation based on tests, reports. Grading system: Letters or numbers. Transcripts are kept for each student.

Enrollment Requirements Program is not open to non-resident foreign students.

Program Costs $127 per credit hour.

Housing and Student Services Housing is not available. Job counseling and placement services are available.

Special Features CLEP credit permitted. Portfolio assessment.

Contact Mr. Joseph A. DiAngelo, D.Ed., Dean of University College, Chester, PA 19013. 215-499-4334.

HUMAN RESOURCES DEVELOPMENT (06.06)
Certificate in Human Resources Management

General Information Unit offering the program: University College. Program content: Business communications, computers, management, personnel, labor relations, social sciences. Available for credit. Certificate signed by the Dean of University College. Certificate applicable to A.S., B.S. in Business Administration.

Program Format Evening, weekend classes offered. Instructional schedule: Once per week. Program cycle: Continuous enrollment. Full program cycle lasts 30 credit hours. Completion of program requires 2.0 GPA.

Evaluation Student evaluation based on tests, reports. Grading system: Letters or numbers. Transcripts are kept for each student.

Enrollment Requirements Program is not open to non-resident foreign students.

Program Costs $127 per credit hour.

Housing and Student Services Housing is not available. Job counseling and placement services are available.

Contact Mr. Joseph A. DiAngelo, D.Ed., Dean of University College, Chester, PA 19013. 215-499-4334.

LAW (22.01)
Certificate in Paralegal Studies

General Information Unit offering the program: University College. Program content: Research, litigation, real estate, business law, estate planning. Available on a non-credit basis.

Endorsed by American Bar Association. Certificate signed by the Dean of University College.

Program Format Daytime, evening classes offered. Instructional schedule: Two evenings or five days per week. Complete program cycle lasts three months (day), nine months (evening).

Evaluation Student evaluation based on tests, reports. Grading system: Letters or numbers. Transcripts are kept for each student.

Enrollment Requirements Thirty-three college credits required. Program is not open to non-resident foreign students.

Program Costs $2100 for the program.

Housing and Student Services Housing is available. Job counseling and placement services are available.

Contact Mr. Joseph A. DiAngelo, D.Ed., Dean of University College, Chester, PA 19013. 215-499-4334.

MANAGEMENT INFORMATION SYSTEMS (06.12)
Certificate in Management Information Systems

General Information Unit offering the program: University College. Program content: Management information systems, accounting, economics, English, mathematics. Available for credit. Certificate signed by the Dean of University College. Certificate applicable to A.S., B.S. in Business Administration.

Program Format Evening classes offered. Instructional schedule: Once per week. Program cycle: Continuous enrollment. Full program cycle lasts 30 credit hours. Completion of program requires 2.0 GPA.

Evaluation Student evaluation based on tests, reports. Grading system: Letters or numbers. Transcripts are kept for each student.

Enrollment Requirements Program is not open to non-resident foreign students.

Program Costs $127 per credit hour.

Housing and Student Services Housing is not available. Job counseling and placement services are available.

Contact Mr. Joseph A. DiAngelo, D.Ed., Dean of University College, Chester, PA 19013. 215-499-4334.

MARKETING MANAGEMENT AND RESEARCH (06.14)
Certificate in Marketing

General Information Unit offering the program: University College. Program content: Economics, statistics, communications, management, research, calculus. Available for credit. Certificate signed by the Dean of University College. Certificate applicable to A.S., B.S. in Business Administration.

Program Format Evening, weekend classes offered. Instructional schedule: Once per week. Program cycle: Continuous enrollment. Full program cycle lasts 30 credit hours. Completion of program requires 2.0 GPA.

Evaluation Student evaluation based on tests, reports. Grading system: Letters or numbers. Transcripts are kept for each student.

Enrollment Requirements Program is not open to non-resident foreign students.

Program Costs $127 per credit hour.

Housing and Student Services Housing is not available. Job counseling and placement services are available.

Special Features CLEP credit permitted. Portfolio assessment.

Contact Mr. Joseph A. DiAngelo, D.Ed., Dean of University College, Chester, PA 19013. 215-499-4334.

TRANSPORTATION AND TRAVEL MARKETING (08.11)
Travel Agency Sales Certificate

General Information Unit offering the program: University College. Program content: Operations, BASIC, sales techniques. Available on a non-credit basis. Certificate signed by the Dean of University College.

Program Format Evening classes offered. Instructional schedule: Twice per week for three hours. Full program cycle lasts 21 weeks.

Evaluation Student evaluation based on tests. Grading system: Letters or numbers. Transcripts are kept for each student.

Enrollment Requirements Thirty college credits, two to three years experience in public service required. Program is not open to non-resident foreign students.

Program Costs $895 for the program.

Housing and Student Services Housing is not available. Job counseling and placement services are not available.

Contact Mr. Joseph A. DiAngelo, D.Ed., Dean of University College, Chester, PA 19013. 215-499-4334.

PUERTO RICO

NUCEA MEMBER
UNIVERSITY OF PUERTO RICO MEDICAL SCIENCES CAMPUS
San Juan, Puerto Rico 00936

DENTAL SERVICES (17.01)
Dental Hygiene

General Information Unit offering the program: Dental Auxiliary Department. Program content: Basic preventive and restorative procedures. Available for credit. Certificate signed by the Chancellor of Medical Sciences Campus. Certificate applicable to associate degree in dental assistance.

Program Format Daytime classes offered. Students enroll once per year. Full program cycle lasts 36 weeks. Completion of program requires 2.00 honor points.

Evaluation Student evaluation based on tests, laboratories, clinical practice. Grading system: Letters or numbers. Transcripts are kept for each student.

Enrollment Requirements Associate degree in expanded functions dental assistance. Program is open to non-resident foreign students.

Program Costs $15 per credit hour.

Housing and Student Services Housing is not available. Job counseling and placement services are not available.

Special Features The program is sponsored by the Medical Sciences Campus (MSC) of the University of Puerto Rico (UPR). The MSC is a highly prestigious health-related institution in Puerto Rico.

Contact Dr. Angel R. Aja, Department Chair, Dental Auxiliary Department, Medical Sciences Campus, GPO Box 5067, San Juan, PR 00936. 809-758-2525 Ext. 1156.

NUCEA MEMBER
UNIVERSITY OF PUERTO RICO, RÍO PIEDRAS
Río Piedras, Puerto Rico 00931

COMPUTER PROGRAMMING (11.02)
Programming Applications Certificate

General Information Unit offering the program: Management Development Center. Program content: History and basic knowledge of computers, analysis and design, operation technique, microcomputer software. Available on a non-credit basis. Certificate signed by the Director, Continuing Education and Extension Division.

Program Format Evening classes offered. Instructional schedule: Twice per week. Students may enroll three times per year. Completion of program requires five courses, grade of C or better.

Evaluation Student evaluation based on tests. Grading system: Letters or numbers. Transcripts are kept for each student.

Enrollment Requirements High school diploma required. Program is open to non-resident foreign students. English language proficiency required.

Program Costs $750 for the program, $150 per course.

Housing and Student Services Housing is not available. Job counseling and placement services are not available.

Special Features The Management Development Center has been offering this type of certificate since 1975. The instructors are Data Processing Center directors or full-time University professors in the data processing area. In 1985 the Continuing Education and Extension Division established a microcomputer laboratory with 20 IBM microcomputers, connected to the mainframe on campus.

Contact Mr. Martín Meléndez Franco, Director, Management Development Center, Continuing Education and Extension Division, Box 23312, UPR Station, Río Piedras, PR 00931-3312. 809-763-7920.

RHODE ISLAND

NUCEA MEMBER
BRYANT COLLEGE
Smithfield, Rhode Island 02917

BUSINESS AND MANAGEMENT, GENERAL (06.01)
Supervisory Management

General Information Unit offering the program: Center for Management Development. Program content: Management, the supervisor and personnel, interpersonal skills. Available on a non-credit basis. Certificate signed by the Director, Center for Management Development.

Program Format Evening classes offered. Instructional schedule: One evening per week. Students may enroll September, January, April. Full program cycle lasts 6 courses.

Evaluation Student evaluation based on tests, papers, reports. Grading system: Letters or numbers. Transcripts are kept for each student.

Program Costs $225 per course.

Housing and Student Services Housing is not available. Job counseling and placement services are not available.

Contact Ms. Rosemary D'Arcy, Associate Director, 450 Douglas Pike, Smithfield, RI 02917-1284. 401-232-6200.

COMPUTER AND INFORMATION SCIENCES, GENERAL (11.01)
Computer Information Systems

General Information Unit offering the program: Center for Management Development. Program content: Computer concepts, BASIC, managing computer-based projects, analysis and design of computerized systems. Available on a non-credit basis. Certificate signed by the Director, Center for Management Development.

Program Format Evening classes offered. Instructional schedule: One evening per week. Students may enroll September, January, April. Full program cycle lasts 5 courses.

Evaluation Student evaluation based on tests, papers, reports. Grading system: Letters or numbers. Transcripts are kept for each student.

Enrollment Requirements Program is open to non-resident foreign students.

Program Costs $205–$235 per course.

Housing and Student Services Housing is not available. Job counseling and placement services are not available.

Contact Ms. Rosemary D'Arcy, Associate Director, 450 Douglas Pike, Smithfield, RI 02917-1284. 401-232-6200.

PERSONNEL AND TRAINING PROGRAMS (07.05)
Certificate in Personnel Administration

General Information Unit offering the program: The Center for Management Development. Program content: Introduction to personnel administration; recruiting, interviewing, and selecting; wage and salary administration; personnel administration and the law. Available on a non-credit basis. Certificate signed by the Director of the Center for Management Development.

Program Format Evening classes offered. Instructional schedule: One evening per week. Students may enroll September, January, April. Full program cycle lasts 6 courses.

Evaluation Student evaluation based on tests, papers, reports. Grading system: Letters or numbers. Transcripts are kept for each student.

Enrollment Requirements English language proficiency required.

Program Costs $205 per course.

Housing and Student Services Housing is not available. Job counseling and placement services are not available.

Contact Ms. Rosemary D'Arcy, Associate Director, 450 Douglas Pike, Smithfield, RI 02917-1284. 401-232-6200.

RHODE ISLAND SCHOOL OF DESIGN
Providence, Rhode Island 02903

DESIGN (50.04)
Certificate in Advertising Design

General Information Unit offering the program: Continuing Education. Program content: Role of the creative director; conceptual, technical, and verbal skills. Available on a non-credit basis. Certificate signed by the Director, Continuing Education.

Program Format Evening, weekend classes offered. Instructional schedule: Once or twice per week for three hours. Program cycle: Continuous enrollment. Completion of program requires grade of C or better, portfolio review.

Evaluation Student evaluation based on papers, reports, critiques, portfolio, verbal presentations. Grading system: Letters or numbers. Transcripts are kept for each student.

Enrollment Requirements High school diploma or equivalent required. Program is open to non-resident foreign students.

Program Costs $4275 for the program, $200–$275 per course.

Housing and Student Services Housing is not available. Job counseling and placement services are available.

Special Features Possibility of waiver for prior experience/education. Part-time flexibility of scheduling. Instructors are working professionals. Portfolio reviews, and career counseling. Lecture series. Courses combine lecture, studio experience, team and individual problem-solving, field trips, slide presentations. Extensive library, clipping file, slide library, studio facilities/equipment. Nationally acclaimed museum.

Contact Continuing Education Office, 2 College Street, Providence, RI 02903. 401-331-3511 Ext. 408.

DESIGN (50.04)
Certificate in Scientific and Technical Illustration

General Information Unit offering the program: Continuing Education. Available on a non-credit basis. Certificate signed by the Director of Continuing Education.

Program Format Evening, weekend classes offered. Instructional schedule: Once or twice per week for three hours. Program cycle: Continuous enrollment. Completion of program requires grade of C or better, portfolio review.

Evaluation Student evaluation based on tests, papers, reports, critiques, portfolio, verbal presentations. Grading system: Letters or numbers. Transcripts are kept for each student.

Enrollment Requirements High school diploma or equivalent required. Program is open to non-resident foreign students.

Program Costs $3600 for the program, $120–$260 per course.

Housing and Student Services Housing is not available. Job counseling and placement services are available.

Special Features Waiver for prior experience/education. Scheduling flexibility. Part-time Instructors are working professionals. Lecture series, workshops. Extensive library, clipping file, slide library, studio facilities. Well-stocked nature lab where specimens may be handled. Nationally acclaimed museum. Student may emphasize scientific or technical illustration. Small enrollment means individual attention.

Contact Continuing Education, 2 College Street, Providence, RI 02903. 401-331-3511 Ext. 408.

FOOD PRODUCTION, MANAGEMENT, AND SERVICES (20.04)
Certificate in Culinary Arts

General Information Unit offering the program: Department of Continuing Education. Available on a non-credit basis. Endorsed by Educational Institute of the American Culinary Federation. Certificate signed by the Director, Office of Continuing Education. Program fulfills requirements for American Culinary Federation.

Program Format Daytime classes offered. Students enroll in September. Full program cycle lasts 2 years. Completion of program requires 2.0 GPA.

Evaluation Student evaluation based on tests, practical. Grading system: Letters or numbers. Transcripts are kept for each student.

Enrollment Requirements High school diploma or GED required.

Program Costs $5550 per semester.

Housing and Student Services Housing is not available. Job counseling and placement services are available.

Contact Dr. Gail Lawson, Assistant Program Director, 2 College Street, Providence, RI 02903. 401-331-3511 Ext. 365.

INTERIOR DESIGN (04.05)
Certificate in Interior Design

General Information Unit offering the program: Continuing Education. Program content: Design process for 3-D spaces, knowledge of construction, legal requirements, designer/client relationship. Available on a non-credit basis. Certificate signed by the Director of Continuing Education. Program fulfills requirements for American Society of Interior Design.

Program Format   Evening, weekend classes offered. Instructional schedule: Once or twice per week for three hours. Program cycle: Continuous enrollment. Completion of program requires grade of C or better, portfolio review.

Evaluation   Student evaluation based on tests, papers, reports, critiques, portfolio, verbal presentations. Grading system: Letters or numbers. Transcripts are kept for each student.

Enrollment Requirements   High school diploma or equivalent required. Program is open to non-resident foreign students.

Program Costs $4000 for the program, $200–$460 per course.

Housing and Student Services   Housing is not available. Job counseling and placement services are available.

Special Features   Waiver for Prior experience/education. Scheduling flexibility. Part-time Instructors are working professionals. Lecture series, workshops, field trips. Extensive library, clipping file, slide library, studio facilities, Nationally acclaimed museum. Based on requirements established by ASID (American Society Interior Design), FIDER (Foundation for Interior Design Education Research) and NCIDQ (National Council for Interior Design Qualifications).

Contact   Continuing Education Office, 2 College Street, Providence, RI 02903. 401-331-3511 Ext. 408.

NUCEA MEMBER
UNIVERSITY OF RHODE ISLAND
Kingston, Rhode Island 02881

FOOD SCIENCES AND HUMAN NUTRITION (19.05)
Dietary Management

General Information   Unit offering the program: Department of Food Science and Nutrition. Program content: Management of nutrition care. Certificate signed by the Associate Dean. Program fulfills requirements for licensure by the Rhode Island Department of Health.

Program Format   Evening classes offered. Program cycle: Continuous enrollment. Full program cycle lasts 2 courses.

Evaluation   Student evaluation based on tests, papers, reports, fieldwork. Grading system: Letters or numbers. Transcripts are kept for each student.

Enrollment Requirements   Limited to dietary managers or supervisors. Program is open to non-resident foreign students.

Program Costs $200 for the program, $100 per course.

Housing and Student Services   Housing is not available. Job counseling and placement services are not available.

Special Features   The certificate program offers a sequence of two courses in the management of nutrition care, which are needed by dietary managers and supervisors in health care facilities and schools by the Rhode Island Department of Health. The courses are designed to meet the qualifications for Medicare/Medicaid membership in HIEFSS, and the membership and certification requirements of the Dietary Managers Association.

Contact   Mr. Joseph P. McGinn, Coordinator, College of Continuing Education, 199 Promenade Street, Providence, RI 02908. 401-277-3810.

HEALTH SERVICES ADMINISTRATION (18.07)
Nursing Home Administration

General Information   Unit offering the program: College of Continuing Education. Program content: Survey, fiscal planning, legal aspects, geriatric overview. Available on a non-credit basis.

Endorsed by Rhode Island Health Care Association. Certificate signed by the Dean, College of Continuing Education.

Program Format   Evening, weekend classes offered. Program cycle: Continuous enrollment. Full program cycle lasts 4 courses. Completion of program requires average grade of C or better.

Evaluation   Student evaluation based on tests, papers, reports. Grading system: Letters or numbers. Transcripts are kept for each student.

Enrollment Requirements   Bachelor's degree required. Program is open to non-resident foreign students.

Program Costs $560 for the program, $140 per course.

Housing and Student Services   Housing is not available. Job counseling and placement services are not available.

Special Features   Nursing Home Administrators' Institute is certificate program offered in cooperation with Rhode Island Health Care Association and Rhode Island Association of Facilities for the Aging. Courses designed to prepare participants for national examination and to increase their knowledge of nursing home administration. Student must successfully complete four of five specialized courses. Program is designed to be completed within one year.

Contact   Mr. Joseph P. McGinn, Coordinator, College of Continuing Education, 199 Promenade Street, Providence, RI 02908. 401-277-3810.

REAL ESTATE (06.17)
Real Estate

General Information   Unit offering the program: College of Continuing Education. Available on a non-credit basis. Endorsed by Rhode Island Association of Realtors. Certificate signed by the Dean, College of Continuing Education. Program fulfills requirements for Sales or Broker's Real Estate License.

Program Format   Evening classes offered. Program cycle: Continuous enrollment. Full program cycle lasts 5 courses. Completion of program requires average grade of C or better.

Evaluation   Student evaluation based on tests, papers, reports. Grading system: Letters or numbers. Transcripts are kept for each student.

Enrollment Requirements   High school diploma required. Program is open to non-resident foreign students.

Program Costs $600 for the program, $120 per course.

Housing and Student Services   Housing is not available. Job counseling and placement services are not available.

Special Features   Designed for those professionally engaged in real estate and those planning to enter the field and for the development of higher standards in the real estate business. Developed by a University-appointed Real Estate Education Advisory Committee and offered in cooperation with the Greater Providence Board of Realtors and the Rhode Island Association of Realtors. Introduced over thirty years ago.

Contact   Mr. Joseph P. McGinn, Coordinator, College of Continuing Education, 199 Promenade Street, Providence, RI 02908. 401-277-3810.

SOUTH CAROLINA

CLEMSON UNIVERSITY
Clemson, South Carolina 29634

NURSING (18.11)
School Nurse Practitioner

General Information   Unit offering the program: Department of Continuing Education in The College of Nursing. Program content: Psychology, health education, nutrition, pediatrics,

School Nurse Practitioner continued

adolescence and childhood problems. Available for credit. Cosponsored by United States Department of Health and Human Services, Division of Nursing. Certificate signed by the Vice Provost.

Program Format two on-campus summer sessions of eight weeks with a nine-month preceptorship in home area. Instructional schedule: All day for two 8-week summer sessions and 4 hours per week for 36 weeks during preceptorship. Students enroll in March. Full program cycle lasts 16 months. Completion of program requires 160 hours contact work, 16 CEUs, 45 hours lab work, 2.0 GPA.

Evaluation Student evaluation based on tests, papers, reports, clinical skill performance. Grading system: Letters or numbers, pass/fail. Transcripts are kept for each student.

Enrollment Requirements Enrollment limited to registered nurses with three years work experience. Program is not open to non-resident foreign students.

Program Costs $1700 for the program (state residents), $3800 for the program (nonresidents).

Housing and Student Services Housing is available. Job counseling and placement services are not available.

Special Features Sixteen-month certificate program funded by federal grant from DHHS for practicing registered nurses interested in school nursing or college health nursing. Focus is on preparation to deliver primary care in ambulatory settings for school-age youth and adolescents. Credit toward baccalaureate degree in nursing as well as continuing education credit available.

Contact Ms. Lorena Downs, Project Director, School Nurse Practitioner Program, 311 College of Nursing, Clemson, SC 29634-1711. 803-656-5524.

COLUMBIA BIBLE COLLEGE AND SEMINARY
Columbia, South Carolina 29230

BIBLE STUDIES (39.02)
Bible Certificate Program

General Information Unit offering the program: Undergraduate Division. Program content: Bible, religious courses. Available for credit. Certificate signed by the President. Certificate applicable to any four-year degree offered at the institution.

Program Format Daytime classes offered. Program cycle: Continuous enrollment. Complete program cycle lasts three quarters, plus three weeks in December and seven weeks in the summer. Completion of program requires 2.0 GPA, 45 quarter units.

Evaluation Student evaluation based on tests, papers. Grading system: Letters or numbers. Transcripts are kept for each student.

Enrollment Requirements High school diploma required. Program is open to non-resident foreign students. English language proficiency required.

Housing and Student Services Housing is available. Job counseling and placement services are available.

Contact Dr. Donald J. Trouten, Dean, Box 3122, Columbia, SC 29230. 803-754-4100 Ext. 226.

BIBLE STUDIES (39.02)
Diploma in Bible Studies

General Information Unit offering the program: Extension Division, Columbia School of Biblical Education. Available for credit. Certificate signed by the President. Certificate applicable to any four-year degree offered at the institution.

Program Format Correspondence, media package (print/audio/video) classes offered. Program cycle: Continuous enrollment. Complete program cycle lasts two to four years. Completion of program requires 2.0 GPA.

Evaluation Student evaluation based on tests, papers. Grading system: Letters or numbers. Transcripts are kept for each student.

Enrollment Requirements High school diploma or GED required. Program is open to non-resident foreign students. English language proficiency required.

Program Costs $2745 for the program.

Special Features The program is designed to enable those in religious ministries to have growth opportunities without going to campus. The program is completely external although courses completed in residence or intensive study modules can apply to program completion.

Contact Dr. James E. Wegner, Dean, Columbia School of Biblical Education, Box 3122, Columbia, SC 29230. 803-754-4100 Ext. 131.

BIBLE STUDIES (39.02)
Graduate Diploma in Biblical Studies

General Information Unit offering the program: Extension Division, Columbia School of Biblical Education. Available for credit. Certificate signed by the President. Certificate applicable to M.Div.

Program Format Correspondence, media package (print/audio/video) classes offered. Program cycle: Continuous enrollment. Complete program cycle lasts two to four years. Completion of program requires 2.0 GPA.

Evaluation Student evaluation based on tests, papers. Grading system: Letters or numbers. Transcripts are kept for each student.

Enrollment Requirements Bachelor's degree required. Program is open to non-resident foreign students. English language proficiency required.

Program Costs $2745 for the program.

Special Features The program is designed to enable those in religious ministries to have growth opportunities without going to campus. The program is completely external although courses completed in residence or intensive study modules can apply to program completion.

Contact Dr. James E. Wegner, Dean, Columbia School of Biblical Education, Box 3122, Columbia, SC 29230. 803-754-4100 Ext. 131.

NUCEA MEMBER
UNIVERSITY OF SOUTH CAROLINA
Columbia, South Carolina 29208

INDIVIDUAL AND FAMILY DEVELOPMENT (19.07)
Certificate in Gerontology

General Information Unit offering the program: College of Social Work, Psychology, and Nursing. Available for credit. Certificate signed by the Dean of Graduate School. Certificate applicable to M.S.W.

Program Format Daytime, evening, weekend classes offered. Program cycle: Continuous enrollment. Complete program cycle lasts two to four semesters. Completion of program requires 18 semester hours.

Evaluation Student evaluation based on tests, papers, reports. Grading system: Letters or numbers. Transcripts are kept for each student.

Enrollment Requirements Bachelor's degree, 2.5 GPA, GRE scores, letters of recommendation required. Program is open to non-resident foreign students.

Program Costs $86 per credit hour.

Housing and Student Services Housing is available. Job counseling and placement services are not available.

Contact Dr. Leon Ginsberg, Chair, Interdisciplinary Program Committee, College of Social Work, Columbia, SC 29208. 803-777-5210.

INDIVIDUAL AND FAMILY DEVELOPMENT (19.07)
Certificate of Graduate Study in Gerontology

General Information Unit offering the program: Graduate School. Available for credit. Certificate signed by the Dean, Graduate School.

Program Format Evening classes offered. Program cycle: Continuous enrollment. Full program cycle lasts 2 semesters.

Evaluation Student evaluation based on tests, papers, reports. Grading system: Letters or numbers. Transcripts are kept for each student.

Enrollment Requirements Bachelor's degree, GRE scores required. Program is open to non-resident foreign students. English language proficiency required.

Program Costs $1548 for the program, $258 per course.

Housing and Student Services Housing is available. Job counseling and placement services are available.

Special Features Provides basic information to multidisciplinary groups of students on issues related to the elderly. There are three required courses and 9 hours of electives in student's area of interest.

Contact Graduate School, 901 Sumter Street, Columbia, SC 29208. 803-777-4243.

MISCELLANEOUS SPECIALIZED AREAS, LIFE SCIENCES (26.06)
Epidemiology and Control of Malaria and Other Vector-Borne Diseases

General Information Unit offering the program: International Center for Public Health Research. Program content: Vector-borne disease control. Available on a non-credit basis. Certificate signed by the Dean, College of Health.

Program Format Daytime classes offered. Students may enroll twice per year. Full program cycle lasts 6 weeks.

Evaluation Student evaluation based on tests, papers, reports. Grading system: Pass/fail. Records are kept for each student.

Enrollment Requirements Training in medicine, engineering, or vector control required. Program is open to non-resident foreign students. Students required to live on campus.

Program Costs $3890 for the program.

Contact Director, International Center for Public Health Research, P.O. Box 699, McClellanville, SC 29458. 803-527-1371.

NURSING (18.11)
Certificate of Graduate Study in Primary Care Nursing

General Information Unit offering the program: College of Nursing. Available for credit. Certificate signed by the President of the University.

Program Format Daytime, evening classes offered. Instructional schedule: Two to three classes per week. Full program cycle lasts 2 years. Completion of program requires 15 credit hours, grade of B or better.

Evaluation Student evaluation based on tests, papers, reports, clinical performance. Grading system: Letters or numbers. Transcripts are kept for each student.

Enrollment Requirements M.N. required. Program is open to non-resident foreign students.

Program Costs $1290 for the program, $258 per course.

Housing and Student Services Housing is available. Job counseling and placement services are available.

Special Features Fifteen semester hours post master's program for part-time students. Emphasis areas are family, adult, child, or gerontological nursing. The adult emphasis areas include correctional, occupational, and psychiatric-mental health. Faculty are nurse practitioners who are doctorally prepared. Graduates of the program are eligible for American Nurses' Association certification as family, adult, child, or gerontological nurse practitioners.

Contact Mr. Mike Hix, Acting Director of Student Services, College of Nursing, Columbia, SC 29208. 803-777-7412.

TEACHER EDUCATION, SPECIFIC SUBJECT AREAS (13.13)
Certificate of Graduate Study in School Health Education

General Information Unit offering the program: Health Promotion and Education. Program content: Drug addiction, nutrition, sexuality, consumer health. Available for credit. Certificate signed by the Dean, Graduate School. Certificate applicable to M.H.Ed. Program fulfills requirements for certification in Health Education from South Carolina Department of Education.

Program Format Daytime, evening classes offered. Program cycle: Continuous enrollment. Full program cycle lasts 18 credit hours. Completion of program requires 3.0 GPA.

Evaluation Student evaluation based on tests, papers, reports. Grading system: Letters or numbers. Transcripts are kept for each student.

Enrollment Requirements Bachelor's degree, three letters of recommendation, GRE scores, letter of intent required. Program is open to non-resident foreign students. English language proficiency required. Minimum TOEFL score required: 550.

Program Costs $1602 for the program, $267 per course.

Housing and Student Services Housing is available. Job counseling and placement services are available.

Special Features Program is intended for teachers active in South Carolina public schools who are teaching health education and/or want to add the health education endorsement to their teaching certificate.

Contact Department Chairman, Department of Health Promotion and Education, Columbia, SC 29208. 803-777-7096.

SOUTH DAKOTA

BLACK HILLS STATE COLLEGE
Spearfish, South Dakota 57783

SECRETARIAL AND RELATED PROGRAMS (07.06)
General Office Secretary Certificate

General Information Unit offering the program: Division of Business. Program content: Typing, shorthand, accounting, clerical, word processing skills. Available for credit. Certificate signed by the President of the College.

General Office Secretary Certificate continued

Program Format Daytime, evening, correspondence classes offered. Program cycle: Continuous enrollment. Full program cycle lasts 2 semesters. Completion of program requires 34 semester hours, average grade of C or better.

Evaluation Student evaluation based on tests, papers, reports. Grading system: Letters or numbers. Transcripts are kept for each student.

Enrollment Requirements College admissions required. Program is open to non-resident foreign students. English language proficiency required. Minimum TOEFL score required: 490.

Program Costs $1600 for the program, $50 per course.

Housing and Student Services Housing is available. Job counseling and placement services are available.

Special Features This one-year program provides students with excellent secretarial and word-processing skills in addition to an introduction to the liberal arts. Program credits can be applied to two- and four-year degree programs in business and are transferable to other colleges and universities.

Contact Dr. Richard Buckles, Chairman, Division of Business, Box 9002, Spearfish, SD 57783. 605-642-6336.

NUCEA MEMBER
NORTHERN STATE COLLEGE
Aberdeen, South Dakota 57401

SECRETARIAL AND RELATED PROGRAMS (07.06)
Office Administration

General Information Unit offering the program: Business Education and Administrative Services. Program content: Business communications, business math, English composition, shorthand, typewriting, word processing, records management. Available for credit. Certificate signed by the Registrar. Certificate applicable to associate or bachelor's degree in office administration.

Program Format Daytime classes offered. Instructional schedule: Three to five classes per week. Full program cycle lasts 2 semesters. Completion of program requires 2.0 GPA.

Evaluation Student evaluation based on tests, papers, reports. Grading system: Letters or numbers. Transcripts are kept for each student.

Enrollment Requirements High school diploma required. Program is open to non-resident foreign students.

Program Costs $1800 for the program.

Housing and Student Services Housing is available. Job counseling and placement services are available.

Special Features Advanced placement in shorthand and typewriting based on education and experience. A 32-semester-hour program with a completion time of two semesters. May carry reduced class load and extend completion time. Teachers hold master's or doctoral degrees. Long-established program leading to job success.

Contact Mr. Ronald L. Johnson, Chair, Business Education and Administrative Services, Box 696, Aberdeen, SD 57401. 605-622-7725.

TENNESSEE

CRICHTON COLLEGE
Memphis, Tennessee 38182

BIBLE STUDIES (39.02)
Life Foundation Certificate

General Information Unit offering the program: Bible Department. Program content: Bible, church ministries, electives. Available for credit. Certificate signed by the Chairman of the Board of Trustees. Certificate applicable to most four-year degrees offered at the institution.

Program Format Daytime, evening classes offered. Program cycle: Continuous enrollment. Full program cycle lasts 2 semesters. Completion of program requires 30 semester hours, average grade of C or better.

Evaluation Student evaluation based on tests, papers, reports. Grading system: Letters or numbers. Transcripts are kept for each student.

Enrollment Requirements College admissions required. Program is open to non-resident foreign students. English language proficiency required.

Program Costs $3900 for the program, $390 per course.

Housing and Student Services Housing is available. Job counseling and placement services are available.

Special Features The broad-based program is generally equivalent to the first year of most programs at the college. The program consists of 18 hours of bible, 6 hours of Christian education and missions and 6 elective hours. It helps prepare the student for limited work in church, missions, or for further college study.

Contact Mr. J. D. Rector, Director of Admissions, 2485 Union Avenue, Memphis, TN 38112. 901-458-7526.

NUCEA MEMBER
EAST TENNESSEE STATE UNIVERSITY
Johnson City, Tennessee 37614

DENTAL SERVICES (17.01)
Dental Assisting

General Information Unit offering the program: Nave Paramedical Center Department/School of Public and Allied Health. Program content: Chairside assisting, dental radiology, dental materials. Available for credit. Endorsed by American Dental Association. Cosponsored by American Dental Assistant Association. Certificate signed by the President of University. Program fulfills requirements for Certified Dental Assistant.

Program Format Daytime classes offered. Instructional schedule: Monday through Friday. Students enroll in the fall. Full program cycle lasts 3 semesters. Completion of program requires clinical contact hours.

Evaluation Student evaluation based on tests, clinical and skill evaluations. Grading system: Letters or numbers. Transcripts are kept for each student.

Enrollment Requirements Minimum ACT score of 16 or SAT score of 720, high school diploma or GED required. Program is open to non-resident foreign students. English language proficiency required.

Program Costs $2181 for the program.

Housing and Student Services Housing is available. Job counseling and placement services are available.

Special Features Dentist is on staff full-time. Program has been accredited since 1980. High percentage of graduates pass national certification examination.

Contact Mr. Victor W. Hopson, D.D.S., Director of Dental Assisting Program, Nave Paramedical Center, 1000 West E Street, Elizabethton, TN 37643. 615-543-2230.

DIAGNOSTIC AND TREATMENT SERVICES (17.02)
Graduate Respiratory Therapy Technician— Cardio-Pulmonary

General Information Unit offering the program: School of Public and Allied Health/Nave Paramedical Center. Program content: Diagnostic and therapeutic procedures in medical setting with care and management of cardio-respiratory impaired. Available on either a credit or non-credit basis. Endorsed by Committee on Allied Health Education and Accreditation (CAHEA). Cosponsored by Joint Review Committee for Respiratory Therapy Education (JRCRTE). Certificate signed by the President of University. Certificate applicable to B.S. in Health Education.

Program Format Daytime classes offered. Instructional schedule: Five days per week. Students enroll in the fall. Full program cycle lasts 12 months. Completion of program requires grade of C or better in all courses, 800 clinical hours.

Evaluation Student evaluation based on tests, papers, proficiency documentation forms. Grading system: Letters or numbers. Transcripts are kept for each student.

Enrollment Requirements Minimum ACT score of 16 or SAT score of 760 required. Program is open to non-resident foreign students. English language proficiency required.

Program Costs $2000 for the program.

Housing and Student Services Housing is available. Job counseling and placement services are available.

Special Features The 12-month certificate Respiratory Therapy Technician program at ETSU allows the graduate to continue in career development towards a bachelor's degree in health education at ETSU or continue an advised career path towards a degree in advanced respiratory therapy. The technician graduate becomes a Certified Respiratory Therapy Technician (CRTT) upon passing the national certification exam.

Contact Mr. Patrick Flaherty, Clinical Director, Nave Paramedical Center, Elizabethton, TN 37643. 615-543-2230.

MISCELLANEOUS ALLIED HEALTH SERVICES (17.05)
Surgical Technology

General Information Unit offering the program: School of Public and Allied Health/Nave Paramedical Center. Program content: Anatomy, terminology, procedures required to function as a team member in the operating room. Available for credit. Endorsed by Committee on Allied Health Education and Accreditation (CAHEA). Cosponsored by Association of Surgical Technologists. Certificate signed by the President. Program fulfills requirements for Certified Surgical Technologist.

Program Format Daytime classes offered. Program cycle: Continuous enrollment. Complete program cycle lasts 11½ months.

Evaluation Student evaluation based on tests, reports, clinical evaluations. Grading system: Letters or numbers. Transcripts are kept for each student.

Enrollment Requirements Minimum ACT score of 16 or SAT score of 720, university admissions required. Program is open to non-resident foreign students. English language proficiency required.

Program Costs $1725 for the program.

Housing and Student Services Housing is available. Job counseling and placement services are available.

Special Features The program has been in effect for twelve years. The instructor/program director is a certified physician's assistant and a certified surgeon's assistant.

Contact Mr. Alan G. Ballard, Surgical Technology Program Director, Nave Paramedical Center, 1000 West E Street, Elizabethton, TN 37643. 615-543-2230.

SECRETARIAL AND RELATED PROGRAMS (07.06)
Administrative Secretarial

General Information Unit offering the program: Office Management. Program content: Office skills, mathematics, accounting, finance. Available for credit. Certificate signed by the President of University. Certificate applicable to bachelor's degree in business administration/office management.

Program Format Daytime, evening classes offered. Program cycle: Continuous enrollment. Full program cycle lasts 2 years. Completion of program requires 2.0 GPA.

Evaluation Student evaluation based on tests, papers, reports. Grading system: Letters or numbers. Transcripts are kept for each student.

Enrollment Requirements High school diploma required. Program is open to non-resident foreign students. English language proficiency required.

Program Costs $687 per semester (state residents); $1215 per semester (nonresidents).

Housing and Student Services Housing is available. Job counseling and placement services are available.

Special Features Eighty percent of faculty hold doctoral degrees. Test-out program is available.

Contact Dr. Don Wilkinson, Chairman, Office Management Department, P.O. Box 23410A, Johnson City, TN 37614. 615-929-4257.

SECRETARIAL AND RELATED PROGRAMS (07.06)
Legal Secretarial

General Information Unit offering the program: Office Management Department. Program content: Office skills, criminal justice, accounting. Available for credit. Certificate signed by the President of University. Certificate applicable to bachelor's degree in business administration/office management.

Program Format Daytime, evening classes offered. Program cycle: Continuous enrollment. Full program cycle lasts 2 years. Completion of program requires 2.0 GPA.

Evaluation Student evaluation based on tests, papers, reports. Grading system: Letters or numbers. Transcripts are kept for each student.

Enrollment Requirements High school diploma required. Program is open to non-resident foreign students. English language proficiency required.

Program Costs $687 per semester (state residents); $1215 per semester (nonresidents).

Housing and Student Services Housing is available. Job counseling and placement services are available.

Special Features Eighty percent of faculty hold doctoral degrees. Test-out program is available.

Contact Dr. Don Wilkinson, Chairman, Office Management Department, P.O. Box 23410A, Johnson City, TN 37614. 615-929-4257.

SECRETARIAL AND RELATED PROGRAMS (07.06)
Medical Secretarial

General Information Unit offering the program: Office Management. Program content: Office skills, accounting, biology, psychology. Available for credit. Certificate signed by the President of University. Certificate applicable to bachelor's degree in business administration/office management.

Medical Secretarial continued

Program Format Daytime, evening classes offered. Program cycle: Continuous enrollment. Full program cycle lasts 2 years. Completion of program requires 2.0 GPA.

Evaluation Student evaluation based on tests, papers, reports. Grading system: Letters or numbers. Transcripts are kept for each student.

Enrollment Requirements High school diploma required. Program is open to non-resident foreign students. English language proficiency required.

Program Costs $687 per semester (state residents); $1215 per semester (nonresidents).

Housing and Student Services Housing is available. Job counseling and placement services are available.

Special Features Eighty percent of faculty hold doctoral degrees. Test-out program is available.

Contact Dr. Don Wilkinson, Chairman, Office Management Department, P.O. Box 23410A, Johnson City, TN 37614. 615-929-4257.

NUCEA MEMBER
MEMPHIS STATE UNIVERSITY
Memphis, Tennessee 38152

REAL ESTATE (06.17)
Certificate in Real Estate

General Information Unit offering the program: Continuing Education Short Courses. Program content: Law, finance, investments appraisal, ethics, contracts. Available on a non-credit basis. Cosponsored by Memphis Board of Realtors. Certificate signed by the Presdient.

Program Format Daytime, evening, weekend classes offered. Full program cycle lasts 7 courses.

Evaluation Student evaluation based on tests. Grading system: Pass/fail. Transcripts are kept for each student.

Program Costs $420–$525 for the program, $60–$75 per course.

Housing and Student Services Housing is not available. Job counseling and placement services are not available.

Contact Ms. Maryann Hicky, Director of Short Courses, Memphis, TN 38152. 901-454-2877.

NUCEA MEMBER
UNIVERSITY OF TENNESSEE, KNOXVILLE
Knoxville, Tennessee 37996

ACCOUNTING, BOOKKEEPING, AND RELATED PROGRAMS (07.01)
Certified Credit Administrator

General Information Unit offering the program: Non-Credit Programs. Program content: Introductory, intermediate, and applied credit management; cases. Available on a non-credit basis. Endorsed by National Institute of Credit (NIC). Cosponsored by National Association of Credit Management (NACM), East Tennessee Chapter. Certificate signed by the Dean. Program fulfills requirements for Certified Credit Administrator.

Program Format Evening classes offered. Instructional schedule: Three hours per week. Program cycle: Continuous enrollment. Completion of program requires four courses.

Evaluation Student evaluation based on tests. Grading system: Letters or numbers. Transcripts are kept for each student.

Enrollment Requirements Program is open to non-resident foreign students. English language proficiency required.

Program Costs $150–$175 per course.

Housing and Student Services Housing is not available. Job counseling and placement services are not available.

Special Features This program has been in existence for approximately ten years. It is designed to meet the needs of credit professionals and to improve the understanding of the fundamentals of credit and financial management.

Contact Ms. Dawn von Weisenstein, Coordinator, Non-Credit Programs, 2016 Lake Avenue, Knoxville, TN 37996-3515. 615-974-6688.

CONSTRUCTION TECHNOLOGY (15.10)
Certified Home Builder

General Information Unit offering the program: Non-Credit Programs. Program content: Construction contracts, business management, sales and marketing. Available on a non-credit basis. Endorsed by National Association of Home Builders. Cosponsored by Home Builders Association of Tennessee. Certificate signed by the Dean.

Program Format Daytime classes offered. Instructional schedule: Three 3-day sessions. Completion of program requires nine courses.

Evaluation Student evaluation based on tests. Grading system: Pass/fail. Transcripts are kept for each student.

Enrollment Requirements Program is open to non-resident foreign students. English language proficiency required.

Program Costs $300–$575 for one 3-day session.

Housing and Student Services Housing is not available. Job counseling and placement services are not available.

Special Features This is the first course offering in this area in Tennessee. The instructors are all qualified in the fields in which they teach, and there is a different instructor for each course.

Contact Ms. Dawn von Weisenstein, Coordinator, Non-Credit Programs, 2016 Lake Avenue, Knoxville, TN 37996-3515. 615-974-6688.

PERSONNEL MANAGEMENT (06.16)
Certified Employee Benefit Specialist

General Information Unit offering the program: Non-Credit Programs. Program content: Group benefit programs, pension plans, social security, savings plans, management principles, legal environment, accounting and information systems, asset management, labor relations, benefit plans and the economy, issues and administration. Available on a non-credit basis. Endorsed by International Foundation of Employee Benefit Plans (IFEBP). Certificate signed by the Dean. Program fulfills requirements for Certified Employee Benefit Specialist.

Program Format Evening classes offered. Instructional schedule: Three hours per week. Program cycle: Continuous enrollment. Completion of program requires ten courses, final exam.

Evaluation Student evaluation based on tests. Grading system: Pass/fail. Transcripts are kept for each student.

Enrollment Requirements Program is open to non-resident foreign students. English language proficiency required.

Program Costs $200 per course.

Housing and Student Services Housing is not available. Job counseling and placement services are not available.

Special Features This program offers an opportunity for career advancement. Bob Cross, the instructor, is a founding principal of the Lincoln-Cross, Inc., agency and has experience as manager of a major international employee benefit consulting firm. This program was developed by the International Foundation of Employee Benefit Plans and the Wharton School of Business.

Contact   Ms. Dawn von Weisenstein, Coordinator, Non-Credit Programs, 2016 Lake Avenue, Knoxville, TN 37996-3515. 615-974-6688.

TEXAS

ABILENE CHRISTIAN UNIVERSITY
Abilene, Texas 79699

INDIVIDUAL AND FAMILY DEVELOPMENT (19.07)
Certificate of Studies in Gerontology

General Information   Unit offering the program: Sociology, Social Work, Gerontology. Available for credit. Endorsed by Association of Gerontology in Higher Education. Certificate signed by the Dean, Graduate School. Certificate applicable to B.S. in Sociology.

Program Format   Daytime classes offered. Students may enroll fall, spring, summer. Full program cycle lasts 15 credit hours. Completion of program requires five courses.

Evaluation   Student evaluation based on tests, papers, class participation. Grading system: Letters or numbers. Transcripts are kept for each student.

Enrollment Requirements   University admissions required. Program is open to non-resident foreign students. English language proficiency required. Minimum TOEFL score required: 550.

Program Costs $2025 for the program.

Housing and Student Services   Housing is available. Job counseling and placement services are available.

Special Features   The undergraduate student, in consultation with the adviser, will design a program of study that will meet the individual student's needs in the area of gerontology. The undergraduate certificate is a nationally recognized credential in the field of gerontological education.

Contact   Dr. C. Bruce Davis, Director, Center for the Study of Aging, Station ACU, Box 8108, Abilene, TX 79699. 915-674-2350.

MISSIONARY STUDIES (39.03)
Certificate for Missionary Preparation (Advanced Study)

General Information   Unit offering the program: Department of Missions. Available for credit. Certificate signed by the Department Chairman. Certificate applicable to B.A., B.S., M.A., M.S., M.Miss. in Missions.

Program Format   Daytime, evening, correspondence classes offered. Program cycle: Continuous enrollment. Completion of program requires 2.6 GPA, 24 credit hours.

Evaluation   Student evaluation based on tests, papers, reports. Grading system: Letters or numbers. Transcripts are kept for each student.

Enrollment Requirements   Bachelor's degree, 2.25 GPA required. Program is open to non-resident foreign students. English language proficiency required. Minimum TOEFL score required: 550.

Program Costs $2250–$3000 for the program, $375 per course.

Housing and Student Services   Housing is available. Job counseling and placement services are available.

Special Features   The program of study is very flexible, allowing for each certificate to be tailored to the specific cultural aspects the student expects to meet.

Contact   Dr. Ed Mathews, Chairman, Department of Missions, ACU Station, Box 7939, Abilene, TX 79699. 915-674-2270.

MISSIONARY STUDIES (39.03)
Certificate for Missionary Preparation (General Study)

General Information   Unit offering the program: Department of Missions. Available for credit. Certificate signed by the Department Chairman. Certificate applicable to B.A., B.S., M.A., M.S., M.Miss. in Missions.

Program Format   Daytime, evening, correspondence classes offered. Program cycle: Continuous enrollment. Completion of program requires 2.6 GPA, 18 credit hours.

Evaluation   Student evaluation based on tests, papers, reports. Grading system: Letters or numbers. Transcripts are kept for each student.

Enrollment Requirements   University admissions required. Program is open to non-resident foreign students. English language proficiency required. Minimum TOEFL score required: 550.

Program Costs $2250–$3000 for the program, $375 per course.

Housing and Student Services   Housing is available. Job counseling and placement services are available.

Special Features   The program of study is very flexible, allowing for each certificate to be tailored to the specific cultural aspects the student expects to meet.

Contact   Dr. Ed Mathews, Chairman, Department of Missions, ACU Station, Box 7939, Abilene, TX 79699. 915-674-2270.

MISSIONARY STUDIES (39.03)
Certificate for Missionary Preparation (Special Study)

General Information   Unit offering the program: Department of Missions. Available for credit. Certificate signed by the Department Chairman. Certificate applicable to B.A., B.S., M.A., M.S., M.Miss. in Missions.

Program Format   Daytime, evening, correspondence classes offered. Program cycle: Continuous enrollment. Completion of program requires 2.6 GPA, 21 credit hours.

Evaluation   Student evaluation based on tests, papers, reports, research project. Grading system: Letters or numbers. Transcripts are kept for each student.

Enrollment Requirements   University admissions required. Program is open to non-resident foreign students. English language proficiency required. Minimum TOEFL score required: 550.

Program Costs $2250–$3000 for the program, $375 per course.

Housing and Student Services   Housing is available. Job counseling and placement services are available.

Special Features   The program of study is very flexible, allowing for each certificate to be tailored to the specific cultural aspects the student expects to meet.

Contact   Dr. Ed Mathews, Chairman, Department of Missions, ACU Station, Box 7939, Abilene, TX 79699. 915-674-2270.

INCARNATE WORD COLLEGE
San Antonio, Texas 78209

EDUCATION, GENERAL (13.01)
Graduate Certificate in Adult Education

General Information   Unit offering the program: Adult Education. Available for credit. Certificate signed by the President. Certificate applicable to M.A. in Adult Education.

Graduate Certificate in Adult Education continued

Program Format Evening classes offered. Program cycle: Continuous enrollment. Complete program cycle lasts two to three semesters. Completion of program requires 15 semester hours.

Evaluation Student evaluation based on tests, papers, reports. Grading system: Letters or numbers. Transcripts are kept for each student.

Enrollment Requirements Bachelor's degree, 2.5 GPA, GRE or GMAT scores required. Program is open to non-resident foreign students. English language proficiency required. Minimum TOEFL score required: 560.

Program Costs $537 per course.

Housing and Student Services Housing is available. Job counseling and placement services are available.

Contact Sr. Mona Smiley, Professor of Adult Education, 4301 Broadway, San Antonio, TX 78209. 512-828-1261.

INDIVIDUAL AND FAMILY DEVELOPMENT (19.07)
Certificate in Aging

General Information Unit offering the program: Interdepartmental. Available on either a credit or non-credit basis. Certificate signed by the Dean of Graduate Studies. Certificate applicable to M.A. in Aging.

Program Format Daytime, evening classes offered. Program cycle: Continuous enrollment. Full program cycle lasts 3 semesters. Completion of program requires 18 semester hours.

Evaluation Student evaluation based on tests, papers, reports, projects. Grading system: Letters or numbers. Transcripts are kept for each student.

Enrollment Requirements Bachelor's degree, 2.5 GPA, satisfactory scores on GRE or MAT required. Program is open to non-resident foreign students. English language proficiency required. Minimum TOEFL score required: 560.

Program Costs $537 per course.

Housing and Student Services Housing is available. Job counseling and placement services are available.

Contact Sr. Margaret Rose Palmer, Director of Institute on Aging, 4301 Broadway, San Antonio, TX 78209. 512-828-1261.

RELIGIOUS EDUCATION (39.04)
Certificate in Pastoral Studies

General Information Unit offering the program: Religious Studies. Program content: Scripture, theology, ministry. Available for credit. Certificate signed by the Academic Dean. Certificate applicable to B.A. in Religious Studies. Program fulfills requirements for Diocesan Catechist Certification.

Program Format Daytime classes offered. Students enroll in June. Full program cycle lasts 16 credit hours.

Evaluation Student evaluation based on tests, papers, reports. Grading system: Letters or numbers. Transcripts are kept for each student.

Enrollment Requirements High school diploma or GED required. Program is open to non-resident foreign students.

Program Costs $2704 for the program, $338 per course.

Housing and Student Services Housing is available. Job counseling and placement services are available.

Special Features Begun in 1968, this program has developed specializations in youth ministry and ministry with Hispanics.

Contact Sr. Eilish Ryan, Director, Pastoral Institute, 4301 Broadway, San Antonio, TX 78209. 512-828-1261.

NUCEA MEMBER
SOUTHERN METHODIST UNIVERSITY
Dallas, Texas 75275

HEALTH SERVICES ADMINISTRATION (18.07)
Healthcare Financial Management Certificate Program

General Information Unit offering the program: School of Continuing Education. Program content: Current trends, finance and management, data processing, economics and politics of health-care industry, third party reimbursement, patients' accounts management. Available on a non-credit basis. Endorsed by Healthcare Financial Management Association, Central Texas Chapter. Certificate signed by the Director, Division of Evening and Summer Studies.

Program Format Evening classes offered. Instructional schedule: One evening per week. Students may enroll three times per year.

Evaluation Student evaluation based on tests, papers, reports. Grading system: Letters or numbers. Records are kept for each student.

Enrollment Requirements Sixty semester hours of college credit or membership in Healthcare Financial Management Association required. Program is open to non-resident foreign students.

Program Costs $195 per course.

Housing and Student Services Housing is not available. Job counseling and placement services are not available.

Contact Office of Healthcare Financial Management Program, SMU Box 275, Dallas, TX 75275-0275. 214-739-3224.

LAW (22.01)
Legal Assistant Certificate

General Information Unit offering the program: Division of Evening and Summer Studies. Program content: Overview of several aspects of law or specialization in family law, litigation, estate planning and probate, real estate, business law. Available on a non-credit basis. Certificate signed by the President of the University.

Program Format Evening, weekend classes offered. Instructional schedule: Once or twice per week. Program cycle: Continuous enrollment. Complete program cycle lasts 2–2½ years. Completion of program requires 16 courses, grade of C or better.

Evaluation Student evaluation based on tests, papers, legal problems. Grading system: Letters or numbers. Records are kep for each student.

Enrollment Requirements Sixty semester hours of college credit required. Program is open to non-resident foreign students.

Program Costs $1700 for the program, $105 per course.

Housing and Student Services Housing is not available. Job counseling and placement services are available.

Special Features No credit given for prior experience. Almost all instructors are practicing attorneys with bachelor's and law degrees. The program started in 1977 with full offerings in 1980 and has had fine acceptance by the Dallas Bar. Attorneys and Dallas Association of Legal Assistants have been willing participants in our special seminars and orientation.

Contact Ms. Lennart V. Larson, Director, Legal Assistant Certificate Program, Dallas, TX 75275. 214-692-2634.

REHABILITATION SERVICES (17.08)
Learning Therapist Certificate Program

General Information Unit offering the program: School of Continuing Education, Department of Psychology. Program content: Training to work with the dyslexic or learning disabled in written language and learning skills. Available on either a credit or non-credit basis. Endorsed by The Academic Language

Therapy Association. Cosponsored by Texas Scottish Rite Hospital for Crippled Children–Child Development Division. Certificate signed by the Director of Continuing Education, Evening and Summer Studies. Certificate applicable to Master of Liberal Arts. Program fulfills requirements for membership in The Academic Language Therapy Association (ALTA).

Program Format Daytime, evening, weekend classes offered. Instructional schedule: All day for one month for two summers. Students enroll in the summer. Full program cycle lasts 2 years. Completion of program requires four courses, grade of B or better, 700 hour-practicum, workshop.

Evaluation Student evaluation based on tests, papers, reports. Grading system: Letters or numbers, pass/fail. Transcripts are kept for each student.

Enrollment Requirements Undergraduate degree, letters of recommendation required. Program is open to non-resident foreign students. English language proficiency required.

Program Costs $459 per course (credit option); $150–$300 per course (non-credit option).

Housing and Student Services Housing is available. Job counseling and placement services are not available.

Special Features Designed for individuals who are interested in working with children or adults who have written language learning disorders (dyslexia or LD). Modeled on the pioneering programs developed by Orton/Gillingham and Texas Scottish Rite Hospital as well as cognitive development and learning strategies from the field of psychology.

Contact Ms. Jamie Williams, Coordinator, Learning Therapist Certificate Program, SMU Box 382-LT, Dallas, TX 75275-0382. 214-369-9556.

SOUTHWESTERN ADVENTIST COLLEGE
Keene, Texas 76059

TYPING, GENERAL OFFICE, AND RELATED PROGRAMS (07.07)
Office Assistant Program

General Information Unit offering the program: Business, Office Administration. Program content: Typing, filing, information processing, office procedures. Available for credit. Certificate signed by the College President. Certificate applicable to A.S. in Office Administration.

Program Format Daytime classes offered. Program cycle: Continuous enrollment. Full program cycle lasts 1 year. Completion of program requires 2.0 GPA.

Evaluation Student evaluation based on tests, papers, reports. Grading system: Letters or numbers. Transcripts are kept for each student.

Enrollment Requirements High school diploma required. Program is open to non-resident foreign students. English language proficiency required. Applicants must pass the MELAB.

Program Costs $5592 for the program, $233 per credit hour.

Housing and Student Services Housing is available. Job counseling and placement services are available.

Contact Ms. Judy Miles, Assistant Professor of Office Administration, Box 567, Keene, TX 76059. 817-645-3921.

WORD PROCESSING (07.08)
Word Processing Program

General Information Unit offering the program: Business, Office Administration. Program content: Typing, filing, office automation, information processing, office procedures. Available for credit. Certificate signed by the College President. Certificate applicable to A.S. in Office Administration.

Program Format Daytime classes offered. Program cycle: Continuous enrollment. Full program cycle lasts 1 year. Completion of program requires 2.0 GPA.

Evaluation Student evaluation based on tests, papers, reports. Grading system: Letters or numbers. Transcripts are kept for each student.

Enrollment Requirements High school diploma required. Program is open to non-resident foreign students. English language proficiency required. Applicants must pass the MELAB.

Program Costs $5592 for the program, $233 per credit hour.

Housing and Student Services Housing is available. Job counseling and placement services are available.

Contact Ms. Judy Miles, Assistant Professor of Office Administration, Box 567, Keene, TX 76059. 817-645-3921.

SUL ROSS STATE UNIVERSITY
Alpine, Texas 79832

SECRETARIAL AND RELATED PROGRAMS (07.06)
Office Occupations

General Information Unit offering the program: Business Administration. Program content: Office skills, secretarial training. Available for credit. Certificate signed by the President of the University.

Program Format Daytime classes offered. Instructional schedule: Classes meet two or three days per week. Program cycle: Continuous enrollment. Completion of program requires 2.0 GPA, 44 credit hours.

Evaluation Student evaluation based on tests. Grading system: Letters or numbers. Transcripts are kept for each student.

Enrollment Requirements University admissions required. Program is open to non-resident foreign students. English language proficiency required. Minimum TOEFL score required: 520.

Program Costs $1298 for the program.

Housing and Student Services Housing is available. Job counseling and placement services are available.

Contact Mrs. Mazie Will, Instructor of Business Administration, Alpine, TX 79832. 915-837-8066.

TEXAS A&M UNIVERSITY AT GALVESTON
Galveston, Texas 77553

MARITIME SCIENCE (MERCHANT MARINE) (28.05)
Certificate of Training

General Information Unit offering the program: Radar Simulator Facility—Coastal Zone Laboratory. Program content: Radar navigation and collision avoidance. Available on either a credit or non-credit basis. Endorsed by U.S. Coast Guard. Certificate signed by the Chief Instructor. Certificate applicable to B.S. in Marine Transportation. Program fulfills requirements for U.S. Merchant Marine, Third Mate Unlimited Tonnage.

Program Format Daytime classes offered. Program cycle: Continuous enrollment. Complete program cycle lasts five or eight days.

Evaluation Student evaluation based on tests, lab work. Grading system: Letters or numbers, pass/fail. Records are kept for each student.

Certificate of Training continued

Enrollment Requirements Program is open to non-resident foreign students. English language proficiency required.

Program Costs $200–$225 for the program.

Housing and Student Services Housing is not available. Job counseling and placement services are not available.

Special Features Several U.S. Merchant Marine licenses require a radar endorsement, which must be renewed at 5-year intervals. The courses satisfy the requirements for both original endorsement and renewal.

Contact Mr. Johnny L. Sneed, Chief Instructor, Radar School, P.O. Box 1675, Galveston, TX 77553. 409-740-4467.

NUCEA MEMBER
TEXAS CHRISTIAN UNIVERSITY
Fort Worth, Texas 76129

AGRICULTURAL BUSINESS AND MANAGEMENT (01.01)
Ranch Management Certificate

General Information Unit offering the program: Ranch Management. Program content: Management principles of land, grass, livestock, and records; marketing; personnel. Available for credit. Certificate signed by the Chancellor. Program fulfills requirements for A.B.S. certification in AI/Palpation/Certified Pesticide Applicator.

Program Format Daytime, evening classes offered. Instructional schedule: Monday through Friday. Students enroll in the fall. Full program cycle lasts 9 months. Completion of program requires 12 courses, 34 credit hours.

Evaluation Student evaluation based on tests, papers, Management Plan. Grading system: Letters or numbers. Transcripts are kept for each student.

Enrollment Requirements Limited to those with farming or ranching experience. Program is open to non-resident foreign students. English language proficiency required. Minimum TOEFL score required: 550.

Program Costs $9980 for the program.

Housing and Student Services Housing is available. Job counseling and placement services are available.

Contact Mr. John Merrill, Director, Ranch Management, Box 30774, Fort Worth, TX 76129. 817-921-7145.

NUCEA MEMBER
TEXAS TECH UNIVERSITY
Lubbock, Texas 79409

BUSINESS AND MANAGEMENT, GENERAL (06.01)
Business Certificate Program

General Information Unit offering the program: Division of Continuing Education, Special Activities. Program content: Accounting, bookkeeping, financial planning, Spanish, supervisory skills, computers, business writing. Available on a non-credit basis. Certificate signed by the Director of Continuing Education.

Program Format Evening classes offered. Students may enroll fall, spring, summer. Full program cycle lasts 2 years. Completion of program requires 85 classroom hours.

Evaluation Student evaluation based on tests. Grading system: Pass/fail. Transcripts are kept for each student.

Enrollment Requirements Program is not open to non-resident foreign students. English language proficiency required.

Program Costs $70 per course.

Housing and Student Services Housing is not available. Job counseling and placement services are not available.

Contact Ms. Helen Otken, Program Coordinator, P.O. Box 4110, Lubbock, TX 79409-2190. 806-742-2352.

LAW (22.01)
Legal Assistant Program

General Information Unit offering the program: Division of Continuing Education, Special Activities. Program content: Family law, client interviewing, legal research, accounting, criminal justice. Available on a non-credit basis. Certificate signed by the Director of Continuing Education.

Program Format Evening classes offered. Students may enroll fall, spring, summer. Full program cycle lasts 2 years. Completion of program requires 85 classroom hours.

Evaluation Student evaluation based on tests. Grading system: Pass/fail. Transcripts are kept for each student.

Enrollment Requirements Program is not open to non-resident foreign students. English language proficiency required.

Program Costs $70 per course.

Housing and Student Services Housing is not available. Job counseling and placement services are not available.

Contact Ms. Helen Otken, Program Coordinator, P.O. Box 4110, Lubbock, TX 79409-2190. 806-742-2352.

NUCEA MEMBER
UNIVERSITY OF HOUSTON
Houston, Texas 77004

BANKING AND FINANCE (06.03)
Certified Financial Planner

General Information Unit offering the program: Center for Executive Development, College of Business Administration. Endorsed by International Board of Standards and Practices for Certified Financial Planners (IBCFP). Certificate signed by the Director, Center for Executive Development. Program fulfills requirements for Certified Financial Planner.

Program Format Evening classes offered. Program cycle: Continuous enrollment. Completion of program requires seven courses.

Evaluation Student evaluation based on tests. Grading system: Pass/fail. Records are kept by College of Business Administration.

Enrollment Requirements High school diploma or GED required. Program is open to non-resident foreign students.

Program Costs $1575 for the program, $225 per course.

Housing and Student Services Housing is not available. Job counseling and placement services are not available.

Special Features Instructors are College of Business Administration professors or financial professionals practicing in their areas of instruction. Many are Certified Financial Planners. The program provides free orientation sessions, comprehensive courses, registration with the IBCFP, one-day intensive reviews for the CFP examinations, and a financial calculator workshop.

Contact Mr. Roger N. Blakeney, Director, Center for Executive Development, College of Business Administration, Houston, TX 77004. 713-749-4176.

LAW (22.01)
Trial Advocacy Institute

General Information Unit offering the program: Law Center, Trial Advocacy Institute. Program content: Hands-on skills in litigation. Available on either a credit or non-credit basis. Certificate signed by the Dean, Law Center. Certificate applicable to J.D.

Program Format Daytime, weekend classes offered. Instructional schedule: All day Friday and Saturday. Students may enroll once (criminal law) or twice (civil law) per year. Full program cycle lasts 5 weeks. Completion of program requires 60 contact hours.

Evaluation Student evaluation based on performance in mock court room. Transcripts are kept for each student.

Enrollment Requirements Limited to third year law students or attorneys admitted to State Bar of Texas within the last three years.

Program Costs $1050 for the program.

Housing and Student Services Job counseling and placement services are available.

Special Features The Trial Advocacy Institute allows law students and practicing attorneys to work with their peers in the community who are at the top in their profession. Instructors are top litigators from major Houston law firms. The program has filled to capacity since its inception eight years ago.

Contact Mr. David Stewart, Assistant Director, Trial Advocacy Institute, Law Center, Houston, TX 77004. 713-749-3947.

SOCIAL WORK (44.07)
Human Services and Gerontology

General Information Unit offering the program: Graduate School of Social Work. Program content: Development, planning, administration, and delivery of professional social services. Available on a non-credit basis. Certificate signed by the Dean, Graduate School of Social Work.

Program Format Daytime, evening, weekend classes offered. Program cycle: Continuous enrollment. Completion of program requires 60 contact hours.

Evaluation Student evaluation based on tests. Grading system: Pass/fail. Record of CEUs kept for each student.

Enrollment Requirements Intended for professionals in human services field. Program is open to non-resident foreign students.

Program Costs $600 for the program.

Housing and Student Services Housing is not available. Job counseling and placement services are not available.

Special Features This program serves a wide variety of human services professionals, including social workers, counselors, psychologists, psychiatrists, and nurses. The Advisory Board is comprised of both faculty of the University's Graduate School of Social Work and top professionals from the city's many institutional and community-based services for the aged.

Contact Mr. William E. Buffum, Assistant Professor, Continuing Education, Graduate School of Social Work, Houston, TX 77004. 713-749-1741.

SOCIAL WORK (44.07)
Human Services Executive Development Program

General Information Unit offering the program: Graduate School of Social Work. Available on a non-credit basis. Certificate signed by the Dean, Graduate School of Social Work.

Program Format Daytime, evening, weekend classes offered. Program cycle: Continuous enrollment. Completion of program requires six courses.

Evaluation Student evaluation based on tests. Grading system: Pass/fail. Record of CEUs kept for each student.

Enrollment Requirements Intended for those in managerial positions. Program is open to non-resident foreign students.

Program Costs $1500 for the program, $250 per course.

Housing and Student Services Housing is not available. Job counseling and placement services are not available.

Special Features This program focuses on executive development of human services professionals, which allows an emphasis on areas unique to this group. The advisory board is composed of community leaders who hold related executive positions in various agencies.

Contact Mr. William Buffum, Assistant Professor, Continuing Education, Graduate School of Social Work, Houston, TX 77004. 713-749-1741.

UNIVERSITY OF TEXAS AT ARLINGTON
Arlington, Texas 76019

BANKING AND FINANCE (06.03)
Mortgage Banking Certificate

General Information Unit offering the program: Mortgage Banking Division–Continuing Education. Program content: Mortgage banking education, on-the-job training. Available on a non-credit basis. Certificate signed by the Director of Continuing Education. Program fulfills requirements for Texas Real Estate Agent.

Program Format Daytime, evening, weekend classes offered. Program cycle: Continuous enrollment. Full program cycle lasts 10 courses. Completion of program requires narrative reports, on-the-job training.

Evaluation Student evaluation based on tests, reports. Grading system: Pass/fail. Computer records are kept for each student.

Enrollment Requirements High school diploma or GED, typing skills required. Program is open to non-resident foreign students. English language proficiency required.

Program Costs $1700 for the program, $75–$375 per course.

Housing and Student Services Job counseling and placement services are available.

Contact Ms. Cheryl Diehl, Mortgage Banking Coordinator, 1022 Border, P.O. Box 19197, Arlington, TX 76019. 817-273-2581.

LAW (22.01)
Legal Assistant Certificate

General Information Unit offering the program: Continuing Education. Available on a non-credit basis. Certificate signed by the Director of Continuing Education.

Program Format Evening, weekend classes offered. Instructional schedule: Once per week for three hours. Program cycle: Continuous enrollment. Completion of program requires 240 contact hours.

Evaluation Student evaluation based on tests, papers, reports. Grading system: Letters or numbers. Transcripts are kept for each student.

Enrollment Requirements High school diploma, English entrance test required. Program is open to non-resident foreign students. English language proficiency required.

Program Costs $1425 for the program, $175 per course.

Housing and Student Services Housing is available. Job counseling and placement services are available.

Special Features Instructors include attorneys, legal assistants, a law librarian, and a legal administrator.

Contact Ms. Melba W. Benson, Ph.D., Coordinator, Legal Assistant Certificate Program, P.O. Box 19197, Arlington, TX 76019. 817-273-2581.

MENTAL HEALTH/HUMAN SERVICES (17.04)
Biofeedback Training Program Certificate

General Information Unit offering the program: Graduate School of Social Work–Human Resource Center. Program content: Psychophysiology and stress, relaxation, instrumentation, hypnotic and imagery techniques, ethical

Biofeedback Training Program Certificate continued
considerations. Available on a non-credit basis. Certificate signed by the Director, Human Resource Center.

Program Format Weekend classes offered. Instructional schedule: Friday evening, all day Saturday and Sunday. Students may enroll fall, spring. Complete program cycle lasts three weekends. Completion of program requires 48 contact hours.

Evaluation Student evaluation based on tests, demonstration of instrumentation skills. Grading system: Pass/fail. Record of CEUs kept for each student.

Enrollment Requirements Undergraduate degree required.

Program Costs $900 for the program.

Housing and Student Services Housing is not available. Job counseling and placement services are not available.

Contact Ms. Cindy Marshall, Director, Human Resource Center, P.O. Box 19197, Arlington, TX 76019. 817-273-2581.

MENTAL HEALTH/HUMAN SERVICES (17.04)
Certificate in Human Services Management

General Information Unit offering the program: Graduate School of Social Work–Human Resource Center. Program content: Leadership, computerized information management, budgeting, personnel, marketing, public relations, accountability. Certificate signed by the Director, Human Resource Center.

Program Format Daytime, weekend classes offered. Full program cycle lasts 2 years. Completion of program requires nine 2-day workshops.

Evaluation Student evaluation based on tests. Grading system: Pass/fail. Record of CEUs kept by Office of Continuing Education.

Enrollment Requirements B.S.W. or M.S.W. required.

Program Costs $95–$145 per course.

Housing and Student Services Housing is not available. Job counseling and placement services are not available.

Contact Ms. Cindy Marshall, Director, Human Resource Center, P.O. Box 19197, Arlington, TX 76019. 817-273-2581.

MENTAL HEALTH/HUMAN SERVICES (17.04)
Drug and Alcohol Counselor Certification Training Program

General Information Unit offering the program: Graduate School of Social Work–Human Resource Center. Program content: Alcohol in perspective, chemical dependency in the adolescent, alcohol and drugs in the workplace and school, counseling, addictive family system, case management and self-care, pharmacology, treatment and rehabilitation. Available on a non-credit basis. Endorsed by Texas Association of Alcoholism and Drug Abuse Counselors. Cosponsored by Dallas Challenge, Inc. Certificate signed by the Director, Human Resource Center. Program fulfills requirements for Certified Alcoholism and Drug Abuse Counselor.

Program Format Daytime classes offered. Instructional schedule: All day for four consecutive days per month. Full program cycle lasts 9 months. Completion of program requires 270 classroom hours.

Evaluation Student evaluation based on tests. Grading system: Pass/fail. Record of CEUs kept by Office of Continuing Education.

Program Costs $135 per course.

Housing and Student Services Housing is not available. Job counseling and placement services are not available.

Contact Ms. Cindy Marshall, Director, Human Resource Center, P.O. Box 19197, Arlington, TX 76019. 817-273-2581.

SECRETARIAL AND RELATED PROGRAMS (07.06)
Office and Secretarial Careers Certificate Program

General Information Unit offering the program: Continuing Education. Available on a non-credit basis. Certificate signed by the Director of Continuing Education.

Program Format Evening, weekend classes offered. Instructional schedule: Once per week for three hours. Program cycle: Continuous enrollment. Completion of program requires 221 contact hours.

Evaluation Student evaluation based on tests, papers, reports. Grading system: Letters or numbers. Transcripts are kept for each student.

Enrollment Requirements High school diploma required. Program is open to non-resident foreign students. English language proficiency required.

Program Costs $1395 for the program.

Housing and Student Services Housing is available. Job counseling and placement services are available.

Special Features Instructors in the program hold graduate degrees and have professional working experience in the field.

Contact Ms. Melba W. Benson, Ph.D., Business Education Director, P.O. Box 19197, Arlington, TX 76019. 817-273-2581.

NUCEA MEMBER

BRIGHAM YOUNG UNIVERSITY
Provo, Utah 84602

HISTORY (45.08)
Certificate in Genealogy

General Information Unit offering the program: Independent Study. Program content: Genealogical research skills. Available for credit. Certificate signed by the Dean–College of Family, Home, and Social Sciences. Certificate applicable to A.A. in Genealogy.

Program Format Correspondence classes offered. Program cycle: Continuous enrollment. Completion of program requires 13–17 credit hours.

Evaluation Student evaluation based on tests. Grading system: Letters or numbers. Transcripts are kept for each student.

Enrollment Requirements Program is open to non-resident foreign students. English language proficiency required.

Program Costs $52 per semester hour.

Special Features Two options are available: the professional option (17 semester hours), for those who wish to learn to research for remuneration, and the personal research option (13 semester hours), for family researchers and hobbyists. Each option requires participation in an approved three-day seminar, the purpose of which is to meet and interact with recognized professionals.

Contact Mr. Ronald F. Malan, Assistant Director, 206 HCEB, Provo, UT 84602. 801-378-4044.

WEBER STATE COLLEGE
Ogden, Utah 84408

BUSINESS AND MANAGEMENT, GENERAL (06.01)
Merchandising Certificate Program

General Information   Unit offering the program: Distributive Technology, Division of Continuing Education. Program content: Sales and retailing. Available for credit. Certificate signed by the Dean, Continuing Education. Certificate applicable to A.A.S. in Sales and Retailing.

Program Format   Correspondence classes offered. Program cycle: Continuous enrollment. Full program cycle lasts 1 year. Completion of program requires 2.0 GPA, six courses.

Evaluation   Student evaluation based on tests, papers, reports. Grading system: Letters or numbers. Transcripts are kept for each student.

Enrollment Requirements   College admissions required. Program is open to non-resident foreign students.

Program Costs $600 for the program, $35 per credit hour.

Housing and Student Services   Housing is available. Job counseling and placement services are available.

Special Features   The entire program can be completed at home anywhere in the world. Each class is specifically designed to improve retail merchandising skills. No prior experience is necessary. The certificate will enhance entry into middle management retail merchandising positions.

Contact   Dr. Dennis A. DeFrain, Program Administrator, Distance Learning, Division of Continuing Education, Ogden, UT 84408-4005. 801-626-6785.

WESTMINSTER COLLEGE OF SALT LAKE CITY
Salt Lake City, Utah 84105

LAW (22.01)
Legal Assistant Training Program

General Information   Unit offering the program: Center for Professional Development. Available on a non-credit basis. Certificate signed by the President of the College.

Program Format   Evening classes offered. Instructional schedule: Three evenings per week. Students enroll in September. Full program cycle lasts 3 semesters. Completion of program requires minimum of 30 units.

Evaluation   Student evaluation based on tests, papers, reports. Grading system: Letters or numbers. Transcripts are kept for each student.

Enrollment Requirements   High school diploma or GED required. Program is not open to non-resident foreign students.

Program Costs $2625 for the program.

Housing and Student Services   Housing is not available. Job counseling and placement services are available.

Special Features   Program began in 1980. Instructors chosen from attorneys or paralegals. Has strict selection of students process (take 40-45 students each year). No open admissions accepted.

Contact   Ms. Elaine Hansen, Program Director, 1840 South 1300 East, Salt Lake City, UT 84105. 801-488-4159.

VERMONT

LYNDON STATE COLLEGE
Lyndonville, Vermont 05851

ACCOUNTING (06.02)
Certified Internal Auditor Preparation

General Information   Unit offering the program: Business Department. Program content: Federal taxation, cost accounting, auditing. Available for credit. Certificate signed by the Associate Academic Dean. Certificate applicable to B.S. in Business Administration, Accounting.

Program Format   Daytime, evening classes offered. Program cycle: Continuous enrollment. Full program cycle lasts 13 courses. Completion of program requires grade of C or better.

Evaluation   Student evaluation based on tests, papers, reports. Grading system: Letters or numbers. Transcripts are kept for each student.

Enrollment Requirements   Bachelor's degree, two years experience required. Program is open to non-resident foreign students. English language proficiency required.

Program Costs $93–$201 per credit hour.

Housing and Student Services   Housing is available. Job counseling and placement services are available.

Special Features   The series fulfills the course requirements for application to take the Certified Internal Auditor examination. In addition, to qualify for the exam, applicants must hold a bachelor's degree and have two years of pertinent work experience.

Contact   Mr. David Bradley, Chair, Business Department, Lyndonville, VT 05851. 802-626-9371.

ACCOUNTING (06.02)
CMA Preparation

General Information   Unit offering the program: Business Department. Program content: Federal taxation, auditing, cost accounting. Available for credit. Certificate signed by the Associate Academic Dean. Certificate applicable to B.S. in Business Administration, Accounting.

Program Format   Daytime, evening classes offered. Program cycle: Continuous enrollment. Full program cycle lasts 16 courses. Completion of program requires grade of C or better.

Evaluation   Student evaluation based on tests, papers, reports. Grading system: Letters or numbers. Transcripts are kept for each student.

Enrollment Requirements   Bachelor's degree, two years experience required. Program is open to non-resident foreign students. English language proficiency required.

Program Costs $93–$201 per credit hour.

Housing and Student Services   Housing is available. Job counseling and placement services are available.

Special Features   Completion of the series of courses prepares the student to take the Certified Management Accountant examination in Vermont. In addition, students must hold a bachelor's degree and have two years of pertinent experience.

Contact   Mr. David Bradley, Chair, Business Department, Lyndonville, VT 05851. 802-626-9371.

ACCOUNTING (06.02)
CPA Preparation

General Information   Unit offering the program: Business Department. Program content: Federal taxation, cost accounting, auditing. Available for credit. Certificate signed by the Associate Academic Dean. Certificate applicable to B.S. in Accounting.

CPA Preparation continued

Program Format Daytime classes offered. Program cycle: Continuous enrollment. Full program cycle lasts 10 courses. Completion of program requires grade of C or better.

Evaluation Student evaluation based on tests, reports. Grading system: Letters or numbers. Transcripts are kept for each student.

Enrollment Requirements High school diploma required. Program is open to non-resident foreign students. English language proficiency required.

Program Costs $93–$201 per credit hour.

Housing and Student Services Housing is available. Job counseling and placement services are available.

Special Features The series of courses fulfills the classroom component requirement for people wishing to take the CPA examination in Vermont. Additional requirements include fulfillment of a period of service with a public accounting firm or comparable experience.

Contact Mr. David Bradley, Chair, Business Department, Lyndonville, VT 05851. 802-626-9371.

BANKING AND FINANCE (06.03)
Finance

General Information Unit offering the program: Business Department. Program content: Federal taxation, accounting, auditing, economics, business law. Available for credit. Certificate signed by the Associate Academic Dean. Certificate applicable to B.S. in Business Administration, Accounting.

Program Format Daytime, evening classes offered. Program cycle: Continuous enrollment. Full program cycle lasts 7 courses. Completion of program requires grade of C or better.

Evaluation Student evaluation based on tests, papers, reports. Grading system: Letters or numbers. Transcripts are kept for each student.

Enrollment Requirements High school diploma required. Program is open to non-resident foreign students. English language proficiency required.

Program Costs $93–$201 per credit hour.

Housing and Student Services Housing is available. Job counseling and placement services are available.

Contact Mr. David Bradley, Chair, Business Department, Lyndonville, VT 05851. 802-626-9371.

BANKING AND FINANCE (06.03)
Financial Planning

General Information Unit offering the program: Business Department. Program content: Investment management, portfolio theory, venture capital, real estate investment. Available for credit. Certificate signed by the Associate Academic Dean. Certificate applicable to B.S. in Business Administration, Accounting.

Program Format Daytime, evening classes offered. Program cycle: Continuous enrollment. Full program cycle lasts 6 courses. Completion of program requires grade of C or better.

Evaluation Student evaluation based on tests, papers, reports. Grading system: Letters or numbers. Transcripts are kept for each student.

Enrollment Requirements High school diploma required. Program is open to non-resident foreign students. English language proficiency required.

Program Costs $93–$201 per credit hour.

Housing and Student Services Housing is available. Job counseling and placement services are available.

Special Features The certificate program is aimed specifically at people who are interested in developing a basic understanding of financial planning for personal or professional development.

Contact Mr. David Bradley, Chair, Business Department, Lyndonville, VT 05851. 802-626-9371.

LAW (22.01)
Paralegal Certificate Program

General Information Unit offering the program: Business Administration. Program content: Litigation legal research; family, estate, and property law. Available for credit. Certificate signed by the Academic Dean. Certificate applicable to A.S., B.S. in Business Administration.

Program Format Daytime, evening classes offered. Full program cycle lasts 3 semesters.

Evaluation Student evaluation based on tests, papers, reports. Grading system: Letters or numbers. Transcripts are kept for each student.

Enrollment Requirements Associate degree or two years legal experience required. Program is open to non-resident foreign students. English language proficiency required.

Program Costs $93–$201 per credit hour.

Housing and Student Services Housing is available. Job counseling and placement services are available.

Special Features A one-year certificate program offered only when a large enough cadre of students is available to take the courses as a group. Therefore, the certificate program is offered infrequently.

Contact Mr. David Bradley, Chair, Business Department, Lyndonville, VT 05851. 802-626-9371.

MANAGEMENT SCIENCE (06.13)
Management Training

General Information Unit offering the program: Business Department. Program content: Business law, marketing, accounting, advertising, investment. Available for credit. Certificate signed by the Associate Academic Dean. Certificate applicable to B.S. in Business Administration.

Program Format Daytime, evening classes offered. Program cycle: Continuous enrollment. Full program cycle lasts 11 courses. Completion of program requires grade of C or better.

Evaluation Student evaluation based on tests, papers, reports. Grading system: Letters or numbers. Transcripts are kept for each student.

Enrollment Requirements High school diploma required. Program is open to non-resident foreign students. English language proficiency required.

Program Costs $93–$201 per credit hour.

Housing and Student Services Housing is available. Job counseling and placement services are available.

Special Features The Lyndon State College Management Training Series provides the local business person with an opportunity to study management sciences as they relate to the successes and failures of American business and industry.

Contact Mr. David Bradley, Chair, Business Department, Lyndonville, VT 05851. 802-626-9371.

MANAGEMENT SCIENCE (06.13)
Manufacturing and Production

General Information Unit offering the program: Business Department. Program content: Accounting, operations management, auditing, information systems. Available for credit. Certificate signed by the Associate Academic Dean. Certificate applicable to B.S. in Business Administration.

Program Format Daytime, evening classes offered. Program cycle: Continuous enrollment. Full program cycle lasts 11 courses. Completion of program requires grade of C or better.

Evaluation Student evaluation based on tests, papers, reports. Grading system: Letters or numbers. Transcripts are kept for each student.

Enrollment Requirements High school diploma required. Program is open to non-resident foreign students. English language proficiency required.

Program Costs $93–$201 per credit hour.

Housing and Student Services Housing is available. Job counseling and placement services are available.

Contact Mr. David Bradley, Chair, Business Department, Lyndonville, VT 05851. 802-626-9371.

MARKETING MANAGEMENT AND RESEARCH (06.14)
Marketing

General Information Unit offering the program: Business Department. Program content: Consumer behavior, sales management, marketing research, advertising. Available for credit. Certificate signed by the Associate Academic Dean. Certificate applicable to B.S. in Business Administration.

Program Format Daytime, evening classes offered. Program cycle: Continuous enrollment. Full program cycle lasts 9 courses. Completion of program requires grade of C or better.

Evaluation Student evaluation based on tests, papers, reports. Grading system: Letters or numbers. Transcripts are kept for each student.

Enrollment Requirements High school diploma required. Program is open to non-resident foreign students. English language proficiency required.

Program Costs $93–$201 per credit hour.

Housing and Student Services Housing is available. Job counseling and placement services are available.

Contact Mr. David Bradley, Chair, Business Department, Lyndonville, VT 05851. 802-626-9371.

PERSONNEL MANAGEMENT (06.16)
Personnel Management

General Information Unit offering the program: Business Department. Program content: Industrial and labor relations, organizational behavior, small business management. Available for credit. Certificate signed by the Associate Academic Dean. Certificate applicable to B.S. in Business Administration.

Program Format Daytime, evening classes offered. Program cycle: Continuous enrollment. Full program cycle lasts 7 courses. Completion of program requires grade of C or better.

Evaluation Student evaluation based on tests, papers, reports. Grading system: Letters or numbers. Transcripts are kept for each student.

Enrollment Requirements High school diploma required. Program is open to non-resident foreign students. English language proficiency required.

Program Costs $93–$201 per credit hour.

Housing and Student Services Housing is available. Job counseling and placement services are available.

Special Features The Personnel Management series is designed for business people, who work in personnel areas or for managers who would like to gain a better understanding of human resources management and theory.

Contact Mr. David Bradley, Chair, Business Department, Lyndonville, VT 05851. 802-626-9371.

SMALL BUSINESS MANAGEMENT AND OWNERSHIP (06.18)
Small Business Management

General Information Unit offering the program: Business Department. Program content: Financial accounting, business ethics, information systems, marketing, economics. Available for credit. Certificate signed by the Associate Academic Dean. Certificate applicable to B.S. in Small Business Management and Entrepreneurship.

Program Format Daytime, evening classes offered. Program cycle: Continuous enrollment. Full program cycle lasts 13 courses. Completion of program requires grade of C or better.

Evaluation Student evaluation based on tests, reports. Grading system: Letters or numbers. Transcripts are kept for each student.

Enrollment Requirements High school diploma required. Program is open to non-resident foreign students. English language proficiency required.

Program Costs $93–$201 per credit hour.

Housing and Student Services Housing is available. Job counseling and placement services are available.

Special Features The courses listed for this certificate program are part of the undergraduate major in Small Business Management and Entrepreneurship, the only such program in Vermont.

Contact Mr. David Bradley, Chair, Business Department, Lyndonville, VT 05851. 802-626-9371.

SPECIAL EDUCATION (13.10)
Special Education Teacher Assistant

General Information Unit offering the program: Psychology and Education Departments. Program content: Educational psychology, reading foundations, reading disabilities, issues and trends in reading. Available for credit. Endorsed by Northeastern Vermont Supervisory Unions. Certificate signed by the Associate Academic Dean. Certificate applicable to B.S. in Special Education.

Program Format Evening classes offered. Program cycle: Continuous enrollment. Full program cycle lasts 2 years. Completion of program requires grade of C or better.

Evaluation Student evaluation based on tests, papers, reports. Grading system: Letters or numbers, pass/fail. Transcripts are kept for each student.

Enrollment Requirements High school diploma or GED required. Program is open to non-resident foreign students. English language proficiency required.

Program Costs $93–$201 per credit hour.

Housing and Student Services Housing is available. Job counseling and placement services are available.

Special Features The Special Education Teacher Assistant Program was designed to meet a specific need requested by Coordinators of Special Education and Chapter I programs in northeastern Vermont. The series of courses provides specific training for teacher assistants.

Contact Office of Continuing Education, Lyndonville, VT 05851. 802-626-9770.

SAINT MICHAEL'S COLLEGE
Winooski, Vermont 05404

BUSINESS ADMINISTRATION AND MANAGEMENT (06.04)
Certificate of Advanced Management Study

General Information Unit offering the program: Graduate Studies Program. Program content: Integration of social and management sciences. Available for credit. Certificate signed by the Academic Dean.

Program Format Evening, weekend classes offered. Program cycle: Continuous enrollment. Complete program cycle lasts two to four semesters. Completion of program requires 3.0 GPA, 18 credit hours.

Evaluation Student evaluation based on tests, papers, reports. Grading system: Letters or numbers. Transcripts are kept for each student.

Enrollment Requirements Master's degree, essay, letters of recommendation, interview required. Program is open to non-resident foreign students. English language proficiency required. Minimum TOEFL score required: 550.

Certificate of Advanced Management Study continued

Program Costs $2340 for the program, $390 per course.

Housing and Student Services   Housing is not available. Job counseling and placement services are available.

Special Features   The program is designed for working professionals who have completed a master's degree in the fields of business or public administration, economics, education administration, computer science, or related areas and who are interested in further developing knowledge and skills in a specific topic area.

Contact   Ms. Deborah Murphy, Director of Graduate Management Programs, Winooski, VT 05404. 802-655-2000 Ext. 2577.

TEACHING ENGLISH AS A SECOND LANGUAGE/FOREIGN LANGUAGE (13.14)
Advanced Teaching English as a Second Language Certificate

General Information   Unit offering the program: Center for International Programs. Available for credit. Certificate signed by the Academic Dean. Certificate applicable to M.A. in Teaching English as a Second Language.

Program Format   Daytime, evening classes offered. Program cycle: Continuous enrollment. Complete program cycle lasts two to three semesters. Completion of program requires 3.0 GPA, 18 credit hours.

Evaluation   Student evaluation based on tests, papers, reports, oral examination. Grading system: Letters or numbers. Transcripts are kept for each student.

Enrollment Requirements   Bachelor's degree required. Program is open to non-resident foreign students. English language proficiency required. Minimum TOEFL score required: 550.

Program Costs $2340 for the program, $390 per course.

Housing and Student Services   Housing is available. Job counseling and placement services are available.

Special Features   Certificate and master's programs provide an overview of current linguistic and second-language theory and practices; applied training in all areas of language skill instruction; experience in testing, curriculum, and materials development; and preparation to assume professional roles or continue graduate studies.

Contact   Mr. Norman Lacharite, Director, TESL Progrm, Winooski, VT 05404. 802-655-2000 Ext. 2300.

THEOLOGICAL STUDIES (39.06)
Certificate of Advanced Specialization

General Information   Unit offering the program: Graduate Theology and Pastoral Ministry. Program content: Scripture, systematic theology. Available for credit. Certificate signed by the President of College.

Program Format   Daytime classes offered. Students enroll in the summer. Full program cycle lasts 18 credit hours.

Evaluation   Student evaluation based on tests, papers. Grading system: Letters or numbers. Transcripts are kept for each student.

Enrollment Requirements   Graduate degree in theology, religious education, or related field; three years experience required. Program is open to non-resident foreign students.

Program Costs $1350 for the program, $225 per course.

Housing and Student Services   Housing is available. Job counseling and placement services are not available.

Contact   Rev. Paul Couture, SSE, Director, Graduate Theology and Pastoral Ministry, Winooski, VT 05404. 802-655-2000 Ext. 2579.

THEOLOGICAL STUDIES (39.06)
Graduate Certificate in Theology

General Information   Unit offering the program: Graduate Theology and Pastoral Ministry. Program content: Old Testament, New Testament, systematics, moral studies, liturgical studies. Available for credit. Certificate signed by the President of College. Certificate applicable to M.A. in Theology and Pastoral Ministry.

Program Format   Daytime classes offered. Students enroll in the summer.

Evaluation   Student evaluation based on tests, papers. Grading system: Letters or numbers. Transcripts are kept for each student.

Enrollment Requirements   Bachelor's degree in arts, science, philosophy, theology, or education; 2.5 GPA; 18 credits in theology or other humanistic discipline required. Program is open to non-resident foreign students.

Program Costs $2340 for the program, $390 per course.

Housing and Student Services   Housing is available. Job counseling and placement services are not available.

Contact   Rev. Paul Couture, SSE, Director, Graduate Theology and Pastoral Ministry, Winooski, VT 05404. 802-655-2000 Ext. 2579.

NUCEA MEMBER
UNIVERSITY OF VERMONT
Burlington, Vermont 05405

CLOTHING, APPAREL, AND TEXTILES MANAGEMENT, PRODUCTION, AND SERVICES (20.03)
Certificate in Fiber Arts and Apparel Design

General Information   Unit offering the program: Merchandising, Consumer Studies, and Design. Available for credit. Certificate signed by the Director, Continuing Education. Certificate applicable to B.S. in Fashion Merchandising, Related Art (Apparel and Textile Design).

Program Format   Daytime, evening classes offered. Instructional schedule: Once per week for three hours. Program cycle: Continuous enrollment. Full program cycle lasts 12 months. Completion of program requires six courses, lab work, graded assignments.

Evaluation   Student evaluation based on tests, papers, reports. Grading system: Letters or numbers. Transcripts are kept for each student.

Enrollment Requirements   Program is open to non-resident foreign students. English language proficiency required.

Program Costs $426 per course (state residents); $1308 per course (nonresidents).

Housing and Student Services   Housing is not available. Job counseling and placement services are not available.

Special Features   Designed for weavers, designers, craftspeople, and business people, certificate composed of five core courses and one elective. Fiber Arts core courses are: Design, Sketching and Illustration, Hand Weaving, Textile Design, and Loom Weaving. Apparel Design core courses are: Design, Sketching and Illustration, Fashion Design and Trend Analysis, Apparel Design I, and Apparel Design II.

Contact   Dr. Suzanne Loker, Department Chair–Merchandising, Consumer Studies, Design, 211 Terrill Hall, Burlington, VT 05401. 802-656-2097.

COMPUTER PROGRAMMING (11.02)
Computer Programming Certificate

General Information   Unit offering the program: Department of Computer Science and Electrical Engineering. Program content:

Programming style and technique with top-down emphasis. Available for credit. Certificate signed by the Director, Continuing Education.

Program Format Evening classes offered. Instructional schedule: One evening per week for three hours. Program cycle: Continuous enrollment. Full program cycle lasts 18 months. Completion of program requires five courses, lab work, graded assignments.

Evaluation Student evaluation based on tests. Grading system: Letters or numbers. Transcripts are kept for each student.

Enrollment Requirements Program is open to non-resident foreign students. English language proficiency required.

Program Costs $426 per course (state residents); $1308 per course (nonresidents).

Housing and Student Services Housing is not available. Job counseling and placement services are not available.

Special Features Designed to provide fundamental knowledge and skills for career as Computer Programmer. Course requirements are Microcomputer Applications, Computer Programming I, Computer Programming II, Introduction to Computer Science, and Structured Business Programming (COBOL). Limited substitutions with approval of department.

Contact Ms. Debbie Worthley, Continuing Education Student Service Adviser, 322 South Prospect Street, Burlington, VT 05401. 802-656-2085.

VIRGINIA

NUCEA MEMBER
GEORGE MASON UNIVERSITY
Fairfax, Virginia 22030

ARCHAEOLOGY (45.03)
Certificate Program in Applied Archaeology

General Information Unit offering the program: Department of Sociology and Anthropology. Program content: Research methods, analysis of social data, field methods in archaeology. Available for credit. Certificate signed by the Registrar. Certificate applicable to B.A. in Anthropology.

Program Format Daytime, evening classes offered. Program cycle: Continuous enrollment. Full program cycle lasts 30 credit hours. Completion of program requires grade of C or better, 150-hour internship.

Evaluation Student evaluation based on tests, papers, reports. Grading system: Letters or numbers. Transcripts are kept for each student.

Enrollment Requirements Bachelor's degree required. Program is open to non-resident foreign students. English language proficiency required. Minimum TOEFL score required: 570.

Program Costs $230 per course (state residents); $460 per course (nonresidents).

Housing and Student Services Housing is available. Job counseling and placement services are available.

Special Features Useful for those seeking employment in cultural resource management, contract archaeology, public archaeology, and museums. Useful for combining archaeological skills with other training in anthropology, history, geology, geography, computer science, and American studies.

Contact Dr. Ann Palkovich, Associate Professor, Department of Sociology and Anthropology, Fairfax, VA 22030. 703-323-3492.

GEOGRAPHY (45.07)
Cartography

General Information Unit offering the program: Geography Program, Department of Public Affairs. Program content: Advanced map design and production. Available for credit. Certificate signed by the College Dean. Certificate applicable to B.A. in Geography.

Program Format Daytime classes offered. Instructional schedule: Two to three classes per week. Program cycle: Continuous enrollment. Full program cycle lasts 3 semesters. Completion of program requires grade of C or better in each course.

Evaluation Student evaluation based on tests, maps, projects. Transcripts are kept for each student.

Enrollment Requirements Bachelor's degree required. Program is not open to non-resident foreign students.

Housing and Student Services Housing is available. Job counseling and placement services are not available.

Special Features The program involves 3 full-time faculty who specialize in cartography and/or remote sensing. Students receive individual attention because class sizes are kept low.

Contact Mr. Robert A. Rundstrom, Assistant Professor, Geography Program, Department of Public Affairs, Fairfax, VA 22030. 703-323-2272.

INDIVIDUAL AND FAMILY DEVELOPMENT (19.07)
Graduate Certificate in Gerontology

General Information Unit offering the program: Office of Individualized Study Degree Programs. Program content: Theoretical and applied aspects of aging. Available for credit. Certificate signed by the Chair of the Gerontology Certificate Program.

Program Format Daytime, evening classes offered. Program cycle: Continuous enrollment. Full program cycle lasts 18 credit hours. Completion of program requires six credits of practicum.

Evaluation Student evaluation based on tests, papers, reports, practicum. Grading system: Letters or numbers. Transcripts are kept for each student.

Enrollment Requirements Master's degree in service-related area required. Program is open to non-resident foreign students. English language proficiency required. Minimum TOEFL score required: 550.

Program Costs $76 per credit hour (state residents); $152 per credit hour (nonresidents).

Housing and Student Services Housing is available. Job counseling and placement services are available.

Special Features Program has been approved by Graduate Council and Dean of the Graduate School. All courses are part of normal university curriculum. Certificate is not awarded until student earns graduate degree. A Gerontology Certificate Program Committee (mandated by the Faculty Senate) oversees and regularly reviews program.

Contact Dr. James F. Sanford, Director, Individualized Study Degree Programs, 4400 University Drive, East Building, Room 124, Fairfax, VA 22030. 703-323-2342.

INDIVIDUAL AND FAMILY DEVELOPMENT (19.07)
Undergraduate Certificate in Gerontology

General Information Unit offering the program: Office of Individualized Study Degree Programs. Program content: Counseling, recreation, social sciences, anatomy, biology. Available for credit. Certificate signed by the Chair of Gerontology Certificate Program.

Program Format Daytime, evening classes offered. Program cycle: Continuous enrollment. Full program cycle lasts 24 credit hours.

Undergraduate Certificate in Gerontology continued

Evaluation Student evaluation based on tests, papers, reports, practicum. Grading system: Letters or numbers. Transcripts are kept for each student.

Enrollment Requirements Bachelor's degree, eight hours of biology, three hours of psychology or sociology required. Program is open to non-resident foreign students. English language proficiency required. Minimum TOEFL score required: 570.

Program Costs $76 per credit hour (state residents); $152 per credit hour (nonresidents).

Housing and Student Services Housing is available. Job counseling and placement services are available.

Special Features Program has been approved by faculty of the participating colleges, the Faculty Senate, and the Vice President for Academic Affairs. All courses are part of normal university curriculum. Certificate is not awarded until student earns baccalaureate degree. A Gerontology Certificate Program Committee (mandated by the Faculty Senate) oversees and regularly reviews program.

Contact Dr. James F. Sanford, Director, Individualized Study Degree Programs, 4400 University Drive, East Building, Room 124, Fairfax, VA 22030. 703-323-2342.

MANAGEMENT INFORMATION SYSTEMS (06.12)
Graduate Certificate in Information Management and Expert Systems

General Information Unit offering the program: School of Business Administration. Program content: Computer systems for management, business expert systems, analysis and design of computer systems. Available for credit. Certificate signed by the Vice President for Academic Affairs. Certificate applicable to M.B.A.

Program Format Daytime, evening classes offered. Program cycle: Continuous enrollment. Full program cycle lasts 15 credit hours.

Evaluation Student evaluation based on tests, papers, reports. Grading system: Letters or numbers. Transcripts are kept for each student.

Enrollment Requirements GMAT score of 500, 2.75 GPA for last 60 hours of bachelor's degree required. Program is open to non-resident foreign students. English language proficiency required. Minimum TOEFL score: 550.

Program Costs $1140 for the program, $228 per course (state residents); $2280 for the program, $456 per course (nonresidents).

Housing and Student Services Housing is available. Job counseling and placement services are available.

Special Features The graduate certificate in Information Management and Expert Systems is intended to help any person who is interested in increasing the productivity of the organization's total information system. While the entrance requirements are rigorous, there is no restriction on the type of previous undergraduate major required to ensure success in the program.

Contact Dr. Ella Gardner, Director of Admissions for IRM, Department of Decision Sciences, 4400 University Drive, Fairfax, VA 22030. 703-323-2758.

MENTAL HEALTH/HUMAN SERVICES (17.04)
Psychology Technician Certificate Program

General Information Unit offering the program: Psychology Department. Program content: Theoretical background and technical skills needed for paraprofessional positions in mental health and human services. Available for credit. Certificate signed by the Academic Vice President.

Program Format Daytime, evening classes offered. Program cycle: Continuous enrollment. Full program cycle lasts 24 credit hours. Completion of program requires grade of B or better in practicum.

Evaluation Student evaluation based on tests, papers, reports, practicum. Grading system: Letters or numbers. Transcripts are kept for each student.

Enrollment Requirements Bachelor's degree in psychology, sociology, or social work required. Program is not open to non-resident foreign students.

Program Costs $1824 for the program, $228 per course.

Housing and Student Services Housing is available. Job counseling and placement services are not available.

Contact Ms. Carol J. Erdwins, Associate Professor, Department of Psychology, Fairfax, VA 22030. 703-323-2206.

NURSING-RELATED SERVICES (17.06)
Graduate Certificate in International Nursing

General Information Unit offering the program: School of Nursing. Available for credit. Certificate signed by the Vice President for Academic Affairs.

Program Format Evening classes offered. Program cycle: Continuous enrollment. Full program cycle lasts 15 credit hours. Completion of program requires 3.0 GPA.

Evaluation Student evaluation based on papers. Grading system: Letters or numbers. Transcripts are kept for each student.

Enrollment Requirements Master's degree in nursing required. Program is open to non-resident foreign students. English language proficiency required. Minimum TOEFL score required: 550.

Program Costs $1140 for the program, $228 per course (state residents); $2280 for the program, $456 per course (nonresidents).

Housing and Student Services Housing is available. Job counseling and placement services are available.

Special Features The Graduate Certificate in International Nursing provides an opportunity for students to enrich their understanding of international health through a sequence of courses including, but not limited to, international nursing, anthropology, international relations, and economics.

Contact Dr. Yuen C. Liu, Coordinator, International Programs, School of Nursing, 4400 University Drive, Fairfax, VA 22030. 703-323-2430.

NURSING-RELATED SERVICES (17.06)
Graduate Certificate in Nursing Administration

General Information Unit offering the program: School of Nursing. Program content: Management and nursing administration. Available for credit. Certificate signed by the Vice President for Academic Affairs.

Program Format Daytime, evening classes offered. Program cycle: Continuous enrollment. Full program cycle lasts 18 credit hours. Completion of program requires 3.0 GPA.

Evaluation Student evaluation based on papers. Grading system: Letters or numbers. Transcripts are kept for each student.

Enrollment Requirements Master's degree in nursing required. Program is open to non-resident foreign students. English language proficiency required. Minimum TOEFL score required: 550.

Program Costs $2052 for the program, $228 per course (state residents); $4104 for the program, $456 per course (nonresidents).

Housing and Student Services Housing is available. Job counseling and placement services are available.

Special Features The Graduate Certificate in Nursing Administration is designed for the student with a master's degree in nursing who wishes formal study in theory and practice in nursing administration in the health care delivery system.

Contact Ms. Jacqueline A. Dienemann, Coordinator, Nursing Administration, School of Nursing, 4400 University Drive, Fairfax, VA 22030. 703-323-2430.

NURSING-RELATED SERVICES (17.06)
Graduate Certificate in Nursing Education

General Information Unit offering the program: School of Nursing. Available for credit. Certificate signed by the Vice President for Academic Affairs.

Program Format Daytime, evening classes offered. Program cycle: Continuous enrollment. Full program cycle lasts 15 credit hours.

Evaluation Student evaluation based on papers, reports. Grading system: Letters or numbers. Transcripts are kept for each student.

Enrollment Requirements Master's degree in nursing required. Program is open to non-resident foreign students. English language proficiency required. Minimum TOEFL score required: 550.

Program Costs $1140 for the program, $228 per course (state residents); $2280 for the program, $456 per course (nonresidents).

Housing and Student Services Housing is available. Job counseling and placement services are available.

Special Features The Graduate Certificate in Nursing Education combines foundation courses in education with courses in the principles and practices of nursing education. The program prepares students to function in nursing educational roles in both academic and nonacademic settings.

Contact Dr. Catherine E. Connelly, Associate Dean, Graduate Programs, School of Nursing, 4400 University Drive, Fairfax, VA 22030. 703-323-2430.

RENEWABLE NATURAL RESOURCES, GENERAL (03.01)
Environmental Management

General Information Unit offering the program: Biology. Program content: Conservation of resources and environment, technical writing, natural science concentration. Available for credit. Certificate signed by the Vice President for Academic Affairs. Certificate applicable to any four-year degree offered at the institution.

Program Format Daytime, evening classes offered. Program cycle: Continuous enrollment. Full program cycle lasts 27 credit hours. Completion of program requires grade of C or better.

Evaluation Student evaluation methods vary by course. Grading system: Letters or numbers. Transcripts are kept for each student.

Enrollment Requirements One year of laboratory science (biology, geology, chemistry) with grade of C or better required. Program is open to non-resident foreign students. English language proficiency required. Minimum TOEFL score required: 550.

Program Costs $76 per credit hour (state residents); $152 per credit hour (nonresidents).

Housing and Student Services Housing is available. Job counseling and placement services are available.

Special Features The curriculum uses a multidisciplinary approach to the biological, physical, and social aspects of environmental problems in order to develop skills for their analysis and resolution. Many opportunities exist for internships in government agencies and in the private sector because of the proximity of the University to Washington, D.C.

Contact Dr. Francis D. Heliotis, Assistant Professor of Biology, Biology Department, Fairfax, VA 22030. 703-323-2181.

TEACHING ENGLISH AS A SECOND LANGUAGE/FOREIGN LANGUAGE (13.14)
Teaching of English as a Second Language

General Information Unit offering the program: Department of English. Program content: Linguistics and grammar. Available for credit. Certificate signed by the Vice President for Academic Affairs. Certificate applicable to M.A. in English, Linguistics.

Program Format Evening classes offered. Program cycle: Continuous enrollment. Full program cycle lasts 15 credit hours. Completion of program requires grade of B or better.

Evaluation Student evaluation based on tests, papers. Grading system: Letters or numbers. Transcripts are kept for each student.

Enrollment Requirements One thousand-word writing sample and two letters of recommendation required. Program is open to non-resident foreign students. English language proficiency required. Minimum TOEFL score required: 550.

Program Costs $1140 for the program, $228 per course (state residents); $2280 for the program, $456 per course (nonresidents).

Housing and Student Services Housing is available. Job counseling and placement services are available.

Special Features The certificate may be pursued concurrently with any of several degree programs offered through the Department of Education, the Department of English, and the Department of Foreign Languages and Literatures, and part of the work toward the certificate may be applicable toward degrees in those departments.

Contact Ms. Deborah E. Kaplan, Graduate Coordinator, Department of English, 4400 University Drive, Fairfax, VA 22030. 703-323-2221.

LYNCHBURG COLLEGE
Lynchburg, Virginia 24501

ACCOUNTING (06.02)
Accounting Certificate

General Information Unit offering the program: School of Business. Available for credit. Certificate signed by the President of the College.

Program Format Daytime, evening classes offered. Program cycle: Continuous enrollment. Full program cycle lasts 45 credit hours. Completion of program requires grade of C or better in all courses.

Evaluation Student evaluation based on tests. Grading system: Letters or numbers. Transcripts are kept for each student.

Enrollment Requirements Bachelor's degree (non-accounting) required. Program is open to non-resident foreign students. English language proficiency required.

Program Costs Part-time students: $450 per course; full-time students over age 25: $450 per course; full-time students age 25 and under: $7300 for the program.

Housing and Student Services Housing is available. Job counseling and placement services are available.

Contact School of Business, Lynchburg, VA 24501. 804-522-8262.

INDIVIDUAL AND FAMILY DEVELOPMENT (19.07)
Graduate Specialist in Gerontology

General Information Unit offering the program: Belle Boone Beard Gerontology Center; Departments of Sociology, Psychology, Biology. Program content: Sociological, psychological, biological aging; gerontological social policy, legislation, community services. Available for credit. Certificate

Graduate Specialist in Gerontology continued
signed by the Dean of the College. Certificate applicable to M.Ed. in Agency Counseling.

Program Format Daytime, evening classes offered. Program cycle: Continuous enrollment. Full program cycle lasts 18 credit hours. Completion of program requires internship.

Evaluation Student evaluation based on tests, papers, reports, oral examination. Grading system: Letters or numbers. Transcripts are kept for each student.

Enrollment Requirements Bachelor's degree, college admissions required. Program is open to non-resident foreign students. English language proficiency required. Minimum TOEFL score required: 550.

Program Costs $2124 for the program, $354 per course.

Housing and Student Services Housing is available. Job counseling and placement services are available.

Special Features Directed toward persons seeking degrees in basic disciplines and wishing to specialize in gerontology; persons who have degrees but want to add gerontology specialization; and persons not seeking or holding degrees who wish to develop nondegree credentials in gerontology. M.Ed. with specialization in agency counseling may combine with gerontology specialist program. Forty-two semester hours is required for both degree and certificate.

Contact Dr. Albert J. E. Wilson III, Director, Belle Boone Beard Gerontology Center, Lynchburg, VA 24501. 804-522-8456.

INDIVIDUAL AND FAMILY DEVELOPMENT (19.07)
Specialist in Gerontology

General Information Unit offering the program: Belle Boone Beard Gerontology Center; Departments of Sociology, Psychology, Biology. Program content: Sociological, psychological, biological aging; gerontological social policy, legislation, community services. Available for credit. Certificate signed by the Dean of the College. Certificate applicable to any four-year degree offered at the institution.

Program Format Daytime, evening classes offered. Program cycle: Continuous enrollment. Full program cycle lasts 18 credit hours. Completion of program requires internship.

Evaluation Student evaluation based on tests, papers, reports. Grading system: Letters or numbers. Transcripts are kept for each student.

Enrollment Requirements College admissions required. Program is open to non-resident foreign students. English language proficiency required. Minimum TOEFL score required: 550.

Program Costs $2700 for the program, $450 per course.

Housing and Student Services Housing is available. Job counseling and placement services are available.

Special Features The Lynchburg College Gerontology Certificate programs are directed toward a) persons who are seeking degrees in one of the basic professions or disciplines and wish to specialize in gerontology; b) persons who already have degrees but want to add a specialization in gerontology; and c) persons not seeking or holding degrees who wish to develop nondegree credentials in gerontology.

Contact Dr. Albert J. E. Wilson III, Director, Belle Boone Beard Gerontology Center, Lynchburg, VA 24501. 804-522-8456.

OLD DOMINION UNIVERSITY
Norfolk, Virginia 23529

COMPUTER AND INFORMATION SCIENCES, GENERAL (11.01)
Certificate in Personal Computing in Business

General Information Unit offering the program: Institute of Management, College of Business and Public Administration. Program content: Lotus 1-2-3, dBase III, WordPerfect, PC-DOS, MS-DOS. Available on a non-credit basis. Certificate signed by the Dean, College of Business and Public Administration.

Program Format Evening classes offered. Instructional schedule: One evening per week. Students may enroll twice per year. Full program cycle lasts 20 weeks. Completion of program requires examinations and exercises.

Evaluation Student evaluation based on tests. Grading system: Pass/fail. Records are kept by Institute of Management.

Enrollment Requirements Program is open to non-resident foreign students.

Program Costs $1195 for the program.

Housing and Student Services Housing is not available. Job counseling and placement services are not available.

Contact Dr. Richard M. Mansfield, Director, Institute of Management, Norfolk, VA 23529-0118. 804-440-4603.

DENTAL SERVICES (17.01)
Certificate Program—Dental Assisting

General Information Unit offering the program: School of Dental Hygiene and Dental Assisting, College of Health Sciences. Program content: Preclinical science, four-handed dentistry, preventive oral health care, selected services as approved by state law. Available on either a credit or non-credit basis. Certificate signed by the Dean, College of Health Sciences. Certificate applicable to B.S. in Dental Hygiene, Interdisciplinary Studies.

Program Format Daytime classes offered. Instructional schedule: Monday through Friday. Students enroll in August. Full program cycle lasts 2 semesters. Completion of program requires average grade of C- or better.

Evaluation Student evaluation based on tests, papers, reports, clinical performance. Grading system: Letters or numbers. Transcripts are kept for each student.

Enrollment Requirements High school diploma or GED, transcripts required. Program is open to non-resident foreign students. English language proficiency required. Minimum TOEFL score required: 500.

Program Costs $2160–$4008 for the program.

Housing and Student Services Housing is available. Job counseling and placement services are available.

Special Features The curriculum is accredited by the American Dental Association, Commission on Dental Accreditation. Students can challenge any course. Students who are successful in this program are eligible for advanced placement in the Dental Hygiene Program.

Contact Ms. Barbara G. McGrady, Coordinator, Dental Assisting Program, School of Dental Hygiene and Dental Assisting, Room 149 Technology Building, Norfolk, VA 23529-0499. 804-440-4310.

EDUCATION ADMINISTRATION (13.04)
Certificate of Advanced Study—Educational Administration

General Information Unit offering the program: Educational Leadership and Services Department. Program content: Advanced graduate level work in educational administration and supervision. Available for credit. Certificate signed by the Rector of the Board of Regents.

Program Format Daytime, evening classes offered. Instructional schedule: Once per week for three hours. Program cycle: Continuous enrollment. Full program cycle lasts 30 credit hours. Completion of program requires writing test, comprehensive examination.

Evaluation Student evaluation based on tests, papers, reports. Grading system: Letters or numbers. Transcripts are kept for each student.

Enrollment Requirements M.S. degree, 3.0 GPA, written recommendation from superiors required. Program is open to non-resident foreign students. English language proficiency required.

Special Features Certificate of Advanced Study is an advanced graduate level degree program which has Virginia State Council Higher Education's approval and has full accreditation by NCATE, the national accrediting agency for educational programs in institutions of higher education. It offers advanced graduate level study in school administration and supervision.

Contact Dr. John P. McSweeney, Graduate Program Director, Administration and Supervision, Norfolk, VA 23529. 804-440-3326.

EDUCATION ADMINISTRATION (13.04)
Certificate of Advanced Study—Vocational and Technical Education Specialty

General Information Unit offering the program: Department of Education Leadership and Service, Department of Vocational and Technical Education. Available for credit. Certificate signed by the President.

Program Format Evening classes offered. Program cycle: Continuous enrollment. Full program cycle lasts 6 semesters.

Evaluation Student evaluation based on tests, papers, reports. Grading system: Letters or numbers. Transcripts are kept for each student.

Enrollment Requirements Master's in vocational education, 3.25 graduate GPA, GRE score of 1000 required. Program is not open to non-resident foreign students. English language proficiency required.

Program Costs $105 per credit hour.

Housing and Student Services Housing is not available. Job counseling and placement services are not available.

Special Features Designed for part-time (evening) study. Students usually employed full-time by public schools.

Contact Mr. Malvern L. Miller, Graduate Program Director, Vocational and Technical Education, Norfolk, VA 23508. 804-440-3307.

INDUSTRIAL PRODUCTION TECHNOLOGIES (15.06)
Certificate Program—Industrial Training

General Information Unit offering the program: Vocational and Technical Education. Program content: Instructional methodology. Available for credit. Certificate signed by the Department Chair. Certificate applicable to B.S. in Secondary Education.

Program Format Daytime classes offered. Program cycle: Continuous enrollment. Full program cycle lasts 8 courses.

Evaluation Student evaluation based on tests, papers, reports. Grading system: Letters or numbers. Transcripts are kept for each student.

Enrollment Requirements Technical background required. Program is open to non-resident foreign students. Students required to live on campus.

Housing and Student Services Housing is available. Job counseling and placement services are available.

Special Features Program is designed to prepare people to be instructors of technical content for business and industry.

Contact Dr. John M. Ritz, Program Leader, Technology Education, Norfolk, VA 23508. 804-440-4305.

INTERNATIONAL RELATIONS (45.09)
Graduate Certificate in the History of Strategy and Policy

General Information Unit offering the program: Department of History. Program content: International relations, military affairs. Available for credit. Certificate signed by the Dean, College of Arts and Letters. Certificate applicable to M.A. in History, International Studies, Humanities.

Program Format Evening classes offered. Program cycle: Continuous enrollment. Complete program cycle lasts 18 months (part-time). Completion of program requires 3.0 GPA.

Evaluation Student evaluation based on tests, papers, reports. Grading system: Letters or numbers. Transcripts are kept for each student.

Enrollment Requirements Bachelor's degree required. Program is open to non-resident foreign students.

Program Costs $1260 for the program, $315 per course.

Housing and Student Services Housing is not available. Job counseling and placement services are available.

Special Features Designed for professional military officers and others wishing to examine political and military decisions in situations involving military force. The program is an extension of the Strategy and Policy curriculum of the Naval War College. Eligible students may transfer 6 credits to the Naval War College toward its diploma.

Contact Mr. Willard C. Frank Jr., Coordinator for Strategy and Policy, Department of History, Norfolk, VA 23508. 804-440-3949.

INVESTMENTS AND SECURITIES (06.10)
Professional Financial Planning

General Information Unit offering the program: Institute of Management, College of Business and Public Administration. Available on a non-credit basis. Certificate signed by the President.

Program Format Evening classes offered. Instructional schedule: One evening per week. Full program cycle lasts 5 courses.

Evaluation Student evaluation based on tests. Records are kept by Institute of Management.

Enrollment Requirements Program is open to non-resident foreign students.

Program Costs $2104 for the program, $495 per course.

Housing and Student Services Housing is not available. Job counseling and placement services are not available.

Contact Dr. Richard M. Mansfield, Director, Institute of Management, Norfolk, VA 23529-0118. 804-440-4603.

OPHTHALMIC SERVICES (17.07)
Certificate Program—Ophthalmic Technology

General Information Unit offering the program: College of Health Sciences. Program content: Ocular anatomy and physiology, optics, ocular disease and pathology, perimetry, contact lens concepts, photography of the retina, advanced diagnostic testing, externships. Available for credit. Cosponsored by Eastern Virginia Medical School–Department of Ophthamology. Certificate signed by the Dean, College of Health Sciences. Certificate applicable to B.S. in Interdisciplinary Studies.

Program Format Daytime, evening classes offered. Instructional schedule: Three to five hours per day, Monday through Friday. Students enroll in September. Full program cycle lasts 22 months. Completion of program requires 2.0 GPA in required courses, externships.

Certificate Program—Ophthalmic Technology continued

Evaluation Student evaluation based on tests, papers, clinical externships, senior project, oral practicals. Grading system: Letters or numbers. Transcripts are kept for each student.

Enrollment Requirements Sixty credits of pre-science, three letters of recommendation, interviews required. Program is open to non-resident foreign students.

Program Costs $2200 per year.

Housing and Student Services Housing is available. Job counseling and placement services are available.

Special Features This joint program, initiated between EVMS and ODU in 1985, is the first of its kind nationally to offer a degree (B.S.) option, along with offering a certificate, in Ophthalmic Technology training. Students are allowed to develop a minor concentration of their own preference through the Interdisciplinary Studies Program.

Contact Ms. Sheila Coyne Nemeth, Program Director, Eastern Virginia Medical School, Lions Sight and Hearing Center, 600 Grosham Drive, Norfolk, VA 23507. 804-628-2100.

PHILOSOPHY (38.01)
Graduate Certificate in Jungian Thought

General Information Unit offering the program: Philosophy Department, Institute of Humanities. Program content: Jung's original works. Available for credit. Certificate signed by the Dean, College of Arts and Letters. Certificate applicable to M.A. in Humanities.

Program Format Daytime, evening, summer retreat classes offered. Instructional schedule: Once per week for three hours. Program cycle: Continuous enrollment. Full program cycle lasts 4 semesters. Completion of program requires 15 credit hours of graduate work in Jungian thought including four core courses.

Evaluation Student evaluation based on papers. Grading system: Letters or numbers. Transcripts are kept for each student.

Enrollment Requirements Bachelor's degree, 3.0 GPA required. Program is open to non-resident foreign students.

Program Costs $1500 for the program, $300 per course.

Housing and Student Services Housing is available. Job counseling and placement services are not available.

Special Features This program has been in existence since 1979, and the certificate has been offered since 1986.

Contact Dr. Douglas Greene, Director, Institute of Humanities, Norfolk, VA 23508. 804-440-3821.

STUDENT COUNSELING AND PERSONNEL SERVICES (13.11)
Certificate of Advanced Study—Guidance and Counseling

General Information Unit offering the program: Guidance and Counseling Program, Department of Education Leadership and Services. Available for credit. Certificate signed by the University President.

Program Format Evening classes offered. Instructional schedule: Three hours per week. Program cycle: Continuous enrollment. Full program cycle lasts 3 semesters. Completion of program requires 3.0 GPA, written comprehensive examination, writing proficiency examination.

Evaluation Student evaluation based on tests, papers, reports, field performance, counseling interviews. Grading system: Letters or numbers, pass/fail. Transcripts are kept for each student.

Enrollment Requirements Master's degree in counseling or related field, 3.25 graduate GPA, minimum combined score of 1000 on the general aptitude section of the GRE, two letters of recommendation, statement of goals and experiences, interview required. Program is open to non-resident foreign students. English language proficiency required. Decisions are made on a case-by-case basis.

Program Costs $3150 for the program. $105 per credit hour.

Housing and Student Services Housing is available. Job counseling and placement services are available.

Special Features The program accepts students with a master's degree in counseling or in a related field of study provided that they have completed prerequisite courses. It is suitable for individuals seeking to enhance their professional preparation and satisfy part of the state licensure requirement as a professional counselor.

Contact Dr. Reiko Schwab, Graduate Program Director, Department of Educational Leadership and Services, Norfolk, VA 23529-0157. 804-440-3221.

WOMEN'S STUDIES (30.07)
Certificate Program—Women's Studies (Graduate)

General Information Unit offering the program: Women's Studies in the College of Arts and Letters. Available for credit. Certificate signed by the Director of Women's Studies. Certificate applicable to M.A. in Humanities.

Program Format Daytime, evening classes offered. Program cycle: Continuous enrollment. Full program cycle lasts 15 credit hours. Completion of program requires 15 credit hours, 3.0 GPA.

Evaluation Student evaluation based on tests, papers, reports. Grading system: Letters or numbers. Transcripts are kept for each student.

Enrollment Requirements Bachelor's degree, 2.5 GPA required. Program is open to non-resident foreign students. English language proficiency required. Students required to live on campus.

Program Costs $1575 for the program, $315 per course.

Housing and Student Services Housing is available. Job counseling and placement services are available.

Contact Dr. Ellen Lewin, Director of Women's Studies, Norfolk, VA 23508. 804-440-3823.

WOMEN'S STUDIES (30.07)
Certificate Program—Women's Studies (Undergraduate)

General Information Unit offering the program: Women's Studies in the College of Arts and Letters. Available for credit. Certificate signed by the Director of Women's Studies.

Program Format Daytime, evening classes offered. Program cycle: Continuous enrollment. Full program cycle lasts 15 credit hours. Completion of program requires 15 credit hours, 2.0 GPA.

Evaluation Student evaluation based on tests, papers, reports. Grading system: Letters or numbers. Transcripts are kept for each student.

Enrollment Requirements Program is open to non-resident foreign students. English language proficiency required. Students required to live on campus.

Program Costs $1350 for the program, $270 per course.

Housing and Student Services Housing is available. Job counseling and placement services are available.

Contact Dr. Ellen Lewin, Director of Women's Studies, Norfolk, VA 23508. 804-440-3823.

NUCEA MEMBER

VIRGINIA COMMONWEALTH UNIVERSITY
Richmond, Virginia 23284

INDIVIDUAL AND FAMILY DEVELOPMENT (19.07)
Certificate in Aging Studies

General Information Unit offering the program: Department of Gerontology. Program content: Overview of gerontology and application of gerontological research. Available for credit. Certificate signed by the Dean, School of Allied Health Professions. Certificate applicable to M.S.W., M.N., M.S. in Psychology, Master of Health Administration.

Program Format Daytime, evening classes offered. Completion of program requires 17 credit hours.

Evaluation Student evaluation based on tests, papers, reports. Grading system: Letters or numbers. Transcripts are kept for each student.

Enrollment Requirements Bachelor's degree, three references, essay required. Program is open to non-resident foreign students. English language proficiency required.

Program Costs $5100 for the program, $300 per credit hour.

Housing and Student Services Housing is available. Job counseling and placement services are available.

Special Features Offered for persons already working with elderly who have no academic training in gerontology and for graduate students in other disciplines. Students share benefits of University's diverse research. These include Geriatric Education Center, Information Resource Center, and Virginia Center on Aging. Research includes cognitive functioning and aging, lifespan development, psychophysiology, pain, suicide, retirement planning and housing, recreation and leisure, rural and minority issues, and sexuality.

Contact Ms. Iris A. Parham, Ph.D., Chair, Box 228 MCV Station, Richmond, VA 23298. 804-786-1565.

MISCELLANEOUS SPECIALIZED AREAS, LIFE SCIENCES (26.06)
Certificate in Environmental Studies

General Information Unit offering the program: Biology, Sociology, Political Science, Urban Studies and Planning. Program content: Social and natural science approaches to the environment. Available for credit. Certificate signed by the Dean, College of Humanities and Sciences.

Program Format Daytime, evening classes offered. Program cycle: Continuous enrollment. Full program cycle lasts 2 semesters. Completion of program requires 30 credit hours, 2.0 GPA.

Evaluation Student evaluation based on tests, papers, reports. Grading system: Letters or numbers. Transcripts are kept for each student.

Enrollment Requirements University admissions required. Program is open to non-resident foreign students. English language proficiency required. Minimum TOEFL score required: 550.

Program Costs $2250 for the program, $225 per course.

Housing and Student Services Housing is available. Job counseling and placement services are available.

Contact Mr. David Hartman, Special Assistant to the Vice Provost, 827 West Franklin, Richmond, VA 23063. 804-367-8421.

PUBLIC ADMINISTRATION (44.04)
Certificate in Public Management

General Information Unit offering the program: Department of Public Administration. Available for credit. Certificate signed by the President. Certificate applicable to M.P.A.

Program Format Daytime, evening classes offered. Instructional schedule: Once per week for three hours. Program cycle: Continuous enrollment. Full program cycle lasts 18 credit hours. Completion of program requires 3.0 GPA.

Evaluation Student evaluation based on tests, papers. Grading system: Letters or numbers. Transcripts are kept for each student.

Enrollment Requirements Bachelor's degree, three years professional experience, references required. Program is open to non-resident foreign students. English language proficiency required.

Program Costs $399 per course.

Housing and Student Services Housing is available. Job counseling and placement services are available.

Special Features A practitioner-oriented program, open only to experienced public service professionals. All instructors are experienced in practical public administration. Off-campus delivery of courses places instruction near students and convenient to their needs.

Contact Mr. Gilbert W. Fairholm, Associate Professor, 816 West Franklin Street, Richmond, VA 23284. 804-367-1046.

TEACHER EDUCATION, GENERAL PROGRAMS (13.12)
Post Baccalaureate Certificate in Montessori Education

General Information Unit offering the program: School of Education, Division of Teacher Education. Program content: Curriculum, materials, methodology. Available for credit. Endorsed by American Montessori Society. Certificate signed by the President. Certificate applicable to Master of Education.

Program Format Daytime, evening classes offered. Instructional schedule: One day and one evening per week, two weekend seminars. Students enroll in June. Full program cycle lasts 1 year. Completion of program requires one-year internship.

Evaluation Student evaluation based on tests, papers, reports, internship. Grading system: Letters or numbers. Transcripts are kept for each student.

Enrollment Requirements Bachelor's degree, experience in working with children (ages 3–6) required. Program is open to non-resident foreign students. English language proficiency required.

Program Costs $4000 for the program.

Housing and Student Services Housing is available. Job counseling and placement services are available.

Special Features The VCU-MTE program prepares sensitive, knowledgeable, and competent Montessori teachers of young children (3–6 years). High-quality education is the emphasis, via expert faculty and small classes. Both the academic and internship phases provide ongoing experiences with children in Montessori settings. Program serves foreign as well as USA trainees.

Contact Dr. Alice M. Pieper, Director, Montessori Teacher Education Program, School of Education, Box 2020, Richmond, VA 23284-2020. 804-367-1324.

NUCEA MEMBER
VIRGINIA POLYTECHNIC INSTITUTE AND STATE UNIVERSITY
Blacksburg, Virginia 24061

BUSINESS AND MANAGEMENT, GENERAL (06.01)
Certified Construction Management

General Information Unit offering the program: Management Development Center. Program content: Project management, communication, quality control, legal liabilities, advanced financial management. Available on a non-credit basis. Endorsed by Associated General Contractors of Virginia, Inc. Certificate signed by the Dean, College of Business.

Program Format Daytime, weekend classes offered. Program cycle: Continuous enrollment. Full program cycle lasts 9 months. Completion of program requires 15 seminar days, certifying examination.

Evaluation Student evaluation based on tests. Transcripts are kept for each student.

Enrollment Requirements Open enrollment. Program is open to non-resident foreign students.

Program Costs $2250 for the program, $135–$170 per course.

Special Features The Associated General Contractors of Virginia with Virginia Tech is one of the first chapters to adopt a certification/diploma approach for developing middle and upper management. The needs assessment, program design, and instructors selection is completed by Virginia Tech.

Contact Dr. R.F. Harshberger, Acting Director, Management Development Center, R.B. Pamplin College of Business, Blacksburg, VA 24061. 703-961-5566.

VIRGINIA WESLEYAN COLLEGE
Norfolk, Virginia 23502

MUSIC (50.09)
Church Music Certificate

General Information Unit offering the program: Adult Studies Program, Music Department. Program content: Choral conducting, children's choir, hymnology, music theory, church music administration, practicum. Available on a non-credit basis. Certificate signed by the President of the College.

Program Format Evening classes offered. Instructional schedule: One evening per week. Program cycle: Continuous enrollment. Full program cycle lasts 1 year. Completion of program requires six courses.

Evaluation Student evaluation based on tests, musical performance, class participation. Grading system: Pass/fail. Record of completion kept by National Registry of Continuing Education.

Enrollment Requirements Musical knowledge and experience as church musician required. Program is not open to non-resident foreign students. English language proficiency required.

Program Costs $720 for the program, $45 per CEU.

Housing and Student Services Housing is not available. Job counseling and placement services are not available.

Special Features Instructors are outstanding local church musicians with strong academic backgrounds. Certificate provides means of professional recognition and personal growth for church musicians.

Contact Ms. Dorothy Hinman, Director, Adult Studies, Wesleyan Drive, Norfolk, VA 23456. 804-461-3232.

WASHINGTON

CITY UNIVERSITY
Bellevue, Washington 98008

ACCOUNTING (06.02)
Certificate in Accounting

General Information Unit offering the program: Continuing Education and Special Programs. Program content: Financial statement analysis, cost accounting, business law. Available for credit. Certificate signed by the President. Certificate applicable to B.S. in Accounting.

Program Format Daytime, evening, weekend, correspondence classes offered. Program cycle: Continuous enrollment. Full program cycle lasts 4 quarters. Completion of program requires 45 credit hours, 2.0 GPA.

Evaluation Student evaluation based on tests, papers, reports. Grading system: Letters or numbers. Transcripts are kept for each student.

Enrollment Requirements Open admissions. Program is open to non-resident foreign students. English language proficiency required. Minimum TOEFL score required: 540.

Program Costs $490 per course.

Housing and Student Services Housing is not available. Job counseling and placement services are not available.

Special Features We offer the prior learning experience portfolio program to fulfill lower division credit. Our instructors are working professionals with a minimum of a master's degree, so our students receive the additional advantage of being taught by an instructor who has a perspective of the real world.

Contact New Student Center, 16661 Northup Way, Bellevue, WA 98008. 800-542-7845.

BUSINESS ADMINISTRATION AND MANAGEMENT (06.04)
Certificate of Advanced Graduate Study in Management

General Information Unit offering the program: Center for Continuing Education and Special Programs. Program content: Accounting, economics, human resources management. Available for credit. Certificate signed by the President. Certificate applicable to M.B.A.

Program Format Daytime, evening, weekend, correspondence classes offered. Program cycle: Continuous enrollment. Full program cycle lasts 4 quarters. Completion of program requires 18 credit hours, 3.0 GPA.

Evaluation Student evaluation based on tests, papers, reports. Grading system: Letters or numbers. Transcripts are kept for each student.

Enrollment Requirements Bachelor's degree or permission of the chief academic officer required. Program is open to non-resident foreign students. English language proficiency required. Minimum TOEFL score required: 540.

Program Costs $410 per course.

Housing and Student Services Housing is not available. Job counseling and placement services are not available.

Special Features We offer the prior learning experience portfolio program to fulfill lower division credit. Our instructors are working professionals with a minimum of a master's degree, so our students receive the additional advantage of being taught by an instructor who has a perspective of the real world.

Contact New Student Center, 16661 Northup Way, Bellevue, WA 98008. 800-542-7845.

BUSINESS AND MANAGEMENT, GENERAL (06.01)
Certificate of Management Studies

General Information   Unit offering the program: Continuing Education and Special Programs. Program content: Labor relations, human resource development, presentations. Available for credit. Certificate signed by the President. Certificate applicable to any four-year degree offered at the institution.

Program Format   Daytime, evening, weekend, correspondence classes offered. Program cycle: Continuous enrollment. Full program cycle lasts 4 quarters. Completion of program requires 35 credit hours, 3.0 GPA.

Evaluation   Student evaluation based on tests, papers, reports. Grading system: Letters or numbers. Transcripts are kept for each student.

Enrollment Requirements   Open admissions. Program is open to non-resident foreign students. English language proficiency required. Minimum TOEFL score required: 540.

Program Costs $490 per course.

Housing and Student Services   Housing is not available. Job counseling and placement services are not available.

Special Features   We offer the prior learning experience portfolio program to fulfill lower division credit. Our instructors are working professionals with a minimum of a master's degree, so our students receive the additional advantage of being taught by an instructor who has a perspective of the real world.

Contact   New Student Center, 16661 Northup Way, Bellevue, WA 98008. 800-542-7845.

COMPUTER PROGRAMMING (11.02)
Certificate in Computer Programming

General Information   Unit offering the program: Center for Continuing Education and Special Programs. Program content: Operating systems, information processing, COBOL. Available for credit. Certificate signed by the President. Certificate applicable to B.S. in Computer Information Services.

Program Format   Daytime, evening, weekend classes offered. Program cycle: Continuous enrollment. Full program cycle lasts 4 quarters. Completion of program requires 35 credit hours, 2.0 GPA.

Evaluation   Student evaluation based on tests, papers, reports. Grading system: Letters or numbers. Transcripts are kept for each student.

Enrollment Requirements   Open admissions. Program is open to non-resident foreign students. English language proficiency required. Minimum TOEFL score required: 540.

Program Costs $490 per course.

Housing and Student Services   Housing is not available. Job counseling and placement services are not available.

Special Features   We offer the prior learning experience portfolio program to fulfill lower division credit. Our instructors are working professionals with a minimum of a master's degree, so our students receive the additional advantage of being taught by an instructor who has a perspective of the real world.

Contact   New Student Center, 16661 Northup Way, Bellevue, WA 98008. 800-542-7845.

CORNISH COLLEGE OF THE ARTS
Seattle, Washington 98102

DRAMATIC ARTS (50.05)
Professional Certificate in Acting

General Information   Unit offering the program: Theater. Program content: Professional actors training program. Available for credit. Certificate signed by the Department Chair. Certificate applicable to B.F.A. in Acting.

Program Format   Daytime, evening classes offered. Instructional schedule: Five days per week. Program cycle: Continuous enrollment. Full program cycle lasts 6 semesters. Completion of program requires 96 credit hours, 2.75 GPA.

Evaluation   Student evaluation based on tests, papers, reports, artistic accomplishment. Grading system: Letters or numbers. Transcripts are kept for each student.

Enrollment Requirements   High school diploma, 2.0 GPA, audition/portfolio review required. Program is open to non-resident foreign students. English language proficiency required. Minimum TOEFL score required: 525.

Program Costs $220 per credit hour, $6100 per year.

Housing and Student Services   Housing is not available. Job counseling and placement services are available.

Special Features   The instructors are active, practicing professional artists. There are performance and internship opportunities. The faculty-student ratio is 1:7.

Contact   Ms. Gretchen Johnston, Director of Admissions and Financial Aid, 710 East Roy, Seattle, WA 98102. 206-323-1400 Ext. 205.

LUTHERAN BIBLE INSTITUTE OF SEATTLE
Issaquah, Washington 98027

BIBLE STUDIES (39.02)
Biblical Studies Certificate

General Information   Available for credit. Certificate signed by the President. Certificate applicable to any two- or four-year degree offered at the institution.

Program Format   Daytime, evening classes offered. Students enroll in September. Full program cycle lasts 2 years. Completion of program requires 90 credits, 2.0 GPA.

Evaluation   Student evaluation based on tests, papers, reports. Grading system: Letters or numbers, pass/fail. Transcripts are kept for each student.

Enrollment Requirements   High school diploma required. Program is open to non-resident foreign students. English language proficiency required. Minimum TOEFL score required: 500.

Program Costs $3855-$6392 per year, $81 per credit hour.

Housing and Student Services   Housing is available. Job counseling and placement services are not available.

Contact   Mr. Rich Fitzer, Director of Admissions, Providence Heights, Issaquah, WA 98027. 800-237-6152.

RELIGIOUS EDUCATION (39.04)
Certificate of Professional Studies

General Information   Unit offering the program: Gerontology, Missiology, Youth Work. Program content: Bible studies, professional studies, Christian life. Available for credit. Certificate signed by the President. Certificate applicable to B.S. in Gerontology, Youth Work; B.A. in Missiology, Biblical Studies.

Program Format   Daytime, evening classes offered. Students enroll in September. Full program cycle lasts 1 year. Completion of program requires 50 credits, 2.0 GPA.

Evaluation   Student evaluation based on tests, papers, reports. Grading system: Letters or numbers, pass/fail. Transcripts are kept for each student.

Enrollment Requirements   Bachelor's degree and/or ministry involvement required. Program is open to non-resident foreign students. English language proficiency required. Minimum TOEFL score required: 500.

Certificate of Professional Studies continued

Program Costs $3855–$6392 for the program, $81 per credit hour.

Housing and Student Services   Housing is available. Job counseling and placement services are available.

Contact   Mr. Rich Fitzer, Director of Admissions, Providence Heights, Issaquah, WA 98027. 800-237-6152.

PUGET SOUND CHRISTIAN COLLEGE
Edmonds, Washington 98020

BIBLE STUDIES (39.02)
Bible Certificate

General Information   Unit offering the program: Bible Department. Program content: Biblical and ministerial studies. Available for credit. Endorsed by American Association of Bible Colleges. Certificate signed by the President of the College. Certificate applicable to any four-year degree offered at the institution.

Program Format   Daytime, evening classes offered. Program cycle: Continuous enrollment. Full program cycle lasts 3 quarters. Completion of program requires 48 credit hours, 2.0 GPA.

Evaluation   Student evaluation based on tests, papers, reports. Grading system: Letters or numbers. Transcripts are kept for each student.

Enrollment Requirements   College admissions required. Program is open to non-resident foreign students. English language proficiency required. Minimum TOEFL score required: 500. Students required to live on campus.

Program Costs $2475 for the program, $80 per credit hour.

Housing and Student Services   Housing is available. Job counseling and placement services are not available.

Special Features   The program was designed to fulfill the needs of students who want one year of Bible College before going to another college or who want more Bible training to be a better worker in the local church. Courses are taken at freshman and sophomore levels.

Contact   Ms. Delores A. Scarbrough, Registrar, 410 4th Avenue North, Edmonds, WA 98020. 206-775-8686.

WEST VIRGINIA

WEST VIRGINIA WESLEYAN COLLEGE
Buckhannon, West Virginia 26201

BUSINESS AND MANAGEMENT, GENERAL (06.01)
Certificate of Business Principles

General Information   Unit offering the program: Outreach Education, Business Department. Program content: Statistics, accounting, marketing, law, communications. Available for credit. Certificate signed by the Dean of Academic Affairs.

Program Format   Correspondence classes offered. Program cycle: Continuous enrollment. Full program cycle lasts 2 semesters. Completion of program requires 18 credit hours, grade of C or better in each course.

Evaluation   Student evaluation based on tests, papers, reports. Grading system: Letters or numbers. Transcripts are kept for each student.

Enrollment Requirements   High school diploma or GED required. Program is open to non-resident foreign students. English language proficiency required.

Program Costs $1525 for the program, $240–$275 per course.

Housing and Student Services   Housing is not available. Job counseling and placement services are not available.

Contact   Ms. Barbara Hinkle, Program Supervisor, Outreach Education, Box 51, Buckhannon, WV 26201. 304-473-8000 Ext. 8430.

WISCONSIN

NUCEA MEMBER
CARTHAGE COLLEGE
Kenosha, Wisconsin 53141

LAW (22.01)
Certificate of Completion, Carthage College Paralegal Program

General Information   Unit offering the program: Department of Continuing Education. Program content: Legal research, survey of law, general practice. Available for credit. Certificate signed by the Academic Dean of the College.

Program Format   Evening, weekend classes offered. Instructional schedule: Two evenings per week and Saturday morning. Program cycle: Continuous enrollment. Full program cycle lasts 14 weeks. Completion of program requires 2.0 GPA.

Evaluation   Student evaluation based on tests, writing legal memoranda and briefs. Grading system: Letters or numbers. Transcripts are kept for each student.

Enrollment Requirements   Satisfactory performance on the Wonderlic Scholastic Level Exam, bachelor's degree or related work experience in a law firm required.

Program Costs $1980 for the program.

Housing and Student Services   Housing is available. Job counseling and placement services are available.

Special Features   The Carthage College Paralegal Program, taught by both practicing attorneys and paralegals, educates mature adults to provide legal assistance for the law profession. The program serves the needs of nontraditional, returning students in career transition who seek to maximize their potential for successful placement in the labor force.

Contact   Ms. Joyce M. Barina, Director of the Paralegal Program, Kenosha, WI 53141. 414-551-8500 Ext. 273.

MILWAUKEE SCHOOL OF ENGINEERING
Milwaukee, Wisconsin 53201

ELECTRICAL AND ELECTRONIC TECHNOLOGIES (15.03)
Basic Electricity and Electronics

General Information   Unit offering the program: Electrical Engineering and Computer Science. Available on either a credit or non-credit basis. Certificate signed by the President. Certificate applicable to A.A.S. in Technical Supervision.

Program Format   Evening classes offered. Instructional schedule: One evening per week. Program cycle: Continuous enrollment. Full program cycle lasts 3 quarters.

Evaluation Student evaluation based on tests, reports, homework, projects. Grading system: Letters or numbers. Transcripts are kept for each student.

Enrollment Requirements High school diploma, college algebra required. Program is open to non-resident foreign students. English language proficiency required. Minimum TOEFL score required: 500.

Program Costs $1305 for the program, $435 per course.

Housing and Student Services Housing is available. Job counseling and placement services are not available.

Special Features Heavy laboratory emphasis.

Contact Mr. Ronald T. Gaudes, Director, Evening College and Extension Programs, P.O. Box 644, Milwaukee, WI 53201-0644. 800-332-MSOE Ext. 7271.

ELECTRICAL AND ELECTRONIC TECHNOLOGIES (15.03)
Digital Troubleshooting and Microprocessor Technology

General Information Unit offering the program: Electrical Engineering and Computer Science. Program content: Electronics, digital logic, troubleshooting, computers, microprocesser-based systems. Available on either a credit or non-credit basis. Certificate signed by the President. Certificate applicable to A.A.S. in Technical Supervision.

Program Format Evening classes offered. Instructional schedule: One evening per week. Program cycle: Continuous enrollment. Full program cycle lasts 3 quarters.

Evaluation Student evaluation based on tests, reports, homework, projects. Grading system: Letters or numbers. Transcripts are kept for each student.

Enrollment Requirements High school diploma, prerequisites required. Program is open to non-resident foreign students. English language proficiency required. Minimum TOEFL score required: 500.

Program Costs $1305 for the program, $435 per course.

Housing and Student Services Housing is available. Job counseling and placement services are not available.

Special Features Heavy laboratory emphasis.

Contact Mr. Ronald T. Gaudes, Director, Evening College and Extension Programs, P.O. Box 644, Milwaukee, WI 53201-0644. 800-332-MSOE Ext. 7271.

ELECTROMECHANICAL INSTRUMENTATION AND MAINTENANCE TECHNOLOGIES (15.04)
Fluid Power Technology

General Information Unit offering the program: Mechanical Engineering. Available on either a credit or non-credit basis. Certificate signed by the President. Certificate applicable to A.A.S. in Technical Supervision.

Program Format Evening classes offered. Instructional schedule: One evening per week. Program cycle: Continuous enrollment. Full program cycle lasts 3 quarters.

Evaluation Student evaluation based on tests, reports, projects. Grading system: Letters or numbers. Transcripts are kept for each student.

Enrollment Requirements High school diploma, college algebra required. Program is open to non-resident foreign students. English language proficiency required. Minimum TOEFL score required: 500.

Program Costs $1305 for the program, $435 per course.

Housing and Student Services Housing is available. Job counseling and placement services are not available.

Special Features Heavy laboratory emphasis. Faculty expertise drawn from employees of The Fluid Power Institute—a nationally recognized research facility located on campus.

Contact Mr. Ronald T. Gaudes, Director, Evening College and Extension Programs, P.O. Box 644, Milwaukee, WI 53201-0644. 800-332-MSOE Ext. 7271.

ENVIRONMENTAL CONTROL TECHNOLOGIES (15.05)
Heating, Ventilating, and Air Conditioning Engineering Technology

General Information Unit offering the program: Mechanical Engineering. Available on either a credit or non-credit basis. Certificate signed by the President. Certificate applicable to A.A.S. in Technical Supervision.

Program Format Evening classes offered. Instructional schedule: One evening per week. Program cycle: Continuous enrollment. Full program cycle lasts 3 quarters.

Evaluation Student evaluation based on tests, reports, projects. Grading system: Letters or numbers. Transcripts are kept for each student.

Enrollment Requirements High school diploma required. Program is open to non-resident foreign students. English language proficiency required. Minimum TOEFL score required: 500.

Program Costs $1305 for the program, $435 per course.

Housing and Student Services Housing is available. Job counseling and placement services are not available.

Special Features Heavy laboratory emphasis with state-of-the-art controls and equipment.

Contact Mr. Ronald T. Gaudes, Director, Evening College and Extension Programs, P.O. Box 644, Milwaukee, WI 53201-0644. 800-332-MSOE Ext. 7271.

QUALITY CONTROL AND SAFETY TECHNOLOGIES (15.07)
Industrial Safety

General Information Unit offering the program: Chemistry Department. Program content: Preventing accidents, improving environmental conditions. Available for credit. Certificate signed by the President. Certificate applicable to A.A.S. in Technical Supervision, B.S. in Industrial Management.

Program Format Evening classes offered. Instructional schedule: Two evenings per week. Program cycle: Continuous enrollment. Full program cycle lasts 5 quarters.

Evaluation Student evaluation based on tests, papers, reports. Grading system: Letters or numbers. Transcripts are kept for each student.

Enrollment Requirements High school diploma required. Program is open to non-resident foreign students. English language proficiency required. Minimum TOEFL score required: 500.

Program Costs $2175 for the program, $435 per course.

Housing and Student Services Housing is available. Job counseling and placement services are available.

Special Features Taught by safety professionals. Helps prepare individuals to become certified safety professionals.

Contact Mr. Ronald T. Gaudes, Director, Evening College and Extension Programs, P.O. Box 644, Milwaukee, WI 53201-0644. 800-322-MSOE Ext. 7271.

QUALITY CONTROL AND SAFETY TECHNOLOGIES (15.07)
Quality Management

General Information Unit offering the program: Mechanical Engineering. Program content: Engineering economy, total quality systems, managing the quality function. Available on either a credit or non-credit basis. Certificate signed by the President. Certificate applicable to B.S. in Mechanical

Quality Management continued

Engineering Technology, Electrical Engineering Technology, Industrial Management.

Program Format   Evening classes offered. Instructional schedule: One evening per week. Program cycle: Continuous enrollment. Full program cycle lasts 3 quarters.

Evaluation   Student evaluation based on tests, reports. Grading system: Letters or numbers. Transcripts are kept for each student.

Enrollment Requirements   College admissions required when taking courses for credit. Program is open to non-resident foreign students. English language proficiency required. Minimum TOEFL score required: 500.

Program Costs $1305 for the program, $435 per course.

Housing and Student Services   Housing is available. Job counseling and placement services are not available.

Special Features   Taught by practicing professionals. Developed with input from the American Society for Quality Control.

Contact   Mr. Ronald T. Gaudes, Director, Evening College and Extension Programs, P.O. Box 644, Milwaukee, WI 53201-0644. 800-322-MSOE Ext. 7271.

QUALITY CONTROL AND SAFETY TECHNOLOGIES (15.07)
Statistical Quality Control

General Information   Unit offering the program: Mechanical Engineering. Program content: Basic and applied statistics, design of experiments, introduction to Taguchi methods. Available on either a credit or non-credit basis. Certificate signed by the President. Certificate applicable to B.S. in Mechanical Engineering Technology, Electrical Engineering Technology, Industrial Management.

Program Format   Evening classes offered. Instructional schedule: One evening per week. Program cycle: Continuous enrollment. Full program cycle lasts 4 quarters.

Evaluation   Student evaluation based on tests, reports. Grading system: Letters or numbers. Transcripts are kept for each student.

Enrollment Requirements   College admissions required when taking courses for credit. Program is open to non-resident foreign students. English language proficiency required. Minimum TOEFL score required: 500.

Program Costs $1740 for the program, $435 per course.

Housing and Student Services   Housing is available. Job counseling and placement services are not available.

Special Features   Taught by individuals (practicing professionals) from industry. Developed with input and direction from the American Society for Quality Control.

Contact   Mr. Ronald T. Gaudes, Director, Evening College and Extension Programs, P.O. Box 644, Milwaukee, WI 53201-0644. 800-332-MSOE Ext. 7271.

MOUNT MARY COLLEGE
Milwaukee, Wisconsin 53222

INDIVIDUAL AND FAMILY DEVELOPMENT (19.07)
Undergraduate Minor in Gerontology

General Information   Unit offering the program: Behavioral Science Department. Program content: Sociology, anthropology, psychology, biology of aging, group work techniques and/or nutrition, optional internship. Available for credit. Certificate signed by the Chairperson, Behavioral Science Department. Certificate applicable to most four-year degrees offered at the institution.

Program Format   Evening classes offered. Instructional schedule: Once per week for three hours. Three courses offered each semester; courses rotate on a two-year basis. Full program cycle lasts 4 semesters. Completion of program requires six courses, 2.3 GPA.

Evaluation   Student evaluation methods vary by course. Grading system: Letters or numbers. Transcripts are kept for each student.

Enrollment Requirements   Bachelor's degree required. Program is open to non-resident foreign students. English language proficiency required. Minimum TOEFL score required: 500.

Program Costs $3060 for the program, $510 per course.

Housing and Student Services   Housing is available. Job counseling and placement services are available.

Special Features   Gerontology students have access to Mount Mary College library's special collection on aging donated by the Milwaukee County Office on Aging.

Contact   Sr. Joanne Poehlman, Chairperson, Behavioral Science Department, 2900 North Menomonee River Parkway, Milwaukee, WI 53222. 414-258-4810.

MUSIC (50.09)
Orff-Schulwerk Level I

General Information   Unit offering the program: Music Department. Program content: Basic Orff, creative movement and dance, recorder instruction. Available for credit. Certificate signed by the Academic Dean. Certificate applicable to undergraduate or graduate programs in music education. Program fulfills requirements for teacher certification update.

Program Format   Daytime classes offered. Instructional schedule: Monday through Friday. Students enroll in the summer. Full program cycle lasts 2 weeks.

Evaluation   Student evaluation based on tests, reports, performance, orchestrations. Grading system: Letters or numbers. Transcripts are kept for each student.

Enrollment Requirements   Basic music training required. Program is open to non-resident foreign students. English language proficiency required. Minimum TOEFL score required: 550.

Program Costs $510 per course.

Housing and Student Services   Housing is available. Job counseling and placement services are not available.

Special Features   Overall course content follows the American Orff-Schulwerk Association "Guidelines for Teacher Training Courses" and has the approval of the AOSA. The faculty includes international and national Orff specialists. The program is intended for the music specialist and/or therapist, classroom teacher, and church musician.

Contact   Sr. Rita Schweitzer, Associate Professor, Music Department, Milwaukee, WI 53222. 414-258-4810.

MUSIC (50.09)
Orff-Schulwerk Level II

General Information   Unit offering the program: Music Department. Program content: Basic Orff, creative movement and dance, recorder instruction. Available for credit. Certificate signed by the Academic Dean. Certificate applicable to undergraduate or graduate programs in music education. Program fulfills requirements for teacher certification update.

Program Format   Daytime classes offered. Instructional schedule: Monday through Friday. Students enroll in the summer. Full program cycle lasts 2 weeks.

Evaluation   Student evaluation based on tests, reports, performance, orchestrations. Grading system: Letters or numbers. Transcripts are kept for each student.

Enrollment Requirements   Basic music training required. Program is open to non-resident foreign students. English language proficiency required. Minimum TOEFL score required: 550.

Program Costs $510 per course.

Housing and Student Services Housing is available. Job counseling and placement services are not available.

Special Features Overall course content follows the American Orff-Schulwerk Association "Guidelines for Teacher Training Courses" and has the approval of the AOSA. The faculty includes international and national Orff specialists. The program is intended for the music specialist and/or therapist, classroom teacher, and church musician.

Contact Sr. Rita Schweitzer, Associate Professor, Music Department, Milwaukee, WI 53222. 414-258-4810.

REHABILITATION SERVICES (17.08)
Post-Baccalaureate Certificate in Art Therapy

General Information Unit offering the program: Art Therapy Department. Program content: Graduate level training in art therapy. Available on a non-credit basis. Endorsed by American Art Therapy Association. Certificate signed by the President. Program fulfills requirements for registration with the American Art Therapy Association.

Program Format Evening, weekend classes offered. Instructional schedule: Two weekends per month, one evening per week. Program cycle: Continuous enrollment. Full program cycle lasts 3 semesters. Completion of program requires 600-hour practicum, three learning contracts.

Evaluation Student evaluation based on projects, practicum. Transcripts are kept for each student.

Enrollment Requirements Bachelor's degree; prerequisite course work in art, art therapy, and behavioral science; letters of recommendation; portfolio required. Program is open to non-resident foreign students.

Program Costs $2750 for the program, $100 per course.

Housing and Student Services Housing is available. Job counseling and placement services are available.

Special Features Courses are taught in a supportive and challenging learning environment by resident faculty and invited guest speakers who are nationally known and respected for their contributions to the field of creative arts therapy.

Contact Ms. Lynn Kapitan, Director, Art Therapy Institute, 2900 North Menomonee River Parkway, Milwaukee, WI 53222. 414-258-4810.

NUCEA MEMBER
UNIVERSITY OF WISCONSIN–MILWAUKEE
Milwaukee, Wisconsin 53201

PUBLIC ADMINISTRATION (44.04)
Certificate in Public Administration

General Information Unit offering the program: Department of Governmental Affairs, Division of Outreach and Continuing Education. Program content: Policy making; local, state, and federal administration. Available on a non-credit basis. Certificate signed by the Dean, Division of Outreach and Continuing Education.

Program Format Daytime, evening classes offered. Program cycle: Continuous enrollment. Complete program cycle lasts 2½ to 3 years. Completion of program requires 150 contact hours.

Evaluation Student evaluation based on papers, oral presentations. Records are kept by Department of Governmental Affairs.

Enrollment Requirements Program is open to non-resident foreign students.

Program Costs $900 for the program.

Housing and Student Services Housing is not available. Job counseling and placement services are available.

Special Features Begun in 1981, the program integrates noncredit offerings of benefit to managers and technicians in area governmental agencies. Instruction is shared between University faculty and knowledgeable ad hoc instructors drawn from administrative settings. Limited transfer credit is accepted for relevant degree and continuing education study completed elsewhere.

Contact Mr. Lynn W. Eley, Professor and Chair, Department of Governmental Affairs, Mitchell Hall 215, P.O. Box 413, Milwaukee, WI 53201. 414-229-4753.

NUCEA MEMBER
UNIVERSITY OF WISCONSIN–OSHKOSH
Oshkosh, Wisconsin 54901

NURSING (18.11)
Graduate Achievement Program in Primary Health Care Nursing

General Information Unit offering the program: Graduate Program, College of Nursing. Available for credit. Certificate signed by the Chancellor.

Program Format Evening classes offered. Instructional schedule: Once per week for two to three hours. Program cycle: Continuous enrollment. Complete program cycle lasts 1½ years.

Evaluation Student evaluation based on papers, reports, clinical performance. Grading system: Letters or numbers. Transcripts are kept for each student.

Enrollment Requirements M.S.N., current RN licensure, three letters of reference required. Program is open to non-resident foreign students. English language proficiency required. Minimum TOEFL score required: 525.

Program Costs $1980 for the program, $330 per course (state residents); $5580 for the program, $930 per course (nonresidents).

Housing and Student Services Housing is available.

Special Features The program consists of courses offered in Master of Science in Nursing program and prepares students to function either as family nurse practitioners or nurse administrators in ambulatory settings. Practicum experiences with qualified preceptors are arranged according to students' career goals and geographic location. Sequential courses result in program taking three semesters to complete (6 credits per semester).

Contact Ms. Louise Rauckhorst, Associate Dean, Director of the Graduate Program, College of Nursing, Oshkosh, WI 54901. 414-424-2106.

TEACHER EDUCATION, SPECIFIC SUBJECT AREAS (13.13)
Graduate Achievement Program in Reading

General Information Unit offering the program: Reading Education Department. Available for credit. Certificate signed by the Dean of Graduate School.

Program Format Daytime, evening classes offered. Instructional schedule: Once per week for three hours. Program cycle: Continuous enrollment. Full program cycle lasts 2 years. Completion of program requires comprehensive examination.

Evaluation Student evaluation based on tests, papers, reports. Grading system: Letters or numbers, pass/fail. Transcripts are kept for each student.

Enrollment Requirements Master's degree required. Program is open to non-resident foreign students.

Program Costs $2057 for the program, $343 per course.

Graduate Achievement Program in Reading continued

Housing and Student Services   Housing is available. Job counseling and placement services are available.

Special Features   The reading program has outstanding resources including a strong graduate faculty, a diagnostic services center, and a reading study center. The program is also offered cooperatively on the UW-Green Bay campus.

Contact   Graduate Office, Dempsey 330, Oshkosh, WI 54901. 414-424-1223.

NUCEA MEMBER

UNIVERSITY OF WISCONSIN–PARKSIDE
Kenosha, Wisconsin 53141

LABOR/INDUSTRIAL RELATIONS (06.11)
Labor Studies Program

General Information   Unit offering the program: Social Science, Labor and Industrial Relations. Program content: Economics, political science, labor history of the United States, contract negotiations. Available for credit. Certificate signed by the Chancellor of the University. Certificate applicable to B.S. in Labor and Industrial Relations.

Program Format   Daytime, evening classes offered. Program cycle: Continuous enrollment. Full program cycle lasts 60 credit hours.

Evaluation   Student evaluation based on tests, papers, reports. Grading system: Letters or numbers. Transcripts are kept for each student.

Enrollment Requirements   University admissions required. Program is open to non-resident foreign students. English language proficiency required.

Program Costs $694 per semester (state residents); $2095 per semester (nonresidents).

Housing and Student Services   Housing is available. Job counseling and placement services are available.

Contact   Mr. Stephen Meyer, Associate Professor, History and Labor Studies, Box 2000, Kenosha, WI 53141. 414-553-2205.

Appendixes

NUCEA Member Institutions

American University, DC
Auburn University at Montgomery, AL
Ball State University, IN
Barry University, FL
Brigham Young University, UT
Bryant College, RI
California State University, Chico, CA
California State University, Dominguez Hills, CA
California State University, Hayward, CA
California State University, Long Beach, CA
California State University, Los Angeles, CA
California State University, Sacramento, CA
Carthage College, WI
Clark University, MA
Colorado State University, CO
Columbus College, GA
East Tennessee State University, TN
Elmhurst College, IL
Emmanuel College, MA
Florida International University, FL
Florida State University, FL
Franklin and Marshall College, PA
George Mason University, VA
George Washington University, DC
Georgia Institute of Technology, GA
Harvard University, MA
Indiana State University, IN
Indiana University at South Bend, IN
Indiana University Bloomington, IN
Indiana University Northwest, IN
Indiana University of Pennsylvania, PA
Johns Hopkins University, MD
Kansas State University, KS
Los Angeles College of Chiropractic, CA
Louisiana State University and Agricultural and Mechanical College, LA
Loyola University of Chicago, IL
Marylhurst College, OR
Memphis State University, TN
New York University, NY
North Carolina State University at Raleigh, NC
Northern Illinois University, IL
Northern Kentucky University, KY

Northern State College, SD
Nova University, FL
Oakland University, MI
Ohio State University, OH
Ohio University–Chillicothe, OH
Old Dominion University, VA
Philadelphia College of Textiles and Science, PA
Pittsburg State University, KS
Purdue University, IN
Rochester Institute of Technology, NY
Roosevelt University, IL
Rutgers, The State University of New Jersey, Cook College, NJ
St. John Fisher College, NY
Saint Louis University, MO
St. Thomas Aquinas College, NY
San Diego State University, CA
San Francisco State University, CA
San Jose State University, CA
School for Lifelong Learning of the University System of New Hampshire, NH
Seton Hill College, PA
Southern Illinois University at Edwardsville, IL
Southern Methodist University, TX
Southern Oregon State College, OR
State University of New York at Albany, NY
State University of New York at Buffalo, NY
Syracuse University, NY
Texas Christian University, TX
Texas Tech University, TX
University of Akron, OH
University of Alabama at Birmingham, AL
University of Arizona, AZ
University of California at Berkeley, CA
University of California, Los Angeles, CA
University of California, San Diego, CA
University of Cincinnati, OH
University of Colorado at Boulder, CO
University of Connecticut, CT
University of Delaware, DE
University of Denver, CO
University of Georgia, GA
University of Hawaii at Manoa, HI
University of Houston, TX

University of Illinois at Urbana-Champaign, IL
University of Iowa, IA
University of Kentucky, KY
University of Lowell, MA
University of Miami, FL
University of Minnesota, Morris, MN
University of Minnesota, Twin Cities Campus, MN
University of Mississippi, MS
University of Missouri–Columbia, MO
University of Nebraska–Lincoln, NE
University of New Hampshire, NH
University of New Haven, CT
University of New Mexico, NM
University of New Orleans, LA
University of North Carolina at Chapel Hill, NC
University of Northern Colorado, CO
University of Oklahoma, OK
University of Pennsylvania, PA
University of Pittsburgh, PA
University of Puerto Rico Medical Sciences Campus, PR
University of Puerto Rico, Río Piedras, PR
University of Rhode Island, RI
University of South Alabama, AL
University of South Carolina, SC
University of Southern California, CA
University of Southern Indiana, IN
University of South Florida, FL
University of Tennessee, Knoxville, TN
University of Vermont, VT
University of Wisconsin–Milwaukee, WI
University of Wisconsin–Oshkosh, WI
University of Wisconsin–Parkside, WI
Virginia Commonwealth University, VA
Virginia Polytechnic Institute and State University, VA
Weber State College, UT
Western Carolina University, NC
Western Michigan University, MI
Western Montana College, MT
West Georgia College, GA
Widener University, Pennsylvania Campus, PA
Worcester State College, MA
Wright State University, OH

Classification of Instructional Programs Taxonomy

Program classifications preceded by a dagger have entries in this book; all other classifications are shown to round out the taxonomy.

01. agribusiness and agricultural production
†01.01 agricultural business and management
01.02 agricultural mechanics
†01.03 agricultural production
†01.04 agricultural products and processing
01.05 agricultural services and supplies
†01.06 horticulture
01.07 international agriculture
01.99 agribusiness and agricultural production, other

02. agricultural sciences
02.01 agricultural sciences, general
02.02 animal sciences
02.03 food sciences
02.04 plant sciences
02.05 soil sciences
02.99 agricultural sciences, other

03. renewable natural resources
†03.01 renewable natural resources, general
03.02 conservation and regulation
03.03 fishing and fisheries
03.04 forestry production and processing
03.05 forestry and related sciences
03.06 wildlife management
03.99 renewable natural resources, other

04. architecture and environmental design
†04.01 architecture and environmental design, general
04.02 architecture
†04.03 city, community, and regional planning
†04.04 environmental design
†04.05 interior design
†04.06 landscape architecture
04.07 urban design
04.08 land use management and reclamation

05. area and ethnic studies
†05.01 area studies
†05.01.02 American studies
†05.01.03 Asian studies, general
†05.02 ethnic studies

06. business and management
†06.01 business and management, general
†06.02 accounting
†06.03 banking and finance
†06.04 business administration and management
†06.05 business economics
†06.06 human resources development
†06.07 institutional management
†06.08 insurance and risk management
†06.09 international business management
†06.10 investments and securities
†06.11 labor/industrial relations
†06.12 management information systems
†06.13 management science
†06.14 marketing management and research
†06.15 organizational behavior
†06.16 personnel management

†06.17 real estate
†06.18 small business management and ownership
†06.19 taxation
†06.20 trade and industrial supervision and management
06.21 computer installation management

07. business (administrative support)
†07.01 accounting, bookkeeping, and related programs
07.02 banking and related financial programs
†07.03 business data processing and related programs
†07.04 office supervision and management
†07.05 personnel and training programs
†07.06 secretarial and related programs
†07.07 typing, general office, and related programs
†07.08 word processing

08. marketing and distribution
†08.01 apparel and accessories marketing
†08.02 business and personal services marketing
†08.03 entrepreneurship
08.04 financial services marketing
08.05 floristry, farm and garden supplies marketing
†08.06 food marketing
†08.07 general marketing
08.08 home and office products marketing
†08.09 hospitality and recreation marketing
08.10 insurance marketing
†08.11 transportation and travel marketing
08.12 vehicles and petroleum marketing

09. communications
†09.01 communications, general
†09.02 advertising
09.03 communications research
†09.04 journalism (mass communications)
†09.05 public relations
09.06 radio/television news broadcasting
†09.07 radio/television, general
†09.08 telecommunications

10. communications technologies
†10.01 communications technologies

11. computer and information sciences
†11.01 computer and information sciences, general
†11.02 computer programming
†11.03 data processing
†11.04 information sciences and systems
†11.05 systems analysis
†11.06 microcomputer applications

12. consumer, personal and miscellaneous services
12.01 drycleaning and laundering services
12.02 entertainment services
12.03 funeral services
†12.04 personal services

13. education
†13.01 education, general
13.02 bilingual/crosscultural education
†13.03 curriculum and instruction
†13.04 education administration
†13.05 educational media
†13.06 evaluation and research
13.07 international and comparative education
†13.08 school psychology

323

13.09	social foundations
†13.10	special education
†13.11	student counseling and personnel services
†13.12	teacher education, general programs
†13.12.02	elementary education
†13.12.04	preelementary education
†13.13	teacher education, specific subject areas
†13.14	teaching English as a second language/foreign language
13.15	teacher assisting

14. engineering

†14.01	engineering, general
14.02	aerospace, aeronautical, and astronautical engineering
14.03	agricultural engineering
14.04	architectural engineering
14.05	bioengineering and biomedical engineering
14.06	ceramic engineering
†14.07	chemical engineering
14.08	civil engineering
†14.09	computer engineering
†14.10	electrical, electronics, and communications engineering
14.11	engineering mechanics
14.12	engineering physics
14.13	engineering science
†14.14	environmental health engineering
14.15	geological engineering
14.16	geophysical engineering
†14.17	industrial engineering
†14.18	materials engineering
14.19	mechanical engineering
14.20	metallurgical engineering
14.21	mining and mineral engineering
14.22	naval architecture and marine engineering
14.23	nuclear engineering
14.24	ocean engineering
14.25	petroleum engineering
14.26	surveying and mapping sciences
14.27	systems engineering
†14.28	textile engineering

15. engineering and engineering related technologies

15.01	architectural technologies
†15.02	civil technologies
†15.03	electrical and electronic technologies
†15.04	electromechanical instrumentation and maintenance technologies
†15.05	environmental control technologies
†15.06	industrial production technologies
†15.07	quality control and safety technologies
†15.07.01	occupational safety and health technology
†15.08	mechanical and related technologies
15.09	mining and petroleum technologies
†15.10	construction technology

16. foreign languages

†16.01	foreign languages, multiple emphasis
16.02	African (non-Semitic) languages
16.03	Asiatic languages
†16.04	Balto-Slavic languages
†16.04.02	Russian
†16.05	Germanic languages
†16.05.01	German
16.06	Greek
16.07	Indic languages
†16.09	Italic languages
†16.09.01	French
†16.09.02	Italian
†16.09.05	Spanish
16.10	native American languages
16.11	Semitic languages

17. allied health

†17.01	dental services
†17.01.01	dental assisting

†17.02	diagnostic and treatment services
†17.02.05	emergency medical technology-ambulance
†17.03	medical laboratory technologies
†17.03.03	clinical animal technology
†17.04	mental health/human services
†17.04.01	alcohol/drug abuse specialty
†17.05	miscellaneous allied health services
†17.05.08	physician assisting
†17.06	nursing-related services
†17.07	ophthalmic services
†17.08	rehabilitation services
†17.08.01	art therapy
†17.08.06	music therapy

18. health sciences

†18.01	audiology and speech pathology
18.02	basic clinical health sciences
†18.03	chiropractic
†18.04	dentistry
†18.07	health services administration
†18.07.03	medical records administration
†18.09	medical laboratory
18.10	medicine
†18.11	nursing
†18.11.03	maternal/child health
†18.12	optometry
18.13	osteopathic medicine
18.14	pharmacy
18.15	podiatry
18.17	predentistry
18.18	premedicine
18.19	prepharmacy
18.20	preveterinary
18.22	public health
18.24	veterinary medicine

19. home economics

19.01	home economics, general
19.02	business home economics
†19.03	family and community services
19.04	family/consumer resource management
†19.05	food sciences and human nutrition
†19.06	human environment and housing
†19.07	individual and family development
†19.07.05	gerontological services
†19.09	textiles and clothing
†19.09.02	fashion design

20. vocational home economics

20.01	consumer and homemaking education
†20.02	child care and guidance management and services
†20.03	clothing, apparel, and textiles management, production, and services
†20.04	food production, management, and services
20.05	home furnishings and equipment management, production, and services
†20.06	institutional, home management, and supporting services

21. industrial arts

21.01	industrial arts

22. law

†22.01	law
†22.01.03	legal assisting

23. letters

23.01	English, general
23.02	classics
23.03	comparative literature
†23.04	composition
†23.05	creative writing
†23.06	linguistics (includes phonetics, semantics, and philology)
†23.07	literature, American
23.08	literature, English
†23.10	speech, debate, and forensics

†23.11	technical and business writing		**39.**	**theology**
†23.12	English as a second language		39.01	biblical languages
			†39.02	Bible studies
24.	**liberal/general studies**		†39.03	missionary studies
†24.01	liberal/general studies		†39.04	religious education
			†39.05	religious music
25.	**library and archival sciences**		†39.06	theological studies
†25.01	library and archival sciences, general			
25.02	archival science		**40.**	**physical sciences**
†25.03	library assisting		40.01	physical sciences, general
†25.04	library science		40.02	astronomy
25.05	museology		40.03	astrophysics
			†40.04	atmospheric sciences and meteorology
26.	**life sciences**		†40.05	chemistry
26.01	biology, general		40.06	geological sciences
26.02	biochemistry and biophysics		40.07	miscellaneous physical sciences
26.03	botany		†40.08	physics
†26.04	cell and molecular biology		40.09	planetary science
26.05	microbiology			
†26.06	miscellaneous specialized areas, life sciences		**41.**	**science technologies**
†26.06.03	ecology		†41.01	biological technologies
26.07	zoology		41.02	nuclear technologies
			†41.03	physical science technologies
27.	**mathematics**			
†27.01	mathematics, general		**42.**	**psychology**
27.02	actuarial sciences		†42.01	psychology, general
†27.03	applied mathematics		†42.02	clinical psychology
27.04	pure mathematics		42.03	cognitive psychology
†27.05	statistics		†42.04	community psychology
			42.05	comparative psychology
28.	**military sciences**		†42.06	counseling psychology
28.01	aerospace science (air force)		42.07	developmental psychology
28.02	Coast Guard science		42.08	experimental psychology
28.03	military science (army)		42.09	industrial and organizational psychology
28.04	naval science (navy, marines)		42.10	personality psychology
†28.05	maritime science (merchant marine)		42.11	physiological psychology
			42.12	psycholinguistics
29.	**military technologies**		42.13	psychometrics
29.01	military technologies		42.14	psychopharmacology
			42.15	quantitative psychology
30.	**multi/interdisciplinary studies**		42.16	social psychology
†30.01	biological and physical sciences			
30.02	clinical pastoral care		**43.**	**protective services**
30.03	engineering and other disciplines		†43.01	criminal justice
†30.04	humanities and social sciences		†43.02	fire protection
30.05	peace studies			
†30.06	systems science		**44.**	**public affairs**
†30.07	women's studies		†44.01	public affairs, general
†30.08	mathematics and computer science		†44.02	community services
30.09	imaging science		†44.03	international public service
			†44.04	public administration
31.	**parks and recreation**		†44.05	public policy studies
31.01	parks and recreation, general		44.06	public works
31.02	outdoor recreation		†44.07	social work
31.03	parks and recreation management			
31.04	water resources		**45.**	**social sciences**
			†45.01	social sciences, general
32.	**basic skills**		†45.02	anthropology
32.01	basic skills		†45.03	archaeology
			45.04	criminology
33.	**citizenship/civic activities**		†45.05	demography
†33.01	citizenship/civic activities		†45.06	economics
			†45.07	geography
34.	**health-related activities**		†45.08	history
†34.01	health-related activities		†45.09	international relations
			†45.10	political science and government
35.	**interpersonal skills**		†45.11	sociology
†35.01	interpersonal skills		†45.12	urban studies
36.	**leisure and recreational activities**		**46.**	**construction trades**
†36.01	leisure and recreational activities		46.01	brickmasonry, stonemasonry, and tile setting
			46.02	carpentry
37.	**personal awareness**		†46.03	electrical and power transmission installation
37.01	personal awareness		†46.04	miscellaneous construction trades and property maintenance
38.	**philosophy and religion**		†46.05	plumbing, pipefitting, and steamfitting
†38.01	philosophy			
†38.02	religion			

47.   **mechanics and repairers**
†47.01   electrical and electronics equipment repair
†47.02   heating, air conditioning, and refrigeration mechanics
†47.03   industrial equipment maintenance and repair
 47.04   miscellaneous mechanics and repairers
 47.05   stationary energy sources
†47.06   vehicle and mobile equipment mechanics and repairers
†47.06.08   aircraft mechanics, powerplant

48.   **precision production**
†48.01   drafting
†48.02   graphic and printing communications
†48.02.03   commercial art
 48.03   leatherworking and upholstery
 48.04   precision food production
†48.05   precision metal work
†48.06   precision work, assorted materials

†48.06.02   jewelry design, fabrication, and repair
†48.07   woodworking

49.   **transportation and material moving**
†49.01   air transportation
 49.02   vehicle and equipment operation
 49.03   water transportation

50.   **visual and performing arts**
†50.01   visual and performing arts, general
†50.02   crafts
 50.03   dance
†50.04   design
†50.04.03   illustration design
†50.05   dramatic arts
†50.06   film arts
†50.07   fine arts
†50.07.03   art history and appreciation
†50.09   music

Indexes

Alphabetical Index by Program Classification

Program classifications are arranged below in alphabetical order by description; institutions offering such programs are listed under each description. The numerical sequence is listed in parentheses. The page number corresponds to the page on which the institution's listing begins; the reader will find a specific program alphabetically among all other entries within the institution. Cross references occur when a program might be expected to be found under another (secondary) classification; the reader will be directed from the secondary to the primary classification assigned to the program.

accounting (06.02)

Albright College, PA 266
Alvernia College, PA 268
American University, DC 84
Baldwin-Wallace College, OH 246
Bentley College, MA 140
Bridgewater State College, MA 143
Calumet College of Saint Joseph, IN 116
City University, WA 314
College of Saint Elizabeth, NJ 180
Felician College, NJ 182
Franklin and Marshall College, PA 270
Franklin Pierce College, NH 174
Golden Gate University, CA 24
Indiana University Northwest, IN 121
Louisiana State University and Agricultural and
Mechanical College, LA 134
Lynchburg College, VA 309
Lyndon State College, VT 303
Marietta College, OH 249
Mercy College, NY 195
Neumann College, PA 272
New Hampshire College, NH 175
North Adams State College, MA 149
Northern Kentucky University, KY 133
Notre Dame College of Ohio, OH 249
Oakland University, MI 158
Otterbein College, OH 252
Pace University, Pleasantville/Briarcliff Campus, NY 216
Philadelphia College of Textiles and Science, PA 275
Robert Morris College, PA 277
St. Francis College, NY 228
Saint Louis University, MO 168
Saint Xavier College, IL 114
San Diego State University, CA 33
Thomas More College, KY 133
University of Baltimore, MD 139
University of California at Berkeley, CA 40
University of California, Los Angeles, CA 47
University of California, Riverside, CA 57
University of California, San Diego, CA 62
University of Cincinnati, OH 256
University of Minnesota, Twin Cities Campus, MN 162
University of Pittsburgh, PA 282
University of Southern Indiana, IN 126
Widener University, Pennsylvania Campus, PA 287

accounting, bookkeeping, and related programs (07.01)

Bentley College, MA 140
California State University, Dominguez Hills, CA 14
Long Island University, C. W. Post Campus, NY 192
Millsaps College, MS 164
New York University, NY 202

St. John Fisher College, NY 229
University of Tennessee, Knoxville, TN 296

advertising (09.02)

Golden Gate University, CA 24
New York University, NY 202
University of Alabama at Birmingham, AL 6
University of California, Los Angeles, CA 47

agricultural business and management (01.01)

Pace University, Pleasantville/Briarcliff Campus, NY 216
Texas Christian University, TX 300

agricultural production (01.03)

Northwest Missouri State University, MO 165

agricultural products and processing (01.04)

Kansas State University, KS 130

aircraft mechanics, powerplant (47.06.08)

See entry under *vehicle and mobile equipment mechanics and repairers (47.06)* for
Northrop University, CA 32

air transportation (49.01)

University of Southern California, CA 70

alcohol/drug abuse specialty (17.04.01)

See entries under *mental health/human services (17.04)* for
Ball State University, IN 115
California State University, Dominguez Hills, CA 14
California State University, Hayward, CA 14
California State University, Sacramento, CA 21
Chapman College, CA 22
College of St. Francis, IL 106
Long Island University, C. W. Post Campus, NY 192
Marycrest College, IA 127
National College of Education, IL 109
New York Institute of Technology, NY 199
Nova University, FL 96
St. Cloud State University, MN 159
Stonehill College, MA 151
University of Akron, OH 252
University of California at Berkeley, CA 40
University of California, Los Angeles, CA 47
University of California, Riverside, CA 57
University of California, San Diego, CA 62
University of California, Santa Barbara, CA 69
University of Miami, FL 100
University of Minnesota, Twin Cities Campus, MN 162
University of Texas at Arlington, TX 301
Western Michigan University, MI 158

American studies (05.01.02)

See entry under *area studies (05.01)* for
Smith College, MA 150

anthropology (45.02)

California State University, Chico, CA 12

apparel and accessories marketing (08.01)

Philadelphia College of Textiles and Science, PA 275

applied mathematics (27.03)

University of New Haven, CT 78

archaeology (45.03)
George Mason University, VA 307

architecture and environmental design, general (04.01)
University of California, San Diego, CA 62

area studies (05.01)
Smith College, MA 150
State University of New York at Albany, NY 234
Wheaton College, IL 115

art history and appreciation (50.07.03)
See entry under *fine arts (50.07)* for
Pace University, Pleasantville/Briarcliff Campus, NY 216

art therapy (17.08.01)
See entries under *rehabilitation services (17.08)* for
College of Notre Dame, CA 23
Mount Mary College, WI 318
Ursuline College, OH 261

Asian studies, general (05.01.03)
See entry under *area studies (05.01)* for
Wheaton College, IL 115

atmospheric sciences and meteorology (40.04)
Creighton University, NE 172

audiology and speech pathology (18.01)
Nova University, FL 96

Balto-Slavic languages (16.04)
American University, DC 84
State University of New York at Albany, NY 234

banking and finance (06.03)
Alvernia College, PA 268
Bentley College, MA 140
Franklin and Marshall College, PA 270
Golden Gate University, CA 24
Lyndon State College, VT 303
Manhattanville College, NY 194
New Hampshire College, NH 175
New York University, NY 202
Notre Dame College of Ohio, OH 249
Nova University, FL 96
Pace University, Pleasantville/Briarcliff Campus, NY 216
St. Francis College, NY 228
Saint Louis University, MO 168
San Diego State University, CA 33
University of Alabama at Birmingham, AL 6
University of California at Berkeley, CA 40
University of California, Los Angeles, CA 47
University of California, San Diego, CA 62
University of Georgia, GA 103
University of Houston, TX 300
University of Texas at Arlington, TX 301

Bible studies (39.02)
Arizona College of the Bible, AZ 10
Calvary Bible College, MO 165
Columbia Bible College and Seminary, SC 292
Crichton College, TN 294
Eastern Christian College, MD 136
Eugene Bible College, OR 264
Faith Baptist Bible College and Seminary, IA 127
Fort Wayne Bible College, IN 118
Hillsdale Free Will Baptist College, OK 263
Lutheran Bible Institute of Seattle, WA 315
North Central Bible College, MN 159
Philadelphia College of Bible, PA 274
Puget Sound Christian College, WA 316
St. Paul Bible College, MN 160
Simpson College, CA 40
Southeastern Bible College, AL 6
United Wesleyan College, PA 282
Western Baptist College, OR 266

biological and physical sciences (30.01)
University of California, Los Angeles, CA 47
University of California, Riverside, CA 57

biological technologies (41.01)
University of Cincinnati, OH 256

business administration and management (06.04)
Alvernia College, PA 268
American University, DC 84
Baruch College of the City University of New York, NY 189
Beaver College, PA 268
City University, WA 314
Elmhurst College, IL 107
Jordan College, MI 153
Marietta College, OH 249
New Hampshire College, NH 175
New York Institute of Technology, NY 199
Northwood Institute, MI 157
Otterbein College, OH 252
St. Joseph's College, NY 230
St. Joseph's College, Suffolk Campus, NY 232
Saint Louis University, MO 168
Saint Michael's College, VT 305
Southern Oregon State College, OR 266
Stevens Institute of Technology, NJ 186
University of California, Los Angeles, CA 47
University of California, Riverside, CA 57
University of California, San Diego, CA 62
University of Minnesota, Morris, MN 161
Washington and Jefferson College, PA 287
Worcester State College, MA 153

business and management, general (06.01)
Alaska Pacific University, AK 8
Albertus Magnus College, CT 76
Albright College, PA 266
American University, DC 84
Anna Maria College for Men and Women, MA 139
Azusa Pacific University, CA 10
Baldwin-Wallace College, OH 246
Baruch College of the City University of New York, NY 189
Bentley College, MA 140
Bridgewater State College, MA 143
Bryant College, RI 289
California State University, Long Beach, CA 16
Calumet College of Saint Joseph, IN 116
City University, WA 314
College of Saint Elizabeth, NJ 180
Creighton University, NE 172
Dominican College of Blauvelt, NY 191
Felician College, NJ 182
Franklin and Marshall College, PA 270
Franklin Pierce College, NH 174
Frostburg State University, MD 136
George Washington University, DC 89
Golden Gate University, CA 24
Harvard University, MA 148
Illinois Benedictine College, IL 108
Indiana University at South Bend, IN 119
Indiana University Northwest, IN 121
Kutztown University of Pennsylvania, PA 271
Long Island University, C. W. Post Campus, NY 192
Louisiana State University and Agricultural and
    Mechanical College, LA 134
Manhattanville College, NY 194
Mars Hill College, NC 239
Marygrove College, MI 156
Mercy College, NY 195
Mount St. Mary's College, CA 32
Neumann College, PA 272
New Hampshire College, NH 175
New York University, NY 202
Notre Dame College of Ohio, OH 249
Nova University, FL 96
Pace University, Pleasantville/Briarcliff Campus, NY 216
Purdue University Calumet, IN 125
Robert Morris College, PA 277

Rochester Institute of Technology, NY 223
Sacred Heart University, CT 77
St. Francis College, NY 228
St. John Fisher College, NY 229
Saint Peter's College, NJ 184
Saint Vincent College, PA 279
Saint Xavier College, IL 114
San Diego State University, CA 33
School for Lifelong Learning of the University System
   of New Hampshire, NH 178
Seton Hill College, PA 280
State University of New York College of Technology
   at Utica/Rome, NY 238
Stonehill College, MA 151
Texas Tech University, TX 300
Thomas More College, KY 133
University of Alabama at Birmingham, AL 6
University of California at Berkeley, CA 40
University of California, Los Angeles, CA 47
University of California, Riverside, CA 57
University of California, San Diego, CA 62
University of Cincinnati, OH 256
University of Indianapolis, IN 126
University of Miami, FL 100
University of Minnesota, Twin Cities Campus, MN 162
University of New Mexico, NM 189
University of Oklahoma, OK 264
University of Pittsburgh, PA 282
University of Southern California, CA 70
Ursuline College, OH 261
Virginia Polytechnic Institute and State University, VA 314
Weber State College, UT 303
West Virginia Wesleyan College, WV 316
Widener University, Pennsylvania Campus, PA 287

business and personal services marketing (08.02)
New York University, NY 202
University of Miami, FL 100

business data processing and related programs (07.03)
Calumet College of Saint Joseph, IN 116
Franklin and Marshall College, PA 270
Jordan College, MI 153
National College of Education, IL 109
New York Institute of Technology, NY 199
New York University, NY 202
Saint Louis University, MO 168
Saint Peter's College, NJ 184

business economics (06.05)
University of New Haven, CT 78

cell and molecular biology (26.04)
San Francisco State University, CA 37
Stevens Institute of Technology, NJ 186

chemical engineering (14.07)
Stevens Institute of Technology, NJ 186

chemistry (40.05)
Calumet College of Saint Joseph, IN 116
Stevens Institute of Technology, NJ 186

child care and guidance management and services (20.02)
California State University, Long Beach, CA 16
College of Mount St. Joseph, OH 248
Jordan College, MI 153
North Adams State College, MA 149
Northwest Missouri State University, MO 165
Rivier College, NH 176
School for Lifelong Learning of the University System
   of New Hampshire, NH 178
Seton Hill College, PA 280
University of Akron, OH 252
University of California, San Diego, CA 62
University of Colorado at Boulder, CO 73
University of Georgia, GA 103
Western Montana College, MT 171

chiropractic (18.03)
Los Angeles College of Chiropractic, CA 31

citizenship/civic activities (33.01)
University of Akron, OH 252

city, community, and regional planning (04.03)
California State University, Chico, CA 12
University of Akron, OH 252
University of California, Los Angeles, CA 47
University of Georgia, GA 103
Wright State University, OH 262

civil technologies (15.02)
University of California, Riverside, CA 57

clinical animal technology (17.03.03)
See entry under *medical laboratory technologies (17.03)*
for
Pace University, Pleasantville/Briarcliff Campus, NY 216

clinical psychology (42.02)
New York Institute of Technology, NY 199
Nova University, FL 96

clothing, apparel, and textiles management, production, and services (20.03)
New York Institute of Technology, NY 199
University of Vermont, VT 306

commercial art (48.02.03)
See entries under *graphic and printing communications (48.02)* for
Pace University, Pleasantville/Briarcliff Campus, NY 216
Southwestern Oklahoma State University, OK 264
University of California, Santa Barbara, CA 69
University of Cincinnati, OH 256
University of Delaware, DE 84
University of South Florida, FL 101

communications, general (09.01)
Baldwin-Wallace College, OH 246
Bentley College, MA 140
Calumet College of Saint Joseph, IN 116
Colorado State University, CO 72
Creighton University, NE 172
Franklin and Marshall College, PA 270
New York University, NY 202
North Carolina State University at Raleigh, NC 240
Rochester Institute of Technology, NY 223
San Jose State University, CA 39
State University of New York at Albany, NY 234
University of Akron, OH 252
University of California at Berkeley, CA 40
University of Denver, CO 74
University of Pennsylvania, PA 282
University of Southern Indiana, IN 126

communications technologies (10.01)
George Washington University, DC 89
Golden Gate University, CA 24

community psychology (42.04)
University of Minnesota, Twin Cities Campus, MN 162

community services (44.02)
Rutgers, The State University of New Jersey, New
   Brunswick, NJ 183
University of Pittsburgh, PA 282

composition (23.04)
University of Akron, OH 252

computer and information sciences, general (11.01)
Albright College, PA 266
American University, DC 84
Baldwin-Wallace College, OH 246
Baruch College of the City University of New York, NY 189

Beaver College, PA ... 268
Bridgewater State College, MA ... 143
Bryant College, RI ... 289
California State University, Bakersfield, CA ... 11
California State University, Sacramento, CA ... 21
Cedar Crest College, PA ... 269
College of Saint Elizabeth, NJ ... 180
College of St. Francis, IL ... 106
Dominican College of Blauvelt, NY ... 191
Fitchburg State College, MA ... 146
Franklin Pierce College, NH ... 174
Goldey Beacom College, DE ... 83
Harvard University, MA ... 148
Hawaii Pacific College, HI ... 106
Manhattanville College, NY ... 194
Mercy College, NY ... 195
New York University, NY ... 202
Nova University, FL ... 96
Old Dominion University, VA ... 310
Otterbein College, OH ... 252
Philadelphia College of Textiles and Science, PA ... 275
Purdue University, IN ... 123
Robert Morris College, PA ... 277
Sacred Heart University, CT ... 77
St. Joseph's College, NY ... 230
St. Joseph's College, Suffolk Campus, NY ... 232
Saint Louis University, MO ... 168
University of Alabama at Birmingham, AL ... 6
University of Baltimore, MD ... 139
University of California, Davis, CA ... 44
University of California, Los Angeles, CA ... 47
University of California, Riverside, CA ... 57
University of California, San Diego, CA ... 62
University of Denver, CO ... 74
University of Kentucky, KY ... 134
University of Minnesota, Twin Cities Campus, MN ... 162
Ursuline College, OH ... 261

computer engineering (14.09)
New York University, NY ... 202
University of California, San Diego, CA ... 62

computer programming (11.02)
Ball State University, IN ... 115
Baruch College of the City University of New York, NY ... 189
California State University, Los Angeles, CA ... 18
City University, WA ... 314
Creighton University, NE ... 172
Dominican College of Blauvelt, NY ... 191
Felician College, NJ ... 182
Fitchburg State College, MA ... 146
Golden Gate University, CA ... 24
Jordan College, MI ... 153
Loyola University of Chicago, IL ... 109
Marygrove College, MI ... 156
New Hampshire College, NH ... 175
New York University, NY ... 202
North Carolina State University at Raleigh, NC ... 240
Oakland City College, IN ... 122
Pace University, Pleasantville/Briarcliff Campus, NY ... 216
Purdue University Calumet, IN ... 125
Saint Peter's College, NJ ... 184
Saint Vincent College, PA ... 279
School for Lifelong Learning of the University System of New Hampshire, NH ... 178
Seton Hill College, PA ... 280
University of California at Berkeley, CA ... 40
University of California, Los Angeles, CA ... 47
University of Cincinnati, OH ... 256
University of Denver, CO ... 74
University of Dubuque, IA ... 127
University of Puerto Rico, Río Piedras, PR ... 289
University of Vermont, VT ... 306
Western New England College, MA ... 153

construction technology (15.10)
Fitchburg State College, MA ... 146
Northwest Missouri State University, MO ... 165

San Diego State University, CA ... 33
University of California, Riverside, CA ... 57
University of Tennessee, Knoxville, TN ... 296

counseling psychology (42.06)
School of the Ozarks, MO ... 170
State University of New York at Albany, NY ... 234
University of California, San Diego, CA ... 62

crafts (50.02)
Rochester Institute of Technology, NY ... 223

creative writing (23.05)
University of California, Los Angeles, CA ... 47
University of Pittsburgh, PA ... 282

criminal justice (43.01)
Calumet College of Saint Joseph, IN ... 116
Florida State University, FL ... 93
Indiana University of Pennsylvania, PA ... 271
Mercy College, NY ... 195
Nova University, FL ... 96
St. Joseph's College, NY ... 230
St. Joseph's College, Suffolk Campus, NY ... 232
University of Akron, OH ... 252
University of New Haven, CT ... 78

curriculum and instruction (13.03)
California State University, Chico, CA ... 12
California State University, Hayward, CA ... 14
National College of Education, IL ... 109
State University of New York at Albany, NY ... 234
University of California, Los Angeles, CA ... 47

data processing (11.03)
Albright College, PA ... 266
Baruch College of the City University of New York, NY ... 189
Felician College, NJ ... 182
Indiana University Northwest, IN ... 121
New York University, NY ... 202
Philadelphia College of Textiles and Science, PA ... 275
Robert Morris College, PA ... 277
University of Cincinnati, OH ... 256
Worcester State College, MA ... 153

demography (45.05)
State University of New York at Albany, NY ... 234

dental assisting (17.01.01)
See entries under *dental services (17.01)* for
East Tennessee State University, TN ... 294
Indiana University Northwest, IN ... 121
Old Dominion University, VA ... 310
University of California, Los Angeles, CA ... 47
University of North Carolina at Chapel Hill, NC ... 244

dental services (17.01)
East Tennessee State University, TN ... 294
Indiana University Northwest, IN ... 121
Old Dominion University, VA ... 310
University of California, Los Angeles, CA ... 47
University of North Carolina at Chapel Hill, NC ... 244
University of Puerto Rico Medical Sciences Campus, PR ... 289

dentistry (18.04)
University of California, Los Angeles, CA ... 47

design (50.04)
College of Mount St. Joseph, OH ... 248
Mercy College, NY ... 195
Pace University, Pleasantville/Briarcliff Campus, NY ... 216
Pacific Northwest College of Art, Oregon Art Institute, OR ... 265
Paier College of Art, Inc., CT ... 76
Pratt Institute, NY ... 222
Rhode Island School of Design, RI ... 290
Ringling School of Art and Design, FL ... 99

Rivier College, NH 176
Rochester Institute of Technology, NY 223
School of the Associated Arts, MN 160
University of California, Los Angeles, CA 47

diagnostic and treatment services (17.02)
California State University, Los Angeles, CA 18
East Tennessee State University, TN 294
Marygrove College, MI 156
Peru State College, NE 174
Southwestern College, KS 132
University of Iowa, IA 127
University of North Carolina at Chapel Hill, NC 244

drafting (48.01)
Northwest Missouri State University, MO 165
Pittsburg State University, KS 130

dramatic arts (50.05)
Cornish College of the Arts, WA 315
Wright State University, OH 262

ecology (26.06.03)
See entry under *miscellaneous specialized areas, life
sciences (26.06)* for
Virginia Commonwealth University, VA 313

economics (45.06)
American University, DC 84

education administration (13.04)
Johns Hopkins University, MD 136
National College of Education, IL 109
Old Dominion University, VA 310
State University of New York at Albany, NY 234
University of Akron, OH 252
University of North Carolina at Chapel Hill, NC 244

educational media (13.05)
Johns Hopkins University, MD 136
San Diego State University, CA 33

education, general (13.01)
Incarnate Word College, TX 297

electrical and electronics equipment repair (47.01)
Indiana Institute of Technology, IN 119
Pittsburg State University, KS 130

electrical and electronic technologies (15.03)
Colorado Technical College, CO 73
Indiana University Bloomington, IN 120
Milwaukee School of Engineering, WI 316
New York University, NY 202
Northwest Missouri State University, MO 165
Stevens Institute of Technology, NJ 186
University of California, Los Angeles, CA 47

electrical and power transmission installation (46.03)
New York University, NY 202

**electrical, electronics, and communications engineering
(14.10)**
University of California, San Diego, CA 62

**electromechanical instrumentation and maintenance
technologies (15.04)**
Milwaukee School of Engineering, WI 316
Northrop University, CA 32

elementary education (13.12.02)
See entry under *teacher education, general programs
(13.12)* for
Bridgewater State College, MA 143

emergency medical technology-ambulance (17.02.05)
See entries under *diagnostic and treatment services
(17.02)* for

Peru State College, NE 174
Southwestern College, KS 132

engineering, general (14.01)
University of California, Los Angeles, CA 47
University of Minnesota, Morris, MN 161
University of Minnesota, Twin Cities Campus, MN 162

English as a second language (23.12)
Georgia Institute of Technology, GA 103
Nova University, FL 96
Pine Manor College, MA 150
Wright State University, OH 262

entrepreneurship (08.03)
California State University, Los Angeles, CA 18
Philadelphia College of Textiles and Science, PA 275

environmental control technologies (15.05)
Milwaukee School of Engineering, WI 316
New York University, NY 202
Southern Illinois University at Edwardsville, IL 114
University of California, Davis, CA 44
University of California, Los Angeles, CA 47
University of California, Riverside, CA 57
University of California, San Diego, CA 62

environmental design (04.04)
University of California, Santa Barbara, CA 69

environmental health engineering (14.14)
Georgia Institute of Technology, GA 103
University of California, San Diego, CA 62

ethnic studies (05.02)
University of Akron, OH 252

evaluation and research (13.06)
Johns Hopkins University, MD 136
State University of New York at Albany, NY 234

family and community services (19.03)
Western Carolina University, NC 246

fashion design (19.09.02)
See entry under *textiles and clothing (19.09)* for
Philadelphia College of Textiles and Science, PA 275

film arts (50.06)
Mercy College, NY 195
New York University, NY 202
Rochester Institute of Technology, NY 223
University of California at Berkeley, CA 40
University of California, Los Angeles, CA 47

fine arts (50.07)
Long Island University, C. W. Post Campus, NY 192
New York University, NY 202
Pace University, Pleasantville/Briarcliff Campus, NY 216
Pacific Northwest College of Art, Oregon Art Institute,
OR 265
Paier College of Art, Inc., CT 76
Ringling School of Art and Design, FL 99
Rochester Institute of Technology, NY 223
School of the Associated Arts, MN 160
University of California at Berkeley, CA 40

fire protection (43.02)
Mercy College, NY 195
San Diego State University, CA 33
University of Akron, OH 252
University of California, Los Angeles, CA 47
University of New Haven, CT 78

food marketing (08.06)
Saint Peter's College, NJ 184

food production, management, and services (20.04)
Alaska Pacific University, AK 8
Indiana University at South Bend, IN 119
New York University, NY 202
Purdue University, IN 123
Rhode Island School of Design, RI 290
Spalding University, KY 133
University of Georgia, GA 103
University of New Haven, CT 78

food sciences and human nutrition (19.05)
Alaska Pacific University, AK 8
University of Iowa, IA 127
University of Rhode Island, RI 291

foreign languages, multiple emphasis (16.01)
Marygrove College, MI 156
New York University, NY 202
Seton Hill College, PA 280
University of Arizona, AZ 10
University of Pittsburgh, PA 282

French (16.09.01)
See entries under *Italic languages (16.09)* for
American University, DC 84
Mercy College, NY 195
Notre Dame College of Ohio, OH 249
Pace University, Pleasantville/Briarcliff Campus, NY 216

general marketing (08.07)
California State University, Los Angeles, CA 18
Franklin and Marshall College, PA 270
Franklin Pierce College, NH 174
Mercy College, NY 195
Neumann College, PA 272
New Hampshire College, NH 175
Nova University, FL 96
Philadelphia College of Textiles and Science, PA 275
Robert Morris College, PA 277
St. Francis College, NY 228
Seton Hill College, PA 280
University of California, Los Angeles, CA 47
University of California, San Diego, CA 62
University of Cincinnati, OH 256
University of South Florida, FL 101

geography (45.07)
George Mason University, VA 307
Wright State University, OH 262

German (16.05.01)
See entries under *Germanic languages (16.05)* for
American University, DC 84
Pace University, Pleasantville/Briarcliff Campus, NY 216

Germanic languages (16.05)
American University, DC 84
Pace University, Pleasantville/Briarcliff Campus, NY 216

gerontological services (19.07.05)
See entries under *individual and family development (19.07)* for
Abilene Christian University, TX 297
Ball State University, IN 115
California State University, Chico, CA 12
Cedar Crest College, PA 269
College of Mount St. Joseph, OH 248
College of Saint Elizabeth, NJ 180
Emmanuel College, MA 145
Florida State University, FL 93
George Mason University, VA 307
Incarnate Word College, TX 297
Lindenwood College, MO 165
Lynchburg College, VA 309
Mars Hill College, NC 239
Medgar Evers College of the City University of New York, NY 195
Mercy College, NY 195

Moravian College, PA 272
Mount Mary College, WI 318
National College of Education, IL 109
North Carolina State University at Raleigh, NC 240
Northern Illinois University, IL 113
Rutgers, The State University of New Jersey, New Brunswick, NJ 183
St. John Fisher College, NY 229
St. Joseph's College, NY 230
St. Joseph's College, Suffolk Campus, NY 232
St. Thomas Aquinas College, NY 234
San Francisco State University, CA 37
Southern Illinois University at Edwardsville, IL 114
Stonehill College, MA 151
University of Akron, OH 252
University of Arizona, AZ 10
University of California, Los Angeles, CA 47
University of Georgia, GA 103
University of Northern Colorado, CO 75
University of South Carolina, SC 292
Virginia Commonwealth University, VA 313
Western Michigan University, MI 158
Wright State University, OH 262
Yeshiva University, NY 239

graphic and printing communications (48.02)
Pace University, Pleasantville/Briarcliff Campus, NY 216
Paier College of Art, Inc., CT 76
Rochester Institute of Technology, NY 223
School of the Associated Arts, MN 160
Southwestern Oklahoma State University, OK 264
University of California at Berkeley, CA 40
University of California, Davis, CA 44
University of California, Riverside, CA 57
University of California, San Diego, CA 62
University of California, Santa Barbara, CA 69
University of Cincinnati, OH 256
University of Delaware, DE 84
University of South Florida, FL 101

health-related activities (34.01)
California State University, Chico, CA 12
University of California, San Diego, CA 62

health services administration (18.07)
California State University, Long Beach, CA 16
Chapman College, CA 22
College of Saint Mary, NE 171
Emmanuel College, MA 145
Golden Gate University, CA 24
Harvard University, MA 148
Illinois Benedictine College, IL 108
Neumann College, PA 272
New York University, NY 202
Nova University, FL 96
Purdue University, IN 123
Saint Peter's College, NJ 184
Southern Methodist University, TX 298
Stephens College, MO 170
University of California, Los Angeles, CA 47
University of Georgia, GA 103
University of Iowa, IA 127
University of Rhode Island, RI 291

heating, air conditioning, and refrigeration mechanics (47.02)
Oakland City College, IN 122
Pittsburg State University, KS 130

history (45.08)
Ball State University, IN 115
Brigham Young University, UT 302
Creighton University, NE 172
University of Pittsburgh, PA 282

horticulture (01.06)
Pace University, Pleasantville/Briarcliff Campus, NY 216
University of California, Los Angeles, CA 47

hospitality and recreation marketing (08.09)
Alaska Pacific University, AK 8
New York University, NY 202
University of Akron, OH 252

human environment and housing (19.06)
Syracuse University, NY 238
University of Akron, OH 252

humanities and social sciences (30.04)
University of Georgia, GA 103

human resources development (06.06)
American University, DC 84
Assumption College, MA 140
Bentley College, MA 140
California State University, Long Beach, CA 16
Chapman College, CA 22
Florida International University, FL 93
Florida State University, FL 93
Golden Gate University, CA 24
Moravian College, PA 272
Neumann College, PA 272
New Hampshire College, NH 175
St. Joseph's College, NY 230
St. Joseph's College, Suffolk Campus, NY 232
University of California at Berkeley, CA 40
University of California, Davis, CA 44
University of Pittsburgh, PA 282
Widener University, Pennsylvania Campus, PA 287

illustration design (50.04.03)
See entries under *design (50.04)* for
Pace University, Pleasantville/Briarcliff Campus, NY ... 216
Paier College of Art, Inc., CT 76
Rhode Island School of Design, RI 290
Ringling School of Art and Design, FL 99
Rochester Institute of Technology, NY 223
School of the Associated Arts, MN 160

individual and family development (19.07)
Abilene Christian University, TX 297
Ball State University, IN 115
California State University, Chico, CA 12
Cedar Crest College, PA 269
College of Mount St. Joseph, OH 248
College of Saint Elizabeth, NJ 180
Emmanuel College, MA 145
Florida State University, FL 93
George Mason University, VA 307
Incarnate Word College, TX 297
Lindenwood College, MO 165
Lynchburg College, VA 309
Mars Hill College, NC 239
Medgar Evers College of the City University of New
York, NY 195
Mercy College, NY 195
Moravian College, PA 272
Mount Mary College, WI 318
National College of Education, IL 109
North Carolina State University at Raleigh, NC .. 240
Northern Illinois University, IL 113
Rutgers, The State University of New Jersey, New
Brunswick, NJ 183
St. John Fisher College, NY 229
St. Joseph's College, NY 230
St. Joseph's College, Suffolk Campus, NY 232
St. Thomas Aquinas College, NY 234
San Francisco State University, CA 37
Southern Illinois University at Edwardsville, IL . 114
Stonehill College, MA 151
University of Akron, OH 252
University of Arizona, AZ 10
University of California, Los Angeles, CA 47
University of Georgia, GA 103
University of Northern Colorado, CO 75
University of South Carolina, SC 292
Ursuline College, OH 261

Virginia Commonwealth University, VA 313
Western Michigan University, MI 158
Wright State University, OH 262
Yeshiva University, NY 239

industrial engineering (14.17)
Louisiana State University and Agricultural and
Mechanical College, LA 134
University of California, Riverside, CA 57

industrial equipment maintenance and repair (47.03)
Pittsburg State University, KS 130

industrial production technologies (15.06)
Ball State University, IN 115
California State University, Los Angeles, CA 18
Fitchburg State College, MA 146
New York Institute of Technology, NY 199
Old Dominion University, VA 310
University of California, Los Angeles, CA 47
University of Cincinnati, OH 256

information sciences and systems (11.04)
Bentley College, MA 140
Dowling College, NY 192
Golden Gate University, CA 24
Jordan College, MI 153
Mercy College, NY 195
Neumann College, PA 272
New York University, NY 202
Pace University, Pleasantville/Briarcliff Campus, NY ... 216
University of California, Los Angeles, CA 47
University of California, San Diego, CA 62

institutional, home management, and supporting services (20.06)
Alaska Pacific University, AK 8

institutional management (06.07)
Dominican College of Blauvelt, NY 191
Golden Gate University, CA 24
New York University, NY 202
University of California, San Diego, CA 62
University of New Haven, CT 78
University of North Carolina at Charlotte, NC ... 245

insurance and risk management (06.08)
University of California, Davis, CA 44
University of Pittsburgh, PA 282

interior design (04.05)
Boston Architectural Center, MA 143
College of Mount St. Joseph, OH 248
Harrington Institute of Interior Design, IL 107
New York Institute of Technology, NY 199
Pace University, Pleasantville/Briarcliff Campus, NY ... 216
Paier College of Art, Inc., CT 76
Philadelphia College of Textiles and Science, PA . 275
Pratt Institute, NY 222
Rhode Island School of Design, RI 290
Ringling School of Art and Design, FL 99
Rochester Institute of Technology, NY 223
Seton Hill College, PA 280
University of California at Berkeley, CA 40
University of California, Riverside, CA 57

international business management (06.09)
California State University, Los Angeles, CA 18
Golden Gate University, CA 24
New York University, NY 202
Nova University, FL 96
University of California, Los Angeles, CA 47
University of Illinois at Urbana-Champaign, IL .. 115
University of Southern California, CA 70

international public service (44.03)
University of Pittsburgh, PA 282

international relations (45.09)
Ohio State University, OH 251
Old Dominion University, VA 310

interpersonal skills (35.01)
School for Lifelong Learning of the University System
of New Hampshire, NH 178

investments and securities (06.10)
New York University, NY 202
Old Dominion University, VA 310
University of California, Davis, CA 44
University of California, Riverside, CA 57

Italian (16.09.02)
See entry under *Italic languages (16.09)* for
Mercy College, NY 195

Italic languages (16.09)
American University, DC 84
Mercy College, NY 195
Notre Dame College of Ohio, OH 249
Pace University, Pleasantville/Briarcliff Campus, NY 216

jewelry design, fabrication, and repair (48.06.02)
See entry under *precision work, assorted materials
(48.06)* for
University of South Florida, FL 101

journalism (mass communications) (09.04)
Calumet College of Saint Joseph, IN 116
Mercy College, NY 195
Moravian College, PA 272
University of California, Los Angeles, CA 47

labor/industrial relations (06.11)
Indiana University Bloomington, IN 120
Indiana University Northwest, IN 121
New York Institute of Technology, NY 199
Pace University, Pleasantville/Briarcliff Campus, NY 216
Rutgers, The State University of New Jersey, Cook
College, NJ 183
Saint Louis University, MO 168
University of California, Davis, CA 44
University of California, Los Angeles, CA 47
University of California, Riverside, CA 57
University of Minnesota, Twin Cities Campus, MN 162
University of Wisconsin–Parkside, WI 320

landscape architecture (04.06)
George Washington University, DC 89
University of California at Berkeley, CA 40
University of California, Los Angeles, CA 47
University of South Florida, FL 101

law (22.01)
Assumption College, MA 140
Barry University, FL 92
Baruch College of the City University of New York, NY 189
Bentley College, MA 140
Bridgewater State College, MA 143
California State University, Bakersfield, CA 11
California State University, Chico, CA 12
California State University, Hayward, CA 14
California State University, Long Beach, CA 16
California State University, Los Angeles, CA 18
Carthage College, WI 316
Cedar Crest College, PA 269
Chapman College, CA 22
College of Mount St. Joseph, OH 248
College of Saint Mary, NE 171
Columbus College, GA 103
Elms College, MA 145
Florida International University, FL 93
George Washington University, DC 89
Humphreys College, CA 31
Indiana State University, IN 119
Indiana University at South Bend, IN 119

Indiana University Bloomington, IN 120
Long Island University, C. W. Post Campus, NY 192
Louisiana State University and Agricultural and
Mechanical College, LA 134
Lyndon State College, VT 303
Manhattanville College, NY 194
Marycrest College, IA 127
Mount Ida College, MA 149
New York University, NY 202
Nova University, FL 96
Rivier College, NH 176
Robert Morris College, PA 277
Russell Sage College, NY 228
Saint Vincent College, PA 279
San Francisco State University, CA 37
San Jose State University, CA 39
Southern Methodist University, TX 298
Stonehill College, MA 151
Syracuse University, NY 238
Texas Tech University, TX 300
University of Alabama at Birmingham, AL 6
University of California, Davis, CA 44
University of California, Los Angeles, CA 47
University of California, Riverside, CA 57
University of California, San Diego, CA 62
University of Cincinnati, OH 256
University of Delaware, DE 84
University of Houston, TX 300
University of Miami, FL 100
University of Mississippi, MS 164
University of New Hampshire, NH 179
University of New Haven, CT 78
University of New Orleans, LA 135
University of Pittsburgh, PA 282
University of South Alabama, AL 8
University of Texas at Arlington, TX 301
Westminster College of Salt Lake City, UT 303
Widener University, Pennsylvania Campus, PA 287
Willamette University, OR 266
William Jewell College, MO 170

legal assisting (22.01.03)
See entries under *law (22.01)* for
Assumption College, MA 140
Barry University, FL 92
Baruch College of the City University of New York, NY 189
Bentley College, MA 140
Bridgewater State College, MA 143
California State University, Bakersfield, CA 11
California State University, Chico, CA 12
California State University, Hayward, CA 14
California State University, Long Beach, CA 16
California State University, Los Angeles, CA 18
Carthage College, WI 316
Cedar Crest College, PA 269
Chapman College, CA 22
College of Mount St. Joseph, OH 248
College of Saint Mary, NE 171
Columbus College, GA 103
Elms College, MA 145
Florida International University, FL 93
George Washington University, DC 89
Humphreys College, CA 31
Indiana State University, IN 119
Indiana University at South Bend, IN 119
Indiana University Bloomington, IN 120
Long Island University, C. W. Post Campus, NY 192
Louisiana State University and Agricultural and
Mechanical College, LA 134
Lyndon State College, VT 303
Manhattanville College, NY 194
Marycrest College, IA 127
Mount Ida College, MA 149
Nova University, FL 96
Rivier College, NH 176
Robert Morris College, PA 277
Russell Sage College, NY 228
Saint Vincent College, PA 279

San Francisco State University, CA 37
San Jose State University, CA 39
Southern Methodist University, TX 298
Stonehill College, MA 151
Syracuse University, NY 238
Texas Tech University, TX 300
University of Alabama at Birmingham, AL 6
University of California, Davis, CA 44
University of California, Los Angeles, CA 47
University of California, Riverside, CA 57
University of California, San Diego, CA 62
University of Cincinnati, OH 256
University of Delaware, DE 84
University of Miami, FL 100
University of Mississippi, MS 164
University of New Hampshire, NH 179
University of New Haven, CT 78
University of New Orleans, LA 135
University of Pittsburgh, PA 282
University of South Alabama, AL 8
University of Texas at Arlington, TX 301
Westminster College of Salt Lake City, UT 303
Widener University, Pennsylvania Campus, PA 287
William Jewell College, MO 170

leisure and recreational activities (36.01)
University of South Florida, FL 101

liberal/general studies (24.01)
American University, DC 84
Johns Hopkins University, MD 136
Mercy College, NY 195
Neumann College, PA 272
Rochester Institute of Technology, NY 223
University of Minnesota, Morris, MN 161
University of Minnesota, Twin Cities Campus, MN 162

library and archival sciences, general (25.01)
Rutgers, The State University of New Jersey, New
   Brunswick, NJ 183
State University of New York at Albany, NY 234

library assisting (25.03)
California State University, Los Angeles, CA 18
School for Lifelong Learning of the University System
   of New Hampshire, NH 178

library science (25.04)
University of Cincinnati, OH 256
University of Missouri–Columbia, MO 170

linguistics (includes phonetics, semantics, and philology) (23.06)
University of Akron, OH 252

literature, American (23.07)
California State University, Chico, CA 12

management information systems (06.12)
Bridgewater State College, MA 143
George Mason University, VA 307
George Washington University, DC 89
Golden Gate University, CA 24
St. Francis College, NY 228
Thomas More College, KY 133
University of California, San Diego, CA 62
Widener University, Pennsylvania Campus, PA 287

management science (06.13)
Golden Gate University, CA 24
Illinois Benedictine College, IL 108
Lyndon State College, VT 303
Pace University, Pleasantville/Briarcliff Campus, NY 216
Philadelphia College of Textiles and Science, PA 275
Saint Louis University, MO 168
University of California, Davis, CA 44
University of Lowell, MA 152

maritime science (merchant marine) (28.05)
Texas A&M University at Galveston, TX 299

marketing management and research (06.14)
Albright College, PA 266
Bridgewater State College, MA 143
College of Saint Elizabeth, NJ 180
Golden Gate University, CA 24
Lyndon State College, VT 303
Notre Dame College of Ohio, OH 249
Pace University, Pleasantville/Briarcliff Campus, NY 216
Saint Louis University, MO 168
Saint Peter's College, NJ 184
University of California at Berkeley, CA 40
University of Pittsburgh, PA 282
Widener University, Pennsylvania Campus, PA 287

materials engineering (14.18)
Stevens Institute of Technology, NJ 186

maternal/child health (18.11.03)
See entry under *nursing (18.11)* for
University of California, Los Angeles, CA 47

mathematics and computer science (30.08)
Stevens Institute of Technology, NJ 186

mathematics, general (27.01)
Creighton University, NE 172
Golden Gate University, CA 24
University of Minnesota, Morris, MN 161

mechanical and related technologies (15.08)
Northwest Missouri State University, MO 165
Stevens Institute of Technology, NJ 186
University of Cincinnati, OH 256

medical laboratory (18.09)
San Francisco State University, CA 37
University of North Carolina at Chapel Hill, NC 244

medical laboratory technologies (17.03)
California State University, Bakersfield, CA 11
Pace University, Pleasantville/Briarcliff Campus, NY 216
University of Iowa, IA 127

medical records administration (18.07.03)
See entry under *health services administration (18.07)* for
Stephens College, MO 170

mental health/human services (17.04)
Ball State University, IN 115
California State University, Dominguez Hills, CA 14
California State University, Hayward, CA 14
California State University, Sacramento, CA 21
Chapman College, CA 22
College of St. Francis, IL 106
George Mason University, VA 307
Long Island University, C. W. Post Campus, NY 192
Marycrest College, IA 127
National College of Education, IL 109
New York Institute of Technology, NY 199
Nova University, FL 96
St. Cloud State University, MN 159
Stonehill College, MA 151
University of Akron, OH 252
University of California at Berkeley, CA 40
University of California, Los Angeles, CA 47
University of California, Riverside, CA 57
University of California, San Diego, CA 62
University of California, Santa Barbara, CA 69
University of Georgia, GA 103
University of Miami, FL 100
University of Minnesota, Twin Cities Campus, MN 162
University of Texas at Arlington, TX 301
Western Michigan University, MI 158

microcomputer applications (11.06)
Baruch College of the City University of New York, NY   189
California State University, Long Beach, CA 16
California State University, Los Angeles, CA 18
Colorado State University, CO 72
Golden Gate University, CA 24
Jordan College, MI 153
Marietta College, OH 249
Pace University, Pleasantville/Briarcliff Campus, NY 216
School for Lifelong Learning of the University System
   of New Hampshire, NH 178
University of California, Los Angeles, CA 47
University of California, Riverside, CA 57
University of Colorado at Boulder, CO 73
University of New Orleans, LA 135

miscellaneous allied health services (17.05)
East Tennessee State University, TN 294
Jordan College, MI 153
Los Angeles College of Chiropractic, CA 31
Marygrove College, MI 156
St. Joseph's College, NY 230
St. Joseph's College, Suffolk Campus, NY 232
University of North Carolina at Chapel Hill, NC 244
University of Southern California, CA 70
Western Michigan University, MI 158

miscellaneous construction trades and property maintenance (46.04)
New York University, NY 202
San Francisco State University, CA 37
University of California, Davis, CA 44
University of Nebraska–Lincoln, NE 174

miscellaneous specialized areas, life sciences (26.06)
Nova University, FL 96
University of South Carolina, SC 292
Virginia Commonwealth University, VA 313

missionary studies (39.03)
Abilene Christian University, TX 297

music (50.09)
Mannes College of Music, NY 194
Marygrove College, MI 156
Mount Mary College, WI 318
North Central Bible College, MN 159
Saint Louis Conservatory of Music, MO 167
San Francisco State University, CA 37
University of California, Los Angeles, CA 47
University of Southern California, CA 70
Virginia Wesleyan College, VA 314

music therapy (17.08.06)
See entry under *rehabilitation services (17.08)* for
Emmanuel College, MA 145

nursing (18.11)
Clemson University, SC 291
University of California, Los Angeles, CA 47
University of South Carolina, SC 292
University of Wisconsin–Oshkosh, WI 319

nursing-related services (17.06)
George Mason University, VA 307
Kansas Newman College, KS 130

occupational safety and health technology (15.07.01)
See entries under *quality control and safety technologies (15.07)* for
Mercy College, NY 195
University of New Haven, CT 78
University of Southern California, CA 70

office supervision and management (07.04)
Auburn University at Montgomery, AL 6
Colorado State University, CO 72
Indiana University Bloomington, IN 120

** **
Mount Ida College, MA 149
New York University, NY 202
Rivier College, NH 176
University of Alabama at Birmingham, AL 6
University of Cincinnati, OH 256

ophthalmic services (17.07)
Old Dominion University, VA 310
University of Minnesota, Twin Cities Campus, MN 162

optometry (18.12)
University of California at Berkeley, CA 40

organizational behavior (06.15)
George Washington University, DC 89
Illinois Benedictine College, IL 108
West Georgia College, GA 105

personal services (12.04)
Jordan College, MI 153

personnel and training programs (07.05)
Bryant College, RI 289
California State University, Long Beach, CA 16
North Carolina State University at Raleigh, NC 240
Stonehill College, MA 151
University of Connecticut, CT 78

personnel management (06.16)
Bentley College, MA 140
Colorado State University, CO 72
Felician College, NJ 182
Illinois Benedictine College, IL 108
Lyndon State College, VT 303
Mercy College, NY 195
New York University, NY 202
Nova University, FL 96
Roosevelt University, IL 113
St. Francis College, NY 228
San Diego State University, CA 33
University of Alabama at Birmingham, AL 6
University of California at Berkeley, CA 40
University of California, Los Angeles, CA 47
University of California, Riverside, CA 57
University of California, San Diego, CA 62
University of Tennessee, Knoxville, TN 296

philosophy (38.01)
Conception Seminary College, MO 165
Old Dominion University, VA 310
St. Hyacinth College and Seminary, MA 150
St. John Vianney College Seminary, FL 100

physical science technologies (41.03)
University of Cincinnati, OH 256

physician assisting (17.05.08)
See entry under *miscellaneous allied health services (17.05)* for
University of Southern California, CA 70

physics (40.08)
Pace University, Pleasantville/Briarcliff Campus, NY 216

plumbing, pipefitting, and steamfitting (46.05)
New York University, NY 202

political science and government (45.10)
George Washington University, DC 89
Golden Gate University, CA 24
Pace University, Pleasantville/Briarcliff Campus, NY 216
University of Akron, OH 252

precision metal work (48.05)
Oakland City College, IN 122
Pittsburg State University, KS 130
Rochester Institute of Technology, NY 223

precision work, assorted materials (48.06)
University of South Florida, FL 101

preelementary education (13.12.04)
See entries under *teacher education, general programs
(13.12)* for
Bridgewater State College, MA 143
California State University, Dominguez Hills, CA 14

psychology, general (42.01)
Creighton University, NE 172
Felician College, NJ 182
Neumann College, PA 272
University of California, Santa Barbara, CA 69

public administration (44.04)
American University, DC 84
California State University, Chico, CA 12
Florida State University, FL 93
Indiana University Northwest, IN 121
North Carolina State University at Raleigh, NC 240
Rutgers, The State University of New Jersey, New
  Brunswick, NJ 183
State University of New York at Albany, NY 234
University of Connecticut, CT 78
University of Hawaii at Manoa, HI 106
University of Wisconsin–Milwaukee, WI 319
Virginia Commonwealth University, VA 313

public affairs, general (44.01)
Golden Gate University, CA 24
University of Georgia, GA 103
University of Pittsburgh, PA 282

public policy studies (44.05)
University of Pittsburgh, PA 282

public relations (09.05)
Bridgewater State College, MA 143
Creighton University, NE 172
George Washington University, DC 89
Golden Gate University, CA 24
New York University, NY 202
Rivier College, NH 176
Rochester Institute of Technology, NY 223
Seton Hill College, PA 280
University of California, Los Angeles, CA 47
University of California, Riverside, CA 57
University of Denver, CO 74

quality control and safety technologies (15.07)
Cogswell Polytechnical College, CA 23
Mercy College, NY 195
Milwaukee School of Engineering, WI 316
School for Lifelong Learning of the University System
  of New Hampshire, NH 178
University of New Haven, CT 78
University of Southern California, CA 70

radio/television, general (09.07)
University of California, Santa Cruz, CA 70
University of New Haven, CT 78

real estate (06.17)
American University, DC 84
Bentley College, MA 140
California State University, Hayward, CA 14
Golden Gate University, CA 24
Johns Hopkins University, MD 136
Memphis State University, TN 296
New York Institute of Technology, NY 199
New York University, NY 202
Robert Morris College, PA 277
Saint Louis University, MO 168
University of California, Los Angeles, CA 47
University of California, Riverside, CA 57
University of California, San Diego, CA 62
University of Cincinnati, OH 256

University of Colorado at Boulder, CO 73
University of Pittsburgh, PA 282
University of Rhode Island, RI 291

rehabilitation services (17.08)
College of Notre Dame, CA 23
Emmanuel College, MA 145
Mercy College, NY 195
Mount Mary College, WI 318
Southern Methodist University, TX 298
Ursuline College, OH 261

religion (38.02)
Creighton University, NE 172
Felician College, NJ 182
Loyola University of Chicago, IL 109
Notre Dame College of Ohio, OH 249
Olivet Nazarene University, IL 113
Patten College, CA 33

religious education (39.04)
Baptist Bible Institute, FL 92
Calumet College of Saint Joseph, IN 116
College of Saint Elizabeth, NJ 180
Emmanuel College, MA 145
Huntington College, IN 118
Incarnate Word College, TX 297
Lutheran Bible Institute of Seattle, WA 315
Notre Dame College of Ohio, OH 249
St. Bonaventure University, NY 228
Saint Joseph Seminary College, LA 135
St. Paul Bible College, MN 160
Stonehill College, MA 151
Trinity Bible College, ND 246
Ursuline College, OH 261
Wesley College, MS 164

religious music (39.05)
Baptist Bible Institute, FL 92
Marylhurst College, OR 265
Seton Hill College, PA 280

renewable natural resources, general (03.01)
George Mason University, VA 307
Jordan College, MI 153

Russian (16.04.02)
See entries under *Balto-Slavic languages (16.04)* for
American University, DC 84
State University of New York at Albany, NY 234

school psychology (13.08)
Johns Hopkins University, MD 136
National College of Education, IL 109
State University of New York at Albany, NY 234

secretarial and related programs (07.06)
Auburn University at Montgomery, AL 6
Black Hills State College, SD 293
Calumet College of Saint Joseph, IN 116
East Tennessee State University, TN 294
Goldey Beacom College, DE 83
Huntington College, IN 118
Jordan College, MI 153
Northern State College, SD 294
Northwest Missouri State University, MO 165
Pace University, Pleasantville/Briarcliff Campus, NY 216
Rivier College, NH 176
School for Lifelong Learning of the University System
  of New Hampshire, NH 178
Southwestern Oklahoma State University, OK 264
Stonehill College, MA 151
Sul Ross State University, TX 299
University of Akron, OH 252
University of Alabama at Birmingham, AL 6
University of Cincinnati, OH 256
University of Texas at Arlington, TX 301
Wright State University, OH 262

small business management and ownership (06.18)
American University, DC 84
Lyndon State College, VT 303
New York University, NY 202
Rochester Institute of Technology, NY 223
University of Akron, OH 252

social sciences, general (45.01)
Mercy College, NY 195

social work (44.07)
University of Houston, TX 300
University of Pittsburgh, PA 282
Western Michigan University, MI 158

sociology (45.11)
St. Joseph's College, Suffolk Campus, NY 232

Spanish (16.09.05)
See entries under *Italic languages (16.09)* for
American University, DC 84
Mercy College, NY 195
Notre Dame College of Ohio, OH 249
Pace University, Pleasantville/Briarcliff Campus, NY 216

special education (13.10)
Johns Hopkins University, MD 136
Lyndon State College, VT 303
National College of Education, IL 109

speech, debate, and forensics (23.10)
University of Akron, OH 252
University of Pittsburgh, PA 282

statistics (27.05)
American University, DC 84
Creighton University, NE 172

student counseling and personnel services (13.11)
California State University, Sacramento, CA 21
Johns Hopkins University, MD 136
Old Dominion University, VA 310

systems analysis (11.05)
Golden Gate University, CA 24
Hawaii Pacific College, HI 106
University of California at Berkeley, CA 40
University of California, San Diego, CA 62

systems science (30.06)
State University of New York at Albany, NY 234

taxation (06.19)
Adelphi University, NY 189
Golden Gate University, CA 24
New York University, NY 202
Pace University, Pleasantville/Briarcliff Campus, NY 216
State University of New York at Buffalo, NY 238
University of California, Riverside, CA 57

teacher education, general programs (13.12)
Bridgewater State College, MA 143
California State University, Dominguez Hills, CA 14
Fitchburg State College, MA 146
Virginia Commonwealth University, VA 313

teacher education, specific subject areas (13.13)
California State University, Hayward, CA 14
California State University, Long Beach, CA 16
California State University, Los Angeles, CA 18
Chapman College, CA 22
Dowling College, NY 192
Fitchburg State College, MA 146
Johns Hopkins University, MD 136
National College of Education, IL 109
San Francisco State University, CA 37
State University of New York at Albany, NY 234
University of California at Berkeley, CA 40

University of California, Riverside, CA 57
University of Cincinnati, OH 256
University of South Carolina, SC 292
University of Wisconsin–Oshkosh, WI 319

teaching English as a second language/foreign language (13.14)
American University, DC 84
Azusa Pacific University, CA 10
George Mason University, VA 307
Saint Michael's College, VT 305
San Diego State University, CA 33
University of Akron, OH 252
University of California at Berkeley, CA 40
University of California, Riverside, CA 57
University of California, San Diego, CA 62
University of California, Santa Barbara, CA 69
University of Pennsylvania, PA 282

technical and business writing (23.11)
American University, DC 84
California State University, Chico, CA 12
Clark University, MA 145
New York Institute of Technology, NY 199
North Carolina State University at Raleigh, NC 240
Robert Morris College, PA 277
San Diego State University, CA 33
San Francisco State University, CA 37
San Jose State University, CA 39
University of Lowell, MA 152
University of South Florida, FL 101
Wright State University, OH 262

telecommunications (09.08)
California State University, Sacramento, CA 21
College of Saint Mary, NE 171
Golden Gate University, CA 24
Marylhurst College, OR 265
Mundelein College, IL 109
New York University, NY 202
San Diego State University, CA 33
State University of New York at Albany, NY 234
University of California at Berkeley, CA 40
University of Miami, FL 100

textile engineering (14.28)
North Carolina State University at Raleigh, NC 240

textiles and clothing (19.09)
Philadelphia College of Textiles and Science, PA 275

theological studies (39.06)
Anderson University, IN 115
Baptist Bible Institute, FL 92
Marylhurst College, OR 265
St. Charles Borromeo Seminary, PA 279
Saint Meinrad College, IN 126
Saint Michael's College, VT 305
Seton Hill College, PA 280

trade and industrial supervision and management (06.20)
Franklin and Marshall College, PA 270
Golden Gate University, CA 24
Indiana University at South Bend, IN 119
Purdue University, IN 123
San Jose State University, CA 39
University of California, Los Angeles, CA 47
University of New Haven, CT 78
University of North Carolina at Charlotte, NC 245

transportation and travel marketing (08.11)
Baruch College of the City University of New York, NY 189
California State University, Sacramento, CA 21
Jones College, FL 95
New York Institute of Technology, NY 199
New York University, NY 202
Purdue University, IN 123
Sacred Heart University, CT 77

St. John Fisher College, NY 229
University of Kentucky, KY 134
Widener University, Pennsylvania Campus, PA 287

typing, general office, and related programs (07.07)
Goldey Beacom College, DE 83
Jones College, FL 95
Oakland City College, IN 122
Ohio University–Chillicothe, OH 251
Pace University, Pleasantville/Briarcliff Campus, NY 216
Southwestern Adventist College, TX 299

urban studies (45.12)
State University of New York at Albany, NY 234
University of Akron, OH 252
University of California, Riverside, CA 57
University of South Florida, FL 101

vehicle and mobile equipment mechanics and repairers (47.06)
Northrop University, CA 32
Oakland City College, IN 122
Pittsburg State University, KS 130

visual and performing arts, general (50.01)
California State University, Long Beach, CA 16

women's studies (30.07)
California State University, Long Beach, CA 16
Florida International University, FL 93
Old Dominion University, VA 310
State University of New York at Albany, NY 234
University of Akron, OH 252
University of Cincinnati, OH 256
University of Pittsburgh, PA 282

woodworking (48.07)
Pittsburg State University, KS 130

word processing (07.08)
Goldey Beacom College, DE 83
Jones College, FL 95
Jordan College, MI 153
Marygrove College, MI 156
Medgar Evers College of the City University of New
    York, NY 195
Robert Morris College, PA 277
Sacred Heart University, CT 77
Southwestern Adventist College, TX 299
University of Akron, OH 252
University of Cincinnati, OH 256

Institutional Index _____

Abilene Christian University, TX 297
Adelphi University, NY 189
Alaska Pacific University, AK 8
Albertus Magnus College, CT 76
Albright College, PA 266
Alvernia College, PA 268
American University, DC 84
Anderson University, IN 115
Anna Maria College for Men and Women, MA 139
Arizona College of the Bible, AZ 10
Assumption College, MA 140
Auburn University at Montgomery, AL 6
Azusa Pacific University, CA 10
Baldwin-Wallace College, OH 246
Ball State University, IN 115
Baptist Bible Institute, FL 92
Barry University, FL 92
Baruch College of the City University of New York, NY 189
Beaver College, PA 268
Bentley College, MA 140
Black Hills State College, SD 293
Boston Architectural Center, MA 143
Bridgewater State College, MA 143
Brigham Young University, UT 302
Bryant College, RI 289
California State University, Bakersfield, CA 11
California State University, Chico, CA 12
California State University, Dominguez Hills, CA 14
California State University, Hayward, CA 14
California State University, Long Beach, CA 16
California State University, Los Angeles, CA 18
California State University, Sacramento, CA 21
Calumet College of Saint Joseph, IN 116
Calvary Bible College, MO 165
Carthage College, WI 316
Cedar Crest College, PA 269
Chapman College, CA 22
City University, WA 314
Clark University, MA 145
Clemson University, SC 291
Cogswell Polytechnical College, CA 23
College of Mount St. Joseph, OH 248
College of Notre Dame, CA 23
College of Saint Elizabeth, NJ 180
College of St. Francis, IL 106
College of Saint Mary, NE 171
Colorado State University, CO 72
Colorado Technical College, CO 73
Columbia Bible College and Seminary, SC 292
Columbus College, GA 103
Conception Seminary College, MO 165
Cornish College of the Arts, WA 315
Creighton University, NE 172
Crichton College, TN 294
Dominican College of Blauvelt, NY 191
Dowling College, NY 192
Eastern Christian College, MD 136
East Tennessee State University, TN 294
Elmhurst College, IL 107
Elms College, MA 145
Emmanuel College, MA 145
Eugene Bible College, OR 264
Faith Baptist Bible College and Seminary, IA 127
Felician College, NJ 182
Fitchburg State College, MA 146
Florida International University, FL 93
Florida State University, FL 93
Fort Wayne Bible College, IN 118
Franklin and Marshall College, PA 270
Franklin Pierce College, NH 174

Frostburg State University, MD 136
George Mason University, VA 307
George Washington University, DC 89
Georgia Institute of Technology, GA 103
Golden Gate University, CA 24
Goldey Beacom College, DE 83
Harrington Institute of Interior Design, IL 107
Harvard University, MA 148
Hawaii Pacific College, HI 106
Hillsdale Free Will Baptist College, OK 263
Humphreys College, CA 31
Huntington College, IN 118
Illinois Benedictine College, IL 108
Incarnate Word College, TX 297
Indiana Institute of Technology, IN 119
Indiana State University, IN 119
Indiana University at South Bend, IN 119
Indiana University Bloomington, IN 120
Indiana University Northwest, IN 121
Indiana University of Pennsylvania, PA 271
Johns Hopkins University, MD 136
Jones College, FL 95
Jordan College, MI 153
Kansas Newman College, KS 130
Kansas State University, KS 130
Kutztown University of Pennsylvania, PA 271
Lindenwood College, MO 165
Long Island University, C. W. Post Campus, NY 192
Los Angeles College of Chiropractic, CA 31
Louisiana State University and Agricultural and
    Mechanical College, LA 134
Loyola University of Chicago, IL 109
Lutheran Bible Institute of Seattle, WA 315
Lynchburg College, VA 309
Lyndon State College, VT 303
Manhattanville College, NY 194
Mannes College of Music, NY 194
Marietta College, OH 249
Mars Hill College, NC 239
Marycrest College, IA 127
Marygrove College, MI 156
Marylhurst College, OR 265
Medgar Evers College of the City University of New
    York, NY 195
Memphis State University, TN 296
Mercy College, NY 195
Millsaps College, MS 164
Milwaukee School of Engineering, WI 316
Moravian College, PA 272
Mount Ida College, MA 149
Mount Mary College, WI 318
Mount St. Mary's College, CA 32
Mundelein College, IL 109
National College of Education, IL 109
Neumann College, PA 272
New Hampshire College, NH 175
New York Institute of Technology, NY 199
New York University, NY 202
North Adams State College, MA 149
North Carolina State University at Raleigh, NC 240
North Central Bible College, MN 159
Northern Illinois University, IL 113
Northern Kentucky University, KY 133
Northern State College, SD 294
Northrop University, CA 32
Northwest Missouri State University, MO 165
Northwood Institute, MI 157
Notre Dame College of Ohio, OH 249
Nova University, FL 96
Oakland City College, IN 122

Oakland University, MI 158
Ohio State University, OH 251
Ohio University–Chillicothe, OH 251
Old Dominion University, VA 310
Olivet Nazarene University, IL 113
Otterbein College, OH 252
Pace University, Pleasantville/Briarcliff Campus, NY 216
Pacific Northwest College of Art, Oregon Art Institute,
    OR 265
Paier College of Art, Inc., CT 76
Patten College, CA 33
Peru State College, NE 174
Philadelphia College of Bible, PA 274
Philadelphia College of Textiles and Science, PA 275
Pine Manor College, MA 150
Pittsburg State University, KS 130
Pratt Institute, NY 222
Puget Sound Christian College, WA 316
Purdue University, IN 123
Purdue University Calumet, IN 125
Rhode Island School of Design, RI 290
Ringling School of Art and Design, FL 99
Rivier College, NH 176
Robert Morris College, PA 277
Rochester Institute of Technology, NY 223
Roosevelt University, IL 113
Russell Sage College, NY 228
Rutgers, The State University of New Jersey, Cook
    College, NJ 183
Rutgers, The State University of New Jersey, New
    Brunswick, NJ 183
Sacred Heart University, CT 77
St. Bonaventure University, NY 228
St. Charles Borromeo Seminary, PA 279
St. Cloud State University, MN 159
St. Francis College, NY 228
St. Hyacinth College and Seminary, MA 150
St. John Fisher College, NY 229
St. John Vianney College Seminary, FL 100
St. Joseph's College, NY 230
St. Joseph's College, Suffolk Campus, NY 232
Saint Joseph Seminary College, LA 135
Saint Louis Conservatory of Music, MO 167
Saint Louis University, MO 168
Saint Meinrad College, IN 126
Saint Michael's College, VT 305
St. Paul Bible College, MN 160
Saint Peter's College, NJ 184
St. Thomas Aquinas College, NY 234
Saint Vincent College, PA 279
Saint Xavier College, IL 114
San Diego State University, CA 33
San Francisco State University, CA 37
San Jose State University, CA 39
School for Lifelong Learning of the University System of
    New Hampshire, NH 178
School of the Associated Arts, MN 160
School of the Ozarks, MO 170
Seton Hill College, PA 280
Simpson College, CA 40
Smith College, MA 150
Southeastern Bible College, AL 6
Southern Illinois University at Edwardsville, IL 114
Southern Methodist University, TX 298
Southern Oregon State College, OR 266
Southwestern Adventist College, TX 299
Southwestern College, KS 132
Southwestern Oklahoma State University, OK 264
Spalding University, KY 133
State University of New York at Albany, NY 234
State University of New York at Buffalo, NY 238
State University of New York College of Technology at
    Utica/Rome, NY 238
Stephens College, MO 170
Stevens Institute of Technology, NJ 186
Stonehill College, MA 151
Sul Ross State University, TX 299
Syracuse University, NY 238

Texas A&M University at Galveston, TX 299
Texas Christian University, TX 300
Texas Tech University, TX 300
Thomas More College, KY 133
Trinity Bible College, ND 246
United Wesleyan College, PA 282
University of Akron, OH 252
University of Alabama at Birmingham, AL 6
University of Arizona, AZ 10
University of Baltimore, MD 139
University of California at Berkeley, CA 40
University of California, Davis, CA 44
University of California, Los Angeles, CA 47
University of California, Riverside, CA 57
University of California, San Diego, CA 62
University of California, Santa Barbara, CA 69
University of California, Santa Cruz, CA 70
University of Cincinnati, OH 256
University of Colorado at Boulder, CO 73
University of Connecticut, CT 78
University of Delaware, DE 84
University of Denver, CO 74
University of Dubuque, IA 127
University of Georgia, GA 103
University of Hawaii at Manoa, HI 106
University of Houston, TX 300
University of Illinois at Urbana-Champaign, IL 115
University of Indianapolis, IN 126
University of Iowa, IA 127
University of Kentucky, KY 134
University of Lowell, MA 152
University of Miami, FL 100
University of Minnesota, Morris, MN 161
University of Minnesota, Twin Cities Campus, MN 162
University of Mississippi, MS 164
University of Missouri–Columbia, MO 170
University of Nebraska–Lincoln, NE 174
University of New Hampshire, NH 179
University of New Haven, CT 78
University of New Mexico, NM 189
University of New Orleans, LA 135
University of North Carolina at Chapel Hill, NC 244
University of North Carolina at Charlotte, NC 245
University of Northern Colorado, CO 75
University of Oklahoma, OK 264
University of Pennsylvania, PA 282
University of Pittsburgh, PA 282
University of Puerto Rico Medical Sciences Campus, PR .. 289
University of Puerto Rico, Río Piedras, PR 289
University of Rhode Island, RI 291
University of South Alabama, AL 8
University of South Carolina, SC 292
University of Southern California, CA 70
University of Southern Indiana, IN 126
University of South Florida, FL 101
University of Tennessee, Knoxville, TN 296
University of Texas at Arlington, TX 301
University of Vermont, VT 306
University of Wisconsin–Milwaukee, WI 319
University of Wisconsin–Oshkosh, WI 319
University of Wisconsin–Parkside, WI 320
Ursuline College, OH 261
Virginia Commonwealth University, VA 313
Virginia Polytechnic Institute and State University, VA 314
Virginia Wesleyan College, VA 314
Washington and Jefferson College, PA 287
Weber State College, UT 303
Wesley College, MS 164
Western Baptist College, OR 266
Western Carolina University, NC 246
Western Michigan University, MI 158
Western Montana College, MT 171
Western New England College, MA 153
West Georgia College, GA 105
Westminster College of Salt Lake City, UT 303
West Virginia Wesleyan College, WV 316
Wheaton College, IL 115
Widener University, Pennsylvania Campus, PA 287

Willamette University, OR 266
William Jewell College, MO 170
Worcester State College, MA 153

Wright State University, OH 262
Yeshiva University, NY 239